WEST ACADEMIC PUBLISHING'S
LAW SCHOOL ADVISORY BOARD

JESSE H. CHOPER
Professor of Law and Dean Emeritus
University of California, Berkeley

JOSHUA DRESSLER
Distinguished University Professor Emeritus, Frank R. Strong Chair in Law
Michael E. Moritz College of Law, The Ohio State University

RENÉE McDONALD HUTCHINS
Dean and Joseph L. Rauh, Jr. Chair of Public Interest Law
University of the District of Columbia David A. Clarke School of Law

YALE KAMISAR
Professor of Law Emeritus, University of San Diego
Professor of Law Emeritus, University of Michigan

MARY KAY KANE
Professor of Law, Chancellor and Dean Emeritus
University of California, Hastings College of the Law

LARRY D. KRAMER
President, William and Flora Hewlett Foundation

JONATHAN R. MACEY
Professor of Law, Yale Law School

DEBORAH JONES MERRITT
Distinguished University Professor, John Deaver Drinko/Baker &
Hostetler Chair in Law
Michael E. Moritz College of Law, The Ohio State University

ARTHUR R. MILLER
University Professor, New York University
Formerly Bruce Bromley Professor of Law, Harvard University

GRANT S. NELSON
Professor of Law Emeritus, Pepperdine University
Professor of Law Emeritus, University of California, Los Angeles

A. BENJAMIN SPENCER
Justice Thurgood Marshall Distinguished Professor of Law
University of Virginia School of Law

JAMES J. WHITE
Robert A. Sullivan Professor of Law Emeritus
University of Michigan

CONTRACTS: TRANSACTIONS AND LITIGATION

Fifth Edition

■ ■ ■

George W. Kuney
Lindsay Young Distinguished Professor of Law,
Director of the Clayton Center for Entrepreneurial Law, and
Director of the L.L.M. Program in United States Business Law
The University of Tennessee College of Law

Robert M. Lloyd
Professor Emeritus
The University of Tennessee College of Law

AMERICAN CASEBOOK SERIES®

WEST
ACADEMIC
PUBLISHING

The publisher is not engaged in rendering legal or other professional advice, and this publication is not a substitute for the advice of an attorney. If you require legal or other expert advice, you should seek the services of a competent attorney or other professional.

American Casebook Series is a trademark registered in the U.S. Patent and Trademark Office.

© West, a Thomson business, 2005, 2008
© 2011 Thomson Reuters
© 2017 LEG, Inc. d/b/a West Academic
© 2020 LEG, Inc. d/b/a West Academic
    444 Cedar Street, Suite 700
    St. Paul, MN 55101
    1-877-888-1330

West, West Academic Publishing, and West Academic are trademarks of West Publishing Corporation, used under license.

Printed in the United States of America

ISBN: 978-1-68467-455-8

ACKNOWLEDGMENTS

The authors and editors express their thanks to the following authors and publishers for permission to reprint portions of the following copyrighted material:

E. Allan Farnsworth and Aspen Publishers; E. Allan Farnsworth, *Contracts* § 12.9 at 766 (4th Ed. 2004).

The American Law Institute; *Restatement of Contracts* (1928) and *Restatement (Second) of Contracts* (1981) and, with the National Conference of Commissioners on Uniform State Laws, the *Uniform Commercial Code* and the *Uniform Electronic Transactions Act*.

The University of Chicago Law Review; Llewellyn, *A Lecture on Appellate Advocacy*, 29 U. CHI. L. REV. 628, 637–38 (1962).

Richard A. Posner and the Texas Law Review Association; Posner, *The Law and Economics of Contract Interpretation*, 83 TEX. L. REV. 1581 (2005).

The authors also thank Sophia Brown and David Cantrell for their administrative, research, problem solving, word processing, and proof reading efforts, as well as our prior students for identifying what was difficult, easy, and useful about contract law.

INTRODUCTION

A contract, by one definition, is "a promise that the law will enforce." These legally enforceable promises make up transactional documents under which property and services are exchanged, risks of loss and uncertainty are allocated, and the profits of human enterprise are divided among the interested parties.

Contracts are everywhere. There are contracts to buy and sell things like homes, boats, and cars; there are employment contracts, apartment leases, settlement agreements, plea bargains, franchise and distributor agreements, property settlements, partnership agreements, merger agreements, licenses to view sporting events, licenses to view or copy intellectual property like books and movies, and more. The federal and state constitutions are contracts between the citizens and the states. At all levels of our society, contracts define relationships between people, both individual people and artificial juridical persons like corporations and limited liability companies. *They specify who shall or may do what, to or for whom, when, and for how long.*

Contracts can be oral, in writing, or both. When the parties cannot agree on what the contract is or what the contract means, if there is enough at stake, the contract is likely to be the subject of litigation or some alternative form of dispute resolution. In any of these processes, the contract will be defined by those pieces of evidence that the courts or other decision-makers allow to be considered. Sometimes whole swaths of contract terms and other evidence are not considered in rendering the decision—they have been ruled "not to count" in the litigation process because, rightly or wrongly, evidence of their existence is barred by a substantive or procedural rule of law, like the parol evidence rule.

Many of the cases that you will read in this book arise from instances where parties or their lawyers did not sufficiently document the parties' deal. In some instances, one party will even deny that a deal was made. In others, their contract did not make provision for a circumstance that later occurred. These contracts ended up in lawsuits.

When a lawyer documents an agreement by drafting a contract, the lawyer should be thinking all the way through the possible courses of performance and changes of circumstance that may come to pass. After conceptualizing all of these possible future events, the lawyer should draft the contract making sufficient provision for each of them. Contracts are an opportunity to both prevent and plan for future disagreement and litigation. They are said to be "private legislation between the parties" or a set of rules that the parties are free to make up to define their relationship.

This includes the rules that will define the demise of the relationship. This is the essence of "freedom of contract."

Too often, in the opinions that follow, the court was faced with a contract that has no provision for a particular circumstance. Unsure of what to do or unhappy with the terms of the contract when the unforeseen circumstance comes to pass, the parties fell into disagreement, neither one wanting to shoulder what they consider to be a disproportionate share of the unanticipated burden. Who wants to be told, after all, that one cannot sell one's land to a newly interested party for twice what one agreed to sell it for just the other day? What business is pleased to learn that its contract appears to require it to continue to supply goods at a price that is suddenly below the cost of manufacturing the goods because the price of oil has almost doubled? It is in these circumstances that the parties often turn to litigation to resolve matters for them—matters that they often could have resolved in advance had they had the foresight to allocate the risk of the circumstance they now face.

This is one area where transactional lawyers can add value to a deal. These lawyers generally specialize in certain types of deals—real estate, public contracting, or entertainment, for example. Because they have seen many deals in their subject-matter specialty, they are able to foresee and provide for risks that their clients might otherwise miss. By tailoring the contract to address these risks, they present the parties with a solution to the problem if it arises. And they create the fodder for litigation should it come to that.

So, contract law is about putting relationships together and defining them, as well as taking them apart or trying to mend or break them. The transactional lawyer is aware of the default rules of law that will apply if the contract does not address the matter and some that may apply even if the drafter tries to vary the rule. The transactional lawyer is planning for what remedies will be available should the deal falter and the parties find themselves on less than pleasant terms in the future. The transactional lawyer is planning, making a record, and providing tools for the litigator and the litigation that may follow.

This text features 29 chapters that explore principles of contract law. Each is organized somewhat non-traditionally for a casebook. Although there is much to be said for forcing students to extract the law from raw cases, this is not the norm in practice. *Practicing attorneys usually turn first to a statute or secondary source like a treatise to find the rules that apply and then turn to cases to illustrate and understand application of the rule. This is the approach used in this text.* In the introductory portion of each chapter, the "black letter law" is discussed. Following this, a number of cases are presented in edited form to illustrate how courts apply these black latter rules. These cases are followed by notes, questions, and problems to reinforce the understanding of how particular rules can be applied. Where appropriate, the text contains references to outside materials for further illustration and exploration.

The challenge for students of contract law is to be actively engaged in the reading and class discussion of the materials. Judicial opinions are working documents, not entertaining stories or objective reports to be swallowed uncritically. In each case, after understanding the court's presentation of the facts, students should seek to understand what rule or standard the court applied, whether there were any alternate rules or standards that could have been applied, and whether (and, if so, how) it would matter if a different rule or standard had been applied. Beyond that, though, students should also be thinking of how the dispute could have been avoided while the contract was being negotiated and documented. How, if at all, can the legal rule or standard be drafted around or incorporated into a contract?

When a lawyer is consulted in the contracting process, there is the opportunity to plan almost every aspect of the relationship or interaction. If the plan—the contract—goes smoothly, there will be no lawsuit and no judicial opinion to read. When things do not go according to plan and a dispute arises, or where there has been a failure to plan, the law steps in with a set of default standards and rules to resolve the dispute. Those rules and standards make up the body of contract law. The rules and standards provide a flexible framework through which to weave the facts that have been created and preserved in order to paint a compelling picture for the decision-maker in later litigation.

In practice, transactional lawyers use a knowledge of what these default rules are to draft around them or to harness them to advance their client's interest. When the relationship has broken down and litigation or other dispute resolution processes are in motion, litigators use the substantive law of contracts and the terms of the contract as drafted with the tools of advocacy, again to advance their client's interests. Counsel is well advised, then, to know contract law, apply it to the terms of a contract when planning and acting in a transactional capacity, and to envision the litigation down-side and how the contract is likely to fare in that process. Contracting is an opportunity to plan the parties' relationship—beginning, middle, and end.

Note on Supplemental Authorities

This book is designed to be used with reference to four bodies of authorities: the Uniform Commercial Code (the "U.C.C."), the Restatement (Second) of Contracts (the "R2d"), the Convention on the International Sale of Goods (the "CISG"), and the UNIDROIT Principles of International Commercial Contracts ("UNIDROIT"). These four sets of rules and standards outline the scope of the modern law of contracts for purposes of this text.

A.   *The United States Materials*

The two sources of United States authority beyond the cases that are presented in this book are the U.C.C. and the R2d.

1.   *The U.C.C.*

The U.C.C. is a series of laws drafted by a group of lawyers and legal scholars for the purpose of facilitating commerce by making the laws governing business transactions rational and uniform throughout the United States. It was drafted after the first Restatement of Contracts and before the R2d. The U.C.C. consists of a dozen articles governing various types of business transactions. It has been adopted more or less uniformly in each of the United States. The only articles covered in this book are Articles 1 and 2, which govern the sale of goods. Articles 1 and 2 have been enacted into law by the legislature of all 50 states except Louisiana, which declined to adopt Article 2 explicitly when it adopted the rest of the U.C.C. but which has incorporated many of the same legal principles in its Civil Code.

Article 1 consists of general provisions applicable across all the other articles. This includes general rules of statutory construction and interpretation and definitions, which are very important. You may want to read through Article 1 early on in your contracts course to get an idea of what is in there—you can always look it up when you need to use it, if you know it is there.

Article 2 is basically a series of statutes setting out rules for contracts for the sale of goods. Article 2 does not provide a rule for all aspects of the sale of goods. In those situations where Article 2 does not provide a contrary rule, the general contracts rules—which are found in a jurisdiction's other statutes or judicial opinions or in the Restatement—apply. Where Article 2 does provide a rule, it usually differs from the common law rule, sometimes in a big way, sometimes only in a very minor way. In some instances, courts in some jurisdictions have changed their general contract law rules so that they follow the Article 2 rule even in cases not involving the sale of goods.

Article 2 only applies to contracts for the sale of "goods." Generally, *goods* are property that is tangible but is not real estate. *See* U.C.C. § 2–101. Thus, Article 2 would apply to a contract for the sale of a car but not to a contract for the sale of a house because a house (at least one that is attached to the land) is "real estate" rather than "goods." Article 2 would, however, apply to a contract for the sale of a mobile home not attached to land.

Article 2 would not apply to a contract for the repair of a car because the repair of a car is a service rather than a sale of goods. This is true even if, as part of the repair job, the mechanic sold the car's owner the parts needed for the repair. In cases involving contracts for a mixture of goods and services, one looks to the predominant purpose of the contract to determine if it is goods or services. If it is the sale of goods with some incidental services, like one for the sale, delivery, and installation of a refrigerator, the U.C.C. applies. If it is a service contract with some incidental goods, like one for servicing an automobile, the U.C.C. does not apply.

There is a common misconception that Article 2 only applies to transactions between businesspeople or "merchants," but it is just that, a misconception. Even though the basic purpose of the U.C.C. is to facilitate business transactions, Article 2 applies to *all* sales of goods. It applies to a law student selling a car to her next-door neighbor just as it applies to General Motors selling a truckload of Chevies to a dealer. Some of the provisions of the U.C.C. are applicable only to "merchants"—a term that is broader than you might expect and is defined in U.C.C. § 2–104—but these special merchant rules are only a small subset of Article 2.

The U.C.C. has an *Official Comment* accompanying each section. In the Official Comment the drafters try to explain the purpose of the section and how it is to work. The Official Comment is not part of the statute. That is, it is not enacted by the legislatures that adopt Article 2 and courts are not required to follow the Official Comment. Nevertheless, where a U.C.C. section applies, courts seldom reach a result contrary to that suggested by the Official Comment. *Whenever you read a U.C.C. section, you should also look at the accompanying Official Comment.*

An important part of the Official Comment is the *Definitional Cross References*. This part of the comment lists words or phrases used in the section in question that are defined elsewhere in the U.C.C. It's extremely important to check the Definitional Cross References because the U.C.C. often gives ordinary words a technical definition that you would not expect.

2.   *The R2d*

The American Law Institute, an organization of law professors, practitioners, and judges formed for the purpose of systematically presenting the state of the law in various fields, produced the *Restatement of the Law of Contracts* in 1932. The Restatement was intended to help courts by presenting the range and pattern of judicial interpretations on various substantive points of contract law. The Restatement was not intended to be enacted by legislatures as law like the U.C.C. The Institute issued the *Restatement (Second) of Contracts* in 1979. In this text we largely make reference to the *Restatement (Second) of Contracts*, or the R2d, rather than the original Restatement.

B. *The International Materials*

The United Nations Convention on Contracts for the International Sale of Goods (the "CISG"), opened for signature April 11, 1980, S. Treaty Doc. No. 9 (1983), 19 I.L.M. 671, reprinted in 15 U.S.C.A. App. at 333 (West 2004), and the UNIDROIT Principles of International Commercial Contracts 2004 are two bodies of contract law principles created with the twin aims of harmonizing the laws of trading nations and producing international rules to govern international commerce.

The CISG is a treaty of the United States and is the law of all 50 of the United States by virtue of the Supremacy Clause of the federal Constitution. In contrast, the UNIDROIT principles have not been enacted or adopted by any nation state and lack the force of law unless affirmatively selected as governing by the parties, either in their contract or afterward. Despite appearing to remain largely "under the radar" in American jurisprudence, the CISG and UNIDROIT Principles are important for lawyers to understand and employ in the increasingly international field of law and business. Also, because they differ from the U.C.C. and the R2d, often in subtle ways, they are useful in the study of contract law and legal reasoning.

1. *The CISG*

As a treaty of the United States, the CISG is the law of the land in the United States for contracts that fall within its scope, unless the parties expressly opt out of its application. This is not as easy as it might seem to be. A choice of law provision that merely selects the law of, say, New York is *not* sufficient to opt out of the CISG—after all, the CISG *is* the law of New York by way of the Supremacy Clause of the United States Constitution. Provisions that explicitly specify that the CISG does not apply and that affirmatively select other law—say, a chosen state's enactment of the U.C.C.—should be effective to accomplish the opt out.

Americans confronting the CISG for the first time may assume that it represents the international version of the U.C.C. This is a mistake. Although there are many similarities, the CISG also has some significant differences from the U.C.C. For example, the two bodies of law have different scopes of applicability. The U.C.C. applies to sales of "goods": all things that are movable at the time of identification to the contract, excluding the monetary purchase price for the goods, investment securities, and causes of action, but including the unborn young of animals, growing crops, and other things attached to land that are to be severed from it. U.C.C. § 2–105. The CISG, on the other hand, applies to contracts of sale of goods between parties whose places of business are in different countries that have adopted the CISG—of which, with some reservations, the United States is one—but does not apply to sales of consumer goods, sales at auction, execution sales and other sales by operation of law, sales of investment securities, sales of ships and aircraft, sales of electricity, or sales where the buyer provides the bulk of the raw material for the production of the goods (as in a "turn-key" or "screw-driver" plant operation). CISG Arts. 1 and 2.

Unlike the U.C.C., the CISG contains no statute of frauds, requirement of a writing, or parol evidence rule. Compare U.C.C. § 2–201(1) (requiring writing for sales of goods over $500) with CISG Art. 11 ("contract of sale need not be concluded in or evidenced by a writing and is not subject to any other requirement of form"); U.C.C. § 2–202 (parol evidence rule) with CISG Art. 11 (the contract "may be proved by any means, including witnesses"). The "battle of the forms" rules for offer and acceptance deal with similar concepts, but are stated with different initial presumptions and may lead to different results. Compare U.C.C. § 2–207 and CISG Art. 19. The U.C.C. and CISG enunciate different standards for consequential damages. *See* CISG Art. 74 ("ought" to have foreseen standard).

A study in 2016 evaluated data from over 5,000 contracts that referenced the CISG. These contracts were filed with the SEC between 1988 and 2014, and involved the sale of securities between corporations and non-professional investors. In 99% of the contracts, the parties' reference the CISG to exclude it from governing their agreement. This study supports the theory that most U.S. companies rarely select the CISG to govern their agreements. It is possible that some U.S. attorneys who select local state laws to govern their agreement are unaware that this choice might result in the CISG governing their agreement anyway. This, in turn, suggests that most U.S. attorneys are not as familiar with the CISG as they are with their own national sales laws, explaining why these attorneys would advise their clients to exclude the CISG from their agreements. *See* John F. Coyle, *The Role of the CISG in U.S. Contract Practice: An Empiracle Study*, U. PA. J. INT'L L., 195 (2016).

2.   *The UNIDROIT Principles*

The Principles of International Commercial Contracts drafted by the International Institute for the Unification of Private Law (the "UNIDROIT Principles") make up a portion of the work of UNIDROIT or the "Rome Institute" known as the Uniform Law of International Commerce. The Principles are not law *per se* but, rather, are closely analogous to the R2d and tend to indicate a consensus opinion about "what the law should be" based in part upon what it is. Thus, they constitute non-binding, persuasive authority that attempts to codify general contract principles across common and civil law jurisdictions. Like the rules of the American Arbitration Association, the UNIDROIT Principles can be contracted for, i.e., the parties may agree that they should apply to the contract to the full extent permitted by the country whose law governs the contract. Unless validly contracted for, the Principles act merely as an interpretative aid for litigants and courts faced with matters that are not addressed by positive governing law such as the U.C.C. or CISG.

Note on Civil Procedure

In most American courts, when an action is instituted by complaint, petition, or other initial filing, a file is created in the court clerk's office. That file is the lawsuit. The parties then prosecute the case, "moving" the court to take actions and make rulings that go into and change the status of the file. A court will generally do little, if anything, on its own to a case (except dismiss it for lack of prosecution), although it may (acting *sua sponte*) should it choose to do so. The index of the motions, orders, and other documents in the file is called the "docket" in most jurisdictions and is increasingly available on-line for review.

In general, the dispositive motions that the parties can bring—those that may result in a closing of the file or portions of the file by dismissal or entry of judgment—proceed from the broad to the narrow. In other words, at the outset of a case, the first motions, like a motion to dismiss under Federal Rule of Civil Procedure 12 for instance, apply a very coarse filter to the plaintiff's claims—they ask whether, assuming everything the plaintiff claims is true, the case should be dismissed and the file closed for a purely legal reason that is beyond factual dispute. For example, under FRCP 12(b)(1), if the court lacks subject matter jurisdiction, then the case should be dismissed, no matter how correct the plaintiff may be regarding how she was wronged by the defendant. Nothing else matters; if the court lacks subject matter jurisdiction, there is no need to proceed further; no relief can be granted. The same is true for lack of personal jurisdiction or expiration of the statute of limitations. These purely legal defenses to the suit are relatively inexpensive to litigate and thus are efficient tools for use in filtering out those lawsuits that should not take up any further judicial resources.

As the litigation proceeds, a series of ever finer and ever more fact-driven filters are applied—a motion for a judgment on the pleadings and a motion for summary judgment, for example. Claims that survive these filters continue (absent settlement) to trial, post-trial motions, and appeals. All of this is very expensive and increasingly resource-intensive for the parties (who supply the ever more detailed facts), for counsel (who develop the ever more detailed facts and applicable law), for judges (who must consider and rule on these ever more detailed facts, rule on the evidentiary motions made to expand or limit the facts, and determine the applicable rules of law), and for juries (who are asked to give up their time for a pittance in jury fees to watch an often disjointed and confusing trial in which these facts are presented and are then asked to make a decision).

Lesson One: If You Can't Get a Summary Judgment, Your Client Has Lost

> We tell our students that most lawsuits are settled before trial. What we often fail to tell them is that in contracts cases, even suits with no merit are settled. It is just too expensive to try a contract case, and in many jurisdictions you can't get to trial in a reasonable time. What is more, contract litigation, much more so than tort litigation, often ties up a business. Moreover, if the case goes to a jury, the outcome can be very hard to predict. So if the business litigator can't get the non-meritorious claim or defense thrown out on summary judgment, the client usually settles.

Robert M. Lloyd, Making Contracts Relevant: Thirteen Lessons for the First-Year Contracts Course, 36 Arizona State Law Journal 257, 257–58 (2004) (internal footnotes and citations omitted).

So, as you read the edited opinions in this book, note the procedural posture of the case. Ask yourself, what is the likelihood of success of the particular cause of action or defense that the opinion is focusing upon? Conversely, how has a plaintiff managed to develop the facts to keep a claim alive so that it can be used to leverage a settlement in the future? The judicial opinions in this book are dispositive documents granting or denying a party's attempts to get something thrown out of the lawsuit file or kept in play pending settlement or judgment. However, they are not the whole story, which, like an iceberg, is mostly out of sight. The litigation action in court swirls around merely the tip of the iceberg that is exposed above water.

Note on Legal Reading

Most first year law students are inundated with hundreds of pages of reading per week. This can often seem to be an overwhelming task, especially after success as an undergraduate with a much lighter page load. However, the task is not an impossible one. Legal reading skills are perhaps the most foundational aspect of a legal education and, like all skills, can be developed through practice and experience.

Research indicates that the development of certain habits or tendencies can improve a person's ability to read cases more effectively and efficiently. These tendencies include placing the case in context (historically and procedurally), reading the case outside of the linear presentation (reading a case out of order), and focusing on the purpose of the reading. This is not an exhaustive list but it hopefully illustrates the idea that reading a case from start to finish is not always the most effective method—in fact, a straight through read is almost never the most effective way to digest a judicial opinion.

Putting a case in context allows the reader to ascertain the underlying issues behind an opinion, which may clarify the holding. Reading outside the order of an opinion—first finding the statement of the issue or issues, then finding the ruling on the issue, then finding the reasoning, then reading the facts to see if they support the reasoning—can provide valuable information (i.e. the holding) which casts light on facts or analysis revealed earlier in the opinion.

Attorneys hone these skills over years of practice. For a first year law student, they may seem difficult or outlandish. But speedy and productive reading can yield favorable results for the client, and attorneys embrace this lesson. It is all part of "working smarter, not harder" as the old canard goes. As first year students, we suggest that you begin to embrace it too.

An Overview of a Working Contract

Before delving into the case law, let's take a brief look at a simple but real contract that will govern the parties' relationship in the purchase and sale of a business in the form of a sale of substantially all its assets. In many of the opinions in this book, the case came about because a matter was not properly provided for in the contract at issue. When reviewing the cases, in addition to thinking about the issue, the rule, the court's application of the rule to the issue and the specific facts, think in terms of how the contract could have been drafted to avoid the dispute. The following discussion of a contract sets the context of transactional work to help you in this process.

A.   The Deal Time Line: Big or Little, Deals Follow a Pattern

A transaction generally follows a standard timeline or chain of events. First, the parties make contact and negotiate. A preliminary agreement is reached and they contact their lawyers, if they have not done so already. Although the key business issues have probably been addressed by the parties, there will often be significant issues left open, some of which will only become apparent to the client after consultation with counsel.

As the parties proceed with full, formal documentation, due diligence (detailed factual and legal investigation) begins, often with one party's production of documents and information relevant to representations and warranties that are being negotiated into the documentation.

The definitive transactional documents are finalized and signed, and further due diligence and other pre-closing activities take place. Then the "closing" occurs; this is the point at which the majority of the consideration changes hands. Deals are either "sign and close"—like a typical sale of goods where the contract to sell is signed, the purchase price is paid, and the goods or a document of title to the goods are delivered—or "delayed closing" deals, like typical real estate transactions where the contract is signed, various due diligence deliveries and inspections are made and then, later, the purchase price is paid and title to the property passes at closing of an "escrow." Payments or deliveries may be made directly, party-to-party, or through an escrow, the preferred route for all but the most basic transactions. Escrows provide the parties with the security of knowing that although they have parted with their consideration, often worth many thousands or millions of dollars, it will not be delivered to the other party until that party's deliveries are complete. In case of a dispute, the escrow agent can hold all consideration already delivered and maintain the status quo pending the dispute's resolution. There may be a post-closing adjustment period as well that will allow the parties to examine what they have purchased or received and adjust price and other compensation to account for unavoidable variations.

For simple transactions, this time line is condensed, and one or more steps may be omitted. On the other hand, in major business transactions, the time line can extend over a year or more. The middle ground of 30 to 90 or 120 days represented by an average residential home purchase and sale transaction is also a typical period in which a small to medium commercial lease or asset purchase transaction might take place.

Keep this timeline in mind when thinking about a contract, drafting one, or considering a contract dispute. Know where the transaction is and where it is going (or where it has stalled). The relative position on this chain of events will affect the pace and the level of detail with which parties draft and define the agreement as well as their litigation goals and available remedies.

Contract negotiation and documentation is often an exercise in *selling:*

(1) Selling the parties on executing the documents;

(2) Selling the parties on voluntary performance, after execution; and

(3) Selling a later court or other entity on enforcement, after voluntary performance has ceased.

As some of the materials in this text will demonstrate, these three sales goals undermine each other to some extent. Consider the tension between selling the parties on execution, which tends to imply plain vanilla documentation with few, if any, "teeth," on the one hand, and selling the parties later on voluntary performance, which is furthered by fairly detailed documents that contain both "carrot" and "stick" provisions in the form of conditions tailored to the particular parties interests. Further, when providing for "teeth," especially when dealing with a contract between a large, sophisticated entity with substantial bargaining power, and a less sophisticated or powerful entity, counsel must be careful not to go too far for fear that a court will use a doctrine like unconscionability to delete or disregard portions of the contract or to re-write the parties' contract.

B. *Contracts Memorialize a Deal*

Contracts are documents that speak as of one particular time (in the case of most, the date of their execution). This means that they are intended to capture the agreements of the parties, and their respective rights and obligations as of that time, and to establish a set of rules that will govern future dealings. They must provide for substantially all the details of the parties' future dealings or they fail in their job. Let's look at the various sections of a basic contract.

Generally, the first page of any transactional document begins with a title in all or initial caps, centered, and underlined. The title identifies the type of contract using a generic term, such as "Lease," "Prenuptial Agreement" or "Asset Purchase Agreement." This is followed by an introductory paragraph that identifies the contract more specifically, often including the date of the agreement, and names the parties, often introducing defined terms for them that are then used throughout the balance of the contract.

The preambles or recitals that follow the title and introductory paragraph set the context for the agreement and are useful in later interpretation. They also provide a place to list related transactional documents and other things that may be part of the transaction as a whole but are otherwise not referenced in the particular agreement itself. The recitals generally include the facts that will help a later reader grasp the nature, purpose, and basis for the agreement—like an introduction to a book. Examples of appropriate facts for recitals include: (i) the history, relationship, and goals of the parties, (ii) the nature of the transaction, and (iii) other transactional documents and things associated with the transaction. The recitals are an excellent place in which to cover factual matters that may be important in applying contract law doctrinal rules at a later date such as the central purpose of the contract, a party's lack of alternatives, or the potential damages faced should one party not perform.

Following the recitals is the substance of the contract. If well-drafted, these provisions are clearly presented in the active voice so the party that is required or permitted to do an act or receive a performance can be easily determined. Also, if well drafted, the contract is not ambiguous; otherwise, a court may be faced with the question of whether or not to allow in various types of evidence to determine what the parties meant. Some of these interpretive rules are discussed in Chapters 15 and 18. Well drafted contracts are also free of unintended vagueness.

The substantive terms include statements of the consideration supporting the contract, discussed in Chapter 5. They will also include representations, warranties, covenants, conditions, and other provisions that serve as the workings of the contract, a legal machine governing the parties, their relationships, and their exchanges. These working provisions are discussed in some detail in Chapters 23 and 24.

C. *An Example: The Simple Asset Purchase Agreement*

ASSET PURCHASE AGREEMENT

This ASSET PURCHASE AGREEMENT AND ESCROW INSTRUCTIONS (the "Agreement") is entered into and effective as of January 5, 2007, at Columbus, Ohio, by and between Joseph Carcello Industries, Inc., a Delaware Corporation (the "Seller"), and Galcar Acquisition Subsidiary 3, a Wyoming limited liability company ("Buyer"), on the basis of the following facts and constitutes (i) a contract of purchase and sale between the Parties, and (ii) escrow instructions to Third American Title Company ("Escrow Agent"), the consent of which appears at the end of this agreement. Buyer and Seller are collectively referred to in this document as the "Parties."

RECITALS

A. Seller has determined that it is in the best interests of its shareholders to enter into this Agreement, whereby Seller will sell to Buyer, for the Purchase Price and on the terms and conditions set forth below, all of the Seller's assets (other than the Excluded Assets, as defined in Section 1.2 below).

B. [*Recitals as appropriate. Recitals are a place to provide general background and context for the rest of the contract. They are also a good place to define, or give short names to, other documents and agreements that may be relevant to the overall transaction and the parties' agreements.*]

AGREEMENT

For good and valuable consideration, the receipt and sufficiency of which is hereby acknowledged, the Parties agree that the above Recitals are true and correct to the best of their knowledge and further agree as follows:

ARTICLE 1

SALE AND PURCHASE

1.1 <u>Sale and Purchase of Seller's Assets.</u> Subject to the terms and conditions below, on the Closing Date (as defined in Section 2.2 below), Seller shall sell, convey, transfer and deliver to Buyer, and Buyer shall purchase from Seller, all of the assets of the Seller, other than those assets specifically excluded under Section 1.2 below (collectively, the "Acquired Assets"). It is expressly understood and agreed that Buyer is purchasing the Acquired Assets subject to all encumbrances thereon existing as of the Close of Escrow.

1.2 <u>Excluded Assets.</u> Buyer will not acquire any interest in the following assets of the Seller's ("Excluded Assets"):

(a)   all of the Seller's cash on hand, deposits in bank accounts and cash equivalent securities or other similar items (collectively, the "Cash Assets") as of the Closing Date; and

(b)   tax refunds and insurance policies related to the Acquired Assets.

1.3 <u>Purchase Price: Payment.</u> Seller shall sell and Buyer shall purchase the Acquired Assets for a total purchase price of $40,000,000 (the "Purchase Price").[1]

1.3.1   <u>Deposit.</u> Upon execution of this Agreement, Buyer shall deliver to Seller an initial deposit (the "Deposit") of $2,000,000 in Cash or Cash Substitute to be applied towards the Purchase Price. "Cash Substitute" means

(i)   a certified or cashier's check, with Buyer as drawer or remitter thereof, drawn and paid through a banking institution acceptable to Seller, currently dated, payable to Seller and honored upon presentation for payment, or

(ii)   an amount credited by wire transfer from an account of Buyer into Seller's bank.

The Deposit will be non-refundable to Buyer pursuant to Article 9 below (subject, however, to Sections 2.2 and 3.1 below). Seller shall hold the Deposit in a separate, segregated, interest-bearing account to be distributed or released as provided herein. Until the Close of Escrow or a default by Buyer (as described in Article 9), the Deposit is not property of the Seller.

1.3.2   <u>Refunds of Deposit.</u> Any refund of the Deposit made under this Agreement will be made to and accepted by Buyer as a corporation.

1.3.3   <u>Grant of Security Interest.</u> Buyer hereby grants to Seller a security interest in the Deposit to secure Buyer's contingent obligation to pay Seller liquidated damages, pursuant to Article 9 below, in the event Buyer defaults.[2]

1.3.4   <u>Additional Cash at Closing.</u> The additional sum of $8,000,000 in cash or Cash Substitute ("Additional Cash") will be delivered by Buyer to Seller at or prior to the Close of Escrow (as more particularly provided in Section 4.1 below).

1.3.5   <u>Note.</u> Prior to the Close of Escrow (as more particularly provided in Section 4.1 below), Buyer shall execute and deliver into Escrow a Promissory Note in the principal amount of $30,000,000 in

---

[1]   Consideration is discussed in Chapter 5.

[2]   Liquidated damages are discussed in Chapter 19.

the form of Exhibit A to this Agreement (the "Note") executed by Buyer. Escrow Agent is hereby instructed to, at the Close of Escrow, date the Note as of the Close of Escrow.

ARTICLE 2

ESCROW[3]

2.1 <u>Opening of Escrow.</u> Within five (5) business days of the execution of this Agreement, Buyer and Seller shall open an Escrow account with an escrow agent reasonably satisfactory to both and shall deposit with Escrow Agent fully executed counterparts of this Agreement for use as escrow instructions. The parties agree to execute Escrow Agent's usual form of supplemental escrow instructions for transactions of this type provided, however, that such escrow instructions will be for the purpose of implementing this Agreement and will not have the effect of modifying this Agreement unless they expressly so state and are initialed by Buyer and Seller. "Opening of Escrow" as used herein means the date when Escrow Agent (i) has received a counterpart or counterparts of this Agreement executed by both Buyer and Seller, (ii) has received notification from Seller that Seller has received the Deposit from Buyer, and (iii) has executed the Consent of Escrow following the signature page of this Agreement.

2.2 <u>Close of Escrow.</u> The closing of the sale and transfer of the Acquired Assets ("Close of Escrow") is to take place on or prior to December 1, 2007 (the "Closing Date"). If the closing has not occurred by that date, either party may terminate this Agreement by providing to the other party and to Escrow Agent five (5) days prior written notice thereof, in which case (i) Seller shall return to Buyer the Deposit, minus the amount of Seller's attorneys' fees and any other costs incurred in connection with the transaction contemplated by this agreement (provided, however, that the total amount of such fees and costs shall not exceed, in the aggregate, $300,000,000), and (ii) the Parties shall have no further obligations under this Agreement.

ARTICLE 3

CONDITIONS TO THE PARTIES' OBLIGATIONS

3.1 <u>Conditions to Buyer's Obligation to Purchase.</u> Buyer's obligation to purchase the Acquired Assets is expressly conditioned upon each of the following:[4]

3.1.1 [*List conditions specific to this deal.*]

---

[3] Escrows and their function are discussed in Chapter 21.

[4] Conditions are critical performance ordering, triggering, and excusing provisions. They are discussed in Chapters 21 and 22.

3.1.2 <u>Seller's Deliveries to Escrow Agent.</u> Timely delivery of those documents required to be delivered to Escrow Agent by Seller pursuant to Article 5 below.

3.2 <u>Conditions to Seller's Obligation to Sell.</u> Seller's obligation to sell the Acquired Assets is expressly conditioned upon each of the following:

3.2.1 <u>Performance by Buyer.</u> Timely performance of each obligation and covenant of, and delivery required of, Buyer hereunder.

3.2.2 <u>Buyer's Deliveries to Seller and Escrow Agent.</u> Timely delivery of the items required to be delivered to Seller and/or Escrow Agent by Buyer pursuant to Article 4 below including, but not limited to, the Deposit, the Additional Cash, the Note, and the Letter of Credit, and the Consent.

ARTICLE 4

BUYER'S DELIVERIES

4.1 <u>Balance of Purchase Price.</u> Buyer shall, at or prior to the Close of Escrow, deliver to Seller cash or Cash Equivalent in the amount of the Additional Cash. Buyer will, at or prior to the Close of Escrow, deliver to Escrow Agent written confirmation, countersigned by Seller, that Buyer has made the delivery required by this Section 4.1.

4.2 <u>Note, Letter of Credit and Consent.</u> Buyer shall, at or prior to the Close of Escrow, deliver to Escrow Agent (i) the Note, in the form attached as Exhibit A and executed by Buyer and (ii) the Letter of Credit, in the form attached as Exhibit B.

4.3 <u>Transfer Documents.</u> Buyer shall, at or prior to the Close of Escrow, deliver to Escrow Agent counterparts, executed by Buyer, of those Transfer Documents set forth in Article 5 below which are required to be executed by Buyer.

4.4 <u>Cash—Prorations.</u> Buyer shall, at or prior to the Close of Escrow, deliver to Escrow Agent cash in the amount, if any, required of Buyer under Article 7 entitled "Proration, Fees and Costs."

ARTICLE 5

SELLER'S DELIVERIES TO ESCROW AGENT

5.1 <u>Transfer Documents.</u> Seller shall, at or prior to the Close of Escrow, deposit into Escrow the following instruments of conveyance and transfer ("Transfer Documents") in order to transfer to Buyer Seller's right, title, and interest in and to the Acquired Assets:

5.1.1 <u>Real Property.</u> With respect to each parcel of real property being transferred, a quitclaim deed in the form of Exhibit C to this Agreement ("Quitclaim Deed") executed and acknowledged by Seller;

5.1.2 <u>Notes.</u> With respect to each debt owed to Seller which is evidenced by a note in favor of Seller ("Note"), an Allonge in the form of Exhibit D to this Agreement, executed by Seller;

5.1.3 <u>Deeds of Trust.</u> With respect to each Note which is secured by a deed of trust under which Seller is the beneficiary, either as original beneficiary or via assignment ("Deed of Trust"), an Assignment of Deed of Trust in the form of Exhibit E to this Agreement, executed and acknowledged by Seller;

5.1.4 <u>Vehicles.</u> With respect to each vehicle owned by Seller, a Department of Motor Vehicles "pink slip" executed by Seller and transferring all of Seller's title in such vehicle to Buyer;

5.1.5 <u>Stock.</u> With respect to all stock owned by a Seller, an Assignment Separate from Certificate in the form of Exhibit F to this Agreement, executed and acknowledged by Seller; and

5.1.6 <u>Personal Property.</u> With respect to all personal property of Seller (including, but not limited to accounts receivable), a bill of sale in the form of Exhibit G to this Agreement (the "Bill of Sale") executed in counterpart by Seller, pursuant to which Seller will transfer all of the personal property of Seller, other than the Excluded Assets, otherwise not transferred pursuant to Sections 5.1.1 through 5.1.5 above.

5.2 <u>Availability of Original Documents.</u> Seller makes no representation or warranty as to the availability of original copies of instruments normally associated with ownership of the Acquired Assets. It is hereby agreed that, except to the extent caused by Seller's gross negligence or willful misconduct, any delay in or ineffectiveness of any transfer of assets contemplated by this Agreement which is caused by the unavailability of such documents shall not constitute a default by Seller hereunder.

ARTICLE 6

BUYER'S REPRESENTATIONS[5]

6.1 <u>Condition of Acquired Assets.</u> BUYER IS TAKING THE ACQUIRED ASSETS IN AN "AS-IS, WHERE-IS, WITH-ALL-FAULTS-AND-ENCUMBRANCES" CONDITION EXISTING AS OF THE CLOSE OF ESCROW, BASED UPON BUYER'S OWN FAMILIARITY THEREWITH AND NOT UPON ANY STATEMENTS, ADVICE, OPINIONS OR REPRESENTATIONS WHICH MAY HAVE BEEN MADE BY SELLER OR SELLER'S AGENTS.

---

[5] Representations and disclaimers of representations are discussed in Chapter 10.

ARTICLE 7

PRORATIONS, FEES AND COSTS

7.1 <u>Prorations.</u> All non-delinquent personal and real property taxes, water, gas, electricity and other utilities, local business or other license fees or taxes and other similar periodic charges payable with respect to the Acquired Assets will be prorated between Buyer and Seller as of the Close of Escrow.

7.2 <u>Seller's Closing Costs.</u> Seller shall pay (i) Seller's own attorneys' fees, (ii) one-half of Escrow Agent's escrow fee, and (iii) one-half of all documentary transfer taxes payable in connection with the recordation of Quitclaim Deeds and Escrow Agent's customary charges to buyers and sellers for document drafting, recording and miscellaneous charges.

7.3 <u>Buyer's Closing Costs.</u> Buyer shall pay (i) Buyer's own attorneys' fees, (ii) one-half of Escrow Agent's escrow fee, and (iii) one-half of all documentary transfer taxes payable in connection with the recordation of Quitclaim Deeds and Escrow Agent's customary charges to buyers and sellers for document drafting, recording and miscellaneous charges, (iv) all sales and use taxes payable as a result of the transactions contemplated by this Agreement, and (v) the cost and expense of any title policies desired by Buyer with respect to the Acquired Assets is not a condition to Buyer's obligations under this Agreement, nor shall Buyer's efforts to acquire such policy or policies in any way delay the Close of Escrow.

ARTICLE 8

RECORDATION: DISTRIBUTION OF FUNDS AND DOCUMENTS

8.1 <u>Form of Disbursements.</u> All disbursements by Escrow Agent will be made by checks of the Escrow Agent or by wire transfer to the account of the receiving party, as such party may direct.

8.2 <u>Recorded Documents.</u> Escrow Agent shall cause the County Recorder of Bigfoot County (the "County Recorder") to record the Quitclaim Deeds and any other documents which are herein expressed to be, or by general usage are, recorded ("Recorded Documents"). After recordation, Escrow Agent shall cause the County Recorder to mail Recorded Documents to the grantee, beneficiary, or person (i) acquiring rights under the Recorded Documents, or (ii) for whose benefit the Recorded Documents were acquired.

8.3 <u>Non-Recorded Documents.</u> Escrow Agent shall, at the Close of Escrow, deliver by United States Mail, (or hold for personal pick-up, if requested), each non-recorded document received hereunder by Escrow Agent to the payee or person (i) acquiring rights under the non-recorded document, or (11) for whose benefit the non-recorded document was acquired.

8.4 Cash Disbursements. Escrow Agent shall, at the Close of Escrow, hold for personal pick-up, or will arrange for wire transfer, (i) to Seller, or order, any excess funds delivered to Escrow Agent by Seller, and (ii) to Buyer, or order, any excess funds theretofore to Escrow Agent by Buyer. Upon Escrow Agent's request, Buyer and Seller shall deposit with Escrow Agent all sums necessary to pay their respective shares of the costs of Closing; provided, however, Buyer and Escrow Agent acknowledge that Seller shall not be required to advance any of its own funds to pay its respective share of the costs of Closing; all such costs will be paid solely out of the Deposit.

8.5 Copies of Documents. Escrow agent shall, at the Close of Escrow, deliver to Buyer and to Seller, copies of the Recorded Documents, conformed to show the recording data.

ARTICLE 9

DEFAULT

9.1 Seller's Remedies. If Buyer defaults under this Agreement and fails to complete the purchase of the Acquired Assets herein provided, then Seller will be released from any further obligations under this Agreement and will be entitled to the following:

> BECAUSE IT WOULD BE EXTREMELY IMPRACTICABLE AND DIFFICULT TO DETERMINE THE DAMAGE AND HARM WHICH SELLER WOULD SUFFER IN THE EVENT BUYER DEFAULTS HEREUNDER, AND BECAUSE A REASONABLE ESTIMATE OF THE TOTAL NET DETRIMENT THAT SELLER WOULD SUFFER IN THE EVENT OF BUYER'S DEFAULT AND FAILURE TO DULY COMPLETE THE ACQUISITION HEREUNDER IS THE SUM OF $2,000,000 PLUS ANY INTEREST ACCRUED THEREON, SELLER WILL BE ENTITLED TO RETAIN THE DEPOSIT OF $2,000,000 PLUS ANY INTEREST ACCRUED THEREON, AS LIQUIDATED DAMAGES. THE PAYMENT OF SUCH AMOUNT AS LIQUIDATED DAMAGES IS NOT INTENDED AS A FORFEITURE OR PENALTY, BUT IS INTENDED TO CONSTITUTE LIQUIDATED DAMAGES TO SELLER.

_____	_____
Buyer's Initials	Seller's Initials

Any fees, costs, or attorneys' fees incurred in the enforcement and collection of liquidated damages as herein provided will not be included in the calculation of liquidated damages and shall be recoverable in addition thereto.[6] Seller's remedies for breach are limited to those provided in this paragraph.

9.2 <u>Buyer's Remedies.</u> If the sale contemplated by this Agreement is not completed according to its terms by reason of any material default of Seller, Buyer will have the right to pursue any remedy at law;[7] provided, however, that upon the occurrence of any material default by Seller, Buyer agrees that it will not (i) record a *lis pendens* or seek any provisional remedies including, but not limited to, the appointment of a receiver, any temporary restraining order, any preliminary injunction or any action for claim and delivery with respect to the Acquired Assets or (ii) request the specific performance of this Agreement.

ARTICLE 10

GENERAL PROVISIONS

10.1 <u>Captions.</u> Captions in this Agreement are asserted for convenience of reference only and do not define, describe, or limit the scope or the intent of this Agreement or any of the terms of this Agreement.

10.2 <u>Exhibits.</u> All exhibits referred to in and attached to this Agreement are a part of this Agreement.

10.3 <u>Entire Agreement.</u>[8] This Agreement contains the final, complete and entire agreement between the Parties and supersedes all prior or contemporaneous agreements, understandings, representations, and statements, oral or written, between the Parties with respect to the subject matter of this Agreement and the transactions contemplated by this Agreement.

10.4 <u>Modification.</u> No modification, waiver, amendment, discharge, or change of this Agreement shall be valid unless the same is in writing and signed by the party against which the enforcement of such modification, waiver, amendment, discharge, or change is or may be sought.

10.5 <u>Attorneys' Fees.</u> Should any party employ an attorney for the purpose of enforcing or construing this Agreement, or obtaining any judgment or court order based on this Agreement, in any legal proceeding whatsoever, including insolvency, bankruptcy, arbitration, declaratory relief, or other litigation, the Prevailing Party (herein defined) shall be entitled to receive from the other party or parties thereto, reimbursement for all attorneys' fees and all costs, including but not limited to service of process, filing fees, and the cost of any bonds, whether taxable or not. Such reimbursement shall be included in any judgment or final order issued in

---

[6]   Liquidated damages clauses are discussed in Chapter 19.

[7]   Remedies are discussed in Chapters 16 to 20.

[8]   Integration clauses such as this and the parol evidence rule are discussed in Chapter 14.

that proceeding. The "Prevailing Party" means the party determined to most nearly prevail and not necessarily the one in whose favor a judgment is rendered. As provided in Article 10 herein, Seller may recover its attorneys' fees in addition to liquidated damages.

10.6   Governing Law. This Agreement is governed by the laws of the State of _____ and federal law, as applicable, without regard to the choice of law provisions of those bodies of law.

10.7   Successors and Assigns. All terms of this Agreement shall be binding upon, inure to the benefit of, and be enforceable by the Parties and their respective legal representatives, successors, and assigns.[9]

10.8   Counterparts. This Agreement may be executed in any number of counterparts, each of which so executed shall be deemed an original, and all of which shall together constitute but one agreement.

10.9   Further Assurances. The Parties shall cooperate with each other and execute any documents reasonably necessary to carry out the intent and purpose of this Agreement.

10.10 Survival of Warranties and Obligations. All warranties and representations contained in this Agreement, and all covenants and duties that are to be performed at a time or times after the Close of Escrow, survive the Close of Escrow.

10.11 Construction. Each party and its counsel have reviewed and revised this Agreement. Any rule of construction to the effect that ambiguities are to be resolved against the drafting party will not apply in the interpretation of this Agreement or any amendments or exhibits hereto.

IN WITNESS WHEREOF, this Agreement has been executed as of the date set forth above.

SELLER: [Name]   BUYER: [Company Name]
Signed:_____   By:_____
Typed:_____   Name:_____
                             Title:_____

Note on the Fifth Edition

The fifth edition of this text features a number of changes from the fourth edition. The principle ones are listed below.

1.   For the majority of cases, we have included a note that translates currency values from the nominal value at the date of the case to 2019 dollar values using a combination of the

---

[9]   Assignment and delegation are discussed in Chapter 29.

Consumer Price Index and the Gross National Product Deflator. These conversions are approximate at best, but much appreciated by students.

2. The "Notes and Questions" have been revised and updated throughout the book.

3. In Chapter 4, *Cook's Pest Control, Inc. v. Rebar* and its accompanying material has been omitted.

4. In Chapter 5, *Frishman v. Canadian Imperial Bank of Commerce* has been omitted for the sake of brevity. Its substance is covered in the notes and questions following Karl N. Llewellyn, A Lecture on Appellate Advocacy.

5. In Chapter 15, a detailed synopsis of the Supreme Court of Tennessee's description of Textual versus Contextual approaches to contract interpretation was added.

6. In Chapter 16, *General Motors Corp. v. Brewer* and its accompanying material has been omitted.

7. In Chapter 17, *Eastern Air Lines, Inc. v. McDonnell Douglas Corp.* and *Poppenheimer v. Bluff City Motor Homes* and their accompanying materials have been omitted.

8. In Chapter 22, *Lumley v. Wagner* has been edited down for the sake of brevity and *Van Wagner Advertising v. S & M Enterprises* and its accompanying material has been omitted.

9. In Chapter 24, *K & G Construction Co. v. Harris* and a short note following *Carter v. Sherburne Corp.* have been omitted.

10. In Chapter 25, *Hemmert Agric. Aviation, Inc. v. Mid-Continent Aircraft Corp.* and *Transcontinental Refrigeration Co. v. Figgins* has been omitted for the sake of brevity. The substance of the latter case has been incorporated into Problem 25-7.

11. In Chapter 26, *Drake v. Wickwire* and its accompanying material has been omitted.

12. In Chapter 28, *Don King Productions v. Douglas* and *Empire Gas Corp. v. American Bakeries Co.* have been omitted.

13. In Chapter 29, *Transportation & Transit Assocs., Inc. v. Morrison Knudsen Corp.*, *Ilkhchooyi v. Best*, *Beattie v. State of Oklahoma, ex rel. Grand River Dam Authority*, and *BIS Computer Solutions, Inc. v. Richmond, Virginia* and their accompanying materials have been omitted.

14. In Chapter 29, *Dolan v. Altice USA, Inc.* has been included. *Dolan* is a new case that deals with a variety of issues covered

in this book, specifically ambiguity, third-party beneficiaries, contract drafting, contract interpretation, and the parol evidence rule.

A Final Introductory Note

This is a casebook designed for a first-year, law-school contract law course that includes material often found in an upper division U.C.C. Sales course, but its goals are not just to teach doctrinal contract law. In fact, if the Contracts course were meant just to teach the "black letter law" of contract, this book would be unnecessary. A commercial outline from any publisher or, better yet, the Restatement (Second) of Contracts and Article 2 of the U.C.C. would suffice.

The rules are only the first step in the dance that is contract law. It is their application to facts (or the facts application to the law) that have been preserved and developed by lawyers that is the real meat of the matter. In addition to the "black letter law," students should focus on developing critical case analysis skills, as well as the use of multi-element and multi-factor standards to state or apply a legal rule. These skills lie at the heart of litigation *and* transactional problem solving in the law of contracts and elsewhere.

After mastering the basic rules, think about how they can be used in a transactional document. Lawyers should seek to draft into or around every law that may affect the transaction. The point is to prepare a document that defines the parties' relationship and will be a useful tool in managing that relationship and in any litigation should that relationship break down. Know the law and how it operates and then deploy that knowledge every step of the way from the parties' first meeting to their last day in court after years of litigation, should it come to that. Pay attention to these bedrock principles as you work through the text and its problems and exercises.

The authors welcome your comments and feedback (gkuney@utk.edu) and more information about them and their school can be found through The University of Tennessee College of Law's website: http://www.law.utk.edu/. Additional materials, including sets of on-line, interactive problems regarding contract damages can be found at the publication page of the website of The Clayton Center for Entrepreneurial Law: http://law.utk.edu/centers/clayton/.

We thank, in particular, David Cantrell (UT Class of 2021) for his detail-oriented assistance in producing this fifth edition. Many others contributed, but his work was integral to the finalization of this casebook.

ABOUT THE AUTHORS

Prior to becoming the Director of The Clayton Center for Entrepreneurial Law at The University of Tennessee College of Law in 2000, George Kuney was a partner in California's Allen Matkins Leck Gamble & Mallory LLP where he concentrated his practice on business law, insolvency, and reorganization matters. Prior to that he received his legal training from the Morrison & Foerster and Howard, Rice (now Arnold & Porter) firms in his home town of San Francisco. In addition to his casebook, Professor Kuney is the author of *California Law of Contracts* (University of California CEB Treatise with Donna C. Looper, *Legal Drafting in a Nutshell* (West, with Donna C. Looper), *Legal Drafting: Processes, Techniques, and Exercises* (West, with Donna C. Looper), *Entrepreneurial Law* (West, with Brian K. Krumm), *A Transactional Matter* (West, with Brian K. Krumm and Donna C. Looper), *Experiencing Remedies* (West), *Bankruptcy in Practice, 4th Ed.* (ABI, with Michael Bernstein), *A Civil Matter* (West, with Donna C. Looper), *The Entrepreneurial Law Clinic Handbook* (West, with Brian K. Krumm), *Judgment Collection in Tennessee* (Center for Entrepreneurial Law, with Wendy Patrick), *Business Reorganizations 3d ed.* (Lexis, with Michael Gerber), *Bamboozled? Bowers v. Baystate and Its Aftermath* (West), *The Elements of Contract Drafting* (West 4th ed.), *Mastering Legal Analysis and Drafting* (Carolina Academic Press, with Donna C. Looper), *Mastering Appellate Advocacy and Process* (Carolina Academic Press, with Donna C. Looper), and a number of articles dealing with contracts, business acquisitions, corporate governance, and reorganization matters. He holds an M.B.A. from the University of San Diego, a J.D. from the University of California's Hastings College of the Law, and a B.A. from the University of California at Santa Cruz.

Robert Lloyd came to The University of Tennessee College of Law in 1983 after a career in commercial law with the Los Angeles firm of Sheppard, Mullin, Richter, & Hampton. He helped to develop the college's Concentration in Business Transactions and served as the first Director of the college's Center for Entrepreneurial Law. Professor Lloyd has had numerous articles on commercial lending transactions published. He holds a J.D. from the University of Michigan and a B.S.E. from Princeton University.

The Clayton Center for Entrepreneurial Law at The University of Tennessee College of Law seeks to improve the training of business lawyers in both transactional and litigation practices through the College of Law curriculum, which combines doctrine and applied skills training, faculty and student scholarship, and presentations for the bar, faculty, and community, both regionally and nationwide. The Center is named for James L. Clayton, a successful Tennessee businessman whose generosity has made the Center possible. Mr. Clayton is a graduate of the College of Law and the founder of Clayton Homes, a national, vertically integrated modular and manufactured housing company that is now a wholly owned subsidiary of Berkshire Hathway, Inc., as well as other successful business ventures. More information on the Center and its programs and activities can be found at: http://law.utk.edu/centers/clayton/.

SUMMARY OF CONTENTS

TABLE OF CONTENTS

TABLE OF CASES

The principal cases are in bold type.

CONTRACTS: TRANSACTIONS AND LITIGATION

Fifth Edition

CHAPTER 1

THE OBJECTIVE THEORY OF CONTRACTS—STANDARDS, ELEMENTS, AND FACTORS

■ ■ ■

For present purposes, a *contract* is "a promise that the law will enforce." The law will not enforce all promises. For instance, the law generally will not enforce promises that are not "supported by consideration." A promise is "supported by consideration" when the promise is made in consideration of (due to) a return promise or performance, i.e., the promisor (the person making the promise) requires something in return for the promise. Consideration and exceptions to these general rules are covered in later chapters. This basic statement is a good working rule for present purposes.

For example, if A says "I promise to give you my car," that's *not* a promise the law will enforce. But if A says "I'll sell you my car for $1,000" (which of course means "I'll give you my car if you'll give me $1,000"), that *is* a promise the law will enforce if the offer is accepted. The requirement for consideration is sometimes referred to as the *bargain requirement*. It is said that the law does not enforce gratuitous promises; it only enforces bargains. Like most broad statements of the law, this statement, while generally true, is subject to exceptions.

Before looking more deeply at consideration in Chapter 5, however, let us turn to another requirement—that, for there to be a contract, there must be an offer and an acceptance. This means that in order to have a contract, one person must offer to enter into a contract and the other must accept that offer. If you say, "I'll sell you my car for $1,000," that's *not* a contract. It's an *offer*. It only becomes a contract when someone responds by saying "Yes, I accept" or "It's a deal" or otherwise indicates a willingness to be bound to the deal.

Most of the time, it is pretty easy to tell when A has made an offer and B has accepted it. But those are not the situations in which people consult lawyers. People consult lawyers when it is not clear whether a particular statement was an offer, or when it is not clear whether a particular response to that statement was an acceptance, or when they want a proposal prepared in such a way that it either is or is not an offer that is capable of immediate acceptance. (Sometimes it is useful to sound out the

1

opposing party with something less than an offer to gauge whether or not one is perhaps setting the price too low or otherwise offering needlessly favorable terms.) Those are the situations this chapter explores.

A group of legal scholars has come up with the following definition of an offer:

> An offer is the manifestation of willingness to enter into a bargain, so made as to justify another person in understanding that his assent to that bargain is invited and will conclude it.

R2d § 24. Broken down, or "exploded" this definition states that an offer has the following mandatory features, which are called "elements:"

> (1) It is "a manifestation" (written, verbal, conduct, by internet posting, etc.);
>
> (2) "of willingness to enter into a bargain" (again, more on bargains later, but note that the willingness applies to a bargain, not a gift);
>
> (3) "so made as to justify another" (note the standard: justifying *another* person; the focus is not on what the offeror intends in her secret heart of hearts, it is what *others are justified in concluding* from the "manifestation of willingness");
>
> (4) "in understanding that"
>
>> (a) "his assent to that bargain is invited" (i.e., is asked for, is desired); and
>>
>> (b) "will conclude it" (i.e. if the offeree responds with a "yes, I accept" there will be a deal with nothing, or at least nothing material, to be worked out).

In working with statutes, like the U.C.C. or CISG, or statements of applicable legal principles, like case law, the R2d, or UNIDROIT, it is extremely useful to perform a two step analysis of the standard being stated:

> *First,* identify whether the standard is made up of a series of required *elements* that all must be present for the standard to be met or a list, often a non-exclusive list, of non-required *factors* to be considered in determining whether the standard has been met. Elements (required) are usually joined with the express or implied conjunction "and," but factors may also be joined with "and." Elements, however, are never joined by the conjunction "or," which indicates that items in a list are alternatives, because, by their nature, elements are all required. Sometimes a standard contains elements that are themselves constituted of factors, and vice versa.

Second, after determining whether the standard consists of elements, factors, or both, mechanically but thoughtfully apply the standard, element-by-element, or factor-by-factor, to the facts. In other words, break down and apply the standard step-by-step, consider alternative interpretations of the facts, and do not jump to conclusions.

Many people who have experienced success in the "real world" have done so because of their ability to instinctively jump to the right conclusion. That skill is not rewarded in law school, although it is in some areas of law practice. Put it aside for now and proceed methodically in the process of applying the standard element-by-element or factor-by-factor to the individual facts at issue. This is the essence of "thinking like a lawyer." The balance of this casebook gives you a chance to do just that.

Introductory Exercise

Applying the standard of R2d § 24, then, determine which of the following constitutes an offer:

(a) I'll sell you my car for $1,000.

(b) I'm thinking about selling my car for $1,000.

(c) I'm going to sell my car for $1,000.

(d) Would you give me $1,000 for my car?

The cases that follow introduce what is called "the objective theory of contracts." This is a way of saying that we look at what the person actually said or did and how a reasonable person would interpret those statements or actions. The term "objective" here is somewhat deceptive and can be confusing. It does not mean an objective measuring device like a ruler or a cup measure—it is really more of a "collective subjective" measurement, based on the decision maker's or makers' conception of a reasonable person. It is not completely subjective—which would represent what the decision maker individually thought—but it is not absolutely objective either. Perhaps this is part of what Justice Sotomayor was alluding to in her 2001 speech at UC Berkeley when she said "I would hope that a wise Latina woman with the richness of her experiences would more often than not reach a better conclusion than a white male who hasn't lived that life."

To put the matter of the objective theory of contract concretely in the context we have been using, we don't look at whether a person intended her statement to be an offer, but rather *we look at whether a reasonable person to whom the statement was addressed would believe it to be an offer*. Think of the objective theory of contracts as the view through a high definition webcam with audio capture floating invisibly above and around the parties. What would a reasonable person viewing the resulting video think had transpired? That is the "objective" theory of contracts—it is one of the first legal fictions you encounter as a law student.

———

LUCY V. ZEHMER
Supreme Court of Virginia
196 Va. 493, 84 S.E.2d 516 (1954)

BUCHANAN, J., delivered the opinion of the court.

[1] This suit was instituted by W. O. Lucy and J. C. Lucy, complainants, against A. H. Zehmer and Ida S. Zehmer, his wife, defendants, to have specific performance of a contract by which it was alleged the Zehmers had sold to W. O. Lucy a tract of land owned by A. H. Zehmer in Dinwiddie county containing 471.6 acres, more or less, known as the Ferguson farm, for $50,000. J. C. Lucy, the other complainant, is a brother of W. O. Lucy, to whom W. O. Lucy transferred a half interest in his alleged purchase.[1]

[2] The instrument sought to be enforced was written by A. H. Zehmer on December 20, 1952, in these words: "We hereby agree to sell to W. O. Lucy the Ferguson Farm complete for $50,000.00, title satisfactory to buyer," and signed by the defendants, A. H. Zehmer and Ida S. Zehmer.

[3] The answer of A. H. Zehmer admitted that at the time mentioned W. O. Lucy offered him $50,000 cash for the farm, but that he, Zehmer, considered that the offer was made in jest; that so thinking, and both he and Lucy having had several drinks, he wrote out "the memorandum" quoted above and induced his wife to sign it; that he did not deliver the memorandum to Lucy, but that Lucy picked it up, read it, put it in his pocket, attempted to offer Zehmer $5 to bind the bargain, which Zehmer refused to accept, and realizing for the first time that Lucy was serious, Zehmer assured him that he had no intention of selling the farm and that the whole matter was a joke. Lucy left the premises insisting that he had purchased the farm.

[4] Depositions were taken and the decree appealed from was entered holding that the complainants had failed to establish their right to specific performance, and dismissing their bill. The assignment of error is to this action of the court.

[5] W. O. Lucy, a lumberman and farmer, thus testified in substance: He had known Zehmer for fifteen or twenty years and had been familiar with the Ferguson farm for ten years. Seven or eight years ago he had

---

[1] [In asking for *specific performance*, the plaintiffs (or "complainants") are asking the court to order the other party to perform its obligations under the contract. This is not the usual remedy in a contracts case. The usual remedy is an award of money. In Chapter 22, you will learn when a party is entitled to have the court order specific performance.—Eds.]

offered Zehmer $20,000 for the farm which Zehmer had accepted, but the agreement was verbal and Zehmer backed out. On the night of December 20, 1952, around eight o'clock, he took an employee to McKenney, where Zehmer lived and operated a restaurant, filling station and motor court. While there he decided to see Zehmer and again try to buy the Ferguson farm. He entered the restaurant and talked to Mrs. Zehmer until Zehmer came in. He asked Zehmer if he had sold the Ferguson farm. Zehmer replied that he had not. Lucy said, "I bet you wouldn't take $50,000.00 for that place."[2] Zehmer replied, "Yes, I would too; you wouldn't give fifty." Lucy said he would and told Zehmer to write up an agreement to that effect. Zehmer took a restaurant check and wrote on the back of it, "I do hereby agree to sell to W. O. Lucy the Ferguson Farm for $50,000 complete." Lucy told him he had better change it to "We" because Mrs. Zehmer would have to sign it too. Zehmer then tore up what he had written, wrote the agreement quoted above and asked Mrs. Zehmer, who was at the other end of the counter ten or twelve feet away, to sign it. Mrs. Zehmer said she would for $50,000 and signed it. Zehmer brought it back and gave it to Lucy, who offered him $5 which Zehmer refused, saying, "You don't need to give me any money, you got the agreement there signed by both of us."

[6]   The discussion leading to the signing of the agreement, said Lucy, lasted thirty or forty minutes, during which Zehmer seemed to doubt that Lucy could raise $50,000. Lucy suggested the provision for having the title examined and Zehmer made the suggestion that he would sell it "complete, everything there," and stated that all he had on the farm was three heifers.

[7]   Lucy took a partly filled bottle of whiskey into the restaurant with him for the purpose of giving Zehmer a drink if he wanted it. Zehmer did, and he and Lucy had one or two drinks together. Lucy said that while he felt the drinks he took he was not intoxicated, and from the way Zehmer handled the transaction he did not think he was either.

[8]   December 20 was on Saturday. Next day Lucy telephoned to J. C. Lucy and arranged with the latter to take a half interest in the purchase and pay half of the consideration. On Monday he engaged an attorney to

---

[2]   [$50,000 in 1952 dollars is roughly the equivalent of $475,000 in 2019 dollars using the Consumer Price Index and the Gross National Product Deflator. The gross national product deflator (the "GNP deflator") is an economic metric that accounts for the effects of inflation in the current year's gross national product by converting its output to a level relative to a base period. The GNP Deflator is calculated with the following formula:

$$\text{GNP Deflator} \quad = \quad \frac{\text{Nominal GNP}}{\text{Real GNP}} \quad \times 100$$

The GNP deflator provides an alternative to the consumer price index (CPI). The CPI is based upon the price of a basket of goods and services while the GNP Deflator incorporates all of the final goods produced by an economy. This allows the GNP Deflator to more accurately capture the effects of inflation since it's not limited to a smaller subset of goods. In this text, we have calculated relative values using both and provide approximate values in 2019 dollars in many of the cases. You can do the same for other values by using the calculator found at http://www.measuringworth.com/uscompare/.—Eds.]

examine the title. The attorney reported favorably on December 31 and on January 2 Lucy wrote Zehmer stating that the title was satisfactory, that he was ready to pay the purchase price in cash and asking when Zehmer would be ready to close the deal. Zehmer replied by letter, mailed on January 13, asserting that he had never agreed or intended to sell.

[9] Mr. and Mrs. Zehmer were called by the complainants as adverse witnesses. Zehmer testified in substance as follows:

[10] He bought this farm more than ten years ago for $11,000. He had twenty-five offers, more or less, to buy it, including several from Lucy, who had never offered any specific sum of money. He had given them all the same answer, that he was not interested in selling it. On this Saturday night before Christmas it looked like everybody and his brother came by there to have a drink. He took a good many drinks during the afternoon and had a pint of his own. When he entered the restaurant around eight-thirty Lucy was there and he could see that he was "pretty high." He said to Lucy, "Boy, you got some good liquor, drinking, ain't you?" Lucy then offered him a drink. "I was already high as a Georgia pine, and didn't have any more better sense than to pour another great big slug out and gulp it down, and he took one too."

[11] After they had talked a while Lucy asked whether he still had the Ferguson farm. He replied that he had not sold it and Lucy said, "I bet you wouldn't take $50,000.00 for it." Zehmer asked him if he would give $50,000 and Lucy said yes. Zehmer replied, "You haven't got $50,000 in cash." Lucy said he did and Zehmer replied that he did not believe it. They argued "pro and con for a long time," mainly about "whether he had $50,000 in cash that he could put up right then and buy that farm."

[12] Finally, said Zehmer, Lucy told him if he didn't believe he had $50,000, "you sign that piece of paper here and say you will take $50,000.00 for the farm." He, Zehmer, "just grabbed the back off of a guest check there" and wrote on the back of it. At that point in his testimony Zehmer asked to see what he had written to "see if I recognize my own handwriting." He examined the paper and exclaimed, "Great balls of fire, I got 'Firgerson' for Ferguson. I have got satisfactory spelled wrong. I don't recognize that writing if I would see it, wouldn't know it was mine."

[13] After Zehmer had, as he described it, "scribbled this thing off," Lucy said, "Get your wife to sign it." Zehmer walked over to where she was and she at first refused to sign but did so after he told her that he "was just needling him [Lucy], and didn't mean a thing in the world, that I was not selling the farm." Zehmer then "took it back over there . . . and I was still looking at the dern thing. I had the drink right there by my hand, and I reached over to get a drink," and he said, "Let me see it." He reached and picked it up, and when I looked back again he had it in his pocket and he dropped a five dollar bill over there, and he said, "Here is five dollars

payment on it." . . . I said, "Hell no, that is beer and liquor talking. I am not going to sell you the farm. I have told you that too many times before."

[14] Mrs. Zehmer testified that when Lucy came into the restaurant he looked as if he had had a drink. When Zehmer came in he took a drink out of a bottle that Lucy handed him. She went back to help the waitress who was getting things ready for next day. Lucy and Zehmer were talking but she did not pay too much attention to what they were saying. She heard Lucy ask Zehmer if he had sold the Ferguson farm, and Zehmer replied that he had not and did not want to sell it. Lucy said, "I bet you wouldn't take $50,000 cash for that farm," and Zehmer replied, "You haven't got $50,000 cash." Lucy said, "I can get it." Zehmer said he might form a company and get it, "but you haven't got $50,000.00 cash to pay me tonight." Lucy asked him if he would put it in writing that he would sell him this farm. Zehmer then wrote on the back of a pad, "I agree to sell the Ferguson Place to W. O. Lucy for $50,000.00 cash." Lucy said, "All right, get your wife to sign it." Zehmer came back to where she was standing and said, "You want to put your name to this?" She said "No," but he said in an undertone, "It is nothing but a joke," and she signed it.

[15] She said that only one paper was written and it said: "I hereby agree to sell," but the "I" had been changed to "We". However, she said she read what she signed and was then asked, "When you read 'We hereby agree to sell to W. O. Lucy,' what did you interpret that to mean, that particular phrase?" She said she thought that was a cash sale that night; but she also said that when she read that part about "title satisfactory to buyer" she understood that if the title was good Lucy would pay $50,000 but if the title was bad he would have a right to reject it, and that was her understanding at the time she signed her name.

[16] On examination by her own counsel she said that her husband laid this piece of paper down after it was signed; that Lucy said to let him see it, took it, folded it and put it in his wallet, then said to Zehmer, "Let me give you $5.00," but Zehmer said, "No, this is liquor talking. I don't want to sell the farm, I have told you that I want my son to have it. This is all a joke." Lucy then said at least twice, "Zehmer, you have sold your farm," wheeled around and started for the door. He paused at the door and said, "I will bring you $50,000.00 tomorrow. . . . No, tomorrow is Sunday. I will bring it to you Monday." She said you could tell definitely that he was drinking and she said to her husband, "You should have taken him home," but he said, "Well, I am just about as bad off as he is."

[17] The waitress referred to by Mrs. Zehmer testified that when Lucy first came in "he was mouthy." When Zehmer came in they were laughing and joking and she thought they took a drink or two. She was sweeping and cleaning up for next day. She said she heard Lucy tell Zehmer, "I will give you so much for the farm," and Zehmer said, "You haven't got that

much." Lucy answered, "Oh, yes, I will give you that much." Then "they jotted down something on paper . . . and Mr. Lucy reached over and took it, said let me see it." He looked at it, put it in his pocket and in about a minute he left. She was asked whether she saw Lucy offer Zehmer any money and replied, "He had five dollars laying up there, they didn't take it." She said Zehmer told Lucy he didn't want his money "because he didn't have enough money to pay for his property, and wasn't going to sell his farm." Both of them appeared to be drinking right much, she said.

[18] She repeated on cross-examination that she was busy and paying no attention to what was going on. She was some distance away and did not see either of them sign the paper. She was asked whether she saw Zehmer put the agreement down on the table in front of Lucy, and her answer was this: "Time he got through writing whatever it was on the paper, Mr. Lucy reached over and said, 'Let's see it.' He took it and put it in his pocket," before showing it to Mrs. Zehmer. Her version was that Lucy kept raising his offer until it got to $50,000.

[19] The defendants insist that the evidence was ample to support their contention that the writing sought to be enforced was prepared as a bluff or dare to force Lucy to admit that he did not have $50,000; that the whole matter was a joke; that the writing was not delivered to Lucy and no binding contract was ever made between the parties.

[20] It is an unusual, if not bizarre, defense. When made to the writing admittedly prepared by one of the defendants and signed by both, clear evidence is required to sustain it.

[21] In his testimony Zehmer claimed that he "was high as a Georgia pine," and that the transaction "was just a bunch of two doggoned drunks bluffing to see who could talk the biggest and say the most." That claim is inconsistent with his attempt to testify in great detail as to what was said and what was done. It is contradicted by other evidence as to the condition of both parties, and rendered of no weight by the testimony of his wife that when Lucy left the restaurant she suggested that Zehmer drive him home. The record is convincing that Zehmer was not intoxicated to the extent of being unable to comprehend the nature and consequences of the instrument he executed, and hence that instrument is not to be invalidated on that ground. 17 C.J.S., Contracts, § 133 b., p. 483; *Taliaferro v. Emery*, 124 Va. 674, 98 S.E. 627. It was in fact conceded by defendants' counsel in oral argument that under the evidence Zehmer was not too drunk to make a valid contract.

[22] The evidence is convincing also that Zehmer wrote two agreements, the first one beginning "I hereby agree to sell." Zehmer first said he could not remember about that, then that "I don't think I wrote but one out." Mrs. Zehmer said that what he wrote was "I hereby agree," but that the "I" was changed to "We" after that night. The agreement that was

written and signed is in the record and indicates no such change. Neither are the mistakes in spelling that Zehmer sought to point out readily apparent.

[23] The appearance of the contract, the fact that it was under discussion for forty minutes or more before it was signed; Lucy's objection to the first draft because it was written in the singular, and he wanted Mrs. Zehmer to sign it also; the rewriting to meet that objection and the signing by Mrs. Zehmer; the discussion of what was to be included in the sale, the provision for the examination of the title, the completeness of the instrument that was executed, the taking possession of it by Lucy with no request or suggestion by either of the defendants that he give it back, are facts which furnish persuasive evidence that the execution of the contract was a serious business transaction rather than a casual, jesting matter as defendants now contend.

[24] On Sunday, the day after the instrument was signed on Saturday night, there was a social gathering in a home in the town of McKenney at which there were general comments that the sale had been made. Mrs. Zehmer testified that on that occasion as she passed by a group of people, including Lucy, who were talking about the transaction, $50,000 was mentioned, whereupon she stepped up and said, "Well, with the high-price whiskey you were drinking last night you should have paid more. That was cheap." Lucy testified that at that time Zehmer told him that he did not want to "stick" him or hold him to the agreement because he, Lucy, was too tight and didn't know what he was doing, to which Lucy replied that he was not too tight; that he had been stuck before and was going through with it. Zehmer's version was that he said to Lucy: "I am not trying to claim it wasn't a deal on account of the fact the price was too low. If I had wanted to sell $50,000.00 would be a good price, in fact I think you would get stuck at $50,000.00." A disinterested witness testified that what Zehmer said to Lucy was that "he was going to let him up off the deal, because he thought he was too tight, didn't know what he was doing." Lucy said something to the effect that "I have been stuck before and I will go through with it."

[25] If it be assumed, contrary to what we think the evidence shows, that Zehmer was jesting about selling his farm to Lucy and that the transaction was intended by him to be a joke, nevertheless the evidence shows that Lucy did not so understand it but considered it to be a serious business transaction and the contract to be binding on the Zehmers as well as on himself. The very next day he arranged with his brother to put up half the money and take a half interest in the land. The day after that he employed an attorney to examine the title. The next night, Tuesday, he was back at Zehmer's place and there Zehmer told him for the first time, Lucy said, that he wasn't going to sell and he told Zehmer, "You know you sold that place fair and square." After receiving the report from his attorney

that the title was good he wrote to Zehmer that he was ready to close the deal.

[26] Not only did Lucy actually believe, but the evidence shows he was warranted in believing, that the contract represented a serious business transaction and a good faith sale and purchase of the farm.

[27] In the field of contracts, as generally elsewhere, "We must look to the outward expression of a person as manifesting his intention rather than to his secret and unexpressed intention. 'The law imputes to a person an intention corresponding to the reasonable meaning of his words and acts.'" *First Nat. Bank v. Roanoke Oil Co.*, 169 Va. 99, 114, 192 S.E. 764, 770 (1937).

[28] At no time prior to the execution of the contract had Zehmer indicated to Lucy by word or act that he was not in earnest about selling the farm. They had argued about it and discussed its terms, as Zehmer admitted, for a long time. Lucy testified that if there was any jesting it was about paying $50,000 that night. The contract and the evidence show that he was not expected to pay the money that night. Zehmer said that after the writing was signed he laid it down on the counter in front of Lucy. Lucy said Zehmer handed it to him. In any event there had been what appeared to be a good faith offer and a good faith acceptance, followed by the execution and apparent delivery of a written contract. Both said that Lucy put the writing in his pocket and then offered Zehmer $5 to seal the bargain. Not until then, even under the defendants' evidence, was anything said or done to indicate that the matter was a joke. Both of the Zehmers testified that when Zehmer asked his wife to sign he whispered that it was a joke so Lucy wouldn't hear and that it was not intended that he should hear.

[29] The mental assent of the parties is not requisite for the formation of a contract. If the words or other acts of one of the parties have but one reasonable meaning, his undisclosed intention is immaterial except when an unreasonable meaning which he attaches to his manifestations is known to the other party.

[30] " . . . The law, therefore, judges of an agreement between two persons exclusively from those expressions of their intentions which are communicated between them . . ." Clark on Contracts, 4 ed., § 3, p. 4.

[31] An agreement or mutual assent is of course essential to a valid contract but the law imputes to a person an intention corresponding to the reasonable meaning of his words and acts. If his words and acts, judged by a reasonable standard, manifest an intention to agree, it is immaterial what may be the real but unexpressed state of his mind.

[32] So a person cannot set up that he was merely jesting when his conduct and words would warrant a reasonable person in believing that he intended a real agreement.

[33] Whether the writing signed by the defendants and now sought to be enforced by the complainants was the result of a serious offer by Lucy and a serious acceptance by the defendants, or was a serious offer by Lucy and an acceptance in secret jest by the defendants, in either event it constituted a binding contract of sale between the parties.

[34] The complainants are entitled to have specific performance of the contracts sued on. The decree appealed from is therefore reversed and the cause is remanded for the entry of a proper decree requiring the defendants to perform the contract in accordance with the prayer of the bill.

NOTES AND QUESTIONS

1. What facts and circumstances led the court to conclude that Lucy and Zehmer had a contract? *actions*

2. What facts and circumstances could be used to argue they did not have a contract? *intentions*

3. At what point in the discussion were Lucy and Zehmer bound to a contract? *Signature + handed back to Lucy*

4. Is what Lucy and Zehmer said and did on Sunday and Monday relevant to the question of whether or not they had formed a contract on Saturday night? *Yes?*

5. Learned Hand, a judge with one of the greatest reputations of all time in the United States, perhaps in part due to the name given to him by his parents, said this:

> A contract has, strictly speaking, nothing to do with the personal, or individual, intent of the parties. A contract is an obligation attached by the mere force of law to certain acts of the parties, usually words, which ordinarily accompany and represent a known intent. If, however, it were proved by twenty bishops that either party, when he used the words, intended something other than the usual meaning which the law imposes upon them, he would still be held. . . .

Hotchkiss v. National City Bank of New York, 200 F. 287, 293 (S.D.N.Y. 1911). The Supreme Court of Oregon once wrote:

> [T]he staunchest "objectivist" would not let a jury hold two parties to an apparently manifested agreement if neither thought the other meant to assent.

Kabil Developments Corp. v. Mignot, 279 Or. 151, 566 P.2d 505 (1977).

If the statement from the *Kabil* case is correct (which it is), is Learned Hand's often-quoted statement from the *Hotchkiss* case really a correct statement of the law? Or is it one of those things you may expect to see all the time in judicial opinions and elsewhere—a generalization that is correct in the context of the case in which it is made but not completely right as a universal statement of the law?

———

EMBRY V. HARGADINE, MCKITTRICK DRY GOODS CO.

Court of Appeals of Missouri
127 Mo. App. 383, 105 S.W. 777 (1907)

GOODE, J.

[1]   The appellant was an employee of the respondent company under a written contract to expire December 15, 1903, at a salary of $2,000 per annum.[3] His duties were to attend to the sample department of respondent, of which he was given complete charge. It was his business to select samples for the traveling salesmen of the company, which is a wholesale dry goods concern, to use in selling goods to retail merchants. Appellant contends that on December 23, 1903, he was reengaged by respondent, through its president, Thomas H. McKittrick, for another year at the same compensation and for the same duties stipulated in his previous written contract. On March 1, 1904, he was discharged, having been notified in February that, on account of the necessity of retrenching expenses, his services and that of some other employees would no longer be required. The respondent company contends that its president never re-employed appellant after the termination of his written contract, and hence that it had a right to discharge him when it chose. The point with which we are concerned requires an epitome of the testimony of appellant and the counter testimony of McKittrick, the president of the company, in reference to the alleged reemployment. Appellant testified: That several times prior to the termination of his written contract on December 15, 1903, he had endeavored to get an understanding with McKittrick for another year, but had been put off from time to time. That on December 23d, eight days after the expiration of said contract, he called on McKittrick, in the latter's office, and said to him that as appellant's written employment had lapsed eight days before, and as there were only a few days between then and the 1st of January in which to seek employment with other firms, if respondent wished to retain his services longer he must have a contract for another year, or he would quit respondent's service then and there. That he had been put off twice before and wanted an understanding or contract at once so that he could go ahead without worry. That McKittrick asked him how

---

³   [$2,000 in 1907 dollars is roughly the equivalent of $55,000 in 2019 dollars using the CPI and the GNP Deflator.—Eds.]

he was getting along in his department, and appellant said he was very busy, as they were in the height of the season getting men out—had about 110 salesmen on the line and others in preparation. That McKittrick then said: "Go ahead, you're all right. Get your men out, and don't let that worry you." That appellant took McKittrick at his word and worked until February 15th without any question in his mind. It was on February 15th that he was notified his services would be discontinued on March 1st. McKittrick denied this conversation as related by appellant, and said that, when accosted by the latter on December 23d, he (McKittrick) was working on his books in order to get out a report for a stockholders' meeting, and, when appellant said if he did not get a contract he would leave, that he (McKittrick) said: "Mr. Embry, I am just getting ready for the stockholders' meeting tomorrow. I have no time to take it up now. I have told you before I would not take it up until I had these matters out of the way. You will have to see me at a later time. I said: Go back upstairs and get your men out on the road. I may have asked him one or two other questions relative to the department, I don't remember. The whole conversation did not take more than a minute."

[2] Embry also swore that, when he was notified he would be discharged, he complained to McKittrick about it, as being a violation of their contract, and McKittrick said it was due to the action of the board of directors, and not to any personal action of his, and that others would suffer by what the board had done as well as Embry. Appellant requested an instruction to the jury setting out, in substance, the conversation between him and McKittrick according to his version, and declaring that those facts, if found to be true, constituted a contract between the parties that defendant would pay plaintiff the sum of $2,000 for another year, provided the jury believed from the evidence that plaintiff commenced said work believing he was to have $2,000 for the year's work. This instruction was refused, but the court gave another embodying in substance appellant's version of the conversation, and declaring it made a contract "if you (the jury) find both parties thereby intended and did contract with each other for plaintiff's employment for one year from and including December 23, 1903, at a salary of $2,000 per annum." Embry swore that, on several occasions when he spoke to McKittrick about employment for the ensuing year, he asked for a renewal of his former contract, and that on December 23d, the date of the alleged renewal, he went into Mr. McKittrick's office and told him his contract had expired, and he wanted to renew it for a year, having always worked under year contracts. Neither the refused instruction nor the one given by the court embodied facts quite as strong as appellant's testimony, because neither referred to appellant's alleged statement to McKittrick that unless he was re-employed he would stop work for respondent then and there.

[3]   It is assigned for error that the court required the jury, in order to return a verdict for appellant, not only to find the conversation occurred as appellant swore, but that both parties intended by such conversation to contract with each other for plaintiff's employment for the year from December, 1903, at a salary of $2,000. If it appeared from the record that there was a dispute between the parties as to the terms on which appellant wanted re-employment, there might have been sound reason for inserting this clause in the instruction; but no issue was made that they split on terms; the testimony of McKittrick tending to prove only that he refused to enter into a contract with appellant regarding another year's employment until the annual meeting of stockholders was out of the way. Indeed, as to the proposed terms McKittrick agrees with Embry, for the former swore as follows: "Mr. Embry said he wanted to know about the renewal of his contract. Said if he did not have the contract made he would leave." As the two witnesses coincided as to the terms of the proposed re-employment, there was no reason for inserting the above-mentioned clause in the instruction in order that it might be settled by the jury whether or not plaintiff, if employed for one year from December 23, 1903, was to be paid $2,000 a year. Therefore it remains to determine whether or not this part of the instruction was a correct statement of the law in regard to what was necessary to constitute a contract between the parties; that is to say, whether the formation of a contract by what, according to Embry, was said, depended on the intention of both Embry and McKittrick. Or, to put the question more precisely: Did what was said constitute a contract of re-employment on the previous terms irrespective of the intention or purpose of McKittrick?

[4]   Judicial opinion and elementary treatises abound in statements of the rule that to constitute a contract there must be a meeting of the minds of the parties, and both must agree to the same thing in the same sense. Generally speaking, this may be true; but it is not literally or universally true. That is to say, the inner intention of parties to a conversation subsequently alleged to create a contract cannot either make a contract of what transpired, or prevent one from arising, if the words used were sufficient to constitute a contract. In so far as their intention is an influential element, it is only such intention as the words or acts of the parties indicate; not one secretly cherished which is inconsistent with those words or acts. The rule is thus stated by a textwriter, and many decisions are cited in support of his text: "The primary object of construction in contract law is to discover the intention of the parties. This intention in express contracts is, in the first instance, embodied in the words which the parties have used and is to be deduced therefrom. This rule applies to oral contracts, as well as to contracts in writing, and is the rule recognized by courts of equity." 2 Paige, Contracts, § 1104. So it is said in another work: "Now this measure of the contents of the promise will be found to coincide in the usual dealings of men of good faith and ordinary competence, both

with the actual intention of the promisor and with the actual expectation of the promisee. But this is not a constant or a necessary coincidence. In exceptional cases a promisor may be bound to perform something which he did not intend to promise, or a promisee may not be entitled to require that performance which he understood to be promised to him." Walds-Pollock, Contracts (3d Ed.) 309. In *Brewington v. Mesker*, 51 Mo.App. 348, 356, it is said that the meeting of minds, which is essential to the formation of a contract, is not determined by the secret intention of the parties, but by their expressed intention, which may be wholly at variance with the former. In *Machine Co. v. Criswell*, 58 Mo.App. 471, an instruction was given on the issue of whether the sale of a machine occurred, which told the jury that an intention on the part of the seller to pass the title, and of the purchaser to receive and accept the machine for the purpose of making it his own, was essential to a sale, and if the jury believed such intention did not exist in the minds of both parties at the time, and was not made known to each other, then there was no sale, notwithstanding the delivery. In commenting on this instruction, the court said: "The latter clause of the instruction is erroneous and misleading. It is true that in every case of purchase the question of sale or no sale is a matter of intention; but such intention must always be determined by the conduct, acts, and express declarations of the parties, and not by the secret intention existing in the mind or minds of the contracting parties. If the validity of such a contract depended upon secret intentions of the parties, then no oral contract of sale could be relied on with safety." *Machine Co. v. Criswell*, 58 Mo., loc. cit. 473. In *Smith v. Hughes*, L.R. 6 Q.B. 597, 607, it was said: "If, whatever a man's real intention may be, he so conducts himself that a reasonable man would believe that he was assenting to the terms proposed by the other party, and that other party upon that belief enters into the contract with him, the man thus conducting himself would be equally bound as if he had intended to agree to the other party's terms." And that doctrine was adopted in *Phillip v. Gallant*, 62 N.Y. 256. In 9 Cyc. 245, we find the following text: "The law imputes to a person an intention corresponding to the reasonable meaning of his words and acts. It judges his intention by his outward expressions and excludes all questions in regard to his unexpressed intention. If his words or acts, judged by a reasonable standard, manifest an intention to agree in regard to the matter in question, that agreement is established, and it is immaterial what may be the real, but unexpressed, state of his mind on the subject." Even more pointed was the language of Baron Bramwell in *Brown v. Hare*, 3 Hurlst. & N.: "Intention is immaterial till it manifests itself in an act. If a man intends to buy, and says so to the intended seller, and he intends to sell, and says so to the intended buyer, there is a contract of sale; and so there would be if neither had the intention." In view of those authorities, we hold that, though McKittrick may not have intended to employ Embry by what transpired between them according to the latter's testimony, yet if what

McKittrick said would have been taken by a reasonable man to be an employment, and Embry so understood it, it constituted a valid contract of employment for the ensuing year.

[5]   The next question is whether or not the language used was of that character, namely, was such that Embry, as a reasonable man, might consider he was re-employed for the ensuing year on the previous terms, and act accordingly. We do not say that in every instance it would be for the court to pronounce on this question, because, peradventure, instances might arise in which there would be such an ambiguity in the language relied on to show an assent by the obligor to the proposal of the obligee that it would be for the jury to say whether a reasonable mind would take it to signify acceptance of the proposal. In *Lancaster v. Elliott*, 28 Mo.App. 86, 92, the opinion, as to the immediate point, reads: "The interpretation of a contract in writing is always a matter of law for determination by the court, and equally so, upon like principles, is the question what acts and words, in nearly every case, will suffice to constitute an acceptance by one party, of a proposal submitted by the other, so that a contract or agreement thereby becomes matured." The general rule is that it is for the court to construe the effect of writings relied on to make a contract, and also the effect of unambiguous oral words. However, if the words are in dispute, the question of whether they were used or not is for the jury. With these rules of law in mind, let us recur to the conversation of December 23d between Embry and McKittrick as related by the former. Embry was demanding a renewal of his contract, saying he had been put off from time to time, and that he had only a few days before the end of the year in which to seek employment from other houses, and that he would quit then and there unless he was reemployed. McKittrick inquired how he was getting along with the department, and Embry said they, i.e., the employees of the department, were very busy getting out salesmen. Whereupon McKittrick said: "Go ahead, you are all right. Get your men out, and do not let that worry you." We think no reasonable man would construe that answer to Embry's demand that he be employed for another year, otherwise than as an assent to the demand, and that Embry had the right to rely on it as an assent. The natural inference is, though we do not find it testified to, that Embry was at work getting samples ready for the salesmen to use during the ensuing season. Now, when he was complaining of the worry and mental distress he was under because of his uncertainty about the future, and his urgent need, either of an immediate contract with respondent, or a refusal by it to make one, leaving him free to seek employment elsewhere, McKittrick must have answered as he did for the purpose of assuring appellant that any apprehension was needless, as appellant's services would be retained by the respondent. The answer was unambiguous, and we rule that if the conversation was according to appellant's version, and he understood he was employed, it constituted in law a valid contract of re-employment, and the court erred in making the formation of a contract

depend on a finding that both parties intended to make one. It was only necessary that Embry, as a reasonable man, had a right to and did so understand.

[6] Some other rulings are assigned for error by the appellant, but we will not discuss them because we think they are devoid of merit. The judgment is reversed, and the cause remanded. All concur.

———

NOTES AND QUESTIONS

1. B sued A for breach of contract. B testified as follows: "A said to me: 'I'll sell you my car for $1,000.' I told him 'It's a deal.' " A testified that what he said was "I'm thinking of selling my car. Do you think I can get $1,000 for it?"

According to the *Embry* court, should the question of whether there was a contract be decided by the judge or by the jury? Is it a question of fact or a question of law? *Jury*

2. "I think we may have a deal." Offer? Acceptance?

———

PROBLEM 1-1

Bobby hears that Andy and Sylvia have broken up, so he asks Sylvia for a date. Needing someone to talk to, Sylvia says yes. Wanting to make a great impression, Bobby spends $600 for a new suit, $400 for two floor-level tickets for the Knicks game, $175 for a limo and $75 for a bottle of champagne. He also has his apartment cleaned for the first time since his girlfriend moved out four months ago. Two hours before she is supposed to meet Bobby, Sylvia reconciles with Andy. She calls Bobby and tells him she can't go out with him. Bobby threatens to sue her for breach of contract.

Does he have a case? *No → acceptance was date not $ spent*

PROBLEM 1-2

Rex and Teresa LeGalley of Albuquerque, New Mexico executed a 16 page "contract" governing virtually all aspects of their marriage. Among other things (many other things) the document provides:

(1) Shoes will be left in the garage when entering the house.

(2) Lights will be turned out at 11:30 p.m. and the parties will rise promptly at 6:30 a.m.

(3) Lunches will be taken to work (not bought) whenever possible.

(4) Gas tanks in vehicles owned by the parties will not be allowed to go below half full, and only premium grade gasoline will be used in these vehicles.

(5) When driving, the parties will maintain separation from the vehicle in front of a distance of at least one car length for each 10 miles per hour of speed.

Suppose that Ms. LeGalley has been tailgating and letting the gas run to a quarter tank or less lately. Can Mr. LeGalley go to court and get an injunction requiring her to keep a safe distance and fill up more often? *Yes*

If the contract has a typical "events of defaults and remedies" section, can Mr. LeGalley give Mrs. LeGalley a notice of default, opportunity to cure the default, and then exercise remedies, which include monetary fines and imposing additional household chores on her?

LEONARD V. PEPSICO, INC.
United States District Court, Southern District, New York
88 F. Supp. 2d 116 (1999)

WOOD, DISTRICT JUDGE.

[1] Plaintiff brought this action seeking, among other things, specific performance of an alleged offer of a Harrier Jet, featured in a television advertisement for defendant's "Pepsi Stuff" promotion. Defendant has moved for summary judgment pursuant to Federal Rule of Civil Procedure 56. For the reasons stated below, defendant's motion is granted.

I.   Background

[2] This case arises out of a promotional campaign conducted by defendant, the producer and distributor of the soft drinks Pepsi and Diet Pepsi. The promotion, entitled "Pepsi Stuff," encouraged consumers to collect "Pepsi Points" from specially marked packages of Pepsi or Diet Pepsi and redeem these points for merchandise featuring the Pepsi logo. Before introducing the promotion nationally, defendant conducted a test of the promotion in the Pacific Northwest from October 1995 to March 1996. A Pepsi Stuff catalog was distributed to consumers in the test market, including Washington State. Plaintiff is a resident of Seattle, Washington. While living in Seattle, plaintiff saw the Pepsi Stuff commercial that he contends constituted an offer of a Harrier Jet.

A.   The Alleged Offer

issue [3] Because whether the television commercial constituted an offer is the central question in this case, the Court will describe the commercial in detail. The commercial opens upon an idyllic, suburban morning, where the chirping of birds in sun-dappled trees welcomes a paperboy on his morning route. As the newspaper hits the stoop of a conventional two-story house, the tattoo of a military drum introduces the subtitle, "MONDAY 7:58 AM." The stirring strains of a martial air mark the appearance of a well-coiffed teenager preparing to leave for school, dressed in a shirt emblazoned with the Pepsi logo, a red-white-and-blue ball. While the teenager confidently preens, the military drumroll again sounds as the subtitle "T-SHIRT 75 PEPSI POINTS" scrolls across the screen. Bursting from his room, the teenager strides down the hallway wearing a leather jacket. The drumroll sounds again, as the subtitle "LEATHER JACKET 1450 PEPSI POINTS" appears. The teenager opens the door of his house and, unfazed by the glare of the early morning sunshine, puts on a pair of sunglasses. The drumroll then accompanies the subtitle "SHADES 175 PEPSI POINTS." A voiceover then intones, "Introducing the new Pepsi Stuff catalog," as the camera focuses on the cover of the catalog.

[4]   The scene then shifts to three young boys sitting in front of a high school building. The boy in the middle is intent on his Pepsi Stuff Catalog, while the boys on either side are each drinking Pepsi. The three boys gaze in awe at an object rushing overhead, as the military march builds to a crescendo. The Harrier Jet is not yet visible, but the observer senses the presence of a mighty plane as the extreme winds generated by its flight create a paper maelstrom in a classroom devoted to an otherwise dull physics lesson. Finally, the Harrier Jet swings into view and lands by the side of the school building, next to a bicycle rack. Several students run for cover, and the velocity of the wind strips one hapless faculty member down to his underwear. While the faculty member is being deprived of his dignity, the voiceover announces: "Now the more Pepsi you drink, the more great stuff you're gonna get."

[5]   The teenager opens the cockpit of the fighter and can be seen, helmetless, holding a Pepsi. "Looking very pleased with himself," the teenager exclaims, "Sure beats the bus," and chortles. The military drumroll sounds a final time, as the following words appear: "HARRIER FIGHTER 7,000,000 PEPSI POINTS." A few seconds later, the following appears in more stylized script: "Drink Pepsi—Get Stuff." With that message, the music and the commercial end with a triumphant flourish.

[6]   Inspired by this commercial, plaintiff set out to obtain a Harrier Jet. Plaintiff explains that he is "typical of the 'Pepsi Generation' . . . he is young, has an adventurous spirit, and the notion of obtaining a Harrier Jet appealed to him enormously." Plaintiff consulted the Pepsi Stuff Catalog. The Catalog features youths dressed in Pepsi Stuff regalia or enjoying Pepsi Stuff accessories, such as "Blue Shades" ("As if you need another reason to look forward to sunny days."), "Pepsi Tees" ("Live in 'em. Laugh in 'em. Get in 'em."), "Bag of Balls" ("Three balls. One bag. No rules."), and "Pepsi Phone Card" ("Call your mom!"). The Catalog specifies the number of Pepsi Points required to obtain promotional merchandise. The Catalog includes an Order Form which lists, on one side, fifty-three items of Pepsi Stuff merchandise redeemable for Pepsi Points. Conspicuously absent from the Order Form is any entry or description of a Harrier Jet. The amount of

Pepsi Points required to obtain the listed merchandise ranges from 15 (for a "Jacket Tattoo" ("Sew 'em on your jacket, not your arm.")) to 3300 (for a "Fila Mountain Bike" ("Rugged. All-terrain. Exclusively for Pepsi.")). It should be noted that plaintiff objects to the implication that because an item was not shown in the Catalog, it was unavailable.

[7]   The rear foldout pages of the Catalog contain directions for redeeming Pepsi Points for merchandise. (See Catalog, at rear foldout pages.) These directions note that merchandise may be ordered "only" with the original Order Form. The Catalog notes that in the event that a consumer lacks enough Pepsi Points to obtain a desired item, additional Pepsi Points may be purchased for ten cents each; however, at least fifteen original Pepsi Points must accompany each order.

[8]   Although plaintiff initially set out to collect 7,000,000 Pepsi Points by consuming Pepsi products, it soon became clear to him that he "would not be able to buy (let alone drink) enough Pepsi to collect the necessary Pepsi Points fast enough." Reevaluating his strategy, plaintiff "focused for the first time on the packaging materials in the Pepsi Stuff promotion," and realized that buying Pepsi Points would be a more promising option. Through acquaintances, plaintiff ultimately raised about $700,000.[4]

B. Plaintiff's Efforts to Redeem the Alleged Offer

[9]   On or about March 27, 1996, plaintiff submitted an Order Form, fifteen original Pepsi Points, and a check for $700,008.50. Plaintiff appears to have been represented by counsel at the time he mailed his check; the check is drawn on an account of plaintiff's first set of attorneys. At the bottom of the Order Form, plaintiff wrote in "1 Harrier Jet" in the "Item" column and "7,000,000" in the "Total Points" column. In a letter accompanying his submission, plaintiff stated that the check was to purchase additional Pepsi Points "expressly for obtaining a new Harrier jet as advertised in your Pepsi Stuff commercial."

[10] On or about May 7, 1996, defendant's fulfillment house rejected plaintiff's submission and returned the check, explaining that:

> The item that you have requested is not part of the Pepsi Stuff collection. It is not included in the catalogue or on the order form, and only catalogue merchandise can be redeemed under this program.

> The Harrier jet in the Pepsi commercial is fanciful and is simply included to create a humorous and entertaining ad. We apologize for any misunderstanding or confusion that you may have experienced and are enclosing some free product coupons for your use.

---

⁴   [$700,000 in 1999 dollars is roughly the equivalent of $1.1 million in 2019 dollars using the CPI and the GNP Deflator.—Eds.]

[11] Plaintiff's previous counsel responded on or about May 14, 1996, as follows:

> Your letter of May 7, 1996 is totally unacceptable. We have reviewed the video tape of the Pepsi Stuff commercial . . . and it clearly offers the new Harrier jet for 7,000,000 Pepsi Points. Our client followed your rules explicitly . . .

> This is a formal demand that you honor your commitment and make immediate arrangements to transfer the new Harrier jet to our client. If we do not receive transfer instructions within ten (10) business days of the date of this letter you will leave us no choice but to file an appropriate action against Pepsi . . .

[12] This letter was apparently sent onward to the advertising company responsible for the actual commercial, BBDO New York ("BBDO"). In a letter dated May 30, 1996, BBDO Vice President Raymond E. McGovern, Jr., explained to plaintiff that:

> I find it hard to believe that you are of the opinion that the Pepsi Stuff commercial ("Commercial") really offers a new Harrier Jet. The use of the Jet was clearly a joke that was meant to make the Commercial more humorous and entertaining. In my opinion, no reasonable person would agree with your analysis of the Commercial.

On or about June 17, 1996, plaintiff mailed a similar demand letter to defendant.

[13] [The court discussed a lot of procedural history not important for our current purposes, including an order made by another court that Leonard pay Pepsi $90,000 to reimburse it for attorneys' fees.—Eds.] The present motion thus follows three years of jurisdictional and procedural wrangling.

II. Discussion

A. *The Legal Framework*

1. *Standard for Summary Judgment*

[14] On a motion for summary judgment, a court "cannot try issues of fact; it can only determine whether there are issues to be tried." *Donahue v. Windsor Locks Bd. of Fire Comm'rs*, 834 F.2d 54, 58 (2d Cir. 1987) (citations and internal quotation marks omitted). To prevail on a motion for summary judgment, the moving party therefore must show that there are no such genuine issues of material fact to be tried, and that he or she is entitled to judgment as a matter of law . . .

* * *

[15] The question of whether or not a contract was formed is appropriate for resolution on summary judgment. As the Second Circuit has recently noted, "Summary judgment is proper when the 'words and actions that allegedly formed a contract [are] so clear themselves that reasonable people could not differ over their meaning.'" *Krumme v. WestPoint Stevens, Inc.*, 143 F.3d 71, 83 (2d Cir. 1998) (quoting *Bourque v. FDIC*, 42 F.3d 704, 708 (1st Cir. 1994)) (further citations omitted).

* * *

B.   Defendant's Advertisement Was Not An Offer

1.   Advertisements as Offers

[The court discussed the question of when an advertisement constitutes an offer, noting the general rule that an ad is not an offer and distinguishing *Lefkowitz v. Great Minneapolis Surplus Store*, which is covered in Chapter 2.—Eds.]

2.   Rewards as Offers

[Here the court distinguished *Carlill v. Carbolic Smoke Ball Co.* covered in Chapter 3.—Eds.]

C.   An Objective, Reasonable Person Would Not Have Considered the Commercial an Offer

[16] Plaintiff's understanding of the commercial as an offer must also be rejected because the Court finds that no objective person could reasonably have concluded that the commercial actually offered consumers a Harrier Jet.

1.   Objective Reasonable Person Standard

[17] In evaluating the commercial, the Court must not consider defendant's subjective intent in making the commercial, or plaintiff's subjective view of what the commercial offered, but what an objective, reasonable person would have understood the commercial to convey. *See Kay-R Elec. Corp. v. Stone & Webster Constr. Co.*, 23 F.3d 55, 57 (2d Cir. 1994) ("We are not concerned with what was going through the heads of the parties at the time [of the alleged contract]. Rather, we are talking about the objective principles of contract law."); *Mesaros*, 845 F.2d at 1581 ("A basic rule of contracts holds that whether an offer has been made depends on the objective reasonableness of the alleged offeree's belief that the advertisement or solicitation was intended as an offer."); Farnsworth, *supra*, § 3.10, at 237; Williston, *supra*, § 4:7 at 296–97.

[18] If it is clear that an offer was not serious, then no offer has been made:

What kind of act creates a power of acceptance and is therefore an offer? It must be an expression of will or intention. It must be an act that leads the offeree reasonably to conclude that a power to *acts done in jest* create a contract is conferred. This applies to the content of the power as well as to the fact of its existence. *It is on this ground that we must exclude* invitations to deal or acts of mere preliminary negotiation, and *acts evidently done in jest* or without intent to create legal relations.

no a legal offer (handwritten)

Corbin on Contracts, § 1.11 at 30 (emphasis added). An obvious joke, of course, would not give rise to a contract. *See, e.g., Graves v. Northern N.Y. Pub. Co.,* 260 A.D. 900, 22 N.Y.S.2d 537 (App. Div. 4th Dept. 1940) (dismissing claim to offer of $1000, which appeared in the "joke column" of the newspaper, to any person who could provide a commonly available phone number). On the other hand, if there is no indication that the offer is "evidently in jest," and that an objective, reasonable person would find that the offer was serious, then there may be a valid offer. *See Barnes,* 549 P.2d at 1155 ("If the jest is not apparent and a reasonable hearer would believe that an offer was being made, then the speaker risks the formation of a contract which was not intended.") *See also Lucy v. Zehmer,* 196 Va. 493, 84 S.E.2d 516, 518, 520 (Va. 1954) (ordering specific performance of a contract to purchase a farm despite defendant's protestation that the transaction was done in jest as "just a bunch of two doggoned drunks bluffing").

(reasoning) (handwritten)

2. *Necessity of a Jury Determination*

[19] Plaintiff also contends that summary judgment is improper because the question of whether the commercial conveyed a sincere offer can be answered only by a jury. Relying on dictum from *Gallagher v. Delaney,* 139 F.3d 338 (2d Cir. 1998), plaintiff argues that a federal judge comes from a "narrow segment of the enormously broad American economic spectrum," *id.* at 342, and, thus, that the question whether the commercial constituted a serious offer must be decided by a jury composed of, inter alia, members of the "Pepsi Generation," who are, as plaintiff puts it, "young, open to adventure, willing to do the unconventional." Plaintiff essentially argues that a federal judge would view his claim differently than fellow members of the "Pepsi Generation."

[20] Plaintiff's argument that his claim must be put to a jury is without merit. *Gallagher* involved a claim of sexual harassment in which the defendant allegedly invited plaintiff to sit on his lap, gave her inappropriate Valentine's Day gifts, told her that "she brought out feelings that he had not had since he was sixteen," and "invited her to help him feed the ducks in the pond, since he was 'a bachelor for the evening.' " *Gallagher,* 139 F.3d at 344. The court concluded that a jury determination was particularly appropriate because a federal judge lacked "the current real-life experience required in interpreting subtle sexual dynamics of the workplace based on nuances, subtle perceptions, and implicit

communications." *Id.* at 342. This case, in contrast, presents a question of whether there was an offer to enter into a contract, requiring the Court to determine how a reasonable, objective person would have understood defendant's commercial. Such an inquiry is commonly performed by courts on a motion for summary judgment. *See Krumme,* 143 F.3d at 83; *Bourque,* 42 F.3d at 708; *Wards Co.,* 761 F.2d at 120.[5]

3.   Whether the Commercial Was "Evidently Done In Jest"

[21] Plaintiff's insistence that the commercial appears to be a serious offer requires the Court to explain why the commercial is funny. Explaining why a joke is funny is a daunting task; as the essayist E.B. White has remarked, "Humor can be dissected, as a frog can, but the thing dies in the process . . ." The commercial is the embodiment of what defendant appropriately characterizes as "zany humor."

[22] First, the commercial suggests, as commercials often do, that use of the advertised product will transform what, for most youth, can be a fairly routine and ordinary experience. The military tattoo and stirring martial music, as well as the use of subtitles in a Courier font that scroll terse messages across the screen, such as "MONDAY 7:58 AM," evoke military and espionage thrillers. The implication of the commercial is that Pepsi Stuff merchandise will inject drama and moment into hitherto unexceptional lives. The commercial in this case thus makes the exaggerated claims similar to those of many television advertisements: that by consuming the featured clothing, car, beer, or potato chips, one will become attractive, stylish, desirable, and admired by all. A reasonable viewer would understand such advertisements as mere puffery, not as statements of fact, *see, e.g., Hubbard v. General Motors Corp.,* 1996 WL 274018, at *6 (S.D.N.Y. May 22, 1996) (advertisement describing automobile as "Like a Rock," was mere puffery, not a warranty of quality); *Lovett,* 207 N.Y.S. at 756; and refrain from interpreting the promises of the commercial as being literally true.

[23] Second, the callow youth featured in the commercial is a highly improbable pilot, one who could barely be trusted with the keys to his parents' car, much less the prize aircraft of the United States Marine Corps. Rather than checking the fuel gauges on his aircraft, the teenager spends his precious preflight minutes preening. The youth's concern for his coiffure appears to extend to his flying without a helmet. Finally, the teenager's comment that flying a Harrier Jet to school "sure beats the bus" evinces an improbably insouciant attitude toward the relative difficulty and danger of piloting a fighter plane in a residential area, as opposed to taking public transportation.

---

[5]   [The premise underlying the court's reasoning seems to be that judges know more about television commercials than they know about gender, interpersonal relationships, and sex. The ramifications of this premise, if true, are beyond the scope of this text.—Eds.]

[24] Third, the notion of traveling to school in a Harrier Jet is an exaggerated adolescent fantasy. In this commercial, the fantasy is underscored by how the teenager's schoolmates gape in admiration, ignoring their physics lesson. The force of the wind generated by the Harrier Jet blows off one teacher's clothes, literally defrocking an authority figure. As if to emphasize the fantastic quality of having a Harrier Jet arrive at school, the Jet lands next to a plebeian bike rack. This fantasy is, of course, extremely unrealistic. No school would provide landing space for a student's fighter jet, or condone the disruption the jet's use would cause.

[25] Fourth, the primary mission of a Harrier Jet, according to the United States Marine Corps, is to "attack and destroy surface targets under day and night visual conditions." United States Marine Corps, Factfile: AV-8B Harrier II (last modified Dec. 5, 1995) http://www.hqmc.usmc.mil/factfile.nsf. Manufactured by McDonnell Douglas, the Harrier Jet played a significant role in the air offensive of Operation Desert Storm in 1991. *See id.* The jet is designed to carry a considerable armament load, including Sidewinder and Maverick missiles. *See id.* As one news report has noted, "Fully loaded, the Harrier can float like a butterfly and sting like a bee— albeit a roaring 14-ton butterfly and a bee with 9,200 pounds of bombs and missiles." Jerry Allegood, Marines Rely on Harrier Jet, Despite Critics, News & Observer (Raleigh), Nov. 4, 1990, at C1. In light of the Harrier Jet's well documented function in attacking and destroying surface and air targets, armed reconnaissance and air interdiction, and offensive and defensive anti-aircraft warfare, depiction of such a jet as a way to get to school in the morning is clearly not serious even if, as plaintiff contends, the jet is capable of being acquired "in a form that eliminates [its] potential for military use." (*See* Leonard Aff. ¶ 20.)

[26] Fifth, the number of Pepsi Points the commercial mentions as required to "purchase" the jet is 7,000,000. To amass that number of points, one would have to drink 7,000,000 Pepsis (or roughly 190 Pepsis a day for the next hundred years—an unlikely possibility), or one would have to purchase approximately $700,000 worth of Pepsi Points. The cost of a Harrier Jet is roughly $23 million dollars, a fact of which plaintiff was aware when he set out to gather the amount he believed necessary to accept the alleged offer. (*See* Affidavit of Michael E. McCabe, 96 Civ. 5320, Aug. 14, 1997, Exh. 6 (Leonard Business Plan).) Even if an objective, reasonable person were not aware of this fact, he would conclude that purchasing a fighter plane for $700,000 is a deal too good to be true.

[27] Plaintiff argues that a reasonable, objective person would have understood the commercial to make a serious offer of a Harrier Jet because there was "absolutely no distinction in the manner" in which the items in the commercial were presented. Plaintiff also relies upon a press release highlighting the promotional campaign, issued by defendant, in which "no mention is made by [defendant] of humor, or anything of the sort." These

arguments suggest merely that the humor of the promotional campaign was tongue in cheek. Humor is not limited to what Justice Cardozo called "the rough and boisterous joke . . . [that] evokes its own guffaws." *Murphy v. Steeplechase Amusement Co.*, 250 N.Y. 479, 483, 166 N.E. 173, 174 (1929). In light of the obvious absurdity of the commercial, the Court rejects plaintiff's argument that the commercial was not clearly in jest.

4. Plaintiff's Demands for Additional Discovery

[28] In his Memorandum of Law, and in letters to the Court, plaintiff argues that additional discovery is necessary on the issues of whether and how defendant reacted to plaintiff's "acceptance" of their "offer"; how defendant and its employees understood the commercial would be viewed, based on test-marketing the commercial or on their own opinions; and how other individuals actually responded to the commercial when it was aired.

[29] Plaintiff argues that additional discovery is necessary as to how defendant reacted to his "acceptance," suggesting that it is significant that defendant twice changed the commercial, the first time to increase the number of Pepsi Points required to purchase a Harrier Jet to 700,000,000, and then again to amend the commercial to state the 700,000,000 amount and add "(Just Kidding)." Plaintiff concludes that, "Obviously, if PepsiCo truly believed that no one could take seriously the offer contained in the original ad that I saw, this change would have been totally unnecessary and superfluous." The record does not suggest that the change in the amount of points is probative of the seriousness of the offer. The increase in the number of points needed to acquire a Harrier Jet may have been prompted less by the fear that reasonable people would demand Harrier Jets and more by the concern that unreasonable people would threaten frivolous litigation. Further discovery is unnecessary on the question of when and how the commercials changed because the question before the Court is whether the commercial that plaintiff saw and relied upon was an offer, not that any other commercial constituted an offer.

[30] Plaintiff's demands for discovery relating to how defendant itself understood the offer are also unavailing. Such discovery would serve only to cast light on defendant's subjective intent in making the alleged offer, which is irrelevant to the question of whether an objective, reasonable person would have understood the commercial to be an offer. *See Kay-R Elec. Corp.*, 23 F.3d at 57 ("We are not concerned with what was going through the heads of the parties at the time [of the alleged contract]."); *Mesaros*, 845 F.2d at 1581; Corbin on Contracts, § 1.11 at 30. Indeed, plaintiff repeatedly argues that defendant's subjective intent is irrelevant. (*See* Pl. Mem. at 5, 8, 13.)

[31] Finally, plaintiff's assertion that he should be afforded an opportunity to determine whether other individuals also tried to accumulate enough Pepsi Points to "purchase" a Harrier Jet is unavailing.

The possibility that there were other people who interpreted the commercial as an "offer" of a Harrier Jet does not render that belief any more or less reasonable. The alleged offer must be evaluated on its own terms. Having made the evaluation, the Court concludes that summary judgment is appropriate on the ground that no reasonable, objective person would have understood the commercial to be an offer.

* * *

[32] For the reasons stated above, the Court grants defendant's motion for summary judgment. The Clerk of Court is instructed to close these cases. Any pending motions are moot.

———

NOTES AND QUESTIONS

1. When Leonard tried to accept the "offer," he was represented by counsel. Should the court then determine whether a reasonable person would have thought his assent to the bargain is invited and would conclude it, or should the standard be whether a reasonable person represented by a reasonable lawyer would have thought so?

2. One professor has suggested that the court should have found a contract in *Leonard* in order to discourage deceptive advertising. Ignore, for purposes of this question, how that is impractical for a variety of reasons and assume for purposes of this question that the ad was deceptive. Should the court then have found there to be a contract?

3. Mr. Leonard would not have ended up with a working jet even had the court found an offer. In 1997, the Pentagon announced that the Harrier was not for sale in flying condition. Before any of the Marine aircraft could be offered to the public, they would have to be "demilitarized" which would have meant removal of all weapons and weapons systems as well as disabling the ability to take off and land vertically, which would make flying one impossible.

———

PROBLEM 1-3

Jodee Berry sued the owners of the restaurant at which she worked for breach of contract. According to the complaint filed in the case, her manager told the waitresses that whoever sold the most food and beverages at each participating location during the month of April would be entered in a drawing for a new Toyota. Over the course of the month, the manager allegedly told the waitresses that he didn't know whether the prize would be a Toyota car, truck, or van, but the winner would have to pay the registration fees on the vehicle. In May, the manager informed Ms. Berry that she was the lucky winner. He blindfolded her and led her to the parking lot. Waiting for her there was a doll

unilateral contract [handwritten note in left margin]

of the Star Wars character "Yoda." Ms. Berry was informed that she was the proud winner of a "toy Yoda."

For some reason, Ms. Berry was unable to see the humor in the situation. She sued. Should she win? *See* Keith A. Rowley, *You Asked For It, You Got It . . . Toy Yoda: Practical Jokes, Prizes, and Contract Law*, 3 NEV. L.J. 526 (2003).

Yes, took jest too far [handwritten]   *Offer and acceptence* [handwritten]

PROBLEM 1-4

Read UNIDROIT article 4.2. Is that standard consistent with the "objective theory of contract" that is the topic of this chapter?

PROBLEM 1-5

Consider an American importer that contracts with a German company to supply it with commercial quantities of chickens, which it intended to resell to restaurant supply companies for resale to their customers. The contract is governed by U.S. law and simply provides for the supply of chicken at various rates for various sizes of birds (e.g., 2.5 to 3 lbs, $120 per 100 lbs.). When the chickens arrive in the U.S., the importer discovers that they are what it would call "old, stewing chickens" and it claims that it had meant young chickens, suitable for broiling and frying. It claims the German company is in breach of its contract. The German company protests that it has supplied just what the contract called for—chickens. How will this dispute be resolved under the objective theory of contracts?

LAWYERING SKILLS PROBLEM:
SUMMARIZING AND SYNTHESIZING

(1) *Summarize.* If you have not done so already, boil down the holdings of each of the cases and problems in this chapter to no more than five, and preferably three, sentences of ordinary length written in plain English. These summaries should be generalizations that can be separated from the specific facts of the cases and problems so you can use them to analyze other sets of facts that may present themselves.

(2) *Synthesize.* Take the summaries from the first part of this exercise and blend them together into a coherent statement of what the law of the objective theory of contract is. You should aim to be able to do this in no more than six to ten sentences of ordinary length written in plain English.

CHAPTER 2

HAS AN OFFER BEEN MADE?

■ ■ ■

There never was a more unfortunate expression used than "meeting of the minds."

—Oliver Wendell Holmes, Jr.

Factors vs. Elements

We return to the subject of legal standards based on factors or elements. In some of your courses, you will be talking in terms of a list of elements, a list of things that have to be satisfied before it will be determined that the tort of "battery," for example, occurred or that the crime of "burglary" was committed. Later on, we'll have a few lists of elements. But the important questions in contracts cannot be answered by going mechanically through a list of elements. They involve more subtle questions that require the consideration of a number of factors, a series of things that may, but need not, all be shown to determine if a particular standard has been met. Elements are requirements; factors are considerations.

Chapter 1 and this chapter deal with the question of whether a communication constitutes an offer. As you have probably already realized, in some situations the briefest statement may be an offer, and in others the most elaborate proposition may not. There is only the basic test, which is articulated in various ways but always with the same basic meaning: "Would another person be justified in believing they could form a contract by assenting to the proposition?"

This is not much of a test to go on. Perhaps the best place to start is to ask yourself, "If I were the person (the offeree) in this case, would I reasonably think I could form a contract by responding to this communication?" One problem with this, of course, is that not everyone thinks the same way. Reasonable minds may—and often do—differ.

We could, of course, let every judge have his or her own opinion as to what constitutes an offer, but there are some problems with this. First, people need to be able to plan their affairs. They need to have some certainty as to whether they have a contract or not without regard to the judge they may draw should litigation ensue. Second, the notion that judges can just make up the law as they see fit is inconsistent with the basic principle of Western democracy that we are governed by laws rather than by the whims of individuals.

So how do we bring some consistency and rationality to the question of whether a communication is an offer? One answer, of course, is that judges have to follow precedent. If there was a prior case with the same facts, the court may be bound by the decision in that case. This is not the place to get into the question of when a prior case is binding on the court and when it is "merely persuasive" or the more difficult question of how persuasive "persuasive authority" really is. The truth of the matter is that most of the time the facts of your case will be different from those of any decided case you can find. It is always frustrating for new lawyers to go to research a case thinking "this must have happened before," only to discover that it hasn't or, if it has, it is not to be found in a reported decision or other recognized authority, in which case it may as well never have happened at all. The reality is that there is an infinite variety of ways in which people can and do mess up their affairs.

One way we bring some sort of order to this situation is to have certain factors that courts take into account in determining whether or not an offer has been made. There is no definitive list. Some of these factors are present in all cases, some in only a few. Some of these factors are very important, others less so.

Look back over the cases we've read so far and see what factors were important and how much weight the courts gave them. As you read the cases that follow, you will see some new factors taken into consideration, and you will see some of the factors from the previous cases dealt with in new ways. The more cases you read and think about, the better you will understand how these factors work.

Although this text is very careful to use the words "elements" and "factors" in the sense that *elements are required* to meet a standard and *factors are considerations* that bear on a standard, not everyone observes that distinction in practice. When you read an opinion referring to factors or elements or analyze a brief or memorandum that does so, make sure to determine whether or not the terms are being used as in this text. Otherwise you may conclude that a requirement is a mere consideration because someone used the term "factor" in the sense of an "element," as in "required factor." Much confusion can be caused by uncritically accepting another's analysis, pigeon-holing, or use of labels without critical reflection.

No matter how many cases you read and study, you will never be able to say for sure in a difficult case whether a particular communication constitutes an offer. That is an uncertainty you'll just have to live with if you want to be a lawyer. Your clients won't like it when you refuse to give a yes-or-no answer but your malpractice carrier will. In one famous case, *Pennzoil v. Texaco*, a client (Texaco) lost about *three billion dollars* because some of the most well regarded lawyers in the country told it there had been no offer and acceptance, and twelve jurors decided otherwise. Because of the size of the verdict (the original jury verdict was $11 billion, but while the case was on appeal and Texaco was in chapter 11 bankruptcy proceedings it was settled for $3 billion) the case has been called "The Texas Common Law Massacre." *See Texaco, Inc. v. Pennzoil, Co.*, 729 S.W.2d 768 (Tex. App.1987); *see also* Robert M. Lloyd, *Pennzoil v. Texaco, Twenty Years After: Lessons for Business Lawyers*, 6 TENN. J. BUS. L. 321 (2005); Kevin J. Delaney, Strategic Bankruptcy (University of California Press 1992, 1998).

————

LONERGAN V. SCOLNICK

District Court of Appeal, Fourth District, California
129 Cal. App. 2d 179, 276 P.2d 8 (1954)

BARNARD, PRESIDING JUSTICE.

[1] This is an action for specific performance or for damages in the event specific performance was impossible.[1]

[2] The complaint alleged that on April 15, 1952, the parties entered into a contract whereby the defendant agreed to sell, and plaintiff agreed to buy a 40-acre tract of land for $2,500; that this was a fair, just and reasonable value of the property; that on April 28, 1952, the defendant repudiated the contract and refused to deliver a deed; that on April 28, 1952, the property was worth $6,081; and that plaintiff has been damaged in the amount of $3,581.[2][3] The answer denied that any contract had been entered into, or that anything was due to the plaintiff.

[3] By stipulation, the issue of whether or not a contract was entered into between the parties was first tried, reserving the other issues for a further trial if that became necessary. The issue as to the existence of a contract was submitted upon an agreed statement, including certain letters between the parties, without the introduction of other evidence.

[4] The stipulated facts are as follows: During March, 1952, the defendant placed an ad in a Los Angeles paper reading, so far as material

---

[1]   [Normally when a contract is breached, the non-breaching party is awarded money damages as compensation. In a few situations, the court compels the breaching party to perform the contract. This is called "specific performance." A contract for the sale of real estate is one of the few situations in which courts regularly grant specific performance. Damages and specific performance are covered in more detail in Chapters 18 to 22.—Eds.]

[2]   [If money damages are awarded for breach of a contract to sell something, the normal measure of damages is the difference between the contract price and the value of the thing to be sold. The idea is to give the non-breaching party the benefit of whatever good deal they were going to get out of the contract. This is another topic covered in Chapter 18.—Eds.]

[3]   [$3,851 in 1954 dollars is roughly the equivalent of $36,000 in 2019 dollars using the CPI and the GNP Deflator.—Eds.]

here, "Joshua Tree vic. 40 acres, . . . need cash, will sacrifice." In response to an inquiry resulting from this ad the defendant, who lived in New York, wrote a letter to the plaintiff dated March 26, briefly describing the property, giving directions as to how to get there, stating that his rock-bottom price was $2,500 cash, and further stating that "This is a form letter." On April 7, the plaintiff wrote a letter to the defendant saying that he was not sure he had found the property, asking for its legal description, asking whether the land was all level or whether it included certain jutting rock hills, and suggesting a certain bank as escrow agent "should I desire to purchase the land." On April 8, the defendant wrote to the plaintiff saying "From your description you have found the property"; that this bank "is O.K. for escrow agent"; that the land was fairly level; giving the legal description;[4] and then saying, "If you are really interested, you will have to decide fast, as I expect to have a buyer in the next week or so." On April 12, the defendant sold the property to a third party for $2,500. The plaintiff received defendant's letter of April 8 on April 14. On April 15 he wrote to the defendant thanking him for his letter "confirming that I was on the right land," stating that he would immediately proceed to have the escrow opened and would deposit $2,500 therein "in conformity with your offer," and asking the defendant to forward a deed with his instructions to the escrow agent. On April 17, 1952, the plaintiff started an escrow and placed in the hands of the escrow agent $100, agreeing to furnish an additional $2,400 at an unspecified time, with the provision that if the escrow was not closed by May 15, 1952, it should be completed as soon thereafter as possible unless a written demand for a return of the money or instruments was made by either party after that date. It was further stipulated that the plaintiff was ready and willing at all times to deposit the $2,400.

[5] The matter was submitted on June 11, 1953. On July 10, 1953, the judge filed a memorandum opinion stating that it was his opinion that the letter of April 8, 1952, when considered with the previous correspondence, constituted an offer of sale which offer was, however, qualified and conditioned upon prompt acceptance by the plaintiff; that in spite of the condition thus imposed, the plaintiff delayed more than a week before notifying the defendant of his acceptance; and that since the plaintiff was aware of the necessity of promptly communicating his acceptance to the defendant his delay was not the prompt action required by the terms of the offer. Findings of fact were filed on October 2, 1953, finding that each and all of the statements in the agreed statement are true, and that all allegations to the contrary in the complaint are untrue. As conclusions of law, it was found that the plaintiff and defendant did not enter into a contract as alleged in the complaint or otherwise, and that the defendant

---

⁴ [A "legal description" is a precise description of the property which allows a person to determine its exact boundaries. If it is in the form of "metes and bounds," it is also a place where you can find practical application for the rule of geometry that the sum of the interior angles of a regular n-sided polygon is 360 degrees.—Eds.]

is entitled to judgment against the plaintiff. Judgment was entered accordingly, from which the plaintiff has appealed.

[6] The appellant contends that the judgment is contrary to the evidence and to the law since the facts, as found, do not support the conclusions of law upon which the judgment is based. It is argued that there is no conflict in the evidence, and this court is not bound by the trial court's construction of the written instruments involved; that the evidence conclusively shows that an offer was made to the plaintiff by the defendant, which offer was accepted by the mailing of plaintiff's letter of April 15; that upon receipt of defendant's letter of April 8 the plaintiff had a reasonable time within which to accept the offer that had been made; that by his letter of April 15 and his starting of an escrow the plaintiff accepted said offer; and that the agreed statement of facts establishes that a valid contract was entered into between the parties. In his briefs the appellant assumes that an offer was made by the defendant, and confined his argument to contending that the evidence shows that he accepted that offer within a reasonable time.

Lone P&fins Argument

[7] There can be no contract unless the minds of the parties have met and mutually agreed upon some specific thing. This is usually evidenced by one party making an offer which is accepted by the other party. Section 25 of the Restatement of the Law on Contracts reads:

26 in R2D Rule

> If from a promise, or manifestation of intention, or from the circumstances existing at the time, the person to whom the promise or manifestation is addressed knows or has reason to know that the person making it does not intend it as an expression of his fixed purpose until he has given a further expression of assent, he has not made an offer.

The language used in *Niles v. Hancock*, 140 Cal. 157, 73 P. 840, 842, "It is also clear from the correspondence that it was the intention of the defendant that the negotiations between him and the plaintiff were to be purely preliminary," is applicable here. The correspondence here indicates an intention on the part of the defendant to find out whether the plaintiff was interested, rather than an intention to make a definite offer to the plaintiff. The language used by the defendant in his letters of March 26 and April 8 rather clearly discloses that they were not intended as an expression of fixed purpose to make a definite offer, and was sufficient to advise the plaintiff that some further expression of assent on the part of the defendant was necessary.

[8] The advertisement in the paper was a mere request for an offer. The letter of March 26 contains no definite offer, and clearly states that it is a form letter.[5] It merely gives further particulars, in clarification of the

---

5   [The court seems to think it's important that this letter is a form letter. Why would that be important?—Eds.]

advertisement, and tells the plaintiff how to locate the property if he was interested in looking into the matter. The letter of April 8 added nothing in the way of a definite offer. It merely answered some questions asked by the plaintiff, and stated that if the plaintiff was really interested he would have to act fast. The statement that he expected to have a buyer in the next week or so indicated that the defendant intended to sell to the first-comer, and was reserving the right to do so. From this statement, alone, the plaintiff knew or should have known that he was not being given time in which to accept an offer that was being made, but that some further assent on the part of the defendant was required. Under the language used the plaintiff was not being given a right to act within a reasonable time after receiving the letter; he was plainly told that the defendant intended to sell to another, if possible, and warned that he would have to act fast if he was interested in buying the land.

[9]   Regardless of any opinion previously expressed, the court found that no contract had been entered into between these parties, and we are in accord with the court's conclusion on that controlling issue. The court's construction of the letters involved was a reasonable one, and we think the most reasonable one, even if it be assumed that another construction was possible.

The judgment is affirmed. [In other words, the court affirms the result on different grounds.—Eds.]

GRIFFIN and MUSSELL, JJ., concur.

NOTES AND QUESTIONS

1.   The way to analyze a case like this one is to look at each communication and determine whether or not it was an offer. Make a table with column headings *Date/Time*, *From*, *To*, *Substance*, and *Analysis*. List each of the communications about the Joshua Tree land on this chart. Make sure that you can explain why each communication here either was or was not an offer using the standards of R2d § 24 and UNIDROIT Article 2.1.2. Be prepared to explain why each communication was or was not an offer under either standard.

2.   Did the trial court think that the letter of April 8 was an offer? Did the court of appeal think it was?

LEFKOWITZ V. GREAT MINNEAPOLIS SURPLUS STORE, INC.

Supreme Court of Minnesota
251 Minn. 188, 86 N.W.2d 689 (1957)

MURPHY, JUSTICE.

[1]   This is an appeal from an order of the Municipal Court of Minneapolis denying the motion of the defendant for amended findings of fact, or, in the alternative, for a new trial. The order for judgment awarded the plaintiff the sum of $138.50[6] as damages for breach of contract.

[2]   This case grows out of the alleged refusal of the defendant to sell to the plaintiff a certain fur piece which it had offered for sale in a newspaper advertisement. It appears from the record that on April 6, 1956, the defendant published the following advertisement in a Minneapolis newspaper:

Saturday 9 A.M. Sharp 3 Brand New Fur Coats Worth to $100.00

First Come First Served $1 Each

makes offer to indefinite

[3]   On April 13, the defendant again published an advertisement in the same newspaper as follows:

Saturday 9 A.M.

2 Brand New Pastel Mink 3-Skin Scarfs Selling for $89.50.

Out they go Saturday. Each . . . $1.00

1 Black Lapin Stole Beautiful, worth $139.50 . . . $1.00

First Come First Served

[4]   The record supports the findings of the court that on each of the Saturdays following the publication of the above-described ads, the plaintiff was the first to present himself at the appropriate counter in the defendant's store and on each occasion demanded the coat and the stole so advertised and indicated his readiness to pay the sale price of $1. On both occasions, the defendant refused to sell the merchandise to the plaintiff, stating on the first occasion that by a "house rule" the offer was intended for women only and sales would not be made to men, and on the second visit that plaintiff knew defendant's house rules.

Facts

[5]   The trial court properly disallowed plaintiff's claim for the value of the fur coats since the value of these articles was speculative and uncertain.[7] The only evidence of value was the advertisement itself to the effect that the coats were "Worth to $100.00," how much less being speculative especially in view of the price for which they were offered for

---

6   [$138.50 in 1957 dollars is roughly the equivalent of $1,240 in 2019 dollars using the CPI and the GNP Deflator.—Eds.]

7   [A party cannot be awarded damages for breach of contract if the amount of the damages is speculative or uncertain. This is covered in Chapter 19.—Eds.]

sale. With reference to the offer of the defendant on April 13, 1956, to sell the "1 Black Lapin Stole . . . worth $139.50 . . ." the trial court held that the value of this article was established and granted judgment in favor of the plaintiff for that amount less the $1 quoted purchase price.

[6]   The defendant contends that a newspaper advertisement offering items of merchandise for sale at a named price is a "unilateral offer" which may be withdrawn without notice. He relies upon authorities which hold that, where an advertiser publishes in a newspaper that he has a certain quantity or quality of goods which he wants to dispose of at certain prices and on certain terms, such advertisements are not offers which become contracts as soon as any person to whose notice they may come signifies his acceptance by notifying the other that he will take a certain quantity of them. Such advertisements have been construed as an invitation for an offer of sale on the terms stated, which offer, when received, may be accepted or rejected and which therefore does not become a contract of sale until accepted by the seller; and until a contract has been so made, the seller may modify or revoke such prices or terms.

* * *

[7]   There are numerous authorities which hold that a particular advertisement in a newspaper or circular letter relating to a sale of articles may be construed by the court as constituting an offer, acceptance of which would complete a contract.

[8]   The test of whether a binding obligation may originate in advertisements addressed to the general public is "whether the facts show that some performance was promised in positive terms in return for something requested." 1 Williston, Contracts (Rev. ed.) sec. 27.

[9]   The authorities above cited emphasize that, where the offer is clear, definite, and explicit, and leaves nothing open for negotiation, it constitutes an offer, acceptance of which will complete the contract. The most recent case on the subject is *Johnson v. Capital City Ford Co.*, La.App., 85 So.2d 75, in which the court pointed out that a newspaper advertisement relating to the purchase and sale of automobiles may constitute an offer, acceptance of which will consummate a contract and create an obligation in the offeror to perform according to the terms of the published offer.

[10] Whether in any individual instance a newspaper advertisement is an offer rather than an invitation to make an offer depends on the legal intention of the parties and the surrounding circumstances. Annotation, 157 A.L.R. 744, 751; 77 C.J.S., Sales, sec. 25b; 17 C.J.S., Contracts, sec. 389. We are of the view on the facts before us that the offer by the defendant of the sale of the Lapin fur was clear, definite, and explicit, and left nothing open for negotiation. The plaintiff having successfully managed to be the

first one to appear at the seller's place of business to be served, as requested by the advertisement, and having offered the stated purchase price of the article, he was entitled to performance on the part of the defendant. We think the trial court was correct in holding that there was in the conduct of the parties a sufficient mutuality of obligation to constitute a contract of sale.

[11] The defendant contends that the offer was modified by a "house rule" to the effect that only women were qualified to receive the bargains advertised. The advertisement contained no such restriction. This objection may be disposed of briefly by stating that, while an advertiser has the right at any time before acceptance to modify his offer, he does not have the right, after acceptance, to impose new or arbitrary conditions not contained in the published offer.

Affirmed.

NOTES AND QUESTIONS

certainty?

1.   What was it that allowed the advertisement in this case to be an offer when the advertisement in *Lonergan* was not an offer? *clear and definite*

2.   This is one of the first examples in this casebook of a common error in legal reasoning: mistaking a proxy for a rule. Here, the rule is the standard of R2d § 24 or some similar common law rule. The proxy is the common conclusion from many cases that various advertisements are not offers. But the rule is not "ads are not offers." The rule is the R2d or common law standard.

COURTEEN SEED CO. V. ABRAHAM

Supreme Court of Oregon
129 Or. 427, 275 P. 684 (1929)

[1]   This is an action for damages, based upon an alleged contract for the sale of a carload of clover seed. The plaintiff, a corporation organized under the laws of Wisconsin, is engaged in the wholesale seed business. The defendant is a warehouseman and grain dealer at Amity, Or. The plaintiff alleges:

> That on October 8, 1927, the said defendant, in writing, sold and agreed to deliver to the plaintiff one carload of red clover seed, at 23 cents per pound, f.o.b. Amity, Oregon, such carload containing approximately 50,000 pounds of red clover . . .

> That this plaintiff had sold and contracted to sell the said seed to others at . . . a profit of 4 cents per pound, after paying freight and charges.

Among other things, the plaintiff then avers:

> Though the defendant has often been requested so to do, yet said defendant has refused to ship or complete the sale of said clover seed to the plaintiff, or any part thereof, and that, by reason of the facts herein set forth, the plaintiff has been damaged in the sum of $2,750.[8]

[2]   The defendant's answer consists of general admissions and denials. On the trial plaintiff secured judgment against defendant for $500, and the defendant appeals.

BROWN, J. (after stating the facts as above).

[3]   The defendant assigns error of the court in overruling his motion for nonsuit in and by which he asserts that the evidence fails to show that defendant ever made a binding offer to plaintiff to sell clover seed.

[4]   Contracts in general are reached by an offer on the one side and acceptance on the other. So it becomes necessary to determine whether the defendant actually offered to sell the clover seed to the plaintiff corporation, and whether it was defendant's intention that contractual relations should exist between them on plaintiff's acceptance.

[5]   The writing upon which the plaintiff relies to show an offer to sell is a telegram sent by defendant to plaintiff on October 8, 1927, which reads: "I am asking 23 cents per pound for the car of red clover seed from which your sample was taken. No. 1 seed, practically no plantain whatever. Have an offer 22 3/4 per pound, f.o.b. Amity."

[6]   Plaintiff's acceptance of the alleged offer reads: "Telegram received. We accept your offer. Ship promptly, route care Milwaukee Road at Omaha."

[7]   A contract should be construed to effect the intention of the parties thereto, as gathered from the entire writings constituting the contract. It is this intent that constitutes the essence of every contract. Giving due consideration to every word contained in the defendant's telegram to plaintiff, we are not prepared to say that that telegram constituted an express offer to sell. It would be poor reasoning to say that the defendant meant to make the plaintiff an offer when he used this language: "I am asking 23 cents per pound for the car of red clover." That does not say, "I offer to you at 23 cents per pound the car of red clover," nor does it say, "I will sell to you the carload of red clover at 23 cents per pound." The writer of the telegram used the word "offer" with reference to some other person when he concluded by saying: "Have an offer 22 3/4 per pound, f.o.b. Amity." Each of the words "offer" and "asking" has its meaning; and we cannot

---

[8]   [$2,750 in 1929 dollars is roughly the equivalent of $40,300 in 2019 dollars using the CPI and the GNP Deflator.—Eds.]

assume that the writer of the telegram meant to use these words in the same sense, nor can we eliminate the word "asking" from the writing.

[8] Now, going back to September 21, 1927, we find that defendant was then mailing out samples of clover seed to divers persons, each sample being inclosed in an envelope on the face of which appeared the following words:

Red clover, 50,000 lbs. like sample. I am asking 24 cents per, f.o.b. Amity, Oregon.

AMITY SEED & GRAIN WAREHOUSE Amity, Oregon

[9] It will be noted that on the envelope the defendant used the language, "I am asking." The plaintiff acknowledged receipt of the sample received by it, and advised the sender that it had accumulated quite a stock of clover seed and preferred to wait a while "before operating further." On October 4th following, owing to rainy weather, which brought about conditions not favorable for hulling the clover seed, the defendant, in search of buyers, wrote the plaintiff, and, on October 8th, plaintiff wired defendant as follows: "Special delivery sample received. Your price too high. Wire firm offer, naming absolutely lowest f.o.b." The defendant then wired, in reply, that he was asking 23 cents per pound, and had received an "offer of 22 3/4." This is the writing upon which the plaintiff rests its case.

[10] It is laid down by eminent authority that information or invitation to negotiate does not constitute an offer. Perhaps one of the most comprehensive discourses on this subject appears in 1 Page on the Law of Contracts; and, for its perspicuity and learning, we set out the following interesting excerpt from section 84 thereof: "The commonest examples of offers meant to open negotiations and to call forth offers in the technical sense are the advertisements, circulars and trade letters sent out by business houses. While it is possible that the offers made by such means may be in such form as to become contracts, they are often merely expressions of a willingness to negotiate."

[Additional discussion from Page on the Law of Contracts is omitted.— Eds.]

[11] The author then refers to and quotes from the leading case of *Nebraska Seed Co. v. Harsh*, 98 Neb. 89, 152 N.W. 310. In that case the defendant wrote the plaintiff company the following:

Lowell, Nebraska, 4–24–1912.

Nebraska Seed Co., Omaha, Neb.—Gentlemen: I have about 1,800 bu. or thereabouts of millet seed of which I am mailing you a sample. This millet is recleaned and was grown on sod and is good seed. I want $2.25 per cwt. for this seed, f. o. b. Lowell.

Yours truly,
H.F. Harsh.

Upon receipt of this letter, the plaintiff wired defendant as follows:

4–26–'12.

H.F. Harsh, Lowell, Nebraska.

Sample and letter received. Accept your offer Millet like sample $2.25 per cwt. Wire how soon can load.

The Nebraska Seed Co.

[12] On the same day the plaintiff wrote the defendant a letter confirming the wire, which stated, among other things:

Have booked purchase of you 1,800 bushels of millet seed to be fully equal to sample you sent us at $2.25 per cwt., your track. Please be so kind as to load this seed at once and ship to us at Omaha. We thank you in advance for prompt attention . . .

The Nebraska Seed Company

[13] The letter was received by defendant at Lowell in due course. After due demand and tender of the purchase price, the defendant refused to deliver the seed. An action followed, in which the alleged contract was set up. Defendant filed a demurrer to the complaint, but his pleading was overruled. On trial plaintiff had verdict. Defendant appealed, and the Supreme Court of Nebraska held that the language, "I want $2.25 per cwt. for this seed, f.o.b. Lowell," did not constitute an offer of sale; that the language was general, and, as such, might be used in an advertisement or circular addressed generally to those engaged in the seed business; and that such language was not an offer by which the defendant was bound, if accepted by any or all of the persons addressed.

The court then quoted with approval from 9 Cyc. 278 E.

[14] In the case of *Moulton v. Kershaw et al.*, 59 Wis. 316, 18 N. W. 172, 48 Am. Rep. 516, the defendant wrote the plaintiff as follows: "In consequence of a rupture in the salt trade, we are authorized to offer Michigan fine salt, in full carload lots of 80 to 95 barrels, delivered at your city, at 85 cts. per barrel, to be shipped per C. & N.W. R.R. Co. only. At this price it is a bargain, as the price in general remains unchanged. Shall be pleased to receive your order."

[15] On the day the plaintiff received this letter, he wired the defendants of his acceptance, and ordered 2,000 barrels of salt. In its disposition of the case, the Supreme Court of Wisconsin held that the letter

upon which the plaintiff relied did not constitute an offer, for the reason that neither the word "sell" nor its equivalent was used therein.

[16] There are many cases of record, the great majority of which seem to follow the doctrine announced in the cases hereinabove discussed. From a review of the decisions, and of the law governing the question at issue in the instant case, we are of opinion that the motion for a nonsuit should have been sustained.

[17] This cause is reversed and remanded, with directions to enter a nonsuit.

BELT and RAND, JJ., concur.

BEAN, J., dissents.

NOTES AND QUESTIONS

1.   The court makes much of the fact that the seller used the word "asking" instead of the word "offer." It should be clear by now that you do not have to use the word "offer" to make an offer. Nobody used that word in *Lucy* or in *Embry*. In fact, in some contexts, "ask" and "offer" are considered synonyms. For instance, stock traders use the term "asked price" for the price at which people are offering to sell a stock. There is something in this case that makes the ask/offer dichotomy important. What is it?

2.   It is often useful to make a *timeline* showing the facts of the case in chronological order, together with the date on which each event occurred. This is especially useful when the facts are complex or when (as in *Courteen Seed*) the court relates them out of chronological order.

3.   Practicing lawyers always prepare timelines or chronological summaries when litigating complex business cases. In the real world, you are not told the facts in the order in which they happen. You learn them bit by bit as you prepare for trial (and, unfortunately, you too often learn some of them during the trial). Putting them down in chronological order makes it easier to see relationships you might otherwise overlook.

4.   This case may have been wrongly decided. There is one crucial fact that the court does not discuss in context. A timeline will make it easier for you to see what that fact is. Do you think the court got it right?

PRACTICE TIP

When drafting a legal document, never use the same phrase twice unless you want it to mean precisely the same thing in both contexts. Conversely, if you want to say the same thing twice, be sure to use identical language in both instances. The English literature academy's glorification of "elegant variation" in which one attempts to vary one's nouns and adjectives when referring repeatedly to the same thing is anathema to the law.

For example, a loan agreement will often provide that the borrower can do certain things "subject to the lender's reasonable approval." If, in one instance, perhaps by oversight, it says that it is "subject to the lender's approval," there is, then, the implication that in that particular instance the lender does not have to be reasonable, perhaps overcoming the presumption that parties to contracts always intend a duty of reasonableness.

SOUTHWORTH V. OLIVER

Supreme Court of Oregon
284 Or. 361, 587 P.2d 994 (1978)

TONGUE, JUSTICE.

[1] This is a suit in equity for a declaratory judgment that defendants "are obligated to sell" to plaintiff 2,933 acres of ranch lands in Grant County.[9] Defendants appeal from a decree of specific performance[10] in favor of plaintiff. We affirm.

[2] Defendants contend on this appeal that a certain "writing" mailed by them to plaintiff was not an offer to sell such lands; that if it was an offer there was no proper acceptance of that offer and that any such offer and acceptance did not constitute a binding contract, at least so as to be specifically enforceable. . . .

---

[9] [A party may bring a declaratory judgment action in a situation where they need a court to declare what their rights are but have no other cause of action to bring. In the usual case, where the parties dispute whether there is a contract, the party claiming that there is a contract will bring a breach of contract action against the other party. In this case it may not have been possible for the plaintiff to bring a breach of contract action against the defendant because even if there was a contract, the time for performance had not yet occurred, so there would have been no breach. In that case, the plaintiff could file a complaint asking for the court to declare that there was in fact a contract. Because of the procedural posture, the party that you might expect to be the defendant in a breach of contract suit is actually the plaintiff in the declaratory judgment action, e.g., the plaintiff may be the party seeking a pre-time-for-performance declaration that there is no contract that she needs to perform. If she waited for the time of performance and did not perform, she would normally be the defendant in a later breach of contract suit.—Eds.]

[10] [A decree of specific performance orders the defendant to perform its obligations under the contract. This is not the normal remedy in a contract case. The normal remedy is to require the defendant to pay a sum of money that will compensate the plaintiff for its loss. A contract for the sale of land is one of the few situations in which a court will normally order specific performance. Chapter 22 covers specific performance.—Eds.]

The parties and the property.

[3]   Defendants are ranchers in Grant County and owned ranches in both the Bear Valley area and also in the John Day valley. In 1976 defendants came to the conclusion that they should "cut the operation down" and sell some of the Bear Valley property, as well as some of their Forest Service grazing permits. Defendant Joseph Oliver discussed this matter with his wife, defendant Arlene Oliver, and also with his son, and the three of them "jointly arrived" at a decision to sell a portion of the Bear Valley property. Joseph Oliver also conferred with his accountant and attorney and, as a result, it was decided that the sale "had to be on terms" rather than cash, for income tax reasons. Defendant Joseph Oliver then had "a discussion with Mr. Southworth (the plaintiff) about the possibility of . . . selling this Bear Valley property." Plaintiff Southworth was also a cattle rancher in Bear Valley. The land which defendants had decided to sell was adjacent to land owned by him and was property that he had always wanted.

The initial meeting between the parties on May 20, 1976.

[4]   According to plaintiff, defendant Joseph Oliver stopped by his ranch on May 20, 1976, and said that he (Oliver) was interested in "selling the ranch" and asked "would I be interested in buying it, and I said 'yes'." Mr. Southworth also testified that "he thought I would be interested in the land and that Clyde (Holliday, also a neighbor) would be interested in the permits" and that "I told him that I was very interested in the land . . ."

[5]   Plaintiff Southworth also testified that at that time defendant Oliver showed him a map, showing land that he "understood them to offer for sale;" that there was no discussion at that time of price or terms of sale, or whether the sale of the land was contingent on sale of any of the permits, but that the conversation terminated with the understanding:

> That he would develop and determine value and price and I would make an investigation to determine whether or not I could find the money and get everything arranged for a purchase. In other words, he was going to do A and then I would do B.

[6]   According to plaintiff Southworth, defendant Oliver said that when he determined the value of the property he would send that information to Southworth so as to give him "notice" of "what he wanted for the land," but did not say that he was also going to give that same information to Mr. Holliday, although he did say that "he planned to talk to Clyde (Holliday) about permits," with the result that plaintiff knew that Oliver "might very well be . . . talking to Clyde about the same thing he talked to you (plaintiff) about" and "give that information to Clyde Holliday as well as yourself."

[7]   According to defendant Joseph Oliver, the substance of that initial conversation with plaintiff was as follows:

> I told him we were going to condense our ranch down and sell some property and that we were in the process of trying to get some figures from the Assessor on it to determine what we wanted to sell and what we might want to do. Whenever we got this information together we were going to send it to him and some of my neighbors and give them the first chance at it. . . .

[8]   Mr. Oliver also testified that plaintiff said that "he was interested;" that he had a map with him; that he mentioned to plaintiff that he "was going to sell some permits," but that there was no discussion "about the permits going with the land at that time" and that he (Oliver) "talked along the lines that Clyde (Holliday) would probably be interested in those permits." On cross-examination Mr. Oliver also answered in the affirmative a question to the effect that the property which he and Mr. Southworth "delineated on the map" during that conversation "was the property" that he "finally decided to sell and made the general offering to the four neighbors."

[9]   Plaintiff also testified that on May 26, 1976, he called Clyde Holliday to ask if he was interested in buying the land and Mr. Holliday said "no," that he was interested only in the permits, but would be interested in trading some other land for some of the land plaintiff was buying from defendants.

The telephone call of June 13, 1976.

[10] Plaintiff testified that on June 13, 1976, he called defendant Oliver by telephone to "ask him if his plans for selling . . . continued to be in force, and he said 'yes,'" that "he was progressing and there had been some delay in acquiring information from the Assessor, but they expected soon to have the information needed to establish the value on the land." Defendant Oliver's testimony was to the same effect, but he also recalled that at that time Mr. Southworth "said everything was in order and that I didn't have to worry, he had the money available and that everything was ready to go."

The letters of June 17, June 21, and June 24, 1976.

Several days later plaintiff received from defendants a letter dated June 17, 1976, as follows:

> Enclosed please find the information about the ranch sales that I had discussed with you previously. These prices are the market value according to the records of the Grant County Assessor. Please contact me if there are any questions.

There were two enclosures with that letter. The first was as follows:

JOSEPH C. and ARLENE G. OLIVER
200 Ford Road
John Day, OR 97845

Selling approximately 2933 Acres in Grant County in T. 16 S., R. 31 E., W.M. near Seneca, Oregon at the assessed market value of:

LAND		$ 306,409
IMPROVEMENTS		18,010
	Total	$ 324,419

Terms available—29% down—balance over 5 years at 8% interest. Negotiate sale date for December 1, 1976 or January 1, 1977.

Available after hay is harvested and arrangements made for removal of hay, equipment and supplies.

ALSO: Selling
Little Bear Creek allotment permit__100 head @ $225
Big Bear Creek allotment permit__200 head @ $250

[11] The second enclosure related to "selling approximately 6365 acres" in Grant County near John Day another ranch owned by the Oliver family.

[12] Defendant Joseph Oliver testified that this letter and enclosures were "drafted" by his wife, defendant Arlene Oliver; that he then read and signed it; that he sent it not only to plaintiff, but also to Clyde Holliday and two other neighbors; that it was sent because "I told them I would send them all this information and we would go from there," that it was "not made as an offer," and that it was his intention that the "property" and "permits" be transferred "together."

[13] Upon receiving that letter and enclosures, plaintiff immediately responded by letter addressed to both defendants, dated June 21, 1976, as follows:

Re the land in Bear Valley near Seneca, Oregon that you have offered to sell; I accept your offer.

[14] Plaintiff testified that on June 23, 1976, Clyde Holliday called and said he needed to acquire a portion of the land "that I had agreed to buy from Joe (Oliver), and I said I have bought the land," and that we would "work out an exchange in accord with what we have previously mentioned," but that "(h)e said he needed more land."

[15] Defendant Joseph Oliver testified that after receiving plaintiff's letter dated June 21, 1976, Clyde Holliday told him that "they (Holliday and plaintiff) were having a little difficulty getting this thing worked out,"

apparently referring to the "exchange" previously discussed between plaintiff and Holliday, and that he (Oliver) then told plaintiff that:

> (T)here seemed to be some discrepancies between what I was getting the two parties and that I didn't exactly want to be an arbitrator or say you are right or you are wrong with my neighbors. I wished they would straighten the thing out, and if they didn't, I really didn't have to sell it, that I would pull it off the market, because I didn't want to get in trouble. I would have to live with my neighbors.

Finally, on June 24, 1976, defendants mailed the following letter to plaintiff:

> "We received your letter of June 21, 1976. You have misconstrued our prior negotiations and written summaries of the lands which we and J. C. wish to sell. That was not made as or intended to be a firm offer of sale, and especially was not an offer of sale of any portion of the lands and permits described to any one person separately from the rest of the lands and permits described.
>
> The memorandum of ours was for informational purposes only and as a starting point for further negotiation between us and you and the others also interested in the properties. It is also impossible to tell from the attachment to our letter of June 17, 1976, as to the legal description of the lands to be sold, and would not in any event constitute an enforceable contract.
>
> We are open to further negotiation with you and other interested parties, but do not consider that we at this point have any binding enforceable contract with you."

This lawsuit then followed.

Defendants' letter of June 17, 1976, was an "offer to sell" the ranch lands.

[16] Defendants first contend that defendants' letter of June 17, 1976, to plaintiff was "not an offer, both as a matter of law and under the facts of this case." In support of that contention defendants say that their testimony that the letter was not intended as an offer was uncontradicted and that similar writings have been held not to constitute offers. Defendants also say that there is "authority for the proposition that all the evidence of surrounding circumstances may be taken into consideration in making that determination" and that the circumstances in this case were such as to require the conclusion that defendants did not intend the letter

as an offer and that plaintiff knew or reasonably should have known that it was not intended as an offer because: *① Legal Theory.*

1.   Defendants obviously did not intend it as an offer.

2.   The wording of the "offer" made it clear that this was "information" that plaintiff had previously expressed an interest in receiving.

3.   It did not use the term offer, but only formally advised plaintiff that defendants are selling certain lands and permits and set forth generally the terms upon which they would consider selling.

4.   Plaintiff knew of the custom of transferring permits with land and had no knowledge from the writing or previous talk that defendants were selling any cattle.

5.   Plaintiff knew and expected this same information to go to others. *② or Fact*

Defendants conclude that:

> Considering the factors determined important by the authorities cited, these factors preponderate heavily that this was not an offer to sell the land only, or to sell at all, and should not reasonably have been so construed by the plaintiff.

[17] In *Kitzke v. Turnidge*, 209 Or. 563, 573, 307 P.2d 522, 527 (1957), this court quoted with approval the following rule as stated in 1 Williston on Contracts 49–50, sec. 22A (1957):

> . . . In the early law of assumpsit stress was laid on the necessity of a promise in terms, but the modern law rightly construes both acts and words as having the meaning which a reasonable person present would put upon them in view of the surrounding circumstances. Even where words are used, "a contract includes not only what the parties said, but also what is necessarily to be implied from what they said." And it may be said broadly that any conduct of one party, from which the other may reasonably draw the inference of a promise, is effective in law as such.

[18] As also stated in 1 Restatement of Contracts sec. 25, Comment (A) (1932) as quoted by this court with approval in *Metropolitan Life Ins. Co. v. Kimball*, 163 Or. 31, 58, 94 P.2d 1101, 1111 (1939):

> It is often difficult to draw an exact line between offers and negotiations preliminary thereto. It is common for one who wishes to make a bargain to try to induce the other party to the intended transaction to make the definite offer, he himself suggesting with more or less definiteness the nature of the contract he is willing to enter into. Besides any direct language indicating an intent to

defer the formation of a contract, the definiteness or indefiniteness of the words used in opening the negotiation must be considered, as well as the usages of business, and indeed all accompanying circumstances.[11]

[19] The difficulty in determining whether an offer has been made is particularly acute in cases involving price quotations, as in this case. It is recognized that although a price quotation, standing alone, is not an offer, there may be circumstances under which a price quotation, when considered together with facts and circumstances, may constitute an offer which, if accepted, will result in a binding contract. It is also recognized that such an offer may be made to more than one person. Thus, the fact that a price quotation is sent to more than one person does not, of itself, require a holding that such a price quotation is not an offer.

[20] We agree with the analysis of this problem as stated in Murray on Contracts 37–40, sec. 24 (1977), as follows:

> If A says to B, "I am going to sell my car for $500," and B replies, "All right, here is $500, I will take it," no contract results, assuming that A's statement is taken at its face value.[12] A's statement does not involve any promise, commitment or undertaking; it is at most a statement of A's present intention . . .

[handwritten margin note: no intent to be bound]

> . . . However, a price quotation or advertisement may contain sufficient indication of willingness to enter a bargain so that the party to whom it is addressed would be justified in believing that his assent would conclude the bargain . . .

> . . . The basic problem is found in the expressions of the parties. People very seldom express themselves either accurately or in complete detail. Thus, difficulty is encountered in determining the correct interpretation of the expression in question. Over the years, some more or less trustworthy guides to interpretation have been developed.

> The first and strongest guide is that the particular expression is to be judged on the basis of what a reasonable man in the position of the offeree has been led to believe. This requires an analysis of what the offeree should have understood under all of the surrounding circumstances, with all of his opportunities for comprehending the intention of the offeror, rather than what the offeror, in fact, intended. This guide may be regarded as simply

---

[11] [This quotation from the Restatement of Contracts is very helpful. It does not try to pretend there is some magic formula for determining whether something is an offer. It recognizes that you just have to take your best shot and live with the uncertainty. (Of course, if you are involved in the transaction early enough, your job is to eliminate, or at least reduce, the uncertainty.)—Eds.]

[12] [Suppose A then says, "It's a deal." Is there then a contract? If so, who made the offer and who accepted?—Eds.]

another manifestation of the objective test. Beyond this universally accepted guide to interpretation, there are other guides which are found in the case law involving factors that tend to recur. The most important of the remaining guides is the language used. If there are no words of promise, undertaking or commitment, the tendency is to construe the expression to be an invitation for an offer or mere preliminary negotiations in the absence of strong, countervailing circumstances. Another guide which has been widely accepted is the determination of the party or parties to whom the purported offer has been addressed. If the expression definitely names a party or parties, it is more likely to be construed as an offer. If the addressee is an indefinite group, it is less likely to be an offer. The fact that this is simply a guide rather than a definite rule is illustrated by the exceptional cases which must be noted. The guide operates effectively in relation to such expressions as advertisements or circular letters. The addressee is indefinite and, therefore, the expression is probably not an offer. However, in reward cases, the addressee is equally indefinite and, yet, the expression is an offer. Finally, the definiteness of the proposal itself may have a bearing on whether it constitutes an offer. In general, the more definite the proposal, the more reasonable it is to treat the proposal as involving a commitment . . .

(Footnotes omitted).

[21] Upon application of these tests to the facts of this case we are of the opinion that defendants' letter to plaintiff dated June 17, 1976, was an offer to sell the ranch lands. We believe that the "surrounding circumstances" under which this letter was prepared by defendants and sent by them to plaintiff were such as to have led a reasonable person to believe that defendants were making an offer to sell to plaintiff the lands described in the letter's enclosure and upon the terms as there stated.

[22] That letter did not come to plaintiff "out of the blue," as in some of the cases involving advertisements or price quotations. Neither was this a price quotation resulting from an inquiry by plaintiff. According to what we believe to be the most credible testimony, defendants decided to sell the lands in question and defendant Joseph Oliver then sought out the plaintiff who owned adjacent lands. Defendant Oliver told plaintiff that defendants were interested in selling that land, inquired whether plaintiff was interested, and was told by plaintiff that he was "very interested in the land," after which they discussed the particular lands to be sold. That conversation was terminated with the understanding that Mr. Oliver would "determine" the value and price of that land, i. e., "what he wanted for the land," and that plaintiff would undertake to arrange financing for the purchase of that land. In addition to that initial conversation, there

was a further telephone conversation in which plaintiff called Mr. Oliver "to ask him if his plans for selling . . . continued to be in force" and was told "yes"; that there had been some delay in getting information from the assessor, as needed to establish the value of the land; and that plaintiff then told Mr. Oliver that "everything was in order" and that "he had the money available and everything was ready to go."

[23] Under these facts and circumstances, we agree with the finding and conclusion by the trial court, in its written opinion, that when plaintiff received the letter of June 17th, with enclosures, which stated a price of $324,419[13] for the 2,933 acres in T. 16 S., R. 31 E., W.M., as previously identified by the parties with reference to a map, and stating "terms" of 29 percent down balance over five years at eight percent interest with a "sale date" of either December 1, 1976, or January 1, 1977, a reasonable person in the position of the plaintiff would have believed that defendants were making an offer to sell those lands to him.

[24] This conclusion is further strengthened by "the definiteness of the proposal," not only with respect to price, but terms, and by the fact that "the addressee was not an indefinite group." *See* Murray, *supra* at 40.

[25] As previously noted, defendants contend that they "obviously did not intend (the letter) as an offer." While it may be proper to consider evidence of defendants' subjective intent under the objective test to which this court is committed, it is the manifestation of a previous intention that is controlling, rather than a "person's actual intent." We do not agree with defendants' contention that it was "obvious" to a reasonable person, under the facts and circumstances of this case that the letter of June 17th was not intended to be an offer to sell the ranch lands to plaintiff.

[26] We recognize, as contended by defendants, that the failure to use the word "offer," the fact that the letter included the "information" previously discussed between the parties, and the fact that plaintiff knew that the same information was to be sent to others, were important facts to be considered in deciding whether plaintiff, as a reasonable person, would have been led to believe that this letter was an "offer." *See also* Murray, *supra*, at 40. We disagree, however, with defendants' contention that these and other factors relied upon by defendants "preponderate" so as to require a holding that the letter of June 17th was not an offer.

[27] The failure to add the word "offer" and the use of the word "information" are also not controlling, and, as previously noted, an offer may be made to more than one person. The question is whether, under all of the facts and circumstances existing at the time that this letter was

---

[13]   [$324,419 in 1978 dollars is roughly the equivalent of $1,250,000 in 2019 dollars using the CPI and the GNP Deflator.—Eds.]

received, a reasonable person in the position of the plaintiff would have understood the letter to be an offer by defendants to sell the land to him.

[28] Defendants also contend that "plaintiff knew of the custom of transferring (Forest Service grazing) permits with the land and had no knowledge from the writing or previous talk that defendants were selling any cattle" (so as to provide such a basis for a transfer of the permits). Plaintiff testified, however, that at the time of the initial conversation, Mr. Oliver told plaintiff that he thought plaintiff "would be interested in the land and that Clyde would be interested in the permits." In addition, defendant Joseph Oliver, in response to questions by the trial judge, although denying that at that time he told plaintiff that he was "going to offer the permits to Mr. Holliday," admitted that he "knew Mr. Holliday was interested in the permits" and "could have" told plaintiff that he was "going to talk to Mr. Holliday about him purchasing the permits."

[29] On this record we believe that plaintiff's knowledge of the facts noted by defendants relating to the transfer of such permits did not require a holding that, as a reasonable man, he did not understand or should not have understood that defendants' letter of June 17th was an offer to sell the ranch lands to him.

[30] Plaintiff's letter of June 21, 1976, was an acceptance of defendants' offer to sell the ranch lands.

[31] The trial court, in a written opinion stating its findings of fact and conclusions of law, held that:

> ... (T)his court finds that the conduct of the defendant together with the words (in Exhibit 3): "Selling ... at the assessed market value ... terms available ... leads to only one reasonable objective conclusion; the defendants were making an offer to sell their property."

[32] As previously stated, we agree with that finding and conclusion. In that same opinion, the trial court then considered the question whether plaintiff's letter of June 21, 1976, was an acceptance of that offer.

[33] As previously stated, plaintiff responded to defendants' letter of June 17, 1976, by a letter dated June 21, 1976, as follows:

> Re the land in Bear Valley near Seneca, Oregon that you have offered for sale; I accept your offer.

* * *

[34] The further fact, as noted by defendants, that plaintiff did not rely on anything in the letter of June 17th as a "document" to "tell whether the permits had to go with the land or not" is also inconclusive, in our opinion. This is because, as previously stated, not only the words of that letter, but all of the facts and circumstances, including the initial conversation

between the parties and their later telephone conversation, were to be considered in making a finding or conclusion that a reasonable person in plaintiff's situation would have understood the letter of June 17th to be an offer by defendants to sell the ranch lands separately from the range permits.

* * *

[35] For all of these reasons, the decree of the trial court is affirmed.

NOTES AND QUESTIONS

1.   When you have only one thing to sell and you send out a communication to a number of people, that's a powerful fact in favor of finding the communication is not an offer. Why wasn't that the case in *Southworth v. Oliver*?

2.   Was the use of the word "information" and the failure to use the word "offer" significant in determining whether or not the communication was an offer?

3.   What factors went into the determination that the June 17 letter was an offer?

4.   Suppose Holliday or one of the other two neighbors who received the letter wanted to buy the land. Does it necessarily follow that the letter would have been an offer as to them?

5.   Do you think the Olivers drafted the letter of June 24, 1976, themselves? Why or why not? What was the purpose of the letter?

6.   Is the Supreme Court of Oregon, which decided both *Courteen Seed* and *Southworth v. Oliver*, being consistent in the two opinions? Or has the law changed between 1929 and 1978? Can the two decisions be harmonized? Or is one of these decisions wrong?

CONTINENTAL LABORATORIES V. SCOTT PAPER CO.
United States District Court, Southern District, Iowa
759 F. Supp. 538 (1990)

VIETOR, CHIEF JUDGE.

[1]   The court has before it defendant Scott Paper Company's (Scott) motion for summary judgment. Plaintiff Continental Laboratories, Inc., (Continental) has resisted and oral arguments have been heard.

Background

A. Facts

[2] During early 1987, representatives of Continental and Scott[14] entered into negotiations concerning a potential supply and distribution agreement whereby Continental would supply hotel amenity products[15] to Scott and Scott would distribute the products within designated areas of the United States. In the course of negotiations, the parties also discussed the possibility of a partial or total acquisition of Continental by Scott, but this possibility was not pursued to fruition. Beginning in May, 1987 and continuing throughout the negotiations period, Scott representatives prepared at least five drafts of a written Supply and Distribution Agreement, which they submitted to Continental. Each new draft incorporated changes which had resulted from negotiations about the prior draft and the subsequent revised draft then became the basis for further negotiations.

[3] On July 19, 1987, Scott, through Jim Smith, announced internally that Scott and Continental had reached a supply and distribution agreement in principle. The parties' representatives exchanged phone calls and participated in numerous meetings between July 29 and August 26, 1987. Mr. Krislov's affidavit and deposition testimony show that Continental representatives believed that a binding oral contract was reached by the parties during a telephone conference call on either August 25 or 26, 1987, between Krislov, Hirsch, Smith, and Steve Ford, Scott's legal counsel. Continental, through Krislov, further believed that Scott representatives would reduce the terms of the allegedly binding oral contract to written form in a document entitled "Supply and Distribution Agreement," as a memorial of the contract. Mr. Smith's affidavit, on the other hand, demonstrates that Scott through Smith never intended to be bound by an oral agreement, but only by a written contract executed by both parties.

[4] Scott representatives sent Continental representatives a copy of a written "Supply and Distribution Agreement" which bears the stamp "DRAFT" and the stamp "REC'D SEP 02 1987." It is believed that Continental employees placed the "REC'D" stamp on the document when they received the copy on September 2, 1987, but the origin of the "DRAFT" stamp is not known for certain. The September 2nd document contains a space for the "Commencement Date," which the Scott representatives left

---

[14] The individuals who represented Continental were: 1. Clinton A. Krislov, who has a legal degree and is also chairman of the board for Continental, 2. David Bequeaith, Continental's vice-president of operations, and 3. Austin Hirsch, legal counsel for Continental. Mr. Hirsch became involved in the negotiations in July, 1987. James Smith, Scott's Director, New Business Development, was the primary representative for Scott.

[15] Hotel amenity products consist of the complimentary, personal sized, health and beauty products that are often provided by hotels to their patrons, i.e., shampoo, bath gel, hand lotion, bar soap, shower caps, shoe polishing cloths, etc.

blank. Although the September 2nd document contains a signature page showing Scott vice-president P.N. White's signature, no officer of Continental ever signed the document.

[5] After Continental representatives received the September 2nd document, the parties' representatives conducted meetings on September 9th and 10th to further discuss implementation of the venture. Subsequent to these meetings, Mr. Smith, on behalf of Scott, prepared a revised copy of the "Supply and Distribution Agreement," which he presented to Mr. Krislov at O'Hare Airport in Chicago. On September 16, 1987, the parties' representatives met in Madrid, Iowa. During the September 16th meeting, Mr. Smith informed the Continental representatives that Scott was no longer interested in the venture and he terminated the meeting and any further discussions regarding the proposed venture.

B. Proceedings

[6] Continental filed suit against Scott in the Iowa District Court for Boone County, alleging that the parties had entered into a final and binding, oral contract during the August telephone conference and that Mr. Smith's actions on September 16, 1987, constituted a breach of that contract by Scott. On April 6, 1988, defendant Scott removed the action to this court on the basis of diversity of citizenship jurisdiction. Defendant Scott has moved for summary judgment on the ground that there was no binding contract. Alternatively, Scott argues that even if there was a binding contract, it contained a condition precedent to Scott's performance, which Continental never fulfilled and Scott properly canceled the contract.

Summary Judgment Standard

[7] Rule 56 of the Federal Rules of Civil Procedure provides that summary judgment "shall be rendered forthwith if the pleadings, depositions, answers to interrogatories, and admissions on file, together with the affidavits, if any, show that there is no genuine issue as to any material fact and that the moving party is entitled to a judgment as a matter of law." To preclude the entry of summary judgment, the nonmovant must make a sufficient showing on every essential element of its case on which it has the burden of proof at trial. Rule 56(e) requires the nonmoving party to go beyond the pleadings and by affidavits, or by the "depositions, answers to interrogatories, and admissions on file," designate "specific facts showing that there is a genuine issue for trial." Fed. R. Civ. P. 56(e). The quantum of proof that the nonmoving party must produce is not precisely measurable, but the nonmoving party must produce enough evidence so that a reasonable jury could return a verdict for the nonmovant. *Anderson v. Liberty Lobby, Inc.*, 477 U.S. 242, 257, 106 S.Ct. 2505, 2514, 91 L.Ed.2d 202 (1986).

[8] On a motion for summary judgment, the court views all the facts in the light most favorable to the nonmoving party, and that party must

also be given the benefit of all reasonable inferences to be drawn from the facts.

Discussion

[9] Under Iowa law, a binding oral contract may exist even though the parties intend to memorialize their agreement in a fully executed document. On the other hand, the parties can make the execution of a written document a condition precedent to the birth of a binding contract. *Elkader Coop. Co. v. Matt*, 204 N.W.2d 873, 875 (Iowa 1973). If either party intends not to be bound in the absence of a fully executed document, no amount of negotiation or oral agreement as to specific terms will result in the formation of a binding contract.

[*Handwritten margin note: Binding oral contract is possible*]

[10] It is the parties' intent which will determine the time of the contract formation. Plaintiff contends that the parties, through their representatives, intended to and did enter into a binding oral contract on August 25 or 26, 1987, during a telephone conference call. Defendant, however, argues that it never intended to be bound until the parties had fully executed a written contract. The court must determine the intent of the parties objectively from their words and actions viewed within the context of the situation and surrounding circumstances.

[11] In ascertaining whether the parties intended to be bound prior to execution of a written document, the court should consider the following factors: 1. whether the contract is of a class usually found to be in writing; 2. whether it is of a type needing a formal writing for its full expression; 3. whether it has few or many details; 4. whether the amount is large or small; 5. whether the contract is common or unusual; 6. whether all details have been agreed upon or some remain unresolved; and 7. whether the negotiations show a writing was discussed or contemplated. After considering these factors in the context of this case, I conclude that the summary judgment record lacks sufficient evidence from which it could be found that Scott intended to be bound in the absence of an executed written contract.

[12] Factors 1 and 2 support Scott's position. The matter was a large and complex commercial undertaking, which is usually put into written form. The parties, who were both represented by legal counsel, negotiated for over seven months and exchanged numerous drafts of a written proposed agreement. Mr. Smith, Scott's representative, stated in his affidavit that he considered the potential relationship with Continental to be a significant matter and that it was Scott's and his own custom and practice to require all significant business agreements to be in writing. The written Agreement does not mention the August 26th phone conference nor does it contain any language which indicates that it is a written memorial of an oral contract. It does, however, contain a clause which states: "[e]xcept as specifically provided herein, this Agreement and the Exhibits

hereto reflect the complete agreement of the parties and there are no other agreements or understandings applicable hereto."

[13] Similarly, factors 3, 4, and 5, support Scott's contention. First, the 12 page contract contains many details and references numerous exhibits. The Agreement addresses such issues as exclusivity of distributorship, products and services supplied, pricing, purchase commitment, payment terms, advance payments, confidentiality, and termination. Additionally, the Agreement references a related agreement between Continental and Redken. Second, the transaction at issue involves a commitment by Scott to purchase a minimum of $2.25 million worth of products from Continental during the term of the contract. Lastly, although supply and distribution agreements are fairly common in the commercial world, this particular contract was unusual for Scott because it involved Scott's entrance into a new market.

[14] Under factor 6, although Mr. Smith announced internally to Scott officials that the parties had reached an agreement in principle in July, 1987, many details were still unresolved. Even after the August telephone conference and the exchange of the September 2nd written agreement, the parties held several meetings in September, 1987, to finalize all of the details regarding manufacture and distribution of the products. On September 14, Mr. Smith even presented Mr. Krislov with another revised draft of the agreement, which Mr. Krislov accepted grudgingly. This evidence suggests that Scott, through Smith, did not consider that there was a final and binding oral agreement.

[15] Finally, an analysis of the summary judgment record under factor 7 also supports Scott's position that it intended to be bound only by a written and executed contract. During the negotiations, the parties had exchanged drafts of proposed written agreements. Also, Scott representatives had left the space for the Commencement Date of the September 2nd Agreement blank, suggesting that they did not consider August 26th to be that date. In the Agreement itself, the parties required that modifications, amendments, terminations, territorial expansions, etc., would all require a writing. *See* Exhibit A to Complaint, p. 2, 4, 8, 9, 10, 11, and 12. It would be strange for Scott to require written modifications without first contemplating a written contract.

[16] Based upon the preceding analysis of the relevant factors, I conclude that Continental has failed to overcome Scott's summary judgment motion. Continental has failed to generate a genuine issue of material fact regarding whether Scott intended to be bound by an oral agreement or only by a written and executed agreement. The summary judgment record shows that, based upon all of the circumstances, Scott communicated its intent to be bound only by a written contract, signed by

both parties. No such contract ever existed. Therefore, defendant's motion for summary judgment IS GRANTED.

Order

[17] IT IS ORDERED that plaintiff's complaint be dismissed.

NOTES AND QUESTIONS

1.　In the first sentence of paragraph 10 under the heading "Discussion," the court says: "It is the parties' intent which will determine the time of their contract formation." Is that a correct statement of the law? Would it be better to say "manifest intent" instead?

2.　The list of seven factors that the court gives is a good example of the type of list NOT to memorize. It's pretty much common sense, and if you want to spend time doing it, you could probably come up with a better list. It all comes down to the basic idea of the objective theory of contracts—what would a reasonable person take into account in deciding whether she was bound before the terms of the deal had been reduced to writing and signed in a big meeting with lawyers running around as if they thought the world was coming to an end? In *Pennzoil v. Texaco*, the fact that a toast had been drunk to celebrate the deal was a major factor leading the jury to decide the parties had made a contract for a multi-billion dollar deal. In that case, all seven of the factors listed in the *Continental Laboratories* opinion would have argued for finding there was no contract, but the jury thought this was outweighed by the Texas tradition of making deals on the basis of a handshake.

3.　Review the *Embry* case in Chapter 1. What was the offer there? What was the acceptance?

PRACTICE TIP

Whenever you are in a course of protracted negotiations like those of the Continental Laboratories case, you should consider the advantages of getting all parties to sign a document stating that there will be no contract until the parties execute formal, final documents setting forth all of the details of the transaction.

METRO-GOLDWYN-MAYER V. SCHEIDER

Supreme Court, New York County, New York
347 N.Y.S.2d 755, 75 Misc. 2d 418 (1972)

FEIN, J.

[1]　Metro-Goldwyn-Mayer, Inc. (MGM) sues Roy Scheider (Scheider), and Roy Scheider Productions, Inc. (Productions), for an injunction enjoining said defendants from entering into agreements which would

require Scheider to perform services for any third party at a time when he is obligated to render services to plaintiff, and enjoining Scheider from rendering services to any third party at a time when he is obligated to render services to plaintiff, and for damages for Scheider's refusal to render services to plaintiff.[16]

[2] MGM is a film producer, under agreement with American Broadcasting Company (ABC), pursuant to which MGM has produced a pilot film entitled "Munich Project." A pilot film is a picture produced for a television network as a demonstration picture with the hope that the network will order a television series based upon the pilot film. During the pendency of this action, ABC has exercised its option, requiring MGM to produce and deliver to ABC a television series based upon the pilot film, for broadcast on the ABC network, beginning in September, 1972. On Sunday, April 30, 1972, during the course of the trial, ABC showed the pilot film on its TV stations.

[3] On September 30, 1971, after meeting and telephone conversations among MGM and ABC representatives, Scheider, and Scheider's agent Joan Scott (Scott), it was agreed: (1) Scheider would appear in and be paid $20,000[17] for making the pilot film; (2) Scheider would be paid, per episode, for his services in any TV series that might result from the pilot; first year, $5,000 per episode; second year, $6,000 per episode; third year, $7,000 per episode; fourth year $9,500 per episode; fifth year, $11,500 per episode; (3) if the pilot film resulted in a television series, MGM would have a one-year option from the date of completion of the pilot for Scheider's services for such series.

[4] Left unresolved in these conversations was Scheider's billing. At that time Scheider was a relatively unknown actor, who had played a major role in a then unreleased picture, "The French Connection," for which he has since gained acclaim and a nomination for an Academy Award as best supporting actor. A preview of that film had been seen by ABC and MGM personnel at that time. Within a few days, it was agreed that Scheider would have second star billing in the pilot and first star billing in the series, should there be a series. These understandings were not reduced to writing, it being agreed that further terms would be worked out between Scheider's attorney and the attorneys for MGM.

---

[16] [What MGM is trying to do with this injunction is force Scheider to work for them. Courts won't usually give injunctions requiring a person to work for another. This arguably violates the constitutional prohibition on involuntary servitude and, more practically, it is likely to involve the court in ongoing disputes about the quality of performance rendered. To achieve the same result indirectly, the courts will sometimes prohibit the defendant from working for anyone else. This relief is often sought and occasionally granted. Injunctions and specific performance are covered in Chapter 22.—Eds.]

[17] [$20,000 in 1972 dollars is roughly the equivalent of $120,000 in 2019 dollars using the CPI and the GNP Deflator.—Eds.]

[5] On this basis, on or about October 6, 1971, Scheider proceeded to Munich, Germany, where, over a six weeks' period, the pilot was filmed. Between that time and up to on or about February 17, 1972, there were negotiations between Scheider's attorney and the attorneys for MGM. On or about February 15, 1972, MGM's attorneys and Scheider's attorney had agreed on all but one of the terms of the proposed agreement in substance, although the language of some agreed upon provisions remained to be drafted. There was disagreement as to the starting date, the date on which Scheider would be required to report to start filming the series. In the conversations between Scott and the MGM representatives, no starting date had been discussed or fixed and at the beginning of the negotiations there was no such discussion. Sometime in late October or early November, 1971, in a telephone conversation between Frederick C. Houghton (Houghton), MGM's attorney, and Daniel Kossow (Kossow), Scheider's attorney, the question of a starting date was first raised.

[6] Kossow pointed out that MGM's one-year option on Scheider's services might interfere with or prevent Scheider's acceptance of other performing assignments for 12 months. Houghton testified that he told Kossow that, if ABC did not exercise its option for a September, 1972 air date, MGM would not require Scheider to report for filming until November 1, 1972.

[7] Kossow testified that he understood Houghton to say that November 1, 1972, was "an outside date before which Mr. Scheider would not be required to render services." Kossow testified that on this basis he told Houghton, "he had a deal," and that he so advised Scheider some time later. However, it is conceded that in subsequent conversations and correspondence with Houghton during the negotiations there was reference to earlier start dates, so that Scheider would have an opportunity to do other work without jeopardizing MGM's network delivery schedule, should ABC exercise its option for a September, 1972 air date for the series, filming would have to begin in the spring of 1972. There were similar discussions between Kossow and Thomas J. Robinson (Robinson), another MGM attorney. In these various conversations and communications, the dates discussed were April and May, 1972 dates, and also June 5, 1972.

[8] It is the custom and practice of the industry that when a pilot is filmed in the fall of the year and shown to the network during the winter, the network has the option for a series to be shown beginning in September of the following year. In such event, filming of the series by the producer must begin in the spring, April or May, or at the latest, early June. If the network determines to show the series beginning in January or February of the next year, a so-called midyear showing, filming of the series takes place in the late fall. It is also the custom and practice that the producing company's option entitles it to require the principal actors in the pilot to

perform in the series, consistent with the network's option to require the producer to produce and deliver a TV series based upon the pilot.

[9] It is undisputed that all of the parties were aware of these customs and practices, and that the ABC-MGM agreement was consistent therewith.

[10] On or about February 17, 1972, Kossow advised MGM that, since MGM had refused to agree to a November 1, 1972 starting date for Scheider, Scheider would not perform in the series and considered that he had no further obligation to MGM, either to negotiate or perform. No written contract was ever executed.

[11] ABC has exercised its option calling upon MGM, to produce a series of eight episodes for air dates commencing September, 1972. MGM has exercised its option requiring Scheider to report on or before June 5, 1972, for filming the series. Scheider has stated that he will not do so.

[12] At issue is whether the terms agreed upon were sufficient to support a finding that the parties made an agreement enforceable under the Statute of Frauds or otherwise.[18]

[13] Whether the terms agreed between Scott and MGM were sufficient to establish a contract, is not free from doubt. There was much testimony on both sides as to the custom and practice of the industry to enter into binding oral arrangements on the basic or essential terms under which a performer will render services in making a pilot film, and for negotiation of a formal contract to continue during the period the actor is performing. There was also testimony as to the custom and practice of embodying such terms in a written "Outline Deal Memo," utilized with respect to Richard Basehart, the other principal actor in the pilot.

[14] There was disagreement as to what terms are considered basic or essential.

[15] It is undisputed that many of the matters left for negotiation, such as residual rights, commercial fees, etc., would substantially affect Scheider's compensation. Moreover, there was never any specific agreement as to a starting date for Scheider's performance, although implicit in MGM's one-year option was the right to exercise the option within the year.

[16] Although plaintiff did not prove that Scheider and his representatives ever agreed on a particular starting date, the record establishes that Scheider and his representatives knew that if ABC exercised its option for a September, 1972 air date, MGM would be compelled to require Scheider to report for filming in the spring or early

---

[18] [The Statute of Frauds provides that certain contracts will not be enforced unless there is a signed record indicating that the parties actually made the contract. The Statute of Frauds is covered in Chapter 13.—Eds.]

summer of 1972. Scheider knew that the MGM option gave it authority to require such a starting date.

[17] It is manifest that many of the essential or basic elements of the contemplated contract were left for future negotiation at the time of the original understanding. Irrespective of any custom or practice of an industry, there is no contract if material financial or time elements involving compensation or other kinds of payment or duration are left undetermined. The court cannot write a contract which the parties have not made.

[18] However, where the parties have completed their negotiations of what they regard as essential elements, and performance has begun on the good faith understanding that agreement on the unsettled matters will follow, the court will find and enforce a contract even though the parties have expressly left these other elements for future negotiation and agreement, if some objective method of determination is available, independent of either party's mere wish or desire. Such objective criteria may be found in the agreement itself, commercial practice or other usage and custom. If the contract can be rendered certain and complete, by reference to something certain, the court will fill in the gaps.

[19] Here, the subsequent agreement of the parties as to all the elements of the contract, except the starting date, provides a basis for finding a complete contract. Although there was no agreement on a start date, this missing element is not dispositive. Implicit in Scheider's agreement to make the pilot and do the series, subject to MGM's one-year option, was a promise to report in time for the filming of the series, in the event ABC picked up the picture for a series with a September, 1972 start. Scheider's agreement was "instinct with an obligation" so to report. (*Wood v. Duff-Gordon,* 222 N.Y. 88, 91, quoting *McCall Co. v. Wright,* 133 App.Div. 62.) Enough had been shown as to the custom and practice of the industry, the understanding of the parties, and their subsequent agreement as to terms, to establish a contract requiring Scheider to report during the spring of 1972 for a September, 1972, air date, if so requested by MGM. This is a reasonable time, which may be implied by law, even if not agreed upon.

[The court went on to hold that the Statute of Frauds rendered the contract unenforceable, but on that issue it was reversed on appeal, and MGM ultimately prevailed.—Eds.]

———

PROBLEM 2-1

Scarlett sends a letter to Rhett in which she says: "If you submit a written offer to buy Tara for $250,000 or more, I will accept your offer." Rhett submits

a written offer to buy Tara for $275,000. Scarlett says: "Rhett, I've changed my mind." Do they have a contract? Look carefully at R2d § 24 and UNIDROIT article 2.1.2 before you answer. Is the answer the same under both standards?

No rejected the offer

PROBLEM 2-2

Read carefully U.C.C. § 2–328, especially subsection (3). In an auction "with reserve," who is the offeror? In an auction "without reserve," who is the offeror and what are the terms of the offer?

PROBLEM 2-3

A rural landlord wants to convince his tenant to locate more cattle on the land that the tenant rents because the rent is measured in terms of cows on the land and goes up as the size of the herd increases. He says to the tenant, "I will see that there will be plenty of water because it never failed here before." The tenant relied upon the statement and acquired more cattle. The water failed. The tenant sued.

Had the landlord made an offer—to see there will be enough water—and, if so, what were the terms of the offer? *No*

See Anderson v. Backlund, 159 Minn. 423, 199 N.W. 90 (1924) (held: remark was in the nature of a prediction, not a representation, warranty, or other contract term).

———

Offers—an Orientation

In determining whether a particular communication constitutes an offer, the analysis begins and ends with the question of whether the offeree was justified in believing that by manifesting her assent, she could form a binding contract. (Many of the cases put it in terms of whether a reasonable person in the position of the offeree would think she could form a contract by manifesting her assent, but the differences between the two formulations are immaterial.) This is, of course, the key to correctly responding to Problem 2-2, above.

In determining whether the offeree would be justified, you should look at any factor that might be relevant. People have put together lists of factors which should be taken into account, but there is no magic in these lists. They are just the author's judgments as to which factors are most often important. Every situation is unique, so there's no right or wrong universal list.

Here are **some** of the factors that will be important in the cases in this book:

1. The Language Used   *Intent to be bound*

Some courts rely heavily on the fact that the language used showed a clear intent to be bound. *See Lucy, Lefkowitz,* and *Courteen Seed.*

On the other hand, sometimes the circumstances under which the communication was made outweigh the language. *See Southworth.*

2. Specificity and Detail

The more specific and detailed the communication is, the more likely it will be construed as an offer. If the person making the communication went to the trouble of spelling out the details, it tends to indicate he intended to be bound, where as if he left important things open, it tends to indicate he thought he would have a chance to negotiate them later. The size of the deal is an important factor here. If the proposal is for a billion dollar merger, the offeree would normally expect that the offeror didn't intend to be bound unless there was an agreement spelling out things in great detail. On the other hand, if the deal is rather small, it would be inefficient to hire a platoon of lawyers to draft an agreement covering every possible contingency.

3. Customs and Practices in the Business

These are important in several different ways. In some businesses, it's customary to regard certain communications as offers, whereas in other businesses a very similar communication would not be considered an offer. For instance, if an auto dealer advertises a particular car at a particular price, he's probably about to sell it to the first person who is willing to pay that price. On the other hand, if somebody advertises her house in the paper for a particular price, she can decide that she doesn't want to sell it or that she will only sell it at a higher price. Why? Because that's the way things are done, and the offeree is expected to know that and take it into account when she forms her belief as to whether her assent will form a contract.

Another way customs and practices become important is by providing "gap fillers" that will allow a communication that otherwise would not be specific enough to be an offer. For instance, in *Lucy*, there were a number of important details left unresolved: what crops, livestock, equipment etc. would be included with the land; who would pay the various expenses involved in the transaction (these expenses, called "closing costs" are often quite substantial in a real estate transaction); when would the deed be delivered; when would the price be paid; what right did the buyer have to back out if he discovered some problem with the property like a toxic waste problem; and the like? In other circumstances, a court might have found that the failure to cover these details kept the parties from forming a contract. In this case, however, the court, though it didn't discuss this, probably was influenced by the fact that in most localities there is a customary way of dealing with these issues when the parties fail to provide for them. *See Scheider* (Hollywood custom supports finding a contract); *compare Continental Laboratories* (the court reached the opposite conclusion, reasoning that in the more staid business of hotel amenity supply, people would want to have all the details worked out before they bound themselves).

4.   The Multiple Acceptance Problem

If a seller has a limited quantity of things to sell and the communication is sent to a number of people, this is an indication that the seller does not intend to be bound but is only soliciting offers from which she can choose. The idea is that the buyer should know the seller wouldn't want to expose herself to the risk that she will have more contracts than she can fulfill. *See Lonergan* (the statement "this is a form letter" perhaps suggests that the letter in *Lonergan* was not an offer); *see also Southworth* (the letter to four potential buyers was an offer to Mr. Southworth even though it had gone out to others).

Sometimes the multiple acceptances problem is avoided if there is an indication that the offer is good only until whatever is being offered is sold. *See Lefkowitz* (ad expressly said "first come, first served").

5.   The Context in Which the Communication Is Made

In *Southworth,* the court was influenced by the fact that Mr. Southworth had been led to believe Mr. Oliver would be sending him an offer. In *Courteen Seed,* the court overlooked a fact that may have allowed it to come to an erroneous conclusion.

––––––

QUESTION

In terms of negotiating leverage and being in control of the substance and structure of a transaction, is it better to be the offeror or the offeree? Is there one right answer to this question? Why or why not?

LAWYERING SKILLS PROBLEM

Your client has received the following letter from a person they have never met who appears to have gotten your client's name and address by searching the city's real property tax records (available online):

Client O. Yours
2525 Elmwood Glen Drive
Anytown, Anystate 55512

RE: 1305 Bridge Avenue; Assessor's Parcel no. 05–24116–008

Dear Mr. or Ms. Yours:

[1] I am interested in acquiring the above-referenced property, which you are listed as owning in the county clerk's records. This letter is an offer to purchase the property from you for $1,100,000.

[2] The property appears to be improved with approximately 50 3-bedroom/2-bathroom apartment units, an onsite laundry facility, and at least 50 standard-sized parking spaces. I estimate, therefore, that there are approximately 150 bedrooms and, estimating rental revenue of $450 per bedroom per month for this sort of low income, itinerant, or student housing, a rent revenue stream of approximately $67,500 per month, or $810,000 per year, assuming 100% occupancy. Deducting $35,000 for operating expenses and a vacancy allowance, then, your property should yield $775,000 per year in net operating income. Given that apartment complexes locally have been recently selling with an imputed capitalization rate of 5%, this means your property is worth $15,500,000.

[3] Because I have some capital that I wish to deploy in the local real estate market in the very near term, I am willing to pay you $16,000,000 for your property, subject to your being able to convey marketable title that is free and clear of all but customary encumbrances. If you accept this offer, the full purchase and sale agreement will include all the standard terms and conditions. No brokerage commission will be paid.

[4] If you accept this offer, please indicate that you do so by signing below where indicated and returning the original to:

IMA Investor, LLC
721 Old Colony Drive

I thank you for your time and consideration in this matter.

Very truly yours,

Dan Gelling

Dan Gelling
President
IMA Investor, LLC

I accept the offer stated above.

Signed: _____   Dated: _____
Name: Client O. Yours
Title: Owner, 1305 Bridge Avenue

(1)   Your client has come to you because, although he does not need to sell the property, being able to sell for more than it is worth is of interest. The client's first question is if this is "for real"—i.e., is this an offer capable of immediate acceptance and, if he signs and returns the letter, will there be a binding contract? Is this an offer under the standards employed in the previous cases and in the R2d? Articulate those standards as a series of factors or elements and indicate what facts support a finding that those factors or elements have or have not been satisfied to support your conclusion.

(2)   Is this an offer under the standards of CISG article 14 (assuming it applied to this transaction)?

(3)   Is this an offer under the standards of UNIDROIT article 2.1.2?

(4)   What is the legal significance of paragraph 2 of the letter, if any? Do you need to understand its details and critically analyze its argument regarding value and the like in order to answer your client's question of whether this letter is an offer?

(5)   What is the legal significance of paragraph 3 of the letter, if any? Do you need to understand its details in order to answer your client's question as to whether this is an offer?

(6)   There are many issues raised by this letter, whether it is an offer or not. What are these issues? Be sure to break them down to their constituent parts. Which issues that you have identified are legal issues? Which are business issues? Are there other issues and, if so, how would you categorize them if they are not legal or business issues?

(7)   In order to accept the offer, must your client sign off on the letter and return it to the sender? If they are not required to accept by doing so, but want to accept, how would you advise them to do so?

CHAPTER 3

HAS THE OFFER BEEN ACCEPTED?

■ ■ ■

Once it has been determined that an offer was made, there is still often a question as to whether the offer was accepted. This is often closely related to the question of whether the offer was still valid at the time the purported acceptance took place. Chapter 4 examines in detail the question of when an offer terminates or ceases to be effective, but you need to understand a few basics of this issue in order to appreciate the material in this chapter. There are four basic ways an offer may terminate. For purposes of illustrating all four, we'll assume A has made the usual offer to B: "I'll sell you my car for $1,000." Any of these terminates the original offer:

The offeree may reject the offer or make a counteroffer, which operates as a rejection (by operation of law). B says to A: "I'm not interested." Or B says to A: "I'll take it if you'll give it to me for $900."

The offer may expire by its own terms, e.g., by lapse of time. If A says: "This offer is good until October 15," B can't accept it on October 16. If, as is often the case, the offer does not say when it expires, it expires after a reasonable time. We'll wait until we get to the next chapter to puzzle over what would be a reasonable time in these circumstances.

The offeror may revoke the offer. A can say: "I've changed my mind." As we'll see in the next chapter, A's right to do so is subject to some limitations.

The offeror or the offeree may die or be adjudicated incompetent. Either event terminates the offeror's capacity to contract and revokes the offer (by operation of law); he or she is no longer capable of making a legally-binding contract.

We can divide offers into three categories:

1. Offers that can be accepted only by performance, forming a unilateral contract;

2. Offers that can be accepted only by a promise, forming a bilateral contract; and

3. Offers that can be accepted either by performance or by a
promise, forming a unilateral or bilateral contract, depending on
the method of acceptance.

Since one of the main reasons we have contracts is to allow people to plan,
to allow them to bind themselves and others to a course of action in the
future, the second category—bilateral contracts—is the most common in
practice. The first and third categories are fairly rare. It is an unusual
situation where the offeror wants to bind herself and leave the offeree free
to accept or not until it is time for the offeree to perform. One situation in
which an offer can be accepted only by performance is a reward type
situation where the offeror wants to entice people to try to perform a task
that they might not be able to accomplish and thus would not want to
promise to perform. (The real estate broker's "open listing," discussed
below, is an example of the reward type situation as is a reward offered for
the return of lost or stolen property.)

Another situation in which an offer might be capable of being accepted
only by performance is where the offeree's promise would not be worth
much. For example, in a famous case that we will look at in a future
chapter, an uncle promised his nephew a large sum of money if the nephew
did not smoke until he was 21. If the nephew made a promise not to smoke
and then broke it, it is unlikely that the uncle would be able to sue the
nephew and prevail, so it seems that the promise would be worthless and
that a person in the nephew's position would be justified in believing that
the offer could be accepted only by performance.

Offers that can be accepted only by performance are unusual outside
of the situations described above. If a law professor wants to ask a question
about an offer that can be accepted only by performance, he or she will
normally make it clear that the situation fits into one of those described
above, or they will make it clear from the language that the offer can be
accepted only by performance. It's usually a rather contrived situation.
(The UNIDROIT principles do not even bother to address the situation
specifically.)

Distinguishing between the other two types of offers is often difficult.
There are two competing considerations. In favor of finding that the offer
can be accepted only by a promise is the fact that people who enter into
contractual relationships generally want to get the other party bound as
soon as possible in order to eliminate uncertainty. This means getting a
promise well ahead of the time that performance is to begin. On the other
hand, R2d § 32 says that in case of doubt, an offer is interpreted as inviting
acceptance either by a promise or by performance.

Fortunately, most of the time, you will not have to decide into which
of these two categories the offer falls. If the offeree accepts by making a
promise (which is what usually happens), it doesn't matter. It's only when

the offeree tries to accept by rendering a performance that you have to ask: "Should it have been clear to the offeree that the offeror was seeking a promise and was not seeking performance?"

PRACTICE TIP: TYPES OF REAL ESTATE BROKERAGE CONTRACTS

Open Listing: This is an offer for a unilateral contract in which the seller promises to pay a commission if (1) the broker produces a buyer ready, willing, and able to purchase under the terms set forth in the agreement (e.g., $100,000 with 20% down and the balance over 10 years at 8% interest) or (2) the broker produces a buyer and the seller sells to that buyer, whether or not at the terms set forth in the brokerage agreement. The purpose of an open listing is to allow the seller to deal with a number of brokers at the same time.

Exclusive Listing: This is a bilateral contract in which the broker promises to use her best efforts to procure a buyer and the seller promises to pay a commission if (1) the broker produces a buyer ready, willing, and able to purchase under the terms set forth in the agreement or (2) the broker produces a buyer and the seller sells to that buyer, whether or not at the terms set forth in the brokerage agreement. The owner agrees not to engage other brokers, but the owner has the right to sell the property herself during the term of the agreement without paying the broker a commission.

Exclusive Right to Sell: This is a bilateral contract in which the broker promises to use her best efforts to produce a buyer and the seller promises to pay a commission if (1) the broker produces a buyer ready, willing, and able to purchase under the terms set forth in the agreement, or (2) the property is sold during the term of the agreement (even if the owner finds the buyer herself), or (3) the seller takes the property off the market during the term of the agreement.

In the cases that follow, the offeree said or did something before the offer was terminated that might or might not have been an acceptance. The court is being called upon to determine whether the offeree's words or actions constitute an acceptance.

As you read the cases, consider R2d § 50(1) and UNIDROIT article 2.1.6(1). The rules seem simple but have some implications you might not expect.

———

EVER-TITE ROOFING CORP. V. GREEN

Court of Appeal of Louisiana
83 So.2d 449 (1955)

AYRES, JUDGE.

Cause of action

[1]   This is an action for damages allegedly sustained by plaintiff as the result of the breach by the defendants of a written contract for the re-roofing of defendants' residence. Defendants denied that their written proposal or offer was ever accepted by plaintiff in the manner stipulated therein for its acceptance, and hence contended no contract was ever entered into. The trial court sustained defendants' defense and rejected plaintiff's demands and dismissed its suit at its costs. From the judgment thus rendered and signed, plaintiff appealed.

Facts

[2]   Defendants executed and signed an instrument June 10, 1953, for the purpose of obtaining the services of plaintiff in re-roofing their residence situated in Webster Parish, Louisiana. The document set out in detail the work to be done and the price therefore to be paid in monthly installments. This instrument was likewise signed by plaintiff's sales representative, who, however, was without authority to accept the contract for and on behalf of the plaintiff. This alleged contract contained these provisions:

Two ways offer accepted

> This agreement shall become binding only upon written acceptance thereof, by the principal or authorized officer of the Contractor, *or upon commencing performance of the work.* This contract is Not Subject to Cancellation. It is understood and agreed that this contract is payable at office of Ever-Tite Roofing Corporation, 5203 Telephone, Houston, Texas. It is understood and agreed that this Contract provides for attorney's fees and in no case less than ten percent attorney's fees in the event same is placed in the hands of an attorney for collecting or collected through any court, and further provides for accelerated maturity for failure to pay any installment of principal or interest thereon when due.
>
> This written agreement is the only and entire contract covering the subject matter hereof and no other representations have been made unto Owner except these herein contained. No guarantee on repair work, partial roof jobs, or paint jobs.

(Emphasis supplied.)

[3]   In as much as this work was to be performed entirely on credit, it was necessary for plaintiff to obtain credit reports and approval from the lending institution which was to finance said contract. With this procedure defendants were more or less familiar and knew their credit rating would have to be checked and a report made. On receipt of the proposed contract

in plaintiff's office on the day following its execution, plaintiff requested a credit report, which was made after investigation and which was received in due course and submitted by plaintiff to the lending agency. Additional information was requested by this institution, which was likewise in due course transmitted to the institution, which then gave its approval.

[4]   The day immediately following this approval, which was either June 18 or 19, 1953, plaintiff engaged its workmen and two trucks, loaded the trucks with the necessary roofing materials and proceeded from Shreveport to defendants' residence for the purpose of doing the work and performing the services allegedly contracted for the defendants. Upon their arrival at defendants' residence, the workmen found others in the performance of the work which plaintiff had contracted to do. Defendants notified plaintiff's workmen that the work had been contracted to other parties two days before and forbade them to do the work.

[5]   Formal acceptance of the contract was not made under the signature and approval of an agent of plaintiff. It was, however, the intention of plaintiff to accept the contract by commencing the work, which was one of the ways provided for in the instrument for its acceptance, as will be shown by reference to the extract from the contract quoted herein above. Prior to this time, however, defendants had determined on a course of abrogating the agreement and engaged other workmen without notice thereof to plaintiff.

[6]   The basis of the judgment appealed was that defendants had timely notified plaintiff before "commencing performance of work." The trial court held that notice to plaintiff's workmen upon their arrival with the materials that defendants did not desire them to commence the actual work was sufficient and timely to signify their intention to withdraw from the contract. With this conclusion we find ourselves unable to agree.

[7]   Defendants' attempt to justify their delay in thus notifying plaintiff for the reason they did not know where or how to contact plaintiff is without merit. The contract itself, a copy of which was left with them, conspicuously displayed plaintiff's name, address and telephone number. Be that as it may, defendants at no time, from June 10, 1953, until plaintiff's workmen arrived for the purpose of commencing the work, notified or attempted to notify plaintiff of their intention to abrogate, terminate or cancel the contract.

[8]   Defendants evidently knew this work was to be processed through plaintiff's Shreveport office. The record discloses no unreasonable delay on plaintiff's part in receiving, processing or accepting the contract or in commencing the work contracted to be done. No time limit was specified in the contract within which it was to be accepted or within which the work was to be begun. It was nevertheless understood between the parties that some delay would ensue before the acceptance of the contract and the

commencement of the work, due to the necessity of compliance with the requirements relative to financing the job through a lending agency. The evidence as referred to hereinabove shows that plaintiff proceeded with due diligence.

Rule+Issue

[9] The general rule of law is that an offer proposed may be withdrawn before its acceptance and that no obligation is incurred thereby. This is, however, not without exceptions. For instance, Restatement of the Law of Contracts stated:

(1) The power to create a contract by acceptance of an offer terminates at the time specified in the offer, or, if no time is specified, at the end of a reasonable time.

What is a reasonable time is a question of fact depending on the nature of the contract proposed, the usages of business and other circumstances of the case which the offeree at the time of his acceptance either knows or has reason to know.

* * *

Holding

[10] Therefore, since the contract did not specify the time within which it was to be accepted or within which the work was to have been commenced, a reasonable time must be allowed therefor in accordance with the facts and circumstances and the evident intention of the parties. A reasonable time is contemplated where no time is expressed. What is a reasonable time depends more or less upon the circumstances surrounding each particular case. The delays to process defendants' application were not unusual. The contract was accepted by plaintiff by the commencement of the performance of the work contracted to be done. This commencement

Holding

began with the loading of the trucks with the necessary materials in Shreveport and transporting such materials and the workmen to defendants' residence. Actual commencement or performance of the work therefore began before any notice of dissent by defendants was given plaintiff. The proposition and its acceptance thus became a completed contract.

[11] By their aforesaid acts defendants breached the contract. They employed others to do the work contracted to be done by plaintiff and forbade plaintiff's workmen to engage upon that undertaking.

* * *

[12] For the reasons assigned, the judgment appealed is annulled, avoided, reversed and set aside and there is now judgment in favor of plaintiff, Ever-Tite Roofing Corporation, against the defendants, G. T. Green and Mrs. Jessie Fay Green, for the full sum of $311.37[1], with 5 per

---

[1]   [$311.37 in 1955 dollars is roughly the equivalent of $2,920 in 2019 dollars using the CPI and the GNP Deflator.—Eds.]

cent per annum interest thereon from judicial demand until paid, and for all costs.

Reversed and rendered.

———

NOTES AND QUESTIONS

1   Read R2d § 30(1). This section reiterates in more formal language the generally-accepted rule that "the offeror is master of her offer." It is mirrored in R2d § 50(1). Suppose A says to B: "I hereby offer to sell you my car for $1,000. You can accept this offer only by standing on your head and whistling The Star-Spangled Banner." B can't accept the offer by saying "It's a deal." B can't accept the offer by paying A $1,000. B can accept the offer only by standing on his head and whistling The Star-Spangled Banner.

2.   Read R2d § 30(2). What was the offer in *Ever-Tite*? How was it accepted? How else could it have been accepted?

3.   The court ignores a powerful argument for the defendants. What is it? (Hint: Remember that we've been talking about the importance of characterizing the facts in a way most favorable to our client. You should also start looking at alternative ways of interpreting language. Could "commencing performance of work" have a meaning other than the one the court gave it? Many attorneys start billing for their time when travel to an engagement starts.)

4.   In *Ever-Tite*, whom did the court regard as specifying how the offer could be accepted? Who really determined how the offer could be accepted? Was the court therefore wrong in the way it decided the case?

5.   UNIDROIT article 2.1.6 corresponds to R2d § 50(1). Are the standards the same?

———

PROBLEM 3-1 *Permitted or Required*

A writes B a letter:

Dear B:

I hereby offer to sell you my collection of Marilyn Monroe memorabilia for $1,000.

Please advise me by mail whether you accept this offer. — *Permitted Manner*

Does not say must or only

Sincerely,

A

Valid offer — intent to be bound
Certainty
Communication

B gets the letter and telephones A telling him she accepts the offer. Has a contract been formed? *See* R2d § 60 ~~Does the~~ Yes

What if B gets the letter and *e-mails* A telling him she accepts the offer? No, depends

———

BEARD IMPLEMENT CO. V. KRUSA

Appellate Court of Illinois
208 Ill. App. 3d 953, 153 Ill. Dec. 387, 567 N.E.2d 345 (1991)

STEIGMANN, J.

[1] This action involves an alleged breach of contract between plaintiff seller, Beard Implement Company, Inc., a farm implement dealership, and defendant buyer, Carl Krusa, a farmer, for the purchase of a 1985 Deutz-Allis N-5 combine. The dispositive issue on appeal is whether the trial court in a bench trial erred in finding a contract existed between the parties. Specifically, defendant contends that plaintiff never accepted defendant's offer to purchase the combine. We agree and reverse.

[2] At trial, defendant testified that between December 20 and December 23, 1985, he had several conversations with plaintiff's representatives concerning the purchase of a new combine. Defendant owned a 1980 Deutz-Allis N-5 combine at that time. In fall 1985, both spindles on his combine had broken and defendant spoke with plaintiff's representatives about repairing them.

[3] On December 23, 1985, defendant met with plaintiff's representatives at plaintiff's office in Arenzville, Illinois. Defendant testified that one of plaintiff's representatives, either Jim Beard or Gerry Beard, filled out a purchase order for a new combine for the price of $52,800[2] cash and the trade-in of the combine defendant then owned. . . . Defendant signed the Allis-Chalmers purchase order, which was dated December 23, 1985. None of plaintiff's representatives signed that order on December 23, 1985, or at any time thereafter. The bottom left corner of this order reads as follows:

———————————————

DEALER'S SALESMAN

This order subject to acceptance by dealer.

Accepted by:

———————————————

DEALER

———

    [2]   [$52,800 in 1991 dollars is roughly equivalent to $97,300 in 2019 dollars using the CPI and the GNP Deflator.—Eds.]

[4] At the same time defendant signed the purchase order, he also signed a counter check drawn on a local bank in the amount of $5,200. Defendant testified that because he did not have his checkbook, plaintiff provided him with the counter check.[3] The check was undated and intended to represent a down payment on the combine. Defendant testified that the check was not dated because he was to call plaintiff later and let plaintiff know if he wanted to proceed with the transaction. At that time, plaintiff would put a date on the check.

[5] Defendant testified that he had misgivings over the Christmas weekend and, after discussing the situation with his wife, telephoned plaintiff's manager, Duane Hess, on December 26, 1985, and told Hess that he did not wish to proceed with the transaction. Defendant explained to Hess that defendant and his wife had determined that "the price was too high" and they "did not want to go further into debt to finance the transaction." Defendant testified that Hess told him that if defendant thought the combine was too expensive, Hess would let defendant out of the deal. Hess did not indicate whether he had signed the order.

[6] Earlier on December 26, 1985, defendant had met with a representative of Cox Implement Company. Defendant identified a copy of the order form that one of Cox's salesman had filled out. This order was dated December 26, 1985, but was signed on December 27. Defendant testified that he told Cox's salesman that his price was too high and that defendant could not go through with either that bid or plaintiff's bid. However, after Cox's quoted price was reduced and the figures on the purchase order were scratched out, defendant signed the purchase order with Cox on December 27, 1985. Defendant stated the agreement with Cox was for the same model combine he was negotiating for with plaintiff but at a lower price. He wanted to consummate the transaction by December 31, 1985, in order to take advantage of the investment tax credit.

[7] Defendant wrote a letter to plaintiff that was dated December 26, 1985, but sent on December 27, 1985. That letter read as follows:

Dec. 26, '85

Dear Sirs:

As I told you by phone on Dec. 26, '85, I do not wish to purchase the 1985–5 combine we talked about so please send me the uncashed counter check on the Bank of Bluffs for the amount of $5,200. Since my "Purchase Order Sheet" had not yet been signed

---

[3] [A counter check is a bank check that does not show the customer's account information and thus can be used by anyone to write a check on their account. At one time, banks often kept them on the counter so that customers could make cash withdrawals from their checking accounts. They are much less common now because banks depend on the magnetically-encoded customer information on the check to process the check. Also, the prevalence of automatic teller machines has reduced the need for such devices.—Eds.]

by the dealer rep, the check wasn't cashed before notification, & the combine wasn't picked up, the [inconvenience] should have been slight.

Feel free to consult my attorney, John D. Coonrod, for details. Again, excuse these changes of events.

Sincerely,

Carl W. Krusa
(FOR "K" FARMS)

[8]   Defendant testified that Jim Beard visited defendant at his farm around lunchtime on December 27, 1985. During this visit, Jim told defendant, "There's no problem, Carl, just please send a check to Tony Thomas for his time explaining the differences between models and options." Defendant recalled that their conversation was friendly and that Jim told him something to the effect that, "Carl, we maybe lost a little bit of commission on this, but don't worry about it. I'll make it up on the next sale." Defendant signed the contract with Cox later that afternoon.

[9]   Defendant testified that when he spoke with Hess on the evening of December 26, Hess did not indicate that he had signed the order that had been signed earlier by defendant. Defendant testified that in his letter to plaintiff, he enclosed a check for $100 made payable to Thomas for Thomas' time. Defendant believed that once this sum was paid, he was released from any obligation to plaintiff seller.

[10] Jim Beard testified that in fall 1985, he approached defendant several times about purchasing a new combine. Jim testified that he again spoke with defendant about purchasing a new combine at plaintiff's Arenzville office at 3:30 or 4 p.m. on December 23, 1985. Gerry Beard was also present. Jim stated that he did not have the authority to sell the combine at a given price; only Gerry and Hess had that authority. The price quoted by Gerry to defendant was $52,800 and the trade-in of defendant's existing combine. Jim identified the purchase order bearing defendant's signature. Jim filled in all the other information on that order.

[11] Jim testified that defendant did not make any statements that he was going to consider the purchase further after signing the purchase order. Jim also stated that defendant did not make any statements to the effect that the purchase order was not to be considered a completed contract.

[12] Jim identified the counter check payable to plaintiff for $5,200. He stated that he filled out the check and defendant signed it, but that he forgot to fill in the date on the check. Jim did not recall any statement made by defendant that the check should be held. Jim recalled that the purchase order and check were signed at approximately 5:30 p.m. He stated that defendant was not threatened or told that he could not leave the office until

he signed the order. Jim stated that he would not have signed the order if defendant had said anything about reserving the right to call back later and cancel the deal.

[13] Jim next spoke with defendant on December 27, 1985. Hess told Jim that defendant did not want to buy the combine and asked Jim to visit defendant. Jim met with defendant that same day and asked defendant why he could not buy the combine. Defendant told him that he could not afford it. Jim stated that defendant did not mention that he had purchased a combine from someone else.

[14] On cross-examination, Jim admitted that he did not sign the purchase order which defendant had signed. He testified that Gerry and Hess are authorized to accept offers on behalf of plaintiff, but that neither one signed the order.

no one signed the purchase order

[15] Gerry Beard testified that defendant came to plaintiff's office in the afternoon of December 23. Gerry stated that he attempted to persuade defendant to purchase a new combine. Gerry testified that he offered to sell the new combine to defendant for $52,800 and that defendant replied, "I'll take the deal." Defendant then signed the order and counter check and left plaintiff's offices.

[16] Gerry stated that he is authorized to accept contracts on behalf of plaintiff. He testified that he accepted the contract with defendant. Gerry stated that defendant did not indicate, after signing the counter check and purchase order, that the transaction was not a completed deal.

[17] On appeal, defendant argues that the trial court erred in finding that a contract existed between him and plaintiff for the purchase of a combine. Defendant argues plaintiff never accepted defendant's offer to purchase the combine because the purchase order defendant signed required a signature by a "dealer" on behalf of plaintiff for acceptance and none of plaintiffs representatives ever signed that order. Accordingly, defendant's subsequent refusal to "go through with the deal" constituted a valid revocation of his offer.

[18] Plaintiff argues that a contract existed between the parties even before their agreement was reduced to writing. Essentially, plaintiff contends that after the verbal agreement was reached, the terms of that agreement were memorialized on the purchase order, which was then signed by defendant. Further, plaintiff argues that this verbal agreement was evidenced by a counter check, which was also signed by defendant and which represented a down payment on the combine. Plaintiff asserts that it accepted both the purchase order and the down payment by placing those documents in its office.

[19] In deciding whether the offer in the present case has been accepted, this court must first identify both the offeror and the offeree. A

treatise on contract law provides some guidance on this issue: "A [ ][4] problem arises when A, through a salesman, has frequently solicited orders from B, the contract to arise when approved by A at A's home office. As we have seen in this situation[,] B is the offeror and A the offeree." J. Calamari & J. Perillo, Contracts § 2–18, at 85 (3d ed. 1987).

[20] In *Foremost Pro Color, Inc. v. Eastman Kodak Co.* (9th Cir.1983), 703 F.2d 534, the court considered whether a contract existed based on two unsigned purchase orders. The district court had concluded that no contract existed because the purchase orders were merely offers to buy, inviting acceptance either by a prompt promise to ship or by prompt or current shipment. (*Foremost*, 703 F.2d at 538.) The court of appeals agreed and stated that the weight of authority suggests that purchase orders are not enforceable contracts until accepted by the offeree. *Foremost*, 703 F.2d at 539.

[21] In the instant case, the purchase order form signed by defendant constitutes an offer made by defendant to plaintiff. Thus, this court needs to determine whether defendant's offer was accepted by plaintiff.

[22] Section 2–206 of the Uniform Commercial Code—Sales (Code) states the following:

(1)   Unless otherwise unambiguously indicated by the language or circumstances

(a)   an offer to make a contract shall be construed as inviting acceptance in any manner and by any medium reasonable in the circumstances;

(b)   an order or other offer to buy goods for prompt or current shipment shall be construed as inviting acceptance either by a prompt promise to ship or by the prompt or current shipment of conforming or non-conforming goods, but such a shipment of non-conforming goods does not constitute an acceptance if the seller seasonably notifies the buyer that the shipment is offered only as an accommodation to the buyer.

(2)   Where the beginning of a requested performance is a reasonable mode of acceptance an offeror who is not notified of acceptance within a reasonable time may treat the offer as having lapsed before acceptance. (Ill. Rev. Stat.1989, ch. 26, par. 2–206.)

[23] For the purposes of the present case, the key word in this statute is the term "unambiguously." If defendant's offer contained on the purchase order is unambiguous in inviting acceptance only by the signature of plaintiff's "dealer," no contract exists until the purchase order is signed accordingly. If, however, defendant's offer is ambiguous in inviting

---

[4]   [The court is using the empty brackets as an indication that it has edited out a word or phrase. Today, we would use an ellipsis (. . .).—Eds.]

plaintiff's acceptance, a contract between plaintiff and defendant could be found to exist.

[24] On appeal, defendant has cited several cases supporting the argument that the purchase order he signed unambiguously invites acceptance only by signature of plaintiff's "dealer." One such case is *Brophy v. City of Joliet* (1957), 14 Ill. App. 2d 443, 144 N.E.2d 816, which involved the sale of revenue bonds. In that case, the court stated that where an offer requires an acceptance to be made in writing, no other form of acceptance can be made. The offer in *Brophy* read as follows:

> The signed acceptance of this proposal shall constitute a contract between the undersigned and the city . . .

> [ ]Accepted for and on behalf of . . . , which is hereby acknowledged by the duly, qualified officials.

> [ ]_____ Mayor

> [ ]_____ City Clerk

Brophy, 14 Ill.App.2d at 448, 144 N.E.2d at 819.

[25] In *La Salle National Bank v. Vega*, 167 Ill. App.3d 154, 520 N.E.2d 1129 (1988), the court dealt with a real estate sales document which was signed by the seller as offeror and clearly stated that a contract would be in full force upon execution by the purchasing trust. The court held that the document did not constitute a valid contract in the absence of acceptance by the written execution of the purchasing trust. The court noted that an offeror has complete control over his offer and its terms of acceptance, and no other mode may be used where a written acceptance is required. *La Salle National Bank*, 167 Ill. App. 3d at 161–62, 520 N.E.2d at 1133.

[The court discussed three more cases with similar facts.—Eds.]

[26] Plaintiff counters defendant's argument by contending that plaintiff was the one to offer the combine to defendant and defendant accepted plaintiff's offer by signing a counter check and giving that check to plaintiff as a down payment on the combine. We are unpersuaded.

[27] We construe section 2–206 of the Code as giving approval to an ancient and cardinal rule of the law of contracts: the offeror is the master of his offer. An offeror may prescribe as many conditions or terms of the method of acceptance as he may wish, including, but not limited to, the time, place, and manner. We also note that contracts are generally construed against the party who drafted the document and that plaintiff drafted the purchase order in the present case, and then gave it to defendant to use for his offer to purchase the combine.

[28] Based on the foregoing, we conclude that the purchase order in this case "unambiguously" required the signature by plaintiff's "dealer" in

order to be a proper acceptance of defendant's offer. Because plaintiff's "dealer" never signed the purchase order, no contract ever existed.

[29] For the reasons stated, the judgment in favor of plaintiff is reversed.

LUND, J., and GREEN, J., concur.

————

NOTES AND QUESTIONS

1.   The dealer argued that an oral contract had been formed before the purchase order was signed. If that had been the case, would it matter whether the "dealer" ever signed the purchase order?

2.   In a case involving facts very similar to the facts of this case, the Los Angeles Rams lost the services of a Heisman Trophy winner because the National Football League's standard player contract form provided that there was no contract until the deal was approved by the league's commissioner. The player, Billy Cannon, signed the Rams' document, but before the commissioner approved, Cannon informed the Rams he was taking a better deal from the Houston Oilers of the newly-formed American Football League (AFL). The court held that Cannon didn't have a contract with the Rams. His signing the form was the offer and it was not accepted until the commissioner gave his approval. *Los Angeles Rams Football Club v. Cannon*, 185 F.Supp. 717 (S.D.Cal.1960). Because the AFL was able to sign stars like Cannon, it was able to become a competitor to the National Football League (NFL). The two leagues later merged to create the present NFL.

3.   Suppose that in the Billy Cannon case, Mr. Cannon had said before he signed the form: "I don't want to hang around waiting for some bureaucrat to approve this. I want to know right now whether we have a contract. So let's just cross out the part that says it has to be approved by the commissioner."

(a) If they had then just signed the form, would they have a contract?

(b) Suppose the League had a rule that no player contract is valid without the signature of the commissioner. Would that affect the outcome?

————

DAVIS V. JACOBY

Supreme Court of California
1 Cal. 2d 370, 34 P.2d 1026 (1934)

PER CURIAM.

[1] Plaintiffs appeal from a judgment refusing to grant specific performance of an alleged contract to make a will. The facts are not in dispute and are as follows:

[2] The plaintiff Caro M. Davis was the niece of Blanche Whitehead, who was married to Rupert Whitehead. Prior to her marriage in 1913 to her co-plaintiff Frank M. Davis, Caro lived for a considerable time at the home of the Whiteheads, in Piedmont, Cal. The Whiteheads were childless and extremely fond of Caro. The record is replete with uncontradicted testimony of the close and loving relationship that existed between Caro and her aunt and uncle. During the period that Caro lived with the Whiteheads, she was treated as and often referred to by the Whiteheads as their daughter. In 1913, when Caro was married to Frank Davis, the marriage was arranged at the Whitehead home and a reception held there. After the marriage Mr. and Mrs. Davis went to Mr. Davis' home in Canada, where they have resided ever since. During the period 1913 to 1931 Caro made many visits to the Whiteheads, several of them being of long duration. The Whiteheads visited Mr. and Mrs. Davis in Canada on several occasions. After the marriage and continuing down to 1931 the closest and most friendly relationship at all times existed between these two families. They corresponded frequently, the record being replete with letters showing the loving relationship.

[3] By the year 1930, Mrs. Whitehead had become seriously ill. She had suffered several strokes and her mind was failing. Early in 1931 Mr. Whitehead had her removed to a private hospital. The doctors in attendance had informed him that she might die at any time or she might linger for many months. Mr. Whitehead had suffered severe financial reverses. He had several sieges of sickness and was in poor health. The record shows that during the early part of 1931 he was desperately in need of assistance with his wife, and in his business affairs, and that he did not trust his friends in Piedmont. On March 18, 1931, he wrote to Mrs. Davis telling her of Mrs. Whitehead's condition and added that Mrs. Whitehead was very wistful. "Today I endeavored to find out what she wanted. I finally asked her if she wanted to see you. She burst out crying and we had great difficulty in getting her to stop. Evidently, that is what is on her mind. It is a very difficult matter to decide. If you come it will mean that you will have to leave again, and then things may be serious. I am going to see the doctor, and get his candid opinion and will then write you again . . . Since writing the above, I have seen the doctor, and he thinks it will help considerably if you come." Shortly thereafter, Mr. Whitehead wrote to Caro

Davis further explaining the physical condition of Mrs. Whitehead and himself. On March 24, 1931, Mr. Davis, at the request of his wife, telegraphed to Mr. Whitehead as follows: "Your letter received. Sorry to hear Blanche not so well. Hope you are feeling better yourself. If you wish Caro to go to you can arrange for her to leave in about two weeks. Please wire me if you think it advisable for her to go." On March 30, 1931, Mr. Whitehead wrote a long letter to Mr. Davis, in which he explained in detail the condition of Mrs. Whitehead's health and also referred to his own health. He pointed out that he had lost a considerable portion of his cash assets but still owned considerable realty, that he needed some one to help him with his wife and some friend he could trust to help him with his business affairs and suggested that perhaps Mr. Davis might come to California. He then pointed out that all his property was community property; that under his will all the property was to go to Mrs. Whitehead; that he believed that under Mrs. Whitehead's will practically everything was to go to Caro. Mr. Whitehead again wrote to Mr. Davis under date of April 9, 1931, pointing out how badly he needed some one he could trust to assist him, and giving it as his belief that if properly handled he could still save about $150,000. He then stated: "Having you [Mr. Davis] here to depend on and to help me regain my mind and courage would be a big thing." Three days later, on April 12, 1931, Mr. Whitehead again wrote, addressing his letter to "Dear Frank and Caro," and in this letter made the definite offer, which offer it is claimed was accepted and is the basis of this action. In this letter he first pointed out that Blanche, his wife, was in a private hospital and that "she cannot last much longer . . . my affairs are not as bad as I supposed at first. Cutting everything down I figure $150,000[5] can be saved from the wreck." He then enumerated the values placed upon his various properties and then continued:

> My trouble was caused by my friends taking advantage of my illness and my position to skin me.
>
> Now if Frank could come out here and be with me, and look after my affairs, we could easily save the balance I mention, provided I don't get into another panic and do some more foolish things.
>
> The next attack will be my end, I am 65 and my health had been bad for years, so, the Drs. don't give me much longer to live. So if you can come, Caro will inherit everything and you will make our lives happier and see Blanche is provided for to the end. My eyesight had gone back on me, I can't read only for a few lines at a time. I am at the house alone with Stanley [the chauffeur] who does everything for me and is a fine fellow. Now, what I want is

---

[5] [$150,000 in 1934 dollars is roughly the equivalent of $2,810,000 in 2019 dollars using the CPI and GNP Deflator.—Eds.]

some one who will take charge of my affairs and see I don't lose any more. Frank can do it, if he will and cut out the booze.

Will you let me hear from you as soon as possible, I know it will be a sacrifice but times are still bad and likely to be, so by settling down you can help me and Blanche and gain in the end. If I had you here my mind would get better and my courage return, and we could work things out.

[4] This letter was received by Mr. Davis at his office in Windsor, Canada, about 9:30 a.m. April 14, 1931. After reading the letter to Mrs. Davis over the telephone, and after getting her belief that they must go to California, Mr. Davis immediately wrote Mr. Whitehead a letter, which, after reading it to his wife, he sent by air mail. This letter was lost, but there is no doubt that it was sent by Davis and received by Whitehead; in fact, the trial court expressly so found. Mr. Davis testified in substance as to the contents of this letter. After acknowledging receipt of the letter of April 12, 1931, Mr. Davis unequivocally stated that he and Mrs. Davis accepted the proposition of Mr. Whitehead and both would leave Windsor to go to him on April 25. This letter of acceptance also contained the information that the reason they could not leave prior to April 25 was that Mr. Davis had to appear in court on April 22 as one of the executors of his mother's estate. The testimony is uncontradicted and ample to support the trial court's finding that this letter was sent by Davis and received by Whitehead. In fact, under date of April 15, 1931, Mr. Whitehead again wrote to Mr. Davis and stated:

Your letter by airmail received this a.m. Now, I am wondering if I have put you to unnecessary trouble and expense, if you are making any money don't leave it, as things are bad here . . . You know your business and I don't and I am half crazy in the bargain, but I don't want to hurt you or Caro.

Then on the other hand if I could get some one to trust and keep me straight I can save a good deal, about what I told you in my former letter.

[5] This letter was received by Mr. Davis on April 17, 1931, and the same day Mr. Davis telegraphed to Mr. Whitehead: "Cheer up—we will soon be there, we will wire you from the train."

[6] Between April 14, 1931, the date the letter of acceptance was sent by Mr. Davis, and April 22, Mr. Davis was engaged in closing out his business affairs, and Mrs. Davis in closing up their home and in making other arrangements to leave. On April 22, 1931, Mr. Whitehead committed suicide. Mr. and Mrs. Davis were immediately notified and they at once came to California. From almost the moment of her arrival Mrs. Davis devoted herself to the care and comfort of her aunt, and gave her aunt constant attention and care until Mrs. Whitehead's death on May 30, 1931.

On this point the trial court found: "From the time of their arrival in Piedmont, Caro M. Davis administered in every way to the comforts of Blanche Whitehead and saw that she was cared for and provided for down to the time of the death of Blanche Whitehead on May 30, 1931; during said time Caro M. Davis nursed Blanche Whitehead, cared for her and administered to her wants as a natural daughter would have done toward and for her mother."

[7] This finding is supported by uncontradicted evidence and in fact is conceded by respondents to be correct. In fact, the record shows that after their arrival in California Mr. and Mrs. Davis fully performed their side of the agreement.

[8] After the death of Mrs. Whitehead, for the first time it was discovered that the information contained in Mr. Whitehead's letter of March 30, 1931, in reference to the contents of his and Mrs. Whitehead's wills was incorrect. By a duly witnessed will dated February 28, 1931, Mr. Whitehead, after making several specific bequests, had bequeathed all of the balance of his estate to his wife for life, and upon her death to respondents Geoff Doubble and Rupert Ross Whitehead, his nephews. Neither appellant was mentioned in his will. It was also discovered that Mrs. Whitehead by a will dated December 17, 1927, had devised all of her estate to her husband. The evidence is clear and uncontradicted that the relationship existing between Whitehead and his two nephews, respondents herein, was not nearly as close and confidential as that existing between Whitehead and appellants.

[9] After the discovery of the manner in which the property had been devised was made, this action was commenced upon the theory that Rupert Whitehead had assumed a contractual obligation to make a will whereby "Caro Davis would inherit everything"; that he had failed to do so; that plaintiffs had fully performed their part of the contract; that damages being insufficient, quasi specific performance should be granted in order to remedy the alleged wrong, upon the equitable principle that equity regards that done which ought to have been done. The requested relief is that the beneficiaries under the will of Rupert Whitehead, respondents herein, be declared to be involuntary trustees for plaintiffs of Whitehead's estate.

[10] It should also be added that the evidence shows that as a result of Frank Davis leaving his business in Canada he forfeited not only all insurance business he might have written if he had remained, but also forfeited all renewal commissions earned on past business. According to his testimony this loss was over $8,000.[6]

[11] The trial court found that the relationship between Mr. and Mrs. Davis and the Whiteheads was substantially as above recounted and that

---

[6] [$8,000 in 1934 dollars is roughly the equivalent of $150,000 in 2019 dollars using the CPI and the GNP Deflator.—Eds.]

the other facts above stated were true; that prior to April 12, 1931, Rupert Whitehead had suffered business reverses and was depressed in mind and ill in body; that his wife was very ill; that because of his mental condition he "was unable to properly care for or look after his property or affairs"; that on April 12, 1931, Rupert Whitehead in writing made an offer to plaintiffs that, if within a reasonable time thereafter plaintiffs would leave and abandon their said home in Windsor, and if Frank M. Davis would abandon or dispose of his said business, and if both of the plaintiffs would come to Piedmont in the said county of Alameda where Rupert Whitehead then resided and thereafter reside at said place and be with or near him, and if Frank M. Davis would thereupon and thereafter look after the business and affairs of said Rupert Whitehead until his condition improved to such an extent as to permit him so to do, and if the plaintiffs would look after and administer to the comforts of Blanche Whitehead and see that she was properly cared for until the time of her death, that, in consideration thereof, Caro M. Davis would inherit everything that Rupert Whitehead possessed at the time of his death and that by last will and testament Rupert Whitehead would devise and bequeath to Caro M. Davis all property and estate owned by him at the time of his death, other than the property constituting the community interest of Blanche Whitehead; that shortly prior to April 12, 1931, Rupert Whitehead informed plaintiffs of the supposed terms of his will and the will of Mrs. Whitehead. The court then finds that the offer of April 12 was not accepted. As already stated, the court found that plaintiffs sent a letter to Rupert Whitehead on April 14 purporting to accept the offer of April 12, and also found that this letter was received by the Whiteheads, but finds that in fact such letter was not a legal acceptance. The court also found that the offer of April 12 was "fair and just and reasonable, and the consideration therefor, namely, the performance by plaintiffs of the terms and conditions thereof, if the same had been performed, would have been an adequate consideration for said offer and for the agreement that would have resulted from such performance; said offer was not, and said agreement would not have been, either harsh or oppressive or unjust to the heirs at law, or devisees, or legatees, of Rupert Whitehead, or to each or any of them, or otherwise."

[12] The court also found that plaintiffs did not know that the statements made by Whitehead in reference to the wills were not correct until after Mrs. Whitehead's death, that after plaintiffs arrived in Piedmont they cared for Mrs. Whitehead until her death and "Blanche Whitehead was greatly comforted by the presence, companionship and association of Caro M. Davis, and by her administering to her wants."

[13] The theory of the trial court and of respondents on this appeal is that the letter of April 12 was an offer to contract, but that such offer could only be accepted by performance and could not be accepted by a promise to perform, and that said offer was revoked by the death of Mr. Whitehead

before performance. In other words, it is contended that the offer was an offer to enter into a unilateral contract, and that the purported acceptance of April 14 was of no legal effect.

Important

[14] The distinction between unilateral and bilateral contracts is well settled in the law. It is well stated in section 12 of the American Institute's Restatement of the Law of Contracts as follows: "A unilateral contract is one in which no promisor receives a promise as consideration for his promise. A bilateral contract is one in which there are mutual promises between two parties to the contract; each party being both a promisor and a promisee." This definition is in accord with the law of California.

[15] In the case of unilateral contracts no notice of acceptance by performance is required. Section 1584 of the Civil Code provides: "Performance of the conditions of a proposal . . . is an acceptance of the proposal."

[16] Although the legal distinction between unilateral and bilateral contracts is thus well settled, the difficulty in any particular case is to determine whether the particular offer is one to enter into a bilateral or unilateral contract. Some cases are quite clear cut. Thus an offer to sell which is accepted is clearly a bilateral contract, while an offer of a reward is a clear-cut offer of a unilateral contract which cannot be accepted by a promise to perform, but only by performance. Between these two extremes is a vague field where the particular contract may be unilateral or bilateral depending upon the intent of the offer and the facts and circumstances of each case. The offer to contract involved in this case falls within this category. By the provisions of the Restatement of the Law of Contracts it is expressly provided that there is a presumption that the offer is to enter into a bilateral contract. Section 31 provides: "In case of doubt it is presumed that an offer invites the formation of a bilateral contract by an acceptance amounting in effect to a promise by the offeree to perform what the offer requests, rather than the formation of one or more unilateral contracts by actual performance on the part of the offeree."

[17] Professor Williston, in his Treatise on Contracts, volume 1, § 60, also takes the position that a presumption in favor of bilateral contracts exists.

[18] In the comment following section 31 of the Restatement the reason for such presumption is stated as follows: "It is not always easy to determine whether an offerer requests an act or a promise to do the act. As a bilateral contract immediately and fully protects both parties, the interpretation is favored that a bilateral contract is proposed."

[19] While the California cases have never expressly held that a presumption in favor of bilateral contracts exists, the cases clearly indicate a tendency to treat offers as offers of bilateral rather than of unilateral contracts.

[20] Keeping these principles in mind, we are of the opinion that the offer of April 12 was an offer to enter into a bilateral as distinguished from a unilateral contract. Respondents argue that Mr. Whitehead had the right as offerer to designate his offer as either unilateral or bilateral. That is undoubtedly the law. It is then argued that from all the facts and circumstances it must be implied that what Whitehead wanted was performance and not a mere promise to perform. We think this is a non sequitur, in fact the surrounding circumstances lead to just the opposite conclusion. These parties were not dealing at arm's length. Not only were they related, but a very close and intimate friendship existed between them. The record indisputably demonstrates that Mr. Whitehead had confidence in Mr. and Mrs. Davis, in fact that he had lost all confidence in everyone else. The record amply shows that by an accumulation of occurrences Mr. Whitehead had become desperate, and that what he wanted was the promise of appellants that he could look to them for assistance. He knew from his past relationship with appellants that if they gave their promise to perform he could rely upon them. The correspondence between them indicates how desperately he desired this assurance. Under these circumstances he wrote his offer of April 12, above quoted, in which he stated, after disclosing his desperate mental and physical condition, and after setting forth the terms of his offer: "Will you let me hear from you as soon as possible—I know it will be a sacrifice but times are still bad and likely to be, so by settling down you can help me and Blanche and gain in the end." By thus specifically requesting an immediate reply Whitehead expressly indicated the nature of the acceptance desired by him, namely, appellants' promise that they would come to California and do the things requested by him. This promise was immediately sent by appellants upon receipt of the offer, and was received by Whitehead. It is elementary that when an offer has indicated the mode and means of acceptance, an acceptance in accordance with that mode or means is binding on the offerer.

[21] Another factor which indicates that Whitehead must have contemplated a bilateral rather than a unilateral contract, is that the contract required Mr. and Mrs. Davis to perform services until the death of both Mr. and Mrs. Whitehead. It is obvious that if Mr. Whitehead died first some of these services were to be performed after his death, so that he would have to rely on the promise of appellants to perform these services. It is also of some evidentiary force that Whitehead received the letter of acceptance and acquiesced in that means of acceptance.

[22] For the foregoing reasons we are of the opinion that the offer of April 12, 1931, was an offer to enter into a bilateral contract which was accepted by the letter of April 14, 1931 . . .

[23] For the foregoing reasons the judgment appealed from is reversed.

———

QUESTIONS

1. According to the court, what was the offer and what was the acceptance? *April 12th letter was offer, April 14th was acceptance*

2. If, after Frank sent the April 14 letter, he and Caro had decided they couldn't leave Canada, would they have been in breach of contract? If, under those circumstances, Mr. Whitehead had sued them, would he have been successful? (This is the sort of thing you should think of before you accept a court's, or your opponent's, or your supervising attorney's characterization of the facts.) *Yes, but for what damages? Nominal? Stakes A for P Vford*

3. The court discusses the fact that by leaving his business in Canada, Frank lost $8,000. Is this important? Why or why not? *Yes, something to lose*

___

PROBLEM 3-2

Queen Victoria's pet Welsh Corgi slips out of the palace and begins to try to make it back home to Wales. Heartbroken, the Queen places an advertisement offering a £100,000 reward to anyone who finds the cuddly little thing and returns him to her. Sherlock Holmes sees the ad and writes the following letter:

Your Majesty:

I promise to find your pet and return it to you.

Your servant,

Sherlock

(a) Under the rule articulated in R.2d §§ 30(2) and 32, has a contract been formed? *No, Unilateral contract*

(b) Under the rule articulated in *Davis v. Jacoby*, has a contract been formed? *No / Uni*

(c) Under the rule articulated in CISG article 18, has a contract been formed? *No?*

(d) Under the rule articulated in UNIDROIT article 2.1.6, has a contract been formed? *No?*

PROBLEM 3-3

MercMart, Inc., "The Company," publishes a mail order catalogue in which it advertises "everything today's mercenary needs to be 100% combat effective." Among other things, the catalogue includes weapons, eavesdropping equipment, and how-to manuals on fighting, breaking and entering, and other criminal activities. You are general counsel for The Company and "The Boss" has asked your advice on the following matters.

[handwritten margin note, left: Contract if 4 days is to be prompt]

(a) Colonel "Mad Mark" Slutzky entered into a contingent fee contract to carry out a revolution in Amerigo, an island nation. On March 1, he ordered 10,000 land mines from The Company, requesting immediate delivery. The land mines were shipped on March 5. That night the colonel had a dream in which an apparition told him "land mines are bad." He immediately called The Company and canceled the contract. The Company told him "Tough. We got a contract." True to The Company's culture, the person who talked to the colonel spoke first and thought about it later. Now she wants to know whether there in fact is a contract obligating the colonel to take the mines. Consult U.C.C. § 2–206 and advise her.

[handwritten margin note, right: Intent to be band. Definiteness certainty. Valid acceptance]

[handwritten note: Contract formed]

[handwritten margin note, left: valid offer]

(b) When Mad Mark's order came in, The Boss immediately called Amerigo's government and offered to sell them 50,000 AK-47 assault rifles. The conversation got nowhere because The Boss and the Minister of Defense couldn't agree on the amount of the Minister's bribe. A short time later, the Minister of Defense sent in a written purchase order for 50,000 AK-47 rifles at MercMart's catalogue price "for immediate delivery." Because of materials shortages, The Company was unable to obtain 50,000 AK-47 assault rifles. Based on what Mad Mark had told The Company, The Boss knew that the government needed weapons immediately, so he shipped the American counterparts of the AK-47, the AR-15 (also known as the M-16). When the rifles arrived at Amerigo's secret warehouse in the United States, the government refused to accept them. The Company took them back and thought no more about it until it was served by Amerigo with a summons and complaint for breach of contract. The Boss says you should explain to the judge that there was no contract to breach because The Company never accepted the government's offer. What is your assessment of the strength of The Boss's position? *See* U.C.C. § 2–206(1)(b).

[handwritten margin note, right: Valid contract but also a breach ↓ need words of accomadation for it not to be a breach ↓ counteroffer]

(c) If you concluded in Part (b) that The Company is in breach, how would you advise The Boss to avoid similar problems in the future?

[handwritten note: Seasonably notify them about accomodation]

PROBLEM 3-4

Law Student has her first call-back interview on Friday. On Monday, she walks into the dry-cleaning establishment she normally patronizes and lays her best conservative, dress-for-success suit on the counter. The cheery clerk says: "Hi, Ms. Student. How are you today?"

Figuring it would be impolite to say that she's three weeks behind in all of her courses, she doesn't even know what's going on in a couple of them, and she thinks she's coming down with the flu, she lies and says: "Pretty good. How are you?"

"Great," says the clerk. "Wednesday OK?"

[handwritten note: counter offeree / counterofforor ↓ Buyer ↓ Company]

"That's fine," says Ms. Student as she walks out wondering if she'd be happier working there instead of a law office.

On Thursday, just before closing time, Ms. Student walks into the dry cleaners and the same friendly clerk is on duty. She returns Ms. Student's suit in the same condition it was in on Monday. Noting the startled look on Ms. Student's face, the clerk says: "The boss got sued last week, and now he hates all lawyers. He says we aren't going to do any cleaning for lawyers any more, and I guess that includes law students as well."

Ms. Student goes to the interview in her second-best outfit, one she knows is a little too trendy for the stodgy law firm where she wants to work. A few weeks later she hears that the people who interviewed her were impressed with her credentials but they thought the way she dressed indicated she "wouldn't fit in here."

Does she have a breach of contract action against the dry cleaner? If so, what was the offer and what was the acceptance?

CARLILL v. CARBOLIC SMOKE BALL CO.

Court of Appeal
1 Q.B. 256 (1893)[7]

APPEAL from decision of HAWKINS, J.

[1] The defendants, who were the proprietors and vendors of a medical preparation called "The Carbolic Smoke Ball," inserted in the Pall Mall Gazette of November 13, 1891, and in other newspapers, the following advertisement:

> "100£ reward will be paid by the Carbolic Smoke Ball company to any person who contracts the increasing epidemic influenza, colds, or any disease caused by taking cold, after having used the ball three times daily for two weeks, according to the printed directions supplied with each ball. 1000£ is deposited with the Alliance Bank, Regent Street, showing our sincerity in the matter.
>
> During the last epidemic of influenza many thousand carbolic smoke balls were sold as preventives against this disease, and in no ascertained case was the disease contracted by those using the carbolic smoke ball.
>
> One carbolic smoke ball will last a family several months, making it the cheapest remedy in the world at the price, 10s., post free. The ball can be refilled at a cost of 5s. Address, Carbolic Smoke Ball Company, 27, Princes Street, Hanover Square, London."

---

[7]   The case was decided in 1892, but the reported opinion appeared in the 1893 volume of reports on opinions of the Queen's Bench.

[2]   The plaintiff, a lady, on the faith of this advertisement, bought one of the balls at a chemist's, and used it as directed, three times a day, from November 20, 1891, to January 17, 1892, when she was attacked by influenza. Hawkins, J., held that she was entitled to recover the 100£.[8] The defendants appealed.

[3]   LINDLEY, L.J. [The Lord Justice stated the facts, and proceeded.] The first observation I will make is that we are not dealing with any inference of fact. We are dealing with an express promise to pay 100£ in certain events. Read the advertisement how you will, and twist it about as you will, here is a distinct promise expressed in language which is perfectly unmistakable—"100£ reward will be paid by the Carbolic Smoke Ball company to any person who contracts the influenza after having used the ball three times daily for two weeks according to the printed directions supplied with each ball."

[4]   We must first consider whether this was intended to be a promise at all, or whether it was a mere puff[9] which meant nothing. Was it a mere puff? My answer to that question is No, and I base my answer upon this passage: "1000£ is deposited with the Alliance Bank, showing our sincerity in the matter." Now, for what was that money deposited or that statement made except to negative the suggestion that this was a mere puff and meant nothing at all? The deposit called in aid by the advertiser as proof of his sincerity in the matter that is, the sincerity of his promise to pay this 100£ in the event which he has specified. I say this for the purpose of giving point to the observation that we are not inferring a promise; there is the promise, as plain as words can make it.

[5]   Then it is contended that it is not binding. In the first place, it is said that it is not made with anybody in particular. Now that point is common to the words of this advertisement and to the words of all other advertisements offering rewards. They are offers to anybody who performs the conditions named in the advertisement, and anybody who does perform the condition accepts the offer. In point of law this advertisement is an offer to pay 100£ to anybody who will perform these conditions, and the performance of the conditions is the acceptance of the offer. That rests upon a string of authorities, the earliest of which is *Williams v. Carwardine*, which has been followed by many other decisions upon advertisements offering rewards.

[6]   But then it is said, "Supposing that the performance of the conditions is an acceptance of the offer, that acceptance ought to have been notified." Unquestionably, as a general proposition, when an offer is made,

---

8   [100£ in 1892 pounds is roughly the equivalent of 10,680£ in 2019 pounds using the Retail Price Index and 11,080£ using the GNP Deflator.—Eds.]

9   [A "puff" is statement about a product so general that a buyer should not rely on it, such as "This is a terrific value." The term "puff" seems particularly appropriate when applied to a smoke ball.—Eds.]

it is necessary in order to make a binding contract, not only that it should be accepted, but that the acceptance should be notified. But is that so in cases of this kind? I apprehend that they are an exception to that rule, or, if not an exception, they are open to the observation that the notification of the acceptance need not precede the performance. This offer is a continuing offer. It was never revoked, and if notice of acceptance is required—which I doubt very much, for I rather think the true view is that which was expressed and explained by Lord Blackburn the case of *Brogden v. Metropolitan Ry. Co.*—if notice of acceptance is required, the person who makes the offer gets the notice of acceptance contemporaneously with his notice of the performance of the condition. If he gets notice of the acceptance before his offer is revoked, that in principle is all you want. I, however, think that the true view, in a case of this kind, is that the person who makes the offer shows by his language and from the nature of the transaction that he does not expect and does not require notice of the acceptance apart from notice of the performance.

[7] We, therefore, find here all the elements which are necessary to form a binding contract enforceable in point of law, subject to two observations. First of all it is said that this advertisement is so vague that you cannot really construe it as a promise—that the vagueness of the language shows that a legal promise was never intended or contemplated. The language is vague and uncertain in some respects, and particularly in this, that the 100£ is to be paid to any person who contracts the increasing epidemic after having used the balls three times daily for two weeks. It is said, When are they to be used? According to the language of the advertisement no time is fixed, and, construing the offer most strongly against the person who has made it, one might infer that any time was meant. I do not think that was meant, and to hold the contrary would be pushing too far the doctrine of taking language most strongly against the person using it. I do not think that business people or reasonable people would understand the words as meaning that if you took a smoke ball and used it three times daily for two weeks you were to be guaranteed against influenza for the rest of your life, and I think it would be pushing the language of the advertisement too far to construe it as meaning that. But if it does not mean that, what does it mean? It is for the defendants to shew what it does mean; and it strikes me that there are two, and possibly three, reasonable constructions to be put on this advertisement, any one of which will answer the purpose of the plaintiff. Possibly it may be limited to persons catching the "increasing epidemic" (that is, then prevailing epidemic), or any colds or diseases caused by taking cold, during the prevalence of the increasing epidemic. That is one suggestion; but it does not commend itself to me. Another suggested meaning is that you are warranted free from catching this epidemic, or colds or other diseases caused by taking cold, whilst you are using this remedy after using it for two weeks. If that is the meaning, the plaintiff is right, for she used the

remedy for two weeks and went on using it till she got the epidemic. Another meaning, and the one which I rather prefer, is that the reward is offered to any person who contracts the epidemic or other disease within a reasonable time after having used the smoke ball. Then it is asked, What is a reasonable time? It has been suggested that there is no standard of reasonableness; that it depends upon the reasonable time for a germ to develop! I do not feel pressed by that. It strikes me that a reasonable time may be ascertained in a business sense and in a sense satisfactory to a lawyer, in this way; find out from a chemist what the ingredients are; find out from a skilled physician how long the effect of such ingredients on the system could be reasonably expected to endure so as to protect a person from an epidemic or cold, and in that way you will get a standard to be laid before a jury, or a judge without a jury, by which they might exercise their judgment as to what a reasonable time would be. It strikes me, I confess, that the true construction of this advertisement is that 100£ will be paid to anybody who used this smoke ball three times daily for two weeks according to the printed directions, and who gets the influenza or cold or other diseases caused by taking cold within a reasonable time after so using it; and if that is the true construction, it is enough for the plaintiff.

[8]   BOWEN, L.J. I am of the same opinion. We were asked to say that this document was a contract too vague to be enforced.

[9]   The first observation which arises is that the document itself is not a contract at all, it is only an offer made to the public. The defendants contend next, that it is an offer the terms of which are too vague to be treated as a definite offer, inasmuch as there is no limit of time fixed for the catching of the influenza, and it cannot be supposed that the advertisers seriously meant to promise to pay money to every person who catches the influenza at any time after the inhaling of the smoke ball. It was urged also, that if you look at this document you will find much vagueness as to the persons with whom the contract was intended to be made—that, in the first place, its terms are wide enough to include persons who may have used the smoke ball before the advertisement was issued; at all events, that it is an offer to the world in general, and, also, that it is unreasonable to suppose it to be a definite offer, because nobody in their senses would contract themselves out of the opportunity of checking the experiment which was going to be made at their own expense. It is also contended that the advertisement is rather in the nature of a puff or a proclamation than a promise or offer intended to mature into a contract when accepted. But the main point seems to be that the vagueness of the document shows that no contract whatever was intended. It seems to me that in order to arrive at a right conclusion we must read this advertisement in its plain meaning, as the public would understand it. It was intended to be issued to the public and to be read by the public. How would an ordinary person reading this document construe it? It was

intended unquestionably to have some effect, and I think the effect which it was intended to have, was to make people use the smoke ball, because the suggestions and allegations which it contains are directed immediately to the use of the smoke ball as distinct from the purchase of it. It did not follow that the smoke ball was to be purchased from the defendants directly, or even from agents of theirs directly. The intention was that the circulation of the smoke ball should be promoted, and that the use of it should be increased. The advertisement begins by saying that a reward will be paid by the Carbolic Smoke Ball Company to any person who contracts the increasing epidemic after using the ball. It has been said that the words do not apply only to persons who contract the epidemic after the publication of the advertisement, but include persons who had previously contracted the influenza. I cannot so read the advertisement. It is written in colloquial and popular language, and I think that it is equivalent to this: "will be paid to any person who shall contract the increasing epidemic after having used the carbolic smoke ball three times daily for two weeks." And it seems to me that the way in which the public would read it would be this, that if anybody, after the advertisement was published, used three times daily for two weeks the carbolic smoke ball, and then caught cold, he would be entitled to the reward. Then again it was said: "How long is this protection to endure? Is it to go on forever, or for what limit of time?" I think that there are two constructions of this document, each of which is good sense, and each of which seems to me to satisfy the exigencies of the present action. It may mean that the protection is warranted to last during the epidemic, and it was during the epidemic that the plaintiff contracted the disease. I think, more probably, it means that the smoke ball will be a protection while it is in use. That seems to me the way in which an ordinary person would understand an advertisement about medicine, and about a specific against influenza. It could not be supposed that after you have left off using it you are still to be protected forever, as if there was to be a stamp set upon your forehead that you were never to catch influenza because you had once used the carbolic smoke ball. I think the immunity is to last during the use of the ball. That is the way in which I should naturally read it, and it seems to me that the subsequent language of the advertisement supports that construction. It says: "During the last epidemic of influenza many thousand carbolic smoke balls were sold, and in no ascertained case was the disease contracted by those using" (not "who had used") "the carbolic smoke ball," and it concludes with saying that one smoke ball will last a family several months (which imports that it is to be efficacious while it is being used), and that the ball can be refilled at a cost of 5s. I, therefore, have myself no hesitation in saying that I think, on the construction of this advertisement, the protection was to ensure during the time that the carbolic smoke ball was being used. My brother, the Lord Justice who preceded me, thinks that the contract would be sufficiently definite if you were to read it in the sense the protection was to be warranted during a reasonable period after use. I have some difficulty myself on that point; but it is not necessary for me to consider it further, because the disease here was contracted during the use of the carbolic smoke ball.

[10] A.L. SMITH, L.J. The first point in this case is, whether the defendants' advertisement which appeared in the Pall Mall Gazette was an offer which, when accepted and its conditions performed, constituted a promise to pay, assuming there was good consideration to uphold that promise, or whether it was only a puff from which no promise could be implied, or, as put by Mr. Finlay, a mere statement by the defendants of the confidence they entertained in the efficacy of their remedy. Or as I might put in the words of Lord Campbell in *Denton v. Great Northern Ry. Co.*, whether this advertisement was mere waste paper. That is the first matter to be determined. It seems to me that this advertisement reads as follows: "reward will be paid by the Carbolic Smoke Ball Company to any person who after having used the ball three times daily for two weeks according to the printed directions supplied with such ball contracts the increasing epidemic influenza, colds, or any diseases caused by taking cold. The ball will last a family several months, and can be refilled at a cost of 5s." If I may paraphrase it, it means this: "If you"—that is one of the public as yet not ascertained, but who, as Lindley and Bowen, L. JJ., have pointed out, will be ascertained by the performing the condition—"will hereafter use my smoke ball three times daily for two weeks according to my printed directions, I will pay you, if you contract the influenza within the period mentioned in the advertisement." Now, is there not a request there? It comes to this: "In consideration of your buying my smoke ball, and then using it as I prescribe, I promise that if you catch the influenza within a certain time I will pay you." It must not be forgotten that this advertisement states that as security for what is being offered, and as proof of the sincerity of the offer, is actually lodged at the bank wherewith to satisfy any possible demands which might be made in the event of the conditions contained therein being fulfilled and a person catching the epidemic so as to entitle him to the reward. How can it be said that such a statement as that embodied only a mere expression of confidence in the wares which the defendants had to sell? I cannot read the advertisement in any such way. In my judgment, the advertisement was an offer intended to be acted upon, and when accepted and the conditions performed constituted a binding promise on which an action would lie, assuming there was consideration for that promise.

_____

NOTES AND QUESTIONS

1. In paragraph 4, Lord Justice Lindley states: " . . . as a general proposition, when an offer is made, it is necessary in order to make a binding

contract, not only that it should be accepted, but that the acceptance should be notified." Is this the rule under R2d § 54? Under U.C.C. § 2–206? Under CISG article 18? UNIDROIT article 2.1.6?

2.   In many contracts books, the *Carbolic Smoke Ball* case is in the chapter on determining what is an offer. The *Leonard* case (the plaintiff who wanted to buy the Harrier jet) served that purpose in this book. Our interest in the *Carbolic Smoke Ball* case is in the method of acceptance of the offer. What were the terms of the offer, and how could it be accepted? There are a couple of different ways of analyzing these questions. The judges don't really address what had to be done to accept because the case comes out the same way no matter how one analyzes these issues, but it might be important if the offer had been withdrawn between the time the plaintiff bought the smoke ball and the time she got sick. Consider the following interpretations of the Carbolic Smoke Ball ad:

Interpretation One

Accept the offer by purchasing a smoke ball. The terms of the contract are that the user gets the hundred pounds if he (1) uses the ball according to directions and (2) gets sick within a reasonable time thereafter.

Interpretation Two

Accept the offer by (1) purchasing a smoke ball and (2) using it according to directions. The terms of the contract are that the user gets the hundred pounds if they get sick within a reasonable time thereafter.

Interpretation Three

To accept the offer, a user must (1) purchase the smoke ball, (2) use it according to directions, and (3) get sick within a reasonable time thereafter.

Assume the offer was withdrawn on January 1. (For purposes of this question, assume that an offer which can be accepted by performance can be revoked at any time before performance is complete. As we'll see later, this is no longer the law in most jurisdictions.)

A purchased the ball on November 15, used it according to directions, completing her two week minimum use on November 29, and got the flu on December 15. Under which of these interpretations would she be allowed to recover the 100 pounds?

B purchased the ball on December 15, used it according to directions, completing her two week minimum use on December 29, and got the flu on January 15. Under which of these interpretations would she be allowed to recover the 100 pounds?

C purchased the ball on December 20, used it according to directions, completing her two week minimum use on January 4, and got the flu on January 7. Under which of these interpretations would she be allowed to recover the 100 pounds?

3.　*Making a silk purse out of a sow's ear.* The *Carbolic Smoke Ball* case is well known and a staple of Contracts courses. Less well known is the company's next move. In a subsequent advertisement, on February 15, 1893, the company renewed and increased its offer, albeit with some careful drafting and limitations, both legal and practical, on liability:

> £100 REWARD was recently offered by the CARBOLIC SMOKE BALL, CO. to anyone who contracted influenza [or various other diseases] after having used the Carbolic Smoke Ball according to the printed directions. Many thousand Carbolic Smoke Balls were sold, but only three persons claimed the reward of £100, thus proving conclusively that this invaluable remedy will prevent and cure the above-mentioned diseases.

> THE CARBOLIC SMOKE BALL CO., Ltd., now offers £200 REWARD to the person who purchases a Carbolic Smoke Ball and afterwards contracts any of the following diseases, viz, INFLUENZA. . . . or any disease caused by taking cold while using the Carbolic Smoke Ball.

> This offer is made to those who have purchased a Carbolic Smoke Ball since January 1, 1893, and is subject to conditions to be obtained upon application, a duplicate of which must be signed and deposited with the Company in London by the applicant before commencing the treatment specified in the conditions [including having to take the three doses each day at corporate headquarters]. This offer will remain open only until March 31, 1893.

PROBLEM 3-5

Jeff had a boathouse on a remote lake. He heard there had been several incidents of vandalism in the area, so, on January 10, he posted a letter to a contractor he knew in a small town near the lake:

> Marcia,

[handwritten margin note: Intent to be bound, and certainty]

> I need a chain link fence with a locked gate around my boathouse. If you can do it for less than $2,500, please start immediately and send me the bill. Use your own judgment as to things like height, placement, etc.

> Jeff

[handwritten note: There was no clear definition as to how to accept offeree can choose how to accept]

Marcia began construction on January 12, as soon as she got the letter (business at the lake is slow in the winter), and she finished two days later. Marcia had become a contractor because she liked building things more than she liked doing paperwork, so she hadn't gotten around to sending a bill (or otherwise telling Jeff she had done the job) before she received his fax on

[handwritten note: Marcia chose to accept by conduct]

January 30 telling her not to build the fence because he was going to sell the boathouse and didn't want "an ugly fence" around it. — *Revocation*

(a) Do the parties have a contract? *See* R2d § 54 and UNIDROIT article 2.1.6.   *Yes/Maybe — accepted valid offer through conduct*

(b) If the parties do have a contract, does Jeff have to pay? *Yes*

There are a number of issues here, so don't jump to conclusions.

Never sent bill so how would he know

The "Mailbox Rule"

A very important, but very basic rule of contract law is the so-called "mailbox rule" or the rule of *Adams v. Lindsell*. The following passages from *Morrison v. Thoelke*, 155 So.2d 889 (Fla.Ct.App.1963), present the rule and its origins.

* * *

[1] A ... leading treatise on the law of contracts, Corbin, Contracts §§ 78 and 80 (1950 Supp. 1961), also devotes some discussion to the "rule" urged by appellants. Corbin writes:

> Where the parties are negotiating at a distance from each other, the most common method of making an offer is by sending it by mail; and more often than not the offeror has specified no particular mode of acceptance. In such a case, it is now the prevailing rule that the offeree has power to accept and close the contract by mailing a letter of acceptance, properly stamped and addressed, within a reasonable time. The contract is regarded as made at the time and place that the letter of acceptance is put into the possession of the post office department.

[2] Corbin negates the effect of the offeree's power to recall his letter:

> The postal regulations have for a long period made it possible for the sender of a letter to intercept it and prevent its delivery to the addressee. This has caused some doubt to be expressed as to whether an acceptance can ever be operative upon the mere mailing of the letter, since the delivery to the post office has not put it entirely beyond the sender's control.

> It is believed that no such doubt should exist ... In view of common practices, in view of the difficulties involved in the process of interception of a letter, and in view of the decisions and printed discussions dealing with acceptance by post, it is believed that the fact that a letter can be lawfully intercepted by the sender should not prevent the acceptance from being operative on mailing. If the offer was made under such circumstances that the offeror should know that the offeree might reasonably regard this

as a proper method of closing the deal, and the offeree does so regard it, and makes use of it, the contract is consummated even though the letter of acceptance is intercepted and not delivered.

[3] The rule that a contract is complete upon deposit of the acceptance in the mails, hereinbefore referred to as "deposited acceptance rule" and also known as the "rule in *Adams v. Lindsell*,"[10] had its origin, insofar as the common law is concerned, in *Adams v. Lindsell*, 1 Barn. & Ald. 681, 106 Eng.Rep. 250 (K.B. 1818). . . .

[4] Examination of the decision in *Adams v. Lindsell* reveals three distinct factors deserving consideration. The first and most significant is the court's obvious concern with the necessity of drawing a line, with establishing some point at which a contract is deemed complete and their equally obvious concern with the thought that if communication of each party's assent were necessary, the negotiations would be interminable. A second factor, again a practical one, was the court's apparent desire to limit but not overrule the decision in *Cooke v. Oxley*, 3 T.R. 653 (1790) that an offer was revocable at any time prior to acceptance. In application to contracts negotiated by mail, this latter rule would permit revocation even after unqualified assent unless the assent was deemed effective upon posting. Finally, having chosen a point at which negotiations would terminate and having effectively circumvented the inequities of *Cooke v. Oxley*, the court, apparently constrained to offer some theoretical justification for its decision, designated a mailed offer as "continuing" and found a meeting of the minds upon the instant of posting assent. Significantly, the factor of the offeree's loss of control of his acceptance is not mentioned.

[5] The justification for the "deposited acceptance" rule proceeds from the uncontested premise of *Adams v. Lindsell* that there must be, both in practical and conceptual terms, a point in time when a contract is complete. In the formation of contracts inter presents this point is readily reached upon expressions of assent instantaneously communicated. In the formation of contracts inter absents by post, however, delay in communication prevents concurrent knowledge of assent and some point must be chosen as legally significant. The problem raised by the impossibility of concurrent knowledge of manifest assent is discussed and a justification for the traditional rule is offered in Corbin, Contracts § 78 (1950).

> A better explanation of the existing rule seems to be that in such cases the mailing of a letter has long been a customary and expected way of accepting the offer. It is ordinary business usage. More than this, however, is needed to explain why the letter is operative on mailing rather than on receipt by the offeror. Even

---

[10] [or the "mailbox rule"—Eds.]

though it is business usage to send an offer by mail, it creates no power of acceptance until it is received. Indeed, most notices sent by mail are not operative unless actually received.

The additional reasons for holding that a different rule applies to an acceptance and that it is operative on mailing may be suggested as follows: When an offer is by mail and the acceptance also is by mail, the contract must date either from the mailing of the acceptance or from its receipt. In either case, one of the parties will be bound by the contract without being actually aware of that fact. If we hold the offeror bound on the mailing of the acceptance, he may change his position in ignorance of the acceptance; even though he waits a reasonable time before acting, he may still remain unaware that he is bound by contract because the letter of acceptance is delayed, or is actually lost or destroyed, in the mails. Therefore this rule is going to cause loss and inconvenience to the offeror in some cases. But if we adopt the alternative rule that the letter of acceptance is not operative until receipt, it is the offeree who is subjected to the danger of loss and inconvenience. He cannot know that his letter has been received and that he is bound by contract until a new communication is received by him. His letter of acceptance may never have been received and so no letter of notification is sent to him; or it may have been received, and the letter of notification may be delayed or entirely lost in the mails. One of the parties must carry the risk of loss and inconvenience. We need a definite and uniform rule as to this. We can choose either rule; but we must choose one. We can put the risk on either party; but we must not leave it in doubt. The party not carrying the risk can then act promptly and with confidence in reliance on the contract; the party carrying the risk can insure against it if he so desires. The business community could no doubt adjust itself to either rule; but the rule throwing the risk on the offeror has the merit of closing the deal more quickly and enabling performance more promptly. It must be remembered that in the vast majority of cases the acceptance is neither lost nor delayed; and promptness of action is of importance in all of them. Also it is the offeror who has invited the acceptance.

[6] The justification suggested by Corbin has been criticized as being anachronistic. Briefly, critics argue that the evident concern with risk occasioned by delay is premised on a time lag between mailing and delivery of a letter of acceptance, which lag, in modern postal systems is negligible. Opponents of the rule urge that if time is significant to either party, modern means of communication permit either party to avoid such delay as the post might cause. *See* Samek, A Reassessment of the Present Rule Relating to Postal Acceptance, *supra. Cf. Rhode Island Tool Co. v. United*

States, supra. At the same time, critics of the rule cannot deny that even in our time delay or misdirection of a letter of acceptance is not beyond the realm of possibility.

[7]   Another justification offered for the rule, related to the argument of expediency discussed by Corbin, is the mixed practical and conceptual argument attributed to Holmes but in reality being manifest in *Adams v. Lindsell* itself. *See* Holmes, The Common Law, 305–307 (1881); Note, 38 Geo. L.J. 106, 110 (1949). This argument proposes that the making of an offer constitutes an expression of assent to the terms of the contract and that the "overt act" of depositing a written acceptance in the post represents the offeror's assent, whereupon the "concluding prerequisite" of a contract, mutual assent, is formed and the contract is complete. Critics of the rule respond by pointing out that the deposit of a letter in the mail is, in and of itself, a neutral factor, charged with legal significance only because the rule makes this particular "overt act" significant: signing a contract but then pocketing it could be, they argue, viewed as equally conclusive.

[8]   At this point and upon the "overt act" theory issue is clearly joined. On the one hand proponents of the rule insist that contracts inter absentes are sui generis and require consideration not in terms of the secondary principles of contract law relating to the necessity of communicating assent and the necessity of an unrecoverable expression of acceptance, but in terms of the essential concept of manifest intent and assent. Opponents of the rule, though no longer encountering conceptual difficulty in the abandonment of the principle of communication, *compare* Langdell, Summary of Law of Contracts, 1–31 (2d ed. 1880) and Williston, Contracts § 81 (1957) *with* Samek, A Reassessment . . . *supra*, argue that absent overriding practical considerations the law relating to acceptance by mail should be harmonized with the law regarding offers by mail and contracts generally, i.e., that the acceptance is ineffective until received. Ultimately then the weight given the "practical considerations" and the emphasis accorded the reliance expectation factors determine the view adopted as to the "deposited acceptance" rule.

[9]   In support of the rule proponents urge its sanction in tradition and practice. They argue that in the average case the offeree receives an offer and, depositing an acceptance in the post, begins and should be allowed to begin reliance on the contract. They point out that the offeror has, after all, communicated his assent to the terms by extending the offer and has himself chosen the medium of communication. Depreciating the alleged risk to the offeror, proponents argue that having made an offer by post the offeror is seldom injured by a slight delay in knowing it was accepted, whereas the offeree, under any other rule, would have to await both the transmission of the acceptance and notification of its receipt before being able to rely on the contract he unequivocally accepted. Finally,

proponents point out that the offeror can always expressly condition the contract on his receipt of an acceptance and, should he fail to do so, the law should not afford him this advantage.

[10] Opponents of the rule argue as forcefully that all of the disadvantages of delay or loss in communication which would potentially harm the offeree are equally harmful to the offeror. Why, they ask, should the offeror be bound by an acceptance of which he has no knowledge? Arguing specific cases, opponents of the rule point to the inequity of forbidding the offeror to withdraw his offer after the acceptance was posted but before he had any knowledge that the offer was accepted; they argue that to forbid the offeree to withdraw his acceptance, as in the instant case, scant hours after it was posted but days before the offeror knew of it, is unjust and indefensible. Too, the opponents argue, the offeree can always prevent the revocation of an offer by providing consideration, by buying an option.

[11] In short, both advocates and critics muster persuasive argument. As Corbin indicated, there must be a choice made, and such choice may, by the nature of things, seem unjust in some cases. Weighing the arguments with reference not to specific cases but toward a rule of general application and recognizing the general and traditional acceptance of the rule as well as the modem changes in effective long-distance communication, it would seem that the balance tips, whether heavily or near imperceptively, to continued adherence to the "rule in *Adams v. Lindsell*." This rule, although not entirely compatible with ordered, consistent and sometime artificial principles of contract advanced by some theorists, is, in our view, in accord with the practical considerations and essential concepts of contract law. *See* Llewellyn, Our Case-Law of Contracts; Offer and Acceptance 11, 48 Yale L.J. 779, 795 (1939). Outmoded precedents may, on occasion, be discarded and the function of justice should not be the perpetuation of error, but, by the same token, traditional rules and concepts should not be abandoned save on compelling ground.

NOTES AND QUESTIONS

1. As the *Morrison v. Thoelke* court points out in paragraph 6, the mailbox rule was developed when postal service was subject to long delays and even uncertain eventual delivery. As such, should it apply today to first class mail? What about express mail or overnight mail services? Why or why not?

2. Should the mailbox rule apply to e-mail, voicemail, or instant messaging? Why or why not? When is a communication that is sent by any of these methods "received"? When it "hits" the addressee's system? Or when it is actually read or heard? Some other time?

3.   Remember, the mailbox rule is a default rule and, the offeror, as the master of the offer, can specify the manner of acceptance and when it is effective. Only if she is silent does the mailbox rule apply.

―――――

PROBLEM 3-6

Seller writes Buyer: "I will sell you my Franklin Mint plate commemorating The Life of Elvis for $400. This offer will expire at noon on July 4." Buyer writes back: "I accept your offer." Buyer's letter is mailed on July 4 at 11 a.m., but because the post office is closed on July 4, it is not postmarked until 2 p.m. on July 5. Do the parties have a contract? *Yes, went in mailbox*

PROBLEM 3-7

Seller writes Buyer: "I will sell you my Sammy Sosa rookie card for $100. This offer will expire on September 18. Your answer must be in my hands by that date." Buyer mails her acceptance on September 17. Seller receives it on September 19. Do they have a contract? *No, offeror is master of offer*

Opt-out of mailbox rule

PROBLEM 3-8

Mr. Kenge sends John Jarndyce an e-mail message offering to convert his fee arrangement in *Jarndyce v. Jarndyce* from hourly billing to a contingency fee. The message states: "This offer will expire at noon tomorrow." At eleven the next morning, Mr. Jarndyce, having cogitated on the offer whilst he took his tea, boots up his computer and sends Mr. Kenge a message purporting to accept the offer. Unfortunately, though neither party knew it, Mr. Jarndyce's internet provider, England On-Line, has suffered a server crash. As a result the message is not delivered for three days. In the meantime, Kenge & Carboy, assuming that Jarndyce has rejected their offer and that they will therefore be able to bill *Jarndyce v. Jarndyce* as they always had, hires a new associate. Does Jarndyce have a contract to change the billing arrangement? *See* R2d §§ 63, 64, 67.

Section 15(a) of the Uniform Electronic Transactions Act provides:

Unless otherwise agreed between the sender and the recipient, an electronic record is sent when it:

    (1)   is addressed properly or is otherwise directed properly to an information processing system that the recipient has designated or uses for the purpose of receiving electronic records or information of the type sent and from which the recipient is able to retrieve the electronic record;

    (2)   is in a form capable of being processed by that system; and

    (3)   enters an information processing system outside the control of the sender or of a person that sent the record on behalf of the

sender or enters a region of the information processing system designated or used by the recipient which is under the control of the recipient.

In the context of providing adequate notice to someone, e-mail, text message, and other forms of electronic notification are common to our 21st Century society. However, they are not without problems, as Justice William W. Bedsworth points out in *Lasalle v. Vogel*, 2019 WL 2428668, at *8 (Cal. Ct. App. June 11, 2019):

> Email has many things to recommend it; reliability is not one of them. Between the ease of mistaken address on the sender's end and the arcane vagaries of spam filters on the recipient's end, email is ill-suited for a communication on which a million dollar lawsuit may hinge. A busy calendar, an overfull in-box, a careless autocorrect, even a clumsy keystroke resulting in a "delete" command can result in a speedy communication being merely a failed one.

PROBLEM 3-9

On March 1, Farmer writes Developer: "I hereby offer to sell you the property known as the 'Jones Farm' for a price of $500,000." Developer receives the letter on March 4. On March 5, Farmer changes her mind and mails (by the U.S. Postal Service) Developer the following: "My offer to sell the farm is hereby revoked." On March 6, Developer mails (by the U.S. Postal Service) a letter purporting to accept the offer. On March 7, Developer receives Farmer's revocation letter. On March 8, Farmer receives Developer's acceptance letter.

Do the parties have a contract? *See* R2d § 42, UNIDROIT article 2.1.4.

PROBLEM 3-10

B has been admiring A's collection of baseball cards. B tells A *[communication #1]*: "If you ever decide to get rid of your Johnny Bench rookie card, I'll trade you my Hank Aaron signed bat." A says he wouldn't part with the Johnny Bench rookie card for a million dollars *[communication #2]*. A couple of weeks later, however, A changes his mind and sends B the following email *[communication #3]*: "I've changed my mind. I'll trade the Bench rookie card on the terms you suggested. If I don't hear otherwise by two weeks from today, I'll assume we have a deal and I'll ship."

B gets the e-mail and decides she's no longer so interested in baseball cards. She plans to e-mail A rejecting the offer, but forgets to do so. On the day he said he would, A mails the rookie card to B (insured for $10,000) *[communication #4]*. Immediately upon receiving the card, B re-wraps it for mailing and encloses a letter saying that she never agreed to the swap. Once again she gets sidetracked with other projects and it's three more weeks until she gets around to mailing the package *[communication #5]*. When A gets the package he is irate. He thought he had a contract, and he sues B for breach of contract. A wants that bat.

How should the court decide the case? Consider R2d §§ 56 and 69, CISG article 18, UNIDROIT articles 2.1.2–2.1.7.

No contract + rejection stopped offer from being acceptable

———

NOTE

Recently, in the debates at the American Law Institute (ALI) regarding the proposal to approve the first Restatement of the Law of Consumer Contracts (RLCC), there were various disagreements among members. However, the primary and most polarizing disagreement involved whether a consumer can assent to terms of an agreement of which he or she is unaware, but of which he or she had reasonable notice of their existence?

Today, consumers regularly consent to the terms of website and software agreements without reading or even looking at the terms that they are agreeing to. Consumers simply click "I agree" and move on with their lives. As a result, some members of the ALI decided businesses should not be required to provide consumers with the option to assent to their terms. Instead, the drafters of the RLCC proposed that if a consumer receives reasonable notice that the agreement exists, and he or she has "a reasonable opportunity to review" those terms, then the consumer is bound by those terms.

The RLCC has attracted heavy criticism from consumer advocates, state attorney generals, politicians, and even major businesses. These opponents argue that the RLCC recommends a new, separate set of contract rules for consumers. Rules not supported by case law precedent or statute. Opponents argue these proposed rules would bind consumers to a website's terms, regardless of whether the consumer agrees to them or even knows they exist. These opponents contend that rules like this undermine the most basic and fundamental principles of contract law.

The Drafters of the RLCC argue the document does not create new contract rules. Rather, the RLCC provides courts and legislatures with a synthesized guide based on current trends in the law and common law precedent.

However, opponents argue that the RLCC is based on a flawed interpretation of the common law doctrine regarding electronic adhesion contracts. As Professor Nancy S. Kim points out:

> Some courts have started to question whether a manifestation of assent is enough to show consent to all the terms, showing signs of requiring specific assent to important, rights-altering terms like mandatory arbitration or recurring fee provisions. In other words, recent cases seem to be swinging the pendulum back toward reasonable expectations, or at least away from unconsented-to terms.

Nancy S. Kim, *The Proposed Restatement of the Law of Consumer Contracts and the Struggle Over the Soul of Contract Law*, JURIST—Academic Commentary, June 2, 2019.

Professor Kim notes that numerous cases that the drafters cite in support of the Restatement, have "overlooked the many factual distinctions that influence [the] holdings."

Many attorneys argue that RLCC ignores that there is no manifestation of assent by the consumer to be bound by the specific terms of the agreement. They emphasize that the ALI is proposing a fundamental shift away from the traditional contract-law premise that silence does not amount to assent.

Perhaps the drafters of the RLCC *are* creating new rules. Or maybe they are applying the same rule differently for contracts between businesses and consumers, and contracts between businesses and businesses. If it is the former, the RLCC ignores the consumer's lack of assent to the terms of the business's agreement; a concept that would likely never constitute a binding agreement between two businesses.

Ultimately, after debating the proposed RLCC for over four hours in 2019, the ALI tabled the proposal for a year.

LAWYERING SKILLS PROBLEM

Sherri was a senior partner in a large law firm. After 25 years of practicing law, she was very wealthy. But she was also burned-out and totally fed up with the practice of law. She wasn't ready to retire, but she wanted to find another career. She had always enjoyed skiing, so she decided that a ski resort would be the ideal business for her.

Among her many contacts was Mario, who was a business broker. He was in the business of helping people like Sherri find businesses to buy. On November 5, when she was cleaning up her desk after a hard day of negotiating on behalf of clients, Sherri wrote Mario the following e-mail:

Mario:

How's my favorite broker? Doing any deals lately?

I've decided to hang it up with the practice of law. I'm going to buy a ski resort. You can make a quick hundred grand if you can find me one that meets my needs. I can pay as much as ten million for the right place if I can get the financing I need.

If you find me the right property, I'll pay you a commission of up to $100,000. I know this is less than you're used to getting, but we're old friends, and I promise that I'll be easy to deal with.

If this is OK, let me know. I'm not going to work with any other brokers, just you. You don't have to commit to spend a lot of time on the deal. Just check out the market and you may earn a quick hundred grand.

Sher

BTW—Disregard the stuff below this. The firm's server puts that on all the e-mails. Don't you just love paranoid lawyers? ;-)

> This communication was sent by the law firm of Cardozo, Gonzales, Chang & Weinstein. It may contain confidential information protected by the attorney-client privilege. If you believe you have received this communication in error, destroy all copies and immediately telephone the sender.
>
> This communication does not reflect an intention by the sender or the sender's client to conduct a transaction or make any agreement by electronic means. Nothing contained in this message or in any attachment shall satisfy the requirements for writing and nothing contained herein or therein shall constitute a contract or a signature.

When Mario got the e-mail, he ignored it because he wasn't interested in ski resorts. He had a couple of hot bio-tech deals going and he wasn't going to be distracted from them for a deal that could only bring him a hundred grand.

About a week later, however, (November 15 to be exact) the weather turned cold and Mario's mind turned to snowboarding. He decided that he would play around with Sherri's idea. He began an intensive study of the winter resort industry. It was mostly to satisfy his own curiosity, but he was thinking there was the possibility he might by chance run across something that would be suitable for Sherri. As sometimes happens, he got carried away with the project and he began spending an inordinate amount of time looking for a deal for Sherri. Finally, he discovered a resort that was exactly what Sherri was looking for. It was a small resort that drew customers from a nearby city. It didn't have much challenging terrain. In fact, it didn't have much terrain at all. But what can you expect for a lousy ten million? Mario first learned of the availability of the resort on November 22, after spending all of that day and most of the previous two days searching on the Internet, telephoning real estate brokers in the mountainous areas of seven states, and checking out a lot of resorts that turned out to be unsuited to Sherri's needs.

On November 23, he sent the following e-mail to Sherri:

Sher:

Found a great property for you. The owner wants too much for it, of course. They always do. But I'm confident we can get him down to your max price and probably a bit below. The geezer is getting old and he wants to retire to Mexico.

Details to follow by snail mail.

Best, Mario

In the meantime, on November 22, Sherri, infuriated by Mario's lack of response to her earlier e-mail and wanting to have tangible written confirmation of her position, Sherri sent the following letter to Mario by the United States Postal Service (registered mail):

Dear Mr. O'Riley:

You have failed to respond as requested to my electronic mail message of November 5. Accordingly, I hereby withdraw any offer which I may have made to you in that message or any other way.

Please direct all future communications to the attorney representing me in this matter, Ralph J. Cardozo, Esq.

Very truly yours,
S. Weinstein, Esq.

Mario received the letter on November 25.

Mario, of course, demanded his $100,000.

Sheri has come to you seeking advice as to whether or not she owes the $100,000 commission. Although Mr. Cardozo has given her his opinion that she does not, she wants someone who will not be paid to litigate the case and is thus more unbiased to give her a legal opinion.

CHAPTER 4

HAS THE OFFER TERMINATED?

■ ■ ■

As stated at the beginning of the last chapter, the basic rules for the termination of offers are:

The offeree may reject the offer or make a counter offer (which operates as a rejection); or

The offer may terminate by its own terms, e.g., by lapse of time; or

The offeror may revoke the offer; or

The offeror or the offeree may die or be adjudged incompetent.

This chapter explores these rules in more detail.

One way the offer can terminate is for the offeree to reject it. Rejection of the offer precludes later acceptance. Unlike acceptance, the "mailbox rule" does not apply to rejections. Rejection is effective when it is actually or constructively received by the offeror. The next cases explore the contours of these rules.

———

MINNESOTA LINSEED OIL CO. v. COLLIER WHITE LEAD CO.
Circuit Court, District of Minnesota
17 F. Cas. 447 (1876)

[1]   This action was removed from the state court and a trial by jury waived. The plaintiff seeks to recover the sum of $2,151.50[1], with interest from September 20, 1875—a balance claimed to be due for oil sold to the defendant. The defendant, in its answer, alleges that on August 3, 1875, a contract was entered into between the parties, whereby the plaintiff agreed to sell and deliver to the defendant, at the city of St. Louis, during the said month of August, twelve thousand four hundred and fifty (12,450) gallons of linseed oil for the price of fifty-eight (58) cents per gallon, and that the plaintiff has neglected and refused to deliver the oil according to the contract; that the market value of oil after August 3rd and during the month was not less than seventy (70) cents per gallon, and therefore claims

---

[1]   [$2,151.50 in 1876 dollars is roughly the equivalent of $52,000 in 2019 dollars using the CPI and the GNP Deflator.—Eds.]

a set-off or counter-claim to plaintiff's cause of action. The reply of the plaintiff denies that any contract was entered into between it and defendant.

[2] The plaintiff resided at Minneapolis, Minnesota, and the defendant was the resident agent of the plaintiff, at St. Louis, Missouri. The contract is alleged to have been made by telegraph.

[3] The plaintiff sent the following dispatch to the defendant: "Minneapolis, July 29, 1875. To Alex. Easton, Secretary Collier White Lead Company, St. Louis, Missouri: Account of sales not enclosed in yours of 27th. Please wire us best offer for round lot named by you—one hundred barrels shipped. Minnesota Linseed Oil Company." —*Request for an offer*

[4] The following answer was received: "St. Louis, Mo., July 30, 1875. To the Minnesota Linseed Oil Company: Three hundred barrels fifty-five cents here, thirty days, no commission, August delivery. Answer. Collier Company."

[5] The following reply was returned: "Minneapolis, July 31, 1875. Will accept fifty-eight cents (58c), on terms named in your telegram. Minnesota Linseed Oil Company." *Counteroffer*

[6] This dispatch was transmitted Saturday, July 31, 1875, at 9:15 p. m., and was not delivered to the defendant in St. Louis, until Monday morning, August 2, between eight and nine o'clock.

[7] On Tuesday, August 3, at 8:53 a. m., the following dispatch was deposited for transmission in the telegraph office: "St. Louis Mo., August 3, 1875. To Minnesota Linseed Oil Company, Minneapolis: Offer accepted-ship three hundred barrels as soon as possible. Collier Company."

[8] The following telegrams passed between the parties after the last one was deposited in the office at St. Louis: "Minneapolis, August 3, 1875. To Collier Company, St. Louis: We must withdraw our offer wired July 31st. Minnesota Linseed Oil Company."

[9] Answered: "St. Louis, August 3, 1875. Minnesota Linseed Oil Company: Sale effected before your request to withdraw was received. When will you ship? Collier Company."

[10] It appeared that the market was very much unsettled, and that the price of oil was subject to sudden fluctuations during the month previous and at the time of this negotiation, varying from day to day, and ranging between fifty-five and seventy-five cents per gallon. It is urged by the defendant that the dispatch of Tuesday, August 3, 1875, accepting the offer of the plaintiff transmitted July 31st, and delivered Monday morning, August 2, concluded a contract for the sale of the twelve thousand four hundred and fifty gallons of oil. The plaintiff, on the contrary, claims, first, that the dispatch accepting the proposition made July 31st, was not

[handwritten margin notes: "Negotiation" (left margin, vertical); "Crazy oil mkt, fluctuated a lot" (bottom left margin, vertical)]

received until after the offer had been withdrawn; second, that the acceptance of the offer was not in due time; third, that the delay was unreasonable; and, therefore, no contract was completed.

[11] NELSON, DISTRICT JUDGE. It is well settled by the authorities in this country, and sustained by the later English decisions, that there is no difference in the rules governing the negotiation of contracts by correspondence through the post-office and by telegraph, and a contract is concluded when an acceptance of a proposition is deposited in the telegraph office for transmission.

[12] The reason for this rule is well stated in *Adams v. Lindsell*, 1 Barn. & Ald. 681. The negotiation in that case was by post. The court said: "That if a bargain could not be closed by letter before the answer was received, no contract could be completed through the medium of the post-office; that if the one party was not bound by his offer when it was accepted (that is, at the time the letter of acceptance is deposited in the mail), then the other party ought not to be bound until after they had received a notification that the answer had been received and assented to, and that so it might go on ad infinitum." In the case at bar the delivery of the message at the telegraph office signified the acceptance of the offer. If any contract was entered into, the meeting of minds was at 8:53 of the clock, on Tuesday morning, August 3, and the subsequent dispatches are out of the case.

[13] This rule is not strenuously dissented from on the argument, and it is substantially admitted that the acceptance of an offer by letter or by telegraph completes the contract, when such acceptance is put in the proper and usual way of being communicated by the agency employed to carry it; and that when an offer is made by telegraph, an acceptance by telegraph takes effect when the dispatch containing the acceptance is deposited for transmission in the telegraph office, and not when it is received by the other party. Conceding this, there remains only one question to decide, which will determine the issues: Was the acceptance of defendant deposited in the telegraph office Tuesday, August 3, within a reasonable time, so as to consummate a contract binding upon the plaintiff?

[14] It is undoubtedly the rule that when a proposition is made under the circumstances in this case, an acceptance concludes the contract if the offer is still open, and the mutual consent necessary to convert the offer of one party into a binding contract by the acceptance of the other is established, if such acceptance is within a reasonable time after the offer was received.

[15] The better opinion is, that what is, or is not, a reasonable time, must depend upon the circumstances attending the negotiation, and the character of the subject matter of the contract, and in no better way can the intention of the parties be determined. If the negotiation is in respect

to an article stable in price, there is not so much reason for an immediate acceptance of the offer, and the same rule would not apply as in a case where the negotiation related to an article subject to sudden and great fluctuations in the market.

[16] The rule in regard to the length of the time an offer shall continue, and when an acceptance completes the contract, is laid down in Parsons on Contracts (volume 1, p. 482). He says: "It may be said that whether the offer be made for a time certain or not, the intention or understanding of the parties is to govern . . . If no definite time is stated, then the inquiry as to a reasonable time resolves itself into an inquiry as to what time it is rational to suppose the parties contemplated; and the law will decide this to be that time which as rational men they ought to have understood each other to have had in mind." Applying this rule, it seems clear that the intention of the plaintiff, in making the offer by telegraph, to sell an article which fluctuates so much in price, must have been upon the understanding that the acceptance, if at all, should be immediate, and as soon after the receipt of the offer as would give a fair opportunity for consideration. The delay here was too long, and manifestly unjust to the plaintiff, for it afforded the defendant an opportunity to take advantage of a change in the market, and accept or refuse the offer as would best subserve its interests.

[17] Judgment will be entered in favor of the plaintiff for the amount claimed. The counter-claim is denied. Judgment accordingly.

KEMPNER v. COHN

Supreme Court of Arkansas
47 Ark. 519, 1 S.W. 869 (1886)

SMITH, J.

[1] Cohn sued Kempner for the non-performance of an alleged agreement to convey a certain lot on Main street, in the city of Little Rock. He claimed damages for the loss of his bargain, for expenses incurred in investigating the title, for the loss of interest upon the money which he had raised by the sale of interest-bearing securities in order to comply with the terms of purchase, and which he had been unable immediately to reinvest to his satisfaction, and for the loss of a profitable lease of the lot which he had made on the faith of getting the lot. The answer denied the existence of any contract between the parties for the sale of the lot. Upon a trial before a jury the plaintiff recovered a verdict and judgment for $611.50[2]. The assignments in the motion for a new trial were the admission of improper evidence, the refusal of the court to give a certain charge to the

------

[2] [$611.50 in 1886 dollars is roughly the equivalent of $16,800 in 2019 dollars using the CPI and the GNP Deflator.—Eds.]

jury, and <u>want of evidence to sustain the verdict.</u> The plaintiff lived in Little Rock; the defendant at Hot Springs. The two cities are about 60 miles apart, and there is communication by mail twice a day. On the twenty-eighth of January the plaintiff wrote the defendant inquiring his terms. The answer was as follows:

HOT SPRINGS, January 30, 1885.

M.M. Cohn, Little Rock, Ark.—DEAR SIR: Yours of the 28th received, and contents noted. In reply will say, in regard to the lot, I will sell you for $10,000 dollars, $5,000 cash and $5,000 for your note, with 10 per cent interest. If that is satisfactory, send the deed, and I will send you properly acknowledged.[3]

Respectfully yours,
John KEMPNER.

[2] This letter was sent in the care of A. Kempner, the defendant's uncle, and agent for the payment of taxes and collection of rents, but who had no authority to contract for the sale of the lot; so that it was not delivered to Cohn until February 2. On February 5th, Cohn told A. Kempner he would take the property, and requested him to inform the defendant. And, in reply to the letter of January 30th, he wrote himself as follows:

LITTLE ROCK, ARK.
February 7, 1885.

J. Kempner, Hot Springs, Ark.—

DEAR SIR:

I hand you herewith the duly acknowledged. In order that I may get possession as soon as possible, I would like for you to return the deed, as well as all the deeds, memorandas, agreements, contracts, etc., that you have in connection with this property, at your earliest convenience,—say by Monday's mail, if you can. I am having the title looked up now, which, if found correct, I will comply with your terms contained in your letter of January 30th, to-wit, $5,000 in cash, and my note for balance or other $5,000. If you should prefer, I will give you Mr. A. Kempner's indorsement, the note to bear 10 per cent. Per annum. You can send the deed to Mr. A. Kempner, if you want to, or to the Merchants' National Bank, if you prefer; though, if convenient, I would rather you would come up because it is always easier to talk than to write.

---

3   [It would appear that something was left out of the last sentence of the letter, but the court reprinted it without comment. "Send the deed, and I will send you properly acknowledged" seems to have been an idiom in use at the time, because there is similar language in the next letter. It appears that Kempner meant that Cohn was to send him a deed in the form that Cohn wanted and Kempner would sign it and acknowledge his signature before a notary public (a requirement for recording the deed in the county land records) and send it back to Cohn.—Eds.]

By the memorandas, agreements, etc., I mean your papers relating to the walls on each side so as to know what to claim. Hoping that you will give this your early attention.

Yours, truly,
M. M. COHN.

[3]   This letter was put in one of the government letter-boxes before Cohn had received any notice that the offer was withdrawn. The envelope is post-marked, "LITTLE ROCK, February 7th, 9 P.M." It reached Kempner on the ninth of February. The defendant, being informed by letter from A. Kempner that Cohn was making his arrangements to buy the property, wrote, on the seventh of February, to Cohn that he had changed his mind, and now declined to sell. Evidence was given, over objection, that Cohn, immediately after receiving the letter of January 30th, had set to work to procure an abstract of the title, paying therefore $11.50, and had employed attorneys to examine the same at a cost of $50; also that he had parted with valuable securities to raise the money for the cash payment, and that after Kempner's refusal to consummate the trade, he had tried unsuccessfully, for some two months, to reinvest the money, whereby he had lost $80 or $100 in interest. It was further proved, without objection, that Cohn, about the time he wrote accepting the offer, had made a contract with another person for a lease of the lot. The property was variously estimated by different witnesses to be worth from $10,000 to $12,500. The plaintiff requested no special directions to the jury.

[4]   The instructions given at the defendant's instance were as follows:

(1)   The court instructs the jury that, before they will be authorized to find damages for plaintiff in any sum whatever, they must believe from a preponderance of the evidence that the contract between plaintiff and defendant for the sale of said lot was definite and complete, and without condition.

(2)   That, before the jury can say that the contract in this case was completed, they must find from the evidence that the offer made by Kempner was accepted by Cohn absolutely, and without qualification, and unless the offer of Kempner was thus accepted you will find for the defendant.

(3)   If the jury finds from the evidence that the letter of Cohn to Kempner, in regard to accepting the offer of said lot, contained any qualification of Kempner's proposition whatever, or that said letter was an absolute acceptance of said proposition, Kempner is not bound, and you will find for defendant.

(4)   Nor would Kempner be bound by the unconditional and unqualified acceptance of his offer, unless the acceptance was made within a reasonable time; and it is for the jury to say what

is a reasonable time, taking into consideration the situation of the parties, and their facilities for communication; and unless you find from the evidence that Kempner's offer was accepted unconditionally, and within a reasonable time, by Cohn, you will find for the defendant, Kempner.

(5) The court instructs the jury that Cohn cannot recover damages for being kept out of the interest of his money, unless he tried to secure investment, and failed, even if there was an absolute contract for the sale of the land.

(6) The court instructs the jury that the statements made by Cohn to A. Kempner, that he, Cohn, would take the property, cannot be considered as an acceptance of J. Kempner's proposition.

[5]   And the court denied the sixth prayer, which was:

If the jury find from the evidence that Kempner rescinded his offer to sell the lot for $10,000, and mailed that revocation before Cohn mailed his acceptance of the offer, they will find for the defendant.

[6]   The most material inquiry is whether the minds of the parties ever met, or mutually assented to the same thing. When parties are conducting a negotiation through the mail, a contract is completed the moment a letter accepting the offer is posted, provided it be done with due diligence after receipt of the letter containing the proposal, and before any intimation is received that the offer is withdrawn.

[7]   Whether an offer remains open is a question of fact. Of course, the proposer may limit the time for acceptance, as every man has the right to dictate the terms upon which he will sell his property. Where the answer by return mail is requested or may be expected from the usage of trade, or nature of the business, the making of the offer is accompanied by an implied stipulation that the answer shall be immediate. But unless the time is limited the proposition is open until it is accepted or rejected, provided an answer is given in a reasonable time.

[8]   The defendant, having caused the question of reasonable time to be submitted to the jury under an instruction drawn by his counsel, and having met with an adverse decision, now asks us to declare, as a matter of law, that Cohn's acceptance was unreasonably delayed. But we think the question was properly resolved in favor of the plaintiff. The subject of negotiation was real estate, which requires more deliberation than if it had been a transaction in cotton or other article of merchandise. It is also less subject to sudden and violent fluctuations in price. Five days was not an unreasonable time within which to come to a determination, have the title looked into, and a conveyance prepared.

[9] Then, as to the attempted retraction: An offer made by letter, which is to be answered in the same way, cannot be withdrawn unless the withdrawal reaches the party to whom it is addressed before he has accepted. An uncommunicated revocation is in law no revocation at all. When Kempner penned his withdrawal of the offer, he did not know that it had been accepted at that time. But it was not necessary that he should know of it, and the acceptance was effectual to complete the contract, not withstanding Kempner had previously mailed a letter to Cohn announcing the retraction of the offer.

[The court held there was error in the admission of certain testimony concerning damages.—Eds.]

[11] If the plaintiff shall, during the present term, enter a *remittitur* upon the usual terms of $100, his judgment will be affirmed; otherwise he must submit to another trial.

PROBLEM 4-1

Suppose that Tom Wolfe (the author of such books as *The Electric Kool-Aid Acid Test* and *The Right Stuff*) wrote a letter to Ted Kaczynski (the mathematician who attempted to assassinate public figures by mailing them bombs, dubbed the "Unibomber" by the press) offering to ghost-write Kaczynski's autobiography in return for half the royalties earned by the book. Suppose further that Kaczynski wrote Wolfe a letter accepting the offer and mailed the letter back to Wolfe along with a bomb. If the bomb exploded and killed Wolfe before he read the acceptance letter, would they have a contract? (Recall that the death of the offeror or the offeree terminates the offer.)

------ *Yes, contract exists when mailed*

DICKINSON V. DODDS
Court of Appeal, Chancery Division
2 Ch. D. 463 (1876)

[1] On Wednesday, the 10th of June, 1874, the Defendant John Dodds signed and delivered to the Plaintiff, George Dickinson, a memorandum, of which the material part was as follows:

> I hereby agree to sell to Mr. George Dickinson the whole of the dwelling-houses, garden ground, stabling, and outbuildings thereto belonging, situated at Croft, belonging to me, for the sum of £800. As witness my hand this tenth day of June, 1874. *Valid*
>
> (Signed)
> John Dodds   *offer*

P.S.—This offer to be left over until Friday, 9 o'clock, A.M., 12th June, 1874

(Signed)
J. Dodds

[2] The bill alleged that Dodds understood and intended that the Plaintiff should have until Friday 9 A.M. within which to determine whether he would or would not purchase, and that he should absolutely have until that time the refusal of the property at the price of $800, and that the Plaintiff in fact determined to accept the offer on the morning of Thursday, the 11th of June, but did not at once signify his acceptance to Dodds, believing that he had the power to accept it until 9 A.M. on the Friday.

[3] In the afternoon of the Thursday the Plaintiff was informed by Mr. Berry that Dodds had been offering or agreeing to sell the property to Thomas Allan, the other Defendant. Thereupon the Plaintiff, at about half-past seven in the evening, went to the house of Mrs. Burgess, the mother-in-law of Dodds, where he was then staying, and left with her a formal acceptance in writing of the offer to sell the property. According to the evidence of Mrs. Burgess this document never in fact reached Dodds, she having forgotten to give it to him.

[4] On the following (Friday) morning, at about seven o'clock, Berry, who was acting as agent for Dickinson, found Dodds at the Darlington railway station, and handed to him a duplicate of the acceptance by Dickinson, and explained to Dodds its purport. He replied that it was too late, as he had sold the property. A few minutes later Dickinson himself found Dodds entering a railway carriage, and handed him another duplicate of the notice of acceptance, but Dodds declined to receive it, saying, "You are too late. I have sold the property."

[5] It appeared that on the day before, Thursday the 11th of June, Dodds had signed a formal contract for the sale of the property to Defendant Allan for £800, and had received from him a deposit of £40.

[6] The bill in this suit prayed that the Defendant Dodds might be decreed specifically to perform the contract of the 10th of June, 1874; that he might be restrained from conveying the property to Allan; that Allan might be restrained from taking any such conveyance; that if any such conveyance had been or should be made, Allan might be declared a trustee of the property for, and might be directed to convey the property to, the Plaintiff; and for damages.

[7] The cause came on for hearing before Vice-Chancellor Bacon on the 25th of January, 1876.

[A decree for specific performance was entered, and the Defendants appealed.—Eds.]

[8]   JAMES, L.J., after referring to the document of the 10th of June, 1874, continued:—

[9]   The document, though beginning "I hereby agree to sell," was nothing but an offer, and was only intended to be an offer, for the Plaintiff himself tells us that he required time to consider whether he would enter into an agreement or not. Unless both parties had then agreed there was no concluded agreement then made; it was in effect and substance only an offer to sell. The Plaintiff, being minded not to complete the bargain at that time, added this memorandum—"This offer to be left over until Friday, 9 o'clock A.M., 12th June, 1874." That shows it was only an offer. There was no consideration given for the undertaking or promise, to whatever extent it may be considered binding, to keep the property unsold until 9 o'clock on Friday morning; but apparently Dickinson was of the opinion, and probably Dodds was of the same opinion, that he (Dodds) was bound by that promise, and could not in any way withdraw from it, or retract it, until 9 o'clock on Friday morning, and this probably explains a good deal of what afterwards took place. But it is clear settled law, on one of the clearest principles of law, that this promise, being a mere nudum pactum, was not binding and that any moment before a complete acceptance by Dickinson of the offer, Dodds was as free as Dickinson himself. Well, that being the state of things, it is said that the only mode in which Dodds would assert that freedom was by actually and distinctly saying to Dickinson, "Now I withdraw of the offer," or what is called a retraction. It must, to constitute a contract, appear that the two minds were at one, at the same moment of time, that is, that there was an offer continuing up to the time of the acceptance. If there was not such a continuing up to the time of the acceptance comes to nothing. Of course it may well be that the one man is bound in some way or other to let the other man know that his mind with regard to the other has been changed; but in this case, beyond all question, the Plaintiff knew that Dodds was no longer minded to sell the property to him as plainly and clearly as if Dodds had told him in so many words, "I withdraw the offer." This is evident from the Plaintiff's own statements in the bill.

[10] The Plaintiff says in effect that, having heard and knowing that Dodds was no longer minded to sell to him, and that he was selling or had sold to someone else, thinking that he could not in point of law withdraw his offer, meaning to fix him to it, and endeavoring to bind him, "I went to the house where he was lodging, and saw his mother-in-law, and left with her an acceptance of the offer, knowing all the while that he had entirely changed his mind. I got an agent to watch for him at 7 o'clock the next morning, and I went to the train just before 9 o'clock the next morning, in order that I might catch him and give him my notice of acceptance just before 9 o'clock, and when that occurred he told my agent, and he told me, you are too late, and he then threw back the paper." It is to my mind quite clear that before there was any attempt at acceptance of the Plaintiff, he

was perfectly well aware that Dodds had changed his mind and that he had in fact agreed to sell the property to Allan. It is impossible, therefore, to say there was ever that existence of the same mind between the two parties which is essential in point of law to making of an agreement. I am of opinion, therefore, that the Plaintiff has failed to prove that there was any binding contract between Dodds and himself.

MELLISH, L.J.

[11] I am of the same opinion. The first question is, whether this document of the 10th of June, 1874, which was signed by Dodds, was an agreement to sell, or only an offer to sell, the property therein mentioned to Dickinson; and I am clearly of the opinion that it was only an offer, although it is in the first part of it, independently of the postscript, worded as an agreement. . . . Well, then, this being only an offer, the law says— and it is a perfectly clear rule of law—that, although it is said that the offer is to be left open until Friday morning at 9 o'clock, that did not bind Dodds. He was not in point of law bound to hold the offer over until 9 o'clock on Friday morning. He was not so bound either in law or in equity. Well, that being so, when on the next day he made an agreement with Allan to sell the property to him, I am not aware of any ground on which it can be said that contract with Allan to have known (there is some dispute about it, and Allan does not admit that he knew of it, but I will assume that he did) that Dodds had made the offer to Dickinson, and had given him till Friday morning at 9 o'clock to accept it, still in point of law that could not prevent Allan from making a more favorable offer than Dickinson, and entering at once into a binding agreement with Dodds.

[12] Dickinson is informed by Berry that the property has been sold by Dodds to Allan. Berry does not tell us from whom he heard it, but he says that he did hear it, that he knew it, and that he informed Dickinson of it. Now, stopping there, the question which arises is this—i.e., an offer has been made for the sale of property, and before that offer is accepted, the person who has made the offer enters into a binding agreement to sell the property to somebody else, and the person to whom the offer was first made receives notice in some way that the property has been sold to another person, can he after that make a binding contract by the acceptance of the offer? I am of opinion that he cannot. The law may be right or wrong in saying that a person who has given to another a certain time within which to accept an offer is not bound by his promise to give that time; but, if he is not bound by that promise, and may still sell the property to someone else, and if it be the law that, in order to make a contract, the two minds must be in agreement at some one time, that is, at the time of the acceptance, how is it possible that when the person to whom the offer has been made knows that the person who has made the offer has sold the property to someone else, and that, in fact, he has not remained in the same mind to sell it to him, he can be at liberty to accept the offer and thereby make a

binding contract? It seems to me that would be simply absurd. If a man makes an offer to sell a particular horse in his stable, and says, "I will give you until the day after to-morrow to accept the offer," and the next day goes and sells the horse to somebody else, and receives the purchase-money from him, can the person to whom the offer was originally made then come and say, "I accept," so as to make a binding contract, and so as to be entitled to recover damages for the nondelivery of the horse? If the rule of law is that a mere offer to sell property, which can be withdrawn at any time, and which is made dependant on the acceptance of the person to whom it is made, is a mere *nudum pactum*, how is it possible that the person to whom the offer has been made can by acceptance make a binding contract after he knows that the person who has made the offer has sold the property to someone else? It is admitted law that, if a man who makes an offer dies, the offer cannot be accepted after he is dead, and parting with the property has very much the same effect as the death of the owner, for it makes the performance of the offer impossible. I am clearly of opinion that, just as when a man who has made an offer dies before it is accepted it is impossible that it can then be accepted, so when once the person to whom the offer was made knows that the property has been sold to someone else, it is too late for him to accept the offer, and on that ground I am clearly of opinion that there was no binding contract for the sale of this property by Dodds to Dickinson, and even if there had been, it seems to me that the sale of the property to Allan was first in point of time. However, it is not necessary to consider, if there had been two binding contracts, which of them would be entitled to priority in equity, because there is no binding contract between Dodds and Dickinson.

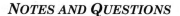

NOTES AND QUESTIONS

1.   Read R2d § 43, which states the generally accepted rule on indirect revocation of acceptance. If the *Dickinson* court had applied that rule, would the offer have been revoked?

2.   Note how casually in paragraph 13 Lord Justice Mellish says the law may be wrong. American judges are much less willing to make such a statement.

3.   At this point in the casebook, most cases we have covered have involved courts applying general contract law to resolve a variety of legal issues. This chapter introduces a few cases where the governing body of law the court applied was the Uniform Commercial Code (U.C.C.), not general contract law as enacted in a particular state. Unlike general contract law, which is created and developed by common law (i.e. case precedent), the U.C.C. represents a body of statutory law that governs important categories of commercial transactions. Article 2 of the U.C.C. establishes the operative rules for the sale of goods, and these rules are supposed to operate more like a civil

law system than a common law system because courts are to look to the statute first for guidance on their decisions, not the caselaw. If the statutory language is ambiguous or vague, the court will refer to relevant caselaw to determine how previous courts have applied and interpreted the statute in similar situations. So, as one professor who teaches U.C.C.-related courses often shouts from the podium when students appear baffled at a U.C.C. problem, "READ THE STATUTE."

Option Contracts

An offer is irrevocable if the promise to keep the offer open is "supported by consideration." Chapter 5 explores the mysteries of consideration, but for the time being we can say that the promise to keep the offer open is "supported by consideration" if the offeree pays the offeror to keep the offer open. Such an irrevocable offer is usually referred to as an *option contract*. It is a separate contract to keep an offer for another contract open.

Option contracts are used widely in business. For instance, a real estate developer who wants to tie up a piece of land until she determines whether she can develop it profitably may enter into an option contract with the owner of the land. The option contract really is an offer by the owner of the land to sell it for a specified price, say $100,000. The offer is irrevocable because the developer pays an amount of money, perhaps $1,000, for the owner's promise not to revoke the offer for a stated period, maybe three months. Another use is in executive compensation. An executive may be given a *stock option* as part of her compensation package. It entitles her to buy stock in the company that employs her. The price of the stock is fixed at the time it is granted, and the holder of the option can purchase the stock at a certain time in the future. The more the price of the stock rises before the option expires, the more valuable the option is. Thus, the executive is given an incentive to work harder to make the stock's price rise.

PROBLEM 4-2

Read carefully U.C.C. § 2–205 dealing with so called "firm offers." Do not ignore definitional cross-references.

John wrote Mary the following letter:

September 15, 2003

Dear Ms. Roe:

I hereby offer to sell you the items on the attached list for a total price of $850,000.

offer

This offer will remain open until November 15 of this year.

Sincerely,

J. Doe

Mary gave no consideration to John for his promise to keep the offer open.

Would the offer be irrevocable if:

(a) The "items on the attached list" were pieces of heavy construction machinery and John and Mary were dealers in used construction machinery.

(b) The "items on the attached list" were comic books and John and Mary were brokers on the New York Comic Book Exchange.

(c) The "items on the attached list" were lots on which homes could be constructed and John and Mary were real estate developers.

(d) The "items on the attached list" were stocks and bonds and John and Mary were stockbrokers.

(e) The "items on the attached list" were antique automobiles and John was a dealer in antique automobiles while Mary was the lead singer in a rock group.

(f) The "items on the attached list" were antique automobiles and Mary was a dealer in antique automobiles while John was the lead singer in a rock group.

(g) The "items on the attached list" were pieces of heavy construction machinery and John and Mary were dealers in used construction machinery, but John typed his name rather than writing it manually in script.

(h) The "items on the attached list" were pieces of heavy construction machinery and John and Mary were dealers in used construction machinery, but the letter stated that the offer would remain open for six months. (If this offer would be irrevocable, for how long would it remain irrevocable?)

PROBLEM 4-3

Read carefully CISG article 16(2) (firm offers). Under the CISG, which of the prior offers would be irrevocable?

————

PETTERSON V. PATTBERG

Court of Appeals of New York
248 N.Y. 86, 161 N.E. 428 (1928)

KELLOGG, J.

[1]   John Petterson, of whose last will and testament the plaintiff is the executrix, was the owner of a parcel of real estate in Brooklyn, known as 5301 Sixth Avenue. The defendant was the owner of a bond[4] executed by Petterson, which was secured by a third mortgage upon the parcel. On April 4, 1924, there remained unpaid upon the principal the sum of $5,450.[5] This amount was payable in installments of $250 on April 25, 1924, and upon a like monthly date every three months thereafter. Thus the bond and mortgage had more than five years to run before the entire sum became due. Under date of the 4th of April, 1924, the defendant wrote Petterson as follows:

> I hereby agree to accept cash for the mortgage which I hold against premises 5301 6th Ave., Brooklyn, N. Y. It is understood and agreed as a consideration I will allow you $780 providing said mortgage is paid on or before May 31, 1924, and the regular quarterly payment due April 25, 1924, is paid when due.

[2]   On April 25, 1924, Petterson paid the defendant the installment of principal due on that date. Subsequently, on a day in the latter part of May, 1924, Petterson presented himself at the defendant's home, and knocked at the door. The defendant demanded the name of his caller. Petterson replied: "It is Mr. Petterson. I have come to pay off the mortgage." The defendant answered that he had sold the mortgage. Petterson stated that he would like to talk with the defendant, so the defendant partly opened the door. Thereupon Petterson exhibited the cash, and said he was ready to pay off the mortgage according to the agreement. The defendant refused to take the money. Prior to this conversation, Petterson had made a contract to sell the land to a third person free and clear of the mortgage to the defendant. Meanwhile, also, the defendant had sold the bond and mortgage to a third party. It therefore became necessary for Petterson to pay to such person the full amount of the bond and mortgage. It is claimed that he thereby sustained a loss of $780, the sum which the defendant agreed to allow upon the bond and mortgage, if payment in full of principal, less that sum, was made on or before May 31, 1924. The plaintiff has had a recovery for the sum thus claimed, with interest.

[3]   Clearly the defendant's letter proposed to Petterson the making of a unilateral contract, the gift of a promise in exchange for the performance

---

[4]   [A bond is an instrument by which a person promises to pay a sum of money. For present purposes it is enough to understand that it is like a promissory note.—Eds.]

[5]   [$5,450 in 1928 dollars is roughly the equivalent of $80,000 in 2019 dollars using the CPI and the GNP Deflator.—Eds.]

of an act.[6] The thing conditionally promised by the defendant was the reduction of the mortgage debt. The act requested to be done, in consideration of the offered promise, was payment in full of the reduced principal of the debt prior to the due date thereof. "If an act is requested, that very act, and no other, must be given." Williston on Contracts, § 73. "In case of offers for a consideration, the performance of the consideration is always deemed a condition." Langdell's Summary of the Law of Contracts, § 4. It is elementary that any offer to enter into a unilateral contract may be withdrawn before the act requested to be done has been performed. A bidder at a sheriff's sale may revoke his bid at any time before the property is struck down to him. The offer of a reward in consideration of an act to be performed is revocable before the very act requested has been done. So, also, an offer to pay a broker commissions, upon a sale of land for the offeror, is revocable at any time before the land is sold, although prior to revocation the broker performs services in an effort to effectuate a sale.

[4] An interesting question arises when, as here, the offeree approaches the offeror with the intention of proffering performance and, before actual tender is made, the offer is withdrawn. Of such a case Williston says:

> The offeror may see the approach of the offeree and know that an acceptance is contemplated. If the offeror can say "I revoke" before the offeree accepts, however brief the interval of time between the two acts, there is no escape from the conclusion that the offer is terminated.

Williston on Contracts, § 60b.

[5] In this instance Petterson, standing at the door of the defendant's house, stated to the defendant that he had come to pay off the mortgage. Before a tender of the necessary moneys had been made, the defendant informed Petterson that he had sold the mortgage. That was a definite notice to Petterson that the defendant could not perform his offered promise, and that a tender to the defendant, who was no longer the creditor, would be ineffective to satisfy the debt. "An offer to sell property may be withdrawn before acceptance without any formal notice to the person to whom the offer is made. It is sufficient if that person has actual knowledge that the person who made the offer has done some act inconsistent with the continuance of the offer, such as selling the property to a third person." *Dickinson v. Dodds*, 2 Ch. Div. 463, headnote. To the same effect is *Coleman v. Applegarth*, 68 Md. 21, 11 A. 284, 6 Am. St. Rep. 417. Thus it clearly appears that the defendant's offer was withdrawn before its acceptance had been tendered. It is unnecessary to determine,

---

6   [Why is it so clear, given the presumption in favor of bilateral contracts? Think of what would happen if you made a bilateral contract under these terms.—Eds.]

therefore, what the legal situation might have been had tender been made before withdrawal. It is the individual view of the writer that the same result would follow. This would be so, for the act requested to be performed was the completed act of payment, a thing incapable of performance, unless assented to by the person to be paid. Williston on Contracts, § 60b. Clearly an offering party has the right to name the precise act performance of which would convert his offer into a binding promise. Whatever the act may be until it is performed, the offer must be revocable. However, the supposed case is not before us for decision. We think that in this particular instance the offer of the defendant was withdrawn before it became a binding promise, and therefore that no contract was ever made for the breach of which the plaintiff may claim damages.

[6] The judgment of the Appellate Division and that of the Trial Term should be reversed, and the complaint dismissed, with costs in all courts.

LEHMAN, J. (dissenting).

[7] The defendant's letter to Petterson constituted a promise on his part to accept payment at a discount of the mortgage he held, provided the mortgage is paid on or before May 31, 1924. Doubtless, by the terms of the promise itself, the defendant made payment of the mortgage by the plaintiff, before the stipulated time, a condition precedent to performance by the defendant of his promise to accept payment at a discount. If the condition precedent has not been performed, it is because the defendant made performance impossible by refusing to accept payment, when the plaintiff came with an offer of immediate performance. "It is a principle of fundamental justice that if a promisor is himself the cause of the failure of performance either of an obligation due him or of a condition upon which his own liability depends, he cannot take advantage of the failure." Williston on Contracts, § 677. The question in this case is not whether payment of the mortgage is a condition precedent to the performance of a promise made by the defendant, but, rather, whether, at the time the defendant refused the offer of payment, he had assumed any binding obligation, even though subject to condition.

[8] The promise made by the defendant lacked consideration at the time it was made. Nevertheless, the promise was not made as a gift or mere gratuity to the plaintiff. It was made for the purpose of obtaining from the defendant something which the plaintiff desired. It constituted an offer which was to become binding whenever the plaintiff should give, in return for the defendant's promise, exactly the consideration which the defendant requested.

[9] Here the defendant requested no counter promise from the plaintiff. The consideration requested by the defendant for his promise to accept payment was, I agree, some act to be performed by the plaintiff. Until the act requested was performed, the defendant might undoubtedly

revoke his offer. Our problem is to determine from the words of the letter, read in the light of surrounding circumstances, what act the defendant requested as consideration for his promise.

[10] The defendant undoubtedly made his offer as an inducement to the plaintiff to "pay" the mortgage before it was due. Therefore, it is said, that "the act requested to be performed was the completed act of payment, a thing incapable of performance, unless assented to by the person to be paid." In unmistakable terms the defendant agreed to accept payment, yet we are told that the defendant intended, and the plaintiff should have understood, that the act requested by the defendant, as consideration for his promise to accept payment, included performance by the defendant himself of the very promise for which the act was to be consideration. The defendant's promise was to become binding only when fully performed; and part of the consideration to be furnished by the plaintiff for the defendant's promise was to be the performance of that promise by the defendant. So construed, the defendant's promise or offer, though intended to induce action by the plaintiff, is but a snare and delusion. The plaintiff could not reasonably suppose that the defendant was asking him to procure the performance by the defendant of the very act which the defendant promised to do, yet we are told that, even after the plaintiff had done all else which the defendant requested, the defendant's promise was still not binding because the defendant chose not to perform.

[11] I cannot believe that a result so extraordinary could have been intended when the defendant wrote the letter. "The thought behind the phrase proclaims itself misread when the outcome of the reading is injustice or absurdity."[7] *See* opinion of Cardozo, C.J., in *Surace v. Danna*, 248 N.Y. 18, 161 N.E. 315. If the defendant intended to induce payment by the plaintiff and yet reserve the right to refuse payment when offered he should have used a phrase better calculated to express his meaning than the words: "I agree to accept." A promise to accept payment, by its very terms, must necessarily become binding, if at all, not later than when a present offer to pay is made.

[12] I recognize that in this case only an offer of payment, and not a formal tender of payment, was made before the defendant withdrew his offer to accept payment. Even the plaintiff's part in the act of payment was then not technically complete. Even so, under a fair construction of the words of the letter, I think the plaintiff had done the act which the defendant requested as consideration for his promise. The plaintiff offered to pay, with present intention and ability to make that payment. A formal tender is seldom made in business transactions, except to lay the foundation for subsequent assertion in a court of justice of rights which spring from refusal of the tender. If the defendant acted in good faith in

---

[7] [Contrast this with the English judge's statement in the last case that the law might be wrong.—Eds.]

making his offer to accept payment, he could not well have intended to draw a distinction in the act requested of the plaintiff in return, between an offer which, unless refused, would ripen into completed payment, and a formal tender. Certainly the defendant could not have expected or intended that the plaintiff would make a formal tender of payment without first stating that he had come to make payment. We should not read into the language of the defendant's offer a meaning which would prevent enforcement of the defendant's promise after it had been accepted by the plaintiff in the very way which the defendant must have intended it should be accepted, if he acted in good faith.

The judgment should be affirmed.

CARDOZO, C.J., and POUND, CRANE, and O'BRIEN, JJ., concur with KELLOGG, J.

LEHMAN, J., dissents in opinion, in which ANDREWS, J., concurs.

Judgments reversed.

NOTES AND QUESTIONS

1.   Did the majority think the offer was one that could be accepted (i) only by a promise, (ii) only by the performance of an act, or (iii) either by a promise or the performance of an act? If it could be accepted by the performance of an act, what was the act?

2.   Did Judge Lehman think the offer was one that could be accepted (i) only by a promise, (ii) only by the performance of an act, or (iii) either by a promise or the performance of an act? If it could be accepted by the performance of an act, what was the act?

3.   Judge Lehman, in paragraph 11, considered the letter in question: "The thought behind the phrase proclaims itself misread when the outcome of the reading is injustice or absurdity." Contrast this with Lord Justice Mellish's statement in *Dickinson v. Dodds* that the law might be wrong. Do you see the different underlying paradigms for thinking about legal and factual issues?

Revocation of Offers for Unilateral Contracts

Revocation of an offer for a bilateral contract doesn't present much of a problem in terms of fairness. If A says to B: "I'll sell you my car for $1,000," and then A revokes the offer, there's no need to feel sorry for B. But it may be a different story if the offer was one that could be accepted only by performance.

In the classic hypothetical, a law professor offers a student: "I'll pay you $500 if you'll walk across the Brooklyn Bridge, and this offer can only be accepted by performance." The law student begins to walk across the bridge and just as he is about to get to the other side, the professor yells: "I revoke!" Because the performance is not complete until the student reaches the other end of the bridge, the classical theory holds that the revocation is effective and the professor doesn't have to pay the $500. This is the rule the court appears to have been applying in *Petterson*.

This sounds a little bit unfair, and in the real world, where a person could expend a great deal of effort (and money) performing the act that constitutes acceptance, some unfairness could result. The drafters of the R2d changed the rules about acceptance by performance. First, as we saw in *Davis v. Jacoby* and the notes following it, they adopted a more flexible rule concerning the method of acceptance. Under the common law, the court had to determine whether the offer was one that could be accepted by a promise or one that could be accepted by performance. It did not admit the possibility that the offeree could choose between accepting the offer by performing the requested act or by accepting the offer by promising to perform the act. As we have seen, the Second Restatement takes a different approach to the question of how an offer may be accepted. Review R2d §§ 30(2) and 32. The UNIDROIT Principles take a similar, albeit vaguer, approach. UNIDROIT article 2.1.6.

The R2d also takes an innovative approach to the question of revoking the offer. Read carefully R2d §§ 45 and 62. *See also* UNIDROIT article 2.1.4.

MINNEAPOLIS & ST. LOUIS RAILWAY V. COLUMBUS ROLLING-MILL CO.

Supreme Court of the United States
119 U.S. 149, 7 S.Ct. 168, 30 L.Ed. 376 (1886)

[1] This was an action by a railroad corporation established at Minneapolis, in the state of Minnesota, against a manufacturing corporation established at Columbus, in the state of Ohio. The petition alleged that on December 19, 1879, the parties made a contract by which the plaintiff agreed to buy of the defendant, and the defendant sold to the plaintiff, 2,000 tons of iron rails, of the weight of 50 pounds per yard, at the price of $54 per ton gross, to be delivered free on board cars at the defendant's rolling-mill in the month of March, 1880, and to be paid for by the plaintiff in cash when so delivered. The answer denied the making of the contract. It was admitted at the trial that the following letters and telegrams were sent at their dates, and were received in due course, by the parties, through their agents:

[2]　December 5, 1879. Letter from plaintiff to defendant: "Please quote me prices for 500 to 3,000 tons 50-lb. steel rails, and for 2,000 to 5,000 tons 50-lb. iron rails, March, 1880, delivery." *- Request for offer*

[3]　December 8, 1879. Letter from defendant to plaintiff: "Your favor of the fifth inst. at hand. We do not make steel rails. For iron rails, we will sell 2,000 to 5,000 tons of 50-lb. rails for fifty-four ($54) dollars per gross ton, for spot cash, F. O. B. cars at our mill, March delivery, subject as follows: In case of strike among our workmen, destruction of or serious damage to our works by fire or the elements, or any causes of delay beyond our control, we shall not be held accountable in damages. If our offer is accepted, shall expect to be notified of same prior to December 20, 1879." *- opt out of mailbox rule*

negotiation

[4]　December 16, 1879. Telegram from plaintiff to defendant: "Please enter our order for twelve hundred tons rails, March delivery, as per your favor of the eighth. Please reply."

Does not mirror

[5]　December 16, 1879. Letter from plaintiff to defendant: "Yours of the 8th came duly to hand. I telegraphed you to-day to enter our order for twelve hundred (1,200) tons 50-lb. iron rails for next March delivery, at fifty-four dollars, ($54,) F. O. B. cars at your mill. Please send contract. Also please send me a template of your 50-lb. rail. Do you make splices? If so, give me prices for splices for this lot of iron."

[6]　December 18, 1879. Telegram from defendant to plaintiff, received same day: "We cannot book your order at present at that price."

[7]　December 19, 1879. Telegram from plaintiff to defendant: "Please enter an order for two thousand tons rails as per your letter of the sixth. Please forward written contract. Reply." The word "sixth" was admitted to be a mistake for "eighth."

[8]　December 22, 1879. Telegram from plaintiff to defendant: "Did you enter my order for two thousand tons rails, as per my telegram of December 19th? Answer."

[9]　After repeated similar inquiries by the plaintiff, the defendant, on January 19, 1880, denied the existence of any contract between the parties.

[10] The jury returned a verdict for the defendant, under instructions which need not be particularly stated; and the plaintiff alleged exceptions, and sued out this writ of error.

[11] Mr. Justice GRAY, after making the foregoing statement of the case, delivered the opinion of the court:

[12] The rules of law which govern this case are well settled. As no contract is complete without the mutual consent of the parties, an offer to sell imposes no obligation until it is accepted according to its terms. So long as the offer has been neither accepted nor rejected, the negotiation remains open, and imposes no obligation upon either party,—the one may decline

to accept, or the other may withdraw his offer; and either rejection or withdrawal leaves the matter as if no offer had ever been made. A proposal to accept, or an acceptance, upon terms varying from those offered, is a rejection of the offer, and puts an end to the negotiation, unless the party who made the original offer renews it, or assents to the modification suggested. The other party, having once rejected the offer, cannot afterwards revive it by tendering an acceptance of it. . . . If the offer does not limit the time for its acceptance, it must be accepted within a reasonable time. If it does, it may, at any time within the limit, and so long as it remains open, be accepted or rejected by the party to whom, or be withdrawn by the party by whom, it was made. . . .

[13] The defendant, by the letter of December 8th offered to sell to the plaintiff 2,000 to 5,000 tons of iron rails on certain terms specified, and added that if the offer was accepted the defendant would expect to be notified prior to December 20th. This offer, while it remained open, without having been rejected by the plaintiff or revoked by the defendant, would authorize the plaintiff to take, at his election, any number of tons not less than 2,000, nor more than 5,000, on the terms specified. The offer, while unrevoked, might be accepted or rejected by the plaintiff at any time before December 20th. Instead of accepting the offer made, the plaintiff, on December 16th, by telegram and letter, referring to the defendant's letter of December 8th, directed the defendant to enter an order for 1,200 tons on the same terms. The mention, in both telegram and letter, of the date and the terms of the defendant's original offer, shows that the plaintiff's order was not an independent proposal, but an answer to the defendant's offer— a qualified acceptance of that offer, varying the number of tons, and therefore in law a rejection of the offer. On December 18th, the defendant, by telegram, declined to fulfill the plaintiff's order. The negotiation between the parties was thus closed, and the plaintiff could not afterwards fall back on the defendant's original offer. The plaintiff's attempt to do so, by the telegram of December 19th, was therefore ineffectual, and created no rights against the defendant. Such being the legal effect of what passed in writing between the parties, it is unnecessary to consider whether, upon a fair interpretation of the instructions of the court, the question whether the plaintiff's telegram and letter of December 16th constituted a rejection of the defendant's offer of December 8th, was ruled in favor of the defendant as matter of law, or was submitted to the jury as a question of fact. The submission of a question of law to the jury is no ground of exception, if they decide it aright. *Pence v. Langdon*, 99 U.S. 578.

Judgment affirmed.

LIVINGSTONE V. EVANS

Alberta Supreme Court
4 D.L.R. 769 (1925)

Valid offer

WALSH, J.

[1] The defendant, T.J. Evans, through his agent, wrote to the plaintiff offering to sell him the land in question for $1,800[8] on terms. On the day that he received this offer the plaintiff wired his agent as follows:— "Send lowest cash price. Will give $1,600 cash. Wire." The agent replied to → *rejection* this by telegram as follows "Cannot reduce price." Immediately upon the receipt of this telegram the plaintiff wrote accepting the offer. It is admitted by the defendants that this offer and the plaintiff's acceptance of it constitute a contract for the sale of this land to the plaintiff by which he is bound unless the intervening telegrams above set out put an end to his offer so that the plaintiff could not thereafter bind him to it by his acceptance of it.

Counter offer

[2] It is quite clear that when an offer has been rejected it is thereby ended and it cannot be afterwards accepted without the consent of him who made it. The simple question and the only one argued before me is whether the plaintiff's counteroffer was in law a rejection of the defendants' offer which freed them from it. *Hyde v. Wrench* (1840), 3 Beav. 334, 49 E.R. 132, a judgment of Lord Langdale, M.R., pronounced in 1840, is the authority for the contention that it was. The defendant offered to sell for £1,000. The plaintiff met that with an offer to pay £950 and (to quote from the judgment at p. 337)—"he thereby rejected the offer previously made by the Defendant. I think that it was not competent for him to revive the proposal of the Defendant, by tendering an acceptance of it."

[3] The plaintiff's telegram was undoubtedly a counter-offer. True, it contained an inquiry as well but that clearly was one which called for an answer only if the counter-offer was rejected. In substance it said:—"I will give you $1,600 cash. If you won't take that wire your lowest cash price." In my opinion it put an end to the defendants' liability under their offer unless it was revived by the telegram in reply to it.

[4] The real difficulty in the case, to my mind, arises out of the defendant's telegram "cannot reduce price." If this was simply a rejection of the plaintiff's counter-offer it amounts to nothing. If, however, it was a renewal of the original offer it gave the plaintiff the right to bind the defendants to it by his subsequent acceptance of it.

[5] With some doubt I think that it was a renewal of the original offer or at any rate an intimation to the plaintiff that he was still willing to treat on the basis of it. It was, of course, a reply to the counter-offer and to the

*Wrong
its a
new offer
not a
renewal*

8　[$1,800 in 1925 dollars is roughly the equivalent of $25,800 in 2019 dollars using the CPI and the GNP Deflator.—Eds.]

inquiry in the plaintiff's telegram. But it was more than that. The price referred to in it was unquestionably that mentioned in his letter. His statement that he could not reduce that price strikes me as having but one meaning, namely, that he was still standing by it and, therefore, still open to accept it.

[6]   I am, therefore, of the opinion that there was a binding contract for the sale of this land to the plaintiff of which he is entitled to specific performance. It was admitted by his counsel that if I reached this conclusion his subsequent agreement to sell the land to the defendant Williams would be of no avail as against the plaintiff's contract.

[7]   There will, therefore, be judgment for specific performance with a declaration that the plaintiff's rights under his contract have priority over those of the defendant Williams under his. The plaintiff will have his costs as agreed by the case. It is silent as to the scale but unless otherwise agreed they should be under C.R., Sch. C., c. 3.

Judgment for the plaintiff.

———————

PROBLEM 4-4

Apply the law of counteroffers as set forth in the two cases above to the following fact situation. Buyer asks Seller to send Buyer a written proposal for the sale of 1,000 heavy-duty stainless steel widgets.[9] Seller sends a written proposal which constitutes an offer to sell 1,000 heavy-duty stainless steel widgets. The fine print on the back of proposal form says "all sales are final" (along with a lot of other terms that are not relevant to our problem). Buyer responds to the proposal with a form headed "Purchase Order." This form contains terms identical to those of the proposal, except that on the reverse side it says "Buyer reserves the right to return any merchandise for full credit within thirty days after delivery." Shortly after receiving the purchase order, Seller ships the widgets. Buyer accepts delivery of the widgets and pays for them. Twenty days after the widgets are delivered, Buyer decides it doesn't need them and ships them back to Seller. They arrive on Seller's loading dock the next day, but Seller refuses to take them back and refuses to give Buyer credit for their price.

Buyer sues. Who wins?

PROBLEM 4-5

Apply the law of counteroffers as set forth in the two cases above to the following fact situation. Buyer asks Seller to send Buyer a written proposal for

———————

[9]   For those unfamiliar with the term, a "widget" is a generic, general purpose term, or placeholder name, for any unspecified device or product. It is commonly used for textbook and other examples where the identity of the product or function is irrelevant and could be distracting.

the sale of 1,000 heavy-duty stainless steel widgets. Seller sends a written proposal which constitutes an offer to sell 1,000 heavy-duty stainless steel widgets. The fine print on the back of the proposal form says "all sales are final" (along with a lot of other terms that are not relevant to our problem). Buyer responds to the proposal with a form headed "Purchase Order." This form contains terms identical to those of the proposal, except that on the reverse side it says "Buyer reserves the right to return any merchandise for full credit within thirty days after delivery." Shortly after receiving the purchase order, Seller sends Buyer a form called "Confirmation." The form is pretty much the same as the proposal except that it has a different heading and begins "We have entered your order for the following merchandise." It then reiterates the terms of the proposal. Like the proposal, it has fine print on the back saying "all sales are final." Shortly thereafter, Seller ships the widgets. Buyer accepts delivery of the widgets and pays for them. Twenty days after the widgets are delivered, Buyer decides it doesn't need them and ships them back to Seller. They arrive on Seller's loading dock the next day, but Seller refuses to take them back and refuses to give Buyer credit for their price.

Buyer sues. Who wins? Why? *Seller wins, sent a counter offer to Buyers counteroffer*

The two problems above illustrate what was called "the last shot advantage." When the parties exchanged forms with conflicting terms, each form after the first was a counter offer. The last form was the offer that was accepted, either when the seller shipped the goods or when the buyer accepted delivery. Thus the person who sent the last form "won" and that form's terms were part of the contract.

U.C.C. § 2–207 was designed to eliminate the last shot advantage. Before you go any further, take a minute to read *carefully* section 2–207 and the accompanying Official Comment. Compare and contrast U.C.C. § 2–207 and CISG article 19.

———

PROBLEM 4-6

Buyer (a merchant) asks Seller (also a merchant) to send Buyer a written proposal for the sale of 1,000 heavy-duty stainless steel widgets. Seller sends a written proposal which constitutes an offer to sell 1,000 heavy-duty stainless steel widgets. The fine print on the back of the proposal form says "all sales are final" (along with a lot of other terms that are not relevant to our problem). Buyer responds to the proposal with a form headed "Purchase Order." This form contains terms identical to those of the proposal, except that on the reverse side it says "Buyer reserves the right to return any merchandise for full credit within thirty days after delivery."

(a)   Under the law of the two cases above, would the parties have a contract at this time?

(b)   Under U.C.C. § 2–207(1), would the parties have a contract at this time? (Don't worry about what the terms of the contract might be, and don't worry about subsections (2) and (3) of § 2–207. They don't apply to the question asked.)

(c)   Under CISG article 19, would the parties have a contract at this time?

(d)   Shortly after Seller receives the purchase order, it ships the widgets. Does Buyer have a right to return the widgets? *See* § 2–207(2).

————

C. ITOH & CO. v. JORDAN INTERNATIONAL CO.

United States Court of Appeals, Seventh Circuit
552 F.2d 1228 (1977)

SPRECHER, CIRCUIT JUDGE.

[1]   The sole issue on this appeal is whether the district court properly denied a stay of the proceedings pending arbitration under section 3 of the Federal Arbitration Act, 9 U.S.C. § 3. [We affirm, albeit on different grounds.—Eds.]

I

[2]   C. Itoh & Co. (America) Inc. ("Itoh") submitted a purchase order dated August 15, 1974 for a certain quantity of steel coils to the Jordan International Company ("Jordan"). In response, Jordan sent its acknowledgment form dated August 19, 1974. On the face of Jordan's form, the following statement appears:

> Seller's acceptance is, however, expressly conditional on Buyer's assent to the additional or different terms and conditions set forth below and printed on the reverse side. If these terms and conditions are not acceptable, Buyer should notify seller at once.

[3]   One of the terms on the reverse side of Jordan's form was a broad provision for arbitration.[10] Itoh neither expressly assented nor objected to the additional arbitration term in Jordan's form until the instant litigation.

---

[10]   The arbitration clause provides:

Any controversy arising under or in connection with the contract shall be submitted to arbitration in New York City in accordance with the rules then obtaining of the American Arbitration Association. Judgment on any award may be entered in any court having jurisdiction. The parties hereto submit to the jurisdiction of the Federal and State courts in New York City, and notice of process in connection with arbitral or judicial proceedings may be served upon the parties by registered or certified mail, with the same effect as if personally served.

[4] Itoh also entered into a contract to sell the steel coils that it purchased from Jordan to Riverview Steel Corporation, Inc. ("Riverview"). The contract between Itoh and Riverview contained an arbitration term which provided in pertinent part:

> Any and all controversies arising out of or relating to this contract, or any modification, breach or cancellation thereof, except as to quality, shall be settled by arbitration . . .

[5] After the steel had been delivered by Jordan and paid for by Itoh, Riverview advised Itoh that the steel coils were defective and did not conform to the standards set forth in the agreement between Itoh and Riverview; for these reasons, Riverview refused to pay Itoh for the steel. Consequently, Itoh brought the instant suit against Riverview and Jordan. Itoh alleged that Riverview had wrongfully refused to pay for the steel; as affirmative defenses, Riverview claimed that the steel was defective and that tender was improper since delivery was late. Itoh alleged that Jordan had sold Itoh defective steel and had made a late delivery of that steel.

[6] Jordan then filed a motion in the district court requesting a stay of the proceedings pending arbitration under section 3 of the Federal Arbitration Act, 9 U.S.C. § 3. The district court concluded that, as between Itoh and Riverview, the issue of whether the steel coils were defective was not referable to arbitration because of the "quality" exclusion in the arbitration provision of the contract between Itoh and Riverview. Since arbitration would not necessarily resolve all the issues raised by the parties, the district court, apparently assuming arguendo that there existed an agreement in writing between Jordan and Itoh to arbitrate their dispute, denied the stay pending arbitration. In the district court's opinion, sound judicial administration required that the entire litigation be resolved in a single forum; since some of the issues relating to quality between Itoh and Riverview were not referable to arbitration, this goal could only be accomplished in the judicial forum.

[7] It is from this denial of a stay pending arbitration that Jordan appeals.[11]

II

[The court held that the district court was wrong in holding that the importance of resolving the entire dispute in a single forum allowed the district court to decide the Jordan-Itoh dispute if there was a valid arbitration agreement. The Federal Arbitration Act required the court to give effect to a valid arbitration agreement.—Eds.]

---

[11] [The court determined that the Federal Arbitration Act requires the courts to permit arbitration any time there is a valid agreement to arbitrate. Thus, the considerations of sound judicial administration were not valid grounds for denying a stay pending arbitration.—Eds.]

III

[8]   Having concluded that the district court had no discretion under section 3 of the Federal Arbitration Act, 9 U.S.C. § 3, to deny Jordan's timely application for a stay of the action pending arbitration if there existed an agreement in writing for such arbitration between Jordan and Itoh, the remaining issue is whether there existed such an agreement.

[9]   The pertinent facts may be briefly restated. Itoh sent its purchase order for steel coils to Jordan which contained no provision for arbitration. Subsequently, Jordan sent Itoh its acknowledgment form which included, inter alia, a broad arbitration term on the reverse side of the form.[12] On the front of Jordan's form, the following statement also appears:

> Seller's acceptance is . . . expressly conditioned on Buyer's assent to the additional or different terms and conditions set forth below and printed on the reverse side. If these terms and conditions are not acceptable, Buyer should notify Seller at once.

[10] After the exchange of documents, Jordan delivered and Itoh paid for the steel coils. Itoh never expressly assented or objected to the additional arbitration term in Jordan's form.

[11] In support of its contention that there exists an agreement in writing to arbitrate, Jordan places some reliance on certain New York decisions interpreting section 2–201 of the Uniform Commercial Code, the UCC Statute of Frauds provision.

[The court then discussed the UCC Statute of Frauds provision, § 2–201, which we will explore in Chapter 13, and determined that it did not apply.]

[12] The instant case, therefore, involves the classic "battle of the forms," and section 2–207, not section 2–201, furnishes the rules for resolving such a controversy. Hence, it is to section 2–207 that we must look to determine whether a contract has been formed by the exchange of forms between Jordan and Itoh and, if so, whether the additional arbitration term in Jordan's form is to be included in that contract.

IV

[13] Section 2–207, Additional Terms in Acceptance or Confirmation, provides:

> (1) A definite and seasonable expression of acceptance or a written confirmation which is sent within a reasonable time operates as an acceptance even though it states terms additional to or different from those offered or agreed upon, unless

---

[12] There is apparently no dispute that, if the arbitration provision is part of a written agreement between the parties, it is sufficiently broad to encompass the instant dispute. Therefore, under 9 U.S.C. sec. 3, if there was an "agreement in writing for . . . arbitration," arbitration should be directed since the underlying controversy is an "issue referable to arbitration" and there is no contention by Itoh that Jordan is "in default in proceeding with such arbitration."

acceptance is expressly made conditional on assent to the additional or different terms.

(2) The additional terms are to be construed as proposals for addition to the contract. Between merchants such terms become part of the contract unless:

    (a) the offer expressly limits acceptance to the terms of the offer;

    (b) they materially alter it; or

    (c) notification of objection to them has already been given or is given within a reasonable time after notice of them is received.

(3) Conduct by both parties which recognizes the existence of a contract is sufficient to establish a contract for sale although the writings of the parties do not otherwise establish a contract. In such case the terms of the particular contract consist of those terms on which the writings of the parties agree, together with any supplementary terms incorporated under any other provisions of this Act.

[14] Under section 2–207 it is necessary to first determine whether a contract has been formed under section 2–207(1) as a result of the exchange of forms between Jordan and Itoh.

[15] At common law, "an acceptance . . . which contained terms additional to . . . those of the offer . . . constituted a rejection of the offer . . . and thus became a counter-offer." *Dorton v. Collins & Aikman Corp*, 453 F.2d 1161, 1166 (6th Cir. 1972). Thus, the mere presence of the additional arbitration term in Jordan's acknowledgment form would, at common law, have prevented the exchange of documents between Jordan and Itoh from creating a contract, and Jordan's form would have automatically become a counter-offer.

[16] Section 2–207(1) was intended to alter this inflexible common law approach to offer and acceptance:

> This section of the Code recognizes that in current commercial transactions, the terms of the offer and those of the acceptance will seldom be identical. Rather, under the current "battle of the forms," each party typically has a printed form drafted by his attorney and containing as many terms as could be envisioned to favor that party in his sales transactions. Whereas under common law the disparity between the fine-print terms in the parties' forms would have prevented the consummation of a contract when these forms are exchanged, section 2–207 recognizes that in many, but not all, cases the parties do not impart such significance to the

terms on the printed forms ... Thus, under subsection (1), a
contract ... (may be) recognized notwithstanding the fact that an
acceptance ... contains terms additional to ... those of the
offer. ... *Id.* at 1166. *See also* Comment 2 to section 2–207; *Air
Products & Chemicals*, *supra*; *John Thallon*, *supra*. And it is now
well-settled that the mere presence of an additional term, such as
a provision for arbitration, in one of the parties' forms will not
prevent the formation of a contract under section 2–207(1).

[17] However, while section 2–207(1) constitutes a sharp departure
from the common law "mirror image" rule, there remain situations where
the inclusion of an additional term in one of the forms exchanged by the
parties will prevent the consummation of a contract under that section.
Section 2–207(1) contains a proviso which operates to prevent an exchange
of forms from creating a contract where "acceptance is expressly made
conditional on assent to the additional ... terms." In the instant case,
Jordan's acknowledgment form contained the following statement:

> Seller's acceptance is ... expressly conditional on Buyer's assent
> to the additional or different terms and conditions set forth below
> and printed on the reverse side. If these terms and conditions are
> not acceptable, Buyer should notify Seller at once.

[18] The arbitration provision at issue on this appeal is printed on the
reverse side of Jordan's acknowledgment, and there is no dispute that Itoh
never expressly assented to the challenged arbitration term.

[19] The Court of Appeals for the Sixth Circuit has held that the
proviso must be construed narrowly:

> Although ... (seller's) use of the words "subject to" suggests that
> the acceptances were conditional to some extent, we do not believe
> the acceptances were "expressly made conditional on (the buyer's)
> assent to the additional or different terms," as specifically
> required under the subsection 2–207(1) proviso. In order to fall
> within this proviso, it is not enough that an acceptance is
> expressly conditional on additional or different terms; rather, an
> acceptance must be expressly conditional on the offeror's assent
> to those terms.

Dorton, supra, at 1168. In *Construction Aggregates Corp. v. Hewitt-Robins,
Inc.*, 404 F.2d 505 (7th Cir. 1968), this court found that an acceptance came
within the ambit of the section 2–207(1) proviso even though the language
employed in the acceptance did not precisely track that of the proviso.
Under either *Construction Aggregates* or *Dorton*, however, it is clear that
the statement contained in Jordan's acknowledgment form comes within
the section 2–207(1) proviso.

[20] Hence, the exchange of forms between Jordan and Itoh did not result in the formation of a contract under section 2–207(1), and Jordan's form became a counteroffer. "(T)he consequence of a clause conditioning acceptance on assent to the additional or different terms is that *as of the exchanged writings, there is no contract.* Either party may at this point in their dealings walk away from the transaction." Duesenberg & King, *supra,* § 3.06(3) at 73. However, neither Jordan nor Itoh elected to follow that course; instead, both parties proceeded to performance: Jordan by delivering and Itoh by paying for the steel coils.

[21] At common law, the "terms of the counter-offer were said to have been accepted by the original offeror when he proceeded to perform under the contract without objecting to the counter-offer." *Dorton, supra,* at 1166. Thus, under pre-Code law, Itoh's performance (i.e., payment for the steel coils) probably constituted acceptance of the Jordan counter-offer, including its provision for arbitration. However, a different approach is required under the Code.

[22] Section 2–207(3) of the Code first provides that "(c)onduct by both parties which recognizes the existence of a contract is sufficient to establish a contract for sale although the writings of the parties do not otherwise establish a contract." As the court noted in *Dorton, supra,* at 1166:

> (W)hen no contract is recognized under subsection 2–207(1) . . . the entire transaction aborts at this point. If, however, the subsequent conduct of the parties particularly, performance by both parties under what they apparently believe to be a contract recognizes the existence of a contract, under subsection 2–207(3) such conduct by both parties is sufficient to establish a contract, notwithstanding the fact that no contract would have been recognized on the basis of their writings alone.

Thus, "(s)ince . . . [Itoh's] purchase order and . . . [Jordan's] counteroffer did not in themselves create a contract, section 2–207(3) would operate to create one because the subsequent performance by both parties constituted 'conduct by both parties which recognizes the existence of a contract.'" *Construction Aggregates, supra,* at 509.

[23] What are the terms of a contract created by conduct under section 2–207(3) rather than by an exchange of forms under section 2–207(1)?[13] As noted above, at common law, the terms of the contract between Jordan and Itoh would be the terms of the Jordan counter-offer. However, the Code has effectuated a radical departure from the common law rule. The second sentence of section 2–207(3) provides that where, as here, a contract has been consummated by the conduct of the parties, "the terms of the particular contract consist of those terms on which the writings of the

---

[13]   If a contract had been formed by the exchange of forms between Jordan and Itoh, it would have been necessary to look to section 2–207(2) to ascertain the terms of that contract.

parties agree, together with any supplementary terms incorporated under any other provisions of this Act." Since it is clear that the Jordan and Itoh forms do not "agree" on arbitration, the only question which remains under the Code is whether arbitration may be considered a supplementary term incorporated under some other provision of the Code.

[24] We have been unable to find any case authority shedding light on the question of what constitutes "supplementary terms" within the meaning of section 2–207(3) and the Official Comments to section 2–207 provide no guidance in this regard. We are persuaded, however, that the disputed additional terms (i.e., those terms on which the writings of the parties do not agree) which are necessarily excluded from a Subsection (3) contract by the language, "terms on which the writings of the parties agree," cannot be brought back into the contract under the guise of "supplementary terms." This conclusion has substantial support among the commentators who have addressed themselves to the issue. As two noted authorities on Article Two of the Code have stated:

> It will usually happen that an offeree-seller who returns an acknowledgment form will also concurrently or shortly thereafter ship the goods. If the responsive document (sent by the seller) contains a printed assent clause, and the goods are shipped and accepted, subsection (3) of section 2–207 comes into play . . . (T)he terms on which the exchanged communications do not agree drop out of the transaction, and reference to the Code is made to supply necessary terms . . . Rather than choosing the terms of one party over those of the other . . . it compels supplying missing terms by reference to the Code . . .

Duesenberg & King, *supra*, § 3.06(4) at 73–74. Similarly, Professors White and Summers have concluded that "contract formation under subsection (3) gives neither party the relevant terms of his document, but fills out the contract with the standardized provisions of Article Two." White & Summers, *supra*, at 29.

[25] Accordingly, we find that the "supplementary terms" contemplated by section 2–207(3) are limited to those supplied by the standardized "gap-filler" provisions of Article Two. *See, e.g.*, section 2–308(a) ("Unless otherwise agreed . . . the place for delivery of goods is the seller's place of business or if he has none his residence"); section 2–309(1) ("The time for shipment or delivery or any other action under a contract if not . . . agreed upon shall be a reasonable time"); section 2–310(a) ("Unless otherwise agreed . . . payment is due at the time and place at which the buyer is to receive the goods even though the place of shipment is the place of delivery"). Since provision for arbitration is not a necessary or missing term which would be supplied by one of the Code's "gap-filler" provisions unless agreed upon by the contracting parties, there is no arbitration term

in the section 2–207(3) contract which was created by the conduct of Jordan and Itoh in proceeding to perform even though no contract had been established by their exchange of writings.

[26] We are convinced that this conclusion does not result in any unfair prejudice to a seller who elects to insert in his standard sales acknowledgment form the statement that acceptance is expressly conditional on buyer's assent to additional terms contained therein. Such a seller obtains a substantial benefit under section 2–207(1) through the inclusion of an "expressly conditional" clause. If he decides after the exchange of forms that the particular transaction is not in his best interest, subsection (1) permits him to walk away from the transaction without incurring any liability so long as the buyer has not in the interim expressly assented to the additional terms. Moreover, whether or not a seller will be disadvantaged under subsection (3) as a consequence of inserting an "expressly conditional" clause in his standard form is within his control. If the seller in fact does not intend to close a particular deal unless the additional terms are assented to, he can protect himself by not delivering the goods until such assent is forthcoming. If the seller does intend to close a deal irrespective of whether or not the buyer assents to the additional terms, he can hardly complain when the contract formed under subsection (3) as a result of the parties' conduct is held not to include those terms. Although a seller who employs such an "expressly conditional" clause in his acknowledgment form would undoubtedly appreciate the dual advantage of not being bound to a contract under subsection (1) if he elects not to perform and of having his additional terms imposed on the buyer under subsection (3) in the event that performance is in his best interest, we do not believe such a result is contemplated by section 2–207. Rather, while a seller may take advantage of an "expressly conditional" clause under subsection (1) when he elects not to perform, he must accept the potential risk under subsection (3) of not getting his additional terms when he elects to proceed with performance without first obtaining buyer's assent to those terms. Since the seller injected ambiguity into the transaction by inserting the "expressly conditional" clause in his form, he, and not the buyer, should bear the consequence of that ambiguity under subsection (3).

* * *

[27] Accordingly, for the reasons stated in this opinion, the decision of the district court is affirmed.

———

PROBLEM 4-7

Buyer sends Acme Foundries a written purchase order (PO) for 10,000 cast iron widgets. The PO does not specify when payment is to be made. Acme sends back a written confirmation with this notation: "Terms: net 30/2% in 10."

In business lingo, this means that the net amount of the price is due 30 days after the date of shipment or invoice and, if paid within 10 days, a 2% discount will apply. Buyer doesn't protest and the widgets are shipped the next day.

(a) Do the parties have a contract? *Yes*

(b) If so, when does payment have to be made? *See* U.C.C. § 2–207, Official Comment 5. *30 days after date of shipment*

PROBLEM 4-8

Purchaser sends Vendor a written PO for 15,000 stainless steel widgets. The PO provides: "Terms: net 45/2% in 10." Vendor sends back a written confirmation which contains the same terms as the PO except that it provides: "Terms: Net 30." Purchaser doesn't protest, and the widgets are shipped in due course.

(a) Is there a contract? *Yes*

(b) If so, when does payment have to be made? *10*

PROBLEM 4-9

Valid offer
Proposed acceptance
2-206 prompt promise to ship

Customer sends Manufacturer a written PO for 20,000 fiberboard widgets. The PO says nothing about the time in which the seller must be notified of defects in the goods. Manufacturer sends back a confirmation which states: "All claims for defects in the goods sold must be <u>made within 5 days after</u> delivery." The norm in the business is that the buyer has at least 30 days in which to give notice of defects. *Need 2-207*

(a) Is there a contract?– *Yes, paragraph explaining why ucc, paragraph about why valid offer, paragraph on acceptance, paragraph on 207*

(b) If so, by what time must buyer inform seller of any defects? *Valid offer, valid acceptance, 2-206/2-207(1), 2-272 but term out*

not a proposal both merchants

PROBLEM 4-10

Developer sends Bank a written offer to purchase the land and building where a soon-to-be-closed branch of the bank is located. Bank writes back: "We accept your offer, but we must be allowed to take with us the chandelier in the lobby." Developer, who has changed her mind, writes back: "The deal is off."

offer rejected by counteroffer

(a) Do the parties have a contract? *NO* — *Paragraph explaining not ucc, service, R+D, law we use is*

(b) If so, who gets the chandelier?

PROBLEM 4-11

ucc   *offer*

Buyer sends Seller a purchase order for 20,000 composite widgets. The PO does not specify when payment is to be made. Seller sends back a written confirmation with the notation: "Terms: net 10." Buyer sends Seller a fax saying: "We object to your 10-day payment terms." Seller ignores the fax, and the widgets are shipped in due course.

agreeing to all items

(a) Do the parties have a contract?

contract under 2-206 and 2-207(1) b/c response was definite seasonable and not conditional

[handwritten margin note top left: if both merchants its in unless buyer objected under 2-207(2)]

[handwritten margin note top right: when confirmation was sent under maibox rule]

(b) If the parties have a contract, when was this contract formed?

(c) If the parties have a contract, when does payment have to be made? *See* U.C.C. § 1–303 (especially subsection (d)) [If you are using the pre-2001 version of Article 1, use 1–205 rather than 1–303], 2–309 and 2–310.

PROBLEM 4-12

[handwritten margin note left: 2-207 (1) analysis would e to demonstrate]

[handwritten margin note right: of il contract formed enforceable]

Grain Exportor calls Corn Broker and orally enters an order for 100,000 bushels of corn at $4.50 per bushel, the then-current market price. Broker tells her: "You got it." Broker sends a written confirmation. The confirmation provides: "All disputes arising out of this contract shall be settled by arbitration in accordance with the rules of the American Arbitration Association." When the corn is delivered, it contains an unacceptably high moisture content. Exporter sues Broker over the high moisture content, and Broker moves to dismiss the suit on the basis that Exporter agreed to arbitrate the dispute.

(a) Is there a contract? *[handwritten: No, Itoh ruling]*

(b) If so, is Exporter compelled to arbitrate?

PROBLEM 4-13

Salesperson calls Homeowner, to whom she has previously given a quote for the installation of vinyl siding on his home. (The quote said nothing about when payment was due, and there is no "industry standard" that would be binding on Homeowner.)

Salesperson: "Do you want to take the siding on the terms of my quote?"

Homeowner: "It's a deal."

Salesperson: "Good. I'll send you a confirmation."

The confirmation that Homeowner receives says "Ten per cent deposit due in 15 days, balance on completion of job." Homeowner does not respond to it.

It's not clear whether Article 2 applies to this transaction, so you need to answer the following questions under the common law and under Article 2.

(a) Is there a contract?

(b) If so, when is payment due?

PROBLEM 4-14

Buyer sends Seller a PO for two boxcar loads of sunflower seeds. The PO provides that freight costs will be paid by the seller. Seller sends back an acknowledgment that provides freight costs will be paid by the buyer. Buyer does not respond to the acknowledgment and the seeds are shipped and accepted. Who has to pay the freight costs?

PROBLEM 4-15

Seller (a merchant) sends Buyer (a non-merchant) an offer to sell an antique knife. The offer provides that Buyer may return the knife for a full refund within 30 days. Buyer sends a letter saying she accepts the offer but she needs 45 days to determine whether to return the knife because she will be out of the country for the entire 30 days following the anticipated date of delivery. Seller does not respond but instead ships the knife. Buyer attempts to return the knife after 35 days. Is she entitled to do so?

———

The law moves slowly and generally lags behind developments in the social and business world. The evaluation of "box-top" or "shrink-wrap" licenses and "in the box" terms in the computer industry—as well as hidden or not-so-hidden terms and conditions that are accepted with the click of a mouse or the tap of a finger—has presented a heretofore unknown context for the application of U.C.C. § 2–207, or not, as the next two cases demonstrate. *See also Step-Saver Data Systems, Inc. v. Wyse Technology*, 939 F.2d 91 (3d Cir. 1991); *but see Taxes of P.R., Inc. v. TaxWorks, Inc.*, 5 F. Supp. 3d 185, 188–189 (D.P.R. 2014) (characterizing *Step-Saver* as dated and predating "the iPhone and widespread use of the internet." Stating further that: "The majority of courts to have considered the enforceability of user agreements have concluded that those agreements are valid and enforceable. *See, e.g., Spivey v. Adaptive Marketing, LLC*, 660 F.Supp.2d 940 (S.D.Ill. 2009); *Meridian Project Systems, Inc. v. Hardin Constr. Co., LLC*, 426 F. Supp. 2d 1101 (E.D.Cal. 2006). *Lexmark Int'l, Inc. v. Static Control Components, Inc.*, 387 F.3d 522, 563 n. 10 (6th Cir. 2004); *Mudd-Lyman Sales & Serv. Corp. v. United Parcel Service, Inc.*, 236 F.Supp.2d 907, 911–12 (N.D.Ill. 2002); *i.LAN Sys., Inc. v. Netscout Serv. Level Corp.*, 183 F.Supp.2d 328 (D.Mass. 2002); *Adobe Sys. Inc. v. Stargate Software Inc.*, 216 F.Supp.2d 1051 (N.D.Cal. 2002); *Adobe Sys. Inc. v. One Stop Micro, Inc.*, 84 F.Supp.2d 1086 (N.D.Cal. 2000); *Pollstar v. Gigmania, Ltd.*, 170 F.Supp.2d 974, 980–81 (E.D.Cal. 2000); *Hill v. Gateway 2000, Inc.*, 105 F.3d 1147 (7th Cir. 1997); *ProCD*, 86 F.3d 1447 (7th Cir.1996). While some courts have characterized user agreements as contracts of adhesion and found them invalid, *see, e.g., Step-Saver Data Systems, Inc.*, 939 F.2d 91 (3d Cir. 1991); *Vault Corp. v. Quaid Software Ltd.*, 847 F.2d 255 (5th Cir. 1988), they are the minority view and we decline to follow their disfavored precedent")).

———

HILL V. GATEWAY 2000, INC.

United States Court of Appeals, Seventh Circuit
105 F.3d 1147 (1997)

EASTERBROOK, CIRCUIT JUDGE.

[1]   A customer picks up the phone, orders a computer, and gives a credit card number. Presently a box arrives, containing the computer and a list of terms, said to govern unless the customer returns the computer within 30 days. Are these terms effective as the parties' contract, or is the contract term-free because the order-taker did not read any terms over the phone and elicit the customer's assent? *Issue*

[2]   One of the terms in the box containing a Gateway 2000 system was an arbitration clause. Rich and Enza Hill, the customers, kept the computer more than 30 days before complaining about its components and performance. They filed suit in federal court arguing, among other things, that the product's shortcomings make Gateway a racketeer (mail and wire fraud are said to be the predicate offenses), leading to treble damages under RICO for the Hills and a class of all other purchasers. Gateway asked the district court to enforce the arbitration clause; the judge refused, writing that "[t]he present record is insufficient to support a finding of a valid arbitration agreement between the parties or that the plaintiffs were given adequate notice of the arbitration clause." Gateway took an immediate appeal, as is its right. 9 U.S.C. § 16(a)(1)(A).

[3]   The Hills say that the arbitration clause did not stand out: they concede noticing the statement of terms but deny reading it closely enough to discover the agreement to arbitrate, and they ask us to conclude that they therefore may go to court. Yet an agreement to arbitrate must be enforced "save upon such grounds as exist at law or in equity for the revocation of any contract." 9 U.S.C. § 2. *Doctor's Associates, Inc. v. Casarotto*, 116 S.Ct. 1652, 134 L.Ed.2d 902 (1996), holds that this provision of the Federal Arbitration Act is inconsistent with any requirement that an arbitration clause be prominent. A contract need not be read to be effective; people who accept take the risk that the unread terms may in retrospect prove unwelcome. *Carr v. CIGNA Securities, Inc.*, 95 F.3d 544, 547 (7th Cir. 1996); *Chicago Pacific Corp. v. Canada Life Assurance Co.*, 850 F.2d 334 (7th Cir. 1988). Terms inside Gateway's box stand or fall together. If they constitute the parties' contract because the Hills had an opportunity to return the computer after reading them, then all must be enforced.

[4]   *ProCD, Inc. v. Zeidenberg*, 86 F.3d 1447 (7th Cir. 1996), holds that terms inside a box of software bind consumers who use the software after an opportunity to read the terms and to reject them by returning the product. Likewise, *Carnival Cruise Lines, Inc. v. Shute*, 499 U.S. 585, 111 S.Ct. 1522, 113 L.Ed.2d 622 (1991), enforces a forum-selection clause that was included among three pages of terms attached to a cruise ship ticket.

ProCD and *Carnival Cruise Lines* exemplify the many commercial transactions in which people pay for products with terms to follow; *ProCD* discusses others. 86 F.3d at 1451–52. The district court concluded in *ProCD* that the contract is formed when the consumer pays for the software; as a result, the court held, only terms known to the consumer at that moment are part of the contract, and provisos inside the box do not count. Although this is one way a contract could be formed, it is not the only way: "A vendor, as master of the offer, may invite acceptance by conduct, and may propose limitations on the kind of conduct that constitutes acceptance. A buyer may accept by performing the acts the vendor proposes to treat as acceptance." *Id.* at 1452. Gateway shipped computers with the same sort of accept-or-return offer ProCD made to users of its software. *ProCD* relied on the Uniform Commercial Code rather than any peculiarities of Wisconsin law; both Illinois and South Dakota, the two states whose law might govern relations between Gateway and the Hills, have adopted the UCC; neither side has pointed us to any atypical doctrines in those states that might be pertinent; *ProCD* therefore applies to this dispute.

[5]   Plaintiffs ask us to limit *ProCD* to software, but where's the sense in that? *ProCD* is about the law of contract, not the law of software. Payment preceding the revelation of full terms is common for air transportation, insurance, and many other endeavors. Practical considerations support allowing vendors to enclose the full legal terms with their products. Cashiers cannot be expected to read legal documents to customers before ringing up sales. If the staff at the other end of the phone for direct-sales operations such as Gateway's had to read the four-page statement of terms before taking the buyer's credit card number, the droning voice would anesthetize rather than enlighten many potential buyers. Others would hang up in a rage over the waste of their time. And oral recitation would not avoid customers' assertions (whether true or feigned) that the clerk did not read term X to them, or that they did not remember or understand it. Writing provides benefits for both sides of commercial transactions. Customers as a group are better off when vendors skip costly and ineffectual steps such as telephonic recitation, and use instead a simple approve-or-return device. Competent adults are bound by such documents, read or unread. For what little it is worth, we add that the box from Gateway was crammed with software. The computer came with an operating system, without which it was useful only as a boat anchor. *See Digital Equipment Corp. v. Uniq Digital Technologies, Inc.,* 73 F.3d 756, 761 (7th Cir.1996). Gateway also included many application programs. So the Hills' effort to limit *ProCD* to software would not avail them factually, even if it were sound legally—which it is not.

[6]   For their second claim, the Hills contend that *ProCD* should be limited to executory contracts (to licenses in particular), and therefore does not apply because both parties' performance of this contract was complete

when the box arrived at their home. This is legally and factually wrong: legally because the question at hand concerns the formation of the contract rather than its performance, and factually because both contracts were incompletely performed. *ProCD* did not depend on the fact that the seller characterized the transaction as a license rather than as a contract; we treated it as a contract for the sale of goods and reserved the question whether for other purposes a "license" characterization might be preferable. 86 F.3d at 1450. All debates about characterization to one side, the transaction in *ProCD* was no more executory than the one here: Zeidenberg paid for the software and walked out of the store with a box under his arm, so if arrival of the box with the product ends the time for revelation of contractual terms, then the time ended in *ProCD* before Zeidenberg opened the box. But of course ProCD had not completed performance with delivery of the box, and neither had Gateway. One element of the transaction was the warranty, which obliges sellers to fix defects in their products. The Hills have invoked Gateway's warranty and are not satisfied with its response, so they are not well positioned to say that Gateway's obligations were fulfilled when the motor carrier unloaded the box. What is more, both ProCD and Gateway promised to help customers to use their products. Long-term service and information obligations are common in the computer business, on both hardware and software sides. Gateway offers "lifetime service" and has a round-the-clock telephone hotline to fulfill this promise. Some vendors spend more money helping customers use their products than on developing and manufacturing them. The document in Gateway's box includes promises of future performance that some consumers value highly; these promises bind Gateway just as the arbitration clause binds the Hills.

[7] Next the Hills insist that *ProCD* is irrelevant because Zeidenberg was a "merchant" and they are not. Section 2–207(2) of the UCC, the infamous battle-of-the-forms section, states that "additional terms [following acceptance of an offer] are to be construed as proposals for addition to a contract. Between merchants such terms become part of the contract unless. . . ." Plaintiffs tell us that *ProCD* came out as it did only because Zeidenberg was a "merchant" and the terms inside ProCD's box were not excluded by the "unless" clause. This argument pays scant attention to the opinion in *ProCD*, which concluded that, when there is only one form, "sec. 2–207 is irrelevant." 86 F.3d at 1452. The question in *ProCD* was not whether terms were added to a contract after its formation, but how and when the contract was formed—in particular, whether a vendor may propose that a contract of sale be formed, not in the store (or over the phone) with the payment of money or a general "send me the product," but after the customer has had a chance to inspect both the item and the terms. *ProCD* answers "yes," for merchants and consumers alike. Yet again, for what little it is worth we observe that the Hills misunderstand the setting of *ProCD*. A "merchant" under the UCC "means a person who deals in goods

of the kind or otherwise by his occupation holds himself out as having knowledge or skill peculiar to the practices or goods involved in the transaction," § 2–104(1). Zeidenberg bought the product at a retail store, an uncommon place for merchants to acquire inventory. His corporation put ProCD's database on the Internet for anyone to browse, which led to the litigation but did not make Zeidenberg a software merchant.

[8] At oral argument the Hills propounded still another distinction: the box containing ProCD's software displayed a notice that additional terms were within, while the box containing Gateway's computer did not. The difference is functional, not legal. Consumers browsing the aisles of a store can look at the box, and if they are unwilling to deal with the prospect of additional terms can leave the box alone, avoiding the transactions costs of returning the package after reviewing its contents. Gateway's box, by contrast, is just a shipping carton; it is not on display anywhere. Its function is to protect the product during transit, and the information on its sides is for the use of handlers rather than would-be purchasers.

[9] Perhaps the Hills would have had a better argument if they were first alerted to the bundling of hardware and legal-ware after opening the box and wanted to return the computer in order to avoid disagreeable terms, but were dissuaded by the expense of shipping. What the remedy would be in such a case—could it exceed the shipping charges?—is an interesting question, but one that need not detain us because the Hills knew before they ordered the computer that the carton would include some important terms, and they did not seek to discover these in advance. Gateway's ads state that their products come with limited warranties and lifetime support. How limited was the warranty—30 days, with service contingent on shipping the computer back, or five years, with free onsite service? What sort of support was offered? Shoppers have three principal ways to discover these things. First, they can ask the vendor to send a copy before deciding whether to buy. The Magnuson-Moss Warranty Act requires firms to distribute their warranty terms on request, 15 U.S.C. § 2302(b)(1)(A); the Hills do not contend that Gateway would have refused to enclose the remaining terms too. Concealment would be bad for business, scaring some customers away and leading to excess returns from others. Second, shoppers can consult public sources (computer magazines, the Web sites of vendors) that may contain this information. Third, they may inspect the documents after the product's delivery. Like Zeidenberg, the Hills took the third option. By keeping the computer beyond 30 days, the Hills accepted Gateway's offer, including the arbitration clause.

[10] The Hills' remaining arguments, including a contention that the arbitration clause is unenforceable as part of a scheme to defraud, do not require more than a citation to *Prima Paint Corp. v. Flood & Conklin Mfg. Co.*, 388 U.S. 395, 87 S.Ct. 1801, 18 L.Ed.2d 1270 (1967). Whatever may be said pro and con about the cost and efficacy of arbitration (which the Hills

disparage) is for Congress and the contracting parties to consider. Claims based on RICO are no less arbitrable than those founded on the contract or the law of torts. *Shearson/American Express, Inc. v. McMahon*, 482 U.S. 220, 238–42, 107 S.Ct. 2332, 2343–46, 96 L.Ed.2d 185 (1987). The decision of the district court is vacated, and this case is remanded with instructions to compel the Hills to submit their dispute to arbitration.

———

NOTES AND QUESTIONS

Is the court right when it says that U.C.C. § 2–207 requires more than one form in order to be applicable? Or is the battle of the forms a subset of more general matters addressed by § 2–207? If the latter, how would you describe the larger set of matters?

———

KLOCEK V. GATEWAY, INC.
United States District Court, District of Kansas
104 F. Supp. 2d 1332 (2000)

VRATIL, DISTRICT JUDGE.

[1]   William S. Klocek brings suit against Gateway, Inc. and Hewlett-Packard, Inc. on claims arising from purchases of a Gateway computer and a Hewlett-Packard scanner. This matter comes before the Court on the Motion to Dismiss (Doc. #6) which Gateway filed November 22, 1999 and Defendant Hewlett-Packard, Inc.'s Motion To Dismiss Or In The Alternative For Stay Of Proceedings (Doc. #16) filed December 22, 1999, the Motion (Doc. #2) to certify a class which plaintiff filed October 29, 1999, the Motion For Sanctions, Expenses and Punitives [sic] (Doc. #11) which plaintiff filed December 3, 1999, the Motion for a Writ of Certiorari (Doc. #12) which plaintiff filed December 6, 1999, and the Motion for Verification (Doc. #24) which plaintiff filed January 25, 2000. For reasons stated below, the Court denies Gateway's motion to dismiss, grants Hewlett-Packard's motion to dismiss, and grants the motions filed by plaintiff.

A.   Gateway's Motion to Dismiss

[2]   Plaintiff brings individual and class action claims against Gateway, alleging that it induced him and other consumers to purchase computers and special support packages by making false promises of technical support. Complaint, PP 3 and 4. Individually, plaintiff also claims breach of contract and breach of warranty, in that Gateway breached certain warranties that its computer would be compatible with standard peripherals and standard internet services. Complaint, PP 2, 5, and 6.

[3] Gateway asserts that plaintiff must arbitrate his claims under Gateway's Standard Terms and Conditions Agreement ("Standard Terms"). Whenever it sells a computer, Gateway includes a copy of the Standard Terms in the box which contains the computer battery power cables and instruction manuals. At the top of the first page, the Standard Terms include the following notice:

NOTE TO THE CUSTOMER:

This document contains Gateway 2000's Standard Terms and Conditions. By keeping your Gateway 2000 computer system beyond five (5) days after the date of delivery, you accept these Terms and Conditions.

[4] The notice is in emphasized type and is located inside a printed box which sets it apart from other provisions of the document. The Standard Terms are four pages long and contain 16 numbered paragraphs. Paragraph 10 provides the following arbitration clause:

DISPUTE RESOLUTION. Any dispute or controversy arising out of or relating to this Agreement or its interpretation shall be settled exclusively and finally by arbitration. The arbitration shall be conducted in accordance with the Rules of Conciliation and Arbitration of the International Chamber of Commerce. The arbitration shall be conducted in Chicago, Illinois, U.S.A. before a sole arbitrator. Any award rendered in any such arbitration proceeding shall be final and binding on each of the parties, and judgment may be entered thereon in a court of competent jurisdiction.[14]

[5] Gateway urges the Court to dismiss plaintiff's claims under the Federal Arbitration Act ("FAA"), 9 U.S.C. § 1 *et seq.* The FAA ensures that written arbitration agreements in maritime transactions and transactions involving interstate commerce are "valid, irrevocable, and enforceable." 9 U.S.C. § 2. Federal policy favors arbitration agreements and requires that we "rigorously enforce" them. *Shearson/American Exp., Inc. v. McMahon*, 482 U.S. 220, 226, 107 S.Ct. 2332 96 L. Ed. 2d 185 (1987).

[6] FAA Section 3 states:

If any suit or proceeding be brought in any of the courts of the United States upon any issue referable to arbitration under an

---

[14] Gateway states that after it sold plaintiff's computer, it mailed all existing customers in the United States a copy of its quarterly magazine, which contained notice of a change in the arbitration policy set forth in the Standard Terms. The new arbitration policy afforded customers the option of arbitrating before the International Chamber of Commerce ("ICC"), the American Arbitration Association ("AAA"), or the National Arbitration Forum ("NAF") in Chicago, Illinois, or any other location agreed upon by the parties. Plaintiff denies receiving notice of the amended arbitration policy. Neither party explains why—if the arbitration agreement was an enforceable contract—Gateway was entitled to unilaterally amend it by sending a magazine to computer customers.

agreement in writing for such arbitration, the court in which such suit is pending, upon being satisfied that the issue involved in such suit or proceeding is referable to arbitration under such agreement, shall on application of one of the parties stay the trial of the action until such arbitration has been had in accordance with the terms of the agreement, providing the applicant for the stay is not in default in proceeding with such arbitration.

9 U.S.C. § 3. Although the FAA does not expressly provide for dismissal, the Tenth Circuit has affirmed dismissal where the applicant did not request a stay. Here, neither Gateway nor plaintiff requests a stay. Accordingly, the Court concludes that dismissal is appropriate if plaintiff's claims are arbitrable.

[7] Gateway bears an initial summary-judgment-like burden of establishing that it is entitled to arbitration. Thus, Gateway must present evidence sufficient to demonstrate the existence of an enforceable agreement to arbitrate. If Gateway makes such a showing, the burden shifts to plaintiff to submit evidence demonstrating a genuine issue for trial. In this case, Gateway fails to present evidence establishing the most basic facts regarding the transaction. The gaping holes in the evidentiary record preclude the Court from determining what state law controls the formation of the contract in this case and, consequently, prevent the Court from agreeing that Gateway's motion is well taken.

[8] Before granting a stay or dismissing a case pending arbitration, the Court must determine that the parties have a written agreement to arbitrate. When deciding whether the parties have agreed to arbitrate, the Court applies ordinary state law principles that govern the formation of contracts. The existence of an arbitration agreement is simply a matter of contract between the parties; arbitration is a way to resolve those disputes—but only those disputes—that the parties have agreed to submit to arbitration. If the parties dispute making an arbitration agreement, a jury trial on the existence of an agreement is warranted if the record reveals genuine issues of material fact regarding the parties' agreement.

[9] Before evaluating whether the parties agreed to arbitrate, the Court must determine what state law controls the formation of the contract in this case. In diversity actions, the Court applies the substantive law, including choice of law rules, that Kansas state courts would apply. Kansas courts apply the doctrine of *lex loci contractus*, which requires that the Court interpret the contract according to the law of the state in which the parties performed the last act necessary to form the contract.

[10] The parties do not address the choice of law issue, and the record is unclear where they performed the last act necessary to complete the contract. Gateway presents affidavit testimony that it shipped a computer to plaintiff on or about August 31, 1997, but it provides no details regarding

the transaction. Plaintiff's complaint alleges that plaintiff lives in Missouri and, if Gateway shipped his computer, it presumably shipped it to Missouri. In his response to Gateway's motion, however, plaintiff states that on August 27, 1997 he purchased the computer in person at the Gateway store in Overland Park, Kansas, and took it with him at that time. Depending on which factual version is correct, it appears that the parties may have performed the last act necessary to form the contract in Kansas (with plaintiff purchasing the computer in Kansas), Missouri (with Gateway shipping the computer to plaintiff in Missouri), or some unidentified other states (with Gateway agreeing to ship plaintiff's catalog order and/or Gateway actually shipping the order).[15]

[11] The Court discerns no material difference between the applicable substantive law in Kansas and Missouri and—as to those two states—it perhaps would not need to resolve the choice of law issue at this time[16]

[12] The Uniform Commercial Code ("UCC") governs the parties' transaction under both Kansas and Missouri law. Regardless whether plaintiff purchased the computer in person or placed an order and received shipment of the computer, the parties agree that plaintiff paid for and received a computer from Gateway. This conduct clearly demonstrates a contract for the sale of a computer. Thus the issue is whether the contract of sale includes the Standard Terms as part of the agreement.

[13] State courts in Kansas and Missouri apparently have not decided whether terms received with a product become part of the parties' agreement. Authority from other courts is split. *Compare Step-Saver*, 939 F.2d 91 (printed terms on computer software package not part of agreement); *Arizona Retail Sys., Inc. v. Software Link, Inc.*, 831 F. Supp. 759 (D. Ariz. 1993) (license agreement shipped with computer software not part of agreement); and *U.S. Surgical Corp. v. Orris, Inc.*, 5 F.Supp.2d 1201 (D. Kan. 1998) (single use restriction on product package not binding agreement); with *Hill v. Gateway 2000, Inc.*, 105 F.3d 1147 (7th Cir.), *cert. denied*, 522 U.S. 808 (1997) (arbitration provision shipped with computer binding on buyer); *ProCD, Inc. v. Zeidenberg*, 86 F.3d 1447 (7th Cir. 1996) (shrinkwrap license binding on buyer);[17] and *M.A. Mortenson Co., Inc. v.*

---

[15]   While Gateway may have shipped the computer to plaintiff in Missouri, the record contains no evidence regarding how plaintiff communicated his order to Gateway, where Gateway received plaintiff's order or where the shipment originated.

[16]   Paragraph 9 of the Standard Terms provides that "this Agreement shall be governed by the laws of the State of South Dakota, without giving effect to the conflict of laws rules thereof." Both Kansas and Missouri recognize choice-of-law provisions, so long as the transaction at issue has a "reasonable relation" to the state whose law is selected. K.S.A. § 84–1–105(1); Mo. Rev. Stat. § 400.1–105(1). At this time, because it must first determine whether the parties ever agreed to the Standard Terms, the Court does not decide whether Kansas or Missouri (or some other unidentified state) would recognize the choice of law provision contained in the Standard Terms.

[17]   The term "shrinkwrap license" gets its name from retail software packages that are covered in plastic or cellophane "shrinkwrap" and contain licenses that purport to become effective as soon as the customer tears the wrapping from the package. *See ProCD*, 86 F.3d at 1449.

Timberline Software Corp., 140 Wn.2d 568, 998 P.2d 305 (Wash. 2000) (following *Hill* and *ProCD* on license agreement supplied with software). It appears that at least in part, the cases turn on whether the court finds that the parties formed their contract *before* or *after* the vendor communicated its terms to the purchaser. *Compare Step-Saver*, 939 F.2d at 98 (parties' conduct in shipping, receiving and paying for product demonstrates existence of contract; box top license constitutes proposal for additional terms under § 2–207 which requires express agreement by purchaser); *Arizona Retail*, 831 F.Supp. at 765 (vendor entered into contract by agreeing to ship goods, or at latest by shipping goods to buyer; license agreement constitutes proposal to modify agreement under § 2–209 which requires express assent by buyer); and *Orris*, 5 F.Supp.2d at 1206 (sales contract concluded when vendor received consumer orders; single-use language on product's label was proposed modification under § 2–209 which requires express assent by purchaser); with *ProCD*, 86 F.3d at 1452 (under § 2–204 vendor, as master of offer, may propose limitations on kind of conduct that constitutes acceptance; § 2–207 does not apply in case with only one form); *Hill*, 105 F.3d at 1148–49 (same); and *Mortenson*, 998 P.2d at 311–314 (where vendor and purchaser utilized license agreement in prior course of dealing, shrinkwrap license agreement constituted issue of contract formation under § 2–204, not contract alteration under § 2–207).

[14] Gateway urges the Court to follow the Seventh Circuit decision in *Hill*. That case involved the shipment of a Gateway computer with terms similar to the Standard Terms in this case, except that Gateway gave the customer 30 days—instead of 5 days—to return the computer. In enforcing the arbitration clause, the Seventh Circuit relied on its decision in *ProCD*, where it enforced a software license which was contained inside a product box. *See Hill*, 105 F.3d at 1148–50. In *ProCD*, the Seventh Circuit noted that the exchange of money frequently precedes the communication of detailed terms in a commercial transaction. *See ProCD*, 86 F.3d at 1451. Citing UCC § 2–204, the court reasoned that by including the license with the software, the vendor proposed a contract that the buyer could accept by using the software after having an opportunity to read the license. *ProCD*, 86 F.3d at 1452. Specifically, the court stated:

> A vendor, as master of the offer, may invite acceptance by conduct, and may propose limitations on the kind of conduct that constitutes acceptance. A buyer may accept by performing the acts the vendor proposes to treat as acceptance.

ProCD, 86 F.3d at 1452. The *Hill* court followed the *ProCD* analysis, noting that "practical considerations support allowing vendors to enclose the full legal terms with their products." *Hill*, 105 F.3d at 1149.[18]

_____

[18]　Legal commentators have criticized the reasoning of the Seventh Circuit in this regard. *See, e.g.*, Jean R. Sternlight, Gateway Widens Doorway to Imposing Unfair Binding Arbitration on Consumers, Fla. Bar J., Nov. 1997, at 8, 10–12 (outcome in Gateway is questionable on federal

[15] The Court is not persuaded that Kansas or Missouri courts would follow the Seventh Circuit reasoning in *Hill* and *ProCD*. In each case the Seventh Circuit concluded without support that UCC § 2–207 was irrelevant because the cases involved only one written form. *See ProCD*, 86 F.3d at 1452 (citing no authority); *Hill*, 105 F.3d at 1150 (citing ProCD). This conclusion is not supported by the statute or by Kansas or Missouri law. Disputes under § 2–207 often arise in the context of a "battle of forms," *see, e.g., Daitom, Inc. v. Pennwalt Corp.*, 741 F.2d 1569, 1574 (10th Cir. 1984), but nothing in its language precludes application in a case which involves only one form. The statute provides:

> Additional terms in acceptance or confirmation.
>
> (1) A definite and seasonable expression of acceptance or a written confirmation which is sent within a reasonable time operates as an acceptance even though it states terms additional to or different from those offered or agreed upon, unless acceptance is expressly made conditional on assent to the additional or different terms.
>
> (2) The additional terms are to be construed as proposals for addition to the contract [if the contract is not between merchants]
>
> . . .

By its terms, § 2–207 applies to an acceptance or written confirmation. It states nothing which requires another form before the provision becomes effective. In fact, the official comment to the section specifically provides that §§ 2–207(1) and (2) apply "where an agreement has been reached orally . . . and is followed by one or both of the parties sending formal memoranda embodying the terms so far agreed and adding terms not discussed." Official Comment 1 of UCC § 2–207. Kansas and Missouri courts have followed this analysis.

---

statutory, common law and constitutional grounds and as a matter of contract law and is unwise as a matter of policy because it unreasonably shifts to consumers search cost of ascertaining existence of arbitration clause and return cost to avoid such clause); Thomas J. McCarthy et al., Survey: Uniform Commercial Code, 53 Bus. Law. 1461, 1465–66 (Seventh Circuit finding that UCC § 2–207 did not apply is inconsistent with official comment); Batya Goodman, Honey, I Shrink-Wrapped the Consumer: The Shrinkwrap Agreement as an Adhesion Contract, 21 Cardozo L. Rev. 319, 344–352 (Seventh Circuit failed to consider principles of adhesion contracts); Jeremy Senderowicz, Consumer Arbitration and Freedom of Contract: A Proposal to Facilitate Consumers' Informed Consent to Arbitration Clauses in Form Contracts, 32 Colum. J.L. & Soc. Probs. 275, 296–299 (judiciary (in multiple decisions, including Hill) has ignored issue of consumer consent to an arbitration clause). Nonetheless, several courts have followed the Seventh Circuit decisions in Hill and ProCD. *See, e.g., Mortenson*, 2000 WL 550845 (license agreement supplied with software); Rinaldi v. Iomega Corp., 1999 WL 1442014, Case No. 98C–09–064–RRC (Del. Sept. 3, 1999) (warranty disclaimer included inside computer Zip drive packaging); Westendorf v. Gateway 2000, Inc., 2000 WL 307369, Case No. 16913 (Del. Ch. March 16, 2000) (arbitration provision shipped with computer); Brower v. Gateway 2000, Inc., 246 A.D.2d 246, 676 N.Y.S.2d 569 (N.Y. App. Div. 1998) (same); Levy v. Gateway 2000, Inc., 1997 WL 823611, 33 U.C.C. Rep. Serv. 2d (Callaghan) 1060 (N.Y. Sup. Ct. August 12, 1997) (same).

[16] In addition, the Seventh Circuit provided no explanation for its conclusion that "the vendor is the master of the offer." *See ProCD*, 86 F.3d at 1452 (citing nothing in support of proposition); *Hill*, 105 F.3d at 1149 (citing *ProCD*). In typical consumer transactions, the purchaser is the offeror, and the vendor is the offeree. While it is possible for the vendor to be the offeror, Gateway provides no factual evidence which would support such a finding in this case. The Court therefore assumes for purposes of the motion to dismiss that plaintiff offered to purchase the computer (either in person or through catalog order) and that Gateway accepted plaintiff's offer (either by completing the sales transaction in person or by agreeing to ship and/or shipping the computer to plaintiff).[19]

[17] Under § 2–207, the Standard Terms constitute either an expression of acceptance or written confirmation. As an expression of acceptance, the Standard Terms would constitute a counter-offer only if Gateway expressly made its acceptance conditional on plaintiff's assent to the additional or different terms. K.S.A. § 84–2–207(1); V.A.M.S. § 400.2–207(1). The conditional nature of the acceptance must be clearly expressed in a manner sufficient to notify the offeror that the offeree is unwilling to proceed with the transaction unless the additional or different terms are included in the contract.[20] Gateway provides no evidence that at the time of the sales transaction, it informed plaintiff that the transaction was conditioned on plaintiff's acceptance of the Standard Terms. Moreover, the mere fact that Gateway shipped the goods with the terms attached did not

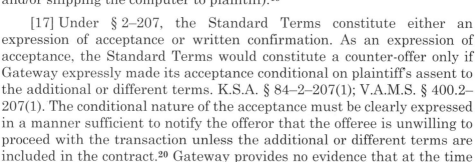

---

[19] UCC § 2–206(b) provides that "an order or other offer to buy goods for prompt or current shipment shall be construed as inviting acceptance either by a prompt promise to ship or by the prompt or current shipment . . ." The official comment states that "either shipment or a prompt promise to ship is made a proper means of acceptance of an offer looking to current shipment." UCC § 2–206, Official Comment 2.

[20] Courts are split on the standard for a conditional acceptance under § 2–207. *See Daitom*, 741 F.2d at 1576 (finding that Pennsylvania would most likely adopt "better" view that offeree must explicitly communicate unwillingness to proceed with transaction unless additional terms in response are accepted by offeror). On one extreme of the spectrum, courts hold that the offeree's response stating a materially different term solely to the disadvantage of the offeror constitutes a conditional acceptance. *See Daitom*, 741 F.2d at 1569 (citing Roto-Lith, Ltd. v. F.P. Bartlett & Co., 297 F.2d 497 (1st Cir. 1962)). At the other end of the spectrum courts hold that the conditional nature of the acceptance should be so clearly expressed in a manner sufficient to notify the offeror that the offeree is unwilling to proceed without the additional or different terms. *See Daitom*, 741 F.2d at 1569 (citing Dorton v. Collins & Aikman Corp., 453 F.2d 1161 (6th Cir. 1972)). The middle approach requires that the response predicate acceptance on clarification, addition or modification. *See Daitom*, 741 F.2d at 1569 (citing Construction Aggregates Corp. v. Hewitt-Robins, Inc., 404 F.2d 505 (7th Cir. 1968)). The First Circuit has since overruled its decision in Roto-Lith, *see* Ionics, Inc. v. Elmwood Sensors, Inc., 110 F.3d 184, and the Court finds that neither Kansas nor Missouri would apply the standard set forth therein. *See* Boese-Hilburn Co. v. Dean Machinery Co., 616 S.W.2d 520 (Mo. App. 1981) (rejecting Roto-Lith standard); Owens-Corning Fiberglas Corp. v. Sonic Dev. Corp., 546 F.Supp. 533, 538 (D. Kan. 1982) (acceptance is not counteroffer under Kansas law unless it is made conditional on assent to additional or different terms (citing Roto-Lith as comparison)); *Daitom*, 741 F.2d at 1569 (finding that Dorton is "better" view). Because Gateway does not satisfy the standard for conditional acceptance under either of the remaining standards (Dorton or Construction Aggregates), the Court does not decide which of the remaining two standards would apply in Kansas and/or Missouri.

communicate to plaintiff any unwillingness to proceed without plaintiff's agreement to the Standard Terms.

[18] Because plaintiff is not a merchant, additional or different terms contained in the Standard Terms did not become part of the parties' agreement unless plaintiff expressly agreed to them. *See* K.S.A. § 84–2–207, Kansas Comment 2 (if either party is not a merchant, additional terms are proposals for addition to the contract that do not become part of the contract unless the original offeror expressly agrees).[21] Gateway argues that plaintiff demonstrated acceptance of the arbitration provision by keeping the computer more than five days after the date of delivery. Although the Standard Terms purport to work that result, Gateway has not presented evidence that plaintiff expressly agreed to those Standard Terms. Gateway states only that it enclosed the Standard Terms inside the computer box for plaintiff to read afterwards. It provides no evidence that it informed plaintiff of the five-day review-and return period as a condition of the sales transaction, or that the parties contemplated additional terms to the agreement.[22] *See Step-Saver*, 939 F.2d at 99 (during negotiations leading to purchase, vendor never mentioned box-top license or obtained buyer's express assent thereto). The Court finds that the act of keeping the computer past five days was not sufficient to demonstrate that plaintiff expressly agreed to the Standard Terms. Thus, because Gateway has not provided evidence sufficient to support a finding under Kansas or Missouri law that plaintiff agreed to the arbitration provision contained in Gateway's Standard Terms, the Court overrules Gateway's motion to dismiss.

[The court's discussion of other issues is omitted.]

NOTES AND QUESTIONS

1.   The court, after casting the consumer as the offeror and Gateway as the offeree, states "As an expression of acceptance, the 'standard terms' would constitute a counteroffer only if Gateway expressly made its acceptance conditional on plaintiff's assent to the additional or different terms." How could Gateway accomplish this task? *follow-up conversation?*

2.   A federal district court, summarizing the state of the law wrote "Courts have held that 'money now, terms later' contracts are enforceable where 1) reference to the binding terms is explicitly made and 2) the purchaser

---

[21] The Court's decision would be the same if it considered the Standard Terms as a proposed modification under UCC § 2–209. *See, e.g., Orris,* 5 F.Supp.2d at 1206 (express assent analysis is same under §§ 2–207 and 2–209).

[22] The Court is mindful of the practical considerations which are involved in commercial transactions, but it is not unreasonable for a vendor to clearly communicate to a buyer—at the time of sale—either the complete terms of the sale or the fact that the vendor will propose additional terms as a condition of sale, if that be the case.

has a clear opportunity to consult those terms and return the product for a refund if he or she is dissatisfied with the conditions of the sale." *Schacter v. Circuit City Stores*, 433 F.Supp. 2d 140, 143 (D. Mass. 2006) (citing *Hill v. Gateway* and other authorities).

3.   The rate of change in commercial contracts and practices is accelerating due, in large part, to the growth of the Internet and other information-science technology. Shrink-wrap, in-the-box, and click-to-accept contracts are increasingly used at all levels of the commercial world. As has historically been the case, the law lags behind these developments for the practical reason that legislatures and courts do not address disputes and other problems until after they arise. Then, typically, the legislature addresses the situation unless a strong constituency favors the status quo and opposes change, which may force the judiciary to address the situation by "making law." Whichever branch of government addresses the problem, a variety of rules and solutions are usually proposed, only a few of which survive to become the dominant or applicable rule. As the preceding cases indicate, things are still working themselves out in this area of law and § 2–207 may prove ill-suited to address box-top licenses and in-the-box terms, both largely unknown when it was drafted.

4.   A note at the end of Chapter 3 briefly discussed the recent proposal by the ALI for a Restatement of Consumer Contracts. In the context of a standard form agreement like the ones in the Gateway cases, consider how those agreements relate to the discussion of the ALI regarding the Restatement of Consumer Contracts.

Business-to-consumer transactions create significant challenges for contract law because of the disparity in information, sophistication, and bargaining power between the two parties. The traditional idea of a contract consists of two parties of similar bargaining power who negotiate, understand, and expressly agree to the terms of their agreement. However, most business-to-consumer agreements are different in that the business drafts the terms of the agreement, which are non-negotiable, then presents them to the consumer on a take-it-or-leave-it basis. Generally, the consumer focuses on very few primary terms of the transaction—price and details about the actual product or service—rather than the standard terms. Many critics of the Restatement of Consumer Contracts worry that if legislatures do not require businesses to present the standard terms to the consumers, businesses may include provisions that are unfair and unfriendly to the consumers.

The Restatement of Consumer Contracts attempts to formalize and make black letter law out of judicial decisions that were, and arguably should continue to be, decided on a case-by-case basis. In these cases, after characterizing the parties as two sophisticated, similarly situated entities, represented by counsel, courts will often strictly construe and enforce the terms of the contract. But, faced with a large business and a consumer, courts appear often to not reach the same strict interpretation and enforcement result, even though the black letter law is the same. An example of this is found in the doctrines of unconscionability and mistake, which we consider in later chapters. *See* Gregory Klass, *Empiricism and Privacy Policies in the Restatement of Consumer Contract Law*, 36 YALE J. ON REG. 45 (2019).

Would it be better to change the black letter law across the board as the supporters of the Restatement of Consumer Contracts appear to recommend? Or is it better to rely upon case-by-case resolution by courts and juries to allow for some discretion in how strictly the law and terms of the contract are interpreted and enforced?

LAWYERING SKILLS PROBLEM

You are a member of the General Counsel's office at Bell Computer, a producer and retailer of personal computer systems and related products. You have been asked to design the legal aspects of an order-taking and product-shipping system that will ensure that, in a later dispute with a customer, the court will find that the customer was the offeree and Bell was the offeror, and that Bell's "in the box" terms—including a mandatory arbitration clause—were part of Bell's offer, which was accepted by the customer when they received their order and retained the product for thirty days without protest. What is your design? Is it practical and workable in the real world of business? Is it legally effective and fool proof?

CHAPTER 5

CONSIDERATION: THE BARGAIN REQUIREMENT

■ ■ ■

Anglo-American law has long taken the position that a promise will not be a legally enforceable contract unless it is "supported by consideration." In essence, this means that something has been given in return for the promise. Another way it is often stated is that "gratuitous promises" (promises that are merely gratuities or gifts) will not be enforced. For example, if an uncle promises his nephew "I'll give you $5,000 when you turn 21," and the uncle asks nothing in return, this is a gratuitous promise and is not enforceable. This *doesn't* mean the uncle *can't* go ahead and give the nephew the money if the uncle wants to. What it does mean, however, is that if the uncle changes his mind, the nephew *can't* use the courts to enforce the promise. He can, of course, use the other members of the family to put moral pressure on the uncle. Most people still believe you should keep your promises, even if they *aren't* legally enforceable.

Once the money has been paid, however, the giver can't take it back on the basis that there's no consideration. It's no longer a matter of contract law because contract law is concerned with promises, which are said to be *executory* (i.e., not yet "executed" or performed). There's no longer any promise involved. Whatever was to be done is done. Whose property the money is becomes the issue. It's now a matter of property—not contract—law. The general rule from property law is that when the property is intentionally turned over ("delivered" with "donative intent") to the recipient, the gift is "complete" or "executed" and the giver can't force the recipient to give it back.

For many law students, understanding exactly what is necessary to have a promise "supported by consideration" is one of the biggest mysteries of the first year. The concept isn't really that difficult but people have conspired to make it hard for you to learn it. First, understand that the purpose of the consideration doctrine is to serve as a screening device to separate those agreements that the law will enforce from those that it won't. In the past, other filters have been used to accomplish this task. For example, previously an agreement that had been sealed with a wax imprint was enforceable (*see* note at end of chapter). Seals are now obsolete and the requirement of consideration remains in its role as a filter separating legally enforceable agreements from those that are not.

Second, if you took a business law course, your business law teacher may have been a member of the conspiracy. To avoid the tough issues, business law teachers sometimes define consideration as "benefit to the promisor or detriment to the promisee." If you learned this definition, unlearn it!

Some of the other members of the conspiracy are dead. They are the judges who wrote the opinions that are still quoted even though they define consideration in outmoded ways. The concept of consideration has changed over the years and many old opinions contain statements about consideration that were correct when they were written but are not correct under the modern concept of consideration.

Modern judges have joined the conspiracy, too. As you have probably figured out by now, many judicial opinions contain loose language that is correct in the context of the particular case but is not correct as a statement of a universal principle of law. This happens with alarming frequency when courts talk about consideration.

The key to understanding consideration is the word "*bargain*." Read carefully R2d § 71(1). It tells us we need two things in order for there to be consideration: (1) The person making the promise must get in return for this promise either (a) another promise *or* (b) a performance *and* (2) the return promise or performance she receives must be "bargained for." The first requirement, phrased in the alternative, is easy. It is the second that has caused mischief in law school for years.

R2d § 71(2) attempts to explain what is meant by the requirement that it be "bargained for." It doesn't mean you have to haggle over it! What it really means is that (1) the promisor *must want it* (the performance or return promise) in return for the promise (that is, the prospect of getting the performance or return promise must be at least part of the reason she is making the promise in the first place) *and* (2) getting this performance or return promise has to be a *condition* to her performing her promise. Put another way, each side of the deal either changed its position or promised to change its position in exchange for the other side's change in position or promise to change position.

A tells B: "I'll give you my car if you'll pay me $1,000." A's promise is supported by consideration because (1) he is making the promise to give his car in order to get (a) the payment of $1,000 or (b) B's return promise to pay $1,000 and (2) A doesn't have to give B the car unless B pays the money or promises to pay it.

Lobbyist tells Congressperson: "I'll contribute $100,000 to your campaign." Let's suppose Lobbyist is doing this only because she believes Congressperson is really the best person for the job. She doesn't expect anything in return. The promise to pay the $100,000 is not enforceable because there was no consideration. There was no consideration because Lobbyist didn't bargain for anything in return.

Now let's get back to the real world. Lobbyist tells Congressperson: "I'll contribute $500,000 to your campaign." Lobbyist promises the contribution because Lobbyist has a bill she wants passed and she knows that Congressperson is more likely to vote for the bill if Lobbyist makes a big campaign contribution. Is there consideration for Lobbyist's promise to make the contribution? No. Even though Lobbyist met the first of our requirements for consideration (she was motivated to make the promise by the prospect of getting Congressperson's vote), she didn't require Congressperson to vote for her bill as a condition to performing her promise.

Suppose Lobbyist tells Congressperson: "I'll contribute $900,000 to your campaign if you'll vote for my bill." Now we have a proposed deal consisting of a promise (to pay $900,000) supported by consideration (the return promise to vote for the bill)! Of course we also have a bribe, and Congressperson and Lobbyist will both go to jail if they are convicted.

The thing that is bargained for may be a promise or a performance. Usually, it's a promise and we have a bilateral contract. R2d § 71(3) explains what we mean when we talk about a bargained-for "performance." Read that section carefully. Performance can be positive (something that is to be affirmatively done) or negative (refraining from doing something). The latter is called a "forbearance." The case that follows the next two problems illustrates what is meant by a "forbearance."

But before we get to the case, let's look a little more at the bargain requirement in a series of problems.

———

PROBLEM 5-1

The owners of a major league baseball team were thinking about moving the franchise. A group of civic boosters wanted a team in their city. The boosters told the team owners, "If you'll move the team to Salt Lake, we'll build a new stadium." The parties agreed to this, and a formal document was executed in which the team agreed to move to Salt Lake City and remain there for at least five years and the city agreed to build a new stadium in accordance with certain specifications set forth in the document.

[handwritten margin note, left: "Offer into bilateral contract – 2 promises"]

[handwritten margin note, right: "Bilateral supported by consideration"]

(a) What was the consideration flowing from the city to the team?

(b) What was the consideration flowing from the team to the city?

[handwritten answer] (a) Promise to build a new stadium

[handwritten answer] (b) promise to move and remain for 5 years

PROBLEM 5-2

The owners of the professional football team were thinking about moving the franchise. A group of civic boosters wanted a team in their city. The boosters told the owners "if you'll move the team to Portland, we'll build a new stadium." The owners said "we're keeping our options open. If you build a new stadium, that will make your city very attractive to us." Over the opposition of citizens who thought the city had needs more pressing than a new stadium, the city government built a new stadium. When the stadium was completed, the team sent the city a letter promising to move the team. The mayor replied with a letter thanking the team but making no promises. (An earlier draft had the city promising all sorts of things, but someone showed it to the city attorney, who edited out all commitments of any kind by the city, saying the mayor had no authority to promise these things without the approval of the city council.)

(a)   Is the team's promise to move binding?

(b)   If so, what is the consideration that makes the promise binding?

NOTES

1.   The preceding problems are made up, but here is a story that is true. The Cincinnati Bengals threatened to leave town because a new stadium had been built for the Cincinnati Reds, but none had been built for the Bengals. So the county built the Bengals a new stadium at a cost of $450 million. The stadium agreement, which the Bengals signed, stated that a half-cent increase in the county's sales tax was needed to keep "competitive and viable major-league football and baseball teams in Cincinnati by construction of a new football stadium."

After the Bengals compiled a terrible record over several seasons, the county commission voted unanimously to ask the county's attorney to look into the question: "Has the [Bengals'] long losing record of poor performances on the field risen to violate the express or implied conditions of the agreement?"

PRACTICE TIP

Be careful of the language you put in your contracts. Think of the way that even innocuous statements like "competitive and viable teams" or "best efforts" might come back to bite you. This may seem like paranoia, but in terms of a legal career, it's a healthy paranoia. As Henry Kissinger, Secretary of State in the Nixon administration, once said: "Even paranoids have enemies."

2.   Although the R2d devotes 10 sections to consideration and 14 sections to contracts without consideration, in the real world, consideration is usually not an issue. And outside the United States, consideration is often not required

at all. Both the CISG and UNIDROIT make no provision for it. It remains a fixture of United States law and the United States law school experience, largely out of tradition and an apparent belief that working with the doctrine is a good method for teaching students how to think like a lawyer.

———

HAMER V. SIDWAY

Court of Appeals of New York
124 N.Y. 538, 27 N.E. 256 (1891)

[1] Appeal from the order of the General Term of the Supreme Court in the fourth judicial department, made July 1, 1890, which reversed a judgment in favor of plaintiff entered upon a decision of the court on trial at Special Term and granted a new trial.

[2] The plaintiff presented a claim [on an alleged contract] to the executor of William E. Story, Sr., for $5,000 and interest from the 6th day of February, 1875. She acquired it through several mesne assignments from William E. Story, 2d.[1] The claim being rejected by the executor, this action was brought. It appears that William E. Story, Sr., was the uncle of William E. Story, 2d; that at the celebration of the golden wedding of Samuel Story and wife, father and mother of William E. Story, Sr., on the 20th day of March, 1869, in the presence of the family and invited guests, he promised his nephew that if he would refrain from drinking, using tobacco, swearing, and playing cards or billiards for money until he became twenty-one years of age he would pay him a sum of $5,000.[2] The nephew assented thereto and fully performed the conditions inducing the promise. When the nephew arrived at the age of twenty-one years and on the 31st day of January, 1875, he wrote to his uncle informing him that he had performed his part of the agreement and had thereby become entitled to the sum of $5,000. The uncle received the letter and a few days later on the sixth of February, [1875,] he wrote and mailed to his nephew the following letter:

W. E. Story, Jr.:

Dear Nephew—

Your letter of the 31st ult. came to hand all right, saying that you had lived up to the promise made to me several years ago. I have no doubt but you have, for which you shall have five thousand dollars as I promised you. I had the money in the bank the day you was 21 years old that I intend for you, and you shall have the

———

[1] ["Several mesne assignments" is an old idiom meaning that it passed through several people before she acquired it.—Eds.]

[2] [$5,000 in 1869 was worth approximately $95,000 in 2019 dollars, computed using the CPI and the GDP Deflator.—Eds.]

money certain. Now, Willie, I do not intend to interfere with this money in any way till I think you are capable of taking care of it and the sooner that time comes the better it will please me. I would hate very much to have you start out in some adventure that you thought all right and lose this money in one year. The first five thousand dollars that I got together cost me a heap of hard work. You would hardly believe me when I tell you that to obtain this I shoved a jackplane many a day, butchered three or four years, then came to this city, and after three months perseverance I obtained a situation in a grocery store. I opened this store early, closed late, slept in the fourth story of the building in a room 30 by 40 feet and not a human being in the building but myself. All this I done to live as cheap as I could to save something. I don't want you to take up with this kind of fare. I was here in the cholera season '49 and '52 and the deaths averaged 80 to 125 daily and plenty of smallpox. I wanted to go home, but Mr. Fisk, the gentleman I was working for, told me if I left then, after it got healthy he probably would not want me. I stayed. All the money I have saved I know just how I got it. It did not come to me in any mysterious way, and the reason I speak of this is that money got in this way stops longer with the fellow that gets it with hard knocks than it does when he finds it. Willie, you are 21 and you have many a thing to learn yet. This money you have earned much easier than I did besides acquiring good habits at the same time and you are quite welcome to the money; hope you will make good use of it. I was ten long years getting this together after I was your age. Now hoping this will be satisfactory, I stop. . . .

Truly Yours,
W. E. Story.

P.S.—You can consider this money on interest.

[3] The nephew received the letter and thereafter consented that the money should remain with his uncle in accordance with the terms and conditions of the letter. The uncle died on the 29th day of January 1887, without having paid over to his nephew any portion of the said $5,000 and interest.

[4] PARKER, J. The question which provoked the most discussion by counsel on this appeal, and which lies at the foundation of plaintiffs asserted right of recovery, is whether by virtue of a contract defendant's testator William E. Story became indebted to his nephew William E. Story, 2d on his twenty-first birthday in the sum of five thousand dollars. The trial court found as a fact that "on the 20th day of March, 1869, . . . William E. Story agreed to and with William E. Story, 2d, that if he would refrain from drinking liquor, using tobacco, swearing, and playing cards or

billiards for money until he should become 21 years of age then he, the said William E. Story, would at that time pay him, the said William E. Story, 2d, the sum of $5,000 for such refraining, to which the said William E. Story, 2d, agreed," and that he "in all things fully performed his part of said agreement."

[5] The defendant contends that the contract was without consideration to support it, and therefore, invalid. He asserts that the promise by refraining from the use of liquor and tobacco was not harmed but benefitted; that which he did was best for him to do independently of his uncle's promise, and insists that it follows that unless the promisor was benefitted, the contract was without consideration. A contention, which if well founded, would seem to leave open for controversy in many cases whether that which the promisee did or omitted to do was, in fact, of such benefit to him as to leave no consideration to support the enforcement of the promisor's agreement. Such a rule could not be tolerated, and is without foundation in the law. The Exchequer Chamber, in 1875, defined consideration as follows: "A valuable consideration in the sense of the law may consist either in some right, interest, profit or benefit accruing to the one party, or some forbearance, detriment, loss or responsibility given, suffered or undertaken by the other." Courts "will not ask whether the thing which forms the consideration does in fact benefit the promisee or a third party, or is of any substantial value to anyone. It is enough that something is promised, done, forborne or suffered by the party to whom the promise is made as consideration for the promise made to him." (Anson's Prin. Of Con. 63.)

[6] "In general a waiver of any legal right at the request of another party is a sufficient consideration for a promise." (Parsons on Contracts, 444.) "Any damage, or suspension, or forbearance of a right will be sufficient to sustain a promise." (Kent, vol. 2,465, 12th ed.)

[7] Pollock, in his work on contracts, page 166, after citing the definition given by the Exchequer Chamber already quoted, says: "The second branch of this judicial description is really the most important one. Consideration means not so much that one party is profiting as that the other abandons some legal right in the present or limits his legal freedom of action in the future as an inducement for the promise of the first."

[8] Now, applying this rule to the facts before us, the promisee used tobacco, occasionally drank liquor, and he had a legal right to do so. That right he abandoned for a period of years upon the strength of the promise of the testator that for such forbearance he would give him $5,000. We need not speculate on the effort which may have been required to give up the use of those stimulants. It is sufficient that he restricted his lawful freedom of action within certain prescribed limits upon the faith of his uncle's agreement, and now having fully performed the conditions imposed, it is of

no moment whether such performance actually proved a benefit to the promissor, and the court will not inquire into it, but were it a proper subject of inquiry, we see nothing in this record that would permit a determination that the uncle was not benefitted in a legal sense. . . .

[9] The order appealed from should be reversed and the judgement of the Special Term affirmed, with costs payable out of the estate.

———

NOTES AND QUESTIONS

1. Willie was not the litigious sort, at least not within the family. After his uncle's death, when money did not seem to be forthcoming from the estate, he sold the right to the money, his claim, to a third party who, it appears, sold it as well and so on (the series of "mesne agreements") until it reached the plaintiff. Discounting and transferring contract claims—taking less than their face amount for them and transferring them on—is an old business that continues today. One of the most powerful inventions of modern business law is the ability to slice, dice, and sell contract rights, debt, equity, and other entitlements to payment streams into different tranches with different priorities and different risks and rates of return. These are the techniques used to "securitize" something. So, remember, if you or your client has a contract claim, there are more than the two alternatives of pursuing it or dropping it; you may also be able to sell it, subject to some restrictions. The sale of personal tort claims is generally prohibited and the purported sale or assignment of those claims will generally have no legal effect.

2. Suppose the uncle had said, "I'll give you $5,000, no strings attached, but hope that out of gratitude you'll refrain from drinking." Would there have been a contract? *No, b/c no bargain on other side?*

3. Suppose the uncle had said, "I'll give you $5,000 right now if you'll promise not to drink until you're 21?" Would there have been a contract? *Yes*

4. What is wrong with the argument that there was no consideration because Willie was benefitted rather than harmed by doing what his uncle wanted?

———

BATSAKIS V. DEMOTSIS

Court of Civil Appeals of Texas
226 S.W.2d 673 (1949)

McGILL, JUSTICE.

[1] This is an appeal from a judgment of the 57th judicial District Court of Bexar County. Appellant was plaintiff and appellee was defendant in the trial court. The parties will be so designated.

[2]   Plaintiff sued defendant to recover $2,000 with interest at the rate of 8% per annum from April 2, 1942, alleged to be due on the following instrument, being a translation from the original, which is written in the Greek language:

Peiraeus
April 2, 1942

Mr. George Batsakis Konstantinou Diadohou #7 Peiraeus

Mr. Batsakis:

I state by my present (letter) that I received today from you the amount of two thousand dollars ($2,000.00) of United States of America money, which I borrowed from you for the support of my family during these difficult days and because it is impossible for me to transfer dollars of my own from America.

The above amount I accept with the expressed promise that I will return to you again in American dollars either at the end of the present war or even before in the event that you might be able to find a way to collect them (dollars) from my representative in America to whom I shall write and give him an order relative to this.

You understand until the final execution (payment) to the above amount an eight per cent interest will be added and paid together with the principal.

I thank you and I remain yours with respects.

The recipient,

(Signed) Eugenia The. Demotsis

[3]   Trial to the court without the intervention of a jury resulted in a judgment in favor of plaintiff for $750.00 principal and interest at the rate of 8% per annum from April 2, 1942 to the date of judgment, totaling $1163.83, with interest thereon at the rate of 8% per annum until paid. Plaintiff has perfected his appeal.

[4]   The court sustained certain special exceptions of plaintiff to defendant's first amended original answer on which the case was tried, and struck there from paragraphs II, III and V. Defendant excepted to such action of the court, but has not cross-assigned error here. The answer, stripped of such paragraphs, consisted of a general denial contained in paragraph I thereof, and of paragraph IV, which is as follows:

IV. That under the circumstances alleged in Paragraph II of this answer, the consideration upon which said written instrument sued upon by plaintiff herein is founded, is wanting and has failed to the extent of $1975.00, and defendant pleads specially under the verification hereinafter made the want and failure of consideration stated, and now tenders, as defendant has heretofore tendered to plaintiff, $25.00 as the value of the loan of money received by defendant from plaintiff, together with interest thereon.

Further, in connection with this plea of want and failure of consideration defendant alleges that she at no time received from plaintiff himself or from anyone for plaintiff any money or thing of value other than, as hereinbefore alleged, the original loan of 500,000 drachmae. That at the time of the loan by plaintiff to defendant of said 500,000 drachmae the value of 500,000 drachmae in the Kingdom of Greece in dollars of money of the United States of America, was $25.00, and also at said time the value of 500,000 drachmae of Greek money in the United States of America in dollars was $25.00. The plea of want and failure of consideration is verified by defendant as follows.

D plead for "want of consideration")

[5] The allegations in paragraph II which were stricken, referred to in paragraph IV, were that the instrument sued on was signed and delivered in the Kingdom of Greece on or about April 2, 1942, at which time both plaintiff [Batsakis] and defendant [Demotsis] were residents of and residing in the Kingdom of Greece, and [Demotsis] avers that on or about April 12, 1942 she owned money and property and had credit in the United States of America, but was then and there in the Kingdom of Greece in straitened financial circumstances due to the conditions produced by World War II and could not make use of her money and property and credit existing in the United States of America. That in the circumstances the plaintiff agreed to and did lend to defendant the sum of 500,000 drachmae, which at that time, on or about April 12, 1942, had the value of $25.00 in money of the United States of America. That the said plaintiff, knowing defendant's financial distress and desire to return to the United States of America, exacted of her the written instrument plaintiff sues upon, which was a promise by her to pay to him the sum of $2,000.00 of United States of America money.

[6] [Batsakis] specially excepted to paragraph IV because the allegations thereof were insufficient to allege either want of consideration or failure of consideration, in that it affirmatively appears therefrom that [Demotsis] received what was agreed to be delivered to her, and that [Batsakis] breached no agreement. The court overruled this exception, and such action is assigned as error. Error is also assigned because of the court's failure to enter judgment for the whole unpaid balance of the principal of the instrument with interest as therein provided.

[7] Defendant testified that she did receive 500,000 drachmae from plaintiff. It is not clear whether she received all the 500,000 drachmae or

only a portion of them before she signed the instrument in question. Her testimony clearly shows that the understanding of the parties was that plaintiff would give her the 500,000 drachmae if she would sign the instrument. She testified:

Q.   Who suggested the figure of $2,000.00?

A.   That was how he asked me from the beginning. He said he will give me five hundred thousand drachmae provided I signed that I would pay him $2,000.00 American money.

[8]   The transaction amounted to a sale by plaintiff of the 500,000 drachmae in consideration of the execution of the instrument sued on, by defendant. It is not contended that the drachmae had no value. Indeed, the judgment indicates that the trial court placed a value of $750.00 on them or on the other consideration which plaintiff gave defendant for the instrument if he believed plaintiff's testimony. Therefore the plea of want of consideration was unavailing. A plea of want of consideration amounts to a contention that the instrument never became a valid obligation in the first place.

[9]   Mere inadequacy of consideration will not void a contract.

[10] Nor was the plea of failure of consideration[3] availing. Defendant got exactly what she contracted for according to her own testimony. The court should have rendered judgment in favor of plaintiff against defendant for the principal sum of $2,000.00 evidenced by the instrument sued on, with interest as therein provided. We construe the provision relating to interest as providing for interest at the rate of 8% per annum. The judgment is reformed so as to award appellant a recovery against appellee of $2,000.00 with interest thereon at the rate of 8% per annum from April 2, 1942. Such judgment will bear interest at the rate of 8% per annum until paid on $2,000.00 thereof and on the balance interest at the rate of 6% per annum. As so reformed, the judgment is affirmed.

Reformed and affirmed.

———

QUESTIONS

1.   The court says "mere inadequacy of consideration will not void a contract." What does that mean?   —   R2D 79

2.   Does it matter whether the 500,000 drachmae had a market value of $25 (as Ms. Demotsis claimed) or $750 (as the trial court found)?

---

[3]   [*Failure* of consideration is a misleading term that courts sometimes use. It does not mean there was no consideration. It means that the promise that constituted consideration was never performed. It has nothing to do with what we're studying. It involves conditions to the obligation to perform, which will be covered in Chapter 7.—Eds.]

3.   Let's assume that (i) the 500,000 drachmae was worth only $25, (ii) the court accepts the R2d's position that nominal consideration will not make a contract enforceable, and (iii) $25 was such a small sum as to be nominal. Would these assumptions change the outcome in the case?

————

Nominal Consideration

The historical rule has been that "courts will not look into the adequacy of consideration." What this means is that as long as there is some consideration, it does not matter that the exchange is grossly unfair. It was even said that one could agree to exchange a great estate for a peppercorn. This sort of consideration where the value of what is given as consideration is not significant in relation to what is received, is called "nominal consideration" or sometimes "peppercorn consideration" because Blackstone used the peppercorn as an example in his 1766 treatise.

"Nominal" doesn't just mean "small" in English; it also means "in name only." Often, things that are offered "in name only" are "small"—so it is easy to adopt "small" as the test, but that is not what the consideration doctrine is focusing upon. So, when you think about "nominal consideration" think in terms of whether the consideration was really bargained for, not its size. Confusion arises when folks notice that consideration that is recited and not really bargained for is often small and then they think that "nominal" is being used in its "small" sense.

As you can imagine, there are very few cases involving nominal consideration. Nevertheless, the use of nominal consideration to support contracts seemed so generally accepted that until fairly recently it used to be common for lawyers to begin the promises in a written contract with the phrase "for $1 in hand paid and other good and valuable consideration, the receipt of which is hereby acknowledged, the undersigned promises . . ." This technique continues to be used, although language of this sort generally marks a lawyer as being rather backward. There are, however, jurisdictions in which a recitation of consideration, even nominal consideration, creates a rebuttable presumption that consideration to support the contract was present. *See, e.g.,* Cal. Civ. Code § 1614.

The justification for allowing enforcement of promises supported by nominal consideration was that it allowed a person to make (or rely on) a promise without having to worry about questions of consideration. It also allowed a person to make an enforceable gift promise. The first Restatement took this position. Illustration 1 to Section 84 read as follows:

> A wishes to make a binding promise to his son B to convey to B Blackacre, which is worth $5,000. Being advised that a gratuitous promise is not binding, A writes to B an offer to sell Blackacre for $1. B accepts. B's promise to pay $1 is sufficient consideration.

The R2d takes a different position. The R2d looks solely at the bargain requirement. The $1 (or the peppercorn) is consideration only if it is actually bargained for, that is only if the person making the promise actually wants it and only if the prospect of receiving it is part of the motivation for entering into the contract. The key to understanding the modern doctrine of consideration, thus, is to focus on the "bargained for" element.

Conversely, if nominal consideration is not bargained for, it will not support a promise as a matter of contract law. Illustration 5 to R2d § 71 reads as follows:

> A desires to make a binding promise to give $1,000 to his son. Being advised that a gratuitous promise is not binding, A offers to buy from B for $1,000 a book worth less than $1. B accepts the offer knowing that the purchase of the book is a mere pretense. There is no consideration for A's promise to pay $1,000.

Is the illustrated "contract" one to pay $1,000 in exchange for a $1 book? Or is it really a promise of a $999 gift? Pay attention to form, but do not let it blind you to substance.

In the limited context of option contracts, however, the R2d does recognize nominal consideration. Read R2d § 87(1) and the Comment following it.

SCHNELL V. NELL

Supreme Court of Indiana
17 Ind. 29 (1861)

PERKINS, JUSTICE.

[1]   Action by J. B. Nell against Zacharias Schnell, upon the following instrument:

> This agreement, entered into this 13th day of February, 1856, between Zacharias Schnell, of Indianapolis, Marion county, State of Indiana, as party of the first part, and J. B. Nell, of the same place, Wendelin Lorenz, of Stilesville, Hendricks county, State of Indiana, and Donata Lorenz, of Frickinger, Grand Duchy of Baden, Germany, as parties of the second part, witnesseth: The said Zacharias Schnell agrees as follows: whereas his wife, Theresa Schnell, now deceased, has made a last will and testament, in which, among other provisions, it was ordained that every one of the above named second parties, should receive the sum of $200; and whereas the said provisions of the will must remain a nullity, for the reason that no property, real or personal,

was in the possession of the said Theresa Schnell, deceased, in her own name, at the time of her death, and all property held by Zacharias and Theresa Schnell jointly, therefore reverts to her husband; and whereas the said Theresa Schnell has also been a dutiful and loving wife to the said Zach. Schnell, and has materially aided him in the acquisition of all property, real and personal, now possessed by him; for, and in consideration of all of this, and the love and respect he bears to his wife; and, furthermore, in consideration of one cent, received by him of the second parties, he then said Zach Schnell, agrees to pay the above named sums of money to the parties of the second part, to wit: $200 to the said J. B. Nell; $200 to the said Wendelin Lorenz; and $200 to the said Donna Lorenz, in the following installment, viz., $200 in one year from the date of these presents; $200 in two years, and $200 in three years; to be divided between the parties in equal portions $66 2/3 each year, or as they may agree, till each one has received his full sum of $200.

And said parties of the second part, for, and in consideration of this, agree to pay the above named sum of money [one cent], and to deliver up to said Schnell, and abstain from collecting any real or supposed claims upon him or his estate, arising from the said last will and testament of the said Theresa Schnell, deceased.

In witness whereof, the said parties on this 13th day of February, 1856, set hereunto their hands and seals

Zacharias Schnell, [SEAL]

J. B. Nell, [SEAL]

Wen. Lorenz, [SEAL]

[2]   The complaint contained no averment of a consideration for the instrument, outside of those expressed in it; and did not aver that the one cent agreed to be paid, had been paid or tendered.

[3]   A demurrer to the complaint was overruled.

[4]   The defendant answered, that the instrument sued on was given for no consideration whatever.

[5]   He further answered, that it was given for no consideration, because his said wife, Theresa, at the time she made the will mentioned, and at the time of her death, owned, neither separately, nor jointly with her husband, or anyone else (except so far as the law gave her an interest in her husband's property), any property, real or personal, etc.

[6]   The will is copied into the record, but need not be into this opinion.

[7]   The Court sustained a demurrer to these answers, evidently on the ground that they were regarded as contradicting the instrument sued

on, which particularly set out the considerations upon which it was executed. But the instrument is latently ambiguous on this point.

[8]   The case turned below, and must turn here, upon the question whether the instrument sued on does express a consideration sufficient to give it legal obligation, as against Zacharias Schnell. It specifies three distinct considerations for his promise to pay $600:

(1)   A promise, on the part of plaintiffs, to pay him one cent.

(2)   The love and affection he bore his deceased wife, and the fact that she had done her part, as his wife, in the acquisition of property.

(3)   The fact that she had expressed her desire, in the form of an inoperative will that the persons named therein should have the sums of money specified.

[9]   The consideration of one cent will not support the promise of Schnell. It is true, that as a general preposition, inadequacy of consideration will not vitiate an agreement. But this doctrine does not apply to a mere exchange of sums of money, of coin, whose value is exactly fixed, but to the exchange of something of, in itself, indeterminate value. In this case, had the one cent mentioned, been some particular one cent, a family piece, or ancient, remarkable coin, possessing an indeterminate value, extrinsic from its simple money value, a different view might be taken. As it is, the mere promise to pay six hundred dollars for one cent, even had the portion of that cent due from the plaintiff been tendered, is an unconscionable contract, void, at first blush, upon its face, if it be regarded as an earnest one. The consideration of one cent is, plainly, in this case, merely nominal, and intended to be so. As the will and testament of Schnell's wife imposed no legal obligation upon him to discharge her bequests out of his property, and as she had done none of her own, his promise to discharge them was not legally binding upon him, on that ground. A moral consideration, only, will not support a promise. And for the same reason, a valid consideration for his promise cannot be found in the fact of a compromise of a disputed claim; for where such claim is legally groundless, a promise upon a compromise of it, or of a suit upon it, is not legally binding. There was no mistake of law or fact in this case, as the agreement admits the will inoperative and void. The promise was simply one to make a gift. The services of his wife, and the love and affection he had borne her, are objectionable as legal considerations for Schnell's promise on two grounds:

> The fact that Schnell loved his wife, and that she had been industrious, constituted no consideration for his promise to pay J. B. Nell, and the Lorenzes, a sum of money. Whether, if his wife in her lifetime, and made a bargain with Schnell, that, in consideration of his promising to pay, after her death, to the

persons named, a sum of money, she would be industrious, and worthy of his affection, such a promise would have been valid and consistent with public policy, we need not decide. Nor is the fact that Schnell now venerates the memory of his deceased wife, a legal consideration for a promise to pay any third person money.

[10] The instrument sued on, interpreted in the light of the facts alleged in the second paragraph of the answer, will not support an action. The demurrer to the answer should have been overruled.

[11] PER CURIAM. The judgment is reversed, with costs. Cause remanded, etc.

QUESTIONS

1.   Is this just an early case rejecting nominal consideration or is there more to it?

2.   Suppose that instead of promising to give the plaintiffs $600 for one cent, Schnell had agreed to sell them 40 acres of land for one cent. Would the result have been different in 1861? Would it be different today?

3.   In the next to last paragraph of the document, the plaintiffs agree to give up any claims they may have under the will. Why isn't this consideration under R2d § 74(1)? Why isn't it consideration under § 74(2)? What do you suppose is the purpose of R2d § 74(2)?

Illusory Promises

Suppose that Young Mr. Story had said to Old Mr. Story: "Promise to pay me $5,000 and I may give up smoking." Would this promise to maybe give up smoking be consideration for the promise to pay $5,000? The answer is no. To be consideration, it has to be a real promise. What Young Mr. Story gave in our hypothetical is sometimes called an "illusory promise." He hasn't bound himself to anything. He has just as much legal right to continue smoking after he makes the deal as he had before. Illusory promises are not consideration.

Conditional Promises

Conditional promises, such as "I promise to pay you $10,000 if X happens," present a more difficult case. But there is a fairly easy basic rule that applies: A conditional promise is consideration if the condition is outside the control of the promisor. One way to understand the reason for this is to consider this case: Suppose I say "I'll promise to pay you $100 if the coin I'm going to flip comes up heads." A mathematician would say that promise is the equivalent of a promise to pay $50, because the mathematical value of a 50–50 chance of getting $100 is $50.

Contracts of the kind described above are called "aleatory contracts." "Aleatory" is another word for "gambling." But aleatory contracts are actually quite important in business. Many people have become very wealthy by devising new types of financial derivatives which were nothing more than very sophisticated aleatory contracts.

One common type of aleatory contract is an insurance policy. The insurance company promises to pay to repair your car if it is damaged (a condition over which the insurance company has no control).

What happens if the condition is within the control of the promissor? That's a more difficult case, and we will consider it after covering some other points.

Alternative Promises

Suppose a person says: "If you promise to pay me $10,000, I'll promise to do either A or B, my choice." Is that promise consideration, or is it an illusory promise? It depends. If both A and B, taken separately, would be consideration, then the promise is consideration. But if either of them would not be consideration, then the promise to do one or the other is not consideration. This makes sense; if one alternative is illusory consideration, then the requirement of consideration is not met.

For example, a real estate developer might want to make sure she has financing lined up before she commits to starting a project. So she could go to a lending institution and enter into an agreement where the lender agrees to make her a loan of ten million dollars and she agrees to repay the loan with interest at the annual rate of six per cent. The consideration for the lender's promise to make the loan would be the borrower's promise to pay interest. But if the borrower thinks that interest rates will be lower at the time the loan is to be made, she may want the freedom to shop for lower rates at that time. In that case, she might negotiate for a deal whereby she agrees to either (i) take the loan and pay the lender interest at the rate of 8 percent per annum or (ii) pay the lender a commitment fee of $100,000. Because either the interest or the commitment fee would be consideration for a promise to loan money, the lender's promise is supported by consideration and the lender's promise is enforceable.

––––––––

PROBLEM 5-3

Term life insurance is the original form of life insurance. It is a temporary policy that builds no cash value and covers only a specific term or period of time. It is earned in exchange for a premium payment and, if the insured dies during the term, the death benefit will be paid to the beneficiary. In a term life insurance policy, what is:

(a) the promise made by the insurance company? *to pay for the death if it happens to the beneficiary*

(b) the consideration for that promise? *the risk incurred / the potential detriment*

PROBLEM 5-4

A real estate developer who is building a project will often require the contractor who is doing the actual building to purchase a "completion bond." (Actually, it is usually the lender who is financing the project who requires the bond in order to ensure that the building will be completed so that, if the lender later forecloses, they are not foreclosing on a half completed building. But to avoid making the problem unnecessarily complex, let's keep the lender out of it for now.) The terms of the bond provide that if the contractor does not finish the project, the bonding company will (at the bonding company's expense) hire another contractor to complete the project. If the bond is a bilateral contract in which the contractor agrees to pay the bonding company a fee (called the "premium"), what is the consideration for the contractor's promise? What is the consideration for the bonding company's promise?

PROBLEM 5-5

In the natural gas industry, "take-or-pay" contracts are common. A gas producer and a pipeline company will enter into a contract under the terms of which the gas producer will promise to sell the pipeline gas at a price of X dollars per million cubic feet of gas. The pipeline company will promise to either (a) take the gas and pay for it *or* (b) pay a cancellation fee of Y dollars. What is the consideration for the producer's promise to sell the gas?

PROBLEM 5-6

Sherlock Holmes lets (rents) his lodgings at 221B Baker Street from Mrs. Hudson at a rent of £4 per month. For many years, Holmes has taken the lodgings on a month-to-month basis, but recently Mrs. Hudson became your client, and you advised her to put Holmes on an annual lease. Holmes insisted that the lease contain a provision allowing him to vacate the premises at any time and have no further obligation for paying any further rent upon the payment of a "cancellation fee." Against your advice, this clause was included in the lease.

Mrs. Hudson has just discovered the secret behind Holmes' high energy level and she has told you in no uncertain terms that you have to find a way to "get that dope fiend out of my house." After reviewing the lease, you discover that you neglected to include a provision that would allow Mrs. Hudson to evict

Holmes on the basis of his pharmacological predilections. Can she avoid the lease on the basis that there is no consideration:

    (a)   if the cancellation fee is £10?

    (b)   if the cancellation fee is sixpence?

[handwritten annotation: Valid as consideration if each alternative independently serves as consideration]

[handwritten annotation: nominal]

More on Conditional Promises

We said that a conditional promise is consideration if the condition is outside the control of the promissor. You now have enough background to consider the question of a condition that is within the control of the promissor.

The easiest way to look at this question is to note that if the condition is within the control of the promissor, what we really have is alternative promises. In other words, suppose the promise is "I'll buy a hundred tons of coal from you if I buy any coal this year." This could be framed as "I'll (1) buy a hundred tons of coal from you, *or* (2) not buy any coal this year." Applying our rule about alternative promises, this promise is consideration only if both of the promises could be consideration. A promise to buy a hundred tons of coal is clearly consideration. The promise to not buy any coal is more of a problem. But we can solve the problem using a nominal consideration analysis. If the promissor is someone who normally buys coal, the promise to not buy any coal this year is a substantial one. It is a major change in his way of doing things. It can then be consideration. If the promissor is someone who does not normally buy coal, then the promise not to buy any (in other words, to just keep doing what he has always done) has no substance and is merely nominal consideration.

PROBLEM 5-7 — *[handwritten: Output Contract]*

Gourmet Cheeses, LLC sells expensive cheeses by mail. To keep its customers happy, it is always looking for new cheeses. It discovered a small family-owned dairy and cheese factory in Iowa that produced a wonderful sharp cheddar. The factory had been in business for more than one hundred years and had over 30 full time employees. Gourmet Cheeses entered into an agreement with the owners of the factory. Under the terms of the agreement, the factory would sell, and Gourmet would purchase, all of the cheese produced by the factory over the next three years at a price specified in the contract. After Gourmet entered into the agreement, it discovered that its customers would not pay Gourmet's premium prices for cheese produced in Iowa. They seemed to think that it could be good cheddar only if it was produced a few miles away in Wisconsin.

Gourmet is now arguing that the agreement is not enforceable because the factory's promise is an illusory promise. The factory can avoid its obligations under the contract by going out of the cheese business for three years. Evaluate that argument.

PROBLEM 5-8

Real estate developer is contracting to purchase parcels of land for a shopping center. Worried that he may not be able to get enough tenants, however, he expressly conditions each of his contracts to purchase on getting leases that he finds are satisfactory to him in his sole discretion within 120 days. When, before 120 days are up, one of his sellers changes her mind and tells him that she is not selling, he sues.

The seller defends the suit based upon an illusory consideration theory. She argues that all she got in return for her agreement to sell was Developer's illusory promise, one which he could get out of merely by claiming that the leases obtained were not satisfactory or by not making any effort to get leases in the first place.

Who should win? *See Mattei v. Hopper*, 51 Cal. 2d 119, 330 P.2d 625 (1958).

WOOD v. LUCY, LADY DUFF-GORDON

Court of Appeals of New York
222 N.Y. 88, 118 N.E. 214 (1917)

CARDOZO, J.

[1] The defendant styles herself "a creator of fashions." Her favor helps a sale. Manufacturers of dresses, millinery, and like articles are glad to pay for a certificate of her approval. The things which she designs, fabrics, parasols, and what not, have a new value in the public mind when issued in her name. She employed the plaintiff to help her to turn this vogue into money. He was to have the exclusive right, subject always to her approval, to place her endorsements on the designs of others. He was also to have the exclusive right to place her own designs on sale, or to license others to market them. In return she was to have one-half of "all profits and revenues" derived from any contracts he might make. The exclusive right was to last at least one year from April 1, 1915, and thereafter from year to year unless terminated by notice of 90 days. The plaintiff says that he kept the contract on his part, and that the defendant broke it. She placed her endorsement on fabrics, dresses, and millinery without his knowledge, and withheld the profits. He sues her for the damages, and the case comes here on demurrer.

[2]   The agreement of employment is signed by both parties. It has a
wealth of recitals. The defendant insists, however, that it lacks the
elements of a contract. She says that the plaintiff does not bind himself to
anything. It is true that he does not promise in so many words that he will
use reasonable efforts to place the defendant's endorsements and market
her designs. We think, however, that such a promise is fairly to be implied.
The law has outgrown its primitive stage of formalism when the precise
word was the sovereign talisman, and every slip was fatal. It takes a
broader view today. A promise may be lacking, and yet the whole writing
may be "instinct with an obligation," imperfectly expressed. (Scott, J., in
McCall Co. v. Wright, 133 App.Div. 62, 117 N.Y. Supp. 775; *Moran v.
Standard Oil Co.*, 211 N.Y. 187, 198, 105 N.E. 217). If that is so, there is a
contract.

[3]   The implication of a promise here finds support in many
circumstances. The defendant gave an exclusive privilege. She was to have
no right for at least a year to place her own endorsements or market her
own designs except through the agency of the plaintiff. The acceptance of
the exclusive agency was an assumption of its duties. We are not to suppose
that one party was to be placed at the mercy of the other. Many other terms
of the agreement point the same way. We are told at the outset by way of
recital that:

> The said Otis F. Wood possesses a business organization adapted
> to the placing of such endorsements as the said Lucy, Lady Duff-
> Gordon, has approved.

[4]   The implication is that the plaintiff's business organization will
be used for the purpose for which it is adapted. But the terms of the
defendant's compensation are even more significant. Her sole
compensation for the grant of an exclusive agency is to be one-half of all
the profits resulting from the plaintiff's efforts. Unless he gave his efforts,
she could never get anything. Without an implied promise, the transaction
cannot have such business "efficacy, as both parties must have intended
that at all events it should have." Bowen, L.J., in the *Moorcock*, 14 P.D. 64,
68. But the contract does not stop there. The plaintiff goes on to promise
that he will account monthly for all moneys received by him, and that he
will take out all such patents and copyrights and trade-marks as may in
his judgment be necessary to protect the rights and articles affected by the
agreement. It is true, of course, as the Appellate Division has said, that if
he was under no duty to try to market designs or to place certificates of
endorsement, his promise to account for profits or take out copyrights
would be valueless. But in determining the intention of the parties the
promise has a value. It helps to enforce the conclusion that the plaintiff
had some duties. His promise to pay the defendant one-half of the profits
and revenues resulting from the exclusive agency and to render accounts

monthly was a promise to use reasonable efforts to bring profits and revenues into existence. For this conclusion the authorities are ample.

[5] The judgment of the Appellate Division should be reversed, and the order of the Special Term affirmed, with costs in the Appellate Division and in this court.

CUDDEBACK, MCLAUGHLIN, and ANDREWS, JJ., concur. HISCOCK, C. J., and CHASE and CRANE, JJ., dissent.

Order reversed, etc.

NOTES AND QUESTIONS

1. There appears to be more than a little misogyny or anti-British sentiment or both underlying Cardozo's opinion in the *Lady Duff-Gordon* case. Consider whether views like these may have had an effect on the outcome of the case.

2. Professor James A. Wooten of the University at Buffalo Law School has noted that the irony of the *Lady Duff-Gordon* case is that Cardozo states that it would place the lady at Wood's mercy if he failed to impute a duty on Wood's part to use best efforts. [para 3]. This is the opposite of the truth: If he did not impose the duty to use best efforts, the contract would fail for lack of consideration, in which case she would be free. It is precisely the imputation of the best efforts clause that puts her at his mercy. Cardozo was, by all accounts, a smart man. We think he knew exactly what he was doing.

KARL N. LLEWELLYN, A LECTURE ON APPELLATE ADVOCACY
29 University of Chicago Law Review 627, 637–38 (1962)

[T]he statement of facts, be it in the brief or be it oral, is the complete guts of your case. And I'm going to give you two statements of fact, one by an utter master, and another in the exactly same case, as an effort to show you how it can be done just the other way on the same facts and the same case.

The statement by the master is Cardozo in *Wood against Lady Duff-Gordon*. And you will get that, as I read it to you. You must remember that Cardozo was a truly great advocate, and the fact that he became a great judge didn't at all change the fact that he was a great advocate. And if you will watch, in the very process of your listening to the facts, you will find two things happening. The one is that according to principle number one, you arrive at the conclusion that the case has to come out one way. And the other is, that it fits into a legal frame that says, "How comfortable it will be, to bring it out that way. No trouble at all. No trouble at all."

"The defendant styles herself"—now watch the way in which she is subtly made into a nasty person—" 'The defendant styles herself 'a creator of fashions.' " Her favor helps a sale. Manufacturers of dresses, millinery, and like articles are glad to pay for a certificate of her approval. The things which she designs, fabrics, parasols, and what not, have a new value in the public mind when issued in her name. She employed the plaintiff to help her turn this vogue into money."

Does this sound—this is an interposition—does this sound like a business deal? Does a business deal sound like a legally enforceable view? Nothing is being said about that. But watch it grow on you. And if I hadn't stopped to tell you about it, it would have grown until you just took it, without a word.

"He was to have the exclusive right"—watch this language—"exclusive right"—what wonderful legal language, to make it legally enforceable—"He was to have the exclusive right . . . to place her own designs on sale, or to license others to market them. In return, she was to have one-half of 'all profits and revenues' derived from any contracts he might make. The exclusive right was to last at least one year from April 1, 1915, and thereafter from year to year unless terminated by notice of ninety days."

My heavens, isn't this legal?

"The plaintiff says that he kept the contract on his part, and that the defendant broke it. She placed her indorsement on fabrics, dresses and millinery. . . ."

"The agreement of employment is signed by both parties. It has a wealth of recitals. The defendant insists, however, that it lacks the elements of a contract. She says that the plaintiff does not bind himself to anything. It is true that he does not promise in so many words that he will use reasonable efforts to place the defendant's indorsement and market her designs."

Now, is there any way to bring that case out, except one? Isn't it obvious that we are going to imply a promise on the part of the plaintiff which will satisfy the requirement of consideration and the decency of the situation.

All right, now try this: "The plaintiff in this action rests his case upon his own carefully prepared form agreement, which has as its first essence his own omission of any expression whatsoever of any obligation of any kind on the part of this same plaintiff. We thus have the familiar situation of a venture in which one party, here the defendant, has an asset, with what is, in advance, of purely speculative value. The other party, the present plaintiff, who drew the agreement, is a marketer eager for profit, but chary of risk. The legal question presented is whether the plaintiff, while carefully avoiding all risk in the event of failure, can nevertheless claim full profit in the event that the market may prove favorable in its response. The law of consideration joins with the principles of business decency in giving the answer. And the answer is no."

Same case. Entirely the same case. But it brings me to the next fundamental point, which is that if you have an intelligent appellant, to rest upon his statement of the facts, if you are the respondent, is suicide. Did you hear me? If he is any good, you're cooked. (Laughter.) You have a positive case to make, and you can only make it by restating the facts so that they fit into your picture of what the whole thing is. And I think with that I can practically stop, can't I, because I've made the fundamental point.

NOTES AND QUESTIONS

1.   At the beginning of this chapter, there was a hypothetical in which a lobbyist tells a congressperson whose vote she wants: "I'll contribute $500,000 to your campaign." Why wouldn't the court imply a return promise in the same way Cardozo did in *Wood v. Lucy, Lady Duff-Gordon*?

2.   In a case that was featured in a prior edition of this casebook, the court examined the situation where a bank had made a loan to a company based, in part, upon the guaranties of five wealthy individuals. Under the guaranties, the guarantors were to pay any unpaid obligations of the company under the loan. The traditional way for such a transaction to be conducted is to have the guarantors sign their guaranties first and deliver them to the bank, which then obtains the borrower's signature on the loan agreement and then funds the loan. This chain of events makes it clear that the guaranties were given in consideration of the loan being funded and that the loan was made in consideration of the guaranties. In this case, however, one of the guarantors did not sign his guaranty before the bank funded the loan. After the company defaulted on the loan, the court held that that guarantor that had not signed before the loan was funded was not liable for the original loan balance and accrued interest due to lack of consideration. The guarantor was, however, liable for additional advances of funds by the bank to the company after he had signed. *Frishman v. Canadian Imperial Bank of Commerce*, 407 F.2d 299 (D.C. Cir. 1968).

Additionally, note that, in situations like the Frishman case, it is a good idea to confirm the authenticity of a signer's signature, perhaps by having it notarized by a notary public. Make sure no one can claim their signature was forged. It's more common than you think for business people to forge signatures of their associates. Sometimes they do it with no thought of defrauding anyone. They figure the person would sign anyway and it's easier to forge the signature than to wait until the person gets back from a trip. Other times it is real fraud.

Martha Stewart's colleague Sam Waksal was sentenced to five years in prison for securities fraud. Part of what he pled guilty to was forging a banker's signature on a letter stating he still owned stock when he had actually sold it. In the Parmalat scandal in Italy, the perps forged a letter from Bank of America saying that one of Parmalat's subsidiaries had a billion dollars on deposit. The accountants accepted the letter, apparently without verifying its accuracy and legitimacy with the bank.

———

PALMER V. DEHN

Court of Appeals of Tennessee
29 Tenn. App. 597, 198 S.W.2d 827 (1946)

BURNETT, JUDGE.

[1] This suit is based on a two count declaration. The first count is to recover damages for personal injuries due to the negligence of the plaintiff in error. The second count is for breach of contract based on a promise of the plaintiff in error to compensate the defendant in error for the personal injuries received in the accident as set forth in the first count.

[2] Pleas of not guilty and non-assumpsit were plead to this declaration.

[3] The case was tried to a jury. At the conclusion of the plaintiff's proof and at the conclusion of all proof the defendant (plaintiff in error) moved specially for a directed verdict as to each count. Both motions were overruled and a verdict was returned by the jury against the defendant.

[4] The facts and legitimate inferences to be drawn therefrom, as viewed from the plaintiff's (defendant in error's) standpoint, are: On October 31, 1944 (summons herein was issued October 24, 1945), Mr. Dehn, a skilled mechanic and traveling representative of Transit Bus Sales Company of St. Louis, Missouri, made one of his quarterly trips to Knoxville. On this trip he contacted Mr. Palmer who had formerly purchased a motor bus from the company Mr. Dehn represented. On being informed that Mr. Palmer was having mechanical trouble with this bus, Dehn went with him to the place the bus was parked. Dehn inspected the bus and told Palmer a belt was too loose. Palmer's driver went away and got the belt tightened. When the driver returned with the tightened belt, the three, Palmer, Dehn and the driver, discussed the matter at length. Dehn was then attempting to show Palmer how tight it should be when the driver started the motor cutting off two of Dehn's fingers. Dehn thought all the time that the driver was out of the car and that no one was inside that could start the motor. Before putting his fingers in their position of peril Dehn did not throw a safety switch which he knew was there so as to prevent injury to him. His explanation for not using this safety switch was

that it was to be used when men were working at opposite ends of the bus and since he thought the driver was with him he did not deem it necessary to take this precaution.

Gift promise –

[5]   Palmer immediately rushed Dehn to a local hospital. On the way to the hospital Palmer said: "I am awful sorry this happened, but don't worry a minute. I will see you are compensated for the loss of your finger, take care of your expenses for the loss of your finger, and all." Later Palmer made a similar assurance.

[6]   It is very earnestly and ably argued that the trial judge should have directed a verdict on behalf of the defendant as to the second count (one based on above contract) because there is no consideration for said promise or contract.

[7]   For there to be a consideration in a contract between parties to the contract it is not necessary that something concrete and tangible move from one to the other. Any benefit to one and detriment to the other may be a sufficient consideration. The jury may draw any reasonable and natural inference from the proof and if by inference from the proof a benefit to the promissor and detriment to the promisee might be inferred this will constitute a valid consideration. In the instant case the jury was justified in inferring that the promisee accepted this promise if it were performed within a reasonable time; that foregoing his right of action for a reasonable time was a good consideration moving to the promissor; they were clearly justified in inferring that the basis of the promise of the promissor was for forbearance in bringing suit. By forbearing he might have readily born a detriment. The promissor might easily have gained a benefit by such a forbearance. *See* 12 Am. Jur., Sec. 85, page 580.

> An agreement to forbear, for a time, proceedings at law or in equity, to enforce a well-founded claim, is a valid consideration for a promise . . . Nor need the agreement to delay be for a time certain, for it may be a reasonable time only, and yet be a sufficient consideration for a promise.

Beasley v. Gregory, 2 Tenn. Ct. App. 378, 382, opinion by Faw, P. J., in which he cites ample authority for the statement.

[8]   It is next insisted that the motion for a directed verdict should have been sustained as to the first count because of the contributory negligence of the plaintiff.

[9]   It is true there was introduced herein very positive proof contrary to that heretofore detailed which tended to show the plaintiff guilty of contributory negligence. This though merely made a question for the jury who under proper instructions on the subject decided in favor of the plaintiff. We think there was material evidence to support the verdict. We must "not lightly . . . assume the primary duty of determining liability or

nonliability, in actions of tort, but ... leave that duty where the Constitution has placed it, with the jury, as triers of facts, and if they act capriciously and arbitrarily to supervise their action." *Jackson v. B. Lowenstein & Bros.*, 175 Tenn. 535, 136 S.W.2d 495, 496; *Wilenzick v. Austin*, 180 Tenn. 591, 177 S. W.2d 548.

[10] The result is all assignments must be overruled and the judgment below affirmed.

HALE, J., concurs.

MCAMIS, JUDGE (dissenting).

[11] I am unable to follow the majority in holding that an enforceable contract arises from the circumstances of the case or the language quoted in the majority opinion.

[12] I cannot think there was any intention to make a binding contract but, if so, there was no consideration moving from plaintiff to defendant. There was no detriment to plaintiff and no benefit to the defendant. The plaintiff had the same right to sue in tort after the promise was made that he had before as indicated by the fact that he is still asserting his tort action in the first count of the declaration and it follows that defendant was not benefitted by being relieved of tort liability.

[13] I can find no basis for holding that there was an inference of a forbearance to sue which would furnish a sufficient supporting consideration. There is no suggestion that this was a condition of the promise and the tort action was not lost to plaintiff as a result of being induced to delay bringing suit beyond the limitation period.

WHITTEN V. GREELEY-SHAW

Supreme Judicial Court of Maine
520 A.2d 1307 (1987)

NICHOLS, JUSTICE.

[1]   On appeal the Defendant, Shirley C. Greeley-Shaw, contends that the Superior Court (Cumberland County) committed error when it entered judgment against her upon a promissory note in favor of the Plaintiff, George D. Whitten, in a foreclosure action, and when the court refused to recognize a certain writing entered into by the parties as a valid contract, that writing being the basis of the Defendant's counterclaim.

[2]   We reject both of the Defendant's claims of error and deny the appeal.

[3]   The Defendant's first claim of error originates from the foreclosure action brought by the Plaintiff. As assignee of a promissory note secured

by a mortgage deed of a home in Harpswell, he sought to foreclose due to the Defendant's failure to pay any portion of the $64,000.00 long since overdue him on the promissory note. The Defendant alleged that she was the owner of the home, that it was given to her by the Plaintiff as an incident of their four-year romantic relationship, and as assistance toward her efforts to start life anew with her fiancée. While the Defendant admits to having executed both the promissory note and the mortgage deed in favor of the Plaintiff's assignor, she argues that neither the Plaintiff, nor his attorney (who was the assignor), had informed her of what the documents were that she was signing, their legal significance, or that she would be responsible for annual payments on the note. She claims that it was not until a week later, when photocopying the documents, that she thoroughly examined them and realized their legal significance. Not until the foreclosure action was commenced, however, did she make known to the Plaintiff her misunderstanding.

[4] The Plaintiff asserts that at all times the funds he advanced to the Defendant to purchase the home was in the form of a loan, and that both he and his attorney made this clear to the Defendant. He testified that he had encouraged her to purchase a home in Maine and that he originally had his attorney's name on the deed and note to save himself possible embarrassment.

[5] While she alleges facts that might possibly give rise to claims of misrepresentation or breach of fiduciary duty, the Defendant does not expressly claim either ground for relief. Based upon evidence adduced at trial, that included the deposition of a second attorney who actually conducted the closing, there was ample evidence to support the finding of the Superior Court that the Defendant was aware of the nature of the documents and her legal responsibilities, and entered into the contract voluntarily. It is to no avail that the Defendant objects to the contents of a contract, that she admits she "barely looked at," despite having been given the opportunity, and indeed encouragement, to read.

[6] Emerging as a counterclaim to the Plaintiff's foreclosure action is the Defendant's request that the court enforce the terms of a written "agreement" entered into by the parties. The parties had engaged in an intermittent extra-marital affair from 1972 until March, 1980. At the time of this writing the Plaintiff, a Massachusetts contractor, had traveled to his Bermuda [Maine] home to vacation with friends, and expected to soon be joined there by his wife. The precise facts surrounding the creation of the agreement are in dispute. However, it is the testimony of the Defendant that she wanted to have "something in writing" because of all the past promises to her that she said the Plaintiff had broken. She testified that the Plaintiff told her, "You figure out what you want and I will sign it." She added that she unilaterally drew up the "agreement" while in Bermuda,

and the Plaintiff signed it without objection. There was an original and a copy, and only he signed the original.

[7]   On his part the Plaintiff testified that he had agreed to visit with the Defendant, who had come to his Bermuda home uninvited, because "[S]he demanded I see her or she would come up and raise hell with my friends" and embarrass him in front of his wife.

[8]   Basically, the "agreement" is a one-page typewritten document, prepared by the Defendant, that begins "I, George D. Whitten . . . agree to the following conditions made by Mrs. Shirley C. Shaw . . ." and then goes on to list four "conditions" required of the Plaintiff. The "conditions" require the Plaintiff to make payments to the Defendant of $500.00 per month for an indeterminate period, make any "major repairs" to the Harpswell home, pay for any medical needs, take one trip with the Defendant and supply her with one piece of jewelry per year, and visit and phone the Defendant at various stated intervals. The only "condition" that approaches the recital of a promise or duty of the Defendant is the statement "[U]nder no circumstances will there be any calls made to my homes or offices without prior permission from me."

[9]   The Plaintiff contends that, inter alia, this writing is unenforceable because of a lack of consideration. The Defendant argues that the writing is enforceable because there is the necessary objective manifestation of assent on each side, supported by the "stated" consideration of the Defendant not to call the Plaintiff without his prior permission, that, she asserts, constituted her "promise."

[10] The Superior Court found that no legally enforceable contract had been created. We agree. Every contract requires "consideration" to support it, and any promise not supported by consideration is unenforceable. The Defendant asks this Court to recognize the "agreement" as an enforceable bilateral contract, where the necessary consideration is the parties' promise of performance. Generally, the Defendant's promise to forbear from engaging in an activity that she had the legal right to engage in, can provide her necessary consideration for the Plaintiffs return promises. However, the Plaintiff's allegation of lack of consideration draws attention to the bargaining process; although the Defendant's promise to forbear could constitute consideration, it cannot if it was not sought after by the Plaintiff, and motivated by his request that the Defendant not disturb him. Of this there was no evidence whatsoever. This clause, the only one that operates in the Plaintiff's favor, was only included in the contract by the Defendant, because, she asserts, she felt the Plaintiff should get something in exchange for his promises. Clearly, this clause was not "bargained for" by the Plaintiff, and not given in exchange for his promises, and as such cannot constitute the consideration necessary to support a contract.

Judgment affirmed.

———

NOTES AND QUESTIONS

1.   The *Hamer* court said that giving up a legal right can be consideration. Did Ms. Greeley-Shaw have a legal right to call Mr. Whitten without prior permission?

2.   In the roofing case, we saw that the customer was deemed to have made the offer even though she just signed a form the roofing company stuck in front of her. Is that a valid analogy? If so, how does it affect the court's reasoning?

3.   Wasn't the real consideration for his signing an implicit agreement that she would not cause a disturbance and embarrass him in front of his wife and friends?

4.   Of the last four cases, there have been two in which the court was willing to imply a return promise and two in which it was not. In each of the cases, try to identify the factors that influenced the court to imply or not to imply a return promise.

5.   The statement in the previous question might not be entirely correct. Is it clear that the *Palmer v. Dehn* court was implying a return promise or is there another way to read the opinion?

———

Implied Promise of Consideration

The cases involving implied promises as consideration (*Wood*, *Frishman*, *Palmer*, and *Whitten*) present a simple legal principle together with a difficult factual determination.

The simple legal principle is this. If A makes a promise in return for B's promise, B's promise is the consideration that makes A's promise binding. On the other hand, if B does not promise anything, A's promise was given without consideration and therefore is not binding.

In most cases, it is easy to tell whether B has made a promise in return. The four cases set out above involve the relatively uncommon situation in which it is not. In each of these cases, one party didn't expressly promise something, but the circumstances were such that by accepting what was offered, the person might have impliedly promised to give something in return. In *Wood*, Col. Wood might have promised to use his best efforts to market the products when he accepted Lady Duff-Gordon's promise of exclusive rights to her creations. In *Frishman*, the bank might have agreed to forbear from making demand on the loan when they accepted Frishman's guarantee. In *Palmer*, the mechanic might have agreed to forbear from suing when he accepted the bus company owner's promise to pay his medical expenses.

Whitten is a little different. In that case there was an express promise not to make any uninvited calls. The court dismisses that as not being bargained for, but it ignores the fact that the real consideration was the mistress's implied promise not to make a scene.

In most of the cases, the court acts as if it is obvious—just common sense—that a promise was (or was not, as the case may be) made. It is not that obvious, as Llewellyn pointed out. The only thing that is obvious is that when you are setting up a deal like this you need to be sure that your client promises the other party something that they want. There is no real test you can apply to determine whether or not a return promise should be implied. The best way to analyze it may be to ask what would happen if the person who allegedly made the implied promise had failed to perform. For instance, in *Wood,* if Col. Wood had induced Lady Duff-Gordon to give him an exclusive right to sell her creations and then done nothing to sell them, a court probably would have found that he promised to make a reasonable effort to sell them and breached that promise. So perhaps Cardozo was right. On the other hand, in *Palmer,* if the mechanic had taken the money and then turned around and sued for more, few courts would have dismissed his suit on the ground that he promised not to sue in return for the promise to pay his medical expenses. *Palmer* seems to be the kind of case that "legal realists" love to talk about. To reach a just result, a court bends the rules of contract law, finding a promise where there was none. *Frishman* can be analyzed the same way. If the bank had accepted Frishman's guaranty and then turned around and declared the loan due and payable, would a court have found that the bank breached an implied promise not to demand payment? It's a tough question, and so it's not surprising that the reported cases involving the *Frishman* fact pattern (there are several—it's one of the few situations in which consideration questions come up in business transactions) have split fairly evenly between those finding an implied promise and those not finding one.

In dealing with cases like these, it's not important whether you decide there was or was not an implied promise. What is important is that you recognize the situation as one where there is consideration for the express promise by one party only if an implied promise on the part of the other party can be found. Note also that each promise must be bargained for. That is, each party must have given their promise in return for the other's promise.

———

KIRKSEY V. KIRKSEY

Supreme Court of Alabama
8 Ala. 131 (1845)

[1] Assumpsit by the defendant, against the plaintiff in error. The question is presented in this Court, upon a case agreed, which shows the following facts:

[2] The plaintiff was the wife of defendant's brother, but had for some time been a widow, and had several children. In 1840, the plaintiff resided on public land, under a contract of lease, she had held over, and was comfortably settled, and would have attempted to secure the land she lived on. The defendant resided in Talladega county, some sixty, or seventy miles off. On the 10th of October, 1840, he wrote to her the following letter:

Dear sister Antillico—

Much to my mortification, I heard, that brother Henry was dead, and one of his children. I know that your situation is one of grief, and difficulty. You had a bad chance before, but a great deal worse now. I should like to come and see you, but cannot with convenience at present. I do not know whether you have a preference on the place you live on, or not. If you had, I would advise you to obtain your preference, and sell the land and quit the country, as I understand it is very unhealthy, and I know society is very bad. If you will come down and see me, I will let you have a place to raise your family, and I have more open land than I can tend; and on the account of your situation, and that of your family, I feel like I want you and the children to do well.

[3] Within a month or two after the receipt of this letter, the plaintiff abandoned her possession, without disposing of it, and removed with her family, to the residence of the defendant, who put her in comfortable houses, and gave her land to cultivate for two years, at the end of which time he notified her to remove, and put her in a house, not comfortable, in the woods, which he afterwards required her to leave.

[4] A verdict being found for the plaintiff, for two hundred dollars, the above facts were agreed, and if they will sustain the action, the judgment is to be affirmed, otherwise it is to be reversed.

[5] ORMOND, J. The inclination of my mind is, that the loss and inconvenience, which the plaintiff sustained in breaking up, and moving to the defendant's a distance of sixty miles, is a sufficient consideration to support the promise, to furnish her with a house, and land to cultivate, until she could raise her family. My brothers, however, think that the promise on the part of the defendant, was a mere gratuity, and that an action will not lie for its breach. The judgment of the Court below must therefore be reversed, pursuant to the agreement of the parties.

NOTE

Kirksey seems like a relic of a bygone day. But a similar case was being litigated just recently. Instead of the uncle inviting his nieces and nephews to come and live close to him, a nephew invited his uncle and aunt to come and live close to him.

According to news reports, Marshall B. Mathers, III was sued by his aunt and uncle, Betti and Jack Schmitt, who alleged that Mr. Mathers agreed to build them a house "worth up to $350,000" on a lot he owned and to pay them $100,000 per year for five years if they would leave their home in Missouri and move to Michigan. The Schmitts claimed Mr. Mathers' motivation was that he wanted them "to be near him and his daughter, while also providing him the intimate support from a loving family member who cared for 'Marshall Mathers' long before the world came to care about Eminem." According to news reports, Mr. Schmitt quit his job after receiving the offer and the couple sold their home and moved to Michigan, where Mr. Mathers bought a lot and built a home for them. But he kept title to the property in his own name, and after they had been living there for two years, he evicted them.

PROBLEM 5-9

Frank hears that his brother Jesse has been shot dead. He writes Jesse's widow and states that if she moves to the state where he lives, he will give her a tract of land and a home to live in until the children are grown. He says he wants her to move "so that my nieces and nephews will be close by. I am getting old and lonely." After she has been there two years, he kicks her off the property. Can she stay until the kids are grown? *Yes — valid contract*

PROBLEM 5-10

The president of a company writes the following letter to a retired employee:

Dear Frank:

Because you worked so hard for the company for so many years, the Board of Directors has authorized me to grant you a pension of Two Thousand Dollars ($2000) per month commencing immediately. Thank you for your faithful service.

Sincerely yours,

ACME MANUFACTURING CORP.

John Acme

President

After Frank has been retired for three years, Acme Manufacturing Corp., now presided over by John's successor, Tom, ceases to pay the pension. Can Frank recover future pension payments? *No — no consideration*

Promissory estoppel

PROBLEM 5-11

A wealthy man sees a homeless person freezing in the cold on the street. He says, "If you'll walk over to that store over there with me, I'll buy you a coat." Is there consideration for his promise? *No 50/50? No benefit to promisor*

PROBLEM 5-12

A grandfather promises to pay his granddaughter $100,000 saying: "None of my grandchildren work, and I am making sure that you don't have to." Is there consideration for his promise? *No*

PROBLEM 5-13

Suppose the grandfather in the previous problem had said: "It's a matter of pride with me that none of my grandchildren work. I'll give you $100,000 so you can quit your job." Is there consideration? _____ *Yes — Promissory Estoppel (PE)*

NOTE ABOUT SEALS

Consideration is a screening device that separates, at least in theory, executory deals the law will enforce from executory deals that it will not. Another device that served this purpose was the seal, a melted bit of wax dripped on a document and then stamped with the promissor's emblem. This formality was sufficiently definite and intentional that the law took it to mean that the promissor really intended to be bound by his promise and, thus, would enforce it (even without consideration). Essentially, the seal ceremony was an elaborate oath swearing ritual.

Over time, the use of seals became more common and steps were taken to make the process of sealing a document more efficient. Today we would say that the market demanded that transaction costs be lowered and transactional attorneys complied. Eventually, the seal was reduced to a printed "L.S." (for "locus sigilli," place of the seal) near the signature line on a contract or other document. As the ceremony of the seal gave way to this mere formality in printing, the seal began to be abolished. By the early 20th century, its significance as a consideration substitute or otherwise was nil in all 50 of the United States. To the extent that seals remain in use (on, for instance, certificates of incorporation), they are meaningless window dressing and have no legal significance.

From time to time, bar examiners and law professors pose a question about seals, which you can respond to with the information in the two paragraphs above. Apart from that, seals are unimportant except as an example of an obsolete mechanism that the law embraced to sort enforceable commitments from unenforceable ones and that, over time, was eroded from a meaningful device to an utterly empty ritual, at which point it was discarded.

LAWYERING SKILLS PROBLEM

You are visiting an old friend, Max, when Max's nephew Shelby stops by with good news. Shelby has been accepted to Cal Tech, his undergraduate institution of choice, where he hopes to major in Physics. Unfortunately, he did not receive a very generous scholarship offer, but Shelby tells Max that, if he can maintain a 3.6 or better GPA in his freshman year, he should be able to obtain a better scholarship package for his sophomore year.

Max tells Shelby how proud he is of him for being accepted to the school and notes that he expects to come into a little money at the close of the quarter, when a company that formerly characterized its equity as a "growth stock" will begin paying a dividend. Max says he would like to contribute to Shelby's college fund with that money. Shelby is very appreciative.

Max says, "let's make this binding, in case I get hit by a bus before the end of the quarter" (Max has always had a somber streak to his humor). He takes some note paper and writes:

For value received, I, Max Faber, promise to pay my nephew, Shelby Lynn, $5,000 on or before June 30, 2011.

He signs his name to the paper and starts to give it to Max, but stops and hands it to you, asking if he has done it right. You ask him, what is the "value received"? He says he doesn't know, but that phrase has been at the start of every promissory note he has ever seen. You explain that consideration doesn't work that way, and that if there isn't any, it won't be enforceable. He offers you the note pad and a pen and says, "You do it for me—I want it to be enforceable."

Can you oblige Max?

"If you promise to attend Cal. Tech, I, Max Faber, promise to pay Shelby Lynn $5,000 on or before June 30, 2011 — conditioned on my company's payment of my dividend."

CHAPTER 6

QUASI-CONTRACTS

■ ■ ■

Quantum Meruit — what one has earned

As one might imagine, there are instances when offer, acceptance, or consideration are lacking, and yet a contract-like recovery is permitted for reasons of public policy. This is most often done through a theory called "implied contract" or "quasi-contract" or "constructive contract." In early common law, one that provided services to another might, in the proper circumstance, recover either their costs expended in the effort or the benefit so conferred. Examples include situations in which medical and other essential services—often termed "necessaries"—were provided without a contract, e.g., to infants, the unconscious, the seriously intoxicated, and the insane, all of whom lack the capacity or ability to contract. The cause of action was called "quantum meruit," and it survives in many jurisdictions to this day. Similarly, "quantum valebat" allowed recovery for providing goods in similar circumstances.

The cases that follow explore these rights of recovery in the nature of contract while avoiding, for the moment, the more difficult question of what the measure of recovery should be if the plaintiff is successful.

COTNAM V. WISDOM

Supreme Court of Arkansas
83 Ark. 601, 104 S.W. 164 (1907)

HILL, C.J.

[1]   The Reporter will state the issues and substance of the testimony, and set out instructions one and two given at instance of appellees, and it will be seen therefrom that instruction one amounted to a peremptory instruction to find for the appellees in some amount.

[2]   The first question is as to the correctness of this instruction. As indicated therein, the facts are that Mr. Harrison, appellant's intestate, was thrown from a street car, receiving serious injuries which rendered him unconscious, and while in that condition the appellees were notified of the accident and summoned to his assistance by some spectator, and performed a difficult operation in an effort to save his life, but they were unsuccessful, and he died without regaining consciousness. The appellant

says: "Harrison was never conscious after his head struck the pavement. He did not and could not, expressly or impliedly, assent to the action of the appellees. He was without knowledge or will power. However merciful or benevolent may have been the intention of the appellees, a new rule of law, of contract by implication of law, will have to be established by this court in order to sustain the recovery." Appellant is right in saying that the recovery must be sustained by a contract by implication of law, but is not right in saying that it is a new rule of law, for such contracts are almost as old as the English system of jurisprudence. They are usually called "implied contracts"; more properly, they should be called *quasi*-contracts or constructive contracts.

[3] The following excerpts from *Sceva v. True*, 53 N. H. 627, are peculiarly applicable here:

> We regard it as well settled by the cases referred to in the briefs of counsel, many of which have been commented on at length by Mr. Shirley for the defendant, that an insane person, an idiot, or a person utterly bereft of all sense and reason by the sudden stroke of an accident or disease, may be held liable, in assumpsit, for necessaries furnished to him in good faith while in that unfortunate and helpless condition. And the reasons upon which this rests are too broad, as well as too sensible and humane, to be overborne by any deductions which a refined logic may make from the circumstance that in such cases there can be no contract or promise in fact—no meeting of the minds of the parties. The cases put it on the ground of an implied contract; and by this is not meant, as the defendant's counsel seems to suppose, an actual contract—that is, an actual meeting of the minds of the parties, an actual, mutual understanding, to be inferred from language, acts and circumstances by the jury—but a contract and promise, said to be implied by the law, where, in point of fact, there was no contract, no mutual understanding, and so no promise. The defendant's counsel says it is usurpation for the court to hold, as a matter of law, that there is a contract and a promise when all the evidence in the case shows that there was not a contract, nor the semblance of one. It is doubtless a legal fiction, invented and used for the sake of the remedy. If it was originally usurpation, certainly it has now become very inveterate, and firmly fixed in the body of the law.

> Illustrations might be multiplied, but enough has been said to show that, when a contract or promise implied by law is spoken of, a very different thing is meant from a contract in fact, whether express or tacit. The evidence of an actual contract is generally to be found, either in some writing made by the parties, or in verbal communications which passed between them, or in their acts and

conduct considered in the light of the circumstances of each particular case. A contract implied by law, on the contrary, rests upon no evidence. It has no actual existence. It is simply a mythical creation of the law. The law says that it shall be taken that there was a promise, when in point of fact, there was none. Of course this is not good logic, for the obvious and sufficient reason that it is not true. It is a legal fiction, resting wholly for its support on a plain legal obligation and a plain legal right. If it were true, it would not be a fiction. There is a class of legal rights, with their correlative legal duties, analogous to the *obligationes quasi ex contractu* of the civil law, which seem to lie in the region between contracts on the one hand, and torts on the other, and to call for the application of a remedy not strictly furnished either by actions *ex contractu* or actions *ex delicto*. The common law supplies no action of *duty*, as it does of assumpsit and trespass; and hence the somewhat awkward contrivance of this fiction to apply the remedy of assumpsit where there is no true contract, and no promise to support it.

[4] . . . . In its practical application, it sustains recovery for physicians and nurses who render services for infants, insane persons and drunkards. And services rendered by physicians to persons unconscious or helpless by reason of injury or sickness are in the same situation as those rendered to persons incapable of contracting, such as the classes above described. The court was therefore right in giving the instruction in question.

[5] The defendant sought to require the plaintiff to prove, in addition to the value of the services, the benefit, if any, derived by the deceased from the operation, and alleges error in the court refusing to so instruct the jury. The court was right in refusing to place this burden upon the physicians. The same question was considered in *Ladd v. Witte*, 116 Wis. 35, where the court said: "That is not at all the test. So that a surgical operation to be conceived and performed with due skill and care, the price to be paid therefore does not depend upon the result. The event so generally lies with the forces of nature that all intelligent men know and understand that the surgeon is not responsible therefore. In absence of express agreement, the surgeon, who brings to such a service due skill and earns the reasonable and customary price therefore, whether the outcome be beneficial to the patient or the reverse."

[6] The court permitted to go to the jury the fact that Mr. Harrison was a bachelor, and that his estate would go to his collateral relatives, and also permitted proof to be made of the value of the estate, which amounted to about $18,500, including $10,000 from accident and life insurance policies. There is a conflict in the authorities as to whether it is proper to prove the value of the estate of a person for whom medical services were rendered, or the financial condition of the person receiving such services.

In *Robinson v. Campbell*, 47 Iowa 625, it was said: "there is no more reason why this charge should be enhanced on account of the ability of the defendants to pay than that the merchant should charge them more for a yard of cloth, or the druggist for filling a prescription, a laborer for a day's work." On the other hand, *see Haley's Succession*, 50 La. Ann. 840; and *Lange v. Kearney*, 4 N.Y.S., 14 which was affirmed by the Court of Appeals, 127 N.Y. 676 holding that the financial condition of the patient may be considered. Whatever may be the true principle governing this matter in contracts, the court is of the opinion that the financial condition of a patient cannot be considered where there is no contract and recovery is sustained on a legal fiction which raises a contract in order to afford a remedy which the justice of the case requires. In *Morrisette v. Wood*, 123 Ala. 384 the court said: "The trial court erred in admitting testimony as to the value of the patient's estate, against the objection of the defendant. The inquiry was as to the value of the professional services rendered by the plaintiff to the defendant's testator, and, as the case was presented below, the amount or value of the latter's estate could shed no legitimate light upon this issue nor aid in its elucidation. The cure or amelioration of disease is as important to a poor man as it is to a rich one, and, *prima facie* at least, the services rendered to one are of the same value as the same services rendered to the other. If there was a recognized usage obtaining in the premises here involved to graduate professional charges with reference to the financial condition of the person for whom such services are rendered, which had been so long established and so universally acted upon as to have ripened into a custom of such character that it might be considered that these services were rendered and accepted in contemplation of it, there is no hint of it in the evidence."

[7]   There was evidence in this case proving that it was customary for physicians to graduate their charges by the ability of the patient to pay, and hence, in regard to that element, this case differs from the Alabama case. But the value of the Alabama decision is the reason given which may admit such evidence, viz., because the custom would render the financial condition of the patient a factor to be contemplated by both parties when the services were rendered and accepted. The same thought, differently expressed, is found in *Lange v. Kearney*, 4 N.Y.Supp. 14. This could not apply to a physician called in an emergency by some bystander to attend a stricken man whom he never saw or heard of before; and certainly the unconscious patient could not, in fact or in law, be held to have contemplated what charges the physician might properly bring against him. In order to admit such testimony, it must be assumed that the surgeon and patient each had in contemplation that the means of the patient would be one factor in determining the amount of the charge for the services rendered. While the law may admit such evidence as throwing light upon the contract and indicating what was really in contemplation when it was made, yet a different question is presented when there is no contract to be

ascertained or construed, but a mere fiction of law creating a contract where none existed in order that there might be a remedy for a right. This fiction merely requires a reasonable compensation for the services rendered. The services are the same, be the patient prince or pauper, and for them the surgeon is entitled to fair compensation for his time, service and skill. It was, therefore, error to admit this evidence and to instruct the jury in the 2nd instruction that in determining what was a reasonable charge they could consider the "ability to pay of the person operated upon."

[8] It was improper to let it go to the jury that Mr. Harrison was a bachelor, and that his estate was left to nieces and nephews. This was relevant to no issue in the case, and its effect might well have been prejudicial. While this verdict is no higher than some of the evidence would justify, yet it is much higher than some of the other evidence would justify, and hence it is impossible to say that this was a harmless error.

[9] Judgment is reversed and cause remanded.

[10] JUSTICES BATTLE and WOOD concur in sustaining the recovery and in holding that it was error to permit the jury to consider the fact that his estate would go to collateral heirs, but they do not concur in holding that it was error to admit evidence of the value of the estate and instructing that it might be considered in fixing the charge.

TOM GROWNEY EQUIPMENT V. ANSLEY

Court of Appeals of New Mexico
119 N.M. 110, 888 P.2d 992 (1994)

BOSSON, JUDGE.

[1] This case presents an issue of first impression in New Mexico. The question is whether an equipment repair shop may recover in restitution for the value of work done where the owner did not authorize or otherwise encourage the repairs. The district court upheld the claim. Being persuaded that the repair shop does not have such an action, we reverse.

Facts

[2] The facts are not in dispute. Jim Ansley ("Owner") sold a backhoe loader on credit to Charles Edwards in 1988. Owner retained a security interest[1] but neglected to record it. In November 1991 Edwards took the

---

[1] [A security interest is like a mortgage on personal property rather than real estate. Essentially both a mortgage and a security agreement are contracts that give a party a present, non-possessory property interest in collateral and, thus, a particular source of payment to support a party's promise to perform under another contract. Should the party fail to perform under the primary contract (like a promissory note, lease, or a purchase agreement), then, under the mortgage or security agreement, the other party may cause the collateral to be sold and the

backhoe to Tom Growney Equipment, Inc. ("Repairer") for repairs. At the time, Edwards had an open account with Repairer. The repairs were duly performed and Repairer released the backhoe to Edwards in exchange for a promissory note. Repairer believed that Edwards owned the backhoe free of any creditor's security interest and was unaware of Edwards' obligation to Owner. Similarly, Owner was unaware of the services provided by Repairer, or that Repairer was owed any money by Edwards.

[3]   Ultimately, Edwards defaulted on both obligations, and in March 1992, Owner repossessed the backhoe from Edwards. Repairer brought suit against both Edwards and Owner for the balance owed on the promissory note. Repairer has not pursued the claim against Edwards. Owner and Repairer filed cross-motions for summary judgment. The district court entered summary judgment against Repairer on claims of open account and lien, finding that Repairer had no contractual relationship with Owner and had waived a claim of lien by releasing the backhoe to Edwards. However, the court did enter summary judgment against Owner "on [Repairer's] claim for quantum merit in the amount of $7,002.53." Owner appeals from that judgment.

Discussion

[4]   Repairer seeks recovery for the value of services performed. Had the services been at Owner's request, Repairer would have had a claim for express contract or perhaps one implied-in-fact. However, Owner was not even aware of the services, and therefore Repairer must look to some other remedy.

[5]   Even without an action in contract, it is reasonably arguable, if not undisputed, that Owner has benefitted to some degree from the repairs. Thus, Repairer may have a claim for restitution based upon a theory of quasi-contract (contract implied-in-law) to prevent unjust enrichment. *See* Dan B. Dobbs, Remedies at 583 ("If recovery is allowed for such unrequested services, it is clear that the recovery is the quasicontract sort, that is, based upon the principle against unjust enrichment and not on contract.") If restitution is available, it would likely result in a measure of damages, quantum meruit, which is significantly different from contract. *See id.* ("When the service was not sought by the defendant, if restitution is allowed at all it is usually measured by the increase in defendant's assets resulting from the service, not by the value of the service itself.").

[6]   New Mexico has recognized a theory of quantum meruit distinct from contract. More recently, our Supreme Court characterized the action as a claim for unjust enrichment. *Hydro Conduit Corp. v. Kemble*, 110 N.M. 173, 176, 793 P.2d 855, 858 (1990). In describing that action, the Supreme Court has identified the theory and rationale: " 'One who has been unjustly

proceeds applied against amounts due under the primary contract. The matter is more complicated than that, but this explanation will serve for present purposes.—Eds.]

enriched at the expense of another may be required by law to make restitution. Restatement of Restitution § 1 comments a, b, c (1937). This quasi-contractual obligation is created by the courts for reasons of justice and equity, notwithstanding the lack of any contractual relationship between the parties.' " *Id.* at 175. In *Danley v. City of Alamogordo*, 91 N.M. 520, 522, 577 P.2d 418, 420 (1978), the Supreme Court applied this theory in determining a city's liability for services performed by a contractor, notwithstanding the city's failure to comply with state purchasing laws which invalidated a contract between the city and the contractor.

[7] These and other New Mexico cases have discussed the theory and rationale in situations where the recipient of the benefit actually knew or should have known of the services performed, which is usually a foundation for relief under an implied-in-fact contract. However, no New Mexico case directly addresses the legal issue presented here, where the services are unsolicited and unknown. In this situation, the provider is left with a restitutionary remedy based upon a contract implied-in-law which serves to alleviate unjust enrichment. Here we must concern ourselves with the fundamental question of whether the resulting enrichment is the equivalent of that characterized by our Supreme Court as "unjust," and thus whether we should impute such a quasi-contract as a matter of law and compel restitution.

[8] In what Professor Dobbs describes as the "orthodox view," restitution is ordinarily not available under the circumstances in this case. *See* Dobbs, *supra*, § 4.9(5), at 701. That general rule is founded upon the owner's fundamental right of free choice: the exclusive right to determine whether his property shall be repaired and if so, by whom. That right of choice necessarily includes the right not to pay for services rendered without knowledge or consent. This principle permeates the equitable foundations of restitution. *See id.* § 4.9(2).

> Underlying most of the cases, however, seems to be a strong double commitment to prevent unjust enrichment on the one hand and to protect the defendant's right of free choice on the other. Where the defendant has a right to choose for himself whether to receive a benefit, and where restitution would deprive him of this choice by requiring payment for a "benefit" the defendant may not want, restitution is often denied. The right of self-determination through personal choices—that is, personal autonomy—is central to personal being and growth as well as to the concept of a free society.

Id. at 683.

[9] This view appears to be consistent with the general rule in the majority of jurisdictions where the owner does not know of or otherwise encourage the repairs provided. Although not all cases express their

theoretical foundations identically, the general principle enjoys fairly uniform support.

[10] We believe this is a fair rule and worthy of adoption in New Mexico. The case at hand falls comfortably within the majority rule. Although there may be some enrichment in terms of the value of those repairs to Owner, we do not believe that Owner has been enriched unjustly. The result may be harsh to Repairer, which is left unpaid for its efforts. In our view, a greater inequity would arise if the law compelled Owner to pay for services he did not request, did not authorize, and possibly did not want. We cannot remedy one wrong by inflicting a still greater injustice on another. *See* Dobbs, *supra*, § 4.9(5), at 702 ("So to require restitution is to require the owner to buy a benefit he did not ask for and may not want.").

* * *

[11] As long as Repairer retained possession of the backhoe, it had a mechanic's statutory lien upon the vehicle for the value of the labor, parts, and repairs rendered. Section 48–3–1(A) provides:

> All artisans and mechanics shall have a lien on things made or repaired by them for the amount due for their work, and may retain possession thereof until said amount is paid. Any person or corporation who repairs any motor vehicle or furnishes parts therefor, at the request or with the consent of any person lawfully in possession of any such motor vehicle, shall have a lien upon such motor vehicle or any part or parts thereof for the sum due for repairing the same, and for labor furnished thereon and for all costs incurred in enforcing such lien and may detain such motor vehicle in possession until such lien be paid.

[12] Under Section 48–3–1 Repairer had a lien for repairs which was superior even to recorded prior liens on the same vehicle, and therefore superior to Owner's interest, as long as the work was ordered by a person lawfully in possession of the vehicle, which would apply here to Edwards. Repairer could have retained the backhoe as security for full payment, but elected not to do so. Under these circumstances, we believe the result is governed by the rule set forth in Restatement of Restitution, *supra*, § 42(2), which states:

> A person who, in the mistaken belief that he or a third person on whose account he acts is the owner, adds value to the chattel of another, is not thereby entitled to restitution from the owner for the value of his services or the increased value given to the chattels; but if the owner brings an action for their conversion the added value or the value of the services, whichever is least, is deducted from the damages.

See Bank of Am., 694 P.2d at 248. Owner did not sue Repairer in conversion, and therefore Repairer has no such claim against Owner.

Conclusion

[13] We reverse the district court's grant of summary judgment in favor of Repairer and remand with instructions to enter judgment in favor of Owner. — Holding

IT IS SO ORDERED.

NOTES AND QUESTIONS

1. The court is being disingenuous when it refers throughout the opinion to Ansley as "Owner." U.C.C. Section 2–401(2) makes it very clear that Ansley was not the owner of the backhoe during the period after he sold it and before he repossessed it. He's just the holder of a lien. By using this terminology, the court makes it seem that there is only one way the case could have come out.

UCC states Ansley was not owner

2. These two cases cannot begin to give you a complete understanding of the complex area of restitution and quasi-contracts. They do, however, give you a basic idea of what the principles and issues are. The concept is explored further in later chapters.

PROBLEM 6-1

Lawyer leaves the office early because it's a nice fall day. When she arrives at her home she finds a man she does not know cleaning the leaves out of her gutters. She is about to ask him what he's doing when she realizes that he works for the yard service her next-door neighbor uses. Apparently the gutter cleaner is new and mistook her house for the house where he was supposed to do the work. Lawyer doesn't like the neighbor or his lawn service. She's had a number of unpleasant conversations with them about the loud leaf blowers the service uses. So she decides to keep quiet and get a free gutter-cleaning to make up for all the times her peace and quiet have been ruined by the leaf blowers.

When the lawn service realizes its mistake, it sends her a bill. Does she have to pay it?

LAWYERING SKILLS PROBLEM

You are an associate general counsel of a nationwide automobile rental firm in 1984. The General Counsel has recently heard of and read the New Mexico court of appeals opinion in *Tom Growney Equipment v. Ansley*, and has become quite concerned. Specifically, the company often rents its cars to travelers at airports who need them for short trips to various cities and other locations. Often, if the renter has a problem with the car and is late or fears he or she will be late to the airport, the renter will abandon the car, take a cab to the airport, and call the company after arriving at the renter's destination, so that the company can pick the car up and close out the billing to the traveler's company. This is, not unsurprisingly, particularly common with lawyers traveling into a locale for a hearing or a meeting and then attempting to jet away quickly to return to their home offices.

The General Counsel's concern is this: What if the renter has work done on the car while he has it but does not pay for the work done or, worse, simply leaves the car in the shop where the work was done? What if the car is picked up and repaired or stored gratuitously by a stranger after being abandoned by the renter? What if it is illegally parked or left in a hotel parking lot and towed and then stored or repaired by the towing company? How can the company be absolutely certain that such a shop would not have a colorable claim for quasi-contractual recovery (quantum meruit or quantum valebat)? The General Counsel has asked you to come up with some suggestions to help prevent such a claim or, if such a claim is brought, ensuring that it can be dismissed early on in the trial court, at or before the summary judgment stage. There is no way that she wants to have to take a case like this (the little, local, helpful garage vs. the big, national, impersonal rent-a-car company) to trial.

What do you suggest?

CHAPTER 7

PRE-EXISTING DUTY AND PAST CONSIDERATION

■ ■ ■

Closely related to quasi-contract is the subject of the pre-existing duty rule and past consideration. Consider a perfectly valid contract, featuring offer, acceptance, and consideration: The agreement of A to sell and B to buy A's car for $14,000. After making this contract, though, A suffers from seller's remorse and tells B, "The car is worth $15,000 and I won't sell it to you for a penny less." Rather than sue for breach, B, who really needs a car, agrees to pay the additional $1,000. Is the new contract supported by consideration?

The answer is "no." The problem is that A was under a pre-existing *Pre* duty to sell the car to B for $14,000, who has now gratuitously agreed to *existing* pay $1,000 more, or a total of $15,000, for it. This situation involves a *Duty* failure of consideration due to "pre-existing duty."

Similarly, what about the situation where a party has benefitted from the actions of another and then agrees to compensate them for the benefit conferred. For example, upon arriving home one day, C finds that D had mowed his lawn under the mistaken belief that she was mowing E's lawn, the subject of a new lawn service contract. C, pleased with the unasked for work, tells D: "No problem—I'll pay you $50 by next Tuesday for today's mowing job." Is C's agreement to pay supported by consideration? *NO*

Again, the answer is "no." Here, D, the party to be paid, is not promising to do or forebear from doing anything. D has already mistakenly and gratuitously performed. There is no consideration because things done in the past generally cannot serve as consideration. *Thing is already done*

The rules in this area are far from consistent. With regard to modifications of contracts that present the pre-existing duty problem, the traditional common law rule was that the contract as modified was not enforceable. The original unmodified contract still had force. This was justified by a policy of preventing "hold-ups," the situation where one party's negotiating leverage increases post-contracting and that party attempts to unilaterally change the terms of the contract to its benefit.

Under the U.C.C. and similar more modern regimes, however, the pre-existing duty rule has been abolished and its place is occupied by a general requirement of good faith. This leaves the hold-up problem to be addressed by other doctrines, notably economic duress (Chapter 11) and even unconscionability (Chapter 12). This means that, in the prior example regarding the sale of A's car, A and B would be able to enforceably modify the contract to provide for that higher price if it was in good faith (e.g., A found out the car was worth more than he had thought, perhaps). Depending on the jurisdiction and the type of contract involved, either the common law or the U.C.C. rule could be applied, as the cases in the first half of this chapter indicate.

In the case of past consideration, the traditional common law approach would also find the contract unsupported by consideration and unenforceable. This could lead to unjust results, especially where there had been part performance by the promissor or reliance by the promissee. For example, an employee might retire from a job and not seek other employment in reliance on another's promise to pay her an annual pension. Enforcement of such contracts based upon part performance or reliance is permitted in various jurisdictions, as the cases in the second half of this chapter demonstrate.

A. THE PRE-EXISTING DUTY RULE

ALASKA PACKERS' ASS'N V. DOMENICO
Circuit Court of Appeals, Ninth Circuit
117 F. 99 (1902)

Appeal from the District Court of the United States for the Northern District of California.

ROSS, CIRCUIT JUDGE.

[1] The libel[1] in this case was based upon a contract alleged to have been entered into between the libelants and the appellant corporation on the 22d day of May, 1900, at Pyramid Harbor, Alaska, by which it is claimed the appellant promised to pay each of the libelants, among other things, the sum of $100 for services rendered and to be rendered. In its answer the respondent denied the execution, on its part, of the contract sued upon, averred that it was without consideration, and for a third defense alleged that the work performed by the libelants for it was performed under other and different contracts than that sued on, and that, prior to the filing of the libel, each of the libelants was paid by the respondent the full amount due him thereunder, in consideration of which

---

[1] [Because the case involved seafarers, it was filed in the federal court under the court's admiralty jurisdiction. In admiralty the document that serves the function of a complaint is called the *libel*. The plaintiff is called the *libelant* and the defendant is the *respondent*.—Eds.]

each of them executed a full release of all his claims and demands against the respondent.

[2] The evidence shows without conflict that on March 26, 1900, at the city and county of San Francisco, the libelants entered into a written contract with the appellants, whereby they agreed to go from San Francisco to Pyramid Harbor, Alaska, and return, on board such vessel as might be designated by the appellant, and to work for the appellant during the fishing season of 1900, at Pyramid Harbor, as sailors and fishermen, agreeing to do "regular ship's duty, both up and down, discharging and loading; and to do any other work whatsoever when requested to do so by the captain or agent of the Alaska Packers' Association." By the terms of this agreement, the appellant was to pay each of the libelants $50 for the season,[2] and two cents for each red salmon in the catching of which he took part.

[3] On the 15th day of April, 1900, 21 of the libelants signed shipping articles by which they shipped as seamen on the Two Brothers, a vessel chartered by the appellant for the voyage between San Francisco and Pyramid Harbor, and also bound themselves to perform the same work for the appellant provided for by the previous contract of March 26th; the appellant agreeing to pay them therefor the sum of $60 for the season, and two cents each for each red salmon in the catching of which they should respectively take part. Under these contracts, the libelants sailed on board the Two Brothers for Pyramid Harbor, where the appellants had about $150,000 invested in a salmon cannery. The libelants arrived there early in April of the year mentioned, and began to unload the vessel and fit up the cannery. A few days thereafter, to wit, May 19th, they stopped work in a body, and demanded of the company's superintendent there in charge $100 for services in operating the vessel to and from Pyramid Harbor, instead of the sums stipulated for in and by the contracts; stating that unless they were paid this additional wage they would stop work entirely, and return to San Francisco. The evidence showed, and the court below found, that it was impossible for the appellant to get other men to take the places of the libelants, the place being remote, the season short and just opening; so that, after endeavoring for several days without success to induce the libelants to proceed with their work in accordance with their contracts, the company's superintendent, on the 22nd day of May, so far yielded to their demands as to instruct his clerk to copy the contracts executed in San Francisco, including the words "Alaska Packers' Association" at the end, substituting, for the $50 and $60 payments, respectively, of those contracts, the sum of $100, which document, so prepared, was signed by the libelants before a shipping commissioner whom they had requested to be brought from Northeast Point; the

---

[2] [$50 in 1900 dollars is roughly the equivalent of $1,540 in 2019 dollars using the CPI and the GNP Deflator—Eds.]

superintendent, however, testifying that he at the time told the libelants that he was without authority to enter into any such contract, or to in any way alter the contracts made between them and the company in San Francisco. Upon the return of the libelants to San Francisco at the close of the fishing season, they demanded pay in accordance with the terms of the alleged contract of May 22nd, when the company denied its validity, and refused to pay other than as provided for by the contracts of March 26th and April 5th, respectively. Some of the libelants, at least, consulted counsel, and, after receiving his advice, those of them who had signed the shipping articles before the shipping commissioner at San Francisco went before that officer, and received the amount due them thereunder, executing in consideration thereof a release in full, and the others paid at the office of the company, also receipting in full for their demands.

[4]   On the trial in the court below, the libelants undertook to show that the fishing nets provided by the respondent were defective, and that it was on that account that they demanded increased wages. On that point, the evidence was substantially conflicting, and the finding of the court was against the libelants the court saying:

> The contention of libelants that the nets provided them were rotten and unserviceable is not sustained by the evidence. The defendants' interest required that libelants should be provided with every facility necessary to their success as fishermen, for on such success depended the profits defendant would be able to realize that season from its packing plant, and the large capital invested therein. In view of this self-evident fact, it is highly improbable that the defendant gave libelants rotten and unserviceable nets with which to fish. It follows from this finding that libelants were not justified in refusing performance of their original contract.

112 Fed. 554.

[5]   The evidence being sharply conflicting in respect to these facts, the conclusions of the court, who heard and saw the witnesses, will not be disturbed.

[6]   The real questions in the case as brought here are questions of law, and, in the view that we take of the case, it will be necessary to consider but one of those. Assuming that the appellant's superintendent at Pyramid Harbor was authorized to make the alleged contract of May 22nd, and that he executed it on behalf of the appellant, was it supported by a sufficient consideration? From the foregoing statement of the case, it will have been seen that the libelants agreed in writing, for certain stated compensation, to render their services to the appellant in remote waters where the season for conducting fishing operations is extremely short, and in which enterprise the appellant had a large amount of money invested;

and, after having entered upon the discharge of their contract, and at a time when it was impossible for the appellant to secure other men in their places, the libelants, without any valid cause, absolutely refused to continue the services they were under contract to perform unless the appellant would consent to pay them more money. Consent to such a demand, under such circumstances, if given, was, in our opinion, without consideration, for the reason that it was based solely upon the libelants' agreement to render the exact services, and none other, that they were already under contract to render. The case shows that they willfully and arbitrarily broke that obligation. As a matter of course, they were liable to the appellant in damages, and it is quite probable, as suggested by the court below in its opinion, that they may have been unable to respond in damages. But we are unable to agree with the conclusions there drawn, from these facts, in these words:

> Under such circumstances, it would be strange, indeed, if the law would not permit the defendant to waive the damages caused by the libelants' breach, and enter into the contract sued upon,—a contract mutually beneficial to all the parties thereto, in that it gave to the libelants reasonable compensation for their labor, and enabled the defendant to employ to advantage the large capital it had invested in its canning and fishing plant.

[7]   Certainly, it cannot be justly held, upon the record in this case, that there was any voluntary waiver on the part of the appellant of the breach of the original contract. The company itself knew nothing of such breach until the expedition returned to San Francisco, and the testimony is uncontradicted that its superintendent at Pyramid Harbor, who, it is claimed, made on its behalf the contract sued on, distinctly informed the libelants that he had no power to alter the original or to make a new contract, and it would, of course, follow that, if he had no power to change the original, he would have no authority to waive any rights thereunder. The circumstances of the present case bring it, we think, directly within the sound and just observations of the supreme court of Minnesota in the case of *King v. Railway Co.*, 61 Minn. 482, 63 N.W. 1105:

[margin note: The company itself did not know]

> No astute reasoning can change the plain fact that the party who refuses to perform, and thereby coerces a promise from the other party to the contract to pay him an increased compensation for doing that which he is legally bound to do, takes an unjustifiable advantage of the necessities of the other party. Surely it would be a travesty of justice to hold that the party so making the promise for extra pay was estopped from asserting that the promise was without consideration. A party cannot lay the foundation of an estoppel by his own wrong, where the promise is simply a repetition of a subsisting legal promise. There can be no consideration for the promise of the other party, and there is no

warrant for inferring that the parties have voluntarily rescinded or modified their contract. The promise cannot be legally enforced, although the other party has completed his contract in reliance upon it.

[8] In *Lingenfelder v. Brewing Co.*, 103 Mo. 578, 15 S.W. 844, the court, in holding void a contract by which the owner of a building agreed to pay its architect an additional sum because of his refusal to otherwise proceed with the contract, said:

It is urged upon us by respondents that this was a new contract. New in what? Jungenfeld was bound by his contract to design and supervise this building. Under the new promise, he was not to do anything more or anything different. What benefit was to accrue to Wainwright? He was to receive the same service from Jungenfeld under the new, that Jungenfeld was bound to tender under the original, contract. What loss, trouble, or inconvenience could result to Jungenfeld that he had not already assumed? No amount of metaphysical reasoning can change the plain fact that Jungenfeld took advantage of Wainwright's necessities, and extorted the promise of five per cent on the refrigerator plant as the condition of his complying with his contract already entered into. Nor had he even the flimsy pretext that Wainwright had violated any of the conditions of the contract on his part. Jungenfeld himself put it upon the simple proposition that "if he, as an architect, put up the brewery, and another company put up the refrigerating machinery, it would be a detriment to the Empire Refrigerating Company," of which Jungenfeld was president. To permit plaintiff to recover under such circumstances would be to offer a premium upon bad faith, and invite men to violate their most sacred contracts that they may profit by their own wrong. That a promise to pay a man for doing that which he is already under contract to do is without consideration is conceded by respondents. The rule has been so long imbedded in the common law and decisions of the highest courts of the various states that nothing but the most cogent reasons ought to shake it. [Citing a long list of authorities.]

[The court then discussed several other cases containing equally vehement language.—Eds.]

[9] It results from the views above expressed that the judgment must be reversed, and the cause remanded, with directions to the court below to enter judgment for the respondent, with costs. It is so ordered.

PROBLEM 7-1

Tired of the condescending attitude of big city wine stewards, a tourist shoots the sommelier in a fancy French restaurant. The Wine Stewards Guild posts a reward of 100,000 francs for the arrest of the perpetrator. A police department detective catches the perp and obtains a confession from him. *– not getting a benefit*

(a)   What does this problem have to do with the principles covered in the *Alaska Packers* case?

(b)   Is the detective entitled to the reward?

(c)   Would it matter that the crime occurred in a precinct other than the detective's and that the detective did the entire investigation during off-duty hours?

already suppose to catch the bad guy

———

NOTES AND QUESTIONS

1.   In law school classes generally and in first year classes in particular, we concentrate on general, big-picture principles. You should be aware, however, that when you're advising clients on real problems there are often special rules, usually statutes but sometimes rules from case law, that give a result you would not expect. For instance, California has a statute that can trap unwary lawyers:

California Civil Code § 1542 (2005)

A general release does not extend to claims which the creditor does not know or suspect to exist in his or her favor at the time of executing the release, which if known by him or her must have materially affected his or her settlement with the debtor.

Most California lawyers are aware of the statute, but out-of-state lawyers often come into the state and pay good money to get a potential plaintiff to sign a release that reads something like this:

19 STATE RELEASE

Releasor hereby releases, acquits and forever discharges Releasee and any other persons and entities of and from any and all actions, causes of action, claims, demands, damages, costs, loss of services, expenses and compensation on account of or in any way growing out of any and all known and unknown personal injuries resulting or to result from the accident that occurred on or about October 31, 2010, at or about Hollywood and Vine Streets in Hollywood, California.

That would seem to cover the problem of injuries discovered after the release is signed, but under the California statute it doesn't. Plaintiffs, of course, later claim they didn't know the extent of their injuries at the time they signed the release.

California law allows the releasor to waive the benefit of the statute, so California lawyers routinely draft releases like this:

CALIFORNIA RELEASE

Releasor hereby releases, acquits and forever discharges Releasee and any other persons and entities of and from any and all actions, causes of action, claims, demands, damages, costs, loss of services, expenses and compensation on account of or in any way growing out of any and all known and unknown personal injuries resulting or to result from the accident that occurred on or about October 31, 2005 at or about Hollywood and Vine Streets in Hollywood, California. Releasor hereby waives the benefits of California Civil Code § 1542, which provides as follows:

> *A general release does not extend to claims which the creditor does not know or suspect to exist in his or her favor at the time of executing the release, which if known by him or her must have materially affected his or her settlement with the debtor.*

_____ (Releasor Initial Here)

This may be a case of the California courts and legislature favoring form over substance. If they really wanted to protect people from settling too cheaply because they don't know the extent of their injuries, they should provide that the benefit of the statute is non-waivable. If they want to make settlements final, they should get the statute repealed. As it is, all that happens is that sharp, local lawyers defeat the purpose of the statute and not-so-sharp, out-of-state lawyers commit malpractice.

There is, however, an argument that the present state of affairs is (1) the only practical way of dealing with the problem, and (2) a very workable compromise between competing policies, much like the *Miranda* warning from constitutional criminal procedure. Can you articulate that argument?

2.   Special rules can bite even sophisticated lawyers. California also has a law making contracts for personal services unenforceable for periods in excess of 7 years. Actor James Gandolfini used a threat that he would invoke this law to get out of his contract when he demanded that Home Box Office network ("HBO") raise his fee for playing the role of Tony Soprano on "The Sopranos" from $400,000 per episode to $800,000 per episode.

3.   Remember not to get too myopically focused on the legal aspects of the parties' relationship. In other words, don't check your common sense at the door of the law school. That would ignore the way contracts are actually modified in the real world. Many times business people solve problems in a way that is both informed and practical, even though it does not fit neatly into legal doctrine. But documenting the modification and keeping matters straight is up to counsel.

4.   The next case explores the relaxation of the pre-existing duty rule to allow for contract modification when unexpected changes in circumstances have arisen.

ANGEL V. MURRAY

Supreme Court of Rhode Island

113 R.I. 482, 322 A.2d 630 (1974)

§ 89 - Modifications

ROBERTS, CHIEF JUSTICE.

[1]   This is a civil action brought by Alfred L. Angel and others against John E. Murray, Jr., Director of Finance of the City of Newport, the city of Newport, and James L. Maher, alleging that Maher had illegally been paid the sum of $20,000 by the Director of Finance and praying that the defendant Maher be ordered to repay the city such sum. The case was heard by a justice of the Superior Court, sitting without a jury, who entered a judgment ordering Maher to repay the sum of $20,000[3] to the city of Newport. Maher is now before this court prosecuting an appeal.

[2]   The record discloses that Maher has provided the city of Newport with a refuse-collection service under a series of five-year contracts beginning in 1946. On March 12, 1964, Maher and the city entered into another such contract for a period of five years commencing on July 1, 1964, and terminating on June 30, 1969. The contract provided, among other things, that Maher would receive $137,000 per year in return for collecting and removing all combustible and noncombustible waste materials generated within the city.

[3]   In June of 1967 Maher requested an additional $10,000 per year from the city council because there had been a substantial increase in the cost of collection due to an unexpected and unanticipated increase of 400 new dwelling units. Maher's testimony, which is uncontradicted, indicates the 1964 contract had been predicated on the fact that since 1946 there had been an average increase of 20 to 25 new dwelling units per year. After a public meeting of the city council where Maher explained in detail the reasons for his request and was questioned by members of the city council, the city council agreed to pay him an additional $10,000 for the year ending on June 30, 1968. Maher made a similar request again in June of 1968 for the same reasons, and the city council again agreed to pay an additional $10,000 for the year ending on June 30, 1969.

[4]   The trial justice found that each such $10,000 payment was made in violation of law. His decision, as we understand it, is premised on two independent grounds. First, he found that the additional payments were unlawful because they had not been recommended in writing to the city council by the city manager. Second, he found that Maher was not entitled to extra compensation because the original contract already required him

trial judge reasoning

---

[3]   [$20,000 in 1974 dollars is roughly the equivalent of $102,000 in 2019 dollars using the CPI and the GNP Deflator.—Eds.]

to collect all refuse generated within the city and, therefore, included the 400 additional units. The trial justice further found that these 400 additional units were within the contemplation of the parties when they entered into the contract. It appears that he based this portion of the decision upon the rule that Maher had a preexisting duty to collect the refuse generated by the 400 additional units, and thus there was no consideration for the two additional payments.

I

[The city manager's failure to recommend additional payments in writing did not make them unlawful.]

II

[5]   Having found that the city council had the power to modify the 1964 contract without the written recommendation of the city manager, we are still confronted with the question of whether the additional payments were illegal because they were not supported by consideration.

A

[6]   As previously stated, the city council made two $10,000 payments. The first was made in June of 1967 for the year beginning on July 1, 1967, and ending on June 30, 1968. Thus, by the time this action was commenced in October of 1968, the modification was completely executed. That is, the money had been paid by the city council, and Maher had collected all of the refuse. Since consideration is only a test of the enforceability of executory promises, the presence or absence of consideration for the first payment is unimportant because the city council's agreement to make the first payment was fully executed at the time of the commencement of this action. However, since both payments were made under similar circumstances, our decision regarding the second payment (Part B, infra) is fully applicable to the first payment.

B

[7]   It is generally held that a modification of a contract is itself a contract, which is unenforceable unless supported by consideration. In *Rose v. Daniels*, 8 R.I. 381 (1866), this court held that an agreement by a debtor with a creditor to discharge a debt for a sum of money less than the amount due is unenforceable because it was not supported by consideration.

[8]   *Rose* is a perfect example of the preexisting duty rule. Under this rule an agreement modifying a contract is not supported by consideration if one of the parties to the agreement does or promises to do something that he is legally obligated to do or refrains or promises to refrain from doing something he is not legally privileged to do. In *Rose* there was no consideration for the new agreement because the debtor was already legally obligated to repay the full amount of the debt.

[9] Although the preexisting duty rule is followed by most jurisdictions, a small minority of jurisdictions, Massachusetts, for example, find that there is consideration for a promise to perform what one is already legally obligated to do because the new promise is given in place of an action for damages to secure performance. *Swartz* is premised on the theory that a promisor's forbearance of the power to breach his original agreement and be sued in an action for damages is consideration for a subsequent agreement by the promisee to pay extra compensation. This rule, however, has been widely criticized as an anomaly.

[10] The primary purpose of the preexisting duty rule is to prevent what has been referred to as the "hold-up game." A classic example of the "hold-up game" is found in *Alaska Packers' Ass'n v. Domenico*, 117 F. 99 (9th Cir. 1902). There 21 seamen entered into a written contract with Domenico to sail from San Francisco to Pyramid Harbor, Alaska. They were to work as sailors and fishermen out of Pyramid Harbor during the fishing season of 1900. The contract specified that each man would be paid $50 plus two cents for each red salmon he caught. Subsequent to their arrival at Pyramid Harbor, the men stopped work and demanded an additional $50. They threatened to return to San Francisco if Domenico did not agree to their demand. Since it was impossible for Domenico to find other men, he agreed to pay the men an additional $50. After they returned to San Francisco, Domenico refused to pay the men an additional $50. The court found that the subsequent agreement to pay the men an additional $50 was not supported by consideration because the men had a preexisting duty to work on the ship under the original contract, and thus the subsequent agreement was unenforceable.

[11] Another example of the "hold-up game" is found in the area of construction contracts. Frequently, a contractor will refuse to complete work under an unprofitable contract unless he is awarded additional compensation. The courts have generally held that a subsequent agreement to award additional compensation is unenforceable if the contractor is only performing work which would have been required of him under the original contract.

[12] These examples clearly illustrate that the courts will not enforce an agreement that has been procured by coercion or duress and will hold the parties to their original contract regardless of whether it is profitable or unprofitable. However, the courts have been reluctant to apply the preexisting duty rule when a party to a contract encounters unanticipated difficulties and the other party, not influenced by coercion or duress, voluntarily agrees to pay additional compensation for work already required to be performed under the contract. For example, the courts have found that the original contract was rescinded, *Linz v. Schuck*, 106 Md. 220, 67 A. 286 (1907); abandoned, *Connelly v. Devoe*, 37 Conn. 570 (1871); or waived, *Michaud v. McGregor*, 61 Minn. 198, 63 N.W. 479 (1895).

[13] Although the preexisting duty rule has served a useful purpose insofar as it deters parties from using coercion and duress to obtain additional compensation, it has been widely criticized as a general rule of law. With regard to the preexisting duty rule, one legal scholar has stated: "There has been a growing doubt as to the soundness of this doctrine as a matter of social policy ... In certain classes of cases, this doubt has influenced courts to refuse to apply the rule, or to ignore it, in their actual decisions. Like other legal rules, this rule is in the process of growth and change, the process being more active here than in most instances. The result of this is that a court should no longer accept this rule as fully established. It should never use it as the major premise of a decision, at least without giving careful thought to the circumstances of the particular case, to the moral deserts of the parties, and to the social feelings and interests that are involved. It is certain that the rule, stated in general and all-inclusive terms, is no longer so well-settled that a court must apply it though the heavens fall." 1A Corbin, *supra*, sec. 171; *see also* Calamari & Perillo, *supra*, § 61.

[14] The modern trend appears to recognize the necessity that courts should enforce agreements modifying contracts when unexpected or unanticipated difficulties arise during the course of the performance of a contract, even though there is no consideration for the modification, as long as the parties agree voluntarily.

[15] Under the Uniform Commercial Code, § 2–209(1), which has been adopted by 49 states, "(a)n agreement modifying a contract (for the sale of goods) needs no consideration to be binding." *See* G.L.1956 (1969 Reenactment) § 6A–2–209(1). Although at first blush this section appears to validate modifications obtained by coercion and duress, the comments to this section indicate that a modification under this section must meet the test of good faith imposed by the Code, and a modification obtained by extortion without a legitimate commercial reason is unenforceable.

[16] The modern trend away from a rigid application of the preexisting duty rule is reflected by section 89D(a) of the American Law Institute's Restatement Second of the Law of Contracts[4] which provides: "A promise modifying a duty under a contract not fully performed on either side is binding (a) if the modification is fair and equitable in view of circumstances not anticipated by the parties when the contract was made . . ."

[17] We believe that section 89D(a) is the proper rule of law and find it applicable to the facts of this case. It not only prohibits modifications obtained by coercion, duress, or extortion but also fulfills society's expectation that agreements entered into voluntarily will be enforced by

---

[4] [The court is actually referring to a draft of the R2d. In the final version, Section 89D became the present R2d § 89.—Eds.]

the courts.[5] *See generally* Horwitz, The Historical Foundations of Modern Contract Law, 87 Harv.L.Rev. 917 (1974). Section 89D(a), of course, does not compel a modification of an unprofitable or unfair contract; it only enforces a modification if the parties voluntarily agree and if (1) the promise modifying the original contract was made before the contract was fully performed on either side, (2) the underlying circumstances which prompted the modification were unanticipated by the parties, and (3) the modification is fair and equitable.

[18] The evidence, which is uncontradicted, reveals that in June of 1968 Maher requested the city council to pay him an additional $10,000 for the year beginning on July 1, 1968, and ending on June 30, 1969. This request was made at a public meeting of the city council, where Maher explained in detail his reasons for making the request. Thereafter, the city council voted to authorize the Mayor to sign an amendment to the 1964 contract which provided that Maher would receive an additional $10,000 per year for the duration of the contract. Under such circumstances we have no doubt that the city voluntarily agreed to modify the 1964 contract.

[19] Having determined the voluntariness of this agreement, we turn our attention to the three criteria delineated above. First, the modification was made in June of 1968 at a time when the five-year contract which was made in 1964 had not been fully performed by either party. Second, although the 1964 contract provided that Maher collect all refuse generated within the city, it appears this contract was premised on Maher's past experience that the number of refuse-generating units would increase at a rate of 20 to 25 per year. Furthermore, the evidence is uncontradicted that the 1967–1968 increase of 400 units "went beyond any previous expectation." Clearly, the circumstances which prompted the city council to modify the 1964 contract were unanticipated. Third, although the evidence does not indicate what proportion of the total this increase comprised, the evidence does indicate that it was a "substantial" increase. In light of this, we cannot say that the council's agreement to pay Maher the $10,000 increase was not fair and equitable in the circumstances.

[20] The judgment appealed from is reversed, and the cause is remanded to the Superior Court for entry of judgment for the defendants.

---

[5]   The drafters of section 89D(a) of the Restatement Second of the Law of Contracts use the following illustrations in comment (b) as examples of how this rule is applied to certain transactions: 1. By a written contract, A agrees to excavate a cellar for B for a stated price. Solid rock is unexpectedly encountered and A so notifies B. A and B then orally agree that A will remove the rock at a unit price which is reasonable but nine times that used in computing the original price, and A completes the job. B is bound to pay the increased amount. . . .

NOTE

Remember that the R2d is not binding on the courts and not every jurisdiction has chosen to abandon the well-established pre-existing duty rule to accept the R2d approach.

———

PROBLEM 7-2

Request for a modification

Susan Acme, President of Acme Manufacturing Company, received a call from Rolf Nadir of Nadir Supply.

"Susan, old friend, how's it going?"

"OK, Rolf. You OK? How are the kids?"

"The kids are fine, Susan, but I got bad news for you. The price of plastic has gone through the roof. I've got to raise the price 50% on that lot you just ordered."

"No way, Rolf. We've got a contract."

"Susan, I could sell that stuff to somebody else for twice what your contract calls for. The only reason I'm only raising the price 50% is that you've been such a good customer. My dad tells me stories about the way your orders saved the company when the bank was threatening to foreclose."

"We've got a contract, Rolf. I'll sue. I mean it."

"You wouldn't really do that. There's not enough money involved. Besides my lawyer would string this thing out for years, and everybody in the industry would find out you sue your old friends."

"Tell you what, Rolf, since we go back such a long time, I'll up the price 25%. Send me a confirming memorandum."

"Done."

Shortly after this conversation took place, Ms. Acme was hit by a bus and killed. The company is now run by her son Jeremy, who never liked Mr. Nadir. Jeremy has asked you whether he can avoid the price increase his mother agreed to, sue Nadir, recover damages, and if possible, wipe that company out of business. Consult U.C.C. § 2–209(1) and advise him.

———

2-209 = Good faith

NOTES

1. One of the most important skills you'll need as a lawyer is the ability to look beyond superficial characterizations of deals and see what, in terms of legal principles, is actually going on. That was what Enron was all about. The company had a lot of ducks. Its lawyers dressed them up like chickens, and the accountants, even though they heard them quack, let Enron carry them on

their financial statements as chickens. The rest, as they say, is history. Arthur Anderson, once one of the most prestigious accounting firms in the world, died in disgrace even though it was partially vindicated on appeal too late to save the firm. *See generally* Enron: Corporate Fiascos and Legal Implications (Foundation Press 2004).

2.   In one case involving Enron's mischaracterization of a deal, J.P. Morgan Chase & Company announced that it had reached a settlement that had cost it approximately a half billion dollars. Eleven insurance companies had guaranteed Morgan against losses on $965 million in sales transactions that Morgan had entered into with an Enron subsidiary. When Enron collapsed, the insurance companies took the position that they were not liable because the transactions that had been represented to them as sales transactions were actually loans. Insurance companies are prohibited by law from guaranteeing loans. The litigation was settled with the insurance companies agreeing to pay 65% of the claim and Morgan agreeing to buy $85 million in worthless bonds from the insurance companies. Bill Lerach, at the time the nation's premier plaintiff's securities litigator, said that the settlement would be useful in cases on behalf of Enron shareholders who claimed they were misled by Enron's lawyers and accountants who, in turn, had mischaracterized the loans. "The evidence that came out is very favorable to our case," Lerach said. "It shows clearly that they were disguised loans and it shows clearly that J.P. Morgan characterized them as disguised loans at the top levels of the company. Of course we will use that evidence." Later, J.P. Morgan and Citicorp agreed to pay almost $300 million dollars in fines and penalties on account of these transactions. The regulators who forced the settlement alleged that the bankers knew that these transactions were really loans but allowed them to be set up to look like sales in order to make Enron's sales look greater than they actually were and to make their debts appear less.

PROBLEM 7-3

Maria Santos operated a lawn maintenance company. When she noticed that the lawn at the Plebeian Yacht Club was not being maintained, she wrote a letter to the board of directors offering to enter into a contract to mow and fertilize the club's lawn for $2,000 a year. In response, the chair of the board (who is authorized to act for the club in all respects) wrote her as follows:

Dear Ms. Santos:

We are unable to accept your offer to enter into a maintenance contract because we are a new club and are trying to make sailing affordable to the masses. We would, however, like to engage your services to cut our grass. If you will cut the grass on our property when, in your professional judgment, it requires cutting, we will pay you $75 per cutting. In determining when our grass needs cutting, please remember that we are a group of working people. We are not Augusta National Country Club.

Sincerely,

PLEBEIAN YACHT CLUB

Joe

President

As soon as her schedule permitted, Ms. Santos went to the club, cut the grass, and submitted a bill, which was paid. This arrangement went on happily for several months until Ms. Santos' mower threw up a piece of stone which damaged a member's car. The member and the board of directors demanded that Ms. Santos pay for repairs to the car, and Ms. Santos refused, saying that the accident was unavoidable on her part because the club, which was too poor to pave its parking lot, had surfaced the lot with coarse crushed stone, much of which had, one way or another, gotten into the lawn. It was therefore impossible to avoid occasionally throwing up pieces of stone while mowing.

The club responded by writing Ms. Santos the following letter:

Dear Ms. Santos:

Because we have been unable to resolve our disagreement otherwise, we are now informing you that in the future you will be liable for any damage caused by objects thrown up by your mowers, regardless of who is at fault. By continuing to mow, you agree that you will reimburse any club member or guest whose person or property is damaged by an object thrown by any of your mowers.

Sincerely,

PLEBEIAN YACHT CLUB

Joseph S. Pack

President

The next time Ms. Santos mowed, her mower threw a stone which damaged a member's new car. Ms. Santos' lawyer has said she is not liable because (1) silence is not acceptance of the offer to modify the parties' contract and (2) there was no consideration for the modification.

Explain whether Ms. Santos is or is not contractually liable. Ignore tort theories of liability.

[handwritten, left margin: Request for a modification]

[handwritten: Yes, modification could have been new offer and was accepted by performance]

B. THE PROBLEM OF PAST CONSIDERATION

MILLS V. WYMAN

Supreme Judicial Court of Massachusetts
20 Mass. (3 Pick.) 207 (1825)

when something happens
and then we make the
promise

[1] This was an action of assumpsit brought to recover a compensation for the board, nursing, etc. of Levi Wyman, son of the defendant, from the 5th to the 20th of February 1821. The plaintiff then lived at Hartford, in Connecticut; the defendant, at Shrewsbury, in this county. Levi Wyman, at the time when the services were rendered, was about 25 years of age, and had long ceased to be a member of his father's family. He was on his return from a voyage at sea, and being suddenly taken sick at Hartford, and being poor and in distress, was relieved by the plaintiff in the manner and to the extent above stated. On the 24th of February, after all the expenses had been incurred, the defendant wrote a letter to the plaintiff, promising to pay him such expenses. There was no consideration for this promise, except what grew out of the relation which subsisted between Levi Wyman and the defendant, and Howe, J., before whom the cause was tried in the Court of Common Pleas, thinking this not sufficient to support the action, directed a nonsuit. To this direction the plaintiff filed exceptions. [We affirm.—Eds.]

[2] PARKER, CHIEF JUSTICE. General rules of law established for the protection and security of honest and fair-minded men, who may inconsiderably make promises without any equivalent, will sometimes screen men of a different character from engagements which they are bound in *foro conscientiae* to perform. This is a defect inherent in all human systems of legislation. The rule that a mere verbal promise, without any consideration, cannot be enforced by action, is universal in its application, and cannot be departed from to suit particular cases in which a refusal to perform such a promise may be disgraceful.

[3] The promise declared on in this case appears to have been made without any legal consideration. The kindness and services toward the sick son of the defendant were not bestowed at his request. The son was in no respect under the care of the defendant. He was twenty-five years old, and had long left his father's family. On his return from a foreign country, he fell sick among strangers, and the plaintiff acted the part of the good Samaritan, giving him shelter and comfort until he died. The defendant, his father, on being informed of this event, influenced by transient feeling of gratitude, promises in writing to pay the plaintiff for the expenses he had incurred. But he was determined to break this promise, and is willing to have his case appear on record as a strong example of particular injustice sometimes necessarily resulting from the operation of general rules.

no underlying, pre-existing legal obligation

Moral obligation consideration is no longer good law

[4]   It is said a moral obligation is sufficient consideration to support an express promise; and some authorities lay down the rule thus broadly; but upon examination of the cases we are satisfied that the universality of the rule cannot be supported, and that there must have been some pre-existing obligation, which has become inoperative by positive law, to form a basis for an effective promise. The cases of debts barred by the statute of limitations, of debts incurred by infants, of debts of bankrupts, are generally put for illustration of the rule. Express promises founded on such pre-existing equitable obligations may be enforced; there is a good consideration for them; they merely remove an impediment created by law to the recovery of debts honestly due, but which public policy protects the debtors from being compelled to pay.[6]

[5]   Without doubt there are great interests of society which justify withholding the coercive arm of the law from these duties of imperfect obligation, as they are called; imperfect, not because they are less binding upon the conscience than those which are called perfect, but because the wisdom of the social law does not impose sanctions upon them.

[6]   A deliberate promise, in writing, made freely and without any mistake, one which may lead the party to whom it is made into contracts and expenses, cannot be broken without a violation of moral duty. But if there was nothing paid or promised for it, the law, perhaps wisely, leaves the execution of it to the conscience of him who makes it. It is only when the party making the promise gains something, or to whom it is made loses something, that the law gives the promise validity. And in the case of the promise of the adult to pay the debt of the infant, of the debtor discharged by the statute of limitations or bankruptcy, the principle is preserved by looking back to the origin of the transaction, where an equivalent is to be found. An exact equivalent is not required by the law; for there being a consideration, the parties are left to estimate its value: though here the courts of equity will step in to relieve from gross inadequacy between the consideration and the promise.

[7]   These principles are deduced from the general current of decided cases upon the subject, as well as from the known maxims of the common law. The general position, that moral obligation is a sufficient consideration for an express promise, is to be limited in its application to cases where at some time or other a good or valuable consideration has existed.   *pre-existing duty*

[8]   A legal obligation is always a sufficient consideration to support either an express or implied promise; such as an infant's debt for

---

[6]   [What the court is referring to here is a rule that if a person promises to pay a debt that is no longer enforceable because the statute of limitations has run on the original contract or has been discharged in bankruptcy, the new promise is enforceable without new consideration. A similar rule applies to debts incurred by a minor that are reaffirmed upon reaching the age of majority.—Eds.]

necessaries, or a father's promise to pay for the support and education of his minor children. But when the child shall have attained to manhood, and shall have become his own agent in the world's business, the debts he incurs, whatever may be their nature, create no obligation; and it seems to follow, that a promise founded upon such a debt has no legally binding force.

[grown man so his debts are not his fathers]

[9] The cases of instruments under seal and certain mercantile contracts, in which consideration need not be proved, do not contradict the principles above suggested. The first import a consideration in themselves, and the second belong to a branch of the mercantile law, which has found it necessary to disregard the point of consideration in respect to instruments negotiable in their nature and essential to the interests of commerce . . .

[10] For the foregoing reasons we are all of opinion that the nonsuit directed by the Court of Common Pleas was right, and that judgment be entered thereon for the costs of the defendant.

————

WEBB v. McGOWIN

Court of Appeals of Alabama
27 Ala. App. 82, 168 So. 196 (1935)

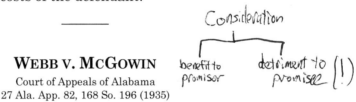

[1] Action by Joe Webb against N. Floyd McGowin and Joseph F. McGowin, as executors of the estate of J. Greeley McGowin, deceased. From a judgment of non-suit, plaintiff appeals.

[2] BRICKEN, JUSTICE. This action is an assumpsit. The complaint as originally filed was amended. The demurrers to the complaint as amended were sustained, and because of this adverse ruling by the court the plaintiff took a nonsuit, and the assignment of errors on this appeal are predicated upon said action or ruling of the court.

[3] A fair statement of the case presenting the questions for decision is set out in appellant's brief, which we adopt.

> On the 3rd day of August, 1925, appellant while in the employ of the W. T. Smith Lumber Company, a corporation, and acting within the scope of his employment, was engaged in clearing the upper floor of mill No. 2 of the company. While so engaged he was in the act of dropping a pine block from the upper floor of the mill to the ground below; this being the usual and ordinary way of clearing the floor, and it being the duty of the plaintiff in the course of his employment to so drop it. The block weighed about 75 pounds.

As appellant was in the act of dropping the block to the ground below, he was on the edge of the upper floor of the mill. As he started to turn the block loose so that it would drop to the ground, he saw J. Greeley McGowin, testator of the defendants, on the ground below and directly under where the block would have fallen had appellant turned it loose. Had he turned it loose it would have struck McGowin with such force as to have caused him serious bodily harm or death. Appellant could have remained safely on the upper floor of the mill by turning the block loose and allowing it to drop, but had he done this the block would have fallen on McGowin and caused him serious injuries or death. The only safe and reasonable way to prevent its coming into contact with McGowin was for appellant to fall with it to the ground below. Appellant did this, and by holding to the block and falling with it to the ground below, he diverted the course of its fall in such way that McGowin was not injured. In thus preventing the injuries to McGowin appellant himself received serious bodily injuries, resulting in his right leg being broken, the heel of his right foot torn off and his right arm broken. He was badly crippled for life and rendered unable to perform physical or mental labor.

On September 1, 1925, in consideration of appellant having prevented him from sustaining death or serious bodily harm and in consideration of the injuries appellant had received, McGowin agreed with him to care for and maintain him for the remainder of appellant's life at the rate of $15[7] every two weeks from the time he sustained his injuries to and during the remainder of appellant's life; it being agreed that McGowin would pay this sum to appellant for his maintenance. Under the agreement McGowin paid or caused to be paid to appellant the sum so agreed on up until McGowin's death on January 1, 1934. After his death the payment were continued to and including January 27, 1934, at which time they were discontinued. Thereupon plaintiff brought suit to recover the unpaid installments accruing up to the time of the bringing of the suit.

[4] The material averment of the different counts of the original complaint and the amended complaint are predicated upon the foregoing statement of facts.

[5] In other words, the complaint as amended averred in substance: (1) That on August 3, 1925, appellant saved J. Greeley McGowin, appellee's testator, from death or grievous bodily harm; (2) that in doing so appellant sustained bodily injury crippling him for life; (3) that in consideration of the services rendered and the injuries received by appellant, McGowin

Material Facts

---

[7] [$15 in 1925 dollars is roughly the equivalent of $215 in 2019 dollars using the CPI and the GNP Deflator.—Eds.]

material facts cont'd

agreed to care for him the remainder of appellant's life, the amount to be paid being $15 every two weeks; (4) that McGowin complied with this agreement until he died on January 1, 1934, and the payments were kept up to January 27, 1934, after which they were discontinued.

[6]   The action was for the unpaid installments accruing after January 27, 1934, to the time of the suit.

[7]   The principal grounds of demurrer to the original and amended complaint are: (1) It states no cause of action; (2) its averments show the contract was without consideration; (3) it fails to allege that McGowin had, at or before the services were rendered, agreed to pay appellant for them; (4) the contract declared on is void under the statute of frauds.

[8]   The averments of the complaint show that appellant saved McGowin from death or grievous bodily harm. This was a material benefit to him of infinitely more value than any financial aid he could have received. Receiving this benefit, McGowin became morally bound to compensate appellant for the services rendered. Recognizing his moral obligation, he expressly agreed to pay appellant as alleged in the complaint and complied with this agreement up to the time of his death; a period of more than 8 years.

[9]   Had McGowin been accidentally poisoned and a physician, without his knowledge or request, had administered an antidote, thus saving his life, a subsequent promise by McGowin to pay the physician would have been valid. Likewise, McGowin's agreement as disclosed by the complaint to compensate appellant for saving him from death or grievous bodily injury is valid and enforceable.

[10] Where the promisee cares for, improves, and preserves the property of the promisor, though done without his request, it is sufficient consideration for the promisor's subsequent agreement to pay for the service, because of the material benefit received. . . .

[11] In *Boothe v. Fitzpatrick*, 36 Vt. 681, the court held that a promise by defendant to pay for the past keeping of a bull which had escaped from defendant's premises and been cared for by plaintiff was valid, although there was no previous request, because the subsequent promise obviated that objection; it being equivalent to a previous request. On the same principle, had the promisee saved the promisor's life or his body from grievous harm, his subsequent promise to pay for the services rendered would have been valid. Such service would have been far more material than caring for his bull. Any holding that saving a man from death or grievous bodily harm is not a material benefit sufficient to uphold a subsequent promise to pay for the service, necessarily rests on the assumption that saving life and preservation of the body from harm have only a sentimental value. The converse of this is true. Life and preservation of the body have material, pecuniary values, measurable in dollars and

cents. Because of this, physicians practice their profession charging for services rendered in saving life and curing the body of its ills, and surgeons perform operations. The same is true as to the law of negligence, authorizing the assessment of damages in personal injury cases based upon the extent of the injuries, earnings, and life expectancies of those injured.

[12] In the business of life insurance, the value of a man's life is measured in dollars and cents according to his expectancy, the soundness of his body, and his ability to pay premiums. The same is true as to health and accident insurance.

[13] It follows that if, as alleged in the complaint, appellant saved J. Greeley McGowin from death or grievous bodily harm, and McGowin subsequently agreed to pay him for the service rendered, it became a valid and enforceable contract.

[14] It is well settled that a moral obligation is a sufficient consideration to support a subsequent promise to pay where the promisor has received a material benefit, although there was no original duty or liability resting on the promisor ... In the case of *State ex rel. Bayer v. Funk, supra,* the court held that a moral obligation is a sufficient consideration to support an executory promise where the promisor has received an actual pecuniary or material benefit for which he subsequently expressly promised to pay.

[15] The case at bar is clearly distinguishable from that class of cases where the consideration is a mere moral obligation or conscientious duty unconnected with receipt by the promisor of benefits of a material or pecuniary nature ... Here the promisor received a material benefit constituting a valid consideration for his promise.

[16] Some authorities hold that, for a moral obligation to support a subsequent promise to pay, there must have existed a prior legal or equitable obligation, which for some reason had become unenforceable, but for which the promisor was still morally bound. This rule, however, is subject to qualification in those cases where the promisor, having received a material benefit from the promisee, is morally bound to compensate him for the services rendered and in consideration of this obligation promises to pay. In such cases the subsequent promise to pay is an affirmance or ratification of the services rendered carrying with it the presumption that a previous request for the service was made. *McMorris v. Herndon,* 2 Bailey (S.C.) 56, 21 Am. Dec. 515; *Chadwick v. Knox,* 31 N.H. 226, 64 Am. Dec. 329; *Kenan v. Holloway,* 16 Ala. 53, 50 Am. Dec. 162; *Ross v. Pearson,* 21 Ala. 473.

[17] Under the decisions above cited, McGowin's express promise to pay appellant for the services rendered was an affirmance or ratification of what appellant had done raising the presumption that the services had been rendered at McGowin's request.

[18] The averments of the complaint show that in saving McGowin from death or grievous bodily harm, appellant was crippled for life. This was part of the consideration of the contract declared on. McGowin was benefitted. Appellant was injured. Benefit to the promisor or injury to the promisee is a sufficient legal consideration for the promisor's agreement to pay. *Fisher v. Bartlett*, 8 Greenl. (Me.) 122, 22 Am.Dec. 225; *State ex rel. Bayer v. Funk, supra.*

[19] Under the averment of the complaint the services rendered by appellant were not gratuitous. The agreement of McGowin to pay and the acceptance of payment by appellant conclusively shows the contrary.

* * *

[20] From what has been said, we are of the opinion that the court below erred in the ruling complained of; that is to say, in sustaining the demurrer, and for this error the case is reversed and remanded.

Reversed and remanded.

[21] SAMFORD, JUSTICE (concurring). The questions involved in this case are not free from doubt, and perhaps the strict letter of the rule, as stated by judges, though not always in accord, would bar recovery by plaintiff, but following the principle announced by Chief Justice Marshall in *Hoffman v. Porter*, Fed.Cas. No. 6,577, 2 Brock. 156, 159, where he says, "I do not think that law ought to be separated from justice, where it is at most doubtful," I concur in the conclusions reached by the court.

\\ One of the last cases where moral obligation plays a role

NOTES AND QUESTIONS

1.   McGowin lived approximately eight and a half years after Webb saved his life, during which he was the president of the W. T. Smith Lumber Company in Chapman, Alabama. He led that company's expansion and diversification as old timber stands were depleted. He was also active in wildlife conservation.

2.   Note that it was not Mr. McGowin who was trying to eliminate the need to pay Webb, the man who saved his life. By the time of the lawsuit, McGowin was dead. It is the executor of his estate, who is under a duty to the estate's other beneficiaries and creditors to object to questionable claims. Note also that it is likely they were the primary beneficiaries of the estate. Executors and other fiduciaries, like trustees and escrow agents, often will seek a declaratory judgment as to the validity of a claim, joining all the other parties in interest, before paying it in order to have the protection of a court order if the payment is questioned in a later lawsuit. It is useful to remember this in practice; a letter of objection to an executor, trustee, or escrow agent prior to a distribution will often cause that party to "freeze" until the parties in interest

settle their differences or an insulating "comfort" order is obtained from a court of competent jurisdiction.

3.   R2d § 86 deals with the situation presented by the cases above. How would each of them have been resolved under R2d § 86?

4.   What differences are there between the rule of R2d § 86 and the rule articulated in *Webb v. McGowin*?

———

PROBLEM 7-4

When the Malibu mansion of billionaire art collector J. Gaul Petty burned, J. Gaul rushed outside screaming "Somebody save my Van Goghs!" Kato, J. Gaul's permanent houseguest and "human pet," rushed into the mansion and attempted to save the paintings. Unfortunately, he was unsuccessful. He was beaten back by the flames and all the paintings were destroyed. When J. Gaul saw that Kato had suffered burns on his face, he told him: "Don't worry. I'll have your face fixed by the world's best plastic surgeon, and I'll have her give you a facelift while she's at it."

Shortly thereafter, J. Gaul and Kato had a falling-out and J. Gaul has come to you to see if he has to pay for Kato's plastic surgery. The scars from the burns aren't very noticeable, but Kato wants that facelift. "The world's best plastic surgeon" (the parties have stipulated as to who was meant by this) has quoted a price of $50,000 for the surgery. Kato's medical insurance will pay the first $1,200. For fixing the scars alone, the price would be $6,000.

How much should J. Gaul have to pay? *See* R2d § 86.

LAWYERING SKILLS PROBLEM: ACCORD
& SATISFACTION VS. NOVATION

When one modifies a contract and one or both parties are released from their obligations under the original contract, the parties that are released are said to have received a "novation."

This stands in contrast to what is known as an "accord and satisfaction" in which the parties enter into a new or modified contract, but the old contract remains in force (perhaps with an extension of time to delay the need for performance) until the new or modified contract is performed. The "accord" is the new or modified agreement. The "satisfaction" is the performance of the accord, and the satisfaction novates the original agreement (or releases the parties from their obligations under the original agreement).

Recall the situation in *Peterson v. Patberg*. Was the modification at issue a modification with a novation or an accord and satisfaction, or either of these things? If you were the creditor in that transaction trying to structure the modification agreement from the outset, which type of modification would you prefer? What if you were the creditor? Why?

CHAPTER 8

PROMISSORY ESTOPPEL

■ ■ ■

Promissory estoppel—"you cannot go back on your promise" for some legal or equitable reason—is relatively new to the common law tradition of contract law. It grew out of equitable estoppel, the notion that, when a person makes a representation of fact that is reasonably relied upon by another, the representing party will not be permitted to deny the truth of the prior representation.

The first opinion in this chapter, *Ricketts v. Scothorn,* took the doctrine of equitable estoppel and expanded it towards promissory estoppels as held in the second case, *Feinberg v. Pfeiffer Co.,* which holds that a promise that the promissor should reasonably expect another to rely upon and to take action or forebear from acting is binding to the extent necessary to avoid injustice.

The next case, *Salsbury v. Northwestern Bell Telephone Co.* addresses the doctrine of promissory estoppel in the context of charitable contributions, an area in which the "reliance inducing action or forbearance" element of classic promissory estoppel is somewhat troublesome. After all, with the exception of gifts pledged for specific purposes, like the construction of a building, charities rarely take action based directly upon a pledge, especially one that is part of a general pledge drive or campaign. This case closes the section of the chapter that presents the expansion and apogee of promissory estoppel.

The last two cases, *Grace v. Taco Tico* and *Loghry v. Unicover,* demonstrate limitations on the doctrine of promissory estoppel that have prevented the doctrine from expanding unfettered. As is noted at the end of the chapter, while promissory estoppel may provide relief to individual people wronged by ill-founded but reasonable reliance on the promises of others, the doctrine has not had much success or acceptance in commercial transactions, especially those involving sophisticated parties.

———

RICKETTS V. SCOTHORN

Supreme Court of Nebraska
57 Neb. 51, 77 N.W. 365 (1898)

SULLIVAN, J.

[1]   In the district court of Lancaster county the plaintiff, Katie Scothorn, recovered judgment against the defendant, Andrew D. Ricketts, as executor of the last will and testament of John C. Ricketts, deceased. The action was based upon a promissory note, of which the following is a copy: "May the first, 1891. I promise to pay to Katie Scothorn on demand, $2,000,[1] to be at 6 percent per annum. J. C. Ricketts." In the petition the plaintiff alleges that the consideration for the execution of the note was that she should surrender her employment as bookkeeper for Mayer Bros., and cease to work for a living. She also alleges that the note was given to induce her to abandon her occupation, and that, relying on it, and on the annual interest, as a means of support, she gave up the employment in which she was then engaged. These allegations of the petition are denied by the administrator.

[2]   The material facts are undisputed. They are as follows: John C. Ricketts, the maker of the note, was the grandfather of the plaintiff. Early in May—presumably on the day the note bears date—he called on her at the store where she was working. What transpired between them is thus described by Mr. Flodene, one of the plaintiff's witnesses:

> A.   Well, the old gentleman came in there one morning about nine o'clock, probably a little before or a little after, but early in the morning, and he unbuttoned his vest, and took out a piece of paper in the shape of a note; that is the way it looked to me; and he says to Miss Scothorn, "I have fixed out something so that you have not got to work anymore." He says, none of my grandchildren work, and you don't have to.
>
> Q.   Where was she?
>
> A.   She took the piece of paper and kissed him, and kissed the old gentleman, and commenced to cry.

[3]   It seems Miss Scothorn immediately notified her employer of her intention to quit work, and that she did soon after abandon her occupation. The mother of the plaintiff was a witness, and testified that she had a conversation with her father, Mr. Ricketts, shortly after the note was executed, in which he informed her that he had given the note to the plaintiff to enable her to quit work; that none of his grandchildren worked, and he did not think she ought to. For something more than a year the plaintiff was without an occupation, but in September, 1892, with the

---

[1]   [$2,000 in 1898 dollars is roughly the equivalent of $62,500 in 2019 dollars using the CPI and the GNP Deflator.—Eds.]

consent of her grandfather, and by his assistance, she secured a position as bookkeeper with Messrs. Funke & Ogden.

[4] On June 8, 1894, Mr. Ricketts died. He had paid one year's interest on the note, and a short time before his death expressed regret that he had not been able to pay the balance. In the summer or fall of 1892 he stated to his daughter, Mrs. Scothorn, that if he could sell his farm in Ohio he would pay the note out of the proceeds. He at no time repudiated the obligation.

[5] We quite agree with counsel for the defendant that upon this evidence there was nothing to submit to the jury, and that a verdict should have been directed peremptorily for one of the parties. The testimony of Flodene and Mrs. Scothorn, taken together, conclusively establishes the fact that the note was not given in consideration of the plaintiff pursuing, or agreeing to pursue, any particular line of conduct. There was no promise on the part of the plaintiff to do, or refrain from doing, anything. Her right to the money promised in the note was not made to depend upon an abandonment of her employment with Mayer Bros., and future abstention from like service. Mr. Ricketts made no condition, requirement, or request. He exacted no quid pro quo. He gave the note as a gratuity, and looked for nothing in return. So far as the evidence discloses, it was his purpose to place the plaintiff in a position of independence, where she could work or remain idle, as she might choose. The abandonment of Miss Scothorn of her position as bookkeeper was altogether voluntary. It was not an act done in fulfillment of any contract obligation assumed when she accepted the note. The instrument in suit, being given without any valuable consideration, was nothing more than a promise to make a gift in the future of the sum of money therein named.

[6] Ordinarily, such promises are not enforceable, even when put in the form of a promissory note. But it has often been held that an action on a note given to a church, college, or other like institution, upon the faith of which money has been expended or obligations incurred, could not be successfully defended on the ground of a want of consideration. In this class of cases the note in suit is nearly always spoken of as a gift or donation, but the decision is generally put on the ground that the expenditure of money or assumption of liability by the donee on the faith of the promise constitutes a valuable and sufficient consideration. It seems to us that the true reason is the preclusion of the defendant, under the doctrine of estoppel, to deny the consideration. Such seems to be the view of the matter taken by the Supreme Court of Iowa in the case of *Simpson Centenary College v. Tuttle*, 71 Iowa 596, 33 N. W. 74, where Rothrock, J., speaking for the court, said: "Where a note, however, is based on a promise to give for the support of the objects referred to, it may still be open to this defense [want of consideration], unless it shall appear that the donee has, prior to any revocation, entered into engagements, or made expenditures based on

such promise, so that he must suffer loss or injury if the note is not paid. This is based on the equitable principle that, after allowing the donee to incur obligations on the faith that the note would be paid, the donor would be estopped from pleading want of consideration." And in the case of *Gans v. Reimensnyder*, 110 Pa. St. 17, 2 Atl. 425, which was an action on a note given as a donation to a charitable object, the court said: "The fact is that, as we may see from the case of *Ryerss v. Trustees*, 33 Pa. St. 114, a contract of the kind here involved is enforceable rather by way of estoppel than on the ground of consideration in the original undertaking." It has been held that a note given in expectation of the payee performing certain services, but without any contract binding him to serve, will not support an action. *Hulse v. Hulse*, 84 E.C.L. 709. But when the payee changes his position to his disadvantage in reliance on the promise, a right of action does arise. *McClure v. Wilson*, 43 Ill. 356; *Trustees v. Garvey*, 53 Ill. 401.

issue

[7] Under the circumstances of this case, is there an equitable estoppel which ought to preclude the defendant from alleging that the note *(consideration)* in controversy is lacking in one of the essential elements of a valid contract? We think there is. An estoppel in pais is defined to be "a right arising from acts, admissions, or conduct which have induced a change of position in accordance with the real or apparent intention of the party against whom they are alleged." Mr. Pomeroy has formulated the following definition:

estoppel

"Equitable estoppel is the effect of the voluntary conduct of a party whereby he is absolutely precluded, both at law and in equity, from asserting rights which might, perhaps, have otherwise existed, either of property, of contract, or of remedy, as against another person who in good faith relied upon such conduct, and has been led thereby to change his position for the worse, and who on his part acquires some corresponding right, either of property, of contract, or of remedy." 2 Pom. Eq. Jur. 804. According to the undisputed proof, as shown by the record before us, the plaintiff was a working girl, holding a position in which she earned a salary of $10 per week. Her grandfather, desiring to put her in a position of independence, gave her the note, accompanying it with the remark that his other grandchildren did not work, and that she would not be obliged to work any longer. In effect, he suggested that she might abandon her employment, and rely in the future upon the bounty which he promised. He doubtless desired that she should give up her occupation, but, whether he did or not, it is entirely certain that he contemplated such action on her part as a reasonable and probable consequence of his gift. Having intentionally influenced the plaintiff to alter her position for the worse on the faith of the note being paid when due, it would be grossly inequitable to permit the maker, or his executor, to resist payment on the ground that the promise was given without consideration.

told her to abandon work

holding

[8] The petition charges the elements of an equitable estoppel, and the evidence conclusively establishes them. If errors intervened at the trial,

they could not have been prejudicial. A verdict for the defendant would be unwarranted. The judgment is right, and is affirmed.

In favor of granddaughter - she quit in reliance of the promise

NOTES AND QUESTIONS

Equitable estoppel is a principle that holds that where a person makes a representation that another relies upon, the person making the representation cannot deny the truth of the fact represented. For instance, A tells B that C is A's agent for the purposes of making a contract to sell A's car. When B makes a contract with C, A cannot claim that he, A, is not bound because he never really appointed C as his agent. How did the *Ricketts* court expand this doctrine?

FEINBERG V. PFEIFFER CO.

Court of Appeals of Missouri
322 S.W.2d 163 (1959)

DOERNER, COMMISSIONER.

[1]   This is a suit brought in the Circuit Court of the City of St. Louis by plaintiff, a former employee of the defendant corporation, on an alleged contract whereby defendant agreed to pay plaintiff the sum of $200 per month for life upon her retirement.[2] A jury being waived, the case was tried by the court alone. Judgment below was for plaintiff for $5,100, the amount of the pension claimed to be due as of the date of the trial, together with interest thereon, and defendant duly appealed.

[2]   The parties are in substantial agreement on the essential facts. Plaintiff began working for the defendant, a manufacturer of pharmaceuticals, in 1910, when she was but 17 years of age. By 1947 she had attained the position of bookkeeper, office manager, and assistant treasurer of the defendant, and owned 70 shares of its stock out of a total of 6,503 shares issued and outstanding. Twenty shares had been given to her by the defendant or its then president, she had purchased 20, and the remaining 30 she had acquired by a stock split or stock dividend. Over the years she received substantial dividends on the stock she owned, as did all of the other stockholders. Also, in addition to her salary, plaintiff from 1937 to 1949, inclusive, received each year a bonus varying in amount from $300 in the beginning to $2,000 in the later years.

[3]   On December 27, 1947, the annual meeting of the defendant's Board of Directors was held at the Company's offices in St. Louis, presided

37 yrs employment

---

2   [$200 in 1959 dollars is roughly the equivalent of $1,720 in 2019 dollars using the CPI and the GNP Deflator.—Eds.]

over by Max Lippman, its then president and largest individual stockholder. The other directors present were George L. Marcus, Sidney Harris, Sol Flammer, and Walter Weinstock, who, with Max Lippman, owned 5,007 of the 6,503 shares then issued and outstanding. At that meeting the Board of Directors adopted the following resolution, which, because it is the crux of the case, we quote in full:

> The Chairman thereupon pointed out that the Assistant Treasurer, Mrs. Anna Sacks Feinberg, has given the corporation many years of long and faithful service. Not only has she served the corporation devotedly, but with exceptional ability and skill. The President pointed out that although all of the officers and directors sincerely hoped and desired that Mrs. Feinberg would continue in her present position for as long as she felt able, nevertheless, in view of the length of service which she has contributed provision should be made to afford her retirement privileges and benefits which should become a firm obligation of the corporation to be available to her whenever she should see fit to retire from active duty, however many years in the future such retirement may become effective. It was, accordingly, proposed that Mrs. Feinberg's salary which is presently $350.00 per month, be increased to $400.00 per month, and that Mrs. Feinberg would be given the privilege of retiring from active duty at any time she may elect to see fit so to do upon a retirement pay of $200.00 per month for life, with the distinct understanding that the retirement plan is merely being adopted at the present time in order to afford Mrs. Feinberg security for the future and in the hope that her active services will continue with the corporation for many years to come. After due discussion and consideration, and upon motion duly made and seconded, it was—

> Resolved, that the salary of Anna Sacks Feinberg be increased from $350.00 to $400.00 per month and that she be afforded the privilege of retiring from active duty in the corporation at any time she may elect to see fit so to do upon retirement pay of $200.00 per month, for the remainder of her life.

[4] At the request of Mr. Lippman his sons-in-law, Messrs, Harris and Flammer, called upon the plaintiff at her apartment on the same day to advise her of the passage of the resolution. Plaintiff testified on cross-examination that she had no prior information that such a pension plan was contemplated, that it came as a surprise to her, and that she would have continued in her employment whether or not such a resolution had been adopted. It is clear from the evidence that there was no contract, oral or written, as to plaintiff's length of employment, and that she was free to quit, and the defendant to discharge her, at any time.

[5] Plaintiff did continue to work for the defendant through June 30, 1949, on which date she retired. In accordance with the foregoing resolution, the defendant began paying her the sum of $200 on the first of each month. Mr. Lippman died on November 18, 1949, and was succeeded as president of the company by his widow. Because of an illness, she retired from that office and was succeeded in October, 1953, by her son-in-law, Sidney M. Harris. Mr. Harris testified that while Mrs. Lippman had been president she signed the monthly pension check paid plaintiff, but fussed about doing so, and considered the payments as gifts. After his election, he stated, a new accounting firm employed by the defendant questioned the validity of the payments to plaintiff on several occasions, and in the Spring of 1956, upon its recommendation, he consulted the Company's then attorney, Mr. Ralph Kalish. Harris testified that both Ernst and Ernst, the accounting firm, and Kalish told him there was no need of giving plaintiff the money. He also stated that he had concurred in the view that the payments to plaintiff were mere gratuities rather than amounts due under a contractual obligation, and that following his discussion with the Company's attorney plaintiff was sent a check for $100 on April 1, 1956. Plaintiff declined to accept the reduced amount, and this action followed. Additional facts will be referred to later in this opinion.

[6] Appellant's first assignment of error relates to the admission in evidence of plaintiff's testimony over its objection, that at the time of trial she was sixty-five and a half years old, and that she was no longer able to engage in gainful employment because of the removal of a cancer and the performance of a colocholecystostomy operation on November 25, 1957. Its complaint is not so much that such evidence was irrelevant and immaterial, as it is that the trial court erroneously made it one basis for its decision in favor of plaintiff. As defendant concedes, the error (if it was error) in the admission of such evidence would not be a ground for reversal, since, this being a jury-waived case, we are constrained by the statutes to review it upon both the law and the evidence, and to render such judgment as the court below ought to have given. We consider only such evidence as is admissible, and need not pass upon questions of error in the admission and exclusion of evidence. However, in fairness to the trial court it should be stated that while he briefly referred to the state of plaintiff's health as of the time of the trial in his amended findings of fact, it is obvious from his amended grounds for decision and judgment that it was not, as will be seen, the basis for his decision.[3]

[7] Appellant's next complaint is that there was insufficient evidence to support the court's findings that plaintiff would not have quit

---

[3] [Is this some sort of coded message and, if so, to whom? What would a legal realist think of this statement? "Me thinks the queen protests too much?" From the time of the original and the amended grounds of decision and then this appellate opinion, the narrative that is the story of this case has hardened in a particular cast.—Eds.]

defendant's employ had she not known and relied upon the promise of defendant to pay her $200 a month for life, and the finding that, from her voluntary retirement until April 1, 1956, plaintiff relied upon the continued receipt of the installments. The trial court so found, and, in our opinion, justifiably so. Plaintiff testified, and was corroborated by Harris, defendant's witness, that knowledge of the passage of the resolution was communicated to her on December 27, 1947, the very day it was adopted. She was told at that time by Harris and Flammer, she stated, that she could take the pension as of that day, if she wished. She testified further that she continued to work for another year and a half, through June 30, 1949; that at that time her health was good and she could have continued to work, but that after working for almost forty years she thought she would take a rest. Her testimony continued:

Q.   Now, what was the reason—I'm sorry. Did you then quit the employment of the company after you—after this year and a half? A. Yes.

Q.   What was the reason that you left? A. Well, I thought almost forty years, it was a long time and I thought I would take a little rest.

Q.   Yes. A. And with the pension and what earnings my husband had, we figured we could get along.

Q.   Did you rely upon this pension? A. We certainly did.

Q.   Being paid? A. Very much so. We relied upon it because I was positive that I was going to get it as long as I lived.

Q.   Would you have left the employment of the company at that time had it not been for this pension? A. No. Mr. Allen: Just a minute, I object to that as calling for a conclusion and conjecture on the part of this witness.

The Court: It will be overruled.

Q.   (Mr. Agatstein continuing): Go ahead, now. The question is whether you would have quit the employment of the company at that time had you not relied upon this pension plan? A. No I wouldn't.

Q.   You would not have. Did you ever seek employment while this pension was being paid to you—A. (interrupting): No.

Q.   Wait a minute, at any time prior—at any other place? A. No, sir.

Q.   Were you able to hold any other employment during that time? A. Yes, I think so.

Q.   Was your health good? A. My health was good.

[8] It is obvious from the foregoing that there was ample evidence to support the findings of fact made by the court below.

[9] We come, then, to the basic issue in the case. While otherwise defined in defendant's third and fourth assignments of error, it is thus succinctly stated in the argument in its brief: " . . . whether plaintiff has proved that she has a right to recover from defendant based upon a legally binding contractual obligation to pay her $200 per month for life."

[10] It is defendant's contention, in essence, that the resolution adopted by its Board of Directors was a mere promise to make a gift, and that no contract resulted either thereby, or when plaintiff retired, because there was no consideration given or paid by the plaintiff. It urges that a promise to make a gift is not binding unless supported by a legal consideration; that the only apparent consideration for the adoption of the foregoing resolution was the "many years of long and faithful service" expressed therein; and that past services are not a valid consideration for a promise. Defendant argues further that there is nothing in the resolution which made its effectiveness conditional upon plaintiff's continued employment, that she was not under contract to work for any length of time but was free to quit whenever she wished, and that she had no contractual right to her position and could have been discharged at any time.

[11] Plaintiff concedes that a promise based upon past services would be without consideration, but contends that there were two other elements which supplied the required element: First, the continuation by plaintiff in the employ of the defendant for the period from December 27, 1947, the date when the resolution was adopted, until the date of her retirement on June 30, 1949. And, second, her change of position, i.e., her retirement, and the abandonment by her of her opportunity to continue in gainful employment, made in reliance on defendant's promise to pay her $200 per month for life.

[12] We must agree with the defendant that the evidence does not support the first of these contentions. There is no language in the resolution predicating plaintiff's right to a pension upon her continued employment. She was not required to work for the defendant for any period of time as a condition to gaining such retirement benefits. She was told that she could quit the day upon which the resolution was adopted, as she herself testified, and it is clear from her own testimony that she made no promise or agreement to continue in the employ of the defendant in return for its promise to pay her a pension. Hence there was lacking that mutuality of obligation which is essential to the validity of a contract.

[13] But as to the second of these contentions we must agree with plaintiff. By the terms of the resolution defendant promised to pay plaintiff the sum of $200 a month upon her retirement. Consideration for a promise

has been defined in the Restatement of the Law of Contracts, Section 75, as:

(1) Consideration for a promise is

    (a) an act other than a promise, or

    (b) a forbearance, or

    (c) the creation, modification or destruction of a legal relation, or

    (d) a return promise,

bargained for and given in exchange for the promise.

[14] As the parties agree, the consideration sufficient to support a contract may be either a benefit to the promisor or a loss or detriment to the promisee.[4]

[15] Section 90 of the Restatement of the Law of Contracts states that: "A promise which the promisor should reasonably expect to induce action or forbearance of a definite and substantial character on the part of the promisee and which does induce such action or forbearance is binding if injustice can be avoided only by enforcement of the promise." This doctrine has been described as that of "promissory estoppel," as distinguished from that of equitable estoppel or estoppel in pais, the reason for the differentiation being stated as follows:

> It is generally true that one who has led another to act in reasonable reliance on his representations of fact cannot afterwards in litigation between the two deny the truth of the representations, and some courts have sought to apply this principle to the formation of contracts, where, relying on a gratuitous promise, the promisee has suffered detriment. It is to be noticed, however, that such a case does not come within the ordinary definition of estoppel. If there is any representation of an existing fact, it is only that the promisor at the time of making the promise intends to fulfill it. As to such intention there is usually no misrepresentation and if there is, it is not that which has injured the promisee. In other words, he relies on a promise and not on a misstatement of fact; and the term "promissory" estoppel or something equivalent should be used to make the distinction.

Williston on Contracts, Rev. Ed., Sec. 139, Vol. 1.

---

4   [Here is that conspiracy at work again misstating the doctrine of consideration. Remember to focus on the modern statement of the consideration doctrine, from R2d § 71, focusing on the "bargained for" concept and do not be misled by language to the contrary in older cases.—Eds.]

[16] In speaking of this doctrine, Judge Learned Hand said in *Porter v. Commissioner of Internal Revenue*, 2d Cir., 60 F.2d 673, 675, that " . . . 'promissory estoppel' is now a recognized species of consideration."

* * *

[17] Was there such an act on the part of plaintiff, in reliance upon the promise contained in the resolution, as will estop the defendant, and therefore create an enforceable contract under the doctrine of promissory estoppel? We think there was. One of the illustrations cited under Section 90 of the Restatement is: "2. A promises B to pay him an annuity during B's life. B thereupon resigns a profitable employment, as A expected that he might. B receives the annuity for some years, in the meantime becoming disqualified from again obtaining good employment. A's promise is binding." This illustration is objected to by defendant as not being applicable to the case at hand. The reason advanced by it is that in the illustration B became "disqualified" from obtaining other employment before A discontinued the payments, whereas in this case the plaintiff did not discover that she had cancer and thereby became unemployable until after the defendant had discontinued the payments of $200 per month. We think the distinction is immaterial. The only reason for the reference in the illustration to the disqualification of A is in connection with that part of Section 90 regarding the prevention of injustice. The injustice would occur regardless of when the disability occurred. Would defendant contend that the contract would be enforceable if the plaintiff's illness had been discovered on March 31, 1956, the day before it discontinued the payment of the $200 a month, but not if it occurred on April 2nd, the day after? Furthermore, there are more ways to become disqualified for work, or unemployable, than as the result of illness. At the time she retired plaintiff was 57 years of age. At the time the payments were discontinued she was over 63 years of age. It is a matter of common knowledge that it is virtually impossible for a woman of that age to find satisfactory employment, much less a position comparable to that which plaintiff enjoyed at the time of her retirement.

[18] The fact of the matter is that plaintiff's subsequent illness was not the "action or forbearance" which was induced by the promise contained in the resolution. As the trial court correctly decided, such action on plaintiff's part was her retirement from a lucrative position in reliance upon defendant's promise to pay her an annuity or pension. In a very similar case, *Ricketts v. Scothorn*, 57 Neb. 51, 77 N.W.365, 367, 42 L.R.A. 794, the Supreme Court of Nebraska said:

> . . . According to the undisputed proof, as shown by the record before us, the plaintiff was a working girl, holding a position in which she earned a salary of $10 per week. Her grandfather, desiring to put her in a position of independence, gave her the note

accompanying it with the remark that his other grandchildren did not work, and that she would not be obliged to work any longer. In effect, he suggested that she might abandon her employment, and rely in the future upon the bounty which he promised. He doubtless desired that she should give up her occupation, but, whether he did or not, it is entirely certain that he contemplated such action on her part as a reasonable and probable consequence of his gift. Having intentionally influenced the plaintiff to alter her position for the worse on the faith of the note being paid when due, it would be grossly inequitable to permit the maker, or his executor, to resist payment on the ground that the promise was given without consideration.

[19] The Commissioner therefore recommends, for the reasons stated, that the judgment be affirmed.

PER CURIAM.

The foregoing opinion by DOERNER, C., is adopted as the opinion of the court. The judgment is, accordingly, affirmed.

WOLFE, P. J., and ANDERSON and RUDDY, JJ., concur.

PRACTICE TIP

This case shows something you need to keep in mind when you're in practice. The person your client is dealing with when they go into the transaction may be a nice person, but there's no guarantee that nice person won't be replaced with someone really nasty or just plain stupid whom your client will have to deal with in the future. Remind your clients of this when they tell you that you don't need to draft protections into the contract because "Joe [or Jane] would never do me wrong."

PROBLEM 8-1

You are planning to file a lawsuit to enforce a promise made to your client. Because you expect the defendant will claim there was no consideration, you want to allege that the promise is enforceable under promissory estoppel. If the jurisdiction applies R2d § 90(1), what elements or factors do you have to plead and prove?

No contract because

SALSBURY V. NORTHWESTERN BELL TELEPHONE

Supreme Court of Iowa
221 N.W.2d 609 (1974)

HARRIS, JUSTICE.

[1] This is the third appeal in which we have considered a claim of charitable subscription following the collapse of an attempt to establish a college in Charles City. In *Pappas v. Hauser*, 197 N.W.2d 607 (Iowa 1972) and *Pappas v. Bever*, 219 N.W.2d 720 (Iowa 1974) we held pledges not legally binding.[5] In this case a letter was sent by the subscriber in lieu of executing the pledge form. The trial court held the letter bound its sender. We affirm.

[2] In this law action for declaratory judgment the trial court's findings have the effect of a jury verdict. Rule 267 and 344(f)(1), Rules of Civil Procedure.

[3] John Salsbury (plaintiff) participated in the efforts to establish Charles City College (the college). He was the first and only chairman of the college's board of trustees. The funding project for the college was described in *Pappas v. Hauser, supra*. As part of the funding drive Peter Bruno, a professional fund raiser, solicited a subscription from Northwestern Bell Telephone Company (defendant). Defendant's office manager in Charles City was Daryl V. Winder who was also active in the campaign to raise money for the college. Bruno negotiated a number of times with Winder for the subscription from defendant.

[4] As a fund solicitor Winder had been given a kit which included pledge forms of the type described in *Pappas v. Hauser, supra*, and *Pappas v. Bever, supra*. Winder lacked authority to bind defendant for a pledge but conveyed the request to superiors in defendant corporation. Winder apparently did not have a pledge form available when he received defendant's consent for the subscription. Accordingly he wrote a letter to Bruno as follows:

> This is to advise you that the contribution from Northwestern Bell Telephone Co. to the Charles City College has been approved by Mr. E. A. McDaniel, District Manager, Mason City.

> The $15,000[6] contribution will be made over a three year period, in three equal payments. Our first $5000 payment will be made in 1968.

---

[5] [The pledge cards stated: "This is a statement of intention and expectation and shall not constitute a legal obligation and shall not be legally binding in any way." *Pappas v. Hauser*, 197 N.W.2d 607, 609 (Iowa 1972).—Eds.]

[6] [$15,000 in 1974 dollars is roughly the equivalent of $76,400 in 2019 dollars using the CPI and the GNP Deflator.—Eds.]

We are very pleased to add our name to the list of contributors to this fine community undertaking.

If I can be of further assistance, please feel free to contact me.

The college and all others treated the letter exactly as another pledge card. In common with executed pledge cards it was assigned to a material supplier of the college. The letter itself was not transmitted to the supplier. A pledge card form was typed-in to reflect the $15,000 pledge though it was not signed by defendant. If any document reflecting defendant's intended contribution was forwarded in connection with the assignment to the supplier it was a copy of the typed-in pledge card.

[5] Plaintiff executed a personal guaranty in order to gain credit from the supplier. Subscription pledges secured the obligation. The supplier then assigned the pledges to American Acceptance Corporation of Philadelphia, Pennsylvania, and finally, after settling with plaintiff, American Acceptance Corporation assigned them to him. In all assignments no copy of the letter was shown or given. Plaintiff conceded he had no knowledge of the letter. He acted in the belief defendant was obligated in the same manner as those who executed pledge cards.

[6] As we have seen in the earlier cases cited the college failed after a short operation. In this appeal we are faced with the question of whether defendant is bound to pay his subscription by reason of the letter. *Pappas v. Bever, supra*, stands as authority defendant would not be bound had it executed only the pledge card.

* * *

[7] Defendant separately assigns the claim the trial court failed to apply fundamental contract principles. It is argued there was a failure of consideration because the college failed before any sums were scheduled for payment under the terms of the letter. It is also claimed the trial court should have given the letter the practical construction adopted by the college when it treated it the same as a pledge card. These assignments presuppose a charitable subscription should be viewed by routine contract standards. Many cases, including our own, have considered charitable subscriptions as desirable but enforceable only upon a showing of consideration sufficient for contractual liability.

[8] Cases throughout the country clearly reflect a conflict between the desired goal of enforcing charitable subscriptions and the realities of contract law. The result has been strained reasoning which has been the subject of considerable criticism. This criticism is directed toward efforts by the courts to secure a substitute for consideration in charitable subscriptions. These efforts were thought necessary to bind the subscriber on a contract theory. Yet, in the nature of charitable subscriptions, it is

presupposed the promise is made as a gift and not in return for consideration. 1 Williston on Contracts, Third Ed., sec.116, page 473.

[9] Consideration sufficient for a binding contract has been found under various criticized theories. *Id.* at 476–79. We have [previously] found consideration in the promises of other subscribers [but this] theory is also criticized:

> . . . The difficulty with this view is its lack of conformity to the facts. It is doubtless possible for two or more persons to make mutual promises that each will give a specified amount to a charity or other object, but in the case of ordinary charitable subscriptions, the promise of each subscriber is made directly to the charity or its trustees, and it is frequently made without any reference to the subscription of others. If induced at all by previous or expected subscriptions, this inducement only affects the motive of the subscriber; it cannot be said that the previous subscriptions were given in exchange for the later one. Indeed the earlier subscriptions would be open to the objection of being past consideration so far as a later subscription was concerned.

1 Williston on Contracts, supra, pages 476–77.

[10] In reaction to this widespread criticism a number of courts have turned to promissory estoppel as an alternative for the consideration requirement.

[11] If promissory estoppel were to be the standard or criterion for enforcement this defendant probably could not be bound on the pledge. Estoppel can never arise unless there has been reliance. Plaintiff relied on defendant's letter but not the form of it. Plaintiff conceded he had not even seen the letter until shortly before trial. And it is the form of the letter that distinguishes it from the pledge cards we have held not to be binding.

[12] We acknowledge as valid the criticism of cases which enforce charitable subscriptions only on a fictional finding of consideration. But we are reluctant to adopt promissory estoppel as the sole alternative basis for such enforcement.

> . . . [W]ide variation in reasoning indicates the difficulty of enforcing a charitable subscription on grounds of consideration. Yet, the courts have generally striven to find grounds for enforcement, indicating the depth of feeling in this country that private philanthropy serves a highly important function in our society.

> Of late, courts have tended to abandon the attempt to utilize traditional contract doctrines to sustain subscriptions and have placed their decision on grounds of promissory estoppel. Surprisingly, however, if promissory estoppel, in its traditional

form, is widely adopted as the grounds upon which such subscriptions are to be tested, fewer subscriptions are likely to be enforced than previously. Under previous holdings, despite the conceptual inadequacy of the reasoning, promises were frequently enforced without regard to detrimental reliance on the promise. It was enough that the promisor had subscribed. If enforcement of charitable subscriptions is a desirable goal, it would seem sounder to view the preponderance of the cases as supporting the proposition that a charitable subscription is enforceable without consideration and without detrimental reliance. This seems to be the position taken in Restatement Second. Recognition of such a rule would also put an end to the flood of needless litigation created by the caution of executors and administrators who, for self-protection against surcharging, will not payout on a subscription without a court decree.

Calamari & Perillo, Law of Contracts, § 103, pages 177–78.

The tentative draft of Restatement of Contracts, Second, includes a new subparagraph 2. Section 90 now reads as follows:

(1) A promise which the promisor should reasonably expect to induce action or forbearance on the part of the promisee or a third person and which does induce such action or forbearance is binding if injustice can be avoided only by enforcement of the promise. The remedy granted for breach may be limited as justice requires.

(2) A charitable subscription or a marriage settlement is binding under Subsection without proof that the promise induced action or forbearance.

[13] We believe public policy supports this view. It is more logical to bind charitable subscriptions without requiring a showing of consideration or detrimental reliance.

[14] Charitable subscriptions often serve the public interest by making possible projects which otherwise could never come about. It is true some fund raising campaigns are not conducted on a plan which calls for subscriptions to be binding. In such cases we do not hesitate to hold them not binding. However where a subscription is unequivocal the pledgor should be made to keep his word.

Affirmed.

———

NOTES AND QUESTIONS

1.   In paragraph 10, the court states that promissory estoppel is an alternative to the consideration requirement in a contract action. This is one approach, in which promissory estoppel is considered to be a consideration substitute. Another approach is to treat promissory estoppel as an entirely independent cause of action with its own elements that must be pleaded and proven and not as a "contract" action. Is this a distinction without a difference? Why would it matter?

2.   Not all courts follow the R2d standard. Some follow the more traditional rule from the original Restatement of Contracts. For example, in *Maryland Nat'l Bank v. United Jewish Appeal Fed'n of Greater Wash., Inc.*, 286 Md. 274, 407 A.2d 1130 (1979), the court discussed R2d § 90's provisions making it easier for charities to collect but decided, instead, to follow the traditional rule.

3.   Haverford College lost a suit to collect four million dollars in charitable pledges from the estate of J. Howard Marshall II. *In re Howard Marshall Charitable Remainder Annuity Trust,* 709 So.2d 662 (La.1998). Marshall, a Texas oil person, is best remembered for having married former Playboy Playmate Anna Nicole Smith when he was 89 years old and she was 27. In addition to graduating from Haverford, Mr. Marshall also graduated from Yale Law School, which may have been what made him attractive to Ms. Smith.

A jury found that Haverford hadn't been injured because it hadn't relied on Mr. Marshall's pledges but instead had named already-funded projects after him. *See* Daniel Golden, *College Finally Got Alumnus to Pledge: Next Job: Collecting,* WALL ST. J., Jul. 29, 2003 at Al, col. 1. It is not clear what effect the court gave R2d 90(2). The estate was represented by Houston lawyer Rusty Hardin, who also represented Arthur Andersen in the document-shredding case that resulted in the demise of that accounting firm.

Mr. Marshall had made a couple of million dollars in gifts to Haverford before, and Haverford had awarded honorary degrees to him and to his first wife, Bettye. It also named its Fine Arts Center for Bettye. The college's case was hampered by lack of written documentation for the pledge. One juror reported being influenced by the fact that the college kept extensive files on the Marshalls, cataloguing such things as their drinking habits. A lesson here is that you have to constantly remind your clients that the documents they generate (electronic as well as paper) will probably be discoverable in litigation and can create impressions that will influence the outcome of litigation. The record is yours to make, within the bounds of propriety, that is, and the opportunity to make a good record should not be wasted.

Mr. Marshall had also made some promises to Yale Law School, but Yale didn't pursue the matter in court. This wasn't the first time that Yale was disappointed. Elihu Yale, for whom the university was named, broke a promise to give it 200£ a year. Other schools have had similar problems. Paul Tulane died without a will, disappointing the New Orleans university named after him in the expectation it would receive his entire estate.

4.   The following case not only illustrates the operation of promissory estoppel in modern, sophisticated transactions, but it also illustrates the structure of these transactions. Take the time to map out the transaction at issue and draw a timeline of the events described. That will help you better understand the case and gain an insight on mergers and acquisitions (M & A) practice.

W.R. GRACE & CO. v. TACO TICO ACQUISITION CORP.

Court of Appeals of Georgia
216 Ga. App. 423, 454 S.E.2d 789 (1995)

BIRDSONG, PRESIDING JUDGE.

[1] W.R. Grace & Co.-Conn. ("Grace") and Del Taco Restaurants, Inc. (collectively "Del Taco"), appeal a judgment, based upon a jury verdict, in favor of Taco Tico Acquisition Corporation, Taco Tico, Inc., George W. Baker, Sr., and R. Gene Smith (collectively "Taco Tico") . . .

[2] The parties operated fast-food Mexican restaurants, Del Taco primarily in the Southeastern United States and Taco Tico primarily in the Midwest and Western United States. In 1990, Taco Tico initiated negotiations directed toward the acquisition of Del Taco. In early and mid-1990's, Taco Tico made various unsuccessful proposals, with differing funding concepts, to acquire the shares of Del Taco owned by Grace and all the publicly held shares of the corporation until finally, in August 1990, the parties executed a non-binding letter of intent that set forth the terms proposed for Taco Tico's acquisition of Del Taco. In significant part, the letter provided that Taco Tico would lease Del Taco's properties for 15 years for $3.5 million annually with an option to purchase at the end of the lease, that Grace would acquire the publicly held shares of Del Taco, and that Taco Tico would pay Grace with a $5.4 million promissory note. Additionally, as collateral for Taco Tico's lease and note payments, Grace would receive a security interest in Taco Tico's properties and warrants to purchase a controlling interest in the new company that would exist after the acquisition. The letter also provided that the agreement would remain contingent on the right of the parties to conduct further investigation of the financial condition of the other. The letter stated that the agreement was in principle only and that neither party would be obligated to complete the transaction until a final agreement was executed by the parties. More significantly, the letter stated:

> Notwithstanding the foregoing . . . or any other past, present or future written or oral indications of assent or indications of results

of negotiation or agreement to some or all matters then under negotiation, it is agreed that no party to the proposed transaction (and no person or entity related to any such party) will be under any legal obligation with respect to the proposed transaction or any similar transaction, and no offer, commitment, estoppel, undertaking or obligation of any nature whatsoever shall be implied in fact, law or equity, unless and until a formal agreement providing for the transaction containing in detailed legal form terms, conditions, representations and warranties (secured by an appropriate escrow) has been executed and delivered by all parties intended to be bound.

This paragraph sets forth the entire understanding and agreement of the parties (and all related persons and entities) with regard to the subject matter of this paragraph and supersedes all prior and contemporaneous agreements, arrangements and understandings related thereto. This paragraph may be amended, modified, superseded or cancelled only by a written instrument which specifically states that it amends this paragraph, executed by an authorized officer of each entity to be bound thereby.

[3] On the same date the parties executed a management services agreement through which Taco Tico agreed to manage the operations of Del Taco and Taco Tico while the parties attempted to complete the acquisition. This agreement provided that Taco Tico would be paid only $10 per month for these management services. Thereafter, Taco Tico began managing Del Taco and Taco Tico.

[4] Changes in economic conditions, however, apparently necessitated alterations in Taco Tico's operations and general financial conditions. As a result, Taco Tico did not attempt to complete the transaction in accordance with the letter of intent, but, instead made proposals concerning Del Taco's continued operation which differed from the terms provided in the letter of intent. Ultimately, Taco Tico was advised that the proposed acquisition would not take place, and the management agreement was terminated.

[5] Subsequently, Taco Tico sued Del Taco asserting claims for fraud and rescission of the agreement, breach of fiduciary duty, violation of the Georgia Securities Act, promissory estoppel (because of representations that the acquisition would be completed), and quantum meruit for services rendered in managing Del Taco. After the trial court granted summary judgment to Del Taco on the claims for breach of fiduciary duty and violation of the Georgia Securities Act, the case proceeded to trial on the remaining claims. Ultimately, the jury found in favor of Del Taco on the claims for fraud and rescission, but awarded damages to Taco Tico on its

claims of promissory estoppel and quantum meruit. The jury also found for Taco Tico on Del Taco's counterclaim.

[6] Del Taco contends the trial court erred by denying its motion for a directed verdict on the promissory estoppel claim because the language of the agreement between the parties specifically disclaimed reliance on future representations by either party concerning their intention to consummate the proposed deal. Del Taco further contends the jury's award of damages for quantum meruit cannot be reconciled with the jury's verdict on the fraud and rescission claims and the explicit contractual provision limiting Taco Tico's management fee to $10 a month. Taco Tico has not appealed the verdict which was adverse to its interests or the earlier grant of summary judgment. Held:

[7] In reviewing the trial court's denial of Del Taco's motion for a directed verdict, this court reviews and resolves the evidence and any doubt or ambiguity in favor of the verdict, and a directed verdict is not proper unless there is no conflict in the evidence as to any material issue and the evidence introduced, with all reasonable deductions therefrom demands a certain verdict.

[8] Del Taco's motion for a directed verdict on Taco Tico's claim for promissory estoppel was based upon Taco Tico's inability to show, as a matter of law, that it reasonably relied on any representations by Del Taco that the acquisition would be completed because the letter of intent disclaimed any reliance on such representations. Under the doctrine of promissory estoppel a "promise which the promisor should reasonably expect to induce action or forbearance on the part of the promisee or a third person and which does induce such action or forbearance is binding if injustice can be avoided only by enforcement of the promise." OCGA § 13–3–44(a). Thus, if Taco Tico could not reasonably rely on any representations made by Del Taco, promissory estoppel would not apply.

[9] Because the letter of intent signed by Taco Tico specifically states that neither party may rely on any representations made by the other party regarding whether the transaction would be consummated, we find that, as a matter of law, Taco Tico could not rely reasonably upon any alleged representations by Del Taco. This court has consistently held that disclaimers in contracts prevent justifiable reliance on other representations purportedly made by the parties ... we perceive no difference between reasonable reliance in promissory estoppel cases and justifiable reliance in other cases sufficient to warrant a different result. Therefore, the evidence presented demanded a verdict for Del Taco on these claims, and the trial court erred by denying Del Taco's motion for a directed verdict. As the cases cited by Taco Tico do not concern disclaimers that applied to both future and past promises, they are not persuasive.

[10] In this appeal, both parties to the negotiations were experienced successful businessmen who were advised by capable attorneys. Therefore, it cannot be reasonably maintained that they did not comprehend the terms of the letter of intent that they signed or that they did not understand the possibility that the transaction would not be completed. Under these circumstances, Taco Tico cannot avoid the responsibility for its actions taken in preparation for the acquisition of Del Taco based on the assumption that the transaction would be completed. Moreover, the record shows that Taco Tico did not attempt to consummate the transaction based on the terms outlined in the letter of intent.

[11] Because of the jury verdict for Del Taco on the claims for fraud and rescission, Taco Tico is bound by the express terms of the contract establishing the payment for the management services provided to Del Taco. Accordingly, we find that the trial court also erred by denying Del Taco's motion for a directed verdict on Taco Tico's claim for quantum meruit because the services for which quantum meruit were claimed were provided under an express contract. Under our law, "there can be no recovery in quantum meruit where an express contract governs all the claimed rights and responsibilities of the parties." *Lord Jeff Knitting Co. v. Lacy,* 195 Ga. App. 287, 288 (393 S.E.2d 55).

[12] The denial of appellants' motions for directed verdict must be reversed and the case remanded to the trial court with direction to enter a directed verdict for appellants on these claims.

[13] Judgment reversed with direction.

NOTE

The next case illustrates the failure of promissory estoppel to expand the protections available even to loyal employees that are hired on an "at-will" basis, by far the most common method of employment.

LOGHRY V. UNICOVER CORP.

Supreme Court of Wyoming
927 P.2d 706 (1996)

GOLDEN, JUSTICE.

[1] Following her discharge, Appellant Corey Loghry brought suit against Appellee Unicover Corporation for breach of her employment contract. In an earlier decision, this Court affirmed the district court's grant of partial summary judgment to Unicover, holding that Unicover's employee handbook did not alter Appellant Corey Loghry's at-will

employment status. *Loghry v. Unicover*, 878 P.2d 510 (Wyo. 1994). Following that decision, Loghry returned to district court pursuing claims of promissory estoppel, breach of the covenant of good faith and fair dealing under a tort theory and a related claim for punitive damages. The district court again entered summary judgment in favor of Unicover and Loghry appeals. We affirm.

Issues

[2] Loghry presents these issues for review: A. Whether the District Court erred in granting Summary Judgment by determining that promissory estoppel could not be available to the employee where a handbook disclaimer exists. B. Whether the District Court erred in granting Summary Judgment on the Plaintiff's contractual breach of the covenant of good faith and fair dealing claim. C. Whether the District Court erred in granting Summary Judgment on the tort claim for the breach of the covenant of good faith and fair dealing and the related punitive damage claim.

[3] Unicover restates the issues as: I. Did Unicover's conspicuous and effective written disclaimers which preserved Loghry's at-will employment relationship with Unicover foreclose Loghry's promissory estoppels claim based upon alleged oral statements made subsequent to her acknowledged receipt of the disclaimers? II. Is there a genuine issue of material fact that a "special relationship of trust and reliance" existed between Unicover and Loghry such to support a tort claim for breach of an "implied covenant of good faith and fair dealing" under Wyoming Law?

Facts

[4] Loghry was an administrative assistant to the director of concept development for Unicover and occasionally worked on creative projects. She developed the Lighthouse Project within the scope of her employment, but before it was marketed a competitor publicized its sale of a similar item. Suspecting that Loghry's supervisor, the director of concept development, had compromised proprietary data to the competitor, corporate officer Brian Hilt, a vice president of Unicover's sister corporation, launched an investigation. Hilt requested that Loghry turn over her files on the Lighthouse Project which she had at her home. Loghry expressed concern over her participation in the investigation of her supervisor and expressed her fear that she would lose her job if she turned over the files for an investigation targeting her supervisor. Hilt assured Loghry that she would not lose her job if she cooperated. Upon receiving Hilt's representation about her job security, Loghry turned over the files to him. In a meeting that afternoon, Hilt informed other officers of his investigation and of his assurances to Loghry. The next Monday, the president of Unicover, Jim Helzer, was informed of Hilt's actions and of Hilt's assurances to Loghry. Helzer informed Loghry's supervisor of the

investigation and the two decided that Loghry's employment should be terminated. Loghry was fired the next morning for a lack of loyalty to her supervisor.

[5] Loghry brought suit and a partial summary judgment was granted to Unicover on the issue of whether she had an implied employment contract. After this Court determined Loghry was an at-will employee and summary judgment should be affirmed on the breach of contract claim, Loghry returned to the district court to pursue claims of promissory estoppel, breach of the covenant of good faith and fair dealing under a tort theory and a related claim of punitive damages. Summary judgment was entered in favor of Unicover and Loghry appeals.

Discussion

Standard of Review

[6] Our review of a grant of summary judgment is the same as the district court. The movant has the burden of clearly demonstrating that there are no genuine issues as to any material fact and that it is entitled to judgment as a matter of law. Finding no such factual issues, we must affirm summary judgment for the appellees unless the district court committed an error of law.

Effect of Disclaimers

[7] Loghry contends that Hilt's promise must be construed as a promise of job security upon which she detrimentally relied and which now entitles her to damages under the theory of promissory estoppel. Unicover argues that promissory estoppel cannot apply as an exception to at-will employment when, at her hiring, Loghry signed a disclaimer which effectively causes her reliance on that later promise to be unreasonable. Unicover contends that the express language of its conspicuous and unambiguous disclaimers prevents the application of promissory estoppel in this case. The employment application disclaimer states:

> In consideration of my employment, I agree to conform to the rules and regulations of the Company and that my employment and compensation can be terminated, with or without cause, and with or without notice, at any time, at the option of either the Company or me. I understand that no employee, manager, or other agent of the Company other than the President of the Company, has any authority to enter into any agreement for employment for any specified period of time, or to make any agreement contrary to the foregoing. Any amendment to the foregoing must be in writing and signed by the President.

The employee handbook disclaimer states:

> The language used in this handbook is not intended to create, nor is it to be construed to constitute, a contract between the Company and any one or all of its employees. You have been hired as an at will employee, and just as you may voluntarily leave at any time, your employment and compensation may be terminated, with or without cause, and with or without notice, at any time by the Company in its sole discretion. There are no promises, express or implied, for continued employment, and no one except the Board of Directors of the Company is authorized to waive or modify these conditions of employment.

[8] The district court ruled that it did not need to decide whether promissory estoppel was an exception to the at-will doctrine because promissory estoppel could not be available to Loghry where the disclaimers effectively defeated the promissory estoppel claim. The district court granted summary judgment to Unicover on this basis. Loghry asserts the district court erred because it is a misstatement of employment law to decide that the at-will doctrine and promissory estoppel are mutually exclusive in this case.

[9] In Wyoming, employers are not obligated to provide for job security. In the absence of a job security provision, employment of an indefinite duration is presumed to be at-will and either the employee or the employer may terminate it at any time for any or no reason. *Loghry v. Unicover*, 878 P.2d 510, 512 (Wyo. 1994). Wyoming has recognized, however, that an employment handbook may imply a contractual term requiring termination for cause. *Id.* Such an implication can be avoided by a conspicuous and unambiguous disclaimer. *Id.* To date, this Court has not recognized promissory estoppel as another exception to the at-will doctrine.

[10] In this case, the application signed by Loghry formed a written, at-will employment contract which eliminated the apparent authority of lower level employees to make promises of job security and which required modification of the contract be in writing by the president of the company. Authorities note that a number of courts have recognized that this type of disclaimer is effective against subsequent oral assurances by unauthorized employees of the employer. The language of the handbook disclaimer clearly and conspicuously informed employees that the manual was not part of their employment contract and that their jobs were terminable at the will of the employer with or without reason. By utilizing these legally effective disclaimers, Unicover did not induce any reasonable expectations of job security and did not give employees any reason to rely on representations of the manual or oral representations of unauthorized employees.

[11] Loghry asserts that an at-will employee can enforce an oral assurance of job security under the theory of promissory estoppel. Wyoming recognizes promissory estoppel as a cause of action in other contexts. In an insurance context, we said, "If an unambiguous promise is made in circumstances calculated to induce reliance, and it does so, the promisee if hurt as a result can recover damages." *Doctors' Co. v. Insurance Corp. of Am.*, 864 P.2d 1018, 1029 (Wyo. 1993) (citations omitted). "The purpose of estoppel is 'to prevent an injury arising from actions or declarations which have been acted on in good faith and which would be inequitable to permit a party to retract.'" *Davis v. Davis*, 855 P.2d 342, 347–48 (Wyo. 1993) (quoting *Jankovsky v. Halladay Motors*, 482 P.2d 129, 132 (Wyo. 1971)). Promissory estoppel claims must show a clear and definite agreement; proof that the party urging the doctrine acted to its detriment in reasonable reliance on the agreement; and the equities support the enforcement of the agreement.

[12] Loghry contends Hilt's promise induced her to change her working relationship and jeopardize her job security and as a result she was unjustly terminated in retaliation for her cooperation in the investigation. Promissory estoppel requires that the promise induce action or forbearance of a definite and substantial character. As an at-will employee, any change of position by Loghry was too insubstantial to amount to reliant conduct. At best, these allegations amount to a claim that Unicover acted with a bad motive. Wyoming recognizes that the bad motives of an employer may be actionable under limited circumstances, particularly for at-will employees. Those allegations of bad motives meeting the legal requirements are actionable under a claim styled as a breach of the covenant of implied good faith and fair dealing. As Loghry pleaded a tort claim for that cause of action, the equities require that Loghry sustain her claim under it, rather than under this element of promissory estoppel.

[13] Even if we were to accept that at-will employment permits application of promissory estoppel and were to further accept that Loghry meets her factual burden on the first two elements of the doctrine, the authorities indicate that the third element requires judicial consideration of what injustice or hardship a promisee will suffer if the promise is not enforced. There is no set criteria as to demonstrating the injustice element; however, generally, a court should at least consider what the promisee's cost of reliance was and whether any other remedy is available to her. Loghry concedes that Hilt's promise that she would not be fired for cooperating in his investigation did not change her status as an at-will employee. Since she could be fired immediately for any reason or no reason, it is impossible to calculate her damages, a necessary part of establishing her promissory estoppel claim. Under the standard that a promise is binding if injustice can only be avoided by enforcement of the promise, Loghry does not demonstrate the requisite harm.

[14] As the preceding analysis demonstrates, application of promissory estoppel in the at-will employment context is not a straightforward proposition. This Court's employment law jurisprudence upholds conspicuous, unambiguous disclaimers by employers as fair notice to employees of what can be expected from the employer. In order to remain consistent, it is our view that resolution of Loghry's promissory estoppels claim requires that we give effect to the disclaimers instead of deciding under our equitable powers. By its use of disclaimers, Unicover clearly intended to protect itself from claims based upon oral representations made to employees concerning job security, and Unicover is entitled to our judgment that the disclaimer provisions are enforceable even against a promissory estoppel claim. The *Chavez* decision aptly states our basis:

> Promissory estoppel requires the party invoking the doctrine to have acted reasonably in justifiable reliance on the promise that was made [I]t was unreasonable for [Loghry] to change [her] position in reliance on oral representations contrary to an express term of an employment contract which provided that their agreement could only be modified in writing [by the President]. Were we to reach a different conclusion, we believe in effect we would be rewriting the terms of the parties' contract, and this we decline to do.

Chavez, 777 P.2d at 374 (citations omitted). There "can be no estoppel as a matter of law when the asserted reliance is not justifiable or reasonable under the circumstances of the case considered as a whole." *Davis*, 855 P.2d at 348; *Roth v. First Sec. Bank*, 684 P.2d 93, 97 (Wyo. 1984). The disclaimer that Loghry signed conspicuously and unambiguously stated that only the president had authority to alter the terms of her employment. By signing such a disclaimer, Loghry signified that she was fully informed that another officer, supervisor, or employee could not secure her position even in an extraordinary situation such as this one. Since this disclaimer informed Loghry that her employment could be terminated for any reason, even an unfair one, and since it informed her that no subsequent, unauthorized statement could alter this, she could not then reasonably rely on Hilt's assurance as a matter of law. Promissory estoppel is not available to Loghry because of the specific disclaimer language.

* * *

Conclusion

[15] Promissory estoppel is not available as a cause of action when an employment contract disclaimer makes reliance on an oral assurance unreasonable . . . The order granting summary judgment to Unicover on all issues is affirmed.

———

NOTE

There has been much academic writing about the use of promissory estoppel in business transactions. In spite of this, it is still very rare. Promissory estoppel has not had a significant impact on commercial transactions. Sidney DeLong, *The New Requirement of Enforcement: Reliance in Commercial Promissory Estoppel*, 1997 WISC. L. REV. 943, 973 (1997). *See also, David v. Snyder, Go Out and Look: The Challenge of Promissory Estoppel and Empirical Scholarship in Contract Law*, 80 TUL. L. REV. 1009 (2006).

LAWYERING SKILLS PROBLEM

Look, again, at R2d § 90(1) and determine what elements or factors need to be proven in order to state a claim under it. When your client is engaging in negotiations and making offers, how can you advise them so that they are protected from claims of promissory estoppel before the negotiation of the contract is complete?

CHAPTER 9

MISUNDERSTANDING & MISTAKE

■ ■ ■

Misunderstanding & mistake are the first of the so-called "formation defenses" that are covered in this text. Essentially, a formation defense is used to avoid finding an enforceable contract when offer, acceptance, and consideration or a valid consideration substitute are present. Other formation defenses in upcoming chapters include Misrepresentation (Chapter 10), Duress (Chapter 11), and Unconscionability (Chapter 12). There are others but they are not specifically covered in this book; they function in the same way.

When the common law lawyers approached the problem of whether or not to enforce a contract where the parties appeared to have entered into it based on a misunderstanding or under a mistaken belief, they tried to solve the problem without appearing to create any new law. They tried to apply the existing principles of contract law in a way that would produce a just result. In the first case that follows, *Raffles v. Wichelhaus*, which is one of the classics of the common law contract tradition, the court may be thought of as taking the position that there was no offer and acceptance because the offeror and the offeree were talking about two different things. This approach is preserved today in R2d § 20(1)(a), addressing the effect of misunderstanding.

If you are not used to reading nineteenth century English case reports, this one will be a little hard to follow. It is not an opinion of the court as we are used to seeing them. Instead, it is a third party account of the oral arguments and the decision the judges rendered orally upon the conclusion of the arguments all of which were conducted publicly. The first three paragraphs are the reporter's summary of the decision below and the pleadings. Then we have the argument of the plaintiff's lawyer (Milward) and that of the defendant's lawyer (Mellish). In these paragraphs, the questions and comments of the judges are shown in brackets.

The procedural posture is interesting, too. In the old pleading practice it was very common to raise a demurrer to a complaint. The demurrer is similar to the modern Federal Rule of Civil Procedure 12(b)(6) motion in that it was a device for dismissing a complaint that failed to state a cause of action for which relief could be granted. Under the old practice, however, demurrers were even more common than are 12(b)(6) motions today. The pleading practice was very rigid. It required that every element of the case to be proved had to be stated in the pleading in the correct manner. Demurrers were often sustained when the complaint contained very minor deficiencies. Originally a case that was dismissed on a demurrer could not be re-filed; in modern terminology, we would say it was "dismissed with prejudice." Many meritorious claims were lost on technicalities of pleading.

There were stories, probably apocryphal, of judges who prided themselves on how seldom they allowed the case to be decided on the merits. Later, it became the practice to sustain demurrers "with leave to amend." This meant the plaintiff could file a new complaint and try to get it right. After this changed, the demurrer was no longer a device for avoiding the merits but it was still (and perhaps is today in its modern FRCP 12(b)(6) form) a device for delay and harassment. Each time a new complaint was filed, the defendant's lawyer could wait until the last day to file before filing his demurrer to the complaint, which would then have to be set for hearing. If the demurrer was sustained, the plaintiff would have to file a new complaint and the defendant would again wait until the last day to file a demurrer. If the plaintiff's lawyer was not a capable and careful pleader, he could be strung out for months or years in this fashion.

In this case we have a more unusual pleading—a demurrer to the answer. This is a pleading that says the answer does not state a valid defense and, thus, the relief requested in the complaint should be summarily granted.

———————

R&D 20

RAFFLES V. WICHELHAUS   — Peerless rule
Court of Exchequer
2 Hurl. & C. 906 (1864)

Facts —

[1] Jan. 20, 1864.—To a declaration for not accepting Surat cotton which the defendant bought of the plaintiff "to arrive ex 'Peerless' from Bombay," the defendant pleaded that he meant a ship called the "Peerless" which sailed from Bombay in October, and the plaintiff was not ready to deliver any cotton which arrived by that ship, but only cotton which arrived by another ship called the "Peerless," which sailed from Bombay in December. Held, [by the court below] on demurrer, that the plea was a good answer [and thus suit was dismissed].

[2] Declaration. For that it was agreed between the plaintiff and the defendants, to wit, at Liverpool, that the plaintiff should sell to the defendants, and the defendants buy of the plaintiff, certain goods, to wit, 125 bales of Surat cotton, guaranteed middling fair merchant's Dhollorah, to arrive ex "Peerless" from Bombay; and that the cotton should be taken from the quay, and that the defendants would pay the plaintiff for the same at a certain rate, to wit, at the rate of 17 1/4d. per pound, within a certain

time then agreed upon after the arrival of the said goods in England. Averments: that the said goods did arrive by the said ship from Bombay in England, to wit at Liverpool, and the plaintiff was then and there ready, and willing and offered to deliver the said goods to the defendants, etc.[1] Breach: that the defendants refused to accept the said goods or pay the plaintiff for them.

[3] Plea: That the said ship mentioned in the said agreement was meant and intended by the defendants to be the ship called the "Peerless," which sailed from Bombay, to wit, in October; and that the plaintiff was not ready and willing and did not offer to deliver to the defendants any bales of cotton which arrived by the last mentioned ship, but instead thereof was only ready and willing and offered to deliver to the defendants 125 bales of Surat cotton which arrived by another and different ship, which was also called the "Peerless," and which sailed from Bombay, to wit, in December.

For the Plaintiff

[4] Milward in support of the demurrer [to the answer—Eds.]. The contract was for the sale of a number of bales of cotton of a particular description, which the plaintiff was ready to deliver. It is immaterial by what ship the cotton was to arrive, long as it was a ship called the "Peerless." The words "to arrive ex 'Peerless,'" only mean that if the vessel is lost on the voyage, the contract is to be at an end. [Pollock, C.B. It would be a question for the jury whether both parties meant the same ship called the "Peerless."] That would be so if the contract was for the sale of a ship called the "Peerless;" but it is for the sale of cotton on board a ship of that name. [Pollock, C.B. The defendant only bought that cotton which was to arrive by a particular ship. It may as well be said, that if there is a contract for the purchase of certain goods in warehouse A., that is satisfied by the delivery of goods of the same description in warehouse B.] In that case there would be goods in both warehouses; here it does not appear that the plaintiff had any goods on board the other "Peerless." [Martin, B. It is imposing on the defendant a contract different from that which he entered into. Pollock, C.B. It is like a contract for the purchase of wine coming from a particular estate in France or Spain, where there are two estates of that name.] The defendant has no right to contradict by parol evidence a written contract good upon the face of it. He does not impute misrepresentation or fraud, but only says that he fancied the ship was a different one. Intentions of no avail, unless stated at the time of the contract; [Pollock, C.B. One vessel sailed in October and the other in December.] The time of sailing is no part of the contract.

---

[1] [Modern usage would call this "tender of the goods."—Eds.]

For the Defendant

[5]   Mellish (Cohen with him), in support of the plea, There is nothing on the Face of the contract to show that any particular ship called the "Peerless" was meant; but the moment it appears that two ships called the "Peerless" were about to sail from Bombay there is a latent ambiguity, and parol evidence may be given for the purpose of showing that the defendant meant one "Peerless," and the plaintiff another. That being so, there was no consensus ad idem, and therefore no binding contract. He was then stopped by the Court.

[6]   PER CURIAM. (A) There must be judgment for the defendants . . . (A) Pollock, C.B., Martin B., and Pigott, B.

NOTES AND QUESTIONS

1.   What was the argument for the plaintiff? For the defendant?

2.   What was the holding of the court?

3.   As noted in the introduction to this chapter, R2d § 20 captures the modern version of the misunderstanding doctrine, structured to cover the situation where neither party knows of the misunderstanding, and where both or only one does.

4.   The case that follows is another of the classics. It presented more of a challenge for the judges who were trying to avoid creating any new doctrine for dealing with a mistake of fact—something different from a simple misunderstanding. The case involves the sale of a cow, and both parties were definitely referring to the same cow, but because they may have both been under a misapprehension as to its breeding capabilities, the majority wanted to avoid finding that a contract had been formed. Watch the way they do it.

SHERWOOD V. WALKER

Supreme Court of Michigan
66 Mich. 568, 33 N.W. 919 (1887)

MORSE, J.

[1]   Replevin for a cow.[2] Suit commenced in justice's court; judgment for plaintiff; appealed to circuit court of Wayne county, and verdict and

---

²   [Replevin is a common law writ for possession of an item of property other than real estate. This sentence is one of the most famous in all of contract law, perhaps because of its brevity and antiquated terminology that renders it both quaint and opaque to the uninitiated, and the fact that *Sherwood v. Walker* has been assigned reading for practically all living lawyers in the United States.—Eds.]

judgment for plaintiff in that court. The defendants bring error, and set out 25 assignments of the same. [We reverse.—Eds.]

[2]   The main controversy depends upon the construction of a contract for the sale of the cow. The plaintiff claims that the title passed, and bases his action upon such claim. The defendants contend that the contract was executory, and by its terms no title to the animal was acquired by plaintiff.[3] The defendants reside at Detroit, but are in business at Walkerville, Ontario, and have a farm at Greenfield, in Wayne county, upon which were some blooded cattle supposed to be barren as breeders. The Walkers are importers and breeders of polled Angus cattle. The plaintiff is a banker living at Plymouth, in Wayne County. He called upon the defendants at Walkerville for the purchase of some of their stock, but found none there that suited him. Meeting one of the defendants afterwards, he was informed that they had a few head upon their Greenfield farm. He was asked to go out and look at them, with the statement at the time that they were probably barren, and would not breed. May 5, 1886, plaintiff went out to Greenfield, and saw the cattle. A few days thereafter, he called upon one of the defendants with the view of purchasing a cow, known as "Rose 2d of Aberlone." After considerable talk, it was agreed that defendants would telephone Sherwood at his home in Plymouth in reference to the price. The second morning after this talk he was called up by telephone, and the terms of the sale were finally agreed upon. He was to pay five and one-half cents per pound, live weight, fifty pounds shrinkage. He was asked how he intended to take the cow home, and replied that he might ship her from King's cattle-yard. He requested defendants to confirm the sale in writing, which they did by sending him the following letter:

WALKERVILLE, May 15, 1886.

T.C. Sherwood, President, etc. DEAR SIR:

We confirm sale to you of the cow Rose 2d of Aberlone, lot 56 of our catalogue, at five and half cents per pound, less fifty pounds shrink. We enclose herewith order on Mr. Graham for the cow. You might leave check with him, or mail to us here, as you prefer.

Yours, truly,
HIRAM WALKER & SONS.

---

[3]   [An *executory* contract is one that has not been performed. If it has been performed, it is referred to as an *executed* contract. When one party has performed but the other has not, the contract is sometimes referred to as being "executory on one side."—Eds.]

The order upon Graham enclosed in the letter read as follows:

WALKERVILLE, May 15, 1886.

George Graham:

You will please deliver at King's cattle-yard to Mr. T.C. Sherwood, Plymouth, the cow Rose 2d of Aberlone, lot 56 of our catalogue. Send halter with the cow, and have her weighed.

Yours truly,

HIRAM WALKER & SONS.

[3]   On the twenty-first of the same month the plaintiff went to defendants' farm at Greenfield, and presented the order and letter to Graham, who informed him that the defendants had instructed him not to deliver the cow. Soon after, the plaintiff tendered to Hiram Walker, one of the defendants, $80, and demanded the cow. Walker refused to take the money or deliver the cow. The plaintiff then instituted this suit. After he had secured possession of the cow under the writ of replevin, the plaintiff caused her to be weighed by the constable who served the writ, at a place other than King's cattle-yard. She weighed 1,420 pounds.

[4]   When the plaintiff, upon the trial in the circuit court, had submitted his proofs showing the above transaction, defendants moved to strike out and exclude the testimony from the case, for the reason that it was irrelevant and did not tend to show that the title to the cow passed, and that it showed that the contract of sale was merely executory. The court refused the motion, and an exception was taken. The defendants then introduced evidence tending to show that at the time of the alleged sale it was believed by both the plaintiff and themselves that the cow was barren and would not breed; that she cost $850, and if not barren would be worth from $750 to $1,000; that after the date of the letter, and the order to Graham, the defendants were informed by said Graham that in his judgment the cow was with calf, and therefore they instructed him not to deliver her to plaintiff, and on the twentieth of May, 1886, telegraphed plaintiff what Graham thought about the cow being with calf, and that consequently they could not sell her. The cow had a calf in the month of October following.

* * *

[5]   It appears from the record that both parties supposed this cow was barren and would not breed, and she was sold by the pound for an insignificant sum as compared with her real value if a breeder. She was evidently sold and purchased on the relation of her value for beef, unless the plaintiff had learned of her true condition, and concealed such knowledge from the defendants. Before the plaintiff secured the possession of the animal, the defendants learned that she was with calf, and therefore of great value, and undertook to rescind the sale by refusing to deliver her.

The question arises whether they had a right to do so. The circuit judge ruled that this fact did not avoid the sale and it made no difference whether she was barren or not. I am of the opinion that the court erred in this holding. I know that this is a close question, and the dividing line between the adjudicated cases is not easily discerned. But it must be considered as well settled that a party who has given an apparent consent to a contract of sale may refuse to execute it, or he may avoid it after it has been completed, if the assent was founded, or the contract made, upon the mistake of a material fact, such as the subject-matter of the sale, the price, or some collateral fact materially inducing the agreement; and this can be done when the mistake is mutual.

[6] If there is a difference or misapprehension as to the substance of the thing bargained for; if the thing actually delivered or received is different in substance from the thing bargained for, and intended to be sold,—then there is no contract; but if it be only a difference in some quality or accident, even though the mistake may have been the actuating motive to the purchaser or seller, or both of them, yet the contract remains binding. "The difficulty in every case is to determine whether the mistake or misapprehension is as to the substance of the whole contract, going, as it were, to the root of the matter, or only to some point, even though a material point, an error as to which does not affect the substance of the whole consideration." *Kennedy v. Panama, etc., Mail Co.*, L.R. 2 Q.B. 580, 587. It has been held, in accordance with the principles above stated, that where a horse is bought under the belief that he is sound, and both vendor and vendee honestly believe him to be sound, the purchaser must stand by his bargain, and pay the full price, unless there was a warranty.

[7] It seems to me, however, in the case made by this record, that the mistake or misapprehension of the parties went to the whole substance of the agreement. If the cow was a breeder, she was worth at least $750; if barren, she was worth not over $80.[4] The parties would not have made the contract of sale except upon the understanding and belief that she was incapable of breeding, and of no use as a cow. It is true she is now the identical animal that they thought her to be when the contract was made; there is no mistake as to the identity of the creature. Yet the mistake was not of the mere quality of the animal, but went to the very nature of the thing. A barren cow is substantially a different creature than a breeding one. There is as much difference between them for all purposes of use as there is between an ox and a cow that is capable of breeding and giving milk. If the mutual mistake had simply related to the fact whether she was with calf or not for one season, then it might have been a good sale, but the mistake affected the character of the animal for all time, and for its present and ultimate use. She was not in fact the animal, or the kind of animal, the

---

[4]   [$80 in 1887 dollars is roughly the equivalent of $2,180 in 2019 dollars using the CPI and the GNP Deflator.—Eds.]

defendants intended to sell or the plaintiff to buy. She was not a barren cow, and, if this fact had been known, there would have been no contract. The mistake affected the substance of the whole consideration, and it must be considered that there was no contract to sell or sale of the cow as she actually was. The thing sold and bought had in fact no existence. She was sold as a beef creature would be sold; she is in fact a breeding cow, and a valuable one. The court should have instructed the jury that if they found that the cow was sold, or contracted to be sold, upon the understanding of both parties that she was barren, and useless for the purpose of breeding, and that in fact she was not barren, but capable of breeding, then the defendants had a right to rescind, and to refuse to deliver, and the verdict should be in their favor.

[8] The judgment of the court below must be reversed, and a new trial granted, with costs of this court to defendants.

CAMPBELL, C.J., and CHAMPLIN, J., concurred.

SHERWOOD, J., (dissenting.)

[9] I do not concur in the opinion given by my brethren in this case. I think the judgments before the justice and at the circuit were right . . .

* * *

[10] There is no question but that the defendants sold the cow representing her of the breed and quality they believed the cow to be, and that the purchaser so understood it. And the buyer purchased her believing her to be of the breed represented by the sellers, and possessing all the qualities stated, and even more. He believed she would breed. There is no pretense that the plaintiff bought the cow for beef, and there is nothing in the record indicating that he would have bought her at all only that he thought she might be made to breed. Under the foregoing facts—and these are all that are contained in the record material to the contract—it is held that because it turned out that the plaintiff was more correct in his judgment as to one quality of the cow than the defendants, and a quality, too, which could not by any possibility be positively known at the time by either party to exist, the contract may be annulled by the defendants at their pleasure. I know of no law, and have not been referred to any, which will justify any such holding, and I think the circuit judge was right in his construction of the contract between the parties.

———

NOTES AND QUESTIONS

1. Mutual mistake? Or a skilled (or lucky) guess and investment by Mr. Sherwood? Did the majority or the dissent get it right?

2.   Rose 2d of Aberlone is a good illustration of business valuation. If she was only "a beef creature" (paragraph 7) to be sold essentially as scrap or for liquidation, she was worth approximately $80. If she could breed and produce milk, she was worth "at least $750" (*Id.*). What explains the $670 differential? The answer is the net present value of the income that Rose could generate over her useful life. In other words, after subtracting the cost of her care, feeding, and housing, she was expected to produce a series of cash flows with a discounted present value of $750 as a breeder but only $80 if she was to go to immediate slaughter. Business assets like Rose, an apartment building, a copyright-protected song, patented process, or a newly-minted associate attorney are viewed, for business purposes, as things that will produce a stream of positive and negative cash flows that, when discounted their net present value, determine their value. Objective as that sounds, valuation is difficult. One must accurately forecast not only the revenues and their timing—in Rose's case, the cash from slaughter or the sales of milk and calves—but also the operating costs—here, Rose's care, feeding, and housing— as well as the appropriate discount rate or required rate of return (to perform the discounting of future dollars into present value dollars). Changing any of these variables changes the indicated value.

3.   Notice the final five words of paragraph 6 in *Sherwood v. Walker*: "unless there was a warranty." A warranty is a statement of fact about the subject matter of a contract in which the warranting party states the condition of the subject matter. If the condition of the subject matter is later proved to be different than as stated, the party in whose favor the warranty runs may seek damages from the warranting party for breach of warranty. Warranties are used in contracts to allocate risk between the parties. They are essentially what are colloquially known as "guarantees" for, say, a car, mattress, or vacuum cleaner. (Legal guaranties like the one at issue in the *Frishman* case in Chapter 5 are different and are never spelled with the double "e" at the end). In many jurisdictions, warranties terminate at the "closing"—when the main consideration is exchanged—unless the contract specifies that they survive.

4.   Plaintiff Sherwood was a gentleman farmer who made his living as president of the Plymouth National Bank at the time of the lawsuit. Later, he would be appointed to be Michigan's first State Commissioner of Banking.

5.   The defendants are the same Hiram Walker & Sons that make alcoholic beverages. Anticipating prohibition in the United States, Mr. Walker built his distillery on the Canadian side of the Detroit River. He proved prescient, if not about 60 years early, in his anticipation. Attempting to stigmatize him, his competitors secured the passage of a law requiring alcoholic beverage manufacturers to label their product with their country of origin. He managed to turn this tactic in his favor through an advertising campaign for the "Canadian Club" brand of whiskey that hinted that Canadian whiskey was superior to its United States counterpart.

6.   After this appeal, on remand a circuit court jury sided with Sherwood. No further appeal was taken and Walker lost Rose. She went on to have five

additional calves. She had previously calved in 1883, but not in 1884 or 1885, the two years prior to the events involved in *Sherwood v. Walker*.

PROBLEM 9-1

It is 1890. You are a lawyer in Michigan. You are representing a party in a case on appeal to the Michigan Supreme Court, which recently decided *Sherwood v. Walker*. The case involves the sale of a mine. At the time the contract of sale was made, both parties believed that there was sufficient commercial grade iron ore in the mine to make the mine worth the contract price. When it was discovered that there was substantially less ore than the parties thought, the buyer tried to back out. At trial, the court issued the following "Findings of Fact:"

1.   The mine contains iron ore, but it does not contain sufficient ore to be commercially viable.

2.   Because the mine does contain iron ore, it is NOT different in substance from what the parties bargained for.

3.   Both parties bargained for a mine that contained sufficient commercial grade iron ore to make the mine worth the contract price.

4.   The buyer would not have entered into the contract if it had known the true facts.

You are bound by the above findings of fact, which the Supreme Court will accept as true. Never mind the fact that some of these "findings of fact" might more properly be categorized as questions of law, which the court could decide *de novo* on appeal. The Court has indicated it will not go into that issue.

Assume that the only reported decision relevant to the case is *Sherwood v. Walker*. Locate, in that case:

(a)   the language most favorable to the buyer.

(b)   the language most favorable to the seller.

WOOD V. BOYNTON

Supreme Court of Wisconsin
64 Wis. 265, 25 N.W. 42 (1885)

TAYLOR, J.

[1]   This action was brought in the circuit court for Milwaukee county to recover the possession of an uncut diamond of the alleged value of

$1,000.[5] The case was tried in the circuit court, and after hearing all the evidence in the case, the learned circuit judge directed the jury to find a verdict for the defendants. The plaintiff excepted to such instruction, and, after a verdict was rendered for the defendants, moved for a new trial upon the minutes of the judge. The motion was denied, and the plaintiff duly excepted, and after judgment was entered in favor of the defendants, appealed to this court. The defendants are partners in the jewelry business. On the trial it appeared that on and before the twenty-eighth of December, 1883, the plaintiff was the owner of and in the possession of a small stone of the nature and value of which she was ignorant; that on that day she sold it to one of the defendants for the sum of one dollar. Afterwards it was ascertained that the stone was a rough diamond, and of the value of about $700. After hearing this fact the plaintiff tendered the defendants the one dollar, and ten cents as interest, and demanded a return of the stone to her. The defendants refused to deliver it, and therefore she commenced this action.

[2]   The plaintiff testified to the circumstances attending the sale of the stone to Mr. Samuel B. Boynton, as follows:

> The first time Boynton saw that stone he was talking about buying the topaz, or whatever it is, in September or October. I went into the store to get a little pin mended, and I had it in a small box,—the pin,—a small earring; . . . this stone, and a broken sleeve-button were in the box. Mr. Boynton turned to give me a check for my pin. I thought I would ask him what the stone was, and I took it out of the box and asked him to please tell me what that was. He took it in his hand and seemed some time looking at it. I told him I had been told it was a topaz, and he said it might be. He says, "I would buy this; would you sell it?" I told him I did not know but what I would. What would it be worth? And he said he did not know; he would give me a dollar and keep it as a specimen, and I told him I would not sell it; and it was certainly pretty to look at. He asked me where I found it, and I told him in Eagle. He asked about how far out, and I said right in the village, and I went out. Afterwards, and about the twenty-eighth of December, I needed money pretty badly, and thought every dollar would help, and I took it back to Mr. Boynton and told him I had brought back the topaz, and he says, "Well, yes; what did I offer you for it?" and I says, "One dollar;" and he stepped to the change drawer and gave me the dollar, and I went out. In another part of her testimony she says: "Before I sold the stone I had no knowledge whatever that it was a diamond. I told him that I had been advised that it was probably a topaz, and he said probably it

---

[5]   [$1,000 in 1885 dollars is roughly the equivalent of $27,000 in 2019 dollars using the CPI and the GNP Deflator.—Eds.]

was. The stone was about the size of a canary bird's egg, nearly the shape of an egg,—worn pointed at one end; it was nearly straw color,—a little darker." She also testified that before this action was commenced she tendered the defendants $1.10, and demanded the return of the stone, which they refused. This is substantially all the evidence of what took place at and before the sale to the defendants, as testified to by the plaintiff herself. She produced no other witness on that point.

[3] The evidence on the part of the defendant is not very different from the version given by the plaintiff, and certainly is not more favorable to the plaintiff. Mr. Samuel B. Boynton, the defendant to whom the stone was sold, testified that at the time he bought this stone, he had never seen an uncut diamond; had seen cut diamonds, but they are quite different from the uncut ones; "he had no idea this was a diamond, and it never entered his brain at the time." Considerable evidence was given as to what took place after the sale and purchase, but that evidence has very little if any bearing upon the main point in the case.

[4] This evidence clearly shows that the plaintiff sold the stone in question to the defendants, and delivered it to them in December, 1883, for a consideration of one dollar. By such sale the title to the stone passed by the sale and delivery to the defendants. How has that title been divested and again vested in the plaintiff? The contention of the learned counsel for the appellant is that the title became vested in the plaintiff by the tender to the Boyntons of the purchase money with interest, and a demand of a return of the stone to her. Unless such tender and demand revested the title in the appellant, she cannot maintain her action. The only question in the case is whether there was anything in the sale which entitled the vendor (the appellant) to rescind the sale and so revest the title in her. The only reasons we know of for rescinding a sale and revesting the title in the vendor so that he may maintain an action at law for the recovery of the possession against his vendee are (1) that the vendee was guilty of some fraud in procuring a sale to be made to him; (2) that there was a mistake made by the vendor in delivering an article which was not the article sold,—a mistake in fact as to the identity of the thing sold with the thing delivered upon the sale. This last is not in reality a rescission of the sale made, as the thing delivered was not the thing sold, and no title ever passed to the vendee by such delivery.

[5] In this case, upon the plaintiff's own evidence, there can be no just ground for alleging that she was induced to make the sale she did by any fraud or unfair dealings on the part of Mr. Boynton. Both were entirely ignorant at the time of the character of the stone and of its intrinsic value. Mr. Boynton was not an expert in uncut diamonds, and had made no examination of the stone, except to take it in his hand and look at it before he made the offer of one dollar, which was refused at the time, and

afterwards accepted without any comment or further examination made by Mr. Boynton. The appellant had the stone in her possession for a long time, and it appears from her own statement that she had made some inquiry as to its nature and qualities. If she chose to sell it without further investigation as to its intrinsic value to a person who was guilty of no fraud or unfairness which induced her to sell it for a small sum, she cannot repudiate the sale because it is afterwards ascertained that she made a bad bargain. There is no pretense of any mistake as to the identity of the thing sold. It was produced by the plaintiff and exhibited to the vendee before the sale was made, and the thing sold was delivered to the vendee when the purchase price was paid. Suppose the appellant had produced the stone, and said she had been told it was a diamond, and she believed it was, but had no knowledge herself as to its character or value, and Mr. Boynton had given her $500 for it, could he have rescinded the sale if it had turned out to be a topaz or any other stone of very small value? Could Mr. Boynton have rescinded the sale on the ground of mistake? Clearly not, nor could he rescind it on the ground that there had been a breach of warranty, because there was no warranty, nor could he rescind it on the ground of fraud, unless he could show that she falsely declared that she had been told it was a diamond, or, if she had been so told, still she knew it was not a diamond.

[6] It is urged, with a good deal of earnestness, on the part of the counsel for the appellant that, because it has turned out that the stone was immensely more valuable than the parties at the time of the sale supposed it was, such fact alone is a ground for the rescission of the sale, and that fact was evidence of fraud on the part of the vendee. Whether inadequacy of price is to be received as evidence of fraud, even in a suit in equity to avoid a sale, depends upon the facts known to the parties at the time the sale is made. When this sale was made the value of the thing sold was open to the investigation of both parties, neither knowing its intrinsic value, and, so far as the evidence in this case shows, both supposed that the price paid was adequate. How can fraud be predicated upon such a sale, even though after investigation showed that the intrinsic value of the thing sold was hundreds of times greater than the price paid? It certainly shows no such fraud as would authorize the vendor to rescind the contract and bring an action at law to recover the possession of the thing sold. Whether that fact would have any influence in an action in equity to avoid the sale we need not consider.

[7] We can find nothing in the evidence from which it could be justly inferred that Mr. Boynton, at the time he offered the plaintiff one dollar for the stone, had any knowledge of the real value of the stone, or that he entertained even a belief that the stone was a diamond. It cannot, therefore, be said that there was a suppression of knowledge on the part of the defendant as to the value of the stone which a court of equity might seize upon to avoid the sale.... The following cases show that, in the

absence of fraud or warranty, the value of the property sold, as compared with the price paid, is no ground for a rescission of a sale. However unfortunate the plaintiff may have been in selling this valuable stone for a mere nominal sum, she has failed entirely to make out a case either of fraud or mistake in the sale such as will entitle her to a rescission of such sale so as to recover the property sold in an action at law.

Holding

[8] The judgment of the circuit court is affirmed.

should be looked at under 153 — should be unilateral not mutual

PROBLEM 9-2

UCC apples are movable 1-103 b; UCC is silent on mistake, bring in 152, 153, 154

Buyer and Seller entered into a contract for the purchase and sale of a quantity of apples. Both Buyer and Seller believed that the apples had little value because they were being stored in a Latin American city that had been surrounded by a rebel army and would rot before the siege was lifted. As a result, the apples were sold for a small fraction of their market price. Unknown to either party, at the time the contract was entered into the local government had already routed the rebels, and the Seller's agents were in the process of arranging shipment of the apples to the United States.

— 154 mutual

(a) How would this case be analyzed under the rule of *Sherwood v. Walker?*

(b) How would this case be analyzed under R2d §§ 152, 154? *under 152 need mutual mistake*

The seller here 154 depends on if one bears the risk of mistake

(c) How would this case be analyzed under UNIDROIT articles 3.4 and 3.5?

(d) Would the result be the same if, at the time the contract was made, the city was still surrounded with no expectation that the siege would be lifted, but shortly after the contract was made the government forces launched a bold and totally unexpected offensive which lifted the siege?

NOTES AND QUESTIONS

1. *The Modern Bases of Mistake*

Contracts are intended to allow parties to plan and, to the extent feasible, to reduce or allocate their risks. It is generally accepted that courts should honor parties' risk allocations. When the parties don't spell out the risk allocation in their agreement, however, the court has to allocate the risk in the way it thinks the parties would have intended had they thought about it. The modern law of mistake is based on the premise that parties entering into a contract do not usually intend to assume the risk of a mutual mistake of fact that materially alters the benefits and burdens of the deal.

Mistake is covered in Chapter 6, sections 151 to 158 of the R2d and articles 3.4 to 3.7 of the UNIDROIT principles.

2. *Fixed Price and Cost-Plus Contracts*

Parties entering into contracts often have to choose between fixed-price and cost-plus contracts. In a fixed-price contract, the person performing the services (usually referred to as the "contractor") agrees to do the job for a set price. In a cost-plus contract, the contractor agrees to do the job for the amount of the costs she incurs (materials, subcontractors, etc.) plus an additional amount (often a percentage of the costs) to cover her overhead and provide a profit.

The main effect of the choice between a fixed-price contract and a cost-plus contract is to allocate the risk that the job will be more (or, theoretically at least, less) difficult than the parties anticipated. A fixed-price contract allocates that risk to the contractor. If the job turns out to be more difficult than expected to complete, the contractor loses. A cost-plus contract allocates that risk to the person employing the contractor. If on a cost-plus contract the job turns out to take more time or materials than expected, the customer bears the extra cost. Because on a fixed-price contract, the contractor assumes the risk that the job will be more expensive than anticipated, courts are very reluctant to let contractors out of their fixed-price contracts on the basis of mistake. To do so would be to deprive the customer of what he bargained for.

It stands to reason that a contractor will charge a higher price on a fixed-price contract than on a cost-plus contract. We'll discuss this more rigorously shortly, but first let's consider why parties might prefer one type of contract over the other. One reason is that one party or the other might be better able to bear the financial risk. For example, a family entering into a contract to have a home built or remodeled might have only a certain amount of money available and they need to be sure the cost won't exceed that amount, so they would need to enter into a fixed-price contract. On the other hand, a company developing a new weapons system or information management system for the government might not have the wherewithal to absorb billions of dollars of losses, so it would need to enter into a cost-plus contract.

A fixed-price contract gives an incentive to the contractor to be efficient. The fact that cost-plus contracts don't provide such an incentive is a criticism often leveled at government cost-plus contracts. As a result, governments and other parties that routinely enter into cost-plus contracts have developed sophisticated variations on the simple cost-plus contract that provide incentives to meet budget goals.

Fixed-price contracts give the customer the opportunity to make potential contractors compete against each other. The customer can solicit several bids and take the lowest one. Usually this is done informally, but in some cases it is done in the manner of a formal auction, usually with sealed bids. Laws often require government contracts to be awarded on the basis of sealed bids. This is done in an attempt to prevent or reduce favoritism and corruption.

Sometimes a customer will get a bid from a contractor, disclose it to a second contractor and ask that contractor to beat it. This is known as "shopping the bid" and is frowned on in most industries. Some contractors will refuse to deal with customers known to be bid shoppers. On the other hand, shopping the bid tends to encourage competition, drive down prices, and benefit consumers, at least if there is a large market and good information involved. Consider how the development of Internet based price comparisons has benefitted consumers of goods and services in just this way by reducing the cost of wide comparison shopping and allowing continuous "bid shopping" through on-line auctions.

An advantage of the cost-plus contract is that it allows for easy modification of the deal. If you decide you want marble instead of linoleum in the entry of the home you're building on a cost-plus basis, you just tell the contractor and she adds the actual cost plus her fee to the price. If you have a fixed-price contract, you have to negotiate the amount of the increased cost every time you make a change. This is one reason that the Department of Defense procures weapons systems on a cost-plus basis. It wants to have the flexibility to improve the technology as the project develops.

3.   *Fixed Fee Contracts in Legal Work*

A considerable amount of legal business is billed on an hourly basis, which is a form of cost-plus contract. The client takes the risk that the matter will take longer than anticipated, which it often does. Clients are putting pressure on lawyers to bill business matters on a fixed-fee basis. Lawyers are generally resisting this. A fixed fee gives the lawyer an incentive to overlook problems rather than find them and fix them. A lawyer on a fixed fee also tends to be less effective as a negotiator. Legal negotiations are often won by the person who is willing to sit and argue until the other person gives in.

On the other hand, lawyers working on a fixed fee basis have a strong incentive to conduct their work efficiently, and conduct only those tasks that have a strong likelihood of resulting in a payoff or acceptable resolution. Once legal services are priced like widgets, the incentive is to produce widgets for less. This has already happened in the insurance defense field and in employer-side labor law practice. It is spreading into standardized commercial finance and lending practice and will probably continue to spread through the legal profession.

4.   *What Alan Greenspan Doesn't Want You to Know*

Aluminum Company of America v. Essex Group, Inc., 499 F.Supp. 53 (W.D. Pa. 1980), is an interesting mistake case involving a large and sophisticated business deal. The parties entered into a long-term (21 years) contract under which ALCOA was to convert ore owned by Essex into aluminum and deliver the finished aluminum to Essex. The price for the conversion was based on a complex formula designed to assure that Essex received aluminum at a price below the normal market price while ALCOA made a reasonable, but not excessive, profit. To develop the formula, the parties hired Alan Greenspan, who later became Chairman of the Federal

Reserve at the close of the 20th Century, but was then an independent consultant. Greenspan's formula provided that part of the price would increase in proportion to ALCOA's average hourly labor cost. This was of course to compensate ALCOA for increases in the cost of the labor expended on the conversion. Another component of the price was to rise in proportion to the Wholesale Price Index. (The Wholesale Price Index, which has since been modified and renamed the Producer Price Index, is like the Consumer Price Index in that it measures increases and decreases in prices. The Consumer Price Index measures how much consumers pay for a range of things consumers regularly purchase. The Wholesale Price Index measured the prices that businesses paid for a range of things that businesses purchase.) This was designed to compensate ALCOA for increases in its non-labor costs.

The formula was designed to give ALCOA a "net income" of between one and seven cents per pound of aluminum processed over and above ALCOA's costs of labor, materials, and other things directly attributable to the processing of the aluminum. This "net income" was to compensate ALCOA for the capital invested in its plants and equipment and for its management and overhead costs. It was also intended to give ALCOA a profit. Essex on the other hand, was intended to have an assured source of aluminum from which it could make wire.

Unfortunately, Mr. Greenspan's formula, for which we can assume he was paid a handsome fee, did not work as advertised. The 1973 oil embargo, an event that may have produced more contract law than any other single event in history, caused electricity prices to rise dramatically. New pollution control regulations added to the increase in electricity prices. Because aluminum production uses huge amounts of electricity, the increase in electricity prices caused ALCOA's non-labor costs to go up much more than the formula compensated them for. Electricity prices went up much more than the Wholesale Price Index did. The result of this was that ALCOA began to suffer huge losses. They estimated that if they were forced to complete the contract they would lose $75 million. At the same time, aluminum prices went up dramatically, largely because of the increase in electricity prices. This gave Essex a windfall. Instead of using all the aluminum to make wire as the parties anticipated, Essex began selling some of it at a huge profit.

ALCOA sued to get out of the contract, claiming mutual mistake (among other things). The court held in favor of ALCOA, relying in part on *Sherwood v. Walker*. Essex asserted that the mistake was not a mistake as to a present fact (which is grounds for relief), but a mistake as to a future event (which is not). The court, however, decided that the mistake was the belief that Mr. Greenspan had created a viable formula. Thus, the court said that because the formula was bad from the beginning, it was a mistake as to a present fact rather than a mistake as to a future event (whether the formula would work). Are you convinced by this distinction? Although it is hard to say categorically that the court was wrong, many are not convinced.

Essex also claimed that ALCOA had assumed the risk by not including in the contract a provision that would have limited its losses if the formula didn't work. The court didn't buy this, either. It said that ALCOA probably just believed that risk was so small that it was not worth the effort to negotiate and draft a provision covering it.

So, now you know something more about contract law and the former chairman of the Federal Reserve—a man whose forward-looking pronouncements have moved markets worldwide. His work is deemed reliable but not guaranteed—that would be an example of irrational exuberance.

JAYNES V. LOUISVILLE & NASHVILLE RAILROAD

United States District Court, Eastern District, Tennessee
560 F. Supp. 57 (1981)

NEESE, DISTRICT JUDGE.

Memorandum Opinion and Orders

[1]   This is an action by a former employee of the defendant railroad to recover damages under the Federal Employers' Liability Act (FELA), 45 U.S.C. §§ 51 et seq., 45 U.S.C. § 56. The defendant moved for a summary judgment on the ground that the claim of the plaintiff is barred by an accord and satisfaction. There being genuine issues of material fact extant between the parties concerning such affirmative defense, summary judgment is not appropriate. See Rule 56(c), Federal Rules of Civil Procedure.

[2]   It is undisputed that on May 6, 1977, in consideration of the sum of $1,312.00[6] paid to him by the defendant, the plaintiff Mr. Jaynes executed a document, agreeing to release the defendant from any claim arising out of the accident which forms the basis of this action. That release specifically encompassed " . . . injuries not now known whether or not the undersigned has been advised by doctors or others in any way."

[3]   The plaintiff seeks to avoid such release, by claiming that such was the result of a mutual mistake of the parties as to the nature of his injury. Cf. Edwards v. Western & Atlantic R., C.A. 5th (1977), 552 F.2d 137, 138 (a mutual mistake as to the expected course of healing of the plaintiff's injury, as opposed to a mutual mistake as to the nature of the injury, is not sufficient to avoid a release).

[4]   The record herein is akin to that before the court in Taylor v. Chesapeake & Ohio Railway Company, C.A. 4th (1975), 518 F.2d 536. In reviewing the granting by the District Court of the railroad's motion for

---

[6]   [$1,312 in 1981 dollars is roughly the equivalent of $3,620 in 2019 dollars using the CPI and the GNP Deflator.—Eds.]

summary judgment, the Court of Appeals stated succinctly the legal principles which govern this Court's consideration of Clinchfield's motion:

* * *

It is axiomatic that summary judgment is never authorized if there is any genuine issue of fact between the parties and that, in determining whether there is any such issue, the facts, including any legitimate inferences therefrom, are to be viewed in the light most favorable to the opposing party. It is equally settled that the validity of a release attacked in a FELA case is governed by federal law, which recognizes mutual mistake as a ground for voiding a release. [Footnote references omitted.—Eds.]

Taylor v. Chesapeake & Ohio Railway Company, supra, 518 F.2d at 536– 37. The question presented thus narrows to, whether there is " . . . sufficient evidence in the record before the Court of mutual mistake to constitute a genuine issue of fact in the case?" 518 F.2d at 537.

[5] Construing the record herein, including any legitimate inferences drawn therefrom, in the light most favorable to the plaintiff, it is possible to conclude that, on May 6, 1977, both Mr. Jaynes and Clinchfield's claim-agent assumed mistakenly that the plaintiff had suffered no serious or permanent injury.[7] There is evidence that some 10 days earlier Clinchfield's physician had released Mr. Jaynes to return to his work. Had these parties understood that the plaintiff's injury was other than minor " . . . it would have been unlikely that a modest settlement, covering substantially little more than lost time to date, would have been made." *Ibid.*, 518 F.2d at 538. These facts, and the reasonable inferences therefrom, are sufficient to raise a genuine issue of material fact as to the validity of the release upon which the defendant relies. *Taylor v. Chesapeake & Ohio Railway Company, supra.*

The motion of the defendant for a summary judgment hereby is DENIED.

NOTES AND QUESTIONS

1. The release stated very clearly that it covered "injuries not now known whether or not the undersigned has been advised by doctors or others in any way." In any other context that language would probably be read as the signer's assumption of the risk that he had injuries he was not aware of. In the case of releases of personal injury claims, however, courts have often been unwilling to use such language to preclude the mistake defense. The courts have had to balance two competing policy considerations. On the one hand,

---

[7] There is evidence in the record which reflects that, in fact, Mr. Jaynes's injury was serious and permanent.

there is a policy of favoring devices (like releases) that allow disputes to be resolved quickly and economically. On the other hand, judges want to protect unsophisticated injured people who may have a need for immediate cash against exploitation by insurance companies who are more knowledgeable because they enter into transactions like these all the time. (Economists call such knowledgeable folks "repeat players" to signify that they have powers and abilities far beyond those of mere mortals.)

The extreme example of this solicitude for people signing releases comes not from a court but from a legislature. California Civil Code § 1542, mentioned earlier in another context provides:

> A general release does not extend to claims which the creditor does not know or suspect to exist in his or her favor at the time of executing the release, which if known by him or her must have materially affected his or her settlement with the debtor.

2.   Suppose a person with a broken leg signs a release in the reasonable belief that the leg will heal and that she will be able to walk normally. If, for reasons that she could not have anticipated, the leg does not heal properly and she can never walk again, the straightforward application of the mistake doctrine holds that she cannot avoid the release on the grounds of mistake. Her mistake is of a future, not a present, fact. What is the rationale for this result?

ANDERSON BROTHERS CORP. v. O'MEARA

United States Court of Appeals, Fifth Circuit
306 F.2d 672 (1962)

JONES, CIRCUIT JUDGE.

[1] The appellant, Anderson Brothers Corporation, a Texas corporation engaged in the business of constructing pipelines, sold a barge dredge to the appellee, Robert W. O'Meara, a resident of Illinois who is an oil well driller doing business in several states and Canada. The appellee brought this suit seeking rescission of the sale or, in the alternative, damages. After trial without a jury, the appellee's prayer of rescission was denied, but damages were awarded. The court denied the appellant's counterclaim for the unpaid purchase price of the dredge. Both parties have appealed. Appellant contends that no relief should have been given to the appellee, and the appellee contends that the damages awarded to him were insufficient.

[2] The dredge which the appellant sold to the appellee was specially designed to perform the submarine trenching necessary for burying a pipeline under water. In particular it was designed to cut a relatively narrow trench in areas where submerged rocks, stumps and logs might be encountered. The dredge could be disassembled into its larger component

parts, moved over land by truck, and reassembled at the job site. The appellant built the dredge from new and used parts in its own shop. The design was copied from a dredge which appellant had leased and successfully used in laying a pipeline across the Mississippi River. The appellant began fabrication of the dredge in early 1955, intending to use it in performing a contract for laying a pipeline across the Missouri River. A naval architect testified that the appellant was following customary practice in pipeline operations by designing a dredge for a specific use. Dredges so designed can be modified, if necessary, to meet particular situations. For some reason construction of the dredge was not completed in time for its use on the job for which it was intended, and the dredge was never used by the appellant. After it was completed, the dredge was advertised for sale in a magazine. This advertisement came to the appellee's attention in early December, 1955. The appellee wanted to acquire a dredge capable of digging canals fifty to seventy-five or eighty feet wide and six to twelve feet deep to provide access to offshore oil well sites in southern Louisiana.

[3] On December 8, 1955, the appellee or someone employed by him contacted the appellant's Houston, Texas, office by telephone and learned that the price of the dredge was $45,000. Terms of sale were discussed, and later that day the appellant sent a telegram to the appellee who was then in Chicago, saying it accepted the appellee's offer of $35,000[8] for the dredge to be delivered in Houston. The appellee's offer was made subject to an inspection. The next day Kennedy, one of the appellee's employees, went to Houston from New Orleans and inspected the dredge. Kennedy, it appears, knew nothing about dredges but was familiar with engines. After inspecting the engines of the dredge, Kennedy reported his findings to the appellee by telephone and then signed an agreement with the appellant on behalf of the appellee. In the agreement, the appellant acknowledged receipt of $17,500. The agreement made provision for payment of the remaining $17,500 over a period of seventeen months. The dredge was delivered to the appellee at Houston on December 11, 1955, and from there transported by the appellee to his warehouse in southern Louisiana. The barge was transported by water, and the ladder, that part of the dredge which extends from the barge to the stream bed and to which the cutting devices are attached, was moved by truck. After the dredge arrived at his warehouse the appellee executed a chattel mortgage in favor of the appellant and a promissory note payable to the order of the appellant. A bill of sale dated December 17, 1955, was given the appellee in which the appellant warranted only title and freedom from encumbrances. Both the chattel mortgage and the bill of sale described the dredge and its component parts in detail.

---

8 [$35,000 in 1962 dollars is roughly the equivalent of $290,000 in 2019 dollars using the CPI and GNP Deflator.—Eds.]

[4]   The record contains much testimony concerning the design and capabilities of the dredge including that of a naval architect who, after surveying the dredge, reported "I found that the subject dredge . . . had been designed for the purpose of dredging a straight trench over a river, lake or other body of water." The testimony shows that a dredge designed to perform sweep dredging, the term used to describe the dredging of a wide channel, must be different in several respects from one used only for trenching operations. The naval architect's report listed at least five major items to be replaced, modified, or added before the dredge would be suited to the appellee's intended use. It is clear that the appellee bought a dredge which, because of its design, was incapable, without modification, of performing sweep dredging.

[5]   On July 10, 1956, about seven months after the sale and after the appellee had made seven monthly payments pursuant to the agreement between the parties, the appellee's counsel wrote the appellant stating in part that "Mr. O'Meara has not been able to put this dredge in service and it is doubtful that it will ever be usable in its present condition." After quoting at length from the naval architect's report, which was dated January 28, 1956, the letter suggested that the differences between the parties could be settled amicably by the appellant's contributing $10,000 toward the estimated $12,000 to $15,000 cost of converting the trenching dredge into a sweep dredge. The appellant rejected this offer and on July 23, 1956, the appellee's counsel wrote the appellant tendering return of the dredge and demanding full restitution of the purchase price. This suit followed the appellant's rejection of the tender and demand.

[6]   In his complaint the appellee alleged breaches of expressed and implied warranty and fraudulent representations as to the capabilities of the dredge. By an amendment he alleged as an alternative to the fraud count that the parties had been mistaken in their belief as to the operations of which the dredge was capable, and thus there was a mutual mistake which prevented the formation of a contract. The appellee sought damages of over $29,000[9], representing the total of principal and interest paid the appellant and expenses incurred in attempting to operate the dredge. In the alternative, the appellee asked for rescission and restitution of all money expended by him in reliance on the contract. The appellant answered denying the claims of the appellee and counterclaiming for the unpaid balance.

[7]   The district court found that:

At the time the dredge was sold by the defendant to the plaintiff, the dredge was not capable for performing sweep dredging operations in shallow water, unless it was modified extensively.

---

[9]   [$29,000 in 1962 dollars is roughly the equivalent of $241,000 in 2019 dollars using the CPI and GNP Deflator.—Eds.]

Defendant had built the dredge and knew the purpose for which it was designed and adapted. None of the defendant's officers or employees knew that plaintiff intended to use the dredge for shallow sweep dredging operations. Gier (an employee of the appellant who talked with the appellee or one of his employees by telephone) mistakenly assumed that O'Meara intended to use the dredge within its designed capabilities.

At the time the plaintiff purchased this dredge he mistakenly believed that the dredge was capable without modification of performing sweep dredging operations in shallow water.

[8]   The court further found that the market value of the dredge on the date of sale was $24,000, and that the unpaid balance on the note given for part of the purchase price was $10,500. Upon its findings the court concluded that:

> The mistake that existed on the part of both plaintiff and defendant with respect to the capabilities of the subject dredge is sufficient to and does constitute mutual mistake, and the plaintiff is entitled to recover the damages he has suffered as a result thereof.

[9]   These damages were found to be "equal to the balance due on the purchase price" plus interest, and were assessed by cancellation of the note and chattel mortgage and vesting title to the barge in the appellee free from any encumbrance in favor of the appellant. The court also concluded that the appellee was "not entitled to rescission of this contract." Further findings and conclusions, which are not challenged in this Court, eliminate any considerations of fraud or breach of expressed or implied warranties. The judgment for damages rests entirely upon the conclusion of mutual mistake. The district court's conclusion that the parties were mutually mistaken "with respect to the capabilities of the subject dredge" is not supported by its findings. "A mutual mistake is one common to both parties to the contract, each laboring under the same misconception." *St. Paul Fire & Marine Insurance Co. v. Culwell*, Tex.Com.App., 62 S.W.2d 100. The appellee's mistake in believing that the dredge was capable, without modification, of performing sweep dredging was not a mistake shared by the appellant, who had designed and built the dredge for use in trenching operations and knew its capabilities. The mistake on the part of the appellant's employee in assuming that the appellee intended to use the dredge within its designed capabilities was certainly not one shared by the appellee, who acquired the dredge for use in sweep dredging operations. The appellee alone was mistaken in assuming that the dredge was adapted, without modification, to the use he had in mind.

[10] The appellee insists that even if the findings do not support a conclusion of mutual mistake, he is entitled to relief under the well-

established doctrine that knowledge by one party to a contract that the other is laboring under a mistake concerning the subject matter of the contract renders it voidable by the mistaken party. As a predicate to this contention, the appellee urges that the trial court erred in finding that "None of defendant's officers or employees knew that plaintiff intended to use the dredge for shallow sweep dredging operations."

[11] There is a conflict in the evidence on the question of the appellant's knowledge of the appellee's intended use, and it cannot be held that the district court's finding is clearly erroneous. It is to be noted that the trial court before whom the appellee testified, did not credit his testimony that he had made a telephone call in which, he said, he personally informed an employee of the appellant of his plans for the use of the dredge.

[12] The appellee makes a further contention that when he purchased the dredge he was laboring under a mistake so grave that allowing the sale to stand would be unconscionable. The ground urged is one which has apparently been recognized in some circumstances. However, the Texas courts have held that when unilateral mistake is asserted as a ground for relief, the care which the mistaken complainant exercised or failed to exercise in connection with the transaction sought to be avoided is a factor for consideration. Although a court of equity will relieve against mistake, it will not assist a man whose condition is attributable to the want of due diligence which may be fairly expected from a reasonable person. This is consistent with the general rule of equity that when a person does not avail himself of an opportunity to gain knowledge of the facts, he will not be relieved of the consequences of acting upon supposition. Whether the mistaken party's negligence will preclude relief depends to a great extent upon the circumstances in each instance.

[13] The appellee saw fit to purchase the dredge subject to inspection, yet he sent an employee to inspect it who he knew had no experience with or knowledge of dredging equipment. It was found that someone familiar with such equipment could have seen that the dredge was then incapable of performing channel type dredging. Although, according to his own testimony, the appellee was conscious of his own lack of knowledge concerning dredges, he took no steps, prior to purchase, to learn if the dredge which he saw pictured and described in some detail in the advertisement, was suited to his purpose. Admittedly he did not even inquire as to the use the appellant had made or intended to make of the dredge, and the district court found that he did not disclose to the appellant the use he intended to make of the dredge. The finding is supported by evidence. The appellee did not attempt to obtain any sort of warranty as to the dredge's capabilities. The only conclusion possible is that the appellee exercised no diligence, prior to the purchase, in determining the uses to which the dredge might be put. Had he sent a qualified person, such as the

naval architect whom he later employed, to inspect the dredge he would have learned that it was not what he wanted, or had even made inquiry, he would have been informed as to the truth or have had a cause of action for misrepresentation if he had been given misinformation and relied upon it. The appellee chose to act on assumption rather than upon inquiry or information obtained by investigation, and, having learned his assumption was wrong, he asks to be released from the resulting consequences on the ground that, because of his mistaken assumption, it would be unconscionable to allow the sale to stand. The appellee seeks this, although the court has found that the appellant was not guilty of any misrepresentation or fault in connection with the transaction.

[14] The appellee should have taken nothing on his claim; therefore, it is unnecessary to consider the question raised by the cross-appeal. The other questions raised by the appellant need not be considered. The case must be reversed and remanded for further proceeding consistent with what we have here held.

Reversed and remanded.

NOTES AND QUESTIONS

1. *Unconscionable vs. material effect.* Under the R2d, a mutual mistake can make a contract voidable only when it has "a material effect on the agreed exchange of performances." The R2d doesn't give us much help in determining when there is a "material effect." It does, however, say: "It is not enough for [the party seeking to void the contract] to prove that he would not have made the contract had it not been for the mistake. He must show that the resulting imbalance in the agreed exchange is so severe that he cannot fairly be required to carry it out." R2d § 152 cmt. c. One example given by the R2d's drafters indicates that where the value of what was sold was half what the parties thought it was, the contract would be voidable. R2d § 152, Illustration 4. Another indicates that where the parties believed that the value of the consideration to be given by one party was $150,000, but in reality it turns out to be $110,000, the contract may be voidable. R2d § 152, Illustration 3.

Section 153 provides that unless the other party to the contract has reason to know of the mistake or is responsible for it, a unilateral mistake will make the contract voidable only if enforcement would be unconscionable. Unconscionability is one of those concepts of which lawyers and judge are likely to say "I can't define it, but I know it when I see it." In other words, you need to read a lot of cases to get a feel for the contours of the doctrine in a particular jurisdiction. One often quoted definition is that an unconscionable bargain is one which "no man in his senses and not under delusion would make on the one hand, and . . . no honest and fair man would accept on the other." It is often attributed to *Hume v. United States*, 132 U.S. 406, 411, 10 S.Ct. 134, 33 L.Ed. 393 (1889), but that opinion was quoting from an old English case, which in turn was quoting from a law dictionary, which was very likely quoting from an even older case.

In any event, the idea is that where there is a unilateral mistake, the party seeking to void the contract should have to meet a much higher standard of unfairness. In *Montgomery v. Strickland*, 384 So. 2d 1085 (Ala. 1980), the court, applying an unconscionability standard to a unilateral mistake case, refused to set aside a contract which called for a seller of land to convey 32 acres where he thought he was selling only 21 or 22 acres.

2.   Parties can allocate the rules of the unknown between them using representations and warranties. Representations and warranties are statements of fact pertinent to a contract. There are distinctions between representations and warranties and the actions that may be brought on them, but that is left for another text. *See* GEORGE W. KUNEY, THE ELEMENTS OF CONTRACT DRAFTING (3d ed. West 2011). For present purposes, it is enough to understand representations and warranties as statements that relate to the character, quality, condition, title to, or rights in the subject matter of a contract. For example, a statement that a sailboat was "carefully well equipped" and "very seaworthy" could be a warranty of its condition in a contract of sale. *See Keith v. Buchanan*, 173 Cal. App. 3d 13, 220 Cal. Rptr. 392 (1985). On the other hand, mere expressions of opinion will not rise to the level of a warranty. *See Williams v. Lowenthal*, 124 Cal. App. 179, 12 P.2d 75 (1932) (statement that a used jukebox "would probably not get out of order" was an opinion, not a warranty). If a statement is a warranty, and it turns out that the facts are not as warranted, then the party in whose favor the warranty runs can recover the cost of making the facts as warranted, the difference in value between what was warranted and what was delivered, or the actual damages caused by the breach of warranty from the warranting party. If a statement is a representation and it is untrue, it may give rise to an option to rescind the contract and recover any consideration already paid or proceed with the contract and bring an action for damages sounding in contract and possibly tort (negligent misrepresentation, misrepresentation, and fraud)— with the potential for punitive damages.

3.   Most contracts prepared by lawyers like the Asset Purchase Agreement in the Introduction to this text have a special section or sections in which all or most of the representations or warranties are collected and expressed. Despite the distinctions between the purpose of representations and warranties, and the different remedies they may support, they are often combined in clauses under which a party represents and warrants that certain facts are true.

4.   Compare and contrast the approaches to mistake in R2d sections 151 to 158 and those in UNIDROIT articles 3.4 to 3.7. Which approach do you find superior in substance? Which do you find superior in terms of organization and drafting? Why?

LAWYERING SKILLS PROBLEM

You are general counsel for an insurance company. The company's standard-form release to be signed by people whom the company is compensating for injuries allegedly caused by its insureds reads:

> Releasor hereby releases, acquits and forever discharges Releasee and any other persons and entities of and from any and all actions, causes of action, claims, demands, damages, costs, loss of services, expenses and compensation on account of or in any way growing out of any and all known and unknown personal injuries resulting or to result from the accident that occurred on or about [date and time], at or about [location].

In spite of the language of the release, a number of courts have held that it does NOT release claims for injuries that the signer does not know she has when she signs the release and accepts the money based on the doctrine of mistake.

You have been asked to re-write the release to make it more likely that courts will interpret it to release claims for injuries not known at the time the release is signed. Explain what you would do and provide specific examples of how you would redraft it.

Don't worry about California Civil Code section 1542 discussed earlier. You will have local counsel draft a California-specific release. You will also, of course, have a law clerk do research to see if there are other states that have unusual requirements. But your job here is just to draft a basic release that will do the job in the ordinary run-of-the-mill state.

CHAPTER 10

MISREPRESENTATION AND FRAUD

■ ■ ■

A "representation" is a statement of fact made by one party upon which the other party may reasonably rely in determining to enter into a contract. A representation is the essence of advertising—it is designed to stimulate one's interest and allay one's concerns about entering into the contract.

When a representation turns out to be false, the other party may be able to "void" the contract, i.e., to treat it as if it had never come into effect. This is also called "rescission" or "rescinding" the contract. This means undoing the contract, which is essentially the same thing as voiding it.

The R2d takes the position that the recipient of the representation may void the contract if the misrepresentation is *either* fraudulent *or* material. (R2d § 164(1)). According to R2d § 162(2), "A misrepresentation is material if it would be likely to induce a reasonable person to manifest his assent, or if the maker knows that it would be likely to induce the recipient to do so." R2d § 162(1) sets out the standards for when a misrepresentation is fraudulent. Essentially, a misrepresentation is fraudulent if it is intentional rather than innocent. So the basic rule is that if the misrepresentation is material, the recipient can void the contract even if the misrepresentation is innocent.

As an alternative to voiding the contract, the recipient can keep the contract in effect and sue for damages. The damages the recipient can recover under contract law for a misrepresentation are the difference between (1) the value of the other party's performance if the statement had been true and (2) the actual value of the other party's performance (i.e., the value given the fact that the statement is actually untrue). For example, suppose Seller sold a business to Buyer, representing that the profits were $1,000,000 per year. In actuality, the profits were only $800,000 per year. At trial, Buyer is able to prove that if the profits had been $1,000,000 per year (as represented) the business would have been worth $5,000,000 and that because the profits are only $800,000, the business is worth only $4,000,000. Then Buyer would be able to recover $1,000,000, the difference between the value of the business as represented and its actual value. If the misrepresentation was fraudulent, Buyer has the option of suing in tort and recovering damages based on a slightly different formula that may include punitive damages.

Because fraudulent intent is usually difficult to prove, misrepresentation is more successfully pled and proven. The two causes of action, however, are generally pleaded together "on information and belief" if that is permitted in the relevant jurisdiction.

Seller Plaintiff ———— *Called Buyer*

HALPERT V. ROSENTHAL

Supreme Court of Rhode Island
107 R.I. 406, 267 A.2d 730 (1970)

KELLEHER, J.

[1] This is a civil action wherein the plaintiff vendor seeks damages for the breach by the defendant vendee of a contract for the sale of real estate. The defendant filed a counter-claim in which he sought the return of his deposit. A jury trial was held in the Superior Court. The jury found for the defendant and judgment followed. The case is before us on the plaintiff's appeal. [We affirm.—Eds.]

[2] On February 21, 1967, the parties hereto entered into a real estate agreement whereby plaintiff agreed to convey a one-family house located in Providence on the southeasterly corner of Wayland and Upton Avenues to defendant for the sum of $54,000. The defendant paid a deposit of $2,000 to plaintiff. The agreement provided for the delivery of the deed and the payment of the balance of the purchase price by June 30, 1967.

[3] On May 17, 1967, a termite inspection was made of the premises, and it was discovered that the house was inhabited by termites. The defendant then notified plaintiff that, because of the termite infestation, he was not going to purchase the property. The defendant did not appear for the title closing which plaintiff had scheduled for June 30, 1967.

D said he wasn't going to buy cause of termites

[4] The plaintiff [seller] immediately commenced this suit. Her complaint prayed for specific performance or monetary damages. When the case came on for trial, the property had been sold to another buyer for the sum of $35,000. The plaintiff then sought to recover from defendant the $19,000[1] difference between the selling price called for in the sales agreement and the actual selling price. The defendant in his answer alleged that plaintiff and her agent had, during the preagreement negotiation, intentionally misrepresented the house as being free of termites. The defendant's counterclaim sought the return of the $2,000 deposit.

[5] At the conclusion of the presentation of all the evidence, plaintiff made a motion for a directed verdict on the issue of the alleged fraudulent

---

[1] [$19,000 in 1970 dollars is roughly the equivalent of $123,000 in 2019 dollars using the CPI and the GNP Deflator.—Eds.]

misrepresentations. The trial justice reserved decision on the motion and submitted the case to the jury. After the jury's verdict, he denied the motion.

[6]　This case is unique in that plaintiff made no motion for a new trial. Her appeal is based for the most part on the trial court's refusal to direct a verdict in her favor on the counterclaim. She has also alleged that the trial justice erred in certain portions of his charge to the jury and in failing to adopt some 15 requests to charge submitted by plaintiff.

[7]　The absence of a motion for a new trial narrows the scope of an inquiry on appeal. Instead of being concerned with the credibility of witnesses or the weight of the evidence as we would be where we reviewing the usual motion for a new trial, we apply the standards applicable to a motion for a directed verdict. In doing so, it is our duty to consider all of the evidence and reasonable inferences deducible therefrom in the light most favorable to defendant.

[8]　Since we consider only the evidence favorable to defendant, we shall set forth defendant's version of three different occasions in 1967 when the alleged misrepresentations relative to absence of any termites were made.

　　1.　In early February, defendant and his wife inspected the Halpert home. They asked the agent about termites and he told them that there was no termite problem and that he had never experienced any termite problem with any of the houses he sold in the East Side section of Providence. *asked realestate agent about termites*

　　2.　Later on in February, defendant, his wife, his sister-in-law and his brother-in-law met plaintiff. The brother-in-law inquired about the presence of termites; plaintiff said that there were no termites in the house. *2nd time asking about T-mites*

　　3.　When defendant was about to sign the purchase and sales agreement, he asked plaintiff's real estate agent whether it might not be advisable if the home be inspected for termites before the agreement was signed. The agent told defendant that such a step was unnecessary because there were no termite problems in the house. *3rd time asking about T-mites*

[9]　The plaintiff contends that any statements or representations attributed to her or her agent were qualified in that when asked about the termites, they replied that to the best of their knowledge or experience the Wayland Avenue property was termite free. What she overlooks is that in our consideration of the correctness of the denial of her motion for a direction, we can consider only that evidence and the reasonable inferences flowing therefrom which favor defendant. We do not weigh the evidence to

determine whether her or her agent's representations were qualified or unqualified.

[10] In contending that she was entitled to a directed verdict, plaintiff contends that to sustain the charge of fraudulent misrepresentation, some evidence had to be produced showing that either she or her agent knew at the time they said there were no termites in the house, that such a statement was untrue. Since the representations made to defendant were made in good faith, she argues that, as a matter of law, defendant could not prevail on his counterclaim.

[11] The defendant concedes that there was no evidence which shows that plaintiff or her agent knowingly made false statements as to the existence of the termites but he maintains that an innocent misrepresentation of a material fact is grounds for rescission of a contract where, as here, a party relies to his detriment on the misrepresentation.

[12] We affirm the denial of the motion for a directed verdict.

[13] The plaintiff, when she made her motion for a directed verdict, stated that her motion was restricted to the issue of "fraud." The word "fraud" is a generic term which embraces a great variety of actionable wrongs. It is a word of many meanings and defies any one all-inclusive definition. Fraud may become important either for the purpose of giving the defrauded person the right to sue for damages in an action for deceit or to enable him to rescind the contract. In this jurisdiction a party who has been induced by fraud to enter into a contract may pursue either one of two remedies. He may elect to rescind the contract to recover what he has paid under it, or he may affirm the contract and sue for damages in an action for deceit.

[14] The distinction between a claim for damages for intentional deceit and a claim for rescission is well defined. Deceit is a tort action, and it requires some degree of culpability on the misrepresenter's part. An individual who sues in an action of deceit based on fraud has the burden of proving that the defendant in making the statements knew they were false and intended to deceive him. On the other hand, a suit to rescind an agreement induced by fraud sounds in contract. It is this latter aspect of fraud that we are concerned with in this case, and the pivotal issue before us is whether an innocent misrepresentation of a material fact warrants the granting of a claim for rescission. We believe that it does.

[15] When he denied plaintiff's motion, the trial justice indicated that a false, though innocent, misrepresentation of a fact made as though of one's knowledge may be the basis for the rescission of a contract. While this issue is one of first impression in this state, it is clear that the trial judge's action finds support in the overwhelming weight of decisional and textual authority which has established the rule that where one induces another to enter into a contract by means of a material misrepresentation, the latter

may rescind the contract. It does not matter if the representation was "innocent" or fraudulent.

In 12 Williston, Contracts, § 1500 at 400–01, Professor Jaeger states:

> It is not necessary, in order that a contract may be rescinded for fraud or misrepresentation, that the party making the misrepresentation should have known that it was false. Innocent misrepresentation is sufficient, for though the representation may have been made innocently, it would be unjust and inequitable to permit a person who has made false representations, even innocently, to retain the fruits of a bargain induced by such representations.

Innocent misrepresentation is sufficient

This statement of law is in accord with Restatement of Contracts, § 476 at 908 which states:

Voidable

> Where a party is induced to enter into a transaction with another party that he was under no duty to enter into by means of the latter's fraud or material misrepresentation, the transaction is voidable as against the latter . . .

Misrepresentation is defined as

> . . . any manifestation by words or other conduct by one person to another that, under the circumstances, amounts to an assertion not in accordance with the facts.

Restatement of Contracts, § 470 at 890–91.

[16] The comment following this section explains that a misrepresentation may be innocent, negligent or known to be false. A misrepresentation becomes material when it becomes likely to affect the conduct of a reasonable man with reference to a transaction with another person. Restatement of Contracts, § 470 (2) at 891. Section 28 of Restatement of Restitution is also in accord with this proposition of law that a transaction can be rescinded for innocent misrepresentation of a material fact.

How misrep becomes material

* * *

[17] It is true that some courts require proof of knowledge of the falsity of the misrepresentation before a contract may be invalidated. However, the weight of authority follows the view that the misrepresenter's good faith is immaterial. We believe this view the better one.

[18] A misrepresentation, even though innocently made, may be actionable, if made and relied on as a positive statement of fact. The question to be resolved in determining whether a wrong committed as the result of an innocent misrepresentation may be rectified is succinctly stated in 12 Williston, *supra*, § 1510, at 462 as follows:

When a defendant has induced another to act by representations false in fact although not dishonestly made, and damage has directly resulted from the action taken, who should bear the loss?

[19] The question we submit is rhetorical. The answer is obvious. Simple justice demands that the speaker be held responsible. Accordingly, we hold that here defendant vendee could maintain his counterclaim.

[20] The plaintiff's second contention is to the effect that even if an innocent misrepresentation without knowledge of its falsity may under certain circumstances entitle the misrepresentee to relief by way of rescission, defendant cannot maintain his action because the sales agreement contains a merger clause. This provision immediately precedes the testimonium clause and provides that the contract " . . . contains the entire agreement between the parties, and that it is subject to no understandings, conditions or representations other than those expressly stated herein." The plaintiff argues that in order to enable a purchaser to rescind a contract containing a merger clause because of a misrepresentation, proof of a fraudulent misrepresentation must be shown. We find no merit in this argument.

P's argument about merger clause is wrong

☆

[21] If, as plaintiff concedes, a merger clause, such as is found within the sales contract now before us, will not prevent a rescission based on a fraudulent misrepresentation, there is no valid reason to say that it will prevent a rescission of an agreement which is the result of a false though innocent misrepresentation where both innocent and fraudulent misrepresentations render a contract voidable. As we observed before, the availability of the remedy of rescission is motivated by the obvious inequity of allowing a person who has made the innocent misrepresentation to retain the fruits of the bargain induced thereby. If we are to permit a party to rescind a contract which is the result of an innocent misrepresentation, the "boiler plate" found in the merger clause shall not bar the use of this remedy.

* * *

[22] Before leaving this phase of plaintiff's appeal, we think it appropriate that we allude to the tendency of many courts to equate an innocent misrepresentation with some species of fraud. Usually the word "fraud" connotes a conscious dishonest conduct on the part of the misrepresenter. Fraud, however, is not present if the speaker actually believes that what he states as the truth is the truth. We believe that it would be better if an innocent misrepresentation was not described as some species of fraud. Unqualified statements imply certainty. Reliance is more likely to be placed on a positive statement of fact than a mere expression of opinion or a qualified statement. The speaker who uses the unqualified statement does so at his peril. The risk of falsity is his. If he is to be liable for what he states, the liability is imposed because he is to be held strictly

[handwritten top margin: Fraudulent = maker intends to induce and is telling a lie. Material = likely to induce you. To get 164 you have to be induced]

accountable for his words. Responsibility for an innocent misrepresentation should be recognized for what it is—an example of absolute liability rather than as many courts have said, an example of constructive fraud.

PROBLEM 10-1

Seller Corporation entered into a contract to sell one of its subsidiaries to Buyer Corporation. The contract contained a representation that all of the subsidiary's patents were valid. Before making the representation, Seller Corporation received assurances from its patent counsel that all of the patents were in fact valid. If, before the time Buyer Corporation is to perform its obligations under the contract (i.e., to pay the purchase price and take title to the stock of the subsidiary), Buyer Corporation discovers that some of the patents are invalid, can it refuse to perform? *See* R2d § 164(1); UNIDROIT articles 3.5–3.8.

[handwritten: Yes, non-disclosure]

[handwritten right margin: not fraudulent but might be material cause a reasonable person can be induced]

PROBLEM 10-2

Seller entered into a contract to sell his small hotel to Buyer. In the course of the negotiations, Seller deliberately overstated the profits in his attempt to induce Buyer to purchase the business. In fact, Buyer was never concerned about the profits of the hotel. She was planning to tear it down and use the land as part of a major resort she was developing.

[handwritten right margin: - misrep]

[handwritten left margin: 167 gives definition]

[handwritten: — M]

Buyer's plans have now fallen apart because she could not get the adjoining landowners to sell and therefore she could not put together a large enough parcel of land for her resort. Can she use Seller's fraudulent misrepresentation to get out of the contract to buy his property? *See* R2d § 164(1); UNIDROIT articles 3.5–3.8.

[handwritten: not induced - contract valid]

[handwritten left margin: Material f. Does not ft under 167.]

LEASCO CORP. V. TAUSSIG

United States Court of Appeals, Second Circuit
473 F.2d 777 (1972)

TIMBERS, CIRCUIT JUDGE:

[1] The essential questions presented on this appeal from a judgment for damages in amount of $669,000[2], entered in this diversity action in favor of plaintiff Leasco Corporation against defendant Peter T. Taussig, following a 4 day nonjury trial in the Southern District of New York, Harold L. Tyler, District Judge, are the propriety of the district court's rulings that

---

[2]   [$669,000 in 1972 dollars is roughly the equivalent of $4,010,000 in 2019 dollars using the CPI and the GNP Deflator.—Eds.]

defendant's claim of rescission based on mutual mistake and misrepresentation was without merit; that defendant had breached his agreement to purchase the stock of one of plaintiff's subsidiaries; and that, defendant having failed specifically to perform such agreement, plaintiff was entitled to damages. Finding no error, we affirm.

I.   Background Facts

[2]   Leasco Corporation (Leasco) is a Delaware corporation with its principal place of business in New York City. Prior to 1969, Leasco had acquired Louis Berger, Inc. (Berger, Inc.), a firm engaged on an international basis in civil engineering and consulting. Louis Berger Associates (Associates), a wholly owned subsidiary of Berger, Inc., also was acquired by Leasco and, together with Berger, Inc., constituted the "Berger division" of Leasco.

[3]   In July 1969, Leasco engaged appellant Peter T. Taussig as vice president and counsel to Berger, Inc. Taussig, a citizen of New Jersey, had civil engineering and law degrees and had practiced law—primarily concerned with construction contracts—in New York City for several years. Leasco hired him through the efforts of Frederick A. Jackson, vice president and corporate counsel for Leasco, who had become acquainted with Taussig when they were both associates in the early 1960's in a New York City law firm.

[4]   Shortly after joining Berger, Inc., Taussig became involved in the efforts of Berger, Inc. to acquire the assets of McCreary-Koretsky Engineers, Inc. (MKE), a California corporation engaged in civil engineering and consulting work. Leasco and Berger, Inc. were interested in acquiring MKE's assets in order to expand Leasco's "Berger division" and to make it more efficient. In late 1969 and early 1970, Taussig was asked to investigate MKE. He examined the service contracts held by MKE, as well as its balance sheets and income statements.

[5]   MKE at that time was facing bankruptcy because of income taxes due the federal government and a major lawsuit brought by one of its clients. A wholly owned subsidiary of Berger, Inc., McCreary-Koretsky International, Inc. (MKI), was able to acquire the contracts and personnel of MKE as part of a reorganization agreement. MKI had been incorporated specifically for the purpose of acquiring the assets of MKE. MKE was to be paid a percentage of the profits made by MKI on the acquired MKE contracts. The reorganization agreement was closed on September 16, 1970, effective as of April 1, 1970.

[6]   Taussig became a vice president of MKI. He acted as a liaison executive between MKI, the Berger companies, and Leasco. His task was to keep Leasco informed about MKI's activities, including its financial condition.

[7] In early December 1970, Leasco began to consider divestiture of its entire Berger division. Leasco's management did not like the severe income fluctuations which are characteristic of the civil engineering and consulting business. They also believed that Leasco did not have enough experience to effectively run these businesses.

[8] When Taussig learned that Leasco intended to divest itself of MKI, he offered to purchase it. In late December 1970, Jackson and Taussig discussed the possibility of a sale to Taussig. Taussig estimated that MKI's pre-tax earnings for the fiscal year ending September 30, 1971 would be about $200,000. Jackson suggested that an appropriate sales price would be 10 times these projected pre-tax earnings, or $2,000,000. They then cut this amount in half, to $1,000,000, because, pursuant to the reorganization agreement with MKE, MKI was required to transfer approximately 50% of its profits to MKE. Taussig generally agreed to these price terms, but suggested a package of $625,000 cash combined with a release by Taussig of Leasco's guarantee of an outstanding loan of $375,000 to MKI from The Bank of America. Jackson agreed to these terms.

[9] With the basic terms agreed upon, the parties began to draft a formal agreement. Taussig at the time was no longer formally employed by Berger, Inc. In April 1970, he had informed Mr. Louis Berger, chief executive of the Berger operations, that he would resign on November 2, 1970. His resignation was finally accepted in late December 1970, but he continued to work unofficially for Leasco. He moved into offices at Leasco in New York and worked closely with Jackson. He thus had access to the same financial data and other information concerning MKI as did the officers of Leasco.

[10] On February 26, 1971, an agreement was entered into for the sale of MKI to Taussig. The closing date was to be April 15, but later was changed by mutual consent to May 28. The price for MKI was $625,000, plus Taussig's release of Leasco from its guarantee to The Bank of America of its outstanding loan of $375,000 to MKI. Two days later, in order to increase the working capital of MKI, Taussig authorized an additional loan of $200,000 by The Bank of America to MKI, with a guarantee by Leasco. Later, another $25,000 was loaned by The Bank of America to MKI and guaranteed by Leasco.

[11] On March 12, 1971, Taussig received the February financial statement for MKI. It disclosed a net loss of $4,702. Taussig traveled to San Francisco where the headquarters of MKI were located. There he learned that a design error in the Fruitvale Bridge job, one of MKI's construction projects, had caused a substantial carry-back loss which accounted for the income loss reflected in the February financial statement. This error also resulted in net losses for the months of March and April.

[12] In April 1971, Taussig, in conversations with Jackson and others, indicated that he might not go through with the purchase. On May 28, a representative of Leasco attended the closing and tendered to Taussig the stock as required by the contract. Taussig refused to accept the tender or to perform as required under the contract.

[13] On June 8, Leasco commenced this action seeking specific performance or damages. It claimed that Taussig had wrongfully refused to purchase all the shares of MKI. Taussig by way of defense claimed rescission of the agreement on the grounds of mutual mistake and misrepresentation with regard to material facts. On September 21, the district court denied Leasco's motion for summary judgment, but ordered discovery limited to the issue of the meaning of certain contract provisions and to the issue of mitigation of damages.

[14] After a nonjury trial in January 1972, the district court filed an opinion on February 23, 1972 holding that there was no misrepresentation or mutual mistake and that Taussig had breached the agreement without factual or legal justification. The court ordered specific performance by Taussig at a reduced price of $169,000, together with a release by Taussig of Leasco from the $500,000 bank loan guarantee; or, if Taussig should fail to perform, a judgment for damages equal to the sales price plus the amount of the loan guarantee, for a total of $669,000. When Taussig failed to perform, a judgment in amount of $669,000 was entered against him.[3]

II.   Defendant's Claim of Rescission

[15] It is undisputed that the contract between Leasco and Taussig was properly executed, and that Leasco made a proper tender of MKI stock on the closing date. Taussig contends here, as he did below, however, that the agreement should be rescinded because the contracting parties were mutually mistaken about a fact material to the agreement or because Leasco negligently misrepresented material facts. These allegedly mistaken or misrepresented facts relate to the projected and actual earnings of MKI.

---

[3]   [The district court ordered Taussig to buy the company for $669,000. When he didn't do so, they ordered him to pay the $669,000 anyway. This is unusual. The normal course would be for Leasco to have sold the company and for Taussig to be liable for the difference between the sale price received from the new buyer and the $669,000 he was supposed to pay. The editors have not been able to determine why the district court increased the price Taussig had to pay. The district court opinion is not officially reported and is apparently not available online. What probably happened is that the company went south even before the district court case was decided. Taussig probably saw this coming and got out of the deal for that reason. His lawyer would then have gone over the deal in detail looking for reasons he could legally avoid the deal and the ones the court discusses below were the best they could come up with. This happens all the time, but as in this case, is settled in most instances. (Over ninety-five percent of all civil cases are settled before trial.)—Eds.]

(A) Alleged Mutual Mistake

[16] When Jackson and Taussig first discussed the sale to Taussig of MKI in late December 1970, Taussig estimated that the projected pretax earnings for MKI for fiscal year 1971 would be about $200,000. MKI's budget in fact showed $197,000 as the anticipated pre-tax earnings for MKI. When Taussig examined Leasco's management reports in January 1971, a graph representing MKI's financial condition showed the line for actual earnings through January approaching the line for anticipated earnings to that date. No doubt the $200,000 estimated earnings figure was one of several factors which determined the sales price of MKI. From these circumstances, Taussig argues that a basic assumption of both parties in negotiating the contract was that they were dealing with a company which would earn $200,000 in the fiscal year ending September 30, 1971. MKI in fact lost $12,000 during that fiscal year. Taussig contends therefore that the agreement should be rescinded because both parties were mistaken about this material fact.

[17] The legal concept of "mistake" is similar to the legal concept of "misrepresentation" in that, under each, a party to a contract may be relieved from his obligations if he was unaware of certain material facts. "Mistake," however, is only such error as is made without representation or deception by the other party to the transaction. Where the mistake is unilateral, the contract is not voidable. But where both parties assume a certain state of facts to exist, and contract on the faith of that assumption, they can be relieved from their obligations if the assumption is erroneous.

[18] In the instant action, we hold that there was no mutual mistake. Both Taussig and Leasco may have hoped, but surely could not have been certain, that MKI would earn $200,000 in fiscal 1971. Neither party intended to allow rescission of the agreement if, as it turned out, one party got a better bargain than had been anticipated. The civil engineering and consulting business is personalized, highly technical, and extremely risky. Neither party could safely assume that the projected earnings would be realized. Both parties had equal access to information indicating that such a projection would be highly unreliable. Indeed, Taussig probably knew more about the business of MKI than anyone else at Leasco since he originally had investigated it, he served as its vice president and he was a liaison executive between Leasco and MKI.

[19] The facts here are analogous to those in *Backus v. MacLaury*, 278 App.Div. 504, 106 N.Y.S.2d 401 (4th Dept. 1951). There the defendant sold a two week old bull calf to the plaintiff who planned to use it for breeding. The price paid, $5,000, was the usual price paid for a breeding bull. Both parties were aware that the earliest at which it can be determined whether a bull is fertile is approximately twelve months. Eighteen months after the sale the plaintiff discovered that the bull was sterile. He sued the

defendant for damages. The court held that, since the parties had equal skill and knowledge on the subject of breeding bulls, a warranty of fitness for purpose could not be implied. With regard to the plaintiff's claim of mutual mistake, the court held determinative the fact that, on the day of sale, both parties were aware that the fertility of the bull was uncertain:

> "Where the parties know that there is doubt in regard to a certain matter and contract on that assumption, the contract is not rendered voidable because one is disappointed in the hope that the facts accord with his wishes. The risk of the existence of the doubtful fact is then assumed as one of the elements of the bargain." 278 App.Div. at 507, 106 N.Y.S.2d at 404, *quoting* Restatement of Contracts § 502(f), at 964 (1934).

[20] In the instant action, the parties cannot be said to have been without doubt that MKI's pre-tax earnings for fiscal 1971 would turn out to be $200,000. As we hold below, there was no warranty by Leasco that MKI actually would earn that amount. Taussig assumed "as one of the elements of the bargain" the risk that a considerably lesser amount would be realized.

[21] We therefore agree with the district court that there was no mutual mistake of fact.

(B) Alleged Misrepresentation

[22] Taussig also contends that MKI's financial statement for the month of January 1971 misrepresented MKI's financial condition. He claims that since this deceptive statement induced him to buy MKI he should be allowed to rescind the agreement.

[23] MKI's January 1971 statement showed earnings of $49,000 for the fiscal year to date. In fact, however, one of the MKI projects had a serious design error that apparently was discovered by MKI project engineers in January but did not come to the attention of MKI's financial officer until February.[4]

[24] The project on which the design error was made was the Fruitvale Bridge. The contract for this bridge was entered into in October 1970. By January 1971, it was determined that it was more than half completed. The accounting treatment for the project was the cost of completion method. Under that method, an accountant determines the revenues earned on the job to date by calculating the percentage of total estimated costs thus far incurred. MKI's financial officer calculated that by January 31 about 59% of the anticipated cost of constructing the bridge had been incurred.

---

[4] In the Leasco organization, financial reports for subsidiaries are prepared by Leasco's controller who tries to get them in the hands of top management twelve business days after the end of the month. It is not clear from the record when the January statement was released, but apparently it was late. It was issued, however, before Taussig entered into the contract with Leasco.

Accordingly, he determined that about 59% of the revenues from the project, or $77,000, should be credited to MKI's earnings. In January, however, MKI's chief project engineer discovered a design error in the bridge sufficiently serious to require that most of the bridge be reconstructed. As a result, MKI's profit and loss statement for February showed a loss of $4,702 primarily attributable to a "prior period adjustment" on the Fruitvale Bridge project. The statement showed a $13,290 reduction in revenue without a corresponding reduction of cost. The March and April statements also showed net losses primarily caused by the design error.

[25] Taussig does not claim that Leasco deliberately failed to disclose the design error. Nor does he contend that those Leasco officers with whom he dealt knew about the design error at the time the contract was entered into. Nevertheless, MKI's January financial statement was misleading. Furthermore, MKI was negligent in failing to discover and to take account of the error. MKI's financial officer failed to check, as he normally did, with MKI's chief engineer before preparing the January statement.

[26] The question is who should bear a loss attributable to an error committed prior to the sale but not reported until after the sale. Under New York law, such a loss often is borne by the seller even if the misrepresentation is innocent. When a person has induced another to act by representations which are false in fact, although not dishonestly made, and damage has resulted directly from the action taken, the person making such representations often bears the loss. Before a court will grant rescission based on unilateral mistake, however, there must be a showing of equitable considerations which favor the party seeking rescission. And the injured person can rescind only if the misstatement induced him to enter into the contract.

[27] In the instant case, the misleading MKI earnings statement did not induce Taussig to enter into the contract. Several facts lead us to this conclusion. Before entering into the agreement, Taussig was well aware that many of the MKI projects received cost of completion accounting treatment.[5] Thus he knew that the profit and loss statements were potentially misleading. He knew that the actual revenues might have been substantially higher or lower than those reported. Taussig also had access, not only to the books and records of MKI, but to its operating personnel as well. He was on Leasco's distribution list for financial statements and short form profit and loss reports. He requested and was given the detailed work sheets from which the December financial reports were prepared. These work sheets disclosed the Fruitvale Bridge project and the accounting treatment of the project. The only restriction imposed upon Taussig was

---

[5] In March 1970, Taussig discussed with Leasco's Assistant Controller the various accounting methods used by MKI with regard to its projects. At trial Taussig admitted knowledge of MKI's accounting methods prior to signing the agreement.

that he could not inform the personnel of MKI that he was purchasing the company, because of the possible disruption this might cause.

[28] If Taussig had taken advantage of the sources of information available to him, he probably would have learned about the design error. Under these circumstances, he should not be heard to complain that he relied upon the financial statements as an accurate and complete description of MKI's financial condition. Moreover, the error in the financial statement was not material. The Fruitvale Bridge project was due for completion in fiscal 1971 and was expected to produce revenues of $130,000. MKI's total projected annual revenues were $2,757,000. Thus, the Fruitvale Bridge project was expected to produce only about 5% of the total revenues. This cannot be said to be material.

[29] We do not rely solely upon these circumstances to support our holding that Taussig was not justified in relying upon MKI's financial statements. The agreement itself specifically disclaimed any warranties or representations concerning MKI's financial condition. *See Danann Realty Corp. v. Harris*, 5 N.Y.2d 317, 184 N.Y.S.2d 599, 157 N.E.2d 597 (1959).

Paragraph 5(d) of the agreement provided:

5.   REPRESENTATIONS AND WARRANTIES OF LEASCO—
Leasco represents and warrants to Taussig as follows:

* * *

(d) Disclaimer—Except as set forth in this Agreement, Leasco makes no other representations and warranties with respect to MKI and the business thereof.

[30] Nowhere in the agreement is there set forth a warranty that the profit and loss or other financial statements accurately represented the financial condition of MKI.

[31] The question as to who should bear the loss attributable to an error committed prior to the sale but not reported until thereafter is not one that the parties failed to consider when the agreement was entered into. The parties in their good faith bargaining anticipated the problem and allocated the risk of loss to Taussig. Absent any showing that this was unfairly done, the obligations assumed by the parties themselves will be enforced.

* * *

[32] We agree with the district court that there was no material misrepresentation relied upon by defendant.

* * *

Affirmed.

DANANN REALTY V. HARRIS
Court of Appeals of New York
5 N.Y.2d 317, 184 N.Y.S.2d 599, 157 N.E.2d 597 (1959)

BURKE, J.

[1] The plaintiff in its complaint alleges, insofar as its first cause of action is concerned, that it was induced to enter into a contract of sale of a lease of a building held by defendants because of oral representations, falsely made by the defendants, as to the operating expenses of the building and as to the profits to be derived from the investment. Plaintiff, affirming the contract, seeks damages for fraud.

[2] At Special Term, the Supreme Court sustained a motion to dismiss the complaint. On appeal, the Appellate Division unanimously reversed the order granting the dismissal of the complaint. Thereafter the Appellate Division granted leave to appeal, certifying the following question: "Does the first cause of action in the complaint state facts sufficient to constitute a cause of action?" We reverse and answer the question: no.

[3] The basic problem presented is whether the plaintiff can possibly establish from the facts alleged in the complaint (together with the contract which was annexed to the complaint) reliance upon the misrepresentations.

[4] We must, of course, accept as true plaintiff's statements that during the course of negotiations defendants misrepresented the operating expenses and profits. Such misrepresentations are undoubtedly material. However, the provisions of the written contract which directly contradict the allegations of oral representations are of equal importance in our task of reaching a decisive answer to the question posed in these cases.

[5] The contract, annexed to and made a part of the complaint, contains the following language pertaining to the particular facts of representations:

> The Purchaser has examined the premises agreed to be sold and is familiar with the physical condition thereof. The Seller has not made and does not make any representations as to the physical condition, rents, leases, expenses, operation or any other matter or thing affecting or related to the aforesaid premises, except as herein specifically set forth, and the Purchaser hereby expressly acknowledges that no such representations have been made, and the Purchaser further acknowledges that it has inspected the premises and agrees to take the premises "as is" ... It is understood and agreed that all understandings and agreements

heretofore had between the parties hereto are merged in this contract, which alone fully and completely expresses their agreement, and that the same is entered into after full investigation, neither party relying upon any statement or representation, not embodied in this contract, made by the other. The Purchaser has inspected the buildings standing on said premises and is thoroughly acquainted with their condition.

[6] Were we dealing solely with a general and vague merger clause, our task would be simple. A reiteration of the fundamental principle that a general merger clause is ineffective to exclude parol evidence to show fraud in inducing the contract would then be dispositive of the issue. To put it another way, where the complaint states a cause of action for fraud, the parol evidence rule is not a bar to showing the fraud—either in the inducement or in the execution—despite an omnibus statement that the written instrument embodies the whole agreement, or that no representations have been made.

[7] Here, however, plaintiff has in the plainest language announced and stipulated that it is not relying on any representations as to the very matter as to which it now claims it was defrauded. Such a specific disclaimer destroys the allegations in plaintiff's complaint that the agreement was executed in reliance upon these contrary oral representations (*Cohen v. Cohen, supra* [1 A.D.2d 586, 151 N.Y.S. 2d 949]). The *Sabo* case, *supra* [*Sabo v. Delman*, 3 N.Y.2d 155, 164 N.Y.S. 2d 714, 143 N.E. 2d 906] dealt with the usual merger clause. The present case, as in the *Cohen* case, additionally, includes a disclaimer as to specific representations.

[8] This specific disclaimer is one of the material distinctions between this case and *Bridger v. Goldsmith, supra* [143 N.Y. 424, 38 N.E. 458] and *Crowell-Collier Pub. Co. v. Josefowitz* (5 N. Y. 2d 998). In the Bridger case, the court considered the effect of a general disclaimer as to representations in a contract of sale, concluding that the insertion of such a clause at the insistence of the seller cannot be used as a shield to protect him from his fraud. Another material distinction is that nowhere in the contract in the *Bridger* case is there a denial of reliance on representations, as there is here. Similarly, in *Crowell-Collier Pub. Co. v. Josefowitz, supra,* decided herewith, only a general merger clause was incorporated into the contract of sale. Moreover, the complaint there additionally alleged that further misrepresentations were made after the agreement had been signed, but while the contract was held in escrow and before it had been finally approved.

[9] Consequently, this clause, which declares that the parties to the agreement do not rely on specific representations not embodied in the

contract, excludes this case from the scope of the *Jackson, Angerosa, Bridger* and *Crowell-Collier* cases, *supra*.

[10] The complaint here contains no allegations that the contract was not read by the purchaser. We can fairly conclude that plaintiff's officers read and understood the contract, and that they were aware of the provision by which they aver that plaintiff did not rely on such extra contractual representations. It is not alleged that this provision was not understood, or that the provision itself was procured by fraud. It would be unrealistic to ascribe to plaintiff's officers such incompetence that they did not understand what they read and signed. Although this court in the *Ernst* case discounted the merger clause as ineffective to preclude proof of fraud, it gave effect to the specific disclaimer of representation clause, holding that such a clause limited the authority of the agent, and hence, plaintiff had notice of his lack of authority. But the larger implication of the Ernst case is that, where a person has read and understood the disclaimer of representation clause, he is bound by it. The court rejected, as a matter of law, the allegation of plaintiff's "that they relied upon an oral statement made to them in direct contradiction of this provision of the contract." The presence of such a disclaimer clause "is inconsistent with the contention that plaintiff relied upon the misrepresentation and was led thereby to make the contract." *Kreshover v. Berger,* 135 App.Div. 27, 28.

[11] It is not necessary to distinguish seriatim the cases in other jurisdictions as they are not, in the main, in point or, in a few instances, clash with the rule followed in the State of New York. The marshaling of phrases plucked from various opinions and references to generalizations, with which no one disagrees, cannot subvert the fundamental precept that the asserted reliance must be found to be justifiable under all the circumstances before a complaint can be found to state a cause of action in fraud. We must keep in mind that "opinions must be read in the setting of the particular cases and as the product of preoccupation with their special facts." *Freeman v. Hewit,* 329 U.S. 249, 252. When the citations are read in the light of this caveat, we find that they are generally concerned with factual situations wherein the facts represented were matters peculiarly within the defendant's knowledge, as in the cases of *Sabo v. Delman, supra,* and *Jackson v. State of New York, supra* [210 App. Div. 115, 205 N.Y.S. 658].

[12] The general rule was enunciated by this court over a half a century ago in *Schumaker v. Mather,* 133 N.Y. 590, 596, that "if the facts represented are not matters peculiarly within the party's knowledge, and the other party has the means available to him of knowing, by the exercise of ordinary intelligence, the truth or the real quality of the subject of the representation, he must make use of those means, or he will not be heard to complain that he was induced to enter into the transaction by misrepresentations."

[13] Very recently this rule was approved as settled law by this court in the case of *Sylvester v. Bernstein,* 283 App.Div. 333, affd. 307 N.Y. 778.

[14] In this case, of course, the plaintiff made a representation in the contract that it was not relying on specific representations not embodied in the contract, while, it now asserts, it was in fact relying on such oral representations. Plaintiff admits then that it is guilty of deliberately misrepresenting to the seller its true intention. To condone this fraud would place the purchaser in a favored position. This is particularly so, where, as here, the purchaser confirms the contract, but seeks damages. If the plaintiff has made a bad bargain he cannot avoid it in this manner.

[15] If the language here used is not sufficient to estop a party from claiming that he entered the contract because of fraudulent representations, then no language can accomplish that purpose. To hold otherwise would be to say that it is impossible for two businessmen dealing at arm's length to agree that the buyer is not buying in reliance on any representations of the seller as to a particular fact.

[16] Accordingly, the order of the Appellate Division should be reversed and that of Special Term reinstated, without costs. The question certified should be answered in the negative.

FULD, J. (dissenting).

[17] If a party has actually induced another to enter into a contract by means of fraud—and so the complaint before us alleges—I conceive that language may not be devised to shield him from the consequences of such fraud. The law does not temporize with trickery or duplicity, and this court, after having weighed the advantages of certainty in contractual relations against the harm and injustice which result from fraud, long ago unequivocally declared that "a party who has perpetrated a fraud upon his neighbor may [not] . . . contract with him in the very instrument by means of which it was perpetrated, for immunity against its consequences, close his mouth from complaining of it and bind him never to seek redress. Public policy and morality are both ignored if such an agreement can be given effect in a court of justice. The maxim that fraud vitiates every transaction would no longer be the rule but the exception." *Bridger v. Goldsmith,* 143 N.Y. 424, 428. It was a concern for similar considerations of policy which persuaded Massachusetts to repudiate the contrary rule which it had initially espoused. "The same public policy that in general sanctions the avoidance of a promise obtained by deceit", wrote that state's Supreme Judicial Court in *Bates v. Southgate,* 308 Mass. 170, 182, "strikes down all attempts to circumvent that policy by means of contractual devices. In the realm of fact it is entirely possible for a party knowingly to agree that no representations have been made to him, while at the same time believing and relying upon representations which in fact have been made and in fact are false but for which he would not have made the agreement. To deny

this possibility is to ignore the frequent instances in everyday experience where parties accept ... and act upon agreements containing ... exculpatory clauses in one form or another, but where they do so, nevertheless, in reliance upon the honesty of supposed friends, the plausible and disarming statements of salesmen, or the customary course of business. To refuse relief would result in opening the door to a multitude of frauds and in thwarting the general policy of the law."

[18] It is impossible, on either principle or reasoning, to distinguish the present case from the many others which this court has decided. As far back as 1894, we decided, in the *Bridger* case, 143 N.Y. 424, *supra*, that the plaintiff was not prevented from bringing an action for fraud, based on oral misrepresentations, even though the written contract provided that it was "understood and agreed" that the defendant seller had not made,

> "for the purpose of inducing the sale * * * or the making of this agreement * * * any statements or representations * * * other than the single one therein set forth. And, just today, we are holding, in the *Crowell-Collier Publishing* case, that the plaintiffs were not barred from suing the defendants for fraud in inducing them to make the contract, despite its recital that

> "This Agreement constitutes the entire understanding between the parties, [and] was not induced by any representations * * * not herein contained".

[19] In addition, in *Jackson v. State of New York,* 210 App.Div. 115, affd. 241 N.Y. 563, *supra*, the contract provided that

> the contractor (plaintiff's predecessor-in-interest) agreed that he had satisfied himself by his own investigation regarding all the conditions of the work to be done and that his conclusion to enter into the contract was based solely upon such investigation and not upon any information or data imparted by the State.

[20] It was held that even this explicit disavowal of reliance did not bar the plaintiff from recovery. In answering the argument that the provision prevented proof either of misrepresentation by the defendant or reliance on the part of the plaintiff, the Appellate Division, in an opinion approved by this court, wrote: "A party to a contract cannot, by misrepresentation of a material fact, induce the other party to the contract to enter into it to his damage and then protect himself from the legal effect of such misrepresentation by inserting in the contract a clause to the effect that he is not to be held liable for the misrepresentation which induced the other party to enter into the contract. The effect of misrepresentation and fraud cannot be thus easily avoided."

[21] Although the clause in the contract before us may be differently worded from those in the agreements involved in the other cases decided

by this court, it undoubtedly reflects the same thought and meaning, and the reasoning and the principles which the court deemed controlling in those cases are likewise controlling in this one. Their application, it seems plain to me, compels the conclusion that the complaint herein should be sustained and the plaintiff accorded a trial of its allegations.

[22] It is said, however, that the provision in this contract differs from those heretofore considered in that it embodies a specific and deliberate exclusion of a particular subject. The quick answer is that the clause now before us is not of such a sort. On the contrary, instead of being limited, it is all-embracing, encompassing every representation that a seller could possibly make about the property being sold and, instead of representing a special term of a bargain, is essentially "boiler plate." *See* Contract of Sale, Standard N.Y.B.T.U. Form 8041; Bicks, Contracts for the Sale of Realty [1956 ed.], pp. 79–80, 94–95. The more elaborate verbiage in the present contract cannot disguise the fact that the language which is said to immunize the defendants from their own fraud is no more specific than the general merger clause in *Sabo v. Delman,* 3 N.Y.2d 155, *supra,* and far less specific than the provision dealt with in the Jackson case, 210 App.Div. 115, *affd.* 241 N.Y. 563, *supra,* or in *Crowell-Collier.*

[23] In any event, though, I cannot believe that the outcome of a case such as this, in which the defendant is charged with fraud, should turn on the particular language employed in the contract. As Judge Augustus Hand, writing for the Federal Court of Appeals, observed, "the ingenuity of draftsmen is sure to keep pace with the demands of wrongdoers, and if a deliberate fraud may be shielded by a clause in a contract that the writing contains every representation made by way of inducement, or that utterances shown to be untrue were not an inducement to the agreement," a fraudulent seller would have a simple method of obtaining immunity for his misconduct. *Arnold v. National Aniline & Chem. Co.,* 20 F.2d 364, 369.

[24] The guiding rule—that fraud vitiates every agreement which it touches—has been well expressed not only by the courts of this state, but by courts throughout the country and by the House of Lords in England. And, in recognizing that the plaintiff may assert a cause of action in fraud, the courts have not differentiated between the type or form of exculpatory provision inserted in the contract. It matters not, the cases demonstrate, whether the clause simply recites that no representations have been made or more fully stipulates that the seller has not made any representations concerning certain enumerated subjects and that the purchaser has made his own investigation and has not relied upon any representation by the seller, not embodied in the writing.

* * *

[25] The rule heretofore applied by this court presents no obstacle to honest business dealings, and dishonest transactions ought not to receive

judicial protection. The clause in the contract before us may lend support to the defense and render the plaintiff's task of establishing its claim more difficult, but it should not be held to bar institution of an action for fraud. Whether the defendants made the statements attributed to them and, if they did, whether the plaintiff relied upon them, whether, in other words, the defendants were guilty of fraud, are questions of fact not capable of determination on the pleadings alone. The plaintiff is entitled to its day in court.

————

NOTES AND QUESTIONS

1. *Why litigators should learn contract drafting.* You may have read accounts of the great job the Justice Department's antitrust litigators did in the Microsoft antitrust trial and settlement of the late 1990s. Now it appears that many of their victories were thrown away in the settlement process by those same lawyers because they didn't understand contract drafting.

Microsoft may have bested the government in the antitrust settlement by using its lawyers' ability to draft precise contracts and by taking advantage of the government lawyers' inability to pick up on the finer points of Microsoft's drafting. *See* John Wilke, *Hard Drive: Negotiating All Night, Tenacious Microsoft Won Many Loopholes,* WALL ST. J., November 9, 2001.

On October 31, 2001, Charles James, antitrust chief of the Justice Department, sought an important concession from Microsoft. He wanted to limit the company's ability to extend its Windows operating-system monopoly into the market for large corporate servers. Without the concession, Mr. James told Microsoft, the settlement was off.

Microsoft resisted, but a court deadline was fast approaching. So Microsoft conceded and its lawyers included a provision agreeing to disclose additional information about how its desktop software related to server software. This was intended to improve rivals' chances of designing programs that were workable with Windows.

But, as the company's lawyers wrote it, the concession was drawn so that, in practice, it required disclosure that would be of little use to competitors—at least according to those competitors.

The pattern was often repeated. The settlement left the company's software monopoly (or at least dominance) intact and is unlikely to stop it from invading and dominating new markets.

The lawyers representing the government may have been very good litigators, but they were weak in drafting and analyzing contracts. So when the substance of the settlement was agreed upon, the Microsoft lawyers drafted the language for the settlement agreement and as one government lawyer realized after the documents had been signed, "the provisions [in favor of the government] were weakened at every turn by qualifying exceptions."

When the Microsoft settlement's terms were disclosed, it was met with "a storm of criticism" from Microsoft's competitors, and some of the states who had been plaintiffs in the case refused to go along with the settlement.

The DOJ, it appears, was "ground down" and lost the war after winning the battle. Remember: It's not over until it is over. Clients may celebrate when a settlement is announced, but good lawyers know the deal isn't done until it is fully documented and signed off on by all interested parties and approved by all necessary courts or regulatory agencies. Opportunities to renegotiate and "adjust" the deal when reducing it to writing exist at every step of the finalization and approval process.

2.   Here is how the drafting and negotiation process for representations and warranties often takes place, using as examples terms that might be found in an asset sale contract like the one in the Introduction.

> *Buyer's Initial Proposal—Phrased in the Absolute:* Seller represents and warrants that there are no claims outstanding against the Seller.

> *Seller's Response—Softened with a Knowledge Limitation:* Seller represents and warrants that, *to the best of Seller's knowledge*, there are no claims outstanding against the Seller.

> *Seller's Response—Softened with a Subject Matter Limitation:* Seller represents and warrants that there are no claims outstanding against the Seller *relating to the Assets to be sold except as stated on schedule 2.3.*

> *Seller's Response—Softened with a Carve Out:* Seller represents and warrants that there are no claims outstanding against the Seller; *provided, however, that this statement does not relate to claims against Seller filed and served upon Seller prior to July 20, 2000.*

> *Seller's Response—Softened with a Basket or Materiality Threshold:* Seller represents and warrants that there are no claims outstanding against the Seller *seeking damages in excess of $50,000.*

These approaches can be combined in a manner that suits the parties in terms of allocating risk.

Further, the negotiation of representations and warranties is, itself, a process of fact discovery and the beginning of due diligence. If the seller won't give an unqualified representation or warranty, why not? Is there something that the buyer should know? Once it is known, should the purchase price or some other term of the deal be adjusted to account for the risk? Note, also, how asking for a representation or warranty as to a matter shifts the cost of the factual investigation of the matter to the party that will make the representation. In other words, instead of the buyer having to beware, the representation shifts the risk to the seller.

Representations and warranties are part of the transactional lawyer's tool box with which to discover risk, to quantify it if possible, and to allocate it between the parties. As to risk—which cannot be eliminated in this world—"Discover it; Quantify it; Allocate it; Box it."

3. How are unilateral mistake and innocent misrepresentation different?

LAWYERING SKILLS PROBLEM

If you want to eliminate—or at least dramatically reduce—the risk that a party to a contract will later be able to successfully assert a claim for misrepresentation or breach of warranty, what can you do in terms of drafting and design of the contract at issue? Are there any limits on this or these techniques? Should there be?

CHAPTER 11

DURESS

■ ■ ■

Another formation defense is that of duress. The law of duress developed in much the same way as the law of mistake. The early common law judges and lawyers wanted to find a way to hold that no contract had been formed, but they also wanted to avoid appearing to create any new law. So they said that because an offer or an acceptance required free will, a person was not capable of forming a binding contract where the other party had robbed him of his free will by a threat of death, imprisonment, or serious physical injury.

The cases that follow demonstrate that the types of threats that will allow a party to avoid a contract have been expanded rather considerably to include, among other things, the notion of economic duress in the face of no alternative source of supply. The courts, however, still hang on to the old language about free will despite the often corporate nature of the parties, which makes the reference rather quaint.

AUSTIN INSTRUMENT, INC. v. LORAL CORP.

Court of Appeals of New York
29 N.Y.2d 124, 324 N.Y.S.2d 22, 272 N.E.2d 533 (1971)

FULD, CHIEF JUDGE.

[1] The defendant, Loral Corporation, seeks to recover payment for goods delivered under a contract which it had with the plaintiff Austin Instrument, Inc., on the ground that the evidence establishes, as a matter of law, that it was forced to agree to an increase in price on the items in question under circumstances amounting to economic duress.

[2] In July of 1965, Loral was awarded a $6,000,000 contract by the Navy for the production of radar sets. The contract contained a schedule of deliveries, a liquidated damages clause applying to late deliveries and a cancellation clause in case of default by Loral.[1] The latter thereupon solicited bids for some 40 precision gear components needed to produce the

---

[1] [A liquidated damages clause provides that if there is a breach, the breaching party will pay a specific ("liquidated") amount in damages. Liquidated damages are covered in Chapter 21.—Eds.]

radar sets, and awarded Austin a subcontract to supply 23 such parts. That party commenced delivery in early 1966.

[3] In May, 1966, Loral was awarded a second Navy contract for the production of more radar sets and again went about soliciting bids. Austin bid on all 40 gear components but, on July 15, a representative from Loral informed Austin's president, Mr. Krauss, that his company would be awarded the subcontract only for those items on which it was low bidder. The Austin officer refused to accept an order for less than all 40 of the gear parts and on the next day he told Loral that Austin would cease deliveries of the parts due under the existing subcontract unless Loral consented to substantial increases in the prices provided for by that agreement—both retroactively for parts already delivered and prospectively on those not yet shipped—and placed with Austin the order for all 40 parts needed under Loral's second Navy contract. Shortly thereafter, Austin did, indeed, stop delivery. After contacting 10 manufacturers of precision gears and finding none who could produce the parts in time to meet its commitments to the Navy,[2] Loral acceded to Austin's demands; in a letter dated July 22, Loral wrote to Austin that "We have feverishly surveyed other sources of supply and find that because of the prevailing military exigencies, were they to start from scratch as would have to be the case, they could not even remotely begin to deliver on time to meet the delivery requirements established by the Government . . . Accordingly, we are left with no choice or alternative but to meet your conditions."

[4] Loral thereupon consented to the price increases insisted upon by Austin under the first subcontract and the latter was awarded a second subcontract making it the supplier of all 40 gear parts for Loral's second contract with the Navy. Although Austin was granted until September to resume deliveries, Loral did, in fact, receive parts in August and was able to produce the radar sets in time to meet its commitments to the Navy on both contracts. After Austin's last delivery under the second subcontract in July, 1967, Loral notified it of its intention to seek recovery of the price increases.

[5] On September 15, 1967, Austin instituted this action against Loral to recover an amount in excess of $17,750 which was still due on the second subcontract. On the same day, Loral commenced an action against Austin claiming damages of some $22,250[3]—the aggregate of the price increases under the first subcontract—on the ground of economic duress. The two actions were consolidated and, following a trial, Austin was awarded the sum it requested and Loral's complaint against Austin was dismissed on the ground that it was not shown that "it could not have

---

[2] The best reply Loral received was from a vendor who stated he could commence deliveries sometime in October.

[3] [$22,250 in 1971 dollars is roughly the equivalent of $138,000 in 2019 dollars using the CPI and the GNP Deflator.—Eds.]

obtained the items in question from other sources in time to meet its commitment to the Navy under the first contract." A closely divided Appellate Division affirmed (35 A.D.2d 387, 316 N.Y.S.2d 528, 532). There was no material disagreement concerning the facts; as Justice Steuer stated in the course of his dissent below, "(t)he facts are virtually undisputed, nor is there any serious question of law. The difficulty lies in the application of the law to these facts." (35 A.D.2d 392, 316 N.Y.S.2d 534.)

[6]   The applicable law is clear and, indeed, is not disputed by the parties. A contract is voidable on the ground of duress when it is established that the party making the claim was forced to agree to it by means of a wrongful threat precluding the exercise of his free will. The existence of economic duress or business compulsion is demonstrated by proof that "immediate possession of needful goods is threatened," *Mercury Mach. Importing Corp. v. City of New York*, 3 N.Y.2d 418, 425, 165 N.Y.S.2d 517, 520, 144 N.E.2d 400, or more particularly, in cases such as the one before us, by proof that one party to a contract has threatened to breach the agreement by withholding goods unless the other party agrees to some further demand. However, a mere threat by one party to breach the contract by not delivering the required items, though wrongful, does not in itself constitute economic duress. It must also appear that the threatened party could not obtain the goods from another source of supply and that the ordinary remedy of an action for breach of contract would not be adequate.

[7]   We find without any support in the record the conclusion reached by the courts below that Loral failed to establish that it was the victim of economic duress. On the contrary, the evidence makes out a classic case, as a matter of law, of such duress.

[8]   It is manifest that Austin's threat—to stop deliveries unless the prices were increased—deprived Loral of its free will. As bearing on this, Loral's relationship with the Government is most significant. As mentioned above, its contract called for staggered monthly deliveries of the radar sets, with clauses calling for liquidated damages and possible cancellation on default. Because of its production schedule, Loral was, in July, 1966, concerned with meeting its delivery requirements in September, October and November, and it was for the sets to be delivered in those months that the withheld gears were needed. Loral had to plan ahead, and the substantial liquidated damages for which it would be liable, plus the threat of default, were genuine possibilities. Moreover, Loral did a substantial portion of its business with the Government, and it feared that a failure to deliver as agreed upon would jeopardize its chances for future contracts. These genuine concerns do not merit the label "self-imposed, undisclosed and subjective" which the Appellate Division majority placed upon them. It was perfectly reasonable for Loral, or any other party similarly placed, to consider itself in an emergency, duress situation.

[9] Austin, however, claims that the fact that Loral extended its time to resume deliveries until September negates its alleged dire need for the parts. A Loral official testified on this point that Austin's president told him he could deliver some parts in August and that the extension of deliveries was a formality. In any event, the parts necessary for production of the radar sets to be delivered in September were delivered to Loral on September 1, and the parts needed for the October schedule were delivered in late August and early September. Even so, Loral had to "work . . . around the clock" to meet its commitments. Considering that the best offer Loral received from the other vendors it contacted was commencement of delivery sometime in October, which, as the record shows, would have made it late in its deliveries to the Navy in both September and October, Loral's claim that it had no choice but to accede to Austin's demands is conclusively demonstrated.

[10] We find unconvincing Austin's contention that Loral, in order to meet its burden, should have contacted the Government and asked for an extension of its delivery dates so as to enable it to purchase the parts from another vendor. Aside from the consideration that Loral was anxious to perform well in the Government's eyes, it could not be sure when it would obtain enough parts from a substitute vendor to meet its commitments. The only promise which it received from the companies it contacted was for commencement of deliveries, not full supply, and, with vendor delay common in this field, it would have been nearly impossible to know the length of the extension it should request. It must be remembered that Loral was producing a needed item of military hardware. Moreover, there is authority for Loral's position that nonperformance by a subcontractor is not an excuse for default in the main contract. In light of all this, Loral's claim should not be held insufficiently supported because it did not request an extension from the Government.

[11] Loral, as indicated above, also had the burden of demonstrating that it could not obtain the parts elsewhere within a reasonable time, and there can be no doubt that it met this burden. The 10 manufacturers whom Loral contacted comprised its entire list of "approved vendors" for precision gears, and none was able to commence delivery soon enough.[4] As Loral was producing a highly sophisticated item of military machinery requiring parts made to the strictest engineering standards, it would be unreasonable to hold that Loral should have gone to other vendors, with whom it was either unfamiliar or dissatisfied, to procure the needed parts. As Justice Steuer noted in his dissent, Loral "contacted all the manufacturers whom it believed capable of making these parts," 35 A.D.2d at 393, 316 N.Y.S.2d at 534, and this was all the law requires.

---

[4] Loral, as do many manufacturers, maintains a list of "approved vendors," that is, vendors whose products, facilities, techniques and performance have been inspected and found satisfactory.

[12] It is hardly necessary to add that Loral's normal legal remedy of accepting Austin's breach of the contract and then suing for damages would have been inadequate under the circumstances, as Loral would still have had to obtain the gears elsewhere with all the concomitant consequences mentioned above. In other words, Loral actually had no choice, when the prices were raised by Austin, except to take the gears at the "coerced" prices and then sue to get the excess back.

[handwritten: Loral had no choice]

[13] Austin's final argument is that Loral, even if it did enter into the contract under duress, lost any rights it had to a refund of money by waiting until July, 1967, long after the termination date of the contract, to disaffirm it. It is true that one who would recover moneys allegedly paid under duress must act promptly to make his claim known. In this case, Loral delayed making its demand for a refund until three days after Austin's last delivery on the second subcontract. Loral's reason—for waiting until that time—is that it feared another stoppage of deliveries which would again put it in an untenable situation. Considering Austin's conduct in the past, this was perfectly reasonable, as the possibility of an application by Austin of further business compulsion still existed until all of the parts were delivered.

[14] In sum, the record before us demonstrates that Loral agreed to the price increases in consequence of the economic duress employed by Austin. Accordingly, the matter should be remanded to the trial court for a computation of its damages.

[15] The order appealed from should be modified, with costs, by reversing so much thereof as affirms the dismissal of defendant Loral Corporation's claim and, except as so modified, affirmed.

[The dissenting opinion of JUDGE BERGAN is omitted.—Eds.]

NOTES

1.   In paragraph 3 the court quotes from Loral's letter of July 22. Review that quoted language. This letter is a perfect example of good lawyering behind the scenes to create a factual record for later litigation. The letter, and the response it elicited, serves as evidence to prove the second main element of economic duress: no alternative source of supply and a need to accede to the wrongful demand.

2.   One of the jobs of a lawyer handling a transaction is to shape the parties' relationship and create a record of events for later litigation should that relationship deteriorate. Not only is this useful when it comes to litigation, but being prepared to litigate can actually help avoid litigation: the other side may sense this preparedness and evaluate the weaknesses in its own position accordingly. Thus, as in rock climbing, counsel should mind the ascent and be forward looking while all the while creating a useful record and preparing to "fall correctly" if falling becomes necessary.

TOTEM MARINE TUG & BARGE, INC. V. ALYESKA PIPELINE SERVICE CO.

Supreme Court of Alaska
584 P.2d 15 (1978)

BURKE, JUSTICE.

[1] This appeal arises from the superior court's granting of summary judgment in favor of defendants-appellees Alyeska Pipeline Services, et al., in a contract action brought by plaintiffs-appellants Totem Marine Tug & Barge, Inc., Pacific, Inc., and Richard Stair.

[2] The following summary of events is derived from the materials submitted in the summary judgment proceedings below.

[3] Totem is a closely held Alaska corporation which began operations in March of 1975. Richard Stair, at all times relevant to this case, was vice-president of Totem. In June of 1975, Totem entered into a contract with Alyeska under which Totem was to transport pipeline construction materials from Houston, Texas, to a designated port in southern Alaska, with the possibility of one or two cargo stops along the way. In order to carry out this contract, which was Totem's first, Totem chartered a barge (the "Marine Flasher") and an ocean-going tug (the "Kirt Chouest"). These charters and other initial operations costs were made possible by loans to Totem from Richard Stair individually and Pacific, Inc., a corporation of which Stair was principal stockholder and officer, as well as by guarantees by Stair and Pacific.

[4] By the terms of the contract, Totem was to have completed performance by approximately August 15, 1975. From the start, however, there were numerous problems which impeded Totem's performance of the contract. For example, according to Totem, Alyeska represented that approximately 1,800 to 2,100 tons of regular uncoated pipe were to be loaded in Houston, and that perhaps another 6,000 or 7,000 tons of materials would be put on the barge at later stops along the west coast. Upon the arrival of the tug and barge in Houston, however, Totem found that about 6,700 to 7,200 tons of coated pipe, steel beams and valves, haphazardly and improperly piled, were in the yard to be loaded. This situation called for remodeling of the barge and extra cranes and stevedores, and resulted in the loading taking thirty days rather than the three days which Totem had anticipated it would take to load 2,000 tons. The lengthy loading period was also caused in part by Alyeska's delay in assuring Totem that it would pay for the additional expenses, bad weather and other administrative problems.

[5] The difficulties continued after the tug and barge left Houston. It soon became apparent that the vessels were traveling more slowly than anticipated because of the extra load. In response to Alyeska's complaints and with its verbal consent, on August 13, 1975, Totem chartered a second tug, the "N. Joseph Guidry." When the "Guidry" reached the Panama Canal, however, Alyeska had not yet furnished the written amendment to the parties' contract. Afraid that Alyeska would not agree to cover the cost of the second tug, Stair notified the "Guidry" not to go through the Canal. After some discussions in which Alyeska complained of the delays and accused Totem of lying about the horsepower of the first tug, Alyeska executed the amendment on August 21, 1975.

[6] By this time the "Guidry" had lost its preferred passage through the Canal and had to wait two or three additional days before it could go through. Upon finally meeting, the three vessels encountered the tail of a hurricane which lasted for about eight or nine days and which substantially impeded their progress.

[7] The three vessels finally arrived in the vicinity of San Pedro, California, where Totem planned to change crews and refuel. On Alyeska's orders, however, the vessels instead pulled into port at Long Beach, California. At this point, Alyeska's agents commenced off-loading the barge, without Totem's consent, without the necessary load survey, and without a marine survey, the absence of which voided Totem's insurance. After much wrangling and some concessions by Alyeska, the freight was off-loaded. Thereafter, on or about September 14, 1975, Alyeska terminated the contract. Although there was talk by an Alyeska official of reinstating the contract, the termination was affirmed a few days later at a meeting at which Alyeska officials refused to give a reason for the termination.

[8] Following termination of the contract, Totem submitted termination invoices to Alyeska and began pressing the latter for payment. The invoices came to something between $260,000 and $300,000. An official from Alyeska told Totem that they would look over the invoices but that they were not sure when payment would be made perhaps in a day or perhaps in six to eight months. Totem was in urgent need of cash as the invoices represented debts which the company had incurred on 10–30 day payment schedules. Totem's creditors were demanding payment and according to Stair, without immediate cash, Totem would go bankrupt. Totem then turned over the collection to its attorney, Roy Bell, directing him to advise Alyeska of Totem's financial straits. Thereafter, Bell met with Alyeska officials in Seattle, and after some negotiations, Totem received a settlement offer from Alyeska for $97,500. On November 6, 1975, Totem, through its president Stair, signed an agreement releasing Alyeska from all claims by Totem in exchange for $97,500.

[9] Five months later, on March 26, 1976, Totem, Richard Stair, and Pacific filed a complaint against Alyeska, which was subsequently amended. In the amended complaint, the plaintiffs sought to rescind the settlement and release on the ground of economic duress and to recover the balance allegedly due on the original contract. In addition, they alleged that Alyeska had wrongfully terminated the contract and sought miscellaneous other compensatory and punitive damages.

[10] Before filing an answer, Alyeska moved for summary judgment against the plaintiffs on the ground that Totem had executed a binding release of all claims against Alyeska and that as a matter of law, Totem could not prevail on its claim of economic duress. In opposition, plaintiffs contended that the purported release was executed under duress in that Alyeska wrongfully terminated the contract; that Alyeska knew that Totem was faced with large debts and impending bankruptcy; that Alyeska withheld funds admittedly owed knowing the effect this would have on plaintiffs and that plaintiffs had no alternative but to involuntarily accept the $97,500 in order to avoid bankruptcy. Plaintiffs maintained that they had thus raised genuine issues of material fact such that trial was necessary, and that Alyeska was not entitled to judgment as a matter of law. Alyeska disputed the plaintiffs' assertions.

[11] On November 30, 1976, the superior court granted the defendant's motion for summary judgment. This appeal followed. [We reverse.—Eds.]

* * *

[12] [A] court's initial task in deciding motions for summary judgment is to determine whether there exist genuine issues of material fact. In order to decide whether such issues exist in this case, we must examine the doctrine allowing avoidance of a release on grounds of economic duress.

[13] This court has not yet decided a case involving a claim of economic duress or what is also called business compulsion. At early common law, a contract could be avoided on the ground of duress only if a party could show that the agreement was entered into for fear of loss of life or limb, mayhem or imprisonment. The threat had to be such as to overcome the will of a person of ordinary firmness and courage. Subsequently, however, the concept has been broadened to include myriad forms of economic coercion which force a person to involuntarily enter into a particular transaction. The test has come to be whether the will of the person induced by the threat was overcome rather than that of a reasonably firm person.

[14] At the outset it is helpful to acknowledge the various policy considerations which are involved in cases involving economic duress. Typically, those claiming such coercion are attempting to avoid the consequences of a modification of an original contract or of a settlement and release agreement. On the one hand, courts are reluctant to set aside

agreements because of the notion of freedom of contract and because of the desirability of having private dispute resolutions be final. On the other hand, there is an increasing recognition of the law's role in correcting inequitable or unequal exchanges between parties of disproportionate bargaining power and a greater willingness to not enforce agreements which were entered into under coercive circumstances.

[15] There are various statements of what constitutes economic duress, but as noted by one commentator, "The history of generalization in this field offers no great encouragement for those who seek to summarize results in any single formula." Dawson, Economic Duress An Essay in Perspective, 45 Mich.L.Rev. 253, 289 (1947). Section 492(b) of the Restatement of Contracts defines duress as:

> any wrongful threat of one person by words or other conduct that induces another to enter into a transaction under the influence of such fear as precludes him from exercising free will and judgment, if the threat was intended or should reasonably have been expected to operate as an inducement.

[16] Professor Williston states the basic elements of economic duress in the following manner:

> 1.   The party alleging economic duress must show that he has been the victim of a wrongful or unlawful act or threat, and

> 2.   Such act or threat must be one which deprives the victim of his unfettered will.

13 Williston on Contracts, § 1617 at 704 (footnotes omitted).

[17] Many courts state the test somewhat differently, eliminating use of the vague term "free will," but retaining the same basic idea. Under this standard, duress exists where: (1) one party involuntarily accepted the terms of another, (2) circumstances permitted no other alternative, and (3) such circumstances were the result of coercive acts of the other party.

> The third element is further explained as follows:

> In order to substantiate the allegation of economic duress or business compulsion, the plaintiff must go beyond the mere showing of reluctance to accept and of financial embarrassment. There must be a showing of acts on the part of the defendant which produced these two factors. The assertion of duress must be proven by evidence that the duress resulted from defendant's wrongful and oppressive conduct and not by the plaintiff's necessities.

W. R. Grimshaw Co., *supra*, 248 F.2d at 904.

[18] As the above indicates, one essential element of economic duress is that the plaintiff show that the other party by wrongful acts or threats,

intentionally caused him to involuntarily enter into a particular transaction. Courts have not attempted to define exactly what constitutes a wrongful or coercive act, as wrongfulness depends on the particular facts in each case. This requirement may be satisfied where the alleged wrongdoer's conduct is criminal or tortious but an act or threat may also be considered wrongful if it is wrongful in the moral sense. Restatement of Contracts, § 492, comment (g); *Gerber v. First National Bank of Lincolnwood*, 30 Ill.App.3d 776, 332 N.E.2d 615, 618 (1975); *Fowler v. Mumford*, 48 Del. 282, 9 Terry 282, 102 A.2d 535, 538 (Del. Super. 1954).

[19] In many cases, a threat to breach a contract or to withhold payment of an admitted debt has constituted a wrongful act. Implicit in such cases is the additional requirement that the threat to breach the contract or withhold payment be done in bad faith.

[20] Economic duress does not exist, however, merely because a person has been the victim of a wrongful act; in addition, the victim must have no choice but to agree to the other party's terms or face serious financial hardship. Thus, in order to avoid a contract, a party must also show that he had no reasonable alternative to agreeing to the other party's terms, or, as it is often stated, that he had no adequate remedy if the threat were to be carried out. What constitutes a reasonable alternative is a question of fact, depending on the circumstances of each case. An available legal remedy, such as an action for breach of contract, may provide such an alternative. Where one party wrongfully threatens to withhold goods, services or money from another unless certain demands are met, the availability on the market of similar goods and services or of other sources of funds may also provide an alternative to succumbing to the coercing party's demands. Generally, it has been said that "(t)he adequacy of the remedy is to be tested by a practical standard which takes into consideration the exigencies of the situation in which the alleged victim finds himself." *Ross Systems*, 173 A.2d at 262.

[21] An available alternative or remedy may not be adequate where the delay involved in pursuing that remedy would cause immediate and irreparable loss to one's economic or business interest. For example, in *Austin Instrument, supra*, and *Gallagher Switchboard Corp. v. Heckler Electric Co.*, 36 Misc.2d 225, 232 N.Y.S.2d 590 (N.Y. Sup. Ct. 1962), duress was found in the following circumstances: A subcontractor threatened to refuse further delivery under a contract unless the contractor agreed to modify the existing contract between the parties. The contractor was unable to obtain the necessary materials elsewhere without delay, and if it did not have the materials promptly, it would have been in default on its main contract with the government. In each case such default would have had grave economic consequences for the contractor and hence it agreed to the modifications. In both, the courts found that the alternatives to agreeing to the modification were inadequate (i.e., suing for breach of

contract or obtaining the materials elsewhere) and that modifications therefore were signed under duress and voidable.

[22] Professor Dalzell, in *Duress By Economic Pressure II*, 20 N. Carolina L. Rev. 340, 370 (1942), notes the following with regard to the adequacy of legal remedies where one party refuses to pay a contract claim:

> Nowadays, a wait of even a few weeks in collecting on a contract claim is sometimes serious or fatal for an enterprise at a crisis in its history. The business of a creditor in financial straits is at the mercy of an unscrupulous debtor, who need only suggest that if the creditor does not care to settle on the debtor's own hard terms, he can sue. This situation, in which promptness in payment is vastly more important than even approximate justice in the settlement terms, is too common in modern business relations to be ignored by society and the courts.

[23] This view finds support in *Capps v. Georgia Pacific Corporation*, 253 Or. 248, 453 P.2d 935 (1969). There, the plaintiff was owed $157,000 as a commission for finding a lessee for defendant's property but in exchange for $5,000, the plaintiff signed a release of his claim against defendant. The plaintiff sued for the balance of the commission, alleging that the release had been executed under duress. His complaint, however, was dismissed. On appeal, the court held that the plaintiff had stated a claim where he alleged that he had accepted the grossly inadequate sum because he was in danger of immediately losing his home by mortgage foreclosure and other property by foreclosure and repossession if he did not obtain immediate funds from the defendant. One basis for its holding was found in the following quote by a leading commentator in the area of economic duress:

> The most that can be claimed (regarding the law of economic duress) is that change has been broadly toward acceptance of a general conclusion that in the absence of specific countervailing factors of policy or administrative feasibility, restitution is required of any excessive gain that results, in a bargain transaction, from impaired bargaining power, whether the impairment consists of economic necessity, mental or physical disability, or a wide disparity in knowledge or experience.

Dawson, Economic Duress—An Essay In Perspective, 45 Mich. L. Rev. 253, 289 (1947).

[24] Turning to the instant case, we believe that Totem's allegations, if proved, would support a finding that it executed a release of its contract claims against Alyeska under economic duress. Totem has alleged that Alyeska deliberately withheld payment of an acknowledged debt, knowing that Totem had no choice but to accept an inadequate sum in settlement of that debt; that Totem was faced with impending bankruptcy; that Totem

was unable to meet its pressing debts other than by accepting the immediate cash payment offered by Alyeska; and that through necessity, Totem thus involuntarily accepted an inadequate settlement offer from Alyeska and executed a release of all claims under the contract. If the release was in fact executed under these circumstances,[5] we think that under the legal principles discussed above that this would constitute the type of wrongful conduct and lack of alternatives that would render the release voidable by Totem on the ground of economic duress. We would add that although Totem need not necessarily prove its allegation that Alyeska's termination of the contract was wrongful in order to sustain a claim of economic duress, the events leading to the termination would be probative as to whether Alyeska exerted any wrongful pressure on Totem and whether Alyeska wrongfully withheld payment from Totem.[6]

REVERSED and REMANDED.

NOTES AND QUESTIONS

1.   The R2d §§ 175 and 176 state the modern law of duress, stripped of all the old common law baggage. Be sure to analyze these two cases under these rules. Would the results be the same?

2.   The UNIDROIT principles cover duress in articles 3.9 (threat) and 3.10 (gross disparity). How do these standards differ from those of the R2d? Be sure to analyze these two cases under the principles, too.

3.   Could the *Alaska Packers* case from Chapter 7 (on pre-existing duty) have been decided as a duress case? If so, does that take away from the policy argument in favor of the pre-existing duty rule?

4.   If *Alaska Packers* and these economic duress cases were decided under the U.C.C. (no pre-existing duty rule but the modification must be in good faith), is there any need for the defense of economic duress? Isn't lack of good faith a lesser, necessarily included standard within economic duress?

PROBLEM 11-1

Mary Inventor developed a new program for screening e-mail to eliminate spam. She got a federally-guaranteed loan from Bank to market the program. Her marketing effort encountered considerable resistance at first, but early in

---

[5]   By way of clarification, we would note that Totem would not have to prove that Alyeska admitted to owing the precise sum Totem claimed it was owed upon termination of the contract but only that Alyeska acknowledged that it owed Totem approximately that amount which Totem sought.

[6]   We make no comment as to whether Alyeska's termination of the contract was wrongful nor as to the truth of Totem's other allegations.

2010 it took off and it began to look as if her product would be a major success. Unfortunately, the government guarantee expired in June 2010, and her loan came due at that time. Bank refused to renew the loan and demanded payment. Ms. Inventor tried a number of other lending institutions, but none of them was willing to lend her the money she needed to pay off the loan from Bank and to continue her marketing efforts because she had neither collateral nor a track record. The only person who would give her the money she needed was Shark, who demanded a 51% percent ownership interest in the business as compensation for the "risk" he was taking. Ms. Inventor reluctantly agreed to the deal Shark proposed. Now the business is doing well and Ms. Inventor has come to you to ask if you can help her "get back all that Shark has pressured me out of."

(a)   Will the doctrine of duress help her case under the approach of the R2d? Under the UNIDROIT principles?

(b)   Does she have a claim against Bank or only against Shark?

PROBLEM 11-2

In 1917, the United States entered World War I. At that time German submarines were inflicting heavy losses on ships crossing the Atlantic. The need to get American troops and supplies to Europe made it imperative for the United States government to get a large number of ships built in the shortest possible time. The government approached the nation's largest shipbuilder and was told that the shipbuilder would build ships for the government only if it was compensated under a plan that provided (i) the shipbuilder was paid the cost of construction plus an additional percentage of cost as its profit, (ii) if the actual cost of construction of any ship was greater than the estimated cost, the government paid the actual cost plus the profit percentage based on the actual cost, (iii) if the actual cost was less than the estimated cost, the shipbuilder got its profit computed on the estimated cost plus it got half the difference between the actual cost and the estimated cost as a bonus for saving the government money, and (iv) the shipbuilder got to estimate the costs all by itself. The government agreed to the contract, and when the shipbuilder made a claim for its enormous profit, the government claimed the defense of duress.

How should the court decide the case under the approach of the R2d? Under the UNIDROIT principles?

LAWYERING SKILLS PROBLEM

You are general counsel for an insurance company (again). The company's standard-form release to be signed by people whom the company has compensated for injuries allegedly caused by its insured reads:

> Releasor hereby releases, acquits and forever discharges Releasee and any other persons and entities of and from any and all actions, causes of action, claims, demands, damages, costs, loss of services, expenses and compensation on account of or in any way growing out

of any and all known and unknown personal injuries resulting or to result from the accident that occurred on or about [date and time], at or about [location].

In spite of the language of the release, you are worried that there are some courts that might hold that it does NOT release claims for injuries, known or unknown, based on the doctrine of duress.

You have been asked to re-write the release to make it more likely that courts will enforce the release as written and reject any duress challenge to it. Explain what you would do. Specific examples of how you would redraft it are preferred.

NOTE: Don't worry about the California Civil Code section discussed earlier in the book. You will have local counsel draft a California-specific release. You will also, of course, have a law clerk do research to see if there are other states that have unusual requirements. But your job here is just to draft a basic release that will do the job in the ordinary run-of-the-mill state.

CHAPTER 12

UNCONSCIONABILITY

■ ■ ■

Unconscionability is a troublesome doctrine. It is the contract law equivalent of constitutional law's now-defunct substantive due process: an ill-defined doctrine with the potential to wreak havoc that, despite the fears of business interests and the hopes of social activists, has been construed so narrowly that, outside of a few key areas, it has hardly any application at all.

If you take nothing else from this chapter apart from the notion that unconscionability is an extreme form of unfairness, remember this: Outside of the David v. Goliath case of the struggling, good-hearted, unfortunate, unlucky individual consumer against the overreaching corporation that is practically the sole source of a particular good or service that is a necessity for the consumer, the doctrine has almost no applicability. When present, it is largely an extreme form of economic duress or a product of a contract of adhesion and is confined to those facts.

That said, what is unconscionability? It is an extreme form of unfairness, such that a court will refuse to enforce the contract despite its meeting all the other requirements of contract law. There are two types of unconscionability: procedural and substantive.

Procedural unconscionability focuses on the element of unfair surprise of a (hidden) term found in a contract prepared by one party and presented to the other on a "take it or leave it" basis (a so called "contract of adhesion"—the 2nd party has no choice but to "adhere" to the terms presented or not contract at all). Procedural unconscionabilty is most often applied to waivers of liability and alternative dispute resolution provisions that may effectively strip any meaningful right of recovery from the weaker party. Procedural unconscionability, based on unfair surprise, lack of meaningful choice, disparate bargaining power, and adhesion contracts, is the form of unconscionability that meets with the most success today.

The other variety, *substantive unconscionability*, had its seeds sown as early as 1870, when it was recognized by the U.S. Supreme Court in *Scott v. United States*, 79 U.S. (12 Wall.) 443, 445, 20 L.Ed. 438 (1870) ("If a contract be unreasonable and unconscionable, but not void for fraud, a court of law will give to the party who sues for its breach damages, not according to its letter, but only such as he is equitably entitled to"), but came to full flower after enactment of the U.C.C. in the turbulent 1960's and 1970's. During this period, corporate enterprise expanded into previously un- and under-served sectors of society, especially the inner city, whose inhabitants had been rendered dependent on government transfer payments by the failed experiments of the Johnson administration's war on poverty. Increasingly isolated from other, more affluent groups by the "white flight" reaction to desegregation's progress "with all deliberate speed" and affluent African-American flight that followed the passage of the Civil Rights Act and similar legislation prohibiting discrimination in housing, employment, and similar fields, these un- and under-served sectors provided opportunities for aggressive sales and credit practices. Some of these aggressive transactions continue today in the form of rent-to-own stores and payday advance lenders, for example.

In the wake of cases like *Williams v. Walker-Thomas Furniture Co.*, the first case in this chapter, which uses substantive unconscionability to invalidate aggressive, unfair financing practices in the inner city, commentators were, variously, delighted or horrified, depending on their perspective. The broad, generalized statement of the doctrine—extreme unfairness under the totality of the circumstances as viewed by the court—suggested more radical outcomes than actually came to pass. The doctrine that appeared to be a threat that could assault freedom of contract and undermine capitalism has, in fact, largely behaved more like a pussycat.

As you read the cases that follow, concentrate on what the underlying rationale of the court appears to be. Is it simple, broad unfairness? Procedural unfairness in the form of a hidden clause in a contract of adhesion when there is an undue differential in bargaining power? Something that shocks the conscience of the court? A combination of these (and other) things?

Remember, in practice, outside of the Consumer-with-no-Alternative v. Big Co. case, unconscionability is far easier to plead than to prove. On the other hand, because of its vague outlines and fact specific nature, it may be a cause of action that is difficult to eliminate through pre-trial motion practice, even though the issue of unconscionability is characterized as a question of law in most if not all jurisdictions, and, thus, may provide plaintiffs with leverage and an increased settlement value based upon, if nothing else, the cost of defense. Although so-called frivolous tort claims make the news, an even bigger problem for American business may be bogus contract claims that cannot be dismissed prior to trial and are often settled without regard to their lack of merit. *See* Robert M. Lloyd, *Making Contracts Relevant: Thirteen Lessons for the First-Year Contracts Course*, 36 ARIZ. ST. L.J. 257, 259–60 (2004).

———

WILLIAMS V. WALKER-THOMAS FURNITURE CO.

United States Court of Appeals, District of Columbia Circuit
350 F.2d 445, 121 U.S. App. D.C. 315 (1965)

J. SKELLY WRIGHT, CIRCUIT JUDGE:

[1] Appclloo, Walker-Thomas Furniture Company, operates a retail furniture store in the District of Columbia. During the period from 1957 to 1962 each appellant in these cases purchased a number of household items from Walker-Thomas, for which payment was to be made in installments. The terms of each purchase were contained in a printed form contract which set forth the value of the purchased item and purported to lease the item to appellant for a stipulated monthly rent payment. The contract then provided, in substance, that title would remain in Walker-Thomas until the total of all the monthly payments made equaled the stated value of the item, at which time appellants could take title. In the event of a default in the payment of any monthly installment, Walker-Thomas could repossess the item.

[2] The contract further provided that "the amount of each periodical installment payment to be made by (purchaser) to the Company under this present lease shall be inclusive of and not in addition to the amount of each installment payment to be made by (purchaser) under such prior leases, bills or accounts; and all payments now and hereafter made by (purchaser) shall be credited pro rata on all outstanding leases, bills and accounts due the Company by (purchaser) at the time each such payment is made." The effect of this rather obscure provision was to keep a balance due on every item purchased until the balance due on all items, whenever purchased, was liquidated. As a result, the debt incurred at the time of purchase of each item was secured by the right to repossess all the items previously purchased by the same purchaser, and each new item purchased automatically became subject to a security interest arising out of the previous dealings.

[3] On May 12, 1962, appellant Thorne purchased an item described as a Daveno, three tables, and two lamps, having total stated value of $391.10. Shortly thereafter, he defaulted on his monthly payments and appellee sought to replevy all the items purchased since the first transaction in 1958.[1]

[4] Similarly, on April 17, 1962, appellant Williams bought a stereo set of stated value of $514.95.[2] She too defaulted shortly thereafter, and

---

[1]   [Replevin is a common law writ for possession of an item of property other than real estate. It seeks a court order commanding the sheriff to take possession of goods and deliver them to the person rightfully entitled to possession. It is most commonly used when a person has defaulted on a loan and the lender wants to repossess the collateral.—Eds.]

[2]   At the time of this purchase her account showed a balance of $164 still owing from her prior purchases. The total of all the purchases made over the years in question came to $1,800. The total payments amounted to $1,400.

appellee sought to replevy all the items purchased since December, 1957. The Court of General Sessions granted judgment for appellee. The District of Columbia Court of Appeals affirmed, and we granted appellants' motion for leave to appeal to this court.

[5] Appellants' principal contention, rejected by both the trial and the appellate courts below, is that these contracts, or at least some of them, are unconscionable and, hence, not enforceable. In its opinion in Williams v. Walker-Thomas Furniture Company, 198 A.2d 914, 916 (1964), the District of Columbia Court of Appeals explained its rejection of this contention as follows:

> Appellant's second argument presents a more serious question. The record reveals that prior to the last purchase appellant had reduced the balance in her account to $164. The last purchase, a stereo set, raised the balance due to $678. Significantly, at the time of this and the preceding purchases, appellee was aware of appellant's financial position. The reverse side of the stereo contract listed the name of appellant's social worker and her $218 monthly stipend from the government. Nevertheless, with full knowledge that appellant had to feed, clothe and support both herself and seven children on this amount, appellee sold her a $514 stereo set.

> We cannot condemn too strongly appellee's conduct. It raises serious questions of sharp practice and irresponsible business dealings. A review of the legislation in the District of Columbia affecting retail sales and the pertinent decisions of the highest court in this jurisdiction disclose, however, no ground upon which this court can declare the contracts in question contrary to public policy. We note that were the Maryland Retail Installment Sales Act, Art. 83 §§ 128–153, or its equivalent, in force in the District of Columbia, we could grant appellant appropriate relief. We think Congress should consider corrective legislation to protect the public from such exploitive contracts as were utilized in the case at bar.

[6] We do not agree that the court lacked the power to refuse enforcement to contracts found to be unconscionable. In other jurisdictions, it has been held as a matter of common law that unconscionable contracts are not enforceable. While no decision of this court so holding has been found, the notion that an unconscionable bargain should not be given full enforcement is by no means novel. In Scott v. United States, 79 U.S. (12 Wall.) 443, 445, 20 L.Ed. 438 (1870), the Supreme Court stated:

> . . . If a contract be unreasonable and unconscionable, but not void for fraud, a court of law will give to the party who sues for its

> breach damages, not according to its letter, but only such as he is equitably entitled to . . .

Since we have never adopted or rejected such a rule, the question here presented is actually one of first impression.

[7] Congress has recently enacted the Uniform Commercial Code, which specifically provides that the court may refuse to enforce a contract which it finds to be unconscionable at the time it was made. 28 D.C. Code § 2–302 (Supp. IV 1965). The enactment of this section, which occurred subsequent to the contracts here in suit, does not mean that the common law of the District of Columbia was otherwise at the time of enactment, nor does it preclude the court from adopting a similar rule in the exercise of its powers to develop the common law for the District of Columbia. In fact, in view of the absence of prior authority on the point, we consider the congressional adoption of § 2–302 persuasive authority for following the rationale of the cases from which the section is explicitly derived. Accordingly, we hold that where the element of unconscionability is present at the time a contract is made, the contract should not be enforced.

[8] Unconscionability has generally been recognized to include an absence of meaningful choice on the part of one of the parties together with contract terms which are unreasonably favorable to the other party. Whether a meaningful choice is present in a particular case can only be determined by consideration of all the circumstances surrounding the transaction. In many cases the meaningfulness of the choice is negated by a gross inequality of bargaining power.[3] The manner in which the contract was entered is also relevant to this consideration. Did each party to the contract, considering his obvious education or lack of it, have a reasonable opportunity to understand the terms of the contract, or were the important terms hidden in a maze of fine print and minimized by deceptive sales practices? Ordinarily, one who signs an agreement without full knowledge of its terms might be held to assume the risk that he has entered a one-sided bargain.[4] But when a party of little bargaining power, and hence little

---

[3] *See* Henningsen v. Bloomfield Motors, Inc., 161 A.2d 69, 86 (N.J. 1960), and authorities there cited. Inquiry into the relative bargaining power of the two parties is not an inquiry wholly divorced from the general question of unconscionability, since a one-sided bargain is itself evidence of the inequality of the bargaining parties. This fact was vaguely recognized in the common law doctrine of intrinsic fraud, that is, fraud which can be presumed from the grossly unfair nature of the terms of the contract. *See* the oft-quoted statement of Lord Hardwicke in Earl of Chesterfield v. Janssen, 28 Eng. Rep. 82, 100 (1751): " . . . (Fraud) may be apparent from the intrinsic nature and subject of the bargain itself; such as no man in his senses and not under delusion would make . . ." And *cf.* Hume v. United States, *supra* note 3, 132 U.S. 406, 413, 10 S.Ct. 134, 137 (1889), where the Court characterized the English cases as "cases in which one party took advantage of the other's ignorance of arithmetic to impose upon him, and the fraud was apparent from the face of the contracts."

[4] *See* Restatement, Contracts § 70 (1932); Note, 63 HARV.L.REV. 494 (1950). *See also* Daley v. People's Building, Loan & Savings Ass'n, 178 Mass. 13, 59 N.E. 452, 453 (1901), in which Mr.

real choice, signs a commercially unreasonable contract with little or no knowledge of its terms, it is hardly likely that his consent, or even an objective manifestation of his consent, was ever given to all the terms. In such a case the usual rule that the terms of the agreement are not to be questioned[5] should be abandoned and the court should consider whether the terms of the contract are so unfair that enforcement should be withheld.

[9] In determining reasonableness or fairness, the primary concern must be with the terms of the contract considered in light of the circumstances existing when the contract was made. The test is not simple, nor can it be mechanically applied. The terms are to be considered "in the light of the general commercial background and the commercial needs of the particular trade or case."[6] Corbin suggests the test as being whether the terms are "so extreme as to appear unconscionable according to the mores and business practices of the time and place." 1 Corbin, op. cit.[7] We think this formulation correctly states the test to be applied in those cases where no meaningful choice was exercised upon entering the contract.

[10] Because the trial court and the appellate court did not feel that enforcement could be refused, no findings were made on the possible unconscionability of the contracts in these cases. Since the record is not sufficient for our deciding the issue as a matter of law, the cases must be remanded to the trial court for further proceedings.

So ordered.

DANAHER, CIRCUIT JUDGE (dissenting):

[11] The District of Columbia Court of Appeals obviously was as unhappy about the situation here presented as any of us can possibly be. Its opinion in the *Williams* case, quoted in the majority text, concludes: "We think Congress should consider corrective legislation to protect the public from such exploitive contracts as were utilized in the case at bar."

Justice Holmes, while sitting on the Supreme Judicial Court of Massachusetts, made this observation:

> . . . Courts are less and less disposed to interfere with parties making such contracts as they choose, so long as they interfere with no one's welfare but their own . . . It will be understood that we are speaking of parties standing in an equal position where neither has any oppressive advantage or power . . .

[5]   This rule has never been without exception. In cases involving merely the transfer of unequal amounts of the same commodity, the courts have held the bargain unenforceable for the reason that "in such a case, it is clear, that the law cannot indulge in the presumption of equivalence between the consideration and the promise." 1 Williston on Contracts § 115 (3d ed. 1957).

[6]   Comment, Uniform Commercial Code § 2–307.

[7]   See Henningsen v. Bloomfield Motors, Inc., *supra* note 2; Mandel v. Liebman, 303 N.Y. 88, 100 N.E.2d 149 (1951). The traditional test as stated in Greer v. Tweed, *supra* note 3, 13 Abb. Pr. N.S. 427, 429 (1872), is "such as no man in his senses and not under delusion would make on the one hand, and as no honest or fair man would accept, on the other."

[12] My view is thus summed up by an able court which made no finding that there had actually been sharp practice. Rather the appellant seems to have known precisely where she stood.

[13] There are many aspects of public policy here involved. What is a luxury to some may seem an outright necessity to others. Is public oversight to be required of the expenditures of relief funds? A washing machine, e.g., in the hands of a relief client might become a fruitful source of income. Many relief clients may well need credit, and certain business establishments will take long chances on the sale of items, expecting their pricing policies will afford a degree of protection commensurate with the risk. Perhaps a remedy when necessary will be found within the provisions of the "Loan Shark" law, D.C. Code 26–601 et seq. (1961).

[14] I mention such matters only to emphasize the desirability of a cautious approach to any such problem, particularly since the law for so long has allowed parties such great latitude in making their own contracts. I dare say there must annually be thousands upon thousands of installment credit transactions in this jurisdiction, and one can only speculate as to the effect the decision in these cases will have.

[15] I join the District of Columbia Court of Appeals in its disposition of the issues.

NOTES AND QUESTIONS

During the late 1950's and early 1960's multiple courts in the District of Columbia struggled to come up with legal ground to cease Walker-Thomas's business practice of combining the cost of his customer's isolated transactions into one lump sum, leaving a balance due on all items purchased until their entire balance was paid in full. If a customer defaulted on a payment, regardless of the aggregate amount she had paid towards the balance due, Walker-Thomas would reposes ALL of the items she had purchased. Three attorneys from the Legal Assistance Office in Washington D.C. decided to "vigorously" represent two defendants in lawsuits against Walker-Thomas Furniture Co. One defendant was named Williams, the other named Thorne, and their attorneys were determined to establish legal precedent that would protect other indigent individuals who were also being taken advantage of by companies like Walker-Thomas.

The attorneys for Williams and Thorne attempted to show a lack of mutual assent, because there was valid precedent supporting that argument. However, the District of Columbia Court of General Sessions reluctantly found for Walker-Thomas, as did the District of Columbia Court of Appeals, who actually wrote in their opinion a call to Congress for "corrective legislation to protect the public from such exploitive contracts." Ultimately, the case was argued before the United States Court of Appeals for the District of Columbia, where the case was reversed and remanded to the general sessions court for proceedings consistent with their opinion (the edited version of which is the case, above).

On remand both cases settled before trial, and both Williams and Thorne were compensated with an amount all parties considered to be a "reasonable value" for the items Walker-Thomas repossessed. After the ruling from the United States Court of Appeals, one of the attorneys who represented Thorne said, "[i]t is hoped that these cases will provide an impetus to civil legal aid offices to challenge exploitation of the poor in the highest court necessary to achieve results for the individual indigent client and to encourage case law which is useful at the trail level for their protection." Dostert, Pierre E., *Appellate Restatement of Unconscionability: Civil Legal Aid at Work.* A.B.A.J. 54, no. 12, 1183, 1186 (1968), http://www.jstor.org/stable/25724619.

———

PROBLEM 12-1

You *Need* $3,000 Wheels!

Christy Chenney, a resident of a desert community in Southern California, lived four days with her car's plastic hubcaps. On day five, armed with three of her boyfriend's pay stubs, a bank statement and the names of references, the unemployed mother of three drove to a strip mall in the suburbs and outfitted her new used-car with a set of gleaming, $57-a-week, rent-to-own chrome wheels. If she makes her payments on time for the next 52 weeks, every 11th payment will be forgiven. In the end, she will have paid $2,736 for a set of $1,800 wheels.

Nothing's worse than plastic hubcaps.

(a) Does Ms. Chenney have an unconscionability claim? Under her "rent-to-own" contract, she can stop payment at any time and have no obligation to pay anything more. She just has to give back the wheels. If she doesn't make all the payments, though, she loses all the money she's paid to date.

(b) Can you think of a way to use the fact that Rent-A-Wheel generously forgives every eleventh payment (providing the other payments are made in a timely manner) into an argument in favor of a finding of unconscionability?

———

[handwritten margin notes: "Substentive ↓ one sided" and "Procedural? Not hidden"]

WEAVER V. AMERICAN OIL CO.

Supreme Court of Indiana
257 Ind. 458, 276 N.E.2d 144 (1971)

ARTERBURN, CHIEF JUSTICE.

[1] In this case the appellee oil company presented to the appellant-defendant lessee, a filling station operator, a printed form contract as a lease to be signed, by the defendant, which contained, in addition to the normal leasing provisions, a "hold harmless" clause which provided in substance that the lessee operator would hold harmless and also indemnify the oil company for any negligence of the oil company occurring on the leased premises. The litigation arises as a result of the oil company's own employee spraying gasoline over Weaver and his assistant and causing them to be burned and injured on the leased premises. This action was initiated by American Oil and Hoffer (Appellees) for a declaratory judgment to determine the liability of appellant Weaver, under the clause in the lease. The trial court entered judgment holding Weaver liable under the lease.

Clause three (3) of the lease reads as follows:

> Lessor, its agents and employees shall not be liable for any loss, damage, injuries, or other casualty of whatsoever kind or by whomsoever caused to the person or property of anyone (including Lessee) on or off the premises, arising out of or resulting from Lessee's use, possession or operation thereof, or from defects in the premises whether apparent or hidden, or from the installation existence, use, maintenance, condition, repair, alteration, removal or replacement of any equipment thereon, whether due in whole or in part to negligent acts or omissions of Lessor, its agents or employees; and Lessee for himself, his heirs, executors, administrators, successors and assigns, hereby agrees to indemnify and hold Lessor, its agents and employees, harmless from and against all claims, demands, liabilities, suits or actions (including all reasonable expenses and attorneys' fees incurred by or imposed on the Lessor in connection therewith) for such loss, damage, injury or other casualty. Lessee also agrees to pay all reasonable expenses and attorneys' fees incurred by Lessor in the event that Lessee shall default under the provisions of this paragraph.

[2] It will be noted that this lease clause not only exculpated the lessor oil company from its liability for its negligence, but also compelled Weaver to indemnify them for any damages or loss incurred as a result of its negligence. The appellate court held the exculpatory clause invalid, 261 N.E.2d 99, but the indemnifying clause valid, 262 N.E.2d 663. In our opinion, both these provisions must be read together since one may be used

to effectuate the result obtained through the other. We find no ground for any distinction and we therefore grant the petition to transfer the appeal to this court.

[3]   This is a contract, which was submitted (already in printed form) to a party with lesser bargaining power. As in this case, it may contain unconscionable or unknown provisions which are in fine print. Such is the case now before this court.

[4]   The facts reveal that Weaver had left high school after one and a half years and spent his time, prior to leasing the service station, working at various skilled and unskilled labor oriented jobs. He was not one who should be expected to know the law or understand the meaning of technical terms. The ceremonious activity of signing the lease consisted of nothing more than the agent of American Oil placing the lease in front of Mr. Weaver and saying "sign," which Mr. Weaver did. There is nothing in the record to indicate that Weaver read the lease; that the agent asked Weaver to read it; or that the agent, in any manner, attempted to call Weaver's attention to the "hold harmless" clause in the lease. Each year following, the procedure was the same. A salesman, from American Oil, would bring the lease to Weaver, at the station, and Weaver would sign it. The evidence showed that Weaver had never read the lease prior to signing and that the clauses in the lease were never explained to him in a manner from which he could grasp their legal significance. The leases were prepared by the attorneys of American Oil Company, for the American Oil Company, and the agents of the American Oil Company never attempted to explain the conditions of the lease nor did they advise Weaver that he should consult legal counsel, before signing the lease. The superior bargaining power of American Oil is patently obvious and the significance of Weaver's signature upon the legal document amounted to nothing more than a mere formality to Weaver for the substantial protection of American Oil.

[5]   Had this case involved the sale of goods it would have been termed an "unconscionable contract" under sec. 2–302 of the Uniform Commercial Code. The statute reads as follows:

19–2–302. Unconscionable contract or clause.

(1)   If the court as a matter of law finds the contract or any clause of the contract to have been unconscionable at the time it was made the court may refuse to enforce the contract, or it may enforce the remainder of the contract without the unconscionable clause, or it may so limit the application of any unconscionable clause as to avoid any unconscionable result.

(2)   When it is claimed or appears to the court that the contract or any clause thereof may be unconscionable the parties shall be afforded a reasonable opportunity to present evidence as to its

commercial setting, purpose and effect to aid the court in making the determination.

[6] According to the Comment to Official Text, the basic test of unconscionability is whether, in light of the general commercial background and the commercial needs of the particular trade or case, the clauses involved are so one-sided as to be unconscionable under the circumstances existing at the time of the making of the contract. Subsection two makes it clear that it is proper for the court to hear evidence upon these questions.

> An "unconscionable contract" has been defined to be such as no sensible man not under delusion, duress or in distress would make, and such as no honest and fair man would accept. There exists here an "inequality so strong, gross and manifest that it is impossible to state it to a man of common sense without producing an exclamation at the inequality of it." "Where the inadequacy of the price is so great that the mind revolts at it the court will lay hold on the slightest circumstances of oppression or advantage to rescind the contract."

It is not the policy of the law to restrict business dealings or to relieve a party of his own mistakes of judgment, but where one party has taken advantage of another's necessities and distress to obtain an unfair advantage over him, and the latter, owing to his condition, has encumbered himself with a heavy liability or an onerous obligation for the sake of a small or inadequate present gain, there will be relief granted. *Stiefler v. McCullough*, 97 Ind.App. 123, 174 N.E. 823 (1931).

[7] The facts of this case reveal that in exchange for a contract which, if the clause in question is enforceable, may cost Mr. Weaver potentially thousands of dollars in damages for negligence of which he was not the cause, Weaver must operate the service station seven days a week for long hours, at a total yearly income of $5,000—$6,000. The evidence also reveals that the clause was in fine print and contained no title heading which would have identified it as an indemnity clause. It seems a deplorable abuse of justice to hold a man of poor education, to a contract prepared by the attorneys of American Oil, for the benefit of American Oil which was presented to Weaver on a "take it or leave it basis."

[8] Justice Frankfurter of the United States Supreme Court spoke on the question of inequality of bargaining power in his dissenting opinion in United States v. Bethlehem Steel Corp. (1942), 315 U.S. 289, 326, 62 S.Ct. 581, 599, 86 L.Ed. 855, 876.

> [I]t is said that familiar principles would be outraged if Bethlehem were denied recovery on these contracts. But is there any principle which is more familiar or more firmly embedded in the history of Anglo-American law than the basic doctrine that the courts will

not permit themselves to be used as instruments of inequity and
injustice? Does any principle in our law have more universal
application than the doctrine that courts will not enforce
transactions in which the relative positions of the parties are such
that one has unconscionably taken advantage of the necessities of
the other?

These principles are not foreign to the law of contracts. Fraud and
physical duress are not the only grounds upon which courts refuse
to enforce contracts. The law is not so primitive that it sanctions
every injustice except brute force and downright fraud. More
specifically, the courts generally refuse to lend themselves to the
enforcement of a "bargain" in which one party has unjustly taken
advantage of the economic necessities of the other . . .

[9]   The traditional contract is the result of free bargaining of parties
who are brought together by the play of the market, and who meet each
other on a footing of approximate economic equality. In such a society there
is no danger that freedom of contract will be a threat to the social order as
a whole. But in present-day commercial life the standardized mass contract
has appeared. It is used primarily by enterprises with strong bargaining
power and position. The weaker party, in need of the good or services, is
frequently not in a position to shop around for better terms, either because
the author of the standard contract has a monopoly (natural or artificial)
or because all competitors use the same clauses.

[10] Judge Frankfurter's dissent was written nearly twenty years ago.
It represents a direction and philosophy which the law, at that time was
taking and is now compelled to accept in our modern society over the old
principle known as the parole evidence rule. The parole evidence rule
states that an agreement or contract, signed by the parties, is conclusively
presumed to represent an integration or meeting of the minds of the
parties. This is an archaic rule from the old common law. The objectivity of
the rule has as its only merit its simplicity of application which is far
outweighed by its failure in many cases to represent the actual agreement,
particularly where a printed form prepared by one party contains hidden
clauses unknown to the other party is submitted and signed. The law
should seek the truth or the subjective understanding of the parties in this
more enlightened age. The burden should be on the party submitting such
"a package" in printed form to show that the other party had knowledge of
any unusual or unconscionable terms contained therein. The principle
should be the same as that applicable to implied warranties, namely that
a package of goods sold to a purchaser is fit for the purposes intended and
contains no harmful materials other than that represented. Caveat lessee
is no more the current law than caveat emptor. Only in this way can justice
be served and the true meaning of freedom of contract preserved. The
analogy is rational. We have previously pointed out a similar situation in

the Uniform Commercial Code, which prohibits unconscionable contract clauses in sales agreements.

[11] When a party can show that the contract, which is sought to be enforced, was in fact an unconscionable one, due to a prodigious amount of bargaining power on behalf of the stronger party, which is used to the stronger party's advantage and is unknown to the lesser party, causing a great hardship and risk on the lesser party, the contract provision, or the contract as a whole, if the provision is not separable, should not be enforceable on the grounds that the provision is contrary to public policy. The party seeking to enforce such a contract has the burden of showing that the provisions were explained to the other party and came to his knowledge and there was in fact a real and voluntary meeting of the minds and not merely an objective meeting.

[12] Unjust contract provisions have been found unenforceable, in the past, on the grounds of being contrary to public policy, where a party has a greater superior bargaining position. In *Pennsylvania Railroad Co. v. Kent* (1964), 136 Ind.App. 551, 198 N.E.2d 615, Judge Hunter, speaking for the court said that although the proposition that "parties may enter into such contractual arrangement as they may desire may be conceded in the general sense; when, however, such special agreement may result in affecting the public interest and thereby contravene public policy, the abrogation of the rules governing common carriers must be zealously guarded against."

[13] We do not mean to say or infer that parties may not make contracts exculpating one of his negligence and providing for indemnification, but it must be done knowingly and willingly as in insurance contracts made for that very purpose.

[14] It is the duty of the courts to administer justice and that role is not performed, in this case, by enforcing a written instrument, not really an agreement of the parties as shown by the evidence here, although signed by the parties. The parole evidence rule must yield to the equities of the case. The appeal is transferred to this court and the judgment of the trial court is reversed with direction to enter judgment for the appellant.

GIVEN, DEBRULER and HUNTER, JJ., concur.

PRENTICE, J., dissents, with opinion.

PRENTICE, JUDGE (dissenting).

[15] My opinion is diametrically opposed to those of both the majority herein and of the Appellate Court as set forth in 261 N.E.2d 99, and 262 N.E.2d 663. There is no law to support the decisions of the Appellate Court . . .

* * *

[16] The decisions of the Appellate Court would not enforce the exculpatory agreement upon the theory that, although this Court has consistently refused to void exculpatory provisions as contrary to public policy, their burdens being unusual and considerable, they should not be enforced unless it appears that the party who assumes the burden under the clause was aware of it and understood its far reaching implications. The burden of proving such awareness, or lack of it, would vary depending upon the relative bargaining positions of the parties. The indemnity provision, however, was held enforceable, by reason of the availability of insurance rendering the risk manageable.

[17] The facts as found, are that although the defendant never read the lease, he had ample opportunity to do so and to obtain counsel. A general rule in effect not only in Indiana but elsewhere, is that a person who signs a contract, without bothering to read the same, will be bound by its terms.

[18] Without regard to whether or not he was aware of its contents, a person will be relieved of his obligations under a contract under circumstances falling into two main categories: (a) where the contract is not enforceable because of occurrences or omissions (fraud, concealment, etc.) surrounding its execution and (b) where the contract is not enforceable because of the nature or subject of the contract (illegality of subject matter). The Appellate Court would have us recognize a third category and excuse performance, at least as to harsh provisions, without a showing that he was aware of and understood the contract provisions and their implications, with the burden of proof upon such issues to vary depending upon the relative bargaining positions of the parties. The objective of such a rule is laudable, but I think it, nevertheless, totally unworkable.

* * *

[19] Chief Justice Arterburn, speaking for a majority of this Court, has concluded that the defendant was in an inferior position with respect to the lease and treats the lease as we might treat an adhesion contract. I find justification for neither. An adhesion contract is one that has been drafted unilaterally by the dominant party and then presented on a "take it or leave it" basis to the weaker party, who has no real opportunity to bargain about its terms. Restatement 2d, Conflict of Law § 332 a, cmt. e; 17 C.J.S. Contracts § 10, at 581. Here we have a printed form contract prepared by American. There was great disparity between the economic positions of American and Defendant; and Defendant was a man of limited educational and business background. However, there is nothing from which we can find or infer that the printed lease provisions were not subject to negotiation or that, with respect to this particular lease, Defendant was not in a bargaining position equal to that of American. The fact that Defendant did not avail himself of the opportunity to read the agreement

but elected to accept it as presented does not warrant the inference that his only options were to "take it or leave it." That the "hold harmless" clause was or might have been in small print, as suggested by the majority, can hardly have significance in light of the claim and finding that the defendant did not read any portion of the document.

* * *

[20] I would accept transfer of this cause, set aside the decision of the Appellate Court, as modified, and affirm the decision of the trial court.

HAINES V. ST. CHARLES SPEEDWAY, INC.

United States Court of Appeals, Eighth Circuit
874 F.2d 572 (1989)

JOHN R. GIBSON, CIRCUIT JUDGE.

[1] Norman and Barbara Haines appeal an adverse summary judgment. Norman Haines was injured when struck in the infield of a racetrack by his own race car while attempting to have it started before an event. He and Barbara, his wife, sued the owner of the racetrack and the promoter of that day's racing event. The district court granted defendants' motions for summary judgment, holding that a release signed by Norman Haines precluded him from pursuing his claims. We affirm.

[2] The facts of this case are essentially undisputed, and in reviewing the district court's decision to grant summary judgment we view the facts in a light most favorable to the nonmoving parties, Norman and Barbara Haines. Norman Haines owned a Stanton sprint car and wished to race it at the St. Charles Speedway of St. Charles, Missouri, on April 26, 1986. Although he hired Mike Thurman to drive the car, Haines desired to enter the infield portion of the Speedway in order to aid in preparing for the race. As he stood in line, waiting with others to enter the infield, Haines was presented with and signed a document entitled "Release and Waiver of Liability and Indemnity Agreement." All those who entered the infield were required to sign this form.

[3] Haines, who has a second or third grade reading ability, signed the document without reading it, as he had done many times before. At no point did he ask his wife Barbara, who was an official of the Midwest Racing Association, or anyone else to explain the significance of the release. Some time after gaining access to the infield, Haines asked that his sprint car be started. During this process, which entailed using a separate auto to push-start the racing car, Haines was struck by his own car and injured.

[4] Haines sued the St. Charles Speedway, Inc. and Bob Wente, the promoter of the event at which Haines was injured. Haines alleged that

they were negligent in permitting an inexperienced driver to operate the push car, in constructing and maintaining the speedway, and in failing to warn him of the dangers presented by the speedway. Norman Haines claimed for damages arising from his injury; his wife Barbara asserted loss of consortium.

[5] The district court granted defendants' motion for summary judgment, holding that the release signed by Haines exculpated the Speedway and Wente from any liability that they may have incurred as a consequence of their alleged negligence. Contending that this was error, Norman and Barbara Haines argue that the release constituted a contract of adhesion under controlling Missouri law and was unenforceable because at the time he signed the release Norman could not have expected that the document would grant the Speedway and promoter Wente unlimited exculpation from liability.

[6] Initially, we observe that the language of the release signed by Haines is both unambiguous and broad in scope:

> RELEASE AND WAIVER OF LIABILITY AND INDEMNITY AGREEMENT IN CONSIDERATION of being permitted to enter for any purpose any RESTRICTED AREA (herein defined as including but not limited to the racing surface, pit areas [and] infield . . .) . . . or for any purpose participate in any way in the event, EACH OF THE UNDERSIGNED . . .
>
>> 1. HEREBY RELEASES, WAIVES, DISCHARGES AND COVENANTS NOT TO SUE the promoter, participants, racing association, sanctioning organization . . ., track operator, track owner, officials, car owners, drivers [and] pit crews . . . from all liability to the undersigned, for any or all loss or damage, and any claim or demands therefor on account of injury to the person or property or resulting in death of the undersigned, whether caused by the negligence of the releasees or otherwise while the undersigned is in or upon the restricted area . . . or for any purpose participating in the event;
>>
>> 2. HEREBY AGREES TO INDEMNIFY AND SAVE AND HOLD HARMLESS the releasees and each of them from any loss, liability, damage, or cost they may incur due to the presence of the undersigned in or upon the restricted area or in any way competing, officiating, observing, or working for, or for any purpose participating in the event and whether caused by the negligence of the releasees or otherwise.
>>
>> 3. HEREBY ASSUMES FULL RESPONSIBILITY FOR AND RISK OF BODILY INJURY, DEATH OR PROPERTY DAMAGE due to the negligence of releasees or otherwise

[handwritten margin note: unambiguous]

while in or upon the restricted area and/or while competing, officiating, observing, or working for or for any purpose participating in the event.

EACH OF THE UNDERSIGNED expressly acknowledges and agrees that the activities of the event are very dangerous and involve the risk of serious injury and/or death and/or property damage. EACH OF THE UNDERSIGNED further expressly agrees that the foregoing release, waiver and indemnity agreement is intended to be as broad and inclusive as is permitted by the law of the Province or State in which the event is conducted and that if any portion thereof is held invalid, it is agreed that the balance shall, notwithstanding, continue in full legal force and effect.

THE UNDERSIGNED HAS READ AND VOLUNTARILY SIGNS THE RELEASE AND WAIVER OF LIABILITY AND INDEMNITY AGREEMENT, and further agrees that no oral representations, statements or inducements apart from the foregoing written agreement have been made.

[7]   The parties, however, debate whether this document constitutes a "contract of adhesion." Missouri law controls in this diversity case. Particularly illuminating are two scholarly opinions crafted by Judge Shangler of the Missouri Court of Appeals for the Western District, one of which provides this definition:

> A contract of adhesion is a form contract submitted by one party and accepted by the other on the basis of *this or nothing*. It is an instrument devised by skilled legal talent for mass and standard industry-wide use which does not allow for idiosyncrasy. It is a transaction not negotiated but one which literally *adheres* for want of choice.

definition

Estrin Constr. Co. v. Aetna Casualty and Sur. Co., 612 S.W.2d 413, 418 n.3 (Mo. App. 1981) (emphasis in original); *see also Spychalski v. MFA Life Ins. Co.*, 620 S.W.2d 388 (Mo. App. 1981). We are satisfied that the document signed by Haines, one obviously crafted by lawyers, printed in small type, and signed by all who desired entry to the infield of the Speedway, constituted a contract of adhesion under this standard. While some such contracts may be enforceable, we are to examine the "total transaction" in determining the intent of the parties, rather than looking only to the literal language of the document. *Id.* at 420.

[8]   Haines contends that the circumstances surrounding his execution of the release mandate that we hold it invalid. He argues that the Speedway knowingly withheld the release form from all track entrants until the moment of entry, and that it had no reason to expect that the

drivers, mechanics, and car owners who frequented the track would appreciate the significance of the release when they signed it.

[9] Here, the district court fully considered the circumstances surrounding the execution of the release. Aware of Haines' claim that he possessed only a second or third grade reading ability, the court stated that, "If Norman Haines is functionally illiterate, it was his duty to procure someone to read or explain the release to him before signing it." In response to Haines' argument that he was "pressured" into signing the release, the district court observed that Haines did not produce any fact establishing that the execution of the release was a product of duress.

[10] Indeed, Norman Haines stated in deposition that he has been involved in racing since 1952, and during that time has owned some 13 sprint cars. In 1954, Haines discontinued participating in racing events as a driver when he started to raise a family. He admits to doing so because of the dangerousness of the sport. He also admits to witnessing, in the past, crashed automobiles roll to the infield portions of the tracks. While we are sensitive to the circumstances now facing Norman Haines, he doubtlessly knew that the sport placed risks on both participants and spectators. Although Haines could have withdrawn from his hobby at any time, he did not do so.

[11] In construing a standardized contract under Missouri law, furthermore, we are "to effectuate the reasonable expectations of the average member of the public who accepts it." *Estrin*, 612 S.W.2d at 419 n.4. To hold that a reasonable person would not realize the significance of the release signed by Haines would be to ignore the unambiguous text of the document.

* * *

Accordingly, the judgment of the district court is affirmed.

ZAPATHA V. DAIRY MART, INC.
Supreme Judicial Court of Massachusetts
381 Mass. 284, 408 N.E.2d 1370 (1980)

WILKINS, JUSTICE.

[1] We are concerned here with the question whether Dairy Mart, Inc. (Dairy Mart), lawfully undertook to terminate a franchise agreement under which the Zapathas operated a Dairy Mart store on Wilbraham Road in Springfield. The Zapathas brought this action seeking to enjoin the termination of the agreement, alleging that the contract provision purporting to authorize the termination of the franchise agreement without cause was unconscionable and that Dairy Mart's conduct was an

unfair and deceptive act or practice in violation of G.L. c. 93A. The judge ruled that Dairy Mart did not act in good faith, that the termination provision was unconscionable, and that Dairy Mart's termination of the agreement without cause was an unfair and deceptive act. We granted Dairy Mart's application for direct appellate review of a judgment that stated that Dairy Mart could terminate the agreement only for good cause and that the attempted termination was null and void. We reverse the judgments.

[2]   Mr. Zapatha is a high school graduate who had attended college for one year and had also taken college evening courses in business administration and business law. From 1952 to May, 1973, he was employed by a company engaged in the business of electroplating. He rose through the ranks to foreman and then to the position of operations manager, at one time being in charge of all metal finishing in the plant with 150 people working under him. In May, 1973, he was discharged and began looking for other opportunities, in particular a business of his own. Several months later he met with a representative of Dairy Mart. Dairy Mart operates a chain of franchised "convenience" stores. The Dairy Mart representative told Mr. Zapatha that working for Dairy Mart was being in business for one's self and that such a business was very stable and secure. Mr. Zapatha signed an application to be considered for a franchise. In addition, he was presented with a brochure entitled "Here's a Chance," which made certain representations concerning the status of a franchise holder.[8]

[3]   Dairy Mart approved Mr. Zapatha's application and offered him a store in Agawam. On November 8, 1973, a representative of Dairy Mart showed him a form of franchise agreement, entitled Limited Franchise and License Agreement, asked him to read it, and explained that his wife would have to sign the agreement as well.

[4]   Under the terms of the agreement, Dairy Mart would license the Zapathas to operate a Dairy Mart store, using the Dairy Mart trademark and associated insignia, and utilizing Dairy Mart's "confidential" merchandising methods. Dairy Mart would furnish the store and the equipment and would pay rent and gas and electric bills as well as certain other costs of doing business. In return Dairy Mart would receive a franchise fee, computed as a percentage of the store's gross sales. The Zapathas would have to pay for the starting inventory, and maintain a minimum stock of saleable merchandise thereafter. They were also responsible for wages of employees, related taxes, and any sales taxes. The

---

[8]   It included the following statements: ". . . you'll have the opportunity to own and run your own business . . ."; "We want to be sure we're hooking up with the right person. A person who sees the opportunity in owning his own business . . . who requires the security that a multi-million dollar parent company can offer him . . . who has the good judgment and business sense to take advantage of the unique independence that Dairy Mart offers its franchisees . . . We're looking for a partner . . . who can take the tools we offer and build a life of security and comfort. . . ."

termination provision, which is set forth in full in the margin,[9] allowed either party, after twelve months, to terminate the agreement without cause on ninety days' written notice. In the event of termination initiated by it without cause, Dairy Mart agreed to repurchase the saleable merchandise inventory at retail prices, less 20%.

[5] The Dairy Mart representative read and explained the termination provision to Mr. Zapatha. Mr. Zapatha later testified that, while he understood every word in the provision, he had interpreted it to mean that Dairy Mart could terminate the agreement only for cause. The Dairy Mart representative advised Mr. Zapatha to take the agreement to an attorney and said "I would prefer that you did." However, he also told Mr. Zapatha that the terms of the contract were not negotiable. The Zapathas signed the agreement without consulting an attorney. When the Zapathas took charge of the Agawam store, a representative of Dairy Mart worked with them to train them in Dairy Mart's methods of operation.

[6] In 1974, another store became available on Wilbraham Road in Springfield, and the Zapathas elected to surrender the Agawam store. They executed a new franchise agreement, on an identical printed form, relating to the new location.

[7] In November, 1977, Dairy Mart presented a new and more detailed form of "Independent Operator's Agreement" to the Zapathas for execution. Some of the terms were less favorable to the store operator than those of the earlier form of agreement.[10] Mr. Zapatha told representatives of Dairy Mart that he was content with the existing contract and had decided not to sign the new agreement. On January 20, 1978, Dairy Mart gave written notice to the Zapathas that their contract was being terminated effective in ninety days. The termination notice stated that Dairy Mart "remains available to enter into discussions with you with respect to entering into a new Independent Operator's Agreement; however, there is no assurance that Dairy Mart will enter into a new

---

[9] The term of this Limited Franchise and License Agreement shall be for a period of Twelve (12) months from date hereof, and shall continue uninterrupted thereafter. If DEALER desires to terminate after 12 months from date hereof, he shall do so by giving COMPANY a ninety (90) day written notice by Registered Mail of his intention to terminate. If COMPANY desires to terminate, it likewise shall give a ninety (90) day notice, except for the following reasons which shall not require any written notice and shall terminate the Franchise immediately:

(a) Failure to pay bills to suppliers for inventory or other products when due.

(b) Failure to pay Franchise Fees to COMPANY.

(c) Failure to pay city, state or federal taxes as said taxes shall become due and payable.

(d) Breach of any condition of this Agreement.

[10] In his testimony, Mr. Zapatha said that he objected to a new provision under which Dairy Mart reserved the option to relocate an operator to a new location and to a requirement that the store be open from 7 A.M. to 11 P.M. every day. Previously the Zapathas' store had been open from 8 A.M. to 10 P.M.

There were other provisions, such as an obligation to pay future increases in the cost of heat and electricity, that were more burdensome to a franchisee. A few changes may have been to the advantage of the franchisee.

Agreement with you, or even if entered into, what terms such Agreement will contain." The notice also indicated that Dairy Mart was prepared to purchase the Zapathas' saleable inventory.

[8]   The judge found that Dairy Mart terminated the agreement solely because the Zapathas refused to sign the new agreement. He further found that, but for this one act, Dairy Mart did not behave in an unconscionable manner, in bad faith, or in disregard of its representations. There is no evidence that the Zapathas undertook to discuss a compromise of the differences that led to the notice of termination.

[9]   On these basic facts, the judge ruled that the franchise agreement was subject to the sales article of the Uniform Commercial Code (G.L. c. 106, art. 2) and, even if it were not, the principles of unconscionability and good faith expressed in that article applied to the franchise agreement by analogy. He further ruled that (1) the termination provision of the agreement was unconscionable because it authorized termination without cause, (2) the termination without cause violated Dairy Mart's obligation of good faith, and (3) the termination constituted "an unfair method of competition and unfair and deceptive act within the meaning of G.L. c. 93A, § 2."

[10] We consider first the question whether the franchise agreement involves a "transaction in goods" within the meaning of those words in article two of the Uniform Commercial Code, and that consequently the provisions of the sales articles of the Uniform Commercial Code govern the relationship between the parties. The Zapathas point specifically to the authority of a court to refuse to enforce "any clause of the contract" that the court finds "to have been unconscionable at the time it was made." [U.C.C. § 2–302]. They point additionally to the obligation of good faith in the performance and enforcement of a contract imposed by [U.C.C.], sec.1–203, and to the specialized definition of "good faith" in the sales article as meaning "in the case of a merchant . . . honesty in fact and the observance of reasonable commercial standards of fair dealing in the trade." [U.C.C.] § 2–103(1)(b).[11]

[11] We need not pause long over the question whether the franchise agreement and the relationship of the parties involved a transaction in goods. Certainly, the agreement required the plaintiffs to purchase goods from Dairy Mart. "Goods" for the purpose of the sales article means generally "all things . . . which are movable." [U.C.C.], § 2–105(1), as appearing in St.1957, c. 765, sec.1. However, the franchise agreement dealt

---

[11]   Generally throughout the Uniform Commercial Code, "good faith" is defined to mean "honesty in fact in the conduct or transaction concerned." G.L. c. 106, [U.C.C.] sec.1–01(19). The definition of "good faith" in the sales article includes a higher standard of conduct by adding a requirement that "merchants" observe "reasonable commercial standards of fair dealing in the trade." G.L. c. 106, [U.C.C.] § 2–103(1)(b). There is no doubt that Dairy Mart is a "merchant" as defined under the sales article. See G.L. c. 106, [U.C.C.] § 2–104.

with many subjects unrelated to the sale of goods by Dairy Mart.[12] About 70% of the goods the plaintiffs sold were not purchased from Dairy Mart. Dairy Mart's profit was intended to come from the franchise fee and not from the sale of items to its franchisees. Thus, the sale of goods by Dairy Mart to the Zapathas was, in a commercial sense, a minor aspect of the entire relationship.[13] We would be disinclined to import automatically all the provisions of the sales article into a relationship involving a variety of subjects other than the sale of goods, merely because the contract dealt in part with the sale of goods. Similarly, we would not be inclined to apply the sales article only to aspects of the agreement that concerned goods. Different principles of law might then govern separate portions of the same agreement with possibly inconsistent and unsatisfactory consequences.

[12] We view the legislative statements of policy concerning good faith and unconscionability as fairly applicable to all aspects of the franchise agreement, not by subjecting the franchise relationship to the provisions of the sales article but rather by applying the stated principles by analogy. This basic common law approach, applied to statutory statements of policy, permits a selective application of those principles expressed in a statute that reasonably should govern situations to which the statute does not apply explicitly.

[13] We consider first the plaintiffs' argument that the termination clause of the franchise agreement, authorizing Dairy Mart to terminate the agreement without cause, on ninety days' notice, was unconscionable by the standards expressed in [U.C.C.] § 2–302.[14] The same standards are set forth in Restatement (Second) of Contracts § 234 (Tent. Drafts Nos. 1–7, 1973). The issue is one of law for the court, and the test is to be made as of the time the contract was made. [U.C.C.] § 2–302(1), and comment 3 of the

---

[12] Where agreements have involved "goods," as defined in the Code, as well as other property or services, courts have attempted to ascertain whether the sale of goods was "their predominant factor, their thrust, their purpose, reasonably stated" (Bonebrake v. Cox, 499 F.2d 951, 960 (8th Cir. 1974)), and, if so, to apply the Code to the agreements. *See* Pittsburgh-Des Moines Steel Co. v. Brookhaven Manor Water Co., 532 F.2d 572, 580 (7th Cir. 1976); De Filippo v. Ford Motor Co., 516 F.2d 1313, 1323 (3d Cir.), *cert. denied*, 423 U.S. 912, 96 S.Ct. 216, 46 L.Ed.2d 141 (1975) (not primarily the sale of goods); Bonebrake v. Cox, supra at 960; Lincoln Pulp & Paper Co. v. Dravo Corp., 436 F. Supp. 262, 275 (D.Me. 1977) (predominantly a service contract); Ranger Constr. Co. v. Dixie Floor Co., 433 F. Supp. 442, 444–45 (D.S.C.1977); Burton v. Artery Co., 279 Md. 94, 102–15, 367 A.2d 935 (1977).

Accordingly, courts have applied the Uniform Commercial Code to distributorship agreements even though such agreements have concerned more than the sale of goods. *See, e. g.*, Corenswet, Inc. v. Amana Refrigeration, Inc., 594 F.2d 129, 134 (5th Cir.), *cert. denied*, 444 U.S. 938, 100 S.Ct. 288, 62 L.Ed.2d 198 (1979).

[13] The essential thrust of the transaction was an exchange of intangible rights, obligations, and services. Viewed in a realistic economic light, the franchise agreement contemplated the licensing by Dairy Mart of an entire "business format," including a trademark, a system of doing business, and the right to occupy a fully equipped store, in return for which it was to receive a franchise fee and the expectation that the Zapathas' efforts, in keeping with their obligations under the agreement, would enhance the goodwill of the Dairy Mart franchise chain as a whole.

[14] The agreement permitted immediate termination on the occurrence of certain conditions which are not involved in this case.

Official Comments. In measuring the unconscionability of the termination provision, the fact that the law imposes an obligation of good faith on Dairy Mart in its performance under the agreement should be weighed.

[14] The official comment to § 2–302 states that "(t)he basic test is whether, in the light of the general commercial background and the commercial needs of the particular trade or case, the clauses involved are so one-sided as to be unconscionable under the circumstances existing at the time of the making of the contract . . . . The principle is one of prevention of oppression and unfair surprise . . . and not of disturbance of allocation of risks because of superior bargaining power." Official Comment 1 to U.C.C. § 2–302.[15] Unconscionability is not defined in the Code, nor do the views expressed in the official comment provide a precise definition. The annotation prepared by the Massachusetts Advisory Committee on the Code states that "(t)he section appears to be intended to carry equity practice into the sales field." *See* 1 R. Anderson, Uniform Commercial Code § 2–302(7) (1970) to the same effect. This court has not had occasion to consider in any detail the meaning of the word "unconscionable" in § 2–302. Because there is no clear, all-purpose definition of "unconscionable," nor could there be, unconscionability must be determined on a case by case basis, giving particular attention to whether, at the time of the execution of the agreement, the contract provision could result in unfair surprise and was oppressive to the allegedly disadvantaged party.

[15] We start with a recognition that the Uniform Commercial Code itself implies that a contract provision allowing termination without cause is not per se unconscionable. Section 2–309(3) provides that "(t)ermination of a contract by one party except on the happening of an agreed event requires that reasonable notification be received by the other party and an agreement dispensing with notification is invalid if its operation would be unconscionable." [U.C.C.] § 2–309. This language implies that termination of a sales contract without agreed "cause" is authorized by the Code, provided reasonable notice is given. There is no suggestion that the ninety days' notice provided in the Dairy Mart franchise agreement was unreasonable.

[16] We find no potential for unfair surprise to the Zapathas in the provision allowing termination without cause. We view the question of unfair surprise as focused on the circumstances under which the agreement was entered into.[16] The termination provision was neither

---

[15] The comment has been criticized as useless and at best ambiguous (J. White & R. Summers, The Uniform Commercial Code, 116 (1972)), and § 2–302 has been characterized as devoid of any specific content. Leff, Unconscionability and the Code (The Emperor's New Clause, 115 U.PA. L.REV. 485, 487–89 (1967)). On the other hand, it has been said that the strength of the unconscionability concept is its abstraction, permitting judicial creativity. *See* Ellinghaus, In Defense of Unconscionability, 78 YALE L.J. 757 (1969).

[16] As we shall note subsequently, the concept of oppression deals with the substantive unfairness of the contract term. This two-part test for unconscionability involves determining

obscurely worded, nor buried in fine print in the contract. *Contrast Williams v. Walker-Thomas Furniture Co.,* 350 F.2d 445, 449 (D.C. Cir.1965). The provision was specifically pointed out to Mr. Zapatha before it was signed; Mr. Zapatha testified that he thought the provision was "straightforward," and he declined the opportunity to take the agreement to a lawyer for advice. The Zapathas had ample opportunity to consider the agreement before they signed it.[17] Significantly, the subject of loss of employment was paramount in Mr. Zapatha's mind. He testified that he had held responsible jobs in one company from 1952 to 1973, that he had lost his employment, and that he "was looking for something that had a certain amount of security; something that was stable and something I could call my own." We conclude that a person of Mr. Zapatha's business experience and education should not have been surprised by the termination provision and, if in fact he was, there was no element of unfairness in the inclusion of that provision in the agreement. *See Fleischmann Distilling Corp. v. Distillers Co.,* 395 F.Supp. 221, 233 ("(i)t is the exceptional commercial setting where a claim of unconscionability will be allowed"). *Contrast Johnson v. Mobil Oil Corp.,* 415 F.Supp. 264, 268–269 (illiterate service station operator incapable of reading dealer contract).

[17] We further conclude that there was no oppression in the inclusion of a termination clause in the franchise agreement. We view the question of oppression as directed to the substantive fairness to the parties of permitting the termination provisions to operate as written. The Zapathas took over a going business on premises provided by Dairy Mart, using equipment furnished by Dairy Mart. As an investment, the Zapathas had only to purchase the inventory of goods to be sold but, as Dairy Mart concedes, on termination by it without cause Dairy Mart was obliged to repurchase all the Zapathas' saleable merchandise inventory, including items not purchased from Dairy Mart, at 80% of its retail value. There was no potential for forfeiture or loss of investment. There is no question here of a need for a reasonable time to recoup the franchisees' initial investment. The Zapathas were entitled to their net profits through the entire term of the agreement. They failed to sustain their burden of showing that the agreement allocated the risks and benefits connected with termination in an unreasonably disproportionate way and that the termination provision

---

whether there was "an absence of meaningful choice on the part of one of the parties, together with contract terms which are unreasonably favorable to the other party." Williams v. Walker-Thomas Furniture Co., 350 F.2d 445, 449 (D.C.Cir.1965). *See* Corenswet, Inc. v. Amana Refrigeration, Inc., 594 F.2d 129, 139 (5th Cir. 1979). The inquiry involves a search for components of "procedural" and "substantive" unconscionability. *See generally* Leff, Unconscionability and the Code The Emperor's New Clause, 115 Pa.L.Rev. 485 (1967). *See also* Johnson v. Mobil Oil Corp., 415 F. Supp. 264, 268 (E.D. Mich. 1976); Fleischmann Distilling Corp. v. Distillers Co., 395 F. Supp. 221, 232–33 (S.D.N.Y. 1975).

[17] This is true as to the initial agreement for the Agawam store and obviously true as to the subsequent identical agreement for the Springfield store.

was not reasonably related to legitimate commercial needs of Dairy Mart. To find the termination clause oppressive merely because it did not require cause for termination would be to establish an unwarranted barrier to the use of termination at will clauses in contracts in this Commonwealth, where each party received the anticipated and bargained for consideration during the full term of the agreement.

[18] The judge concluded that bad faith was also manifested by Dairy Mart's introductory brochure, which made representations of "security, comfort, and independence." Although this brochure and Mr. Zapatha's mistaken understanding that Dairy Mart could terminate the agreement only for cause could not be relied on to vary the clear terms of the agreement, the introductory brochure is relevant to the question of good faith. However, although the brochure misstated a franchisee's status as the owner of his own business, it shows no lack of honesty in fact relating to the right of Dairy Mart to terminate the agreement. Furthermore, by the time the Zapathas executed the second agreement, and even the first agreement, they knew that they would operate the franchise, but that they would not own the assets used in the business (except the goods to be sold); that the franchise agreement could be terminated by them and, at least in some circumstances, by Dairy Mart; and that in fact the major investment of funds would be made by Dairy Mart. We conclude that the use of the brochure did not warrant a finding of an absence of "honesty in fact." *See Corenswet, Inc. v. Amana Refrigeration, Inc.*, 594 F.2d 129, 138 (5th Cir. 1979); *Mason v. Farmers Ins. Cos.*, 281 N.W.2d 344, 347 (Minn. 1979).

Zapathas knew abt the clause; it was very clear.

* * *

Judgments reversed.

───────

NOTE ON ECONOMIC ANALYSIS

The court talks about the allocation of risks and benefits. This is one of the "big ideas" in contracts discourse. Here's how it works.

I'm a farmer. I grow hops. You're a brewery. You brew beer. We enter into a contract where I agree to sell you 100 thousand bushels of hops next year. Why would we do this? Why not just wait until next year when my hops crops comes in and you need hops for your beer?

The traditional answer has been we want certainty. But a better way to look at it is to say we are both trying to reduce our risk. You're probably saying: "Isn't that the same thing? Isn't risk just the opposite of certainty?" Yes it is, but looking at it from the risk point of view allows us to be a bit more sophisticated.

You, the brewer, are trying to reduce your risk that you will not be able to get any hops. I, the farmer, am trying to reduce the risk that I will not have a market for my hops. But by trying to reduce the risks we also create new ones. I now have the risk that I will not be able to grow 100,000 bushels of hops. I also have the risk that the price of hops will double between now and next year.

You, the brewer, have the same sort of risk. Suppose you decide you no longer want to take part in destroying lives through the demon of alcohol. So you decide from now on you're going to brew nothing but herb tea. This means that NASCAR team you sponsor is going to have to take off the sign that says "Jennifer's Wicked Ale" and replace it with one that says "Jennifer's Herb Tea." When I deliver my hops you will not be able to say "I'm sorry we don't use those anymore." You're stuck.

Now suppose you foresee this. You could say when we make the contract, "I'd like a provision that lets me out of the contract if I ever stop brewing beer."

If I am smart I will say one of two things: "I'm not willing to take the risk that you'll stop brewing beer and I'll be stuck with 100,000 bushels of hops." Or "Fine, we can do that, but I want something in return." What I want in return might be more money, but it could be something like a right to get out of the contract if a drought wipes out my hops crop.

Zapatha is based in part on the idea that when Zapatha took the risk that Dairy Mart would terminate him, he got something in return for it. The idea is that if he was concerned about getting terminated, he could have gone to some other franchisor and gotten a better deal.

But what if all franchisors have similar clauses? That must mean that it is pretty important to franchisors. If it were not, somebody would offer franchises that can't be terminated in return for a slightly larger percentage of the profits. It might work like this: Suppose Dairy Mart charges Zapatha 10% of his gross sales as a franchise fee. If I have a chain of convenience stores I might be willing to be stuck with a franchisee for life if I could get 12%. So I might start a chain and take away a lot of Dairy Mart's franchisees who wanted security.

But if the franchisors—the Dairy Marts of this world—value having that clause in there more than the franchisees value taking it out, then it stays in. The franchisors want at least (say) 14% for taking it out, but the franchisees are only willing to pay 12% to have it taken out. So it stays in, which is in everyone's best interest, at least if their individual evaluations of what it's worth are correct.

And therein lies the rub. If you subscribe to traditional microeconomic analysis, you might believe that the parties' evaluations of worth would be accurate, given the usual stipulation of a so-called "perfect market"—featuring many participants, low transaction costs, perfect information, and the like. But the real market is not perfect and it is not static. Remember all those other parties on the supply and demand curves who are not at market equilibrium at the snapshot moment of our pretty little microeconomic analysis. Remember that the market, and all the information in it, are in constant flux as to the quality, quantity, and accuracy of information. Remember that there are substantial costs of gathering, analyzing, and using this information, providing a disincentive for doing so. And remember that in most markets there are not an infinite number of buyers and sellers who are free from a compulsion to buy or sell.

The market is not perfect and the risk-allocation decisions will not be "right" for every party—but if properly documented, they will be binding on the parties and will govern the parties' relationship. This is the essence of the modern institution of contract.

NOTE ON ALTERNATIVE DISPUTE RESOLUTION

Starting in the 1980s, faced with exploding litigation costs and interminable delays in processing cases due to crowded dockets, businesses began to embrace the concept of ADR and include mandatory arbitration provisions in their contracts to the extent that some courts began to invalidate these provisions on unconscionability grounds. These clauses are often deeply embedded in the contract, and unsophisticated parties were seen to have little chance of discovering or understanding them. Plaintiffs were often subject to extra costs, significant penalties in the event of breach, and stripped of many of legal rights (like choice of forum, joinder, and class action in some cases). Furthermore, it appears to many that the business would usually gain significant advantages with arbitrators based upon the "repeat customer" preference.

In *Tillman v. Commercial Credit Loans, Inc.*, 362 N.C. 93, 655 S.E.2d 362 (2008) the North Carolina Supreme Court refused to enforce an arbitration clause for many of these same reasons. The provision was so lopsided that the court refused to sever the clause and instead invalidated the entire agreement. The following opinion illustrates the potential unfairness of arbitration clauses in an employment setting.

COOPER V. MRM INVESTMENT CO.

United States District Court, Middle District of Tennessee
199 F. Supp. 2d 771 (2002)

NIXON, DISTRICT JUDGE.

[1] Pending before the Court is Defendants' Motion to Dismiss or, in the Alternative, to Compel Arbitration and Stay Proceedings. Plaintiff has now responded to this Motion. The Court heard oral arguments in this matter on April 8, 2002. For the reasons discussed below, Defendants' Motion will be denied.

I. Background

[2] This case arises from the employment of Plaintiff by Defendant MRM Investment Co. ("MRM"), a Kentucky Fried Chicken ("KFC") franchisee. Ms. Cooper was hired by MRM to work at its Waverly, Tennessee KFC on or about January 3, 2000. Plaintiff alleges that, while working for MRM, she was sexually harassed by Defendant Terry Rogers, one of the owners of MRM, and was constructively discharged by Defendants on or about August 2000.

[3] As part of her employment contract, and prior to commencing work at KFC, Plaintiff signed a document entitled "Arbitration of Employee Rights." The document provides:

> . . . KFC and I agree to use confidential binding arbitration for any claims that arise between me and KFC, its related companies and/or their current or former employees. Such claims would include any concerning compensation, employment including, but not limited to any claims concerning (sexual harassment), or termination or employment . . . In any arbitration, the prevailing rules of the American Arbitration Association and, to the extent not inconsistent, the prevailing rules of the Federal Arbitration Act will apply.

(Doc. No. 16, Exh. A) (herein, "KFC Arbitration Agreement").

[4] Defendants now argue that Plaintiff and Defendants have bargained for mandatory arbitration, and thus her claims under Title VII of the Civil Rights Act of 1964, 42 U.S.C. §§ 2000e et seq. ("Title VII"), and the Tennessee Human Rights Act, Tenn. Code Ann. §§ 4–21–1401 et seq. are subject to arbitration. Plaintiff responds that there is no agreement to arbitrate between herself and these particular Defendants, and, even if there is an agreement, that agreement is unenforceable because it require the Plaintiff to pay a portion of the costs associated with arbitration.

II. Legal Standards

[5] The Supreme Court has recently held that agreements to arbitrate employment disputes as a condition of employment are almost universally enforceable under the Federal Arbitration Act, 9 U.S.C. §§ 1, et seq. ("FAA"), *Circuit City Stores, Inc. v. Adams*, 532 U.S. 105, 149 L. Ed. 2d 234, 121 S.Ct. 1302 (2001). Nevertheless, arbitration agreements may be attacked under "such grounds as exist at law or in equity for the revocation of a contract." 9 U.S.C. § 2.

[6] The Sixth Circuit has consistently held that pre-dispute mandatory arbitration agreements are valid. *Haskins v. Prudential Ins. Co. of Am.*, 230 F.3d 231, 239 (6th Cir. 2000); *Willis v. Dean Witter Reynolds, Inc.*, 948 F.2d 305, 310 (6th Cir. 1991). Specifically, the Sixth Circuit has held that the employees may be required, as a condition of employment, to

waive their right to bring future Title VII claims in court. *Willis, supra.* Almost every other Circuit to consider this issue has agreed with the Sixth Circuit.

[7] However, although the Supreme Court and lower courts endorse the use of arbitration, courts continue to emphasize that an employee cannot be required to forfeit any "substantive rights" as a condition of employment. *See Gilmer v. Interstate/Johnson Lane Corp.,* 500 U.S. 20, 28, 114 L. Ed. 2d 26, 111 S.Ct. 1647 (1991). Thus, " . . . even if arbitration is generally a suitable forum for resolving a particular statutory claim, the specific arbitral forum provided under an arbitration agreement must nevertheless allow for the effective vindication of that claim." *Floss v. Ryan's Family Steak Houses, Inc.,* 211 F. 3d 306 (6th Cir. 2000).

[8] Some courts have held that requiring a plaintiff to pay for the right to vindicate their federal substantive rights would amount to an insurmountable obstacle. *See e.g., Paladino v. Avnet Computer Tech., Inc.,* 134 F.3d 1054 (11th Cir. 1999); *Shankle v. B-G Maint. Mgmt. of Colo., Inc.,* 163 F. 3d 1230 (10th Cir. 1999) (finding that requiring the Plaintiff to pay costs renders the arbitral format invalid).

[9] Additionally, although mandatory arbitration is presumed valid, the waiver of any rights (substantive or procedural), must be both knowing and clear. *See K.M.C. Co., Inc. v. Irving Trust Co.,* 757 F.2d 752 (6th Cir. 1985); *Trumbull v. Century Marketing Corp.,* 12 F. Supp.2d 683, 687 (N.D. Ohio. 1998) ("to conclude that there was a waiver of [the right to a jury trial], there must at least be evidence that the plaintiff intended such waiver.").

[10] Finally, and most fundamentally, an agreement to arbitrate Title VII rights must comport with the principles of contract law. In deciding whether the arbitration agreements are enforceable, state-law contract principles control.

[11] First, although courts may not invalidate arbitration agreements under state laws that only apply to arbitration provisions, general contract defenses may still operate to invalidate an arbitration agreement. The Sixth Circuit has held that a contractual agreement to arbitrate may be invalidated by a showing of fraud, duress, mistake, unconscionability or any other ground upon which a contract may be set aside. *Haskins,* 230 F.3d at 239; accord *Steven M. Burton v. J.C. Bradford & Co., L.L.C.,* No. 3:97–0153 (March 13, 1998, Nixon, J.).

[12] Most importantly, an arbitration agreement may not be upheld if it is unconscionable. As a Tennessee Court recently observed:

> Unconscionability may arise from a lack of a meaningful choice on the part of one party (procedural unconscionability) or from contract terms that are unreasonably harsh (substantive

unconscionability). *Williams v. Walker-Thomas Furniture Co.,* 121 U.S. App.D.C. 315, 350 F.2d 445 (D.C. Cir. 1965). In Tennessee we have tended to lump the two together and speak of unconscionability resulting when inequality of the bargain is so manifest as to shock the judgment of a person of common sense, and where the terms are so oppressive that no reasonable person would make them on one hand, and no honest and fair person would accept them on the other.

Trinity Indus., Inc. v. McKinnon Bridge Co., Inc., 2001 WL 1504827 (Tenn. Ct. App. 2001)

[13] Furthermore, Tennessee law disfavors adhesion contracts. The Tennessee Supreme Court recently observed that an adhesion contract is a

standardized form offered to consumers . . . on essentially a "take it or leave it" basis, without affording the consumer a realistic opportunity to bargain and under such conditions that the consumer cannot obtain the desired product or service except by acquiescing to the form of the contract.

Buraczynski v. Erying, 919 S.W.2d 314, 320 (Tenn. 1996) (quoting Black's Law Dictionary 40 (6th ed. 1990)). However, in Tennessee, an adhesion contract is only unenforceable when the terms of the contract are "beyond the reasonable expectation of an ordinary person, or oppressive or unconscionable." *Id.* (citation omitted). In the mandatory arbitration or employment disputes context, the Ninth Circuit recently held, on remand, that the arbitration agreement at issue was unconscionable "because it is a contract of adhesion . . ." and was substantively one-sided, lacking a "modicum of bilaterality.'" *Circuit City Stores, Inc. v. Adams,* 279 F.3d 889 (9th Cir. 2002) ("Circuit City II") (citation omitted).

[14] Second, the Sixth Circuit has also held that in order for a mandatory arbitration agreement to be valid, there must be adequate consideration. *Floss,* 211 F.3d at 315. In deciding whether contracts are enforceable, federal courts must look to state contract law. In Tennessee, consideration is an essential element of every contract. Hence, a promise is legally enforceable only if the promisor receives an act, forbearance or a promise thereof, in return for that promise. In essence, there must be a mutuality of obligation.

[15] Finally, as with all contracts, it is axiomatic that in order for there to be a valid contract the parties must manifest their assent to a bargain in order to be bound by it.

III. Discussion

A.   Is there an Arbitration Agreement Between these Parties?

[16] Plaintiff initially argues that there is no enforceable contract between Plaintiff and Defendants because she did not agree to arbitrate employment disputes with the particular defendants, but only with KFC. Since Plaintiff was actually employed by MRM Investment Company, she claims that she is not bound by the arbitration agreement in this case, since KFC is not a named defendant. Although the Arbitration Agreement specifically includes KFC's "related companies . . . and/or their current or former employees," Plaintiff asserts that MRM is not a related company and Terry Rogers and Larry Mays are not current or former employees of KFC or its related companies. Defendants contend that, for the purposes of this contract, MRM and KFC are synonymous, and, even if this were not the case, MRM is a "related company" of KFC.

[17] The court rejects Plaintiff's contention that she did not have a contract with MRM. Clearly, a franchise of KFC is a "related company" under the plain meaning of the contract. Furthermore, Mays and Rogers are "current or former" employees of KFC or its related companies—*i.e.,* MRM. Thus, there is an agreement to arbitrate between Plaintiff and the Defendants.

B.   Are there any Reasons to Set Aside
the Arbitration Agreement?

[18] As discussed above, agreements to arbitrate are favored by the courts, and will only be set aside where there is a showing of traditional legal and equitable reasons for refusing to enforce the agreements. Therefore, the Court will analyze the contractual agreement to arbitrate and determine its validity. The court will also consider whether any defenses to the formation of a contract are applicable.

1.   Unconscionability

[19] Having already analyzed the Arbitration Agreement and determined that it constitutes an agreement between Plaintiff and the Defendants, the Court will next determine whether any state law defenses to the contract are applicable. First, while the Court is not aware of any fraud or duress associated with the formation of this contract, the defense of unconscionability may be applicable to mandatory arbitration agreements in the employment discrimination context. *Circuit City II*, 279 F.3d 889.

[20] In *Circuit City II*, the Ninth Circuit found that the arbitration agreement at issue was a contract of adhesion, and therefore it was procedurally unconscionable. The Court also found that the agreement was substantively unconscionable because the mandatory arbitration

agreement only applied to the employees; the employer was not bound to arbitrate its claims.

[21] The Ninth Circuit considered California Law in making its determination, which, as interpreted by that Court, varies somewhat from Tennessee law. In Tennessee, a contract of adhesion is only invalid if it is unconscionable. *Buraczynski*, 919 S.W.2d at 320. Thus, this Court must first determine whether the KFC Arbitration Agreement is a contract of adhesion and, if so, whether it is unconscionable.

[22] The Court finds that, applying the Tennessee law discussed above, the KFC Arbitration Agreement is a contract of adhesion. In *Buracdzynski*, the Tennessee Supreme Court surveyed the law to find that "Courts generally agree that 'the distinctive feature of a contract of adhesion is that the weaker party has no realistic choice as to its terms.'" 919 S.W.2d at 321, citing *Broemmer v. Abortion Serv. of Phoenix, Ltd.*, 173 Ariz. 148, 840 P. 2d 1013, 1013 (Ariz. 1992). The Buraczynski Court found that the arbitration agreements at issue were contracts of adhesion because the agreements were "standardized form contracts prepared by the contracting party with superior knowledge of the subject matter . . . [and] offered . . . on a 'take it or leave it' basis." 919 S.W.2d at 320. The same is true of the KFC Arbitration Agreement. In fact, MRM's attorney conceded as much at the April 8, 2002 hearing. This agreement is a form contract, drafted by KFC's attorneys, offered to Plaintiff on a "take it or leave it" basis. Plaintiff had no choice.[18] She either had to accept the job based on the terms outlined in the KFC Arbitration Agreement, or she had to find another job. *See Trumbull*, 12 F. Supp.2d at 686 ("employment contracts rarely result from bargaining between the parties. Rather, an employee is given a contract to sign on a take-it-or-leave-it basis"). Especially in today's economy, the choice to 'leave it' often amounts to no choice at all. Indeed, if she 'leaves it,' she probably forgoes the opportunity for employment.[19] *Id*. Hence, the KFC Arbitration Agreement is a contract of adhesion.

[23] A contract of adhesion is only invalid if it is also unconscionable. In Tennessee, courts will only refuse to enforce a contract of adhesion where "the terns of the agreement are beyond the reasonable expectations

---

[18] It is important to note that this case involves employment at a fast food establishment, not a brokerage house. Many of the cases involving mandatory arbitration have involved mandatory arbitration under Securities Registration Form U-4, a form used by the major stock exchanges. *See e.g., Gilmer; Haskins; Willis*. However, the precedential value of those cases is undermined by the clear difference between employees seeking employment at Dean Witter or Prudential, and those seeking employment at KFC. The bargaining position of the latter is, on average, weaker than the bargaining position of employees at brokerage firms. While this difference is not determinative, it certainly informs the Court's thinking.

[19] The Court notes the increasing trend toward mandatory arbitration in employment contracts. Thus, prospective employees often have no choices at all—that is, even if they decide to walk away from one mandatory arbitration contract, they will often have no choice but to accept another employment contract that mandates arbitration as well. *See John A. Gray. Have the Foxes Become the Guardian of the Chickens? The Post-Gilmer Legal Status of Predispute Mandatory Arbitration as a Condition of Employment*, 37 VILL. L. REV. 113, 115 (1992).

of an ordinary-person, or oppressive or unconscionable." *Buraczynski*, 919 S.W.2d at 320. The Tennessee Supreme Court also recognized that "Courts will not enforce adhesion contracts which are oppressive to the weaker party. . . ." *Id.*

[24] The Court finds that the KFC Arbitration Agreement is both oppressive to the weaker party and unconscionable. Although the Buraczynski Court found that the arbitration agreements at issue in that case were not oppressive or unconscionable, that case is distinguishable on a number of grounds. First, *Buraczynski* concerned a physician-patient arbitration agreement, not an employment agreement. The pressure facing a prospective employee coupled with the uniform incongruity in bargaining positions between the employer and employee renders the KFC Arbitration Agreement different from a physician-patient agreement. Second, the Buraczynski Court emphasized that the agreement at issue specified, "in ten point capital letter red type, directly above the signature line, that 'by signing this contract you are giving up your right to a jury or court trial. . . .' " 919 S.W.2d at 321. No such language is present in the KFC Arbitration Agreement. A court in this circuit has recognized that the waiver of the right to a jury trial must be both knowing and clear. *Trumbull*, 12 F. Supp.2d at 687. If the employee is not clearly made aware of the rights she is waiving, that waiver is not only invalid, but the entire agreement is rendered unduly oppressive.

[25] Nevertheless, even if the KFC Arbitration Agreement contained all of the various rights Plaintiff waived by "agreeing" to arbitrate her future dispute in CAPITALIZED TWELVE POINT FONT, the Court would still find that this Arbitration Agreement is oppressive and unconscionable, both on its face and inherently.[20] This court is particularly concerned with the encroachment upon Plaintiff's liberty interest. Thus, for the reasons discussed below, the Court finds that this arbitration contract is unconscionable.

[26] As discussed above, in Tennessee a contract is unconscionable if "the inequality of the bargain is so manifest as to shock the judgment of a person of common sense, and where the terms are so oppressive that no reasonable person would make them on the one hand, and no honest and fair person would accept them on the other." *Haun v. King*, 690 S.W.2d at 872. If the ordinary employee were informed of the consequences of signing the arbitration agreement, and if that employee were informed of the consequences of signing the arbitration agreement, and if that employee had a choice, she would not sign that agreement. However, in the employment context, the employee simply has no choice. As the D.C. Circuit recognized in Williams, "when a party of little bargaining power,

---

[20] Therefore, employers cannot simply make the arbitration agreement longer and more detailed in order to "correct" the inherent problems associated with many pre-dispute mandatory arbitration agreements.

and hence little real choice, signs a commercially unreasonable contract with little or no knowledge of its terms, it is hardly likely that his consent, or even an objective manifestation of his consent, was ever given to all the terms." 350 F.2d at 450. Additionally, the attorneys that drafted the KFC Arbitration Agreement would certainly never sign that agreement if they were in Plaintiff's shoes.[21] Thus, considering all of the surrounding circumstances, this Court finds that not only would an ordinary person be shocked by the oppressive terms of his Arbitration Agreement, but no honest and fair person would accept these terms, knowing the full ramifications of doing so.[22]

[27] However, the KFC Arbitration Agreement does contain a measure of what the California courts have termed a "modicum of bilaterality." *Circuit City II*, citing *Armendariz v. Found Health Psychcare Servs., Inc.,* 24 Cal. 4th 83, 6 P.3d 669, 692 (Cal. 2000). In *Circuit City II*, the Ninth Circuit found that the Circuit City arbitration agreement was substantively unconscionable because, although the employee is compelled to arbitrate his or her claims, the employer remains free to litigate its own claims. As the California Supreme Court observed, where the employer is not bound to arbitrate its claims, and there is no clear justification for this lack of mutuality of obligations, arbitration functions "less as a forum for neutral dispute resolution and more as a means of maximizing employer advantage." *Armendariz*, 6 P.3d at 692. At oral arguments, MRM's counsel confirmed that the KFC Arbitration Agreement imposes mandatory arbitration on the employee and the employer. Thus, the KFC Arbitration Agreement is not as asymmetrical as the agreement invalidated by the Circuit City II Court. Nevertheless, the agreement was still drafted by KFC, and imposed on a prospective employee precisely at the time that he or she is most willing to sign anything just to get a job. Although the KFC Arbitration Agreement binds both parties, only the Defendant is aware of the ramifications of the agreement. Furthermore, only the Defendant is aware of the myriad of the Title VII rights and remedies that Plaintiff forgoes by "agreeing" to arbitrate her disputes. *See id.* at 614 (noting that under the agreement, Plaintiff has been "stripped of her right to a judicial forum for a Title VII violation and . . . stripped of numerous remedies under

---

[21] In the words of President Kennedy, "the heart of the question is whether all Americans are to be afforded equal rights and equal opportunities, whether we are going to treat our fellow Americans as we want to be treated." *President John F. Kennedy's Radio and Television Report to the American People on Civil Rights* (June 11, 1963), Pun. Papers 468, 469 (1963).

[22] This Court is aware of the difficulties facing employers, who must deal with many employment discrimination claims, many of which are ultimately found to be without merit. The Court is also mindful of the large number of employment discrimination cases in the federal court system. However, this Court will not overlook the clear unconscionability of these arbitration agreements in order to achieve greater efficiency or convenience. This issue is simply too important. These cases do not "clog" the federal docket—they belong in federal court. Employees must not be forced to either forgo employment or forgo their right to a day in court, and Courts must not use the perceived problems associated with employment discrimination to prevent employees, and society at large, from vindication the rights that Congress enshrined in the Civil Rights Acts.

Title VII," and finding the agreement unconscionable). Therefore, this Court finds that there is an insufficient "modicum of bilaterality" present in this case. In other words, there is an asymmetry born out of a difference in bargaining power that pervades the resulting arbitration agreement. Thus, for all of these reasons, the Court finds that the KFC Arbitration Agreement is unconscionable.

2.   Plaintiff's Substantive Rights

[28] Even if this Court found no contractual defenses to the enforcement of the KFC Arbitration Agreement, Plaintiff's substantive rights are affected by the agreement. Courts have recognized that, although arbitration agreements are generally favored, they will not be enforced if they affect an individual's substantive rights. Where an individual is unable to vindicate his or her rights because of an obstacle erected by an arbitration agreement, the court may not enforce that arbitration agreement.

[29] Courts have held that requiring the plaintiff to pay for the right to vindicate their federal substantive rights would amount to an insurmountable obstacle. However, the agreement specifically indicates that the American Arbitration Association's ("AAA") rules would govern the arbitration proceedings. The AAA rules impose a number of fees and costs that Plaintiff would have to bear as the "initiating party." Requiring a party to pay fees and costs, over and above what they party would have to pay in a court, may deprive that party of the right to vindicate his or her rights.

[30] In *Cole*, the D.C. Circuit observed that "it would undermine Congress' intent to prevent employees who are seeking to vindicate statutory rights form gaining access to a judicial forum and then require them to pay for the services of an arbitrator when they would never be required to pay for a judge in Court." 105 F.3d at 1484. The Supreme Court recently observed that "where . . . a party seeks to invalidate an arbitration agreement on the ground that arbitration would be prohibitively expensive, that party bears of the burden of showing the likelihood of incurring such costs." *Green Tree Fin. Corp.-Ala. v. Randolph,* 531 U.S. 79, 148 L. Ed. 2d 373, 121 S.Ct. 513(2000).[23]

[31] Although the Supreme Court held that requiring Plaintiff to pay a share of the arbitration costs does not automatically render an arbitration clause invalid, the Court need not ultimately address this issue. In this case, Plaintiff's affidavit convinces the Court that she will be unable to pay the high costs of arbitration. The KFC Arbitration Agreement

---

[23] A federal court recently held that, under *Green Tree*, an employee need only show a likelihood that he or she will be responsible for significant costs associated with the arbitral forum, rather than focusing on that employee's specific financial situation. Ball v. SFX Broad., Inc., 165 F. Supp. 2d 230, 239–40 (N.D.N.Y. 2001).

specifies that AAA arbitration rules would apply. AAA rules impose a number of fees and costs on the parties, (AAA Rules 38–41, Doc. No. 16, Exh. B), although the rules do not clearly prescribe the specific allocation of responsibility for payment of those fees and costs. Plaintiff's 2001 W-2 form shows that she received total net income of $7253.74 last year. Plaintiff, and others similarly situated, often cannot afford to pay the high costs of arbitration.[24]

[32] Furthermore, arbitration proceedings are private proceedings, and in order to retain an arbitrator, Plaintiff (or her attorney) would be required to pay at least part of that arbitrator's fee.[25] The AAA also specifies various other fees that surpass the most filing fees charged by the federal courts. Although AAA may waive some of its fees, "the mere fact that [plaintiff] might obtain some relief from the significant fees . . . does not prohibit the conclusion that she has shown the 'likelihood' of incurring such fees, as required by the Supreme Court's *Green Tree* decision." *Ball,* 165 F. Supp.2d at 240, n. 10. In this case, Plaintiff will not be able to pay the costs of arbitrating her employment dispute. Since this fact might prevent her from being able to vindicate her federal statutory rights, Supreme Court precedent mandates that this court may not compel arbitration.

[33] Defendants maintain that even if this Court were to find that fees associated with arbitration are excessive, Plaintiff's argument relating to costs is moot because MRM has now agreed to pay all of the costs associated with arbitration. Plaintiff responds that this Court should not allow the Defendants to sever an invalid provision of the contract after the Court has found that provision to be invalid. *Citing Perez v. Globe Airport Sec. Serv., Inc.,* 253 F.3d 1280 (11th Cir. 2001), [vacated, *Perez v. Globe Airport Sec. Serv.,* 294 F.3d 1275 (11th Cir. 2002)—Eds.] Plaintiff stresses that allowing an employer to include unlawful provisions in their arbitration agreements and sever those provisions when challenged, would encourage the employer to overreach. In other words, as the Perez Court notes:

> To sever the costs and fees provision and force the employee to arbitrate a Title VII claim despite the employer's attempt to limit the remedies available would reward the employer for its actions and fail to deter similar conduct by others

253 F.3d at 1287. Plaintiff noted at oral argument that allowing the employer to overreach initially would result in the creation of a disincentive to the Plaintiff's vindication of her Title VII rights. The Court agrees. The KFC Arbitration Agreement may deter some employees from initiating proceedings in the first place because the agreement, under the

---

[24] Costs of arbitrating Plaintiff's dispute may very well exceed her yearly salary for 2001.

[25] Other than paying her taxes, Plaintiff is not required to pay part of my salary as a federal judge.

AAA Rules, mandates fee splitting. Therefore, Plaintiff was forced to file suit in federal court in order to have this Court hold that the fee splitting provision is invalid. The Defendants will not be allowed, at this point, to abandon a provision that KFC's attorneys carefully drafted, in order to "save" the Arbitration Agreement. If Defendants could sever invalid provisions from their contracts, the Court would create an incentive for employers to craft questionable arbitration agreements, require plaintiffs to jump through hoops in order to invalidate those agreements, and ultimately allow the defendants to jettison questionable provisions from the arbitration agreements. Allowing Defendants to do so at this point would be inequitable.

3. Societal Rights

[34] In addition to the individual substantive rights that are deprived by the KFC Arbitration Agreement, there are a number of societal rights that this mandatory Arbitration Agreement curtails. Federal Courts, and courts in general, have a very important role in the Civil Rights context. As the Supreme Court observed:

> When the Civil Rights Act of 1964 was passed, it was evident that enforcement would prove difficult and that the Nation would have to rely in part upon private litigation as a means of securing broad compliance with the law. [Thus, a Plaintiff acts not only for] himself alone but also as a "private attorney general," indicating a policy that Congress considered of the highest priority.

Newman v. Piggie Park Enterprises, Inc., 390 U.S. 400, 402, 19 L. Ed. 2d 1263, 88 S.Ct. 964 (1968) (per curiam). Therefore, mandatory pre-dispute arbitration deprives this Plaintiff of her right to not only vindicate her own rights, but also society's right to condemn "invidious bias" in the workplace through a private attorney general. *McKennon v. Nashville Banner Publ'g Co.*, 513 U.S. 352, 357, 130 L. Ed. 2d. 852, 115 S.Ct. 879 (1995).

IV. Conclusion

[35] Therefore, the Court will neither dismiss this case at this time nor compel arbitration. A federal court is the proper forum for Plaintiff to seek to vindicate her rights under the Civil Rights Act and the Tennessee Human Rights Act. Thus, Defendants' motion is hereby DENIED, and this case will proceed before this Court.

NOTES

1. The District Court in *Cooper v. MRM Investment Co.* was reversed on appeal despite its hard work in attempting to craft a thorough opinion based upon multiple grounds. *Cooper v. MRM Investment Co.*, 367 F.3d 493 (6th Cir. 2004). The Court of Appeals vacated the judgment to the extent it held that

the likely costs of arbitration were so high that they would deter the employee from exercising the right to arbitrate and remanded the case for a determination as to the effect of a new set of AAA rules on arbitration. In all other respects, the Court of Appeals reversed the judgment. Notably, the Court of Appeals found that the definition of adhesion contract used by the District Court was limited to consumer contracts for goods and services, not employment contracts.

2.   Are we a long way from *Walker Thomas Furniture*? District Judge Nixon appears to have tried to resurrect J. Skelly Wright's earlier opinion from the beginning of this chapter but the Sixth Circuit Court of Appeals would have none of it, at least in the employment context.

––––––––––

WARNING: Don't Get Carried Away with Unconscionability

Generally, the documents mean what they say. Really. Don't get carried away with what the unconscionability cases say.

Casebook authors appear to love the cases where distinguished jurists use attractive rhetoric to let folks out of contracts. This is not the way the world works.

Outside of the context of overreaching arbitration or other alternative dispute resolution provisions tucked into a contract of adhesion, it is virtually impossible and unheard of for even a moderately sophisticated party or one represented by counsel to win an unconscionability defense to enforcement of a contract.

> Yes, you can win an unconscionability case if your client is poor and uneducated, and if the other party is a sleazy organization that preys on poor people, and if you're able to afford [to prosecute or defend] an appeal, and if you get Skelly Wright on the bench. But absent these circumstances, the client is going to be stuck with the documents she signs.

Robert M. Lloyd, *Making Contracts Relevant: Thirteen Lessons for the First Year Contracts Course*, 36 ARIZ. ST. L. J. 257, 267 (2004).

So, to repeat, don't get carried away with unconscionability.

LAWYERING SKILLS PROBLEM

You are general counsel for an insurance company. The company's standard-form release to be signed by people whom the company has compensated for injuries allegedly caused by its insured reads:

> Releasor hereby releases, acquits and forever discharges Releasee and any other persons and entities of and from any and all actions, causes of action, claims, demands, damages, costs, loss of services, expenses and compensation on account of or in any way growing out of any and all known and unknown personal injuries resulting or to

result from the accident that occurred on or about [date and time], at or about [location].

Releasor and Releasee agree to use confidential binding arbitration for any claims that arise between themselves, including disputes that involve third parties. In any arbitration, the prevailing rules of the American Arbitration Association and, to the extent not inconsistent with those rules, the prevailing rules of the Federal Arbitration Act will apply.

In spite of the language of the release, you are worried that there are some courts that might refuse to enforce the arbitration clause based on the doctrine of unconscionability.

You have been asked to re-write the release to make it more likely that courts will enforce the arbitration clause as written and reject any unconscionability challenge to it. Explain what you would do. Specific examples of how you would redraft it are preferred.

CHAPTER 13

THE STATUTE OF FRAUDS

■ ■ ■

The statute of frauds was born in England in 1677. Generally speaking, it requires either that the entire contract or its essential terms be represented in a writing "signed by the party to be charged"—i.e., the party against whom enforcement is sought—if the contract is:

(1) for the sale of land;

(2) for the sale of goods for over $500 (U.C.C. version);

(3) to be performed in over one year;

(4) to answer for the debt of another (i.e., a guarantee or surety arrangement);

(5) in consideration of marriage.

The purpose of the statute was to avoid fraud by false claims of oral contracts for these "major" types of contracts and the legislative determination that a writing requirement would eliminate or substantially suppress this sort of fraud. The marriage provision also serves a personal decision cautionary function. As so often occurs, the law of unintended consequences took hold and, instead of preventing fraud, the statute was soon used to perpetuate a different kind of fraud: wrongful *denial* of actual oral contracts that fall within its scope. Squeezing a lightly inflated balloon does not remove the air from it, it just moves it around; just so with human behaviors like fraud when subjected to legislation.

The statute has found considerable criticism and has been largely repealed worldwide, including in its birthplace, England, in the 1950s. The CISG, for example, provides explicitly that a contract may be proven in any manner possible—in addition to eliminating the parol evidence rule to be covered in Chapter 14, this provision eliminates the statute of frauds for contracts covered by the CISG. The UNIDROIT Principles are in accord with the CISG.

Despite this, the statute of frauds remains part of the law of the United States. Law students are thus obligated to learn the rule and its permutations, which are a favorite of law professors and bar examiners nationwide. The cases that follow illustrate its application. As you read them, note how the analysis has four steps: (1) does the statute appear to apply to the transaction at hand?; (2) if so, is there a "technical" argument that removes the contract from the statute's coverage (e.g., a contract that will, but is not required to, take more than a year to perform)?; (3) is there a writing that is sufficient to meet the statute's requirements? and (4), if not, is there an argument for waiver, estoppel or some other evasionary doctrine to ameliorate what would otherwise be a harsh application of the statute?

Read carefully Restatement (Second) §§ 110 and 130.

NOTE

The case that follows deals with the U.C.C. Article 2's statute of frauds, section 2–201. At the time Article 2 was written, the statute of frauds had been the subject of a great deal of criticism. Rather than eliminating any writing requirement entirely, the drafters decided to draft a provision that would retain the benefits of the statute of frauds but eliminate many of the problems associated with it. Read section 2–201 carefully to see how it differs from the general statute of frauds provisions in R2d § 110 and 130.

AZEVEDO V. MINISTER

Supreme Court of Nevada
86 Nev. 576, 471 P.2d 661 (1970)

MOWBRAY, J.

[1]   This case centers about the enforceability of an oral agreement to purchase 1,500 tons of hay. The principal issue presented for our determination is whether the periodic accountings prepared by the seller and sent to the buyer covering the sale of the hay constituted confirming memoranda within the provisions of NRS 104.2201(2)[1] of the Uniform Commercial Code and, if so, whether the seller sent them within a reasonable time as required by that statute so that the oral agreement is not barred by the statute of frauds. The district judge ruled that the mandates of NRS 104.2201(2) had been satisfied, and he upheld the validity of the agreement. We agree, and we affirm the judgment of the lower court.

1.   The Facts.

[2]   Appellant J. L. Azevedo is a rancher who buys and sells hay. He is licensed to do so, and he is bonded by appellant United States Fidelity and Guaranty Company.[2] Respondent Bolton F. Minister operates the

---

[1]   [This is a reference to U.C.C. § 2–201(2) as enacted in Nevada's statutes.—Eds.]

[2]   [As a condition to licensing people to engage in certain businesses, states often require that they post a surety bond. In essence, a surety bond is an insurance policy issued in favor of any

Minister Ranch near Yerington, Nevada, where he raises and sells large quantities of hay.

[3] In early November 1967, Azevedo approached Minister for the purpose of buying hay. Terms were discussed. Several days later an agreement was reached by telephone. Both parties acknowledge that Azevedo agreed to purchase hay from Minister at a price of $26.50 per ton for the first and second cuttings and $28 per ton for the third cutting and that the parties opened an escrow account in a Yerington bank in Minister's favor, where Azevedo agreed to deposit sufficient funds to cover the cost of *[handwritten: issue simplified]* the hay as he hauled it from the Minister Ranch. The parties are in dispute as to the total quantity of hay Azevedo agreed to purchase. Minister claims Azevedo contracted to purchase 1,500 tons. Azevedo maintains that they never had an agreement as to quantity. Soon after this telephone conversation, Azevedo deposited $20,000 in the designated escrow account and began hauling hay from the Minister Ranch. As Azevedo hauled the hay, Minister furnished him with periodic accountings, commencing December 4, which specified the dates the hay was hauled, names of the truckers, bale count, and weight. This arrangement was satisfactory to the parties, and it continued until the latter part of March 1968, when Minister loaded only two of four trucks sent by Azevedo for hay, because the funds on deposit in the escrow account were insufficient to cover all four loads. *[handwritten: Compel Azevedo to buy more hay]* Azevedo then refused to buy any more hay, and Minister commenced this action in district court.

2. The Statute of Frauds.

[4] The determination of the legal issues presented for our consideration will turn on our interpretation of NRS 104.2201(2) of the Uniform Commercial Code. Since the enactment of the Uniform Commercial Code, sweeping changes have been effectuated in the law of commercial transactions. NRS 104.2201 provides:

> 1. Except as otherwise provided in this section a contract for the sale of goods for the price of $500 or more is not enforceable [sic] by way of action or defense unless there is some writing sufficient to indicate that a contract for sale has been made between the parties and signed by the party against whom enforcement is sought or by his authorized agent or broker. A writing is not insufficient because it omits or incorrectly states a term agreed upon but the contract is not enforceable [sic] under this subsection beyond the quantity of goods shown in such writing.

> 2. Between merchants if within a reasonable time a writing in confirmation of the contract and sufficient against the sender is

---

member of the public who might be damaged by the licensee's dishonesty, insolvency, or, in some cases, incompetence. When Azevedo didn't pay for the hay, Minister apparently sued not only him, but also the company that issued his bond.—Eds.]

received and the party receiving it has reason to know its contents, it satisfies the requirements of subsection 1 against such party unless written notice of objection to its contents is given within 10 days after it is received.

3.   A contract which does not satisfy the requirements of subsection 1 but which is valid in other respects is enforceable [sic]:

> (a) If the goods are to be specially manufactured for the buyer and are not suitable for sale to others in the ordinary course of the seller's business and the seller, before notice of repudiation is received and under circumstances which reasonably indicate that the goods are for the buyer, has made either a substantial beginning of their manufacture or commitments for their procurement; or

> (b) If the party against whom enforcement is sought admits in his pleading, testimony or otherwise in court that a contract for sale was made, but the contract is not enforceable [sic] under this provision beyond the quantity of goods admitted; or

> (c) With respect to goods for which payment has been made and accepted or which have been received and accepted (NRS 104.2606).

[5] As with all codifications, it was impossible for the Uniform Commercial Code to encompass every conceivable factual situation. Realizing this limitation, its drafters couched much of the language of the text and comments in broad generalities, leaving many problems to be answered by future litigation.

[6] The development of the action of assumpsit in the fourteenth century gave rise to the enforceability of the oral promise. Although parties to an action could not be witnesses, the alleged promise could be enforced on the strength of oral testimony of others not concerned with the litigation. Because of this practice, a party could readily suborn perjured testimony, resulting in marked injustice to innocent parties who were held legally obligated to promises they had never made. The statute of frauds was enacted to preclude this practice.[3] The passage of the statute did not eliminate the problem, but rather, has precipitated a controversy as to the relative merits of the statute. Those favoring the statute of frauds insist that it prevents fraud by prohibiting the introduction of perjured testimony. They also suggest that it deters hasty action, in that the formality of a writing will prevent a person from obligating himself without

---

[3]   Statute of Frauds, 1677, 29 Car. 2, c. 3 (repealed). The amount of the transaction necessary to bring the sale within the statute was 10 pounds.

contract
for sale goods ~~~~ *signed* *specify quantity*

a full appreciation of the nature of his acts. Moreover, it is said, since business customs almost entirely conform to the mandates of the statute, an abolition of the statute would seriously disrupt such affairs.

[7] On the other hand, in England the statute of frauds has been repealed. The English base their position upon the reasoning that the assertion of the technical defense of the statute aids a person in breaking a contract and effects immeasurable harm upon those who have meritorious claims.

[8] It is further maintained by the advocates of the English position that the rationale for the necessity of the statute has been vitiated, because parties engaged in litigation today may testify as witnesses and readily defend against perjured testimony.

[9] The Uniform Commercial Code, however, has attempted to strike a balance between the two positions by seeking to limit the defense of the statute to only those cases where there is a definite possibility of fraud.

[10] It is in the light of this historical background that we turn to consider whether the oral agreement of the parties in this case is barred by the statute of frauds.

[11] There is no question that the Azevedo-Minister agreement was oral and that its enforceability is governed by NRS 104.2201(2), *supra*. The sale of hay is included within the definition of the sale of "goods" as defined by NRS 104.2105(1) and NRS 104.2107(2), which when read together provide that the sale of "growing crops," when they are to be "severed by the buyer or by the seller," constitutes the sale of goods within the definition of that expression in the Uniform Commercial Code. The parties agree that they are "merchants" within the meaning of that term as defined in the Code.

[12] It is also true that the statute of frauds is no defense to that portion of the contract that has been performed under the provisions of NRS 104.2201(3)(c), *supra*, which makes enforceable an oral contract "[w]ith respect to goods . . . which have been received and accepted."

[13] The legal issues are, therefore, (1) whether Minister's accountings constituted confirming memoranda within the standards of NRS 104.2201(2) and, if so, (2) whether Minister sent them within a reasonable time as required by the statute. [We answer these questions "yes" and "yes."—Eds.]

3.   The Confirming Memoranda.

(a) The accounting of January 21, 1968.

[14] In addition to the data set forth in the periodic accountings covering the dates on which hay was hauled, the names of the truckers,

and the bale counts and weights, Minister added the following statement in his January 21 accounting to Azevedo:

letter indicating terms of oral agreement

> From your original deposit of $20,000.00 there is now a balance of $1819.76. At this time there remains [sic] approximately 16,600 bales of hay yet to be hauled on your purchase, about 9200 of which are first crop, 7400 of which are second crop.
>
> We would appreciate hearing when you plan to haul the balance of the hay. Also please make a deposit to cover the hay, sufficient in amount to pay for the hay you will be currently hauling. At this time you have only about $2.25 deposit per ton on the remaining balance of the hay, and we cannot permit a lower deposit per ton and still consider the hay as being sold.

silent

[15] Azevedo did not challenge or reply to Minister's accountancy of January 21. Rather, he deposited an additional $3,000 in the escrow account and continued hauling hay.

(b)   The accounting of February 22, 1968.

[16] In the regular accounting of February 22, Minister added the following: "Balance of deposit on approximately 14,000 bales remaining to be hauled—$1635.26."

[17] Azevedo did not challenge or reply to the February 22 accounting.

[18] It is these two accountings that the district judge found constituted confirming memoranda within the meaning of NRS 104.2201(2). There is little authority articulating the meaning of a confirming memorandum as used in the Code. The official Comment, Uniform Laws Annotated, Uniform Commercial Code § 2–201 (1968), states at 90, 91:

Confirming memoranda 3 req

> Only three definite and invariable requirements as to the [confirming] memorandum are made by this subsection. First, it must evidence a contract for the sale of goods; second, it must be "signed," a word which includes any authentication which identifies the party to be charged; and third, it must specify a quantity.

The parties concede that the memoranda were "signed" within the meaning of the statute, but appellant Azevedo urges that neither memorandum confirms the existence of an oral contract.

[19] While § 2–201(2) of the Code is entirely new in the commercial law field, its only effect is to eliminate the defense of the statute of frauds. The party alleging the contract still has the burden of proving that an oral contract was entered into before the written confirmation. The purpose of the subsection of the Code is to rectify an abuse that had developed in the law of commerce. The custom arose among business people of confirming

oral contracts by sending a letter of confirmation. This letter was binding as a memorandum on the sender, but not on the recipient, because he had not signed it.[4] The abuse was that the recipient, not being bound, could perform or not, according to his whim and the market, whereas the seller had to perform.[5] Obviously, under these circumstances, sending any confirming memorandum was a dangerous practice. Subsection (2) of section 2–201 of the Code cures the abuse by holding a recipient bound unless he communicates his objection within 10 days.

[20] Appellant urges that the January and February accountings do not meet the standards of the subsection because neither memorandum makes reference to any oral agreement between the parties. A fair reading of the memoranda shows otherwise. The January memorandum states that, "At this time there remains [sic] approximately 16,600 bales of hay yet to be hauled on your purchase," and, further, that, "We [Minister] would appreciate hearing when you plan to haul the balance of the hay." Although neither the January nor the February memorandum refers to the previous November agreement by telephone, the language clearly demonstrates that the referred-to agreement between the parties was not an in future arrangement, but a pre-existing agreement between Azevedo and Minister. As the court said in *Harry Rubin & Sons, Inc. v. Consolidated Pipe Co.*, 153 A.2d 472, 476 (Pa. 1959), in ruling on a case involving subsection (2) of section 2–201: "Under the statute of frauds as revised in the Code[,] 'All that is required is that the writing afford a basis for believing that the offered oral evidence rests on a real transaction.'" (footnote omitted.)

[21] The district judge found that it did so in the instant case, and the record supports his finding.

4. The "Reasonable Time" Factor.

[22] Subsection 2 of NRS 104.2201 provides that the confirming memorandum must be sent within a reasonable time after the oral contract is made. Appellant argues that the delay of 10 weeks (November 9 to January 21) as a matter of law is an unreasonable time. We do not agree. What is reasonable must be decided by the trier of the facts under all the circumstances of the case under consideration. Subsection 2 of NRS 104.1204 provides:

> What is a reasonable time for taking any action depends on the nature, purpose and circumstances of such action.

[23] In this case, the parties commenced performance of their oral agreement almost immediately after it was made in early November. Azevedo deposited $20,000 in the designated escrow account and began

---

[4]   As indicated in the instant case, Minister, who signed the memorandum, could be held to deliver to Azevedo the balance of the hay on the terms indicated.

[5]   The record reflects the price of hay was lower in March than in the previous November, when the parties had agreed on a tonnage price.

hauling hay. Minister commenced sending his periodic accounting reports to Azevedo on December 14.[6] It is true that the accounting containing the confirming memorandum was not sent until January 21. It was at that time that Azevedo's deposit of $20,000 was nearing depletion. Minister so advised Azevedo in the January memorandum. Azevedo responded by making an additional deposit. He did not object to the memorandum, and he continued to haul the hay until the latter part of March. Under "the nature, purpose and circumstances" of the case, we agree with the district judge that the delay was not unreasonable.

[24] The judgment is affirmed.

———

PROBLEM 13-1

A young Hollywood star and the star's personal trainer enter into an oral contract under the terms of which the trainer will work for the star for the rest of his life. Is this contract subject to the statute of frauds?

Is there an unclear pronoun reference in the statement of this problem's facts? If so, does it affect the answer?

PROBLEM 13-2

A world renowned operatic tenor and an elderly opera fan enter into an oral contract under the terms of which the tenor will be paid $499 for performing at the fan's 80th birthday party. The fan is now 78 years old. Is this contract subject to the statute of frauds?

PROBLEM 13-3

Buyer and Seller enter into an oral contract for the sale of a vacant lot that Seller owns. Buyer sends Seller a signed letter that states:

This will confirm our agreement that you will sell to me and I will buy from you the lot at 123 Main Street, legally described as "Lot 99 in the Toxic Waste Subdivision, as per Map 44 recorded in the office of the Register of Deeds of Bigfoot County, California." The price will be $100,000 and all other terms will be as we have previously agreed.

Seller receives the letter but does not respond to it.

Can the contract be enforced against Seller? Can the contract be enforced against Buyer?

---

[6]   Azevedo concedes that he never challenged or replied to any of the accountings.

PROBLEM 13-4

[handwritten: No signature from seller]

Buyer and Seller enter into an oral contract for the sale of a vacant lot that Seller owns. Buyer sends Seller a signed letter that states:

[handwritten: unless we point to 129 which is reasonable reliance]

> This will confirm our agreement that you will sell to me and I will buy from you the lot at 123 Main Street, legally described as "Lot 99 in the Toxic Waste Subdivision, as per Map 44 recorded in the office of the Register of Deeds of Bigfoot County, California."

The letter goes on to spell out in detail all of the important terms of the transaction. Seller receives the letter but does not respond to it.

Can the contract be enforced against Seller? Can the contract be enforced against Buyer?

PROBLEM 13-5

[handwritten: need a writing or exception]

Farmer and Broker enter into an oral contract for the purchase and sale of 10,000 bushels of hops at a price of $3.00 per bushel. Broker sends Farmer a note that reads in full: *[handwritten: More than $500　goods—so UCC]*

> This will confirm our agreement that you will sell me 10,000 bushels of hops at $2.75 a bushel.
>
> *Sleazy C. Broker*

[handwritten: — Merchants exception? Depends if farmer is merchant]

[handwritten left margin: Change the price — additional of different term]

Farmer does not respond to the note. Farmer decides he doesn't want to deal with someone whose word can't be trusted, and he refuses to deliver the hops. Broker sues, and Farmer defends on the basis that the statute of frauds precludes enforcement of the contract. Will this defense be successful?

[handwritten: 10 days no writing]

PROBLEM 13-6

Farmer and Broker enter into an oral contract for the purchase and sale of 10,000 bushels of hops at a price of $3.00 per bushel. Broker sends Farmer a note that reads in full:

> This will confirm our agreement that you will sell me 10,000 bushels — *[handwritten: written objection]* of hops at $2.75 a bushel.

Farmer mails the note back to Broker with the following annotation:

> "The price was 3 bucks—you jerk." /s/ Farmer. *[handwritten: — acknowledging the contract]*

[handwritten: needs to come within 10 days of receipt]

Farmer decides he doesn't want to deal with someone whose word can't be trusted, and he refuses to deliver the hops. Broker sues, and Farmer defends on the basis that the statute of frauds precludes enforcement of the contract. Will this defense be successful?

[handwritten left margin: write this one out ↑]

——————

[handwritten: Under 2-207(2) the additional term is dropped out]

WADDLE V. ELROD

Supreme Court of Tennessee, at Nashville
367 S.W.3d 217 (2012)

[1]   In this appeal we must determine whether the Statute of Frauds, Tenn.Code Ann. § 29–2–101(a)(4) (Supp.2011), applies to a settlement agreement requiring the transfer of an interest in real property; and, if so, whether emails exchanged by the parties' attorneys satisfy the Statute of Frauds under the Uniform Electronic Transactions Act ("UETA"), Tenn.Code Ann. §§ 47–10–101 to –123 (2001 & Supp.2011). We hold that the Statue of Frauds applies to settlement agreements requiring the transfer of an interest in real property and that the emails, along with a legal description of the property contained in the cross-claim, satisfy the Statute of Frauds. Accordingly, we affirm the judgment of the Court of Appeals enforcing the settlement agreement.

Facts and Procedural History

[2]   On January 29, 2007, Regent Investments 1, LLC ("Regent") sued octogenarian Earline Waddle, and her niece, Lorene Elrod. According to the allegations of the complaint, Regent contracted to purchase from Ms. Waddle approximately four acres of real property located at 2268 Prim Lane, in Rutherford County, Tennessee ("the Prim Lane property"), for $230,000. Regent paid Ms. Waddle $10,000 earnest money when the contract was signed. However, in preparing to close the deal, Regent learned of a quitclaim deed by which Ms. Waddle had conveyed one-half of her interest in the Prim Lane property to Ms. Elrod. Regent sued Ms. Waddle, alleging breach of contract, fraud, and intentional and negligent misrepresentation. Regent requested specific performance, $1,000,000 in damages, attorney's fees, costs, and pre-judgment interest. Regent also asked the trial court to set aside the quitclaim deed, arguing that Ms. Elrod had wrongfully obtained her one-half interest by exercising undue influence over Ms. Waddle.

[3]   On May 14, 2007, Ms. Waddle filed a cross-claim against Ms. Elrod, also alleging that Ms. Elrod had acquired her one-half interest in the Prim Lane property through undue influence. The cross-claim included a legal description of the Prim Lane property. According to the allegations of the cross-claim, after Ms. Waddle's husband of more than fifty years died on February 12, 2001, Ms. Elrod began frequently visiting Ms. Waddle. In early March 2001, Ms. Elrod arranged for her own attorney, whom Ms. Waddle did not know, to draft both the quitclaim deed conveying a one-half interest in the Prim Lane property to Ms. Elrod and a durable power of attorney naming Ms. Elrod as Ms. Waddle's attorney-in-fact. On March 15, 2001, Ms. Elrod drove Ms. Waddle to the attorney's office and persuaded her to sign both documents. Ms. Waddle alleged that she did not have the benefit of independent legal counsel prior to signing the documents, that

Ms. Elrod provided no money or consideration for the interest she acquired in the Prim Lane property, that she did not willingly or knowingly intend to convey any interest in the Prim Lane property to Ms. Elrod, and that the power of attorney executed contemporaneously with the quitclaim deed created a confidential relationship giving rise a to presumption of undue influence with respect to the quitclaim deed. Ms. Waddle asked the trial court to set aside the quitclaim deed and to award her "any and all damages" caused by Ms. Elrod's undue influence, including, and in particular, the damages resulting from Ms. Waddle's inability to convey Regent marketable title to the Prim Lane property.

[4] On July 10, 2007, Ms. Elrod filed an answer to the cross-claim, denying all allegations of undue influence and wrongdoing and arguing that the assistance she had provided Ms. Waddle served as consideration for the quitclaim deed.

[5] On April 28, 2009, Regent agreed to dismiss with prejudice its claims against Ms. Waddle and Ms. Elrod. In exchange, Ms. Waddle agreed to return Regent's $10,000 earnest money, and both Ms. Waddle and Ms. Elrod agreed that Regent would not be responsible for any portion of the court costs Ms. Waddle's cross-claim against Ms. Elrod remained pending, however, with a jury trial scheduled for June 2 to June 4, 2009.

[6] The day before trial, Ms. Elrod's attorney, Mr. Gregory Reed, advised Ms. Hagan, counsel for Ms. Waddle, that Ms. Elrod was willing to return her one-half interest in the Prim Lane property to avoid going to trial if Ms. Waddle would settle the case and release all other claims against her. Through her attorney, Ms. Waddle agreed to settle the case on the condition that she would not be responsible for any of the court costs. Around 4:00 p.m., Mr. Reed advised Ms. Hagan that Ms. Elrod had agreed to settle the case with Ms. Waddle's condition. At 4:34 p.m., Ms. Hagan sent the following email to Mr. Reed:

> Greg,
>
> This confirms that we have settled this case on the following terms:
>
> Elrod deeds property interest back to Waddle, Both [sic] parties sign full release, Waddle bears no court costs.
>
> Let me know if I have correctly stated our agreement.
>
> Thanks,
>
> Mary Beth

[7] At 5:02 p.m., Mr. Reed responded:

That is the agreement. I understand that you will draft the deed and take a shot at the court's order. No admission of guilt is to be included.

Greg Reed

[8] The attorneys thereafter advised the trial court of the terms of the agreement. Believing that a settlement had been reached and that a written order memorializing the settlement would be entered later, the trial court cancelled the jury trial and excused prospective jurors. Counsel for Ms. Waddle prepared and forwarded the settlement documents to counsel for Ms. Elrod. Ms. Waddle, understanding that the settlement had returned sole ownership of the Prim Lane property to her, paid all outstanding property taxes. Approximately three weeks later, however, Ms. Elrod advised her attorney that she had changed her mind and no longer wanted to settle the case. When Ms. Elrod refused to sign the settlement documents, Mr. Reed moved to withdraw from further representation, and the trial court granted Mr. Reed's motion.

[9] On July 13, 2009, Ms. Waddle filed a motion asking the trial court to enforce the settlement agreement. On September 2, 2009, Ms. Elrod filed a response, arguing that the discussions on June 1, 2009, resulted merely in an agreement to agree, with many important material terms unresolved. Alternatively, Ms. Elrod argued that the Statute of Frauds, Tenn.Code Ann. § 29–2–101 (Supp.2011), bars enforcement of the settlement agreement because it required the transfer of an interest in real property and was not evidenced by a writing signed by Ms. Elrod or her attorney describing with specificity the terms of the agreement and the property at issue. Relying on the Uniform Electronic Transactions Act ("UETA"), *see* Tenn.Code Ann. §§ 47–10–101 to –123 (2001 & Supp.2011), Ms. Waddle argued in response that the email from Ms. Elrod's attorney, which confirmed the terms of the settlement and included Mr. Reed's typewritten name, constituted a writing signed by an agent of the party to be charged and satisfied the Statute of Frauds.

[10] Following a hearing, the trial court entered an order on September 15, 2009, enforcing the settlement agreement. The trial court found that Ms. Elrod had agreed through her attorney and authorized agent to settle the case on the terms set out in June 1, 2009 email. As a result, the trial court divested Ms. Elrod of any right, title, or interest in the Prim Lane property and vested ownership of the property in Ms. Waddle. The trial court also dismissed with prejudice Ms. Waddle's remaining claims against Ms. Elrod, ordered each party to bear her own attorney's fees and discretionary costs, and taxed court costs to Ms. Waddle. The trial court's order did not expressly address either Ms. Elrod's argument that the Statute of Frauds precluded enforcement of the

settlement or Ms. Waddle's argument that the emails constituted writings signed by the party to be charged under the UETA and satisfied the Statute of Frauds.

[11] Ms. Elrod appealed, but she did not challenge the trial court's factual finding that the parties had reached an agreement to settle the case. Rather, she argued that the Statute of Frauds precludes enforcement of the settlement agreement. The Court of Appeals rejected this argument and affirmed the trial court's judgment enforcing the settlement agreements, reasoning that the Statute of Frauds applies only to "any contract for the *sale* of lands," Tenn.Code Ann. § 29–2–101(a)(4) (emphasis added), and does not apply to a settlement agreement requiring the transfer of an interest in real property.

[12] We granted Ms. Elrod's application for permission to appeal.

[13] As the Court of Appeals recognized, Ms. Elrod does not dispute that the parties reached an agreement; rather, she argues that the Statute of Frauds applies and precludes enforcement of the settlement agreement because it required the transfer of an interest in real property. In contrast, Ms. Waddle argues that the Court of Appeals' judgment should be affirmed because the relevant portion of the Statute of Frauds applies only to contracts for the sale of land. Alternatively, Ms. Waddle maintains that the emails counsel exchanged and the legal description of the Prim Lane property in Ms. Waddle's cross-claim satisfy the Statute of Frauds.

[14] A settlement agreement made during the course of litigation is a contract between the parties, and as such, contract law governs disputes concerning the formation, construction, and enforceability of the settlement agreement. Like other contracts, a settlement agreement may be subject to the Statute of Frauds. The Statute of Frauds precludes actions to enforce certain types of patrol contracts unless the action is supported by written evidence of the parties' agreement.

[15] The settlement agreement in the present case requires a conveyance of real property. With respect to real property, Tennessee's Statute of Frauds provides:

> No action shall be brought . . . [u]pon any contract for the sale of lands, tenements, or hereditaments, . . . unless the promise or agreement, upon which such action shall be brought, or some memorandum or note thereof, shall be in writing, and signed by the party to be charged therewith, or some other person lawfully authorized by such party. In a contract for the sale of lands, tenements, or hereditaments, the party to be charged is the party against whom enforcement of the contracts is sought.

Tenn.Code Ann. § 29–2–101(a)(4).

[16] The primary purpose of the Statute of Frauds is to reduce the risk of fraud and perjury associated with oral testimony. The Statutes of Frauds also fosters certainty in transactions by ensuring that contract formation is not based upon loose statements or innuendoes long after witnesses have become unavailable or when memories of the precise agreement have been dimmed by the passage of time. Another purpose of the Statute of Frauds is to protect property owners against hasty or inconsiderate agreements concerning a valuable species of property and misunderstandings as to the nature and extent of such agreements.

[17] While this Court has long emphasized that the Statute of Frauds should be strictly adhered to and construed to accomplish its intended purposes, *Newman v. Carroll*, 11 Tenn. (3 Yer.) 18, 26 (1832), the Statute of Frauds is an affirmative defense. *See* Tenn. R. Civ. P. 8.03. In other words, parol agreements within the Statute of Frauds are not void ab initio, and enforcement of such agreements may be barred only if a party pleads the Statute of Frauds. Parties may choose to abide by parol contracts for the sale of land. Indeed, the Statute of Frauds was not enacted for the purpose of permitting a person to avoid a contract. Its object was not to grant a privilege to a person to refuse to perform what he has agreed to do. It was not enacted as a shield to the dishonest.

[18] The word "sale," used in the statutory phrase "contract for the sale of lands, tenements, or hereditaments," has long been broadly interpreted to mean any alienation of real property, including even a donation of realty. This Court has previously explained that such a broad construction is consistent both with the purposes of the Statute of Frauds and with the common law understanding of the term:

> The word "sale in our statute of frauds (section 3142, Shannon's Code) means alienation, and an action on a parol contract made by the owner binding him to give or donate land to another, would, we think, fall within the terms of that statute. A contrary holding would open a wide door to perjury and fraud, and defeat, as we think, one of the purposes of the statute.
>
> . . .
>
> Plaintiff insists that a parol done of land does not, in legal contemplation, stand upon a parity with a parol vendee. . . . We cannot assent to this proposition. . . . At common law the word "purchase" in its largest and most extensive sense is defined by Littleton to be the possession of lands and tenements which a man hath as by his own act or agreement, and not by descent by any of his ancestors or kindred. In this sense it is contradistinguished from acquisition by right of blood, and includes every other method of coming to an estate by but merely that of inheritance, wherein the title is vested in a person, not by his own act or

agreement, but by the single operation of law. And says Mr. Blackstone: "Purchase, indeed, in its vulgar and confined acceptation, is applied only to such acquisitions of land as are to be obtained by way of bargain and sale for money, or some other valuable consideration; but this falls far short of the legal idea of purchase, for if I give land freely to another, he is in the eyes of the law a purchaser, and falls within Littleton's definition, for he comes to the estate by his own agreement; that is, he consents to the gift."

[Citation omitted.—Eds.]

[19] In the century since the Tennessee General Assembly has not amended the Statute of Frauds to ascribe a more narrow meaning to the word "sale." Relying on a legal dictionary, Ms. Waddle asks this Court to construe "sale" as meaning "[t]he transfer of property or title for *a price . . . in money paid or promised." See Black's Law Dictionary* 1364 (8th ed.2004) (emphasis added). However, Ms. Waddle has failed to provide any persuasive rationale for overruling our past precedent and we decline to do so. We conclude that the Court of Appeals erred by holding that the Statute of Frauds does not apply to this settlement agreement.

[20] Consistent with the rule applied by a majority of jurisdictions, we hereby hold that the Statute of Frauds applies to any settlement agreement requiring a transfer of an interest in real property. [Extensive string citation omitted.—Eds.] We emphasize, however, that in determining whether the Statute of Frauds applies, courts must consider the terms of the settlement agreement, not the subject matter of the litigation. Settlement agreements arising from litigation that involves real property are subject to the Statute of Frauds only if the terms of the settlement agreement herein required Ms. Elrod to transfer her one-half interest in the Prim Lane property to Ms. Waddle, the Statute of Frauds applies.

[21] We next consider whether the Statute of Frauds bars enforcement of the settlement agreement at issue in this appeal. As already explained, parol contracts are enforceable if "some memorandum or note thereof, shall be in writing and signed by the party to be charged therewith, or some other person lawfully authorized by such party." Tenn.Code Ann. § 29–2–101(a)(4). The Statute of Frauds does not require a written contract, only a written memorandum or note evidencing the parties' agreement. Additionally, while the writing required by the Statute of Frauds must contain the essential terms of the contract, it need not be in a single document. *See Lambert v. Home Fed. Sav. & Loan Ass'n*, 481 S.W.2d 770, 773 (Tenn.1972). As this Court explained in *Lambert*:

> The general rule is that the memorandum, in order to satisfy the statute, must contain the essential terms of the contract, expressed with such certainty that they may be understood from

the memorandum itself or some other writing to which it refers or with which it is connected, without resorting to parol evidence. A memorandum disclosing merely that a contract had been made, without showing what the contract is, is not sufficient to satisfy the requirement of the Statute of Frauds that there be a memorandum in writing of the contract.

[22] Of course, even if one or more memoranda are produced sufficiently describing the terms of a parol agreement, the Statute of Frauds also requires that one of the writings be signed by the party to be charged or by some other person authorized to act on that party's behalf. The authority of the agent or the evidence of his agency need not be in writing, however. While the Statute of Frauds does not define "signed," many years ago the Court of Appeals considered whether a party's printed name on a bill of sale satisfied the signature requirement. *See Gessler v. Winton*, 24 Tenn. App. 411, 145 S.W.2d 789 (1940). In holding that the printed name was sufficient, the Court of Appeals stated:

> The [S]tatute [of frauds] does not specify any particular form of signing. It merely requires that the party to be charged shall have signed the memorandum. It has been held that a cross mark is a good signature; also initials; even numerals, when used with the intention of constituting a signature; and a typewritten name or imprint made by a rubber stamp has the same effect; and this is equally true, though the typewriting or stamp impression be made by another, if the person to be charged has directed it.
>
> . . .
>
> This has been the law in England for more than a century, and has been followed quite generally in this country.

Id. at 794 (citations and internal quotation marks omitted).

[23] While *Gessler* predates email, its holding appears broad enough to encompass typed names appearing in emails. However, we need not rely upon *Gessler* to determine whether the email that includes the name of Ms. Elrod's attorney satisfies the Statutes of Frauds requirement of a writing signed by the party to be charged. In 2001 the General Assembly enacted the UETA. Ms. Waddle relied upon the UETA in the trial court when arguing that the email constituted a writing for purposes of the Statute of Frauds and that Mr. Reed's name on the email constitutes the signature of an agent of Ms. Elrod, the party to be charged. She has continued to advance these arguments on appeal.

[24] The UETA "applies to electronic records and electronic signatures relating to a transaction." Tenn.Code Ann. § 47–10–103(a). The General Assembly has declared that the UETA:

Must be construed and applied to:

(1) Facilitate electronic transactions consistent with other applicable law;

(2) Be consistent with reasonable practices concerning electronic transactions and with the continued expansion of those practices; and

(3) Effectuate its general purpose to make uniform the law with respect to the subject of [the UETA] among states enacting it.

Tenn.Code Ann. § 47–10–106. The UETA does not require parties to conduct transactions by electronic means. Tenn.Code Ann. § 47–10–105(a). Rather, the UETA governs "transactions between parties each of which has agreed to conduct transactions by electronic means. Whether the parties agree to conduct a transaction by electronic means is determined from the context and surrounding circumstances, including the parties' conduct." Tenn.Code Ann. § 47–10–105(a)–(b). "Transaction means an action or set of actions occurring between two (2) or more persons relating to the conduct of business, commercial, or governmental affairs." Tenn.Code Ann. § 47–10–102(16). Under the UETA:

(a) A record or signature may not be denied legal effect or enforceability solely because it is in electronic form.

(b) A contract may not be denied legal effect or enforceability sole because an electronic record was used in its formation.

(c) If a law requires a record to be in writing, an electronic record satisfies the law.

(d) If a law requires a signature, an electronic signature satisfies the law.

Tenn. Code Ann. § 47–10–107(a)–(d). "Electronic signature" includes "an electronic sound, symbol, or process attached to or logically associated with a record and executed or adopted by a person with the intent to sign the record. Tenn.Code Ann. § 47–10–102(8); *see also id.* cmt. 7 ("[T]he mere inclusion of one's name as part of an email message" qualifies as an electronic signature "so long as in each case the signer executed or adopted the symbol with the intent to sign.").

[25] Applying the foregoing principles, we conclude that the Statute of Frauds does not bar enforcement of the settlement agreement at issue in this appeal. The parties, through their attorneys, evidenced an intent to finalize the settlement by electronic means; thus, the UETA applies. Pursuant to section 47–10–107(c), the emails counsel exchanged constitute a signed memorandum, note, or writing for purposes of the Statute of Frauds.

[26] Additionally, under the principles discussed in *Lambert*, the emails, considered along with the legal description of the Prim Lane property in the cross-claim, described the terms of the parol agreement with sufficient specificity to satisfy the Statute of Frauds. In particular, the emails described the following four material terms of the settlement: (1) Ms. Elrod would convey her interest "in the property" back to Ms. Waddle; (2) each party would sign a release giving up any claims she may have had against the other party; (3) Ms. Waddle would not be responsible for court costs; and (4) Ms. Elrod would not admit guilt. Ms. Elrod's attorney confirmed the settlement, responding electronically "[t]hat is our agreement." While the emails referred only to "the property," the Prim Lane property was the only realty at issue in the litigation, and Ms. Waddle's cross-claim included a full legal description of the Prim Lane property. As stated in *Lambert*, a writing is sufficient if the terms of the agreement may be understood either from the writing itself or from some other writing connected with it. The emails and cross-claim satisfy this standard.

[27] Furthermore, although Ms. Elrod did not sign the email, there is no dispute that Mr. Reed was acting as her agent when he negotiated the settlement. He had written his signature on a printed version of the email, rather than typed his name at the end of the email, his signature would undoubtedly have been sufficient to satisfy the Statute of Frauds. The UETA, recognizing that all sorts of transactions are now routinely conducted by electronic means on a daily basis, obviates the need for a handwritten signature. Mr. Reed's typed name at the end of the email constitutes an "electronic signature." Tenn.Code Ann. § 47–10–107(d). As the agent of Ms. Elrod, Mr. Reed's electronic signature on the email confirming the terms of the settlement agreement satisfies the signature requirement of the Statute of Frauds.

Conclusion

[28] The Statute of Frauds applies to settlement agreements requiring the transfer of an interest in real property. However, the Statute of Frauds does not bar enforcement of the settlement agreement at issue in this appeal. The emails counsel for the parties exchanged, along with the legal description of the Prim Lane property included in the cross-claim, constitute a sufficiently definite writing, note, or memorandum, and the email confirming the terms of the settlement agreement included the electronic signature of the attorney and authorized agent of Ms. Elrod, the party to be charged. Thus, on these alternate grounds we affirm the Court of Appeals' judgment enforcing the settlement agreement, including the taxing of court costs to Ms. Elrod. Costs of this appeal also are taxed to Ms. Elrod, for which execution may issue if necessary.

NOTE

1. Not since the days of the telegraph have we had as many disputes about offer, acceptance, and the statute of frauds based upon uncontroverted facts as we do in the e-mail and Internet age. Once the telephone was invented, much business was conducted verbally, which generated often conflicting notes and memories of the conversations involved and the practice of sending self-serving confirming letters. But with the rise of e-mail, people are contemporaneously documenting their conversations and events all around them, creating a robust record that can be used to document or litigate over a contract just as was the case in the telegraph offer and acceptance cases featured earlier in this text. Keep this in mind when e-mailing, texting, instant messaging or otherwise posting words and images on the Internet. You are making a record that can be used for or against you or your client.

2. What happens if a written agreement or memorandum is lost or destroyed? Can it still be used to satisfy the statute of frauds? Would it make sense to allow verbal testimony to establish the former existence and terms of such a writing? The Nevada Supreme Court thought so in *Khan v. Bakhsh*, 306 P.3d 411 (Nev. 2013).

3. Satisfying the strict electronic signature requirement of the UETA is not always as simple as the previous case makes it appear. In *Waddle*, the court found that "the parties, through their attorneys, evidenced an intent to finalize the settlement by electronic means; thus, the UETA applies." But, it is not always that simple.

In *J.B.B. Investment Partners, Ltd. v. Fair*, 232 Cal. App. 4th 974 (Cal. Ct. App. 2014), a California trial court granted plaintiff investors' motion to enforce a settlement agreement between the plaintiffs and defendants, limited liability companies and their principal. The court determined that the defendant satisfied the electronic signature requirement under California's Uniform Electronic Transaction Act (UETA) because the principal printed his name at the bottom of his e-mail responding to the plaintiff's e-mail containing the settlement offer. *See* Civ. Code, § 1633.1–1633.17. On appeal, the Court of Appeal of California reviewed the case to determine whether the defendant's signature on this email satisfied the strict signature requirement of the UETA.

> Under [the] UETA . . . an electronic record satisfies the requirement that a record be in writing, and an electronic signature satisfies the requirement that the writing be signed. 'An electronic record or electronic signature is attributable to a person if it was the act of the person . . . . [A]n 'electronic signature' [is defined] as 'an electronic sound, symbol, or process attached to or logically associated with an electronic record and executed or adopted by a person with the intent to sign the electronic record. [The] UETA applies, however, only when the parties consent to conduct the transaction by electronic means. Whether the parties consent to conduct a contract by electronic means is determined from the context and surrounding circumstances, including the parties' conduct.

The plaintiffs invested $250,000 in Boulevard and Cameron, a business owned by the defendant, Tom Fair (who besides being a businessman was also a licensed attorney). After discovering that Fair had made various fraudulent misrepresentations and omissions to them regarding their investment and his business, the plaintiffs had their attorneys contact Fair and attempt to negotiate a settlement to avoid filing a civil suit against him and his company.

The parties had been negotiating back and forth via email, and on July 4, Russo, counsel for one plaintiff, emailed Fair a ten paragraph settlement agreement. The last paragraph of the settlement agreement contained the following language: "WE require a YES or NO on this proposal; you need to say '*I accept.*' . . . Anything less shifts all focus to litigation . . . ." This settlement agreement did not include a signature line or signature block, and the signatures of the plaintiffs were also not on the document.

On July 5, at 10:17 a.m., Fair replied to Russo's email: ". . . *I agree.* Tom [F]air."

Haliburton, counsel for the other plaintiff, promptly replied to Fair via e-mail asking him to provide a less ambiguous response because he could not decide whether Fair was accepting or rejecting their settlement offer. Also, Haliburton advised Fair that he was prepared to file the complaint against him unless Fair provided them with a clear, unambiguous acceptance.

The plaintiffs filed the complaint against Fair on July 5, just before noon. Haliburton and Russo emailed a copy of the complaint to Fair at 12:25 p.m.

At 1:02 p.m., Fair responded to Haliburton via text message saying: "I said I agree. Took wording right from [Russo's] e-mail. I agree." After sending this text message, Fair promptly called Haliburton and left the following voicemail: "Hey, I just got your email . . . I thought I was quite clear on my first response, I made another response by e-mail, I said I agree with [plaintiffs' counsel's] terms. You know? So, that's it."

At 1:07 p.m., Fair sent yet another text message to Haliburton saying: "I do not believe you gave proper notice. Also, I agreed with your terms. You should not have filed. We clearly have an agreement. [T]om [F]air."

At 1:36 p.m., Fair sent a text message to Russo that said: "Filing does not obviate agreement/acceptance. Pls acknowledge."

At 1:53 p.m., Russo responded to Fair via e-mail saying:

This confirms full agreement. I will work on the formal settlement paperwork which will confirm to the settlement agreement made today based on the 10 numbered paragraphs below with no admission of liability or wrongdoing by anyone. I will seek to get that settlement paperwork to you for review by Monday with the goal of getting it all finalized and signed next week. The settlement is otherwise binding . . . .

Two minutes later, at 1:55 p.m., Fair sent Haliburton the following text message: "I have accepted by phone, and [e-mail]. Stop proceeding. I said *accept* which is the same as 'agree.' You must stop and you must tell the court we have an agreement."

On July 11, Haliburton sent Fair a written draft of the final settlement agreement which contained the names of the plaintiffs and defendants. "It advised that the agreement could be 'signed and delivered by facsimile' and that it could be 'electronically signed' by each party." It also included signature blocks for each party, but neither plaintiff had signed the agreement.

Fair never signed the July 11 settlement agreement. The plaintiffs sued Fair to enforce the settlement agreement.

The Court of Appeal pointed out that the trial court ignored a provision in the UETA requiring the electronic signature be "executed or adopted by a person with the intent to sign the electronic record." See § 1633.2(h). Regarding the e-mail Fair sent on July 5 at 10:17 a.m., Fair testified that he believed he had agreed to the terms that Russo suggested in an e-mail that morning, but because the plaintiffs filed the lawsuit those terms became moot and he changed his mind. He also stated that he did not consider his name at the bottom of the e-mail to be a signature to a settlement agreement because he never signed important documents, like settlement agreements, without his attorney present.

The Court of Appeal concluded, "as a matter of law, that [the record] does not show that Fair printed his name at the end of his e-mail with any intent to formalize an electronic transaction. Indeed, substantial evidence in the record refutes such a finding." The court concluded that the e-mail exchange between the parties indicated that they agreed to negotiate via e-mail, but nothing more.

The July 4 settlement offer did not contain a statement indicating that the parties agreed to enter into a final settlement by electronic means. The plain language of the July 4 offer clarified that no signature was requested as the offer did not include a signature line or signature block, nor did it contain a signature by either of the plaintiffs, and advised that future paperwork was forthcoming.

The Court of Appeal ultimately held, as a matter of law, the record contained insufficient evidence to conclude that Fair electronically signed the settlement agreement, and it reversed the trial court's judgment.

LAWYERING SKILLS PROBLEM

One law firm's computer system adds the following disclaimer on every e-mail its lawyers send:

> This communication does not reflect an intention by the sender or the sender's client or principal to conduct a transaction or make any agreement by electronic means. Nothing contained in this message or in any attachment shall satisfy the requirements for a writing, and nothing contained herein shall constitute a contract or electronic

signature under the Electronic Signatures in Global and National Commerce Act, any version of the Uniform Electronic Transactions Act or any other statute governing electronic transactions.

What do you do if you receive an e-mail from an attorney in this firm stating that she agrees to give you an additional 10 days to file an answer to her complaint?

CHAPTER 14

THE PAROL EVIDENCE RULE

■ ■ ■

The parol evidence rule is traditionally one of, if not the, most difficult doctrines of a law school first-year contracts course. The rule is fairly simply stated, but is riddled with exceptions and seeming exceptions that have grown up around it as the courts have wrestled with circumstances in which strict application of the rule would seem to produce unjust results. Like the statute of frauds and the rule against perpetuities, the parol evidence rule is now largely a creature of American law, having been adopted in the R2d and the U.C.C. and excluded from the CISG and UNIDROIT as well as the laws of the civil law countries. *See* CISG article 11, UNIDROIT article 1.2.

Keep in mind that "parol evidence" is the same thing as "extrinsic evidence"—it is evidence of any sort (not just oral statements) that is not a part of the writing that is claimed to be an integrated agreement. The parol evidence rule concerns whether or not a court will admit evidence of prior or contemporaneous agreements when determining what the terms of the parties' agreement are when there is a written contract.

If the written contract was intended by the parties as the final and complete expression of the terms (the R2 refers to this as a "completely integrated agreement"), then no terms from any prior or contemporaneous agreement are relevant, even if they address issues not dealt with in the written document. The completely integrated agreement essentially wipes out all those prior or contemporaneous agreements. If the written document was intended to be the final expression of some but not all of the terms (the R2d refers to this as a "partially integrated agreement"), then terms from prior or contemporaneous agreements will not be given effect if they are inconsistent with the terms of the written document, but they may be given effect if they deal with issues not dealt with in the written document.

For example, Holmes and Watson make a deal for Watson's purchase of Holmes' Stradivarius. They sign a document setting out most of the terms of the deal but failing to address the issue of when the violin will be delivered. If the court determines that the document is only partially integrated, it can give effect to Holmes' testimony that before they signed the document they agreed that Holmes could keep the violin until the

Queen's birthday. If the document is completely integrated, this prior agreement has no effect.

In *Individual Healthcare Specialists, Inc. v. BlueCross BlueShield of Tennessee, Inc.*, the Supreme Court of Tennessee noted the significant policy reasons for the parol evidence rule:

> A strict enforcement of [the parol evidence] rule tends to greater security and safety in business transactions, and leaves less opportunity for dishonesty and false swearing, induced, perhaps, by a change of purpose or a failure to obtain the result that was anticipated when the transaction was originally consummated and reduced to writing.

Individual Healthcare Specialists, Inc. v. BlueCross BlueShield of Tennessee, Inc., 566 S.W.3d. 671, 695 (Tenn. 2019) (quoting *McGannon v. Farrell*, 141 Tenn. 631, 214 S.W. 432, 433 (Tenn. 1919)).

From these general statements of the parameters of the rule, then, a number of sub-issues present themselves and are explored in the cases and problems that follow. Remember:

1.   *The parol evidence rule is concerned with what evidence will be admitted to prove what the terms of an integrated agreement are.* It does not bar parol evidence proffered for another purpose (such as to prove a defense to formation like misrepresentation, fraud, or duress; or to prove whether the agreement is integrated, partially or completely, or not). As such, although it is a substantive rule of law, it is one to be applied by the court as a preliminary evidentiary matter and is not a question for the jury.

2.   *The parol evidence rule applies only to integrated agreements: those intended by the parties to express either the final terms agreed to about a portion of their arrangements or relationship (partial integration) or the full scope of their arrangements or relationship regarding a particular subject matter (complete integration).* If the agreement is not integrated, the rule has no application. An integration or merger clause—one stating that the agreement constitutes the parties' entire agreement with regard to its subject matter and that all prior and contemporaneous agreements regarding its subject matter, if any, are discharged and of no further force or effect—is compelling but not dispositive evidence of integration.

Thus, the general parol evidence rule analysis should proceed as:

A.   Is the proffered parol evidence of a prior or contemporaneous agreement?

B.   If so, is it offered to prove the *terms* of the parties' contract?

C.   If so, is the written agreement partially or completely integrated? If partially integrated, the evidence is barred to the extent it would vary or contradict the terms, but may be admissible to supplement or explain the terms. If the agreement is completely integrated, the evidence is barred.

The steps of this analysis can also be inverted and performed C, B, A. The specific formulation of this analysis varies between the R2d, the U.C.C., and the case law of various jurisdictions. The exact language of the relevant jurisdiction for each step should be substituted as appropriate. The cases that follow illustrate the parol evidence rule in action.

FEDERAL DEPOSIT INSURANCE CORP.[1] V. HADID

United States Court of Appeals, Fourth Circuit
947 F.2d 1153 (1991)

NIEMEYER, CIRCUIT JUDGE.

[1]   On a complaint filed by the National Bank of Washington (NBW) to collect on two promissory notes that Mohammed Anwar M. Hadid guaranteed, a jury found in favor of Hadid, crediting his testimony of an oral agreement by which his guarantees would become null and void if he were not given control of stock which secured the notes. On NBW's motion for judgment notwithstanding the verdict, the district court found that the oral agreement violated the parol evidence rule and entered judgment against Hadid in the amount of $1,854,875.03 on the notes plus $272,035.26 in attorneys' fees. The Federal Deposit Insurance Corporation (FDIC) succeeded to the judgment when it declared NBW insolvent in August 1990. Hadid contends on appeal that the facts surrounding application of the parol evidence rule were properly submitted to the jury and should have been left for the jury to determine.

[2]   For the reasons that follow, we affirm the judgment of the district court on the notes but reverse with respect to the amount of the award for attorneys' fees.

I

[3]   As evidence of the debt arising from two loans made by NBW to Keystone Financial Corporation (Keystone) and P.S. Investment Co., Inc. (P.S. Investment) in 1986, NBW accepted two promissory notes. The one

---

[1]   [In this case, the FDIC has stepped in to represent the failed bank, National Bank Washington, and is prosecuting this action to maximize the recovery of the failed bank's assets. To the extent there is a shortfall of assets to cover insured deposits at the bank, the FDIC will use government depository insurance funds to make up the shortfall.—Eds.]

signed by Keystone was in the amount of $1,314,209.75 and its repayment was secured by a pledge of the common stock in McDowell Enterprises, Inc. Repayment of that note was also guaranteed by Dr. P.S. Prasad and Bert Lance.[2] The second, signed by P.S. Investment, was in the amount of $200,000.00, and its repayment was guaranteed by Dr. Prasad and his wife. Dr. Prasad owned both Keystone and P.S. Investment.

[4]   The loans, which were short-term, were extended by NBW on several occasions in 1986 and early 1987, but in August 1987 NBW demanded full repayment. At that time, Dr. Prasad proposed several arrangements for restructuring the loans, one of which provided that Hadid would become a new guarantor. Hadid was a well-known customer of NBW, whose creditworthiness was known to the bank. The bank therefore accepted the proposal. The agreed terms for the restructuring of the loans were set forth in two written Renewal and Extension Agreements dated November 30, 1987.

[5]   The Renewal and Extension Agreement for each loan is prefaced by introductory provisions which describe the history of the loan, the security, the guarantors and the request for restructuring. In addition to setting forth the terms of restructuring, each agreement refers to a new promissory note and guarantee to be executed simultaneously. Both agreements provide that District of Columbia law shall govern. The Renewal and Extension Agreement applicable to the Keystone loan contains an additional section that provides that the pledge agreement granting NBW a security interest in the McDowell stock "shall remain in full force and effect." J.A. 221.

[6]   Despite the extensions granted by the Renewal and Extension Agreements, the loans were not paid by either the principals or guarantors and NBW filed suit to enforce the notes and guarantees. Hadid defended the claims against him by alleging that he should be released from his guarantees because NBW failed to release to him the McDowell stock that had been pledged to NBW. He alleged that an oral agreement was reached when the Renewal and Extension Agreements were negotiated, that he would be given control over the stock and, if not, his guarantee would be null and void. NBW disputed this claim. In addition to denying that any such agreement was ever made, NBW presented evidence that Hadid never asserted the existence of any oral agreement at any time after the Renewal and Extension Agreements were executed, including each occasion when demand on the notes was made and when thereafter he made payments of interest and gave assurances of repayment. Crediting Hadid's oral agreement, the jury returned a verdict in his favor.

---

[2]   [Bert Lance served as Director of the Office of Management and Budget under President Jimmy Carter—Eds.]

[7]   Before the commencement of trial, NBW filed a motion in limine[3] seeking a ruling that the parol evidence rule barred Hadid from introducing evidence at trial that NBW had orally agreed to release the stock to him. The district court took the matter under advisement so that it could receive evidence on the issue. When NBW renewed this defense in a motion for a directed verdict, the district court again deferred ruling, stating that it would let the case be presented to the jury and would take up the question "on a post-trial motion if the verdict is adverse to [NBW]." J.A. 164. When the jury returned a verdict in favor of Hadid, the district court granted NBW's motion for a judgment notwithstanding the verdict, finding: 1) that the Renewal and Extension Agreements were fully integrated agreements and 2) that the proffered oral agreement conflicted with the express terms of the written ones. Applying the parol evidence rule applicable in the District of Columbia, the district court rejected Hadid's defense based on the oral agreement as a matter of law and entered judgment in favor of NBW on the notes.

* * *

[8]   After judgment was entered in this case, the Controller of the Currency declared NBW insolvent, closed the bank and appointed the FDIC as receiver. On August 23, 1990, the district court substituted FDIC for NBW in this action.

II

[9]   "[The parol evidence] rule provides that when parties to a contract have executed a completely integrated written agreement, it supersedes all other understandings between the parties. Thus, the writing itself is viewed as the expression of the parties' intent." [*Ozerol v. Howard University*] 545 A.2d at 641 (citing Restatement (Second) of Contracts § 213 (1979)). Those principles, moreover, are not atypical. Professor Williston has more generally summarized the principle: " 'Where parties, without fraud or mistake, have reduced to writing a contract, it is presumed alone to express the final conclusion reached, and all previous and contemporaneous oral discussion, or written memoranda, are assumed to be either rejected or merged in it.' " 4 S. Williston, A Treatise on the Law of Contracts § 632A, at 984 (3d ed. 1961). Williston goes on to point out that when the writing is complete on its face and is certain and definite as to the objects of the agreement, the writing is "conclusively presumed" to be the entire contract between the parties, which cannot be contradicted or modified by parol or extrinsic evidence. *Id.* at 985.

[10] Whether an agreement is integrated is a factual question that "depends on the intent of the parties [as revealed by the writing itself], the conduct and language of the parties, and the surrounding circumstances."

---

[3]   [A motion *in limine* is a pre-trial motion to exclude certain evidence that for one reason or another should not be heard by the jury.—Eds.]

Ozerol, 545 A.2d at 641. The application of the parol evidence rule, however, is a question for resolution by the court, not the jury, and, as is the case with any question for the court, it is the court and not the jury which resolves disputed facts on the point. *See id.* at 643 ("question of integration . . . is for the trial court to determine as 'a question of fact. . . .'") (quoting Restatement (Second) of Contracts § 209 cmt. c (1979)). If, after resolving disputed facts, the court finds that the transaction is intended to be covered by the writing, only the writing is considered by the jury in resolving liability. The court does not, and need not, decide that the oral agreement was not made. Rather, it decides only that the oral agreement is irrelevant to liability on the writing. Similarly, if the court concludes that the writing is not integrated, it does not decide that the oral agreement was made. It commits that issue to the jury. *Id.* at 642.

[11] While the preferred practice under District of Columbia law is to make and resolve any objection on parol evidence preliminarily, it nevertheless permits the issue to be raised for the first time on a motion for directed verdict, since the rule is a matter of substantive law and not merely a rule of evidence. In any event, when the trial court resolves the factual question of whether the written agreement is integrated, our standard of review, as a matter of federal law, is whether the findings are clearly erroneous.

[12] In this case we cannot, and do not, conclude that the trial court's findings are clearly erroneous. The court found first, on the basis of all the evidence presented at trial, that the Renewal and Extension Agreements dated November 30, 1987, were fully integrated agreements. All prior understandings between the parties, including the promissory notes, the pledge agreements, and the guarantees, were reduced to formal written agreements, and no evidence suggests that any understanding prior to the Renewal and Extension Agreements was governed by oral agreements. As sophisticated businessmen, the parties not only documented their understandings on virtually all points, they retained attorneys to draft documents and have them executed formally, with witnessing and, in the case of corporations, attestation. Particularly in light of the fact that one of the formal agreements between the parties specifically addressed the continuation of the McDowell stock-pledge agreement, one would expect that other agreements reached at the time of negotiations regarding the role of the McDowell stock would also have been reduced to writing if the parties intended them to be legally binding. A different analysis would make written instruments of little value and increase the temptation to commit perjury or simply to restate agreements to the liking of the parties.

[13] The district court also determined that even if the agreements were not fully integrated, the oral agreement proffered by Hadid conflicted with the terms of the written Renewal and Extension Agreement for the Keystone loan. Hadid testified that an oral agreement, reached at the time

he signed the Renewal and Extension Agreements, provided that he would receive "control over the McDowell stock" so that he could "sell it" if necessary, and if he did not receive control over the McDowell stock, the guarantees were null and void. The purported oral agreement to give Hadid "control over the McDowell stock" is directly inconsistent with the express language of the Renewal and Extension Agreement for the Keystone loan providing that the pledge agreement involving the McDowell stock in favor of NBW "shall remain in full force and effect." To continue the perfection of the pledge agreement and NBW's security interest in the stock, NBW would have to retain possession of the stock. *See* 28 D.C. Code Ann. § 9–304(1) (1991) (D.C.'s version of the Uniform Commercial Code). Any control by Hadid, therefore, would have conflicted with NBW's security interest as preserved by the written instruments.[4]

AFFIRMED IN PART, REVERSED IN PART, AND REMANDED WITH INSTRUCTIONS.

NOTES AND QUESTIONS

1.   Read carefully R2d §§ 213(1), 213(2), 209, and 210, which define "integrated agreement" and "completely integrated agreement." As stated this way, the parol evidence rule is fairly straightforward. The tough issues are (1) when is an agreement "completely integrated"? (2) when is the prior agreement "inconsistent"? and (3) when is the prior agreement "within the scope" of a completely integrated agreement?

2.   In the first paragraph of the *FDIC v. Hadid* opinion, the court says "the district court found that the oral agreement violated the parol evidence rule." Can an agreement "violate the parol evidence rule" or was the court being sloppy in its language?

3.   You should always, always, *always* put a merger or integration clause in your documents. If there had been one in the guaranties that Mr. Hadid signed, the bank (and the FDIC) might well have been able to avoid the expense of a trial and an appeal. Historically, for an unknown reason, guaranties have often not featured merger clauses. This began to change after the savings and loan crisis of the late 1980s during which not all the cases were resolved in favor of the banks or the government receivers.

---

4   [Here, the court may be disingenuous. There is a difference between ownership of a thing and having control over a thing. At any one time, these two types of rights can be held by different entities. Thus, even if NBW were to have perfected its security interest in the stock through possession, there could be nothing inconsistent with the pledge agreement giving Mr. Hadid the right to control the disposition of the stock and cause the proceeds to be applied, under the pledge, to the principal indebtedness, thus decreasing his exposure to liability under the renewal and extension agreements. This line of reasoning, however, is more appropriate to a course in commercial law dealing with article 9 of the U.C.C.—Eds.]

4.   A typical merger or integration clause reads:

This Agreement is the final, complete, and exclusive expression of the terms of the Agreement between the parties pertaining to [describe scope of agreement, e.g., the lease of 1401 Laurel Avenue] and supersedes all prior and contemporaneous understandings or agreements of the parties.

Note how the language used in the clause tracks the language of R2d §§ 209 and 210 and U.C.C. § 2–202. This is an example of drafting a contract provision to incorporate or trigger a legal standard or doctrine. If you know a legal rule, you generally either want to fall squarely within its application or to avoid it entirely. Uncertainty of coverage is time consuming and expensive in negotiations and litigation.

5.   Note that it may be possible to defeat an integration clause and the parol evidence rule by pleading fraudulent inducement to enter into the contract in the first place. *See Riverisland Cold Storage, Inc. v. Fresno-Madera Credit Assn.*, 55 Cal. 4th 1169 (2013).

6.   Another doctrine, called the D'oench (pronounced "D-ench") doctrine also bars evidence of secret side agreements to defend against claims by banks and other institutions that have come under receivership or otherwise been taken over by federal regulators. *See Winterbrook Realty, Inc. v. FDIC*, 820 F. Supp. 27 (D.N.H. 1993) (discussing evolution, application, and policy justifications for D'oench doctrine); *see also* 12 U.S.C. § 1823(e) (limiting enforcement of secret or side agreements). In these situations, it is said that the doctrine determines which of the two "innocents"—the FDIC or the bank customer—should bear the costs of the failed institution's wrongs. If the customer bears any blame for his or her own predicament (e.g., by failing to get the side agreement in writing), the scales tip in favor of the FDIC, and the D'oench doctrine bars the claim or defense.

7.   The parol evidence rule is not just a rule for commercial or civil lawyers. It applies to criminal cases involving agreements, most notably settlement or plea bargain agreements, as the next case demonstrates.

———

UNITED STATES V. FENTRESS
United States Court of Appeals, Fourth Circuit
792 F.2d 461 (1986)

WILKINSON, CIRCUIT JUDGE:

[1] Robert Mark Fentress appeals from judgments of conviction entered by the U.S. District Court for the Western District of North Carolina upon Fentress' guilty pleas. He argues that the prosecution breached a plea agreement by recommending to the court that Fentress be compelled to compensate the victims of his crimes and by further

recommending that Fentress' prison sentence begin after he had completed his current period of incarceration for an unrelated felony. Fentress also argues that the district court erred in the process by which it accepted his pleas and ordered him to make restitution. As we find no prosecutorial violation of the agreement and no prejudicial departure from proper plea procedures, we affirm.

I

[2] On March 4, 1985, Fentress and his lawyer entered into a written plea bargain with an Assistant United States Attorney. In the agreement, Fentress promised to plead guilty to one armed bank robbery in violation of 18 U.S.C. § 2113(a) in the case docketed as C–CR–84–118, and to one bank robbery in violation of 18 U.S.C. § 2113(b) in the case docketed as C–CR–84–119. Fentress also promised to plead guilty to six other violations of 18 U.S.C. § 2113(b). Conviction under § 2113(a) authorizes a fine not exceeding $5000, a term of imprisonment not exceeding twenty years, or both of these punishments; conviction under § 2113(b) authorizes a fine not exceeding $5000, a term of imprisonment not exceeding ten years, or both of these punishments. For either offense, the court may order the perpetrator to make restitution to the victims of the theft. *See* 18 U.S.C. § 3579.

[3] The prosecution promised in the plea agreement to suggest to the court that any sentence imposed in case C–CR–84–119 "not exceed 5 years imprisonment, thereby recommending that the term of imprisonment for the two counts to which the defendant pleads guilty in indictments C–CR–84–118 and C–CR–84–119 should not exceed 25 years." It was thus expressly contemplated that those two terms would run consecutively. For the other six violations of 18 U.S.C. § 2113(b), the prosecution promised to "recommend that the sentences imposed upon defendant's plea of guilty . . . be made to run concurrently with each other and to also run concurrently with any sentence imposed upon defendant's plea of guilty to Indictments in cases numbered C–CR–84–118 and C–CR–84–119." These were the only positions to which the prosecution bound itself on the punishment of Fentress. Nothing was mentioned about the relationship between the proposed sentence here and a twelve-year federal sentence that Fentress was already serving for a bank robbery in Georgia. The agreement specifically provided that "This document contains the full and complete agreement between the parties, and no promises or representations have been made except as are incorporated herein."

[4] The Assistant United States Attorney presented the parties' deal to the district court and introduced testimony showing the factual basis for the guilty pleas, including a report that Fentress had stolen $37,844.61,

but the government had recovered only $239.00. Alluding to this evidence in his comments on the appropriate sentence, the prosecutor argued that

> [T]he agreement does not speak to other forms of punishment, in addition to the time limits or time frame that's stated in the agreement. The agreement does not speak to the other forms of punishment that you might impose, such as restitution. Any amount of money this man makes during prison, for example, might be appropriately used to offset the amount of money that he took. The fine itself is about $40,000.00[5] in this case as it relates to the eight bank robberies, eight times the $5,000.00 for each one. Those are other possibilities, Judge, that I would bring to your attention, as I'm sure you have already considered. We do urge you to run whatever time you impose on [case C–CR–84–119] consecutively to the time that is imposed on [case C–CR–84–118], and we urge the Court to run all this time consecutively to the time that he is facing in Georgia, the twelve years that he faces down there.

[5]   The district court subsequently did sentence Fentress in C–CR–84–118 to a twenty-year term of imprisonment that would be followed by a five-year term of imprisonment for the charge in C–CR–84–119. This time would be in addition to that served for the Georgia felony. For each of the other six robberies, the court ordered five-year sentences to be served concurrently with the incarceration under C–CR–84–118 and C–CR–84–119. The court also ordered Fentress to make restitution to each of the robbed banks. Fentress now appeals.

II

[6]   Fentress first protests that the prosecution breached the plea agreement by asking the district court to order restitution and consecutive sentences. Evaluation of this argument turns on the correct interpretation of the agreement in which the parties defined their commitments. In that analysis, "we must apply fundamental contract and agency principles to plea bargains as the best means to fair enforcement of the parties' agreed obligations." *United States v. McIntosh*, 612 F.2d 835, 837 (4th Cir. 1979). Accordingly, "any dispute over the terms of the agreement is to be resolved by objective standards." *United States v. Krasn*, 614 F.2d 1229, 1233 (9th Cir.1980).

[7]   These standards indicate that the prosecutor's comments did not violate the plea bargain. Everything the government promised to do, it did. The government kept its promises on the proposed length of imprisonment for C–CR–84–119 and on the proposed overlap among the sentences for violation of 18 U.S.C. § 2113(b). The government simply made no other

---

[5]   [$40,000 in 1986 dollars is roughly the equivalent of $91,600 in 2019 dollars using the CPI and the GNP Deflator.—Eds.]

guarantees about its conduct, as Fentress himself acknowledged when he agreed to the "merger" clause of the plea bargain instrument. Perhaps for that reason, Fentress did not object when the Assistant United States Attorney argued for restitution and consecutive sentences or when the district court imposed these penalties. Certainly Fentress has never suggested that the prosecution articulated any further representations. Fundamental contract principles establish that the written plea bargain was "adopted by the parties as a complete and exclusive statement of the terms of the agreement." Restatement (Second) of Contracts § 210 (1981). As a fully integrated agreement, the described exchange may not be supplemented with unmentioned terms. *Id.* at § 216. Fentress' newly suggested provision, that the prosecution would offer no recommendations other than those identified in the plea bargain instrument, therefore cannot stand.

[8]   This conclusion from the law of contracts carries over to the law of criminal procedure. The prosecution owed Fentress no duty but that of fidelity to the agreement. Neither the Constitution nor the Federal Rules of Criminal Procedure requires that a plea agreement must encompass all of the significant actions that either side might take. If the agreement does not establish a prosecutorial commitment on the full range of possible sanctions, we should recognize the parties' limitation of their assent. Courts have regularly upheld analogous prosecutorial measures that were not precluded by agreement. While the government must be held to the promises it made, it will not be bound to those it did not make. To do otherwise is to strip the bargaining process itself of meaning and content.

[9]   As the Supreme Court noted in *Santobello v. New York*, 404 U.S. at 261, 92 S.Ct. at 498, the considerations underlying enforcement of a plea bargain "presuppose fairness in securing agreement between an accused and a prosecutor." Fentress received fair treatment in this case. He was represented by an attorney throughout the negotiations and he has not questioned that the lawyer provided effective assistance within the sense described by *Hill v. Lockhart*, 474 U.S. 52, 106 S.Ct. 366, 88 L.Ed.2d 203 (1985). Fentress also brought to the plea negotiations, along with counsel, bargaining leverage that was commensurate with that of the prosecution, namely his right to force the prosecution to trial. Because Fentress' deal was thus no less voluntary than any other bargained-for exchange, we abide by the precise terms of the agreement and find that the prosecution made no promises that were violated in the request for restitution and consecutive sentences.

NOTES AND QUESTIONS

1.   The term "merger clause" comes from the idea that the prior agreements and discussions are merged forward into the written agreement. These clauses are also called "integration clauses" because they show the intent to have a completely integrated agreement.

2.   In another criminal case, Enricho Navarroli was charged by the state of Illinois with drug dealing. The state attorney general indicated to Mr. Navarroli that it would reduce the charges against him if he would assist in breaking up the drug operation. He accepted the offer, acted as an undercover operative for the state and, before the time came for him to plead guilty, the state had a change of heart and decided not to go easy on him. He objected and the trial court agreed, finding that he had relied on the bargain he had made with the state and had performed much of his duties under that contract. The Illinois Supreme Court reversed, holding that the state was not bound by the contract for reasons of public policy. *People v. Navarroli*, 121 Ill.2d 516, 118 Ill.Dec. 414, 521 N.E.2d 891 (1988). Had Navarroli completed his performance and pleaded guilty to whatever charges were brought, his due process rights should have protected him from a later change of heart by the state. The lesson here: if you are representing defendants, attempt to lock down the plea agreement as early as you can and, to the extent possible, obtain judicial approval or implementation of that agreement before allowing the defendant to substantially perform in reliance on the agreement. *See generally* E. Allen Farnsworth, *Changing Your Mind: The Law of Regretted Decisions*, at 2 and 203 (1998).

MASTERSON V. SINE

Supreme Court of California
68 Cal. 2d 222, 65 Cal. Rptr. 545, 436 P.2d 561 (1968)

TRAYNOR, CHIEF JUSTICE.

[1]   Dallas Masterson and his wife Rebecca owned a ranch as tenants in common. On February 25, 1958, they conveyed it to Medora and Lu Sine by a grant deed "Reserving unto the Grantors herein an option to purchase the above described property on or before February 25, 1968" for the "same consideration as being paid heretofore plus their depreciation value of any improvements Grantees may add to the property from and after two and a half years from this date." Medora is Dallas' sister and Lu's wife. Since the conveyance Dallas has been adjudged bankrupt. His trustee in bankruptcy and Rebecca brought this declaratory relief action to establish their right to enforce the option.[6]

---

[6]   [The court doesn't make it clear, but what is happening is this: When a person files for relief under the bankruptcy laws, all their assignable, nonexempt property becomes the property of a bankruptcy "estate" controlled by a trustee. The trustee's job is to collect and liquidate the

[2] The case was tried without a jury. Over defendants' objection the trial court admitted extrinsic evidence that by "the same consideration as being paid heretofore" both the grantors and the grantees meant the sum of $50,000[7] and by "depreciation value of any improvements" they meant the depreciation value of improvements to be computed by deducting from the total amount of any capital expenditures made by defendants grantees the amount of depreciation allowable to them under United States income tax regulations as of the time of the exercise of the option.

[3] The court also determined that the parol evidence rule precluded admission of extrinsic evidence offered by defendants to show that the parties wanted the property kept in the Masterson family and that the option was therefore personal to the grantors and could not be exercised by the trustee in bankruptcy.

[4] The court entered judgment for plaintiffs, declaring their right to exercise the option, specifying in some detail how it could be exercised, and reserving jurisdiction to supervise the manner of its exercise and to determine the amount that plaintiffs will be required to pay defendants for their capital expenditures if plaintiffs decide to exercise the option.

[5] Defendants appeal. They contend that the option provision is too uncertain to be enforced and that extrinsic evidence as to its meaning should not have been admitted. The trial court properly refused to frustrate the obviously declared intention of the grantors to reserve an option to repurchase by an overly meticulous insistence on completeness and clarity of written expression. It properly admitted extrinsic evidence to explain the language of the deed. The trial court erred, however, in excluding the extrinsic evidence that the option was personal to the grantors and therefore nonassignable.

[6] When the parties to a written contract have agreed to it as an "integration"—a complete and final embodiment of the terms of an agreement—parol evidence cannot be used to add to or vary its terms. When only part of the agreement is integrated, the same rule applies to that part, but parol evidence may be used to prove elements of the agreement not reduced to writing.

---

property and distribute the proceeds pro rata among the creditors in strict priority under the rules of the bankruptcy code and otherwise applicable law. Historically, these distributions have averaged about 10 cents on the dollar. Here, the trustee is trying to exercise the option so he can turn around and sell the ranch in order to raise money for the creditors, the ranch apparently being worth a lot more than the option price. Dallas Masterson preferred that the ranch belong to his sister and her husband rather than to his (Dallas's) creditors. As a result, he granted the sister and husband the land and reserved to himself what he asserts is a "personal" option that was unassignable and did not become property of his bankruptcy estate and, thus, could not be exercised by the trustee for the benefit of creditors. The dissenting opinion makes a great deal of this.—Eds.]

[7] [$50,000 in 1968 dollars is roughly the equivalent of $361,000 in 2019 dollars using the CPI and the GNP Deflator.—Eds.]

[7] The crucial issue in determining whether there has been an integration is whether the parties intended their writing to serve as the exclusive embodiment of their agreement. The instrument itself may help to resolve that issue. It may state, for example, that "there are no previous understandings or agreements not contained in the writing," and thus express the parties' "intention to nullify antecedent under standings or agreements." (*See* 3 Corbin, Contracts (1960) sec. 578, p. 411.) Any such collateral agreement itself must be examined, however, to determine whether the parties intended the subjects of negotiation it deals with to be included in, excluded from, or otherwise affected by the writing. Circumstances at the time of the writing may also aid in the determination of such integration.

[8] California cases have stated that whether there was an integration is to be determined solely from the face of the instrument, and that the question for the court is whether it "appears to be a complete . . . agreement . . ." Neither of these strict formulations of the rule, however, has been consistently applied. The requirement that the writing must appear incomplete on its face has been repudiated in many cases where parol evidence was admitted "to prove the existence of a separate oral agreement as to any matter on which the document is silent and which is not inconsistent with its terms"—even though the instrument appeared to state a complete agreement. Even under the rule that the writing alone is to be consulted, it was found necessary to examine the alleged collateral agreement before concluding that proof of it was precluded by the writing alone. It is therefore evident that "The conception of a writing as wholly and intrinsically self-determinative of the parties' intent to make it a sole memorial of one or seven or twenty-seven subjects of negotiation is an impossible one." (9 Wigmore, Evidence (3d ed. 1940) sec. 2431, p. 103.) For example, a promissory note given by a debtor to his creditor may integrate all their present contractual rights and obligations, or it may be only a minor part of an underlying executory contract that would never be discovered by examining the face of the note.

[9] In formulating the rule governing parol evidence, several policies must be accommodated. One policy is based on the assumption that written evidence is more accurate than human memory. This policy, however, can be adequately served by excluding parol evidence of agreements that directly contradict the writing. Another policy is based on the fear that fraud or unintentional invention by witnesses interested in the outcome of the litigation will mislead the finder of facts. McCormick has suggested that the party urging the spoken as against the written word is most often the economic underdog, threatened by severe hardship if the writing is enforced. In his view the parol evidence rule arose to allow the court to control the tendency of the jury to find through sympathy and without a dispassionate assessment of the probability of fraud or faulty memory that

the parties made an oral agreement collateral to the written contract, or that preliminary tentative agreements were not abandoned when omitted from the writing. (*See* McCormick, Evidence (1954) sec. 210.) He recognizes, however, that if this theory were adopted in disregard of all other considerations, it would lead to the exclusion of testimony concerning oral agreements whenever there is a writing and thereby often defeat the true intent of the parties. (*See* McCormick, *op. cit. supra*, sec. 216, p. 441.)

[10] Evidence of oral collateral agreements should be excluded only when the fact finder is likely to be misled. The rule must therefore be based on the credibility of the evidence. One such standard, adopted by section 240(1)(b) of the Restatement of Contracts, permits proof of a collateral agreement if it "is such an agreement as might naturally be made as a separate agreement by parties situated as were the parties to the written contract." (*see* McCormick, Evidence (1954) sec. 216, p. 441.) The draftsmen of the Uniform Commercial Code would exclude the evidence in still fewer instances: "If the additional terms are such that, if agreed upon, they would certainly have been included in the document in the view of the court, then evidence of their alleged making must be kept from the trier of fact." (Com. 3, sec. 2–202, italics added.)[8]

[11] The option clause in the deed in the present case does not explicitly provide that it contains the complete agreement, and the deed is silent on the question of assignability. Moreover, the difficulty of accommodating the formalized structure of a deed to the insertion of collateral agreements makes it less likely that all the terms of such an agreement were included. The statement of the reservation of the option might well have been placed in the recorded deed solely to preserve the grantors' rights against any possible future purchasers and this function could well be served without any mention of the parties' agreement that the option was personal. There is nothing in the record to indicate that the parties to this family transaction, through experience in land transactions or otherwise, had any warning of the disadvantages of failing to put the whole agreement in the deed. This case is one, therefore, in which it can be said that a collateral agreement such as that alleged "might naturally be made as a separate agreement." A fortiori, the case is not one in which the parties "would certainly" have included the collateral agreement in the deed.

[12] It is contended, however, that an option agreement is ordinarily presumed to be assignable if it contains no provisions forbidding its

---

[8]   Corbin suggests that, even in situations where the court concludes that it would not have been natural for the parties to make the alleged collateral oral agreement, parol evidence of such an agreement should nevertheless be permitted if the court is convinced that the unnatural actually happened in the case being adjudicated. (3 Corbin, Contracts, sec. 485, pp. 478, 480.) This suggestion may be based on a belief that judges are not likely to be misled by their sympathies. If the court believes that the parties intended a collateral agreement to be effective, there is no reason to keep the evidence from the jury.

transfer or indicating that its performance involves elements personal to the parties . . . In the absence of a controlling statute the parties may provide that a contract right or duty is nontransferable. Moreover, even when there is no explicit agreement—written or oral—that contractual duties shall be personal, courts will effectuate presumed intent to that effect if the circumstances indicate that performance by substituted person would be different from that contracted for.

[13] In the present case defendants offered evidence that the parties agreed that the option was not assignable in order to keep the property in the Masterson family. The trial court erred in excluding that evidence.

The judgment is reversed.

PETERS, TOBRINER, MOSK, and SULLIVAN, JJ., concur.

BURKE, JUSTICE.

[1] I dissent. The majority opinion:

(1) Undermines the parol evidence rule as we have known it in this state since at least 1872 by declaring that parol evidence should have been admitted by the trial court to show that a written option, absolute and unrestricted in form, was intended to be limited and nonassignable;

(2) Renders suspect instruments of conveyance absolute on their face;

(3) Materially lessens the reliance which may be placed upon written instruments affecting the title to real estate; and

(4) Opens the door, albeit unintentionally, to a new technique for the defrauding of creditors.

[2] The opinion permits defendants to establish by parol testimony that their grant to their brother (and brother-in-law) of a written option, absolute in terms, was nevertheless agreed to be nonassignable by the grantee (now bankrupt), and that therefore the right to exercise it did not pass, by operation of the bankruptcy laws, to the trustee for the benefit of the grantee's creditors.

[3] And how was this to be shown? By the proffered testimony of the bankrupt optionee himself! Thereby one of his assets (the option to purchase defendants' California ranch) would be withheld from the trustee in bankruptcy and from the bankrupt's creditors. Understandably the trial court, as required by the parol evidence rule, did not allow the bankrupt by parol to so contradict the unqualified language of the written option.

[4] The court properly admitted parol evidence to explain the intended meaning of the "same consideration" and "depreciation value" phrases of the written option to purchase defendants' land, as the intended

meaning of those phrases was not clear. However, there was nothing ambiguous about the granting language of the option and not the slightest suggestion in the document that the option was to be nonassignable. Thus, to permit such words of limitation to be added by parol is to contradict the absolute nature of the grant, and to directly violate the parol evidence rule.

* * *

[5] The majority opinion arrives at its holding via a series of false premises which are not supported either in the record of this case or in such California authorities as are offered.

* * *

[6] At the outset the majority in the present case reiterated that the rule against contradicting or varying the terms of a writing remains applicable when only part of the agreement is contained in the writing, and parol evidence is used to prove elements of the agreement not reduced to writing. But having restated this established rule, the majority opinion inexplicably proceeds to subvert it.

[7] Each of the three cases cited by the majority holds that although parol evidence is admissible to prove the parts of the contract not put in writing, it is not admissible to vary or contradict the writing or prove collateral agreements which are inconsistent therewith. The meaning of this rule (and the application of it found in the cases) is that if the asserted unwritten elements of the agreement would contradict, add to, detract from, vary or be inconsistent with the written agreement, then such elements may not be shown by parol evidence.

[8] The contract of sale and purchase of the ranch property here involved was carried out through a title company upon written escrow instructions executed by the respective parties after various preliminary negotiations. The deed to defendant grantees, in which the grantors expressly reserved an option to repurchase the property within a ten-year period and upon a specified consideration, was issued and delivered in consummation of the contract. In neither the written escrow instructions nor the deed containing the option is there any language even suggesting that the option was agreed or intended by the parties to be personal to the grantors, and so nonassignable. The trial judge, on at least three separate occasions, correctly sustained objections to efforts of defendant optionors to get into evidence the testimony of Dallas Masterson (the bankrupt holder of the option) that a part of the agreement of sale of the parties was that the option to repurchase the property was personal to him, and therefore unassignable for benefit of creditors. But the majority hold that that testimony should have been admitted, thereby permitting defendant optionors to limit, detract from and contradict the plain and unrestricted

terms of the written option in clear violation of the parol evidence rule and to open the door to the perpetration of fraud.

[9] Options are property, and are widely used in the sale and purchase of real and personal property. One of the basic incidents of property ownership is the right of the owner to sell or transfer it ... Moreover, the right of transferability applies to an option to purchase, unless there are words of limitation in the option forbidding its assignment or showing that it was given because of a peculiar trust or confidence reposed in the optionee.

[10] The right of an optionee to transfer his option to purchase property is accordingly one of the basic rights which accompanies the option unless limited under the language of the option itself. To allow an optionor to resort to parol evidence to support his assertion that the written option is not transferable is to authorize him to limit the option by attempting to restrict and reclaim rights with which he has already parted. A clearer violation of two substantive and basic rules of law—the parol evidence rule and the right of free transferability of property—would be difficult to conceive.

* * *

V

[11] Upon this structure of incorrect premises and unfounded assertions the majority opinion arrives at its climax: The pronouncement of "several policies (to) be accommodated . . . (i)n formulating the rule governing parol evidence." Two of the "policies" as declared by the majority are: Written evidence is more accurate than human memory; fraud or unintentional invention by interested witnesses may well occur.

[12] I submit that these purported "policies" are in reality two of the basic and obvious reasons for adoption by the Legislature of the parol evidence rule as the policy in this state. Thus the speculation of the majority concerning the views of various writers on the subject and the advisability of following them in this state is not only superfluous but flies flatly in the face of established California law and policy. It serves only to introduce uncertainty and confusion in a field of substantive law which was codified and made certain in this state a century ago.

[13] However, despite the law which until the advent of the present majority opinion has been firmly and clearly established in California and relied upon by attorneys and courts alike, that parol evidence may not be employed to vary or contradict the terms of a written instrument, the majority now announce that such evidence "should be excluded only when the fact finder is likely to be misled," and that "The rule must therefore be based on the credibility of the evidence." But was it not, inter alia, to avoid misleading the fact finder, and to further the introduction of only the

evidence which is most likely to be credible (the written document), that the Legislature adopted the parol evidence rule as a part of the substantive law of this state?

[The dissenting opinion continues on in this vein, attacking each of the majority's premises.—Eds.]

[14] Comment hardly seems necessary on the convenience to a bankrupt of such a device to defeat his creditors. He need only produce parol testimony that any options (or other property, for that matter) which he holds are subject to an oral "collateral agreement" with family members (or with friends) that the property is nontransferable "in order to keep the property in the family" in the friendly group. In the present case the value of the ranch which the bankrupt and his wife held an option to purchase has doubtless increased substantially during the years since they acquired the option. The initiation of this litigation by the trustee in bankruptcy to establish his right to enforce the option indicates his belief that there is substantial value to be gained for the creditors from this asset of the bankrupt. Yet the majority opinion permits defeat of the trustee and of the creditors through the device of an asserted collateral oral agreement that the option was "personal" to the bankrupt and nonassignable "in order to keep the property in the family"![9]

* * *

[15] I would hold that the trial court ruled correctly on the proffered parol evidence, and would affirm the judgment.

McCOMB, J., concurs.

Rehearing denied; McCOMB and BURKE, JJ., dissenting.

NOTES AND QUESTIONS

1.   If the trial court used the parol evidence rule to exclude the testimony showing the option was personal to the grantors, why did it not exclude the evidence that "same consideration" meant $50,000 and the evidence as to how the depreciation value was to be computed?

2.   Note carefully the way Justice Traynor uses the word "integration." Is he using it the same way the R2d uses "integrated agreement?"

3.   In *Hadid*, the court says: "Williston goes on to point out that when the writing is complete on its face and is certain and definite as to the objects of the agreement, the writing is 'conclusively presumed' to be the entire contract between the parties, which cannot be contradicted or modified by

---

[9]   As noted at the outset of this dissent, it was by means of the bankrupt's own testimony that defendants (the bankrupt's sister and her husband) sought to show that the option was personal to the bankrupt and thus not transferable to the trustee in bankruptcy.

parol or extrinsic evidence." Is this the test Justice Traynor is applying in the majority opinion?

———

HUNT FOODS V. DOLINER

Supreme Court of New York, Appellate Division
26 A.D.2d 41, 270 N.Y.S.2d 937 (1966)

STEUER, JUSTICE.

[1] In February 1965 plaintiff corporation undertook negotiations to acquire the assets of Eastern Can Company. The stock of the latter is owned by defendant George M. Doliner and his family to the extent of 73%. The balance is owned by independent interests. At a fairly early stage of the negotiations agreement was reached as to the price to be paid by plaintiff ($5,922,500[10] if in cash, or $5,730,000 in Hunt stock), but several important items, including the form of the acquisition, were not agreed upon. At this point it was found necessary to recess the negotiations for several weeks. The Hunt negotiators expressed concern over any adjournment and stated that they feared that Doliner would use their offer as a basis for soliciting a higher bid from a third party. To protect themselves they demanded an option to purchase the Doliner stock. Such an option was prepared and signed by George Doliner and the members of his family and at least one other person associated with him who were stockholders. It provides that Hunt has the option to buy all of the Doliner stock at $5.50 per share. The option is to be exercised by giving notice on or before June 1, 1965, and if notice is not given the option is void. If given, Hunt is to pay the price and the Doliners to deliver their stock within seven days thereafter. The agreement calls for Hunt to pay $1,000 for the option, which was paid. To this point there is substantial accord as to what took place.

[2] Defendant claims that when his counsel called attention to the fact that the option was unconditional in its terms, he obtained an understanding that it was only to be used in the event that he solicited an outside offer; and that plaintiff insisted that unless the option was signed in unconditional form negotiations would terminate. Plaintiff contends there was no condition. Concededly, on resumption of negotiations the parties failed to reach agreement and the option was exercised. Defendants declined the tender and refused to deliver the stock.

[3] Plaintiff moved for summary judgment for specific performance. We do not believe that summary judgment lies. Plaintiff's position is that

———

[10] [$5,922,500 in 1966 dollars is roughly the equivalent of $45,800,000 in 2019 dollars using the CPI and the GNP Deflator.—Eds.]

the condition claimed could not be proved under the parol evidence rule and, eliminating that, there is no defense to the action.

[4]   The parol evidence rule, at least as that term refers to contracts of sale,[11] is now contained in Section 2–202 of the Uniform Commercial Code, which reads:

> Terms with respect to which the confirmatory memoranda of the parties agree or which are otherwise set forth in a writing intended by the parties as a final expression of their agreement with respect to such terms as are included therein may not be contradicted by evidence of any prior agreement or of a contemporaneous oral agreement but may be explained or supplemented

> * * *

> (b)   by evidence of consistent additional terms unless the court finds the writing to have been intended also as a complete and exclusive statement of the terms of the agreement.

[5]   The term (that the option was not to be exercised unless Doliner sought outside bids), admittedly discussed but whose operative effect is disputed, not being set out in the writing, is clearly "additional" to what is in the writing. So the first question presented is whether that term is "consistent" with the instrument. In a sense any oral provision which would prevent the ripening of the obligations of a writing is inconsistent with the writing. But that obviously is not the sense in which the word is used. To be inconsistent the term must contradict or negate a term of the writing. A term or condition which has a lesser effect is provable.

[6]   The Official Comment prepared by the drafters of the Code contains this statement:

> If the additional terms are such that, if agreed upon, they would certainly have been included in the document in the view of the court, then evidence of their alleged making must be kept from the trier of fact.

(McKinney's Uniform Commercial Code, Part 1, p. 158)

[7]   Special Term interpreted this language as not only calling for an adjudication by the court in all instances where proof of an "additional oral term" is offered, but making that determination exclusively the function of the court. We believe the proffered evidence to be inadmissible only where the writing contradicts the existence of the claimed additional term. The conversations in this case, some of which are not disputed, and the

---

[11]   While article 2 of the Uniform Commercial Code which contains this section does not deal with the sale of securities, this section applies to article 8, dealing with securities. All parties and Special Term so regarded it.

expectation of all the parties for further negotiations, suggest that the alleged oral condition precedent cannot be precluded as a matter of law or as factually impossible. It is not sufficient that the existence of the condition is implausible. It must be impossible.

[8] The order should be reversed on the law and the motion for summary judgment denied with costs and disbursements to abide the event.

[9] Order and judgment (one paper) unanimously reversed, on the law, with $50 costs and disbursements to abide the event, and plaintiff's motion for summary judgment denied. All concur.

LURIA BROS. & CO. V. PIELET BROS. SCRAP IRON & METAL, INC.

United States Court of Appeals, Seventh Circuit
600 F.2d 103 (1979)

FAIRCHILD, CHIEF JUDGE.

[1] This is a diversity action for breach of contract. Most of the events giving rise to this litigation occurred in Illinois and we accept the parties' assumption that Illinois law is applicable. The action below was tried before a jury which returned a verdict in the amount of $600,000, having found that a contract for the purchase of barge scrap steel existed between plaintiff, Luria Brothers & Co., Inc. (hereinafter referred to as "Luria") and defendant, Pielet Brothers Scrap Iron & Metal, Inc. (hereinafter referred to as "Pielet"), and that Luria was damaged as a consequence of Pielet's failure to deliver. Defendant appeals, arguing among other things that no enforceable agreement was ever made, and therefore, plaintiff was not entitled to damages. We affirm.

[2] A consideration of the issues requires a statement of the facts in some detail. Luria, in its capacity as both a broker and a dealer is in the business of buying, selling, and processing scrap metal. Pielet is in the same business. The parties had done business with each other on a number of occasions prior to the transaction giving rise to this litigation. In fact, Lawrence Bloom, who represented Pielet in this matter had formerly been employed by Luria as a scrap trader.

[3] Most of the facts surrounding the subject transaction are not in dispute and were stipulated to at trial. In mid-September, 1973, Bloom, a vice-president of Pielet, telephoned Richard Fechheimer, a vice-president of Luria. Bloom informed Fechheimer that Pielet might offer a substantial quantity of scrap metal for sale. Bloom inquired as to whether Luria would be interested in purchasing the metal and Fechheimer said that it would be. Subsequent telephone conversations took place between Bloom and

Fechheimer in which price quotations and other matters were discussed. The quantity was to be 35,000 net tons of scrap steel from old barges cut into sections measuring five feet by five feet by twenty feet. The shipment date was to be on or before December 31, 1973. The price was set at $42 per net ton if Luria took delivery in Houston or $49 if Luria took delivery in Brownsville (Texas). This transaction was unusual in two respects. First, the amount of scrap involved was much larger than that in a typical scrap transaction. Secondly, while the type or grade of scrap was not unusual, the dimensions were. Luria intended to process the scrap for resale as "No. 1 heavy melting" scrap by reducing it to a size that would fit into a steel furnace, generally in pieces at least 1/4 inch thick and not more than 5 feet long by 18 inches wide.

[4] Shortly after the foregoing conversations between Bloom and Fechheimer, Fechheimer telephoned Mr. Forlani, an account executive at Luria's Chicago office, to discuss the purchase of scrap from Pielet. Forlani made some handwritten notes on a worksheet which Luria uses in connection with buying and selling scrap. These notes related to the terms of the barge scrap transaction between Pielet and Luria. Subsequently, and sometime before September 24, Forlani made a telephone call to Bloom to discuss this scrap transaction. At some point, but before September 24, Bloom made some handwritten notes on a worksheet Pielet employed in connection with buying and selling scrap.

[5] On September 24, 1973, Bloom caused to be prepared a sales confirmation relating to the scrap transaction between Pielet and Luria. The following information was typed on the confirmation form:

Quantity: Thirty-five thousand (35,000) net tons

Material: Steel barges cut 5' X 5' X 20' free of non metallics

Price: $42.00 per net ton F.O.B. Shipping point barge Houston,

Texas or $49.00 per net ton delivered Brownsville, Texas

Shipment: On or before December 31, 1973

Terms: 90% Advance on receipt of surveyor's weights and bill of lading

[6] Bloom signed the sales confirmation and mailed the original and one copy to Forlani. The copy bore the printed words "confirmation copy." The following words are printed at the bottom of both the original and the confirmation copy of Pielet's confirmation form: "PLEASE SIGN AND RETURN THE COPY OF THIS CONFIRMATION FOR OUR FILES. FAILURE TO RETURN COPY DOES NOT VOID CONTRACT." Neither Forlani nor any officer or other employee of Luria ever signed or returned the confirmation copy to Bloom or anyone else at Pielet.

[7]   In the ordinary course of business when Luria makes a purchase of scrap, information regarding the purchase is typed or written on its own purchase confirmation form. On or about October 4, 1973, Forlani caused to be prepared a purchase confirmation containing the same terms as in Pielet's form, except with respect to the delivery date and mode of shipment. The delivery date typed on the form was by October 31, 1973 and the mode of shipment appeared to be left to the discretion of Luria. On the reverse side of this form are printed standard terms including ones referring to warranties, insurance, and taxes, as well as one stating "This order constitutes the entire contract between the parties." The original and one copy of this form are sent to the seller. These bear in red letters the words "RETURN ACCEPTANCE COPY IMMEDIATELY" in the lower right hand corner. There were no other words on this document to indicate any condition as to the existence of a contract.

[8]   Forlani sent the original and a copy of the October 4th purchase confirmation to Bloom. Bloom testified that upon receipt of this document, he immediately or shortly thereafter called Forlani to inform him that the Luria confirmation was erroneous with respect to delivery date and mode of shipment. Forlani agreed that the confirmation was erroneous in these two particulars. Bloom asked Forlani to send him an amendment correcting these errors, but Forlani never did. Neither Bloom nor any other officer or employee of Pielet ever signed or returned the acceptance copy to Luria.

[9]   During late October and November, Forlani called Bloom several times to ask why Pielet had not begun to deliver the steel. Although the delivery date stated in Pielet's confirmation form and orally agreed upon was on or before December 31, 1973, it is "common trade practice" to space deliveries out during the contract period, especially where the quantity involved is very large. On December 3, 1973, Forlani wrote a letter to Pielet saying Luria had not received notification of shipment and requesting that prompt attention be given. On February 6, 1974 representatives of Luria met with Bloom. Bloom stated he was having trouble with his supplier, and further mentioned that his supplier could not obtain the propane necessary for the torches used to cut the barges. On February 13, a week after the meeting, Luria wrote a letter to Bloom to make it clear that the matter had to be resolved. Luria never received a reply and Pielet never delivered the scrap. Luria filed its complaint in the district court on April 25, 1974.

[The court determined that the evidence established a contract.—Eds.]

II

[10] Next, Pielet contends that even if the evidence is sufficient to establish the existence of a binding contract between the parties, it was error for the district court to exclude evidence that the sales contract was expressly conditional upon Pielet obtaining the scrap metal from a

particular supplier. In an offer of proof, Bloom testified that in their first conversation in September, he told Fechheimer "I was doing business with people that I had never heard of, that they were fly-by-night people, that I was worried about shipment and if I didn't get shipment, I didn't want any big hassle, but if I got the scrap, he would get it." Trans. at 268.[12]

[11] In excluding this offered testimony, the district court relied on the Uniform Commercial Code's parol evidence rule, sec. 2–202, which provides:

> Terms with respect to which the confirmatory memoranda of the parties agree or which are otherwise set forth in a writing intended by the parties as a final expression of their agreement with respect to such terms as are included therein may not be contradicted by evidence of any prior agreement or of a contemporaneous oral agreement but may be explained or supplemented
>
> (a) By course of dealing or usage of trade (sec. 1–205) or by course of performance (sec. 2–208); and
>
> (b) By evidence of consistent additional terms unless the court finds the writing to have been intended also as a complete and exclusive statement of the terms of the agreement.

[12] The determination that the writings of the parties were intended to be a final expression of their agreement is to be made by the trial court. In light of Luria's acceptance of the terms stated in the Pielet writing, we agree with the district court's conclusion that the Pielet sales confirmation brought sec. 2–202 into play to bar Bloom's testimony.

[13] Nevertheless, Pielet contends that sec. 2–202 is not applicable to this case. According to Pielet, Luria sued on an oral contract and therefore the parol evidence rule is not applicable because the writings of the parties were not the basis of the action but only collateral to it.

[14] It is true that although these writings were relied on to satisfy the Code's Statute of Frauds, sec. 2–201, and to exclude parol evidence, Luria had to go outside these writings to prove to the jury the existence of an enforceable sales contract. But the writings are insufficient in themselves only because of two differing terms and are directly related to the contract sought to be proved.

[15] As noted in 1 Anderson, Uniform Commercial Code sec. 2–202(3) (2d 1970), sec. 2–202 of the Code "extends (the operation of the parol

---

[12] During the presentation of Luria's case, Bloom did testify on cross-examination that in conversations subsequent to the writings he told Forlani "if I get it (the scrap), you will get it." We agree with Pielet that in that context, the jury would take this statement as an excuse for not delivering rather than as a condition of the contract. Therefore, if Bloom's testimony relating to his first conversation with Fechheimer was wrongfully excluded, the harm would be prejudicial.

evidence rule) to some degree to writings which are not the complete contract of the parties." The code itself refers to this fact in sec. 2–207(3) which provides that where a contract is established by the conduct of the parties, the terms of the contract consist, at least, of those terms on which the writings agree even though "the writings of the parties do not otherwise establish a contract."

[16] In a case construing Illinois law, the court in *Jones & McKnight Corp. v. Birdsboro Corporation*, 320 F.Supp. 39 (N.D. Ill., E.D.1970) noted that where the existence of a sales contract was clear (in that case because of the actual delivery of goods and payment), sec. 2–202 "obviates the necessity of determining . . . whether the contract was oral or written." *Id.* at 42. Evidence of an alleged prior oral agreement cannot be used to contradict the terms on which the writings of the parties agree.

[17] In this case, of course, the existence of a sales contract was in issue. At first glance, it is troublesome that Luria was allowed to introduce testimony of the September conversations between the parties to help establish its case while Pielet was denied the opportunity to introduce statements made in the course of those same conversations. However, the fairness of this result becomes clear upon examination of why it was necessary for Luria to use parol evidence to prove the existence of the sales contract. Pielet's sales confirmation and Luria's purchase confirmation differed on two important terms, delivery date[,] and mode of shipment. Luria used undisputed parol evidence that there had been a "meeting of the minds" as to these terms prior to the confirmatory memoranda to support its position that these two discrepancies were due to inadvertence and clerical error on Luria's part rather than disagreement between the parties. If the writings had agreed on these two important terms, Pielet would be hard pressed to argue that no contract for sale existed. In fact, Bloom testified that had the Luria purchase confirmation been correct on these points he would have signed and returned it. (Trans. at 67.) Allowing one party to use parol evidence to clarify a mistake in a writing, does not open the flood gates to any and all parol evidence bearing on the agreement.[13]

[18] Having found sec. 2–202 applicable, the next question is whether the excluded evidence contradicts or is inconsistent with the terms of the writings. Pielet argues that the offered testimony did not "contradict" but instead "explained or supplemented" the writings with "consistent additional terms." For this contention, Pielet relies upon *Hunt Foods & Industries, Inc. v. Doliner*, 26 A.D.2d 41, 270 N.Y.S.2d 937 (1966). In

---

[13] Pielet cites McCormick on Evidence sec. 56 (2d ed. 1972) for the proposition that once one party has introduced part of a conversation, the other party automatically has the right to introduce the remainder of the conversation relating to the same subject. This is a general rule of evidence based on materiality and relevance. The parol evidence rule, on the other hand, is a rule of substantive law. Evidence is excluded not because it is not credible or not relevant but because of a policy favoring the reliability of written representations of the terms of a contract.

reversing the trial court's summary judgment for plaintiff, the court in Hunt held that evidence of an oral condition precedent did not contradict the terms of a written stock option which was unconditional on its face. Therefore evidence of the condition precedent should not have been barred by U.C.C. sec. 2–202. "In a sense any oral provision which would prevent the ripening of the obligations of a writing is inconsistent with the writing. But that obviously is not the sense in which the word is used. (Citation omitted.) To be inconsistent the term must contradict or negate a term of the writing." *Id.* at 43, 270 N.Y.S.2d at 940. This reasoning in *Hunt* was followed in *Michael Schiavone & Sons, Inc. v. Securalloy Co.*, 312 F.Supp. 801 (D.Conn. 1970). In that case, the court found that parol evidence that the quantity in a sales contract was "understood to be up to 500 tons cannot be said to be inconsistent with the terms of the written contract which specified the quantity as '500 Gross Ton.'" *Id.* at 804.

[19] The narrow view of inconsistency espoused in these two cases has been criticized. In *Snyder v. Herbert Greenbaum & Assoc., Inc.*, 38 Md.App. 144, 380 A.2d 618 (1977), the court held that parol evidence of a contractual right to unilateral rescission was inconsistent with a written agreement for the sale and installation of carpeting. The court defined "inconsistency" as used in sec. 2–202(b) as "the absence of reasonable harmony in terms of the language and respective obligations of the parties." *Id.* at 623 (citing U.C.C. sec. 1–205(4)). *See also Southern Concrete v. Mableton Contractors*, 407 F.Supp. 581 (N.D.Ga. 1975), *aff'd memo.*, 569 F.2d 1154 (5th Cir. 1978).

[20] We adopt this latter view of inconsistency and reject the view expressed in Hunt. Where writings intended by the parties to be a final expression of their agreement call for an unconditional sale of goods, parol evidence that the seller's obligations are conditioned upon receiving the goods from a particular supplier is inconsistent and must be excluded.

[21] Had there been some additional reference such as "per our conversation" on the written confirmation indicating that oral agreements were meant to be incorporated into the writing, the result might have been different. *See Ralston Purina v. Rooker*, 346 So.2d 901 (Miss. 1977), *distinguishing Paymaster Oil Mill Company v. Mitchell*, 319 So.2d 652 (Miss. 1975).

[22] We also note that Comment 3 of the Official Comment to sec. 2–202 provides, among other things:

> If the additional terms are such that, if agreed upon, they would certainly have been included in the document in the view of the court, then evidence of their alleged making must be kept from the trier of fact.

[23] Pielet makes much of the fact that this transaction was an unusual one due to the size and the amount of scrap involved. Surely a

term relieving Pielet of its obligations under the contract in the event its supplier failed it would have been included in the Pielet sales confirmation.

* * *

The judgment appealed from is affirmed.

———

NOTES AND QUESTIONS

1. Was there an integrated agreement (as the R2d uses that term) in this case? If so, what document or documents constituted the integrated agreement?

2. Suppose the writings had said nothing about who had to pay for the insurance on the shipment. Should the court let in oral testimony to the effect that the parties had agreed that the seller would pay for the insurance? *Yes, there'd be the absence of harmony on this issue – MD.*

———

ZELL V. AMERICAN SEATING CO.

United States Court of Appeals, Second Circuit
138 F.2d 641 (1943)

FRANK, CIRCUIT JUDGE.

[1] On defendant's motion for summary judgment, the trial court, after considering the pleadings and affidavits, entered judgment dismissing the action. From that judgment, plaintiff appeals.

[2] On a motion for summary judgment, where the facts are in dispute, a judgment can properly be entered against the plaintiff only if, on the undisputed facts, he has no valid claim; if, then, any fact asserted by the plaintiff is contradicted by the defendant, the facts as stated by the plaintiff must, on such a motion, be taken as true. Accordingly for the purpose of our decision here, we take the facts as follows:

[3] Plaintiff, by a letter addressed to defendant company dated October 17, 1941, offered to make efforts to procure for defendant contracts for manufacturing products for national defense or war purposes, in consideration of defendant's agreement to pay him $1,000 per month for a three months' period if he were unsuccessful in his efforts, but, if he were successful, to pay him a further sum in an amount not to be less than 3% nor more than 8% of the "purchase price of said contracts." On October 31, 1941, at a meeting in Grand Rapids, Michigan, between plaintiff and defendant's President, the latter, on behalf of his company, orally made an agreement with plaintiff substantially on the terms set forth in plaintiff's letter, one of the terms being that mentioned in plaintiff's letter as to commissions; it was orally agreed that the exact amount within the two

percentages was to be later determined by the parties. After this agreement was made, the parties executed, in Grand Rapids, a written instrument dated October 31, 1941, appearing on its face to embody a complete agreement between them; but that writing omitted the provision of their agreement that plaintiff, if successful, was to receive a bonus varying from three to eight per cent; instead, there was inserted in the writing a clause that the $1,000 per month "will be full compensation, but the company may, if it desires, pay you something in the nature of a bonus." However, at the time when they executed this writing, the parties orally agreed that the previous oral agreement was still their actual contract, that the writing was deliberately erroneous with respect to plaintiff's commissions, and that the misstatement in that writing was made solely in order to "avoid any possible stigma which might result" from putting such a provision "in writing," the defendant's President stating that "his fears were based upon the criticism of contingent fee contracts." Nothing in the record discloses whose criticism the defendant feared; but plaintiff, in his brief, says that defendant was apprehensive because adverse comments had been made in Congress of such contingent-fee arrangements in connection with war contracts. The parties subsequently executed further writings extending, for two three-month periods, their "agreement under date of October 31, 1941." Through plaintiff's efforts and expenditures of large sums for traveling expenses, defendant, within this extended period, procured contracts between it and companies supplying aircraft to the government for war purposes, the aggregate purchase price named in said contracts being $5,950,000.[14] The defendant has refused to pay the plaintiff commissions thereon in the agreed amount (i.e., not less than three per cent) but has paid him merely $8,950 (at the rate of $1,000 a month) and has offered him, by way of settlement, an additional sum of $9,000 which he has refused to accept as full payment.

[4] Defendant argues that the summary judgment was proper on the ground that, under the parol evidence rule, the court could not properly consider as relevant anything except the writing of October 31, 1941, which appears on its face to set forth a complete and unambiguous agreement between the parties. If defendant on this point is in error, then, if the plaintiff at a trial proves the facts as alleged by him, and no other defenses are successfully interposed, he will be entitled to a sum equal to 3% of $5,950,000.

* * *

[5] It is not surprising that confusion results from a rule called "the parol evidence rule" which is not a rule of evidence, which relates to extrinsic proof whether written or parol, and which has been said to be

---

[14] [$5,950,000 in 1943 dollars is roughly the equivalent of $86,400,000 in 2019 dollars using the CPI and the GNP Deflator.—Eds.]

virtually no rule at all. As Thayer said of it, "Few things are darker than this, or fuller of subtle difficulties." The rule is often loosely and confusingly stated as if, once the evidence establishes that the parties executed a writing containing what appears to be a complete and unambiguous agreement, then no evidence may be received of previous or contemporaneous oral understandings which contradict or vary its terms. But, under the parol evidence rule correctly stated, such a writing does not acquire that dominating position if it has been proved by extrinsic evidence that the parties did not intend it to be an exclusive authoritative memorial of their agreement. If they did intend it to occupy that position, their secret mutual intentions as to the terms of the contract or its meaning are usually irrelevant, so that parties who exchange promises may be bound, at least "at law" as distinguished from "equity," in a way which neither intended, since their so-called "objective" intent governs. When, however, they have previously agreed that their written promises are not to bind them, that agreement controls and no legal obligations flow from the writing. It has been held virtually everywhere, when the question has arisen that (certainly in the absence of any fraudulent or illegal purpose) a purported written agreement, which the parties designed as a mere sham, lacks legal efficacy, and that extrinsic parol or other extrinsic evidence will always be received on that issue. So the highest court of Michigan has several times held. It has gone further: In *Woodard v. Walker*, 192 Mich. 188, 158 N.W. 846, that court specifically enforced against the seller an oral agreement for the sale of land which had been followed by a sham written agreement, for sale of the same land at a higher price, intended to deceive the seller's children who were jealous of the buyer.

[6] We need not here consider cases where third persons have relied on the delusive agreement to their detriment or cases in other jurisdictions (we find none in Michigan) where the mutual purpose of the deception was fraudulent or illegal. For the instant case involves no such elements. As noted above, the pleadings and affidavits are silent as to the matter of whom the parties here intended to mislead, and we cannot infer a fraudulent or illegal purpose. Even the explanation contained in plaintiff's brief discloses no fraud or illegality: No law existed rendering illegal the commission provision of the oral agreement which the parties here omitted from the sham writing; while it may be undesirable that citizens should prepare documents so contrived as to spoil the scent of legislators bent on proposing new legislation, yet such conduct is surely not unlawful and does not deserve judicial castigation as immoral or fraudulent; the courts should not erect standards of morality so far above the customary. *Woodard v. Walker* leaves no doubt that the Michigan courts would hold the parol evidence rule inapplicable to the facts as we have interpreted them.

[7] Candor compels the admission that, were we enthusiastic devotees of that rule, we might so construe the record as to bring this case

within the rule's scope; we could dwell on the fact that plaintiff, in his complaint, states that the acceptance of his offer "was partly oral and partly contained" in that October 31 writing, and could then hold that, as that writing unambiguously covers the item of commissions, the Plaintiff is trying to use extrinsic evidence to "contradict" the writing. But the plaintiff's affidavit, if accepted as true and liberally construed, makes it plain that the parties deliberately intended the October 31 writing to be a misleading, untrue, statement of their real agreement.

[8] We thus construe the record because we do not share defendant's belief that the rule is so beneficent, so promotive of the administration of justice, and so necessary to business stability, that it should be given the widest possible application. The truth is that the rule does but little to achieve the ends it supposedly serves[15] Although seldom mentioned in modern decisions, the most important motive for perpetuation of the rule is distrust of juries, fear that they cannot adequately cope with, or will be unfairly prejudiced by, conflicting "parol" testimony. If the rule were frankly recognized as primarily a device to control juries, its shortcomings would become obvious, since it is not true that the execution by the parties of an unambiguous writing, "facially complete," bars extrinsic proof. The courts admit such "parol" testimony (other than the parties' statements of what they meant by the writing) for a variety of purposes: to show "all the operative usages" and "all the surrounding circumstances prior to and contemporaneous with the making" of a writing; to show an agreed oral condition, nowhere referred to in the writing, that the writing was not to be binding until some third person approved; to show that a deed, absolute on its face, is but a mortgage. These and numerous other exceptions have removed most of that insulation of the jury from "oral" testimony which the rule is said to provide.

---

[15] That this fear was one of the causes of the creation of the rule. *See* THAYER, A PRELIMINARY TREATISE ON EVIDENCE 409, 410 (1898); 9 Wigmore on Evidence § 2446 (3d ed.).

Formalism was also a causal factor. *See* 9 Wigmore, ibid. However, for criticism of over-emphasis on the formalism of the so-called "strict period of law," *see* United States v. Forness, 125 F.2d 928, 935–36 (2d Cir. 1942).

Another factor was veneration for the written word. *See* Wigmore, ibid. Paul Radin, Primitive Man as Philosopher (1927) 59–60, says: "Much if not all of the magical quality and potency possessed by the word is derived from its connection with the written script. That is quite intelligible. Granted a dynamic and ever-changing world, then the written word with its semi-permanence and its static character was a much desired oasis ... But culturally and psychologically it possessed even a greater significance, for it completed the victory of the visual-minded man over his competitors. From that time on, at least for the literate man, the main verities were the visual verities."

The perpetuation of the parol evidence rule doubtless owes much to inertia. Any profession, the medical as well as the legal, possessed of a monopoly in its field, tends to develop what are today called "bureaucratic" habits of strong disinclination to alter its established ways. Unconscious sadism perhaps, too, influences some of the academic praise of the parol evidence rule: some cloistered scholars seem to take satisfaction in "hard cases" which, they feel should not lead to deviations from "good law."

[9]   The rule, then, does relatively little to deserve its much advertised virtue of reducing the dangers of successful fraudulent recoveries and defenses brought about through perjury. The rule is too small a hook to catch such a leviathan. Moreover, if at times it does prevent a person from winning, by lying witnesses, a lawsuit which he should lose, it also, at times, by shutting out the true facts, unjustly aids other persons to win lawsuits they should and would lose, were the suppressed evidence known to the courts. Exclusionary rules, which frequently result in injustice, have always been defended—as was the rule, now fortunately extinct, excluding testimony of the parties to an action—with the danger-of-perjury argument.[16] Perjury, of course, is pernicious and doubtless much of it is used in our courts daily with unfortunate success. The problem of avoiding its efficacious use should be met head on. Were it consistently met in an indirect manner—in accordance with the viewpoint of the adulators of the parol evidence rule—by wiping out substantive rights provable only through oral testimony, we would have wholesale destruction of familiar causes of action such as, for instance, suits for personal injury and for enforcement of wholly oral agreements.

[Several long and even less relevant paragraphs of this rant are omitted.—Eds.]

[10] In sum, a rule so leaky cannot fairly be described as a stout container of legal certainty. John Chipman Gray, a seasoned practical lawyer, expressed grave doubts concerning the reliance of businessmen on legal precedents generally. If they rely on the parol evidence rule in particular, they will often be duped. It has been seriously questioned whether in fact they do so to any considerable extent. We see no good reason why we should strain to interpret the record facts here to bring them within such a rule.

Reversed and remanded.

———

NOTES

1.   Judge Jerome Frank, the author of this opinion, is considered to have been one of the most extreme followers of the Legal Realist school of jurisprudence. In an attempt to emphasize the importance of the judge's subjective impressions to the outcome of litigation, he once said that the

---

[16]   Perjury is one of the great bugaboos of the law. Every change in procedure by which the disclosure of the truth has been made easier has raised the spectra of perjury to frighten the profession. It was only in 1851 that Lord Brougham's Act for the first time made the parties to civil actions competent to testify in the higher courts of England. There was great dread of the Act, lest the interest of the parties should prove too powerful an incentive to false swearing . . . But the fear that the temptation to perjury would ruin the value of the testimony of interested parties has so completely vanished that no one would seriously think of restoring the disqualification. Sunderland, *Scope and Method of Discovery Before Trial*, 42 YALE L.J. (1933) 863, 867.

outcome of cases could depend on what the judge ate for breakfast. This led critics to refer to Legal Realism as "gastronomic jurisprudence."

2.   Learned Hand, considered one of the greatest American judges of all time, was on the panel that decided *Zell* and joined in the opinion. This fact should not be taken too seriously, however. When Hand was asked about Frank's long opinions, he reportedly said: "I see how [Frank] comes out and pay no attention to the shit." Laura Kalman, Legal Realism at Yale, 1927– 1960, 284 n.02 (1986), quoted in Paul Brickner, *Book Review* Comment, *The Lemon Test and Subjective Intent in Establishment Clause Analysis: The Case for Abandoning the Purpose Prong,* 76 KY. L.J. 1061, 1082 (1988).

3.   Judge Frank is also reputed to have said: "most lawsuits are won on a balance of the perjury." (quoted in *S.G. Supply Co. v. Greenwood Int'l, Inc.,* 769 F.Supp. 1430, 1442 (N.D.Ill. 1991)). Strange words from someone who wanted to abolish a rule designed to protect against perjured testimony.

4.   Some judges and legal commentators argue that when courts are construing a parties' agreement, one should generally consider both the language of the parties' agreement and extrinsic evidence to properly determine the intent of the parties and the contractual meaning (Contextualists). However, there are many who disagree with that approach and instead argue that extrinsic evidence—such as preliminary negotiations, the surrounding circumstances, course of performance, course of dealing, and usage of trade—is of little importance, and courts should construe only the language of the parties' agreement without these additional materials (Textualists). The justification for the latter position is allowing parties to introduce extrinsic evidence results in more litigation over the meaning of the contracts than if the courts only considered the four corners of the agreement.

However, an empirical study that sought to determine if enforcement costs were higher under either approach found very little support that either approach results in more litigation or higher enforcement costs. *See* Joshua Silverstein, *Contract Interpretation Enforcement Costs: An Empirical Study of Textualism Versus Contextualism Conducted via the West Key Number System,* 47 HOFSTRA L. REV. 1011 (2019).

LAWYERING SKILLS PROBLEM

Imagine that the parol evidence a rule has been abolished. What would be the effect of this development? Specifically, if you were a sophisticated lawyer documenting a deal, how would this affect your drafting, if at all?

CHAPTER 15

INTERPRETATION OF CONTRACTS

■ ■ ■

Interpretation of the contract, i.e., what the contract means, is by far the most litigated issue in contract law. There are many rules or "canons" or "maxims" that courts have articulated in an attempt to rationalize the process that they go through in deciding what the words mean, *see, e.g.,* R2d §§ 200–204; UNIDROIT articles 4.1–4.8. But they're not very helpful. For each rule, there is an exception and a counter rule. They are most often employed as support for an interpretation that has been decided upon for other reasons, so we're not going to spend time on them here. Those interested in the interpretive rules should read Llewellyn, *Remarks on the Theory of Appellate Decision and How the Rules or Canons about Statutes Are To Be Construed*, 3 VAND. L. REV. 395 (1950), which is no less timely today than when it was written. *See also* THOMAS R. HAGGARD AND GEORGE W. KUNEY, LEGAL DRAFTING IN A NUTSHELL, *Chapter 4, The Rules of Interpretation* (4th ed. 2016).

This chapter deals with a more limited set of issues: When may a court look at extrinsic evidence to help determine what the written document means, and when must it go by the document alone? Note that this is *not* the same inquiry as that of the parol evidence rule. That rule concerned what evidence could be considered to determine what the terms of the contract *were*, not necessarily what they *meant*. (This is classic legal reasoning that drives non-lawyers wild! "What do you mean the evidence can come in to prove what the term means when it can't come in to prove the term itself?") This chapter concerns the inquiry as to meaning, which some would argue has allowed a truck-sized hole to be punched in the parol evidence rule by Justice Traynor of the California Supreme Court and others, as the *Trident Center v. Connecticut General Life Insurance* case demonstrates.

The traditional interpretation analysis appears straightforward. The common law presumed that the parties' writing and the official law of contract are the definitive elements of the agreement and one need look no further to interpret the contract. One is to confine oneself to the "four corners" of the document, unless an ambiguity in the language is found. If an ambiguity presents itself, then one may turn to extrinsic evidence to determine its meaning. As noted above, this traditional four-corners approach has come under attack in some jurisdictions and, under the

419

U.C.C., evidence of the parties' experience and industry practice can now support incorporation of different meanings to serve the intent of the parties, as the following case demonstrates.

PRACTICE TIP: VAGUENESS AND AMBIGUITY

The terms "ambiguity" and "vagueness" should not be confused.

Ambiguity occurs when a word or phrase is capable of meaning two or more things. For example, if a contract provides that one party "shall pay x and y $500,000." It is unclear whether x and y are each to receive $500,000 or if x and y are to receive a total of $500,000 to share. Another common source of ambiguity is the unclear pronoun reference. When drafting or reviewing and revising contracts, when you see a pronoun, it is best to ask whether a defined term for a party or third party cannot be inserted in its place. Defined terms are, after all, a sort of very specific, private pronoun created by the drafter.

Vagueness, on the other hand, is a lack of clarity. It is often intentionally used in legal drafting when the parties are unable to agree on a provision governing what is thought to be a rare or unexpected event without incurring costs that are not justified due to the low probability of the event happening. Consider, for example, the standard prevailing party attorneys' fee shifting clause, which provides for an award of "reasonable fees and costs." While one party may want to quantify or cap the amount of a fee award by specifying a not-to-exceed figure, this is likely to be unacceptable to the other party. Rather than run up their current fees negotiating a provision that everyone hopes will never be used—everyone is optimistic at the inception of most deals—the attorneys compromise on the "reasonable attorney's fee" language.

But vagueness can cause problems if it is used inadvertently or unintentionally. Lawyers should closely examine their documents and question the impact and wisdom of including every "reasonable" or "material" or similar word. In fact, a good general rule is to examine and question the impact of and need for all adverbs or adjectives in a transactional document. Any surplus words should be removed lest some later court apply the maxim that every part of the contract should be construed to have some effect and give the word meaning where none was intended.

[handwritten: P Hired Thomas]

PACIFIC GAS & ELECTRIC CO. V. G. W. THOMAS DRAYAGE & RIGGING CO.

[handwritten: - Unambiguous Contract]

Supreme Court of California
69 Cal. 2d 33, 69 Cal. Rptr. 561, 442 P.2d 641 (1968)

[handwritten: court had to decide to allow Parties offering evidence]

TRAYNOR, CHIEF JUSTICE.

[handwritten: Cause of Action]

[1] Defendant appeals from a judgment for plaintiff in an action for damages for injury to property under an indemnity clause of a contract.

[handwritten: Facts]

[2] In 1960 defendant entered into a contract with plaintiff to furnish the labor and equipment necessary to remove and replace the upper metal cover of plaintiff's steam turbine. Defendant agreed to perform the work "at (its) own risk and expense" and to "indemnify" plaintiff "against all loss, damage, expense and liability resulting from . . . injury to property, arising out of or in any way connected with the performance of this contract." Defendant also agreed to procure not less than $50,000 insurance to cover liability for injury to property. Plaintiff was to be an additional named insured, but the policy was to contain a cross-liability clause extending the coverage to plaintiff's property.

[handwritten: - Terms]
[handwritten: - Terms]

[handwritten: Facts]

[3] During the work the cover fell and injured the exposed rotor of the turbine. Plaintiff brought this action to recover $25,144.51[1], the amount it subsequently spent on repairs. During the trial it dismissed a count based on negligence and thereafter secured judgment on the theory that the indemnity provision covered injury to all property regardless of ownership.

[handwritten: Sounds like outside of dealing]

[handwritten: though it reads for 3rd parties, plain language says it should cover injuries to P's property]

[4] Defendant offered to prove by admissions of plaintiff's agents, by defendant's conduct under similar contracts entered into with plaintiff, and by other proof that in the indemnity clause the parties meant to cover injury to property of third parties only and not to plaintiff's property. Although the trial court observed that the language used was "the classic language for a third party indemnity provision" and that "one could very easily conclude that . . . its whole intendment is to indemnify third parties," it nevertheless held that the "plain language" of the agreement also required defendant to indemnify plaintiff for injuries to plaintiff's property. Having determined that the contract had a plain meaning, the court refused to admit any extrinsic evidence that would contradict its interpretation. *[handwritten: — Court refused to admit extrinsic evidence.]*

[handwritten: Only to 3rd parties not Plaintiff properties]

[5] When a court interprets a contract on this basis, it determines the meaning of the instrument in accordance with the " . . . extrinsic evidence of the judge's own linguistic education and experience." (3 Corbin on Contracts (1960 ed.) (1964 Supp. sec. 579, p. 225, fn. 56).) The exclusion of testimony that might contradict the linguistic background of the judge reflects a judicial belief in the possibility of perfect verbal expression. This

---

[1] [$22,144.51 in 1968 dollars is roughly the equivalent of $160,000 in 2019 dollars using the CPI and the GNP Deflator.—Eds.]

[handwritten: Accident occurred during Project]

belief is a remnant of a primitive faith in the inherent potency[2] and inherent meaning of words.[3]

[6] The test of admissibility of extrinsic evidence to explain the meaning of a written instrument is not whether it appears to the court to be plain and unambiguous on its face, but whether the offered evidence is relevant to prove a meaning to which the language of the instrument is reasonably susceptible.

[7] A rule that would limit the determination of the meaning of a written instrument to its four-corners merely because it seems to the court to be clear and unambiguous, would either deny the relevance of the intention of the parties or presuppose a degree of verbal precision and stability our language has not attained.

[8] Some courts have expressed the opinion that contractual obligations are created by the mere use of certain words, whether or not there was any intention to incur such obligations. Under this view, contractual obligations flow, not from the intention of the parties but from the fact that they used certain magic words. Evidence of the parties' intention therefore becomes irrelevant.

[9] In this state, however, the intention of the parties as expressed in the contract is the source of contractual rights and duties. A court must ascertain and give effect to this intention by determining what the parties meant by the words they used. Accordingly, the exclusion of relevant, extrinsic evidence to explain the meaning of a written instrument could be justified only if it were feasible to determine the meaning the parties gave to the words from the instrument alone.

[10] If words had absolute and constant referents, it might be possible to discover contractual intention in the words themselves and in the manner in which they were arranged. Words, however, do not have absolute and constant referents. "A word is a symbol of thought but has no arbitrary and fixed meaning like a symbol of algebra or chemistry. . . ." (*Pearson v. State Social Welfare Board* (1960) 54 Cal.2d 184, 195, 5 Cal.Rptr. 553, 559, 353 P.2d 33, 39.) The meaning of particular words or groups of words varies with the " . . . verbal context and surrounding circumstances and purposes in view of the linguistic education and

---

[2] *E.g.,* "The elaborate system of taboo and verbal prohibitions in primitive groups; the ancient Egyptian myth of Khern, the apotheosis of the word, and of Thoth, the Scribe of Truth, the Giver of Words and Script, the Master of Incantations; the avoidance of the name of God in Brahmanism, Judaism and Islam; totemistic and protective names in mediaeval Turkish and Finno-Ugrian languages; the misplaced verbal scruples of the 'Pre cieuses'; the Swedish peasant custom of curing sick cattle smitten by witchcraft, by making them swallow a page torn out of the psalter and put in dough. . . ." from ULLMAN, THE PRINCIPLES OF SEMANTICS 43 (1963 ed.). *See also* OGDEN AND RICHARDS, THE MEANING OF MEANING, 24–47 (rev. ed. 1956).

[3] "Rerum enim vocabula immutabilia sunt, homines mutabilia," (Words are unchangeable, men changeable) from Dig. XXXIII, 10, 7, § 2, de sup. leg. as quoted in 9 WIGMORE ON EVIDENCE187 § 2461.

experience of their users and their hearers or readers (not excluding judges) . . . A word has no meaning apart from these factors; much less does it have an objective meaning, one true meaning." (Corbin, The Interpretation of Words and the Parol Evidence Rule (1965) 50 Cornell L.Q. 161, 187.) Accordingly, the meaning of a writing "can only be found by interpretation in the light of all the circumstances that reveal the sense in which the writer used the words. The exclusion of parol evidence regarding such circumstances merely because the words do not appear ambiguous to the reader can easily lead to the attribution to a written instrument of a meaning that was never intended." (Citations omitted.)

[11] Although extrinsic evidence is not admissible to, add to, detract from, or vary the terms of a written contract, these terms must first be determined before it can be decided whether or not extrinsic evidence is being offered for a prohibited purpose. The fact that the terms of an instrument appear clear to a judge does not preclude the possibility that the parties chose the language of the instrument to express different terms. That possibility is not limited to contracts whose terms have acquired a particular meaning by trade usage,[4] but exists whenever the parties' understanding of the words used may have differed from the judge's understanding.

* * *

[12] In the present case the court erroneously refused to consider extrinsic evidence offered to show that the indemnity clause in the contract was not intended to cover injuries to plaintiff's property. Although that evidence was not necessary to show that the indemnity clause was reasonably susceptible of the meaning contended for by defendant, it was nevertheless relevant and admissible on that issue. Moreover, since that clause was reasonably susceptible of that meaning, the offered evidence was also admissible to prove that the clause had that meaning and did not cover injuries to plaintiff's property.[5] Accordingly, the judgment must be reversed.

---

[4] Extrinsic evidence of trade usage or custom has been admitted to show that the term "United Kingdom" in a motion picture distribution contract included Ireland (Ermolieff v. R.K.O. Radio Pictures, 19 Cal.2d 543, 549–52, 122 P.2d 3 (1942)); that the word "ton" in a lease meant a long ton or 2,240 pounds and not the statutory ton of 2,000 pounds (Higgins v. Cal. Petroleum, etc., Co., 120 Cal. 629, 630–32, 52 P. 1080 (1898)); that the word "stubble" in a lease included not only stumps left in the ground but everything "left on the ground after the harvest time" (Callahan v. Stanley, 57 Cal. 476, 477–79 (1881)); that the term "north" in a contract dividing mining claims indicated a boundary line running along the "magnetic and not the true meridian" (Jenny Lind Co. v. Bower & Co., 11 Cal. 194, 197–99 (1858)) and that a form contract for purchase and sale was actually an agency contract (Body-Steffner Co. v. Flotill Products, 63 Cal.App.2d 555, 558–62, 147 P.2d 84 (1944)).

[5] The court's exclusion of extrinsic evidence in this case would be error even under a rule that excluded such evidence when the instrument appeared to the court to be clear and unambiguous on its face. The controversy centers on the meaning of the word "indemnify" and the phrase "all loss, damage, expense and liability." The trial court's recognition of the language as typical of a third party indemnity clause and the double sense in which the word "indemnify" is

Textualist Approach vs. Contextualist Approach

In the following passages from *Individual Healthcare Specialists, Inc. v. BlueCross BlueShield of Tennessee, Inc.*, 566 S.W.3d. 671, 695 (Tenn. 2019), the court thoroughly described both the textual and contextual approach to contract interpretation, as well as the origins of these approaches and their rise, fall, and regeneration over time:

* * *

[1] . . .BlueCross asserts globally that the trial court erred in admitting extrinsic evidence to construe the parties' agreements. It maintains that all of the contractual provisions at issue were clear and unambiguous on the face of the document, noting that the trial court said as much in its order denying IHS's motion for partial summary judgment, in which it found "no ambiguities in the parties' contract documents." Having made that threshold determination, BlueCross insists, the trial court was thereafter obliged to reject IHS's request to admit extrinsic evidence on the proper interpretation of the agreements and instead look only to the written agreements themselves. From a policy standpoint, BlueCross argues that, for contracts that include an integration clause, this Court should require trial courts to interpret contracts based on their written language only, without resort to extrinsic evidence.

[2] IHS argues the inverse. It maintains that the testimony on the parties' intent and their course of dealing over the years was key to proper interpretation of the agreements. IHS maintains that the Court of Appeals erred in holding that the trial court should have excluded extrinsic evidence on the question of whether IHS was entitled to an award of attorney fees under the indemnification provision. A strict "plain meaning" rule that precludes the use of extrinsic evidence, it contends, is at odds with

---

used in statutes and defined in dictionaries demonstrate the existence of an ambiguity. (Compare Civ.Code, § 2772, "Indemnity is a contract by which one engages to save another from a legal consequence of the conduct of one of the parties, or of some other person," with Civ. Code, § 2527, "Insurance is a contract whereby one undertakes to indemnify another against loss, damage, or liability, arising from an unknown or contingent event.") Black's Law Dictionary (4th ed. 1951) defines "indemnity" as "A collateral contract or assurance, by which one person engages to secure another against an anticipated loss or to prevent him from being damnified by the legal consequences of an act or forbearance on the part of one of the parties or of some third person." STROUD'S JUDICIAL DICTIONARY (2d ed. 1903) defines it as a "Contract . . . to indemnify against a liability. . . ."

the courts' obligation to interpret contracts in a way that comports with the parties' intent.[6]

[3] As explained in more detail below, in so framing their arguments, it can be said that BlueCross urges us to adopt a "textual" approach to contract interpretation while IHS advocates for a "contextual" approach. As the name suggests, the *textual approach* is text-centered; under it, the court interprets a contract by focusing on the plain meaning of the text, ascertained from the written agreement only, to the exclusion of any evidence extrinsic to it. In contrast, under the *contextual approach*, the court interprets a contract based on a broad understanding of the context of the agreement and the parties' intent, taken from evidence of extrinsic matters such as the circumstances of their negotiation. *See generally* Lawrence A. Cunningham, *Contract Interpretation 2.0: Not Winner-Take-All but Best-Tool-for-the-Job*, 85 GEO. WASH. L. REV. 1625 (Nov. 2017) (hereinafter "Cunningham, 85 GEO. WASH. L. REV. at ___"); Ronald J. Gilson, Charles F. Sabel, & Robert E. Scott, *Text and Context: Contract Interpretation as Contract Design*, 100 CORNELL L. REV. 23 (Nov. 2014) (hereinafter "Gilson et al., 100 CORNELL L. REV. at ___").

[4] We first offer some background on how these two competing approaches to contract interpretation and extrinsic evidence evolved. Next we review how Tennessee courts have used them, with particular focus on the parol evidence rule. Finally, we apply the appropriate law to the facts in this case.

Historical Overview

[5] "Historically, the English common law applied two different sets of doctrines to interpret a disputed contract." Gilson et al., 100 CORNELL L. REV. at 46. In the law courts, contracts were enforced in accordance with a set of objective rules. A precursor to the textual approach, this formalistic method focused on the text of the contract at issue without reference to any evidence outside of the written document. *Id.* at 47. The objective rules or doctrines "were administered strictly, without exceptions for cases in which the application of the rule appeared to defeat its purpose." *Id.*

[6] In contrast, the English chancery courts, courts of equity, interpreted contracts by applying broad equitable principles that were "administered loosely and [ ] designed to provide exceptions to the common law interpretive rules." *Id.* The equitable principles "were generally cast in subjective terms and therefore

---

6   Amicus Curiae Professor George Kuney is in general alignment with this position, arguing that a court's consideration of the context of an agreement as well as its language is more likely to result in interpretation that reflects the intentions of the parties.

required judges to exercise such judgment by evaluating the context of the particular transaction." *Id.*

[7] Over time, the chancery courts and the common law courts began to exercise overlapping jurisdiction in contractual disputes; however, each tribunal continued to view cases from its own perspective. *Id.* (quoting J.H. Baker, An Introduction to English Legal History 12–14 (4th ed. 2002)). The two competing systems often had "incompatible procedural and substantive doctrines." *Id.* at 48–49. Eventually, courts of law and courts of equity were merged in England and in the United States. "The result was an uncomfortable combination of legal and equitable doctrines; and it was this awkward amalgam that formed the matrix of American contract law." *Id.* at 49.

[8] Roughly up to the middle of the twentieth century, most American courts predominantly applied the textual approach to contract interpretation, rejecting all evidence extrinsic to the written document. Cunningham, 85 GEO. WASH. L. REV. at 1628. The textual approach is essentially based on three familiar rules of contract interpretation: the plain meaning rule,[7] the four corners rule,[8] and the parol evidence rule.[9] All of these limit the use of extrinsic evidence in contract interpretation.[10]

[9] A widely-cited New York case provides an example of the strict textualist approach. In *Hotchkiss v. National City Bank of New York,* 200 F. 287 (S.D.N.Y. 1911), the New York court refused to consider witness testimony on custom associated with a contract, stating that the witness's testimony was "not competent evidence at all, since it in effect usurps the court's function." *Hotchkiss,* 200 F. at 293. Rejecting all extrinsic evidence, the court

---

[7] In general, under the plain meaning rule, if language in a contract is initially deemed unambiguous, its "plain meaning" should be used, without recourse to matters extraneous to the text of the agreement. *See* Black's Law Dictionary 1336 (10th ed. 2014).

[8] As discussed below, the four corners rule appears to be stated in two ways; first, that a contract's meaning is gathered from the entire document rather than its isolated parts, and second, that extraneous evidence is not used to interpret a contract that is deemed unambiguous. *See* Black's Law Dictionary 772 (10th ed. 2014).

[9] Formulations of the so-called "parol evidence rule" vary, but in general it provides that "a writing intended by the parties to be a final embodiment of their agreement cannot be modified by evidence of earlier or contemporaneous agreements that might add to, vary, or contradict the writing." Black's Law Dictionary 1292 (10th ed. 2014).

[10] The term "extrinsic evidence" includes any "[e]vidence relating to a contract but not appearing on the face of the contract because it comes from other sources, such as statements between the parties or the circumstances surrounding the agreement." Black's Law Dictionary 675 (10th ed. 2014). Unless a particular type of extrinsic evidence is at issue, courts often refer to all extra-contractual evidence as "extrinsic evidence."

explained: "A contract has, strictly speaking, nothing to do with the personal, or individual, intent of the parties."[11] *Id.*

[10] In the mid-twentieth century, jurists and scholars began to question strict adherence to the textual rules. Professor Arthur Corbin, a well-known scholar and author of a popular contracts treatise, wondered, "How could any writing prove its own completeness and how can any word or document prove its own meaning[?]" Cunningham, 85 GEO. WASH. L. REV. at 1628. Corbin and like-minded jurists advocated a broader approach. "Start with the writing," they urged, "but determine meaning according to all probative circumstances," including extrinsic evidence such as the structure of the contract, the parties' bargaining history, the circumstances surrounding the formation of the contract, and the parties' course of performance.[12] *Id.*

[11] In response, a number of jurists moved toward what came to be known as a contextual approach. In a widely-cited example, the California Supreme Court in *Pacific Gas*, cited by the trial court below, embraced broad use of interpretive extrinsic evidence. 442 P.2d at 644–46. In *Pacific Gas*, the trial court had held that the parties' contract had a "plain meaning" and thereafter refused to admit any extrinsic evidence to contradict its initial interpretation. *Id.* at 642. The California Supreme Court criticized the trial court's approach. "A rule that would limit the determination of the meaning of a written instrument to its four-corners merely because it seems to the court to be clear and unambiguous," the *Pacific Gas* Court said, "would either deny the relevance of the intention of the parties or presuppose a degree of verbal precision and stability our language has not attained." *Id.* at 644. It held that, if extrinsic evidence shows that the contract language is susceptible to more than one meaning, it can be admitted to prove the parties' actual intent. *Id.* at 645.

[handwritten: Pacific Gas embraced the contextual approach]

[handwritten: Holding of PA]

[12] The influence of contextualism found its way into the Restatement (Second) of Contracts. Cunningham, 85 GEO. WASH. L. REV. at 1629. Section 202 of the Restatement, on rules of contract

---

[11] The sometimes harsh results resulting from the textual rules engendered numerous exceptions to rigid enforcement. *See, e.g., Hines v. Wilcox,* 96 Tenn. 148, 33 S.W. 914, 914–15 (Tenn. 1896) (listing multiple exceptions to the parol evidence rule).

[12] In addition, some judges and commentators came to criticize the "ambiguous versus unambiguous" dichotomy used in textualism an arbitrary barrier to the use of important tools for interpreting contracts and statutes. *See* Lawrence M. Solan, *Pernicious Ambiguity in Contracts and Statutes,* 79 Chi.-Kent L. Rev. 859, 859 (2004) ("The problem, perhaps ironically, is that the concept of ambiguity is itself perniciously ambiguous."); Ward Farnsworth et al., *Ambiguity About Ambiguity: An Empirical Inquiry into Legal Interpretation,* 2 J. LEGAL ANALYSIS 257, 276 (2010) ("If one person says that both proposed readings of [legal text] seem plausible, and a colleague disagrees, finding one reading too strained, what is there to do about it but for each to stamp his foot?").

interpretation, provides that the words of the contract "and other conduct are interpreted in the light of all the circumstances, and if the principal purpose of the parties is ascertainable it is given great weight." Restatement (Second) of Contracts § 202(1) (1981). Section 212, specifically applicable to integrated agreements, provides: "The interpretation of an integrated agreement is directed to the meaning of the terms of the writing or writings *in light of the circumstances* . . . ." Restatement (Second) of Contracts § 212(1) (1981) (emphasis added). The comments to section 212 explain that "extrinsic evidence cannot change the plain meaning of a writing," but the meaning of contractual terms "can almost never be plain except in a context." *Id.* § 212 cmt. b.

[13] Thus, many elements of contextualism gained wide acceptance. "By the 1990s, . . . contextualism, [had] softened the parol evidence rule, loosened the four corners doctrine, and diluted the plain meaning rule." Cunningham, 85 GEO. WASH. L. REV. at 1629.

[14] However, as had happened at times with an overly rigid textualist approach, contextualism was also taken to extremes. Some courts took it as a license to disregard the written words of the contract. Under an extreme contextualist approach, if extrinsic evidence indicates that the contractual language does not comport with the intent of the parties, the court may "override" the text if "doing so is necessary to substantially 'correct' or complete the parties' written contract by realigning it with its 'true' meaning." Gilson et al., 100 CORNELL L. REV. at 36. This extreme application of contextualism prompted a correction of sorts, some resurgent support for textualism—particularly in commercial contracts.[13] Cunningham, 85 GEO. WASH. L. REV. at 1629.

[15] Any attempt to discern where the modern majority of jurisdictions falls on the question of "textual versus contextual" approach to contract interpretation gives way to frustration because of "the reality that different settings warrant different approaches." Cunningham, 85 GEO. WASH. L. REV. at 1627. In any given state, caselaw "evades tidy classification as textualist or contextualist because, rather than wedded to one school, courts often choose the more suitable doctrine given the interpretation task at hand." *Id.* & Appendix (comparing contradictory intra-jurisdiction cases); *see also* Eric A. Posner, *The Parol Evidence*

---

[13]   *See, e.g., Trident Ctr. v. Conn. Gen. Life Ins. Co.,* 847 F.2d 564, 569 (9th Cir. 1988); *Gen. Tire & Rubber Co. v. Firestone Tire & Rubber Co.,* 489 F.2d 1105, 1123–24 (6th Cir. 1973); *Alameda Cnty. Flood Control & Water Conservation Dist. v. Dep't of Water Res.,* 213 Cal. App. 4th 1163, 1188–89, 152 Cal. Rptr. 3d 845 (2013).

Rule, The Plain Meaning Rule and The Principles of Contractual Interpretation, 146 U. PA. L. REV. 533, 553 (1998) ("No jurisdiction has a bright-line [parol evidence rule]. Courts might state one or the other as a general rule, but all sorts of subsidiary doctrines provide exceptions."). "Many differences in this juxtaposition can be explained on various, somewhat technical grounds—such as date, state versus federal law, high state court or low, degree of clarity, and so on. But ultimately the best explanation for these and innumerable other such apparent anomalies is the inherent untidiness of the cases." Cunningham, 85 GEO. WASH. L. REV. at 1630.

* * *

The Court in *BlueCross* described how early Tennessee caselaw favored the contextualist approach to contract interpretation even when the contract's language was clear, and that elements of textualism were found in only a small percentage of cases. At that time, the vast majority of courts across the country took the opposite approach favoring textualism over contextualism.

> For example, in 1895, [the Supreme Court of Tennessee] stated that "[t]he intention is the governing principle of construction. In ascertaining the intention, the situation of the parties, the motives that led to the agreement, and the objects designed to be effected by it, may all be looked to by the court." *Nunnelly, 29 S.W. at 127; see also Taylor v. Neblett,* 51 Tenn. 491, 493 (1871) ("The governing principle of construction of contracts is the intention of the parties. The sense in which they mutually understood it is that which must control in its enforcement. To ascertain the intention of parties, it is legitimate to look to their situation at the time and to the surrounding circumstances."); *Jones,* 42 Tenn. at 583 ("The governing principle of construction is the intention of the parties. That intention may be ascertained by looking to the situation of the parties, the motives which induced the agreement, and the object and purpose designed to be effected by it."). Some recited contextual principles after determining that the contract language was "ambiguous," *see, e.g., Mills,* 59 Tenn. at 457–58, and others did so without first finding ambiguity, *see, e.g., Nunnelly,* 29 S.W. at 127.

Id. at 688.

Over time, Tennessee courts relied more and more on textualist principles, particularly when courts found the language of the contract was unambiguous. This resulted in more courts interpreting contracts as written and in accordance with the plain terms of the agreement. This shift towards textualist principles indicated that the Tennessee courts rejected the broad and extreme contextualist principles applied by the California Supreme Court in *Pacific Gas*. Rather, more recent Tennessee caselaw reflects a greater balance between both textualist and contextualist principles:

Modern Tennessee approach

> [The cases] demonstrate a definite focus on the written words in the parties' contract, but they also consider evidence related to the situation of the parties and the circumstances of the transaction in interpreting those words. For example, in *Penske Truck Leasing Co. v. Huddleston*, the Court said: "The intention of the parties is to be determined by a fair construction of the terms and provisions of the contract, by the subject matter to which it has reference, by the circumstances of the particular transaction giving rise to the question, and by the construction placed on the agreement by the parties in carrying out its terms." 795 S.W.2d 669, 671 (Tenn. 1990). Following *Penske*, the Court in *Hughes v. New Life Development Corp.* stated, "The search for the parties' intent should focus on the four corners of the contract, the circumstances in which the contract was made, and the parties' actions in carrying out the contract." 387 S.W.3d 453, 465 (Tenn. 2012).

Id. at 692.

Other states have gone through similar processes of flux in terms of textualism and contextualism and it is likely that this will continue going forward.

NOTE

The next case explores the ramifications of Judge Traynor's legacy found in *Pacific Gas & Electric Co. v. G. W. Thomas Drayage & Rigging Co.* Traynor waged a war against the effect of the parol evidence and four-corners rule and, by Judge Kozinski's assessment, won. Note that later developments, noted after the case, somewhat soften Traynor's victory while never directly overruling *PG&E*.

TRIDENT CENTER V. CONNECTICUT GENERAL LIFE INSURANCE CO.

United States Court of Appeals, Ninth Circuit
847 F.2d 564 (1988)

KOZINSKI, CIRCUIT JUDGE:

[1] The parties to this transaction are, by any standard, highly sophisticated business people: Plaintiff is a partnership consisting of an

insurance company and two of Los Angeles' largest and most prestigious law firms; defendant is another insurance company. Dealing at arm's length and from positions of roughly equal bargaining strength, they negotiated a commercial loan amounting to more than $56 million[14]. The contract documents are lengthy and detailed; they squarely address the precise issue that is the subject of this dispute; to all who read English, they appear to resolve the issue fully and conclusively.

[2]　Plaintiff nevertheless argues here, as it did below, that it is entitled to introduce extrinsic evidence that the contract means something other than what it says. This case therefore presents the question whether parties in California can ever draft a contract that is proof to parol evidence. Somewhat surprisingly, the answer is no.

Facts

[3]　The facts are rather simple. Sometime in 1983 Security First Life Insurance Company and the law firms of Mitchell, Silberberg & Knupp and Manatt, Phelps, Rothenberg & Tunney formed a limited partnership for the purpose of constructing an office building complex on Olympic Boulevard in West Los Angeles. The partnership, Trident Center, the plaintiff herein, sought and obtained financing for the project from defendant, Connecticut General Life Insurance Company. The loan documents provide for a loan of $56,500,000 at 12 ¼ percent interest for a term of 15 years, secured by a deed of trust on the project. The promissory note provides that "[m]aker shall not have the right to prepay the principal amount hereof in whole or in part" for the first 12 years.

[4]　Everything was copacetic for a few years until interest rates began to drop. The 12 ¼ percent rate that had seemed reasonable in 1983 compared unfavorably with 1987 market rates and Trident started looking for ways of refinancing the loan to take advantage of the lower rates. Connecticut General was unwilling to oblige, insisting that the loan could not be prepaid for the first 12 years of its life, that is, until January 1996.

[5]　Trident then brought suit in state court seeking a declaration that it was entitled to prepay the loan now, subject only to a 10 percent prepayment fee. Connecticut General promptly removed to federal court and brought a motion to dismiss, claiming that the loan documents clearly and unambiguously precluded prepayment during the first 12 years. The district court agreed and dismissed Trident's complaint. The court also "sua sponte, sanction[ed] the plaintiff for the filing of a frivolous lawsuit." Order of Dismissal, No. CV 87–2712 JMI (Kx), at 3 (C.D. Cal. June 8, 1987). Trident appeals both aspects of the district court's ruling.

---

[14]　[$56,000,000 in 1968 dollars is roughly the equivalent of $404,000,000 in 2019 dollars using the CPI and the GNP Deflator.—Eds.]

Discussion

I

Trident's Arguments

[6]   Trident makes two arguments as to why the district court's ruling is wrong. First, it contends that the language of the contract is ambiguous and proffers a construction that it believes supports its position. Second, Trident argues that, under California law, even seemingly unambiguous contracts are subject to modification by parol or extrinsic evidence. Trident faults the district court for denying it the opportunity to present evidence that the contract language did not accurately reflect the parties' intentions.

A.   *The Contract*

The 12 year rule was clearly stated

[7]   As noted earlier, the promissory note provides that Trident "shall not have the right to prepay the principal amount hereof in whole or in part before January 1996." Note at 6. It is difficult to imagine language that more clearly or unambiguously expresses the idea that Trident may not unilaterally prepay the loan during its first 12 years. Trident, however, argues that there is an ambiguity because another clause of the note provides that "[i]n the event of a prepayment resulting from a default hereunder or the Deed of Trust prior to January 10, 1996 the prepayment fee will be ten percent (10%)." Note at 6–7. Trident interprets this clause as giving it the option of prepaying the loan if only it is willing to incur the prepayment fee. *Why Trident believes it could add extrinsic evidence*

Holding→

[8]   We reject Trident's argument out of hand. In the first place, its proffered interpretation would result in a contradiction between two clauses of the contract; the default clause would swallow up the clause prohibiting Trident from prepaying during the first 12 years of the contract. The normal rule of construction, of course, is that courts must interpret contracts, if possible, so as to avoid internal conflict.

[9]   In any event, the clause on which Trident relies is not on its face reasonably susceptible to Trident's proffered interpretation. Whether to accelerate repayment of the loan in the event of default is entirely Connecticut General's decision. The contract makes this clear at several points. *See* Note at 4 ("in each such event [of default], the entire principal indebtedness, or so much thereof as may remain unpaid at the time, shall, *at the option of Holder*, become due and payable immediately" (emphasis added)); *id.* at 7 ("[i]n the event Holder exercises its *option to accelerate* the maturity hereof . . ." (emphasis added)); Deed of Trust ¶ 2.01, at 25 ("in each such event [of default], Beneficiary *may* declare all sums secured hereby immediately due and payable . . ." (emphasis added)). Even if Connecticut General decides to declare a default and accelerate, it "may rescind any notice of breach or default." *Id.* ¶ 2.02, at 26. Finally, Connecticut General has the option of doing nothing at all: "Beneficiary reserves the right at its sole option to waive noncompliance by Trustor with

any of the conditions or covenants to be performed by Trustor hereunder." *Id.* ¶ 3.02, at 29.

[10] Once again, it is difficult to imagine language that could more clearly assign to Connecticut General the exclusive right to decide whether to declare a default, whether and when to accelerate, and whether, having chosen to take advantage of any of its remedies, to rescind the process before its completion.

[11] Trident nevertheless argues that it is entitled to precipitate a default and insist on acceleration by tendering the balance due on the note plus the 10 percent prepayment fee. The contract language, cited above, leaves no room for this construction. It is true, of course, that Trident is free to stop making payments, which may then cause Connecticut General to declare a default and accelerate. But that is not to say that Connecticut General would be required to so respond. The contract quite clearly gives Connecticut General other options: It may choose to waive the default, or to take advantage of some other remedy such as the right to collect "all the income, rents, royalties, revenue, issues, profits, and proceeds of the Property." Deed of Trust ¶ 1.18, at 22. By interpreting the contract as Trident suggests, we would ignore those provisions giving Connecticut General, not Trident, the exclusive right to decide how, when and whether the contract will be terminated upon default during the first 12 years.

[12] In effect, Trident is attempting to obtain judicial sterilization of its intended default. But defaults are messy things; they are supposed to be. Once the maker of a note secured by a deed of trust defaults, its credit rating may deteriorate; attempts at favorable refinancing may be thwarted by the need to meet the trustee's sale schedule; its cash flow may be impaired if the beneficiary takes advantage of the assignment of rents remedy; default provisions in its loan agreements with other lenders may be triggered. Fear of these repercussions is strong medicine that keeps debtors from shirking their obligations when interest rates go down and they become disenchanted with their loans.[15] That Trident is willing to suffer the cost and delay of a lawsuit, rather than simply defaulting, shows far better than anything we might say that these provisions are having their intended effect. We decline Trident's invitation to truncate the lender's remedies and deprive Connecticut General of its bargained-for protection.

B.   Extrinsic Evidence

[13] Trident argues in the alternative that, even if the language of the contract appears to be unambiguous, the deal the parties actually struck is

---

[15] This provides a symmetry with the situation where interest rates go up and it is the lender who is stuck with a loan it would prefer to turn over at market rates. In an economy where interest rates fluctuate, it is all but certain that one side or the other will be dissatisfied with a long-term loan at some time. Mutuality calls for enforcing the contract as written no matter whose ox is being gored.

in fact quite different. It wishes to offer extrinsic evidence that the parties had agreed Trident could prepay at any time within the first 12 years by tendering the full amount plus a 10 percent prepayment fee. As discussed above, this is an interpretation to which the contract, as written, is not reasonably susceptible. Under traditional contract principles, extrinsic evidence is inadmissible to interpret, vary or add to the terms of an unambiguous integrated written instrument.

[14] Trident points out, however, that California does not follow the traditional rule. Two decades ago the California Supreme Court in *Pacific Gas & Electric Co. v. G.W. Thomas Drayage & Rigging Co.*, 69 Cal.2d 33, 442 P.2d 641, 69 Cal.Rptr. 561 (1968), turned its back on the notion that a contract can ever have a plain meaning discernible by a court without resort to extrinsic evidence. The court reasoned that contractual obligations flow not from the words of the contract, but from the intention of the parties. "Accordingly," the court stated, "the exclusion of relevant, extrinsic evidence to explain the meaning of a written instrument could be justified only if it were feasible to determine the meaning the parties gave to the words from the instrument alone." 69 Cal.2d at 38, 442 P.2d 641, 69 Cal.Rptr. 561. This, the California Supreme Court concluded, is impossible: "If words had absolute and constant referents, it might be possible to discover contractual intention in the words themselves and in the manner in which they were arranged. Words, however, do not have absolute and constant referents." *Id.* In the same vein, the court noted that "[t]he exclusion of testimony that might contradict the linguistic background of the judge reflects a judicial belief in the possibility of perfect verbal expression. This belief is a remnant of a primitive faith in the inherent potency and inherent meaning of words." *Id.* at 37, 442 P.2d 641, 69 Cal.Rptr. 561 (citation and footnotes omitted).[16]

[15] Under *Pacific Gas*, it matters not how clearly a contract is written, nor how completely it is integrated, nor how carefully it is negotiated, nor how squarely it addresses the issue before the court: the contract cannot be rendered impervious to attack by parol evidence. If one side is willing to claim that the parties intended one thing but the agreement provides for another, the court must consider extrinsic evidence of possible ambiguity. If that evidence raises the specter of ambiguity where there was none before, the contract language is displaced and the intention of the parties must be divined from self-serving testimony offered by partisan witnesses whose recollection is hazy from passage of time and colored by their conflicting interests. We question whether this approach is more likely to

---

[16]   In an unusual footnote, the court compared the belief in the immutable meaning of words with " '[t]he elaborate system of taboo and verbal prohibitions in primitive groups . . . [such as] the Swedish peasant custom of curing sick cattle smitten by witchcraft, by making them swallow a page torn out of the psalter and put in dough . . .' " *Id.* n. 2 (quoting ULLMAN, THE PRINCIPLES OF SEMANTICS 43 (1963)).

divulge the original intention of the parties than reliance on the seemingly clear words they agreed upon at the time.

[16] *Pacific Gas* casts a long shadow of uncertainty over all transactions negotiated and executed under the law of California. As this case illustrates, even when the transaction is very sizeable, even if it involves only sophisticated parties, even if it was negotiated with the aid of counsel, even if it results in contract language that is devoid of ambiguity, costly and protracted litigation cannot be avoided if one party has a strong enough motive for challenging the contract. While this rule creates much business for lawyers and an occasional windfall to some clients, it leads only to frustration and delay for most litigants and clogs already overburdened courts.

Everything the PA rule does

PA rule leads to frustration

[17] It also chips away at the foundation of our legal system. By giving credence to the idea that words are inadequate to express concepts, *Pacific Gas* undermines the basic principle that language provides a meaningful constraint on public and private conduct. If we are unwilling to say that parties, dealing face to face, can come up with language that binds them, how can we send anyone to jail for violating statutes consisting of mere words lacking "absolute and constant referents"? How can courts ever enforce decrees, not written in language understandable to all, but encoded in a dialect reflecting only the "linguistic background of the judge"? Can lower courts ever be faulted for failing to carry out the mandate of higher courts when "perfect verbal expression" is impossible? Are all attempts to develop the law in a reasoned and principled fashion doomed to failure as "remnant[s] of a primitive faith in the inherent potency and inherent meaning of words"?

[18] Be that as it may. While we have our doubts about the wisdom of *Pacific Gas*, we have no difficulty understanding its meaning, even without extrinsic evidence to guide us. As we read the rule in California, we must reverse and remand to the district court in order to give plaintiff an opportunity to present extrinsic evidence as to the intention of the parties in drafting the contract.[17] It may not be a wise rule we are applying, but it is a rule that binds us. *Erie R.R. Co. v. Tompkins*, 304 U.S. 64, 78, 58 S.Ct. 817, 822, 82 L.Ed. 1188 (1938).

Has to reverse and remand based on PA rule in Cali.

II

[19] In imposing sanctions on plaintiff, the district court stated:

Pursuant to Fed. R. Civ. P. 11, the Court, sua sponte, sanctions the plaintiff for the filing of a frivolous lawsuit. The Court

---

[17] Nothing we say should be construed as foreclosing Connecticut General from moving for summary judgment after completion of discovery; given the unambiguous language of the contract itself, such a motion would succeed unless Trident were to come forward with extrinsic evidence sufficient to render the contract reasonably susceptible to Trident's alternate interpretation, thereby creating a genuine issue of fact resolvable only at trial.

concludes that the language in the note and deed of trust is plain and clear. No reasonable person, much less firms of able attorneys, could possibly misunderstand this crystal-clear language. Therefore, this action was brought in bad faith.

Order of Dismissal at 3. Having reversed the district court on its substantive ruling, we must, of course, also reverse it as to the award of sanctions. While we share the district judge's impatience with this litigation, we would suggest that his irritation may have been misdirected. It is difficult to blame plaintiff and its lawyers for bringing this lawsuit. With this much money at stake, they would have been foolish not to pursue all remedies available to them under the applicable law. At fault, it seems to us, are not the parties and their lawyers but the legal system that encourages this kind of lawsuit. By holding that language has no objective meaning, and that contracts mean only what courts ultimately say they do, *Pacific Gas* invites precisely this type of lawsuit.[18] With the benefit of 20 years of hindsight, the California Supreme Court may wish to revisit the issue. If it does so, we commend to it the facts of this case as a paradigmatic example of why the traditional rule, based on centuries of experience, reflects the far wiser approach. *Traditional rule is wiser approach*

Conclusion

[20] The judgment of the district court is REVERSED. The case is REMANDED for reinstatement of the complaint and further proceedings in accordance with this opinion. The parties shall bear their own costs on appeal.

Why couldn't court reverse? the PA rule and set new precedents. B/of ERC Doctrine

NOTES

1. When Trident locked itself into a loan at an interest rate of 12 ¼%, inflation seemed out of control and interest rates were rising faster than they had in anyone's memory. It seemed to everyone that they would go on rising. This may have been the reason that Trident agreed to what seems in hindsight to have been a very bad deal. One lesson to take from this case is that as a lawyer negotiating deals and drafting documents you need to think of the ways in which conditions might change and make sure your client is protected if they do.

2. The California Supreme Court limited *Pacific Gas & Electric* in *Dore v. Arnold Worldwide, Inc.*, 39 Cal.4th 384, 46 Cal.Rptr.3d 668, 139 P.3d 56

---

[18] This is not to say, of course, that all lawsuits seeking to challenge the interpretation of facially unambiguous contracts are necessarily immune from imposition of sanctions. Even under *Pacific Gas*, a party urging an interpretation lacking any objectively reasonable basis in fact might well be subject to sanctions for bringing a frivolous lawsuit. [Practically speaking, this is a largely un-meetable standard.—Eds.]

Deals with how courts started to limit the PG rule

(2006). In the process of hiring an account executive, an ad agency wrote him a letter which provided in part:

> Brook, please know that as with all of our company employees, your employment with Arnold Communications, Inc. is at will. This simply means that Arnold Communications has the right to terminate your employment with Arnold Communications, Inc. at any time.

The agency required the executive to sign the letter. When he was terminated, the executive sued, alleging not only breach of contract, but also fraud and intentional infliction of emotional distress. His contract claim was that various oral representations, conduct, and documents had created an implied-in-fact contract that provided he would not be discharged except for cause.

The trial court granted summary judgment for the ad agency on the implied-in-fact contract claim. The Court of Appeal reversed, stating that the letter did not specifically state he could be terminated without cause. The California Supreme Court reversed the Court of Appeals. The majority opinion noted that under *Pacific Gas* extrinsic evidence may be admitted only if the language is susceptible of the meaning proffered. It said: "As a matter of simple logic, [the phrase 'at any time'] entails the notion of 'with or without cause.' "

Justice Baxter said in his concurring opinion that while the majority "to their credit" had chosen to apply *Pacific Gas* narrowly, it was susceptible to the broader interpretation given it in *Trident Center*. He quoted from that opinion and noted other criticisms of the opinion, including the later misgivings of Justice Mosk, who had joined in the *Pacific Gas* majority. Justice Baxter concluded that "it may be time for a fuller reconsideration of the meaning and scope of *Pacific Gas*."

A few years later, the California Court of Appeals further limited *Pacific Gas & Electric* in *Abers v. Rounsavell*, 189 Cal.App.4th 348, 116 Cal.Rptr.3d. 860 (2010). In *Abers*, the Court of Appeals did not acknowledge the broad "test of admissibility of extrinsic evidence" applied by the court in *Pacific Gas*, and instead followed the narrow application of *Pacific Gas* as applied by the Court in *Dore*. Quoting Justice Baxter's concurrence, the *Abers* court noted that, "Written agreements whose language appears clear in the context of the parties' dispute are not open to claims of 'latent' ambiguity." *Id. at 356.* Concluding that "[i]f there is no patent or latent ambiguity, " 'the case is over.' " *Id. at 357.*

Furthermore, the *Dore* and *Abers* courts elected not to use the language cited by the court in *Pacific Gas* which permitted the use of extrinsic evidence to prove language that was "fairly susceptible" to more than one meaning. Instead, these two courts only used the phrase "reasonably susceptible" regarding ambiguity in the contract language, and both courts seem to take a more four-corners approach to interpretation, which was the approach the *Pacific Gas* court intentionally avoided.

3.   Even more recently, in *Hot Rods, LLC v. Northrop Grumman Sys. Corp.*, 242 Cal. App. 4th 1166, 1176 (2015), the court held that a sentence in an integration clause stating " 'no extrinsic evidence whatsoever may be introduced in any judicial proceedings involving this Agreement' " expressed the intent of the parties "to bypass the general rule that consistent extrinsic evidence is admissible to explain the meaning of a contractual provision." Attorneys are word people and will be held to mean what they say, especially in a written document.

————

FRIGALIMENT IMPORTING V. B.N.S. INTERNATIONAL SALES

United States District Court for the Southern District of New York
190 F. Supp. 116 (1960)

FRIENDLY, CIRCUIT JUDGE.

How to interpret chicken

[1] The issue is, what is chicken? Plaintiff says "chicken" means a young chicken, suitable for broiling and frying. Defendant says "chicken" means any bird of that genus that meets contract specifications on weight and quality, including what it calls "stewing chicken" and plaintiff pejoratively terms "fowl." Dictionaries give both meanings, as well as some others not relevant here. To support it, plaintiff sends a number of volleys over the net; defendant essays to return them and adds a few serves of its own. Assuming that both parties were acting in good faith, the case nicely illustrates Holmes' remark "that the making of a contract depends not on the agreement of two minds in one intention, but on the agreement of two sets of external signs—not on the parties' having meant the same thing but on their having said the same thing." The Path of the Law, in Collected Legal Papers, p. 178. I have concluded that plaintiff has not sustained its burden of persuasion that the contract used "chicken" in the narrower sense.

[2] The action is for breach of the warranty that goods sold shall correspond to the description. Two contracts are in suit. In the first, dated May 2, 1957, defendant, a New York sales corporation, confirmed the sale to plaintiff, a Swiss corporation, of

> US Fresh Frozen Chicken, Grade A, Government Inspected, Eviscerated 2 1/2–3 lbs. and 1 1/2–2 lbs. each all chicken individually wrapped in cryovac, packed in secured fiber cartons or wooden boxes, suitable for export scheduled May 10, 1957 pursuant to instructions from Penson & Co., New York.

Terms →

> 75,000   lbs. 2 ½–3 lbs . . . . @ $33.00
> 25,000   lbs. 1 ½–2 lbs . . . . @ $36.50
>   per 100 lbs. FAS New York

The second contract, also dated May 2, 1957, was identical save that only 50,000 lbs. of the heavier "chicken" were called for, the price of the smaller birds was $37 per 100 lbs., and shipment was scheduled for May 30. The initial shipment under the first contract was short but the balance was shipped on May 17. When the initial shipment arrived in Switzerland, plaintiff found, on May 28, that the 2 1/2–3 lbs. birds were not young chicken suitable for broiling and frying but stewing chicken or "fowl"; indeed, many of the cartons and bags plainly so indicated. Protests ensued. Nevertheless, shipment under the second contract was made on May 29, the 2 1/2–3 lbs. birds again being stewing chicken. Defendant stopped the transportation of these at Rotterdam.

[3]   This action followed . . .

[4]   Since the word "chicken" standing alone is ambiguous, I turn first to see whether the contract itself offers any aid to its interpretation. Plaintiff says the 1 1/2–2 lbs. birds necessarily had to be young chicken since the older birds do not come in that size, hence the 2 1/2–3 lbs. birds must likewise be young. This is unpersuasive—a contract for "apples" of two different sizes could be filled with different kinds of apples even though only one species came in both sizes. Defendant notes that the contract called not simply for chicken but for "US Fresh Frozen Chicken, Grade A, Government Inspected." It says the contract thereby incorporated by reference the Department of Agriculture's regulations, which favor its interpretation; I shall return to this after reviewing plaintiff's other contentions.

[called for US chicken]

[5]   The first hinges on an exchange of cablegrams which preceded execution of the formal contracts. The negotiations leading up to the contracts were conducted in New York between defendant's secretary, Ernest R. Bauer, and a Mr. Stovicek, who was in New York for the Czechoslovak government at the World Trade Fair. A few days after meeting Bauer at the fair, Stovicek telephoned and inquired whether defendant would be interested in exporting poultry to Switzerland. Bauer then met with Stovicek, who showed him a cable from plaintiff dated April 26, 1957, announcing that they "are buyer" of 25,000 lbs. of chicken 2 1/2–3 lbs. weight, Cryovac packed, grade A Government inspected, at a price up to 33 cents per pound, for shipment on May 10, to be confirmed by the following morning, and were interested in further offerings. After testing the market for price, Bauer accepted, and Stovicek sent a confirmation that evening. Plaintiff stresses that, although these and subsequent cables between plaintiff and defendant, which laid the basis for the additional quantities under the first and for all of the second contract, were predominantly in German, they used the English word "chicken"; it claims this was done because it understood "chicken" meant young chicken whereas the German word, "Huhn," included both "Brathuhn" (broilers) and "Suppenhuhn" (stewing chicken), and that defendant, whose officers

were thoroughly conversant with German, should have realized this. Whatever force this argument might otherwise have is largely drained away by Bauer's testimony that he asked Stovicek what kind of chickens were wanted, received the answer "any kind of chickens," and then, in German, asked whether the cable meant "Huhn" and received an affirmative response . . .

[6]   Plaintiff's next contention is that there was a definite trade usage that "chicken" meant "young chicken." Defendant showed that it was only beginning in the poultry trade in 1957, thereby bringing itself within the principle that "when one of the parties is not a member of the trade or other circle, his acceptance of the standard must be made to appear" by proving either that he had actual knowledge of the usage or that the usage is "so generally known in the community that his actual individual knowledge of it may be inferred." 9 Wigmore, Evidence (3d ed. § 1940) 2464. Here there was no proof of actual knowledge of the alleged usage; indeed, it is quite plain that defendant's belief was to the contrary. In order to meet the alternative requirement, the law of New York demands a showing that "the usage is of so long continuance, so well established, so notorious, so universal and so reasonable in itself, as that the presumption is violent that the parties contracted with reference to it, and made it a part of their agreement." *Walls v. Bailey*, 1872, 49 N.Y. 464, 472–73.

[7]   Plaintiff endeavored to establish such a usage by the testimony of three witnesses and certain other evidence. Strasser, resident buyer in New York for a large chain of Swiss cooperatives, testified that "on chicken I would definitely understand a broiler." However, the force of this testimony was considerably weakened by the fact that in his own transactions the witness, a careful businessman, protected himself by using "broiler" when that was what he wanted and "fowl" when he wished older birds. Indeed, there are some indications, dating back to a remark of Lord Mansfield, Edie v. East India Co., 2 Burr. 1216, 1222 (1761), that no credit should be given "witnesses to usage, who could not adduce instances in verification." 7 Wigmore, Evidence (3d ed. 1940), § 1954; *see McDonald v. Acker, Merrall & Condit Co.*, 2d Dept.1920, 192 App.Div. 123, 126, 182 N.Y.S. 607. While Wigmore thinks this goes too far, a witness' consistent failure to rely on the alleged usage deprives his opinion testimony of much of its effect. Niesielowski, an officer of one of the companies that had furnished the stewing chicken to defendant, testified that "chicken" meant "the male species of the poultry industry. That could be a broiler, a fryer or a roaster," but not a stewing chicken; however, he also testified that upon receiving defendant's inquiry for "chickens," he asked whether the desire was for "fowl or frying chickens" and, in fact, supplied fowl, although taking the precaution of asking defendant, a day or two after plaintiff's acceptance of the contracts in suit, to change its confirmation of its order from "chickens," as defendant had originally prepared it, to "stewing chickens."

Dates, an employee of Urner-Barry Company, which publishes a daily market report on the poultry trade, gave it as his view that the trade meaning of "chicken" was "broilers and fryers." In addition to this opinion testimony, plaintiff relied on the fact that the Urner-Barry service, the Journal of Commerce, and Weinberg Bros. & Co. of Chicago, a large supplier of poultry, published quotations in a manner which, in one way or another, distinguish between "chicken," comprising broilers, fryers and certain other categories, and "fowl," which, Bauer acknowledged, included stewing chickens. This material would be impressive if there were nothing to the contrary. However, there was, as will now be seen.

[8] Defendant's witness Weininger, who operates a chicken eviscerating plant in New Jersey, testified "Chicken is everything except a goose, a duck, and a turkey. Everything is a chicken, but then you have to say, you have to specify which category you want or that you are talking about." Its witness Fox said that in the trade "chicken" would encompass all the various classifications. Sadina, who conducts a food inspection service, testified that he would consider any bird coming within the classes of "chicken" in the Department of Agriculture's regulations to be a chicken. The specifications approved by the General Services Administration include fowl as well as broilers and fryers under the classification "chickens." Statistics of the Institute of American Poultry Industries use the phrases "Young chickens" and "Mature chickens," under the general heading "Total chickens." and the Department of Agriculture's daily and weekly price reports avoid use of the word "chicken" without specification.

[9] Defendant advances several other points which it claims affirmatively support its construction. Primary among these is the regulation of the Department of Agriculture, 7 C.F.R. § 70.300–70.370, entitled, "Grading and Inspection of Poultry and Edible Products Thereof." And in particular 70.301 which recited:

Chickens. The following are the various classes of chickens:

  (a) Broiler or fryer . . .

  (b) Roaster . . .

  (c) Capon . . .

  (d) Stag . . .

  (e) Hen or stewing chicken or fowl . . .

  (f) Cock or old rooster. . . .

[10] Defendant argues, as previously noted, that the contract incorporated these regulations by reference. Plaintiff answers that the contract provision related simply to grade and Government inspection and did not incorporate the Government definition of "chicken," and also that the definition in the Regulations is ignored in the trade. However, the

latter contention was contradicted by Weininger and Sadina; and there is force in defendant's argument that the contract made the regulations a dictionary, particularly since the reference to Government grading was already in plaintiff's initial cable to Stovicek.

[11] Defendant makes a further argument based on the impossibility of its obtaining broilers and fryers at the 33 cents price offered by plaintiff for the 2 1/2–3 lbs. birds. There is no substantial dispute that, in late April, 1957, the price for 2 1/2–3 lbs. broilers was between 35 and 37 cents per pound, and that when defendant entered into the contracts, it was well aware of this and intended to fill them by supplying fowl in these weights. It claims that plaintiff must likewise have known the market since plaintiff had reserved shipping space on April 23, three days before plaintiff's cable to Stovicek, or, at least, that Stovicek was chargeable with such knowledge. It is scarcely an answer to say, as plaintiff does in its brief, that the 33 cents price offered by the 2 ½–3 lbs. "chickens" was closer to the prevailing 35 cents price for broilers than to the 30 cents at which defendant procured fowl. Plaintiff must have expected defendant to make some profit—certainly it could not have expected defendant deliberately to incur a loss.

[12] Finally, defendant relies on conduct by the plaintiff after the first shipment had been received. On May 28 plaintiff sent two cables complaining that the larger birds in the first shipment constituted fowl. Defendant answered with a cable refusing to recognize plaintiff's objection and announcing "We have today ready for shipment 50,000 lbs. chicken 2 1/2–3 lbs. 25,000 lbs. broilers 1 1/2–2 lbs.," these being the goods procured for shipment under the second contract, and asked immediate answer "whether we are to ship this merchandise to you and whether you will accept the merchandise." After several other cable exchanges, plaintiff replied on May 29 "Confirm again that merchandise is to be shipped since resold by us if not enough pursuant to contract chickens are shipped the missing quantity is to be shipped within ten days stop we resold to our customers pursuant to your contract chickens grade A you have to deliver us said merchandise we again state that we shall make you fully responsible for all resulting costs."[19] Defendant argues that if plaintiff was sincere in thinking it was entitled to young chickens, plaintiff would not have allowed the shipment under the second contract to go forward, since the distinction between broilers and chickens drawn in defendant's cablegram must have made it clear that the larger birds would not be broilers. However, plaintiff answers that the cables show plaintiff was insisting on delivery of young chickens and that defendant shipped old ones at its peril. Defendant's point would be highly relevant on another disputed issue—whether if liability were established, the measure of damages should be the difference in market value of broilers and stewing chicken in

---

[19] These cables were in German; "chicken," "broilers" and, on some occasions, "fowl," were in English.

BNS was new to the trade

Frigaliment construed the term chicken subjectively

New York or the larger difference in Europe, but I cannot give it weight on the issue of interpretation. Defendant points out also that plaintiff proceeded to deliver some of the larger birds in Europe, describing them as "poulets"; defendant argues that it was only when plaintiff's customers complained about this that plaintiff developed the idea that "chicken" meant "young chicken." There is little force in this in view of plaintiff's immediate and consistent protests.

[13] When all the evidence is reviewed, it is clear that defendant believed it could comply with the contracts by delivering stewing chicken in the 2 1/2–3 lbs. size. Defendant's subjective intent would not be significant if this did not coincide with an objective meaning of "chicken." Here it did coincide with one of the dictionary meanings, with the definition in the Department of Agriculture Regulations to which the contract made at least oblique reference, with at least some usage in the trade, with the realities of the market, and with what plaintiff's spokesman had said. Plaintiff asserts it to be equally plain that plaintiff's own subjective intent was to obtain broilers and fryers; the only evidence against this is the material as to market prices and this may not have been sufficiently brought home. In any event it is unnecessary to determine that issue. For plaintiff has the burden of showing that "chicken" was used in the narrower rather than in the broader sense, and this it has not sustained. This opinion constitutes the Court's findings of fact and conclusions of law. Judgment shall be entered dismissing the complaint with costs.

Rule for BNS — court looked to external factors to determine proper interpretation

NOTES AND QUESTIONS

1.   More recently, ambiguity about the meaning of a German word led to litigation in the United States. An officer of Deutsche Bank, a large German bank, told an interviewer from DER SPIEGEL, a German publication, that Deutsche Bank and Bankers Trust Corp., a large U.S. Bank had been were not involved in "Übernahmegespräche." Shortly thereafter, Deutsche Bank took over Bankers Trust. At the time of the interview, the two banks were engaged in preliminary talks about the takeover.

After the takeover a group of investors sued in New York claiming damages for false and misleading statements made in violation of United States securities laws. They claimed that the German term "Übernahmegespräche" is the equivalent of the English term "takeover talks" (which is its literal translation) and that the parties were clearly engaged in takeover talks at the time of the interview. The defendants claimed that "Übernahmegespräche" is not the equivalent of the English "takeover talks." They said that the English term "takeover talks" encompasses any talks about a corporate takeover, whereas, the German term, "Übernahmegespräche" is used only to describe formal and structured talks in which the parties share confidential information.

In April, 2002, a federal court refused to grant the defendants a summary judgment, saying that the meaning of the word was a question of fact that would have to be decided at trial. *Buxbaum v. Deutsche Bank AG*, 196 F. Supp.2d 367 (S.D.N.Y. 2002). The case was thereafter settled, but only after the parties had conducted extensive (and expensive) discovery. *See Buxbaum v. Deutsche Bank AG*, 216 F.R.D. 72 (S.D.N.Y. 2003).

2. The Supreme Court of Delaware has explained the principles governing contract interpretation as follows:

> The principles governing contract interpretation are well settled. Contracts must be construed as a whole, to give effect to the intentions of the parties. Where the contract language is clear and unambiguous, the parties' intent is ascertained by giving the language its ordinary and usual meaning. Courts consider extrinsic evidence to interpret the agreement only if there is an ambiguity in the contract. *Northwestern Nat'l. Ins. Co. v. Esmark, Inc.*, 672 A.2d 41, 43 (Del. 1996).

The court must determine whether a contract is ambiguous by reviewing the entire contract. *Pisano v. Delaware Solid Waste Auth.*, 2006 WL 3457686 (Del. Super. Ct. 2006). "Ambiguity only exists when the contract's terms are 'reasonably or fairly susceptible of different interpretations' or if the terms may have more than one meaning." *Id.* (quoting *Rhone-Poulenc Basic Chemicals Co. v. American Motorists, Ins. Co.*, 616 A.2d 1192, 1195 (Del.Supr. 1992)). The court will not create ambiguity where the ordinary meaning of the terms leaves no room for uncertainty. *Id.* (citing *Rhoune*, 616 A.2d at 1197). "If the language is clear and unequivocal, the parties are bound by its plain meaning." *Id.* (citing *Emmons v. Hartford Underwriters Ins. Co.*, 697 A.2d 742, 745 (Del. 1997)).

3. The four-corners rule is, in many ways, the product of the objective theory of contracts that was introduced in Chapter 1 and that underlies many of the other concepts covered in following chapters. The objective theory of contracts is the bedrock of Anglo-American, common-law contract doctrine. It stands in marked contrast to the approach of jurisdictions governed by the civil law. For example, the German Civil Code, section 133, provides, in translation: "In the interpretation of a declaration of will, the real intention is to be ascertained, and the literal sense of what is expressed is not to be followed." Similarly, the French Civil Code, article 1156, states "One must in agreement seek what the common intention of the contracting parties was, rather than pay attention to the literal meaning of terms." Thinking back on Justice Traynor's opinion in the *Pacific Gas and Electric* case, was he embracing the civil law system and rejecting the common-law objective theory of contracts?

4. A fairly recent California case may have significant effects on the way contract interpretation cases are decided. The court in *City of Hope Nat'l Med. Ctr. v. Genentech*, 43 Cal.4th 375, 181 P.3d 142, 75 Cal.Rptr.3d 333 (Cal. 2008), questioned the role juries should play in determining the validity of conflicting extrinsic evidence and how the resulting ambiguities should be construed. The court held that the jury could properly decide both issues or decide the evidence

question alone and allow the judge to decide against whom the conflict should be interpreted. So drafters wishing to avoid jury interpretation of a contract may want to include boilerplate that provides for arbitration or judicial review of conflicting evidence.

5. It is fairly common for contract boilerplate to include an acknowledgement that the document has been mutually negotiated in an attempt to block application of the maxim that ambiguities are to be construed against the drafter. Whether or not such a self-serving provision will be enforced will depend upon the facts of each case; but the argument can only be made if the provision is present.

6. *Is a burrito a sandwich?* The question was litigated in Worchester, Mass., in 2006. When a shopping center that already leased space to a Panera bakery decided to lease space to Qdoba Mexican Grill, Panera pointed to a restrictive use covenant in its lease that prohibited the center from leasing to another sandwich shop. Panera took the position that a burrito was the Mexican equivalent of a sandwich and took the matter to court, seeking an injunction to prevent Qdoba from setting up its operations. Expert witnesses from the culinary world submitted declarations on both sides of the issue. The court ruled that a burrito is not a sandwich. *See* Jenn Abelson, *Arguments Spread Thick: Rivals Aren't Serving Same Food, Judge Rules,* WORCHESTER GLOBE (November 10, 2006). Thinking about the "objectivity" of the objective theory of contracts, one may wonder if the decision would have been the same in Imperial Beach, California, or Tucson, Arizona. And what about the humble "wrap"? Is that a sandwich? It sure looks like a burrito.

7. Judge Posner once posited that the goals of a system of contract interpretation should be to minimize transaction costs. He divides these transaction costs into two types or stages of costs, drafting-stage costs and litigation stage costs. Faced with a gap in meaning caused by an omission or ambiguity in the parties' drafting of the contract, he describes five approaches that the court might take, each with attendant costs and benefits:

1. Try to determine what the parties really meant; assume that they had covered the issue but failed to incorporate it into the contract.

2. Try to determine what resolution the parties would have agreed to if they had thought about the issue when negotiating the contract.

3. Pick the economically efficient solution and assume that is what the parties intended.

4. Treat the matter as a toss-up and use some rule like "construe the contract against the drafter" to resolve the matter.

5. Pretend that written agreements are always complete integrations and exclude all other evidence.

Richard A. Posner, *The Law and Economics of Contract Interpretation*, 83 TEX. L. REV. 1581 (2005). Which approach do you think is superior? Why?

8.   In *Individual Healthcare Specialists, Inc. v. BlueCross BlueShield of Tennessee, Inc.*, 566 S.W.3d 671 (Tenn. 2019), one of the issues being litigated involved an indemnity provision that was substantially the same as the one from *Pacific Gas* which began this chapter. Individual Healthcare Specialists, Inc. (IHS) argued that an inter-party indemnity provision was a "key issue" during their negotiations with BlueCross (BC), because IHS (a much smaller corporation) wanted to ensure they could recover attorney fees from BC in case of litigation. BC argues that "if the parties wanted to impose fee-shifting obligations in litigation between themselves, it was incumbent on them to adopt a contractual provision clearly and unequivocally doing so." The Tennessee Supreme Court agreed with BC, and held that the parties' agreement failed to do so.

The question before the court was whether the language in the indemnity provision was sufficiently specific enough to apply to the recovery of attorney fees in this inter-party lawsuit, which the court ultimately held it was not. It is interesting to note that in the 50+ years from *Pacific Gas* to *BlueCross*, attorneys are still drafting indemnity clauses that are ambiguous as to whether they are third-party, or inter-party clauses. There is a lot of bad lawyering going on out there, and you should focus on how to avoid this and similar problems, because these clauses should not have to go all the way to the Supreme Courts of various states.

(a)   How should you draft an indemnity clause if your client wants to indemnify only third parties, to ensure you avoid this issue?

(b)   How should you draft an indemnity clause if your client wants to indemnify the other party to the agreement, to ensure you avoid this issue?

(c)   Should one have to specify if attorneys' fees are within the scope of indemnity? Historically, attorneys' fees have been treated differently than other forms of damages in the United States. Do you think that distinction makes sense?

LAWYERING SKILLS PROBLEM

This is less of a problem than a story that illustrates how important punctuation can be to contract interpretation—and how a misplaced comma cost one company $2.13 million:

In 2002, Rogers Communications Inc. signed a contract with Aliant Inc., meaning to have entered into a long term agreement at a favorable rate. In 2005 they were surprised, therefore, when Aliant implemented a rate hike and were supported in this effort by the Canadian regulatory body with jurisdiction over the matter.

On page 7 of the contract a provision stated that the agreement "shall continue in force for a period of five years from the date it is made, and thereafter for successive five year terms, unless and until terminated by one year prior notice in writing by either party."

The problem, you see, is with the second comma in the quoted provision, which makes the contract terminable "at any time, without cause, upon one-year's written notice" in the words of the Canadian regulators. Without the second comma, the termination provision would apply only to successive terms, not to the original five-year term, which appears to be what the folks at Rogers Communication had in mind. But Aliant read the contract and sought to enforce its literal terms, and the regulators agreed.

The lesson is clear. Due to the parol evidence rule and the four corners rule, careful wording and punctuation in contracts is critical to transactional practice, and mistakes in these areas provide ample fodder for litigation over the interpretation of contracts.

Attention to detail is essential to the successful practice of law.

CHAPTER 16

WARRANTY LIABILITY – *Only under UCC*

■ ■ ■

Warranties

A warranty is a promise that certain facts are true. Warranties can be express (based on statements of a party) or implied (based on conduct of a party or by operation of law).

A breached or incorrect warranty will support an action for damages. The measure of damages is the difference between (a) the value of the contract performance as warranted and (b) the value of the contract performance as it was actually performed. The non breaching party may also be able to recover additional amounts (known as consequential or incidental damages) under rules discussed in later chapters.

PRACTICE TIP

Warranties are generally drafted in this form:

"[Buyer, Seller, other defined term] warrants that [warranted facts carefully stated as to scope and substance]."

Just about any statement of present or past fact can be warranted, and warranties are often coupled with representations (which, if incorrect, support recision of the contract and possibly tort damages, including punitive damages). Typical representations and warranties in business transactions include that (1) the party is duly organized, in good standing, and authorized to enter in the transaction, (2) the transaction is not a breach of any other agreement and does not violate the law, (3) a seller or lessor has good title to all assets being sold or leased, and those assets are free of liens and encumbrances, (4) all material facts have been disclosed, and (5) goods being sold conform to certain standards.

Unlike representations, which are focused on the truth of the matter stated, warranties are really about allocating risk, which implicates pricing. In other words, when thinking about the warranty function of a provision, the focus is on who bears the loss if the fact does not exist as warranted, not whether or not it is true. The amount of risk impacts the purchase price or interest rate to be charged. This is different from a representation, which is wholly concerned with whether a fact is true or not, a binary go/no-go

---

> *function that may allow a party to rescind the contract and face no*
> *obligation to close the transaction. Thus, it may be appropriate for*
> *a party to make a warranty but not a representation concerning the*
> *particular fact at issue.*

The U.C.C. Approach

In a sale of goods contract covered by the Uniform Commercial Code, any "affirmation of fact or promise made by the seller to the buyer which relates to the goods and becomes part of the basis of the bargain creates an express warranty that the goods shall conform to the affirmation or promise." U.C.C. § 2–313(1)(a). This approach blurs the distinction between the classic definitions of representations, warranties, and covenants.

As stated in *Daugherty v. American Honda Motor Co.*, 144 Cal. App. 4th 824, 830, 51 Cal. Rptr. 3d 118 (2006):

> A warranty is a contractual promise from the seller that the goods conform to the promise. If they do not, the buyer is entitled to recover the difference between the value of the goods accepted by the buyer and the value of the goods had they been as warranted. A seller may limit its liability for defective goods by disclaiming or modifying a warranty. The general rule is that an express warranty does not cover repairs made after the applicable time or mileage periods have elapsed . . . . Several courts have expressly rejected the proposition that a latent defect, discovered outside the limits of a written warranty, may form the basis for a valid express warranty claim [even] if the warrantor knew of the defect at the time of sale. [internal citations and quotation marks omitted.—Eds.]

There are two major questions that arise under § 2–313:

(1) Is the purported warranty an "affirmation of fact" (2–313(a)) and not just puffing? The cases on this point are in conflict and often this may appear to be decided on the basis of court's view of the equities.

(2) What does the statute mean by the requirement that the purported warranty be part of the "basis of the bargain?" This requires a showing of knowledge of the warranty and reliance on the warranty. Generally speaking, the case law provides a rebuttable presumption of reliance.

Finally, keep in mind that warranty liability is strict liability in contract. If a party makes a warranty, it is bound even though the fact or promise that was warranted was out of that party's control. In fact, that is the whole point of a warranty. Under the U.C.C., warranties are presumed to relate to the condition of the goods when they are delivered unless the contract provides otherwise.

PRACTICE TIP: DISCLAIMERS

Consider including a broad provision that eliminates or disclaims as far as legally possible all express or implied warranties except as expressly provided for in the contract. But see U.C.C. § 2–316(1) (disclaimer or limitation of warranty inconsistent with an express warranty will be inoperative if consistent construction not reasonable); U.C.C. § 2–316(2)–(3) (disclaimer of implied warranties with specific disclaimers, general disclaimers, buyer inspections, and course of performance). A disclaimer of warranties, however, may be subject to court scrutiny that may reflect some hostility to overreaching disclaimers and releases obtained by economically dominant parties. You should also include a merger or integration clause so that evidence of any prior or contemporaneous statements that could be construed as representations or warranties will be excluded.

A. EXPRESS WARRANTY

ROYAL BUSINESS MACHINES V. LORRAINE CORP.

United States Court of Appeals, Seventh Circuit
633 F.2d 34 (1980)

[1] This is an appeal from a judgment of the district court entered after a bench trial awarding Michael L. Booher and Lorraine Corp. (Booher) $1,171,216.16 in compensatory and punitive damages against Litton Business Systems, Inc. and Royal Business Machines, Inc. (Royal). The judgment further awarded Booher attorneys' fees of $156,800.00. It denied, for want of consideration, the recovery by Royal of a $596,921.33 indebtedness assessed against Booher earlier in the proceedings in a summary judgment. The judgment also granted Royal a set-off of $12,020.00 for an unpaid balance due on computer typewriters.

[2] The case arose from commercial transactions extending over a period of 18 months between Royal and Booher in which Royal sold and Booher purchased 114 RBC I and 14 RBC II plain paper copying machines. In mid-August 1976, Booher filed suit against Royal in the Indiana courts claiming breach of warranties and fraud. On September 1, 1976, Royal sued Booher on his financing agreements in the district court and also removed the state litigation to the district court where the cases were consolidated.

[3] The issues in the cases arise under Indiana common law and under the UCC as adopted in Indiana. The contentions urged by Royal on appeal are that:

[handwritten: What Royal argued on appeal]

(1) substantial evidence does not support the findings that Royal made certain express warranties or that it breached any express warranty and, as a matter of law, no warranties were made; and

(2) substantial evidence does not support the findings that Royal breached the implied warranties of merchantability and fitness for a particular purpose; and

(3) substantial evidence does not support the finding that Booher made timely revocation of acceptance of the goods sold; and

(4) substantial evidence does not support the findings upon which the awards of compensatory damages were made and that certain awards constituted a double recovery; and

(5) substantial evidence does not support the findings upon which the awards of punitive damages were made.

[handwritten: Holding]

[4] We reverse and remand for a new trial on the grounds set forth in this opinion.

EXPRESS WARRANTIES

[handwritten: Issue]

[5] We first address the question whether substantial evidence on the record supports the district court's findings that Royal made and breached express warranties to Booher. The trial judge found that Royal Business Machines made and breached the following express warranties: *[handwritten: Trial court found these to be EW]*

[handwritten: All express warranties?]

(1) that the RBC Model I and II machines and their component parts were of high quality; *[handwritten: – opinion]*

(2) that experience and testing had shown that frequency of repairs was very low on such machines and would remain so; *[handwritten: –opinion]*

(3) that replacement parts were readily available; *[handwritten: future goods – NO EW]*

(4) that the cost of maintenance for each RBC machine and cost of supplies was and would remain low, no more than 1/2 cent per copy; *[handwritten: – future goods – NO EW]*

(5) that the RBC machines had been extensively tested and were ready to be marketed; *[handwritten: – factual affirmation]*

(6) that experience and reasonable projections had shown that the purchase of the RBC machines by Mr. Booher and Lorraine Corporation and the leasing of the same to customers would return substantial profits to Booher and Lorraine; *[handwritten: – opinion]*

(7) that the machines were safe and could not cause fires; and *[handwritten: – factual aff (rms)]*

[handwritten: Does it relate to the goods – is it part of the basis of the bargain]

Lorraine says Royal breached the express warranties

(8) that service calls were and would be required for the RBC Model II machine on the average of every 7,000 to 9,000 copies, including preventive maintenance calls. *— factual affirmation*

[6] Substantial evidence supports the court's findings as to Numbers 5, 7, 8, and the maintenance aspect of Number 4, but, as a matter of law, Numbers 1, 2, 3, 6, and the cost of supplies portion of Number 4 cannot be considered express warranties. *— 1, 2, 3, 6 are not EW*

Express warranties governed by UCC 2-313

[7] Paraphrasing UCC § 2–313 as adopted in Indiana, an express warranty is made up of the following elements: (a) an affirmation of fact or promise, (b) that relates to the goods, and (c) becomes a part of the basis of the bargain between the parties. When each of these three elements is present, a warranty is created that the goods shall conform to the affirmation of fact or to the promise. *Rule Proof*

[8] The decisive test for whether a given representation is a warranty or merely an expression of the seller's opinion is whether the seller asserts a fact of which the buyer is ignorant or merely states an opinion or judgment on a matter of which the seller has no special knowledge and on which the buyer may be expected also to have an opinion and to exercise his judgment. General statements to the effect that good are "the best," or are "of good quality," or will "last a lifetime" and be "in perfect condition," are generally regarded as expressions of the seller's opinion or "the puffing of his wares" and do not create an express warranty. *opinion or puffing*

[9] No express warranty was created by Royal's affirmation that both RBC machine models and their component parts were of high quality. This was a statement of the seller's opinion, the kind of "puffing" to be expected in any sales transaction, rather than a positive averment of fact describing a product's capabilities to which an express warranty could attach.

[10] Similarly, the representations by Royal that experience and testing had shown that the frequency of repair was "very low" and would remain so lack the specificity of an affirmation of fact upon which a warranty could be predicated. These representations were statements of the seller's opinion. *Sellers opinion - not warranty*

[11] The statement that replacement parts were readily available is an assertion of fact, but it is not a fact that relates to the goods sold as required by [UCC §] 2–313(1)(a) and is not an express warranty to which the goods were to conform. Neither is the statement about the future costs of supplies being 1/2 cent per copy an assertion of fact that relates to the goods sold, so the statement cannot constitute the basis of an express warranty. *future*

[12] It was also erroneous to find that an express warranty was created by Royal's assurances to Booher that purchase of the RBC machines would bring him substantial profits. Such a representation does not describe the goods within the meaning of UCC § 2–313(1)(b), nor is the representation

an affirmation of fact relating to the goods under UCC § 2–313(1)(a). It is merely sales talk and the expression of the seller's opinion. *See Regal Motor Products v. Bender*, 102 Ohio App. 447, 139 N.E.2d 463, 465 (1956) (representation that goods were "readily saleable" and that the demand for them would create a market was not a warranty).

[13] On the other hand, the assertion that the machines could not cause fires is an assertion of fact relating to the goods, and substantial evidence in the record supports the trial judge's findings that the assertion was made by Royal to Booher.[1] The same may be said for the assertion that the machines were tested and ready to be marketed. *See Bemidji Sales Barn v. Chatfield*, 312 Minn. 11, 250 N.W.2d 185 (1977) (seller's representation that cattle "had been vaccinated for shipping fever and were ready for the farm" constituted an express warranty). *See generally* R. Anderson, Uniform Commercial Code § 2–313:36 (2d ed. 1970) (author asserts that seller who sells with seal of approval of a third person, *e.g.*, a testing laboratory, makes an express warranty that the product has been tested and approved and is liable if the product was in fact not approved). The record supports the district court's finding that Royal represented that the machines had been tested.[2]

[14] As for findings 8 and the maintenance portion of Number 4, Royal's argument that those statements relate to predictions for the future and cannot qualify as warranties is unpersuasive.[3] An expression of future capacity or performance can constitute an express warranty. In *Teter v. Shultz*, 110 Ind. App. 541, 39 N.E.2d 802, 804 (1942), the Indiana courts held that a seller's statement that dairy cows would give six gallons of milk per day was an affirmation of fact by the seller relating to the goods. It was not a statement of value nor was it merely a statement of the seller's opinion. The Indiana courts have also found that an express warranty was created by a seller's representation that a windmill was capable of furnishing power to grind 20 to 30 bushels of grain per hour in a moderate

---

[1]   Michael Booher testified at trial that in February or March of 1975 he called the service department at Royal Typewriter Company and spoke with either Bruce Lewis, national service manager, or with Joe Miller. Booher testified that he told the Royal representative that he had received a report of a fire in an RBC I machine at a customer's office. Booher then testified. "They told me that that couldn't happen." (Tr. Vol. IV. pp. 457–59).

[2]   The trial court's findings speak of "RBC machines" with reference to the testing warranty. The court's specific findings, however, refer only to the RBC II machine. On retrial, it would clarify matters if the specific machine intended were named.

Michael Booher testified at trial that Tom Gavel had assured Booher the Royal Bond Copier machine had been tested: "He [Gavel] said. 'They have been well tested.' and said, 'They are great machines.' " (Tr. Vol. III, p. 292).

Booher also testified that Jack Airey, a Royal representative, had stated at a promotional meeting that the RBC 11 had been extensively tested and was ready to market: "They [Royal] were now ready to market it [RBC II]; that it had been extensively tested." (Tr. Vol. 111, p. 317).

[3]   In Number 4, the trial court found that the appellant warranted that the cost of maintenance for each RBC machine and cost of supplies was and would remain low, no more than 1/2 cent per copy, and in Number 8 that service calls were and would be required for the RBC Model II machine approximately every 7,000 to 9,000 copies.

wind and with a very light wind would pump an abundance of water. *Smith v. Borden*, 160 Ind. 223, 66 N.E. 681 (1903). Further, in *General Supply and Equipment Co. v. Phillips, supra*, the Texas courts upheld the following express warranties made by a seller of roof panels: (1) that tests show no deterioration in 5 years of normal use; (2) that the roofing panels won't turn black or discolor . . . even after years of exposure; and (3) that the panels will not burn, rot, rust, or mildew. *Snow's Laundry and Dry Cleaning v. Georgia Power Co.*, 61 Ga. App. 402, 6 S.E.2d 159 (1939), impliedly recognized that a warranty as to future gas consumption following installation of gas equipment was possible. In holding that no warranty was created in that particular case, the Georgia court noted: "The statements made by Spencer were denominated by him as estimates, and nowhere did he warrant or guarantee that the gas consumption would not exceed $230.50 per month." 61 Ga. App. at 405, 6 S.E.2d at 162. See *Matlack, Inc. v. Butler Mfg. Co.*, 253 F. Supp. 972 (E.D. Pa. 1966).

[15] Whether a seller affirmed a fact or made a promise amounting to a warranty is a question of fact reserved for the trier of fact. Substantial evidence in the record supports the finding that Royal made the assertion to Booher that maintenance cost for the machine would run 1/2 cent per copy and that this assertion was not an estimate but an assertion of a fact of performance capability.[4]

[16] Finding Number 8, that service calls on the RBC II would be required every 7,000 to 9,000 copies, relates to performance capability and could constitute the basis of an express warranty. There is substantial evidence in the record to support the finding that this assertion was also made.[5]

[17] While substantial evidence supports the trial court's findings as to the making of those four affirmations of fact or promises, the district court failed to make the further finding that they became part of the basis of the bargain. Ind. Code § 26–1–2–313(1) (1976). While Royal may have

---

[4] Michael Booher testified at trial that Mr. Gavel, a Royal representative, told Booher in April 1974, at a meeting in Booher's Indianapolis office, that cost for service on the RBC I machine would be a half cent. (Tr. Vol. 111, pp. 29498). Booher further testified that in July 1974, at a meeting in Chicago sponsored by Royal, he was told by Jack Airey, a Royal representative, that maintenance costs for the RBC II machine would be the same as on the RBC I, except that service costs should actually be a little less due to the reliability of the machine. (Tr. Vol. 111. pp. 320–21).

Gavel testified by deposition taken on May 27, 1977, which was admitted into evidence at trial, that he told Booher that service costs for the RBC I machine would be half a cent (Gavel Dep., p. 28). He further testified in reference to the costs quoted to dealers on the RBC II machines that "[n]obody ever implied they were estimates." (Gavel Dep., p. 110).

[5] Michael Booher testified at trial that at the Chicago meeting Royal representatives, Jack Airey and Roland Schultz, told him that the RBC II machines would require a service call, a customer-related call about every nine thousand copies, and that "we would have preventative maintenance calls about every twenty to twenty-one thousand copies. . . ." (Tr. Vol. III, p. 325).

made such affirmations to Booher, the question of his knowledge or reliance is another matter.[6]

[18] This case is complicated by the fact that it involved a series of sales transactions between the same parties over approximately an 18-month period and concerned two different machines. The situations of the parties, their knowledge and reliance, may be expected to change in light of their experience during that time. An affirmation of fact which the buyer from his experience knows to be untrue cannot form a part of the basis of the bargain. Therefore, as to each purchase, Booher's expanding knowledge of the capacities of the copying machines would have to be considered in deciding whether Royal's representations were part of the basis of the bargain. The same representations that could have constituted an express warranty early in the series of transactions might not have qualified as an express warranty in a later transaction if the buyer had acquired independent knowledge as to the fact asserted.

[19] The trial court did not indicate that it considered whether the warranties could exist and apply to each transaction in the series. Such an analysis is crucial to a just determination. Its absence renders the district court's findings insufficient on the issue of the breach of express warranties.

[20] Since a retrial on the questions of the breach of express warranties and the extent of damages is necessary, we offer the following observations. The court must consider whether the machines were defective upon delivery. Breach occurs only if the goods are defective upon delivery and not if the goods later become defective through abuse or neglect.

---

[6]   The requirement that a statement be part of the basis of the bargain in order to constitute an express warranty is essentially a reliance requirement and is inextricably intertwined with the initial determination as to whether given language may constitute an express warranty since affirmations, promises and descriptions tend to become a part of the basis of the bargain. It was the intention of the drafters of the U.C.C. not to require a strong showing of reliance. In fact, they envisioned that all statements of the seller become part of the basis of the bargain unless clear affirmative proof is shown to the contrary. *See* Official Comments 3 and 8 to U.C.C. § 2–313. Sessa v. Riegle, 427 F. Supp. 760, 766 (E.D. Pa. 1977), *aff'd without op.*, 568 F.2d 770 (3d Cir. 1978).

Cf. Woodruff v. Clark County Farm Bureau Coop. Ass'n, 153 Ind. App. 31, 286 N.E.2d 188 (1972) where the court stated: "Whether such assertions [statements by the seller] constituted express warranties and whether [the buyer] relied upon these assertions are material issues of fact to be determined by the trier of fact. 286 N.E.2d at 199; Stamm v. Wilder Travel Trailers, 44 Ill. App. 3d 530, 358 N E.2d 382 (1976) (reliance necessary in order to give rise to an express warranty).

"(F)or all practical purposes it is suggested that no great change was wrought by the Code. Whether one speaks of reliance or basis of the bargain, little difference exists between the two. In neither case should the statement be required to have been the sole factor leading the buyer to purchase. In either case, the statement should, at least, be one of such factors. What is really crucial is whether the statement was made as an affirmation of fact, the goods did not live up to the statement and the defect was not so apparent that the buyer could not be held to have discovered it for himself." Bender's U.C.C. Service, Dusenberg & King, *Sales and Bulk Transfers* § 6.01, n. 2. (Matthew Bender & Co. 1980).

[21] In considering the promise relating to the cost of maintenance, the district court should determine at what stage Booher's own knowledge and experience prevented him from blindly relying on the representations of Royal. A similar analysis is needed in examining the representation concerning fire hazard in the RBC I machines. The court also should determine when that representation was made. If not made until February 1975, the representation could not have been the basis for sales made prior to that date.

Remanded for an new trial regarding the Statements that had express warranty potential

NOTES AND QUESTIONS

1. How did the court justify its conclusion that no express warranty was created by the statements that the machines "were of high quality?" Are you convinced by this? Suppose the seller had said, "This is Grade A merchandise." Suppose the seller had said, "These are Grade A eggs." Would these statements create express warranties?

2. In *Jones v. Kellner*, 5 Ohio App. 3d 242, 451 N.E.2d 548, 36 U.C.C. Rep. Serv. 784 (1982), a private party seller's oral statement that a used car was "in 'A-1' condition mechanically" was held to be an express warranty. In *Chrysler-Plymouth City Inc. v. Guerrero*, 620 S.W.2d 700 (Tex. Civ. App. 1981) the court held that the words, "top quality" constituted an express warranty.

3. How does the court reach the conclusion that the statement that replacement parts were readily available was not an express warranty? Would the court's reasoning support a conclusion that the statement, "replacement parts for this machine are readily available," is not an express warranty but "this is a machine for which replacement parts are readily available" is such a warranty? Regardless of how the statement was actually phrased, what do you suppose the seller was really trying to tell the buyer?

4. How does the court reach the conclusion that two identical statements could be made with respect to the first copier purchased and the last, and an express warranty would be created with respect to the first copier but not with respect to the last?

5. What does U.C.C. § 2–313 mean when it says the affirmation or promise must become "part of the basis of the bargain?" Under the old, now superseded Uniform Sales Act a statement could become an express warranty only "if the buyer purchases the goods relying thereon."

———

BAYLINER MARINE CORP. v. CROW

Supreme Court of Virginia
257 Va. 121, 509 S.E.2d 499 (1999)

[1] In this appeal, the dispositive issue is whether there was sufficient evidence to support the trial court's ruling that the manufacturer of a sport fishing boat breached an express warranty and implied warranties of merchantability and fitness for a particular purpose.

[2] In the summer of 1989, John R. Crow was invited by John Atherton, then a sales representative for Tidewater Yacht Agency, Inc. (Tidewater), to ride on a new model sport fishing boat known as a 3486 Trophy Convertible, manufactured by Bayliner Marine Corporation (Bayliner). At that time, Tidewater was the exclusive authorized dealer in southeastern Virginia for this model Bayliner boat. During an excursion lasting about 20 minutes, Crow piloted the boat for a short period of time but was not able to determine its speed because there was no equipment on board for such testing.

[3] When Crow asked Atherton about the maximum speed of the boat, Atherton explained that he had no personal experience with the boat or information from other customers concerning the boat's performance. Therefore, Atherton consulted two documents described as "prop matrixes," which were included by Bayliner in its dealer's manual.

[4] Atherton gave Crow copies of the "prop matrixes," which listed the boat models offered by Bayliner and stated the recommended propeller sizes, gear ratios, and engine sizes for each model. The "prop matrixes" also listed the maximum speed for each model. The 3486 Trophy Convertible was listed as having a maximum speed of 30 miles per hour when equipped with a size "20x20" or "20x19" propeller. The boat Crow purchased did not have either size propeller but, instead, had a size "20x17" propeller.

[5] At the bottom of one of the "prop matrixes" was the following disclaimer: "This data is intended for comparative purposes only, and is available without reference to weather conditions or other variables. All testing was done at or near sea level, with full fuel and water tanks, and approximately 600 lb. passenger and gear weight."

[6] Atherton also showed Crow a Bayliner brochure describing the 1989 boat models, including the 3486 Trophy Convertible. The brochure included a picture of that model fully rigged for offshore fishing, accompanied by the statement that this model "delivers the kind of performance you need to get to the prime offshore fishing grounds."

[7] In August 1989, Crow entered into a written contract for the purchase of the 3486 Trophy Convertible in which he had ridden. The purchase price was $120,000, exclusive of taxes. The purchase price included various equipment to be installed by Tidewater including a

Bought boat with smaller propeller and added 2000 lbs of equipment

generator, a cockpit cover, a "Bimini top," a winch, a spotlight, radar, a navigation system, an icemaker, fishing outriggers, an automatic pilot system, extra fuel gauges, a second radio, and air conditioning and heating units. The total weight of the added equipment was about 2,000 pounds. Crow did not test drive the boat after the additional equipment was installed or at any other time prior to taking delivery.

After using the boat he noticed it was slow

[8] When Crow took delivery of the boat in September 1989, he piloted it onto the Elizabeth River. He noticed that the boat's speed measuring equipment, which was installed in accordance with the contract terms, indicated that the boat's maximum speed was 13 miles per hour. Crow immediately returned to Tidewater and reported the Problem.

only max of 13 mph. Reported issue to Tidewater

The performance presented was incorrect

[9] During the next 12 to 14 months, while Crow retained ownership and possession of the boat, Tidewater made numerous repairs and adjustments to the boat in an attempt to increase its speed capability. Despite these efforts, the boat consistently achieved a maximum speed of only 17 miles per hour, except for one period following an engine modification when it temporarily reached a speed of about 24 miles per hour. In July 1990, a representative from Bayliner wrote Crow a letter stating that the performance representations made at the time of purchase were incorrect, and that 23 to 25 miles per hour was the maximum speed the boat could achieve.

After repairs the boat could only go max 17mph

[10] In 1992, Crow filed a suit against Tidewater, Bayliner, and Brunswick Corporation, the manufacturer of the boat's diesel engines. Crow alleged, among other things, that Bayliner breached express warranties, and implied warranties of merchantability and fitness for a particular purpose.

[11] At a bench trial in 1994, Crow, Atherton, and Gordon W. Shelton, III, Tidewater's owner, testified that speed is a critical quality in boats used for offshore sport fishing in the Tidewater area of Virginia because of the distance between the coast and the offshore fishing grounds. According to these witnesses, a typical offshore fishing site in that area is 90 miles from the coast. Therefore, the speed at which the boat can travel to and from fishing sites has a major impact on the amount of time left in a day for fishing.

[12] Crow testified that because of the boat's slow speed, he could not use the boat for offshore fishing, that he had no other use for it, and that he would not have purchased the boat if he had known that its maximum speed was 23 to 25 miles per hour. Crow testified that he had not used the boat for fishing since 1991 or 1992. He admitted, however, that between September 1989, and September 1994, the boat's engines had registered about 850 hours of use. Bob Schey, Bayliner's manager of yacht testing, testified that a pleasure boat in a climate such as Virginia's typically would register 150 engine hours per year.

Crows argument

[13] The trial court entered judgment in favor of Crow against Bayliner on the counts of breach of express warranty and breach of implied warranties of merchantability and fitness for a particular purpose. The court awarded Crow damages of $135,000, plus prejudgment interest from June 1993. The court explained that the $135,000 award represented the purchase price of the boat, and about $15,000 in "damages" for a portion of the expenses Crow claimed in storing, maintaining, insuring, and financing the boat.

[14] On appeal, we review the evidence in the light most favorable to Crow, the prevailing party at trial. We will uphold the trial court's judgment unless it is plainly wrong or without evidence to support it. [We reverse.—Eds.]

[15] Crow argues that the "prop matrixes" he received created an express warranty by Bayliner that the boat he purchased was capable of a maximum speed of 30 miles per hour. We disagree.

[16] [U.C.C.] § 2–313 provides, in relevant part:

Express warranties by the seller are created as follows:

(a) Any affirmation of fact or promise made by the seller to the buyer which relates to the goods and becomes part of the basis of the bargain creates an express warranty that the goods shall conform to the affirmation or promise.

(b) Any description of the goods which is made a part of the basis of the bargain creates an express warranty that the goods shall conform to the description.

[17] The issue whether a particular affirmation of fact made by the seller constitutes an express warranty is generally a question of fact. See id., Official Comment 3. In Daughtrey, we examined whether a jeweler's statement on an appraisal form constituted an express warranty. We held that the jeweler's description of the particular diamonds being purchased as "v.v.s. quality" constituted an express warranty that the diamonds were, in fact, of that grade.

[18] Unlike the representation in Daughtrey, however, the statements in the "prop matrixes" provided by Bayliner did not relate to the particular boat purchased by Crow, or to one having substantially similar characteristics. By their plain terms, the figures stated in the "prop matrixes" referred to a boat with different sized propellers that carried equipment weighing substantially less than the equipment on Crow's boat. Therefore, we conclude that the statements contained in the "prop matrixes" did not constitute an express warranty by Bayliner about the performance capabilities of the particular boat purchased by Crow.

[19] Crow also contends that Bayliner made an express warranty regarding the boat's maximum speed in the statement in Bayliner's sales brochure that this model boat "delivers the kind of performance you need to get to the prime offshore fishing grounds." While the general rule is that a description of the goods that forms a basis of the bargain constitutes an express warranty, [U.C.C.] § 2–313(2) directs that "a statement purporting to be merely the seller's opinion or commendation of the goods does not create a warranty."

[20] The statement made by Bayliner in its sales brochure is merely a commendation of the boat's performance and does not describe a specific characteristic or feature of the boat. The statement simply expressed the manufacturer's opinion concerning the quality of the boat's performance and did not create an express warranty that the boat was capable of attaining a speed of 30 miles per hour. Therefore, we conclude that the evidence does not support the trial court's finding that Bayliner breached an express warranty made to Crow.

[The court's discussions of the implied warranty issues are reprinted later in this chapter.—Eds.]

QUESTIONS

1. If you were representing Bayliner, what additional language would you want to add to the prop matrixes to beef up the disclaimer?

2. Assuming that the disclaimer keeps the prop matrixes from being an express warranty by Bayliner, is it still possible to make a good argument that by giving the buyer the document, the dealer made a warranty?

3. Would there have been a breach of an express warranty if it were shown that when Bayliner did the tests upon which the prop matrixes were based, the boat had defective speed measuring equipment and was only making 25 mph rather than the 30 mph stated in the matrixes? Would Bayliner be liable? Would the dealer?

4. How might Crow have been able to overcome the argument that the prop matrixes related to boats not configured the way his was?

PROBLEM 16-1

Buyer went to Seller's used car lot looking for a car. She found one she liked and asked Seller: "How are the tires on this one?"

Seller replied: "It has good tires."

Buyer decided to take the car, and she and Seller signed a contract that was silent as to the subject of warranties.

A few days later, the right front tire, which had been defectively re-treaded, blew out while Buyer was on the Interstate. Buyer was injured and sued Seller, alleging breach of an express warranty. At trial Seller proved that he bought the tires from a reputable dealer who warranted to Seller that the tires were "better than new." Seller also proved that he had bought at least 200 tires from the same dealer and had never before had problems with them. The court found that the written contract was NOT a "fully integrated agreement."

Which is Seller's best defense? Why?

(a) The written contract didn't say anything about the tires.

(b) The buyer didn't rely on his statement. — *Don't need to rely*

(c) The seller took all reasonable precautions to insure that the tires were in fact good tires. *Doesn't matter— warranty liability is strict liability*

(d) The statement was "just puffing" rather than an affirmation of fact.

PROBLEM 16-2

Grower bought several bags of seeds, planning to grow his crop in the normal manner, using 600 pounds of fertilizer per acre. When he got home, he *— after the sale* opened one of the bags and found inside a brochure that stated (among other things): "These are new and improved seeds. Because of advances in seed science, these seeds require only 300 pounds of fertilizer per acre, half the amount required with ordinary seeds." Grower followed the directions and used only 300 pounds of fertilizer. His crop failed. Surveying his neighbors, he discovered that those who believed the brochure and used only 300 pounds of fertilizer per acre also had crop failures, while those who ignored it and used 600 pounds had successful crops. Does Grower have a cause of action for breach of express warranty? *See* Official Comment 7 to U.C.C. § 2–313. *No, b/c it was included after the fact*

Cannot be after contract is formed b/c it is not basis of the bargain

B. IMPLIED WARRANTY OF MERCHANTABILITY

Read carefully U.C.C. § 2–314 and the comments. Then read carefully Restatement (Third) of Torts §§ 1–3, and 21, which are reproduced below. How are they alike? How do they differ? Which provides the most protection?

Restatement (Third) of Torts

§ 1. *Liability of Commercial Seller or Distributor for Harm Caused by Defective Products.*

One engaged in the business of selling or otherwise distributing products who sells or distributes a defective product is subject to liability for harm to persons or property caused by the defect.

§ 2. *Categories of Product Defect*

A product is defective when, at the time of sale or distribution, it contains a manufacturing defect, is defective in design, or is defective because of inadequate instructions or warnings. A product:

> (a) contains a manufacturing defect when the product departs from its intended design even though all possible care was exercised in the preparation and marketing of the product;

> (b) is defective in design when the foreseeable risks of harm posed by the product could have been reduced or avoided by the adoption of a reasonable alternative design by the seller or other distributor, or a predecessor in the commercial chain of distribution, and the omission of the alternative design renders the product not reasonably safe;

> (c) is defective because of inadequate instructions or warnings when the foreseeable risks of harm posed by the product could have been reduced or avoided by the provision of reasonable instructions or warnings by the seller or other distributor, or a predecessor in the commercial chain of distribution, and the omission of the instructions or warnings renders the product not reasonably safe.

§ 3. *Circumstantial Evidence Supporting Inference of Product Defect*

It may be inferred that the harm sustained by the plaintiff was caused by a product defect existing at the time of sale or distribution, without proof of a specific defect, when the incident that harmed the plaintiff:

> (a) was of a kind that ordinarily occurs as a result of product defect; and

> (b) was not, in the particular case, solely the result of causes other than product defect existing at the time of sale or distribution.

§ 21. *Definition of "Harm to Persons or Property": Recovery for Economic Loss*

For purposes of this Restatement, harm to persons or property includes economic loss if caused by harm to:

> (a)   the plaintiff's person; or

> (b)   the person of another when harm to the other interferes with an interest of the plaintiff protected by tort law; or

> (c)   the plaintiff's property other than the defective product itself.

goods [handwritten]

merchant seller [handwritten]

PROBLEM 16-3

Consumer buys a dozen eggs at the grocery store. When he gets them home, he discovers they are rotten. *— not merchantable* [handwritten]

(a) Does he have a claim under U.C.C. § 2–314? If so, which of the specific tests in U.C.C. § 2–314 does it fail to satisfy?

(b) Does he have a claim under the Restatement (Third) of Torts?

PROBLEM 16-4

Sir Galahad bought a shield from Sir Mordred, a wandering knight who spends most of his time wandering from castle to castle, mooching off the local barons. In the course of his sales pitch, Mordred told Galahad: "this shield will never break." *— opinion or warranty — should be warranty* [handwritten]

The first time Galahad went into combat with the shield, it was shattered by a single blow of his adversary's sword, and Galahad was severely wounded.

Does Galahad have a claim for breach of express warranty, implied warranty of merchantability, neither, or both?

PROBLEM 16-5

merchant? [handwritten]

merchantability? [handwritten]

Samantha purchased a used taxi with 212,000 miles on it from Executive's Taxi Company. Within two weeks after she purchased it, the transmission in the car failed, and Samantha had to spend $1,000 to have it repaired. Samantha sued and alleged a breach of the implied warranty of merchantability.

Can Executive Taxi Company prevail with the argument that no implied warranty of merchantability arose because it was not "a merchant with respect to goods of that kind?" *See* U.C.C. § 2–104. *— have to look at facts* [handwritten]

Merchant [handwritten]

BAYLINER MARINE CORP. v. CROW

Supreme Court of Virginia
257 Va. 121, 509 S.E.2d 499 (1999)

[Please refer back to the facts of the case earlier in this chapter.—Eds.]

Did it breach an implied warranty? [handwritten]

[1] We next consider whether the evidence supports the trial court's conclusion that Bayliner breached an implied warranty of merchantability. Crow asserts that because his boat was not capable of achieving a maximum speed of 30 miles per hour, it was not fit for its ordinary purpose as an offshore sport fishing boat. Bayliner contends in response that, although the boat did not meet the needs of this particular sport fisherman, there was no evidence from which the trial court could conclude that the

Crow never told Atherton he needed the boat for the specific purpose of 30 mph — thus Bayliner did not breach its IW [handwritten]

*[handwritten top margin: * Court finds that Bayliner didn't breach IW b/c no evidence it was not merchantable for offshore fishing, just not 30 mph.]*

boat generally was not merchantable as an offshore fishing boat. We agree with Bayliner's argument.

[2] [U.C.C. §] 2–314 provides that, in all contracts for the sale of goods by a merchant, a warranty is implied that the goods will be merchantable. To be merchantable, the goods must be such as would "pass without objection in the trade" and as "are fit for the ordinary purposes for which such goods are used." [U.C.C.] § 2–314(2)(a),(c). The first phrase concerns whether a "significant segment of the buying public" would object to buying the goods, while the second phrase concerns whether the goods are "reasonably capable of performing their ordinary functions." *Federal Signal Corp. v. Safety Factors, Inc.,* 125 Wash. 2d 413, 886 P.2d 172, 180 (Wash. 1994). In order to prove that a product is not merchantable, the complaining party must first establish the standard of merchantability in the trade. Bayliner correctly notes that the record contains no evidence of the standard of merchantability in the offshore fishing boat trade. Nor does the record contain any evidence supporting a conclusion that a significant portion of the boat-buying public would object to purchasing an offshore fishing boat with the speed capability of the 3486 Trophy Convertible.

[3] Crow, nevertheless, relies on his own testimony that the boat's speed was inadequate for his intended use, and Atherton's opinion testimony that the boat took "a long time" to reach certain fishing grounds in the Gulf Stream off the coast of Virginia. However, this evidence did not address the standard of merchantability in the trade or whether Crow's boat failed to meet that standard. Thus, we hold that Crow failed to prove that the boat would not "pass without objection in the trade" as required by Code § 8.2–314(2)(a).

[handwritten left margin: The boat was fit or the ordinary purposes under 2-314]

[handwritten right margin: no evidence in offshore fishing industry that boat was not merchantable]

[handwritten: SCT reversed Trial court on EW and IW claims]

ADAMS v. AMERICAN CYANAMID CO.

Nebraska Court of Appeals
1 Neb. App. 337, 498 N.W.2d 577 (1992)

[handwritten right: Implied Warranty Case]

I. Introduction

[1] This appeal arises from an action based on theories of strict liability and breach of warranty of merchantability under the Uniform Commercial Code. William Timothy "Tim" Adams and Carol Adams brought suit against American Cyanamid Company and Panhandle cooperative Association for damages sustained to a crop of edible beans which was lost after a herbicide manufactured by American Cyanamid was applied to the Adamses' fields. The jury awarded a judgment for the Adams in the amount of $193,500 against American Cyanamid. American Cyanamid appeals. We affirm in part, and in part reverse and remand for a new trial.

[handwritten left margin: cause of action]

[handwritten right margin: Pro History]

[handwritten bottom: The Adams' brought suit against Cyanamid for damages to a crop of beans. Trial awarded J to Adams. CTA affirmed and reverse and remanded]

II.   Factual Background

[2]   In 1989, Tim Adams planned to grow beans on 860 acres of center-pivot irrigated fields. He sought the services of Glenn Johnson of Servi-Tech crop consultants to inspect his fields, to make recommendations as to fertilizers, herbicides, and seed, and to observe the crop through the growing season. Johnson recommended a combination of the herbicides Eptam and Prowl. Prowl herbicide is manufactured by the defendant, American Cyanamid. Adams purchased these herbicides from Panhandle Co-op, whose employee applied the herbicides at the application rate specified by Johnson. In early June, the fields were planted with great northern and pinto beans.

[3]   At first, the bean crop grew well, but after the first of July, Adams noticed that the plants in field No. 8 began to look weakened, and plants in the other fields followed suit. The beans flourished in a strip of field No. 1 where no herbicide had been applied due to a parked center pivot. The beans also flourished in a 10-acre area of field No. 5 where no herbicide was applied because the sod had recently been brought under cultivation.

[4]   Prowl, the trade name for the herbicide used, is a dinitroaniline herbicide, which can destroy plants by causing a swollen hypocotyl, i.e., the plant's main root stem, and a reduction of the secondary root system.

[5]   Prowl was applied in combination with Eptam, a thiocarbamate herbicide. A thiocarbamate herbicide produces a type of plant injury different from that produced by a dinitroaniline herbicide. A thiocarbamate herbicide causes early leaf effect and lasts in the soil for a few weeks. The Adamses' expert was able to exclude the possibility that Eptam had caused the plant injury.

[6]   The jury entered a general verdict for the Adamses for $193,500, the amount of the lost crop. The jury entered special verdicts finding that the defendant was strictly liable in tort and had breached the warranty of merchantability. The defendant moved for judgment notwithstanding the verdict and for a new trial, which motions were overruled. [This court reverses as to strict liability but affirms on merchantability.—Eds.]

III.   Assignment of Errors

[7]   The defendant's assignments of error may be reduced to the following claims: (1) The court erred in failing to sustain the defendant's motions for a directed verdict and motion for judgment notwithstanding the verdict because there was insufficient evidence for the jury to find that the defendant was strictly liable for the damage to the plaintiffs' crops; (2) the court erred in failing to sustain the defendant's motions for a directed verdict and motion for judgment notwithstanding the verdict because there was insufficient evidence for the jury to find that the herbicide sold to the plaintiffs was not merchantable; (3) the court erred in instructing the jury

to determine whether the disclaimer was conspicuous, contrary to Neb. UCC § 1–201(10) (Cum. Supp. 1990); (4) the court erred in failing to sustain the defendant's motions for a directed verdict and motion for judgment notwithstanding the verdict because the herbicide label contained a conspicuous disclaimer of the implied warranty of merchantability as a matter of law; (5) the court erred in failing to sustain the defendant's motions for a directed verdict and motion for judgment notwithstanding the verdict because the plaintiffs' knowledge of the disclaimer on the herbicide label, through their agent, excluded the implied warranty of merchantability as a matter of law; and (6) the court erred in failing to rule on the unconscionability of the limitation of damages clause on the herbicide label, pursuant to Neb. UCC § 2–302 (Reissue 1980), thereby failing to find and instruct the jury that the limitation of damages clause in the herbicide label excluded the plaintiffs' recovery of consequential damages from breach of warranty.

IV. Analysis

1. Directed Verdict and Judgment Notwithstanding the Verdict

[8] Generally, the defendant claims that the trial court erred by failing to sustain its motions for directed verdict and for judgment notwithstanding the verdict because there was insufficient evidence to support the jury's verdict finding the defendant liable on theories of strict liability and breach of warranty of merchantability. These assignments will be considered together because they must be reviewed under the same standards.

[9] A trial court should direct a verdict as a matter of law only when the facts are conceded, undisputed, or such that reasonable minds can draw but one conclusion therefrom. The party against whom the motion is made is entitled to have every controverted fact resolved in his or her favor and to have the benefit of every inference which can reasonably be drawn from the evidence. If there is any evidence which will sustain a finding for the party against whom the motion is made, the case may not be decided as a matter of law.

[10] On a motion for judgment notwithstanding the verdict, the moving party is deemed to have admitted as true all the material and relevant evidence admitted which is favorable to the party against whom the motion is directed, and, further, the party against whom the motion is directed is entitled to the benefit of all proper inferences which can be deduced therefrom.

(a) Strict Liability

[11] The defendant claims the trial court erred in overruling its motions for a directed verdict and for judgment notwithstanding the verdict because there was insufficient evidence for a jury to find the

defendant liable on a theory of strict liability. The Adamses' suit was based on Restatement (Second) of Torts § 402 A at 347–48 (1965), which in relevant part provides: "(1) One who sells any product in a defective condition unreasonably dangerous to the user or consumer or to his property is subject to liability for physical harm thereby caused to the ultimate user or consumer, or to his property." The elements in a prima facie case in strict liability depend on the type of defect that is asserted. The Supreme Court has said:

> In products liability litigation the notion of a defective product embraces two separate concepts. The first, commonly labeled a manufacturing defect, is one in which the product differs from the specifications and plan of the manufacturer. . . .

> The second concept of a defective product is one in which the product meets the specifications of the manufacturer but the product nonetheless poses an unreasonable risk of danger. This condition is generally characterized as a design defect. . . .

> While a particular design may pose such an unreasonable risk of danger, liability for this danger differs, depending upon the theory of recovery presented by the plaintiff. . . .

> In a strict liability cause of action it is generally proposed that the focus of the court's inquiry should be on the product itself and not the manufacturer. Thus, a finding that the product poses an unreasonable risk of danger is sufficient.

Nerud v. Haybuster Mfg., 215 Neb. 604, 610–11, 340 N.W.2d 369, 373–74 (1983).

[12] The Adamses did not claim that American Cyanamid's product was subject to a manufacturing defect, or stated differently, they concede that Prowl did conform to the chemical description on the label. Therefore, the question is whether the evidence is sufficient to support the jury's finding on strict liability for a design defect. According to *Rahmig v. Mosley Machinery Co.*, 226 Neb. 423, 441, 412 N.W.2d 56, 69 (1987), to recover on a claim of strict liability in tort for a defectively designed product, a plaintiff must prove the following by a preponderance of the evidence:

> (1) The defendant placed the product on the market for use and knew, or in the exercise of reasonable care should have known, that the product would be used without inspection for defects; (2) the product was in a defective condition when it was placed on the market and left the defendant's possession; (3) the defect was the proximate or a proximately contributing cause of plaintiff's injury sustained while the product was being used in the way and for the general purpose for which it was designed and intended; (4) the defect, if existent, rendered the product unreasonably dangerous

and unsafe for its intended use . . . and (6) plaintiff's damages were a direct and proximate result of the alleged defect.

[13] In the instant case, there is no question that it was foreseeable to American Cyanamid that its product would be used by a farmer without inspection. Moreover, if the product was defective, it was defective when it was placed on the market and left American Cyanamid's possession. Nevertheless, no evidence was adduced to show that Prowl was unreasonably dangerous. The Supreme Court has stated:

> This court has defined the term "unreasonably dangerous" to mean that the product has a propensity for causing physical harm beyond that which would be contemplated by the ordinary user or consumer who purchases it, with the ordinary knowledge common to the foreseeable class of users as to its characteristics.

Rahmig v. Mosley Machinery Co., 226 Neb. at 440, 412 N.W.2d at 69 (quoting *Nerud v. Haybuster Mfg., supra*).

[14] Because the Adamses have failed to make a prima facie case that the herbicide was unreasonably dangerous, their cause of action for strict liability must fail. Accordingly, we hold that it was error for the court to overrule the defendant's motions for directed verdict and for judgment notwithstanding the verdict on this count. Our holding makes it unnecessary to consider the defendant's assignment of error based on its motion to strike the strict liability count.

(b)   Breach of Warranty

[15] The defendant also claims that the Adamses presented insufficient evidence to prove there was a breach of the implied warranty of merchantability and that the trial court erred by failing to direct a verdict against the Adamses on this theory of recovery. [We affirm.—Eds.]

Neb. UCC § 2–314 (Reissue 1980) provides:

> (1)   Unless excluded or modified (Section 2–316), a warranty that the goods shall be merchantable is implied in a contract for their sale if the seller is a merchant with respect to goods of that kind. . . .
>
> (2)   Goods to be merchantable must be at least such as
>
>   . . . .
>
>   (c)   are fit for the ordinary purposes for which such goods are used.

There is no question that American Cyanamid is a merchant, i.e., one that deals in the goods of the kind involved in the transactions under consideration. *See* Neb. UCC § 2–104 (Reissue 1980).

[16] After goods are accepted, the buyer has the burden of establishing any breach with respect to those goods. *Laird v. Scribner Coop*, 237 Neb. 532, 466 N.W.2d 798 (1991).

[17] The plaintiffs' prima facie case for breach of warranty of merchantability has been described in *Delgado v. Inryco, Inc.*, 230 Neb. 662, 433 N.W.2d 179 (1988):

> There must be proof that there was a deviation from the standard of merchantability at the time of sale and that such deviation caused the plaintiff's injury both proximately and in fact. Thus, a breach of the warranty has been found to exist where the item sold failed to perform adequately because of a lack of quality inherent within the item itself.

Id. at 668, 433 N.W.2d at 183–84 (quoting *O'Keefe Elevator v. Second Ave. Properties*, 216 Neb. 170, 343 N.W.2d 54 (1984)).

[18] The Delgado court also stated, "In proving a deviation from the standard of merchantability, some proof of noncompliance with the warranty must be presented." *Id.* at 668, 433 N.W.2d at 184. A plaintiff may not rely on the sole fact that an accident occurred. *See Delgado v. Inryco, Inc., supra.*

[19] In the case at bar, the defendant argues that "there was no proof by the plaintiffs that the risk of harm from the Prowl herbicide was any greater than herbicides in its class generally, and there was no evidence as to any breach of a standard of merchantability." Brief for appellant at 30.

[20] In *Laird v. Scribner Coop, supra,* the Supreme Court held that " 'reliance on eyewitnesses alone is not fatal when the defect is obvious to a layman, but when standards of performance of the product are not generally known, other evidence, usually expert testimony, is necessary to prove proper or acceptable standards of performance.' " (Emphasis in original.) *Id. at 539, 466 N.W.2d at 804* (quoting *Durrett v. Baxter Chrysler-Plymouth, Inc.*, 198 Neb. 392, 253 N.W.2d 37 (1977)).

[21] It would seem apparent to a layperson that the standard of merchantability for herbicides is that they should not damage the crops to which they are applied. Therefore, expert testimony was not required to establish a standard of merchantability.

[22] As to the existence of a breach of the standard, the evidence at trial was in conflict. Prof. Eugene Heikes, called by the Adamses, testified that a dinitroaniline herbicide affects plants through their root system, attacking the hypocotyl, or main root, and the secondary roots which branch therefrom. He also testified that the growth of the bean plants he inspected was stunted because of their swollen hypocotyl and the lack of a secondary root system.

[23] Dr. Raymond Ward, a soil testing specialist called by the defendant, testified that the injury to the root system was not caused by the herbicide, but by the quality of water from the deep wells used to irrigate the fields. He testified that the irrigation water contained sodium, chlorides, and boron and that dry beans are especially susceptible to injury from the concentration of such salts in the soil.

[24] Whether there was a breach of implied warranty of merchantability is a factual question for jury determination. Professor Heikes testified that injury to the plants was caused by the effects of dinitroaniline substances. [It was undisputed that Prowl contained dinitroaniline.] Professor Heikes' testimony was sufficient for the jury to have concluded that the herbicide in question was not suitable for its ordinary use in controlling weeds in dry beans.

Breach of IW is a for jury

[25] Therefore, we hold that the Adamses presented sufficient evidence as to a breach of a standard of merchantability. Accordingly, we affirm that portion of the court's judgment overruling the motions for directed verdict and for judgment notwithstanding the verdict to the Adamses' theory of recovery based on implied warranty of merchantability.

NOTE

In case you're wondering how the court held that a product that killed a farmer's crop was not "unreasonably dangerous," the definition, as the quote from the *Rahmig* case shows, requires "physical harm." While the court doesn't define that term, it has often been limited in a products liability context to mean damage *caused by a sudden traumatic event* rather than by a gradual process as would be the case with an herbicide of this type.

SUMINSKI V. MAINE APPLIANCE WAREHOUSE, INC.

Supreme Court of Maine
602 A.2d 1173 (1992)

ROBERTS, J.

[1] Defendant Maine Appliance Warehouse, Inc. appeals from a judgment of the Superior Court (Androscoggin County, Alexander, J.) affirming the judgment of the District Court (Lewiston, Beliveau, J.) in favor of the plaintiff Paul Suminski. The District Court held that Maine Appliance breached the implied warranty of merchantability under the Maine Uniform Commercial Code (UCC), 11 M.R.S.A. § 2–314 (1964), when it sold Suminski a defective television set for $713.97 and that Maine Appliance's conduct amounted to a violation of the Maine Unfair Trade

Practices Act (UTPA), 5 M.R.S.A. § 206–214 (1989). The District Court ordered that Maine Appliance fully reimburse Suminski and pay $1,000 in attorneys' fees. Maine Appliance contends inter alia that the District Court erred in finding a violation of the UTPA and that the evidence was insufficient to prove a breach of the implied warranty of merchantability. Although we reject the first contention, we agree with the second and vacate the judgment.

[2] Suminski purchased a brand new television set from Maine Appliance in May 1988. In June 1989 the set began to turn off by itself, although the picture would come on when the plaintiff turned the set off and on. Suminski called Maine Appliance and was told that his set was out of warranty, but was given the name of a repairperson. Suminski called the repairperson who requested that he look for someone else to repair the set. About two months later, the set did not turn on at all. Suminski called again to Maine Appliance, and a salesperson repeated that the set was out of warranty and that Suminski would have to talk to the sales manager for any further assistance. Suminski requested that the manger call him the next morning. After not hearing back the next morning, Suminski called in the afternoon and spoke with manager Ray Picard. Picard stated that Maine Appliance's only obligation was to provide the name of a repairperson and that the store would charge Suminski for any work that it might do on the set.

[3] Suminski then contacted attorney Stephen Wade who telephoned Picard. Picard repeated his assertion that the express warranty was the store's only obligation to Suminski, although he offered to give the name of a repairperson. Picard stated that Suminski was not being treated differently than any other Maine Appliance customer. In addition, Picard stated that he had been in the electronics business for a long time and had never heard of an implied warranty of merchantability. When Wade requested that Picard contact his attorney to confirm the existence of the implied warranty of merchantability, Picard abruptly hung up.

[4] Suminski brought suit against Maine Appliance for a breach of the implied warranty of merchantability and violation of the UTPA. After the trial, the District Court found that Maine Appliance had breached the implied warranty of merchantability and violated the UTPA. The Superior Court affirmed the judgment of the District Court but denied Suminski's motion for attorneys' fees on appeal. Maine Appliance now appeals, and Suminski cross-appeals, from the Superior Court rulings. Suminski also requests attorneys' fees for this appeal.

[5] Maine Appliance contends that, because no exclusion or modification of an implied warranty was made at the time of sale, the District Court erred in finding a violation of the UTPA, citing *State ex rel. Tierney v. Ford Motor Co.,* 436 A.2d 866, 873 (Me. 1981). We disagree.

Although we stated in *Ford Motor* that a violation of the statutory warranties, such as the implied warranty of merchantability, is not a *per se* violation of the UTPA, we stressed "that given the proper circumstances a defendant's failure to honor the statutory warranties may well be evidence of a violation of the UTPA." *Id.* To trigger the UTPA, we require more than a mere failure to honor the statutory warranty. The defendant's conduct must be unfair or deceptive. *Id.* at 874.

[6]   In this case, the court could find that Maine Appliance continually refused to take responsibility for repairing the television set once the express warranty had expired and that the sales manager even denied the existence of Maine's implied warranty of merchantability. Suminski testified that he was told by a salesperson and by Picard that all Maine Appliance was required to do was to provide Suminski with the name of a repairperson. Moreover, there was evidence that this conduct was consistent with the regular practices of Maine Appliance. The District Court rationally could find that the practice of Maine Appliance involved such unfair or deceptive behavior that it violated the UTPA. *Id.*

[7]   Fatal to Suminski's claim, however, is his failure to establish a breach of the implied warranty of merchantability. Maine's version of Article 2 of the UCC provides that "a warranty that the goods shall be merchantable is implied in a contract for their sale if the seller is a merchant with respect to goods of that kind." 11 M.R.S.A. § 2–314(1) (1964). The District Court concluded that the television set bought by Suminski "was not fit for the ordinary purposes for which such goods are used," and, therefore, was not merchantable under 11 M.R.S.A. 314(2)(c). On appeal, we view the evidence of a breach of the implied warranty of merchantability, together with all justifiable inferences drawn therefrom, in the light most favorable to the plaintiff. *See Sylvain v. Masonite Corp.,* 471 A.2d 1039, 1041 (Me. 1984).

[8]   The District Court heard evidence that Suminski bought a new expensive television set which began to turn off automatically after thirteen months. No evidence was presented concerning the specific defect in the product. In some circumstances a breach of the implied warranty of merchantability under the UCC may be established by circumstantial evidence. In the case at bar, however, the television set was in all respects satisfactory during approximately thirteen months after it was purchased. For all that appears in the record, the malfunction at that time may have resulted from a defective switch, repairable at a small cost. We conclude that the sale of a major appliance with a switch that fails more than a year later, cannot support a finding that the entire appliance was unmerchantable when sold. To use an automotive example, an unmerchantable battery may not render an entire vehicle unmerchantable.

[9] We need not discuss any other issue raised by Maine Appliance nor Suminski's cross-appeal for attorney fees.

Judgment vacated.

NOTES AND QUESTIONS

1. In each of the preceding cases, think of how the court characterized the product and its intended use. Was there an alternative way of characterizing these things that might have changed the outcome of the case, or alternatively, one that might have made the decision even easier?

2. The characterization of the product's intended use was outcome determinative in *Daniell v. Ford Motor Co.*, 581 F.Supp. 728 (D.N.M. 1984). Connie Daniell felt "overburdened," so she attempted to commit suicide by locking herself in the trunk of her Ford LTD. At some point after she incarcerated herself, she changed her mind and discovered that she couldn't get out. Nine days later, she did get out. The opinion doesn't say how. She sued Ford, alleging, among other things, breach of the implied warranty of merchantability. The court said "the usual and ordinary purpose of an automobile trunk is to transport and store goods, including the automobile's spare tire. Plaintiff's use of the trunk was highly extraordinary, and there is no evidence that the trunk was not fit for the ordinary purpose for which it was intended." *Id.* at 731. The court also rejected the plaintiff's claim that Ford had breached a duty to warn her of the danger, saying: "the potential efficacy of any warning, given the plaintiff's use of the automobile trunk compartment for a deliberate suicide attempt, is questionable." *Id.*

C. IMPLIED WARRANTY OF FITNESS FOR A PARTICULAR PURPOSE

LEWIS v. MOBIL OIL CORP.

United States Court of Appeals, Eighth Circuit
438 F.2d 500 (1971)

GIBSON, J.

[1] In this diversity case the defendant appeals from a judgment entered on a jury verdict in favor of the plaintiff in the amount of $89,250 for damages alleged to be caused by use of defendant's oil.

[2] Plaintiff Lewis has been doing business as a sawmill operator in Cove, Arkansas, since 1956. In 1963, in order to meet competition, Lewis decided to convert his power equipment to hydraulic equipment. He purchased a hydraulic system in May 1963, from a competitor who was installing a new system. The used system was in good operating condition at the time Lewis purchased it. It was stored at his plant until November

1964, while a new mill building was being built, at which time it was installed. Following the installation, Lewis requested from Frank Rowe, a local Mobil oil dealer, the proper hydraulic fluid to operate his machinery. The prior owner of the hydraulic system had used Pacemaker oil supplied by Cities Service, but plaintiff had been a customer of Mobil's for many years and desired to continue with Mobil. Rowe said he didn't know what the proper lubricant for Lewis' machinery was, but would find out. The only information given to Rowe by Lewis was that the machinery was operated by a gear-type pump; Rowe did not request any further information. He apparently contacted a Mobil representative for a recommendation, though this is not entirely clear, and sold plaintiff a product known as Ambrex 810. This is a straight mineral oil with no chemical additives.

[3] Within a few days after operation of the new equipment commenced, plaintiff began experiencing difficulty with its operation. The oil changed color, foamed over and got hot. The oil was changed a number of times, with no improvement. By late April 1965, approximately six months after operations with the equipment had begun, the system broke down, and a complete new system was installed. The cause of the breakdown was undetermined, but apparently by this time there was some suspicion of the oil being used. Plaintiff Lewis requested Rowe to be sure he was supplying the right kind of oil. Ambrex 810 continued to be supplied.

[4] From April 1965 until April 1967, plaintiff continued to have trouble with the system, principally with the pumps which supplied the pressure. Six new pumps were required during this period, as they continually broke down. During this period, the kind of pump used was a Commercial pump which was specified by the designer of the hydraulic system. The filtration of oil for this pump was by means of a metal strainer, which was cleaned daily by the plaintiff in accordance with the instruction given with the equipment.

[5] In April 1967, the plaintiff changed the brand of pump from a Commercial to a Tyrone pump. The Tyrone pump, instead of using the metal strainer filtration alone, used a disposable filter element in addition. Ambrex 810 oil was also recommended by Mobil and used with this pump, which completely broke down three weeks later. At this point, plaintiff was visited for the first time by a representative of Mobil Oil Corporation, as well as a representative of the Tyrone pump manufacturer.

[6] On the occasion of this visit, May 9, 1967, plaintiff's system was completely flushed and cleaned, a new Tyrone pump installed, and on the pump manufacturer's and Mobil's representative's recommendation, a new oil was used which contained certain chemical additives, principally a "defoamant." Following these changes, plaintiff's system worked satisfactorily up until the time of trial, some two and one-half years later.

*P and
D's arguments*

[7]   Briefly stated, plaintiff's theory of his case is that Mobil supplied him with an oil which was warranted fit for use in his hydraulic system, that the oil was not suitable for such use because it did not contain certain additives, and that it was the improper oil which caused the mechanical breakdowns, with consequent loss to his business. The defendant contends that there was no warranty of fitness, that the breakdowns were caused not by the oil but by improper filtration, and that in any event there can be no recovery of loss of profits in this case.

I.   The Existence of Warranties

*Warranty
of fitness
not merchantability*

[8]   Defendant maintains that there was no warranty of fitness in this case, that at most there was only a warranty of merchantability and that there was no proof of breach of this warranty, since there was no proof that Ambrex 810 is unfit for use in hydraulic systems generally. We find it unnecessary to consider whether the warranty of merchantability was breached, although there is some proof in the record to that effect, since we conclude that there was a warranty of fitness.

[9]   Plaintiff Lewis testified that he had been a longtime customer of Mobil Oil, and that his only source of contact with the company was through Frank Rowe, Mobil's local dealer, with whom he did almost all his business. It was common knowledge in the community that Lewis was converting his sawmill operation into a hydraulic system. Rowe knew this, and in fact had visited his mill on business matters several times during the course of the changeover. When operations with the new machinery were about to commence, Lewis asked Rowe to get him the proper hydraulic fluid. Rowe asked him what kind of a system he had, and Lewis replied it was a Commercial-pump type. This was all the information asked or given. Neither Lewis nor Rowe knew what the oil requirements for the system were, and Rowe knew that Lewis knew nothing more specific about his requirements. Lewis also testified that after he began having trouble with his operations, while there were several possible sources of the difficulty the oil was one suspected source, and he several times asked Rowe to be sure he was furnishing him with the right kind.

[10] Rowe's testimony for the most part confirmed Lewis'. It may be noted here that Mobil does not contest Rowe's authority to represent it in this transaction, and therefore whatever warranties may be implied because of the dealings between Rowe and Lewis are attributable to Mobil. Rowe admitted knowing Lewis was converting to a hydraulic system and that Lewis asked him to supply the fluid. He testified that he did not know what should be used and relayed the request to a superior in the Mobil organization, who recommended Ambrex 810. This is what was supplied.

[11] When the first Tyrone pump was installed in April 1967, Rowe referred the request for a proper oil recommendation to Ted Klock, a Mobil engineer. Klock recommended Ambrex 810. When this pump failed a few

weeks later, Klock visited the Lewis plant to inspect the equipment. The system was flushed out completely and the oil was changed to DTE-23 and Del Vac Special containing several additives. After this, no further trouble was experienced.

[12] This evidence adequately establishes an implied warranty of fitness. Arkansas has adopted the Uniform Commercial Code's provision for an implied warranty of fitness [U.C.C. § 2–315]:

> Where the seller at the time of contracting has reason to know any particular purpose for which the goods are required and that the buyer is relying on the seller's skill or judgment to select or furnish suitable goods, there is unless excluded or modified under the next section an implied warranty that the goods shall be fit for such purpose. . . .

Under this provision of the Code, there are two requirements for an implied warranty of fitness: (1) that the seller have "reason to know" of the use for which the goods are purchased, and (2) that the buyer relies on the seller's expertise in supplying the proper product. Both of these requirements are amply met by the proof in this case. Lewis' testimony, as confirmed by that of Rowe and Klock, shows that the oil was purchased specifically for his hydraulic system, not for just a hydraulic system in general, and that Mobil certainly knew of this specific purpose. It is also clear that Lewis was relying on Mobil to supply him with the proper oil for the system, since at the time of his purchases, he made clear that he didn't know what kind was necessary.

[13] Mobil contends that there was no warranty of fitness for use in his particular system because he didn't specify that he needed an oil with additives, and alternatively that he didn't give them enough information for them to determine that an additive oil was required. However, it seems that the circumstances of this case come directly within that situation described in the first comment to this provision of the Uniform Commercial Code:

> 1.   Whether or not this warranty arises in any individual case is basically a question of fact to be determined by the circumstances of the contracting. Under this section the buyer need not bring home to the seller *actual knowledge of the particular purpose* for which the goods are intended or of his reliance on the seller's skill and judgment, if the circumstances are such that the seller has reason to realize the purpose intended or that the reliance exists. . . . (emphasis added).

Here Lewis made it clear that the oil was purchased for his system, that he didn't know what oil should be used, and that he was relying on Mobil to supply the proper product. If any further information was needed, it was incumbent upon Mobil to get it before making its recommendation. That it could have easily gotten the necessary information is evidenced by the fact that after plaintiff's continuing complaints, Mobil's engineer visited the plant, and, upon inspection, changed the recommendation that had previously been made.

[14] Additionally, Mobil contends that even if there were an implied warranty of fitness, it does not cover the circumstances of this case because of the abnormal features which the plaintiff's system contained, namely an inadequate filtration system and a capacity to entrain excessive air. There are several answers to this contention. First of all, the contention goes essentially to the question of causation—i.e., whether the damage was caused by a breach of warranty or by some other cause—and not to the existence of a warranty of fitness in the first place. Secondly, assuming that certain peculiarities in the plaintiff's system did exist, the whole point of an implied warranty of fitness is that a product be suitable for a specific purpose, and that a seller should not supply a product which is not so suited. Thirdly, there is no evidence in the record that the plaintiff's system was unique or abnormal in these respects. It operated satisfactorily under the prior owner, and the new system has operated satisfactorily after it was adequately cleaned and an additive type oil used.

[15] While we will discuss these problems more completely in the question of causation, it may be briefly noted here that the proof shows that plaintiff's filtration system was installed and maintained in strict accordance with the manufacturer's recommendations, that this was a standard system, and that any hydraulic system has a certain unavoidable capacity to entrain air. . . . It is sufficient to note here that there was no evidence that the plaintiff's system was in any way unique in this respect. Thus, Mobil's defense that there was no warranty of fitness because of an "abnormal use" of the oil is not appropriate here. . . .

[The opinion also considered Mobil's contentions relating to (1) causation and (2) damages. The court concluded, inter alia, that the record did not support recovery for loss of profits of the dimension reflected in the verdict for plaintiff of $89,250, and remanded the case for a new trial on the issue of damages—Eds.]

NOTE

Lewis shows how easy it is to create an implied warranty of fitness when the sales person is dealing face-to-face with a customer. For this reason, most sellers include in their sales receipts and other documentation very explicit disclaimers of this warranty. In the next chapter, we'll see what is necessary to make such disclaimers effective.

BAYLINER MARINE CORP. V. CROW

Supreme Court of Virginia
257 Va. 121, 509 S.E.2d 499 (1999)

[Please refer back to the facts of the case earlier in this chapter.—Eds.]

[1] Crow contends that the "particular purpose" for which the boat was intended was use as an offshore fishing boat capable of traveling at a maximum speed of 30 miles per hour. However, to establish an implied warranty of fitness for a particular purpose, the buyer must prove as a threshold matter that he made known to the seller the particular purpose for which the goods were required. The record before us does not support a conclusion that Crow informed Atherton of this precise requirement. Although Crow informed Atherton that he intended to use the boat for offshore fishing and discussed the boat's speed in this context, these facts did not establish that Atherton knew on the date of sale that a boat incapable of travelling at 30 miles per hour was unacceptable to Crow. Thus, we conclude that the evidence fails to support the trial court's ruling that Bayliner breached an implied warranty of fitness for a particular purpose.

[handwritten margin note: Crow never told he needed boat to go 30 mph]

[handwritten note: never made known the particular purpose]

NOTES AND QUESTIONS

1.　What is the court's stated reason for holding there was no breach of the implied warranty of fitness for a particular purpose?

2.　Suppose that Crow had come to Atherton and said "I need a boat for offshore fishing. It'll be based in the Tidewater." Atherton said "I think the Bayliner 3486 is just what you need."

(a)　Would that create an express warranty?

(b)　Would it create an implied warranty of fitness for a particular purpose?

(c)　If there was created a warranty of fitness for a particular purpose, was it breached?

3.　In the *Daniell* case—the one involving attempted suicide in the trunk of a Ford car—discussed earlier in the chapter, the plaintiff also alleged breach of the warranty of fitness for a particular purpose. The court rejected this as well. There was no evidence that the seller had reason to know the plaintiff intended to use the car to commit suicide.

PROBLEM 16-6

Gwen developed a fever and red spots on her face. Art went to Merlin, described Gwen's symptoms, and asked Merlin to prepare a potion to cure her. Merlin told him, "For five shillings I can give you a potion that will fix her right up." Art paid the five shillings and Merlin mixed up a batch of his world-renowned chicken pox potion. Gwen took the potion but remained sick for two weeks until a wandering monk called at the castle and said a blessing over her. At that point, she began to get better. Subsequently, it was determined that Gwen had measles, rather than chicken pox.

Art has sought your advice as court solicitor. First, he wants to know if there has been a breach of the implied warranty of fitness for a particular purpose. What do you tell him?

PROBLEM 16-7

Now let us look at the same question in Problem 16-6 from the standpoint of express warranty.

On the same facts, now Art wants to know if there has been a breach of any express warranty. What do you tell him?

LAWYERING SKILLS PROBLEM

Buyer, a logger, entered into a contract to log a tract of land in which a substantial portion of the timber was located in swampland. Buyer had never logged swampland before, but he knew of another logger, Seller, who had. Buyer telephoned Seller and asked him what kind of tractor Buyer should purchase in order to log the swampland. Seller told Buyer, "You're in luck. I have a tractor that I'm selling and it's just what you need." After some negotiations, Buyer purchased the tractor. The tractor failed to meet Buyer's expectations, and Buyer sued, alleging breaches of express warranties, the implied warranty of merchantability, and the implied warranty of fitness for a particular purpose. In the course of discovery:

Seller sent Buyer the following Request for Admissions under Fed. R. Civ. P. 36:

   1.   Seller is **NOT** a "merchant" as that term is defined in the U.C.C. with respect to tractors.

Buyer sent Seller the following Requests for Admissions under Fed. R. Civ. P. 36:

   1.   By a contract entered into on January 14, 2004, Seller sold Buyer a tractor, which Buyer intended to use for the purpose of logging swampland.

   2.   Seller had actual knowledge that Buyer required the tractor for the purpose of logging swampland.

3.   Buyer relied on Seller's skill and judgment to select a suitable tractor and Buyer purchased the tractor in reliance on Seller's skill and judgment.

4.   The sale contract contained no effective disclaimer of the implied warranty of merchantability or the implied warranty of fitness for a particular purpose.

5.   There is no course of performance, course of dealing, or usage of trade that would exclude or modify any implied warranty of merchantability or any warranty of fitness for a particular purpose arising in this transaction.

6.   Buyer's inspection of the tractor would not exclude or modify any implied warranty of merchantability or any warranty of fitness for a particular purpose arising in this transaction.

7.   The tractor is not fit for the purpose of logging swampland.

8.   The tractor is not fit for the ordinary purpose for which such goods are used.

ALL of these Requests were admitted.

Solely on the basis of the requests for admissions, Buyer and Seller have both moved for partial summary judgment on the issues of (1) breach of the implied warranty of merchantability and (2) breach of the implied warranty of fitness for a particular purpose. Explain how the court should decide the motions. In other words, can the court decide—solely on the basis of the Requests for Admissions—if either of the implied warranties has or has not been breached? Explain why the court can or cannot decide each of the issues.

CHAPTER 17

DEFENSES TO WARRANTY LIABILITY

■ ■ ■

The implied warranties of merchantability and fitness arise automatically if the requirements of U.C.C. §§ 2–314 and 2–315 are satisfied. Article 2, however, gives sellers the ability to keep those warranties out of their transactions. As noted in the introduction to Chapter 16, clauses that prevent these warranties from arising are often called "disclaimers" because they disclaim the warranties.

Even more common than disclaimers are limitations on remedies, often referred to as "exclusionary clauses." These are addressed in U.C.C. § 2–719. These clauses may be used in place of disclaimers, they may be used with limited disclaimers (those which disclaim some but not all warranties), or they may be used as "belt and suspenders lawyering" to protect the seller should the disclaimer for some reason be ineffective.

Exclusionary clauses state that the buyer's remedies for breach of the contract are limited. Some merely say that the seller will not be liable for consequential damages. Other say that the buyer's only remedy is replacement of the defective goods. For instance, if your wedding pictures don't turn out because of defective photographic film, they'll buy you some new film. (You can use it for your next wedding.)

PROBLEM 17-1

Read carefully U.C.C. § 2–316(2) & (3).

(a)   Is it possible to have an oral disclaimer of the warranty of fitness for a particular purpose? What about merchantability?

(b)   Is the warranty of merchantability excluded by the statement: "There are no warranties which extend beyond the description on the face hereof?"

As you read the case that follows, look for the differences between disclaimers and exclusionary clauses.

———

SCHROEDER V. FAGEOL MOTORS

Supreme Court of Washington
86 Wash. 2d 256, 544 P.2d 20 (1975)

HUNTER, J.

[1] In June of 1970, the plaintiff (respondent), John Schroeder, purchased a used 1970 White truck from the defendant (petitioner), Fageol Motors, Inc., to be used in the hauling of automobiles between California and Washington. The odometer showed 6,180 miles, and Fageol assured the plaintiff that the original warranty, which was still in effect, would cover the vehicle for an additional 94,000 miles. The new truck warranties were set out in an "Owner Book" which was separate from the purchase order signed by the plaintiff. While the plaintiff admitted that he would not have purchased the truck without the warranties, it is evident that Fageol did not go through the "Owner Book" and explain the intricacies of the warranties and the various disclaimers. In fact, the plaintiff was not advised of the existence of any disclaimers or exclusionary clauses. Upon signing the order, the plaintiff was given his "Owner Book" and directed to place it in the glove box.

[2] On October 5, 1970, while the truck was in California, the engine exploded. At this time the vehicle still had more than 50,000 miles remaining on the warranty. The plaintiff notified Cummins Engine Co., Inc., also a defendant (petitioner) herein, whose separate warranty appeared in the "Owner Book." At its direction, the plaintiff took the truck to a local Cummins dealer, who undertook repairs without cost to the plaintiff. It was then determined that the engine failure was the result of a casting defect in a piston rod cap.

[3] Upon completion of the repairs, the truck was returned to the plaintiff, yet it never functioned properly. The plaintiff, experiencing heating and vibration Problems, made repeated complaints to both Cummins and Fageol. While numerous attempts were made to correct the Problems, neither defendant was ever successful.

[4] The plaintiff ultimately brought suit against Fageol and Cummins for damages resulting from the defendants' failure to properly effectuate repairs in accordance with their own respective warranties. The complaint alleged that the plaintiff had incurred $8,431.45 in repair bills, and $12,160 in lost profits. The trial court concluded that the defendants had both made independent express warranties to repair the vehicle and that the damages alleged were proximately caused by a failure to fulfill these warranties. In reaching its decision, the court refused to recognize Fageol's claim that it was protected from any consequential damages due to an exclusionary clause contained in the White truck comprehensive warranty, which stated in normal size print: "In no event shall the Seller be liable for special or consequential damages." Relying on *Berg v.*

Stromme, 79 Wash. 2d 184, 484 P.2d 380 (1971), the court held that there had been no discussion nor explicit negotiations between Fageol and the plaintiff regarding limitations or disclaimers of liability, but rather that the plaintiff had merely been handed the "Owner Book" and instructed to keep it in the truck. Furthermore, there was no showing of a bargain and the clause was neither conspicuous nor were the limitations set forth with particularity. Secondly, the trial court held that Fageol was not entitled to indemnity against Cummins since both defendants had actively attempted, and failed, to make proper repairs.

[5]   The Court of Appeals affirmed all of the holdings of the trial court, *Schroeder v. Fageol*, 12 Wash. App. 161, 528 P.2d 992 (1974), and this court granted the defendants' petition for review.

[6]   The facts of this case present a question of first impression arising under the Washington state adaptation of the Uniform Commercial Code, to wit: whether a clause excluding consequential damages under [U.C.C. §] 2–719(3) must be negotiated between the parties and set forth with particularity in a conspicuous manner. Put another way, do the requirements set forth in *Berg v. Stromme, supra* apply with equal force to an exclusionary clause under [U.C.C. §] 2–719(3)?[1] The defendant Fageol contends that the criteria utilized by the trial court is limited to cases arising under [U.C.C. §] 2–316, and is not intended to apply to cases pertaining to [U.C.C. §] 2–719(3). Furthermore, the defendant argues that "negotiations" and "conspicuousness" are only relevant in those instances involving consumers as opposed to a purely commercial transaction between businessmen.

[7]   We agree that the trial court and the Court of Appeals failed to properly distinguish between disclaimer and exclusionary clauses.

> A disclaimer clause is a device used to exclude or limit the seller's warranties; it attempts to control the seller's liability by reducing the number of situations in which the seller can be in breach. An exclusionary clause, on the other hand, restricts the remedies available to one or both parties once a breach is established.

J. White & R. Summers, *Handbook of the Law under the Uniform Commercial Code*, § 12–11, at 383–84 (1972). The functional purpose of RCW 62A.2–719(3) is to allow the parties to allocate their risks. Official Comment 1, [U.C.C. §] 2–719.

[8]   While the two sections are clearly distinguishable, they are not mutually exclusive, since both disclaimers and exclusionary clauses can be invalidated upon being declared unconscionable under [U.C.C. §] 2–302. In fact, by its use of the word "unconscionable," [U.C.C. §] 2–719(3) conditions

---

[1]   [*Berg v. Stromme*, a pre-U.C.C. case, held ineffective a disclaimer printed in small type on the back side of an automobile sales contract.—Eds.]

the validity of an exclusionary clause on one factor—the standards set forth in [U.C.C. §] 2–302. Therefore, once placed in its proper perspective, the true issue becomes whether "conspicuousness" and "the presence of negotiation" are relevant when defining the elusive concept of *unconscionability.*

Unconscionable Thomas Walker analysis

[9] While it is extremely difficult to articulate an operational definition of unconscionability, those cases interpreting the doctrine appear to fall within two classifications: (1) substantive unconscionability; and (2) procedural unconscionability. Substantive unconscionability involves those cases where a clause or term in the contract is alleged to be one-sided or overly harsh, while procedural unconscionability relates to impropriety during the process of forming a contract. J. White & R. Summers, *Handbook of The Law under the Uniform Commercial Code*, § 4–2, at 117 (1972). In *Williams v. Walker-Thomas Furniture Co.*, 121 U.S. App. D.C. 315, 350 F.2d 445 (1965), the court pronounced that procedural unconscionability was best described as a lack of "meaningful choice." In discussing the various factors to be considered in determining whether a meaningful choice is present, the court noted that consideration must be given to "all the circumstances surrounding the transaction," including "[t]he manner in which the contract was entered," whether each party had "a reasonable opportunity to understand the terms of the contract," and whether "the important terms [were] hidden in a maze of fine print . . ." *Williams v. Walker-Thomas Furniture Co., supra* at 449. It is readily apparent that both "conspicuousness" and "negotiations" are factors, albeit not conclusive, which are certainly relevant when determining the issue of conscionability in light of *all the surrounding circumstances.* Furthermore, the question of un-conscionability cannot be judged in the abstract, but rather it must be determined in light of the general commercial setting. *Kohlenberger Inc. v. Tyson's Foods Inc.*, 510 S.W.2d 555 (Ark. 1974); *Dow Corning Corp. v. Capitol Aviation Inc.*, 411 F.2d 622 (7th Cir. 1969). Therefore, several additional factors which must be considered, especially in purely commercial transactions, are prior course of dealings between the parties and usage of trade. RCW 62A.1–205(1) and (2); *Reynolds v. Preferred Mutual Ins. Co., supra.* Placing the above criteria within the context of the instant case, we must consider whether the plaintiff and Fageol, through prior contracts had established a consistently adhered to policy of excluding consequential damages, or whether it is a recognized practice within the trade to exclude consequential damages. The presence of either of these elements, unless the trade practice as related to the plaintiff was clearly unreasonable,[2] would support a finding of

Important Question

usage of trade?

---

[2] "(I)t is essential that 'trade custom' be considered a rule of thumb, to be disregarded when the crucial analysis of relative bargaining positions indicates that the consumer has been disadvantaged." (Footnote omitted.) Terry and Fauvre, *The Unconscionability Offense*, 4 GA. L. REV. 469, 503 (1970).

conscionability in spite of a lack of "negotiations" or the "inconspicuous" appearance of the clause.

[10] We are fully aware that the rule enunciated in *Berg v. Stromme, supra* was premised predominately on policy grounds. However, this does not support Fageol's contention that the *Berg* rule is limited to disclaimer cases involving innocent consumers as contrasted with purely commercial transactions involving businessmen. In *Dobias v. Western Farmers Ass'n,* 6 Wash. App. 194, 491 P.2d 1346 (1971), the Court of Appeals applied *Berg* to a commercial transaction, and in *Baker v. Seattle,* 79 Wash.2d 198, 484 P.2d 405 (1971), a case involving an injured consumer, we recognized that this public policy regarding disclaimers of liability, extended to cases involving exclusionary clauses under RCW 62A.2–719(3). We now find no persuasive reason why this same public policy should not extend to cases arising under RCW 62A.2–719(3), in which the litigants are both businessmen.

* * *

[11] The issue of unconscionability presents a question of law for the court; not an issue of fact for the jury. [U.C.C. §] 2–302 states:

(1) If the court as a matter of law finds the contract or any clause of the contract to have been unconscionable at the time it was made the court may refuse to enforce the contract, or it may enforce the remainder of the contract without the unconscionable clause, or it may so limit the application of any unconscionable clause as to avoid any unconscionable result.

(2) When it is claimed or appears to the court that the contract or any clause thereof may be unconscionable *the parties shall be afforded a reasonable opportunity to present evidence as to its commercial setting, purpose and effect to aid the court in making the determination.*

(Italics ours.)

[12] In accordance with the requisites set forth above, a court is not authorized to dispose of this issue under the rules governing summary judgment. Instead, [U.C.C. §] 2–302 envisions a full hearing at which time each party will have a "reasonable opportunity" to present evidence bearing on the question of unconscionability. Since exclusionary clauses in purely commercial transactions are prima facie conscionable, the burden of establishing that a clause is unconscionable lies upon the party attacking it. In view of the fact that the trial court based its decision entirely on *Berg v. Stromme, supra,* without addressing the fundamental question of

---

It is the unreasonableness and unfairness of a contract term which is the primary target of U.C.C. § 2–302. *See* Spanogle, *Analyzing Unconscionability Problems,* 117 U. PA. L. REV. 931, 943 (1969).

Burden of establishing a EC unconscionable is on party attacking it

unconscionability in a manner required under the provisions of RCW 62A.2–302, we hold that the decisions of the trial court and the Court of Appeals are reversed, and this cause is remanded for a hearing consistent with the requirements set forth herein.

Remanded b/c Trial and CTA did not look at FC through lens of unconscionability

NOTES AND QUESTIONS

1.   What is the difference between a disclaimer and an exclusionary clause?

2.   Most commentators agree that Article 2 treats disclaimers and exclusionary clauses as two different animals. Disclaimers are governed by section U.C.C. § 2–316, which is in Part 3 of Article 2, the same part that governs the creation of warranties. (Do you see how the organization of the article can be important to its interpretation?) Exclusionary clauses are governed by U.C.C. § 2–719, which is in Part 7, the remedies part. But does this result necessarily follow from the language of the particular sections? Consider an exclusionary clause that prevents the buyer from obtaining any real recovery for a breach of the implied warranty of merchantability. Isn't it within the express language of U.C.C. § 2–316(2)? *See* U.C.C. § 2–316(4) and comment 2. How much weight should be given this comment?

Read the Statute!

As stated in Chapter 4, U.C.C. contract law often differs greatly from general contract law principals. The U.C.C. is more of a civil law system because it is a statutory system rather than a common law, case law system like the general law of contracts. When applying a U.C.C. statute to the facts of a case, you should look first and primarily to the statute for guidance unless the statute is ambiguous or vague. If the statute is ambiguous or vague, turn to case law for guidance on resolving the issue.

Generally, then, one resolves U.C.C. statutory issues by looking at the language of the statute. For example, as you know from Problem 17-1, if a party is trying to disclaim warranties of fitness for a particular purpose, he or she MUST do so in writing, and it must be conspicuous. One can make this determination by simply reading U.C.C. § 2–316(2) carefully. However, what if the question is whether the written disclaimer was conspicuous? Section 2–316(2) does not define "conspicuousness," but U.C.C. § 1–201(10) does. So, one would refer to the statutory definition of the term and interpret and apply it without reference to caselaw for guidance. To bolster the analysis, one could also turn to case law for supporting interpretations, but the primary analysis should begin with the statute.

Also, following most sections of the U.C.C. (and sometimes in the version of the U.C.C. that has been enacted in a particular state) is a section titled, "Official Comments." These comments provide additional guidance and explanation of the meaning and application of the statutes. Although these comments do not have the same authority as the statutes themselves, many courts and legal scholars frequently cite to these comments as persuasive authority.

So, when dealing with issues under the U.C.C., the first thing to you do is ask yourself, "what does the statute say?" If the statute is clear and unambiguous, then apply and interpret the language of the statute to the facts of your case. Avoid being the reason a law school professor (or a judge for that matter) yells across the room, "READ THE STATUTE!" They do not care what a reasonable person would generally do in a similar situation (unless the statute uses that standard). They care about what the statute says, and so should you.

PROBLEM 17-2

A manufacturer's standard form agreement for a farm tractor provides:

Manufacturer's sole obligation with respect to the warranties arising out of the sale of this vehicle is limited to the repair of the vehicle and the replacement of defective parts for a period of 24 months from the date of purchase. In no event shall Manufacturer be liable for any consequential loss or damage of any nature arising from any cause whatsoever. *[handwritten: If consumer good A is prima facie unconscionable]*

Is this clause subject to the requirements of U.C.C. § 2–316(2)? Is this clause prima facie unconscionable under U.C.C. § 2–719(3)? If so, is it substantive or procedural unconscionability?

PROBLEM 17-3

Unbeknownst to her wicked step-sisters, Cinderella has been running an Internet auction site from her dismal quarters in the basement. As a result, when the Prince's ball was announced, she had more than enough ready cash to buy a coach and six horses to pull it. She went to Honest Earls Used Coaches and picked out a coach and six horses to pull it. The sales contract she signed provided in large red letters:

IN THE EVENT THAT THE GOODS SOLD SHALL PROVE DEFECTIVE OR OTHERWISE FAIL TO CONFORM TO THE CONTRACT, BUYER'S SOLE REMEDY SHALL BE THE REFUND OF THE PURCHASE PRICE PAID. IT IS EXPRESSLY UNDERSTOOD THAT THIS IS IN LIEU OF ALL OTHER REMEDIES AND THAT IN NO EVENT SHALL SELLER BE LIABLE FOR CONSEQUENTIAL DAMAGES.

Cindy took the coach to the ball and the Prince was entranced by her charms. Sometime after midnight (it's not clear exactly when; they had both consumed considerable champagne) the Prince escorted Cindy back to her coach, dropping subtle hints about marriage and not-so-subtle hints that they should take a ride together in the country. When they got to the spot where the coach was parked, however, they discovered that the coach had turned into a pumpkin and the horses into mice.

Cindy has, of course, sued Honest Earl. She is seeking damages for the humiliation she suffered and also for the loss of the chance to become wife of the ruler of the principality. (It was a small principality, but it had considerable mineral resources.) Honest Earl has asked for a ruling that even if Cindy prevails on her argument that the coach and horses were unmerchantable (something Earl is not yet willing to concede) the most Cindy would be entitled to recover is the amount she paid for the coach and horses.

How should the court rule on this motion?

PROBLEM 17-4

A clause in a contract for the sale of a used car provides, "This vehicle is not warranted in any way." The clause is in small print on the back of the form, but the seller specifically draws the buyer's attention to the clause. Is it adequate to exclude the implied warranty of merchantability? *See Harriman School Dist. v. Southwestern Petroleum*, 757 S.W.2d 669 (Tenn. Ct. App. 1988), and *Hull-Dobbs, Inc. v. Mallicoat*, 57 Tenn. App. 100, 415 S.W.2d 344 (1966).

JASKEY FINANCE & LEASING V. DISPLAY DATA CORP.

United States District Court, Eastern District of Pennsylvania
564 F. Supp. 160 (1983)

[1] In this diversity action, defendant, Display Data Corporation ("Display Data"), a Maryland corporation with its principal place of business in Maryland, moves to dismiss pursuant to Fed. R. Civ. P. 12(b)(6) the claims of plaintiffs, Jaskey Finance and Leasing ("Jaskey") and Samrus Corporation ("Samrus"), both Pennsylvania corporations with their principal places of business in Pennsylvania, for breach of express warranties, warranties of fitness and for negligent design of a computer system. For the reasons set forth in this memorandum, the Court will grant the defendant's motion to dismiss the express warranty claims, the implied warranty of fitness claims, and the negligent design claim.

[2] The subject of this suit is a 32K computer purchased by Jaskey and Samrus from Display Data in October 1977. The parties entered into two contracts, one for the sale of the equipment, programming and installation services and another for maintenance of the computer system. Plaintiffs, who were dissatisfied with the operation of the computer, sued

The computer did not operate right

alleging that the computer and its component parts failed to operate properly, resulting in damages and the further economic loss of obtaining alternate computer time. In their lawsuit, plaintiffs allege that defendant's conduct amounted to a breach of contract, a breach of express warranties, misrepresentation and negligence.

[3] Two contracts are concerned: (a) an Equipment, Programming and Installation Services Contract, and (b) a Maintenance Contract. Each of these contracts is comprised of a single sheet of paper printed on both sides. The front side of the contracts contains blank spaces on which the name of the parties, the quantity, model number and the price of the goods were filled in. The bottom of the front side of the contracts states in bold type "Terms and Conditions on Reverse Side Are Part of This Contract." Immediately under this phrase the signatures of the parties appear. The reverse side of the Equipment, Programming and Installation Services Contract is titled "Terms and Conditions" and contains six separately numbered and titled paragraphs. Two of the paragraphs are relevant to the present case. The first is paragraph 5 which is titled "warranties" and within it is the following warranty and disclaimer:

Paragraph 5 is relevant to the case

Warranty (a) Seller warrants that it will provide maintenance service for Purchaser according to the terms and conditions of the separate maintenance contract executed by and between the parties.

Warranty (b) For a period of one (1) year after the program is delivered, Seller will make every reasonable effort to remedy or correct any errors in the program which are brought to the attention of the Seller.

Disclaimers (c) EXCEPT AS SPECIFICALLY PROVIDED HEREIN, THERE ARE NO WARRANTIES, EXPRESS OR IMPLIED, WHICH EXTEND BEYOND THE DESCRIPTION ON THE FACE OR REVERSE SIDE HEREOF.

Exclusionary clause (d) IN NO EVENT SHALL SELLER BE LIABLE TO PURCHASER FOR LOSS OF PROFITS OR OTHER ECONOMIC LOSS, INCLUDING SPECIAL, CONSEQUENTIAL OR OTHER SIMILAR DAMAGES ARISING OUT OF ANY CLAIMED BREACH BY SELLER OF ITS OBLIGATIONS THEREUNDER.

The other relevant provision in the Equipment, Programming and Installation Services Contract is under paragraph 6 which is entitled "Miscellaneous" and reads "This contract contains the entire agreement between the parties, and shall be binding upon both parties and their respective heirs, successors and/or assigns." The Maintenance Contract in paragraph 7 contains a similar disclaimer clause which reads "EXCEPT AS SPECIFICALLY PROVIDED HEREIN, THERE ARE NO WARRANTIES, EXPRESS OR IMPLIED, WHICH EXTEND BEYOND

Disclaimer

It was written no IW's or EW's

THE DESCRIPTION CONTAINED HEREIN." The contracts between the parties contain provisions that Maryland law governs the agreement. . . .

[4] As to the plaintiff's express warranty claim, it is clear that the words employed in the disclaimer clause in the Equipment Contract, along with the integration clause, are sufficient to preclude express warranties. Plaintiff alleges that Display Data expressly warranted that the computer and programs which it was selling and leasing constituted a "turnkey" system that required plaintiff to perform only routine maintenance; was a system which was particularly suitable for use by an automobile dealership; was a system which was adaptable to businesses other than automobile dealerships and was a system in which all errors and malfunctions would be eliminated within a specified time period thereby resulting in an error-free system. The written contractual agreements described previously do not contain any of these alleged express warranties. The Equipment Contract warrants that the seller will provide maintenance service for the purchaser subject to the terms in the Maintenance Contract and that for a period of one year after the program is delivered, seller will make every reasonable effort to correct any errors in the program. These are the only express warranties that are created by the contracts. Moreover, the contracts expressly exclude any other express warranties. Paragraph 5(c) of the Equipment Contract reads "EXCEPT AS SPECIFICALLY PROVIDED HEREIN, THERE ARE NO WARRANTIES, EXPRESS OR IMPLIED, WHICH EXTEND BEYOND THE DESCRIPTION ON THE FACE OR THE REVERSE SIDE HEREOF."

[5] Paragraph 7 of the Maintenance Contract contains almost identical language. Although the parties have not brought to the Court's attention any Maryland cases which are dispositive of the express warranty issue, Maryland has adopted the Uniform Commercial Code and cases in other states applying the Uniform Commercial Code are almost unanimous in holding that provisions disclaiming express warranties by the use of language similar to that in this case are effective disclaimers of express warranties. . . .

[6] It is true, as plaintiff contends, that Maryland's Commercial Code does not require that express warranties be made part of the written agreement but rather provides that "[a]ny affirmation of fact or promise made by the seller to the buyer which relates to the goods and becomes part of the basis of the bargain creates an express warranty that the goods shall conform to the affirmation or promise." Md. [Com. Law] Code Ann. § 2–313(1)(a). Plaintiff in its brief states that the express warranties alleged were contained in advertising or promotional material that was received by the plaintiff. However, the plaintiff ignores the effect of the parol evidence rule on this transaction. Under Maryland's Commercial Code if the parties intended the written contract to be a "final" expression of their agreement, then it may not be contradicted by evidence of any prior

[handwritten top margin: If disclaimer is in contract, and the warranty is parole evidence, it will not be brought in, but can still file suit under Misrepresentation]

agreement or contemporaneous oral agreement, and if the parties intended the contract to be the "complete and exclusive" statement of their agreement, it may not be supplemented even by non-contradictory terms. Md. [Com. Law] Code Ann. §§ 2–316(1), 2–202. *[handwritten: Maryland PER Issue]*

[7]   The Equipment Contract contains an integration provision which reads in relevant part, "[t]his contract contains the entire agreement between the parties." Thus, the contract plainly states that it constitutes the entire understanding between the parties. Courts applying the Uniform Commercial Code's provisions to similar integration provisions have found that such language is sufficient to render the contract the final and exclusive agreement of the parties, thereby preventing the introduction of parol evidence to vary the contract's terms. . . . In reaching the same conclusion, this Court has considered that the parties involved are merchants who had equal bargaining power with respect to the subject matter of their transaction. There is no suggestion that the plaintiffs were unaware of the significance of the disclaimer and integration clauses which were part of the contracts. Because allowing plaintiffs to base an express warranty claim on language not present in the contract would be inconsistent with the integration clause, plaintiff's express warranty claim fails to state a claim upon which relief may be granted and will be dismissed pursuant to Rule 12(b)(6) of the Federal Rules of Civil Procedure. *[handwritten right margin: EW claim is based on language not in contract]*

PROBLEM 17-5

Mr. and Ms. Bear went to Grimm Bros. Discount Furniture to buy a chair for their cub. Mr. Bear saw an official NFL-sponsored child's chair with the logo of his favorite team (the Chicago Bears) on it. He told Ms. Bear "now Teddy can pull up his chair next to my recliner when the ball games come on and we can engage in some male bonding." Ms. Bear was not so impressed. She expressed concern that one of Papa Bear's buddies might have a little too much to drink one night and sit in the kid's chair. *[handwritten: goods]*

"Not to worry," said the sales associate, "this chair will hold an adult. It's not nearly as flimsy as it looks. It's made of new space-age particle board." *[handwritten: 2-316? prob warenty]*

[handwritten left margin: Reliance] Based on the sales associate's assurance, Ms. Bear reluctantly agreed to the purchase of the chair. Mr. and Ms. Bear signed a sales contract that said in large red letters just above the signature line: *[handwritten right margin: PER we need to know if contract was integrated]*

EXCEPT AS EXPRESSLY SET FORTH IN THIS CONTRACT, THIS PRODUCT IS SOLD WITHOUT ANY WARRANTIES, EXPRESS OR IMPLIED. *[handwritten: Store will say disclaimer is valid]* *[handwritten right margin: PER would black it]*

A few days later, the Bear family returned from an outing and discovered that an intruder had sat in the child's NFL-endorsed chair and broken it while eating porridge. The chair was made of ordinary particle board, and, while it

[handwritten bottom: Since it was not written the disclaimer is valid]
[handwritten bottom: The EW was oral - the disclaimer was not conspicuous]

was quite satisfactory for use by a small child, there was no way it would support an adult or even a young golden-haired woman.

Has there been a breach of an express warranty?

PROBLEM 17-6

Ms. Muffett, a dairy products broker, entered into a contract with In The Dell Farms, Inc. The contract calls for In The Dell Farms, Inc. to deliver "one thousand gallons of USDA Number 1 curds and whey." The contract contained a clause which conspicuously provided:

Seller disclaims all warranties, express and implied, including without limitation all warranties of merchantability or fitness.

In The Dell Farms, Inc. delivered 1000 gallons of USDA Number 2 curds and whey. Number 2 curds and whey are less valuable than Number 1 curds and whey.

Does Ms. Muffett have a breach of warranty claim? *See* U.C.C. §§ 2–313(1) and 2–316(1).

PROBLEM 17-7

IW of merchantability

Your client sold one of his customers a drill bit for oil drilling. (These bits are expensive. Howard Hughes was as rich as he was because his father had founded Hughes Tool Company, which made bits like the one in question.) The bit broke the first time the customer tried to use it, and the customer immediately brought it back and demanded the return of his money. Your client, being a typical oil patch good old boy, told the customer exactly what he could do with the broken drill bit.

Not surprisingly, the customer sued, alleging breach of the implied warranty of merchantability. You asked the client what documentation there was for the sale, and he showed you his standard invoice. It contained no warranties, no disclaimers, and no exclusionary clauses. When you asked why these terms were not in the document, he told you that everybody in the oil business knew that when you buy a drill bit you get an "Oklahoma warranty." You overcame your reluctance to admit your ignorance, and you asked what an "Oklahoma warranty" was. He explained with some condescension that "if it breaks, you got two bits instead of one. You don't whine about it. You just buy another one from somebody else." Your investigation indicates that this is in fact the way things are done in the oil patch.

usage of trade could create a course of dealing limitation on warranty

What is the effect, if any, of the fine tradition that is the "Oklahoma Warranty" if the buyer doesn't take his medicine but instead hires a big-city lawyer and sues? *See* U.C.C. § 2–316(3)(c).

and would prevent Plaintiff from recovering

Consequential Damages

2-719 — Failed its essential purpose

BISHOP LOGGING CO. V. JOHN DEERE INDUSTRIAL EQUIPMENT CO.

South Carolina Court of Appeals
317 S.C. 520, 455 S.E.2d 183 (1995)

Pro History

[1] Respondent Bishop Logging Company (Bishop Logging) brought this action against John Deere Industrial Equipment Company (John Deere), Construction Equipment Sales, Inc. (CES), and Denharco, f/k/a Hurricana Metals, charging fraud, negligent misrepresentation, and breach of express warranty in connection with the sale of several pieces of heavy forestry equipment which were to be utilized in a novel swamp logging operation. The jury returned a verdict for Bishop Logging on each cause of action against John Deere, and awarded Bishop Logging $1,000,000 in actual damages and $1,200,000 in punitive damages. The trial court denied John Deere's post-trial motions for judgment n.o.v., new trial, and new trial nisi. We affirm in part and reverse in part.

Facts

[2] Bishop Logging Company is a large, family owned logging contractor formed in 1980 in the low country of South Carolina. Bishop Logging has traditionally harvested pine timber. However, in 1988 Bishop Logging began investigating the feasibility of a fully mechanized hardwood swamp logging operation when its main customer, Stone Container Corporation, decided to expand hardwood production. In anticipating an increased demand for hardwood in conjunction with the operation of a new paper machine, Stone Container requested that Bishop Logging harvest and supply hardwood for processing at its mill. In South Carolina, most suitable hardwood is located deep in the swamplands. Because of the high accident risk in the swamp, Bishop Logging did not want to harvest hardwood by the conventional method of manual felling of trees.[3] Since Bishop Logging had already been successful in its totally mechanized pine logging operation, it began a search for improved methods of hardwood swamp logging centered on mechanizing the process in order to reduce labor, minimize personal injury and insurance costs, and improve efficiency and productivity.

[3] A fully mechanized swamp logging operation was a new concept in hardwood logging. As planned, it consisted of three components. First, a feller-buncher would cut the timber. The feller-buncher was a tractor-mounted mobile saw which would travel through the swamp to the timber. Second, a mobile stroke delimber would travel behind the feller-buncher to

---

[3] Conventional hardwood logging is very labor intensive requiring workers to walk through the woods and manually cut and delimb trees with a chainsaw. A tractor-like machine called a cable skidder approaches the cut tree and the operator of the skidder gets off the machine and manually places a cable around the log and hooks it up to the machine. The operator then gets back on the skidder and drags the tree to a log deck, which is a marshalling area for cut trees, and unloads.

the felled tree. It would remove the limbs, top the tree, and prepare it to be dragged from the swamp. Finally, grapple skidders would remove the logs from the swamp to log trucks.

[4] As Bishop Logging knew that no fully mechanized swamp logging package of equipment was available for purchase, it launched a campaign to design a package to suit its needs. Its search began with a number of equipment companies and manufacturers. Adrian Bishop, the president of Bishop Logging, approached representatives of John Deere, Hurricana, and CES to determine if existing equipment could be modified to work in a swamp environment. In cooperation with the sales representatives, Bishop Logging investigated various types of equipment, including observing some of the equipment operating in different conditions.

[5] Bishop Logging ultimately purchased several pieces of John Deere equipment to comprise the system. This equipment included a Model 693D excavator on which a Koehring feller-buncher was attached, a Model 690D excavator with an attached Hurricana stroke delimber, and three Model 548D grapple skidders with oversized tires. The gross sales price of the machinery was $608,899. All the equipment came with a written John Deere "New Equipment Warranty," whereby John Deere agreed only to repair or replace the equipment during the warranty period, and did not warrant the suitability of the equipment. Hoping to sell more equipment if the Bishop Logging system was successful, however, John Deere agreed to assume part of the risk of the new enterprise by extending its standard equipment warranties notwithstanding the unusual use and modifications to the equipment.

All came with John Deere warranty

[6] Soon after being placed in operation in the swamp, the machinery began to experience numerous mechanical Problems. John Deere, through CES, made over $110,000 in warranty repairs on the equipment. However, Bishop Logging contended the swamp logging system failed to operate as represented by John Deere and, as a result, it suffered a substantial financial loss.[4]

* * *

[7] . . . . John Deere contends the court erred in failing to grant its trial motions on the cause of action for breach of express warranty. Specifically, John Deere claims the court erred in allowing Bishop Logging to receive lost profits and consequential damages for breach of express warranty because it effectively disclaimed express and implied warranties other than those contained in the John Deere "New Equipment Warranty," and those warranty provisions limited Bishop Logging's remedies for breach of the warranty to repair or replacement of defective parts, and

John Deere's Arguments

---

[4] According to its expert witness, the total financial loss to Bishop Logging was either $540,921 or $723,320 for the three year estimated life of the equipment. The difference depended upon the price Bishop Logging received per cord of wood logged by it.

explicitly excluded liability for consequential damages. Bishop Logging, on the other hand, maintains the exclusive remedy as limited "failed of its essential purpose," *S.C. Code Ann. § 36–2–719(2)*, thus entitling it to other remedies available under the Code, including consequential damages.

[8] Following delivery of the equipment, Bishop Logging experienced many mechanical Problems, and although parts were replaced, the equipment continued to malfunction. Benizzi admitted that the equipment had a lot of down time. Barry Smith, who had sixteen years of experience and had driven all of the equipment, testified he had never seen equipment break down more times than this. He further testified the equipment malfunctioned continuously, John Deere unsuccessfully attempted on many occasions to repair it, and as a result Bishop Logging could never make production.

[9] James E. Lyons, a mechanic responsible for warranty repairs to Bishop Logging's swamp logging package, was qualified as an expert in heavy equipment repair. He testified that Bishop Logging always had Problems with the carrier on the Model 690 excavator, and it was a total failure for this application. He further testified the most chronic failure was the Model 548D skidders which experienced substantial breakdowns within a few weeks of being placed in the field. In Mr. Lyons's view, the 548 skidders deteriorated because of the stress resulting from the forty four inch tires which had been approved by John Deere. The skidders were never "repaired to where they would work on a long term basis," and according to Lyons, they simply were not durable in the swamp logging application.

[10] In the "New Equipment Warranty," John Deere expressly provided: (1) John Deere would repair or replace parts which were defective in material or workmanship; (2) a disclaimer of any express warranties or implied warranties of merchantability or fitness for a particular purpose; (3) an exclusion of all incidental or consequential damages; and (4) no authority for the dealer to make any representations, promises, modifications, or limitations of John Deere's written warranty. John Deere argues that under this limited warranty, replacement of parts and repair of equipment were all that was required by it, and that this was, in fact, promptly performed upon request by Bishop with over $110,000 in warranty repairs.

[11] Under the South Carolina Uniform Commercial Code (UCC), it is clear that the parties to a contract may establish exclusive, limited written warranties and limitation of damages as a remedy for breach thereof. *S.C. Code Ann. § 36–2–719 (1977). Section 36–2–719(1)* of the Code provides that the agreement may limit the buyer's remedies to repair or replacement of nonconforming goods or parts, and if such remedy is expressly agreed to be exclusive, it is the sole remedy. *Section 36–2–719(3)* states that

consequential damages may be limited or excluded unless the limitation or exclusion is unconscionable.

[12] Despite the exclusive remedy provisions in *§ 36–2–719*, in certain circumstances a party may nonetheless be entitled to the general remedies of the UCC. *Section 36–2–719(2)* states that when circumstances cause an exclusive remedy to "fail of its essential purpose, remedy may be had as provided in this Act." The official comments under *§ 36–2–719* further provide that "under subsection (2), where an apparently fair and reasonable clause because of circumstances fails in its purpose or operates to deprive either party of the substantial value of the bargain, it must give way to the general remedy provisions of this Article." Id. *§ 36–2–719 comment 1.*

[13] The purpose of the exclusive remedy of replacement or repair of defective parts from John Deere's viewpoint was to give it an opportunity to make the equipment conform with the contract while limiting the risks to which it was subject by excluding direct and consequential damages that might otherwise arise. From Bishop Logging's perspective, it was to insure that the equipment would be operable in the swamp application and if the equipment did not function properly, to insure John Deere would cure any defects within a reasonable time after they were discovered. Where a seller is given a reasonable chance to correct defects and the equipment still fails to function properly, the buyer is deprived of the benefits of the limited remedy and it therefore fails of its essential purpose. *Beal v. General Motors Corp.,* 354 F.Supp. 423, 426 (D. Del. 1973). In such circumstances, § 36–2–719(2) permits the buyer to pursue the other remedies provided by the UCC if the defect substantially affects the value of the buyer's bargain. *S.C. Code Ann. § 36–2–719 comment 1*; see also *Clark v. Int'l Harvester Co.,* 99 Idaho 326, 581 P.2d 784, 798 (Idaho 1978).

[14] In *Riley v. Ford Motor Co.,* 442 F.2d 670 (5th Cir. 1971), the United States Fifth Circuit Court of Appeals held that under the circumstances of that case, which also involved a seller's express warranty limiting the buyer's recourse to the repair or replacement of defective parts, it was "unable to conclude that the jury was unjustified in its implicit finding that the warranty operated to deprive the purchaser 'of the substantial value of the bargain.'" Like the instant case, Riley concerned a seller's inability to remedy numerous major and minor defects within a reasonable time. Similarly, in *Murray v. Holiday Rambler, Inc.,* 83 Wis. 2d 406, 265 N.W.2d 513 (Wis. 1978), it was held that a warrantor's limited remedy to repair or replace defective parts failed in its essential purpose where the cumulative effect of a substantial number of defects substantially impaired the value of the goods to the buyer.

[15] The evidence at trial was clearly sufficient for the jury to determine that John Deere did not effectively perform its obligation to

repair the equipment properly and within a reasonable time, and as a result, Bishop Logging was deprived of the substantial value of the equipment it contracted for. We therefore affirm the jury's verdict on the warranty claim implicitly finding that the limited warranty failed in its essential purpose so as to deprive Bishop Logging of the substantial value of the bargain, and, as a consequence, gave Bishop Logging the right to pursue other remedies provided by the UCC.

Holding

[16] Notwithstanding Bishop Logging's ability to recover direct damages for breach of the warranty on the equipment due to the failure of its essential purposes, John Deere argues that the limitation of consequential damages expressed in the warranty has independent significance and should be effective to disclaim such damages under the facts of this case unless to do so would be unconscionable. In a purely commercial setting, as in this case, John Deere maintains that limitations on consequential damages are routinely upheld against challenges of unconscionability. Contrary to John Deere's assertion, Bishop Logging contends the premise of "certainty of repair" underlies the entire contract, and consequently "the exclusion of consequential damages logically refers to losses incurred only during a reasonable time before which repairs are successful." Since the attempted repairs never cured the defects in the equipment or made it operable as contemplated by the limited warranty, Bishop Logging argues the exclusion of consequential damages is inapplicable to those damages caused by John Deere's breach of its obligation to repair or replace the defective equipment.

[17] The effect of the failure of a limited remedy under § 36–2–719(2) upon a clause excluding liability for consequential damages is a major issue that has not been resolved by the appellate courts of this State. One line of cases holds that the exclusion of consequential damages is part of the limited remedy which has failed and hence allows the buyer to recover consequential damages. A second line of cases holds that the clause excluding consequential damages is entitled to independent significance and remains enforceable despite a failure of essential purpose unless the buyer can establish that the clause is unconscionable.

[18] In *Waters v. Massey-Ferguson, Inc.,* 775 F.2d 587 (4th Cir. 1985), the Fourth Circuit Court of Appeals, applying South Carolina law, addressed the issue of the effect that the failure of a repair or replacement remedy had upon the exclusion of consequential damages. In that case, Waters, a soybean farmer, purchased a Massey-Ferguson tractor to assist in his farming operation. He received a limited warranty with language limiting remedies similar in all practical respects with the John Deere Warranty. The tractor suffered chronic hydraulic failures, and the seller was unable to remedy its defects. Walters in turn suffered serious planting delays and alleged the defective tractor was responsible for consequential damages in the form of lost profits on his crops.

[19] Although the court held that the plaintiff-buyer could recover consequential damages, the court neither held that the exclusion was part of the failed limited remedy nor that the exclusion was unconscionable. Rather, the court interpreted the exclusion of consequential damages as applying only to those damages flowing directly from the breach of the warranty of quality and as inapplicable to those damages caused by the seller's breach of its obligation to repair or replace the defective parts. *Id.* at 591–592. In reaching this conclusion, the court declared that the threshold inquiry was one of contractual construction, and in ascertaining the intent of the parties, the court sought to determine what expectations were aroused in the parties by their written language in light of the surrounding circumstances. The court examined the contract from three different interpretive perspectives: (1) the language used in the text of the written agreement; (2) the creative context of the contract to determine which party drafted the written terms in question in order to place upon that party the duty to articulate the agreement precisely; and (3) the commercial context with emphasis upon the precise nature and purpose of the contract and the type of goods involved. Id. The court concluded that the exclusion of consequential damages did not extend to the situation in which the seller failed to repair the tractor as required by the warranty, since the contract indicated that the parties contemplated repair would be possible, and thus, the parties did not anticipate any need to limit damages from the failure of this remedy. *Id.* at 592.

[20] Likewise, the parties in the present case assumed that any mechanical Problems in the equipment could be corrected. In the context of the commercial nature of the transaction, John Deere's agent knew the equipment would be used in the swamp application and knew that regular, certain repair was promised and expected in order that all of the equipment could be used for its purpose. In negotiating the sale, John Deere's agent assured Bishop Logging that "those units would function properly in [the swamp] environment," and that he would have "at [his] beck and call . . . factory support to make sure that the equipment functioned properly." Therefore, we must interpret the exclusion of consequential damages in light of this premise of "certainty of repair" which underlies the entire contract. The parties obviously agreed to exclude consequential damages in the event that John Deere performed its obligation to repair or replace defects. However, Bishop Logging could reasonably have expected to recover consequential damages when, as here, the defects were never adequately corrected and the limited remedy proved ineffectual.

[21] The failure of the limited remedy in this case materially altered the balance of risk set by the parties in the agreement. Therefore, we conclude that the court was correct in disregarding the other limitations and exclusions on John Deere's warranties, and allowing the full array of remedies provided by the UCC, including recovery of consequential

allowed full array of remedies, failed its essential purpose

damages and incidental losses under *S.C. Code Ann. §§ 36–2–714* and *2–715.*

[22] *Section 36–2–714* sets forth the normal measure of direct damages for breach of warranty. The formula for calculating direct damages is the value of the goods as warranted less the value of the goods as accepted. In addition to the recovery of direct damages, *§ 36–2–714(3)* also provides for the recovery of incidental and consequential damages. Incidental damages resulting from the sellers' breach include expenses reasonably incurred in inspection, receipt transportation, and care and custody of goods rightfully rejected as well as expenses incident to effecting cover. See *S.C. Code Ann. § 36–2–715(1)*. Consequential damages include:

> (a) any loss resulting from general or particular requirements and needs of which the seller at the time of contracting had reason to know and which could not reasonably be prevented by cover or otherwise; and

> (b) injury to person or property proximately resulting from any breach of warranty.

See *S.C. Code Ann. § 36–2–715(2)*. Profits lost as a result of the breach are recoverable under this section as consequential damages. In *Marshall and Williams Co. v. General Fibers and Fabrics, Inc.*, 270 S.C. 247, 241 S.E.2d 888 (1978) the court indicated that consequential damages could also include additional operating expenses caused by the breach. The burden of proving the extent of loss incurred by way of consequential damages is on the buyer. *S.C. Code Ann. § 36–2–715, comment 4.*

[23] In the present case, the losses suffered by Bishop Logging were primarily lost anticipated profits. There was no personal injury and there was no injury to other property owned by Bishop Logging. According to Bishop Logging's expert witness who was hired to make a study of the economic loss in this case, the total financial loss to Bishop Logging was either $540,921 or $723,323 for the three year estimated life of the equipment. The difference depended upon the price Bishop Logging received per cord of wood logged by it. The one million dollar actual damage award recovered by Bishop Logging, however, was not only for lost profits from not meeting expected production schedules, but also other unspecified damages which the jury awarded. Although mathematical precision is not required in the proof of loss, we believe the jury's actual damage award lacked relation to the testimony in the record offered to establish damages and apparently included impermissible, noneconomic damages. To that extent, the actual damage award is reduced to the maximum total of economic damages claimed by Bishop Logging, $723,323. See *Wiggins v. Todd*, 296 S.C. 432, 373 S.E.2d 704 (Ct. App. 1988) (We may modify a judgment to reduce an award of damages where certain damages improperly allowed can be segregated).

consequential damages were not unconscionable, allowed the damages out of fairness towards the buyer

[handwritten margin note top: UCC - movable at the time of identification of contract]

PROBLEM 17-8

Trucker purchased a truck with a warranty that read as follows:

[handwritten margin: Warranty]

Manufacturer warrants to the owner each part of this vehicle to be free under normal use and service from defects in material and workmanship for a period of 12 months from the date of original retail delivery or first use.

[handwritten margin: exclusionary clause]
[handwritten margin: Disclaimer →]

Manufacturer's obligation under this warranty shall be limited to the repair of the vehicle and the replacement of defective parts. *[handwritten: 2-719(1) repair or replace]*

The warranties herein expressed are **IN LIEU OF** any other express or implied warranty, including without limitation any implied **WARRANTY** of **MERCHANTABILITY** or **FITNESS**, and of any other obligation on the part of Manufacturer or Dealer. In no event shall Manufacturer or Dealer be liable for any consequential loss or damage of any nature arising from any cause whatsoever. *[handwritten: 2-719 -(3) consequents)]*

[handwritten margin: Exclusionary clause]

The contract also called for Trucker to pay for the truck in monthly installments over a period of three years.

During the first year, the truck was in Dealer's shop for a total of 60 days to remedy a variety of Problems, some major and some minor. Trucker loses $300 in profits every day the truck was in the shop. At the end of the year, seeing his warranty coverage coming to an end and his mechanical Problems not coming to an end, Trucker stopped making payments and returned the truck to Dealer. Is Trucker liable for the loan balance? See § 2–608(2). Is Dealer liable for consequential damages? See § 2–719(2).

[handwritten margin: Did it fail of essential purpose?]
[handwritten: too late to revoke]

[handwritten: Appellant]   *[handwritten: Apellee]*

VAN DEN BROEKE v. BELLANCA AIRCRAFT CORP.

United States Court of Appeals, Fifth Circuit
576 F.2d 582 (1978)

[1] In this diversity action, appellant contends that the district court erred in granting appellee's [Bellanca Aircraft Corp.'s] motion for summary judgment. The district court held that express disclaimers of warranty precluded appellant's [Broeke's] reliance on implied warranties of merchantability and fitness and negligence in design. Because we hold that the disclaimers were not shown to be part of the agreement, however, we reverse.

[handwritten margin: Disclaimers were not part of agreement]

[2] The facts are simple. In April of 1973, appellant ordered an airplane from appellee through Abide Aero Service. In arriving at his decision to purchase this plane for use as a commercial crop duster, appellant was relying on advertising by Bellanca representing such a use.

[handwritten bottom: Commercial good - unconscionable test if consequential damages]

Additionally, he made his purpose known to the agent at Abide Aero. When the aircraft was delivered on June 6, 1973 a warranty certificate purporting to disclaim implied warranties and limit damages was also delivered. A postcard notifying Bellanca of the purchase for the purpose of activating warranties was also delivered. This card was returned to Bellanca either by appellant's office or by Abide Aero. Subsequently, appellant began experiencing mechanical difficulties with the aircraft and after absorbing business losses, sold the plane. Appellant then brought suit alleging breach of warranties and negligence in construction. Appellant asked for damages to include lost profits, cost of repairs, and loss on the resale of the aircraft. The district court granted appellee's motion for summary judgment holding that appellee's disclaimers of warranties precluded recovery. Appellant then appealed to this court.

[3]   Because this is a diversity case we, of course, apply Mississippi's law. The particular law we look to is Mississippi's version of the Uniform Commercial Code, Miss. Code Ann. (1972) § 75–1–101 *et seq.* Appellant bases his right to recovery under the Code on § 75–2–314, providing generally for implied warranties, and on § 75–2–315, providing for warranty of fitness for a particular purpose. Appellant also contended that the plane was negligently manufactured. Appellee contended, and the lower court agreed, however, that these warranties were excluded by virtue of the disclaimers in the warranty document, and that remedies were limited, pursuant to § 75–2–719, to preclude recovery for consequential damages or negligence.

[4]   The law with respect to limitation on exclusion of warranties in Mississippi was unclear at the time of the purchase of the airplane. Although both § 75–2–314 and § 75–2–315 provide that the implied warranties shall arise unless "excluded or modified," the legislature failed to enact § 2–316, the section normally dealing with exclusion or modification of warranties. Happily, however, we need not purport to decide whether and to what limit warranties may have been able to be disclaimed in Mississippi, because we hold that the disclaimers were not shown to have become part of the contract.

[5]   Both historically and under the Code, the time for determining the terms of the contract is when the bargain is struck. Disclaimers of warranty are no different. Therefore, unless the disclaimers are disclosed prior to the agreement and agreed upon, thereby made part of the contract, they are not binding. In the instant situation this is reflected by the language of § 75–2–315 which refers to the time of contracting as the operative time, and by that of § 75–2–719 which requires agreement on the limitation of remedies. It is evident that under Mississippi authority, the time of contracting is the relevant point to determine limitations on warranties. As the record was developed below, the warranty was not delivered apparently until after the agreement had been made. The record

does not adequately reflect the time at which the contract was made in this case, and thus does not reveal whether the warranty document limiting warranties and remedies was delivered before the time of contracting or after that time. The parties are free to develop this factual issue on remand.

[6] The requirements for modification are also provided by the Code, § 75–2–209. Because the aircraft in question cost in excess of $500, the sales contract is subject to § 75–2–201, the Code "statute of frauds." Because the underlying contract is subject to § 75–2–201, § 75–2–209(1) and (3) requires a signed modification agreement. In the instant case, there appears to be neither an agreement by appellant accepting a modified warranty scheme, nor a signature of appellant signifying such acceptance. A warranty card was mailed notifying Bellanca of appellant's purchase. This postcard, however, did not contain the warranty disclaimer, did not incorporate them by reference, and was not signed by appellant. Therefore, it would be impossible for us to hold that the mere action of returning a notice-type postcard was a modification of a contract.

[7] Even though the postcard was ineffective to operate as a modification, § 75–2–209(3) provides that such an ineffective attempt can, under the proper facts, operate as a waiver. According to its accepted definition, a waiver is a voluntary and intentional relinquishment of a known right. Judged by this standard it would be impossible for us to hold that the sending of the postcard constituted a waiver as a matter of law. The postcard, by its terms merely notifies Bellanca that a sale has been made. Although it is denoted as a "Warranty Registration" and states "To place your Bellanca Warranty into effect you must mail this card to the factory within 7 days of delivery to original user or purchaser" there is nothing evidencing an intent on the part of appellant to relinquish his other warranties in favor of the Bellanca Warranty. The probable intent of the appellant, if indeed he sent the card, was to insure hassle-free service for whatever would be covered by the Bellanca Warranty. Because no one actively desires a law suit, until one is necessary it is eminently practical to give notice in order to insure that those repairs which may fortunately fall under the limited warranty would be promptly effected. The mere fact that one seeks to avoid a lawsuit until it is practically necessary however, should not imply the intent to waive other contractual rights. Based upon the record as developed, we therefore hold that appellant did not waive the implied warranties and remedies that arose upon the purchase of the aircraft.[5]

Because the disclaimers were ineffective for the reasons states above, we REVERSE and REMAND.

---

[5] Of course, appellee is free to prove on remand that appellant, as a matter of fact, did waive implied warranties. We merely hold that, on the record before us, appellee did not prove appellant's waiver.

PROBLEM 17-9

Homer purchased a new sports car from Dealer. While he was driving a curving mountain road, wondering why it wasn't as much fun as the television commercials made it seem, the car's steering failed. Both Homer and the car were damaged in the resulting crash. Homer filed suit against Dealer alleging breach of the warranty of merchantability. Upon receipt of the summons and complaint, Dealer forwarded a copy to Manufacturer (from whom Dealer had purchased the car) along with a letter that read in full as follows:

July 21, 2010

Manufacturer
99–1/2 Jitney Blvd.
Detroit, Michigan 48100

Gentlemen:

Enclosed is a copy of a summons and complaint served upon us in connection with an allegedly defective automobile that you manufactured. Demand is hereby made that you appear in and defend in this action on behalf of my dealership.

Very truly yours,
/s/ Dealer

Having better things to do, Manufacturer ignored the letter. The case was tried and judgment was entered against Dealer. The jury found as facts (1) the steering mechanism in the car was defective, and (2) this defect had caused the injury. Dealer then filed a separate action against Manufacturer for breach of the implied warranty of merchantability.

In the Dealer-Manufacturer litigation, will Manufacturer be able to argue successfully that under § 2–607(5) it is not bound by the prior jury's determinations that the steering mechanism was defective and that that defect caused the accident? Why or why not? *See Bendix-Westinghouse Automotive Air Brake Co. v. Swan Rubber Co.*, 55 Cal. App. 3d 256, 127 Cal.Rptr. 571 (1976).

NOTE

In *Uniroyal, Inc. v. Chambers Gasket and Manufacturing Co.*, 177 Ind.App. 508, 380 N.E.2d 571 (1978), the court explained the purpose of the "vouching-in" procedure:

The common-law right of a defendant to "vouch-in" a person liable over to him was set forth in the leading case of *Littleton v. Richardson*, 34 N.H. 179, 66 Am. Dec. 759, 760 (1856):

[W]hen a person is responsible over to another, either by operation of law or by express contract . . . and he is duly notified of the pendency of the suit, and requested to take upon him the defense of it, he is no longer regarded as a stranger, because he has the right to appear and defend the action, and has the same means and advantages of contravening the claim as if he was the real and nominal party upon the record. In every such case, if due notice is given to such person, the judgment, if obtained without fraud or collusion . . . will be conclusive against him, whether he has appeared or not. . . .

"Voucher to warranty" has deep roots in common-law emanating from England. (*See* Comment, 29 ARK. L. REV. 486 (1976)). Its application in America has flourished. In 1963, the General Assembly saw fit to codify the practice as it relates to the law of sales concerning "middlemen" by enacting § 2–607: [The court then quoted § 2–607(5).] Vouching-in is a "simple and expedient way for defendants who have a right over against another to avoid the necessity of relitigating the issues of liability to the plaintiff in the first suit." IB Moore's Federal Practice 0.405[9]. It has the unique advantage of not requiring personal service of process. *Id.*

Statute of Limitations

PROBLEM 17-10

On July 8, 2007, Aerostar Aircraft purchased an aircraft engine from Oceanic Engines. The engine sat in Aerostar's warehouse until 2009, when it was installed in a new airplane. The airplane was sold to Dealer, and it sat on Dealer's lot until August 15, 2011, when it was sold to Purchaser. The first time Purchaser flew the plane, the engine failed. Purchaser made a crash landing in a cornfield. He was uninjured but the aircraft suffered extensive damage. So did the cornfield. It was determined that the cause of the crash was Oceanic's failure to install a cotter key on a crucial nut. The cotter key is required by Federal Aviation Regulations, and because it was not installed the nut came loose in flight. Is Purchaser's U.C.C. § 2–314 claim against Oceanic barred by U.C.C. § 2–725?

PROBLEM 17-11

On March 1, 2005, Purchaser purchased a set of tires with a warranty that provides:

> "Manufacturer warrants that these tires will perform satisfactorily in normal service for a period of five years or until 50,000 miles have been driven on them, whichever comes first."

There were no disclaimers, exclusionary clauses, or other provisions concerning warranties in the sales contract.

[Handwritten top margin: 4 years when breach should have or was discovered if language of warranty is extended for future performance]

[Handwritten left margin: accrues when breach was discovered ~ 4 years from time tire blew up]

[Handwritten right margin: Merchantability - barred b/c SOL is 4 years of tender if delivery]

(a) On September 1, 2009, the right front tire blew out causing a minor accident resulting in $4,000 worth of damage to Purchaser's Mercedes. Purchaser replaced the right front tire, and the other three tires logged their 50,000th mile on December 1, 2009. Purchaser has sued, alleging a breach of the implied warranty of merchantability. Is his claim barred by § 2–725? (Read the question carefully.)

(b) Suppose that on June 1, 2007, when the tires had been driven 55,000 miles a blowout occurred, causing a serious accident. The tires still had plenty of tread left, and the cause of the accident was determined to be a manufacturing defect. Could Purchaser assert a breach of warranty claim? If so, when would the statute run?

[Handwritten: beyond 5 years or 50,000]

[Handwritten: NO, over 50,000 miles]

Using Other Law to Circumvent Warranty Defenses

If the sellers have defenses to warranty claims, it may still be possible to recover under tort law. To do so, however, the plaintiff needs a basis for a tort law cause of action. Personal injury, wrongful death, or property damage is usually necessary. For the most part tort law does not allow recovery for "pure economic loss," i.e., lost profits and the like not associated with personal injury or property damage.

Restatement (Third) of Torts

§ 18. *Disclaimers, Limitations, Waivers, and Other Contractual Exculpations as Defenses to Products Liability Claims for Harm to Persons*

Disclaimers and limitations of remedies by product sellers or other distributors, waivers by product purchasers, and other similar contractual exculpations, oral or written, do not bar or reduce otherwise valid products liability claims against sellers or other distributors of new products for harm to persons.

* * *

§ 21. *Definition of "Harm to Persons or Property:" Recovery for Economic Loss*

For purposes of this Restatement, harm to persons or property includes economic loss if caused by harm to:

(a) the plaintiff's person; or

(b) the person of another when harm to the other interferes with an interest of the plaintiff protected by tort law; or

(c) the plaintiff's property other than the defective product itself.

Comment:

f.   Harm to other property: disclaimers and limitations of remedies. Although recovery for harm to property other than the defective product itself is governed by this Restatement, the Institute leaves to developing case law the questions of whether and under what circumstances contracting parties may disclaim or limit remedies for harm to other property. Of course, such contractual limitations would be effective only between the parties themselves. When a defective product causes harm to property owned by third persons, the contractual arrangements between the contracting parties should not shield the seller from liability to the third party. However, contractual limitations on tort liability for harm to property, when fairly bargained for, may provide an effective way for the contracting parties efficiently to allocate risks of such harm between themselves.

PROBLEM 17-12

(a) Manufacturer purchased a furnace from Furnace Co. and had it installed in its factory. The sale contract provided: "In no event shall Furnace Co. be liable for consequential loss or damage arising from any cause whatsoever." The following January, a small but vital part in the furnace malfunctioned and the furnace stopped heating. Manufacturer was forced to close its plant for two weeks until a replacement part could be found. Can Manufacturer recover for the profits lost while the furnace was down?

(b) What would be the result in Part (a) if the furnace exploded and destroyed Manufacturer's computer system and the destruction of the computer system was the reason for the shutdown?

(c) What would be the answer in Part (a) if the furnace exploded but did not damage anything other than the furnace itself?

MORRIS V. MACK'S USED CARS

Supreme Court of Tennessee
824 S.W.2d 538 (1992)

[1] The purchaser, Darrell Morris, sued the seller, Mack's Used Cars & Parts, Inc., for compensatory, treble, and punitive damages, alleging fraudulent concealment, breach of express warranty of title under T.C.A. § 47–2–312, breach of express warranty of description under T.C.A. § 47–2–313, breach of implied warranty of merchantability under T.C.A. § 47–2–314, and violation of the Tennessee Consumer Protection Act forbidding unfair or deceptive acts under T.C.A. § 47–18–104(b)(6), (7).

[2]   The facts were not disputed. In September 1985 the defendant sold to Morris a vehicle described on the bill of sale as a 1979 Ford pickup truck. An older truck was traded in as a down payment, and the balance of the purchase price was financed over a term of three years with a retail installment contract and security agreement, pursuant to which the certificate of title was delivered by the defendant-seller directly to the lender. The bill of sale contained the following statement immediately above the purchaser's signature, "This unit sold as is. No warranties have been expressed or implied." At the time of sale, the truck had been wrecked or dismantled and was a "reconstructed" vehicle within the meaning of Title 55, Chapter 3, Part 2[6] of Tennessee Code Annotated. The seller knew but did not disclose to the purchaser that the pickup was a reconstructed vehicle. The purchaser obtained this information three years later when he received the certificate of title after paying the final installment on the sales contract. Being reconstructed reduced the vehicle's fair market value 30 to 50 percent.

[3]   The seller's defense was that the disclaimer contained in the bill of sale avoided any liability for its not disclosing to the purchaser the condition of the vehicle as revealed by the certificate of title.

[4]   The trial court agreed with the seller and dismissed the suit. On appeal of the count charging violation of the Consumer Protection Act, the Court of Appeals affirmed, stating,

> To hold the Defendant liable under the Tennessee Consumer Protection Act would, in effect, be creating liability under an "as is" sale which is waived under T.C.A. § 47–2–316(3)(a).

The Court of Appeals held, in the words of Judge Franks, dissenting, "[T]here can be no claim for unfair or deceptive trade practices whenever a seller disclaims warranties under the Uniform Commercial Code . . . with an 'as is' clause." [We reverse.—Eds.]

[5]   The trial court and the Court of Appeals misconstrued these statutes as they relate to the Consumer Protection Act. Disclaimers permitted by § 47–2–316 of the Uniform Commercial Code (UCC) may limit or modify liability otherwise imposed by the code, but such disclaimers do not defeat separate causes of action for unfair or deceptive acts or practices under the Consumer Protection act, T.C.A. § 47–18–101 to –5002.

[6]   The UCC contemplates the applicability of supplemental bodies of law to commercial transactions. Section 47–1–103, T.C.A., provides the following:

> Unless displaced by the particular provisions of chapters 1 through 9 of this title, the principles of law and equity, including

---

6   [This part covers certificates of title for wrecked, dismantled, or rebuilt motor vehicles.—Eds.]

the law merchant and the law relative to capacity to contract, principal and agent, estoppel, fraud, misrepresentation, duress, coercion, mistake, bankruptcy, or other validating or invalidating cause shall supplement its provisions.

Also, the supplementary nature of the Consumer Protection Act is made clear by T.C.A. § 47–18–112, which states:

The powers and remedies provided in this part shall be cumulative and supplementary to all other powers and remedies otherwise provided by law. The invocation of one power or remedy herein shall not be construed as excluding or prohibiting the use of any other available remedy.

[7]   A seller may disclaim all implied warranties pursuant to T.C.A. § 47–2–316, which provides in pertinent part:

Exclusion or modification of warranties . . . (3)(a) unless the circumstances indicate otherwise, all implied warranties are excluded by expressions like "as is," "with all faults" or other language which in common understanding calls the buyer's attention to the exclusion of warranties and makes plain that there is no implied warranty.

[8]   The Consumer Protection Act recognizes this right of exclusion or modification of warranties under the UCC. Section 47–18–113, T.C.A., provides:

Waiver of Rights. (a) No provision of this part may be limited or waived by contract, agreement, or otherwise, notwithstanding any other provision of law to the contrary; provided, however, the provisions of this part shall not alter, amend, or repeal the provisions of the Uniform Commercial Code relative to express or implied warranties or the exclusion or modification of such warranties.

The above provision, however, also specifically precludes disclaimer of liability under the Consumer Protection Act. Furthermore, the UCC, pursuant to T.C.A. § 47–1–203, imposes an obligation of good faith in the performance or enforcement of every contract. Under T.C.A. § 47–1–102(3), this obligation may not be disclaimed.

[9]   Claims under the UCC and the Consumer Protection Act are distinct causes of action, with different components and defenses. The Consumer Protection Act is applicable to commercial transactions, also regulated by the UCC. The Court of Appeals in *Skinner v. Steele*, 730 S.W.2d 335 (Tenn. Ct. App. 1987), reached a similar conclusion with regard to the regulation of the insurance industry. The court held that the mere existence of a separate statute regulating the insurance industry does not create exemption from the Consumer Protection Act. 730 S.W.2d at 338.

[10] Other states have recognized that the disclaimer of warranty liabilities under the UCC does not preclude the advancement of non-warranty claims based on unfair trade practices. In *V.S.H. Realty, Inc. v. Texaco, Inc.*, 757 F.2d 411 (1st Cir. 1985), the buyer of an oil storage facility under an "as is" contract sued the seller alleging misrepresentation, non-disclosure, and violation of the Massachusetts statute prohibiting unfair or deceptive practices. The district court dismissed the statutory claim on the basis of the "as is" disclaimer. The First Circuit Court of Appeals reversed, stating:

> We believe the district court's view of the law regarding "as is" clauses is incorrect. Although the Uniform Commercial Code does expressly permit disclaimers in the sale of goods between merchants, § 2–316 refers specifically to disclaimers of implied warranties, suggesting to us that it was intended only to permit a seller to limit or modify the contractual bases of liability which the Code would otherwise impose on the transaction. The section does not appear to preclude claims based on fraud or other deceptive conduct.

757 F.2d at 417.

[11] Automobile sales cases from other jurisdictions have held that an "as is" disclaimer of warranties does not bar an action for deceptive trade practices. In *Metro Ford Sales, Inc. v. Davis*, 709 S.W.2d 785 (Tex. Ct. App.—Fort Worth 1986), the buyer of a used truck brought an action against the seller under the Texas Deceptive Trade Practices Consumer Protection Act (DTPA). The buyer alleged that the salesman falsely represented that the truck was in "top" condition and had not been wrecked. The seller contended that the warranty disclaimer signed by the buyer was admissible to counter the DTPA cause of action. The court concluded,

> We hold that the waiver of warranty did not waive [the buyer's] cause of action for misrepresentation under the DTPA and that the waiver was properly excluded.

709 S.W.2d at 790. In *Attaway v. Tom's Auto Sales, Inc.*, 242 S.E.2d 740 (Ga. Ct. App. 1978), the buyer of a used car brought suit against the seller, alleging breach of warranty and violation of the Georgia Fair Business Practices Act (Act). The sales contract provided "all cars sold as is . . . no guarantee." The court stated that "the language in the contract would appear to prevent [the buyer] from recovering on the grounds of express or implied warranty" and concluded that "although [the buyer] might not be able to rescind the contract or otherwise set it aside, the Act itself is in no

way tied to contractual rights and is wholly self-sustaining." 242 S.E.2d at 742. The court concluded:

> From an overview of [the Act], we find that there is thereby created a separate and distinct cause of action under its provisions. A consumer who is damaged thereby has an independent right to recover under the Act, regardless of any other theory of recovery.

Id.

[12] The Tennessee Consumer Protection Act is to be liberally construed to protect consumers and others from those who engage in deceptive acts or practices. *Haverlah v. Memphis Aviation, Inc.*, 674 S.W.2d 297, 305 (Tenn. Ct. App. 1984). In a case similar to the one before the Court, the seller's failure to disclose to the buyer that the vehicle had been in an accident and had been repaired constituted a violation of the Consumer Protection Act. *See Patty v. Herb Adcox Chevrolet Co.*, 756 S.W.2d 697 (Tenn. Ct. App. 1988). To allow the seller here to avoid liability for unfair or deceptive acts or practices by disclaiming contractual warranties under the UCC would contravene the broad remedial intent of the Consumer Protection Act.

[13] In summary, disclaimers permitted by T.C.A. § 47–2–316 do not prevent application of the Consumer Protection Act. The Consumer Protection Act creates a separate and distinct cause of action for unfair or deceptive acts or practices.

[14] The judgments of the trial court and Court of Appeals dismissing the alleged violation of the Consumer Protection Act, therefore, are reversed and the case is remanded. The costs are taxed to the appellee.

LAWYERING SKILLS PROBLEM

In 2006, Penny King purchased a used 1995 model Ranch-Aire aerobatic airplane (one that is specially-designed for loops, rolls, and other air show-type maneuvers) from Uncle Sky's Aircraft Sales, a dealer in new and used aircraft. Penny operates a small flying school, just herself and two or three part-time instructors. The part-time instructors turn over regularly as they get airline jobs (or give up trying to get airline jobs, as the case may be). At any given time Penny would own two or three aircraft. Typically, she would keep an eye out for good deals in used aircraft and when she saw a good deal, she would buy the plane, use it for a couple of years and sell it when something better came along.

As an aviation professional, Penny knew that an aircraft that has been damaged (ever) is much less valuable than one that has never been damaged. Therefore, Penny required that the bill of sale she received from Uncle Sky provide "subject aircraft has never been damaged."

Similarly, Penny knew that aircraft are subject to *airworthiness directives*. The Federal Aviation Administration from time to time issues airworthiness directives when it discovers unsafe design features in a particular type of airplane. These are like automobile recall notices, but with a couple of major differences—the *owner* (not the manufacturer) of the aircraft has to pay for the work done on the aircraft and it is *illegal* to fly the aircraft if the airworthiness directive has not been complied with. To make sure that there weren't any airworthiness directives that had been issued with respect to the Ranch-Aire and not already incorporated into her airplane, Penny made sure that the bill of sale she got from Uncle Sky provided "all airworthiness directives pertaining to this aircraft have been complied with."

In 2010, Penny decided it was time to sell the old Ranch-Aire. Penny's middle-aged body no longer took kindly to the g-forces generated by beginners incompetently attempting barrel rolls. Penny placed the following ad in an aviation magazine:

> 1195 Ranch-Aire. Fun aerobatic airplane. New radios. Never damaged. All airworthiness directives complied with. Call 865.974.0681.

Mike Grey saw the ad. He called Penny and told her he had seen the ad. She gave him a demonstration flight, and he decided he had to have the aircraft. They entered into a contract where he agreed to buy the aircraft subject to the express condition precedent that "Buyer shall be satisfied with the results of an inspection of the aircraft and its log books performed by a Federal Aviation Administration-licensed aircraft mechanic."

The contract was one page long and was prepared by Penny. The last line in the contract, in ordinary type, directly above the signature line, read: "no warranties."

After signing the contract, Mike hired a mechanic to inspect the aircraft and its log books. The inspection of the log books was important because federal regulations require that a log book be maintained for every aircraft and that all damage to the aircraft and all repairs to the aircraft be recorded in the log books, which are always transferred along with an airplane.

Prior to signing the contract for the purchase of the aircraft, Mike glanced at the log book, but he did not review it thoroughly because he intended to have his mechanic, who knew better what to look for, take a very close look at it.

The mechanic inspected the aircraft and its log book, and told Mike that there appeared to be nothing wrong with either. Mike thereupon paid for the airplane and took possession of it.

Two years later, Mike went to sell the plane to buy a plane that was newer and more powerful. When his buyer had the plane inspected, her mechanic found two major problems with the plane. First, he found that the airplane had, in fact, been damaged some years earlier, before Penny bought the plane. The damage had been repaired so that it was not detectable even by the most careful inspection of the plane, but the repairs were logged in the log book, and a careful reading of the log book by Penny, Mike, or the mechanics who inspected the airplane when Penny and Mike made their purchases would have revealed the damage. Unfortunately, none of these folks read the log book that carefully, and in spite of the quality of the repair, the fact that the aircraft had suffered this damage reduced its value. Also, the buyer's mechanic discovered there was an airworthiness directive that had been issued three years before Penny bought the plane. The airworthiness directive required adding a stiffener to the wing to reduce metal fatigue in the wing. It would cost $2,000 comply with the airworthiness directive, and the fact that the airplane had flown so many years without the stiffener meant that the wing had suffered more than the usual amount of metal fatigue and this further detracted from the value of the plane.

Mike's mechanic could not have determined that there was an airworthiness directive that had not been complied with solely by looking at the log book, but a careful mechanic making an inspection such as this would have obtained a list of airworthiness directives applying to this particular model of aircraft and checked against the log book, where each repair made to comply with an airworthiness directive is logged, to make sure that every one of them had been complied with. Instead, Mike's mechanic relied on entries made by Penny's mechanic when he did his annual inspections of the aircraft. At each annual inspection, Penny's mechanic had written in the log book: "All airworthiness directives complied with." When he made this notation he did not actually check that all the airworthiness directives ever issued against the plane had been complied with. Instead, he went back to the similar entry made at the last annual inspection and then just checked to make sure no airworthiness directives had come out since that date or that if one had, it had been complied with. A very careful mechanic would have obtained a list of all the airworthiness directives ever issued against this model and checked that compliance with them had been logged in the log book before he made this notation the first time, but Penny's mechanic had not done this. Instead he relied on the entry made by the previous owner's mechanic and only looked for airworthiness directives issued since that entry. The previous owner's mechanic had done the same thing. He had relied on the entries made by the mechanic before him. An earlier mechanic had overlooked an airworthiness directive, and nobody had picked it up.

The discovery of these defects means that Mike won't be able to sell the plane except at a much reduced price. He has come to you to see if he has any breach of warranty claims against Penny. Please advise him.

CHAPTER 18

PRINCIPLES OF CONTRACT DAMAGES

. . . *compensating nonbreaching party for its loss*

Before the specifics of damages, a few general principles need to be covered. First, in breach of contract cases, Anglo-American law generally aims at compensating the non-breaching party rather than making the breaching party perform. A decree of *specific performance,* a court order requiring the breaching party to perform, is the norm in some legal systems, and, as we shall see, is sometimes available in Anglo-American courts, but most of the time the non-breaching party is entitled only to an award of money damages.

Second, contract damages are about compensation, not punishment or any other goal. The amount of the damages is not intended to punish the breaching party for breaching the contract, but only to compensate the non-breaching party for its loss. The basic measure of damages is *the amount of money that will place the non-breaching party in as good a monetary position as she would have been in had the contract been performed*. This, generally, excludes non-monetary damages of a "personal" or emotional nature that might be compensable under other fields of law like torts.

For example, suppose that Buyer and Seller enter into a contract for the sale of a million barrels of oil at $50 a barrel, delivery to be made in thirty days. If war breaks out in the Middle East and the price of oil is $90 a barrel at the time for delivery and Seller breaches, Buyer is entitled to damages of $40 million ($40 a barrel) because that's the profit he would have made on the deal if the contract had been performed. (Contract Price = $50; Market Price = $90; Lost Profit = $40) It doesn't matter one bit that it's purely a windfall for Buyer, who did nothing to deserve it (other than being lucky enough to have made a contract at the right time).

On the other hand, suppose that Vendor and Purchaser enter into a contract for the sale of wheat at $3 a bushel, delivery to be made in August. It turns out that Vendor is a really nasty person. He breaches the contract just because he has it in for Purchaser. Nevertheless, the price of wheat drops to $2.50 a bushel and Purchaser is able to get the wheat for less money than she would have had to pay to Vendor. Purchaser is not entitled to recover anything in the way of damages because she didn't suffer any monetary loss.

Similarly, consider two people developing real property in a southeastern beach resort town. The first is a real estate developer who is renovating a group of five cottages that will each rent for a net profit after expenses of $2,000 per month. The second is a widow with four children who wants to retire to the beach resort from her small home in Michigan that she owns free and clear and who hopes that her children will come and visit her often if she has four extra bungalows in which they may stay. Both enter into contracts with Contractor to renovate and develop their parcels of property into five functional one-bedroom/bathroom units. Unbeknownst to either of them, Contractor rarely completes a contract on time. The average delay is six months. If Contractor performs up to its average and is six months late on both projects, the developer may be entitled to up to $60,000 in damages (representing 5 units x $2,000 profit per unit per month x 6 months). But if the widow stays in Michigan waiting for completion and incurs no additional costs as a result of the delays, she may be entitled to nothing for the breach of contract, even though she must stay north for another dreary winter.

The first two cases in this chapter illustrate the general contracts approach to damages. Later cases and problems explore the computation of specific damages in detail, first under the common law/R2d approach and, second under the U.C.C. The UNIDROIT principles and the CISG are largely analogous to the R2d and U.C.C. in this area and are not separately examined. *See* UNIDROIT articles 7.4.1–7.4.8. Keep in mind that those authorities should be specifically referenced if they are applicable to a particular transaction or dispute.

MENZEL V. LIST

Court of Appeals of New York.
24 N.Y.2d 91, 298 N.Y.S.2d 979, 246 N.E.2d 742 (1969)

BURKE, J.

[1]   In 1932 Mrs. Erna Menzel and her husband purchased a painting by Marc Chagall at an auction in Brussels, Belgium, for 3,800 Belgian francs (then equivalent to about $150). When the Germans invaded Belgium in 1940, the Menzels fled and left their possessions, including the Chagall painting, in their apartment. They returned six years later and found that the painting had been removed by the German authorities and that a receipt for the painting had been left. The location of the painting between the time of its removal by the Germans in 1941 and 1955 is unknown. In 1955 Klaus Perls and his wife, the proprietors of a New York art gallery, purchased the Chagall from a Parisian art gallery for $2,800. The Perls knew nothing of the painting's previous history and made no inquiry concerning it, being content to rely on the reputability of the Paris gallery as to authenticity and title. In October, 1955 the Perls sold the painting to Albert List for $4,000. However, in 1962, Mrs. Menzel noticed

a reproduction of the Chagall in an art book accompanied by a statement that the painting was in Albert List's possession. She thereupon demanded the painting from him but he refused to surrender it to her.

[2] Mrs. Menzel then instituted a replevin action against Mr. List and he, in turn, impleaded the Perls, alleging in his third-party complaint that they were liable to him for breach of an implied warranty of title. At the trial, expert testimony was introduced to establish the painting's fair market value at the time of trial. The only evidence of its value at the time it was purchased by List was the price which he paid to the Perls. The trial court charged the jury that, if it found for Mrs. Menzel against List, it was also to "assess the value of said painting at such an amount as you believe from the testimony represents its present value." The jury returned a verdict for Mrs. Menzel and she entered a judgment directing the return of the painting to her or, in the alternative, that List pay to her the value of the painting, which the jury found to be $22,500. (List has, in fact, returned the painting to Mrs. Menzel.) In addition, the jury found for List as against the Perls, on his third-party complaint, in the amount of $22,500[1], the painting's present value, plus the costs of the Menzel action incurred by List.

[3] The Perls appealed to the Appellate Division, First Department, from that judgment and the judgment was unanimously modified, on the law, by reducing the amount awarded to List to $4,000 (the purchase price he had paid for the painting), with interest from the date of the purchase. In a memorandum, the Appellate Division held that the third-party action was for breach of an implied warranty of quiet possession and, accordingly, held that the Statute of Limitations had not run on List's claim since his possession was not disturbed until the judgment for Mrs. Menzel. In addition, the court held that the "applicable measure of damages was the price List paid for the painting at the time of purchase, together with interest."

[4] List filed a notice of appeal as of right from the unanimous modification insofar as it reduced the amount of his judgment to $4,000, with interest from the date of purchase . . . .

[5] List's appeal and the Perls' cross appeal present only questions of law for resolution, the facts having been found by the jury and affirmed by the Appellate Division (its modification was on the law as to the proper measure of damages and the running of interest). The issue on the main appeal is simply what is or should be the proper measure of damages for the breach of an implied warranty of title (or quiet possession) in the sale of personal property. . . .

---

[1] [$22,500 in 1969 dollars is roughly the equivalent of $154,000 in 2019 dollars using the CPI and the GNP Deflator.—Eds.]

[6]   At the time of the sale to List and at the commencement of the *Menzel* replevin action, there was in effect [a statute] which provided that "In a contract to sell or a sale, unless contrary intention appears, there is

> 1.   An implied warranty on the part of the seller that . . . he has a right to sell the goods . . .
>
> 2.   An implied warranty that the buyer shall have and enjoy quiet possession of the goods as against any lawful claims existing at the time of the sale."

[7]   In addition, [another statute] provided: "The measure of damages for breach of warranty is the loss directly and naturally resulting, in the ordinary course of events, from the breach of warranty. . . ."[2] The Perls contend that the only loss directly and naturally resulting, in the ordinary course of events, from their breach was List's loss of the purchase price. List, however, contends that loss is the present market value of the painting, the value which he would have been able to obtain if the Perls had conveyed good title. The Perls support their position by reference to the damages recoverable for breach of the warranty of quiet possession as to real property. However, this analogy has been severely criticized by a leading authority in these terms: "This rule [limiting damages to the purchase price plus interest] virtually confines the buyer to rescission and restitution,[3] a remedy to which the injured buyer is undoubtedly entitled if he so elects, but it is a violation of general principles of contracts to deny him in an action on the contract such damages *as will put him in as good a position as he would have occupied had the contract been kept.*" 11 Williston, Contracts [3d ed.], § 1395A, p. 484 [emphasis added]. Clearly, List can only be put in the same position he would have occupied if the contract had been kept by the Perls if he recovers the value of the painting at the time when, by the judgment in the main action, he was required to surrender the painting to Mrs. Menzel or pay her the present value of the painting. Had the warranty been fulfilled, i.e., had title been as warranted by the Perls, List would still have possession of a painting currently worth $22,500 and he could have realized that price at an auction or private sale. If List recovers only the purchase price plus interest, the effect is to put him in the same position he would have occupied *if the sale had never been made.* Manifestly, an injured buyer is not compensated when he recovers only so much as placed him in *status quo ante* since such a recovery implicitly denies that he had suffered any damage . . . [Awarding the buyer the value of the property] reflects what the buyer has actually lost and it

---

[2]   [Expectancy damages for breach of warranty in a sale are equal to the value of the things as warranted less the value of the thing actually received in the sale. We recommend that you commit their simple formula to memory.—Eds.]

[3]   [Recission and restitution is a remedy which entitles the non-breaching party to terminate the contract and receive the return of any money or other benefits it has conferred on the other party.—Eds.]

awards to him only the loss which has directly and naturally resulted, in the ordinary course of events, from the seller's breach of warranty.

[8]   An objection raised by the Perls to this measure of damages is that it exposes the innocent seller to potentially ruinous liability where the article sold has substantially appreciated in value. However, this "potential ruin" is not beyond the control of the seller since he can take steps to ascertain the status of title so as to satisfy himself that he himself is getting good title. (Mr. Perls testified that to question a reputable dealer as to his title would be an "insult." Perhaps, but the sensitivity of the art dealer cannot serve to deprive the injured buyer of compensation for a breach which could have been avoided had the insult been risked.) Should such an inquiry produce no reasonably reliable information as to the status of title, it is not requiring too much to expect that, as a reasonable businessman, the dealer would himself either refuse to buy or, having bought, inform his vendee of the uncertain status of title. Furthermore, the seller could modify or exclude the warranties since they arise only "unless contrary intention appears". Had the Perls taken the trouble to inquire as to title, they could have sold to List subject to any existing lawful claims unknown to them at the time of the sale. Accordingly, the "prospects of ruin" forecast as flowing from the rule are not quite as ominous as the argument would indicate. Accordingly, the order of the Appellate Division should be reversed as to the measure of damages and the judgment awarding List the value of the painting at the time of trial of the *Menzel* action should be reinstated.

* * *

[9]   Order reversed, with costs to third-party plaintiff-appellant-respondent, and case remitted to Supreme Court, New York County, for further proceedings in accordance with the opinion herein.

UNITED STATES NAVAL INSTITUTE V. CHARTER COMMUNICATIONS

United States Court of Appeals, Second Circuit
936 F.2d 692 (1991)

KEARSE, CIRCUIT JUDGE:

[1]   This case returns to us following our remand in *United States Naval Institute v. Charter Communications, Inc.*, 875 F.2d 1044 (2d Cir. 1989) ("*Naval I*"), to the United States District Court for the Southern District of New York, Pierre N. Leval, Judge, for the fashioning of relief in favor of plaintiff United States Naval Institute ("Naval") against defendant Charter Communications, Inc., and Berkley Publishing Group (collectively "Berkley"), for breach of an agreement with respect to the publication of the paperback edition of *The Hunt For Red October* ("*Red October*" or the

"Book"). On remand, the district court awarded Naval $35,380.50[4] in damages, $7,760.12 as profits wrongfully received by Berkley, and $15,319.27 as prejudgment interest on the damages awarded, plus costs. Naval appeals from so much of the judgment as failed to award a greater amount as profits . . . . For the reasons below, we reverse the award of profits; we affirm the award of damages . . .

I.   Background

[2]   Naval, as the assignee of the author's copyright in *Red October*, entered into a licensing agreement with Berkley in September 1984 (the "Agreement"), granting Berkley the exclusive license to publish a paperback edition of the Book "not sooner than October 1985." Berkley shipped its paperback edition to retail outlets early, placing those outlets in position to sell the paperback prior to October 1985. As a result, retail sales of the paperback began on September 15, 1985, and early sales were sufficiently substantial that the Book was near the top of paperback best-seller lists before the end of September 1985.

[3]   Naval commenced the present action when it learned of Berkley's plans for early shipment, and it unsuccessfully sought a preliminary injunction. After trial, the district judge dismissed the complaint. He ruled that Berkley had not breached the Agreement because it was entitled, in accordance with industry custom, to ship prior to the agreed publication date. On appeal, we reversed. Though we upheld the district court's finding that the Agreement did not prohibit the early shipments themselves, we concluded that if the "not sooner than October 1985" term of the Agreement had any meaning whatever, it meant at least that Berkley was not allowed to cause such voluminous paperback retail sales prior to that date, and that Berkley had therefore breached the Agreement. Accordingly, we remanded for entry of a judgment awarding Naval appropriate relief.

[4]   In a Memorandum and Order dated July 17, 1990 ("July 17 Order"), the district judge rejected Berkley's claim that "its premature publication of the paperback edition constituted only a contract violation and not an infringement of Naval's copyright." He found that Naval's copyright was infringed by the early publication . . . He concluded that Naval was entitled to recover damages for copyright infringement, comprising actual damages suffered by Naval plus Berkley's profits "attributable to the infringement." 17 U.S.C. § 504(b).

[5]   The court calculated Naval's "actual damages from Berkley's wrongful pre-October 'publication'" as the profits Naval would have earned from hardcover sales in September 1985 if the competing paperback edition had not then been offered for sale. July 17 Order at 8. Noting the downward trend of hardcover sales of the Book from March through August 1985, the

---

4   [$35,380.50 in 1991 dollars is roughly the equivalent of $65,200 in 2019 dollars using the CPI and the GNP Deflator.—Eds.]

court found that there was no reason to infer that Naval's September 1985 sales would have exceeded its August 1985 sales. The court calculated Naval's lost sales as the difference between the actual hardcover sales for those two months, and awarded Naval $35,380.50 as actual damages.

[6] The district judge held that Berkley's profits "attributable to the infringement" were only those profits that resulted from "sales to customers who would not have bought the paperback but for the fact it became available in September." July 17 Order at 10. He found that most of the September paperback sales were made to buyers who would not have bought a hardcover edition in September, and therefore only those September sales that displaced hardcover sales were attributable to the infringement. Berkley's profit on the displacing copies totaled $7,760.12, and the court awarded that amount to Naval.

[7] The court awarded Naval prejudgment interest (totaling $15,319.27) on the $35,380.50 awarded as actual damages but denied such interest on the award of Berkley's profits. It also denied Naval's request for attorney's fees.

[8] Judgment was entered accordingly, and these appeals followed.

II. Discussion

[9] For the reasons below, we conclude that Naval is not entitled to recover for copyright infringement or to be awarded attorney's fees. Naval is, however, entitled to recover for breach of contract, and we affirm the district court's award of actual damages and of prejudgment interest.

A. Naval's Claim of Copyright Infringement

[The court held that Berkley's acts did not constitute copyright infringement.—Eds.]

B. Contract Damages

* * *

[10] The damages awarded by the district court on remand had two components: (1) Naval's lost profits resulting from Berkley's early publication of the paperback edition of the Book, and (2) Berkley's profits attributable to its assumed infringement. For the reasons discussed above, the latter component of the award cannot stand. The former component, however, may properly measure damages under a breach-of-contract theory.

[11] Since the purpose of damages for breach of contract is to compensate the injured party for the loss caused by the breach, those damages are generally measured by the plaintiff's actual loss. While on occasion the defendant's profits are used as the measure of damages, this generally occurs when those profits tend to define the plaintiff's loss, for an

award of the defendant's profits where they greatly exceed the plaintiff's loss and there has been no tortious conduct on the part of the defendant would tend to be punitive, and punitive awards are not part of the law of contract damages. *See generally* Restatement (Second) of Contracts § 356 comment *a* ("The central objective behind the system of contract remedies is compensatory, not punitive"); *id.* comment *b* (agreement attempting to fix damages in amount vastly greater than what approximates actual loss would be unenforceable as imposing a penalty); *id.* § 355 (punitive damages not recoverable for breach of contract unless conduct constituting the breach is also a tort for which such damages are recoverable).

[12] Here, the district court found that Berkley's alleged $724,300 profits did not define Naval's loss because many persons who bought the paperback in September 1985 would not have bought the book in hardcover but would merely have waited until the paperback edition became available. This finding is not clearly erroneous, and we turn to the question of whether the district court's finding that Naval suffered $35,380.50 in actual damages was proper.

[13] In reaching the $35,380.50 figure, the court operated on the premise that, but for the breach by Berkley, Naval would have sold in September the same number of hardcover copies it sold in August. Berkley challenges that premise as speculative and argues that since Naval presented no evidence as to what its September 1985 sales would have been, Naval is entitled to recover no damages. It argues alternatively that the court should have computed damages on the premise that sales in the second half of September, in the absence of Berkley's premature release of the paperback edition, would have been made at the same rate as in the first half of September. Evaluating the district court's calculation of damages under the clearly erroneous standard of review, we reject Berkley's contentions.

[14] The record showed that, though there was a declining trend of hardcover sales of the Book from March through August 1985, Naval continued to sell its hardcover copies through the end of 1985, averaging some 3,000 copies a month in the latter period. It plainly was not error for the district court to find that the preponderance of the evidence indicated that Berkley's early shipment of 1,400,000 copies of its paperback edition, some 40% of which went to retail outlets and led to the Book's rising close to the top of the paperback best-seller lists before the end of September 1985, caused Naval the loss of some hardcover sales prior to October 1985.

[15] As to the quantification of that loss, we think it was within the prerogative of the court as finder of fact to look to Naval's August 1985 sales. Though there was no proof as to precisely what the unimpeded volume of hardcover sales would have been for the entire month of September, any such evidence would necessarily have been hypothetical.

But it is not error to lay the normal uncertainty in such hypotheses at the door of the wrongdoer who altered the proper course of events, instead of at the door of the injured party. *See, e.g.,* Restatement (Second) of Contracts § 352 comment *a* ("Doubts are generally resolved against the party in breach."). The court was not required to use as the starting point for its calculations Naval's actual sales in the first half of September, *i.e.,* those made prior to the first retail sale of the paperback edition. Berkley has not called to our attention any evidence in the record to indicate that the sales in a given month are normally spread evenly through that month. Indeed, it concedes that "to a large degree, book sales depend on public whim and are notoriously unpredictable. . . ." (Berkley brief on appeal at 31 n.15.). Thus, nothing in the record foreclosed the possibility that, absent Berkley's breach, sales of hardcover copies in the latter part of September would have outpaced sales of those copies in the early part of the month. Though the court accurately described its selection of August 1985 sales as its benchmark as "generous[ ]," it was not improper, given the inherent uncertainty, to exercise generosity in favor of the injured party rather than in favor of the breaching party.

[16] In all the circumstances, we cannot say that the district court's calculation of Naval's damages was clearly erroneous.

* * *

Conclusion

[17] We have considered all the arguments made by both parties in support of their respective positions on these appeals and, except as indicated above, have found them to be without merit. For the foregoing reasons, we reverse so much of the judgment as granted Naval $7,760.12 as an award of Berkley's profits. In all other respects, the judgment is affirmed.

NOTE

The Hunt For Red October was a Cold War-era novel about a Soviet submarine crew that defected to the United States. Some say it was the book that created the techno-thriller as a fiction genre. The author, Tom Clancy was a small-town insurance agent. At the time he wrote the novel, he had never been aboard a submarine or even served in the military in any capacity. The novel was nevertheless so realistic that when commercial publishers turned it down, it was published by the United States Naval Institute Press, a non-profit, whose stated mission is "to provide an open forum for the exchange of ideas, to disseminate and advance the knowledge of sea power, and to preserve our naval and maritime heritage." Its normal stock in trade is such page-turners as *Naval Shiphandling*, and *The Marine Officer's Guide*. It had never before published a work of fiction.

The Hunt For Red October got a huge boost when the President publicly praised it, calling it "the perfect yarn." It became the basis for a successful motion picture and started Tom Clancy's career as a novelist, a career that made him so wealthy he purchased part ownership of the Baltimore Orioles baseball team and attempted to purchase the Minnesota Vikings football team.

Remedies Under the R2d and the Common Law of Contracts

[handwritten margin note: Restatement Provision for Damages]

Section 347 of the R2d provides that the measure of damages is:

(a) the loss in the value to [a party] of the other party's performance caused by its failure or deficiency, PLUS *[margin: loss involve plus]*

(b) any other loss, including incidental or consequential loss, caused by the breach, LESS *[margin: any other loss]*

(c) any cost or other loss that he has avoided by not having to perform. *[margin: Less cost avoided]*

The amount in clause (a) of R2d § 347 is the value of the performance which was not given. For example, if Vendor breaches a contract whereby she is to convey property to Purchaser for a price of $1,000,000, Purchaser's loss in value is the market value of the property (not necessarily $1,000,000). If Contractor and Homeowner enter into a contract whereby Contractor is to do a remodeling job on Homeowner's house for an agreed price of $10,000 and Contractor fails to do any work at all, Homeowner's loss in value is the market price for having another contractor do the same work. If Contractor does all the work except for the last coat of paint, Homeowner's loss in value is the market price for having another contractor do this painting.

In incidental and consequential damages (terms used in clause (b) of R2d § 347) include additional costs incurred after the breach in a reasonable attempt to avoid loss, even if unsuccessful. Examples include a broker's fee paid to find a replacement buyer and seller for goods when a contract of sale is breached. Consequential damages include damage to person or property caused by the breach. If, for example, services contracted for are defective and cause damage to property, that loss is recoverable. *The terms used are not that important; the bottom line is that the loss caused by the breach is recoverable.*

The "cost avoided" includes such things as payment to the breaching party of the contract price, cost of doing the work required by the contract, and the value of the property to be transferred under the contract. Naturally, these are treated as a cost avoided only to the extent the non-breaching party cannot terminate her performance and avoid the loss. For example, in our Contractor-Homeowner hypothetical, if Homeowner refuses to pay because Contractor fails to show up, she has a cost avoided of $10,000. On the other hand, if she had already paid a deposit of $2,000, her cost avoided would only be $8,000.

Here's another example: Developer and Paver enter into a contract under the terms of which Paver is to pave the roads in a new subdivision that Developer is building at a cost of $200,000. After the contract has been signed and before Paver does any work, Developer breaches. At trial, Paver is able to show that if she had completed the paving according to the contract, it would have cost her $180,000. Paver's loss in value (paragraph (a)) is $200,000, her cost avoided (paragraph (c)) is $180,000, and there are no "other losses" (paragraph (b)). Thus, Paver is entitled to damages of $20,000. We say that Paver is entitled to "the benefit of the bargain." She made a good deal, and she's entitled to the benefit of it regardless of whether the other party breaches. *[margin note: Benefit of bargain]*

There's another way to calculate the damages that many people find easier than using the R2d formula. It's based on the principle that you give the non-breaching party an amount of money that will put her in the same position that performance would have. You begin by calculating the financial position that the non-breaching party would have been in if the contract had been performed. In other words you add up the value of what they would have received and subtract the value of what they would have given up. Here Paver would have received $200,000 and had to spend $180,000. So she would have been $20,000 ahead. Then, in the same way, you calculate the position she is in after the breach. In this case, Paver is just breaking even. Then you determine how much money it would take to move the non-breaching party from where she actually is after the breach to where she would be if the contract had been fully performed. In this case, it would take $20,000 to put her in the position that performance would have, so that is how much she should be awarded. *[margin note: easier than R2D]*

Try both methods on the problems that follow. *The only way to really learn how to compute contract damages is to work through problems and examples.* For those of you that thought you could avoid mathematical word problems by going to law school, you were wrong.

———

PROBLEM 18-1

Remodeler and Homeowner enter into a contract for the remodeling of Homeowner's kitchen with a price of $10,000. Before Homeowner pays anything or Remodeler does any work, Homeowner breaches. At trial, Remodeler is able to prove that if she had been allowed to perform the contract,

L in vabe = 10
no other losses
cost avoid = 8

2,000

she could have done it for $8,000. How much is Remodeler entitled to recover in damages from Homeowner? *2,000 to put her in place if K was performed*

PROBLEM 18-2

L in vabe = 5,500
no other losses
cost avoided = 5200 = 300

Roofer and Owner enter into a contract for the roofing of Owner's building for a price of $6,000. Owner makes a $500 down payment and then breaches. At trial Roofer is able to show that if he had performed the contract it would have cost him $5,200. How much is Roofer entitled to recover in damages from Owner? *300* *Loss in value 5,500 to go*

Profit of 800 if K is performed has 500 so needs 300 to get what he deserves

PROBLEM 18-3

Would have been up 100 already spent 75

Painter and Farmer enter into a contract for the painting of Farmer's barn for a price of $800. Farmer makes no down payment. After Painter has spent $75 on the job, Farmer breaches. At trial, Painter is able to show that if he had been allowed to finish the job, it would have cost him a total of $700 (i.e., the $75 spent to date plus an additional $625). How much is Painter entitled to recover in damages from Farmer? *175 - 75 behind and deserves to be 100 ahead needs 175 to do that*

800
625
175

PROBLEM 18-4

K price minus payments = 3000 + 0 = 4800 = 2200 + 1000 he's down = 2200

Slumlord and Electrician enter into a contract for the re-wiring of Slumlord's building for a price of $6,000. After Electrician has spent $4,000 on the job and Slumlord has made $3,000 in progress payments to Electrician, Slumlord breaches. At trial Electrician is able to show that if he had been allowed to complete the job, it would have cost him an additional $800 (in addition to the $4,000 spent to date) to complete the job. How much is Electrician entitled to recover in damages from Slumlord? *would have been up now if performed* *down 1000* *deserves to be up now = pay him 2200 to do that* *down 1000*

PROBLEM 18-5

17,000 ahead if K is performed

Bank and Programmer enter into a contract under the terms of which Programmer agrees to re-program Bank's computer to alert management to any hacking attempts for a price of $3,000. Before Bank has paid Programmer any money and before Programmer has done any work or incurred any expenses, Programmer realizes that the job is a lot bigger than she thought. She tells Bank to forget about it. (This is a breach of the contract.) Bank contacts a number of programmers and finds that the best price any of them will give is $20,000, so Bank has its computer reprogrammed at a cost of 20 grand. How much is Bank entitled to recover in damages from Programmer? *17,000?*

PROBLEM 18-6

Promoter and Singer enter into a contract under the terms of which Singer will perform at Promoter's concert for a fee of $10,000. Before Singer has been paid any money, Singer breaches the contract. In order to get a comparable entertainer as a replacement for Singer, Promoter has to pay $15,000. He also incurs $3,000 in additional transportation costs in order to get the replacement

5,000 profit, down 8,000 now

Loss in value of 10
cost lost = 8
- cost avoid = 10 2/000

[handwritten margin note, top: Loss in value = 10, other loses = 8, cost avoided = 10, 18 - 10 = 8,000]

entertainer to the concert on time. How much is Promoter entitled to recover in damages from Singer? *[handwritten: Was going to get $8 down 3, pay 8,000]*

PROBLEM 18-7

Power Company and Construction Company enter into a contract under the terms of which Construction Company agrees to build a power plant for a cost of $100 million. Before any money has been paid or any work has been done, Construction Company discovers that because of rising labor and materials costs, it will cost Construction Company $125 million to build the plant. Construction Company breaches the contract. Power Company hires another company to build the plant at a cost of $110 million. How much is Power Company entitled to recover in damages from Construction Company? *[handwritten right margin: would have been 25 ahead now only 10 need 15]*

[handwritten: down 15 million to 25 only up 10 — pay 15]

PROBLEM 18-8 *[handwritten: skip]*

You are representing the plaintiff in a breach of contract case. Your client, a builder, entered into a contract to sell for $300,000 a home he had recently completed. The buyer defaulted. Your client sold the home some time later for $250,000. On cross-examination of your client by the lawyer for the defaulting buyer, the following exchange occurred:

Q: Are you a good judge of the value of a home?

A: Yes, I am.

Q: Do you normally try to sell your homes for more than they're worth?

A: I try to sell my homes for a fair price.

Q: Fair market value?

A: Yeah.

What is the defendant's lawyer going to argue in her summation? What would you ask on re-direct to minimize its effect? *[handwritten: My client is down 50,000 b/c of buyer breach]*

_____

Remedies Under the U.C.C.

One of the beauties of the U.C.C.'s Article 2 is that it introduced a market-based mechanism as an optional way to fix damages. Rather than rely upon valuation testimony, under Article 2, if the non-breaching party wishes to invoke its market-based damage fixing provisions, and does so properly, the relevance of valuation technology can be eliminated. Read U.C.C. § 2–706 and the accompanying comments and § 2–708(1). Then apply all that good stuff to the problems that follow.

_____

PROBLEM 18-9

Heinz operates a nightclub, Studio 57, in downtown Pittsburgh. When the bloom goes off the business, he decides to switch to welding as a career, and he enters into a contract to sell the furniture and sound system to French for $12,000. French breaches the contract and Heinz gives the proper notice (§ 2–706(3)) and resells the goods to English in a commercially reasonable manner for $8,000. At trial, French shows that at the time and place for tender (i.e., when and where Heinz was to turn over the goods) the market price for such goods was $10,000.

(a) If the court finds that notice was proper and the resale was "commercially reasonable," what are Heinz's damages?

(b) If the court finds that the sale was not commercially reasonable, what are Heinz's damages?

(c) If the court finds that notice was not given, what are Heinz's damages?

(d) How can the sale be commercially reasonable if it's at less than the going market price?

(e) If Heinz decides to keep the goods, what are his damages?

PROBLEM 18-10

Petty runs the local Chevrolet dealership. Except for the cost of the cars he sells, all his costs are fixed, i.e., they remain the same regardless of whether he sells one car or one hundred. (Remember these problems are referred to as "hypotheticals"). Foyt comes in and orders a new 'Vette for $55,000, which is the market price. It costs Petty $53,000 to purchase the car from GM. A few days later Foyt repudiates. But within the hour, Oldfield comes in and orders a new 'Vette for $55,000. Instead of canceling the order for Foyt's car, Petty just sells that car to Oldfield. In an action for damages against Foyt, what is Petty entitled to recover under 2–706? Assuming (everyone seems to) that "market price" means retail market price, what are Petty's damages under 2–708(1)? Section 1–106 says the U.C.C. remedies should put the aggrieved party in as good a position as if the other party had performed the contract. Does either of these measures of damages do this? For a suggested method of analysis, read *VERY CAREFULLY* U.C.C. § 2–708(2) and Comment 2 following it. The case that follows should also be helpful.

LOCKS V. WADE

New Jersey Superior Court, Appellate Division
36 N.J. Super. 128, 114 A.2d 875 (1955)

CLAPP, S.J.A.D.

cause of action

[1] Defendant appeals from a county district court judgment taken against him for breach of contract. Contract and breach are admitted or assumed on appeal; the only issue is damages.

[2] Under the contract plaintiff leased to defendant an automatic phonograph, a juke box, for two years and agreed to supply records and replace parts wearing out. Proceeds of the operation were to be shared on a specified basis, but with a minimum of $20 per week to be paid plaintiff by defendant. Defendant, it is claimed, repudiated the contract; and plaintiff never installed the machine.

[3] The court gave plaintiff judgment for $836—that is, the sum of $20 per week for two years, less apparently the costs plaintiff would have been put to, had he performed the contract, less also depreciation on the machine.

[4] Defendant makes two points. The first rests on plaintiff's testimony that the component parts of the very machine he had intended to lease defendant were, after the breach, rented to others. Defendant argues that the amount plaintiff thus realized should have been credited on the claim sued upon.

[5] Defendant would have us apply here the rule obtaining on the breach of an agreement to lease realty; that is, he claims the measure of the lessor's damages here is the difference between the agreed rental and the rental value of the property. His contention further is that even though under the agreement before us, the lessor is obliged to perform some personal services, he, in order to establish the rental value, has the burden of proving what he received on a reletting.

[6] Plaintiff, passing the questions (or most of them), meets the argument by referring to his testimony, not contradicted, that:

[7] "The equipment called for by this agreement was readily available in the market. But locations were very hard to get."

[8] We think the position plaintiff takes on the matter is sound. Where, as here, a plaintiff lessor agrees to lease an article of which the supply in the market is for practical purposes not limited, then the law would be depriving him of the benefit of his bargain if on the breach of the agreement, it required his claim against the lessee to be reduced by the amount he actually did or reasonably could realize on a reletting of the article. For if there had been no breach and another customer had appeared, the lessor could as well have secured another such article and

entered into a second lease. In case of the breach of the first lease, he should have the benefit of both bargains or not—in a situation where the profit on both would be the same—be limited to the profit on the second of them.

[9]   An illustration with figures may make this more graphic. If the agreed rental under the lease amounts to $2,040, the cost of installation and of furnishing records and parts to $500, and the depreciation on the juke box over the period of the lease to $700, the lessor stands to make $840 on the deal. If another customer presents himself, the lessor will buy another juke box, which he is entitled to enter on his books at cost and depreciate in the same way as he does with the first. Thus, if he makes the same agreement with the second customer, he will make another $840 on the second lease. If the first lessee repudiates his agreement, the purchase of an additional machine will, of course, be unnecessary, because the first machine can be leased to the second customer. In such a situation, under defendant's theory, the lessor would receive as damages for this repudiation only the $2,040 rental agreed on under the first lease, less the $2,040 rental for the same machine under the second lease, or nothing. This would leave the lessee only the $840 profit he will make under the second lease; whereas had the first lessee lived up to his bargain, the lessor's profits would have been $840 on each of two leases, or $1,680.

[10] We conclude that the proper measure of damages here is the difference between the contract price and the cost of performing the first contract, as the court apparently held below. In the case of realty which (unlike the juke box) is specific and not to be duplicated on the market, the lessor could not properly lease it to another for the same period unless the first lease were broken or terminated. In such a case the lessor should not be awarded two profits merely because of the first lessee's default.

[11] So in general we may say that gains made by a lessor on a lease entered into after the breach are not to be deducted from his damages unless the breach enabled him to make the gains. The recoverable damages in the case of a contract are such as may reasonably be within the contemplation of the parties at the time of the contract, and with that in view, we should not in the present case deny lessor the benefit of his bargain.

* * *

Affirmed.

————

NOTE

People like the plaintiff in the above case have been referred to as "lost volume sellers." This means that when the buyer defaults, they aren't just faced with the prospect of re-selling the goods at a lower price; they lose all the profit they would have made on the sale. That is the reason sections 2–706 and 2–708(1) don't give them adequate compensation, and they must be compensated under 2–708(2).

PROBLEM 18-11

Dealer sells new Volvos for $30,000 each. It costs Dealer $25,000 to purchase each vehicle and prepare it for sale. The market price for new Volvos of this type is $30,000. Lawyer enters into a contract to purchase a new Volvo for $30,000. Lawyer breaches, and Dealer sells the car to Accountant in a commercially reasonable manner after giving Lawyer the proper notice. The sale to Accountant is for $30,000. What are Dealer's damages? (P.S., Volvo will supply Dealer with as many of these cars as he needs to fill his orders.) *[handwritten: 10,000]*

[handwritten: unlimited supply]   *[handwritten: needs profit for both]*

PROBLEM 18-12

Dealer sells antique cars. Dealer enters into a contract to sell a 1903 Oldsmobile (the kind with a tiller instead of a steering wheel) to Collector for $110,000. The market price for such a car is $110,000. Dealer purchased the *[handwritten: 30,000 profit]* car three months ago from Sucker for $80,000. Collector breaches the contract. Dealer sells the car to Enthusiast for $110,000 after giving Collector proper notice. The sale is made in a commercially reasonable manner. What are Dealer's damages? (P.S., there are no other 1903 Oldsmobiles available on the market.) *[handwritten: 30,000 b/c he is not lost volume seller!]*

PROBLEM 18-13

Dealer sells new motorbikes for $400 each. Dealer can get an unlimited supply of motorbikes for $300 each. Professor agrees to buy a new motorbike from Dealer for $375. (We professors are tough negotiators.) The fair market value of the motorbike is $400. Professor defaults and, after giving the proper notice, Dealer sells the motorbike in a commercially reasonable manner for $400. What are Dealer's damages? *[handwritten: 200? 100 profit, lost 100 b/c of Professor]*

PROBLEM 18-14 *[handwritten: Skip]*

Dealer sells new Econoboxes for $8,000 each. Dealer can get an unlimited supply of Econoboxes for $7,000 each. Civil Servant agrees to buy an Econobox from Dealer for $8,500. Civil Servant defaults. What are Dealer's damages?

PROBLEM 18-15 *[handwritten: Skip]*

Dealer sells new Maseratis for $150,000 each. Dealer can get an unlimited supply of these examples of fine Italian craftsmanship for $140,000 each. Developer agrees to buy a Maserati for $150,000 and makes a $5,000 down payment. Developer defaults. What are Dealer's damages? Read U.C.C. §§ 2–

712 and 2–713 and the accompanying comments and apply them to the next problem.

PROBLEM 18-16

Farmer contracts to deliver 5,000 bushels of wheat to Elevator Co. on September 15 at a price of $2.00 a bushel. On September 15, when the market price is $4.00 a bushel, Farmer fails to show up. It takes Elevator Co. until September 18 to get in contact with Farmer, who doesn't admit until September 21 that he is not going to deliver. It then takes until September 22 for the Elevator Co. to make a substitute contract. On September 21 and 22, the market price for wheat is $4.50 a bushel, and Elevator Co. purchases wheat from another grower at $4.50 a bushel in substitution for the wheat Farmer failed to deliver.

(a) What can Elevator Co. recover as damages?

(b) Suppose that Elevator Co. had chosen not to buy any wheat in substitution for the wheat it was supposed to get from Farmer. What would its damages be then?

CHAPTER 19

LIMITATIONS ON CONTRACT DAMAGES

■ ■ ■

The basic rules of expectancy damages for breach of contract are subject to three principal limitations: foreseeability, certainty, and avoidability. Under the foreseeability limitation, damages are disallowed unless they were foreseen or reasonably foreseeable to the parties at the time of contracting. This rule of foreseeability thus draws on the objective theory of contract to define and then respect the risk allocations that the parties reasonably and objectively made when they entered into the contract. If, for example, you know that my profit of $1,000 depends on your delivery of a certain part to my Chicago customers in 24 hours and you undertake to provide overnight delivery without limiting or disclaiming liability for delay, you have probably assumed the risk and can be held to pay me my lost $1,000 in profits should you breach and fail to deliver the part in a timely manner. If, on the other hand, you are not aware of the time-sensitive nature of the delivery, it is difficult to fairly charge you for those damages.

The second limitation is certainty. It is considered unfair to award damages that are speculative, insofar as one is entitled to the benefit one *would have* received for one's bargain—not the benefit one *might have* received. Certainty, however, is a relative term that does not require absolute certainty, just reasonable certainty. Further, uncertainty is generally part of the defense's burden and, if unable to carry this burden, the plaintiff's initial proof of the expectancy interest will carry the day.

Finally, there is the limit of avoidability. Put another way, there is a duty on the part of the non-breaching party to behave reasonably and minimize damages. This is just good policy, as providing an incentive to minimize loss is more efficient than maximizing it, no matter who must bear the burden of compensation.

The cases in this chapter explore the parameters of these limiting doctrines on expectancy damages.

A. FORESEEABILITY

HADLEY V. BAXENDALE

Court of Exchequer
9 Ex. 341 (1854)

[1] At the trial before Crompton, J., at the last Gloucester Assizes, it appeared that the plaintiffs carried on an extensive business as millers at Gloucester; and that, on the 11th of May, their mill was stopped by a breakage of the crank shaft by which the mill was worked. The steam-engine was manufactured by Messrs. Joyce & Co., the engineers, at Greenwich, and it became necessary to send the shaft as a pattern for a new one to Greenwich. The fracture was discovered on the 12th, and on the 13th, the plaintiffs sent one of their servants to the office of the defendants, who are the well known carriers trading under the name of Pickford & Co., for the purpose of having the shaft carried to Greenwich. The plaintiff's servant told the clerk that the mill was stopped, and that the shaft must be sent immediately; and in answer to the inquiry when the shaft would be taken, the answer was, that if it was sent up by twelve o'clock any day, it would be delivered at Greenwich on the following day. On the following day the shaft was taken by the defendants, before noon, for the purpose of being conveyed to Greenwich, and the sum of 2£. 4s. was paid for its carriage for the whole distance; at the same time the defendant's clerk was told that a special entry, if required, should be made to hasten its delivery. The delivery of the shaft at Greenwich was delayed by some neglect; and the consequence was, that the plaintiffs did not receive the new shaft for several days after they would otherwise have done, and the working of their mill was thereby delayed and they thereby lost the profits they would otherwise have received.

[2] [The defendants] object that these damages were too remote, and that the defendants were not liable with respect to them. The learned Judge left the case generally to the jury, who found a verdict with 25£ damages beyond the amount paid into Court.

[3] *Whateley*, in last Michaelmas Term, obtained a rule nisi for a new trial, on the ground of misdirection.

[4] *Keating and Dowdeswell* (Feb. 1) showed cause.—The plaintiffs are entitled to the amount awarded by the jury as damages. These damages are not too remote, for they are not only the natural and necessary consequence of the defendants' default, but they are the only loss which the plaintiffs have actually sustained. The principle upon which damages are assessed is founded upon that of rendering compensation to the injured

Baxendale only liable for reasonably forseeable damages at the time of contracting

party . . . [PARKE, B.[1]—The sensible rule appears to be that which has been laid down in France, and which is declared in their code [and] translated in Sedgwick: "The damages due to the creditor consist in general of the loss that he has sustained, and the profit which he has been prevented from acquiring . . . The debtor is only liable for the damages foreseen, or which might have been foreseen, at the time of the execution of the contract, when it is not owing to his fraud that the agreement has been violated. Even in the case of nonperformance of the contract, resulting from the fraud of the debtor, the damages only comprise so much of the loss sustained by the creditor, and so much of the profit which he has been prevented from acquiring, as directly and immediately results from the non-performance of the contract."] If that rule is to be adopted, there was ample evidence in the present case of the defendants' knowledge of such a state of things as would necessarily result in the damage of the plaintiffs suffered through the defendant's default. . . .

[5] ALDERSON, B. We think that there ought to be a new trial in this case; but in so doing, we deem it to be expedient and necessary to state explicitly the rule which the Judge, at the next trial, ought, in our opinion, to direct the jury to be governed by when they estimate the damages. It is, indeed, of the last importance that we should do this; for if the jury are left without any definite rule to guide them, it will, in such cases as these, manifestly lead to the greatest injustice . . .

[6] Now we think the proper rule in such a case as the present is this:—Where two parties have made a contract which one of them has broken, the damages which the other party ought to receive in respect of such breach of contract should be such as may fairly and reasonably be considered either arising naturally, i.e., according to the usual course of things, from such breach of contract itself, or such as may reasonably be supposed to have been in the contemplation of both parties, at the time they made the contract, as the probable result of the breach of it. Now, if the special circumstances under which the contract was actually made were communicated by the plaintiffs to the defendants, and thus known to both parties, the damages resulting from the breach of such a contract, which they would reasonably contemplate, would be the amount of injury which would ordinarily follow from a breach of contract under these special circumstances so known and communicated. But, on the other hand, if these special circumstances were wholly unknown to the party breaking the contract, he, at the most, could only be supposed to have had in his contemplation the amount of injury which would arise generally, and in the great multitude of cases not affected by any special circumstances, from such a breach of contract. For, had the special circumstances been known,

consequential damages are those that arise naturally of the breach if

---

[1] [This is a question by Baron Parke. In the old English reports, questions from the bench were enclosed in brackets. The judges of The Court of Exchequer were called "barons" because it was believed that the Magna Carta allowed only barons to sit on this court.—Eds.]

Hadley never told Pickford about what a delay would do

Not forseeable that P only had one shaft

the parties might have specially provided for the breach of contract by special terms as to the damages in that case; and of this advantage it would be very unjust to deprive them. Now the above principles are those by which we think the jury ought to be guided in estimating the damages arising out of any breach of contract. It is said, that other cases such as breaches of contract in the nonpayment of money, or in the not making a good title to land, are to be treated as exceptions from this, and as governed by a conventional rule. But as, in such cases, both parties must be supposed to be cognizant of that well-known rule, these cases may, we think be more properly classed under the rule above enunciated as to cases under known special circumstances, because there both parties may reasonably be presumed to contemplate the estimation of the amount of damages according to the conventional rule.

[7] Now, in the present case, if we are to apply the principles above laid down, we find that the only circumstances here communicated by the plaintiffs to the defendants at the time the contract was made, were, that the article to be carried was the broken shaft of a mill, and that the plaintiffs were the millers of that mill. But how do these circumstances show reasonably that the profits of the mill must be stopped by an unreasonable delay in the delivery of the broken shaft by the carrier to the third person? Suppose the plaintiffs had another shaft in their possession put up or putting up at the time, and that they only wished to send back the broken shaft to the engineer who made it; it is clear that this would be quite consistent with the above circumstances, and yet the unreasonable delay in the delivery would have no effect upon the intermediate profits of the mill. Or, again, suppose, that, at the time of the delivery to the carrier, the machinery of the mill had been in other respects defective, then, also, the same results would follow. Here it is true that the shaft was actually sent back to serve as a model for a new one, and that the want of a new one was the only cause of the stoppage of the mill, and that the loss of profits really arose from the delay in delivering the broken one to serve as a model. But it is obvious that, in the great multitude of cases of millers sending off broken shafts to third persons by a carrier under ordinary circumstances, such consequences would not, in all probability, have occurred; and these special circumstances were here never communicated by the plaintiffs to the defendants. It follows, therefore, that the loss of profits here cannot reasonably be considered such a consequence of the breach of contract as could have been fairly and reasonably contemplated by both the parties when they made this contract. For such loss would neither have flowed naturally from the breach of this contract in the great multitude of such cases occurring under ordinary circumstances, nor were the special circumstances, which, perhaps, would have made it a reasonable and natural consequence of such breach of contract, communicated to or known by the defendants. The Judge ought, therefore, to have told the jury that, upon the facts then before them, they ought not to take the loss of profits

P could've had another shaft or could've had multiple defective parts

They never told this to Ds,

new trial

into consideration at all in estimating the damages. There must therefore be a new trial in this case.

Rule absolute.

———

NOTES AND QUESTIONS

The foreseeability limitation of *Hadley v. Baxendale* is found in section 351 of the R2d and article 7.4.4 of the UNIDROIT Principles. One is phrased in the negative, the other in the positive. Apart from this, is the standard that is expressed the same? Is there a difference in meaning caused by stating the standard in the positive or the negative?

———

MARQUETTE CEMENT MANUFACTURING V. LOUISVILLE & NASHVILLE R.R.

United States District Court, Eastern District, Tennessee
281 F. Supp. 944 (1967)

WILSON, DISTRICT JUDGE.

[Marquette Cement sold cement to Vulcan Materials. Vulcan had two divisions: Rock Products, which made Ready-Mix concrete and Concrete Pipe, which made Concrete Pipe. Concrete Pipe always purchased air-entrained cement and Rock Products never did. Rock Products added its own air to specification after it received the cement. Because of a mistake by a railroad clerk, a carload of air-entrained cement intended for the Concrete Pipe Division was routed to the Rock Products Division.—Eds.]

[railroad clerk makes mistake]

[1] The carload of "air-entrained" cement was delivered to the Rock Products Division and was used by it in its ready-mix cement plant. At the time Rock Products Division had under order from Marquette more than one carload of cement. However, Rock Products Division did not expect to receive "air-entrained" cement and it is not possible to determine merely from appearance whether cement already contains an air-entraining agent or not. Accordingly, the Rock Products Division added an air-entraining agent to the cement after it had been unloaded and before receiving the notice of delivery from the L & N Railroad which would show that the cement was already air-entrained. On March 31st the cement was processed by Rock Products Division and delivered to certain job sites in and around Chattanooga. The majority of it went to the construction site of the Calsted Nursing Home in Chattanooga to be used by the H. E. Collins Contracting Company in the structural floor system thereof. Another portion of the concrete went to the J. C. Miller Construction Company for the purpose of constructing a small cement floor in a garage. The concrete

⋆ Concrete use had visual deficiencies

what damages is he entitled to?

used in both of these jobs showed deficiencies and it was necessary that the same be removed in each instance.

[2] The bill of lading showed that the cement was air-entrained, but the train clerk at the L & N who re-routed the shipment from Concrete Pipe to Rock Products had not noted that the cement was air-entrained, and in fact was uninformed as to what the designation meant. He was likewise uninformed as to what use the Vulcan Materials Company made of the concrete it received at either of its two divisions or as to any difference in the concrete received at the two divisions.

All the damages as expectation remedy

[3] The value of the carload of cement was $1,408.16 and the freight charges amounted to $91.10. The cost to the plaintiffs for replacing the Calsted Nursing Home floor slab was $9,558.30 and the cost of replacing the floor slab in the garage was $167.00. The plaintiffs incurred additional costs of $197.00 to a concrete testing laboratory. The plaintiffs seek to recover damages in the total sum of $11,416.56,[2] being the total of the above items of cost, plus interest.   *11,421.56*

100% Breach

[4] First, there can be no doubt that the defendant is liable unto the plaintiffs for breach of contract by virtue of its misdelivery of the carload of cement. It was the duty of the carrier to deliver the freight at the destination designated in the contract of shipment. The error in routing instructions would not relieve the carrier of the duty of making delivery to the destination designated on the bill of lading, nor permit the carrier to change the destination. The real question with which we are here concerned is the damages to which plaintiffs are entitled by virtue of the breach. Before discussing the rules governing the measure of damage in a breach of contract action for misdelivery, it is appropriate to consider the plaintiffs' alternate contention that a negligence action would also lie for misdelivery. No authority is cited by the plaintiff in support of its tort theory. While a contract may create a state of affairs in which a general duty arises the breach of which may constitute actionable negligence, negligence will not lie where the only duty breached is one created by contract. It is only where there is a breach of a general duty, even though it may arise out of a relationship created by contract, that breach of duty may constitute actionable negligence. Here the only duty breached was the duty to deliver under a contract of carriage. Accordingly, the Court need not consider the rules of law governing the measure of damage in a tort action.

No tort claim bc only breach of contract is

[5] Returning to the plaintiffs' claim for damage for breach of contract, the plaintiffs claim the following elements of damages: (1) the cost of shipping charges ($91.10), (2) the value of the carload of air-entrained cement ($1,408.16), (3) the cost of removing the adulterated concrete from

---

[2] [$11,416.56 in 1967 dollars is roughly the equivalent of $85,800 in 2019 dollars using the CPI and the GNP Deflator.—Eds.]

Cost of the shipping charge + cost of bad cement

the construction sites ($9,725.30), and (4) the cost of the tests performed by the laboratory ($197.00).

[6] The Court had occasion to examine the rules with respect to damages for breach of contract in the case of *Clark v. Ferro Corp.*, 237 F.Supp. 230 (D.C.Tenn., 1964). To summarize briefly the principles involved, the general purpose of the law is to place the plaintiff in the position he would have been in had the contract been fulfilled in accordance with its terms. More specifically, under the rule of *Hadley v. Baxendale*, 9 Ex. 341, 156 Eng. Reprint 145, 5 Eng.Rul.Cas. 502 (1854), damages recoverable for breach of contract are (1) such as may fairly and reasonably be considered as arising in the usual course of events from the breach of the contract itself or (2) such as may reasonably be supposed to have been in the contemplation of the parties at the time they made the contract. This is the rule in Tennessee. The rule has been stated in terms of "foreseeability" in the Restatement of Contracts (Sec. 330):

> In awarding damages, compensation is given for only those injuries that the defendant had reason to foresee as a probable result of his breach when the contract was made. If the injury is one that follows the breach in the usual course of events, there is sufficient reason for the defendant to foresee it; otherwise it must be shown specifically that the defendant had reason to know the facts and to foresee the injury.

[7] The statement providing for "special" or "consequential" damages is merely a further extension of "foreseeability." McCormick, in speaking of the rule of *Hadley v. Baxendale*, observes:

> This standard is in the main an objective one. It takes account of what the defendant who made the contract might then have foreseen as a reasonable man, in the light of the facts known to him, and does not confine the inquiry to what he actually did foresee. It the loss claimed is unusual, then it becomes necessary to ascertain whether the defaulting party was notified of the special circumstances'

McCormick on Damages, p. 565, sec. 138.

[The court then discussed and rejected arguments that special rules, rather the common law rules of contract damages, should apply.—Eds.]

[8] There remains to be considered which of the elements of damage claimed by the plaintiff fall within the common law rules of damage for breach of contract. In this regard it would appear clear that the plaintiff would be entitled to recover any damages sustained by it which may fairly be supposed to have been within the contemplation of the parties at the time the contract was made. These would be such damages as might naturally be expected to follow the breach of contract and would include

the value of the shipment and the transportation charges paid thereon. Thus the plaintiff would be entitled to recover the sum of $1,408.16 as the value of the shipment and the sum of $91.10 as the cost of shipment paid.

[9] With respect to the remaining items of damage claimed by the plaintiffs, that is the cost of testing and removing the defective concrete from construction sites, such damages may only be considered as special or consequential damages. With respect to their recovery the issue then arises as to whether the special circumstances giving rise to the damages were communicated to or known by the defendant at the time the contract of carriage was made. In order to recover special damages under the circumstances of this case, it must appear that at the time of the making of the contract of carriage the defendant had reasonable notice or knowledge of the special conditions rendering such damages the natural and probable result of the breach. The Court is of the opinion that the evidence does not establish such notice or knowledge upon the part of the defendant. It is true that the bill of lading did designate the shipment as "air-entrained cement." This information is not sufficient, however, to put the carrier on notice as to the use for which it was to be put. Nor was it sufficient to put the carrier on notice that an additional air-entraining agent would be added to the cement by the plaintiff, thereby rendering it unsuited for structural use. The notice here received by the carrier by the inclusion of the words "air-entrained cement" upon the bill of lading was not sufficient to render reasonably foreseeable the subsequent events which resulted in the expenses incurred by the plaintiff in testing and in removing the defective concrete. The defendant accordingly would not be liable for the sum of $197.00 incurred by the plaintiff in having concrete tests performed nor the sum of $9,725.30 incurred by the plaintiff in having defective concrete removed. The plaintiff would be entitled to recover the value of the shipment of cement and the shipping costs paid thereon, or the total sum of $1,499.26.

A judgment will enter accordingly.

STROH BREWERY V. GRAND TRUNK WESTERN R.R.

United States District Court, Eastern District Michigan
513 F. Supp. 827 (1981)

COOK, JR., JUDGE.

Memorandum Opinion

[1] This is an action for damages brought against a common carrier under the provisions of 49 U.S.C. § 20(11), which is often referred to as the Carmack Amendments. Plaintiff, The Stroh Brewery Company (Stroh), is an Arizona corporation which does business within the State of Michigan.

Grand Trunk Western Railroad Company (Grand Trunk), is a Michigan corporation which does business within the State of Michigan.

[2] On or about September 14, 1976, a carload of "Stroh Bulk Type Malt," which had been ordered by Stroh from the Rahr Malting Company in Shakopee, Minnesota, was placed in hopper car number CNW 172379 (Stroh Malt Car) and shipped by rail to Detroit. The malt was to be delivered to Stroh at Greater Northern Feed, Inc. (Great Northern) which, in addition to being a wholly owned subsidiary, was Stroh's agent for taking delivery of railroad cars.

[3] On or about September 9, 1976, a carload of barley, which had been ordered by Rickel Malting Company, Inc. (Rickel) from Fleischmann Malting Company, in Minneapolis, Minnesota, was placed in hopper car number CNW 173379 (Rickel Barley Car) and shipped by rail to Rickel.

[4] Both cars were transferred to the Grand Trunk line in Chicago. Thereafter, they were transported to Grand Trunk's Farnsworth Siding in Detroit, Michigan, arriving on or about September 20, 1976. Farnsworth Siding has eight tracks upon which Grand Trunk stores railroad cars until delivery. The only "hopper cars" that were stored on the Farnsworth Siding were those cars which were scheduled for delivery to Stroh and Rickel.

[5] Simultaneously with, or prior to, the arrival of the Stroh Malt Car and the Rickel Barley Car at Farnsworth Siding, Grand Trunk sent "Constructive Placement Notices" (which had been prepared from inbound billings) to Stroh and Rickel, informing them that their respective cars had arrived. (These inbound billings described the respective contents as "Bulk Stroh Type Malt" and "Bulk Barley.")

[6] During the morning of September 21, 1976, Stroh called William Abbey, the Yardmaster of the Farnsworth Yard and an employee of Grand Trunk, and, according to the usual practices of these two parties, requested delivery of eight cars (six hopper cars and two empty boxcars) in a specific order at Great Northern. The Stroh Malt Car was included in that list of cars. Abbey transcribed the car numbers on his "Switch List" in the order, as requested by Stroh. In the afternoon of September 21st, a copy of the "Switch List" was given to the switch crew (Joseph Lippai, John Wrubel, a third unknown individual and an engineer). Instead of delivering the Stroh Malt Car at Great Northern as requested, the switch crew mistakenly placed the Rickel Barley Car upon the Great Northern Siding for use and consumption by Stroh.

[7] Although Great Northern had expected delivery of the Stroh Malt Car, its employees did not notice that the Rickel Barley Car had been delivered in its place. On Wednesday, September 22, 1976, Parrinello, a Stroh employee, was instructed to unload all of the cars. Stroh's standard procedures for unloading cars at Great Northern were as follows:

Covered hopper cars of malt or grits are placed on GNFI (Great Northern Feed, Inc.) rail siding for unloading into malt and grit storage bins. Before unloading procedure begins, material is inspected in each compartment of each car. Car numbers are checked to ensure each car is placed on siding in sequence for unloading. Records are kept such as a "Daily Loading & Unloading" track sheet which the employees fill out as they unload cars, recording the seal numbers, card number and bin number. One sample is taken from each compartment and labeled appropriately as to the car number, date unloaded, supplier, type of material and compartment number.

Deposition Exhibit 6.

[8] At all times that are relevant hereto, Stroh had the correct car number on its business records. It had an opportunity to discover that (1) one of the cars bore the wrong car number and (2) the contents within the car was barley, not malt.

[9] The content from the Rickel Barley Car was unloaded, transported to Stroh and placed into the brewing process where it was mixed with existing Rahr Malt, which resulted in the contamination of the Rahr Malt and the burning out of certain grinding engines due to the texture of the barley. All of the contaminated Rahr Malt had to be removed from the bin by vacuum, and the grinding engines were replaced. On September 24, 1976, Stroh ultimately received the Stroh Malt Car. Stroh subsequently sold the contaminated malt-barley mixture as feed and paid Rickel for the value of the bulk barley.

[10] At all times that are pertinent to this inquiry, including the time at which the contracts of carriage were executed, the Yardmaster and members of the switch crew who misdelivered the Rickel Barley Car to Stroh at Great Northern knew that (1) the only hopper cars that were stored in Farnsworth Yard were those which had been consigned to Stroh or Rickel, (2) the Rickel hopper cars contained only barley, (3) the Stroh hopper cars, which were scheduled for delivery at Great Northern, contained only malt or corn grits, (4) the only hopper cars at Great Northern which contained either malt or corn grits, were for use by Stroh, (5) Rahr, Ladisch, Shrot and Lauhoff were names of some of the manufacturers of the malt and corn grits, (6) all of the Stroh hopper cars had to be delivered in a specific order because of the different contents in the cars, (7) Great Northern had two unloading pits over which the hopper cars would be placed by Grand Trunk, (8) each car would be emptied into one of two pits and then, by means of a screw elevator, its contents would be placed in a separate above ground storage bin from which the malt or corn grits would be deposited in a truck for delivery to Stroh, (9) the malt and corn grits would be utilized in the process of brewing Stroh's beer, and

(10) the malt and corn grits would be returned wet to Great Northern after the brewing process as a byproduct ("spent grain Mash") where it would then be dried, blown into Grand Trunk boxcars and shipped to a specific designation.

[11] Plaintiff has two claims for breach of contract against Defendant. The first contract of carriage involved the shipment of the Stroh Malt Car and the wrongful delivery of the Rickel Barley Car. Damages sought for this breach are for those out of pocket costs (e.g., the cost of the Rahr malt which was contaminated when mixed with the bulk barley; the cost of removing that mixture from brewing facility; the cost of the bulk barley delivered, less the amount received for the malt-barley mixture) which were allegedly caused by the misdelivery. Inasmuch as Stroh did receive the Stroh Malt Car, no claim has been made for the value of its contents.

[12] The second breach of contract of carriage is based upon Defendant's alleged failure to deliver the Rickel Barley Car to Rickel. Damages for both claims amount to $19,198.99.

[13] The damages sought for the breach of the Stroh contract of carriage are considered special or consequential damages and must be decided upon the ability of a "reasonable man" to foresee the damages. The principles involved regarding the issue of "foreseeability" are aptly summarized in *Marquette Cement Manufacturing Company v. Louisville and Nashville Railroad Company*, 281 F.Supp. 944 (E.D. Tenn.1967):

> Under the rule of *Hadley v. Baxendale*, (1854) 9 Ex. 314, 156 Eng. Reprint 145, 5 Eng.Rul.Cas. 502, damages recoverable for breach of contract are (1) such as may fairly and reasonably be considered as arising in the usual course of events from the breach of the contract itself or (2) such as may reasonably be supposed to have been in the contemplation of the parties at the time they made the contract . . . The rule has been stated in terms of "foreseeability" in the Restatement of Contracts (Sec. 330):
>
>> In awarding damages, compensation is given for only those injuries that the defendant had reason to foresee as a probable result of his breach when the contract was made. If the injury is one that follows the breach in the usual course of events, there is sufficient reason for the defendant to foresee it; otherwise it must be shown specifically that the defendant had reason to know the facts and to foresee the injury.
>
> The statement providing for "special" or "consequential" damages is merely a further extension of "foreseeability." McCormick, in speaking of the rule of *Hadley v. Baxendale*, observes:

> This standard is in the main an objective one. It takes account of what the defendant who made the contract might have foreseen as a reasonable man, in the light of the facts known to him, and does not confine the inquiry to what he actually did foresee. I(f) the loss claimed is unusual, then it becomes necessary to ascertain whether the defaulting party was notified of the special circumstances.

McCormick on Damages, p. 565, sec. 138.

[14] Defendant had vast experience in the hauling and the delivery of grain. It, through employees, knew the importance of the order in which the cars were to be delivered, and that Stroh received malt and corn grits for the purpose of making beer.

[15] Thus, applying the *Marquette* principles to the instant cause, the Court is of the opinion that the damages, which resulted from the misdelivery of barley to Stroh, were reasonably foreseeable.

[16] The reasonable foreseeableness that the mistake would not be caught is increased because of the similarities in the numbers on the cars and the similarities in the appearance of the contents within the cars.

[17] Although it is clearly obvious that Plaintiff was not free from negligence, the Court disagrees with Defendant's position that the only foreseeable consequence which would normally arise from the misdelivery of the cars was that (1) Stroh would have discovered the wrong car and (2) rejected delivery, resulting in only a minor inconvenience to Stroh and Grand Trunk. The Court believes that implicit in such a defense is the admission that it was also foreseeable that the mistake would not be caught by Stroh.

[18] The Court believes that the *Marquette* case, wherein the Plaintiffs' claims for special or consequential damages under the Carmack Amendment was not allowed by the Court, is similar to, but distinguishable from, the instant case. In *Marquette*, the plaintiff regularly sold and shipped cement to Vulcan Materials Company at its two separate Chattanooga plants. One of the plants manufactured ready-mix concrete while the other manufactured only concrete pipe. A carload of "air-entrained" cement, suitable only for utilization in making concrete pipe, was shipped by Marquette via a bill of lading consigning it to Vulcan's concrete pipe division. Due to an error in routing, the railroad misdelivered the carload of "air-entrained" cement, sending it to Chattanooga Rock Products, the ready-mix concrete division. The ready-mix concrete made from this cement was defective and had to be replaced. Chattanooga Rock Products and Marquette then brought suit against the railroad to recover the damages which resulted when the contents of the misdelivered shipment were used in the manufacturing process for which they were unsuited. The Court awarded the Plaintiff the value of the shipment and

the freight charges but refused to award any other damages. With regard to the special or consequential damages that were not awarded, the Court stated as follows:

> With respect to the remaining items of damage claimed by the plaintiffs, that is the cost of testing and removing the defective concrete from construction sites, such damages may only be considered as special or consequential damages. With respect to their recovery the issue then a rises as to whether the special circumstances giving rise to the damages were communicated to or known by the defendant at the time the contract of carriage was made. In order to recover special damages under the circumstances of this case, it must appear that at the time of the making of the contract of carriage the defendant had reasonable notice or knowledge of the special conditions rendering such damages the natural and probable result of the breach. The Court is of the opinion that the evidence does not establish such notice or knowledge upon the part of the defendant. It is true that the bill of lading did designate the shipment as "air-entrained cement." This information is not sufficient, however, to put the carrier on notice as to the use for which it was to be put. Nor was it sufficient to put the carrier on notice that an additional air-entraining agent would be added to the cement by the plaintiff, thereby rendering it unsuited for structural use. The notice here received by the carrier by the inclusion of the words "air-entrained cement" upon the bill of lading was not sufficient to render reasonably foreseeable the subsequent events which resulted in the expenses incurred by the plaintiff in testing and removing the defective concrete.

At Pages 950, 951.

[19] In *Marquette*, unlike the case at bar, the only knowledge or notice that the defendant had with regard to the operation of the plaintiffs, the shipment or its intended use was the bill of lading which include the words "air-entrained" cement:

> The bill of lading showed that the cement was air-entrained, but the train clerk at the L & N who rerouted the shipment from Concrete Pipe to Rock Products had not noted that the cement was air-entrained, and in fact was uninformed as to what the designation meant. He was likewise uninformed as to what use the Vulcan Materials Company made of the concrete it received at either of its two divisions or as to any difference in the concrete received at the two divisions.

[20] In the instant case, Defendant had that much knowledge and more. It is not necessary that Defendant have detailed knowledge of the

damages incurred. On the other hand, it is sufficient that Defendant possess sufficient notice of the facts and circumstances which would render damages probable.

[21] In *L. E. Whitlock Truck Service, Inc. v. Regal Drilling Company, supra*, the Court affirmed an Order of the district court which granted an award of special damages of lost profits for delay in delivery. In that case, an oil rig was being transported by a carrier who specialized in, and was experienced in, hauling oil rigs. The carrier knew it was the shipper's only oil rig. In finding for the shipper, the Court reasoned as follows:

> There is adequate testimony in the record to support the award of special damages. The appellant specialized in and was experienced in the hauling of oil well equipment and was aware of the importance of time to those engaged in the drilling business. There is adequate evidence in the record to support the finding that the appellant knew of the need and the importance to the appellee of delivery of the rig on time and of damages which would result in the event appellee did not have the use of it. The appellant knew that the appellee had only the one drilling rig. Thus the appellant knew the circumstances upon which the special damages here awarded are based.

At Page 492.

[22] Based upon the foregoing analysis, it is, therefore, ordered that Stroh shall be, and is, allowed to recover the sum of $19,198.99[3] from Grand Trunk for the breach of the Stroh and Rickel contracts of carriage.

[23] The foregoing constitutes the Court's findings of fact and conclusions of law as required by Fed. R. Civ. P. 52.

———

NOTES AND QUESTIONS

Stroh Brewery Company was founded in 1949 and closed down after a 50-year run in 1999. In 1996, it had about 10% of the United States beer market, producing its own brands like Stroh's, Augsburger, and Northern Plains, and serving as a contract brewer for August Brewery, Boston Beer Company, Fischer Brewing, and Pete's Brewing Company.

———

---

[3]   [$19,198.99 in 1981 dollars is roughly the equivalent of $53,000 in 2019 dollars using the CPI and the GNP Deflator.—Eds.]

LINC EQUIPMENT SERVICES V. SIGNAL MEDICAL SERVICES

United States Court of Appeals, Seventh Circuit
319 F.3d 288 (2003)

EASTERBROOK, CIRCUIT JUDGE.

[1]   Signal Medical leased from Linc Equipment a mobile magnetic resonance imager (MRI), an expensive device that had a monthly net rental in the $30,000 range. (The "net" signifies that Signal covered expenses, including insurance and taxes, on top of the $30,000.) Signal promised to return the MRI at the end of the lease in good condition, less normal wear and tear. Signal, which like Linc is a merchant in the business of renting medical equipment, subleased this MRI to a hospital, which later returned the machine directly to Linc. Unfortunately, the MRI was left on during transit, which damaged the magnet and required the machine to be taken out of service for 10 months while it was repaired. The repairs, which cost about $130,000, were paid for by the insurance carrier. Linc sued in state court both Signal and the firm that handled the machine's transportation; the insurer intervened to make a third-party claim in subrogation against Signal.

[2]   After the parties agreed to a bench trial, the district judge tackled damages ahead of the merits. The judge assumed that Signal is responsible for any harm to the MRI and held a hearing to explore the question whether it is liable for consequential damages (repair costs already having been resolved). As the judge understood Illinois law, which the parties agree governs, consequential damages may be awarded only if the signatories "expressly contemplated" them. The contract does not in so many words entitle Linc to consequential damages, and at the evidentiary hearing the persons who negotiated the lease testified that they had not discussed or thought about this subject. As a result, the judge concluded, consequential damages could not have been "expressly contemplated." This finding led to judgment on the merits in Signal's favor.

[3]   We doubt that Illinois requires "express contemplation" of consequential damages—or that, if it does, this phrase implies a subjective as opposed to an objective inquiry. Although the district judge and the parties did not mention it, *Hadley v. Baxendale*, 9 Ex. 341, 156 Eng. Rep. 145 (1854), remains the dominant source of law on the recovery of consequential damages for breach of contract, and we have held that Illinois follows *Hadley*'s approach. What *Hadley* holds is that a consequential loss is compensable only if "reasonably foreseeable," not that it must be "expressly contemplated." Although the phrase "expressly contemplated" crops up in some Illinois cases, that state's judiciary has explained that it is used as a synonym for foreseeability. Signal, which like Linc was a merchant in the medical-equipment-rental business, reasonably could have foreseen that return of the MRI in bad condition would cost Linc

rental revenue while it was being repaired. That the lease excluded consequential damages in an action by Signal, but not in an action by Linc, shows that the parties must have understood this possibility.

[4] What is more, it is hard to see why income lost because of inability to rent a chattel should be classified as "consequential" damages at all. Lost rental value is a direct outcome of the broken promise and does not depend on the details of Linc's business or any idiosyncratic way that Linc would employ the MRI—things that Signal might not know and therefore could not consider when deciding how much care to take with Linc's machine. To see this, suppose that Linc wanted to sell rather than rent the MRI immediately after its return from Signal's customer. The selling price of a MRI depends on expected net income (rental or billings to patients, less costs), plus scrap value at the end of its economically useful life, all discounted to present value. Suppose that this MRI in good condition would have had 60 months of service remaining before becoming obsolete. The same machine, with the damage actually sustained, would have had only 50 months' service remaining (deferred for 10 months) and required a $130,000 capital investment to repair. It therefore would have sold for less than the same machine in operable condition. The difference between what the MRI would have fetched in a sale immediately after its return in damaged condition, and what it could have been sold for had Signal kept its promise to return it in good condition, is the real economic loss caused by transporting the machine with the magnet on. It fits nicely within standard measures of damages in contract cases. See generally E. Allan Farnsworth, III Farnsworth on Contracts § 12.9 (2d ed. 1990).

[5] Because the market price of rental equipment capitalizes the expected rental stream—not only reducing cash flows to present value but also taking into account the probability that some months will not fetch rentals, when machines are between customers or demand is slack—it would be double counting to award a lessor anything extra for lost rental income. Consider what should happen if one of Hertz's customers has an accident and the car must be taken out of the fleet for a month while being repaired. Would Hertz recover not only the cost of repair (say, $1,000) but also the $50 daily rental during that month ($50 x 30 = $1,500)? Such a measure frequently would overcompensate the lessor. If the accident caused the value of the used car to decline by, say, $1,500 (from $15,000 in good condition to $13,500 with repairs pending), Hertz could sell the damaged car for $13,500, invest an extra $1,500, buy a used car equal in value to the one it expected to receive at the end of the rental, and rent *that* car for $50 per day. Its full loss would be $1,500 (the difference in resale prices); if Hertz neglected to cover in the market, and instead claimed a loss of $2,500, it would be met with the defense that it had failed to mitigate damages. Just so with Linc. If it had a ready market for MRI machines, it could have covered when it learned of the problem and leased out the newly

purchased machine; then its full loss would have been the difference between the cost of cover and the amount it could have realized when selling the damaged machine.

[6]   One must consider as well the possibility that MRI machines have lives that depend on accumulated use (wear and tear) rather than technological obsolescence. In that event, taking the machine out of service did not cost Linc ten months' rental but only postponed its receipt. Then damages would be limited to the time value of money (that is, to interest on the deferral of income). The magnet's rebuilding might even have extended the machine's useful life. All of this is captured automatically in the difference between the sale prices of sound and damaged MRI devices, which makes this calculation preferable to judicial attempts to determine how likely it was that a particular machine would have been rented during these particular months, what its expected useful life may have been, and so on. Best to take advantage of market prices that reflect this information, rather than try to generate the information on the witness stand. We know that this MRI *was* sold for $475,000 immediately after the repairs were completed; such a price for a fully functional MRI, with many future months of rental in store, strongly implies that $300,000[4] would be an excessive award for the loss of 10 months' use.

[7]   So the district court was right to conclude that Linc is not entitled to damages measured by the monthly rental times the number of months required for repair, but wrong to think that the cost of making repairs sets a cap on damages. The judgment is vacated, and the case is remanded for further proceedings consistent with this opinion.

———

PROBLEM 19-1

Precision Sound, Inc. ("Seller") enters into a contract to sell an item of recording equipment to Solid Gold Recording Studios ("Buyer"). A few days later, Seller learns that Buyer needs this piece of equipment in order to fulfill its obligations under a major contract. Seller had no reason to foresee this at the time the contract was made. Shortly after learning this fact, Seller's general manager places the order for the equipment with the manufacturer. He makes a mistake in filling out the order form, and the manufacturer ships the wrong equipment. By the time the mistake has been rectified, the time for Seller to deliver the equipment to Buyer has passed and Buyer has lost the big contract. Can Buyer recover damages resulting from the loss of the contract? What is the policy behind this result?

———

---

4   [$300,000 in 2003 dollars is roughly the equivalent of $409,000 in 2019 dollars using the CPI and the GNP Deflator.—Eds.]

B. CERTAINTY

CHICAGO COLISEUM CLUB V. DEMPSEY
Court of Appeals of Illinois
265 Ill. App. 542 (1932)

MR. JUSTICE WILSON delivered the opinion of the court.

[1] Chicago Coliseum Club, a corporation, as plaintiff, brought its action against William Harrison Dempsey, to recover damages for breach of a written contract executed March 13, 1926, but bearing date of March 6 of that year.

[2] Plaintiff was incorporated as an Illinois corporation for the promotion of general pleasure and athletic purposes and to conduct boxing, sparring and wrestling matches and exhibitions for prizes or purses. The defendant William Harrison Dempsey was well known in the pugilistic world and, at the time of the making and execution of the contract in question, held the title of world's Champion Heavy Weight Boxer.

[3] Under the terms of the written agreement, the plaintiff was to promote a public boxing exhibition in Chicago or some suitable place to be selected by the promoter, and had engaged the services of one Harry Wills, another well known boxer and pugilist, to engage in a boxing match with the defendant Dempsey for the championship of the world. By the terms of the agreement Dempsey was to receive $10, receipt of which was acknowledged, and the plaintiff further agreed to pay to Dempsey the sum of $30,000 on the 5th day of August 1926—$500,000 in cash at least 10 days before the date fixed for the contest, and a sum equal to 50 per cent of the net profits over and above the sum $2,000,000 in the event the gate receipts should exceed that amount. In addition the defendant was to receive 50 per cent of the net revenue derived from moving picture concessions or royalties received by the plaintiff, and defendant agreed to have his life and health insured in favor of the plaintiff in a manner and at a place to be designated by the plaintiff. Defendant further agreed not to engage in any boxing match after the date of the agreement and prior to the date on which the contest was to be held. Certain agreements previously entered into by the defendant with one Floyd Fitzsimmons for a Dempsey-Wills boxing match were declared to be void and of no force and effect. Certain other mutual agreements were contained in the written contract which are not necessary in a consideration of this case.

[4] March 6, 1926, the plaintiff entered into an agreement with Harry Wills, in which Wills agreed to engage in a boxing match with the Jack Dempsey named in the agreement hereinbefore referred to. Under this agreement the plaintiff, Chicago Coliseum Club was to deposit $50,000 in escrow in the National City Bank of New York City, New York, to be paid over to Wills on the 10th day prior to the date fixed for the holding of the

boxing contest. Further conditions were provided in said contract with Wills, which, however, are not necessary to set out in detail. There is no evidence in the record showing that the $50,000[5] was deposited nor that it has ever been paid, nor is there any evidence in the record showing the financial standing of the Chicago Coliseum Club, a corporation, plaintiff in this suit. This contract between the plaintiff and Wills appears to have been entered into several days before the contract with Dempsey.

[5] March 8, 1926, the plaintiff entered into a contract with one Andrew C. Weisberg, under which it appears that it was necessary for the plaintiff to have the services of an experienced person skilled in promoting boxing exhibitions and that the said Weisberg was possessed of such qualifications and that it was necessary for the plaintiff to procure his help in the promoting of the exhibition. It appears further from the agreement that it was necessary to incur expenditures in the way of traveling expenses, legal services and other costs in and about the promotion of the boxing match, and Weisberg agreed to investigate, canvass and organize the various hotel associations and other business organizations for the purpose of securing accommodations for spectators and to procure subscriptions and contributions from such hotels and associations and others for the erection of an arena and other necessary expense in order to carry out the enterprise and to promote the boxing match in question. Under these agreements Weisberg was to furnish the funds for such purposes and was to be reimbursed out of the receipts from the sale of tickets for the expenses incurred by him, together with a certain amount for his services.

[6] Both the Wills contract and the Weisberg contract are referred to at some length, inasmuch as claims for damages by plaintiff are predicated upon these two agreements. Under the terms of the contract between the plaintiff and Dempsey and the plaintiff and Wills, the contest was to be held during the month of September, 1926.

[7] July 10, 1926, plaintiff wired Dempsey at Colorado Springs, Colorado, stating that representatives of life and accident insurance companies would call on him for the purpose of examining him for insurance in favor of the Chicago Coliseum Club, in accordance with the terms of his contract, and also requesting the defendant to begin training for the contest not later than August 1, 1926. In answer to this communication plaintiff received a telegram from Dempsey, as follows:

BM Colorado Springs Colo B. E. Clements July 10th 1926

President Chicago Coliseum Club Chgo Entirely too busy training for my coming Tunney match to waste time on insurance

---

[5] [$50,000 in 1932 dollars is roughly the equivalent of $919,000 in 2019 dollars using the CPI and the GNP Deflator.—Eds.]

repudiate of agreement

representatives stop as you have no contract suggest you stop kidding yourself and me also.

Jack Dempsey

[8] We are unable to conceive upon what theory the defendant could contend that there was no contract, as it appears to be admitted in the proceeding here and bears his signature and the amounts involved are sufficiently large to have created a rather lasting impression on the mind of anyone signing such an agreement. It amounts, however, to a repudiation of the agreement and from that time on Dempsey refused to take any steps to carry out his undertaking. It appears that Dempsey at this time was engaged in preparing himself for a contest with Tunney to be held at Philadelphia, Pennsylvania, sometime in September, and on August 3, 1926, plaintiff, as complainant, filed a bill in the superior court of Marion county, Indiana, asking to have Dempsey restrained and enjoined from engaging in the contest with Tunney, which complainant was informed and believed was to be held on the 16th day of September, and which contest would be in violation of the terms of the agreement entered into between the plaintiff and defendant at Los Angeles, March 13, 1926.

[9] Personal service was had upon the defendant Dempsey in the proceeding in the Indiana court and on August 27, 1926, he entered his general appearance, by his attorneys, and filed his answer in said cause. September 13, 1926, a decree was entered in the superior court of Marion county, finding that the contract was a valid and subsisting contract between the parties, and that the complainant had expended large sums of money in carrying out the terms of the agreement, and entering a decree that Dempsey be perpetually restrained and enjoined from in any way, wise, or manner, training or preparing for or participating in any contracts or engagements in furtherance of any boxing match, prize fight or any exhibition of like nature, and particularly from engaging or entering into any boxing match with one Gene Tunney, or with any person other than the one designated by plaintiff.

[10] It is insisted among other things that the costs incurred by the plaintiff in procuring the injunctional order in Marion county, Indiana, were properly chargeable against Dempsey for his breach of contract and recoverable in this proceeding. Under the evidence in the record in this proceeding there appears to have been a valid subsisting agreement between the plaintiff and Dempsey, in which Dempsey was to perform according to the terms of the agreement and which he refused to do, and the plaintiff, as a matter of law, was entitled at least to nominal damages. For this reason, if for no other, judgment should have been for the plaintiff.

[11] During the proceeding in the circuit court of this county it was sought to introduce evidence for the purpose of showing damages, other

than nominal damages, and in view of the fact that the case has to be retried, this court is asked to consider the various items of expense claimed to have been incurred and various offers of proof made to establish damages for breach of the agreement. Under the proof offered, the question of damages naturally divides itself into the four following propositions:

1st. Loss of profits which would have been derived by the plaintiff in the event of the holding of the contest in question;

2nd. Expenses incurred by the plaintiff prior to the signing of the agreement between the plaintiff and Dempsey;

3rd. Expenses incurred in attempting to restrain the defendant from engaging in other contests and to force him into a compliance with the terms of his agreement with the plaintiff; and

4th. Expenses incurred after the signing of the agreement and before the breach of July 10, 1926.

[12] *Proposition 1.* Plaintiff offered to prove by one Mullins that a boxing exhibition between Dempsey and Wills held in the City of Chicago on September 22, 1926, would bring a gross receipt of $3,000,000, and that the expense incurred would be $1,400,000, leaving a net profit to the promoter of $1,600,000. The court properly sustained an objection to this testimony. The character of the undertaking was such that it would be impossible to produce evidence of a probative character sufficient to establish any amount which could be reasonably ascertainable by reason of the character of the undertaking. The profits from a boxing contest of this character, open to the public, is dependent upon so many different circumstances that they are not susceptible of definite legal determination. The success or failure of such an undertaking depends largely upon the ability of the promoters, the reputation of the contestants and the conditions of the weather at and prior to the holding of the contest, the accessibility of the place, the extent of the publicity, the possibility of other and counter attractions and many other questions which would enter into consideration. Such an entertainment lacks utterly the element of stability which exists in regular organized business. This fact was practically admitted by the plaintiff by the allegation of its bill filed in the Marion county court of Indiana asking for an injunction against Dempsey. Plaintiff in its bill in that proceeding charged, as follows:

[13] "That by virtue of the premises aforesaid, the plaintiff will, unless it secures the injunctive relief herein prayed for, suffer great and irreparable injury and damages, not compensable by any action at law in damages, the damages being incapable of commensuration, and plaintiff, therefore, has no adequate remedy at law."

[14] Compensation for damages for a breach of contract must be established by evidence from which a court or jury are able to ascertain the

extent of such damages by the usual rules of evidence and to a reasonable degree of certainly. We are of the opinion that the performance in question is not susceptible of proof sufficient to satisfy the requirements and that the damages, if any, are purely speculative.

[15] *Proposition 2:* Expenses incurred by the plaintiff prior to the signing of the agreement between the plaintiff and Dempsey.

[16] The general rule is that in an action for a breach of contract a party can recover only on damages which naturally flow from and are the result of the act complained of. The Wills contract was entered into prior to the contract with the defendant and was not made contingent upon the plaintiff's obtaining a similar agreement with the defendant Dempsey. Under the circumstances the plaintiff speculated as to the result of his efforts to procure the Dempsey contract. It may be argued that there had been negotiations pending between plaintiff and Dempsey which clearly indicated an agreement between them, but the agreement in fact was never consummated until sometime later. The action is based upon the written agreement which was entered into in Los Angeles. Any obligations assumed by the plaintiff prior to that time are not chargeable to the defendant. Moreover, an examination of the record discloses that the $50,000 named in the contract with Wills, which was to be payable upon a signing of the agreement, was not and never has been paid. There is no evidence in the record showing that the plaintiff is responsible financially, and, even though there were, we consider that it is not an element of damage which can be recovered for breach of the contract in question.

[17] *Proposition 3:* Expenses incurred in attempting to restrain the defendant from engaging in other contests and to force him into a compliance with the terms of his agreement with the plaintiff.

[18] After the repudiation of the agreement by the defendant, plaintiff was advised of defendant's match with Tunney which, from the evidence, it appears, was to take place in Philadelphia in the month of September and was in direct conflict with the terms of the agreement entered into between plaintiff and defendant. Plaintiff's bill, filed in the superior court of Marion county, Indiana, was an effort on the part of the plaintiff to compel defendant to live up to the terms of his agreement. The chancellor in the Indiana court entered his decree, which apparently is in full force and effect, and the defendant in violating the terms of that decree, after personal service, is answerable to that court for a violation of the injunctional order entered in said proceeding. The expenses incurred, however, by the plaintiff in procuring that decree are not collectible in an action for damages in this proceeding; neither are such similar expenses as were incurred in the trips to Colorado and Philadelphia, nor the attorney's fees and other expenses thereby incurred. The plaintiff having been informed that the defendant intended to proceed no further under his

agreement, took such steps at its own financial risk. There was nothing in the agreement regarding attorney's fees and there was nothing in the contract in regard to the services of the defendant from which it would appear that the action for specific performance would lie. After the clear breach of contract by the defendant, the plaintiff proceeded with this character of litigation at its own risk. We are of the opinion that the trial court properly held that this was an element of damages which was not recoverable.

[19] *Proposition 4:* Expenses incurred after the signing of the agreement and before the breach of July 10, 1926.

[20] After the signing of the agreement plaintiff attempted to show expenses incurred by one Weisberg in and about the furtherance of the project. Weisberg testified that he had taken an active part in promoting sports for a number of years and was in the employ of the Chicago Coliseum Club under a written contract during all of the time that his services were rendered in furtherance of this proposition. This contract was introduced in evidence and bore the date of March 8, 1926. Under its terms Weisberg was to be reimbursed out of the gate receipts and profits derived from the performance. His compensation depended entirely upon the success of the exhibition. Under his agreement with the plaintiff there was nothing to charge the plaintiff unconditionally with the costs and expenses of Weisberg's services. The court properly ruled against the admissibility of the evidence.

[21] We find in the record, however, certain evidence which should have been submitted to the jury on the question of damages sustained by the plaintiff. The contract on which the breach of the action is predicated shows a payment of $10 by the plaintiff to the defendant and the receipt acknowledged. It appears that the stadium located in the South Park District, known as Soldier's Field, was considered as a site for the holding of the contest and plaintiff testified that it paid $300 to an architect for plans in the event the stadium was to be used for the performance. This item of damage might have been made more specific and may not have been the best evidence in the case but, standing alone, it was sufficient to go to the jury. There were certain elements in regard to wages paid assistant secretaries which may be substantiated by evidence showing that they were necessary in furtherance of the undertaking. If these expenses were incurred they are recoverable if in furtherance of the general scheme. The defendant should not be required to answer in damages for salaries paid regular officials of the corporation who were presumed to be receiving such salaries by reason of their position, but special expenses incurred are recoverable. The expenses of Hoffman in going to Colorado for the purpose of having Dempsey take his physical examination for insurance, if before the breach and reasonable, are recoverable. The railroad fares for those who went to Los Angeles for the purpose of procuring the signing of the

agreement are not recoverable as they were incurred in a furtherance of the procuring of the contract and not after the agreement was entered into. The services of Shank in looking after railroad facilities and making arrangements with the railroad for publicity and special trains and accommodations were items which should be considered and if it develops that they were incurred in a furtherance of the general plan and properly proven, are items for which the plaintiff should be reimbursed.

[22] The items recoverable are such items of expense as were incurred between the date of the signing of the agreement and the breach of July 10, 1926, by the defendant and such as were incurred as a necessary expense in furtherance of the performance. Proof of such items should be made subject to the usual rules of evidence.

[23] For the reasons stated in this opinion the judgment of the circuit court is reversed and the cause remanded for a new trial.

Judgment reversed and cause remanded.

HEBEL, P. J., and FRIEND, J., concur.

———

NOTES AND QUESTIONS

1.   In the 1920s, a heavyweight championship fight was America's leading sporting event, what the Super Bowl is today. Jack Dempsey was, with the possible exception of Babe Ruth, the leading sports celebrity of the day. If you were Dempsey's manager, what would you have done to make sure that Dempsey (and of course, Dempsey's manager is reputed to have taken an outsize portion of Dempsey's pay), rather than the promoter, got most of the profits from the fight?

2.   Around 1970, a group of oil company engineers identified a phenomenon that has come to be called "the winner's curse." The engineers noticed that every time their company won an auction for an oil lease, it ended up losing money on the deal. As they thought about it, the engineers realized that because no one knew exactly how much oil was recoverable under the lease, some bidders would overestimate the oil and some would underestimate it. The winner of the auction would normally be the company that overestimated by the largest margin and thus bid too much. Since that time the winner's curse has been the subject of several books and numerous Ph.D. dissertations. Businesses have hired consultants to help them structure their bids to avoid the winner's curse. But when the Chicago Coliseum Club signed its contract, no one had heard of the winner's curse. Is it possible Dempsey did the plaintiff a favor by breaching the contract?

3.   The certainty limitation is found in section 352 of the R2d and article 7.4.3 of the UNIDROIT principles. They are phrased differently. What are the

substantive differences? Which is likely to lead to greater recovery by the non-breaching party?

4.   Under the so-called "American Rule" attorneys' fees incurred in obtaining and enforcing a contract damage judgment are not recoverable absent a provision providing for them as allowable damages in the contract itself. This is in contrast with the so-called "English Rule" under which the prevailing party may recover its attorneys' fees from the other party. As a result of the American Rule, contract clauses providing for attorneys fees are common in American contracts. They are often, but need not be, in the form of a prevailing party attorneys' fee clause, which operates like the English Rule. But some contracts provide for attorneys' fee recovery for only one party to the contract. Should such "one way" clauses be enforceable? Some states say, "yes, but." For instance, the California Civil Code's section 1717 converts a one way clause into a bilateral clause allowing recovery by either party—so the clause is enforceable as modified by the statute. Is this good policy? What sort of incentives does the presence or absence of an enforceable attorneys' fee provision produce?

————

ERICSON V. PLAYGIRL

Court of Appeal of California
73 Cal. App. 3d 850, 140 Cal. Rptr. 921 (1977)

FLEMING, ACTING P.J.

[1]   Were damages awarded here for breach of contract speculative and conjectural, or were they clearly ascertainable and reasonably certain, both in nature and in origin?

[2]   The breach of contract arose from the following circumstances: plaintiff John Ericson, in order to boost his career as an actor, agreed that defendant Playgirl, Inc., could publish without compensation as the centerfold of its January 1974 issue of Playgirl photographs of Ericson posing naked at Lion Country Safari. No immediate career boost to Ericson resulted from the publication. In April 1974 defendant wished to use the pictures again for its annual edition entitled Best of Playgirl, a publication with half the circulation of Playgirl and without advertising. Ericson agreed to a rerun of his pictures in Best of Playgirl on two conditions: that certain of them be cropped to more modest exposure, and that Ericson's photograph occupy a quarter of the front cover, which would contain photographs of five other persons on its remaining three-quarters. Defendant honored the first of these conditions but not the second, in that as the result of an editorial mixup Ericson's photograph did not appear on the cover of Best of Playgirl. Ericson thereupon sued for damages, not for invasion of privacy from unauthorized publication of his pictures, but for

loss of the publicity he would have received if defendant had put Ericson's picture on the cover as it had agreed to do.

[3]   All witnesses testified that the front cover of a magazine is not for sale, that a publisher reserves exclusive control over the front cover because its format is crucial to circulation, that consequently it is impossible to quote a direct price for front cover space. Witnesses also agreed that a picture on the front cover of a national magazine can provide valuable publicity for an actor or entertainer, but that it is difficult to put a price on this publicity. Analogies were sought in the cost of advertising space inside and on the back cover of national magazines. In July 1974 a full-page advertisement in Playgirl cost $7,500 to $8,000, a quarter page $2,500, and the back cover $11,000. However, Best of Playgirl carried no advertising and enjoyed only half the circulation of its parent magazine.

[4]   The trial court awarded plaintiff damages of $12,500,[6] expressly basing its award on the testimony of Richard Cook, western advertising manager for TV Guide. According to Cook, the value to an entertainer of an appearance on the cover of a national magazine is "probably close to $50,000, and I base that on this: That magazine lays on the newsstand, a lot of people that never buy it see it, and everybody that does buy it certainly sees it." Cook said that the circulation of a magazine affects the value of a cover appearance, as does the magazine's demographics, i.e., the specific audience it reaches. He based his opinion on his knowledge of Playgirl, for he had no knowledge of the circulation, demographics, or even existence of Best of Playgirl. He also quantified his opinion by stating that if the picture only occupied a quarter of the cover instead of the full cover, the value of the appearance would be only a fourth of $50,000, which was the figure used by the trial court in fixing plaintiff's damages for loss of publicity at $12,500.

I

[5]   On appeal the sole substantial issue is that of damages, for it is clear the parties entered a contract which defendant breached.[7]

[6]   In reviewing the issue of damages we first note that the cause of action is for breach of contract and not for a tort such as invasion of privacy. Defendant is not charged with committing a civil wrong but merely with failing to keep its promise. From this classification of the action as breach

---

[6]   [$12,500 in 1977 dollars is roughly the equivalent of $51,800 in 2019 dollars using the CPI and the GNP Deflator.—Eds.]

[7]   The contract consisted of the following letter:

"I, John Ericson, hereby release to Playgirl the use of my centerfold, cropped to eliminate genital exposure, to appear as a fold-out in 'The Best of Playgirl.' Also, it is understood that a head shot of me will appear on the front cover of 'The Best of Playgirl', lower left. I further release all other pictures which appeared in the January centerfold section for use in The Best of Playgirl."

of contract, three important consequences affecting the measure of damages follow:

1.   Damages may not be punitive or exemplary and may not be imposed as a form of chastisement.

2.   Damages are limited to losses that might reasonably be contemplated or foreseen by the parties.

3.   Damages must be clearly ascertainable and reasonably certain, both in their nature and origin.

[7] In each of these respects damages for breach of contract differ from damages in tort; accordingly, tort precedents on the measure of damages have no direct relevancy here. Of limited application, too, is the tort rule that when calculation of the fact and amount of damages has been made difficult by defendant's wrong, courts will adopt whatever means are at hand to right the wrong.

[8] Plaintiff's claim of damages for breach of contract was based entirely on the loss of general publicity he would have received by having his photograph appear, alongside those of five others, on the cover of Best of Playgirl. Plaintiff proved that advertising is expensive to buy, that publicity has value for an actor. But what he did not prove was that loss of publicity as the result of his nonappearance on the cover of Best of Playgirl did in fact damage him in any substantial way or in any specific amount. Plaintiff's claim sharply contrasts with those few breach of contract cases that have found damages for loss of publicity reasonably certain and reasonably calculable, as in refusals to continue an advertising contract. In such cases the court has assessed damages at the market value of the advertising, less the agreed contract price. Plaintiff's claim for damages more closely resembles those which have been held speculative and conjectural, as in the analogous cases of *Jones v. San Bernardino Real Estate Board* (1959) 168 Cal.App.2d 661, 665, where the court declined to award purely conjectural damages for loss of commissions, contacts, business associations, and clientele allegedly occasioned by plaintiff's expulsion from a local realty board; and of *Fisher v. Hampton* (1975) 44 Cal.App.3d 741, where the court rejected an award of damages for defendant's failure to drill a $35,000 oil well when geological reports opined that oil would not be found and no evidence whatever established that plaintiff had been damaged. Under normal legal rules plaintiff's claim for damages failed to satisfy the requirements of reasonable foreseeability and reasonable certainty, and therefore took on a punitive hue.

[The court discussed special damage rules applicable to entertainers and decided they didn't help the plaintiff.—Eds.]

III

[9] Plaintiff, however, is entitled to recover nominal damages for breach of contract. We evaluate plaintiff's right to nominal damages by analogy to Civil Code section 3344, which provides minimum statutory damages of $300 for knowing commercial use of a person's name or likeness without his consent. The statute's obvious purpose is to specify an amount for nominal damages in situations where actual damages are impossible to assess. Accordingly, although we find no support for any assessment of compensatory damages in plaintiff's favor because of the wholly speculative nature of the detriment suffered by plaintiff as a result of his nonappearance on a fourth of the cover of Best of Playgirl, plaintiff is entitled to nominal damages for breach of contract, which we fix in the sum of $300.

[10] The judgment is modified to reduce the amount of damages to $300, and, as so modified, the judgment is affirmed. Costs on appeal to plaintiff.

———

FERA v. VILLAGE PLAZA INC.

Supreme Court of Michigan
396 Mich. 639, 242 N.W.2d 372 (1976)

KAVANAGH, C.J.

[1] Plaintiffs received a jury award of $200,000[8] for loss of anticipated profits in their proposed new business as a result of defendants' breach of a lease. The Court of Appeals reversed. 52 Mich. App. 532, 218 N.W.2d 155 (1974). We reverse and reinstate the jury's award.

Facts

[2] On August 20, 1965 plaintiffs and agents of Fairborn-Village Plaza executed a ten-year lease for a "book and bottle" shop in defendants' proposed shopping center. This lease provided for occupancy of a specific location at a rental of $1,000 minimum monthly rent plus 5% of annual receipts in excess of $240,000. A $1,000 deposit was paid by plaintiffs.

[3] After this lease was executed, plaintiffs gave up approximately 600 square feet of their leased space so that it could be leased to another tenant. In exchange, it was agreed that liquor sales would be excluded from the percentage rent override provision of the lease.

[4] Complications arose, including numerous work stoppages. Bank of the Commonwealth received a deed in lieu of foreclosure after default by

---

[8] [$200,000 in 1976 dollars is roughly the equivalent of $882,000 in 2019 dollars using the CPI and the GNP Deflator.—Eds.]

Fairborn and Village Plaza. Schostak Brothers managed the property for the bank.

[5] When the space was finally ready for occupancy, plaintiffs were refused the space for which they had contracted because the lease had been misplaced, and the space rented to other tenants. Alternative space was offered but refused by plaintiffs as unsuitable for their planned business venture.

[6] Plaintiffs initiated suit in Wayne Circuit Court, alleging *inter alia* a claim for anticipated lost profits. The jury returned a verdict for plaintiffs against all defendants for $200,000.

[7] The Court of Appeals reversed and remanded for new trial on the issue of damages only, holding that the trial court "erroneously permitted lost profits as the measure of damages for breach of the lease." 52 Mich. App. 532, 542, 218 N.W.2d 155, 160.

[8] In *Jarrait v. Peters,* 145 Mich. 29, 31–32, 108 N.W. 432 (1906), plaintiff was prevented from taking possession of the leased premises. The jury gave plaintiff a judgment which included damages for lost profits. This Court reversed:

> It is well settled upon authority that the measure of damages when a lessor fails to give possession of the leased premises is the difference between the actual rental value and the rent reserved. 1 Sedgwick on Damages (8th ed.), § 185. Mr. Sedgwick says:
>
>> If the business were a new one, since there could be no basis on which to estimate profits, the plaintiff must be content to recover according to the general rule.
>
> The rule is different where the business of the lessee has been interrupted.
>
> * * *
>
> The evidence admitted tending to show the prospective profits plaintiff might have made for the ensuing two years should therefore have been excluded under the objections made by defendant, and the jury should have been instructed that the plaintiff's damages, if any, would be the difference between the actual rental value of the premises and the rent reserved in the lease.

[9] Six years later, in *Isbell v. Anderson Carriage Co,* 170 Mich. 304, 318, 136 N.W. 457 (1912), the Court wrote:

> It has sometimes been stated as a rule of law that prospective profits are so speculative and uncertain that they cannot be recognized in the measure of damages. This is not because they

are profits, but because they are so often not susceptible of proof to a reasonable degree of certainty. Where the proof is available, prospective profits may be recovered, when proven, as other damages. But the jury cannot be asked to guess. They are to try the case upon evidence, not upon conjecture.

[10] These cases and others since should not be read as stating a rule of law which prevents *every* new business from recovering anticipated lost profits for breach of contract. The rule is merely an application of the doctrine that "[i]n order to be entitled to a verdict, or a judgment, for damages for breach of contract, the plaintiff must lay a basis for a reasonable estimate of the extent of his harm, measured in money." 5 Corbin on Contracts, § 1020, p. 124. The issue becomes one of sufficiency of proof. "The jury should not [be] allowed to speculate or guess upon this question of the amount of loss of profits." *Kezeli v. River Rouge Lodge IOOF,* 195 Mich. 181, 188, 161 N.W. 838 (1917).

> Assuming, therefore, that profits prevented may be considered in measuring the damages, are profits to be divided into classes and kinds? Does the term "speculative profits" express one of these classes, differing in nature from nonspeculative profits? Do "uncertain" profits differ in kind from "certain" profits? The answer is assuredly, No. There is little that can be regarded as "certain," especially with respect to what would have happened if the march of events had been other than it in fact has been. Neither court nor jury is required to attain "certainty" in awarding damages; and this is just as true with respect to "value" as with respect to "profits." Therefore, the term "speculative and uncertain profits" is not really a classification of profits, but is instead a characterization of the evidence that is introduced to prove that they would have been made if the defendant had not committed a breach of contract. The law requires that this evidence shall not be so meager or uncertain as to afford no reasonable basis for inference, leaving the damages to be determined by sympathy and feelings alone. The amount of evidence required and the degree of its strength as a basis of inference varies with circumstances.

5 Corbin on Contracts, § 1022, pp. 139–40.

[11] The rule was succinctly stated in *Shropshire v. Adams,* 40 Tex.Civ.App. 339, 344, 89 S.W. 448, 450 (1905):

> Future profits as an element of damage are in no case excluded merely because they are profits but because they are uncertain. In any case when by reason of the nature of the situation they may be established with reasonable certainty they are allowed.

[12] It is from these principles that the "new business"/"interrupted business" distinction has arisen.

> If a business is one that has already been established a reasonable prediction can often be made as to its future on the basis of its past history . . . If the business . . . has not had such a history as to make it possible to prove with reasonable accuracy what its profits have been in fact, the profits prevented are often but not necessarily too uncertain for recovery.

5 Corbin on Contracts, § 1023, pp. 147, 150–51.

[13] The Court of Appeals based its opinion reversing the jury's award on two grounds. First, that a new business cannot recover damages for lost profits for breach of a lease. We have expressed our disapproval of that rule. Secondly, the Court of Appeals held plaintiffs barred from recovery because the proof of lost profits was entirely speculative. We disagree.

[14] The trial judge in a thorough opinion made the following observations upon completion of the trial.

> On the issue of lost profits, there were days and days of testimony. The defendants called experts from the Michigan Liquor Control Commission and from Cunningham Drug Stores, who have a store in the area, and a man who ran many other stores. The plaintiffs called experts and they, themselves, had experience in the liquor sales business, in the book sales business and had been representatives of liquor distribution firms in the area.

> The issue of the speculative, conjectural nature of future profits was probably the most completely tried issue in the whole case. Both sides covered this point for days on direct and cross-examination. The proofs ranged from no lost profits to two hundred and seventy thousand dollars over a ten-year period as the highest in the testimony. A witness for the defendants, an expert from Cunningham Drug Company, testified the plaintiffs probably would lose money. Mr. Fera, an expert in his own right, testified the profits would probably be two hundred and seventy thousand dollars. The jury found two hundred thousand dollars. This is well within the limits of the high and the low testimony presented by both sides, and a judgment was granted by the jury.

> The court cannot invade the finding of fact by the jury, unless there is no testimony to support the jury's finding. There is testimony to support the jury's finding. We must realize that witness Stein is an interested party in this case, personally. He is an officer or owner in Schostak Brothers. He may personally lose money as a result of this case. The jury had to weigh this in determining his credibility. How much credibility they gave his

testimony was up to them. How much weight they gave to counter-evidence was up to them. . . .

The court must decide whether or not the jury had enough testimony to take this fact from the speculative-conjecture category and find enough facts to be able to make a legal finding of fact. This issue [damages for lost profits] was the most completely tried issue in the whole case. Both sides put in testimony that took up days and encompassed experts on both sides. This fact was adequately taken from the category of speculation and conjecture by the testimony and placed in the position of those cases that hold that even though loss of profits is hard to prove, if proven they should be awarded by the jury. In this case, the jury had ample testimony to make this decision from both sides.

The jury award was approximately seventy thousand dollars less than the plaintiffs asked and their proofs showed they were entitled to. The award of the jury was well within the range of the proofs and the court cannot legally alter it, as determination of damages is a jury function and their finding is justified by the law in light of the evidence in this case.

The loss of profits are often speculative and conjectural on the part of witnesses. When this is true, the court should deny loss of profits because of the speculative nature of the testimony and the proofs. However, the law is also clear that where lost profits are shown, and there is ample proof on this point, they should not be denied merely because they are hard to prove. In this case, both parties presented testimony on this issue for days. This testimony took the lost profits issue out of the category of speculation and conjecture. The jury was given an instruction on loss of profits and what the proofs must show, and the nature of the proofs, and if they found them to be speculative they could not award damages therefor. The jury, having found damages to exist, and awarded the same in this case in accord with the proper instructions, the court cannot, now, overrule the jury's finding.

[15] As Judge Wickens observed, the jury was instructed on the law concerning speculative damages. The case was thoroughly tried by all the parties. Apparently, the jury believed the plaintiffs. That is its prerogative.

[16] The testimony presented during the trial was conflicting. The weaknesses of plaintiffs' specially prepared budget were thoroughly explored on cross-examination. Defendants' witnesses testified concerning the likelihood that plaintiffs would not have made profits if the contract had been performed. There was conflicting testimony concerning the availability of a liquor license. All this was spread before the jury. The jury

weighed the conflicting testimony and determined that plaintiffs were entitled to damages of $200,000.

* * *

[17] The Court of Appeals is reversed and the trial court's judgment on the verdict is reinstated.

[18] Costs to plaintiffs.

COLEMAN, J. (concurring in part, dissenting in part).

[19] Although anticipated profits from a new business may be determined with a reasonable degree of certainty such was not the situation regarding loss of profits from liquor sales as proposed by plaintiffs.

[20] First, plaintiffs had no license and a Liquor Control Commission regional supervisor and a former commissioner testified that the described book and bottle store could not obtain a license. Further, the proofs of possible profits from possible liquor sales—if a license could have been obtained—were too speculative. The speculation of possible licensing plus the speculation of profits in this case combine to cause my opinion that profits from liquor sales should not have been submitted to the jury.

[21] I agree with Judge O'Hara in his Court of Appeals dissent and would have allowed proof of loss from the bookstore operation to go to the jury, but not proof of loss from liquor sales. His remedy is also approved. I would affirm the trial court judgment conditioned upon plaintiffs' consenting within 30 days following the release of this opinion, to "remitting that portion of the judgment in excess of $60,000. Otherwise, the judgment should be reversed and a new trial had." Plaintiffs are also entitled to the $1,000 deposit.

QUESTION

Have you ever seen a "book and bottle" shop in your neighborhood? Does that tell you something about the plaintiffs' business model?

C. AVOIDABILITY

Restatement (Second) Section 350[9] reads as follows:

Avoidability as a Limitation on Damages

(1) Except as stated in Subsection (2), damages are not recoverable for loss that the injured party could have avoided without undue risk, burden or humiliation.

(2) The injured party is not precluded from recovery by the rule stated in Subsection (1) to the extent that he has made reasonable but unsuccessful efforts to avoid loss.

IN RE WORLDCOM, INC.

United States Bankruptcy Court, Southern District of New York
361 B.R. 675 (2007)

ARTHUR J. GONZALEZ, BANKRUPTCY JUDGE.

Introduction

[1] Before the Court are cross-motions for summary judgment separately brought by Michael Jordan ("Jordan") and WorldCom, Inc. (hereafter referred to as the "Debtors" or "MCI").

Background

[2] On or about July 10, 1995, Jordan and the Debtors entered into an endorsement agreement (the "Agreement"). At that time, Jordan was considered to be one of the most popular athletes in the world. The Agreement granted MCI a ten-year license to use Jordan's name, likeness, "other attributes," and personal services to advertise and promote MCI's telecommunications products and services beginning in September 1995 and ending in August 2005. The Agreement did not prevent Jordan from endorsing most other products or services, although he could not endorse the same products or services that MCI produced. In addition to a $5 million signing bonus, the Agreement provided an annual base compensation of $2 million for Jordan. The Agreement provided that Jordan would be treated as an independent contractor and that MCI would not withhold any amount from Jordan's compensation for tax purposes. The Agreement provided that Jordan was to make himself available for four days, not to exceed four hours per day, during each contract year to produce television commercials and print advertising and for promotional appearances. The parties agreed that the advertising and promotional materials would be submitted to Jordan for his approval, which could not

---

[9] Copyright 1981 by the American Law Institute.

be unreasonably withheld, fourteen days prior to their release to the general public. From 1995 to 2000, Jordan appeared in several television commercials and a large number of print ads for MCI.

[3]   On July 1, 2002, MCI commenced a case under chapter 11 of [the Bankruptcy Code. In the case, Jordan sought compensation for MCI's breach of his endorsement contract.—Eds.]

The Parties' Contentions[10]

[4]   MCI asserts two bases for disallowance of the Claim. One, MCI contends that the Agreement is an "employment contract" within the meaning of section 502(b)(7) of the Bankruptcy Code and that Jordan's claim is "capped" pursuant to that section. Second, MCI argues that Jordan had an obligation to mitigate his damages and failed to do so. MCI argues that these two bases entitle it to summary judgment with respect to its objection to the Claim, and assert that either under section 502(b)(7) or as a result of Jordan's failure to mitigate damages following the Debtors' rejection, the Claim should be reduced to $4 million. MCI argues that it is under no obligation to pay Jordan for contract years 2004 and 2005.

[5]   Jordan argues for summary judgment allowing the Claim in full and overruling and dismissing MCI's objections to the Claim. Jordan argues that because he was not an "employee" of MCI and because the Agreement was not an "employment agreement," section 502(b)(7) does not apply to cap his claim. Regarding MCI's mitigation argument, Jordan argues that the objection should be overruled and dismissed for three independent reasons (1) Jordan was a "lost volume seller" and thus mitigation does not apply, (2) there is no evidence that Jordan could have entered into a "substantially similar" endorsement agreement, and (3) Jordan acted reasonably when he decided not to pursue other endorsements after MCI's rejection of the Agreement.

mitigation counter [handwritten margin note]

Discussion

A. *Summary Judgment Standard*

[6]   Under Federal Rule of Civil Procedure 56(c), made applicable to this proceeding by Federal Rule of Bankruptcy 7056, summary judgment is only appropriate where the record shows that "there is no genuine issue as to any material fact and that the moving party is entitled to judgment as a matter of law." *See* Fed. R. Civ. P. 56(c)

* * *

B. *Application of Section 502(b)(7)*

[7]   Jordan argues that section 502(b)(7) does not apply to his claim because he was an independent contractor and not an employee of MCI.

---

[10]   References to arguments made, or positions asserted, by MCI or Jordan are to arguments made by the attorneys for each.

MCI argues that section 502(b)(7) does apply to the Claim because the Agreement was an Employment Contract and Jordan was an "employee" within the meaning of that statute.

* * *

[8] Based upon a review of aforementioned, most specifically the factors cited in the case law, the Court finds that Jordan was not an "employee" and the Agreement was not an "employment contract" pursuant to section 502(b)(7). Therefore, there being no genuine issue of material facts as to Jordan's status, the Court grants summary judgment to Jordan on this point and holds that this basis for MCI's objection to the Claim is overruled and denied.

C.   *Mitigation*

[9] The doctrine of avoidable consequences, which has also been referred to as the duty to mitigate damages, bars recovery for losses suffered by a non-breaching party that could have been avoided by reasonable effort and without risk of substantial loss or injury. The burden of proving that the damages could have been avoided or mitigated rests with the party that committed the breach.

applying D.C. law

[10] Jordan argues that as a "lost volume seller" he was under no obligation to mitigate damages. Alternatively, Jordan argues that MCI failed to establish that Jordan could have entered a "substantially similar" endorsement contract and that Jordan acted reasonably in not entering another endorsement agreement after MCI's breach. MCI counters that Jordan is not a lost volume seller and that MCI has shown that Jordan failed to take reasonable steps to mitigate damages.

[11] The damages for a contract's rejection are determined in accordance with the law that would govern the value of the claim outside the context of bankruptcy.

[12] The Court will look to the District of Columbia ("D.C.") as the applicable state law for mitigation and other consequences of MCI's rejection of the Agreement. The parties, under Section 16 of the Agreement, "Arbitration; Governing Law," provided that any controversy would be submitted to arbitration to be governed in accordance with D.C. law.

but not enough DC law

[13] The Court was not furnished nor did research reveal D.C. cases precisely on point. Therefore, the Court will discuss and rely on cases from other jurisdictions where needed.

1.   *Whether Jordan Was a "Lost Volume Seller"*

[14] Jordan argues that MCI's mitigation defense does not apply here because Jordan is akin to a "lost volume seller." Jordan points to testimony demonstrating that he could have entered into additional endorsement contracts even if MCI had not rejected the Agreement. Thus, he argues,

any additional endorsement contracts would not have been substitutes for the Agreement and would not have mitigated the damages for which MCI is liable.

[15] "A lost volume seller is one who has the capacity to perform the contract that was breached in addition to other potential contracts due to unlimited resources or production capacity." Precision Pine & Timber, Inc. v. United States, 72 Fed.Cl. 460, 490 (Fed.Cl.2006). A lost volume seller does not minimize its damages by entering into another contract because it would have had the benefit of both contracts even if the first were not breached. The lost volume seller has two expectations, the profit from the breached contract and the profit from one or more other contracts that it could have performed at the same time as the breached contract. "The philosophical heart of the lost volume theory is that the seller would have generated a second sale irrespective of the buyer's breach" and that "[i]t follows that the lost volume seller cannot possibly mitigate damages." D. Matthews, *Should the Doctrine of Lost Volume Seller Be Retained? A Response to Professor Breen,* 51 U. MIAMI L.REV. 1195, 1214 (July 1997).

[16] The lost volume seller theory is recognized in the Restatement (2d) of Contracts, §§ 347, 350 (1981) (the "Restatement (2d)").[11] The lost volume seller theory applies to contracts for services as well as goods. *See* Restatement (2d), § 347, ill. 16

[17] This case offers a twist on the typical lost volume seller situation. In what the Court regards as the typical situation, the non-breaching seller has a near-inexhaustible supply of inventory. In the typical situation, when a buyer breaches an agreement to buy a good or service from the seller, the item is returned to inventory and the lost volume seller continues in its efforts to sell its goods or services. However, the transactions that occur following the breach are not necessarily the result of the breach but fundamentally the result of the seller continuing efforts to market its goods and services. It is this continuous effort coupled with a virtually limitless supply that warrants the lost volume exception to mitigation. As stated above, the transactions that may occur after the breach would in the

---

[11] Comment f to § 347 states in part:

"Lost volume." Whether a subsequent transaction is a substitute for the broken contract sometimes raises difficult questions of fact. If the injured party could and would have entered into the subsequent contract, even if the contract had not been broken, and could have had the benefit of both, he can be said to have "lost volume" and the subsequent transaction is not a substitute for the broken contract. The injured party's damages are then based on the net profit that he has lost as a result of the broken contract.

Comment d to § 350 states:

"Lost volume." The mere fact that an injured party can make arrangements for the disposition of the goods or services that he was to supply under the contract does not necessarily mean that by doing so he will avoid loss. If he would have entered into both transactions but for the breach, he has "lost volume" as a result of the breach. *See* Comment f to § 347. In that case the second transaction is not a "substitute" for the first one. *See* Illustrations 9 and 10.

context of the lost volume seller have occurred independent of the breach. Here, Jordan lacked a nearly limitless supply and had no intention of continuing to market his services as a product endorser.[12]

[18] Although not addressed by a D.C. court, the majority of cases hold that Jordan bears the burden of proving that he is a lost volume seller.

[19] To claim lost volume seller status, Jordan must establish that he would have had the benefit of both the original and subsequent contracts if MCI had not rejected the Agreement. Although there is no definitive set of elements that the non-breaching party must show, many cases seem to follow the language from the Restatement (2d), Section 347, that the non-breaching party must show that it "could and would have entered into" a subsequent agreement.

[20] In his arguments, Jordan focuses primarily on his *capacity* to enter subsequent agreements, arguing that the loss of MCI's sixteen-hour annual time commitment hardly affected his ability to perform additional endorsement services. On this prong alone, Jordan likely would be considered a lost volume seller of endorsement services because he had sufficient time to do multiple endorsements. Although he does not have the "infinite capacity" that some cases discuss, a services provider does not need unlimited capacity but must have the requisite capacity and intent to perform under multiple contracts at the same time. *See Gianetti*, 266 Conn. at 561–62, 833 A.2d 891 (plastic surgeon could be considered a lost volume seller if it were determined that he had the capacity and intent to simultaneously work out of three or four hospitals profitably).

[21] Contrary to Jordan's analysis, courts do not focus solely on the seller's capacity. The seller claiming lost volume status must also demonstrate that it *would* have entered into subsequent transactions. Jordan has not shown he could and *would have* entered into a subsequent agreement. Rather, the evidence shows that Jordan did not have the "subjective intent" to take on additional endorsements. The testimony from Jordan's representatives establishes that although Jordan's popularity enabled him to obtain additional product endorsements in 2003, Jordan desired to scale back his level of endorsements. Jordan's financial and business advisor, Curtis Polk ("Polk"), testified that at the time the Agreement was rejected, Jordan's desire was "not to expand his spokesperson or pitchman efforts with new relationships." Polk testified that had Jordan wanted to do additional endorsements after the 2003 rejection, he could have obtained additional deals. Jordan's agent, David

---

[12] On one hand, the "lost volume seller" exception does not appear to be available to a product endorser because of the understandable concern over dilution through overexposure. However, if an endorser has not approached what would be his or her endorsement limit, prior to dilution, it would seem that the continuous effort then to obtain more endorsements would be akin to the traditional lost volume seller, and the defense then available. As will be discussed herein, Jordan's situation is not indicative of a lost volume seller under any analysis.

Falk ("Falk"), testified that "there might have been twenty more companies that in theory might have wanted to sign him" but that Jordan and his representatives wanted to avoid diluting his image. Jordan's Memorandum for Summary Judgment stated that at the time the Agreement was rejected, Jordan had implemented a strategy of not accepting new endorsements because of a belief that new deals would jeopardize his ability to achieve his primary goal of National Basketball Association ("NBA") franchise ownership.

* * *

2.   *Whether Jordan Made Reasonable Efforts to Mitigate*

[The court held that the rule requiring a discharged employee to accept only "substantially similar" employment did not apply here. The court distinguished the famous case of *Parker v. Twentieth Century-Fox Film Corp.*, 474 P.2d 689 (Cal.1970), in which the California Supreme Court ruled that Shirley MacLaine, a leading actor of her day, did not have to accept a role in a Western movie to be filmed in Australia to mitigate the damages caused when the studio canceled *Bloomer Girl*, a Civil War era musical in which she was to play the lead.—Eds.]

3.   *Whether Jordan's Beliefs that Another Endorsement Would Dilute His Impact as an Endorser or Harm His Reputation Were Reasonable Justifications for not Mitigating Damages*

[22] Jordan cites the risk that entering another endorsement contract could dilute his impact as an endorser or damage his reputation or business interests.

a.   *Dilution*

[23] Jordan's dilution argument is not convincing. Jordan's agent Falk testified that although there were no "fixed numbers" for the amount of endorsements, Jordan and his representatives were wary about dilution and sensitive about "protecting the brand" of Jordan. Jordan does not set forth any facts showing that Jordan's image was at risk of dilution. MCI convincingly responds that adding an agreement to replace a lost one is merely maintaining the status quo, not a dilution of Jordan's impact by addition. MCI's expert stated that Jordan had previously had sixteen endorsement agreements in place, which further weakens Jordan's dilution argument and casts doubt on Falk's statement that Jordan and his advisors "always felt that less is more" in terms of endorsements. While the Court recognizes that Jordan's image is the true commodity here and its market value could be diluted from overexposure, MCI has shown that Jordan's image was not at risk of dilution by replacing the MCI endorsement agreement with another one. The only statements Jordan offers to support his argument that he behaved reasonably by not seeking another endorsement in 2003 because of a concern with diluting his image are

conclusory in nature and contradicted by the available evidence. The contention that pursuing an endorsement opportunity would dilute the image Jordan wished to cultivate as one befitting an NBA team owner, also discussed under Point 4 below, may well raise factual issues regarding the impact an endorsement may have on a team owner's image but that impact is irrelevant to Jordan's duty to mitigate damages for his "rejected" endorsement contract. There is no genuine issue of material fact that dilution did not excuse Jordan's duty to mitigate damages.

  b. *Risk to Reputation*

[24] Under the risk to reputation theory Jordan cites, an injured party is not allowed to recover from a wrongdoer those damages that the injured party "could have avoided without undue risk, burden or humiliation." *See* Restatement (2d), § 350(1). Jordan's "harm to reputation" argument is flawed because the envisioned harm to Jordan's reputation does not rise to the level of harm found in the cited case law.

[25] The cases cited by Jordan illustrate the harm to reputation that will excuse a party's duty to mitigate. In *Eastman Kodak Co. v. Westway Motor Freight, Inc.,* 949 F.2d 317 (10th Cir.1991), Kodak shipped a load of sensitized photographic material on a truck operated by the defendant. Most of the material was destroyed in transit because of the defendant's mishandling. The Tenth Circuit held that Kodak was not required to sell the damaged merchandise to mitigate damages, stating that the record revealed that Kodak's reputation, which it spent considerable resources in developing, "could be harmed if it was required to sell damaged merchandise in order to mitigate damages." *Id.* at 320.

[The court explained how the other cases cited by Jordan were similar.— Eds.]

[26] Those cases show the uncontroversial maxim that a plaintiff faced with the choice of (1) selling a sub-standard product to the public to mitigate damages caused by the breach of another and (2) doing nothing— can choose to do nothing, but Jordan was not confronted with those circumstances. While Jordan's reputation is considerable and obviously the result of careful development, there are no factual assertions that support the proposition that Jordan's choosing another endorsement opportunity is akin to being forced to sell damaged goods, as was the case in *Eastman Kodak. . . .*

  4. *Whether Focusing on NBA Ownership Was a Reasonable Decision*

[27] Jordan cites his goal of owning an NBA team as a reasonable justification for his decision not to enter additional endorsement agreements.

[28] In support, Jordan cites cases that hold if a non-breaching plaintiff chooses a reasonable course of action despite the existence of

another course of action that, in hindsight, would have been better at lessening harm, the plaintiff's damages are not reduced. A closer examination at such cases reveals that they are not applicable to Jordan's situation. Cases that Jordan cites, such as *Novelty Textile Mills, Inc. v. C.T. Eastern, Inc.,* 743 F.Supp. 212 (S.D.N.Y.1990), and *Fed. Ins. Co. v. Sabine Towing & Transp. Co.,* 783 F.2d 347 (2d Cir.1986), share a common theme not present in the instant matter: the non-breaching party faced a choice between two reasonable courses of action right after the breach or tort that inflicted the damage, and made a choice to lessen the damage that appeared reasonable at the time. *See, e.g., Novelty Textile Mills,* 743 F.Supp. at 219 ("If the course of conduct chosen by the plaintiff was reasonable, the plaintiff can recover despite the existence of another reasonable course of action that would have further lessened the plaintiff's damages"). Jordan's choice to focus on NBA team ownership, in contrast, *was not done to lessen the damage from MCI's rejection,* but was done for other, unrelated business reasons.

[29] In *Novelty Textile Mills,* the plaintiff hired the defendant to ship its fabric, but while the defendant had the fabric in its possession, a liquid contaminant damaged the goods. The court held that, given the circumstances, the plaintiff's decision to salvage the damaged goods rather than attempting to clean them was reasonable. The court considered factors such as the resale cost, the low value of the goods, and that the goods were no longer fit for their intended use.

[30] In *Tennessee Valley Sand & Gravel Co. v. M/V Delta,* 598 F.2d 930 (5th Cir.1979), the plaintiff's barge sank after the defendant towed it. The plaintiff decided to raise the barge from the river bottom, rather than abandoning it and contacting the U.S. Army Corps of Engineers, who would have removed it and sought recovery from the negligent party. The trial court concluded that the sinking resulted entirely from the defendant's lack of due care. But at the time the plaintiff made the decision to raise the barge, the defendant denied liability, so the plaintiff faced the possibility that it could be liable for the costs of removal and for any damage the abandoned vessel caused to third parties if it did not act. The court found the decision to remove the barge to be a reasonable one. "In determining whether the victim's conduct falls within the range of reasonableness, the court must consider that the necessity for decision-making was thrust upon him by the defendant, and judgments made at time of crisis are subject to human error." *Id.* at 933.

[31] Those cases demonstrate that a court will not sharply second-guess the decisions made by a non-breaching party when it attempts to mitigate the damages caused by the breaching party. The cases differ from Jordan's situation because his decision to focus on NBA team ownership was independent of MCI's rejection and was not contemplated as one that would lessen the harm of that rejection. Such a decision was unrelated to

the duty to mitigate damages resulting from a rejected agreement as a product endorser. In short, the argument that Jordan acted reasonably by focusing solely on his efforts to become an NBA team owner is a red herring. It may have been reasonable for Jordan to focus on becoming an NBA team owner in the scope of Jordan's overall future desires but that does not mean it can support a determination that he was relieved of his obligation to mitigate damages in response to MCI's rejection of the Agreement.

[32] Furthermore, Jordan did not have to pursue *any* endorsement, such as one that would be beneath a celebrity of Jordan's stature, e.g., endorsing a product likely to be distasteful to Jordan or his fans. Jordan had the duty to take reasonable efforts to mitigate, such as by seeking another endorsement for an established, reputable company for compensation near to what he received from MCI. MCI has established that there is no genuine issue as to whether Jordan made reasonable efforts to do so. The Court finds that as a matter of law Jordan has failed to mitigate damages.

———

PROBLEM 19-2

In 1994, the owner of a lot in East Flatbush, Brooklyn, New York, enters into a lease of the lot to a nationally recognized owner-operator and franchisor of Mexican-themed fast food outlets. The fast food company had inquired about purchasing the property, but the owner was adamant that the property was not for sale, although he would enter into a 99-year lease. The lot owner, delighted to have a long term lease of the property with a financially well-heeled, class "A" tenant, gave notice to the prior tenant—a used car lot—that its lease would not be renewed at the end of the term in 60 days. The used car lot owner, therefore, vacated the lot at the end of the term, relocating a couple of blocks away.

Then, apparently for the first time, the fast food company discovered that there was crime in New York City that might adversely affect the operation of the restaurant. In fact, the local Crime Prevention Officer for the precinct informed the fast food company that the area experienced excessive drug trafficking, violence, and firearm use, and the proposed restaurant would likely be robbed frequently. Seeking to back out of the long term lease, the fast food company contacts the lot owner, tells him that it no longer wishes to lease the property, and that it will provide the lot owner with a substitute tenant, a shell corporation with no assets except for a franchise agreement from another, grade "B" Mexican fast food franchisor.

(a) Under the duty to mitigate, must the owner accept the substitute tenant?

(b) Does it matter whether or not the grade "B" substitute tenant sublets the lot from the nationally recognized owner-operator and franchisor of Mexican-themed fast food outlets?

(c) Does it matter whether the nationally recognized owner-operatory and franchisor of Mexican-themed fast food outlets is proposing to assign the long term lease to the substitute tenant and receive a novation from the lot owner?

(d) Does it matter whether or not the rent specified in the lease is a particular sum or has a percentage of sales component?

PROBLEM 19-3 *PPT Test*

The County Highway Department enters into a contract with Builder for the construction of a bridge for $250,000. The bridge is to be built on a new highway which will connect the airport and a prosperous suburb. When Builder has expended $175,000 and has received $125,000 in progress payments, the county, in breach of the contract, announces that it is not going to build the highway and tells Builder to stop work. Builder expends another $35,000 and completes the bridge at a total cost of $210,000. Since the highway is not built, the county now has a bridge out in the middle of a cotton field. Builder sues for $125,000. How much is she entitled to? *90 K*

cost avoided

was supposed to get 40 – when stopped, down 50 would take 90 to get him in position

125 − 35 = 90

_____

NOTES AND QUESTIONS

1. The traditional rule in Anglo-American law is that physical pain and suffering or emotional distress damages are not recoverable as damages under a breach of contract theory. Read R2d section 353, which generally embodies this rule. Compare UNIDROIT article 7.4.2. Which do you think is the better rule? *Why?*

2. Parties may include waivers of consequential and incidental damages in their contracts in order to allocate the risk of non-performance. For example, a contract could provide:

> In no event will either party be liable for loss of profits or any special, incidental, or consequential damages, regardless of their cause, amount, or severity, and regardless of whether either party has or should have knowledge of the potential for such damages or whether they were reasonably foreseeable at the time of contracting or otherwise.

Note how the clause is drafted precisely around *Hadley v. Baxendale*, excluding "incidental, or consequential damages" as well as "reasonably foreseeable" damages, and also goes beyond those standards so as to narrowly circumscribe the damages that can be awarded due to breach.

Could a similar provision relieve the parties of a duty to mitigate damages? Should such a provision be enforced? If enforceable, how would you draft the provision?

Transactional lawyers are incorporating case law into their contracts constantly, adjusting the language to embrace or draft around language that has been blessed or damned by the courts. This is a different, continuous form of legal research than that often practiced by litigators, who generally have the comparative luxury of waiting until after the dispute has arisen to hit the books (or the Internet). The transactional lawyer should be focused on proactive drafting in light of changes in applicable law to shape and control the relationship of the parties at its conception, during the relationship's life, and its ultimate demise. Litigation, all too often, is focused on reactive drafting and advocacy over the remains of a relationship that is dead or needs to be put out of its misery.

Draft into the law or around it. Draft to make the record that you want.

CHAPTER 20

OTHER MEASURES OF RECOVERY AND A REVIEW OF DAMAGES

■ ■ ■

A. THE RELIANCE INTEREST

When the non-breaching party cannot recover expectancy or benefit of the bargain damages due to, for example, a lack of certainty, recovery can still be had under a "reliance" measure of damages. Put simply, in that case, the non-breaching party can recover expenses that were foreseeable at the time of entering into the contract such as expenses of preparation or part performance. R2d § 349[1] provides:

> As an alternative to "expectation damages," the injured party has a right to damages based on his reliance interest, including expenditures made in preparation for performance or in performance, less any loss that the party in breach can prove with reasonable certainty the injured party would have suffered had the contract been performed.

The next case illustrates the reliance measure in action in a case where the breach of contract resulted in a loss of uncertain profits and, thus, expectancy damages could not be awarded.

———

SECURITY STOVE & MANUFACTURING V. AMERICAN RAILWAY EXPRESS

Court of Appeals of Missouri
227 Mo. App. 175, 51 S.W.2d 572 (1932)

BLAND, J.

[1] This is an action for damages for the failure of defendant to transport, from Kansas City to Atlantic City, New Jersey, within a reasonable time, a furnace equipped with a combination oil and gas burner. The cause was tried before the court without the aid of a jury, resulting in

———

[1] Copyright 1981 by the American Law Institute. Reprinted with permission. All rights reserved.

a judgment in favor of plaintiff in the sum of $801.50 and interest, or in a total sum of $1,000.00[2]. Defendant has appealed.

[2] The facts show that plaintiff manufactured a furnace equipped with a special combination oil and gas burner it desired to exhibit at the American Gas Association Convention held in Atlantic City in October, 1926. The president of plaintiff testified that plaintiff engaged space for the exhibit for the reason "that the Henry L. Dougherty Company was very much interested in putting out a combination oil and gas burner; we had just developed one, after we got through, better than anything on the market and we thought this show would be the psychological time to get in contact with the Dougherty Company"; that "the thing wasn't sent there for sale but primarily to show"; that at the time the space was engaged it was too late to ship the furnace by freight so plaintiff decided to ship it by express, and, on September 18th, 1926, wrote the office of the defendant in Kansas City, stating that it had engaged a booth for exhibition purposes at Atlantic City, New Jersey, from the American Gas Association, for the week beginning October 11th; that its exhibit consisted of an oil burning furnace, together with two oil burners which weighed at least 1,500 pounds; that, "In order to get this exhibit in place on time it should be in Atlantic City not later than October the 8th. What we want you to do is to tell us how much time you will require to assure the delivery of the exhibit on time."

[3] Mr. Bangs, chief clerk in charge of the local office of the defendant, upon receipt of the letter, sent Mr. Johnson, a commercial representative of the defendant, to see plaintiff. Johnson called upon plaintiff taking its letter with him. Johnson made a notation on the bottom of the letter giving October 4th, as the day that defendant was required to have the exhibit in order for it to reach Atlantic City on October 8th.

[4] On October 1st, plaintiff wrote the defendant at Kansas City, referring to its letter of September 18th, concerning the fact that the furnace must be in Atlantic City not later than October 8th, and stating what Johnson had told it, saying: "Now Mr. Bangs, we want to make doubly sure that this shipment is in Atlantic City not later than October 8th and the purpose of this letter is to tell you that you can have your truck call for the shipment between 12 and 1 o'clock on Saturday, October 2nd for this." On October 2nd, plaintiff called the office of the express company in Kansas City and told it that the shipment was ready. Defendant came for the shipment on the last mentioned day, received it and delivered the express receipt to plaintiff. The shipment contained 21 packages. Each package was marked with stickers backed with glue and covered with silica of soda,

---

to prevent the stickers being torn off in shipping. Each package was given a number. They ran from 1 to 21.

[5] Plaintiff's president made arrangements to go to Atlantic City to attend the convention and install the exhibit, arriving there about October 11th. When he reached Atlantic City he found the shipment had been placed in the booth that had been assigned to plaintiff. The exhibit was set up, but it was found that one of the packages shipped was not there. This missing package contained the gas manifold, or that part of the oil and gas burner that controlled the flow of gas in the burner. This was the most important part of the exhibit and a like burner could not be obtained in Atlantic City.

[6] Wires were sent and it was found that the stray package was at the "over and short bureau" of defendant in St. Louis. Defendant reported that the package would be forwarded to Atlantic City and would be there by Wednesday, the 13th. Plaintiff's president waited until Thursday, the day the convention closed, but the package had not arrived at the time, so he closed up the exhibit and left. About a week after he arrived in Kansas City, the package was returned by the defendant.

[7] Bangs testified that the reasonable time for a shipment of this kind to reach Atlantic City from Kansas City would be four days; that if the shipment was received on October 4th, it would reach Atlantic City by October 8th; that plaintiff did not ask defendant for any special rate; that the rate charged was the regular one; that plaintiff asked no special advantage in the shipment; that all defendant, under its agreement with plaintiff was required to do was to deliver the shipment at Atlantic City in the ordinary course of events; that the shipment was found in St. Louis about Monday afternoon or Tuesday morning; that it was delivered at Atlantic City at the Ritz Carlton Hotel, on the 16th of the month. There was evidence on plaintiff's part that the reasonable time for a shipment of this character to reach Atlantic City from Kansas City was not more than three or four days.

[8] The petition upon which the case was tried alleges that plaintiff, on October 2d, 1926, delivered the shipment to the defendant; that defendant agreed, in consideration of the express charges received from plaintiff, to carry the shipment from Kansas City to Atlantic City, and to deliver the same to plaintiff at Atlantic City, New Jersey, on or before October 8th, 1926, the same being the reasonable and proper time necessary to transport said shipment to Atlantic City, in as good condition as when received . . .

* * *

That relying upon defendant's promise and the promises of its agents and servants, that said parcels would be delivered at

Atlantic City by October 8th, 1926, if delivered to defendant by October 4th, 1926, plaintiff herein hired space for an exhibit at the American Gas Association Convention at Atlantic City, and planned for an exhibit at said Convention and sent men in the employ of this plaintiff to Atlantic City to install, show and operate said exhibit, and that these men were in Atlantic City ready to set up this plaintiff's exhibit at the American Gas Association Convention on October 8th, 1926

That defendant, in violation of its agreement, failed and neglected to deliver one of the packages to its destination on October 8th, 1926.

That the package not delivered by defendant contained the essential part of plaintiff's exhibit which plaintiff was to make at said convention on October 8th, was later discovered in St. Louis, Missouri, by the defendant herein, and that plaintiff, for this reason, could not show his exhibit.

[9] Plaintiff asked damages, which the court in its judgment allowed as follows: $147.00 express charges (on the exhibit); $45.12 freight on the exhibit from Atlantic City to Kansas City; $101.39 railroad and pullman fares to and from Atlantic City, expended by plaintiff's president and a workman taken by him to Atlantic City; $48.00 hotel room for the two; $150.00 for the time of the president; $40.00 for wages of plaintiff's other employee and $270.00 for rental of the booth, making a total of $801.51.

[10] Defendant contends that its instructions in the nature of demurrers to the evidence should have been given for the reason that the petition and plaintiff's evidence show that plaintiff has based its cause of action on defendant's breach of a promise to deliver the shipment at a specified time and that promise is non-enforceable and void under the Interstate Commerce Act; that the court erred in allowing plaintiff's expenses as damages; that the only damages, if any, that can be recovered in cases of this kind, are for loss of profits and that plaintiff's evidence is not sufficient to base any recovery on this ground.

* * *

[11] We think, under the circumstances in this case, that it was proper to allow plaintiff's expenses as its damages. Ordinarily the measure of damages where the carrier fails to deliver a shipment at destination within a reasonable time is the difference between the market value of the goods at the time of the delivery and the time when they should have been delivered. But where the carrier has notice of peculiar circumstances under which the shipment is made, which will result in an unusual loss by the shipper in case of delay in delivery, the carrier is responsible for the real damage sustained from such delay if the notice given is of such character,

and goes to such extent, in informing the carrier of the shipper's situation, that the carrier will be presumed to have contracted with reference thereto. *Central Trust Co. of New York v. Savannah & W. R. Co.*, 69 F. 683, 685.

[12] In the case at bar defendant was advised of the necessity of prompt delivery of the shipment. Plaintiff explained to Johnson the "importance of getting the exhibit there on time." Defendant knew the purpose of the exhibit and ought to respond for its negligence in failing to get it there. As we view the record this negligence is practically conceded. The undisputed testimony shows that the shipment was sent to the over and short department of the defendant in St. Louis. As the packages were plainly numbered this, prima facie, shows mistake or negligence on the part of the defendant. No effort was made by it to show that it was not negligent in sending it there, or not negligent in not forwarding it within a reasonable time after it was found.

[13] There is no evidence of claim in this case that plaintiff suffered any loss of profits by reason of the delay in the shipment. In fact defendant states in its brief:

> The plaintiff introduced not one whit of evidence showing or tending to show that he would have made any sales as a result of his exhibit but for the negligence of the defendant. On the contrary Blakesley testified that the main purpose of the exhibit was to try to interest the Henry L. Dougherty Company in plaintiff's combination oil and gas burner, yet that was all the evidence that there was as to the benefit plaintiff expected to get from the exhibit.

> As a matter of evidence, it is clear that the plaintiff would not have derived a great deal of benefit from the exhibit by any stretch of the imagination . . .

> No where does plaintiff introduce evidence showing that the Henry L. Dougherty Company in all probability would have become interested in the combination oil and gas burner and made a profitable contract with the plaintiff.

[14] There is evidence that the exhibit was not sent to make a sale.

* * *

[15] Defendant contends that plaintiff "is endeavoring to achieve a return of the status quo in a suit based on a breach of contract. Instead of seeking to recover what he would have had, had the contract not been broken, plaintiff is trying to recover what he would have had, had there never been any contract of shipment;" that the expenses sued for would have been incurred in any event. It is no doubt, the general rule that where there is a breach of contract the party suffering the loss can recover only that which he would have had, had the contract not been broken, and this

is all the cases decided upon which defendant relies, including *C., M. & St. P. Ry. v. McCaull-Dinsmore Co.*, 253 U.S. 97, 100, 40 S.Ct. 504, 64 L.Ed. 801 (1920). But this is merely a general statement of the rule and is not inconsistent with the holdings that, in some instances, the injured party may recover expenses incurred in relying upon the contract, although such expenses would have been incurred had the contract not been breached.

[16] In *Sperry et al. v. O'Neill-Adams Co.*, 185 F. 231 (1911), the court held that the advantages resulting from the use of trading stamps as a means of increasing trade are so contingent that they cannot form a basis on which to rest a recovery for a breach of contract to supply them. In lieu of compensation based thereon the court directed a recovery in the sum expended in preparation for carrying on business in connection with the use of the stamps. The court said, loc. cit. 239:

> Plaintiff in its complaint had made a claim for lost profits, but, finding it impossible to marshal any evidence which would support a finding of exact figures, abandoned that claim. Any attempt to reach a precise sum would be mere blind guesswork. Nevertheless a contract, which both sides conceded would prove a valuable one, had been broken and the party who broke it was responsible for resultant damage. In order to carry out this contract, the plaintiff made expenditures which otherwise it would not have made . . . The trial judge held, as we think rightly, that plaintiff was entitled at least to recover these expenses to which it had been put in order to secure the benefits of a contract of which defendant's conduct deprived it.

* * *

[17] The case at bar was not to recover damages for loss of profits by reason of the failure of the defendant to transport the shipment within a reasonable time, so that it would arrive in Atlantic City for the exhibit. There were no profits contemplated. The furnace was to be shown and shipped back to Kansas City. There was no money loss, except the expenses, that was of such a nature as any court would allow as being sufficiently definite or lacking in pure speculation. Therefore, unless plaintiff is permitted to recover the expenses that it went to, which were a total loss to it by reason of its inability to exhibit the furnace and equipment, it will be deprived of any substantial compensation for its loss. The law does not contemplate any such injustice. It ought to allow plaintiff, as damages, the loss in the way of expenses that it sustained, and which it would not have been put to if it had not been for its reliance upon the defendant to perform its contract. There is no contention that the exhibit would have been entirely valueless and whatever it might have accomplished defendant knew of the circumstances and ought to respond for whatever damages plaintiff suffered. In cases of this kind the method

of estimating the damages should be adopted which is the most definite and certain and which best achieves the fundamental purpose of compensation. 17 C. J. p. 846; *Miller v. Robertson*, 266 U.S. 243, 257, 45 S.Ct. 73, 78, 69 L.Ed. 265. Had the exhibit been shipped in order to realize a profit on sales and such profits could have been realized, or to be entered in competition for a prize, and plaintiff failed to show loss of profits with sufficient definiteness, or that he would have won the prize, defendant's cases might be in point. But as before stated, no such situation exists here.

[18] While, it is true that plaintiff already had incurred some of these expenses, in that it had rented space at the exhibit before entering into the contract with defendant for the shipment of the exhibit and this part of plaintiff's damages, in a sense, arose out of a circumstance which transpired before the contract was even entered into, yet, plaintiff arranged for the exhibit knowing that it could call upon defendant to perform its common law duty to accept and transport the shipment with reasonable dispatch. The whole damage, therefore, was suffered in contemplation of defendant performing its contract, which it failed to do, and would not have been sustained except for the reliance by plaintiff upon defendant to perform it. It can, therefore, be fairly said that the damages or loss suffered by plaintiff grew out of the breach of the contract, for had the shipment arrived on time, plaintiff would have had the benefit of the contract, which was contemplated by all parties, defendant being advised of the purpose of the shipment.

The judgment is affirmed.

All concur.

B. THE RESTITUTIONARY INTEREST

Another way of measuring the plaintiff's damages is to ask "what is the value of the benefit the plaintiff conferred upon the defendant?" We refer to this as the plaintiff's restitutionary interest. Just as a criminal defendant may have to make restitution of any gains from her crime, a contract breacher may have to make restitution of any gains from the contract he breached. Under the old rules of pleading, the plaintiff would ask for "rescission and restitution," the breach giving her the right to rescind the contract and take back any benefits she had conferred on the defendant.

In a simple case where all the plaintiff has done is make a payment to the defendant, calculating her damages on a restitution basis would give the same recovery as would calculating her damages on a reliance basis. In most cases, however, the plaintiff is better off with a reliance-based recovery because the restitution measure will allow the plaintiff to recover only those expenditures which directly benefitted the defendant, whereas the reliance measure will allow the plaintiff to recover all her expenditures, including payments made to third parties. For example, in *Security Stove*, a restitution measure would have allowed the plaintiff to recover only the freight charges, whereas a reliance measure allowed it to recover hotel charges, transportation costs of the individuals, etc.

Note that the election of quantum meruit claims rather than expectancy damages is that of the *non*-breaching party. The plaintiff is entitled to have her damages calculated using whichever measure gives her the largest recovery. There will be rare occasions when the restitution measure gives the plaintiff more in damages because the benefit that the defendant received was more than the cost the plaintiff incurred to confer that benefit. The case that follows is one of those rare cases.

SOUTHERN PAINTING COMPANY OF TENNESSEE V. UNITED STATES, EX REL. SILVER

United States Court of Appeals, Tenth Circuit
222 F.2d 431 (1955)

HUXMAN, J.

Cause of action

[1]   This is an appeal by the defendants, Southern Painting Company of Tennessee, Inc., and the United Pacific Insurance Company, from a judgment of $13,000 rendered by the United States District Court for the District of Kansas in favor of the appellee, E. M. Silver, doing business as Silver Plumbing and Heating, in an action by the United States for the use of E. M. Silver, under the Miller Act, 40 U.S.C.A. § 270a, etc.

[2]   The complaint alleged that Southern Painting Company of Tennessee, Inc., herein called Southern, hired Silver as a subcontractor to furnish all labor, material and supervision in connection with the plumbing and heating specifications under two contracts which Southern had with the United States; that after he had practically completed such work under the contract, Southern breached the contract by refusing to allow him to finish the work; that because of such breach he was entitled to sue for the reasonable value of the work he had performed under quantum meruit. He asked for judgment in the sum of $72,000.[3]

[3]   In its answer Southern alleged that Silver wrongfully breached the contract, forcing Southern at great cost to get another contractor to complete the work; that Silver had been paid more than his services were worth; that Silver had entered into a settlement with Southern as to the portion of work covered by Contract 999, and that the action was in the

---

[3]   [$72,000 in 1955 dollars is roughly the equivalent of $675,000 in 2019 dollars using the CPI and the GNP Deflator.—Eds.]

nature of a breach of contract and as such could not be maintained under the Miller Act; hence the court was without jurisdiction.

Contract info

[4] The terms of the contract are without dispute and only a short reference will be made thereto. Southern held two contracts with the Government, No. ENG 999 and ENG 1052 for rehabilitation work on Government camps near Salina. Under the subcontract with Silver, he was to furnish all labor and material necessary to do the plumbing and heating work under the two contracts. Southern agreed to reimburse Silver for all material, labor, taxes, insurance, etc., and agreed to purchase tools and equipment necessary to do the work. Silver was to receive $6,000 lump sum for the work under Contract 999 and $4,000 lump sum for work under Contract 1052, plus a fair percentage of the net profit on all additional extra plumbing and heating work.

[5] The parties are in disagreement as to who breached the contract. Southern claimed Silver did. It is sufficient to say that the court found that Southern breached the contract. We are satisfied that the evidence clearly sustains this finding. Apparently more than 90% of all the work under the subcontract was completed at the time of the breach by Southern. Silver had been paid $7,000 of his fee under the subcontract. The court found the fair and reasonable value of Silver's services under the contract and found that in addition to what he had received he was entitled to receive an additional $13,000, together with interest from July 15, 1952, until paid, that being the day on which Silver was wrongfully discharged, according to the court's finding.

* * *

[6] It is . . . contended that the judgment of the court is grossly excessive and that the findings and judgment are not supported by competent evidence. It is contended that plaintiff's Exhibit 24 offered to establish value of the services was improperly received in evidence. Without describing the exhibit in detail, we are inclined to agree that it was improperly received. But plaintiff's proof of the value of the services was not predicated alone on Exhibit 24. Delbert W. Robertson, an experienced plumbing contractor, testified for plaintiff as to the value of the services performed by plaintiff. His evidence was competent and was sufficient to sustain the findings of the court with respect to the reasonable value of the services. Neither do we feel that the record clearly shows that the court relied alone on Exhibit 24 in reaching its conclusions as to the value of Silver's services. We think the findings of the court and its judgment except as hereinafter pointed out find support in the record.

PROBLEM 20-1

[handwritten left margin: 10,000 in progress]

Buyer and Seller enter into a contract for the sale of a house for $100,000. Seller breaches after Buyer has made a $10,000 down payment. The house is worth $100,000. How much is Buyer entitled to recover? Is Buyer's recovery based on a restitutionary or a reliance theory? Do we care?

[handwritten: would have got 100]

PROBLEM 20-2

[handwritten: 10's pre contract position]

Same facts as the immediately preceding problem except that the proof shows conclusively that the house was worth $95,000. How much is Buyer entitled to recover? *See* Restatement (Second) § 349.

———

The cases and presentation above regarding reliance and restitution only scrape the surface of the doctrinal law in these areas, but is sufficient to acquaint you with these alternative remedial measures. To pursue these theories further, consider taking a "Remedies" course. For now, it is enough to just scratch the surface.

———

C. REVIEW OF DAMAGES

[handwritten left margin: damages that are reasonably foreseeable]

PROBLEM 20-3

Owner puts her house on the market, asking $180,000 for it. Buyer offers $150,000 for the house. Owner accepts the offer, and they enter into a contract for the purchase and sale of the house at a price of $150,000. In connection with the sale, Owner becomes obligated to pay Broker a commission of $9,000. This commission is not refundable in the event of Buyer's breach. Buyer does in fact breach the contract. Seller pays Broker the commission. Evidence at trial shows that at the time title to the house was to be transferred, the fair market value of the house was $140,000. (And Owner in fact re-sells the house for that price, paying no brokerage commission.) How much is Owner entitled to receive as damages?

[handwritten left margin: 140 is cost avoided]

[handwritten: 150 − 9 = 141,000 if no breach   140 − 9 = 131 9(0 = 14)]

PROBLEM 20-4

Owner puts her house on the market, asking $180,000 for it. Buyer offers $150,000 for the house. Owner accepts the offer, and they enter into a contract for the purchase and sale of the house at a price of $150,000. In connection with the sale, Owner becomes obligated to pay Broker a commission of $9,000. This commission, however, is payable only in the event Buyer completes the sale and pays Owner the purchase price. Buyer breaches the contract. Seller does not pay Broker the commission. Evidence at trial shows that at the time title to the house was to be transferred, the fair market value of the house was

[handwritten bottom: L in value − 150 − 149 = 1,000]

[handwritten bottom: House worth 140 − give him 1000 to put him in position]

$140,000. (And Owner in fact re-sells the house for that price, paying no brokerage commission.) How much is Owner entitled to receive as damages?

PROBLEM 20-5

Owner puts her house on the market, asking $180,000 for it. Buyer offers $150,000 for the house. Owner accepts the offer, and they enter into a contract for the purchase and sale of the house at a price of $150,000. The contract between Owner and Broker provides that if the sale is completed and Buyer pays Owner the purchase price, Owner will pay Broker a commission of $9,000. This contract further provides (as is the custom in many parts of the country) that if Buyer breaches, Owner only has to pay broker half the commission ($4,500). Buyer does in fact breach the contract. Seller pays Broker the $4,500. Evidence at trial shows that at the time title to the house was to be transferred, the fair market value of the house was $140,000. (And Owner in fact re-sells the house for that price, paying no brokerage commission.) How much is Owner entitled to receive as damages? Lin Value = 150

PROBLEM 20-6

Developer enters into a contract with Paver for the paving of Developer's parking lot for a price of $25,000. Developer breaches the contract at a time when Paver has spent $12,000 on the job and received a total of $10,000 in progress payments. If Paver had to finish the job, it would have cost her a total of $19,000 (the $12,000 she has already spent plus an additional $7,000). The fair market value of the work Paver has done to date is $11,000. How much is Paver entitled to receive in damages?

PROBLEM 20-7

Landlord and Painter enter into a contract under the terms of which Painter will paint Landlord's building for a price of $10,000. (Painter intends to do all the labor himself. No employees or subcontractors will be involved.) Landlord pays Painter a down payment of $2,000, and Painter spends $1,500 of it to purchase all the paint necessary for the job. Before Painter starts work, Underbid contacts Landlord and offers to do the job for $7,000. Landlord takes her up on it and tells Painter to forget the gig. Painter attempts to return the paint and is told it cannot be returned because it is a custom color. Then he attempts to dispose of the paint and is told that he has to pay a $50 fee to have it disposed of in an environmentally-responsible manner. Painter's brother-in-law offers to sneak the paint into the landfill at night in exchange for a $7.29 six pack of Sam Adams, but Painter, perhaps because he has been inhaling too many fumes, declines the offer and pays the $50. Painter is unable to find any other work to do during the six weeks he had set aside to do Landlord's job, so he takes his family to Disney World. The cost of the trip is $3,800.

How much is Painter entitled to receive in damages?

PROBLEM 20-8

When Trader made a killing in the stock market, she bought herself an airplane at a cost of $300,000. Recently, the market has been even better to her, so she decided to buy a new plane. She hired Broker to sell the airplane for her and agreed to pay Broker a commission of $20,000 in connection with the sale. The contract between Trader and Broker required Trader to pay the commission only if a buyer located by Broker actually completed the sale and Trader was paid for the plane. After several months of advertising and dozens of long-distance calls to potential buyers (all at Broker's expense), Broker found Buyer, who entered into a contract to purchase the plane for $180,000.

After entering into the contract, Buyer realized that the fair market value of the plane was only $150,000. He thereupon informed Trader that he would not honor his contract. Tired of fooling around, Trader hired Auctioneer to sell the plane at a public auction. Buyer was given notice of the sale and the plane was sold at auction for $135,000. Auctioneer was paid a fee of $2,000, and Broker never got his $20,000 because the buyer he found (Buyer) never completed the deal.

Trader sued Buyer for breach of contract. At trial, there were two major issues: (1) Was the sale by auction made in good faith and in a commercially reasonable manner? (2) What was the market price of the airplane at the time and place for tender? On the latter issue, Broker, testifying for Trader, testified that the market price was $130,000. Buyer's lawyer hired two appraisers. Highball said the airplane was worth $200,000. Lowball said the airplane was worth $140,000. Buyer's lawyer paid Lowball his fee, stamped his report "Confidential—Attorney's Work Product" and stuffed it in the file, never to see the light of day again. She hired Highball to testify at trial. The judge found as a fact that the market price of the airplane at the time and place for tender was $155,000.

(a) How much should Trader recover in damages if the court finds that the sale was conducted in good faith and in a commercially reasonable manner?

(b) How much should Trader recover in damages if the court finds that the sale was NOT conducted in a commercially reasonable manner? (Consider this. If the sale is not commercially reasonable, should Trader be able to claim the $2,000 auctioneer's fee as an element of incidental damages?)

D. PROBLEMS TO REVIEW ON YOUR OWN

Answers for these problems are on the pages following the problems. You'll get more out of the problems if you work them before you look at the answers.

1. Seller and Buyer enter into a contract for the sale of Seller's house to Buyer at a price of $100,000. No real estate commissions or other expenses are involved in the sale. Buyer breaches and the court determines that the fair market value of the house is $92,000. How much can Seller recover in damages?

2. Sailor and Contractor enter into a contract under the terms of which Contractor is to build a boathouse on Sailor's property for a price of $5,000. Contractor breaches before any work has been done or any money has been paid. Sailor discovers that it will cost her $6,500 to have the work done by another contractor. How much is Sailor entitled to recover as damages?

3. Sailor and Contractor enter into a contract under the terms of which Contractor is to build a boathouse on Sailor's property for a price of $15,000. Contractor breaches before any work has been done, but after Sailor has paid Contractor an initial payment of $5,000. Sailor discovers that it will cost her $19,000 to have the work done by another contractor. How much is Sailor entitled to recover as damages?

4. Sailor and Contractor enter into a contract under the terms of which Contractor is to build a boathouse on Sailor's property for a price of $8,000. Sailor repudiates before any work has been done or any money has been paid. Contractor proves that it would have cost her $6,000 to build the boathouse. How much is Contractor entitled to recover as damages?

5. Sailor and Contractor enter into a contract under the terms of which Contractor is to build a boathouse on Sailor's property for a price of $12,000. Sailor repudiates before any work has been done, but after Sailor has paid Contractor $3,000 as a deposit. It is established that it would have cost Contractor $10,000 to build the boathouse. How much is Contractor entitled to recover as damages?

6. Grower and Broker enter into a contract under the terms of which it is agreed that Broker will purchase Grower's wheat crop for a price of $3.00 per bushel. At the time and place for delivery, the market price for wheat is $3.25 per bushel. Broker waits for Grower to show up with her wheat. When Grower fails to show up, Broker investigates and determines that Grower has sold her crop elsewhere. Without unreasonable delay, Broker purchases some wheat to replace the wheat she had expected to get from Grower, but by the time she can act the price has gone up and she has to pay $3.40 per bushel. How much (per bushel) is she entitled to recover in damages?

7.   Grower and Broker enter into a contract under the terms of which it is agreed that Broker will purchase Grower's wheat crop for a price of $3.00 per bushel. At the time and place for delivery, the market price for wheat is $3.25 per bushel. Broker waits for Grower to show up with her wheat. When Grower fails to show up, Broker investigates and determines that Grower has sold her crop elsewhere. Broker gets so fed up she decides to quit the wheat business and become a beach bum. How much (per bushel) is she entitled to recover in damages?

8.   Dealer agrees to buy Collector's Expressionist painting for $2 million. Dealer repudiates the contract. Collector re-sells the painting in good faith and in a commercially reasonable manner to another art gallery for $1.5 million and sues Dealer for breach of contract. At trial it is determined that the fair market value of the painting was $1.8 million dollars. How much is Collector entitled to recover as damages?

9.   Dealer agrees to buy Collector's Expressionist painting for $2 million. Dealer repudiates the contract. The fair market value of the painting at the time it was to be delivered is $1.8 million, but Collector decides she no longer wants to sell the painting, so she keeps it. How much is Collector entitled to recover as damages?

10. Wholesaler and Grocery Store enter into a contract under the terms of which Grocery Store agrees to buy a ton of apples from Wholesaler for $1,000. Wholesaler can get as many apples as it wants for $900 a ton. Grocery Store breaches its contract with Wholesaler, and Wholesaler in good faith and in a commercially reasonable manner re-sells the apples it had planned to sell to Grocery Store to Kroger for $975 a ton. How much is Wholesaler entitled to recover in damages?

11. Farmer and Broker enter into a contract under the terms of which Broker agrees to buy Farmer's entire apple crop for $1,000 a ton. It costs Farmer $900 a ton to grow the apples. Broker breaches its contract with Farmer, and Farmer in good faith and in a commercially reasonable manner re-sells the apples she had planned to sell to Broker to Health Food Store for $975 a ton, giving proper notice, of course. How much is Farmer entitled to recover in damages?

Answers to Problems to Review on Your Own

Problem 1: $8,000

Loss in value is $100,000. Cost avoided is $92,000.

If the contract had been performed, Seller would have $100,000 in cash. Now she has a $92,000 house. The difference is $8,000.

Problem 2: $1,500

Loss in value is $6,500. Cost avoided is $5,000.

If the contract had been performed, she would have had a boathouse and been out $5,000. Now she has the boathouse but it will cost her $6,500. She needs to get $1,500 to get where she would have been.

Problem 3: $9,000

Loss in value is $19,000. Cost avoided is $10,000. (That is the amount owing on the contract that she would have had to pay if it hadn't been breached).

If the contract had been performed, she would have had a boathouse and been out $15,000. Now she has the boathouse but is out $24,000 ($5,000 to Contractor and $19,000 to the person who actually built the boathouse).

Problem 4: $2,000

Loss in value is $8,000. Cost avoided is $6,000.

If the contract had been performed, she would have made $2,000. As it is now, she has nothing.

Problem 5: $0. We'll discuss in a later chapter whether or not she might have to give something back.

Loss in value is $9,000. Cost avoided is $10,000.

If the contract had been performed, she would have made $2,000. As it is, she has $3,000.

Problem 6: 40 cents a bushel

Section 2–712 allows the non-breaching buyer to recover the difference between the cost of cover ($3.40—she can get the higher price because she purchased "without unreasonable delay") and the contract price ($3.00) together with incidental or consequential damages (there weren't any) but less expenses saved in consequence of the breach (there weren't any).

Problem 7: 25 cents a bushel

Section 2–713 allows the buyer who has not covered to recover the difference between the market price ($3.25) and the contract price ($3.00) together with incidental and consequential damages (none) less expenses saved (none).

Problem 8: $500,000

Section 2–706 allows the non-breaching seller to recover the difference between the resale price ($1,500,000) and the contract price ($2,000,000) together with incidental damages (none) less expenses saved (none).

Problem 9: $200,000

If the non-breaching seller does not re-sell, § 2–708(1) gives her as damages the difference between the market price ($2,000,000) and the unpaid contract price ($1,800,000) together with incidental damages (none) less expenses saved (none).

Problem 10: $100 a ton

Because Wholesaler can get as many apples as it can sell, it is a "lost volume seller" and is entitled to the profit it would have made on the contract that was breached.

Problem 11: $25 a ton

Because Farmer has a limited supply of apples, her damages are determined by § 2–706 which gives her the difference between the resale price and the contract price.

CHAPTER 21

LIQUIDATED DAMAGES

■ ■ ■

It often makes sense for the parties to agree in the contract how much money will be awarded if there is a breach of the contract. These agreed-upon damages are referred to as "liquidated damages."

Provisions for liquidated damages allow the non-breaching party to recover when a limiting doctrine, such as the requirement that damages be proven with certainty, would otherwise make it impossible to recover a meaningful amount of damages. Alternatively, by acting as an agreed-upon limitation of liability, they can allow a party to limit its potential exposure so that it can safely enter into a contract without worrying that an inadvertent breach would expose it to damages out of all proportion to the profit it was making from the deal. Liquidated damages provisions also reduce litigation costs. Proving damages is often costly and fraught with uncertainty, requiring extensive investigation by accountants, financial experts, economists, and the like.

Present-day courts are usually favorably disposed toward liquidated damages clauses, in part because they save resources by reducing litigation and in part because giving effect to them furthers the general principle of freedom of contract. But if you took the language of the opinions—even recent ones—too literally you might think that courts are hostile to liquidated damages. Courts will often recite older, traditional rules limiting liquidated damages clauses and then uphold clauses that seem to violate these rules. The reason for this, as for most anomalies in law, is historical.

Early in the history of contract law, parties ensured the performance of contracts with a penal bond. The bond was a sealed instrument in which the promisor promised to pay a sum of money, but the bond provided that the obligation to pay would become "null and void" if the promisor performed his obligations under the accompanying contract. The amount of the bond was often a substantial sum intended to ensure that the contract was performed. For example, a wool merchant might promise to deliver 10 bushels of wool at Cardiff, and the bond might be a promise to pay several times the value of the wool if he failed to deliver it.

In the 1600's, courts of equity began enjoining the enforcement of penal bonds and requiring that the non-breaching party institute a suit at law for the determination of his loss. Thus, the principle emerged that a penalty designed to coerce performance was unenforceable, but a reasonable attempt to estimate damages that would be difficult to prove with sufficient certainty was valid and enforceable. This principle continues to be repeated in case law today.

Valid unless unreasonable

At first, courts were jealous of their prerogatives—including the fixing of damages—and viewed liquidated damages clauses with hostility. More recently, however, courts have become susceptible to arguments in favor of economic efficiency, and liquidated damages clauses are met with favor. Some legislatures have joined the fold. For example, California has amended its Civil Code to create a presumption that a liquidated damages clause is valid in a non-consumer contract unless it is proven that the clause is "unreasonable." Cal. Civ. Code § 1671. That is probably the case in other jurisdictions as well, but most other jurisdictions aren't so forthcoming about it. They go on quoting rules from the old cases but apply them in such a way that the result is as if they had adopted the California rule.

As a practical matter, one of the authors advises students and clients that, in a non-consumer context, a liquidated damages clause is very likely to be enforced if it is not procedurally unconscionable and amounts to no more than 10% of the contract's overall value. Further, it is likely—not "very likely," just "likely"—to be enforced if it is not procedurally unconscionable and amounts to no more than 20–25% of the value of the contract. Liquidated damages clauses of over 20–25% of the contract's value are anyone's guess as to whether a court will enforce them, and require a totality of the circumstances analysis.

One caveat is in order, however. A liquidated damages provision is likely to be struck down if it gives the non-breaching party a sum that clearly puts it in a better position than it would be in if the contract were performed. Also, a lawyer is asking for trouble if she doesn't attempt to tailor the damages to the severity of the breach. For instance, absent unusual circumstances, liquidated damages for a tenant's breach of a lease should vary according to the term remaining at the time of breach. A lease that gave the same amount of damages whether the tenant breached in the first month or the last would normally not be a reasonable attempt to estimate damages and would not pass muster. Similarly, per-day late charges in a contract for construction or supply of a product are more likely to be enforced than a one-size-fits-all default fee.

If the court does invalidate the liquidated damages provision, the non-breaching party is of course entitled to recover damages calculated in the usual manner unless the terms of the contract dictate otherwise. Further, if the liquidated damage clause is upheld and was drafted to be a baseline or minimum measure of damages rather than the exclusive remedy, additional damages may be pled, proven, and recovered in the usual manner.

The R2d recites the traditional standards for liquidated damages in section 356. The comparable UNIDROIT provision is article 7.4.13.

———

DIFFLEY V. ROYAL PAPERS, INC.

Court of Appeals of Missouri
948 S.W.2d 244 (1997)

CRANE, P.J.

[1]   Plaintiffs, pension plan trustees, filed an action to collect $210.80, which represented a late fee of 10% of total contributions due, against defendant employer for making late contributions to the pension plan in two months in 1995. After hearing the trustees' and employer's motions for summary judgment, the trial court entered summary judgment in employer's favor. The trustees appeal. We affirm on the grounds that the late fee is an unenforceable penalty.

[2]   The undisputed facts before the court on the motions for summary judgment were as follows: Defendant, Royal Papers, Inc., (employer) had a collective bargaining agreement with Teamsters Local #688 covering its warehouse employees. Pursuant to this agreement, employer contributes $31.00 per week, per employee, to the Teamsters Negotiated Pension Plan (the Pension Plan). The Pension Plan is administered by the Trustees pursuant to the Trust Agreement which is incorporated by reference into the collective bargaining agreement. The collective bargaining agreement and the Trust Agreement do not provide for a penalty for late payments to the Pension Plan. On May 9, 1994 the Trustees issued a Memorandum to all contributing employers of the Pension Plan which established a policy for late contributions. The memorandum provided:

> Effective February 15, 1994, the Trustees of the Teamsters Negotiated Pension Plan adopted a policy regarding employers who are delinquent in contributions to the Fund. A late penalty of ten percent (10%), unless specified otherwise in the collective bargaining agreement, of the total contributions due for the month will be assessed against an employer who is fifteen (15) days late in submitting reports and contributions to the Fund office (to be mailed to: Teamsters Insurance & Welfare Fund Administrative Office, P.O. Box 503092, St. Louis, MO. 63150–3092).

> A completed report form and contribution check is due in the Teamsters Negotiated Pension Fund office (address listed above) not later than fifteen (15) days after the end of the month being

Trustees want fee from employer

no later than 30 days after the end of the month

reported. Therefore, in order to avoid a late penalty, a contribution must be received by the Fund not later than thirty (30) days after the end of the month being reported.

[3] Plaintiff Richard Diffley signed as the Union Trustee and Allan Barton signed as the Employer Trustee. Employer subsequently made two late contributions to the Pension Plan. According to the Trustees' motion, the September payment, which was due on October 30, 1995, was not received until November 9, 1995. The October payment, which was due on November 30, 1995 was not received until December 6, 1995.

2 late contributions

No Consideration?

[4] The Trustees appeal from the trial court's entry of summary judgment against them. They contend that the 10% late penalty was a valid liquidated damages provision which the trial court should have enforced. We disagree.

* * *

Trustees argument

[5] Under state law, the Trustees argue that the 10% late fee is a proper liquidated damages provision which is entitled to enforcement. Employer, who also does not concede that the May 9th memorandum is a binding contract, argues that the late fee is an unenforceable penalty provision. We do not need to address the question of whether the May 9th memorandum is binding on employer because even if it is, the 10% late fee contained therein is unenforceable as a penalty clause.

LD is valid — Penalty not valid

[6] Liquidated damages clauses are valid and enforceable, while penalty clauses are invalid. A penalty provision specifies a punishment for default. On the other hand, liquidated damages are a measure of compensation which, at the time of contracting, the parties agree will represent damages in case of breach.

intention of parties

[7] For a damage clause to be valid as fixing liquidated damages: (1) the amount fixed as damages must be a reasonable forecast for the harm caused by the breach; and (2) the harm must be of a kind difficult to accurately estimate. Furthermore, in determining whether an agreement sets forth a penalty or liquidated damages, we look to the intention of the parties as ascertained from the contract as a whole. The provision must be fixed on the basis of compensation, otherwise it is construed as a penalty clause designed primarily to compel performance. While the label the parties attach to a provision is not conclusive, it is a circumstance to be considered when deciding whether the provision is to be considered liquidated damages or a penalty.

[8] In this case the penalty of 10% of total contributions due for the month is a penalty provision and not a liquidated damages clause. The fee is termed a "late penalty." The amount of the penalty, 10% of all monthly contributions due, is far more than the loss of market interest on the monthly contributions during the time the payment is unpaid and is not a

10% fee is a Penalty provision not an LD clause

10/10 is for more than the loss of market interest on the monthly contributions - not reasonable

reasonable forecast of the harm caused by the breach. The harm caused by late payments is easily measurable in terms of loss of interest or investment return during the time the payment is unpaid and the expense of administrative costs incurred in pursuing collection. The trial court did not err in entering summary judgment in employer's favor.

The judgment of the trial court is affirmed.

NOTES AND QUESTIONS

1.   In the quoted portion of the Trustees' Memorandum, the language used is a "late *penalty* of ten percent (10%)." This was an unfortunate and uninformed choice of words due to the case law regarding unenforceable penalties discussed in the introduction to this chapter. A well drafted contract will say the sum is payable "as liquidated damages and not as a penalty." Although courts are supposed to look through the form of the transaction and base their decision on substance, using words that the other side can turn against you is never wise.

2.   In paragraph 7, the court states: "The provision must be fixed on the basis of compensation, otherwise it is construed as a penalty clause designed primarily to compel performance." The court seems to be saying that the fact that the clause is intended to compel performance makes it an unenforceable penalty. Watch how the next opinion treats that issue.

DJ MANUFACTURING CORP. v. UNITED STATES

United States Court of Appeals, Federal Circuit
86 F.3d 1130 (1996)

BRYSON, CIRCUIT JUDGE.

[1]   DJ Manufacturing Corporation (DJ) appeals from a decision of the United States Court of Federal Claims granting summary judgment to the government. DJ argued that the liquidated damages clause in the contract between the parties was unenforceable as a penalty. The trial court rejected that argument, as do we.

I

[2]   In January 1991, the government solicited an offer from DJ for 283,695 combat field packs to support troops who were then participating in Operation Desert Storm. The solicitation documents set forth a delivery schedule, sought accelerated delivery if possible, and provided for liquidated damages for late delivery. The parties negotiated a contract, which became effective on February 14, 1991. Like the underlying solicitation documents, the contract provided that, for each article

delivered after the date fixed in the contract, liquidated damages would be assessed at 1/15 of one percent of the contract price for each day of delay.

[3] DJ missed several delivery deadlines. In accordance with the liquidated damages clause, the government withheld payment in the amount of $663,266.92,[1] a reduction of about 8 percent of the total contract price of $8,493,828.

[4] DJ filed suit in the Court of Federal Claims to recover the withheld amount, contending that the liquidated damages clause constituted an unenforceable penalty. The government moved for summary judgment. In support of its motion, the government submitted a declaration by an Army logistics management specialist, who stated that possession of the field packs was essential to the troops' combat readiness. In addition, the government submitted a declaration from the contracting officer, who stated that all contracts for items to be used in Operation Desert Shield/Desert Storm contained liquidated damages clauses for late delivery because of the need to get war items to the soldiers quickly.

[5] In response to the government's motion, DJ produced an affidavit of its president, who stated that the rate set forth in the liquidated damages clause "does not seem related to any specific need with respect to the item in question or the time-frame, but, rather, seems to be a fairly standard rate used in many solicitations for many different items." The affidavit listed several other government contracts and solicitations that allegedly contained clauses setting liquidated damages at the same rate. DJ argued that there was therefore a disputed issue of material fact as to whether the contracting officer had "used a standard rate, historically employed by [the agency]" and had made "no attempt to forecast just compensation."

[6] The Court of Federal Claims granted the government's motion. At the outset, the court held that DJ bore the burden of establishing that the liquidated damages clause was unenforceable, and that in order to avoid summary judgment DJ had to point to evidence raising a triable question of fact with respect to that issue. The court then recited the rule that a liquidated damages clause is enforceable if the harm that would be caused by a breach is difficult to estimate and the amount or rate fixed as liquidated damages is a reasonable forecast of the loss that may be caused by the breach.

[7] As to the first element, the court characterized this case as presenting "a paradigmatic example of a situation where accurate estimation of the damages resulting from delays in delivery is difficult, if not impossible." As to the second element, the court rejected DJ's argument that in order to determine the reasonableness of the liquidated damages,

---

[1] [$663,266.92 in 1996 dollars is roughly the equivalent of $1,060,000 in 2019 dollars using the CPI and the GNP Deflator.—Eds.]

it was necessary to inquire into the process that the contracting officer followed in reaching the amount that was inserted into the contract. The inquiry, the court explained, is an objective one. "The proper inquiry focuses on whether the amount itself is a reasonable forecast, not whether, as [DJ] seems to suggest, the individual responsible for proposing the rate engaged in a reasonable attempt to forecast damages." Because DJ failed to offer any evidence that the liquidated damages rate agreed upon in the contract was "greater than that which the government could reasonably suffer as a result of the delayed delivery of the field packs," the court granted the government's motion and ordered DJ's complaint to be dismissed.

II

[8] By fixing in advance the amount to be paid in the event of a breach, liquidated damages clauses save the time and expense of litigating the issue of damages. Such clauses "serve a particularly useful function when damages are uncertain in nature or amount or are unmeasurable," *Priebe & Sons v. United States,* 332 U.S. 407, 411, 92 L.Ed. 32, 68 S.Ct. 123 (1947), which is often the case when there is a delay in the completion of a contract for the government. Id.; *United States v. Bethlehem Steel Co.,* 205 U.S. 105, 120, 51 L.Ed. 731, 27 S.Ct. 450 (1907); *Jennie-O Foods, Inc. v. United States,* 217 Ct.Cl. 314, 580 F.2d 400, 413 (Ct.Cl.1978) ("Costs to the public convenience and the temporary thwarting of the public goals . . . are hard to measure with precision.").

[9] When damages are uncertain or difficult to measure, a liquidated damages clause will be enforced as long as "the amount stipulated for is not so extravagant, or disproportionate to the amount of property loss, as to show that compensation was not the object aimed at or as to imply fraud, mistake, circumvention or oppression." *Wise v. United States,* 249 U.S. 361, 365, 63 L.Ed. 647, 39 S.Ct. 303 (1919); *see United States v. Bethlehem Steel Co.,* 205 U.S. at 121 ("The amount is not so extraordinarily disproportionate to the damage which might result from the [breach], as to show that the parties must have intended a penalty and could not have meant liquidated damages."). With that narrow exception, "there is no sound reason why persons competent and free to contract may not agree upon this subject as fully as upon any other, or why their agreement, when fairly and understandingly entered into with a view to just compensation for the anticipated loss, should not be enforced." *Wise v. United States,* 249 U.S. at 365; *see also Sun Printing & Publishing Ass'n v. Moore,* 183 U.S. 642, 674, 22 S.Ct. 240, 46 L.Ed. 366 (1902) (except where "the sum fixed is greatly disproportionate to the presumed actual damages," a court "has no right to erroneously construe the intention of the parties, when clearly expressed, in the endeavor to make better contracts for them than they have made for themselves").

[10] A party challenging a liquidated damages clause bears the burden of proving the clause unenforceable. That burden is an exacting one, because when damages are uncertain or hard to measure, it naturally follows that it is difficult to conclude that a particular liquidated damages amount or rate is an unreasonable projection of what those damages might be. See Restatement (Second) of Contracts § 356 cmt. b (1981) ("The greater the difficulty either of proving that loss has occurred or of establishing its amount with the requisite certainty . . . the easier it is to show that the amount fixed is reasonable."); 5 Samuel Williston, A Treatise on the Law of Contracts § 783 (W. Jaeger ed. 1961).

[11] While some state courts are hostile to liquidated damages clauses, federal law "does not look with disfavor upon 'liquidated damages' provisions in contracts." *Priebe & Sons, Inc. v. United States,* 332 U.S. at 411. The few federal cases in which liquidated damages clauses have been struck down provide some indication of how rare it is for a federal court to refuse to enforce the parties' bargain on this issue. For example, in *Priebe & Sons, Inc. v. United States*, the Supreme Court struck down a liquidated damages clause when it was "certain when the contract was made" that the breach in question "plainly would not occasion damage." 332 U.S. at 413. The contract in *Priebe* contained two liquidated damages clauses: one for delay in the delivery of eggs and a second for failure to have the eggs inspected and ready for delivery by a specific time prior to the delivery date. The contractor was late in meeting the inspection requirement, but delivered the eggs on time. Thus, only the second liquidated damages clause was at issue in the case. As the Court viewed that clause, a delay in inspection that did not result in a delay in delivery could not cause any loss to the government. At the same time, however, the Court stated that if the breach had involved "failure to get prompt performance when delivery was due," the Court would have had "no doubt of the validity of the provision for 'liquidated damages' when applied under those circumstances." *Id.* at 412.

* * *

III

[12] In light of these principles, the trial court was correct to grant summary judgment to the government. DJ argues that the government should bear the burden of proving the clause enforceable and that the evidence before the trial court did not establish the government's right to recovery as a matter of law. That argument, however, flies in the face of settled law regarding the burden of proof and the standards for granting summary judgment.

[13] As noted above, it was DJ's burden to prove that the liquidated damages clause was unenforceable. When a party moves for summary judgment on an issue as to which the other party bears the burden of proof,

the moving party need not offer evidence, but may obtain summary judgment merely by pointing out to the court "that there is an absence of evidence to support the nonmoving party's case." *Celotex Corp. v. Catrett*, 477 U.S. 317, 325, 91 L. Ed. 2d 265, 106 S.Ct. 2548 (1986).

[14] The only evidence that DJ produced at the summary judgment stage was the affidavit of its president, which alleged that the liquidated damages rate was a "standard" rate, rather than a rate selected specifically for the field pack contract. In addition, DJ relies on the declaration of the contracting officer, which stated that the liquidated damages clause was put into the field pack contract, as well as other contracts for items to be used in Operations Desert Shield/Desert Storm "due to the almost overwhelming need to get war items, such as field packs, into the soldiers' possession as soon as possible."

[15] Neither of those two items of evidence raises an issue of material fact requiring a trial. DJ argues that the contracting officer's statement about the need to get war items into the soldiers' possession quickly shows that the liquidated damages clause was designed to be a "spur to performance" and thus was an unenforceable penalty. That assertion, however, is at odds with several Supreme Court decisions, which make clear that a liquidated damages clause is not rendered unlawful simply because the promisee hopes that it will have the effect of encouraging prompt performance by the promisor. In *Robinson v. United States*, for example, the Court explained that in the case of construction contracts, "a provision giving liquidated damages for each day's delay is *an appropriate means of inducing due performance*, or of giving compensation, in case of failure to perform." 261 U.S. 486, 488 (1928) (emphasis added). Similarly, in *Wise v. United States*, the Court stated that courts should "look with candor, if not with favor," on liquidated damages clauses "*as promoting prompt performance of contracts* and because adjusting in advance, and amicably, matters the settlement of which through courts would often involve difficulty, uncertainty, delay and expense." 249 U.S. at 366 (emphasis added). And in *United States v. Bethlehem Steel Co.*, the Court held that a liquidated damages clause may provide "*security for the proper performance of the contract* as to time of delivery" unless the amount of the liquidated damages is "*extraordinarily disproportionate* to the damage which might result from the [breach]." 205 U.S. at 121 (emphasis added).

* * *

[16] There is no inconsistency in a promisee's seeking assurance of performance through a guarantee of fair compensation for breach. As Williston noted with respect to standard (and legitimate) liquidated damages provisions, "there can be no doubt that these provisions are intended not merely as a provision for an unfortunate and unexpected contingency but also to secure the promisee in the performance of the main

obligation and to make the promisor more reluctant to break it." 5 Samuel Williston, *supra*, § 778, at 692. In this respect, at least, Corbin was in agreement. *See* 5 Arthur J. Corbin, Corbin on Contracts § 1058, at 339–40 (1964 ed.) ("The purpose of providing for a money payment in case of breach, whether it be called a penalty, a forfeiture, liquidated damages, or merely a sum of money, is primarily to secure the performance promised. . . . Penalties are said to be *in terrorem* to induce performance as promised; in large measure the same is true of liquidated damages"). What the policy against penalties is designed to prevent is a penal sanction that is so disproportionate to any damage that could be anticipated that it seeks "to enforce performance of the main purpose of the contract *by the compulsion of this very disproportion*." 5 Samuel Williston, *supra*, § 776, at 668 (emphasis added). Nothing that DJ offered or pointed to in the evidence before the trial court remotely suggested that the liquidated damages clause in this case is of that character.

* * *

[17] Finally, DJ argues that there was a triable issue as to whether the liquidated damages rate that the parties agreed upon in the field pack contract was unreasonable. Once again, DJ bore the burden of pointing to evidence establishing a material factual dispute on that issue, and the trial court correctly held that DJ failed to carry that burden.

[18] The damages that are likely to flow from delays in the delivery of goods is often difficult to assess, particularly when the goods are to be produced in the uncertain setting of wartime. As the Third Circuit put the matter in *United States v. Le Roy Dyal Co.,* 186 F.2d 460, 463 (3d Cir. 1950), *cert. denied,* 341 U.S. 926, 95 L. Ed. 1357, 71 S.Ct. 797 (1951), "in dealing with some matters pertaining to governmental activities, the question of ascertaining how much pecuniary loss is caused by failure of one contracting with the government to keep his promise is especially difficult." To illustrate the point, that court cited a colorful English case that is closely analogous here (*id.*):

> But how much damage could accrue to the Spanish government because a shipyard failed to deliver, at the time agreed upon, four torpedo-boat destroyers? This question was involved in testing the validity of a provision for liquidated damages for delay in the House of Lords decision in *Clydebank Engineering and Shipbuilding Co., Ltd. v. Castaneda.* How could the damages be accurately determined? As Lord Halsbury said in an opinion upholding the provision . . . "in order to do that properly and to have any real effect upon any tribunal determining that question, one ought to have before one's mind the whole administration of the Spanish Navy."

* * *

[19] In this case, not only did DJ fail to raise a triable question with respect to the difficulty of forecasting damages at the outset, but it also failed to raise any factual issue casting doubt on the reasonableness of the stipulated damages rate. Nor is there anything inherently unreasonable about that rate—a reduction in the contract price of 1/15 of one percent per day, or two percent per month, on a contract that was supposed to be completed within a period of only a few months.

* * *

AFFIRMED.

NOTES AND QUESTIONS

1.   In paragraph 6 of the opinion the circuit court states (with apparent approval) the rule that the trial court applied. Read carefully R2d § 356. How does the Restatement rule differ from the rule the trial court applied?

2.   Why have rules such as these? Why not allow freedom of contract where the parties can agree to whatever damage provisions they want?

3.   A Federal Communications Commission decision synthesized and summarized the law of liquidated damages as follows:

> When parties enter into a contract, the law allows them to apportion risk through the establishment of a liquidated damages clause. A liquidated damage clause will be enforced as long as the amount stipulated for is not so extravagant, or disproportionate to the amount of property loss, as to show that compensation was not the object aimed at or to imply fraud, mistake, circumvention, or oppression. With that narrow exception, there is no sound reason why persons competent and free to contract may not agree upon this subject as fully as upon any other, or why their agreement, when fairly and understandingly entered into with a view to just compensation for the anticipated loss, should not be enforced.

In re BDPCS, Inc., 15 F.C.C.R. 17590, 17610 (2000) (footnotes and internal citations omitted).

VANDERBILT UNIVERSITY V. DINARDO
United States District Court, Middle District, Tennessee
974 F. Supp. 638 (1997)

ECHOLS, DISTRICT JUDGE.

[1] Presently pending before the Court is Defendant's Motion for Summary Judgment, to which Plaintiff has responded in opposition.

[handwritten top margin: P filed cross motion]

Plaintiff has also filed a Cross-Motion for Summary Judgment, to which Defendant has responded in opposition. For the reasons outlined herein, Defendant's Motion is DENIED and Plaintiff's Motion is GRANTED.

[handwritten left margin: alleged breach of employment contract]

[2] Plaintiff, Vanderbilt University, filed this Complaint against Defendant, Gerry DiNardo, seeking damages arising from Defendant's alleged breach of an employment contract. Defendant filed a Motion for Summary Judgment asserting that he is entitled to judgment as a matter of law because the liquidated damage provision contained in the employment contract upon which Plaintiff's claim is based is: 1) an unlawful penalty provision under Tennessee law, and/or 2) inapplicable because Defendant was given permission to breach the employment contract.[2]

[handwritten left margin: Coach's argument]

[handwritten: LD is a penalty provision – unenforceable]

[3] Plaintiff also filed a Motion for Summary Judgment contending that it is entitled to judgment in its favor because the liquidated damage provision at issue is enforceable as a matter of law.

[handwritten: University thinks its a valid LD]

* * *

[handwritten left margin: Football Coach]

[4] The facts upon which Plaintiff's claim is based are as follows: On December 3, 1990, Defendant, Gerry DiNardo, and Plaintiff, Vanderbilt University, executed an employment contract ("Contract") under which Defendant was employed as Plaintiff's head football coach. The original termination date of the Contract was January 5, 1996. Section 8 of the Contract provided as follows:

[handwritten left margin: Clause 8 shows coach knew of importance]

> Section 8. Mr. DiNardo recognizes that his promise to work for the University for the entire term of this 5-year Contract is of the essence of this Contract to the University. Mr. DiNardo also recognizes that the University is making a highly valuable investment in his continued employment by entering into this Contract and its investment would be lost were he to resign or otherwise terminate his employment as Head Football Coach with the University prior to the expiration of this Contract.[3] Accordingly, Mr. DiNardo agrees that in the event he resigns or otherwise terminates his employment as Head Football Coach (as opposed to his resignation or termination from another position at the University to which he may have been reassigned), prior to the expiration of this Contract, and is employed or performing services for a person or institution other than the University, he will pay to the University as liquidated damages an amount equal to his Base Salary, less amounts that would otherwise be deducted

[handwritten left margin: Liquidated damages provision]

---

[2] Defendant also claims that the damage provision is not a liquidated damages clause but instead is a thinly-disguised covenant not to compete. The Court disagrees that the damage clause should be so characterized. The clause provides for specific damages for a breach of contract if Defendant becomes employed elsewhere. However, the clause is applicable even if Defendant procures employment in a completely unrelated field.

[3] [Why say all of this? Doesn't the next sentence do the job all by itself?—Eds.]

or withheld from his Base Salary for income and social security tax purposes, multiplied by the number of years (or portion(s) thereof) remaining on the Contract.

[5] During the negotiations, the language of Section 8 was modified at the request of Defendant so that any liquidated damages would be calculated based on Defendant's net pay, rather than on his gross pay.

[6] Defendant's base salary was initially set at $100,000 per year. By amendment to the Contract dated June 25, 1992, Plaintiff increased Defendant's base salary to $110,000, effective January 1, 1992. By amendment dated June 25, 1993, the base salary was increased to $125,000 per year. In April 1994, Plaintiff increased Defendant's base salary to $135,000 per year retroactive to January 1, 1994.

[7] In November 1994, near the end of the 1994 football season, Joe Dean, the Athletic Director at Louisiana State University ("LSU"), asked [Vanderbilt Athletic Director Paul] Hoolahan for permission to speak with Defendant about a possible job at LSU. Defendant also asked Hoolahan for permission to speak with LSU regarding possible employment. Hoolahan verbally granted permission for LSU and Defendant to speak about the matter. On December 12, 1994, Defendant announced his decision to accept the job as LSU's head football coach and he resigned from his employment as head football coach at Vanderbilt University.

[8] Defendant contends that the liquidated damage provision contained in the employment contract is an unlawful penalty under Tennessee law. It is well established that parties to a contract may stipulate to an amount of liquidated damages. . . . Courts will not enforce liquidated damage provisions, however, where the provision is a penalty that punishes the defaulting party. In order to determine whether a liquidated damage provision is a penalty, the Court must consider "whether the amount stipulated was reasonable in relation to the amount of damages that could be expected to result from the breach." (*Harmon*, 699 S.W.2d at 163). If the provision is a reasonable estimate of the damages that would occur from a breach, then the provision is normally construed as an enforceable stipulation for liquidated damages. The Court must also determine whether the parties contemplated that such damages would flow from a failure to perform the contract, and that such damages would be indeterminate or difficult to ascertain.

[9] In the present case, under Section 8 of the Contract, upon breach, Defendant would be required to pay an amount equal to his base salary, less that which would otherwise be deducted or withheld from his base salary for income and social security tax purposes multiplied by the number of years remaining on the Contract. At the time that Defendant

terminated his employment, he was receiving a gross base salary of $135,000 and a net salary of $91,781.60 per year. Defendant terminated his Contract on December 12, 1994. The Contract with the Addendum expired on January 5, 1998. As such, the liquidated damage provision provided that Defendant pay Plaintiff $281,886.43.

[10] It is the opinion of the Court that the liquidated damage provision in the Contract is not an unlawful penalty and that the established damages in the sum of $281,886.43[4] are reasonable when compared to the potential actual damages to be suffered by Vanderbilt on account of Defendant's breach. According to Vanderbilt, expenses associated with recruiting a new head coach amounted to more than $27,000. Moreover, because Defendant took his coaching staff with him to LSU, Vanderbilt had to pay $86,840 in order to move the new coaching staff to Nashville and into Vanderbilt facilities. The yearly compensation for the new coaching staff was $770,000, while the DiNardo coaching staff was paid $708,563, a difference of $61,437. If this amount is multiplied by the three years remaining in the Contract, it totals $184,311.[5] Furthermore, the aforementioned specific damages sustained by Vanderbilt do not include the potentially extensive other damages to Vanderbilt which may result in having to suddenly replace a head football coach. Such damages are difficult to quantify, but may include damage to reputation and public relations, lost profits from reduced football ticket sales, lost talents of resigning assistant coaches, broken promises and relationships with players, lost recruits and future recruiting opportunities, reduced membership in athletic clubs and alumni support, decline in donations to the athletic program, redesigning publicity, media guides, logos and uniforms, etc.

[11] Under the circumstances of this case, the Court finds the use of the formula based on Defendant's salary to determine the amount of liquidated damages is reasonable. Although DiNardo's base salary is not specifically related to any specific anticipated damages in the event he resigns, it is reasonable given the nature of the unquantifiable damages in this case. The potential damage to Plaintiff extends far beyond the cost of merely hiring a new head football coach. It is this uncertain potentiality that the parties sought to address by providing for a sum certain to apply towards anticipated expenses and losses. It is impossible to estimate how the loss of a head football coach will affect alumni relations, public support, football ticket sales, contributions, etc. Indeed, the success and reputation

---

[4]　[$281,886.43 in 1997 dollars is roughly the equivalent of $441,000 in 2019 dollars using the CPI and the GNP Deflator.—Eds.]

[5]　In response to Plaintiff's Statement of Undisputed Facts, Defendant denies that Plaintiff had to pay for the moving expense for a new head coach, etc. However, while Plaintiff submitted admissible evidence in support of its allegations regarding damages incurred, Defendant merely denied that Plaintiff's allegations are correct without citing to any admissible evidence contained in the record. Conclusory denials are insufficient to raise a genuine issue of material fact.

earned by the resigning coach, as well as that of the new coach may dramatically impact the situation. As such, to require a precise formula for calculating damages resulting from the breach of contract by a college head football coach would be tantamount to barring the parties from stipulating to liquidated damages in advance. In addition, the damage provision of the Contract does reflect a projected declining loss to Plaintiff based upon the length of service remaining on the coach's contract. This decrease is reasonable given Vanderbilt's concern about the stability of its football program and the investment made into DiNardo's "continued employment" as head football coach.[6]

[12] Defendant asserts that in determining whether the liquidated damage clause is reasonable, the Court may not consider the consequential damages sustained by Vanderbilt, and instead is limited to consideration of the actual cost of replacing him as head coach. This argument is without merit. Parties to a contract may include consequential damages and even damages not usually awarded by law in a liquidated damage provision provided that they were contemplated by the parties.

[13] In the present case, it is clear from the plain language of the Contract that the parties contemplated that the effect of a breach of contract by Defendant would have an impact beyond the cost of simply replacing his services. As quoted in Section 8 of the Contract, the liquidated damage provision, "the University is making a highly valuable investment in [DiNardo's] continued employment by entering into this Contract and its investment would be lost were he to resign or otherwise terminate his employment as Head Football Coach with the University prior to the expiration of this Contract." Furthermore, the Contract also provided that "a long-term commitment by Mr. DiNardo [was] important to the University's desire for a stable intercollegiate football program." As such, the parties contemplated damages other than the mere cost of replacement services that could result from Defendant's breach and the effect such a breach would have on Plaintiff's football program.

[14] In further support of the reasonableness of the liquidated damage clause is the fact that the Contract was the result of arms-length negotiations. Not only was Defendant represented by counsel during the contract negotiation process, Defendant's counsel was successful in negotiating a substantial reduction in the liquidated damage provision by providing that the measure of damages would be Defendant's net rather than gross salary. Under the circumstances of Defendant's breach, this reduces the amount of liquidated damages by over $100,000.[7]

---

[6] It is also reasonable that the amount of damages increased when the Addendum was executed as Vanderbilt made yet another commitment into the DiNardo football program.

[7] It is interesting to note that the Contract contained a similar liquidated damage provision in favor of Defendant in the event Plaintiff terminated the contract prior to its expiration date.

[15] For the foregoing reasons, the Court finds that the liquidated damage clause in Section 8 of the Contract is reasonable, and thus enforceable, under the circumstances of this case.

LD.'s enforceable   * * *

[16] In conclusion, the Court finds the liquidated damage clause contained in Defendant's employment contract is reasonable as a matter of law. Since this clause provides designated damages of $281,886.43 as discussed in this Memorandum, Plaintiff's Motion is GRANTED, and judgment is entered in favor of Plaintiff in the amount of $281,886.43. For the reasons stated herein, Defendant's motion is denied.

NOTES AND QUESTIONS

1. Review section 8 of DiNardo's contract. What is the point of the first sentence? Doesn't the next sentence contain the operative language of the parties' agreement?

2. In paragraph 6 of the opinion, the court notes that the language of section 8 was "modified at the request of" DiNardo. What is the point, if any, of this?

3. This case perhaps underscores the importance of a forum selection clause in a contract. Vanderbilt would probably prefer to sue to collect its liquidated damages in Nashville rather than in Baton Rouge. Assuming that one is well regarded in one's community, it is generally preferable to sue or be sued at home. The rule of law is, to some degree, as you have probably guessed, a malleable one. In any event, don't ignore the elephant in the corner that nobody is talking about. Or the Commodore. Or the Tiger.

4. In October, 2003, ESPN.com reported that the $47 million contract between the San Diego Chargers and wide receiver David Boston provided the team could recover liquidated damages of up to $3 million if Mr. Boston committed certain specified infractions, including being suspended for "conduct detrimental to the team." In recent years, such clauses have become quite common in professional sports contracts. Jim Trotter, *Boston's stay here might be a short one*, UNION TRIBUNE, Mar. 9, 2004.

MONSANTO CO. v. MCFARLING

United States Court of Appeals, Federal Circuit
363 F.3d 1336 (2004)

CLEVENGER, CIRCUIT JUDGE.

[1] The United States District Court for the Eastern District of Missouri entered summary judgment against defendant Homan McFarling and in favor of the Monsanto Company ("Monsanto") under Federal Rule of Civil Procedure 54(b) on some, but not all, of the claims being litigated. The district court held that, when McFarling replanted some of Monsanto's patented ROUNDUP READY® soybeans that he had saved from his prior year's crop, McFarling breached the Technology Agreement that he had signed as a condition of his purchase of the patented seeds. The district court also held that McFarling had failed to demonstrate a genuine issue of material fact that prevented entry to summary judgment on any of his counterclaims or his defenses to Monsanto's breach-of-contract claim. Finally, the district court held that a liquidated damages provision in the Technology Agreement was valid and enforceable under Missouri law and entered a judgment in the amount of $780,000. McFarling appeals the district court's rulings on several of his counterclaims and defenses, as well as its ruling on the contractual damages provision. We affirm the district court on the counterclaims and defenses, but we vacate the district court's judgment as it relates to the damages provision and remand for a determination of Monsanto's actual damages.

[2] Monsanto manufactures ROUNDUP® herbicide. ROUNDUP® contains glyphosate, a chemical that indiscriminately kills vegetation by inhibiting the metabolic activity of a particular enzyme, 5-enolpyruvyl-shikimate-3-phosphate synthase ("EPSPS"). EPSPS is necessary for the conversion of sugars into amino acids—and thus for growth—in many plants and weeds.

[3] Monsanto also markets ROUNDUP READY® genetic-modification technology. In soybean seeds, the ROUNDUP READY® technology operates by inserting the gene sequence for a variant of EPSPS that is not affected by the presence of glyphosate but that still performs the sugar-conversion function required for cell growth. Thus, ROUNDUP READY® soybean seeds produce both a "natural" version of EPSPS that is rendered ineffective in the presence of the glyphosate in ROUNDUP® herbicide, and a genetically modified version of EPSPS that permits the soybean seeds to grow nonetheless. ROUNDUP®, or other glyphosate-based herbicides, can thus be sprayed over the top of an entire field, killing the weeds without harming the ROUNDUP READY® soybeans.

[4] Monsanto licenses its proprietary ROUNDUP READY® technology through two interrelated licensing schemes. First, it licenses the patented gene to seed companies that manufacture the glyphosate-

tolerant seeds that are sold to farmers. Under this license, seed companies gain the right to insert the genetic trait into the germplasm of their own seed (which can differ from seed company to seed company), and Monsanto receives the right to a royalty or "technology fee" of $6.50 for every 50-pound bag of seed containing the ROUNDUP READY® technology sold by the seed company. Monsanto also owns several subsidiary seed companies that comprise approximately 20 percent of the market for ROUNDUP READY® soybeans.

[5]   Second, Monsanto requires that seed companies execute licenses, rather than conduct unconditional sales, with their farmer customers. The 1998 version of this "Monsanto Technology Agreement" (the "Technology Agreement") between Monsanto and the soybean farmers using ROUNDUP READY® soybeans places several conditions on the soybean farmers' use of the licensed soybeans. In exchange for the "opportunity to purchase and plant seed containing" the ROUNDUP READY® technology, soybean farmers agree, *inter alia*:

> To use the seed containing Monsanto gene technologies for planting a commercial crop only in a single season.
>
> To not supply any of this seed to any other person or entity for planting, and to not save any crop produced from this seed for replanting, or supply saved seed to anyone for replanting.
>
> To not use this seed or provide it to anyone for crop breeding, research, generation of herbicide registration data or seed production.

[6]   The technology Agreement also contains a clause specifying damages in the event of the breach by the farmer:

> In the event that the Grower saves, supplies, sells or acquires seed for replant in violation of the Agreement and license restriction, in addition to other remedies available to the technology provider(s), the Grower agrees that damages will include a claim for liquidated damages, which will be based on 120 times the applicable Technology Fee.

[7]   Homan McFarling operates a 5000-acre farm in Pontotoc County, Mississippi. In 1998, McFarling executed the Technology Agreement in connection with the license of 1000 bags of ROUNDUP READY® soybean seed. McFarling concedes that he saved 1500 bushels of seed from his 1998 crop, enough to plant approximately 1500, acres, and that he replanted them in 1999. He subsequently saved 3075 bags of soybeans from his 1999 crop, replanting them in 2000.

[8]   Soybeans destined for replanting are apparently cleaned after harvest. When McFarling sent his seeds saved from 1998 season to a third party for cleaning, Monsanto had some samples taken, had genetic makeup

of the seeds tested at Mississippi State University, and thus learned that McFarling was saving ROUNDUP READY® seeds.

[9]   In January 2000, Monsanto filed suit against McFarling, alleging, *inter alia*, infringement of the '435 and '605 patents and breach of the Technology Agreement, and seeking a preliminary injunction prohibiting McFarling from "planting, transferring or selling the infringing articles to a third party." In his answer, McFarling raised affirmative defenses (styled alternatively as counterclaims when possible) both to liability— including, *inter alia*, violations of the Plant Variety Protection Act ("PVPA"), 84 Stat. 1542, as amended, 7 U.S.C. § 2321 *et seq.*, the federal antitrust laws, the patent misuse doctrine, and the patent exhaustion and first sales doctrines—and to damages as calculated under the 120 multiplier in the Technology Agreement. He did not, however, challenge the validity of Monsanto's patents. Because McFarling's only connection with Missouri was a forum selection clause in the Technology Agreement, McFarling also brought a motion to dismiss based on a lack of personal jurisdiction.

[10] The district court held that the forum selection clause was valid and entered a preliminary injunction against McFarling. On appeal, we affirmed the district court on both issues. *See Monsanto Co. v. McFarling*, 302 F.3d 1291, 1296, 1299–300 (Fed. Cir. 2002) *("McFarling I")*. Addressing Monsanto's likelihood of success on the merits, we held that the district court did not err in finding that McFarling had not demonstrated a reasonable likelihood of success on his affirmative defenses. *Id.* at 1297– 99.

[11] Back in the district court, Monsanto moved for summary judgment on the infringement claim under the '605 patent, the breach of the Technology Agreement claim, and all of McFarling's affirmative defenses. The district court granted summary judgment in favor of Monsanto on all of McFarling's defenses as well as on liability with respect to Monsanto's '605 patent infringement claim and the Technology Agreement claim. On damages, however, the district court denied Monsanto's summary judgment motion. It left the damages issue regarding infringement of the '605 patent for trial. Additionally, although it held the liquidated damages clause in the Technology Agreement to be valid and enforceable (provided the 120 multiplier was applied to the number of bags of seed purchased rather than the number replanted), it concluded that there was insufficient evidence of the number of bags purchased by McFarling in 1998 to enter judgment on damages on the breach-of-contract claim. After McFarling stipulated that he purchased 1000 bags of ROUNDUP READY® soybean seed in 1998, the district court entered final judgment pursuant to Federal Rule of Civil Procedure 54(b) on Monsanto's breach-of-contract claim only in the amount of $780,000.00 (120 × $6.50 × 1000), and against McFarling on his counterclaims.

[12] In the district court, Monsanto had argued that the 120 multiplier in the liquidated damages clause should be interpreted to produce damages of 120 times the technology fee times the number of bags of seed replanted by McFarling. The district court rejected that formula, reasoning that it would constitute an unlawful penalty because it simply imposes a multiple of the liquidated damages, clause, the district court fashioned a formula that multiplies 120 times the licensing fee times the number of bags of seed purchased.

[The court discussed several procedural matters and rejected McFarling's argument based on federal patent law and antitrust law.—Eds.]

[13] Finally, McFarling argues that the district court erred in holding that 120 multiplier on the technology fee in the Technology Agreement was a valid and enforceable liquidated damages clause under Missouri law. Upon independent review, *see Robert Blond Meat Co. v. Eisenberg*, 273 S.W.2d 297, 299 (Mo. 1954) (holding that the validity of a liquidated damages clause is a question of law and reviewing it without reference), we agree with McFarling that the liquidated damages clause in the Technology Agreement is invalid and unenforceable under Missouri law as it applies to McFarling's breach of replanting of saved seed.

[14] Missouri law distinguishes between liquidated damages clauses, which are valid and enforceable, and penalty clauses, which are neither. *See Diffley v. Royal Papers, Inc.*, 948 S.W.2d 244, 246 (Mo. Ct. App. 1997); *Paragon Group, Inc. v. Ampleman*, 878 S.W.2d 878, 880–81 (Mo. Ct. App. 1994); *Burst v. R.W. Beal & Co.*, 771 S.W.2d 87, 90 (Mo. Ct. App. 1989); *Grand Bissell Towers, Inc. v. Joan Gagnon Enters., Inc.*, 657 S.W.2d 378, 379 (Mo. Ct. App. 1983).

* * *

[15] One long-standing litmus test that the Missouri courts use to determine whether a contractual provision determining damages is a reasonable estimate of the anticipated harm is what we term the "anti-one-size rule":

> [A] court may consider whether the agreement contains various stipulations of various degrees of importance, the breaches of which would be easy to calculate in damages as to some and difficult as to others, in which the event the sum specified would be construed as a penalty and not as liquidated damages "even though the parties in express terms have declared the contrary."

Wilt v. Waterfield, 273 S.W.2d 290, 295 (1954) (quoting *Sylvester Watts Smyth Realty Co. v. Am. Sure. Co. of N.Y.*, 292 Mo. 423, 238 S.W. 494, 499 (Mo. 1921)).

[16] This fixed rule of Missouri Contract law is not unusual. Variations on this anti-one-size rule are applied in a number of jurisdictions.

[17] The anti-one-size rule is an intuitive corollary of the two-prong Missouri test that applies when a single formula for liquidated damages applies to multiple provisions pertains. It reminds us that the validity of a damages clause must be measured on a provision-by-provision basis; the fact that the harm flowing from the breach of one provision may be difficult to measure does not validate a contractual damages provision as it applies to the breach of another provision. Additionally, the anti-one-size rule provides a rule of thumb assay to determine if a contractual damage provision was fixed on the basis of compensation: If the same formula is used to calculate damages for breaches of two different provisions that would be expected to require two substantially different methods of compensation, then the contract on its face admits that the parties did not view the specified damages as compensatory. In some cases, this evidence intrinsic to the contract may provide a more reliable measure of the parties' intent than a hindsight comparison of the sum specified in the contract and the damage award required to compensate the nonbreaching party for the damages actually sustained.

[18] We conclude that the 120 multiplier in the Technology Agreement is not valid under Missouri law. It was not, at the time of contracting, a reasonable estimate of the harm that Monsanto would likely suffer in the event that McFarling breached the contractual prohibition on saving ROUNDUP READY® soybeans.

[19] Monsanto's principal argument to the contrary is that ROUNDUP READY® soybeans can self-replicate at an exponential rate. One bag of soybean seed can yield 36 bags of soybean seed to save for the following season, although this figure may vary with different types of crops, seed varieties, geographic growing locations, planting rates, cultural practices, and growing conditions, among other factors. Based on this figure together with assumptions of infinite acreage on which to plant and no commercial sale of any soybeans, a farmer planting one bag of soybeans in year one would reap 36 bags to replant in year two, 1296 bags to replant in year three, and 46,656 bags to replant in year four. This simple narrative is forceful insofar it illustrates the potential magnitude of the harm that Monsanto could suffer from losing control of its proprietary technology. However, an illustration that breach of the Technology Agreement under particular conditions may be reasonably expected to lead to harm of great magnitude is not sufficient to uphold the validity of the damages clause in its entirety. The damages clause is not valid as applied to the provision of the technology Agreement that prohibits saving soybean seed and that was breached by McFarling. In other words, the 120 multiplier does not pass muster under Missouri's anti-one-size rule.

[20] The 120 multiplier in the Technology Agreement also violates the anti-one-size rule because it specifies the same measure of damages in the event of breach of several different restrictive provisions of the contract that led to different types of damages. The license can trigger the 120 multiplier in the Technology Agreement by violating any one of several distinct provisions: "In the event that the Grower *saves, supplies, sells or acquires seed for replant* in violation of this Agreement and license restriction . . . the Grower agrees that damages will include a claim for liquidated damages . . ." (emphasis added). We conclude that the nature of the harm to Monsanto flowing from breach of the provision prohibiting seed saving is fundamentally different from the nature of the harm to Monsanto flowing from breach of the provision prohibiting seed supplying and seed selling.

[21] In fact, Monsanto repeatedly acknowledged the importance of the distinction between seed saving by the farmer for replant on his own farm and seed transfer to third parties for replant. Monsanto argues in its brief that "whether an infringer saves seed for himself only or transfer saved seed to other growers . . . significantly impacts the multiplier effect and the harm to Monsanto." Additionally, the following exchange occurred at oral argument between the court and Monsanto's attorney:

> Court: The character or quality of the breach when [McFarling] breaches on his own farm is really different from Monsanto's perspective than the quality of the breach if he goes to the county fair and sells 5000 bags to 5000 different purchasers. Am I right?

> Counsel: Absolutely. And that's why the 120 times multiple is so reasonable.

* * *

[22] Under the anti-size-one rule, a liquidated damages clause is invalid if even one breach covered by the clause fails to qualify for enforceability as liquidated damages. Since the breach of seed saving cannot warrant liquidated damages, for the reasons we state, we need not consider the consequences of the breach of acquiring seed for replant. Proof of loss is of course substantially more difficult when the breaching farmer supplies or sells the seed to another farmer in violation of the agreement. If a farmer transfers seed to a third-party for replant, Monsanto not only has no privity of contract with the purchasers, but it also faces difficulty tracing the seed, location and deposing the individuals who purchased it, and thus determining the amount of harm caused by the breach. In this situation, the difficulty of proof of loss would be considerable. However, if a farmer saves seed for replant in a future growing season, the number of bags planted is more readily ascertainable from a single defendant who is in privity with Monsanto.

[23] Monsanto's expectations of the compensable loss flowing from the breach should also be lower when the breaching farmer replants on his own farm. The testimony of Monsanto's own damages expert suggests that a distinction between replanting and transferring is in part due to different rates of seed-replication in each scenario. The acreage of an individual grower for replanting is finite, placing a brake on the replication rate, whereas the geographical area available to plant resold seed is practically unlimited. Monsant[o]'s damages expert assumed that soybeans self-replicated at a linear rather than an exponential rate in his only example demonstrating the harm to Monsanto that could flow from a farmer breaching by replanting seed rather than by transferring seed. The damages expert presumed that the farmer would save the same amount of seed each year, likely just enough to plant the farm's acreage.

* * *

[24] When a damages clause is a penalty clause, the clause is unenforceable under Missouri law and only actual damages are available. We therefore remand to the district court to compute actually damages based on the number of bags of seed saved and replanted.

NOTE

More than 90% of the soybeans and 70% of the corn and cotton produced in the United States come from Roundup Ready seeds. But evolution has produced several varieties of Roundup Ready resistant weeds. *See* https://www.chem.purdue.edu/courses/chm333/Spring%202012/Handouts/Roundup%20resistant%20weeds%20USATODAY%20DEC%202010.pdf *(". . . the problem is spreading quickly across the Corn Belt and beyond, with Roundup now proving unreliable in killing at least 10 weed species in at least 22 states").*

———

PROBLEM 21-1

Read carefully U.C.C. §§ 2–719(1)(a) and 2–719(3) and Restatement (Second) § 356. Which of the following clauses limiting remedies would be upheld? *None of them ?*

(a) The contract for the sale of a burglar alarm provides that damages for the failure of the burglar alarm are limited to $100. The alarm fails to function and $50,000 worth of jewelry and antiques are stolen from the buyer's home. *upheld!*

(b) The contract for the sale of photographic film provides that if the film is defective, the buyer's remedies are limited to a return of the purchase price. The film is defective and the buyer is left without any pictures of her wedding, the first ever wedding on the summit of Mount Everest.

17K × 150 = 2,550,000

(c) The contract for the delivery of an overnight package provides that if the package is not delivered on time, the shipper's only remedy is the return of her money. The package fails to arrive on time, a billion dollar corporate merger is delayed, and the lawyer who sent the package goes from being on the fast track for partnership to looking for a job.

PROBLEM 21-2

Reconsider the *Diffley* case. If you had been representing the Teamsters, what could you have done to give your liquidated damages provision a good shot at being enforceable while still making it a strong incentive for employers to get their money in on time?

PROBLEM 21-3

A general contractor had a contract to build an office building. The general contract provided that if completion of the building was delayed, the general contractor would pay liquidated damages of $1,000 a day. The lowest bid on the electrical work was from a new and rather small company. The general contractor told the electrical contractor he would like to give them the job, but he could not take the risk that the sub would be late in completing the electrical work and throw the whole project off schedule. The electrical sub therefore suggested that the electrical subcontract provide for liquidated damages of $2,000 per day. The head of the electrical sub stated that the reason for this provision was "to show that we have confidence we can perform." At the time the parties entered into the subcontract, they both knew that each day of delay in the completion of the electrical work would result in no more than one day's delay in the completion of the entire project, and there was a substantial likelihood that the delay in the completion of the entire project would be even less.

As it turned out, the electrical work was completed 30 days late. The project was completed 21 days late, and if the electrical work had been completed on time, the project still would have been 15 days late.

How much is the general contractor entitled to recover as damages?

30 grand?

PROBLEM 21-4

A law professor and law book publisher entered into a contract under the terms of which the professor would revise a chapter in the publisher's treatise on contract damages. The contract provided that the professor's fee would be $600 if the manuscript were delivered by March 1, $450 if it were delivered by April 15, and $200 if it were delivered at any time thereafter.

Is there a problem with this provision?

PROBLEM 21-5

Mark Dove, a law student, entered into an employment contract with Rose Acre Farms, a large agri-business concern. Under the terms of the contract, Mr. Dove would work for Rose Acre Farms for ten weeks during the summer for the sum of $7,500. The contract provided that if a certain construction project on which Mr. Dove was to be working in a supervisory capacity was not completed on time OR if Mr. Dove was late for work even one time, Mr. Dove would pay "as liquidated damages and not as a penalty," the sum of $5,000.

Is the liquidated damages provision enforceable? *No, disproportionate / penalty*

PROBLEM 21-6

Mark Dove, a law student, entered into an employment contract with Rose Acre Farms, a large agri-business concern. Under the terms of the contract, Mr. Dove would work for Rose Acre Farms for ten weeks during the summer for the sum of $2,500. The contract provided that if a certain construction project on which Mr. Dove was to be working in a supervisory capacity was completed on time and if Mr. Dove was not late for work even one time, Mr. Dove would receive a bonus of $5,000.

Mr. Dove was late for work one morning because his car wouldn't start. (He planned to use the bonus to buy a new one). Because he was late, he didn't get the bonus and he sued to recover it. Should he win? *No → bonus ≠ damages*

PROBLEM 21-7

Your client has agreed to pay liquidated damages of $200,000 if it fails to perform its part of a contract. It wants to be sure it is not required to pay more. What provisions would you put into the contract to make sure its exposure is limited to $200,000? *Merger clause*

LAWYERING SKILLS PROBLEM

When Trista Rehn was chosen to be The Bachelorette on the reality-based television program of that name, she was required to sign a contract of 17 single-spaced pages. One clause provided:

> F.   **Liquidated Damages:** I agree that any breach or violation by me of any of the terms or provisions of this Agreement shall result in substantial damages and injury to Producer and/or the Network, the precise amount of which would be extremely difficult or impracticable to determine. Accordingly, Producer and I have made a reasonable endeavor to estimate a fair compensation for potential losses and damages to Producer and/or the Network which would result from any breach by me of any material term of this Agreement, including, but not limited to paragraph IV D. [paragraph IV D. provides that she assumes the risk of all the dangers and hazards she will encounter on the show, including the risk of pregnancy and sexually-

transmitted diseases—as we'll see in the next two chapters, it's not clear how one would breach a clause like this; possibly she could do it by suing on account of damage from one of the risks she assumed] and, therefore, I further agree that, in addition to the remedies set forth hereinabove, I will also be obligated to pay, and I agree to pay to Producer and/or the Network, the sum of Five Million Dollars ($5,000,000) as a reasonable and fair amount of liquidated damages to compensate Producer and/or the Network for any loss or damage resulting from each breach by me of the terms hereof. I further agree that such sum bears a reasonable and proximate relationship to the actual damages which Producer and/or the Network will or may suffer from each breach by me.

This clause was separately initialed by Ms. Rehn, as were most of the other significant clauses in the contract. There were a total of 35 provisions in the contract to be initialed by Ms. Rehn. Among the provisions, the breach of which would trigger the liquidated damages clause, were:

Paragraph I A. requiring her to appear on news shows, talk shows etc. "when and where designated by Producer in its sole discretion."

Paragraph II A. requiring her to refrain from taking photographs during the period of the show's taping without the permission of the producer.

Paragraph VI A. requiring her to refrain from using the series name in any publicity except as provided in the agreement.

Paragraph VI B. requiring her to refrain from taking refuge in any place where the series cameras cannot photograph her.

Paragraph VI C. requiring her to refrain from wearing any apparel with a nationally recognized logo unless it has been provided by the producer and further requiring her to "abide by . . . all U.S. laws and all applicable local laws."

(1) If Ms. Rehn were arrested for speeding while wearing her Mickey Mouse wristwatch, could the producer get a judgment for five million? (Or could they get ten million? She's breached two provisions.)

(2) If Ms. Rehn breached the contract in a way that caused the producer damage that was serious but not provable with reasonable certainty, how would you argue that Ms. Rehn is not liable for the five million?

(3) What is the intended effect of the provision that states "Producer and I have made a reasonable endeavor to estimate a fair compensation for potential losses and damages . . . ?" Can you think of an unintended effect it may have?

CHAPTER 22

SPECIFIC PERFORMANCE

■ ■ ■

Specific performance, or a mandatory (positive) injunction or order of a court instructing a party to perform its contractual obligations, is the exception to the rule. Many reasons have been advanced for this, including policies against voluntary or involuntary servitude and the difficulties and unwillingness of judges to supervise and evaluate the adequacy of performance. Parties to a breach of contract suit are often acrimonious— imagine expending precious public, judicial resources on forcing them to "play nice" rather than just ordering payment of damages and leaving enforcement to the parties and the sheriff. Parties to a contract dispute can generally be expected to act like four year olds if given the chance.

Also possible, of course, is a prohibitory (negative) injunction, ordering the parties not to do anything but perform the contract. We saw one of these at issue in *MGM v. Scheider* in Chapter 2. This sort of decree is easier to enforce but remains tedious and is largely considered a waste of judicial resources if money damages will suffice. Thus, the basic rule: specific performance is only available when money damages are inadequate to compensate the non-breaching party.

This "inadequacy" rule historically led to a few categorical rules. The most common is the rule that contracts for the purchase of real property could be specifically enforced by the purchaser as land was considered "unique." Combining this rule with the principle of mutuality of remedy leads to the rule applicable in some jurisdictions, like Tennessee, that a contract for the purchase or sale of real estate is specifically enforceable against either the buyer or the seller.

While this assumption that land was unique may have been true in an agrarian-based or feudal society, it is certainly subject to doubt in modern America where real estate has largely been turned into a commodity with the spread of suburban sprawl, housing developments, shopping malls, and the rise of the condominium and other forms of shared and fractionalized real estate ownership and control. A member of the American Institute of Appraisers would be hard pressed to find even 5% of the property in the United States that could not be appraised and given a market value through a melding of the comparison approach, the income approach, and the replacement cost approach. The value that a proximate interstate off ramp will bring to your acre of real estate can be measured with precision, commercial or residential, up or down, long before the ramp is ever built.

Thus, the categorical rules, like specific performance of land sales, may be on their way out—but they are not out yet. As the cases in this chapter indicate, the focus of the rules on availability of specific performance and other equitable, non-money-damages relief should return once again to the first principles: the inadequacy of money damages to appropriately compensate the non-breaching party for his or her loss.

As noted above, whatever the direction in which the law is moving in this area, the historical, categorical rules remain in force in most jurisdictions. They also provide easy testing targets for law professors and bar examiners.

The R2d covers specific performance in sections 357 to 369. The UNIDROIT provisions are found in articles 7.2.3 to 7.2.5.

SP   *Available when $ damages does NOT make P whole*

CENTEX HOMES CORP. V. BOAG

Superior Court of New Jersey, Chancery Division
128 N.J. Super. 385, 320 A.2d 194 (1974)

GELMAN, J.

[1] Plaintiff Centex Homes Corporation (Centex) is engaged in the development and construction of a luxury high-rise condominium project in the Boroughs of Cliffside Park and Fort Lee. The project when completed will consist of six 31-story buildings containing in excess of 3,600 condominium apartment units, together with recreational buildings and facilities, parking garages and other common elements associated with this form of residential development. As sponsor of the project Centex offers the condominium apartment units for sale to the public and has filed an offering plan covering such sales with the appropriate regulatory agencies of the States of New Jersey and New York.

[2] On September 13, 1972, defendants Mr. and Mrs. Eugene Boag executed a contract for the purchase of apartment unit No. 2019 in the building under construction and known as "Winston Towers 200." The contract purchase price was $73,700, and prior to signing the contract defendants had given Centex a deposit in the amount of $525. At or shortly after signing the contract defendants delivered to Centex a check in the amount of $6,870 which, together with the deposit, represented approximately 10% of the total purchase of the apartment unit. Shortly thereafter Boag was notified by his employer that he was to be transferred to the Chicago, Illinois, area. Under date of September 27, 1972 he advised Centex that he "would be unable to complete the purchase" agreement and stopped payment on the $6,870 check. Centex deposited the check for

collection approximately two weeks after receiving notice from defendant, but the check was not honored by defendants' bank. On August 8, 1973 Centex instituted this action in Chancery Division for specific performance of the purchase agreement or, in the alternative, for liquidated damages in the amount of $6,870.[1] The matter is presently before this court on the motion of Centex for summary judgment.

[3] Both parties acknowledge, and our research has confirmed, that no court in this State or in the United States has determined in any reported decision whether the equitable remedy of specific performance will lie for the enforcement of a contract for the sale of a condominium apartment. The closest decision on point is *Silverman v. Alcoa Plaza Associates,* 37 A.D. 2d 166, 323 N.Y.S. 2d 39 (App. Div. 1971), which involved a default by a contract-purchaser of shares of stock and a proprietary lease in a cooperative apartment building. The seller, who was also the sponsor of the project, retained the deposit and sold the stock and the lease to a third party for the same purchase price. The original purchaser thereafter brought suit to recover his deposit, and on appeal the court held that the sale of shares of stock in a cooperative apartment building, even though associated with a proprietary lease, was a sale of personalty and not of an interest in real estate. Hence, the seller was not entitled to retain the contract deposit as liquidated damages.[2]

[4] As distinguished from a cooperative plan of ownership such as involved in *Silverman*, under a condominium housing scheme each condominium apartment unit constitutes a separate parcel of real property which may be dealt with in the same manner as any real estate. Upon closing of title the apartment unit owner receives a recordable deed which confers upon him the same rights and subjects him to the same obligations as in the case of traditional forms of real estate ownership, the only difference being that the condominium owner receives in addition an undivided interest in the common elements associated with the building and assigned to each unit.

[5] Centex urges that since the subject matter of the contract is the transfer of a fee interest in real estate, the remedy of specific performance is available to enforce the agreement under principles of equity which are well-settled in this state.

[6] The principle underlying the specific performance remedy is equity's jurisdiction to grant relief where the damage remedy at law is inadequate. The text writers generally agree that at the time this branch of equity jurisdiction was evolving in England, the presumed uniqueness of land as well as its importance to the social order of that era led to the

---

[1] [$6,870 in 1974 dollars is roughly the equivalent of $35,000 in 2019 dollars using the CPI and the GNP Deflator.—Eds.]

[2] Under New York law, if the contract was deemed to be for the sale of realty, the seller could retain the deposit in lieu of damages.

conclusion that damages at law could never be adequate to compensate for the breach of a contract to transfer an interest in land. Hence specific performance became a fixed remedy in this class of transactions. The judicial attitude has remained substantially unchanged and is expressed in Pomeroy as follows:

> [I]n applying this doctrine the courts of equity have established the further rule that in general the legal remedy of damages is inadequate in all agreements for the sale or letting of land, or of any estate therein; and therefore in such class of contracts the jurisdiction is always exercised, and a specific performance granted, unless prevented by other and independent equitable considerations which directly affect the remedial right of the complaining party. . . .

1 Pomeroy, Equity Jurisprudence (5th ed. 1941), § 221(b)

[7] While the inadequacy of the damage remedy suffices to explain the origin of the vendee's right to obtain specific performance in equity, it does not provide a rationale for the availability of the remedy at the instance of the vendor of real estate. Except upon a showing of unusual circumstances or a change in the vendor's position, such as where the vendee has entered into possession, the vendor's damages are usually measurable, his remedy at law is adequate and there is no jurisdictional basis for equitable relief. *But see* Restatement, Contracts § 360, cmt. c.[3] The early English precedents suggest that the availability of the remedy in a suit by a vendor was an outgrowth of the equitable concept of mutuality, i.e., that equity would not specifically enforce an agreement unless the remedy was available to both parties.

[8] So far as can be determined from our decisional law, the mutuality of remedy concept has been the prop which has supported equitable jurisdiction to grant specific performance in actions by vendors of real estate. The earliest reported decision in this State granting specific performance in favor of a vendor is *Rodman v. Zilley,* 1 N.J. Eq.320 (Ch. 1831), in which the vendee (who was also the judgment creditor) was the highest bidder at an execution sale. In his opinion Chancellor Vroom did not address himself to the question whether the vendor had an adequate remedy at law. The first reported discussion of the question occurs in *Hopper v. Hopper,* 16 N.J. Eq. 147 (Ch. 1863), which was an action by a

---

[3] The Restatement's reasoning, as expressed in § 360, comment c, amounts to the inconsistent propositions that (1) because the vendor may not have sustained any damage which is actionable at law, specific performance should be granted, and (2) he would otherwise sustain damage equal to the loss of interest on the proceeds of the sale. Yet loss of interest is readily measurable and can be recovered in an action at law, and to the extent that the vendor has sustained no economic injury, there is no compelling reason for equity to grant to him the otherwise extraordinary remedy of specific performance. At the end of the comment, the author suggests that the vendor is entitled to specific performance because that remedy should be mutual, a concept which is substantially rejected as a decisional basis in §§ 372 and 373 of the Restatement.

SP is an equitable remedy

vendor to compel specific performance of a contract for the sale of land. In answer to the contention that equity lacked jurisdiction because the vendor had an adequate legal remedy, Chancellor Green said (at p. 148):

> It constitutes no objection to the relief prayed for, that the application is made by the vendor to enforce the payment of the purchase money, and not by the vendee to compel a delivery of the title. The vendor has not a complete remedy at law. Pecuniary damages for the breach of the contract is not what the complainant asks, or is entitled to receive at the hands of a court of equity. He asks to receive the price stipulated to be paid in lieu of the land. The doctrine is well established that the remedy is mutual, and that the vendor may maintain his bill in all cases where the purchaser could sue for a specific performance of the agreement.

[9] No other rationale has been offered by our decisions subsequent to Hopper, and specific performance has been routinely granted to vendors without further discussion of the underlying jurisdictional issue.

[10] Our present Supreme Court has squarely held, however, that mutuality of remedy is not an appropriate basis for granting or denying specific performance. *Fleischer v. James Drug Stores,* 1 N.J. 138 (1948); *see also,* Restatement, Contracts § 372; 11 Williston, Contracts (3d ed. 1968), § 1433. The test is whether the obligations of the contract are mutual and not whether each is entitled to precisely the same remedy in the event of a breach. In *Fleischer* plaintiff sought specific performance against a cooperative buying and selling association although his membership contract was terminable by him on 60 days' notice. Justice Heher said:

must be mutual

> And the requisite mutuality is not wanting. The contention contra rests upon the premise that, although the corporation "can terminate the contract only in certain restricted and unusual circumstances," any "member" may withdraw at any time by merely giving notice.

> Clearly, there is mutuality of obligation, for until his withdrawal complainant is under a continuing obligation of performance in the event of performance by the corporation. It is not essential that the remedy of specific performance be mutual . . . The modern view is that the rule of mutuality of remedy is satisfied if the decree of specific performance operates effectively against both parties and gives to each the benefit of a mutual obligation . . .

> The fact that the remedy of specific enforcement is available to one party to a contract is not in itself a sufficient reason for making the remedy available to the other; but it may be decisive when the adequacy of damages is difficult to determine and there is no other reason for refusing specific enforcement. It is not

necessary, to serve the ends of equal justice, that the parties shall have identical remedies in case of breach.

[11] The disappearance of the mutuality of remedy doctrine from our law dictates the conclusion that specific performance relief should no longer be automatically available to a vendor of real estate, but should be confined to those special instances where a vendor will otherwise suffer an economic injury for which his damage remedy at law will not be adequate, or where other equitable considerations require that the relief be granted. As Chancellor Vroom noted in *King v. Morford,* 1 N.J. Eq.274, 281–282 (Ch. Div. 1831), whether a contract should be specifically enforced is always a matter resting in the sound discretion of the court and considerable caution should be used in decreeing the specific performance of agreements, and . . . the court is bound to see that it really does the complete justice which it aims at, and which is the ground of its jurisdiction.

[12] Here the subject matter of the real estate transaction—a condominium apartment unit—has no unique quality but is one of hundreds of virtually identical units being offered by a developer for sale to the public. The units are sold by means of sample, in this case model apartments, in much the same manner as items of personal property are sold in the market place. The sales prices for the units are fixed in accordance with schedule filed by Centex as part of its offering plan, and the only variance as between apartments having the same floor plan (of which six plans are available) is the floor level or the building location within the project. In actuality, the condominium apartment units, regardless of their realty label, share the same characteristics as personal property.

[13] From the foregoing one must conclude that the damages sustained by a condominium sponsor resulting from the breach of the sales agreement are readily measurable and the damage remedy at law is wholly adequate. No compelling reasons have been shown by Centex for the granting of specific performance relief and its complaint is therefore dismissed as to the first count.

[14] Centex also seeks money damages pursuant to a liquidated damage clause in its contract with the defendants. It is sufficient to note only that under the language of that clause (which was authored by Centex) liquidated damages are limited to such moneys as were paid by defendant at the time the default occurred. Since the default here consisted of the defendant's stopping payment of his check for the balance of the down-payment, Centex's liquidated damages are limited to the retention of the "moneys paid" prior to that date, or the initial $525 deposit. Accordingly, the second count of the complaint for damage relief will also be dismissed.

NOTES AND QUESTIONS

1.   A condominium is a form of ownership of real estate in which the owner of each unit owns parts of the real estate herself. She owns a fee simple interest in the three-dimensional space which she occupies and a proportional interest in the "common areas" (halls, walls, floor, roof, grounds, etc.) as a tenant-in-common with the owners of the other units. In a cooperative apartment building, the owner does not really own his apartment. Instead, the entire building is owned by a corporation. When the buyer "buys an apartment" in a co-op (in the terminology used) he actually gets stock in the corporation and a perpetual lease of his individual apartment. The co-op form of ownership evolved before condominium ownership. The condominium form of ownership is generally considered to be superior, but in New York and other East coast jurisdictions, cooperatives were prevalent before condominiums were established and lawyers still use the cooperative form of ownership because it is customary, they are used to it, and there is a great deal of case law to rely on. The condominium form of ownership is prevalent in Florida and on the West Coast and is generally the form of shared ownership that is being adopted in areas that are experiencing growth of this sort and lack a historical bias toward cooperatives.

2.   Good lawyers are always on the lookout for situations where people are trying to "elevate form over substance." For example, suppose that Fish approaches Shark for a Loan, offering to give Shark a mortgage on Fish's home as security. Shark wants to avoid laws regulating loans and mortgages, so he tells Fish: "I'll buy your house for $100,000. You can buy it back from me any time in the next year for $120,000. In the meantime, you can continue to live in it rent free." A court would have no trouble deciding that although this transaction was in *form* a sale, lease, and option to repurchase, it was in *substance* a loan and mortgage. The court would normally apply to it all the laws pertaining to loans and mortgages, including laws limiting the amount of interest that can be charged.

3.   In the case discussed in paragraph 3, was the court elevating form over substance? Can you think of a good reason why the court might be justified in elevating form over substance in that situation?

WALGREEN CO. v. SARA CREEK PROPERTY CO.

United States Court of Appeals, Seventh Circuit
966 F.2d 273 (1992)

POSNER, CIRCUIT JUDGE.

[1] This appeal from the grant of a permanent injunction raises fundamental issues concerning the propriety of injunctive relief. The essential facts are simple. Walgreen has operated a pharmacy in the Southgate Mall in Milwaukee since its opening in 1951. Its current lease,

signed in 1971 and carrying a 30-year, 6-month term, contains, as had the only previous lease, a clause in which the landlord, Sara Creek, promises not to lease space in the mall to anyone else who wants to operate a pharmacy or a store containing a pharmacy. . . .[4] [We affirm.—Eds.]

[2] In 1990, fearful that its largest tenant—what in real estate parlance is called the "anchor tenant"—having gone broke was about to close its store, Sara Creek informed Walgreen that it intended to buy out the anchor tenant and install in its place a discount store operated by Phar-Mor Corporation, a "deep discount" chain, rather than, like Walgreen, just a "discount" chain. Phar-Mor's store would occupy 100,000 square feet, of which 12,000 would be occupied by a pharmacy the same size as Walgreen's. The entrances to the two stores would be within a couple of hundred feet of each other.

[3] Walgreen filed this diversity suit for breach of contract against Sara Creek and Phar-Mor and asked for an injunction against Sara Creek's letting the anchor premises to Phar-Mor. After an evidentiary hearing, the judge found a breach of Walgreen's lease and entered a permanent injunction against Sara Creek's letting the anchor tenant premises to Phar-Mor until the expiration of Walgreen's lease. He did this over the defendants' objection that Walgreen had failed to show that its remedy at law—damages—for the breach of the exclusivity clause was inadequate. Sara Creek had put on an expert witness who testified that Walgreen's damages could be readily estimated, and Walgreen had countered with evidence from its employees that its damages would be very difficult to compute, among other reasons because they included intangibles such as loss of goodwill.

[4] Sara Creek reminds us that damages are the norm in breach of contract as in other cases. Many breaches, it points out, are "efficient," in the sense that they allow resources to be moved into a more valuable use. Perhaps this is one—the value of Phar-Mor's occupancy of the anchor premises may exceed the cost to Walgreen of facing increased competition. If so, society will be better off if Walgreen is paid its damages, equal to that cost, and Phar-Mor is allowed to move in rather than being kept out by an

---

[4]   [A provision like this might read as follows:

For so long as Walgreen occupies or leases space in the Parcel, it is expressly agreed that neither all nor any portion of the Parcel shall be used, directly or indirectly, for any one or more of the following purposes: (i) the operation of a drug store or a so-called prescription pharmacy or for any other purpose requiring a qualified pharmacist or other person authorized by law to dispense medicinal drugs, directly or indirectly, for a fee or remuneration of any kind; (ii) the sale of so-called health and/or beauty aids and/or drug sundries; (iii) the operation of a business in which greeting cards and/or gift wrap shall be offered for sale; (iv) the operation of a business in which food shall be sold for off premises consumption; (v) the sale of alcoholic beverages; (vi) the operation of a medical diagnostic lab, and/or (vii) the operation of a business in which photofinishing services and/or photographic film are offered for sale.

The quoted provision is from a Walgreen transactional document in an unrelated deal.—Eds.]

injunction. That is why injunctions are not granted as a matter of course, but only when the plaintiff's damages remedy is inadequate. Walgreen's is not, Sara Creek argues; the projection of business losses due to increased competition is a routine exercise in calculation. Damages representing either the present value of lost future profits or (what should be the equivalent) the diminution in the value of the leasehold have either been awarded or deemed the proper remedy in a number of reported cases for breach of an exclusivity clause in a shopping-center lease. [The court cited 7 cases and an A.L.R. annotation.—Eds.] Why, Sara Creek asks, should they not be adequate here?

[5] Sara Creek makes a beguiling argument that contains much truth, but we do not think it should carry the day. For if, as just noted, damages have been awarded in some cases of breach of an exclusivity clause in a shopping-center lease, injunctions have been issued in others. [Here, the court cited six cases.—Eds.] The choice between remedies requires a balancing of the costs and benefits of the alternatives. The task of striking the balance is for the trial judge, subject to deferential appellate review in recognition of its particularistic, judgmental, fact-bound character. As we said in an appeal from a grant of a preliminary injunction—but the point is applicable to review of a permanent injunction as well—"The question for us [appellate judges] is whether the [district] judge exceeded the bounds of permissible choice in the circumstances, not what we would have done if we had been in his shoes." *Roland Machinery Co. v. Dresser Industries, Inc.,* 749 F.2d 380, 390 (7th Cir. 1984).

[6] The plaintiff who seeks an injunction has the burden of persuasion—damages are the norm, so the plaintiff must show why his case is abnormal. But when, as in this case, the issue is whether to grant a permanent injunction, not whether to grant a temporary one, the burden is to show that damages are inadequate, not that the denial of the injunction will work irreparable harm. "Irreparable" in the injunction context means not rectifiable by the entry of a final judgment. It has nothing to do with whether to grant a permanent injunction, which, in the usual case anyway, is the final judgment. The use of "irreparable harm" or "irreparable injury" as synonyms for inadequate remedy at law is a confusing usage. It should be avoided. Owen M. Fiss & Doug Rendleman, Injunctions 59 (2d ed. 1984).

[7] The benefits of substituting an injunction for damages are twofold. First, it shifts the burden of determining the cost of the defendant's conduct from the court to the parties. If it is true that Walgreen's damages are smaller than the gain to Sara Creek from allowing a second pharmacy into the shopping mall, then there must be a price for dissolving the injunction that will make both parties better off. Thus, the effect of upholding the injunction would be to substitute for the costly processes of forensic fact determination the less costly processes of private negotiation.

[handwritten margin note: Court has issued both remedies]

Second, a premise of our free-market system, and the lesson of experience here and abroad as well, is that prices and costs are more accurately determined by the market than by government. A battle of experts is a less reliable method of determining the actual cost to Walgreen of facing new competition than negotiations between Walgreen and Sara Creek over the price at which Walgreen would feel adequately compensated for having to face that competition.

[8]   That is the benefit side of injunctive relief but there is a cost side as well. Many injunctions require continuing supervision by the court, and that is costly. . . . Some injunctions are problematic because they impose costs on third parties. A more subtle cost of injunctive relief arises from the situation that economists call "bilateral monopoly," in which two parties can deal only with each other: the situation that an injunction creates. The sole seller of widgets selling to the sole buyer of that product would be an example. But so will be the situation confronting Walgreen and Sara Creek if the injunction is upheld. Walgreen can "sell" its injunctive right only to Sara Creek, and Sara Creek can "buy" Walgreen's surrender of its right to enjoin the leasing of the anchor tenant's space to Phar-Mor only from Walgreen. The lack of alternatives in bilateral monopoly creates a bargaining range, and the costs of negotiating to a point within that range may be high. Suppose the cost to Walgreen of facing the competition of Phar-Mor at the Southgate Mall would be $1 million, and the benefit to Sara Creek of leasing to Phar-Mor would be $2 million. Then at any price between those figures for a waiver of Walgreen's injunctive right both parties would be better off, and we expect parties to bargain around a judicial assignment of legal rights if the assignment is inefficient. R.H. Coase, "The Problem of Social Cost," 3 J. Law & Econ. 1 (1960). But each of the parties would like to engross as much of the bargaining range as possible—Walgreen to press the price toward $2 million, Phar-Mor to depress it toward $1 million. With so much at stake, both parties will have an incentive to devote substantial resources of time and money to the negotiation process. The process may even break down, if one or both parties wants to create for future use a reputation as a hard bargainer; and if it does break down, the injunction will have brought about an inefficient result. All these are in one form or another costs of the injunctive process that can be avoided by substituting damages.

[9]   The costs and benefits of the damages remedy are the mirror of those of the injunctive remedy. The damages remedy avoids the cost of continuing supervision and third-party effects, and the cost of bilateral monopoly as well. It imposes costs of its own, however, in the form of diminished accuracy in the determination of value, on the one hand, and of the parties' expenditures on preparing and presenting evidence of damages, and the time of the court in evaluating the evidence, on the other.

[10] The weighing up of all these costs and benefits is the analytical procedure that is or at least should be employed by a judge asked to enter a permanent injunction, with the understanding that if the balance is even the injunction should be withheld. The judge is not required to explicate every detail of the analysis and he did not do so here, but as long we are satisfied that his approach is broadly consistent with a proper analysis we shall affirm; and we are satisfied here. The determination of Walgreen's damages would have been costly in forensic resources and inescapably inaccurate. The lease had ten years to run. So Walgreen would have had to project its sales revenues and costs over the next ten years, and then project the impact on those figures of Phar-Mor's competition, and then discount that impact to present value. All but the last step would have been fraught with uncertainty.

[11] To summarize, the judge did not exceed the bounds of reasonable judgment in concluding that the costs (including forgone benefits) of the damages remedy would exceed the costs (including forgone benefits) of an injunction. We need not consider whether, as intimated by Walgreen, exclusivity clauses in shopping-center leases should be considered presumptively enforceable by injunctions. Although we have described the choice between legal and equitable remedies as one for case-by-case determination, the courts have sometimes picked out categories of cases in which injunctive relief is made the norm. The best-known example is specific performance of contracts for the sale of real property. The rule that specific performance will be ordered in such cases as a matter of course is a generalization of the considerations discussed above. Because of the absence of a fully liquid market in real property and the frequent presence of subjective values (many a homeowner, for example, would not sell his house for its market value), the calculation of damages is difficult; and since an order of specific performance to convey a piece of property does not create a continuing relation between the parties, the costs of supervision and enforcement if specific performance is ordered are slight. The exclusivity clause in Walgreen's lease relates to real estate, but we hesitate to suggest that every contract involving real estate should be enforceable as a matter of course by injunctions. Suppose Sara Creek had covenanted to keep the entrance to Walgreen's store free of ice and snow, and breached the covenant. An injunction would require continuing supervision, and it would be easy enough if the injunction were denied for Walgreen to hire its own ice and snow remover and charge the cost to Sara Creek. On the other hand, injunctions to enforce exclusivity clauses are quite likely to be justifiable by just the considerations present here—damages are difficult to estimate with any accuracy and the injunction is a one-shot remedy requiring no continuing judicial involvement. So there is an argument for

making injunctive relief presumptively appropriate in such cases, but we need not decide in this case how strong an argument.

AFFIRMED.

Campbell Soup Co. v. Wentz
United States Court of Appeals, Third Circuit
172 F.2d 80 (1948)

Goodrich, J.

[1] These are appeals from judgments of the District Court denying equitable relief to the buyer under a contract for the sale of carrots . . .

[2] The transactions which raise the issues may be briefly summarized. On June 21, 1947, Campbell Soup Company (Campbell), a New Jersey corporation, entered into a written contract with George B. Wentz and Harry T. Wentz, who are Pennsylvania farmers, for delivery by the Wentzes to Campbell of all the Chantenay red cored carrots to be grown on fifteen acres of the Went farm during the 1947 season. Where the contract was entered into does not appear. The contract provides, however, for delivery of the carrots at the Campbell plant in Camden, New Jersey. The prices specified in the contract ranged from $23 to $30 per ton according to the time of delivery. The contract price for January, 1948 was $30 a ton.

[3] The Wentzes harvested approximately 100 tons of carrots from the fifteen acres covered by the contract. Early in January, 1948, they told a Campbell representative that they would not deliver their carrots at the contract price. The market price at that time was at least $90 per ton, and Chantenay red cored carrots were virtually unobtainable. The Wentzes then sold approximately 62 tons of their carrots to the defendant Lojeski, a neighboring farmer. Lojeski resold about 58 tons on the open market, approximately half to Campbell and the balance to other purchasers.

[4] On January 9, 1948, Campbell, suspecting that Lojeski was selling it "contract carrots," refused to purchase any more, and instituted these suits against the Wentz brothers and Lojeski to enjoin further sale of the contract carrots to others, and to compel specific performance of the contract. The trial court denied equitable relief. We agree with the result reached, but on a different ground from that relied upon by the District Court.

[5] The case has been presented by both sides as though *Erie Railroad v. Tompkins,* 1938, 304 U.S. 64, 58 S.Ct. 817, 82 L.Ed. 1188, 114 A.L.R. 1487, and *Klaxon Company v. Stentor Electric Manufacturing Co., Inc.,* 1941, 313 U.S. 487, 61 S.Ct. 1020, 85 L.Ed. 1477, had never been

decided. We are not advised as to the place of the contract, although as we have pointed out in other cases, the Pennsylvania conflict of laws rule, which binds us here, refers matters concerning the validity and extent of obligation of the contract to the place of making. In this instance, however, the absence of data on which to base a rule of reference does not preclude the decision of the case. We have said several times in this Circuit that the question of the form of relief is a matter for a federal court to decide. But neither federal decisions nor the law of New Jersey or Pennsylvania as expressed in the Uniform Sales Act differ upon this point. A party may have specific performance of a contract for the sale of chattels if the legal remedy is inadequate. Inadequacy of the legal remedy is necessarily a matter to be determined by an examination of the facts in each particular instance.

[6] We think that on the question of adequacy of the legal remedy the case is one appropriate for specific performance. It was expressly found that at the time of the trial it was "virtually impossible to obtain Chantenay carrots in the open market." This Chantenay carrot is one which the plaintiff uses in large quantities, furnishing the seed to the growers with whom it makes contracts. It was not claimed that in nutritive value it is any better than other types of carrots. Its blunt shape makes it easier to handle in processing. And its color and texture differ from other varieties. The color is brighter than other carrots. The trial court found that the plaintiff failed to establish what proportion of its carrots is used for the production of soup stock and what proportion is used as identifiable physical ingredients in its soups. We do not think lack of proof on that point is material. It did appear that the plaintiff uses carrots in fifteen of its twenty-one soups. It also appeared that it uses these Chantenay carrots diced in some of them and that the appearance is uniform. The preservation of uniformity in appearance in a food article marketed throughout the country and sold under the manufacturer's name is a matter of considerable commercial significance and one which is properly considered in determining whether a substitute ingredient is just as good as the original.

[7] The trial court concluded that the plaintiff had failed to establish that the carrots, "judged by objective standards," are unique goods. This we think is not a pure fact conclusion like a finding that Chantenay carrots are of uniform color. It is either a conclusion of law or of mixed fact and law and we are bound to exercise our independent judgment upon it. That the test for specific performance is not necessarily "objective" is shown by the many cases in which equity has given it to enforce contracts for articles—family heirlooms and the like—the value of which was personal to the plaintiff.

[8] Judged by the general standards applicable to determining the adequacy of the legal remedy, we think that on this point the case is a

proper one for equitable relief. There is considerable authority, old and new, showing liberality in the granting of an equitable remedy. We see no reason why a court should be reluctant to grant specific relief when it can be given without supervision of the court or other time-consuming processes against one who has deliberately broken his agreement. Here the goods of the special type contracted for were unavailable on the open market, the plaintiff had contracted for them long ahead in anticipation of its needs, and had built up a general reputation for its products as part of which reputation uniform appearance was important. We think if this were all that was involved in the case specific performance should have been granted.

[9]   The reason that we shall affirm instead of reversing with an order for specific performance is found in the contract itself. We think it is too hard a bargain and too one-sided an agreement to entitle the plaintiff to relief in a court of conscience. For each individual grower the agreement is made by filling in names and quantity and price on a printed form furnished by the buyer. This form has quite obviously been drawn by skillful draftsmen with the buyer's interests in mind.

[10] Paragraph 2 provides for the manner of delivery. Carrots are to have their stalks cut off and be in clean sanitary bags or other containers approved by Campbell. This paragraph concludes with a statement that Campbell's determination of conformance with specifications shall be conclusive.

[11] The defendants attack this provision as unconscionable. We do not think that it is, standing by itself. We think that the provision is comparable to the promise to perform to the satisfaction of another and that Campbell would be held liable if it refused carrots which did in fact conform to the specifications.

[12] The next paragraph allows Campbell to refuse carrots in excess of twelve tons to the acre. The next contains a covenant by the grower that he will not sell carrots to anyone else except the carrots rejected by Campbell nor will he permit anyone else to grow carrots on his land. Paragraph 10 provides liquidated damages to the extent of $50 per acre for any breach by the grower. There is no provision for liquidated or any other damages for breach of contract by Campbell.

[13] The provision of the contract which we think is the hardest is paragraph 9, set out in the margin.[5] It will be noted that Campbell is

---

[5]   Grower shall not be obligated to deliver any Carrots which he is unable to harvest or deliver, nor shall Campbell be obligated to receive or pay for any Carrots which it is unable to inspect, grade, receive, handle, use or pack at or ship in processed form from its plants in Camden (1) because of any circumstance beyond the control of Grower or Campbell, as the case may be, or (2) because of any labor disturbance, work stoppage, slow-down, or strike involving any of Campbell's employees. Campbell shall not be liable for any delay in receiving Carrots due to any of the above contingencies. During periods when Campbell is unable to receive Grower's Carrots,

excused from accepting carrots under certain circumstances. But even under such circumstances the grower, while he cannot say Campbell is liable for failure to take the carrots, is not permitted to sell them elsewhere unless Campbell agrees. This is the kind of provision which the late Francis H. Bohlen[6] would call "carrying a good joke too far." What the grower may do with his product under the circumstances set out is not clear. He has covenanted not to store it anywhere except on his own farm and also not to sell to anybody else.

[14] We are not suggesting that the contract is illegal. Nor are we suggesting any excuse for the grower in this case who has deliberately broken an agreement entered into with Campbell. We do think, however, that a party who has offered and succeeded in getting an agreement as tough as this one is, should not come to a chancellor and ask court help in the enforcement of its terms. That equity does not enforce unconscionable bargains is too well established to require elaborate citation.

[15] The plaintiff argues that the provisions of the contract are separable. We agree that they are, but do not think that decisions separating out certain provisions from illegal contracts are in point here. As already said, we do not suggest that this contract is illegal. All we say is that the sum total of its provisions drives too hard a bargain for a court of conscience to assist.

[16] This disposition of the problem makes unnecessary further discussion of the separate liability of Lojeski, who was not a party to the contract, but who purchased some of the carrots from the Wentzes.

The judgments will be affirmed.

———

NOTE

After the end of the 1959 college football regular season the New York Giants of the National Football League attempted to sign University of Mississippi star Charlie Flowers to an NFL contract before he could sign with the rival American Football League (later merged into the NFL as the AFC). Flowers balked because NCAA rules barred a player who had signed a pro contract from bowl games. To allow Flowers to play in the Sugar Bowl (where he played against Billy Cannon, whose contract problems are described in a note following *Beard Implement Company* in Chapter 3), the Giants agreed to keep the contract secret. Upon receiving assurances that the contract would be

---

Grower may, with Campbell's written consent, dispose of his Carrots elsewhere. Grower may not, however, sell or otherwise dispose of any Carrots which he is unable to deliver to Campbell.

6   [Francis H. Bohlen was at one time the Dean of the University of Pennsylvania Law School. Apparently he was well-known at the time this opinion was written.—Eds.]

kept secret, Flowers signed and received a bonus of $3,500.[7] (This is not a typo. That's what players made in those days.) Like Mr. Cannon's contract, this contract also provided that it became valid and binding only upon approval by the Commissioner of the National Football League. Part of the deal between Flowers and the Giants was that the Giants would not submit the contract to the commissioner until after the Sugar Bowl. Flowers had a change of heart, and in early December, he told the Giants he wanted to get out of the deal. The Giants responded by submitting the contract to the commissioner, who approved it on December 15 with the understanding that the approval wouldn't be announced until after the Sugar Bowl. On December 29, three days before the Sugar Bowl, Mr. Flowers negotiated a better deal with the Los Angeles Chargers of the American Football League (now the San Diego Chargers of the NFL). This contract was not formally executed until after the Sugar Bowl. Also on December 29, Mr. Flowers wrote the Giants a letter telling them the deal was off and returning their bonus check uncashed.

The Giants sued Mr. Flowers and the Chargers in federal court, seeking specific performance of his contract with them, or, in the alternative, an injunction prohibiting him from playing for the Chargers. The trial court held that the commissioner's approval of the Flowers/Giants contract was not effective because the contract had been submitted to him in violation of the parties' understanding.

On appeal the Fifth Circuit took a different approach:

> Without considering the legal issues on the merits, we affirm the judgment of the trial court. We do so by application of the age-old, but sometimes overlooked doctrine that "he who comes into equity must come with clean hands." . . . That doctrine is rooted in the historical concept of the court of equity as a vehicle for affirmatively enforcing the requirements of conscience and good faith. This presupposes a refusal on its part to be the abettor of inequity.

New York Football Giants, Inc. v. Los Angeles Chargers Football Club, Inc., 291 F.2d 471, 473–74 (5th Cir. 1961). The court said that the "deceit" practiced by the Giants barred them from being the beneficiaries of any equitable remedy.

———

LUMLEY V. WAGNER

Lord Chancellor's Court
1 De. G.M. & G. 604, 42 Eng. Rep. 687 (1852)

[1]   LORD ST. LYONS, LORD CHANCELLOR. The question which I have to decide in the present case arises out of a very simple contract, the effect of which is, that the Defendant Johanna Wagner should sing at Her Majesty's Theatre for a certain number of nights, and that she should not

---

[7] $3,500 in 1959 dollars is roughly the equivalent of $30,000 in 2019 dollars using the CPI and the GNP Deflator.

sing elsewhere (for that is the true construction) during that period. As I understand the points taken by the Defendant's counsel in support of this appeal they in effect come to this, namely, that a Court of Equity ought not to grant an injunction except in cases connected with specific performance, or where the injunction being to compel a party to forbear from committing an act (and not to perform an act), that injunction will complete the whole of the agreement remaining unexecuted.

[2]   Wherever this court has not proper jurisdiction to enforce specific performance, it operates to bind men's consciences, as far as they can be bound, to a true and literal performance of their agreements; and it will not suffer them to depart from their contracts at their pleasure, leaving the party with whom they have contracted to the mere chance of any damages which a jury may give. The exercise of this jurisdiction has, I believe, had a wholesome tendency towards the maintenance of that good faith which exists in this country to a much greater degree perhaps than in any other; and although the jurisdiction is not to be extended, yet a Judge would desert his duty who did not act up to what his predecessors have handed down as the rule for his guidance in the administration of such an equity.

[3]   It was objected that the operation of the injunction in the present case was mischievous, excluding the Defendant J. Wagner from performing at any other theatre while this Court had no power to compel her to perform at Her Majesty's Theatre. It is true that I have not the means of compelling her to sing, but she has no cause of complaint if I compel her to abstain from the commission of an act which she has bound herself not to do, and thus possibly cause her to fulfil her engagement. The jurisdiction which I now exercise is wholly within the power of the Court, and being of opinion that it is a proper case for interfering, I shall leave nothing unsatisfied by the judgment I pronounce. The effect, too, of the injunction is restraining J. Wagner from singing elsewhere may, in the event of an action being brought against her by the Plaintiff, prevent any such amount of vindictive damages being given against her as a jury might probably be inclined to give if she had carried her talents and exercised them at the rival theatre: the injunction may also, as I have said, tend to the fulfillment of her engagement; though, in continuing the injunction, I disclaim doing indirectly what I cannot do directly.

[4]   Referring again to the authorities, I am well aware that they have not been uniform, and that there undoubtedly has been a difference of decision on the question now revived before me; but, after the best consideration which I have been enabled to give to the subject, the conclusion at which I have arrived is, I conceive, supported by the greatest weight of authority.

———

NOTES AND QUESTIONS

The remedies clause in Trista Rehn's contract for the reality-based television program "The Bachelorette," which we looked at when discussing liquidated damages in the previous chapter, is a little one-sided:

> E. *Remedies*: I acknowledge and agree that the rights I have granted hereunder and my participation related thereto are unique, unusual, special and extraordinary, the loss of which would not be adequately compensable in damages in an action at law. I further agree that, in addition to any rights or remedies which Producer may have under this Agreement or otherwise, Producer therefore would be entitled to all available equitable remedies in case of my breach or threatened breach of this Agreement. Any remedies, rights, undertakings and obligations contained in this Agreement shall be cumulative. No remedies, rights, undertakings, or obligations shall be in limitation of any other remedy, rights, undertaking, or obligation of either party. No breach of this Agreement shall entitle me to terminate or rescind the rights granted to Producer or the Network herein. I hereby waive the right, in the event of any such breach by Producer or the Network, to equitable relief or to enjoin, restrain or interfere with the exercise of any of the Granted Rights, it being my understanding that my sole remedy shall be the right to recover monetary damages with respect to any such breach.

The term "Granted Rights" is defined in the contract to include all the rights granted to the producer and the network under the contract, which are pretty broad:

> The unconditional right throughout the universe in perpetuity to use, simulate or portray (and to authorize others to do so) or to refrain from using, simulating or portraying, my name, likeness (whether photographic or otherwise), voice, personality, personal identification or personal experiences (including without limitation, whether I am clothed, partially clothed or naked, whether I am aware of or unaware of such photographing, videotaping, filming, or recording, and by requiring me to wear a microphone at all times), my life story, biographical data, incidents, situations and events which heretofore occurred or hereafter occur, including without limitation the right to use, or to authorize others to use any of the foregoing in or in connection with the Series (or any episode or portion thereof) and the distribution, exhibition, advertising, promoting or publicizing of the Series or any Series episode by Producer, the Network, its operations, activities or programming services and with any merchandise, tie-in, product or service of any kind where such use is made in conjunction with a reference to the Series by Producer, the Network, or any of its programming services, but not so as to constitute a direct endorsement of any other product or service.

1.   How would you explain to Ms. Rehn what the remedies clause means?

2.   Suppose you were representing the producer in a suit against Ms. Rehn and the producer wanted to get equitable relief. How would you distinguish *Campbell Soup Co. v. Wentz*?

LAWYERING SKILLS PROBLEM

Suppose that you want to draft a contract so as to make it more likely that a court will specifically enforce an agreement. What sort of provisions would you draft in light of the case law on the subject? Remember, the key is to read the cases to see what the courts were looking for in order to grant specific performance and then to draft into that standard and out of or around any prohibitions on the remedy.

CHAPTER 23

EXPRESS CONDITIONS

. . .

Read R2d § 224. There is no specific corollary in the UNIDROIT Principles.

If there is one contract law concept that is used everyday in the practice of law, it is express conditions. Express conditions, and their close relatives, events of default and remedies, are what put "teeth" in contracts and protect clients each step along the way as a deal progresses. The beauty of express conditions is their simplicity—properly drafted, they are like a club; crude, perhaps, but effective. If *x*, then *y*; if not *x*, then no *y*, [and then *z*].

used in everyday practice of law.

To be effective, conditions must be carefully drafted and integrated into the rest of the contract. First, one must take care to clearly draft the condition so its terms are clear. Conditions generally trigger duties (found in clauses using the verb "shall") or rights (found in clauses using the word "may"). The reader of the contract must be able to determine when the condition is satisfied and, if it is satisfied or not, what consequences follow. Historically, conditions have not been favored by the law and have been strictly construed against the party attempting to rely on one, particularly if that party drafted the agreement. Thus, precise word choice is key.

In most contract negotiations, one party will seek to include many conditions, especially conditions to closing or to other points at which substantial rights are transferred or vest, and the other party will try to limit the number of conditions to the absolute minimum. For example, in a purchase and sale agreement like the one in the Introduction to this text, the seller will try to limit the conditions to closing to as few *objective* conditions as possible, such as any needed third party approvals and the lack of any prohibitory injunction or other adverse ruling by governing bodies. By doing so, the seller is seeking to lock the buyer into the deal and allow as little wiggle room as possible to avoid having the buyer back out (or threaten to do so unless they receive better terms and additional consideration).

The buyer, on the other hand, will want to build in as many conditions, and to keep these conditions as *subjective* and dependent upon the buyer's own judgment, as possible. By doing so, the buyer can more easily walk away if due diligence[1] reveals that things are other than as expected or, alternatively enjoy the opportunity to later renegotiate terms in exchange for a waiver of the condition. For example, buyers may seek to include the condition that due diligence will conclude with satisfactory results as judged by the buyer "in its sole discretion." This sort of condition can also be framed as "lack of material adverse change" condition to closing. *See generally* In re IBP, Inc. Shareholders Litig., 789 A.2d 14 (Del. Ch. 2001) (refusing to allow party to invoke a material adverse change provision to cancel merger and discussing case law regarding similar provisions). In such a clause it is important to define what "material" and "adverse" and even "change" means and who determines whether the condition has been met. To the extent that vagueness remains, it should be vagueness in favor of your client, not the other side.

Parties can waive and courts can ignore conditions. Contracts are often full of clauses providing that a party's failure to act or enforce a right or remedy shall not be deemed to be a waiver of that right, and that any waiver of a current right shall not be a waiver of any other right or a future incidence of the same right.

Thus, express conditions are some of the most important tools that lawyers use to protect their clients' interests. They are not foolproof, however, as a court must be willing to enforce them. The case that follows demonstrates how effective they can be when strictly enforced.

P appeals — won at trial level

DOVE v. ROSE ACRE FARMS

Court of Appeals of Indiana
434 N.E.2d 931 (1982)

NEAL, JUDGE.

Cause of action

[1] Plaintiff-appellant Mark Dove (Dove) appeals a negative judgment of the Decatur Circuit Court in favor of defendant-appellee Rose Acre Farms, Inc. in a trial before the court without the intervention of a jury.

We affirm.

Statement of the Facts

Dove employed by. D

[2] The evidence most favorable to support the judgment and the facts found specially by the trial court are as follows. Dove had been employed by Rose Acre Farms, operated by David Rust (Rust), its president and principal owner, in the summers and other times from 1972 to 1979. The

---

[1] "Due diligence" refers to the process by which the buyer and its agents (attorneys, accountants, building inspectors, etc.) investigate "with due diligence" the property that is being purchased or other aspects of the deal.

business of Rose Acre was the production of eggs, and, stocked with 4,000,000 hens and staffed with 300 employees, it produced approximately 256,000 dozen eggs per day. Rust had instituted and maintained extensive bonus programs, some of which were for one day only, or one event or activity only. For example, one bonus was the white car bonus; if an employee would buy a new white car, keep it clean and undamaged, place a Rose Acre sign on it, commit no tardiness or absenteeism, and attend one management meeting per month, Rose Acre would pay $100 per month for 36 months as a bonus above and beyond the employee's regular salary, to apply on payments. Any slight violation, such as being a minute late for work, driving a dirty or damaged car, or missing work for any cause, would work a forfeiture of the bonus. Other bonuses consisted of egg production bonuses, deed conversion bonuses, house management bonuses, and a silver feather bonus. This last bonus program required the participant to wear a silver feather, and a system of rewards and penalties existed for employees who participated. While the conditions of the bonuses varied, one condition existed in all bonus programs: during the period of the bonus, the employee must not be tardy for even a minute, and must not miss work any day for any cause whatever, even illness. If the employee missed any days during the week, he was sometimes permitted to make them up on Saturday and/or Sunday. Any missed work not made up within the same week worked a forfeiture of the bonus. These rules were explained to the employees and were stated in a written policy. The bonus programs were voluntary, and all the employees did not choose to participate in them. When a bonus was offered a card was issued to the participant stating his name and the terms and amount of the bonus. Upon completion of the required tasks, the card was attached to the pay sheet, and the bonus was added to the paycheck. Rust was strict about tardiness and absenteeism, whether an employee was on a bonus program or not. If an employee was tardy, his pay would be docked to the minimum wage, or he would be sent home and lose an entire day. A minute's tardiness would also deprive the employee of a day for purposes of seniority. As was stated in the evidence, bonuses were given for the "extra mile" or actions "above and beyond the call of duty." The purpose of the bonus programs and penalties was to discourage absenteeism and tardiness, and to promote motivation and dependability.

[3] In June 1979, Rust called in Dove and other construction crew leaders and offered a bonus of $6,000 each if certain detailed construction work was completed in 12 weeks. As Dove conceded in his own testimony, the bonus card indicated that in addition to completing the work, he would be required to work at least five full days a week for 12 weeks to qualify for the bonus. On the same day Dove's bonus agreement, by mutual consent, was amended to ten weeks with a bonus of $5,000 to enable him to return to law school by September 1. Dove testified that there was no ambiguity in the agreement, and he understood that to qualify for the bonus he would

have to work ten weeks, five days a week, commencing at starting time and quitting only at quitting time. Dove testified that he was aware of the provisions concerning absenteeism and tardiness as they affected bonuses, and that if he missed any work, for any reason, including illness, he would forfeit the bonus. The evidence disclosed that no exception had ever been made except as may have occurred by clerical error or inadvertence.

[4] In the tenth week Dove came down with strep throat. On Thursday of that week he reported to work with a temperature of 104 degrees, and told Rust that he was unable to work. Rust told him, in effect, that if he went home, he would forfeit the bonus. Rust offered him the opportunity to stay there and lay on a couch, or make up his lost days on Saturday and/or Sunday. Rust told him he could sleep and still qualify for the bonus. Dove left to seek medical treatment and missed two days in the tenth week of the bonus program.

[5] Rust refused Dove the bonus based solely upon his missing the two days of work. While there was some question of whether the construction job was finished, Rust does not seem to have made that issue the basis of his refusal. Bonuses to other crew leaders were paid. The trial court denied Dove's recovery and, in the conclusions of law, stated that Dove had not shown that all of the conditions of the bonus contract had been met. Specifically, Dove failed to work five full days a week for ten weeks.

* * *

[6] Dove argues that the bonus agreement was implemented to (1) insure his presence on the construction site, and (2) cut the cost of construction through maximum production by workers. He next contends that Rose Acre got what it bargained for, that is, the completion of the project. He argues that he was present on the job, including the hours he worked late, at least 750 hours during the ten weeks, while regular working hours would amount to only 500 hours. Therefore, he concludes, there was substantial compliance with the agreement, and he should not be penalized because he failed to appear on the last two days because of illness. Rust disputes that Dove worked any significant amount of overtime.

[7] Investigation of authority in bonus situations reveals that a bonus arrangement is contractually enforceable where it is shown that an employee has done or has foregone something which he was not otherwise obligated to do or forego. However, Rose Acre does not contest the existence of a valid bonus contract. It defends its judgment on the grounds that the conditions designated in the contract were not fulfilled because Dove did

not work five days a week for ten weeks. It is stated in 56 C.J.S. Master and Servant sec. 98:

> An employee is not entitled to a bonus until after the time stipulated in the contract for its payment, or until other conditions designated in the contract for its payment have been fulfilled, in the absence of evidence establishing a modification or waiver of the conditions, and unless the nonfulfillment is due to the employer's act or omission.

Conditions not met

* * *

[8] We are constrained to observe, in the case before us, that the bonus rules at Rose Acre were well known to Dove when he agreed to the disputed bonus contract. He certainly knew Rust's strict policies and knew that any absence for any cause whatever worked a forfeiture of the bonus. With this knowledge he willingly entered into this bonus arrangement, as he had done in the past, and he must be held to have agreed to all of the terms upon which the bonus was conditioned. If the conditions were unnecessarily harsh or eccentric, and the terms odious, he could have shown his disdain by simply declining to participate, for participation in the bonus program was not obligatory or job dependent. *not obligated*

[9] Contrary to Dove's assertion that completion of a task was the central element of the bonus program, we are of the opinion that the rules regarding tardiness and absenteeism were a central theme. Rust stated that the purpose of the bonus program was to discourage tardiness and absenteeism and to promote motivation and dependability. Indeed, some of the bonus programs such as the white car bonus and the silver feather bonus were apparently an effort on the part of Rust to establish among the employees an identity with Rose Acre and to create an esprit de corps. The direct tangible benefits to Rose Acre would be unmeasurable, and the burden upon the employees would be equally unmeasurable. Yet, Rust was willing to pay substantial bonuses in the implementation of his program, and the employees, including Dove, were quite as willing to take the money.

[10] No fraud or bad faith has been shown on the part of Rose Acre, and no public policy arguments have been advanced to demonstrate why the bonus contract should not be enforced as agreed between the parties. We are not at liberty to remake the contract for the parties. *no fraud or bad faith*

not entitled to bonus *No Quasi b/c no unjust enrichment*

NOTES AND QUESTIONS

1. Lest you have the impression that Rose Acre Farms is a small operation run by quirky Farmer Rust and that this sort of thing would never happen in a commercial operation, think again. Rose Acre Farms, Inc. began as a single-layer hen farm with 1,800 hens, and today is a highly integrated

table egg production system with multiple eight-layer hen farms and millions of hens. It is one of the largest egg producers in the United States. *See Rose Acre Farms v. United States*, 55 Fed. Cl. 643, 647 (2003).

2. Take a look at R2d § 229. Does that section suggest that the court should or could have reached a different result?

———

Tobacco crop grower

insured Tobacco crop

HOWARD V. FEDERAL CROP INSURANCE CORP.

United States Court of Appeals, Fourth Circuit
540 F.2d 695 (1976)

WIDENER, CIRCUIT JUDGE:

Cause of action

[1] Plaintiff-Appellants sued to recover for losses to their 1973 tobacco crop due to alleged rain damage. The crops were insured by the defendant-appellee, Federal Crop Insurance Corporation (FCIC). Suits were brought in state court in North Carolina and removed to the United States District Court. The three suits are not distinguishable factually so far as we are concerned here and involve identical questions of law. They were combined for disposition in the district court and for appeal. The district court granted summary judgment for the defendant and dismissed all three actions. We remand for further proceedings. Since we find for the plaintiffs as to the construction of the policy, we express no opinion on the procedural questions.

insurance policies

[2] FCIC, an agency of the United States, in 1973, issued three policies to the Howards, insuring their tobacco crops, to be grown on six farms, against weather damage and other hazards.

gross loss to plaintiffs

plowed before inspector could come

[3] The Howards (plaintiffs) established production of tobacco on their acreage, and have alleged that their 1973 crop was extensively damaged by heavy rains, resulting in a gross loss to the three plaintiffs in excess of $35,000. The plaintiffs harvested and sold the depleted crop and timely filed notice and proof of loss with FCIC, but, prior to inspection by the adjuster for FCIC, the Howards had either plowed or disked under the tobacco fields in question to prepare the same for sowing a cover crop of rye to preserve the soil. When the FCIC adjuster later inspected the fields, he found the stalks had been largely obscured or obliterated by plowing or disking and denied the claims, apparently on the ground that the plaintiffs had violated a portion of the policy which provides that the stalks on any acreage with respect to which a loss is claimed shall not be destroyed until the corporation makes an inspection. *Express Condition*

[4] The holding of the district court is best capsuled in its own words:

The inquiry here is whether compliance by the insured with this provision of the policy was a condition precedent to the recovery.

The court concludes that it was and that the failure of the insured to comply worked a forfeiture of benefits for the alleged loss.[2]

[5] There is no question but that apparently after notice of loss was given to defendant, but before inspection by the adjuster, plaintiffs plowed under the tobacco stalks and sowed some of the land with a cover crop, rye. The question is whether, under paragraph 5(f) of the tobacco endorsement to the policy of insurance, the act of plowing under the tobacco stalks forfeits the coverage of the policy. Paragraph 5 of the tobacco endorsement is entitled Claims. Pertinent to this case are subparagraphs 5(b) and 5(f), which are as follows:

5(b) It shall be a condition precedent to the payment of any loss that the insured establish the production of the insured crop on a unit and that such loss has been directly caused by one or more of the hazards insured against during the insurance period for the crop year for which the loss is claimed, and furnish any other information regarding the manner and extent of loss as may be required by the Corporation.

5(f) The tobacco stalks on any acreage of tobacco of types 11a, 11b, 12, 13, or 14 with respect to which a loss is claimed shall not be destroyed until the Corporation makes an inspection.

[6] The arguments of both parties are predicated upon the same two assumptions. First, if subparagraph 5(f) creates a condition precedent, its violation caused a forfeiture of plaintiffs' coverage. Second, if subparagraph 5(f) creates an obligation (variously called a promise or covenant) upon plaintiffs not to plow under the tobacco stalks, defendant may recover from plaintiffs (either in an original action, or, in this case, by a counterclaim, or as a matter of defense) for whatever damage it sustained because of the elimination of the stalks. However, a violation of subparagraph 5(f) would not, under the second premise, standing alone, cause a forfeiture of the policy.

[7] Generally accepted law provides us with guidelines here. There is a general legal policy opposed to forfeitures. When it is doubtful whether words create a promise or a condition precedent, they will be construed as creating a promise. The provisions of a contract will not be construed as conditions precedent in the absence of language plainly requiring such construction.

---

[2] The district court also relied upon language in subparagraph 5(b), *infra*, which required as a condition precedent to payment that the insured, in addition to establishing his production and loss from an insured case, "furnish any other information regarding the manner and extent of loss as may be required by the Corporation." The court construed the preservation of the stalks as such "information." We see no language in the policy or connection in the record to indicate this is the case.

[8]   Plaintiffs rely most strongly upon the fact that the term "condition precedent" is included in subparagraph 5(b) but not in subparagraph 5(f). It is true that whether a contract provision is construed as a condition or an obligation does not depend entirely upon whether the word "condition" is expressly used. However, the persuasive force of plaintiffs' argument in this case is found in the use of the term "condition precedent" in subparagraph 5(b) but not in subparagraph 5(f). Thus, it is argued that the ancient maxim to be applied ["expressio unis, exclusio alterus," in Latin.—Eds.] is that the expression of one thing is the exclusion of another.

* * *

[9]   The Restatement of the Law of Contracts states:

Section 261. INTERPRETATION OF DOUBTFUL WORDS AS PROMISE OR CONDITION.

Where it is doubtful whether words create a promise or an express condition, they are interpreted as creating a promise; but the same words may sometimes mean that one party promises a performance and that the other party's promise is conditional on that performance.

[The comparable provision in the Restatement (Second) is § 227. Read it carefully and make sure you understand what it means.—Eds.] Two illustrations (one involving a promise, the other a condition) are used in the Restatement:

2.   A, an insurance company, issues to B a policy of insurance containing promises by A that are in terms conditional on the happening of certain events. The policy contains this clause: "provided, in case differences shall arise touching any loss, the matter shall be submitted to impartial arbitrators, whose award shall be binding on the parties." This is a promise to arbitrate and does not make an award a condition precedent of the insurer's duty to pay.

3.   A, an insurance company, issues to B an insurance policy in usual form containing this clause: "In the event of disagreement as to the amount of loss it shall be ascertained by two appraisers and an umpire. The loss shall not be payable until 60 days after the award of the appraisers when such an appraisal is required." This provision is not merely a promise to arbitrate differences but makes an award a condition of the insurer's duty to pay in case of disagreement.

[10] We believe that subparagraph 5(f) in the policy here under consideration fits illustration 2 rather than illustration 3. Illustration 2 specifies something to be done, whereas subparagraph 5(f) specifies something not to be done. Unlike illustration 3, subparagraph 5(f) does not

state any conditions under which the insurance shall "not be payable," or use any words of like import. We hold that the district court erroneously held, on the motion for summary judgment, that subparagraph 5(f) established a condition precedent to plaintiffs' recovery which forfeited the coverage.

[11] From our holding that defendant's motion for summary judgment was improperly allowed, it does not follow the plaintiffs' motion for summary judgment should have been granted, for if subparagraph 5(f) be not construed as a condition precedent, there are other questions of fact to be determined. At this point, we merely hold that the district court erred in holding, on the motion for summary judgment, that subparagraph 5(f) constituted a condition precedent with resulting forfeiture. *Did NOT*

[12] The explanation defendant makes for including subparagraph 5(f) in the tobacco endorsement is that it is necessary that the stalks remain standing in order for the Corporation to evaluate the extent of loss and to determine whether loss resulted from some cause not covered by the policy. However, was subparagraph 5(f) inserted because without it the Corporation's opportunities for proof would be more difficult, or because they would be impossible? Plaintiffs point out that the Tobacco Endorsement, with subparagraph 5(f), was adopted in 1970, and crop insurance goes back long before that date. Nothing is shown as to the Corporation's prior 1970 practice of evaluating losses. Such a showing might have a bearing upon establishing defendant's intention in including 5(f). Plaintiffs state, and defendant does not deny, that another division of the Department of Agriculture, or the North Carolina Department, urged that tobacco stalks be cut as soon as possible after harvesting as a means of pest control. Such an explanation might refute the idea that plaintiffs plowed under the stalks for any fraudulent purpose. Could these conflicting directives affect the reasonableness of plaintiffs' interpretation of defendant's prohibition upon plowing under the stalks prior to adjustment? *FDIC Argument*

[13] We express no opinion on these questions because they were not before the district court and are mentioned to us largely by way of argument rather than from the record. No question of ambiguity was raised in the court below or here and no question of the applicability of paragraph 5(c) to this case was alluded to other than in the defendant's pleadings, so we also do not reach those questions. Nothing we say here should preclude FCIC from asserting as a defense that the plowing or disking under of the stalks caused damage to FCIC if, for example, the amount of the loss was thereby made more difficult or impossible to ascertain whether the plowing or disking under was done with bad purpose or innocently. To repeat, our narrow holding is that merely plowing or disking under the stalks does not of itself operate to forfeit coverage under the policy.

Does not forfeit coverage

[14] The case is remanded for further proceedings not inconsistent with this opinion.

VACATED AND REMANDED.

———

NOTES AND QUESTIONS

1.   This case illustrates an important principle of drafting: Never use different phrases to convey the same meaning. If you make even the smallest change, it may (in fact, it should) be interpreted as an indication you mean something different than what you meant when you used similar language in another part of the document.

2.   An article on the front page of *The Wall Street Journal* on May 5, 2003, entitled *Abuses Plague Crop Insurance*, discussed the problem of fraud in the federal crop insurance program. A headline said the "system is proving easy to fool." It described one farmer alleged to have defrauded the government out of at least $4 million.

3.   Redraft Paragraph 5(f) to make sure the government doesn't have to pay if a farmer destroys the tobacco stalks.

———

On Transactional Practice

To understand how practicing lawyers use conditions to make sure their clients get what they bargain for, it helps to understand how large sales, mergers, and the like are actually structured. The best way to start is by understanding how a typical sale of a single-family home is handled.

A Typical Residential Real Estate Sale

The first step is for the buyer and the seller to enter into a contract for the purchase and sale of the property. The contract will have certain conditions precedent to the obligations of the parties. Because these contracts are usually drafted by real estate brokers or by unsophisticated lawyers, they will typically use language such as "this contract is subject to the following contingencies." The contract will then list conditions precedent such as the buyer obtaining a loan, the buyer selling her present home, inspections showing the property free from physical defects, termites, etc.

If the contract is well-drafted, it will label the conditions as "conditions precedent" rather than as "contingencies," and it will list separately those conditions that are conditions precedent to the buyer's obligation to purchase the property and those conditions that are conditions precedent to the seller's obligation to sell the property. This is the approach used in the Asset Purchase Agreement in the Introduction. It will also spell out which conditions may be waived, by whom they may be waived, and how a waiver is to be documented. The contract should also say whose duty it is to make sure the conditions are satisfied and how that person can go about satisfying that duty.

A poorly-written contract might say:

This contract is subject to Buyer's ability to obtain satisfactory financing.

A thorough contract would say:

Buyer's obligation to purchase is subject to the condition precedent that within thirty days of the date of this agreement Buyer shall have obtained from a financial institution satisfactory to Buyer (in Buyer's reasonable discretion) a loan in an amount of not less than $300,000 with a term of not less than 20 years, an interest rate of not more than 7% per annum, closing costs of not more than $6,000 and other terms and conditions satisfactory to Buyer (in Buyer's reasonable discretion). This condition is solely for the benefit of Buyer and may be waived by Buyer. Within seven days after the date of this Agreement, Buyer shall make application to at least four financial institutions making loans of the type described above in the area in which the property is located. If Buyer shall fail to make such applications or fail to cooperate in the approval process, Buyer shall be deemed to have waived this condition.

The contract can go on in even more detail, but you get the idea. Exactly how much detail the contract will have will depend on a number of factors: how much money is involved, how much the client is willing to pay, how much detail the other parties to the transaction are willing to put up with, how much the parties trust each other, how much detail is customary in similar transactions in this particular area, etc.

Once the contract has been signed, the parties will open an escrow. An escrow is a transactional device for holding instruments, other documents, and money while the conditions are being satisfied. Essentially, to satisfy conditions, consideration, documents, instruments and the like are given to the escrow holder and, when all conditions to the "close of escrow" have been met, the escrow agent distributes the contents of the escrow to the appropriate parties. In a residential and estate transaction, the seller (or the seller's bank) gets the money and the buyer gets the deed to the house. In some parts of the country there are businesses that specialize in holding escrows. In others, persons involved in the deal may act as escrow holders.

Each party to the transaction will deliver money and/or documents to the escrow holder together with "escrow instructions," which are in reality themselves contracts between that party and the escrow holder. The seller's escrow instructions will be the simplest. The seller will give the escrow holder a deed conveying the property to the buyer. The seller's escrow instructions will tell the escrow holder that the escrow holder may file the deed with the appropriate office (in effect transferring title to the property to the buyer) if the escrow holder holds a certain sum of money for delivery to the seller. (This sum will normally be the purchase price less the "closing costs" to be paid by the seller.) The buyer will deliver to the escrow holder the purchase price with instructions that the escrow holder may deliver that money to the seller when certain conditions spelled out in the escrow instructions have been satisfied. These conditions will be based on the conditions in the purchase agreement. For example, there might be a condition that the escrow holder has received a report from a licensed pest control operator showing that the property is free from termites. Alternatively, the condition might be phrased to require a letter from the buyer saying that the buyer has received satisfactory assurances that there are no termites. The sale contract will almost always provide that the seller is to deliver clear title to the property, free of any liens or encumbrances except those the buyer has agreed to. This may be implemented in the escrow instructions through a condition requiring the escrow holder to have a commitment from a title insurance company to issue an insurance policy in effect guaranteeing that the buyer will (upon recording of the deed) have that clear title to the property.

Often there will be mortgages involved, and that will complicate things a little more. Typically, the seller has a mortgage on the property and that mortgage will be paid off as part of the transaction. The holder of that mortgage will deliver to the escrow holder a document releasing the mortgage along with instructions telling the escrow holder that the escrow holder's right and duty to record the release (i.e., to make the release effective) are subject to the condition precedent that the escrow holder "is in a position" to pay the mortgage holder the money due it on the loan secured by the mortgage.

Similarly, the buyer will normally be borrowing money to buy the property, and that loan will be secured by a new mortgage to be recorded against the property. The new lender will deliver to the escrow holder the loan proceeds (the money), with instructions that it can pay them to the old lender and/or the seller, as appropriate, subject to the condition precedent that it is in a position to record the mortgage in favor of the new lender and that a title insurance company is in a position to guarantee the priority of the new mortgage.

When all of the conditions set out in everybody's escrow instructions have been satisfied, the escrow "closes." The escrow holder delivers all the money and documents to the appropriate places and has no more duties. This is where the phrase "to close a deal" comes from. Business people, particularly brokers, claim to have "closed" the deal when they have an agreement with the other party, but lawyers know the deal isn't really done until the definitive deal documents have been signed, due diligence is complete, all of the conditions have been satisfied, the requisite filings have been made, and escrow has been closed. This reflects tension between lawyers and brokers. Brokers figure they're entitled to a commission as soon as they get the buyer and the seller to shake hands, while lawyers know that a lot of escrows never close because the buyer can't get financing or because an unknown toxic waste dump is found on the property, or for one of a hundred other reasons. Brokers see these things as "technicalities" conjured up by "deal-killing lawyers."

Bigger Deals

The "house closing," as this sort of transaction is often called, is the model for all sorts of large and complex business deals. For instance, when two corporations merge, they will go through the same process. There will be an initial contract where the heads of the two corporations agree to merge and there will be closing when all the conditions precedent in the initial agreement have been satisfied and the two companies actually become one. The initial agreement will often have (literally) dozens of conditions precedent to the closing and the parties' obligation to merge. These will include approval of the requisite percentage of shareholders of each corporation (as required by the by-laws or the corporate laws of the relevant jurisdiction), approval of governmental authorities, satisfaction of each corporation that the business and financial condition of the other is as was represented at the time they made the agreement, opinion letters from corporate attorneys to the effect that the merger is legal and has been validly documented, opinion letters from tax attorneys as to the tax consequences of the merger, etc. When both sides conclude that the conditions are satisfied or have been waived, they will have a ceremony called a "closing" in which the documents effecting the merger are signed and delivered. They call it a "closing" after the escrow closing, even though there may be no actual escrow. Often the closing is also a negotiating session in which business people and lawyers, short-tempered from lack of sleep, hammer out and document last-minute details.

———

APPEAL OF EDWIN J. SCHOETTLE CO.

Supreme Court of Pennsylvania
390 Pa. 365, 134 A.2d 908 (1957)

BENJAMIN R. JONES, JUSTICE.

[1] This is an appeal from a judgment entered upon an arbitrator's award in a proceeding under the Act of 1957.[3]

[2] In June 1954 the Edwin J. Schoettle Co., a Pennsylvania corporation, and its six subsidiaries were available for purchase. Lester L. Kardon, interested in purchasing the company and five of its subsidiaries, opened negotiations for that purpose. The negotiations extended from June 24, 1954 to September 17, 1954, on which latter date the parties entered into a written agreement under the terms of which Kardon[4] (hereinafter called the buyer) purchased all the issued and outstanding capital stock of Schoettle Co. and all its subsidiaries (hereinafter called sellers). The total purchase price set forth in the agreement of sale (excluding certain real estate) was $2,100,000 of which amount $187,863.60 was set aside under paragraph 11 of the agreement to be held by the Provident Trust Company of Philadelphia as escrow agent to indemnify the buyer against "the liabilities of sellers by reason of any and all provisions of this agreement."

[3] The present litigation arises from the fact that the buyer has presented a claim against the escrow fund for $69,998.42 as a "liability" of the seller under the agreement. Payment of this claim having been disputed by the sellers, both parties, under the provisions of the agreement, submitted to arbitration and Judge Gerald F. Flood was selected as arbitrator. On October 26, 1956 Judge Flood, as arbitrator, and, after hearing, awarded to the buyer $3,182.88.[5] Buyer's motion to correct the arbitrator's award was dismissed by the Code of Common Pleas No. 6 of Philadelphia County and judgment was entered in the amount of $3,182.88 in conformity with the arbitrator's award. From that judgment this appeal ensued.

[4] The resolution of this controversy depends upon the interpretation of certain portions of the 25-page written agreement of

---

[3] [In this case, be sure to distinguish between the date of the agreement (the court calls it the "purchase date") and the closing date, which is when the parties get together and exchange the money for the stock. Here, as in most business transactions, it's a critical distinction. The case is complex, so you'll need to make careful notes as you read.—Eds.]

[4] Kardon later assigned all his rights under the agreement to a new corporation, Edwin J. Schoettle Company, Inc., and it was this corporation which presented the claim against the escrow fund.

[5] The buyer's claim is based largely on the proposition that sellers had warranted the company's net worth. The amount allowed by the arbitrator—$3,182.88—represented an error in computing state taxes, additional taxes and water rent. This amount is undisputed as a proper claim against the fund.

September 17, 1954. The pertinent portions of this agreement are paragraphs 5(g), 9(a), 9(b), 9(c), 10(d), and 15, which read as follows:

5.   *Representations and Warranties.*

Sellers *represent and warrant* as follows: [Emphasis supplied.]

* * *

5(g) Absence of certain changes. Since June 30, 1954, there have not been (i) any changes in Company's or its subsidiaries' financial condition, assets, liabilities, or businesses, other than changes in the ordinary course of business, none of which have been materially adverse, and changes required or permitted hereunder; (ii) any damage, destruction, or loss, whether or not covered by insurance, materially and adversely affecting the properties or businesses of Company and its subsidiaries as an entirety; (iii) any declaration, or setting aside, or payment of any dividend or other distribution in respect of Company's capital stock or that of any subsidiary (except that prior to the date hereof, Company has declared and paid a dividend of Sixteen and Two Thirds Cents ($0.16 2/3) per share on all issued and outstanding shares of its said capital stock), or any direct or indirect redemption, purchase, or other acquisition of any such stock; or (iv) any increase in the compensation payable or to become payable by Company or any subsidiary to any of their officers, employees, or agents, or any bonus payment or arrangement made to or with any of them.

* * *

9.   *Conditions precedent.*

All obligations of Buyer under this agreement are subject to the fulfillment, prior to or at the closing of each of the following *conditions*: [Emphasis supplied.]

(a)   *Financial condition at closing.* As of the time of closing the financial condition of the Company and its subsidiaries in the aggregate shall be no less favorable than the financial condition shown on the statements of said corporations dated June 30, 1954 and warranted to be true and complete in paragraph 5(e) hereof.

(b)   *Representations and warranties true at closing.* Sellers' representations and warranties contained in this agreement shall be true at the time of closing as though such representations and warranties were made at such time.

(c)   *Performance.* Sellers shall have performed and complied with all agreements and conditions required by this agreement to be performed or complied with by them prior to or at the closing.

* * *

10. *Indemnification.* Sellers shall indemnify and hold harmless Buyer, subject to the limitations of paragraph 11 hereof, against and in respect of:

* * *

(d) Any damage or deficiency resulting from any misrepresentation, breach of warranty, or nonfulfillment of any agreement on the part of Sellers, or any of them, under this agreement, or from any misrepresentation in or omission from any certificate or other instrument furnished or to be furnished to Buyer hereunder;

* * *

15. *Survival of representations.* All representations, warranties and agreements made by Sellers and Buyer in this agreement or pursuant hereto shall survive closing, subject to the provisions of paragraph 11 hereof.

[5] The buyer (appellant) contends that the financial condition on the date of purchase—September 17, 1954—was less favorable than that reflected in the company's financial statement of June 30, 1954 and, therefore, he is entitled to reimbursement out of the escrow fund for the amount of the deficiency. Sellers (appellees) deny any reduction in the financial condition and further argue that, even if there were any reduction, buyer has no right to reimbursement under the agreement unless such reduction resulted from occurrences outside the ordinary course of business or which caused a materially adverse change in the company's financial condition. Actually the buyer's position is that paragraph 9(a), *supra*, constituted a "warranty" on the sellers' part that the financial condition of the company and its subsidiaries was not less favorable than demonstrated by the financial statement of June 30, 1954 and, therefore, sellers having breached the warranty the buyer is entitled to claim the difference between the net worth on June 30, 1954 and September 17, 1954. On the other hand, sellers take the position that their engagement under paragraph 9(a) constituted a "condition" and not a warranty and the buyer had simply the right to refuse a consummation of the sale if the "condition" was not fulfilled; when the buyer elected to consummate the sale it waived the "condition."

[6] At the hearing before the arbitrator the buyer introduced certain evidence for the purpose of proving that it was the parties intent that the sellers would warrant that the financial condition of the company and its subsidiaries would be no less favorable on the date of closing than on June 30, 1954. Such evidence consisted of the original letter opening negotiations, a memorandum prepared by the Provident Trust Company

acting for the sellers, an interim draft of a proposed form of agreement containing interlineations and marginal notations made by one of buyer's counsel, an accountant's calculation reflecting the condition of the company and its subsidiaries from June 30 to the date of closing, together with an itemization of buyer's claim and accountant's report showing the financial condition of the company on June 30, 1954 and September 17, 1954. The buyer urges that a proper interpretation of this agreement requires a consideration of all this evidence in order to ascertain the parties' intent.

* * *

[7]   The language of the instant agreement is clear and unambiguous. The buyer's evidence would tend to prove that in the negotiations leading up to the integrated agreement it was intended that the sellers warrant the company's and its subsidiaries' financial condition, whereas the language of the agreement plainly expresses a contrary intent. The admission of such evidence would vary and change the language of the agreement and its exclusion was eminently proper under the circumstances.

[8]   This written agreement was carefully and meticulously prepared by able and competent counsel after long and thorough negotiations. Each general paragraph of the agreement is headed by a title descriptive of the contents of each paragraph. Paragraph 5, entitled "Representations and Warranties", expressly states that the sellers "represented and warranted" fifteen separate and carefully spelled out factual situations. Paragraph 9, entitled "Conditions precedent" expressly states that "All obligations of buyer under this agreement are subject to the fulfillment, prior to or at the closing, of each of the following conditions." It is to be noted that included among the "conditions" was the financial condition of the company and its subsidiaries at the time of closing, that the fulfillment of the "conditions" was to take place not subsequent to but "prior to or at the closing" and that the buyer's obligations, not the sellers', were made subject to the fulfillment of the condition. This agreement, in distinct and indubitable language, distinguishes between such engagements on the sellers' part as constitute "Warranties" and such engagements as constitute "Conditions."

[9]   Assuming, arguendo, that the company and its subsidiaries' financial condition was less favorable on September 17, 1954 than the financial condition shown on the statement dated June 30, 1954, what under this agreement was the buyer's remedy? The buyer claims that such fact constituted a breach of warranty which gave to him the right to recover the amount of the reduced net worth, while the sellers claim that the buyer had the choice on September 17, 1954 either to accept the situation or to refuse to proceed under the agreement.

[10] The buyer argues that it was impossible to ascertain at the date of closing whether or not the net worth of the company and its subsidiaries

had been reduced, and that only by an examination after date of closing could this fact be ascertained and, therefore, both parties must have intended that the buyer have a reasonable time after the date of closing to ascertain this fact. Such an argument not only finds no support in the wording of the agreement but, on the contrary, is in direct conflict with the express terms of the agreement. Such a contention would require that we read into the agreement that which is in direct variance with the clear and unambiguous language employed to express the parties' intent.

[11] In determining this controversy we have no need to draw a distinction between "warranties" and "conditions" generally—a field in which there is great confusion.[6] The parties themselves to this agreement have by its express terms drawn a clear distinction between the sellers' obligations in the nature of warranties and their obligations in the nature of conditions and among the latter have included the financial condition of the company and its subsidiaries. Sellers made no representation or warranty concerning the financial condition.

[12] The arbitrator concluded that to construe paragraph 9(a) as creative of a promise for the breach of which the buyer could recover damages—i.e., a warranty—would be inconsistent with paragraph 5(g). With this conclusion we are in full agreement. The sellers in paragraph 5(g) represented and warranted, inter alia, that there had not been any changes in the financial condition of the company or its subsidiaries other than changes in the ordinary course of business, none of which had been materially adverse and were changes required or permitted under the agreement. Paragraph 9(a) covers an entirely different situation in that it referred to such changes in the financial condition of the company and its subsidiaries in the ordinary course of business which were materially adverse and not permitted under the agreement; if this situation arose the agreement specifically provided that the buyer was under no obligation to complete the purchase. A comparison of paragraph 5(g) with paragraph 9(a) clearly leads to this conclusion; to place upon paragraph 9(a) any other construction than that placed upon it by the arbitrator would amount to a redundancy.

---

[6] Lord Abinger in Charter v. Hopkins, 4 M. & W. 399, has said "Two things have been confounded together. A warranty is an express or implied statement of something which the party undertakes shall be part of a contract; and, though part of the contract, yet collateral to the express object of it. But in many of the cases, some of which have been referred to, the circumstances of a party selling a particular thing by its proper description has been called a warranty, and a breach of such contract a breach of warranty, but it would be better to distinguish such cases as a noncompliance with a contract which a party has engaged to fulfill; as, if a man offers to buy peas of another, and he sends him beans, he does not perform his contract; but that is not a warranty; there is no warranty that he should sell him peas; the contract is to sell peas, and if he sell him anything else in their stead it is a non-performance of it. So, if a man were to order copper for sheathing ships—that is, a particular copper, prepared in a particular manner—if the seller sent him a different sort, in that case he does not comply with the contract; and though this may have been ranged under the class of cases relating to warranties, yet it is not properly so."

[13] A resolution of the instant controversy depends entirely upon an interpretation of the language of this agreement. The language employed by the parties is manifestly indicative of that which was intended and the meaning of the agreement—free as it is of ambiguity and doubt—is to be determined by what the agreement states. The parties carefully and scrupulously delineated between the sellers' undertakings which were intended to be "warranties" and those which were intended to be "conditions." It is crystal clear that the undertaking under paragraph 9(a) was simply a "condition" and not a "warranty" and once the buyer elected to accept this agreement the provisions of paragraph 9(a) ceased to be operative and the buyer had no right to recover any damages.

[14] The judgment of the Court below is affirmed. Costs to be paid by appellant.

———

NOTES AND QUESTIONS

1.   Suppose a provision in the construction contract in question had read: "The obligation of the general contractor to make payment to the subcontractor for any work is subject to the condition precedent that the general contractor shall have received payment for such work from the owner or the owner's agent." If the owner declared bankruptcy and did not pay the general contractor, would the general contractor have to pay the sub-contractor? *See Gulf Construction Co. v. Self*, 676 S.W.2d 624 (Tex. App. 1984). If you're not sure, how would you draft the provision to make sure it did? Or is that possible?

2.   The conditions we've seen so far had to occur before a contract came into being or a duty became effective. These are called conditions precedent (pronounced "pre SEED n't"). They are by far the most common type of condition. But there is a second type of condition called a *condition subsequent*. If a condition subsequent occurs, a duty that is already in effect is discharged or modified. The case that follows illustrates this.

———

GRAY V. GARDNER
Supreme Court of Massachusetts
17 Mass. 188 (1821)

[1] ASSUMPSIT on a written promise to pay the plaintiff 5198 dollars, 87 cents, with the following condition annexed, *viz.*, "on the condition that if a greater quantity of sperm oil should arrive in whaling vessels at *Nantucket* and *New Bedford*, on or between the first day of April and the first day of October of the present year, both inclusive, than arrived at said places, in whaling vessels, on or within the same term of time the last year, then this obligation to be void." Dated April 14, 1819.

[2]   The consideration of the promise was a quantity of oil, sold by the plaintiff to the defendants. On the same day another note unconditional had been given by the defendants, for the value of the oil, estimated at sixty cents per gallon; and the note in suit was given to secure the residue of the price, estimated at eighty five cents, to depend on the contingency mentioned in the said condition.

[3]   At the trial before the chief justice, the case depended upon the question whether a certain vessel, called the *Lady Adams*, with the cargo of oil, arrived at *Nantucket* on the first day of October, 1819, about which fact the evidence was contradictory. The judge ruled that the burden of proving the arrival within the time was on the defendants; and further that, although the vessel might have, within the time, gotten within the space which might be called *Nantucket Roads*, yet it was necessary that she should have come to anchor, or have been moored, somewhere within that space before the twelve following the first day of October, in order to have *arrived*, within the meaning of the contract.

[4]   The opinion of the chief justice on both these points was objected to by the defendants, and the questions were saved. If it was wrong on either point, a new trial was to be had; otherwise judgement was to be rendered on the verdict, which was found for the plaintiff.

[5]   PARKER, C. J. The very words of the contract show that there was a promise to pay, which was to be defeated by the happening of an event, *viz.*, the arrival of a certain quantity of oil, at the specified places, in a given time. It is like a bond with a condition; if the obligor would avoid the bond, he must show performance of the condition. The defendants, in this case, promise to pay a certain sum of money, on condition that the promise shall be void on the happening of an event. It is plain that the burden of proof is upon them; and if they fail to show that the event has happened, the promise remains good.

[6]   The other point is equally clear for the plaintiff. Oil is to arrive at a given place before twelve o'clock at night.

[7]   A vessel with oil heaves in sight, but she does not come to anchor before the hour is gone. In no sense can the oil be said to have arrived. The vessel is coming until she drops anchor, or is moored. She may sink, or take fire, and never arrive, however near she may be to her port. It is so in contracts of insurance; and the same reason applies to a case of this sort. Both parties put themselves upon a nice point in this contract; it was a kind of wager as to be quantity of oil which should arrive at the ports mentioned, before a certain period. They must be held strictly to their contract, there being no equity to interfere with the terms of it.

Judgment on the verdict.

NOTE

The next case presents a "void as against public policy" attack on a notice condition. It failed.

INMAN V. CLYDE HALL DRILLING CO., INC.

Supreme Court of Alaska
369 P.2d 498 (1962)

DIMOND, JUSTICE.

[1] This case involves a claim for damages arising out of an employment contract. The main issue is whether a provision in the contract, making written notice of a claim a condition precedent to recovery, is contrary to public policy.

[2] Inman worked for the Clyde Hall Drilling Company as a derrickman under a written contract of employment signed by both parties on November 16, 1959. His employment terminated on March 24, 1960. On April 5, 1960, he commenced this action against the Company claiming that the latter fired him without justification, that this amounted to a breach of contract, and that he was entitled to certain damages for the breach. In its answer the Company denied that it had breached the contract, and asserted that Inman had been paid in full the wages that were owing him and was entitled to no damages. Later the Company moved for summary judgment on the ground that Inman's failure to give written notice of his claim,[7] as required by the contract, was a bar to his action based on the contract.[8] The motion was granted, and judgment was entered in favor of the Company. This appeal followed.

[3] A fulfillment of the thirty-day notice requirement is expressly made a "condition precedent to any recovery." Inman argues that this provision is void as against public policy. In considering this first question we start with the basic tenet that competent parties are free to make contracts and that they should be bound by their agreements. In the

---

[7] The fact that Inman did not give written notice was not disputed.

[8] The portion of the contract with which we are concerned reads:

You agree that you will, within thirty (30) days after any claim (other than a claim for compensation insurance) that arises out of or in connection with the employment provided for herein, give written notice to the Company for such claim, setting forth in detail the facts relating thereto and the basis for such claim; and that you will not institute any suit or action against the Company in any court or tribunal in any jurisdiction based on any such claim prior to six (6) months after the filing of the written notice of claim hereinabove provided for, or later than one (1) year after such filing. Any action or suit on any such claim shall not include any item or matter not specifically mentioned in the proof of claim above provided. It is agreed that in any such action or suit, proof by you of your compliance with the provisions of this paragraph shall be a condition precedent to any recovery.

absence of a constitutional provision or statute which makes certain contracts illegal or unenforceable, we believe it is the function of the judiciary to allow men to manage their own affairs in their own way.[9] As a matter of judicial policy the court should maintain and enforce contracts, rather than enable parties to escape from the obligations they have chosen to incur.[10]

[4]   We recognize that "freedom of contract" is a qualified and not an absolute right, and cannot be applied on a strict, doctrinal basis. An established principle is that a court will not permit itself to be used as an instrument of inequity and injustice. As Justice Frankfurter stated in his dissenting opinion in *United States v. Bethlehem Steel Corp.*, "The fundamental principle of law that the courts will not enforce a bargain where one party has unconscionably taken advantage of the necessities and distress of the other has found expression in an almost infinite variety of cases."[11] In determining whether certain contractual provisions should be enforced, the court must look realistically at the relative bargaining positions of the parties in the framework of contemporary business practices and commercial life. If we find those positions are such that one party has unscrupulously taken advantage of the economic necessities of the other, then in the interest of justice—as a matter of public policy—we would refuse to enforce the transaction. But the grounds for judicial interference must be clear. Whether the court should refuse to recognize and uphold that which the parties have agreed upon is a question of fact upon which evidence is required.

[5]   The facts in this case do not persuade us that the contractual provision in question is unfair or unreasonable. Its purpose is not disclosed. The requirement that written notice be given within thirty days after a claim arises may have been designed to preclude stale claims; and the further requirement that no action be commenced within six months thereafter may have been intended to afford the Company timely opportunity to rectify the basis for a just claim. But whatever the objective was, we cannot find in the contract anything to suggest it was designed from an unfair motive to bilk employees out of wages or other compensation justly due them.

[6]   There was nothing to suggest that Inman did not have the knowledge, capacity or opportunity to read the agreement and understand it; that the terms of the contract were imposed upon him without any real freedom of choice on his part; that there was any substantial inequality in bargaining positions between Inman and the Company. Not only did he

---

[9]   Dr. Miles Medical Co. v. John D. Park & Sons, 220 U.S. 373, 411, 31 S.Ct. 376, 55 L.Ed. 502, 520 (1911) (Justice Holmes, dissenting).

[10]   Baltimore & Ohio S. W. Ry. v. Voigt, 176 U.S. 498, 505, 20 S.Ct. 385, 44 L.Ed. 560, 565 (1900).

[11]   315 U.S. 289, 327–28, 62 S.Ct. 581, 600, 86 L.Ed. 855, 877 (1942).

attach a copy of the contract to his complaint, which negatives any thought that he really wasn't aware of its provisions, but he also admitted in a deposition that at the time he signed the contract he had read it, had discussed it with a Company representative, and was familiar with its terms. And he showed specific knowledge of the thirty-day notice requirement when, in response to a question as to whether written notice had been given prior to filing suit, he testified:

A.   Well, now, I filed—I started my claim within 30 days, didn't I, from the time I hit here. I thought that would be a notice that I started suing them when I first came to town.

Q.   You thought that the filing of the suit would be the notice?

A.   That is right.

[7]   Under these circumstances we do not find that such a limitation on Inman's right of action is offensive to justice. We would not be justified in refusing to enforce the contract and thus permit one of the parties to escape his obligations. It is conceivable, of course, that a thirty-day notice of claim requirement could be used to the disadvantage of a workman by an unscrupulous employer. If this danger is great, the legislature may act to make such a provision unenforceable. But we may not speculate on what in the future may be a matter of public policy in this state. It is our function to act only where an existence public policy is clearly revealed from the facts and we find that it has been violated. That is not the case here.

[8]   Inman's claim arose on March 24, 1960. His complaint was served on the Company on April 14. He argues that since the complaint set forth in detail the basis of his claim and was served within thirty days, he had substantially complied with the contractual requirement.

[9]   Service of the complaint probably gave the Company actual knowledge of the claim. But that does not serve as an excuse for not giving the kind of written notice called for by the contract. Inman agreed that no suit would be instituted "prior to six (6) months after the filing of the written notice of claim." If this means what it says (and we have no reason to believe it does not), it is clear that the commencement of an action and service of the complaint was not an effective substitute for the kind of notice called for by the agreement. To hold otherwise would be to simply ignore an explicit provision of the contract and say that it had no meaning. We are not justified in doing that.

* * *

The judgment is affirmed.

———

NOTE

In *Vintage Rodeo Parent, LLC v. Rent-a-Center, Inc.*, No. CA 2018–0927–SG, 2019 WL1223026 (Del. Ch. Mar. 14, 2019), Vintage Capital Management (Vintage), a private equity firm, agreed to buy Rent-a-Center for $15 per share, a total deal of about $1.37 billion. Because Vintage owned a similar rent-to-own business, the deal would likely be subject to a lengthy antitrust review by the FTC. Thus, the parties agreed to include a provision in their agreement that if they could not close the deal by Dec. 17 (termination date), either party had the option to terminate the agreement at will. However, if the parties were still waiting for approval from the FTC, either party could extend the termination date by three months by providing the other party with notice to extend, before the termination date.

The agreement also included a provision that entitled Rent-a-Center to "a breakup fee." If Vintage chose not to extend the termination date and either party exercised their option to terminate the agreement, Vintage had to pay Rent-a-Center a $126 million breakup fee.

Shortly after the parties signed the merger agreement, Rent-a-Center's business improved, and their stock price went up almost 50% from the $15 per share price they agreed to sell to Vintage. Also, at this point, it was clear the merger would not have FTC approval by the termination date. After some discussion among Rent-a-Center Board members, they decided they wanted out of the deal. They also wanted to collect the $126 million breakup fee from Vintage. For both to happen, Vintage or B. Riley Financial (Vintage's banker on the deal) would have to forget to send notice to extend the termination date to Rent-a-Center by the Dec. 17 deadline.

Unfortunately for Vintage, they forgot. Sure enough, Rent-a-Center terminated the agreement after Dec. 17 and requested their $126 million breakup fee from Vintage. Vintage refused and filed suit against Rent-a-Center in Delaware court, arguing that the conduct of both parties in continuing to pursue the merger in good faith until the termination date was evidence that both parties wanted to extend the termination date. However, as the judge noted, that was not the parties' deal. The judge held that these two sophisticated parties, who had negotiated over this agreement, were bound by its terms:

> Vintage was entitled to extend the End Date simply by sending Rent-a-Center notice of election to do so by a date certain, Vintage and B. Riley personnel, in the context of this $1 billion-plus merger, simply forgot to give such notice. As one B. Riley principal messaged another, immediately upon learning of the failure of notice, "We are [prejudiced in the extreme]."

In practice, if you or your client signs a merger or other agreement, and the agreement explicitly says that the agreement will terminate unless you do certain things to extend it, you better do everything it says if you plan on extending it. Make a checklist of tasks you must accomplish by certain dates and follow that checklist! Set reminders in your smartphone or on your computer, write them on a sticky note and put them on your desk or monitor, do whatever you have to do to ensure that nothing on your checklist slips your mind.

CLARK V. WEST

Court of Appeals of New York
193 N.Y. 349, 86 N.E. 1 (1908)

[1] On February 12, 1900, the plaintiff and defendant entered into a written contract, under which the former was to write and prepare for publication for the latter a series of law books, the compensation for which was provided in the contract. After the plaintiff had completed a three-volume work known as "Clark & Marshall on Corporations," the parties disagreed. The plaintiff claimed that the defendant had broken the contract by causing the book to be copyrighted in the name of a corporation which was not a party to the contract, and he brought this action to recover what he claims to be due him, for an accounting and other relief. The defendant demurred to the complaint on the ground that it did not state facts sufficient to constitute a cause of action. The Special Term overruled the demurrer, but upon an appeal to the Appellate Division that decision was reversed and the demurrer sustained.

[2] Those portions of the contract which are germane to the present stage of the controversy are as follows: The plaintiff agreed to write a series of books relating to specified legal subjects. The manuscript furnished by him was to be satisfactory to the defendant. The plaintiff was not to write or edit anything that would interfere with the sale of books to be written by him under the contract, and he was not to write any other books unless requested so to do by the defendant in which latter event he was to be paid $3,000 a year. The contract contained a clause which provided that "the first party (the plaintiff) agrees to totally abstain from the use of intoxicating liquors during the continuance of this contract, and that the payment to him in accordance with the terms of this contract of any money in excess of $2 per page is dependent on the faithful performance of this as well as the other conditions of this contract. . . ." In a later paragraph it further recited that, "in consideration of the above promises of the first party (the plaintiff), the second party (the defendant) agrees to pay to the first party $2 per page, . . . on each book prepared by the first party under this contract and accepted by the second party, and if said first party abstains from the use of intoxicating liquor and otherwise fulfills his agreements as hereinbefore set forth, he shall be paid an additional $4 per page in manner hereinbefore stated." This was followed by a specification of the method and times of payment, in which it was agreed that: "When a

completed chapter or completed chapters amounting to not less than 125 pages, to be delivered, the second party shall pay to the first party $2 per page, but he shall not be required to pay more than $250 in any one month prior to the acceptance by him of a completed book. These advance payments are to be made as soon as the completed chapters are delivered as above stated, but if, after such delivery and payment, the manuscript shall not be regarded by the second party as satisfactory, no further payment shall be made until the first party shall have made the same satisfactory to the second party. All payments on account of parts of books are to be treated as payments on account, against the books previously completed and accepted. They are for accommodation of first party only. After the publication of any book or books prepared by the first party under this contract, he shall at the end of every six months be entitled to receive, and the second party agrees to pay him, an amount equal to one-sixth of the net receipts from the combined sales of all books which shall have been prepared by the said first party and published by the said second party under this contract, less any and all payments previously made, said first party and all money then due to the second party from the first party, until the amount of $6 per page of each book shall have been paid, after which the first party shall have no right, title or interest in said books or the receipts from the sale thereof."

[3] The plaintiff in his complaint alleges completion of the work on Corporations and publication thereof by the defendant, the sale of many copies thereof from which the defendant received large net receipts, the number of pages it contained (3,469), for which he had been paid at the rate of $2 per page, amounting to $6,938, and that defendant has refused to pay him any sum over and above that amount, or any sum in excess of $2 per page. Full performance of the agreement on plaintiff's part is alleged, except that he "did not totally abstain from the use of intoxicating liquor during the continuance of said contract; but such use by the plaintiff was not excessive and did not prevent or interfere with the due and full performance by the plaintiff of all the other stipulations in said contract." The complaint further alleges a waiver on the part of the defendant of the plaintiff's stipulation to totally abstain from to use of intoxicating liquors, as follows: "(12) That defendant waived plaintiff's breach of the stipulation to totally abstain from the use of intoxicating liquors during the continuance of said contract; that long prior to the completion of said manuscript on Corporation, and its delivery to and acceptance by the defendant, the defendant had full knowledge and well knew of plaintiff's said use of intoxicating liquor during the continuance of said contract, but nevertheless acquiesced in and failed to object thereto, and did not terminate the contract on account thereof; that with full knowledge of said breach by the plaintiff defendant continued to exact and require of the plaintiff performance of all the other stipulations and conditions of said contract, and treated the same as still in force, and continued to receive,

and did receive, installments of manuscript under said contract, and continued to make and did make payments to plaintiff by way of advancements, and finally accepted and published said manuscript as aforesaid; that at no time during the performance of said contract by the plaintiff did the defendant notify or intimate to the plaintiff that defendant would insist upon strict compliance with said stipulation to totally abstain from the use of intoxicating liquor, or that defendant intended to take advantage of plaintiff's said breach, and on account and by reason thereof refuse to pay plaintiff the royalty stipulated in said contract; that, on the contrary, and with full knowledge of plaintiff's said use of intoxicating liquors, defendant repeatedly avowed and represented to the plaintiff that he was entitled to and would receive said royalty payment, and plaintiff believed and relied on said representation, and in reliance thereon continued in the performance of said contract until the time of the breach thereof by the defendant, as hereinafter specifically alleged, and at all times during the writing of said treatise on Corporations, and after as well as before publication thereof, as aforesaid, it was mutually understood, agreed, and intended by the parties hereto that, notwithstanding plaintiff's said use of intoxicating liquors, he was nevertheless entitled to receive and would receive said royalty as the same accrued under said contract." The defendant's breach of the contract is then alleged, which is claimed to consist in his having taken out a copyright upon the plaintiff's work on Corporations in the name of a publishing company which had not relation to the contract and the relief asked for is that the defendant be compelled to account, and that the copyright be transferred to the plaintiff, or that he recover its value.

[4] The appeal is by permission of the Appellate Division, and the following questions have been certified to us: (1) Does the complaint herein state facts sufficient to constitute a cause of action? (2) Under the terms of the contract alleged in the complaint, is the plaintiff's total abstinence from the use of intoxicating liquors a condition precedent which can be waived so as to render defendant liable upon the contract notwithstanding plaintiff's use of intoxicating liquors? (3) Does the complaint herein allege facts constituting a valid and effective waiver of plaintiff's nonperformance of such condition precedent?

[5] WERNER, J. (after stating the facts as above). The contract before us, stripped of all superfluous verbiage, binds the plaintiff to total abstention from the use of intoxicating liquors during the continuance of the work which he was employed to do. The stipulations relating to the plaintiff's compensation provide that if he does not observe this condition he is to be paid at the rate of $2 per page, and if he does comply therewith he is to receive $6 per page. The plaintiff has written one book under the contract known as "Clark & Marshall on Corporations," which has been accepted, published, and copies sold in large numbers by the defendant.

The plaintiff admits that while he was at work on the book he did not entirely abstain from the use of intoxicating liquors. He has been paid only $2 per page for the work he has done. He claims that, despite his breach of this condition, he is entitled to the full compensation of $6 per page, because the defendant, with full knowledge of plaintiff's nonobservance of this stipulation as to total abstinence, has waived the breach thereof and cannot now insist upon strict performance in this regard. This plea of waiver presents the underlying question which determines the answers to the questions certified.

[6] Briefly stated, the defendant's position is that the stipulation as to plaintiff's total abstinence is the consideration for the payment of the difference between $2 and $6 per page, and therefore could not be waived except by a new agreement to that effect based upon a good consideration; that the so-called waiver alleged by the plaintiff is not a waiver, but a modification of the contract in respect of its consideration. The plaintiff, on the other hand, argues that the stipulation for his total abstinence was merely a condition precedent, intended to work a forfeiture of the additional compensation in case of a breach, and that it could be waived without any formal agreement to that effect based upon a new consideration.

[7] The subject matter of the contract was the writing of books by the plaintiff for the defendant. The duration of the contract was the time necessary to complete them all. The work was to be done to the satisfaction of the defendant, and the plaintiff was not to write any other books except those covered by the contract, unless requested so to do by the defendant, in which latter event he was to be paid for that particular work by the year. The compensation for the work specified in the contract was to be $6 per page, unless the plaintiff failed to totally abstain from the use of intoxicating liquors during the continuance of the contract, in which event he was to receive only $2 per page. That is the obvious import of the contract construed in the light of the purpose for which it was made, and in accordance with the ordinary meaning of plain language. It is not a contract to write books in order that the plaintiff shall keep sober, but a contract containing a stipulation that he shall keep sober so that he may write satisfactory books. When we view the contract from this standpoint, it will readily be perceived that the particular stipulation is not the consideration for the contract, but simply one of its conditions which fits in with those relating to time and method of delivery of manuscript, revision of proof, citation of cases, assignment of copyrights, keeping track of new cases and citations for new editions, and other details which might be waived by the defendant, if he saw fit to do so. This is made clear, it seems to us, by the provision that, "in consideration of the above promises," the defendant agrees to pay the plaintiff $2 per page on each book prepared by him, and if he "abstains from the use of intoxicating liquor and otherwise

fulfills his agreements as hereinbefore set forth, he shall be paid an additional $4 per page in manner hereinbefore stated." The compensation of $2 per page, not to exceed $250 per month, was an advance or partial payment of the whole price of $6 per page, and the payment of the two-thirds, which was to be withheld pending the performance of the contract, was simply made contingent upon the plaintiff's total abstention from the use of intoxicants during the life of the contract. It is possible, of course, by segregating that clause of the contract from the context, to give it a wider meaning and a different aspect than it has when read in conjunction with other stipulations; but this is also true of other paragraphs of the contract. The paragraph, for instance, which provides that after the publication of any of the books written by the plaintiff he is to receive an amount equal to one-sixth of the net receipts from the combined sales of all the books which shall have been published by the defendant under the contract, less any and all payments previously made, "until the amount of $6 per page of each book shall have been paid, after which the first party (plaintiff) shall have no right, title, or interest in said books or the receipts from the sales thereof."

[8] That section of the contract, standing alone, would indicate that the plaintiff was to be entitled, in any event, to the $6 per page to be paid out of the net receipts of the copies of the book sold. The contract, read as a whole, however, shows that it is modified by the preceding provisions, making the compensation in excess of the $2 per page dependent upon the plaintiff's total abstinence, and upon the performance by him of the other conditions of the contract. It is obvious that the parties thought that the plaintiff's normal work was worth $6 per page. That was the sum to be paid for the work done by the plaintiff, and not for total abstinence. If the plaintiff did not keep to the condition as to total abstinence, he was to lose part of that sum. Precisely the same situation would have risen if the plaintiff had disregarded any of the other essential conditions of the contract. The fact that the particular stipulation was emphasized did not change its character. It was still a condition which the defendant could have insisted upon, as he has apparently done in regard to some others, and one which he could waive just as he might have waived those relating to the amount of the advance payments, or the number of pages to be written each month. A breach of any of the substantial conditions of the contract would have entailed a loss or forfeiture similar to that consequent upon a breach of the one relating to total abstinence, in case of the defendant's insistence upon his right to take advantage of them. This, we think, is the fair interpretation of the contract, and it follows that the stipulation as to the plaintiff's total abstinence was nothing more nor less than a condition precedent. If that conclusion is well founded, there can be no escape from the corollary that this condition could be waived; and, if it was waived, the defendant is clearly not in a position to insist upon the forfeiture which his waiver was intended to annihilate. The forfeiture must

stand or fall with the condition. If the latter was waived, the former is no longer a part of the contract. Defendant still has the right to counterclaim for any damages which he may have sustained in consequence of the plaintiff's breach, but he cannot insist upon strict performance.

[9] This whole discussion is predicated, of course upon the theory of an express waiver. We assume that no waiver could be implied from the defendant's mere acceptance of the books and his payment of the sum of $2 per page without objection. It was the defendant's duty to pay that amount in any event after acceptance of the work. The plaintiff must stand upon his allegation of an express waiver, and if he fails to establish that he cannot maintain his action.

[10] The theory upon which the defendant's attitude seems to be based is that, even if he has represented to the plaintiff that he would not insist upon the condition that the latter should observe total abstinence from intoxicants, he can still refuse to pay the full contract price for his work. The inequity of this position becomes apparent when we consider that this contract was to run for a period of years, during a large portion of which the plaintiff was to be entitled only to the advance payment of $2 per page; the balance being contingent, among other things, upon publication of the books and returns from sales. Upon this theory the defendant might have waived the condition while the first book was in process of production, and yet, when the whole work was completed, he would still be in a position to insist upon the forfeiture because there had not been strict performance. Such a situation is possible in a case where the subject of the waiver is the very consideration of a contract (*Organ v. Stewart*, 60 N.Y. 413, 420), but not where the waiver relates to something that can be waived. In the case at bar, as we have seen, the waiver is not of the consideration or subject-matter, but of an incident to the method of performance. The consideration remains the same. The defendant has had the work he bargained for, and it is alleged that he has waived one of the conditions as to the manner in which it was to have been done. He might have insisted upon literal performance, and then he could have stood upon the letter of his contract. If, however, he has waived that incidental condition, he has created a situation to which the doctrine of waiver very precisely applies.

[11] The cases which present the most familiar phases of the doctrine of waiver are those which have arisen out of litigation over insurance policies where the defendants have claimed a forfeiture because of the breach of some condition in the contract, but it is a doctrine of general application which is confined to no particular class of cases. A "waiver" has been defined to be the intentional relinquishment of a known right. It is voluntary and implies an election to dispense with something of value, or forego some advantage which the party waiving it might at its option have demanded or insisted upon, and this definition is supported by many cases in this and other states. In the recent case of *Draper v. Oswego Co. Fire R.*

Assn, 190 N.Y. 12, 15, 82 N.E. 755, Chief Judge Cullen, in speaking for the court upon this subject, said: "While that doctrine and the doctrine of equitable estoppel are often confused in insurance litigation, there is a clear distinction between the two. A 'waiver' is the voluntary abandonment or relinquishment by a party of some right or advantage. As said by my Brother Vann in the *Kiernan Case*, 150 N.Y. 190, 44 N.E. 698: 'The law of waiver seems to be a technical doctrine introduced and applied by the court for the purpose of defeating forfeitures . . . While the principle may not be easily classified, it is well established that, if the words and acts of the insurer reasonably justify the conclusion that with full knowledge of all the facts it intended to abandon or not to insist upon the particular defense afterwards relied upon, a verdict or finding to that effect establishes a waiver, which, if it once exists, can never be revoked.' The doctrine of equitable estoppel, or estoppel in pais, is that a party may be precluded by his acts and conduct from asserting a right to the detriment of another party who, entitled to rely on such conduct, has acted upon it . . . As already said, the doctrine of waiver is to relieve against forfeiture. It requires no consideration for a waiver, nor any prejudice or injury to the other party." To the same effect, *see Knarston v. Manhattan Life Ins. Co.*, 140 Cal. 57, 73 Pac. 740.

[12] It remains to be determined whether the plaintiff has alleged facts which, if proven, will be sufficient to establish his claim of an express waiver by the defendant of the plaintiff's breach of the condition to observe total abstinence. In the 12th paragraph of the complaint, the plaintiff alleges facts and circumstances which we think, if established, would prove defendant's waiver of plaintiff's performance of that contract stipulation. These facts and circumstances are that, long before the plaintiff had completed the manuscript of the first book undertaken under the contract, the defendant had full knowledge of the plaintiff's nonobservance of that stipulation, and that with such knowledge he not only accepted the completed manuscript without objection, but "repeatedly avowed and represented to the plaintiff that he was entitled to and would receive said royalty payments (i.e., the additional $4 per page), and plaintiff believed and relied upon such representations, . . . and at all times during the writing of said treatise on Corporations, and after as well as before publication thereof as aforesaid, it was mutually understood, agreed, and intended by the parties hereto that, notwithstanding plaintiff's said use of intoxicating liquors, he was nevertheless entitled to receive and would receive said royalty as the same accrued under said contract." The demurrer not only admits the truth of these allegations, but also all that can by reasonable and fair intendment be implied therefrom. Under the modern rule, pleadings are not to be construed against the pleader, but averments which sufficiently point out the nature of the plaintiff's claim are sufficient, if under them he would be entitled to give the necessary evidence. Tested by these rules, we think it cannot be doubted that the

allegations contained in the twelfth paragraph of the complaint, if proved upon the trial, would be sufficient to establish an express waiver by the defendant of the stipulation in regard to plaintiff's total abstinence.

[13] The three questions certified should be answered in the affirmative, the order of the Appellate Division reversed the interlocutory judgment of the Special Term affirmed, with costs in both courts, and defendant be permitted to answer the complaint within 20 days upon payment of costs.

CULLEN, C.J., and EDWARD T. BARTLETT, HAIGH, VANN, HISCOCK, and CHASE, J.J., concur.

Order reversed, etc.

———

NOTES AND QUESTIONS

1. In the fall of 1899, about four months before he entered into the contract in question, Mr. Clark was dismissed from his position as a law professor at Washington & Lee University, a position he had only had for a month or two. The university president explained that Professor Clark was "addicted to drinking beyond what would be proper in a college professor."

2. In the next case, the difficulty of administering contracts, conditions, and waivers of conditions in practice is illustrated. The best-laid contracts and plans can easily go awry.

———

BURGER KING V. FAMILY DINING, INC.

United States District Court, Eastern District, Pennsylvania
426 F. Supp. 485 (1977)

Memorandum and Order

HANNUM, DISTRICT JUDGE.

[1] Presently before the Court is defendant's motion for an involuntary dismissal in accordance with Rule 41(b), Federal Rules of Civil Procedure, advanced at the close of plaintiff's case. The trial is before the Court sitting without a jury.

[2] In bringing the suit plaintiff seeks a determination under the Declaratory Judgment Act, Title 28, United States Code § 2201, that a contract between the parties, by its own terms, is no longer of any force and effect. A request for declaratory relief is appropriate in a case such as this where the primary question is whether such a termination has occurred.

[3] Jurisdiction of the parties is based on diversity of citizenship in accordance with Title 28, United States Code § 1332(a).

Facts Established in Plaintiff's Case

[4] Plaintiff Burger King Corporation (hereinafter "Burger King") is a Florida corporation engaged in franchising the well-known Burger King Restaurants. In 1954, James W. McLamore, founder of Burger King Restaurants, Inc. (the corporate predecessor of Burger King) built the first Burger King Restaurant in Miami, Florida. In 1961 the franchise system was still relatively modest size having only about 60 or 70 restaurants in operation outside of Florida. By 1963, however, Burger King began to experience significant growth and was building and operating, principally through franchisees, 24 restaurants per year. It was also at this time that Burger King's relationship with defendant Family Dining, Inc., (hereinafter "Family Dining") was created.

[5] Family Dining is a Pennsylvania corporation which at the present time operates ten Burger King Restaurants (hereinafter "Restaurant") in Bucks and Montgomery Counties in Pennsylvania. Family Dining was founded and is currently operated by Carl Ferris who had been a close personal friend of McLamore's for a number of years prior to 1963. In fact they had attended Cornell University together in the late 1940's. It would seem that this friendship eventually led to the business relationship between Burger King and Family Dining which was conceived in the "Burger King Territorial Agreement" (hereinafter "Territorial Agreement") entered on May 10, 1963.

[6] In accordance with the Territorial Agreement Burger King agreed that Family Dining would be its sole licensee, and thus have an "exclusive territory," in Bucks and Montgomery Counties provided Family Dining operated each Restaurant pursuant to Burger King license agreements[12] and maintained a specified rate of development. Articles I and II of the Territorial Agreement (Plaintiff's Exhibit P-2) are pertinent to this dispute. They provide as follows:

I

For a period of one year, beginning on the date hereof, Company will not operate or license others for the operation of any BURGER KING restaurant within the following described territory hereinafter referred to as "exclusive territory," to-wit:

The counties of Bucks and Montgomery, all in the State of Pennsylvania

---

[12] Each restaurant is opened pursuant to a separate Burger King license agreement.

as long as licensee operates each BURGER KING restaurant pursuant to BURGER KING restaurant licenses with Company and faithfully performs each of the covenants herein contained.

This agreement shall remain in effect and Licensee shall retain the exclusive territory for a period of ninety (90) years from the date hereof, provided that at the end of one, two, three, four, five, six, seven, eight, nine and ten years from the date hereof, and continuously thereafter during the next eighty years, Licensee has the following requisite number of BURGER KING restaurants in operation or under active construction, pursuant to Licenses with Company:

One (1) restaurant at the end of one year;

Two (2) restaurants at the end of two years;

Three (3) restaurants at the end of three years;

Four (4) restaurants at the end of four years;

Five (5) restaurants at the end of five years;

Six (6) restaurants at the end of six years;

Seven (7) restaurants at the end of seven years;

Eight (8) restaurants at the end of eight years;

Nine (9) restaurants at the end of nine years;

Ten (10) restaurants at the end of ten years;

and continually maintains not less than ten (10) restaurants during the next eighty (80) years.

Licensee and company may mutually agree to the execution of a restaurant license to a person other than the Licensee, herein, if such restaurant license is executed same will count as a requisite number as set forth in paragraph above.

II

If at the end of either one, two, three, four, five, six, seven, eight, nine or ten years from the date hereof, or anytime thereafter during the next eighty (80) years, there are less than the respective requisite number of BURGER KING operations or under active construction in the "exclusive territory" pursuant to licenses by Company, this agreement shall terminate and be of no further force and effect. Thereafter, Company may operate or license others for the operation of BURGER KING Restaurants anywhere within the exclusive territory, so long as such restaurants are not within the "Protected Area", as set forth in any BURGER KING Restaurant License to which the Licensee herein is a party.

[7] The prospect of exclusivity for ninety years was clearly intended to be an inducement to Family Dining to develop the territory as prescribed and it appears that it had exactly this effect as Family Dining was to become one of Burger King's most successful franchisees. While Burger King considered Carl Ferris to be somewhat of a problem at various times and one who was overly meticulous with detail, it was nevertheless through his efforts which included obtaining the necessary financing and assuming significant risks, largely without assistance from Burger King, that enabled both parties to benefit from the arrangement.

[8] On August 16, 1963, Family Dining opened the First Restaurant at 588 West DeKalb Pike in King of Prussia, Pennsylvania. The second Restaurant was opened on July 2, 1965, at 409 West Ridge Pike, Conshohocken, Pennsylvania, and the third Restaurant was opened October 19, 1966, at 2561 West Main Street, Norristown, Pennsylvania.

[9] However, by April, 1968, Family Dining had not opened or begun active construction on a fourth Restaurant which, in accordance with the development rate, should have been accomplished by May 10, 1967, and it was apparent that a fifth Restaurant would not be opened by May 10, 1968, the date scheduled. On May 1, 1968, the parties entered into a Modification of the Territorial Agreement (hereinafter "Modification") whereby Burger King agreed to waive Family Dining's failure to comply with the development rate. (Plaintiff's Exhibit P-4.) There is nothing contained in the record which indicates that Burger King received anything of value in exchange for entering this agreement. However, McLamore testified that if the fourth and fifth Restaurants would be built nearly in compliance with the development rate for the fifth year he would overlook the year or so default in the fourth Restaurant. (N.T. 39). This attitude seems to be consistent with his overall view toward the development rate with respect to which, he testified, was "designed to insure the company of an orderly process of growth which would also enable the company to produce a profit on the sale of its franchises and through the collection of royalties that the restaurants would themselves produce." (N.T. 35.)

[10] The fourth Restaurant was opened on July 1, 1968, at 1721 North DeKalb Pike, Norristown, Pennsylvania, and the fifth Restaurant was opened on October 17, 1968, at 1035 Bustleton Pike in Feasterville, Pennsylvania.

[11] On April 18, 1969, Ferris forwarded a letter to McLamore pertaining to certain delays in site approval and relating McLamore's earlier statement that there would be no problem in waiving the development schedule for the sixth Restaurant. (Plaintiff's Exhibit P-5.) The letter expressed Ferris' concern regarding compliance with the

development rate. By letter dated April 26, 1969, from Howard Walker of Burger King, Ferris was granted a month extension in the development rate. (Plaintiff's Exhibit P-6.) With respect to this extension McLamore testified that "it never crossed my mind to call a default of this agreement on a technicality." (N.T. 47.)

[12] On October 1, 1969, the sixth Restaurant was opened at 1515 East High Street in Pottstown, Pennsylvania. The seventh Restaurant was opened on February 2, 1970, ahead of schedule, at 560 North Main Street in Doylestown, Pennsylvania.

[13] At this point in time Burger King was no longer a modest sized franchise system. It had became a wholly owned subsidiary of the Pillsbury Company and had, in fact, evolved into a complex corporate entity. McLamore was elevated to Chairman of the Board of Burger King and, while he remained the chief executive officer for a time, Arthur A. Rosewall was installed as Burger King's President. Ferris was no longer able to expect the close, one to one relationship with McLamore that had previously obtained in his dealings with the company. It seems clear that as a result Family Dining began to experience difficulties in its day to day operations with Burger King.

[14] One of the problem areas which arose concerned site selection. In a typical situation when a franchisee would seek approval for a building site an application would be submitted to the National Development Committee comprised of various Burger King officials. Based on Ferris' prior showing regarding site selection it could be expected that he would have little difficulty in obtaining their approval. In McLamore's view, Ferris was an exceptionally fine franchisee whose ability to choose real estate locations was exceptional. (N.T. 61.) However, in August, 1970, a Frankford Avenue location selected by Ferris was rejected by the National Development Committee. The reasons offered in support of the decision to reject are not entirely clear and it seems that for the most part it was an exercise of discretion. The only plausible reason, given Ferris' expertise, was that the site was 2.7 miles from another Burger King franchise operated by Pete Miller outside Family Dining's exclusive territory. Yet Burger King chose not to exercise its discretion in similar circumstances when it permitted another franchisee to build a Restaurant in Devon, Pennsylvania, approximately 3 miles away from an existing Family Dining Restaurant.

[15] In his August 25, 1970, memo to the Carl Ferris file McLamore observed that Burger King "had sloppy real estate work involved in servicing him and that (Burger King was) guilty of many follow up delinquencies." (Defendant's Exhibit D-7.) This was during a time, as Burger King management was well aware, where it was one thing to select a location and quite another to actually develop it. That is, local governing

bodies were taking a much stricter view toward allowing this type of development. It was also during this time, as McLamore's memo points out, Burger King realized that the Bucks-Montgomery territory was capable of sustaining substantially more Restaurants than originally thought.

[16] Amidst these circumstances, the eighth Restaurant was opened ahead of schedule on October 7, 1970, at 601 South Broad Street in Lansdale, Pennsylvania. And in December, 1971, Burger King approved Family Dining's proposed sites for two additional Restaurants in Ambler, Pennsylvania and Levittown, Pennsylvania.

[17] In early 1972, Arthur Rosewell became the chief executive officer of Burger King. At this time it also became apparent that the ninth Restaurant would not be opened or under construction by May 10, 1972. On April 27, 1972, in a telephone conversation with McLamore, Ferris once again expressed his concern to Burger King regarding compliance with the development rate. Burger King's position at that time is evidenced by McLamore's Memo to the Carl Ferris file dated April 28, 1972, wherein he provides that "Ferris' territorial arrangement with the company is such that he must have his ninth store (he has eight open now) under construction next month. I indicated to him that, due to the fact that he was in the process of developing four sites at this time, the company would consider he had met, substantially, the requirements of exclusivity." (Plaintiff's Exhibit P-7.) McLamore testified that at that time he had in mind a further delay of 3 to 6 months. (N.T. 55.)

[18] In April, 1973, Burger King approved Family Dining's proposed site for a Restaurant in Warminster, Pennsylvania. However, as of May 10, 1973, neither the ninth or the tenth Restaurant had been opened or under active construction.

[19] A letter dated May 23, 1973, from Helen D. Donaldson, Franchise Documents Administrator for Burger King, was sent to Ferris. (Plaintiff's Exhibit P-10.) The letter provides as follows:

> Dear Mr. Ferris:
>
> During a periodic review of all territorial agreements we note that as of this date your development schedule requiring ten restaurants to be open or under construction by May 10, 1973, has not been met. Our records reflect eight stores open in Bucks and/or Montgomery County, and one site approved but not manned.
>
> Under the terms of your territorial agreement failure to have the required number of stores in operation or under active construction constitutes a default of your agreement.
>
> If there are extenuating circumstances about which this office is not aware, we would appreciate your earliest advice.

[20] It is doubtful that the Donaldson letter was intended to communicate to Ferris that the Territorial Agreement was terminated. The testimony of both Rosewall (N.T. 187) and Leslie W. Paszat (N.T. 256), an executive of Burger King, who worked closely with Rosewall on the Family Dining matter indicates that even Burger King had not settled its position at this time. Ferris' letter dated July 27, 1973, to Rosewall (Defendant's Exhibit D-10), and Rosewall's reply dated August 3, 1973 (Plaintiff's Exhibit P-11) also fail to demonstrate any understanding that the Territorial Agreement was terminated.

[21] It seems that throughout this period Burger King treated the matter as something of a "hot potato" subjecting Ferris to contact with several different Burger King officials. Much of Ferris' contact with Rosewall was interrupted by Rosewall's month long vacation and a meat shortage crisis to which he had to devote a substantial amount of his time. Ultimately Paszat was given responsibility for Family Dining and it appears that he provided Ferris with the first clear indication that Burger King considered the Territorial Agreement terminated in his letter of November 6, 1973 (Plaintiff's Exhibit P-14). Burger King's corporate structure had become so complex that the question of who, when or where the decision was made could not be answered. The abrupt manner in which Burger King's position was communicated to Family Dining, under the circumstances, was not straightforward.[13]

[22] From November, 1973, until some point early in 1975, the parties attempted to negotiate their differences with no success. The reason for the lack of success is understandable given that Burger King from the outset considered exclusivity a non-negotiable item. It was during this period on September 7, 1974, that Family Dining began actual construction of the ninth Restaurant in Warminster, Pennsylvania.

[23] Several months before the instant litigation was begun Family Dining informed Burger King that it intended to open a ninth Restaurant on or about May 15, 1975, on Street Road, Warminster, Pennsylvania. In February, 1975, Burger King notified Family Dining that a franchise agreement (license) had to be entered for the additional Restaurant without which Family Dining would be infringing Burger King's trademarks. A similar notice was given in April, 1975, in which Burger King indicated it would retain counsel to protect its rights. Nevertheless Family Dining proceeded with its plans to open the Warminster Restaurant.

[24] In May, 1975, Burger King filed a complaint, which was the inception of this lawsuit, seeking to enjoin the use of Burger King

---

[13]   [The lesson here is that the failure to look the person in the eye and say "there's a problem here" can have both business and legal consequences. If you can't do it, hire someone to do it for you.—Eds.]

trademarks by Family Dining at the Warminster Restaurant. The Court granted a Temporary Restraining Order until a hearing on the complaint could be held. On May 13, 1975, the parties reached an agreement on terms under which the Burger King trademarks could be used at the Warminster Restaurant. Pursuant to the agreement Burger King filed an amended complaint seeking the instant declaratory relief. Subsequently and also pursuant to this agreement Family Dining opened its tenth Restaurant in Willow Grove, Pennsylvania, the construction of which began on March 28, 1975.

Discussion

[25] Family Dining raises several arguments in support of its motion pursuant to Rule 41(b). One of its principal arguments is that the termination provision should be found inoperative because otherwise it would result in a forfeiture to Family Dining. For reasons which have become evident during the presentation of Burger King's case the Court finds Family Dining's position compelling both on legal and equitable grounds and is thus persuaded that the Territorial Agreement should not be declared terminated. Under Rule 41(b) when a plaintiff in an action tried by the Court without a jury has completed the presentation of his evidence, the defendant, without waiving his right to offer evidence in the event the motion is not granted, may move for a dismissal on the ground that upon the facts and the law plaintiff has shown no right to relief. Inasmuch as termination is the only relief sought by Burger King, it follows that dismissal of the action is appropriate.

[26] In bringing this suit Burger King maintains that the Territorial Agreement is a divisible contract wherein Family Dining promised to open or have under active construction one new Restaurant in each of the first ten years of the contract in exchange for which Burger King promised to grant one additional year of exclusivity for each new Restaurant. This, to be followed by an additional eighty years of exclusivity provided the first ten Restaurants were built on time. In support Burger King relies on the opening language of Article I of the Territorial Agreement which provides that "(f)or a period of one year, beginning on the date hereof, Company will not operate or license . . ." It is thus argued that since Family Dining clearly failed to perform its promises the Court must, in accordance with the express language of Article II, declare the contract terminated. Burger King further argues that because Family Dining did not earn exclusivity beyond the ninth year, upon termination, it could not be found that Family Dining would forfeit anything in which it had an interest.

[27] Contrary to the analysis offered by Burger King, the Court considers the development rate a condition subsequent, not a promise, which operates to divest Family Dining of exclusivity. Where words in a contract raise no duty in and of themselves but rather modify or limit the

promisees' right to enforce the promise such words are considered to be a condition. Whether words constitute a condition or a promise is a matter of the intention of the parties to be ascertained from a reasonable construction of the language used, considered in light of the surrounding circumstances. It seems clear that the true purpose of the Territorial Agreement was to create a long-term promise of exclusivity to act as an inducement to Family Dining to develop Bucks and Montgomery Counties within a certain time frame. A careful reading of the agreement indicates that it raises no duties, as such, in Family Dining. Both Article I and Article II contain language which refers to ninety years of exclusivity subject to limitation. For instance, Article I provides in part that "(t)his Agreement shall remain in effect and licensee shall retain the exclusive territory for a period of ninety (90) years from the date hereof, provided that at the end of one, two. . . ." Failure to comply with the development rate operates to defeat liability on Burger King's promise of exclusivity. Liability, or at least Family Dining's right to enforce the promise, arose upon entering the contract. The fact that Burger King seeks affirmative relief premised on the development rate and the fact that it calls for a specified performance by Family Dining tend to obscure its true nature. Nevertheless, in the Court's view it is a condition subsequent.

* * *

[28] The question arises whether Burger King has precluded itself from asserting Family Dining's untimeliness on the basis that Burger King did not demand literal adherence to the development rate throughout most of the first ten years of the contract. Nothing is commoner in contracts than for a promisor to protect himself by making his promise conditional. Ordinarily a party would be entitled to have such an agreement strictly enforced, however, before doing so the Court must consider not only the written contract but also the acts and conduct of the parties in carrying out the agreement. As Judge Kraft, in effect, provided in *Dempsey v. Stauffer*, 182 F.Supp. 806, 810 (E.D. Pa. 1960), after one party by conduct indicates that literal performance will not be required, he cannot without notice and a reasonable time begin demanding literal performance.

[29] In the early going Burger King did not demand that Family Dining perform in exact compliance with the development schedule. It failed to introduce any evidence indicating that a change in attitude had been communicated to Family Dining. At the time of the Donaldson letter Family Dining's non-compliance with the development rate was no worse than it was with respect to the fourth and fifth Restaurants. The letter itself was sent by a documents administrator rather than a Burger King official and it seems to imply that the Territorial Agreement would not be terminated. Assuming that at some point between May and November, or even at the time of the Donaldson letter, Ferris realized literal performance would be required, the circumstances of this type of development are such

that Burger King was unreasonable in declaring a termination such a short time after, if not concurrent with, notice that literal performance would be required.

[30] Considerable time was consumed in negotiations between November, 1973, until shortly before suit although it appears that these efforts were an exercise in futility given Burger King's view on exclusivity. Moreover, it could be expected that Burger King would have sued to enjoin any further progress by Family Dining, during this lengthy period, just as it did when Family Dining attempted to get the ninth Restaurant under way. The upshot being that the hiatus in development from November, 1973, until active construction began on the ninth and tenth Restaurants is not fully chargeable to Family Dining.

[31] Based on the foregoing the Court concludes that Burger King is not entitled to have the condition protecting its promise strictly enforced.

[32] Moreover and more important, even though a suit for declaratory relief can be characterized as neither legal nor equitable, giving strict effect to the termination provision involves divesting Family Dining of exclusivity, which, in the Court's view, would amount to a forfeiture. As a result the Court will not ignore considerations of fairness and believes that equitable principles, as well, ought to govern the outcome of this suit.

[33] The Restatement, Contracts, sec. 30[14] provides:

A condition may be excused without other reason if its requirement

    (a) will involve extreme forfeiture or penalty, and

    (b) its existence or occurrence forms no essential part of the exchange for the promisor's performance.

[34] Taking the latter consideration first, it seems clear that throughout the early duration of the contract Burger King was more concerned with a general development of the territory than it was with exact compliance with the terms of the development rate. Burger King offered no evidence that it ever considered literal performance to be critical. In fact, the evidence indicates quite the contrary. Even though McLamore testified that he never contemplated a delay of the duration which occurred with the ninth and tenth Restaurants, he felt a total delay of approximately 19 months with respect to the fourth and fifth Restaurants was nearly in compliance. On the basis of his prior conduct and his testimony considered in its entirety his comments on this point command little weight.

[35] Clearly Burger King's attitude with respect to the development rate changed. Interestingly enough it was sometime after Burger King realized Bucks and Montgomery Counties could support substantially

---

[14] [The substance of this is now contained in § 229 of the R2d.—Eds.]

more than ten Restaurants as had been originally thought. It was also at a time after Rosewall replaced McLamore as chief executive officer.

[36] Burger King maintains that Ferris' conduct indicates that he knew strict compliance with the development rate was required. This is based on the several occasions where Ferris expressed concern over noncompliance. However, during the presentation of Burger King's evidence it was established that Ferris was an individual who was overly meticulous with details which caused him to be, in many respects, ignored by Burger King officials. Given this aspect of his personality and Burger King's attitude toward him very little significance can be attached to Ferris' expressions of concern. In short, the evidence fails to establish that either Burger King or Family Dining considered the development rate critical. If it eventually did become critical it was not until very late in the first ten years and in such a way that, in conscience, it cannot be used to the detriment of Family Dining.

[37] As previously indicated, the Court believes that if the right of exclusivity were to be extinguished by termination it would constitute a forfeiture. In arguing that by termination Family Dining will lose nothing that it earned, Burger King overlooks the risks assumed and the efforts expended by Family Dining, largely without assistance from Burger King, in making the venture successful in the exclusive territory. While it is true that Family Dining realized a return on its investment, certainly part of this return was the prospect of continued exclusivity. Moreover, this is not a situation where Burger King did not receive any benefit from the relationship.

[38] In making the promise of exclusivity Burger King intended to induce Family Dining to develop its Restaurants in the exclusive territory. There is no evidence that the failure to fulfill the time feature of this inducement was the result of any intentional or negligent conduct on the part of Family Dining. And at the present time there are ten Restaurants in operation which was all the inducement was intended to elicit. Assuming all ten were built on time Burger King would have been able to expect some definable level of revenue, a percentage of which it lost due to the delay. Burger King did not, however, attempt to establish the amount of this loss at trial.

[39] In any event if Family Dining were forced to forfeit the right of exclusivity it would lose something of incalculable value based on its investment of time and money developing the area, the significant risks assumed and the fact that there remains some 76 years of exclusivity under the Territorial Agreement. Such a loss would be without any commensurate breach on its part since the injury caused to Burger King by the delay is relatively modest and within definable limits. Thus, a

termination of the Territorial Agreement would result in an extreme forfeiture to Family Dining.

[40] In accordance with the foregoing the Court finds that under the law and based upon the facts adduced in Burger King's case, it is not entitled to a declaration that the Territorial Agreement is terminated. Therefore, Family Dining's Rule 41(b) motion for an involuntary dismissal is granted.

NOTES AND QUESTIONS

1.   What was the condition involved in this case and what was the duty which arose or ceased if the condition occurred?

2.   Suppose that in May, 1973, when the letter quoted in paragraph 19 was being written, you had been asked to give legal advice to Burger King. What would you have told them to do with Mr. Ferris?

CANTRELL-WAIND & ASSOCIATES V. GUILLAUME MOTORSPORTS, INC.

Court of Appeals of Arkansas
62 Ark. App. 66, 968 S.W.2d 72 (1998)

SAM BIRD, JUDGE.

[1]   Cantrell-Waind & Associates, Inc., has appealed from a summary judgment entered for appellee Guillaume Motorsports, Inc., in its action to recover a real estate brokerage commission. Because we agree with appellant that the circuit judge erred in his interpretation of the applicable law and because genuine issues of material fact remain to be tried, we reverse and remand.

[2]   On August 1, 1994, appellee, represented by its president and sole stockholder Todd Williams, agreed to lease real property in Bentonville to Kenneth Bower and Kay Bower. The lease gave the Bowers an option to purchase and provided for the payment of a commission to appellant, the real estate broker in this transaction, as follows:

> In the event of the exercise of this option within the first twenty-four (24) month period, ten per cent (10%) of the monthly rental payments shall apply to the purchase price. Thereafter, this credit shall reduce two per cent (2%) per year until the expiration of the original lease term hereof, to the effect that the credit will be eight per cent (8%) during the third year, six per cent (6%) during the fourth year, and four per cent (4%) during the fifth year. The sales

price shall be $295,000.00. GUILLAUME MOTORSPORTS, INC., agrees [to] pay CANTRELL-WAIND & ASSOCIATES, INC., a real estate commission of $15,200.00 upon closing of sale of the property under this Option to Purchase, provided the closing occurs within two (2) years from the date of execution of the Lease with Option to Purchase.

[3] The Bowers' attorney, Charles Edward Young, III, notified Williams in writing on April 23, 1996, that the Bowers chose to exercise the option to purchase, and that they anticipated closing at the earliest possible date. Young also sent a copy of this letter to Samuel Reeves, appellee's attorney. Soon after this, Williams approached Mr. Bower and offered to credit him with one-half of the appellant's $15,200 commission if he would agree to delay closing until after August 1, 1996. Mr. Bower declined this offer.

[4] Ruth Ann Whitehead, a loan officer at the Bank of Bentonville, notified Mr. Bower on July 19, 1996, that the loan had been approved and that she awaited notification of a closing date. In his deposition, Young said that he attempted to set a July closing date on behalf of the Bowers but had been told by Ms. Whitehead, Reeves, and a representative of the title company that Williams had told them he would be out of the country in late July and unavailable for closing until after August 1.

[5] Young also said that he had asked Reeves if Williams would utilize a power of attorney for closing before August 1 but Williams refused. Williams did not leave the country and was in Bentonville July 22 through 25. Closing occurred on August 14, 1996, and the commission was not paid.

[6] Appellant filed a complaint against Guillaume Motorsports, Inc., on August 12, 1996, for breach of contract. Appellee moved for summary judgment on the ground that it was under no obligation to close the transaction before August 1. In support of its motion, appellee filed the affidavits of Ms. Whitehead and Mr. Carroll, who stated that, to their knowledge, a closing date was not scheduled before August 14, 1996.

[7] Appellee Williams also filed his affidavit stating that a closing date was not established before August 14, 1996, and that the Bowers had not demanded an earlier closing date. Further, he admitted: "While I did in fact approach Kenneth Bower with a proposal to reduce the purchase price if he would agree to establish a closing date after August 1, 1996, my offer was not accepted and no such agreement was made." He said although it would not have bothered him to put the closing off until after August 1, he did not think it was a "conscious decision" not to be available until after August 1.

[8] In a hearing on the motion for summary judgment, counsel for appellee argued that neither the corporation nor Williams was under any obligation to close prior to August 1. He contended there was no bad faith

to be inferred by the deliberate avoidance of a real estate commission that is keyed to a "drop-dead" date. He said the real estate broker agreed to the terms of the contract and was bound by it. Counsel pointed out the two separate terms used in the contract when referring to the option to purchase and the closing. The contract stated that to get the maximum discount in the purchase price the Bowers had to exercise the option before August 1, 1996. However, the clause referring to the commission stated that the transaction had to close by August 1. Counsel stated, "I believe my client had every right to do anything within his power, short of breaching his contract with this buyer, to see that this closing didn't occur earlier than that date so he would not owe the commission."

[9] In response to appellee's motion for summary judgment, appellant argued that appellee (by Williams) had a duty to act in good faith and that, in taking steps to prevent the transaction from closing before August 1, 1996, appellee had not acted in good faith. Appellant contended that all contingencies and requirements for the loan had been satisfied by July 19, 1996, and that Mr. and Ms. Bower had attempted to establish a closing date before August 1, but had been deliberately prevented from doing so by Williams's misrepresentations that he would be out of the country and unavailable to close until after August 1. Appellant attached as exhibits excerpts from the depositions of Ms. Whitehead, Mr. Young, Laura Tway (who assisted with closing), Mrs. Bower, Mr. Bower, Williams, and Mr. Carroll. Also attached was a copy of Mr. Young's May 28, 1996, letter to Mr. Reeves. In a supplemental response to the motion for summary judgment, appellant also requested summary judgment against appellee.

[10] In his order granting summary judgment, the judge stated that appellee had no obligation to appellant to arrange for a closing date that would have entitled appellant to a commission and said that the real estate commission was "clearly avoidable" by appellee.

[11] On appeal appellant argues that the trial court erred in ignoring Williams's prevention of a condition precedent as a material fact and that the trial court erred in granting summary judgment in appellee's favor. Appellant argues that, although appellee had no duty to insure that closing occurred before August 1, 1996, it did have a duty not to actively hinder or prevent the transaction from closing before that date. Appellee contends that the circuit court acted appropriately in refusing to extend its obligations beyond those created by the express terms of the contract and that Williams was under no obligation to make himself available for a closing date that would have entitled appellant to a commission.

[12] The term of the contract providing that a commission would be due appellant only if closing occurred before August 1, 1996, is a condition precedent. When a contract term leaves a decision to the discretion of one

party, that decision is virtually unreviewable; however, courts will become involved when the party making the decision is charged with bad faith.

[13] In *Willbanks v. Bibler*, 216 Ark. 68, 224 S.W.2d 33 (1949), the Arkansas Supreme Court held that "he who prevents the doing of a thing shall not avail himself of the nonperformance he has occasioned." *Id.* at 72, 224 S.W.2d at 35. *See also* Samuel Williston, The Law of Contracts sec. 677 (3d ed. 1961). This principle is expressed in 17A Am. Jur. 2d Contracts § 703 (1991):

> One who prevents or makes impossible the performance or happening of a condition precedent upon which his liability by the terms of a contract is made to depend cannot avail himself of its nonperformance. Even more broadly, where a promisor prevents or hinders the occurrence, happening, or fulfillment of a condition in a contract, and the condition would have occurred except for such hindrance or prevention, the performance of the condition is excused and the liability of the promisor is fixed regardless of the failure to perform the condition. Moreover, while prevention by one party to a contract of the performance of a condition precedent excuses the nonperformance of the condition, it must be shown that the nonperformance was actually due to the conduct of such party; if the condition would not have happened whatever such conduct, it is not dispensed with.

[14] A party has an implied obligation not to do anything that would prevent, hinder, or delay performance.

[15] Comment b to section 225 of the Restatement (Second) of Contracts (1981) provides that the non-occurrence of a condition of a duty is said to be "excused" when the condition need no longer occur in order for performance of the duty to become due: "It may be excused by prevention or hindrance of its occurrence through a breach of the duty of good faith and fair dealing." The Restatement (Second) of Contracts sec. 205 (1981) states: "Every contract imposes upon each party a duty of good faith and fair dealing in its performance and its enforcement." This legal principle also applies to contracts providing for the payment of commissions to real estate agents. Accordingly, we hold that the circuit court erred in failing to recognize that a duty of good faith and fair dealing was included in this contract and, therefore, appellee was obligated to not deliberately avoid closing the transaction before August 1, 1996.

[16] Our above holding requires a determination of whether there is a genuine issue of material fact as to whether appellee's actions prevented or hindered the occurrence of the condition precedent. The burden of sustaining a motion for summary judgment is on the moving party. On appeal, we must view the evidence in the light most favorable to the non-moving party. It is our task to determine whether the evidentiary items

presented by the moving party in support of the motion left a material question of fact unanswered. Summary judgment is not proper where evidence, although in no material dispute, reveals aspects from which inconsistent hypotheses might reasonably be drawn and reasonable minds might differ. It is not the role of summary judgment to weigh and resolve conflicting testimony but to simply decide whether such questions exist to be resolved at trial. A summary judgment analysis does not evaluate evidence beyond the question of whether a dispute exists.

[17] Appellant presented evidence that all of the requirements for the transaction to close had occurred by July 19, 1996, and that Mr. and Ms. Bower were eager to close before August 1; that Williams was aware that closing could occur before August 1; and that Williams had stated to Ms. Whitehead that he would be unavailable to close the transaction until after August 1 because he would be out of the country. In his deposition, and in his answers to appellant's requests for admission, appellee Williams admitted that he was in fact in Bentonville from July 22 through 25 and that he did not leave the country.

[18] In its brief, appellant asserts that it was entitled to summary judgment. We note, however, that appellant did not move for summary judgment but simply requested such relief in the conclusion to its supplemental response to appellee's motion for summary judgment. Consequently, even if the trial court had applied the correct principle of law, and if appellant had properly moved for summary judgment, we could not agree that summary judgment was warranted. In his deposition, appellee Williams testified that he was ready, willing, and able to close and would have closed the transaction before August 1 if he had been contacted. He also stated that, although he was in Bentonville on July 22 through 25, he was not aware until the afternoon of the 25th that the Bowers wanted to close the transaction as soon as possible. In our opinion, genuine issues of material fact remained for trial. Accordingly, we reverse the circuit judge's entry of summary judgment for appellee and remand this case for trial.

Reversed and remanded.

ROBBINS, C.J., and ROAF, J., agree.

_____

WESTERN HILLS, OREGON, LTD. V. PFAU

Supreme Court of Oregon
265 Or. 137, 508 P.2d 201 (1973)

MCALLISTER, J.

[1] This is a suit to compel specific performance of an agreement to purchase real property. The plaintiff, the owner of the property, is a limited

partnership. Defendants are members of a joint venture, formed for the purpose of purchasing the property from plaintiff and developing it. The trial court found that plaintiff was entitled to specific performance of the agreement, and entered its decree accordingly. Defendants appeal, contending that they were excused from performing by a failure of a condition contained in the agreement, and that the agreement is too indefinite to permit specific enforcement.

[2] Plaintiff Western Hills owned a tract of approximately 286 acres in Yamhill County which it had listed for sale with a Salem real estate firm. Defendant Pfau, who is also a real estate broker, heard about this listing early in 1970. He contacted the other defendants, and they jointly submitted a proposal to purchase the property. Their original proposal was not accepted, but negotiations with Western Hills took place which culminated, on or about March 6, 1970, in the execution of the written agreement which is the subject of this suit. The agreement consists of a filled-in form entitled "Exchange Agreement" together with several attached documents. Generally, it provides that in exchange for the Yamhill County property, defendants agreed to pay Western Hills $15,000 in cash, to convey to Western Hills four parcels of real property "subject to appraisal and acceptance" by Western Hills, and to pay a balance of $173,600 on terms specified in the agreement. In addition to other terms not material to this appeal, the agreement provides:

> Closing of transaction is subject to ability of purchasers to negotiate with City of McMinnville as to a planned development satisfactory to both first and second parties within 90 days from date. A reasonable extension not to exceed 6 months to be granted if necessary.

[3] Defendants made preliminary proposals for a planned development to the McMinnville Planning Commission, but, although the Commission's reaction to these proposals was favorable, defendants abandoned their attempts to secure approval of a development plan. In September, 1970, defendant Pfau, who represented the other defendants in the transaction, met with some of the partners in Western Hills and notified them that defendants did not wish to go through with the purchase. Western Hills refused to release defendants from the agreement. This suit followed.

[4] Defendants contend that their obligation to purchase the property never became absolute because the condition quoted above was never fulfilled. It appears from the evidence that defendants did not proceed with their application for Planning Commission approval of a planned development because they believed the development would be too expensive, primarily because city sewers would not be available to serve the property for several years. Immediate development would have

required the developers to provide a private system of sewage treatment and disposal.

[5] It also appears that at the time they executed the agreement, defendants knew that city sewers would not be available for some time. Defendants' initial offer of purchase included a proposal that the closing of the transaction be subject to satisfactory sewer development. This term was deleted from the final agreement because, according to plaintiff's witnesses, the parties knew that sewers would not be available. Pfau testified that he agreed to the deletion of that term because he was led to believe that the provision for approval of a planned development accomplished the same thing.

[6] The question is whether defendants were excused from performing their agreement to purchase the property because they never secured the city's approval of a "satisfactory" planned development, when the evidence shows that they abandoned their application for an approved planned development because the expense of providing an alternative sewer system made the development financially unattractive. In *Anaheim Co. v. Holcombe,* 246 Or. 541, 426 P.2d 743 (1967) we considered an earnest money agreement which contained a provision making the purchaser's offer "contingent on obtaining a loan of $25,000." We held that when an agreement contains such a term, it imposes upon the vendee an implied condition that he make a reasonable effort to procure the loan. In the present case defendants had a similar duty, arising by implication, to make a reasonable effort to secure the city's approval of a planned development. As related above, defendants abandoned their attempt to secure the approval of the city Planning Commission in spite of that body's favorable reaction to their initial proposals. There was never any indication that defendants' plan was likely to be rejected.

[7] The condition required, however, not only approval of a planned development, but of a development which was "satisfactory" to the parties. When a contract makes a party's duty to perform conditional on his personal satisfaction the courts will give the condition its intended effect. Discussing such contracts, this court said in *Johnson v. School District No. 12,* 210 Or. 585, 590–591, 312 P.2d 591 (1957):

Such contracts are generally grouped into two categories:

(1) Those which involve taste, fancy or personal judgment, the classical example being a commission to paint a portrait. In such cases the promisor is the sole judge of the quality of the work, and his right to reject, if in good faith, is absolute and may not be reviewed by court or jury.

(2) Those which involve utility, fitness or value, which can be measured against a more or less objective standard. In these cases, although there is some conflict, we think the better view is

that performance need only be "reasonably satisfactory," and if the promisor refuses the proffered performance, the correctness of his decision and the adequacy of his grounds are subject to review.

[8]   The condition with which we are concerned in this case properly belongs in the first of these categories as it requires the exercise of the parties' personal judgment. There is no objective test by which a court or jury could determine whether a particular development plan ought to be "satisfactory" to reasonable men in defendants' position. The condition is similar to that in *Mattei v. Hopper,* 51 Cal. 2d 119,330 P.2d 625 (1958) in which the purchaser's duty under a land sale contract was "subject to Coldwell Banker & Company obtaining leases satisfactory to the purchaser." In a suit by the purchaser to compel specific performance, the seller contended that because of this provision there was no mutuality of obligation. The court held that there was a valid contract. Discussing the two types of "satisfaction" clauses, the court said:

> However, it would seem that the factors involved in determining whether a lease is satisfactory to the lessor are too numerous and varied to permit the application of a reasonable man standard as envisioned by this line of cases. . . .

> This multiplicity of factors which must be considered in evaluating a lease shows that this case more appropriately falls within the second line of authorities dealing with "satisfaction" clauses, being those involving fancy, taste, or judgment. Where the question is one of judgment, the promisor's determination that he is not satisfied, when made in good faith, has been held to be a defense to an action on the contract. . . .

330 P.2d at 627.

[9]   The condition in the present case is similar to that in Mattei in another respect as well. In that case as in this one the question of satisfaction was not concerned with the quality of the other party's performance. The court in *Mattei* held that the general rule was nevertheless applicable:

> Even though the "satisfaction" clauses discussed in the above-cited cases dealt with performances to be received as parts of the agreed exchanges, the fact that the leases here which determined plaintiff's satisfaction were not part of the performance to be rendered is not material. The standard of evaluating plaintiff's satisfaction—good faith—applies with equal vigor to this type of condition. . . .

Id.

[10] As in *Mattei* we are concerned in this case with a "satisfaction" clause of the type requiring the exercise of personal judgment as to a

matter which was not part of the other party's agreed performance. The test, as indicated, is the promisor's real, not feigned, dissatisfaction.

[11] It is clear from the authorities, however, that this dissatisfaction must be not only bona fide and in good faith, but also must relate to the specific subject matter of the condition. General dissatisfaction with the bargain will not suffice.

> . . . Where a promise is conditional, expressly or impliedly, on his own satisfaction, he must give fair consideration to the matter. A refusal to examine the . . . performance, or a rejection of it, not in reality based on its unsatisfactory nature but on fictitious grounds or none at all, will amount to prevention of performance of the condition and excuse it.

5 Williston, op. cit. 203–04.

[12] As Corbin points out, although the promisor is under no duty if, in good faith, he is dissatisfied with a performance to be rendered to his personal satisfaction, nevertheless

> [n]ot infrequently it is possible to prove that the defendant is satisfied in fact, that the work has been done exactly as he specified, and that his dissatisfaction is either with his own specifications or merely with having to pay money that he prefers to use otherwise . . .

3A Corbin, op. cit. 92.

[13] It is inherent in the requirement that dissatisfaction be bona fide and in good faith that the promisor cannot be allowed to base a claim of dissatisfaction on circumstances which were known or anticipated by the parties at the time of contracting. In the present case the evidence is clear that the defendants entered the agreement with full knowledge that city sewer service would not be immediately available and that their development of the property would have to include a sewage disposal system of some kind. The *Brydon* case is in point and its reasoning is persuasive. Although defendants were entitled under the contract to be the judges of their own satisfaction with any development plan that might be approved by the city, they should not be permitted to rely on the "satisfaction" clause in order to reject the contract because of an expense known and contemplated at the time of contracting. We hold, therefore, that defendants were not justified in abandoning their attempts to secure city approval of a development plan simply because of the expense of providing a sewer system which they knew when they entered the contract would have to be provided as a part of the development. Not having performed their duty to use reasonable diligence to obtain city approval of a development plan, defendants may not rely on the nonoccurrence of the condition. *Anaheim Co. v. Holcombe, supra.*

This contract was made after some negotiations between the parties. It cannot be a matter of doubt that both parties intended that the coal should be furnished from the plaintiff's mine. As a matter of course it was not expected that it should be equal in quality to that which came from the Big Vein Mines; and no just construction of the contract can give to it such a meaning. It was, however, to be satisfactory to the officers who were named. But this term of the contract did not give them a capricious or arbitrary discretion to reject it . . . Certainly they were not obliged to accept the coal, if they thought it was not fit for the uses contemplated by the contract; neither on the other hand would they be justified in rejecting it for the reason that it did not possess qualities, which at the time of the contract it was known by the parties that it did not possess. . . .

65 Md. at 220.

* * *

The decree of the trial court is affirmed.

PRACTICE TIP

This chapter has emphasized the need to think through the deal and draft express conditions to protect the client. Obviously, this can be overdone. "Overlawyering" takes the lawyers' time, wastes the clients' money, and carries with it the risk that one of the parties will get frustrated and walk away from the deal. It takes judgment, experience, and a good bit of intuition to know when it's best to hammer out all the details and when and if it's best to cover things generally and leave the details to be worked out when disputes arise. You don't want to be known as a deal-killer. On the other hand, it's a lot cheaper to resolve questions at the contract drafting stage.

A good example is the case of the aborted domed stadium in Buffalo. In an attempt to get a sports stadium that would revive the area's dying economy, Erie County entered into a contract with some real estate developers. The contract called for the developers to give the county land on which to build the stadium and for the county to build the stadium and lease it to the developers. The contract was only five pages long, and most of it dealt with the terms of the lease. As to the building of the stadium, it just said: "The county shall construct domed facilities comparable to the Houston Astrodome."

When the county put the construction contract out for bids, it discovered that it would cost $72 million to get the stadium built instead of the $50 million the county had budgeted. The county

> *decided it didn't want a stadium that much. The developers sued, and because there were no conditions to the county's obligation, the county conceded the liability issue. The damages phase of the trial lasted 9 months, and the transcript was 25,000 pages long. The developers were awarded $24 million in damages. The damage award was reversed on appeal because the trial court had misapplied New York's idiosyncratic version of the Hadley v. Baxendale test. A second trial awarded the developers $6.5 million. This was reversed on appeal and the plaintiffs were able to recover only the money they actually expended in reliance and mitigation.*
>
> *The litigation went on for 18 years, and it all could have been avoided if the lawyers had included a condition dealing with the rather obvious possibility that the stadium would cost more than anticipated. The case caption is Kenford Co. v. County of Erie. The most important appellate opinions are at 489 N.Y.S.2d 939, 493 N.Y.S.2d 234, 526 N.Y.S.2d 282, and 540 N.Y.S.2d 1.*

LAUREL RACE COURSE, INC. V. REGAL CONSTRUCTION CO.

Court of Appeals of Maryland
274 Md. 142, 333 A.2d 319 (1975)

LEVINE, J., delivered the opinion of the Court.

[1] The dispute which has resulted in this appeal was spawned from the lofty but earnest ambition of appellant, Laurel Race Course, Inc. (Laurel), to build "the best [race] track in the United States." To the extent that it might not have fully attained such preeminence, it undoubtedly faults appellee, Regal Construction Company, Inc. (Regal), with whom it had contracted to rebuild its track. Its dissatisfaction with the quality of Regal's performance under that contract led to Laurel's refusal to pay a portion of the sum claimed for those services. As a consequence, Regal brought suit and, following a nonjury trial in the Circuit Court for Prince George's County (Bowen, J.), obtained a judgment against Laurel in the amount of $67,276.17. This appeal followed.

[2] As the first step in its quest, Laurel, in March 1972, engaged an internationally renowned engineering firm, Watkins and Associates, Inc. (Watkins) of Lexington, Kentucky. Later that spring, Laurel and Watkins entered into a contract whereby the latter agreed to design a plan for the reconstruction of the Laurel track and the installation of a complete drainage system. Watkins had achieved success in designing such "all-weather" tracks for a number of racing courses throughout the world. In addition to preparing a design, a set of specifications and other similar documents, Watkins was to have personnel in attendance during the construction phase.

[3]   In June 1972, Regal submitted a bid proposal for the construction work. In doing so, it agreed to perform "in strict accordance with the terms and conditions of the specifications and contract documents . . . and the plans . . . and do such other work incidental thereto as [might] be ordered by the Engineer, at the unit or lump sum prices quoted in the attached 'Bid Schedule.' " It also declared that it had "examined the site of the work and informed [it]self fully in regard to all conditions pertaining to the place where the work [was] to be done; [and] that [it had] examined the plans, specifications, and contract documents. . . ." It also agreed to "substantially complete all work on or before September 1, 1972, and to finish the job by September 15, 1972." This document and the contract itself expressly made time of the essence.

[4]   After becoming the successful bidder, Regal executed the usual panoply of documents which regularly attend such transactions. Among them was the "General Conditions" which defined Watkins's status as the "Engineer." It was to "have general inspection and direction of the work as the authorized representative of the owner [Laurel]." It had "authority to reject work and materials which [did] not conform to the plans, specifications and contract documents, . . . [and to] decide all engineering questions. . . ." It was also charged with the duty to "interpret the meaning and requirements" of those documents and to "decide all disputes" that might arise thereunder.

[5]   In order to "protect itself from loss," Laurel was permitted to withhold partial payments from Regal if the latter failed "to remedy defective work" and for "other causes which in the opinion of the Engineer would justify [Laurel] in withholding such . . . payments." In addition, the General Conditions allowed Laurel to "retain not less than [ten percent] of the amount [of each partial payment] until final completion and acceptance of all work covered by this contract." The General Conditions concluded with a guarantee by Regal of "all construction against defective materials, equipment and workmanship for a period of twelve months. . . ." This included a commitment to "replace such defective parts without cost to the Owner."

[6]   Essentially, the work to be performed by Regal consisted of the rehabilitation of both the dirt and turf tracks, and the installation of a surface and underground drainage system, including proposed lakes, most of which was designed primarily to provide a "faster" track under "all-weather" conditions. The specifications detailed rather minutely the gradation requirements for the various materials to be used in the base, sub-base and cushion of the main track. In this connection, the specifications provided: "If any over-size rock, or other deleterious materials that could be harmful to a running horse, are incorporated within the base material during the storage, mixing, or hauling of the base soil, such harmful material shall be removed by the Contractor at his own

expense." With respect to the storm drainage system, the specifications provide that "[a]ll pipes shall be laid with ends abutting and true to line and grade," and that the "space between pipes shall be filled with a concrete mortar of proper consistency" as therein specified.

[7]　Both the subbase and blended base materials were to "be paid for at the contract unit price in-place and compacted to the required density." Payment under the entire contract was to be made on a "unit price" basis, whereby the total amount to be paid Regal was to be determined by applying the unit prices contained in the bid proposal to the actual quantities "certified by the Engineer for the items enumerated in the Bid Schedule. . . ."

[8]　The contract was dated July 3, 1972, and Regal apparently commenced its work shortly thereafter. Performance was neither substantially completed by September 1 nor fully completed by September 15. Regal professes to have substantially completed the work in accordance with the contract terms by September 25, and claims that it ultimately rendered complete performance. On September 28, 1972, after "turning over" the track to Laurel on the 25th, Regal received a "punch list" of 18 items requiring its attention. After Regal claimed in late November that it had remedied those deficiencies and therefore demanded payment in full, Watkins forwarded its recommendation that payment be withheld because:

> During the construction of the base the Contractor permitted a large amount of rock and oversize material to become mixed with the clay and sand which were hauled from the source of supply and, in spite of repeated requests, did not make a reasonable effort to remove this material from the base while it was being placed . . . [I]t has been necessary for [Laurel's] crew to perform a large amount of maintenance work that would not have been required had the base been properly blended and compacted.

> The condition of the track for the first three weeks resulted in justifiable complaints from the horsemen and could be traced directly to the failure of the Contractor to obtain adequate compaction and proper shaping of the inside ditch and drainage.

Watkins recommended witholding

[9]　Having received the recommendation from Watkins that payment of the balance due be retained, Laurel refused to pay the sum of $110,931.91, representing the amount then claimed by Regal as the unpaid balance on the total contract amount of $786,401.35. The latter brought suit for this amount plus interest in February 1973. By the time of the trial in April 1974, the amount claimed by Regal under the written contract had been reduced to $49,648 plus interest because Laurel had made additional payments during the intervening period.

[10] In its declaration, Regal sought payment under two express contracts. For its first cause of action, it claimed the $49,648 under the

Regal wanted remaining $ and $ from oral agreement

original contract to which we have alluded. The other claim, amounting to $42,657.48, was based on a verbal contract allegedly entered into during late December 1972, when a conference was held between the parties to resolve the impasse which had arisen. The essence of this claim is that Laurel agreed to pay Regal for such additional work as the latter would thereafter perform, provided it was not found to have been necessitated by defective or incomplete performance under the basic written contract. Regal claimed that it was entitled to recovery under this theory for additional work it subsequently had performed in the summer of 1973.

[11] At the trial, Regal's witnesses claimed that the blended soil base material which it had supplied not only had met the contract specifications, but also had been approved by Watkins, whose personnel had been present throughout the construction stage. With respect to the 24-inch pipe which had been installed as part of the drainage system, Regal conceded that it had become separated in some places and was "out of alignment both horizontally and vertically," but insisted that originally it had been "laid true to grade." It recognized the likelihood, however, that the bed supporting the pipe had not been properly reinforced, and that not all the joints had been mortared.

[12] In regard to the verbal contract, Laurel claimed at the trial that rather than an additional agreement, what had emerged from the December 1972 conference was a request by Regal for a further opportunity to comply with the specifications under the original contract. Laurel maintained that shortly after Regal "turned over" the track on September 25, 1972, stones were observed on the cushion of the track that had "worked up from the base." This was initially observed during the training season which had preceded the racing season. To assuage the horsemen, who were fearful of injuries to the horses and the jockeys, Laurel found it necessary to perform a considerable amount of work with its own employees and equipment. Laurel sought to recoup the expenses incurred for this labor and equipment by backcharging Regal. This claim also included a charge for Laurel equipment that was used by Regal in an effort to bring the track into conformity with the specifications.

Laurel had to correct some of Regal's work

[13] When Regal returned to the site in the summer of 1973, it did some additional work on the base of the track in the form of "remixing and reblending." Expert soil engineers employed by Watkins testified that these efforts had improved the quality of the track, but had not brought it into compliance with the specifications because of stones and excessive clay content. They pointed out that any stone greater than 3/8 of an inch was too large for a racetrack, and that such stones were "coming out of" the ten-inch soil base. The principal difficulty caused by the excessive clay content is that in rainy weather it expands and slows up the horses because it drains poorly. The witnesses acknowledged that they had observed the oversize stones in the material being installed by Regal in 1972, but were

stones too big

repeatedly assured by the latter's construction superintendent, who said "'I'll get them out.'" There had been testimony that during the construction stage, Regal employees were "out with buckets, they were handpicking [the stones]."

[14] The expert testimony on behalf of Laurel was that only the part of the 24-inch pipe which did not run under the track could be unearthed, but an inspection of that part indicated it had not been laid true to grade; that the joints were not closed tightly and had not been mortared; and the "lifting holes had not been plugged." Hence, the pipe had not been installed in accordance with the specifications and was not functioning correctly.

[15] At the conclusion of the trial, the court said with respect to the stones, "I hold everybody accountable for that: the contractor, the racetrack owner and the engineers." Thus, it refused to recognize the presence of the stones as a deviation from contract performance. In regard to the refusal of the engineer to furnish the certificate, the court found that "[Regal] had performed substantially all that [it] was asked or instructed to do"; and that the track was "substantially in conformance with what was expected." Hence, it allowed the entire balance claimed under the written contract— $49,648. It also allowed $12,724.01 for the work which Regal had allegedly performed pursuant to the verbal contract. The court refused to allow Laurel any amount for the back-charges, although they were not controverted by any evidence. In addition to the total principal sum of $62,372.01, the court allowed Regal interest in the amount of $4,904.16. A portion of this interest was on part of the judgment itself, and the remainder was on the sums which Laurel had paid during the period intervening between the filing of suit and the trial.

[16] In urging reversal, Laurel advances these arguments:

(1) That the trial court erred in overruling Laurel's demurrer to count I of the declaration in which Regal had sought recovery upon the written contract. The demurrer was bottomed on the failure to allege production of the engineer's final certificate—a condition precedent to Laurel's liability.

Laurel appeal

* * *

[17] Following the trial court's ruling on the demurrer, the case was tried on an amended declaration which included a claim under the written contract in count I and upon the oral contract in count II. At the trial, Laurel persisted in its contention, to no avail, that Regal failed to produce a certificate of the engineer as a condition precedent to liability under the written contract. As we have indicated, the same argument is pressed on appeal.

[18] Almost a century ago, our predecessors held in *Gill v. Vogler*, 52 Md. 663, 666 (1879), where work was "to be done . . . to the satisfaction of

the City Commissioner [of Baltimore]," and payments during the progress of the work were to be made only in accordance with his "monthly estimates," that those estimates were a condition precedent to recovery of such payments, absent bad faith or collusion.

[19] From that holding has emerged the general rule, followed uniformly by decisions of this Court, that where payments under a contract are due only when the certificate of an architect or engineer is issued, production of the certificate becomes a condition precedent to liability of the owner for materials and labor in the absence of fraud or bad faith. Apart from fraud or bad faith, the only other exceptions to this rule are waiver or estoppel.

[20] The durability of this rule may be more readily appreciated when one considers the emphasis with which it was enunciated by our predecessors. For example, in *Lynn v. B. & O. R.R. Co.*, 60 Md. 404 (1883), Judge Miller said for this Court:

> So, in the case before us, it was not enough that the jury might believe from the evidence that Legge unreasonably rejected the ice, or that he was grossly wrong in his judgment . . . ; they must go further, and actually infer and find fraud or bad faith. By this contract, which is perfectly lawful, the parties expressly agreed to submit the question whether the ice to be supplied was "good, clear, and solid," to the judgment of this third party, and his judgment, no matter how erroneous or mistaken it may be, or how unreasonable it may appear to others, is conclusive between the parties, unless it be tainted with fraud or bad faith. To substitute for it the opinions and judgments of other persons, whether judge, jury or witnesses, would be to annul the contract, and make another in its place.

60 Md. at 415.

[21] There is no question but that under subsection 24 of the General Conditions, payment of the "balance due . . . including the percentage retained during the construction period" is expressly conditioned upon production of the engineer's "Final Certificate."[15] It is equally clear that the amount awarded by the trial court under count I of the declaration was the

---

[15] In pertinent part, subsection 24 provides:

Upon notice that the work is ready for final inspection and acceptance, the Engineer shall make such inspection; and when he finds the work acceptable under the Contract and the Contract fully performed, he shall promptly issue a 'Final Certificate' over his signature stating in effect that the work provided for in the Contract has been satisfactorily completed and recommending its acceptance by the Owner.

The balance due the Contractor, including the percentage retained during the construction period, will then be paid to the Contractor by the Owner. This final payment will be made within sixty days after date of the Engineer's 'Final Certificate,' and said final payment shall evidence the Owner's acceptance of work unless it is accepted in writing prior to said final payment.

alleged "balance due . . . including the percentage retained." Nor is there any contention advanced by Regal that any of the exceptions to the general rule—fraud, bad faith, waiver or estoppel—were established here.

[The court then rejected arguments that this was not a proper interpretation of the contract.—Eds.]

NOTES AND QUESTIONS

1. The litany continues: Time or another term is of the essence; Nonseverability; No amendment or waiver by conduct; All amendments and waivers must be in writing; Recitations that both parties have been represented by counsel, or at least had the opportunity to consult with counsel, have read the agreement and understand it. All these provisions are attempts by the parties to avoid having a court later refuse to enforce a condition by finding that is was waived by conduct, was unconscionable, would otherwise lead to a forfeiture, and the like. A determined court can generally find some way to excuse a failed condition should it choose to do so, and can often do so in a ruling that is so fact-based that it is largely immune on appeal, at least if counsel has done her job and presented the judge with an adequate record to protect the ruling. (Why are fact-based decisions more immune on appeal than purely legal determinations? Consider the applicable standards of review).

Counsel can best guard against this result by: (a) drafting the consequences of failure of a condition explicitly into the same provision, not just leaving it to the default and remedy provisions of the agreement, (b) employing good boilerplate to attempt to document the parties' intention that all the terms of the document be strictly construed, and (c) explicitly stating the reason that the condition was included and that it was a fundamental inducement for one or more of the parties to enter into the transaction. This is not foolproof, but it is a good start.

Clients, further, should be guided through the process of documenting waivers of conditions so that each waiver is as limited as possible and so that client conduct does not undo the results that would otherwise be obtained through careful drafting and contracting. The best lawyerly solution or structure can be undone by a client's subsequent actions, so designing a legal structure that is usable by the client is critical to its success.

2. When reviewing or analyzing conditions, focus on what is likely to occur if the condition is not met. Does the client have an appropriate course of action—or cause of action—to pursue under the terms of the contract? If not, one should be provided. Also, consider whether this test is met for the opposing party. If not, is it better for your client if this remains the case? Or is it better to attempt to fix the potential problem and fill the void? Answers to these last questions will vary enormously depending on the circumstances.

LAWYERING SKILLS PROBLEM

Your client is a trade organization of building contractors. You have been hired to draft a standard-form contract that contractors and their customers will use on building projects that are too small to make it economical for both of the parties to hire a lawyer to negotiate and draft on their behalf. The contract is to be between the owner and the contractor and is to cover such things as when various phases of the work are to be completed and when progress payments are to be made. The standard form contract has to be fairly evenhanded (i.e., it can't give the contractor an unfair advantage) because the people the contractors will be dealing with are sophisticated enough that they will not sign a one-sided contract. Explain how you would use express conditions to limit the risks to which the parties are exposed.

CHAPTER 24

CONSTRUCTIVE CONDITIONS

. . .

Express conditions are fairly straightforward. Constructive conditions, on the other hand, are not. You may question why one is so clear and the other so fuzzy and filled with uncertainty. The answer is that constructive conditions are things that are implied by the courts when the parties have not adequately documented their arrangements and the relationships of their various performances and failures to perform or to perform completely. As such, the rules are deliberately fuzzy so as to provide courts with principles to apply in resolving the dispute but the flexibility to avoid forfeiture and to attempt to do substantial justice.

Constructive conditions, like express conditions, are important because they delineate the relationship between individual performances within a contract. They answer the question left unanswered by the drafters: What happens to the other performances called for by the contract if one performance is not carried out, is incompletely carried out, or is affected by an unforeseen circumstance? Are the other performances excused? Or must they be performed, subject to some right to recover any shortfall resulting from the failed performance? A court will use constructive conditions and the concepts of material breach and substantial performance to resolve the dispute if the parties don't.

Some definitions to orient you:

Remember, constructive conditions are about the unspecified, undocumented relationships between covenants (promises) in a contract. Covenants can be divided into three categories:

Independent Covenants—Promises that are not linked by conditions express or implied. Failure of one party to perform the promise does not excuse the other from performing its independent promise.

Mutual, Dependent Covenants—Promises that are linked by an express or implied condition that failure of a party to perform one promise will (or may) excuse performance of the other promise.

Mutual, Simultaneous Covenants—Essentially the same as mutual, dependent covenants, except that performance of each promise is to take place at the same time, rather than seriatim (one after another).

In addition to these characterizations of conditions and the covenants to which they relate are some terms regarding the degree of a breach of a covenant:

> A *total or material breach* of a covenant is an unexcused failure to perform that either goes to the heart of the contract or is so severe, or both, that it excuses performance of mutual, dependent or simultaneous covenants on the other side of the contract. A *total or material breach* gives rise to an excuse of performance and an action for damages on the part of the non-breaching party. (Later in this chapter we will distinguish between a material breach, which temporarily suspends the other party's duty to perform counter-performance and may be cured, and a *total breach*, which is what a material breach can ripen into over a period of time, and which may not be cured and truly excuses the other party's performance forever. *See* R2d § 242. But for now we will lump them together.)

> An *immaterial breach* of a covenant is an unexcused failure to perform that does not go to the heart of the contract and is not so severe that it excuses executory counter-performance of mutual, dependent or simultaneous covenants on the other side of the contract. An immaterial breach does not excuse performance but does give rise to an action for damages on the part of the nonbreaching party.

> *Substantial performance* of a covenant is performance that is sufficient to lead to the conclusion that the breach of the covenant is immaterial. In other words, it is the opposite of material breach.

The cases that follow explore these concepts. As the notes that follow indicate, the precise characterization of covenants and the conditions that link them is often unnecessary, but understanding material breach, immaterial breach, and substantial performance and their implications is crucial, as suggested by the materials on express conditions.

Recall that express conditions are some of the principal tools in the transactional attorney's tool box. In each of the cases in this chapter, one or more express conditions was missing, forcing (or freeing) the court to interpret the contract for the parties by imposing a constructive condition. In these instances, one party, at least, is always unhappy with the result. If the parties use express conditions at the time of contracting, they can be the ones to allocate risk and price that allocation into their contract themselves—and that is always a superior result when compared to a forced, post-breach allocation by a court informed only through the distorted lens of litigation.

So, when reading each case, consider what express condition or other contractual terms could have been included at the time of contracting to prevent the sorry state of affairs that the parties faced in court. Most of the cases in this book would not have arisen if the contracts were drafted by competent counsel who had included an express clause to deal with the problem. ROBERT M. LLOYD, *Making Contracts Relevant: Thirteen Lessons for the First Year Contracts Course*, 36 ARIZ. ST. L.J. 257, 275 (2004) (citing Randy E. Barnett, *The Sound of Silence: Default Rules and Contractual Consent*, 78 VA. L. REV. 821, 825–26 (1992)).

———

Apprentice

KINGSTON V. PRESTON

silk merchant
said will sell business to Kingston

Court of King's Bench
2 Doug. 689 (1773)

[1] This was an action of debt for non-performance of covenants contained in certain articles of agreement between the plaintiff and the defendant. The declaration stated: That, by articles made the 24th of March, 1770, the plaintiff, for the considerations thereinafter mentioned, covenanted with the defendant to serve him for one year and a quarter next ensuing, as a covenant servant, in his trade of a silk-mercer, at £200 a year, and, in consideration of the premises, the defendant covenanted that, at the end of the year and a quarter, he would give up his business of a mercer to the plaintiff, and a nephew of the defendant, or some other person to be nominated by the defendant, and give up to them his stock in trade, at a fair valuation; and that, between the young traders, deeds of partnership should be executed for fourteen years, and from and immediately after the execution of the said deeds the defendant would permit the said young traders to carry on the said business in the defendant's house. Then the declaration stated a covenant by the plaintiff, that he would accept the business and stock-in-trade, at a fair valuation, with the defendant's nephew, or such other person, etc., and execute such deeds of partnership, and, further, that the plaintiff should and would, at and before the sealing and delivery of the deeds cause and procure good and sufficient security to be given to the defendant, to be approved of by the defendant, for the payment of £250 monthly to the defendant, in lieu of a moiety [a 1/2 share.—Eds.] of the monthly produce of the stock in trade, until the value of the stock should be reduced to £4,000. Then the plaintiff averred that he had performed and been ready to perform his covenants, and assigned for breach on the part of the defendant, that he had refused to surrender and give up his business at the end of the said year and a quarter. The defendant pleaded: 1. That the plaintiff did not offer sufficient security; and, 2. That he did not give sufficient security for the payment of the £250, etc. And the plaintiff demurred generally to both pleas. On the part of the plaintiff, the case was argued by Mr. Buller, who contended that the covenants were mutual and independent, and therefore a plea of the breach of one of the covenants to be performed by the plaintiff was no bar to an

P argued were mutual + independent

argued they were dependent contract — D

action for a breach by the defendant of one which he had bound himself to perform, but that the defendant might have his remedy for the breach by the plaintiff in a separate action. On the other side, Mr. Grose insisted that the covenants were dependent in their nature, and therefore performance must be alleged. The security to be given for the money was manifestly the chief object of the transaction, and it would be highly unreasonable to construe the agreement so as to oblige the defendant to given up a beneficial business, and valuable stock-in-trade, and trust to the plaintiff's personal security (who might, and indeed was admitted to be worth nothing), for the performance of his part.

3 kinds

[2] In delivering the judgment of the Court, LORD MANSFIELD expressed himself to the following effect: There are three kinds of covenants: 1. Such as are called mutual and independent, where either party may recover damages from the other for the injury he may have received by a breach of covenants in his favor, and where it is no excuse for the defendant to allege a breach of the covenants on the part of the plaintiff. 2. There are covenants which are conditions and dependent, in which the performance of one depends on the prior performance of another, and therefore till this prior condition is performed, the other party is not liable to an action on his covenant. 3. There is also a third sort of covenants, which are mutual conditions to be performed at the same time; and in these, if one party was ready and offered to perform his part, and the other neglected or refused to perform his, he who was ready and offered has fulfilled his engagement, and may maintain an action for the default of the other though it is not certain that either is obliged to do the first act. His lordship then proceeded to say, that the dependence or independence of covenants was to be collected from the evident sense and meaning of the parties, and that, however transposed they might be in the deed, their precedency must depend on the order of time in which the intent of the transaction requires their performance. That, in the case before the Court, it would be the greatest injustice if the plaintiff should prevail. The essence of the agreement was, that the defendant should not trust to the personal security of the plaintiff, but before he delivered up his stock and business, should have good security for the payment of the money. The giving of such security, therefore, must necessarily be a condition precedent. Judgment was accordingly given for the defendant, because the part to be performed by the plaintiff was clearly a condition precedent.

Dependent

NOTES AND QUESTIONS

Prior to *Kingston v. Preston*, English law presented the following anomalous situation: Suppose Builder and Owner entered into a contract whereby Builder promised to build a house on Owner's land and Owner agreed to pay Builder £100. Builder then, instead of building the house, went off and got drunk (a not uncommon occurrence). When Builder sobered up he could go to a solicitor and have a suit filed against Owner, alleging that Owner had breached his promise to pay the £100. If Owner had failed to put an express condition in the contract, making his promise to pay the money conditional upon the building actually being built, Builder would have a good cause of action. (Owner would of course have a cause of action against Builder, but he would have to get a lawyer and go through the hassle of a lawsuit. Even then he might not be able to prove that the building would have been worth £100, so he might have come out on the short end.)

After *Kingston v. Preston*, the courts began imposing constructive conditions where the parties neglected to put express conditions in their contracts. Constructive conditions are generally conditions that the other party perform her obligations under the contract, or at least that she be ready, willing, and able to do so (called "tender" of performance). For example, suppose Seller and Buyer contract for the purchase and sale of a car. Seller being ready, willing, and able to deliver the car is a constructive condition to Buyer's obligation to pay the money. Likewise, Buyer being ready, willing, and able to deliver the money is a constructive condition to Seller's obligation to deliver the car. Thus if Seller fails to deliver the car, Buyer not only has an action for breach of contract, she is also relieved of her obligation to pay the money. Seller's delivery of the car is a constructive condition to Buyer's obligation to pay the money and Buyer's payment of the money is a constructive condition to Seller's obligation to deliver the car.

Where it is possible for the parties' performances to be rendered simultaneously, they are to be rendered simultaneously unless the language or the circumstances indicate to the contrary. *See* R2d § 234(1). Thus in our example of the delivery of the car, the presumption would be that the car would be delivered at the same time the full purchase price is paid. But the contract could provide that the buyer has to make a deposit ahead of time or that she is to be given extra time in which to pay all or part of the purchase price.

Sometimes one of the performances takes place over time. For instance, it takes time to build a house. The rule here is that, unless the parties intend otherwise, where one performance takes time, that performance is required before the other party's performance is due. *See* R2d § 234(2). It has been said that the theory behind the development of this rule is that the performance that takes time is usually some sort of labor (like building a house) whereas the performance that can be rendered instantaneously is usually paying money, and the people that had money were more dependable than those that did the work. In other words, the builder might take the money, get drunk, and never build the house. There may have been some truth in that, especially in England in the eighteenth and nineteenth centuries, where the rule developed. Nevertheless, some will seize upon the explanation that the judges in those days came from the monied class, and they were simply looking out for their own.

The rule isn't as harsh as it seems. Builders can and do protect themselves by requiring the owner to make "progress payments" as the construction proceeds. (Well-drafted agreements make these payments express conditions to the duty of the builder to do any further work.) So the rule requiring the person whose performance will take time to complete to fully perform before being paid anything is only a default rule. It only applies if the parties don't provide differently in their agreement.

The two cases that follow illustrate one important difference between constructive conditions and express conditions. As we saw in *Dove v. Rose Acre Farms*, express conditions have to be performed precisely and to the letter. Constructive conditions, however, only have to be "substantially performed."

JACOB & YOUNGS, INC. V. KENT

Court of Appeals of New York
230 N.Y. 239, 129 N.E. 889 (1921)

CARDOZO, J.

[1] The plaintiff built a country residence for the defendant at a cost of upwards of $77,000, and now sues to recover a balance of $3,483.46[1], remaining unpaid. The work of construction ceased in June, 1914, and the defendant then began to occupy the dwelling. There was no complaint of defective performance until March, 1915. One of the specifications for the plumbing work provides that—

> All wrought-iron pipe must be well galvanized, lap welded pipe of the grade known as "standard pipe" of Reading manufacture.

[2] The defendant learned in March, 1915, that some of the pipe, instead of being made in Reading, was the product of other factories. The plaintiff was accordingly directed by the architect to do the work anew. The plumbing was then encased within the walls except in a few places where it had to be exposed. Obedience to the order meant more than the substitution of other pipe. It meant the demolition at great expense of substantial parts of the completed structure. The plaintiff left the work untouched, and asked for a certificate that the final payment was due. Refusal of the certificate was followed by this suit.

[3] The evidence sustains a finding that the omission of the prescribed brand of pipe was neither fraudulent nor willful. It was the result of the oversight and inattention of the plaintiff's subcontractor. Reading pipe is distinguished from Cohoes pipe and other brands only by the name of the manufacturer stamped upon it at intervals of between six and seven feet. Even the defendant's architect, though he inspected the

---

[1] [$3,483.46 in 1921 dollars is roughly the equivalent of $49,000 in 2019 dollars using the CPI and the GNP Deflator.—Eds.]

architect failed to notice discrepancy

pipe upon arrival, failed to notice the discrepancy. The plaintiff tried to
show that the brands installed, though made by other manufacturers, were
the same in quality, in appearance, in market value, and in cost as the
brand stated in the contract—that they were, indeed, the same thing,
though manufactured in another place. The evidence was excluded, and a
verdict directed for the defendant. The Appellate Division reversed, and
granted a new trial.

P suggests the same sh∂

[4]   We think the evidence, if admitted, would have supplied some
basis for the inference that the defect was insignificant in its relation to the
project. The courts never say that one who makes a contract fills the
measure of his duty by less than full performance. They do say, however,
that an omission, both trivial and innocent, will sometimes be atoned for
by allowance of the resulting damage, and will not always be the breach of
a condition to be followed by a forfeiture. The distinction is akin to that
between dependent and independent promises, or between promises and
conditions. Some promises are so plainly independent that they can never
by fair construction be conditions of one another. Others are so plainly
dependent that they must always be conditions. Others, though dependent
and thus conditions when there is departure in point of substance, will be
viewed as independent and collateral when the departure is insignificant.
Considerations partly of justice and partly of presumable intention are to
tell us whether this or that promise shall be placed in one class or in
another. The simple and the uniform will call for different remedies from
the multifarious and the intricate. The margin of departure within the
range of normal expectation upon a sale of common chattels will vary from
the margin to be expected upon a contract for the construction of a mansion
or a "skyscraper." There will be harshness sometimes and oppression in the
implication of a condition when the thing upon which labor has been
expended is incapable of surrender because united to the land, and equity
and reason in the implication of a like condition when the subject-matter,
if defective, is in shape to be returned. From the conclusion that promises
may not be treated as dependent to the extent of their uttermost minutiae
without a sacrifice of justice, the progress is a short one to the conclusion
that they may not be so treated without a perversion of intention. Intention
not otherwise revealed may be presumed to hold in contemplation the
reasonable and probable. If something else is in view, it must not be left to
implication. There will be no assumption of a purpose to visit venial faults
with oppressive retribution.

immaterial

[5]   Those who think more of symmetry and logic in the development
of legal rules than of practical adaptation to the attainment of a just result
will be troubled by a classification where the lines of division are so
wavering and blurred. Something, doubtless, may be said on the score of
consistency and certainty in favor of a stricter standard. The courts have
balanced such considerations against those of equity and fairness, and

found the latter to be the weightier. The decisions in this state commit us to the liberal view, which is making its way, nowadays, in jurisdictions slow to welcome it. Where the line is to be drawn between the important and the trivial cannot be settled by a formula. "In the nature of the case precise boundaries are impossible." 2 Williston on Contracts, § 841. The same omission may take on one aspect or another according to its setting. Substitution of equivalents may not have the same significance in fields of art on the one side and in those of mere utility on the other. Nowhere will change be tolerated, however, if it is so dominant or pervasive as in any real or substantial measure to frustrate the purpose of the contract. There is no general license to install whatever, in the builder's judgment, may be regarded as "just as good." The question is one of degree, to be answered, if there is doubt, by the triers of the facts, and, if the inferences are certain, by the judges of the law. We must weigh the purpose to be served, the desire to be gratified, the excuse for deviation from the letter, the cruelty of enforced adherence. Then only can we tell whether literal fulfillment is to be implied by law as a condition. This is not to say that the parties are not free by apt and certain words to effectuate a purpose that performance of every term shall be a condition of recovery. That question is not here. This is merely to say that the law will be slow to impute the purpose, in the silence of the parties, where the significance of the default is grievously out of proportion to the oppression of the forfeiture. The willful transgressor must accept the penalty of his transgression. For him there is no occasion to mitigate the rigor of implied conditions. The transgressor whose default is unintentional and trivial may hope for mercy if he will offer atonement for his wrong.

[6] In the circumstances of this case, we think the measure of the allowance is not the cost of replacement, which would be great, but the difference in value, which would be either nominal or nothing. Some of the exposed sections might perhaps have been replaced at moderate expense. The defendant did not limit his demand to them, but treated the plumbing as a unit to be corrected from cellar to roof. In point of fact, the plaintiff never reached the stage at which evidence of the extent of the allowance became necessary. The trial court had excluded evidence that the defect was unsubstantial, and in view of that ruling there was no occasion for the plaintiff to go farther with an offer of proof. We think, however, that the offer, if it had been made, would not of necessity have been defective because directed to difference in value. It is true that in most cases the cost of replacement is the measure. The owner is entitled to the money which will permit him to complete, unless the cost of completion is grossly and unfairly out of proportion to the good to be attained. When that is true, the measure is the difference in value. Specifications call, let us say, for a foundation built of granite quarried in Vermont. On the completion of the building, the owner learns that through the blunder of a subcontractor part of the foundation has been built of granite of the same quality quarried in

New Hampshire. The measure of allowance is not the cost of reconstruction. "There may be omissions of that which could not afterwards be supplied exactly as called for by the contract without taking down the building to its foundations, and at the same time the omission may not affect the value of the building for use or otherwise, except so slightly as to be hardly appreciable." *Handy v. Bliss*, 204 Mass. 513, 519, 90 N.E. 864, 134 Am. St. Rep. 673. The rule that gives a remedy in cases of substantial performance with compensation for defects of trivial or inappreciable importance has been developed by the courts as an instrument of justice. The measure of the allowance must be shaped to the same end.

[7]　The order should be affirmed, and judgment absolute directed in favor of the plaintiff upon the stipulation, with costs in all courts.

MCLAUGHLIN, J.

[8]　I dissent. The plaintiff did not perform its contract. Its failure to do so was either intentional or due to gross neglect which, under the uncontradicted facts, amounted to the same thing, nor did it make any proof of the cost of compliance, where compliance was possible.

[9]　Under its contract it obligated itself to use in the plumbing only pipe (between 2,000 and 2,500 feet) made by the Reading Manufacturing Company. The first pipe delivered was about 1,000 feet and the plaintiff's superintendent then called the attention of the foreman of the subcontractor, who was doing the plumbing, to the fact that the specifications annexed to the contract required all pipe used in the plumbing to be of the Reading Manufacturing Company. They then examined it for the purpose of ascertaining whether this delivery was of that manufacture and found it was. Thereafter, as pipe was required in the progress of the work, the foreman of the subcontractor would leave word at its shop that he wanted a specified number of feet of pipe, without in any way indicating of what manufacture. Pipe would thereafter be delivered and installed in the building, without any examination whatever. Indeed, no examination, so far as appears, was made by the plaintiff, the subcontractor, defendant's architect, or any one else, of any of the pipe except the first delivery, until after the building had been completed. Plaintiff's architect then refused to give the certificate of completion, upon which the final payment depended, because all of the pipe used in the plumbing was not of the kind called for by the contract. After such refusal, the subcontractor removed the covering or insulation from about 900 feet of pipe which was exposed in the basement, cellar, and attic, and all but 70 feet was found to have been manufactured, not by the Reading Company, but by other manufacturers, some by the Cohoes Rolling Mill Company, some by the National Steel Works, some by the South Chester Tubing Company, and some which bore no manufacturer's mark at all. The balance

of the pipe had been so installed in the building that an inspection of it could not be had without demolishing, in part at least, the building itself.

[10] I am of the opinion the trial court was right in directing a verdict for the defendant. The plaintiff agreed that all the pipe used should be of the Reading Manufacturing Company. Only about two-fifths of it, so far as appears, was of that kind. If more were used, then the burden of proving that fact was upon the plaintiff, which it could easily have done, since it knew where the pipe was obtained. The question of substantial performance of a contract of the character of the one under consideration depends in no small degree upon the good faith of the contractor. If the plaintiff had intended to, and had, complied with the terms of the contract except as to minor omissions, due to inadvertence, then he might be allowed to recover the contract price, less the amount necessary to fully compensate the defendant for damages caused by such omissions. But that is not this case. It installed between 2,000 and 2,500 feet of pipe, of which only 1,000 feet at most complied with the contract. No explanation was given why pipe called for by the contract was not used, nor was any effort made to show what it would cost to remove the pipe of other manufacturers and install that of the Reading Manufacturing Company. The defendant had a right to contract for what he wanted. He had a right before making payment to get what the contract called for. It is no answer to this suggestion to say that the pipe put in was just as good as that made by the Reading Manufacturing Company, or that the difference in value between such pipe and the pipe made by the Reading Manufacturing Company would be either "nominal or nothing." Defendant contracted for pipe made by the Reading Manufacturing Company. What his reason was for requiring this kind of pipe is of no importance. He wanted that and was entitled to it. It may have been a mere whim on his part, but even so, he had a right to this kind of pipe, regardless of whether some other kind, according to the opinion of the contractor or experts, would have been "just as good, better, or done just as well." He agreed to pay only upon condition that the pipe installed were made by that company and he ought not to be compelled to pay unless that condition be performed. The rule, therefore, of substantial performance, with damages for unsubstantial omissions, has no application.

[11] What was said by this court in *Smith v. Brady, supra,* is quite applicable here:

> I suppose it will be conceded that every one has a right to build his house, his cottage or his store after such a model and in such style as shall best accord with his notions of utility or be most agreeable to his fancy. The specifications of the contract become the law between the parties until voluntarily changed. If the owner prefers a plain and simple Doric column, and has so provided in the agreement, the contractor has no right to put in

its place the more costly and elegant Corinthian. If the owner, having regard to strength and durability, has contracted for walls of specified materials to be laid in a particular manner, or for a given number of joists and beams, the builder has no right to substitute his own judgment or that of others. Having departed from the agreement, if performance has not been waived by the other party, the law will not allow him to allege that he has made as good a building as the one he engaged to erect. He can demand payment only upon and according to the terms of his contract, and if the conditions on which payment is due have not been performed, then the right to demand it does not exist. To hold a different doctrine would be simply to make another contract, and would be giving to parties an encouragement to violate their engagements, which the just policy of the law does not permit.

(17 N.Y. 186, 72 Am. Dec. 442).

[12] I am of the opinion the trial court did not err in ruling on the admission of evidence or in directing a verdict for the defendant.

[13] For the foregoing reasons I think the judgment of the Appellate Division should be reversed and the judgment of the Trial Term affirmed.

HISCOCK, C. J., and HOGAN and CRANE, JJ., concur with CARDOZO, J.

POUND and ANDREWS, JJ., concur with MCLAUGHLIN, J.

Order affirmed, etc.

On motion for reargument:

PER CURIAM. The court did not overlook the specification [that] provides that defective work shall be replaced. The promise to replace, like the promise to install, is to be viewed, not as a condition, but as independent and collateral, when the defect is trivial and innocent. The law does not nullify the covenant, but restricts the remedy to damages.

The motion for a reargument should be denied.

HISCOCK, C. J., and CARDOZO, POUND, MCLAUGHLIN, CRANE, and ANDREWS, JJ., concur.

Motion denied.

––––––––

Excerpts from the *Jacobs & Youngs* Contract and Its "Specifications"[2]

Art. II. It is understood and agreed by and between the parties hereto that the work included in this contract is to be done under the direction of

––––––––

[2] Reprinted with permission from RICHARD DANZIG & GEOFFREY R. WATSON, THE CAPABILITY PROBLEM IN CONTRACT LAW (2d ed. 2004).

the said Architect, and that his decision as to the true construction and meaning of the drawings and specifications shall be final. It is also understood and agreed by and between the parties hereto that such additional drawings and explanations as may be necessary to detail and illustrate the work to be done are to be furnished by said Architect, and they agree to conform to and abide by the same so far as they may be consistent with the purpose and intent of the original drawings and specifications referred to in Art. I.

* * *

Art. III. No alterations shall be made in the work except upon written order of the Architect; the amount to be paid by Owner or allowed by the Contractors by virtue of such alterations to be stated in said order. Should the Owner and Contractors not agree as to amount to be paid or allowed, the work shall go on under the order required above, and in case of failure to agree, the determination of said amount shall be referred to arbitration, as provided for in Art. XII of this contract.

Art. IV. The Contractors shall provide sufficient, safe and proper facilities at all times for the inspection of the work by the Architect or his authorized representatives; shall, within twenty-four hours after receiving written notice from the Architect to the effect, proceed to remove from the grounds or buildings all materials condemned by him, whether worked or unworked, and to take down all portion of the work which the Architect shall by like written notice condemn as unsound or improper, or as in any way failing to conform to the drawings and specifications, and shall make good all work damaged or destroyed thereby.

Art. V. Should the Contractors at any time refuse or neglect to supply a sufficiency of properly skilled workmen, or of materials of the proper quality, or fail in any respect to prosecute the work with promptness and diligence, or fail in the performance of any of the agreements herein contained, such refusal, neglect or failure being certified by the Architect, the Owner shall be at liberty, after three days written notice to the Contractors, to provide any such labor or materials, and to deduct the cost thereof from any money then due or thereafter to become due to the Contractors under this contract; and if the Architect shall certify that such refusal, neglect or failure is sufficient ground for such action, the Owner shall also be at liberty to terminate the employment of the Contractors for the said work and to enter upon the premises and take possession, for the purpose of completing the work included under this contract, of all materials, tools and appliances thereon, and to employ any other person or persons to finish the work, and to provide the materials therefor; and in case of such discontinuance of the employment of the Contractors they shall not be entitled to receive any further payment under this contract expect that which shall exceed the expense incurred by the owner in finishing the work, such excess shall be paid by the owner to the Contractors; but if such expense shall exceed such unpaid balance, the Contractors shall pay the difference to the Owner. The expense incurred by the Owner as herein provided, either for furnishing materials or for finishing the work, and any damage incurred through such default, shall be audited and certified by the Architect, whose certificate thereof shall be conclusive upon the parties.

Art. VI. The Contractors shall complete the several portions and the whole of the work comprehended in this Agreement by and at the time or times hereinafter stated, to wit, December 15th, 1913.

Art. VII. Should the Contractors be delayed in the prosecution or completion of the work by the act, neglect or default of the Owner, of the Architect, or of any other contractor employed by the Owner upon the work, or by any damage caused by fire or other casualty for which the Contractors are not responsible, or by combined action of workmen in no wise caused by or resulting from default or collusion on the part of the Contractors, then the time herein fixed for the completion of the work shall be extended for a period equivalent to the time lost by reason of any or all the causes aforesaid, which extended period shall be determinate and fixed by the Architect; but no such allowance shall be made unless a claim therefor is presented in writing to the Architect within forty-eight hours of the occurrence of such delay.

* * *

Art. IX. It is hereby mutually agreed between the parties hereto that the sum to be paid by the Owner to the Contractors for said work and materials shall be Seventy thousand five hundred ($70,500) dollars, subject to additions and deductions as hereinbefore provided, and that such sum shall be paid by the Owner to the Contractors, in current funds, and only upon certificates of the Architect, as follows:

On or about the first day of each month a certificate will be given by the architect to the contractors for a payment on account of value of the work finished and erected at the site, which represents in his judgment a fair proportion to the whole of the contract price less a fifteen per cent (15%) margin which shall be withheld until after the completion and acceptance of the entire work.

The final payment, or 15% of the total amount of this contract, shall be made within thirty days after the completion of the work included in this contract, and all payments shall be due when certificates for the same are issued.

* * *

Art. XII. In case the Owner and Contractors fail to agree in relation to matters of payment, allowance or loss referred to in Arts. III or VIII of this contract, or should either of them dissent from the decision of the Architect referred to in Art. VII of this contract, which dissent shall have been filed in writing with the Architect within ten days of the announcement of such decision, then the matter shall be referred to a Board of Arbitration to consist of one person selected by the Owner, and one person selected by the Contractors, these two to select a third. The decision of any two of this Board shall be final and binding on both parties hereto. Each party hereto shall pay one half of the expense of such reference.

* * *

(Extracts from Specifications.)

General Conditions

(19) The Contractor is responsible for, and must make good any defects arising or discovered in his work within two years after completion of work and acceptance, or faults in labor or material, unless hereinafter changed.

* * *

(22) Where any particular brand of manufactured article is specified, it is to be considered as a standard. Contractors desiring to use another shall first make application in writing to the Architect, stating the difference in cost, and obtain their written approval of the change.

* * *

Character of Work and Labor:

(24) The decision of the Architect as to the character of any material or labor furnished by the Contractor is to be final and conclusive on both Contractor and Owner.

Access to Works:

(25) The Architect or his authorized agents are to have free access at all times to the works or to any place where any of the material for the same is in preparation.

* * *

Certificates:

(28) For each and every payment the Architect will issue his regular form or certificate, and the term "Entitled to" which appears on the certificate is hereby understood by each and all of the parties signing the contract to mean that in the Architect's judgment the work called for under said payment has been satisfactorily executed, entitling the Contractor to the money.

* * *

The payment by the Owner of such certificates, including the final certificate, will not constitute an acceptance of the work thus paid for as far as the Contractor is concerned, and the Owner shall hold the Contractor solely responsible for any and all defects that may appear in said work, at any time, before or after said payments, excepting such as may result from imperfections in the plans and specifications. Each certificate of payment to be issued by the Architect within not less than ten (10) days after the receipt of a written request from the Contractor for such payment, provided the Architect considers such payment due.

Approved material:

(225) The approval of the quality of any material will not be considered as acceptance of the work when installed should such material or work prove defective.

* * *

Wrought iron pipe:

(227) All wrought iron pipe must be well galvanized lap welded pipe of the grade known as "Standard Pipe" of Reading manufacture. Burrs formed in cutting must be reamed out. Fittings shall be extra heavy, galvanized, malleable iron fittings.

NOTES AND QUESTIONS

1.   Assume that the specification of "Reading Pipe" was part of a very detailed set of specifications and procedures for building the custom home at issue. Assume further that these specifications and procedures had been dickered over and negotiated as part of the contract. In light of these assumptions, do you think the majority or the dissent got it right? Why or why not?

2.   Justice Cardozo, author of the opinion in the *Lucy, Lady Duff Gordon* case, was willing to imply a "reasonable efforts to perform" term into that contract. Is that consistent with his willingness to excuse strict compliance with the detailed provisions in their contract and its specifications in this case?

3.   What could Mr. Kent, a successful New York lawyer, have done to ensure that he got Reading Pipe and that his other specifications were followed?

4.   How can you contract for perfect performance? Would a clause providing that (a) the contractor's strict performance of the contract with regard to each and every covenant and specification was at the heart of the contract, (b) strict performance was an express condition precedent to owner's duty to pay, and (c) failure of the contractor to perform strictly in accordance with the contract terms was intended by the parties to result in a forfeiture of

the contractor's right to payment work? *Consider* R2d § 229. Is there no way to require perfect performance?

5.   What is the downside, if any, of including a condition that may, at least in hindsight, appear over-reaching? Is it just that the court may blue line (cross out) that one provision?

PRACTICE TIP

Where there is a provision in a contract that a court might not enforce because it appears to be overreaching, counsel can greatly increase the chances of its enforcement by explaining why the provision is necessary or critical to the deal. The recitals at the beginning of the contract are a good place to do this. Explaining the provision not only shows (as opposed to just telling) the court that it was a material part of the consideration for the party in whose favor it runs, it also shows that the other party understood this and agreed to this allocation of performance and risk.

This technique is, thus, similar in operation to the U.C.C.'s requirement of a clear and conspicuous disclaimer of the implied warranty of merchantability. See U.C.C. § 2–316(2).

---

6.   Assume that Mr. Kent could not have cared less about the installation of non-Reading Pipe that was of the same quality. Assume that he was unhappy with other aspects of the job—like how long it took to perform or some undocumented detail like the precise type of spark arrester in the chimney. Does that affect his claim for failure to meet specifications? Legally? Ethically? Morally? What if he was perfectly happy with the job but just wanted a lower price based on the failure to perform to the letter of the contract? Or based on his ability to conjure up an argument? Does that affect anything?

O. W. GRUN ROOFING & CONSTRUCTION CO. V. COPE

Court of Civil Appeals of Texas
529 S.W.2d 258 (1975)

CADENA, J.

[1]   Plaintiff, Mrs. Fred M. Cope, sued defendant, O. W. Grun Roofing & Construction Co., to set aside a mechanic's lien filed by defendant and for damages in the sum of $1,500.00[3] suffered by plaintiff as a result of the alleged failure of defendant to perform a contract calling for the installation of a new roof on plaintiff's home. Defendant, in addition to a general denial,

---

³ [$1,500 in 1975 dollars is roughly the equivalent of $7,000 in 2019 dollars using the CPI and the GNP Deflator.—Eds.]

Difference between 770.60 — Contract price   *770.60 - 648*
= 122.60

filed a cross-claim for $648.00, the amount which plaintiff agreed to pay defendant for installing the roof, and for foreclosure of the mechanic's lien on plaintiff's home.

cope —

[2] Following trial to a jury, the court below entered judgment awarding plaintiff $122.60 as damages for defendant's failure to perform the contract; setting aside the mechanic's lien; and denying defendant recovery on its cross-claim. It is from this judgment that defendant appeals.

[3] The jury found (1) defendant failed to perform his contract in a good and workmanlike manner; (2) defendant did not substantially perform the contract; (3) plaintiff received no benefits from the labor performed and the materials furnished by defendant; the reasonable cost of performing the contract in a good and workmanlike manner would be $777.60. Although the verdict shows the cost of proper performance to be $777.60, the judgment describes this finding as being in the amount of $770.60, and the award of $122.60 to plaintiff is based on the difference between $770.60 and the contract price of $648.00.

Procedural History

[4] By its first point, defendant questions the factual and legal sufficiency of the evidence to support the jury's findings. The argument under this point (defendant's brief contains no statement following each point), is limited to the contention that all of the elements of "substantial performance" were established.

[5] We find no assignments of error in the motion for new trial specifically calling the trial court's attention to the complaint that the evidence is insufficient to support the finding that defendant did not perform the contract in a good and workmanlike manner (issue no. 1), or that the finding that defendant did not substantially perform the contract (issue no. 2) was contrary to the overwhelming weight and preponderance of the evidence.

[6] The only questions, therefore, which we can consider under defendant's first point are that there is no evidence to support the finding that defendant did not perform in a good and workmanlike manner and that the evidence establishes as a matter of law that defendant substantially performed the contract. In considering these "no evidence" points, we look only to the evidence supporting the verdict.

[7] The written contract required defendant to install a new roof on plaintiff's home for $648.00. The contract describes the color of the shingles to be used as "russet glow," which defendant defined as a "brown varied color." Defendant acknowledges that it was his obligation to install a roof of uniform color. *— was D's obligation*

[8] After defendant had installed the new roof, plaintiff noticed that it had streaks which she described as yellow, due to a difference in color or shade of some of the shingles. Defendant agreed to remedy the situation

D installed different shingle

and he removed the nonconforming shingles. However, the replacement shingles do not match the remainder, and photographs introduced in evidence clearly show that the roof is not of a uniform color. Plaintiff testified that her roof has the appearance of having been patched, rather than having been completely replaced. According to plaintiff's testimony, the yellow streaks appeared on the northern, eastern and southern sides of the roof, and defendant only replaced the non-matching shingles on the northern and eastern sides, leaving the southern side with the yellow streaks still apparent. The result is that only the western portion of the roof is of uniform color.

[9] When defendant originally installed the complete new roof, it used 24 "squares" of shingles. In an effort to achieve a roof of uniform color, five squares were ripped off and replaced. There is no testimony as to the number of squares which would have to be replaced on the southern, or rear, side of the house in order to eliminate the original yellow streaks. Although there is expert testimony to the effect that the disparity in color would not be noticeable after the shingles have been on the roof for about a year, there is testimony to the effect that, although some nine or ten months have elapsed since defendant attempted to achieve a uniform coloration, the roof is still "streaky" on three sides. One of defendant's experts testified that if the shingles are properly applied the result will be a "blended" roof rather than a streaked roof.

[10] In view of the fact that the disparity in color has not disappeared in nine or ten months, and in view of the fact that there is testimony to the effect that it would be impossible to secure matching shingles to replace the nonconforming ones, it can reasonably be inferred that a roof of uniform coloration can be achieved only by installing a completely new roof.

[11] The evidence is undisputed that the roof is a substantial roof and will give plaintiff protection against the elements.

[12] The principle which allows recovery for part performance in cases involving dependent promises may be expressed by saying that a material breach or a breach which goes to the root of the matter or essence of the contract defeats the promisor's claim despite his part performance, or it may be expressed by saying that a promisor who has substantially performed is entitled to recover, although he has failed in some particular to comply with his agreement. The latter mode of expressing the rule is generally referred to as the doctrine of substantial performance and is especially common in cases involving building contracts, although its application is not restricted to such contracts.

[13] It is difficult to formulate [a] definitive rule for determining whether the contractor's performance, less than complete, amounts to "substantial performance," since the question is one of fact and of degree, and the answer depends on the particular facts of each case. But, although

the decisions furnish no rule of thumb, they are helpful in suggesting guidelines. One of the most obvious factors to be considered is the extent of the nonperformance. The deficiency will not be tolerated if it is so pervasive as to frustrate the purpose of the contract in any real or substantial sense. The doctrine does not bestow on a contractor a license to install whatever is, in his judgment, "just as good." The answer is arrived at by weighing the purpose to be served, the desire to be gratified, the excuse for deviating from the letter of the contract and the cruelty of enforcing strict adherence or of compelling the promisee to receive something less than for which he bargained. Also influential in many cases is the ratio of money value of the tendered performance and of the promised performance. In most cases the contract itself at least is an indication of the value of the promised performance, and courts should have little difficulty in determining the cost of curing the deficiency. But the rule cannot be expressed in terms of a fraction, since complete reliance on a mathematical formula would result in ignoring other important factors, such as the purpose which the promised performance was intended to serve and the extent to which the nonperformance would defeat such purpose, or would defeat it if not corrected. *See generally*, 3A Corbin, Contracts §§ 700–07 (1960).

[14] Although definitions of "substantial performance" are not always couched in the same terminology and, because of the facts involved in a particular case, sometimes vary in the recital of the factors to be considered, the following definition by the Commission of Appeals in *Atkinson v. Jackson Bros.*, 270 S.W. 848, 849 (Tex. Com. App. 1925), is a typical recital of the constituent elements of the doctrine:

> To constitute substantial compliance the contractor must have in good faith intended to comply with the contract, and shall have substantially done so in the sense that the defects are not pervasive, do not constitute a deviation from the general plan contemplated for the work, and are not so essential that the object of the parties in making the contract and its purpose cannot, without difficulty, be accomplished by remedying them. Such performance permits only such omissions or deviations from the contract as are inadvertent and unintentional, are not due to bad faith, do not impair the structure as a whole, and are remediable without doing material damage to other parts of the building in tearing down and reconstructing.

[15] What was the general plan contemplated for the work in this case? What was the object and purpose of the parties? It is clear that, despite the frequency with which the courts speak of defects that are not "pervasive," which do not constitute a "deviation from the general plan," and which are "not so essential that the object of the parties in making the contract and its purpose cannot, without difficulty, be accomplished by remedying them," when an attempt is made to apply the general principles to a

particular case difficulties are encountered at the outset. Was the general plan to install a substantial roof which would serve the purpose which roofs are designed to serve? Or, rather, was the general plan to install a substantial roof of uniform color? Was the object and purpose of the contract merely to furnish such a roof, or was it to furnish such a roof which would be of a uniform color? It should not come as a shock to anyone to adopt a rule to the effect that a person has, particularly with respect to his home, to choose for himself and to contract for something which exactly satisfies that choice, and not to be compelled to accept something else. In the matter of homes and their decoration, as much as, if not more than, in many other fields, mere taste or preference, almost approaching whimsy, may be controlling with the homeowner, so that variations which might, under other circumstances, be considered trifling, may be inconsistent with that "substantial performance" on which liability to pay must be predicated. Of course mere incompleteness or deviations which may be easily supplied or remedied after the contractor has finished his work, and the cost of which to the owner is not excessive and readily ascertainable, present less cause for hesitation in concluding that the performance tendered constitutes substantial performance, since in such cases the owner can obtain complete satisfaction by merely spending some money and deducting the amount of such expenditure from the contract price.

[16] In the case before us there is evidence to support the conclusion that plaintiff can secure a roof of uniform coloring only by installing a completely new roof. We cannot say, as a matter of law, that the evidence establishes that in this case that a roof which so lacks uniformity in color as to give the appearance of a patch job serves essentially the same purpose as a roof of uniform color which has the appearance of being a new roof. We are not prepared to hold that a contractor who tenders a performance so deficient that it can be remedied only by completely redoing the work for which the contract called has established, as a matter of law, that he has substantially performed his contractual obligation.

* * *

The judgment of the trial court is affirmed.

NOTES AND QUESTIONS

1. If a party has not substantially performed, we say that they have committed a *material breach*. It follows from the concept of constructive conditions that if one party has committed a material breach, the other party has no further duty to perform until the breach has been remedied. There are no precise standards for determining whether a party has committed a material breach. Read R2d § 241, which lists five "circumstances" that are "significant" in determining whether there has been a material breach. This

very helpful

list of factors should not be considered exhaustive. In determining whether there has been a material breach (or a failure to substantially perform, which is basically the same thing), a court should consider any factor that bears on the question of whether the non-breaching party should be excused from her duty to perform (and, as the next case shows, allowed to walk away from the contract) or whether she should be required to perform and left with only a claim for damages on account of the breach.

2.   A material breach only suspends the non-breaching party's obligation to perform. That is, the non-breaching party doesn't have to do anything now, but she may have to perform later if the breaching party cures the default within a reasonable time. If there is no cure within a *reasonable time*, the material breach ripens into a *total breach*. A total breach discharges the non-breaching party's obligation to perform and gives rise to a damage claim for breach of the whole contract. R2d § 242 sets forth the factors to be taken into account in determining whether a breach is a total breach. As with a material breach, the test is flexible and open-ended. In trying to determine whether or not there has been a total breach, consider any fact that bears on the question of whether it is fair to require the non-breaching party to give the breaching party more time before declaring the contract is at an end and taking steps to mitigate his damages.

good law summary

3.   Determining whether there has been a total breach is one of the toughest decisions you will have to make as a practicing lawyer. There will be times when your client is incurring losses it may never be able to recover (either because of problems of proof or because the breaching party may go bankrupt), but if the client terminates the contract too soon, the client will be the one committing the total breach and the one held liable.

CARTER V. SHERBURNE CORP.

Supreme Court of Vermont
132 Vt. 88, 315 A.2d 870 (1974)

SHANGRAW, CHIEF JUSTICE.

[1]   This is an appeal by the defendant from a judgment of the Rutland County Court. The subject matter of the litigation is work done and materials furnished by the plaintiff in connection with a development of the defendant's near Sherburne Mountain. The plaintiff claimed that he was not fully paid for labor and materials furnished under written contracts, and that he was entitled to further amounts on a quantum meruit basis for labor and materials furnished without express agreement as to price. The defendant claimed defective performance and payment for everything due, and asserted a counterclaim for expense necessitated by plaintiff's alleged failure to fulfill contractual commitments. The Court found that the plaintiff was in substantial compliance under his contracts,

that the defendant had no right to terminate the contracts, and that the defendant's counterclaim was without foundation. The Court also found that the plaintiff performed other work for the defendant without compensation under a promise for additional work which was not fulfilled by the defendant. Plaintiff was awarded various sums for unpaid invoices, payment for other work done for the defendant, and interest. The defendant corporation has appealed.

[2] The facts as found by the Court are, in substance, as follows:

There were four written contracts between the parties covering (a) the furnishing and placing of gravel on one road, (b) the drilling and blasting of rock on various residential roads, (c) road construction, and (d) the cutting and grubbing of a gondola lift-line. The contracts called for weekly progress payments based upon work completed with a provision for retaining 10% until ten days after final acceptance. The billings from the plaintiff to the defendant amounted to $52,571.25, of which $41,368.05 was paid by the defendant. The difference between the $52,571.25 billed, and $41,368.05 paid, comprised $4,596.45 retained by the defendant under its holdback provision, and adjustments claimed by the defendant of $6,606.75. The Court found that adjustments in the amount of $4,747.25[4] was improperly taken by the defendant and that amount was decreed to the plaintiff. In addition the Court found that the plaintiff was entitled to all the retainage held by the defendant.

* * *

[3] The defendant's primary contention is that the Court's ruling that the plaintiff was in substantial compliance under his contracts is error. The contention is that this ruling was based on the erroneous conclusion that time was not of the essence of the contracts, and that as time was of the essence and plaintiff failed to perform within the time specified, plaintiff was not in substantial compliance and defendant is entitled to the amounts withheld as retainage.

[4] Where time is of the essence, performance on time is a constructive condition of the other party's duty, usually the duty to pay for the performance rendered. Time may be made of the essence of a contract by a stipulation to that effect, or by any language that expressly provides that the contract will be void if performance is not within a specified time. Where the parties have not expressly declared their intention, the determination as to whether time is of the essence depends on the intention

---

4 [$4,747.25 in 1974 dollars is roughly the equivalent of $24,200 in 2019 dollars using the CPI and the GNP Deflator.—Eds.]

of the parties, the circumstances surrounding the transaction, and the subject matter of the contract.

[5] As a general rule, time is not of the essence in a building or construction contract in the absence of an express provision making it such. "Construction contracts are subject to many delays for innumerable reasons, the blame for which may be difficult to assess. The structure . . . becomes part of the land and adds to the wealth of its owner. Delays are generally foreseen as probable; and the risks thereof are discounted . . . The complexities of the work, the difficulties commonly encountered, the custom of men in such cases, all these lead to the result that performance at the agreed time by the contractor is not of the essence." 3A A. Corbin, Contracts § 720, at 377 (1960).

[6] We conclude, then, that time was not of the essence of any of the contracts considered here. None of the four contracts included express language making time of the essence, and we can find nothing in the circumstances surrounding these contracts that would lift them out of the operation of the general rule. Two of the contracts called for completion dates and forfeitures for non-completion on schedule, but the inclusion of dates in construction contracts does not make time of the essence. *DeSombre v. Bickel*, 18 Wis.2d 390, 118 N.W.2d 868 (1963). Moreover, the inclusion of penalty or forfeiture provisions for noncompletion on schedule is strong evidence that time is not of the essence and that performance on time is not a condition of the other party's duty to accept and pay for the performance rendered. 3A A. Corbin, Contracts § 720 (1960).

[7] Ordinarily, in contracts where time is not of the essence, a failure to complete the work within the specified time will not terminate the contract, but it will subject the contractor to damages for the delay. However, in this case, most of the delays were due to the actions of the defendant corporation in constantly shifting the plaintiff's activities from one contract to another. Delay in the performance of a contract will, as a rule be excused where it is caused by the act or default of the opposite party, or by the act or default of persons for whose conduct the opposite party is responsible. Where this is the case, the contractor will not be held liable, under a provision for liquidated damages or otherwise, for his non-compliance with the terms of the contract; and his non-compliance will not be considered a breach. An obligation of good faith and fair dealing is an implied term in every contract, and a party may not obstruct, hinder, or delay a contractor's work and then seek damages for the delay thus occasioned.

[8] Defendant also disputes the Court's conclusions with respect to the gondola lift-line contract. Defendant informed the plaintiff in April, 1968, that no more progress payments would be made on the gondola contract. At that time, plaintiff had completed a substantial portion of the

delayed progress payments NOT whole contract

contracted work, but had not yet invoiced it. After defendant's notice, plaintiff continued to work on the lift-line, but was forced to stop for financial reasons. Defendant claims that the plaintiff is not entitled to recover for work done or invoiced after the notice concerning termination of payments.

[9] Defendant's April notice concerned only the progress payments due the plaintiff. It was not a notice of contract termination. In the absence of a total disavowal of the contract, failure of payment does not require an immediate cessation of performance. The contracts between the plaintiff and the defendant were not terminated until June of 1968. The termination was without legal justification, and the plaintiff is entitled to recover the contract price for all work done before the termination date.

[10] As to the defendant's contentions regarding the parties' contract for additional work, it is clear that the parties entered into an express, although unformalized, contract for good consideration. The Court's findings and conclusions with respect to the contract itself are entirely proper. The consideration rendered by the plaintiff was legally sufficient in that the work performed was independent of the parties' previous agreements, and, contrary to the defendant's contention, the parol evidence rule does not preclude, as between original parties, proof of failure of consideration.

* * *

Judgment affirmed.

PRACTICE TIP

Contracts often contain clauses stating "time is of the essence." These clauses can sometimes turn a non-material breach into a material breach or a total breach. You should be careful about putting too much faith in these clauses, however. They are so common that courts often don't take them seriously. The better, more professional way to do it is to use express conditions, events of default, and remedies to say when the client can suspend its performance and when it can terminate the contract.

PROBLEM 24-1

Developer and Construction Company had a contract under the terms of which Construction Company was to build twenty houses in Developer's subdivision for a price of $2,000,000. Construction was to be completed by March 1. The contract provided that "time is of the essence." The contract further provided that Developer would make periodic progress payments as construction progressed. The progress payments would be pro-rated so that Construction Company would be paid for 90% of the work completed to date, with a 10% "retainage" to be paid when the project was fully completed and all of the discrepancies on Developer's "punch list" had been rectified.

On March 1, the situation stood as follows: All of the houses had been completed except for the interior painting in fifteen of them. The interior painting had been delayed because Construction Company had had difficulty with its painting subcontractor and had had to replace it with a different sub. (The difficulties were primarily due to poor performance on the part of the sub, but Construction Company was not entirely blameless in the matter). Because the market for painters was a little tight at the time, Construction Company had been unable to find a sub who could complete the job on time. Prior to March 1, Developer had paid Construction Company $1,600,000 for work completed through the time of the last progress payment. On March 1, Construction Company was entitled to another $150,000 for work completed since the last progress payment. Developer was entitled to withhold $50,000 on account of the work not yet completed, and there was the $200,000 retainage to be paid when the job was fully completed.

Developer has consulted you. She says: "Let's kick these jerks off the job and not pay them another cent. I can get the painting finished for next to nothing and save close to four hundred grand. That'll cover my alimony payments for the next year and a half."

(a)　Express in the terms used by the *Carter* opinion the argument that you would make if you were in front of the Supreme Court of Vermont (the folks who decided *Carter*).

(b)　Express the same argument under §§ 241 and 242 of the Restatement.

(c)　Suppose that instead of saying "Time is of the essence," the contract had said, "Completion by March 1, 2002 of all work to be completed hereunder shall be a condition precedent to Developer's duty to pay any outstanding sums due and failure to complete all work by March 1, 2002 shall entitle Developer to terminate this contract and recover damages."

(i)　Would this improve Developer's position?

(ii)　Would you expect a contractor to sign a contract with a provision like this?

————

Playing in the Band: Constructive Conditions, Substantial Performance, and Material Breach

To understand the interplay between express conditions, promises, constructive conditions, material breach, and total breach, consider the following. Band and Promoter have a contract for Band to play a concert. The contract provides that Promoter will provide at least 25 security personnel, two of whom shall be stationed at Band's dressing room and one of whom shall be stationed at Band's bus. The contract could (and probably should) have provided that this was a condition precedent to Band's obligation to perform. In that case, Band would not have been required to perform unless and until the heavies were in place. But the contract did not clearly designate the provision as an express condition, so it will probably be construed as a promise. We'll assume that it will be construed as a promise and not as an express condition.

Suppose that Band shows up for the concert and there are only 15 security personnel available. Promoter tells Band's manager that she can only supply one guard for the dressing room and the bus will be safe without a guard. "After all, this is a '70s Rock show. If these geezers got rowdy, they'd all have heart attacks." Because the provision for the number of security personnel is a promise, Promoter will be liable for damages. Band will probably be able to recover damages only if they are injured or their property is damaged or stolen. They may suffer nervous indigestion worrying about overzealous groupies in the audience, but the requirement that contract damages be proved with reasonable certainty will preclude any recovery for that.

Band's obligation to perform is also subject to the constructive condition that Promoter substantially performs her promises. If she has not substantially performed, we say that she has materially breached. The effect of a failure to substantially perform[5] (or a material breach— "material breach" is just another way of saying "failure to substantially perform") is to relieve Band of the duty to perform its obligations. (The constructive condition hasn't been satisfied.) To determine whether Promoter has substantially performed, what the court really does is ask "is Promoter's failure so severe that Band should not have to perform?" In this case, Band's manager (or her counsel) has to guess how a court will come out on the question. If Promoter's failure to provide security (along with Promoter's other failures to perform her promises) constitutes a material breach then Band can withhold its performance until Promoter gets sufficient security in place. If the breach by Promoter is a total breach, Band can stay in its bus and head for the next show. Assuming that the breach is a material breach, whether it is a total breach will probably depend on whether Promoter is willing and able to get sufficient security in place by show time.

---

[5] The rule against splitting infinitives is archaic and is largely a matter of taste. Here, splitting the infinitive is vastly superior to the alternative. Pardon the split infinitive, but it's easier to understand if it is said that way.

PROBLEM 24-2

Homer and Marge ("H & M") entered into a contract with Builder, who was to build a home for them. Because H & M are now getting a million dollars an episode for their cable television show, it was to be quite a place. The contract provided for progress payments to be made as construction progressed. The last payment of $100,000 was to be made when construction was completed. The house was finished two months late. When it was finally done, H & M went for their last walk-through and discovered that the painting in the living room was so badly done that the room would have to be repainted. Builder refused to do the repainting and H & M hired a painter to do it at a cost of $2,000. H & M also incurred additional rent of $5,000 because construction was late. H & M are now living in the house. They haven't paid Builder the last $100,000.

(a)   If Builder's breach was a total breach, what are H & M's rights and obligations? *They don't need to pay the 100 grand?* ✓

(b)   If Builder's breach was not a material breach, what are H & M's rights and obligations? *pay but sue for damages → recover 7k* ✓

BRITTON V. TURNER

Superior Court of Judicature of New Hampshire
6 N.H. 481 (1834)

PARKER, J. delivered the opinion of the court.

[1] It may be assumed, that the labor performed by the plaintiff, and for which he seeks to recover a compensation in this action, was commenced under a special contract to labor for the defendant the term of one year, for the sum of one hundred and twenty dollars, and that the plaintiff has labored but a portion of that time, and has voluntarily failed to complete the entire contract.

[2] It is clear, then, that he is not entitled to recover upon the contract itself, because the service, which was to entitle him to the sum agreed upon, has never been performed.

[3] But the question arises, can the plaintiff, under these circumstances, recover a reasonable sum for the service he has actually performed, under the count in *quantum meruit*.

[4] Upon this, and questions of a similar nature, the decisions to be found in the books are not easily reconciled.

[5] It has been held, upon contracts of this kind for labor to be performed at a specified price, that the party who voluntarily fails to fulfill the contract by performing the whole labor contracted for, is not entitled to recover any thing for the labor actually performed, however much he may

have done towards the performance, and this has been considered the settle rule of law upon this subject . . .

[6] That such [a] rule in its operation may be very unequal, not to say unjust, is apparent.

[7] A party who contracts to perform certain specified labor, and who breaks his contract in the first instance, without any attempt to perform it, can only be made liable to pay the damages which the other party has sustained by reason of such non-performance, which in many instances may be trifling—whereas a party who, in good faith, has entered upon the performance of his contract, and nearly completed it, and then abandoned the further performance—although the other party had had the full benefit of all that has been done, and has perhaps sustained no actual damage—is in fact subjected to a loss of all which has been performed, in the nature of damages for the non-fulfilment of the remainder, upon the technical rule, that the contract must be fully performed in order to a recovery of any part of the compensation.

[8] By the operation of this rule, then, the party who attempts performance may be placed in a much worse situation than he who wholly disregards his contract, and the other party may receive much more, by the breach, and more than he could be entitled to were he seeking to recover damages by an action.

[9] The case before us presents an illustration. Had the plaintiff in this case never entered upon the performance of his contract, the damage could not probably have been greater than some small expense and trouble incurred in procuring another to do the labor which he had contracted to perform. But having entered upon the performance, and labored nine and a half months, the value of which labor to the defendant as found by the jury, is ninety-five dollars, if the defendant can succeed in this defense, he in fact receives nearly five sixths of the value of a whole year's labor, by reason of the breach of contract by the plaintiff a sum not only utterly disproportionate to any probable, not to say possible damage, which could have resulted from the neglect of the plaintiff to continue the two and a half months, but altogether beyond any damage which could have been recovered by the defendant, had the plaintiff done nothing towards the fulfilment of his contract.

[10] Another illustration is furnished in *Lantry v. Parks*, 8 Cow. 63. There the defendant hired the plaintiff for a year, at ten dollars per month. The plaintiff worked ten and a half months, and then left, saying he would work no more for him. This was on Saturday; on Monday the plaintiff returned, and offered to resume his work, but the defendant said he would employ him no longer. The court held that the refusal of the defendant on Saturday was a violation of his contract, and that he could recover nothing for the labor performed . . .

[11] We hold, then, that where a party undertakes to pay upon a special contract for the performance of labor, or the furnishing of materials, he is not to be charged upon such special agreement until the money is earned according to the terms of it, and where the parties have made an express contract the law will not imply and raise a contract different from that which the parties have entered into, except upon some farther transaction between the parties.

[12] In case of a failure to perform such special contract, by the default of the party contracting to do the service, if the money is not due by the terms of the special agreement he is not entitled to recover for his labor, or for the materials furnished, unless the other party receives what has been done, or furnished, and upon the whole case derives a benefit from it. *Taft v. Montague*, 14 Mass. 282 [7 Am. Dec. 215]; 2 Stark. Ev. 644.

[13] But if, where a contract is made of such a character, a party actually receives labor, or materials, and thereby derives a benefit and advantage, over and above the damage which has resulted from the breach of the contract by the other party, the labor actually done, and the value received, furnish a new consideration, and the law thereupon raises a promise to pay to the extent of the reasonable worth of such excess. This may be considered as making a new case, one not within the original agreement, and the party is entitled to "recover on his new case, for the work done, not as agreed, but yet accepted by the defendant." 1 Dane Abr. 224.

[14] If, on such failure to perform the whole, the nature of the contract be such that the employer can reject what has been done, and refuse to receive any benefit from the part performance, he is entitled so to do, and in such case is not liable to be charged, unless he has before assented to and accepted of what has been done, however much the other party may have done towards the performance. He has in such case received nothing, and having contracted to receive nothing but the entire matter contracted for, he is not bound to pay, because his express promise was only to pay on receiving the whole, and having actually received nothing, the law cannot and ought not to raise an implied promise to pay. But where the party receives value, takes and uses the materials, or has advantage from the labor, he is liable to pay the reasonable worth of what he has received. *Farnsworth v. Garrard*, 1 Camp. 38. And the rule is the same, whether it was received and accepted by an assent subsequent to the performance of all which was in fact done. If he received it under such circumstances as precluded him from rejecting it afterwards, that does not alter the case; it has still been received by his assent.

[15] In fact, we think the technical reasoning, that the performance of the whole labor is a condition precedent, and the right to recover anything dependent upon it; that the contract being entire, there can be no

if condition precedent to finish contract it

apportionment; and that there being an express contract no other can be implied, even upon the subsequent performance of service, is not properly applicable to this species of contract, where a beneficial service has been actually performed; for we have abundant reason to believe, that the general understanding of the community is, that the hired laborer shall be entitled to compensation for the service actually performed, though he do not continue the entire term contracted for, and such contracts must be presumed to be made with reference to that understanding, unless an express stipulation shows the contrary.

[16] Where a beneficial service has been performed and received, therefore, under contracts of this kind, the mutual agreements cannot be considered as going to the whole of the consideration, so as to make them mutual conditions, the one precedent to the other, without a specific proviso to that effect . . . It is easy, if parties so choose, to provide by an express agreement that nothing shall be earned, if the laborer leaves his employer without having performed the whole service contemplated, then there can be no pretense for a recovery if he voluntarily deserts the service before the expiration of the time.

[17] The amount, however, for which the employer ought to be charged, where the laborer abandons his contract, is only reasonable worth, or the amount of advantage he receives upon the whole transaction. *Wadleigh v. Sutton*; and, in estimating the value of the labor, the contract price for the service cannot be exceeded. . . .

Employer can sue for damages from nonperformance

[18] If a person makes a contract fairly he is entitled to have it fully performed, and if this is not done he is entitled to damages. He may maintain a suit to recover the amount of damage sustained by the nonperformance.

[19] The benefit and advantage which the party takes by the labor, therefore, is the amount of value which he receives, if any, after deducting the amount of damage; and if he elects to put this in defense he is entitled so to do, and the implied promise which the law will raise, in such case, is to pay such amount of the stipulated price for the whole labor, as remains after deducting what it would cost to procure a completion of the residue of the service, and also any damage which has been sustained by reason of the non-fulfilment of the contract.

[20] If, in such case it be found that the damages are equal to, or greater than the amount of the labor performed so that the employer, having a right to the full performance of the contract, has not upon the whole case received a beneficial service, the plaintiff cannot recover.

[21] This rule, by binding the employer to pay the value of the service he actually receives, and the laborer to answer in damages where he does not complete the entire contract, will leave no temptation to the former to drive the laborer from his service, near the close of his term, by ill-

treatment, in order to escape from payment; nor to the latter to desert his service before the stipulated time, without a sufficient reason; and it will, in most instances, settle the whole controversy in one action, and prevent a multiplicity of suits and cross actions.

[22] There may be instances, however, where the damage occasioned is much greater than the value of the labor performed, and if the party elects to permit himself to be charged for the value of the labor, without interposing the damages in defense, he is entitled to do so, and may have an action to recover his damages for the non-performance, whatever, they may be. *Crowninshield v. Robinson*, 1 Mason 93.

[23] And he may commence such action at any time after the contract is broken, notwithstanding no suit has been instituted against him; but if he elects to have the damages considered in the action against him, he must be understood as conceding that they are not to be extended beyond the amount of what he has received, and he cannot afterwards sustain an action for farther damages.

[24] Applying the principles thus laid down to this case, the plaintiff is entitled to judgment on the verdict.

[25] The defendant sets up a mere breach of the contract in defense of the action, but this cannot avail him. He does not appear to have offered evidence to show that he was damned by such breach, or to have asked that a deduction should be made upon that account. The direction to the jury was therefore correct, that the plaintiff was entitled to recover as much as the labor performed was reasonably worth; and the jury appear to have allowed a *pro rata* compensation, for the time which the plaintiff labored in the defendant's service.

[26] As the defendant has not claimed or had any adjustment of damages, for the breach of the contract, in this action, if he has actually sustained damage he is still entitled to a suit to recover the amount . . .

Judgment on the verdict.

———

PROBLEM 24-3

Owner and Roofer enter into a contract for the re-roofing of Owner's home. The contract provides that the price will be $4,000. Roofer spends $3,000 doing the job. Owner claims the roof is the wrong color. She refuses to pay, and gets second roofer to re-roof the house. She pays the second roofer $4,200. Roofer sues and it is determined that Roofer committed a total breach of the contract by putting on the wrong color of shingles. It is also determined that the value of the work done by roofer was $3,500. Case law in the jurisdiction provides that in the proper circumstances a party who has committed a total breach can recover under quantum meruit. How much is Roofer entitled to recover from Owner? (To date, Owner has made no payments to Roofer.)

    a. $4,000   b. $3,500   c. $3,000   d.   Nothing

[handwritten: Quant. mer. not applicable]

PROBLEM 24-4

Contractor and Sub entered into a contract under the terms of which Sub was to do part of the construction on a dam project for a price of $2.5 million. There was a great deal of friction on the project. Contractor claimed that Sub's work did not meet specifications. Sub countered that its work did meet specifications and even if it did not, it was the fault of Contractor for furnishing defective plans, failing to properly prepare the site, and denying it access to the project at certain times.

Finally, Contractor and Sub got into a major dispute, and Contractor threw Sub off the job. Contractor got another sub to finish the job for $500,000. At the time it left the job, Sub had spent $2.8 million, and it would have had to spend another $400,000 to complete the job. It had been paid $1.5 million. The court found as a fact that the value of the work Sub had done prior to its dismissal was $3.2 million.

(a) How much is Sub entitled to recover if it is determined that Sub was the party who committed the first total breach? (The answer is in *Britton v. Turner*.)   *[handwritten: None]*

(b) How much is Sub entitled to recover if it is determined that Contractor was the party who committed the first total breach? (*See Southern Painting Co.* in Chapter 20.)   *[handwritten: 1.7 million $]*

[handwritten: 3.2 − 1.5 = 1.7]

NOTE

Because the law of implied conditions is so fuzzy, good contracts use events of default, declarations of default, opportunities to cure, and specifications of remedies to address the situation. Every contract carries within it the implied covenant by each party to provide a remedy to the other in case of breach. The parties are free, however, to make this covenant express and use conditions to do so. It is far superior to provide for a detailed remedies section in the contract rather than leave the matter wholly to the common law, the statutes, and the courts.

For example, in a secured loan agreement, the following could be events of default:

(a)   breach of warranty;

(b)   failure to pay on time;

(c)   failure to perform any other obligation in a timely manner;

(d) grant of a subordinate security interest in collateral;

(e) sale of collateral without paying over the proceeds or obtaining consent;

(f) material impairment of the value of the collateral;

(g) violation of financial covenants such as a debt ratio.

If an event of default occurs, the lender can choose to declare a default, or it may be automatic. In truth, some sort of notice will always be required, even for "automatic" defaults.

There may be a cure period for the event—a time period in which the defaulting party can perform to "undo" the event of default—usually triggered by the notice of default from the other party. Some parties don't like to grant cure periods at all or grant only short ones. They often convince the other side that they won't call a default for minor problems—this gives them the whip hand if they need it later. Remember, while the friendly loan officer selling you the loan may be someone that you would trust with a whip, her buddy in collections may be someone that you would not want to meet in a dark alley or otherwise.

Specified remedies can include: cessation of future advances of funds, acceleration of obligations, obtaining possession of collateral or other property, requiring the debtor to assemble collateral, allowing for inspections, conducting an auction (that shall be deemed commercially reasonable). *Can you think of what remedies could be provided for in a real property lease? A personal property lease? An intellectual property license? A franchise agreement?*

CHAPTER 25

SALES: CONTRACT PERFORMANCE UNDER THE UNIFORM COMMERCIAL CODE

■ ■ ■

A. THE PERFECT TENDER RULE

Article 2's provisions on performance are deceptive. Upon a casual reading, it appears that the drafters merely restated the obvious, hedging their bets even further by liberally peppering their sentences with wishy-washy phrases like "reasonably" and "seasonably." In fact, however, there are some real zingers in Article 2. Even though the drafters used some terms like "reasonably" and "seasonably" to provide some expansion joints, the law of sales is still statutory law, and the statutes must be read precisely. As an example, read carefully § 2–601 and apply it to the problems that follow.

2-601 — reject or accept where accept any commercial unit or units and reject the rest

———

PROBLEM 25-1

Kent, a wealthy lawyer, contracts with Jacob & Youngs Mobile Homes, Inc. to have two mobile homes custom built. One is to be airlifted to a remote area of the Adirondack Mountains, where Kent plans to use it as a hunting and fishing retreat. The other is to be transported to a remote island in the Caribbean, where Kent plans to use it as a winter hideaway. The contract provides that all pipe used in the mobile homes "must be well galvanized, lap welded pipe of the grade known as 'standard pipe' of Reading Manufacture."

When the mobile homes are completed, Kent goes to the factory to inspect them prior to having them transported to their sites by another contractor. He discovers that they conform to the contract in every respect except that one home has about half the plumbing done with pipe manufactured by the Cohoes Pipe Company rather than with pipe manufactured by the Reading Pipe Company.

(a) Does Article 2 apply to this transaction? Isn't building a structure like this a service rather than a sale? Aren't these houses real estate rather than goods? (Regardless of how you come out on this point, assume for the questions that follow that Article 2 does apply.)

PPT— mostly goods, homes movable at time of identification to contract

(b)   Which of the following courses of action are open to Kent?

    (i)   accept both homes ✓

    (ii)   reject both homes ✓

    (iii)   accept the home with the conforming pipe and reject the one with the non-conforming ✓

    ?(iv)   accept the home with the non-conforming pipe and reject the one with the conforming

    ?(v)   reject the non-conforming pipe and accept both homes otherwise

(c)   Read § 2–714(1). May Kent accept the homes and then sue for damages? *Yes*

(d)   Refresh your recollection of *Jacob & Youngs v. Kent*, 230 N.Y. 239, 129 N.E. 889 (1921), from Chapter 24, above. Does the U.C.C. change the result? How?

PROBLEM 25-2

goods
\ Single lot - 2-601 PTR

The Mad Hatter ordered 100 yards of gray wool felt from Black Sheep Wool Products, LLC. It was to be delivered in one shipment on September 1. When the wool was delivered, Mr. Hatter discovered that about 10 yards of it was of a slightly darker color than called for by the contract specifications. He can reject the wool felt (choose one):

C?
nonconforming

(a)   only if the discrepancy constitutes a material (no pun intended) breach of the contract.

(b)   only if the discrepancy substantially impairs the value of the felt to him. *– Revocation and not installment contract*

2-601 can reject if seller fails to tender and goods do not conform in any way

(c)   as long as the goods failed to conform to the contract in any way and he acted in good faith.

(d)   under no circumstances. There's no way he can reject the felt on the basis of such a minor discrepancy.

PROBLEM 25-3

Suppose the Mad Hatter in Problem 25–2 wanted to keep the 90 yards that had the right color and reject the off-color 10 yards. Could he do that?

is it commercial unit? depends if wool can be divided into?

PROBLEM 25-4

Black Sheep Wool Products LLC learned its lesson. It made sure the wool in the next shipment was perfect in every way. (Of course, it also charged the Mad Hatter a little extra to make up for the increased costs of additional quality control inspectors. Everything has a price.)

The contract called for the felt to be delivered on November 1, but it was a few days late. Can the Mad Hatter use the perfect tender rule of section 2–601 to reject the felt on the ground that the delivery was late?

In thinking about this problem, consider *Harlow & Jones, Inc. v. Advance Steel Co.*, 424 F. Supp. 770 (E.D. Mich. 1976), which presented interesting issues about the perfect tender rule. Harlow was an importer of steel. It entered into an oral contract to sell Advance 1,000 tons of cold-rolled German steel. The contract provided that the steel was to be shipped from European ports during September—October, 1974. Harlow's confirmation form had a provision that stated: "All delivery dates are approximate and not guaranteed." It also had *force majeure* clauses which provided that Harlow was not responsible for delays beyond its control.

The steel was shipped from Europe in three shipments. The first shipment was shipped in September and arrived in October. The second was shipped in October and arrived in early November. The third was shipped in mid-November and arrived in late November. Advance rejected the last shipment because of late delivery. Harlow sued, claiming the delivery was not late. The court rejected Harlow's argument that the terms in its confirmation form were controlling, holding that under U.C.C. § 2–207 they did not become part of the contract. The court did, however, hold that the last shipment conformed to the contract terms because "according to an accepted steel importing trade usage, shipment in September—October means delivery in October—November." Thus, because the last of the steel had been delivered before the end of November it conformed to the contract.

The case illustrates a couple of important points about the perfect tender rule. First, the perfect tender rule is a default rule. Where the parties would prefer that there be a less strict standard, they can agree to that. In this case, the seller wanted a less strict standard, but it didn't want it enough to insist on it as a condition to the formation of a contract. The second point is that even though the perfect tender rule requires strict compliance with the terms of the contract, the terms of the contract may be something other than what a person who is not in the business would expect from a literal reading. So a lawyer who gets involved in a sales contract has to make sure she understands all the trade usages. This often means grilling the client on all the trade usages that they take for granted.

So, what result does that imply for the Mad Hatter and the right to reject the felt because it was a few days late?

B. CURE

It has been suggested that the perfect tender rule does not exist in the real world. The basis for saying so is that the Code makes so many exceptions to it, that the seller can usually find exceptions within which she can fit. Where the seller cannot find an exception, courts are likely to apply some sort of a judicially created *de minimis* rule to protect the good faith seller from minor and technical nonconformities. Whether there really is a perfect tender rule is something you can decide for yourself as we explore the materials that follow.

Perhaps the most important buffer on the effect of the perfect tender rule is the seller's right to cure defective performance. Read carefully U.C.C. § 2–508 and the Official Comment and apply them to the problems that follow.

———

2-508 cure [handwritten]

Goods - single lot [handwritten]

PROBLEM 25-5

Can accept reject, or accept 10 Does seller have cure? the cure is not the thing asked for [handwritten left margin]

Simple Simon operates a chain of organic coffee houses. They serve only food grown without the use of pesticides. Simon's usual pie supplier is closed by a strike, so Simon places and order for "100 pies, assorted flavors" with The Pieman, LLC. The contract provides that all of the pies are to be made from ingredients grown without pesticides. It also provides that delivery is to be made prior to 10 a.m. on Friday the 13th.

nonconforming [handwritten]

Knew that he would not want fruit with pesticides [handwritten left margin]

The Pieman is unable to obtain organic raspberries, so it includes in the shipment 10 pies made with raspberries grown using pesticides. The rest of the pies are all made entirely from organic ingredients. The pies are delivered at 8:30, and when Simon learns about the raspberries (the pies were accompanied by a letter explaining about the raspberry problem), he telephones The Pieman LLC and demands that it send someone to "pick up all of your poisonous pies before we throw them in the dumpster!" *Rejection* [handwritten]

The Pieman responds by saying, "Before 10 am we'll deliver 10 organic apple pies to replace the raspberry." Simon doesn't think this is fair. He wants your advice as to whether he has to accept this tender of The Pieman's wares.

What do you tell him? *See* § 2–508(1). *was not surprise rejection to buyer* [handwritten]

PROBLEM 25-6

seller can cure never specified just raspberry [handwritten]

2-508(2) [handwritten]

The farmer's wife damaged her butcher knife while defending herself from three vision-impaired rodents. So she goes to the Sonoma-Williams website and checks out the model 1682 butcher knife. The site informs her that the model 1682 ships within 24 hours. In reliance on that assurance, Ms. Farmer places an order for a model 1682. She pays extra for expedited shipping because she fears that further rodent attacks may be imminent.

1870 was better/more expensive non-conforming [handwritten left margin]

The knife arrives two days later, no rodent attacks having occurred in the interim. When Ms. Farmer examines the knife, she discovers that it is a model 1870, rather than the model 1682 that she had ordered. She calls Sonoma-Williams, and they tell her that because of a shortage of model 1682 knives, they have been shipping model 1870 knives, which are actually a more expensive model at no additional charge. When Ms. Farmer insists that she wants a model 1682, the customer service associate is very apologetic.

2-508(2) seller had reason to believe the non-conforming would be accepted [handwritten]

seller gets further reasonable time to cure [handwritten]

The customer service associate tells her that a model 1682 will be shipped that day and that she can use the model 1870 to defend herself against any rodent attacks that occur prior to the delivery of the model 1682. "Just be sure to wipe any blood off before you return it," he tells her. "The people in the returns department don't have a sense of humor." Ms. Farmer says she'll think about it. After some discussions with her daughter, who is active in the animal rights movement, Ms. Farmer decides she really doesn't want a new butcher knife. She'll try reasoning with the creatures instead.

She wants advice on her rights. *See* § 2–508(2). Which of these pieces of advice would you give her?

(a) Actually, if they had insisted on your accepting a model 1870, you would have been stuck. Consider yourself lucky you're going to get a model 1682. *– No*

(b) The seller has a right to cure, so you have to accept the model 1682 they've offered. *– Not complete, D better answer*

(c) Under the facts you've related to me, the seller has no right to cure and you don't have to accept the model 1682. *- No*

– (d) If the seller had reasonable grounds to believe that the model 1870 would be acceptable, you have to take the model 1682 if they get it to you within a reasonable time. *2-508(2), 1870 was better model so seller had reason to believe*

PROBLEM 25-7

The owner of a meat market and a salesman for a commercial refrigeration manufacturer entered into a sales agreement for two new refrigerated display cases. The owner liked the 3000 model because of its wood grained panel sides, so, on August 18, the parties executed a lease and shipping order and the owner wrote the salesman a check for the down payment. The next day, the salesman discovered and informed the owner that the 3000 model was not available in wood grain; the only model in wood grain was called MD. The salesman informed the owner that the MD model would "do the job," so the owner agreed to change the order to two MD cases.

The display cases were shipped to the owner on September 3 and installed on September 7. The 3000 unit was significantly different from the MD model in that the former used a passive gravity coil system and no fans, and the MD model had three fans that blew cold air over the surface of the meat. The owner noticed that these fans quickly dried out and discolored his meat so he called the manufacturer to complain. The manufacturer recommended some adjustments, but when the problem continued, it sent some condensation pans to the owner to fill with water and place in the units to increase humidity as a possible remedy. The condensations pans did not adequately address the problem.

The meat market's owner's attorney wrote a letter to the manufacturer on October 6, informing them that the display cases were not suitable for the purposes which they were purchased, and offered to return the cases in exchange for the down payment. The letter stated that the owner had already purchased new cases from another supplier, which the owner did not actually purchase for approximately another three weeks. On November 15, the owner removed the cases from his market, and on November 17, the owner served a formal notice of cancellation and rescission on the manufacturer. *See Transcontinental Refrigeration Co. v. Figgins*, 179 Mont. 12, 585 P.2d 1301 (1978).

(a) Is the seller's right to cure governed by § 2–508(1) or § 2–508(2)? Which do you think? Does it matter?

(b) Suppose the sale agreement was silent as to the date the display cases were to be delivered. How long would the seller have to cure? *See* § 2–309(1).

(c) How diligent was the lessor about curing the defect? Should how diligent the lessor was about curing the defect be a factor in determining how much time it has to cure?

ZABRISKIE CHEVROLET, INC. V. SMITH

New Jersey Superior Court, Law Division
99 N.J. Super. 441, 240 A.2d 195 (1968)

DOAN, J.D.C. (temporarily assigned).

[1] This action arises out of the sale by plaintiff to defendant of a new 1966 Chevrolet automobile. Within a short distance after leaving the showroom the vehicle became almost completely inoperable by reason of mechanical failure. Defendant the same day notified plaintiff that he canceled the sale and simultaneously stopped payment on the check he had tendered in payment of the balance of the purchase price. Plaintiff sues on the check and the purchase order for the balance of the purchase price plus incidental damages and defendant counterclaims for the return of his deposit and incidental damages. The facts are not complex nor do they present any serious dispute.

[2] On February 2, 1967 defendant signed a form purchase order for a new 1966 Chevrolet Biscayne Sedan which was represented to him to be a brand-new car that would operate perfectly. On that occasion he paid plaintiff $124 by way of deposit. On February 9, 1967 defendant tendered plaintiff his check for $2,069.50 representing the balance of the purchase price ($2,064) and $5.50 for license and transfer fees. Delivery was made to defendant's wife during the early evening hours of Friday, February 10, 1967, at which time she was handed the keys and the factory package of printed material, including the manual and the manufacturer-dealer's warranty, none of which she or her husband ever read before or after the

sale was made, nor were the details thereof specifically explained to or agreed to by defendant. While en route to her home, about 2 1/2 miles away, and after having gone about 7/10 of a mile from the showroom, the car stalled at a traffic light, stalled again within another 15 feet and again thereafter each time the vehicle was required to stop. When about halfway home the car could not be driven in "drive" gear at all, and defendant's wife was obliged to then propel the vehicle in "low-low" gear at a rate of about five to ten miles per hour, its then maximum speed. In great distress, defendant's wife was fearful of completing the journey to her home and called her husband, who thereupon drove the car in "low-low" gear about seven blocks to his home. Defendant, considerably upset by this turn of events, thereupon immediately called his bank (which was open this Friday evening), stopped payment on the check and called plaintiff to notify them that they had sold him a "lemon," that he had stopped payment on the check and that the sale was cancelled. The next day plaintiff sent a wrecker to defendant's home, brought the vehicle to its repair shop and after inspection determined that the transmission was defective.

Stop payment

[3]   Plaintiff's expert testified that the car would not move, that there was no power in the transmission and in that condition the car could not move. Plaintiff replaced the transmission with another one removed from a vehicle then on plaintiff's showroom floor, notifying defendant thereafter of what had been done. Defendant refused to take delivery of the vehicle as repaired and reasserted his cancellation of the sale. Plaintiff has since kept the vehicle in storage at his place of business. Within a short period following these occurrences plaintiff and defendant began negotiations for a new 1967 Chevrolet, but these fell through when plaintiff insisted that a new deal could only be made by giving defendant credit for the previously ordered 1966 Chevrolet. This defendant refused to do because he considered the prior transaction as cancelled.

[The court determined that the Joneses had not "accepted" the car. Acceptance is discussed in the next section of this chapter.—Eds.]

[4]   Lastly, plaintiff urges that under the Code, N.J.S. 12A:2–508, N.J.S.A. it had a right to cure the nonconforming delivery. N.J.S. 12A:2–508, N.J.S.A. states:

P's argument

(1)   Where any tender or delivery by the seller is rejected because non-conforming, and the time for performance has not yet expired, the seller may seasonably notify the buyer of his intention to cure and may then within the contract time make a conforming delivery.

(2)   Where the buyer rejects a non conforming tender which the seller had reasonable grounds to believe would be acceptable with or without money allowance the seller may if he seasonably

2-508

is there time to cure?

notifies the buyer have a further reasonable time to substitute a conforming tender.

The New Jersey Study Comment to 12A:2–508 reads:

> 3.   Subsection 2–508(2) has been applauded as a rule aimed at ending "forced breaches" . . . Section 2–508 prevents the buyer from forcing the seller to breach by making a surprise rejection of the goods because of some minor non-conformity at a time at which the seller cannot cure the deficiency within the time for performance.

The Uniform Commercial Code Comment to 12A:2–508 reads:

> 2.   Subsection (2) seeks to avoid injustice to the seller by reason of a surprise rejection by the buyer. However, the seller is not protected unless he had "reasonable grounds to believe" that the tender would be acceptable.

[5]   It is clear that in the instant case there was no "forced breach" on the part of the buyer, for he almost immediately began to negotiate for another automobile. The inquiry is as to what is intended by "cure," as used in the Code. This statute makes no attempt to define or specify what a "cure" shall consist of. It would appear, then, that each case must be controlled by its own facts. The "cure" intended under the cited section of the Code does not, in the court's opinion, contemplate the tender of a new vehicle with a substituted transmission, not from the factory and of unknown lineage from another vehicle in plaintiff's possession. It was not the intention of the Legislature that the right to "cure" is a limitless one to be controlled only by the will of the seller. A "cure" which endeavors by substitution to tender a chattel not within the agreement or contemplation of the parties is invalid.

[6]   For a majority of people the purchase of a new car is a major investment, rationalized by the peace of mind that flows from its dependability and safety. Once their faith is shaken, the vehicle loses not only its real value in their eyes, but becomes an instrument whose integrity is substantially impaired and whose operation is fraught with apprehension. The attempted cure in the present case was ineffective.

[7]   Accordingly, and pursuant to N.J.S. 12A:2–711, N.J.S.A., judgment is rendered on the main case in favor of defendant. On the counterclaim judgment is rendered in favor of defendant and against plaintiff in the sum of $124, being the amount of the deposit, there being no further proof of damages.

[8]   Defendant shall, as part of this judgment, execute for plaintiff, on demand, such documents as are necessary to again vest title to the vehicle in plaintiff.

Something to Think About

As stated by Judge Richard Posner in *MindGames, Inc. v. Western Publishing Co.*, 218 F.3d 652, 656–57 (7th Cir. 2000):

> The objection has to do with the difference between *rule* and *standard* as methods of legal governance. A rule singles out one or a few facts and makes it or them conclusive of legal liability; a standard permits consideration of all or at least most facts that are relevant to the standard's rationale. A speed limit is a rule; negligence is a standard. Rules have the advantage of being definite and of limiting factual inquiry but the disadvantage of being inflexible, even arbitrary, and thus overinclusive, or of being underinclusive and thus opening up loopholes (or of being *both* over- and underinclusive!). Standards are flexible, but vague and open-ended; they make business planning difficult, invite the sometimes unpredictable exercise of judicial discretion, and are more costly to adjudicate—and yet when based on lay intuition they may actually be more intelligible, and thus in a sense clearer and more precise, to the persons whose behavior they seek to guide than rules would be. No sensible person supposes that rules are always superior to standards, or vice versa, though some judges are drawn to the definiteness of rules and others to the flexibility of standards. But that is psychology; the important point is that some activities are better governed by rules, others by standards.

U.C.C. Article 9 and Article 3 are primarily composed of rules. There are, of course, some exceptions, such as the standards for commercially reasonable sales. Article 2 has a lot of rules, but the big questions in Article 2 generally involve standards.

C. ACCEPTANCE, REJECTION, REVOCATION OF ACCEPTANCE

PROBLEM 25-8

On February 1, the Mad Hatter received another shipment of felt. This time the color was off on the entire shipment. Because he was in the middle of a large order, he put the shipment aside, intending to ship it back to Black Sheep Wool Products LLC by return post.

By this time, however, the mercury nitrate used in the felt and hat production process had affected his brain, and he forgot about rejecting the wool until February 21, when he sent the wool back along with the a nasty letter telling Black Sheep Wool Products LLC that just because they could sell

[handwritten margin note: Is the mad-hatter a merchant?]

inferior products to the little boy who cries in the lane didn't mean they could deal so cavalierly with "a person of my stature." *[handwritten: 20 days reasonable?]*

Does Black Sheep Wool Products have to take the wool back? *See* U.C.C. § 2–602(1) and U.C.C. § 2–606. *[handwritten: 20 days for wool is reasonable, not perishable]*

PRACTICE TIP

You can minimize disputes over the question of whether notice was timely by including in the sale contract (e.g., in your seller client's standard acknowledgment sent in response to purchase orders) a provision that all defects must be reported within a certain number of days of delivery.

PROBLEM 25-9

[handwritten: Buyer has accepted]

Suppose Mr. Hatter's rejection is not effective. Then what happens? *See* U.C.C. § 2–607(1) and U.C.C. § 2–714. *[handwritten: Must pay at contract rate]*

PROBLEM 25-10

[handwritten margin note: Installment? - NO]

Hi-Ho Dairy Stores placed an order with In The Dells Farms, Inc. for a thousand gallons of fat-free skim milk. When the milk was delivered, the manager of Hi-Ho's packaging facility asked the driver of the tank truck, "Are you sure this is fat-free skim milk? It smells like one percent to me."

The driver, Simon Simple, an authorized agent of In The Dells Farms, Inc., assured the manager that it was. On that basis, the manager said that Hi-Ho Dairy Stores would accept the milk and told Mr. Simple to pump the milk into one of Hi-Ho's empty tanks.

[handwritten margin note: He can't use the milk]

Believing it now to be one percent milk, Hi-Ho Dairy Stores would like to revoke its acceptance of the milk. It can use the milk because it sells one percent milk as well as fat-free skim, but it would like to revoke the acceptance "to teach those corporate agri-business people a lesson."

Assuming that it accepted the milk, can Hi-Ho Dairy Stores revoke its acceptance? *See* § 2–608. *[handwritten: Does non-conformity substantially impair]*

PROBLEM 25-11

[handwritten: Merchant]

Big City Edison ("Big Ed") contracts to buy 500,000 barrels of fuel oil from Abdul, an oil broker operating in the "spot market." The contract requires that the oil have a maximum sulfur content of 0.50%. Big Ed notifies Abdul it will not accept delivery of oil with a sulfur content in excess of 0.50%. When he bought the oil, Abdul received a certificate from a reputable independent testing laboratory showing that the sulfur content of the oil was 0.48%. The contract calls for delivery on or before June 1. The oil is actually delivered and pumped into Big Ed's tanks on May 30. On June 4, a test by Big Ed's chemist shows a sulfur content of 0.53%. This is confirmed by independent laboratories.

[handwritten: Non-Conforming]

(a) Does Big Ed have to accept the oil? *See* U.C.C. § 2–601. *[handwritten: — NO]*

(b) Does Abdul have a right to cure under U.C.C. § 2–508(2)? *[handwritten: if reasonable time]*

(c) Suppose that Big Ed mixes 100,000 barrels of the oil delivered by Abdul with oil having a higher sulfur content. Can it reject (i) all 500,000 barrels, (ii) 400,000 barrels or (iii) none? *See* §§ 2–601, 2–606, and 2–607(2). Would it matter whether the oil was mixed before or after Big Ed received its lab results? *[handwritten: Yes; yes; — No]*

(d) Suppose that Big Ed fails to notify Abdul of its rejection until June 10. Would it matter that the world oil price had fallen between June 1 and June 10? *See* U.C.C. § 2–602. *[handwritten: Yes might not be reasonable as a merchant must sell or follow instructions]*

(e) Suppose that Big Ed accepted the oil on the basis of the test results from the independent laboratory. Could it revoke its acceptance when it gets its own lab results? Would it matter whether it got the independent lab's report (i) from Abdul, as part of Abdul's effort to induce it to accept the oil and pay for it, or (ii) directly from the independent lab, paying the independent lab a separate fee as part of Big Ed's acceptance, verification and quality control procedure? *See* U.C.C. § 2–608.

(f) Would it matter to your answer to question (e) whether federal regulations prohibited Big Ed from burning oil with a sulfur content greater than 0.50? Would that fact matter to your answer to question (a)?

(g) Can acceptance be revoked as to the 100,000 barrels mixed with the high sulfur oil? *[handwritten: Yes]*

PROBLEM 25-12

Ahmed contracts to deliver one 50,000 barrel shipment to Golf Oil each month for 2 years. The contract calls for oil with a sulfur content not to exceed 0.90%. *[handwritten: Installment]*

(a) Ahmed's second shipment has a sulfur content of 0.96%. The oil is less valuable than it would be if it conformed to the contract, but Golf can still use it. Can it nevertheless reject the shipment? *See* U.C.C. § 2–612. *[handwritten: If it substantially impairs]*

(b) Ahmed's first shipment and his third through eighth shipments have sulfur contents of less than 0.90%, but his ninth shipment has a sulfur content so high Golf can't use the oil. Can Golf reject the shipment? Can it cancel the contract? Would it affect your answer if the high sulfur oil had been shipped in the first shipment rather than the ninth? *[handwritten: Can it be cured? Yes, because it is 9th shipment, cant cancel whole contract b/c first 8 were conforming and does not substantially impair]*

KEEN v. MODERN TRAILER SALES, INC.
Colorado Court of Appeals
40 Colo. App. 527, 578 P.2d 668 (1978)

[1] Plaintiffs, Charles F. and Shirley A. Keen, appeal from a judgment denying their claim for rescission of a contract for the purchase of a mobile home. We reverse and remand for further proceedings.

[2] The trial court's findings of fact, which are not disputed here, relate that on April 20, 1974, plaintiffs went to the sales lot of defendant, Modern Trailer Sales, Inc. After informing one of the defendant's salesmen that they sought to purchase a three bedroom home, 14 feet in width and 70 feet in length, and priced from $9,000 to $9,500, plaintiffs were shown several mobile homes, some of which, unknown to the plaintiffs, were models smaller than the requested size. The following day, accompanied by their son, plaintiffs returned to the lot and made a final selection. At that time, the salesman assured the plaintiffs' son that the selected model was 14 by 70 feet in size.[1]

[3] The parties subsequently executed a written contract, detailing the plaintiffs' requirements and the purchase price. Although that agreement specified the selected model's width as 14 feet, the length of the home was omitted. Documents referencing the length of the subject home were readily available to defendant's salesman, however, and he, in fact, knew the home was not the size requested by the plaintiffs. Nonetheless, the manufacturer's statement of origin and an application for title subsequently sent to them by defendant also listed the home as 14 by 70 feet.

[4] Within a month of delivery, the mobile home drifted off its footings. After defendant refused to assist in correcting the problem, plaintiffs arranged for reskirting of the sides by a third party. Consequently, they discovered that the length of the home was in fact only 64 feet, and thus lacked six feet in length and 84 square feet of living space. When complaints to defendant were ignored, plaintiffs instituted this action.

[5] Based on the above findings of fact, the trial court concluded that by failing to deliver a mobile home 14 by 70 feet in size the defendant breached its contract with plaintiffs. And, in a ruling which is not challenged here, the trial court dismissed plaintiffs' claim for damages. Treating plaintiffs' request for rescission as seeking revocation of acceptance under the Uniform Commercial Code, § 4–2–608, C.R.S. 1973, ... the court also denied plaintiffs' claim for cancellation of the contract and return of the purchase price.

---

[1] [14 × 70 = 980 sq. ft.—Eds.]

[6]   Section 4–2–608(1)(b), C.R.S. 1973, authorizes a buyer to revoke his acceptance of a nonconforming item, if his acceptance without discovery of the item's nonconformity "was reasonably induced either by the difficulty of discovery before acceptance or by the seller's assurances," a precondition not in dispute here, and if the item's "nonconformity substantially impairs its value to him." Reasoning in part that "[t]he Keens occupancy of the mobile home from the end of April 1974, to date, clearly shows that the value of the mobile home to the Keens was not substantially impaired," the trial court determined that the latter requisite of substantial impairment was not made out by defendant's breach here. Since we view the court's premise as erroneous, we remand for reconsideration of its factual determination.

* * *

[7]   To aid the court in its consideration on remand we add the following. The test of "substantial impairment" justifying revocation of acceptance is "whether the nonconformity is such as will in fact cause substantial impairment of value to the buyer though the seller had no advance knowledge as the buyer's particular circumstances." [U.C.C.] Section 2–608 (Official Comment 2). This section creates a subjective test in the sense that the requirements of the particular buyer must be examined and deferred to. Yet, since the rationale of the substantial impairment requisite is to bar revocation for trivial defects or defects which may be easily corrected, the impairment of the buyer's requirements must be substantial in objective terms.

[8]   Accordingly, the determinative issues before the trial court are whether the plaintiffs sought to purchase mobile home of specified dimensions for their particular living needs, and whether the nonconformity here—the delivered mobile home's lacking approximately 8% of the total living space warranted by the defendant—is substantial in an objective sense.

* * *

The judgment is reversed and the cause is remanded for the trial court's redetermination of the propriety of plaintiffs' revocation of acceptance.

QUESTION

Could the Keens have argued they had rejected the mobile home? If they had, how would it have changed the burden of proof? See U.C.C. § 2–607(4).

CHAPTER 26

ANTICIPATORY REPUDIATION

■ ■ ■

If one party to a contract decides not to perform under the contract, must the other party wait until the time for performance to either sue for breach or to make other arrangements to mitigate damages? No.

Anticipatory repudiation—equivalent to a breach of a contract before performance is due—occurs when a party unequivocally communicates an intention not to perform or, by actions, renders performance impossible by, for example, selling to a third party a unique item that is the subject of the contract. To constitute repudiation, the prospective non-performance must substantially impair the value of the contract to the non-repudiating party. Upon repudiation, the other parties to the contract may either wait a reasonable time for performance or treat the contract as breached and resort to their remedies. The other parties may also suspend further performance of their duties, whether they elect to treat the repudiation as a breach or merely wait a reasonable time before doing so.

The R2d outlines the common law of repudiation in sections 250 to 257. UNIDROIT articles 7.3.3 and 7.3.4 do the same in a more summary fashion. The Uniform Commercial Code codified the rules regarding anticipatory repudiation in sections 2–610 and 2–611 and the CISG does so in articles 71 to 73; both codes are substantially similar in this area.

The acts or statements that constitute sufficient unequivocal communication of an intention not to perform vary from case to case. It has been characterized as an overt communication of intention that renders performance impossible or demonstrates a clear determination not to continue performance. Performance need not be absolutely, utterly impossible. If a party states that it will not perform unless it receives a performance to which it is not entitled (or fails to provide adequate assurance of performance when that has been properly demanded under U.C.C. section 2–609), repudiation has occurred. After repudiation, the aggrieved party may immediately resort to any remedy provided the actions are undertaken in good faith.

An anticipatory repudiation can itself be retracted up to the moment that the repudiating party's next performance under the contract is due so long as the non-repudiating party has not yet cancelled the contract or materially changed his position or otherwise indicated that he considers the repudiation final. Retraction may be by any method that indicates clearly to the other party that the previous repudiation is withdrawn and the party now intends to perform. A retraction must include any assurance of future performance justifiably demanded by the nonrepudiating party.

These are good, common sense rules that appear to provide a reasonable framework within which the parties can operate when one fears that one or more of the parties may not perform. The following cases trace the development of the doctrine and illustrate its modern application. This is another area where it is critical that the communications with the other side be handled in a coordinated, calculated fashion. It is all too easy for a party that thought it was the non-repudiating party to be characterized as the repudiating party because of overly hasty or inadequately documented actions. Lawyers should be thinking about creating an adequate record to stand on to support the claim that the other side anticipatorily repudiated.

HOCHSTER V. DE LA TOUR

Queen's Bench
2 El. & Bl. 678, 118 Eng. Rep. 922 (1853)

[1] LORD CAMPBELL C. J. now delivered the judgment of the Court. On this motion in arrest of judgment,[1] the question arises, Whether, if there be an agreement between A. and B., whereby B. engages to employ A. on and from a future day for a given period of time, to travel with him into a foreign country as a courier, and to start with him in that capacity on that day, A. being to receive a monthly salary during the continuance of such service, B. may, before the day, refuse to perform the agreement and break and renounce it, so as to entitle A. before the day to commence an action against B. to recover damages for breach of the agreement; A. having been ready and willing to perform it, till it was broken and renounced by B. The defendant's counsel very powerfully contended that, if the plaintiff was not contented to dissolve the contract, and to abandon all remedy upon it, he was bound to remain ready and willing to perform it till the day when the actual employment as courier in the service of the defendant was to begin; and that there could be no breach of the agreement, before that day, to give a right of action. But it cannot be laid down as a universal rule that, where by agreement an act is to be done on a future day, no action can be brought for a breach of the agreement till the day for doing the act has arrived. If a man promises to marry a woman on a future day, and before that day marries another woman, he is instantly liable to an action for breach of promise of marriage; *Short v. Stone* (8 Q.B. 358). If a man contracts to execute a lease on and from a future day for a certain term,

---

[1] [A motion in arrest of judgment was a motion to stay a judgment on the ground that it was clear from the record that the judgment was wrong.—Eds.]

and, before that day, executes a lease to another for the same term, he may be immediately sued for breaking the contract; *Ford v. Tiley* (6 B. & C. 325). So, if a man contracts to sell and deliver specific goods on a future day, and before the day he sells and delivers them to another, he is immediately liable to an action at the suit of the person with whom he first contracted to sell and deliver them; *Bowdell v. Parsons* (10 East, 359). One reason alleged in support of such an action is, that the defendant has, before the day, rendered it impossible for him to perform the contract at the day: but this does not necessarily follow; for, prior to the day fixed for doing the act, the first wife may have died, a surrender of the lease executed might be obtained, and the defendant might have repurchased the goods so as to be in a situation to sell and deliver them to the plaintiff. Another reason may be, that, where there is a contract to do an act on a future day, there is a relation constituted between the parties in the meantime by the contract, and that they impliedly promise that in the meantime neither will do anything to the prejudice of the other inconsistent with that relation. As an example, a man and woman engaged to marry are affianced to one another during the period between the time of the engagement and the celebration of the marriage. In this very case, of traveler and courier, from the day of the hiring till the day when the employment was to begin, they were engaged to each other; and it seems to be a breach of an implied contract if either of them renounces the engagement. This reasoning seems in accordance with the unanimous decision of the Exchequer Chamber in *Elderton v. Emmens*, which we have followed in subsequent cases in this Court. The declaration in the present case, in alleging a breach, states a great deal more than a passing intention on the part of the defendant which he may repent of, and could only be proved by evidence that he had utterly renounced the contract, or done some act which rendered it impossible for him to perform it. If the plaintiff has no remedy for breach of the contract unless he treats the contract as in force, and acts upon it down to the 1st June 1852, it follows that, till then, he must enter into no employment which will interfere with his promise "to start with the defendant on such travels on the day and year," and that he must then be properly equipped in all respects as a courier for a three months' tour on the continent of Europe. But it is surely much more rational, and more for the benefit of both parties, that, after the renunciation of the agreement by the defendant, the plaintiff should be at liberty to consider himself absolved from any future performance of it, retaining his right to sue for any damage he has suffered from the breach of it. Thus, instead of remaining idle and laying out money in preparations which must be useless, he is at liberty to seek service under another employer, which would go in mitigation of the damages to which he would otherwise be entitled to for a breach of the contract. It seems strange that the defendant, after renouncing the contract, and absolutely declaring that he will never act under it, should be permitted to object that faith is given to his assertion, and that an opportunity is not left to him of changing his mind. If the plaintiff is barred of any remedy by entering into an engagement inconsistent with starting as a courier with the defendant on the 1st June, he is prejudiced by putting faith in the defendant's assertion: and it would be more consonant with principle, if the defendant were precluded from saying that he had not broken the contract when he declared that he entirely renounced it. Suppose that the defendant, at the time of his renunciation, had embarked on a voyage for Australia, so as to render it physically impossible for him to employ the plaintiff as a courier on the continent of Europe in the months of June, July and August 1852: according to decided cases, the action might have been brought before the 1st June; but the renunciation may have been founded on other facts, to be given in evidence, which would equally have rendered the defendant's performance of the contract impossible. The man who wrongfully renounces a contract into which he has deliberately entered cannot justly complain if he is immediately sued for a compensation in damages by the man whom he has injured: and it seems reasonable to allow an option to the injured party, either to sue immediately, or to wait till the time when the act was to be done, still holding it as prospectively binding for the exercise of this option, which may be advantageous to the innocent party, and cannot be prejudicial to the wrongdoer. An argument against the action before the 1st of June is urged from the difficulty of calculating the damages: but this argument is equally strong against an action before the 1st of September, when the three months would expire. In either case, the jury in assessing the damages would be justified in looking to all that had happened, or was likely to happen, to increase or mitigate the loss of the plaintiff down to the day of trial.

* * *

[2] Upon the whole, we think that the declaration in this case is sufficient. It gives us great satisfaction to reflect that, the question being on the record, our opinion may be reviewed in a Court of Error. In the meantime we must give judgment for the plaintiff.

Judgment for plaintiff.

NOTES AND QUESTIONS

1.   The *Hochster* opinion, among other things, should make it plain how important paragraphs and headings can be in making text easily readable. The opinion featured neither and is not. Remember that when taking exams.

2.   *Hochster v. De La Tour* is considered the seminal or ovular case for the doctrine of anticipatory repudiation. What two things does it allow a party to a contract to do upon the other party's repudiation?

3. At the time this case was decided, it was well accepted that courts didn't make law; they found it among the already-established rules. How does this court explain that anticipatory repudiation is not really a new rule, but just an application of well-established rules?

————

AMF, INC. V. MCDONALD'S CORP.

ucc 3

United States Court of Appeals, Seventh Circuit
536 F. 2d 1167 (1976)

CUMMINGS, CIRCUIT JUDGE.

[1] AMF, Incorporated, filed this case in the Southern District of New York in April 1972. It was transferred to the Northern District of Illinois in May 1973. AMF seeks damages for the alleged wrongful cancellation and repudiation of McDonald's Corporation's ("Mc-Donald's") orders for sixteen computerized cash registers for installation in restaurants owned by wholly-owned subsidiaries of McDonald's and for seven such registers ordered by licensees of McDonald's for their restaurants. In July 1972, McDonald's of Elk Grove, Inc. sued AMF to recover the $20,385.28[2] purchase price paid for a prototype computerized cash register and losses sustained as a result of failure of the equipment to function satisfactorily. Both cases were tried together during a fortnight in December 1974. A few months after the completion of the bench trial, the district court rendered a memorandum opinion and order in both cases in favor of each defendant. The only appeal is from the eight judgment orders dismissing AMF's complaints against McDonald's and the seven licensees. We affirm.

[2] The district court's memorandum opinion and order are unreported. Our statement of the pertinent facts is culled from the 124 findings of fact contained therein or from the record itself.

[3] In 1966, AMF began to market individual components of a completely automated restaurant system, including its model 72C computerized cash register involved here. The 72C cash register then consisted of a central computer, one to four input stations, each with a keyboard and cathode ray tube display, plus the necessary cables and controls.

[4] In 1967, McDonald's representatives visited AMF's plant in Springdale, Connecticut, to view a working "breadboard" model 72C to decide whether to use it in McDonald's restaurant system. Later that year, it was agreed that a 72C should be placed in a McDonald's restaurant for evaluation purposes.

———

[2] [$20,385.28 in 1976 dollars is roughly the equivalent of $90,000 in 2019 dollars using the CPI and the GNP Deflator.—Eds.]

[5] In April 1968, a 72C unit accommodating six input stations was installed in McDonald's restaurant in Elk Grove, Illinois. This restaurant was a wholly-owned subsidiary of McDonald's and was its busiest restaurant. Besides functioning as a cash register, the 72C was intended to enable counter personnel to work faster and to assist in providing data for accounting reports and bookkeeping. McDonald's of Elk Grove, Inc. paid some $20,000 for this prototype register on January 3, 1969. AMF never gave McDonald's warranties governing reliability or performance standards for the prototype.

[6] At a meeting in Chicago on August 29, 1968, McDonald's concluded to order sixteen 72C's for its company-owned restaurants and to cooperate with AMF to obtain additional orders from its licensees. In December 1968, AMF accepted McDonald's purchase orders for those sixteen 72C's. In late January 1969, AMF accepted seven additional orders for 72C's from McDonald's licensees for their restaurants. Under the contract for the sale of all the units, there was a warranty for parts and service. AMF proposed to deliver the first unit in February 1969, with installation of the remaining twenty-two units in the first half of 1969. However, AMF established a new delivery schedule in February 1969, providing for deliveries to commence at the end of July 1969 and to be completed in January 1970, assuming that the first test unit being built at AMF's Vandalia, Ohio, plant was built and satisfactorily tested by the end of July 1969. This was never accomplished.

[7] During the operation of the prototype 72C at McDonald's Elk Grove restaurant, many problems resulted, requiring frequent service calls by AMF and others. Because of its poor performance, McDonald's had AMF remove the prototype unit from its Elk Grove restaurant in late April 1969.

[8] At a March 18, 1969, meeting, McDonald's and AMF personnel met to discuss the performance of the Elk Grove prototype. AMF agreed to formulate a set of performance and reliability standards for the future 72C's, including "the number of failures permitted at various degrees of seriousness, total permitted downtime, maximum service hours and cost." Pending mutual agreement on such standards, McDonald's personnel asked that production of the twenty-three units be held up and AMF agreed.

[9] On May 1, 1969, AMF met with McDonald's personnel to provide them with performance and reliability standards. However, the parties never agreed upon such standards. At that time, AMF did not have a working machine and could not produce one within a reasonable time because its Vandalia, Ohio, personnel were too inexperienced. After the May 1st meeting, AMF concluded that McDonald's had canceled all 72C orders. The reasons for the cancellation were the poor performance of the prototype, the lack of assurances that a workable machine was available

and the unsatisfactory conditions at AMF's Vandalia, Ohio, plant where the twenty-three 72C's were to be built.

[10] On July 29, 1969, McDonald's and AMF representatives met in New York. At this meeting it was mutually understood that the 72C orders were canceled and that none would be delivered.

[11] In its conclusions of law, the district court held that Mc-Donald's and its licensees had entered into contracts for twenty-three 72C cash registers but that AMF was not able to perform its obligations under the contracts. *Citing* Section 2–610 of the Uniform Commercial Code (Ill. Rev. Stats. (1975) ch. 26, § 2–610) and Comment 1 thereunder, the court concluded that on July 29, McDonald's justifiably repudiated the contracts to purchase all twenty-three 72C's.

[12] Relying on Section 2–609 and 2–610 of the Uniform Commercial Code (Ill. Rev. Stats. (1975) ch. 26, §§ 2–609 and 2–610),the court decided that McDonald's was warranted in repudiating the contracts and therefore had a right to cancel the orders by virtue of Section 2–711 of the Uniform Commercial Code. (Ill. Rev. Stats. (1975) ch. 26, § 2–711). Accordingly, judgment was entered for McDonald's. *repudiated*

[13] The findings of fact adopted by the district court were a mixture of the court's own findings and findings proposed by the parties, some of them modified by the court. AMF has assailed ten of the 124 findings of fact, but our examination of the record satisfies us that all have adequate support in the record and support the conclusions of law.

[14] Whether in a specific case a buyer has reasonable grounds for insecurity is a question of fact. Comment 3 to UCC § 2–609; Anderson, Uniform Commercial Code, § 2–609 (2d ed. 1971). On this record, McDonald's clearly had "reasonable grounds for insecurity" with respect to AMF's performance. At the time of the March 18, 1969, meeting, the prototype unit had performed unsatisfactorily ever since its April 1968 installation. Although AMF had projected delivery of all twenty-three units by the first half of 1969, AMF later scheduled delivery from the end of July 1969 until January 1970. When McDonald's personnel visited AMF's Vandalia, Ohio, plant on March 4, 1969, they saw that none of the 72C systems was being assembled and learned that a pilot unit would not be ready until the end of July of that year. They were informed that the engineer assigned to the project was not to commence work until March 17th. AMF's own personnel were also troubled about the design of the 72C, causing them to attempt to reduce McDonald's order to five units. Therefore, under Section 2–609 McDonald's was entitled to demand adequate assurance of performance by AMF.

[15] However, AMF urges that Section 2–609 of the UCC is inapplicable because McDonald's did not make a written demand of adequate assurance of due performance. In *Pittsburgh-Des Moines Steel*

Co. v. Brookhaven Manor Water Co., 532 F.2d 572, 581 (7th Cir. 1976), we noted that the Code should be liberally construed[3] and therefore rejected such "a formalistic approach" to Section 2–609. McDonald's failure to make a written demand was excusable because AMF's Mr. Dubosque's testimony and his April 2 and 18, 1969, memoranda about the March 18th meeting showed AMF's clear understanding that McDonald's had suspended performance until it should receive adequate assurance of due performance from AMF (Tr. 395; AMF Exhibit 79; McD. Exhibit 232).

[16] After the March 18th demand, AMF never repaired the Elk Grove unit satisfactorily nor replaced it. Similarly, it was unable to satisfy McDonald's that the twenty-three machines on order would work. At the May 1st meeting, AMF offered unsatisfactory assurances for only five units instead of twenty-three. The performance standards AMF tendered to McDonald's were unacceptable because they would have permitted the 72C's not to function properly for 90 hours per year, permitting as much as one failure in every fifteen days in a busy McDonald's restaurant. Also, as the district court found, AMF's Vandalia, Ohio, personnel were too inexperienced to produce a proper machine. Since AMF did not provide adequate assurance of performance after McDonald's March 18th demand, UCC Section 2–609(1) permitted McDonald's to suspend performance. When AMF did not furnish adequate assurance of due performance at the May 1st meeting, it thereby repudiated the contract under Section 2–609(4). At that point, Section 2–610(b) permitted McDonald's to cancel the orders pursuant to Section 2–711, as it finally did on July 29, 1969.

* * *

JUDGMENT AFFIRMED.

NOTES AND QUESTIONS

1.   The R2d contains a provision similar to U.C.C. § 2–609, R2d § 251, as does the CISG, article 71(3), and UNDROIT, article 7.3.4. These authorities do NOT require the demand for assurances to be in writing as the U.C.C. does.

2.   Not all courts are this liberal when confronted with the explicit statutory requirement of a writing contained in U.C.C. § 2–609. In fact most are not, as many lawyers who have failed to follow the statutory requirements have found. Eastern Airlines won a $25 million judgment against McDonnell Douglas on account of late deliveries of airplanes that put Eastern at a severe competitive disadvantage. The judgment was reversed because Eastern had not followed all the statutory formalities in giving McDonnell Douglas notice

---

[3]   UCC § 1–102(1) provides that the Code "shall be liberally construed and applied to promote its underlying purposes and policies" (Ill. Rev. Stats. ch. 26, § 1–102(1) (1975)). [This provision is now section 1–103(a). The language has been changed slightly.—Eds.]

that they had defaulted. *Eastern Air Lines v. McDonnell Douglas Corp.*, 532 F.2d 957 (5th Cir. 1976). On the specific question of whether a demand for adequate assurance under Article 2 must be in writing, the majority of the courts that have addressed the issue have held that it must. The Illinois Appellate Court said: "The record contains no indication that [the buyer] at any time placed a demand for assurances of future performance on the part of [the seller] in writing, and a demand for assurances of future performance is ineffectual unless placed in writing." *Bodine Sewer, Inc. v. Eastern Illinois Precast, Inc.*, 143 Ill. App. 3d 920, 97 Ill. Dec. 898, 493 N.E.2d 705, 1 UCC Rep. Serv. 2d 1480, 1489 (1986). U.C.C. § 2–609 is very explicit and should be followed mechanically in *every case*; unfortunately, commercial lawyers and clients, like police required to "Mirandize" their suspects, all too often fail to do so properly, with serious results.

<hr>

HOPE'S ARCHITECTURAL PRODUCTS, INC. v. LUNDY'S CONSTRUCTION, INC.

United States District Court, District of Kansas
781 F. Supp. 711 (1991)

LUNGSTRUM, J.

Memorandum and Order

[1]   This case presents a familiar situation in the field of construction contracts. Two parties, who disagreed over the meaning of their contract, held their positions to the brink, with litigation and loss the predictable result of the dispute. What is rarely predictable, however, (and what leads to a compromise resolution of many construction disputes when cool heads hold sway) is which party will ultimately prevail. The stakes become winner-take-all.

[2]   Plaintiff Hope's Architectural Products (Hope's) is a New York corporation that manufactures and installs custom window fixtures. Defendant Lundy's Construction (Lundy's) is a Kansas corporation that contracted to buy windows from Hope's for a school remodeling project. Defendant Bank IV Olathe (Bank IV) is a national banking organization with its principal place of business in Kansas. Bank IV acted as surety for a statutory bond obtained by Lundy's for the remodeling project.[4]

[3]   Hope's contends that Lundy's breached the contract to buy windows, entitling Hope's to damages in the amount of the contract price

---

4   [On a construction project, a person who supplies materials and is not paid is entitled to a *materialman's lien* on the property as security for any amounts owed it. If the property is owned by the government, the materialman's lien is not available. To give suppliers comparable protection, statutes provide that the contractor post a *payment bond*. This is in essence an insurance policy that assures that all of the materialmen will be paid. A materialman who is not paid has a cause of action against the issuer of the bond, which is why Bank IV is a defendant.—Eds.]

of $55,000.[5] Hope's also contends that Bank IV wrongfully refused to pay Hope's on the bond when Lundy's breached the contract. Hope's has sued for breach of contract, and in the alternative, for recovery under the theory of quantum meruit. A trial to the Court was held December 4 and 5, 1991. Two issues emerged as pivotal to the resolution of this case: (1) when was delivery of the windows due, and (2) if delivery was late, could Hope's lawfully suspend performance and demand certain assurances, (including ultimately, a demand for prepayment in full) that Lundy's would not back charge for the late delivery under the authority of K.S.A. § 84–2–609? Because the Court finds that a determination of these issues leads to the conclusion that Hope's was the party in breach of this contract, the plaintiff's request for relief is denied.

I.   Facts

[4] The following findings of fact are entered pursuant to Fed. R. Civ. P. 52. On June 13, 1988, defendant Lundy's entered into a contract with the Shawnee Mission School District as general contractor for the construction of an addition to the Rushton Elementary School. Lundy's provided a public works bond in connection with the Rushton project as required by K.S.A. § 60–1111 (1983). The purpose of the bond was to insure that Lundy's paid any outstanding indebtedness it incurred in the construction of the project. The statutory bond was secured through defendant Bank IV.

[5] Plaintiff Hope's is a manufacturer of custom-built windows. The initial contact between Hope's and Lundy's occurred through Mr. Richard Odor, a regional agent for Hope's in Kansas City. On June 29, 1988, Hope's contracted with Lundy's to manufacture ninety-three windows for the Rushton project. The contract price, including the cost of labor and materials for the windows, was $55,000.

[6] Although the contract included a term pertaining to the time for delivering the windows, there is some controversy over the meaning of this provision. Even under the most favorable interpretation to Hope's, however, delivery was due twelve to fourteen weeks after Hope's received approved shop drawings from Lundy's on July 18. Thus, delivery was due no later than October 24, 1988.

[7] During the late summer and fall of 1988, several discussions took place between Hope's and Lundy's concerning when the windows would be delivered to the job site. Production of the windows was delayed by events that, according to the testimony of Mr. Odor, were not the fault of Lundy's. On September 27, 1988, Mark Hannah, vice president of Lundy's, wrote to Hope's requesting that installation of the windows begin by October 19, and be completed by October 26. On October 14 Hannah again wrote to

---

[5] [$55,000 in 1991 is roughly the equivalent of $101,000 in 2019 dollars using the CPI and the GNP Deflator.—Eds.]

Hope's, threatening to withhold "liquidated damages" from the contract price if Hope's did not comply with these deadlines. Although there was no provision in the contract for liquidated damages, Hope's did not make any response to the October 14 letter.

[8]   The windows were shipped from Hopes' New York plant to Kansas City on October 28. Delivery to the Rushton site was anticipated on November 4. On November 1, Hannah called Hopes' office in New York to inquire about the windows. He spoke to Kathy Anderson, Hopes' customer service manager. The substance of this conversation is disputed. Hope's claims that Hannah threatened a back charge of $11,000 (20% of the contract price) for late delivery of the windows. Hannah testified, however, that although the possibility of a back charge was discussed, no specific dollar amount was mentioned. Hannah specifically denies that he threatened to withhold $11,000 from the contract.

[9]   After her conversation with Hannah, Anderson immediately informed Chris Arvantinos, vice president of Hope's, of the threatened back charge. Arvantinos called Hannah to discuss the back charge, but he does not recall hearing Hannah mention the $11,000 figure. Arvantinos requested that Hannah provide assurances that Lundy's would not back charge Hope's, but Hannah was unwilling to provide such assurances.

[10] In a letter written on November 2, Arvantinos informed Hannah that Hope's was suspending delivery of the windows until Lundy's provided assurances that there would be no back charge. Hannah received this letter on the morning of November 3, shortly before Mr. Odor visited Hannah at Lundy's. Odor, who had spoken with Arvantinos about the back charge, issued a new demand that Lundy's had to meet before Hope's would deliver the windows. He gave Hannah an invoice for the full amount of the contract price, demanding prepayment before the windows would be delivered.

[11] Odor set out three ways that Lundy's could meet this demand: (1) payment of the contract price in full by cashier's check; (2) placement of the full contract price in an escrow account until the windows were installed; or (3) delivery of the full contract amount to the architect to hold until the windows were installed. All three options required Lundy's to come up with $55,000 before the windows would be delivered. Hannah believed that the demand presented by Odor superseded the letter from Arvantinos he received earlier that morning.

[12] Hannah informed Odor that there was no way for Lundy's to get an advance from the school district at that time to comply with Hopes' request. The meeting ended, Lundy's did not prepay, and Hope's did not deliver the windows. On November 7, 1988, Lundy's terminated the contract with Hope's. Thereafter, Lundy's obtained an alternate supplier of the windows.

[13] On February 15, 1989, Hope's notified defendant Bank IV of Lundy's failure to pay the contract price and demanded payment from Bank IV on the public works bond. Bank IV refused to pay Hopes' claim. This action was filed by Hope's on March 20, 1989. Jurisdiction of the matter rests with this Court pursuant to 28 U.S.C. § 1332.

II. Discussion

[14] At the outset, the Court concludes that the Uniform Commercial Code (UCC) governs this transaction. Article 2 of the UCC applies to transactions in goods. K.S.A. § 84–2–102 (1983). The contract at issue in this case involved a mixed goods/services transaction. Whether the UCC applies to hybrid transactions such as this depends upon " 'whether their predominant factor, their thrust, their purpose, reasonably stated, is the rendition of service, with goods incidentally involved or is a transaction of sale, with labor incidentally involved.' " *Systems Design & Management Information, Inc. v. Kansas City Post Office Employees Credit Union,* 14 Kan. App. 2d 266, 270–71, 788 P.2d 878 (1990). If the UCC applies, it applies to all facets of the transaction. The transaction at issue in this case primarily involved a sale of windows, with installation and manufacturing services provided as an incidental component. Therefore, the UCC applies.

A. Plaintiff's Contract Claim Against Defendant Lundy's

[15] This case turns on the resolution of two central and interrelated issues: (1) when was delivery due under the contract, and (2) could Hope's lawfully demand the assurances it demanded from Lundy's under K.S.A. § 84–2–609 [UCC § 2–609]. If the demands for assurances were proper, then Hope's would have been justified in suspending its performance and withholding delivery and Lundy's failure to provide assurances and subsequent termination of the contract amounted to a total breach. If, however, the demands for assurances were not proper under [§ 2–609], then Hope's breached the contract by wrongfully withholding delivery of the windows and Lundy's was entitled to cancel the contract. The delivery date issue is addressed first because the matter of whether or not Hope's was already in breach for late delivery goes directly to the propriety of its demand for assurances.

1. Delivery Date

[16] Even under Hope's interpretation of the delivery term, delivery of the windows was not timely.[6] At trial, Chris Arvantinos, Hope's vice president, testified that Hope's committed to deliver the windows twelve to

---

[6] "Delivery" is defined by Black's Law Dictionary as "the act by which the res or substance thereof is placed within the actual or constructive possession or control of another . . . What constitutes delivery depends largely on the intent of the parties." Black's Law Dictionary 385 (5th ed. 1979). In this case, the parties bargained for more than mere shipment of the windows. Arvantinos testified that Hope's committed to delivering the windows to the job site between October 10 and October 24. Thus, delivery was to occur under the parties' agreement when the windows arrived in Kansas City and were available for installation at the Rushton job site.

fourteen weeks after July 18, 1988, the day Hope's received approved shop drawings. This would make delivery due between October 10 and October 24. In fact, the windows did not arrive in Kansas City until November 4, fifteen and one-half weeks after July 18. Hope's claims that this delay was "immaterial" and did not excuse Lundy's from its duties under the contract. Hope's is unable to cite any controlling authority to support this argument, however. Moreover, this argument misses the point. Even if an "immaterial" delay did not excuse future performance by Lundy's, no performance was due from Lundy's until the windows were delivered to the job site, which never occurred.

[17] Hope's also argues, almost in passing, that the delay was caused by problems that were outside of its control, thus excusing Hope's from responsibility for the late delivery. Under a clause in the contract, Hope's disclaimed responsibility "for delayed shipments and deliveries occasioned by strikes, fires, accidents, delays of common carriers or other causes beyond our control . . ." (Plaintiff's exhibit 11, para. 3). During the course of production, Hope's experienced problems with its "bonderizing" and prime paint system, which resulted in a delay in production of approximately two weeks. (Defendants' exhibit 403). Hope's produced no evidence at trial, however, to show that this was a matter which was beyond its control. Moreover, it is interesting to note that Hope's did not contemporaneously seek from Lundy's any extension of the delivery date under this provision or notify Lundy's that it might result in a delay beyond October 24. It appears that reference to this clause is more of an afterthought born of litigation than a bona fide excuse for modifying the delivery date.

[18] Hope's also contends that a three to four day delay resulted when Lundy's asked for a change in the design of the windows to include "weep holes" after production had already begun. However, Hopes' representative, Odor, testified that nothing Lundy's did delayed Hopes' manufacturing. Moreover, even accounting for this delay, Hope's was a week late delivering the windows.

2.   *Section 2–609 Demand for Assurances*

[19] The framework for judging demands for assurances under [§ 2–609] was set forth in *LNS Investment Co., Inc. v. Phillips 66 Co.*, 731 F. Supp. 1484, 1487 (D. Kan. 1990):

> To suspend its performance pursuant to [§ 2–609], defendant must (1) have had reasonable grounds for insecurity regarding plaintiff's performance under the contract, (2) have demanded in writing adequate assurance of plaintiff's future performance and (3) have not received from plaintiff such assurance.

[20] White and Summers note that what constitutes a "reasonable ground" for insecurity and an "adequate assurance" are fact questions. J.

White & R. Summers, Uniform Commercial Code § 6–2, at 236 (3d ed. 1988). Reasonableness and adequacy are determined according to commercial standards when, as is the case here, the parties are merchants. [U.C.C. § 2–609] K.S.A. § 84–2–609(2) (1983).

[21] Although nothing in the record indicates that Hope's expressly claimed any rights under [§ 2–609] during the course of this transaction, Hope's asserted at trial that the October 14 letter from Lundy's demanding delivery by October 16 and threatening liquidated damages gave Hope reasonable grounds for insecurity. Delivery was not due until October 24 under Hopes' version of the parties' agreement, and Lundy's had no right to demand performance early, let alone broach the withholding of liquidated damages. This letter might have justified a demand for assurances under [§ 2–609]. However, Hope's made no such demand after receiving the letter. Instead of invoking its rights under [2–609], Hope's chose not to respond at all to Lundy's threat of liquidated damages. This event merely came and went without any legal consequence.

[22] Hope's in effect invoked its rights under [§ 2–609] in response to Lundys' threat of a back charge during the November 1 phone conversations. Two separate demands for assurances were made in response to this threat. Initially, Chris Arvantinos demanded assurances that Lundy's would not back charge Hope's for the delayed shipment in a telephone conversation with Mark Hannah later in the day on November 1. Arvantinos memorialized this demand in a letter composed on that day and mailed on the second of November. In their telephone conversation, Hannah refused to provide assurances that Lundy's would not back charge Hope's.

[23] Hope's made a second demand for assurances on November 3, when Richard Odor presented Hopes' invoice to Hannah demanding payment in full. Thus, Hope's demanded assurances that it would not be back charged on November 1, and when that demand was refused, Hope's made a second demand on November 3. The Court finds that Hope's was not entitled to invoke [§ 2–609] on either occasion.

[24] When Hope's made its first demand for assurances on November 1, it was already in breach of the parties' agreement. Delivery of the windows was due by October 24, but the windows did not arrive in Kansas City until November 4. A party already in breach is not entitled to invoke section 2–609 by demanding assurances. *United States v. Great Plains Gasification Associates*, 819 F.2d 831, 835 (8th Cir. 1987); cf. *Sumner v. Fel-Air, Inc.*, 680 P.2d 1109 (Alaska 1984) (2–609 does not apply after a breach has already occurred). To hold otherwise would allow a party to avoid liability for breaching its contract by invoking 2–609 to extract from the nonbreaching party an assurance that no damages will be sought for the breach. A nonbreaching party in need of prompt performance could be

coerced into giving up its right to damages for the breach by giving in to the demands in order to receive the needed performance. This Court refuses to endorse such a result.

[25] The assurances which Hope's demanded, moreover, were excessive. "What constitutes 'adequate assurance' is to be determined by factual conditions; the seller must exercise good faith and observe commercial standards; his satisfaction must be based upon reason and must not be arbitrary or capricious." *Richmond Leasing Co. v. Capital Bank, N.A.,* 762 F.2d 1303, 1310 (5th Cir. 1985). "If the assurances he demands are more than 'adequate' and the other party refuses to accede to the excessive demands, the court may find that the demanding party was in breach or a repudiator." J. White & R. Summers, *supra,* § 6–2, at 236.

[26] Lundy's argues that Hopes' demand for assurances in the November 2 letter from Arvantinos was overly broad and unreasonable. The letter informed Lundy's that Hope's would not deliver the windows to the job site until it received assurances that it would not "be backcharged or otherwise held responsible for liquidated damages, delay charges *or any extra costs on account of time of delivery of the windows.*" ((Plaintiff's exhibit 23) (emphasis added)). When this demand was made, the windows had not yet arrived in Kansas City. Therefore, the parties did not know at this time whether the proper quantity of windows had been shipped, whether the windows were the correct size, or whether they otherwise met Lundy's specifications. If there were any nonconformities in the shipment, there could have been another delay in the time of delivery while Hope's corrected the problem. Yet, Hope's demanded a blanket assurance that it would not be held responsible for any extra costs incurred because of "time of delivery of the windows." This demand was overly broad on its face and unreasonable under [§ 2–609].

[27] The assurances Hope's demanded on November 3 were also excessive. In his meeting with Mark Hannah, Richard Odor insisted that Lundy's prepay the contract price, deliver a cashier's check to the architect, or place the full contract price in an escrow account before the windows would be delivered. Yet, Lundy's never gave any indication that it was unable or unwilling to pay the amount it owed to Hope's when the windows were delivered and the bond stood as security for Lundy's obligation. Such a demand was unreasonable and amounted to a breach by Hope's. *See Pittsburgh-Des Moines Steel v. Brookhaven Manor Water Co.,* 532 F.2d 572, 578–82 (7th Cir. 1976) (demanding under § 2–609 a personal guarantee of payment from a shareholder, or that other party escrow the entire amount of the contract price before it was due, absent any showing of an inability to pay, was unreasonable); *Scott v. Crown,* 765 P.2d 1043 (Colo. Ct. App. 1988) (demanding payment in full before it was due was unreasonable demand under § 2–609 and amounted to anticipatory breach). The payment terms under the contract were "Progress payments by the 10th of

each month covering 90% of the total value of materials delivered and installation performed during the previous month with final payment upon completion of our [Hopes'] work." (Plaintiff's exhibit 11.) By demanding prepayment, Hope's essentially attempted to rewrite this term of the contract. *Pittsburgh-Des Moines Steel,* 532 F.2d 572 at 578–82 (§ 2–609 may not be used to force a contract modification); *Scott,* 765 P.2d 1043 (same).

[28] Although Hope's contends that a threatened back charge of $11,000 for a one week delay in shipment justified its demand for prepayment, the Court is not persuaded that Lundy's made any specific demand for $11,000. The testimony on this issue was controverted, but only Kathy Anderson, Hopes' customer service manager, testified, in a perfunctory manner, that an $11,000 back charge was threatened. Mark Hannah specifically denied making such a demand. Neither Chris Arvantinos nor Richard Odor testified to recalling receiving such a demand. There was also testimony at trial from one witness for Hope's that the threatened back charge was in the amount of $5,000. The Court is not persuaded that Lundy's went beyond making unspecified threats of a back charge for possible damages it would incur because of Hopes' delay.

[29] By threatening to withhold damages from the contract price, Lundy's was merely exercising its rights under K.S.A. § 84–2–717 [UCC § 2–717] which entitles a buyer to deduct from the amount owing on the contract any damages from the seller's breach. Giving notice of its intention to avail itself of a legal right did not indicate that Lundy's was unwilling or unable to perform under the contract. Indeed, the very nature of the right invoked by Lundy's manifests an intention that it would continue performing and pay the contract price due, less damages caused by Hopes' delay. Thus, the demand for prepayment was unreasonably excessive when there was no indication that Lundy's would not pay Hope's when performance was due.

[30] Both Hopes' delay in delivering the windows and Hopes' excessive demands entitled Lundy's to treat Hope's as in breach and to cancel the contract, which it did on November 7, 1988. K.S.A. § 84–2–711 (1983) ("Where the seller fails to make delivery or repudiates . . . the buyer may cancel . . ."). Thus, Hope's is not entitled to recover under its claim for breach of contract.

* * *

B. *Plaintiff's Quantum Meruit Claim*

[31] Hope's also claims that it is entitled to compensation from Lundy's under the theory of quantum meruit. "Quantum meruit," which literally means "as much as he deserves," is a phrase used often in older cases to describe an equitable doctrine premised on the theories of unjust

enrichment and restitution. Black's Law Dictionary 1119 (5th ed. 1979). Recovery was allowed under this theory when a benefit had been received by a party and it would be inequitable to allow the party to retain it. E. Farnsworth, Contracts § 2.20, at 103 n.4 (2d ed. 1990). Instead of labeling it quantum meruit, courts today speak in terms of restitution. *See Pioneer Operations Co. v. Brandeberry*, 14 Kan. App. 2d 289, 789 P.2d 1182 (1990).

[32] To recover in restitution, a breaching plaintiff must have conferred a benefit on the nonbreaching party. *See Walker v. Ireton*, 221 Kan. 314, 559 P.2d 340 (1977) (right to restitution limited to expenditures or services that benefitted disregard other party); Restatement (Second) of Contracts § 374 (1979). The burden is on the breaching party to prove the extent of the benefit conferred, and doubts will be resolved against him. Restatement (Second) of Contracts § 374 cmt. b (1977).

[33] In this case, Hope's conferred no benefit on Lundy's. The windows manufactured by Hope's were never used in the Rushton project, and the Court is not persuaded that the installation advice provided by Christiansen Steel Erection for Hope's improved the project. Hope's admits that the only labor it claims to have provided at the Rushton job site was consultation work performed by Christiansen Steel Erection, a company Hope's subcontracted with to install the windows. Mike and John Christiansen visited the job site on several occasions to advise Lundy's on how to prepare the window openings for installation. The advice they provided, however, related to the installation of windows that were never used on the project. When Lundy's canceled its contract with Hope's, it obtained an alternate supplier of a different type of windows. These windows did not require the same careful preparation of the window openings as the Hope's windows. Lundy's job foreman testified that the Christiansens' advice became moot when the alternate supplier was obtained. "[A] party's expenditures in preparation for performance that do not confer a benefit on the other party do not give rise to a restitution interest." Restatement (Second) of Contracts § 370 cmt. a (1977). Thus, because no benefit was conferred upon Lundy's, Hope's has no valid claim to restitution.

III. Conclusion

[34] After careful consideration of the facts and law, this Court holds that Hope's breached the contract in question. Therefore, defendant Lundy's was entitled to cancel its performance and defendant Bank IV was not obligated to pay Hope's under the statutory bond.

[35] IT IS THEREFORE ORDERED that plaintiff's claims for relief are hereby denied, and judgment is entered in favor of defendants.

NOTES AND QUESTIONS

1.   Re-read the first paragraph of the opinion. As it indicates, situations very similar to that presented by the case are likely to come up in *your* practice.

2.   What would have been the effect of the October 14 letter discussed in paragraph 7 if: (a) the contract did not require Hope's to meet those deadlines or (b) the contract did require Hope's to meet them?

———

PROBLEM 26-1

Grower had a contract to deliver carrots to Soup Company for $300 a ton. Because of a drought, Grower's crop was much smaller than usual. He still had enough carrots to perform his contract with Soup Company, but he didn't have many left over to sell on the open market. As a result, it looked as if he was going to suffer a loss for the year. Because of the drought, the market price for this type of carrot was $450 a ton. If he could sell the carrots for $450 a ton, he could make enough of a profit to keep his daughter in law school. He consulted with his daughter, who told him that the doctrine of impracticability relieved him of his obligations under the contract. Unfortunately, the daughter was wrong when she told her father he could get out of the contract on the basis of impracticability.

Grower called Soup Company's purchasing manager and told her that "on advice of counsel," he didn't have to perform, and he wouldn't perform if she didn't agree to amend the contract to raise the price to $400 a ton. The purchasing manager told him, "We expect your carrots to be delivered in accordance with our contract. If not, we'll see you in court."

(a)   Did Grower's threat constitute a repudiation? *No, not definite + final*

(b)   Does Soup Company have to take steps to mitigate its damages, or can it just wait to see if Grower delivers his carrots? *See* U.C.C. § 2–610. *needs to mitigate*

(c)   If there are no further communications between Grower and Soup Company and Grower delivers the carrots the day before the last day for performance under the contract, can Soup Company refuse to accept them? *See* U.C.C. § 2–611. *no*

(d)   If the purchasing manager decided that Grower probably wasn't going to perform and purchased substitute carrots from a farm in Brazil, is there any need to give Grower notice of this fact? *yes*

Performance Defenses

CHAPTER 27

IMPOSSIBILITY, IMPRACTICABILITY, AND FRUSTRATION OF PURPOSE

■ ■ ■

This chapter looks at classic common law excuses for failure to perform because of events that are outside the control of the parties. Once you conclude there is a contract (because there was offer, acceptance, and consideration), and you have interpreted the contract and determined what conditions there are to performance, and whether those conditions have been satisfied, then the time is ripe for performance. When the time is ripe, performance must occur or be excused, or else there is a breach. This chapter examines the first three doctrines we will look at constituting excuse of performance or, put another way, performance defenses.

Before looking at the excuses of impossibility, impracticability, and frustration of purpose, it bears keeping in mind that these excuses of performance have very, very limited application in contracts with any degree of sophistication at all. Rather, transactional lawyers address these excuses of performance by allocating the risk of loss from something outside the parties' control with explicit clauses such as "force majeure" and "hell or high water" clauses. A typical force majeure clause reads as follows:

> If any party fails to perform its obligations because of strikes, lockouts, labor disputes, embargoes, acts of God, inability to obtain labor or materials or reasonable substitutes for labor or materials, governmental restrictions, governmental regulations, governmental controls, judicial orders, enemy or hostile governmental action, civil commotion, fire or other casualty, or other causes beyond the reasonable control of the party obligated to perform, then that party's performance shall be excused for so long as the cause for failure to perform persists. Despite anything to the contrary in this paragraph, if the cause of a party's failure to perform results from any act by that party, then such cause shall not excuse the performance of the provisions of this Agreement by that party.

Conversely, a "hell or high water" clause, often found in equipment leases, is a clause that obligates the lessee to pay rent for the entire term of the lease, regardless of any event affecting the equipment or any change in circumstances.

With these express provisions to cope with the risk of events outside the parties' control in mind, we turn to the classic excuses of impossibility of performance, impracticability, and frustration of purpose that may be applied when the parties do not contract around them in advance.

TAYLOR V. CALDWELL

D — rented Hall to P

King's Bench
122 Eng. Rep. 309 (1863)

let P use gardens and Hall

[1] BLACKBURN, J. In this case the plaintiffs and defendants had, on the 27th May, 1861, entered into a contract by which the defendants agreed to let the plaintiffs have the use of The Surrey Gardens and Music Hall on four days then to come, *viz.*, the 17th June, 5th July, 5th August and 19th August, for the purpose of giving a series of four grand concerts, and day and night fetes at the Gardens and Hall on those days respectively; and the plaintiffs agreed to take the Gardens and Hall on those days, and pay £100 for each day.

[2] The parties inaccurately call this a "letting," and the money to be paid a "rent;" but the whole agreement is such as to shew that the defendants were to retain the possession of the Hall and Gardens so that there was to be no demise of them, and that the contract was merely to Give the plaintiffs the use of them on those days. Nothing however, in our opinion, depends on this. The agreement then proceeds to set out various stipulations between the parties as to what each was to supply for these concerts and entertainments, and as to the manner in which they should be carried on. The effect of the whole is to shew that the existence of the Music Hall in the Surrey Gardens in a state fit for a concert was essential for the fulfilment of the contract—such entertainments as the parties contemplated in their agreement could not be given without it.

[3] After the making of the agreement, and before the first day on which a concert was to be given, the Hall was destroyed by fire. This destruction, we must take it on the evidence, was without the fault of either party, and was so complete that in consequence the concerts could not be given as intended. And the question we have to decide is whether, under these circumstances, the loss which the plaintiffs have sustained is to fall upon the defendants. The parties when framing their agreement evidently had not present to their minds the possibility of such a disaster, and have made no express stipulation with reference to it, so that the answer to the question must depend upon the general rules of law applicable to such a contract.

issue

Hall destroyed by fire

Taylor could no longer perform

[4]   There seems no doubt that where there is a positive contract to do a thing, not in itself unlawful, the contractor must perform it or pay damages for not doing it, although in consequence of unforeseen accidents, the performance of his contract has become unexpectedly burthensome or even impossible. The law is so laid down in 1 Rol. Abr. 450, Condition (G), and in the note (2) to *Walton v. Waterhouse* (2 Wms. Saund. 421 a. 6th ed.), and is recognized as the general rule by all the Judges in the much discussed case of *Hall v. Wright* (E.B. & E. 746). But this rule is only applicable when the contract is positive and absolute, and not subject to any condition either express or implied. and there are authorities which, as we think establish the principle that where, from the nature of the contract, it appears that the parties must from the beginning have known that it could not be fulfilled unless when the time for the fulfilment of the contract arrived some particular specified thing continued to exist, so that, when entering into the contract, they must have contemplated such continuing existence as the foundation of what was to be done; there, in the absence of any express or implied warranty that the thing shall exist, the contract is not to be construed as a positive contract, but as subject to an implied condition that the parties shall be excused in case, before breach, performance becomes impossible from the perishing of the thing without default of the contractor.

[5]   There seems little doubt that this implication tends to further the great object of making the legal construction such as to fulfil the intention of those who entered into the contract. For in the course of affairs men in making such contracts in general would, if it were brought to their minds, say that there should be such a condition. . . .

[6]   There is a class of contracts in which a person binds himself to do something which requires to be performed by him in person; and such promises, e.g., promises to marry, or promises to serve for a certain time, are never in practice qualified by an express exception of the death of the party; and therefore in such cases the contract is in terms broken if the promisor dies before fulfilment. Yet it was very early determined that, if the performance is personal, the executors are not liable; *Hyde v. The Dean of Windsor* (Cro. Eliz. 552, 553). *See* 2 Wms. Exors. 1560, 5th ed., where a very apt illustration is given. "Thus," says the learned author, "if an author undertakes to compose a work, and dies before completing it, his executors are discharged from this contract: for the undertaking is merely personal in its nature, and, by the intervention of the contractor's death, has become impossible to be performed." For this he cites a dictum of Lord Lyndhurst in *Marshall v. Broadhurst* (1 Tyr. 348, 349), and a case mentioned by Patterson J. in *Wentworth v. Cock* (10 A. & E. 42, 45–46). In *Hall v. Wright* (E.B. & E. 746, 749), Crompton J., in his judgment, puts another case. "Where a contract depends upon personal skill, and the act of God renders it impossible, as, for instance, in the case of a painter employed to paint a

picture who is struck blind, it may be that the performance might be excused."

[7] It seems that in those cases the only ground on which the parties, or their executors, can be excused from the consequences of the breach of the contract, is that from the nature of the contract there is an implied condition of the continued existence of the life of the contractor, and perhaps in the case of the painter of his eyesight.

[8] It may, we think, be safely asserted to be now English law, that in all contracts of loan of chattels or bailments if the performance of the promise of the borrower or bailee to return the things lent or bailed, becomes impossible because it has perished, this impossibility (if not arising from the fault of the borrower or bailee from some risk which he has taken upon himself) excuses the borrower or bailee from the performance of his promise to redeliver the chattel.

[9] The great case of *Coggs v. Bernard* (1 Smith's L.C. 171, 5th ed.; 2 L. Raym. 909) is now the leading case on the law of bailments, and Lord Holt, in that case, referred so much to the Civil law that is might perhaps be thought this principle was there derived direct from the civilians, and was not generally applicable in English law except in the case of bailments; but the case of *Williams v. Lloyd* (W. Jones, 179), above cited, shows that the same law had been already adopted by the English law as early as The Book of Assizes. The principle seems to us to be that, in contracts in which the performance depends on the continued existence of a given person or thing, a condition is implied that the impossibility of performance arising from the perishing of the person or thing shall excuse the performance.

[10] In none of these cases is the promise in words other than positive, nor is there any express stipulation that the destruction of the person or thing shall excuse the performance; but that excuse is by law implied, because from the nature of the contract it is apparent that the parties contracted on the basis of the continued existence of the particular person or chattel. In the present case, looking at the whole contract, we find that the parties contracted on the basis of the continued existence of the Music Hall at the time when the concerts were to be given; that being essential to their performance.

[11] We think, therefore, that the Music Hall having ceased to exist, without fault of either party, both parties are excused, the plaintiffs from taking the gardens and paying the money, the defendants from performing their promise to give the use of the Hall and Gardens and other things. Consequently, the rule must be absolute to enter the verdict for the defendants.

Rule absolute.

— MINERAL PARK LAND CO. V. HOWARD —

Supreme Court of California
172 Cal. 289, 156 P. 458 (1916)

constuct a bridge

SLOSS, J.

cause of action

[1] The defendants appeal from a judgment in favor of plaintiff for $3,650.[1] The appeal is on the judgment roll alone.

[2] The plaintiff was the owner of certain land in the ravine or wash known as the Arroyo Seco, in South Pasadena, Los Angeles county. The defendants had made a contract with the public authorities for the construction of a concrete bridge across the Arroyo Seco. In August, 1911, the parties to this action entered into a written agreement whereby the plaintiff granted to the defendants the right to haul gravel and earth from plaintiff's land, the defendants agreeing to take therefrom all of the gravel and earth necessary in the construction of the fill and cement work on the proposed bridge, the required amount being estimated at approximately 114,000 cubic yards. Defendants agreed to pay 5 cents per cubic yard for the first 80,000 yards, the next 10,000 yards were to be given free of charge, and the balance was to be paid for at the rate of 5 cents per cubic yard.

[3] The complaint was in two counts. The first alleged that the defendants had taken 50,131 cubic yards of earth and gravel, thereby becoming indebted to plaintiff in the sum of $2,506.55, of which only $900 had been paid, leaving a balance of $1,606.55 due. The findings support plaintiff's claim in this regard, and there is no question of the propriety of so much of the judgment as responds to the first count. The second count sought to recover damages for the defendants' failure to take from plaintiff's land any more than the 50,131 yards.

D failed to take more gravel (80K) ↓ took it from somewhere else

[4] It alleged that the total amount of earth and gravel used by defendants was 101,000 cubic yards, of which they procured 50,869 cubic yards from some place other than plaintiff's premises. The amount due the plaintiff for this amount of earth and gravel would, under the terms of the contract, have been $2,043.45. The count charged that plaintiff's land contained enough earth and gravel to enable the defendants to take therefrom the entire amount required, and that the 50,869 yards not taken had no value to the plaintiff. Accordingly the plaintiff sought, under this head, to recover damages in the sum of $2,043.45.

remaining gravel = no value to P

[5] The answer denied that the plaintiff's land contained any amount of earth and gravel in excess of the 50,131 cubic yards actually taken, and alleged that the defendants took from the said land all of the earth and gravel available for the work mentioned in the contract.

D "took all available gravel"

---

[1] [$3,650 in 1916 dollars is roughly the equivalent of $86,000 in 2019 dollars using the CPI and the GNP Deflator.—Eds.]

[6] The court found that the plaintiff's land contained earth and gravel far in excess of 101,000 cubic yards of earth and gravel, but that only 50,131 cubic yards, the amount actually taken by the defendants, was above the water level. No greater quantity could have been taken "by ordinary means," or except by the use, at great expense, of a steam dredger, and the earth and gravel so taken could not have been used without first having been dried at great expense and delay. On the issue raised by the plea of defendants that they took all the earth and gravel that was available the court qualified its findings in this way: It found that the defendants did take all of the available earth and gravel from plaintiff's premises, in this, that they took and removed "all that could have been taken advantageously to defendants, or all that was practical to take and remove from a financial standpoint"; that any greater amount could have been taken only at a prohibitive cost, that is, at an expense of 10 or 12 times as much as the usual cost per yard. It is also declared that the word "available" is used in the findings to mean capable of being taken and used advantageously. It was not "advantageous or practical" to have taken more material from plaintiff's land, but it was not impossible. There is a finding that the parties were not under any mutual misunderstanding regarding the amount of available gravel, but that the contract was entered into without any calculation on the part of either of the parties with reference to the amount of available earth and gravel on the premises.

[7] The single question is whether the facts thus found justified the defendants in their failure to take from the plaintiff's land all of the earth and gravel required. This question was answered in the negative by the court below. The case was apparently thought to be governed by the principle—established by a multitude of authorities—that where a party has agreed, without qualification, to perform an act which is not in its nature impossible of performance, he is not excused by difficulty of performance, or by the fact that he becomes unable to perform.

[8] It is, however, equally well settled that, where performance depends upon the existence of a given thing, and such existence was assumed as the basis of the agreement, performance is excused to the extent that the thing ceases to exist or turns out to be nonexistent. Thus, where the defendants had agreed to pasture not less than 3,000 cattle on plaintiff's land, paying therefor $1 for each and every head so pastured, and it developed that the land did not furnish feed for more than 717 head, the number actually put on the land by defendant, it was held that plaintiff could not recover the stipulated sum for the difference between the cattle pastured and the minimum of 3,000 agreed to be pastured. *Williams v. Miller*, 68 Cal. 290, 9 Pac. 166. Similarly, in *Brick Co. v. Pond*, 38 Ohio St. 65, where the plaintiff had leased all the "good No. 1 fire clay on his land," subject to the condition that the lessees should mine or pay for not less than 2,000 tons of clay every year, paying therefor 25 cents per ton, the court

held that the lessees were not bound to pay for 2,000 tons per year, unless there was No. 1 clay on the land in such quantities as would justify its being taken out. In *Ridgely v. Conewago Iron Co.*, 53 Fed. 988, the holding was that a mining lease requiring the lessee to mine 4,000 tons of ore annually, and to pay therefor a fixed sum per ton, or, failing to take out such quantity, to pay therefore, imposed no obligation on the lessee to pay for such stipulated quantity after the ore in the demised premises had become exhausted. There are many other cases dealing with mining leases of this character, and the general course of decision is to the effect that the performance of the obligation to take out a given quantity or to pay royalty thereon, if it be not taken out, is excused if it appears that the land does not contain the stipulated quantity.

[9]   We think the findings of fact make a case falling within the rule of these decisions. The parties were contracting for the right to take earth and gravel to be used in the construction of the bridge. When they stipulated that all of the earth and gravel needed for this purpose should be taken from plaintiff's land, they contemplated and assumed that the land contained the requisite quantity, available for use. The defendants were not binding themselves to take what was not there. And, in determining whether the earth and gravel were "available," we must view the conditions in a practical and reasonable way. Although there was gravel on the land, it was so situated that the defendants could not take it by ordinary means, nor except at a prohibitive cost. To all fair intents then, it was impossible for defendants to take it.

[10]   "A thing is impossible in legal contemplation when it is not practicable; and a thing is impracticable when it can only be done at an excessive and unreasonable cost." 1 Beach on Contr. § 216. We do not mean to intimate that the defendants could excuse themselves by showing the existence of conditions which would make the performance of their obligation more expensive than they had anticipated, or which would entail a loss upon them. But, where the difference in cost is so great as here, and has the effect, as found, of making performance impracticable, the situation is not different from that of a total absence of earth and gravel.

[11] On the facts found, there should have been no recovery on the second count.

[12] The judgment is modified by deducting therefrom the sum of $2,043.45, and, as so modified, it stands affirmed.

We concur: SHAW, J.; LAWLOR, J.

NOTE

Don't let this case mislead you into thinking that courts routinely grant relief when events are not as expected. It has to be something extraordinary. In this case, it was extremely unlikely that the parties would have foreseen that there would be water in the Arroyo Seco for an extended period. The name "Arroyo Seco" means "dry ravine." The area through which it runs (Pasadena to Los Angeles) is basically a desert. The Arroyo Seco runs right past Dodger stadium, where for the first 20 years of the stadium's existence no baseball game was ever cancelled on account of rain.

AMERICAN TRADING AND PRODUCTION CORP. V. SHELL INTL. MARINE LTD.

United States Court of Appeals, Second Circuit
453 F.2d 939 (1972)

MULLIGAN, CIRCUIT JUDGE.

[1] This is an appeal by American Trading and Production Corporation (hereinafter "owner") from a judgment entered on July 29th, 1971, in the United States District Court for the Southern District of New York, dismissing its claim against Shell International Marine Ltd. (hereinafter "charterer") for additional compensation in the sum of $131,978.44[2] for the transportation of cargo from Texas to India via the Cape of Good Hope as a result of the closing of the Suez Canal in June, 1967 . . . The action was tried on stipulated facts and without a jury before Hon. Harold R. Tyler, Jr. who dismissed the claim on the merits in an opinion dated July 22, 1971.

[2] We affirm.

[3] The owner is a Maryland corporation doing business in New York and the charterer is a United Kingdom corporation. On March 23, 1967, the parties entered into a contract of voyage charter in New York City which provided that the charterer would hire the owner's tank vessel, WASHINGTON TRADER, for a voyage with a full cargo of lube oil from Beaumont/Smiths Bluff, Texas to Bombay, India. The charter party provided that the freight rate would be in accordance with the then prevailing American Tanker Rate Schedule (ATRS), $14.25 per long ton of cargo, plus seventy-five percent (75%), and in addition there was a charge of $.85 per long ton for passage through the Suez Canal. On May 15, 1967 the WASHINGTON TRADER departed from Beaumont with a cargo of 16,183.32 long tons of lube oil. The charterer paid the freight at the invoiced sum of $417,327.36 on May 26, 1967. On May 29th, 1967 the owner

---

2   [$131,978.44 in 1972 dollars is roughly the equivalent of $792,000 in 2019 dollars using the CPI and the GNP Deflator.—Eds.]

advised the WASHINGTON TRADER by radio to take additional bunkers at Ceuta due to possible diversion because of the Suez Canal crisis. The vessel arrived at Ceuta, Spanish Morocco on May 30, bunkered and sailed on May 31st, 1967. On June 5th the owner cabled the ship's master advising him of various reports of trouble in the Canal and suggested delay in entering it pending clarification. On that very day, the Suez Canal was closed due to the state of war which had developed in the Middle East. The owner then communicated with the charterer on June 5th through the broker who had negotiated the charter party, requesting approval for the diversion of the WASHINGTON TRADER which then had proceeded to a point about 84 miles northwest of Port Said, the entrance to the Canal. On June 6th the charterer responded that under the circumstances it was "for owner to decide whether to continue to wait or make the alternative passage via the Cape since Charter Party obliges them to deliver cargo without qualification." In response the owner replied on the same day that in view of the closing of the Suez, the WASHINGTON TRADER would proceed to Bombay via the Cape of Good Hope and "we [are] reserving all rights for extra compensation." The vessel proceeded westward, back through the Straits of Gibraltar and around the Cape and eventually arrived in Bombay on July 15th (some 30 days later than initially expected), traveling a total of 18,055 miles instead of the 9,709 miles which it would have sailed had the Canal been open. The owner billed $131,978.44 as extra compensation which the charterer has refused to pay.

[4] On appeal and below the owner argues that transit of the Suez Canal was the agreed specific means of performance of the voyage charter and that the supervening destruction of this means rendered the contract legally impossible to perform and therefore discharged the owner's unperformed obligation (Restatement of Contracts § 460 (1932)). Consequently, when the WASHINGTON TRADER eventually delivered the oil after journeying around the Cape of Good Hope, a benefit was conferred upon the charterer for which it should respond in *quantum meruit*. The validity of this proposition depends upon a finding that the parties contemplated or agreed that the Suez passage was to be the exclusive method of performance, and indeed it was so argued on appeal. We cannot construe the agreement in such a fashion. The parties contracted for the shipment of the cargo from Texas to India at an agreed rate and the charter party makes absolutely no reference to any fixed route. It is urged that the Suez passage was a condition of performance because the ATRS rate was based on a Suez Canal passage, the invoice contained a specific Suez Canal toll charge and the vessel actually did proceed to a point 84 miles northwest of Port Said. In our view all that this establishes is that both parties contemplated that the Canal would be the probable route. It was the cheapest and shortest, and therefore it was in the interest of both that it be utilized. However, this is not at all equivalent to an agreement that it be the exclusive method of performance. The charter party does not

so provide and it seems to have been well understood in the shipping industry that the Cape route is an acceptable alternative in voyages of this character.

[5]   The District of Columbia Circuit decided a closely analogous case, *Transatlantic Financing Corp. v. United States*, 124 U.S. App. D.C. 183, 363 F.2d 312 (1966). There the plaintiff had entered into a voyage charter with defendant in which it agreed to transport a full cargo of wheat on the CHRISTOS from a United States port to Iran. The parties clearly contemplated a Suez passage, but on November 2, 1956 the vessel reduced speed when war blocked the Suez Canal. The vessel changed its course in the Atlantic and eventually delivered its cargo in Iran after proceeding by way of the Cape of Good Hope. In an exhaustive opinion Judge Skelly Wright reviewed the English cases which had considered the same problem and concluded that "the Cape route is generally regarded as an alternative means of performance. So the implied expectation that the route would be via Suez is hardly adequate proof of an allocation to the promisee of the risk of closure. In some cases, even an express expectation may not amount to a condition of performance." *Transatlantic Financing Corp. v. United States, supra*, 363 F.2d at 317 (footnote omitted).

[6]   Appellant argues that *Transatlantic* is distinguishable since there was an agreed upon flat rate in that case unlike the instant case where the rate was based on Suez passage. This does not distinguish the case in our view. It is stipulated by the parties here that the only ATRS rate published at the time of the agreement from Beaumont to Bombay was the one utilized as a basis for the negotiated rate ultimately agreed upon. This rate was escalated by 75% to reflect whatever existing market conditions the parties contemplated. These conditions are not stipulated. Had a Cape route rate been requested, which was not the case, it is agreed that the point from which the parties would have bargained would be $17.35 per long ton of cargo as against $14.25 per long ton.

[7]   Actually, in *Transatlantic* it was argued that certain provisions in the P. & I. Bunker Deviation Clause referring to the direct and/or customary route required, by implication, a voyage through the Suez Canal. The court responded "actually they prove only what we are willing to accept—that the parties expected the usual and customary route would be used. The provisions in no way condition performance upon non-occurrence of this contingency." *Transatlantic Financing Corp. v. United States, supra*, 363 F.2d at 317 n. 8. We hold that all that the ATRS rate establishes is that the parties obviously expected a Suez passage but there is no indication at all in the instrument or *dehors* that it was a condition of performance.

[8]   This leaves us with the question as to whether the owner was excused from performance on the theory of commercial impracticability

(Restatement of Contracts § 454 (1932)). Even though the owner is not excused because of strict impossibility, it is urged that American law recognizes that performance is rendered impossible if it can only be accomplished with extreme and unreasonable difficulty, expense, injury or loss.[3] There is no extreme or unreasonable difficulty apparent here. The alternate route taken was well recognized, and there is no claim that the vessel or the crew or the nature of the cargo made the route actually taken unreasonably difficult, dangerous or onerous. The owner's case here essentially rests upon the element of the additional expense involved— $131,978.44. This represents an increase of less than one third over the agreed upon $417,327.36. We find that this increase in expense is not sufficient to constitute commercial impracticability under either American or English authority.

[9] Mere increase in cost alone is not a sufficient excuse for nonperformance (Restatement of Contracts § 467 (1932)). It must be an "extreme and unreasonable"[4] expense (Restatement of Contracts § 454 (1932)).[5] While in the *Transatlantic* case *supra*, the increased cost amounted to an increase of about 14% over the contract price, the court did cite with approval the two leading English cases *Ocean Tramp Tankers Corp. v. V/O Sovfracht (The Eugenia)*, [1964] 2 Q.B. 226, 233 (C.A. 1963) (which expressly overruled *Societe Franco Tunisienne D'Armement v. Sidermar S.P.A. (The Messalia)*, [1961] 2 Q.B. 278 (1960), where the court had found frustration because the Cape route was highly circuitous and involved an increase in cost of approximately 50%), and *Tsakiroglou & Co. Lt. v. Noblee Thorl G.m.b.H.*, [1960] 2 Q.B. 318, 348, aff'd, [1962] A.C., 93 (1961) where the House of Lords found no frustration though the freight costs were exactly doubled due to the Canal closure.[6]

---

3   This is the formula utilized in the Restatement of Contracts § 454 (1932).

4   The Restatement gives some examples of what is "extreme and unreasonable"— Restatement of Contracts § 460, Illus. 2 (tenfold increase in costs) and Illus. 3 (costs multiplied fifty times) (1932); compare § 467, Illus. 3. *See generally* G. Grismore, Principles of the Law of Contracts § 179 (rev. ed. J. E. Murray 1965).

5   Both parties take solace in the Uniform Commercial Code which in comment 4 to Section 2–615 states that the rise in cost must "alter the essential nature of the performance. . . ." This is clearly not the case here. The owner relies on a further sentence in the comment which refers to a severe shortage of raw materials or of supplies due to "war, embargo, local crop failure, unforeseen shutdown of major sources of supply or the like, which either causes a marked increase in cost. . . ." Since this is not a case involving the sale of goods but transportation of a cargo where there was an alternative which was a commercially reasonable substitute (*see* U.C.C. § 2–614(1)) the owner's reliance is misplaced.

6   While these are English cases and refer to the doctrine of "frustration" rather than "impossibility" as Judge Skelly Wright pointed out in *Transatlantic, supra*, 363 F.2d at 320 n. 16 the two are considered substantially identical, 6 A. Corbin, Contracts § 1322, at 327 n. 9 (rev. ed. 1962). While *Tsakiroglou* and *The Eugenia* are criticized in Schegal, Of Nuts, and Ships and Sealing Wax, Suez, and Frustrating Things—The Doctrine of Impossibility of Performance, 23 RUTGERS L. REV. 419, 448 (1969), apparently on the theory that the charterer is a better loss bearer, the overruled *Sidermar* case was previously condemned in Berman, Excuse for Nonperformance in the Light of Contract Practices in International Trade, 63 COLUM. L. REV. 1413, 1424–27 (1963).

[10] Appellant further seeks to distinguish *Transatlantic* because in that case the change in course was in the mid-Atlantic and added some 300 miles to the voyage while in this case the WASHINGTON TRADER had traversed most of the Mediterranean and thus had added some 9000 miles to the contemplated voyage. It should be noted that although both the time and the length of the altered passage here exceeded those in the *Transatlantic*, the additional compensation sought here is just under one third of the contract price. Aside from this however, it is a fact that the master of the WASHINGTON TRADER was alerted by radio on May 29th, 1967, of a "possible diversion because of Suez Canal crisis," but nevertheless two days later he had left Ceuta (opposite Gibraltar) and proceeded across the Mediterranean. While we may not speculate about the foreseeability of a Suez crisis at the time the contract was entered, there does not seem to be any question but that the master here had been actually put on notice before traversing the Mediterranean that diversion was possible. Had the WASHINGTON TRADER then changed course, the time and cost of the Mediterranean trip could reasonably have been avoided, thereby reducing the amount now claimed.

* * *

[11] Matters involving impossibility or impracticability of performance of contract are concededly vexing and difficult. One is even urged on the allocation of such risks to pray for the "wisdom of Solomon." 6 A. Corbin, Contracts § 1333, at 372 (1962). On the basis of all of the facts, the pertinent authority and a further belief in the efficacy of prayer, we affirm.

PUBLICKER INDUSTRIES V. UNION CARBIDE CORP.

United States District Court, Eastern District, Pennsylvania
17 U.C.C. Rep. Serv. (Callaghan) 989 (1975)

WEINER, DISTRICT JUDGE.

[1] This case presents the problem of whether a seller's performance under a contract has become impracticable because its costs have nearly doubled due allegedly to unforeseeable events arising out of the 1973 Middle East War.

[2] In July of 1972, Union Carbide Corporation and Publicker Industries, entered into a contract whereby Union Carbide was to supply Publicker with a substance called "Spirits Grade Ethanol" for a period of three years. The price was to be determined by a detailed formula set forth in the contract. Essentially the price was to be adjusted once at the beginning of each year of the contract to reflect any change in the seller's cost. The major cost element of Ethanol is Ethylene, a type of natural gas,

and the following clause indicates how fluctuations in its cost was to affect the selling price.

> (d) The contract price of $.2450 per gallon shall be adjusted by four-tenths of one cent ($.004) per gallon for each one-tenth of one cent ($.001) per pound increase or decrease from the "base value" in the average of Seller's Standard Cost for Ethylene used in the manufacture of Ethanol at its Texas City, Texas plant during the calendar year immediately preceding the then current calendar year. The "base value" referred to above shall be the average of Seller's Standard Cost for Ethylene used in the production of Ethanol at its Texas City, Texas plant during the calendar year 1972. Seller's Standard Cost for Ethylene shall mean the charge UNION CARBIDE makes to all of its Gulf Coast internal consumers for Gulf Coast produced Ethylene.

complex price caps

> In no event, however, shall the amount of said increase in the contract price for Ethanol 190 Proof, based upon Seller's increased Standard Cost for Ethylene, cause the price to be paid for Ethanol 190 Proof to exceed the price listed below:

> During the calendar year 1974 $.2550 per gallon*
> During the calendar year 1975 $.2650 per gallon*
> During the calendar year 1976 $.2750 per gallon*
> During the calendar year 1977 $.2850 per gallon*

> * plus the amount of any increase, or minus the amount of any decrease, pursuant to paragraphs (a)(b) and (c) above.[7]

[3] By July of 1974, the price of Ethylene had risen so much that Union Carbide informed Publicker that it would insist on amending the contract to remove the price ceilings from the Ethylene price escalator provision quoted above. In August of 1974, Union Carbide told Publicker that unless it agreed to the proposed changes, it would cease supplying it with Ethanol. Thereupon, Publicker brought this action to require that Union Carbide specifically perform the contract.

[4] After preliminary proceedings, it was agreed that until this suit was resolved, Union Carbide would continue to supply Publicker but at the higher price it had demanded. It was further agreed that the court would make an initial ruling on whether it had the power to alter the terms of the contract. That is the question that is presently before us. Essentially we must determine whether Union Carbide's refusal to honor the contract was

---

[7] Paragraphs (a), (b), and (c) of the contract are price escalator provisions for the other cost elements of Ethanol.

justified, and if so, whether the contract can be enforced but at a higher price to be set by the court.

[5] Defendant, Union Carbide, argues that the very substantial and allegedly unforeseen rise in the price of Ethylene excused it from further performance on two grounds: (1) that it was the type of occurrence which under the "force majeure" clause of the contract relieved it of its duty to perform; and (2) that as a matter of general commercial law, the price rise was of such a nature as to render further performance impracticable (U.C.C. § 2–615).

[6] The "force majeure" clause provided in relevant part that:

> Neither party shall be liable for its failure to perform hereunder if said performance is made impracticable due to any occurrence beyond its reasonable control, including acts of God, fires, floods, wars, sabotage, accidents, labor disputes or shortages, governmental laws, ordinances, rules and regulations, ..., inability to obtain material, equipment or transportation, and any other similar or different occurrence. The party whose performance is made impracticable by any such occurrence shall have the right to omit during the period of such occurrence all or any portion of the quantity deliverable during such period. ...

[7] It is comparable to that portion of the Uniform Commercial Code also relied upon by defendant which provides that:

> Delay in delivery or non-delivery in whole or in part by a seller ... is not a breach of his duty under a contract for sale if performance as agreed has been made impracticable by the occurrence of a contingency the non-occurrence of which was a basic assumption on which the contract was made. ...

> Delay in delivery or non-delivery by a seller ... is not a breach of his duty under a contract for sale if performance as agreed has been made impracticable by the occurrence of a contingency the nonoccurrence of which was a basic assumption on which the contract was made. ...

12 A. Pa. Stat. Ann. § 2–615 (Purdon's 1970).

[8] Under either of the theories put forth by the defendant, the key to success is a finding by us that performance under the terms of the contract would be "impracticable." This would essentially require us to find that increased costs alone are sufficient to render performance impracticable. Comment 4 to § 2–615 quoted above indicates that:

> Increased cost alone does not excuse performance unless the rise in cost is due to some unforseen contingency which alters the essential nature of the performance. Neither is a rise in the

market in itself a justification, for that is exactly the type of business risk which business contracts cover. But a severe shortage of raw materials or of supplies due to a contingency such as war, embargo, local crop failure, unforseen shutdown of major sources of supply or the like, which either causes a marked increase in cost or altogether prevents the seller from securing supplies necessary to his performance, is within the contemplation of this section.

[9] Union Carbide argues that it has suffered excessive cost increases as a result of allegedly unprecedented Arab price hikes. Testimony was presented to show the connection between oil prices and natural gas prices. Various experts testified that at the time of the contract, it was completely unforeseeable that the oil producing nations would bring about such exorbitant price increases. Union Carbide's experts further testified that the price ceiling established for 1974 in the contract was based upon their forecast that the Ethylene price for 1974 would be 3.75 cents a pound but that in fact by July 1974 the price had risen to 7 cents a pound. As a result, defendant's cost per gallon of Ethanol rose from 21.2 cents a gallon in 1973 to 37.2 cents a gallon by the middle of 1974. Confronted with a contract sale price fixed at 26.5 gallons for 1974, defendant was losing over 10 cents a gallon at the time it refused to continue performance. It now alleges that if it is forced to complete performance under the present contract, it will suffer an aggregate loss in excess of 5.8 million dollars.

[10] However, plaintiff Publicker contends that because the oil producing nations had joined together in 1971 to effect a 25% price increase, further price increases of the same kind were not unforeseeable at the time of the contract. Furthermore, it argues that the precise purpose of the ceiling provision in the contract was to place upon Union Carbide the risk of any unusual rise in the price of Ethylene. It is contended that in any event, the mere fact that the cost of performance has doubled does not make such performance impracticable.

[11] We agree with the plaintiff. We are not aware of any cases where something less than a 100% percent cost increase has been held to make a seller's performance "impracticable." It is clear that in the present case, the contract contemplated that foreseeable cost increases would be passed on to the buyer. However, the existence of a specific provision which put a ceiling on contract price increases resulting from a rise in the cost of Ethylene impels the conclusion that the parties intended that the risk of a substantial and unforeseen rise in its cost would be borne by the seller, Union Carbide.

> While it may be an overstatement to say that increased cost and difficulty of performance never constitute impracticability, to justify relief there must be more of a variation between expected

cost and the cost of performing by an available alternative than is present in this case, where the promisor can legitimately be presumed to have accepted some degree of abnormal risk, and where impracticability is urged on the basis of added expense alone.

Transatlantic Financing Corporation v. United States, 363 F.2d 312, 319 (D. C. Cir. 1966). While *Transatlantic* involved a much smaller cost increase, we feel that its reasoning is equally applicable here.

[12] As a finding that performance would be impracticable is necessary for defendant to prevail under either of the theories it has advanced, our conclusion that performance was not made impracticable puts defendant in breach of the contract. While not necessary to our holding, we also note that we have some doubt as to whether the Arab oil price rises were a "contingency the non-occurrence of which was a basic assumption on which the contract was made" or whether because of the rule of ejusdem generis[8] they would be covered by the "force majeure" clause of the contract.

[13] This opinion is filed in lieu of any findings of fact and conclusions of law that might be required under Fed. R. Civ. P. 52(a).

———

UNITED STATES V. WEGEMATIC CORP.

United States Court of Appeals, Second Circuit
360 F.2d 674 (1966)

FRIENDLY, CIRCUIT JUDGE.

[1] The facts developed at trial in the District Court for the Southern District of New York, fully set forth in a memorandum by Judge Graven, can be briefly summarized: In June 1956 the Federal Reserve Board invited five electronics manufacturers to submit proposals for an intermediate-type, general-purpose electronic digital computing system or systems; the invitation stressed the importance of early delivery as a consideration in determining the Board's choice. Defendant, a relative newcomer in the field, which had enjoyed considerable success with a smaller computer known as the ALWAC III-E, submitted a detailed proposal for the sale or lease of a new computer designated as the ALWAC 800. It characterized the machine as "a truly revolutionary system utilizing all of the latest technical advances," and featured that "maintenance problems are minimized by the use of highly reliable magnetic cores for not only the high

---

[8] [The *ejusdem generis* rule provides that where general words follow a list of specifics, the general words are not to be construed in their widest meaning, but are to be construed as relating only to things of the same nature as those in the list. Read the force majure clause carefully. Has the drafter negated the *ejusdem generis* rule? After all, it's only supposed to be a rule of interpretation.—Eds.]

specd memory but also logical elements and registers." Delivery was offered nine months from the date the contract or purchase order was received. In September the Board acted favorably on the defendant's proposal, ordering components of the ALWAC 800 with an aggregate cost of $231,800. Delivery was to be made on June 30, 1957, with liquidated damages of $100 per day for delay. The order also provided that in the event the defendant failed to comply "with any provision" of the agreement, "the Board may procure the services described in the contract from other sources and hold the Contractor responsible for any excess cost occasioned thereby." Defendant accepted the order with enthusiasm.

[2] The first storm warning was a suggestion by the defendant in March 1957 that the delivery date be postponed. In April it informed the Board by letter that delivery would be made on or before October 30 rather than as agreed, the delay being due to the necessity of "a redesign which we feel has greatly improved this equipment"; waiver of the stipulated damages for delay was requested. The Board took the request under advisement. On August 30 defendant wrote that delivery would be delayed "possibly into 1959"; it suggested use of ALWAC III-E equipment in the interim and waiver of the $100 per day "penalty." The Board also took this request under advisement but made clear it was waiving no rights. In mid-October defendant announced that "due to engineering difficulties it has become impracticable to deliver the ALWAC 800 Computing System at this time"; it requested cancellation of the contract without damages. The Board set about procuring comparable equipment from another manufacturer; on October 6, 1958, International Business Machines Corporation delivered an IBM 650 computer, serving substantially the same purpose as the ALWAC 800, at a rental of $102,000 a year with an option to purchase for $410,450.

[3] In July 1958 the Board advised defendant of its intention to press its claim for damages; this suit followed. The court awarded the United States $46,300 for delay under the liquidated damages clause, $179,450 for the excess cost of the IBM equipment, and $10,056 for preparatory expenses useless in operating the IBM system—a total of $235,806[9], with 6% interest from October 6, 1958.

[4] The principal point of the defense, which is the sole ground of this appeal, is that delivery was made impossible by "basic engineering difficulties" whose correction would have taken between one and two years and would have cost a million to a million and a half dollars, with success likely but not certain. Although the record does not give an entirely clear notion what the difficulties were, two experts suggested that they may have stemmed from the magnetic cores, used instead of transistors to achieve a solid state machine, which did not have sufficient uniformity at this stage

---

[9]   [$235,806 in 1966 dollars is roughly the equivalent of $1,820,000 in 2019 dollars using the CPI and the GNP Deflator.—Eds.]

of their development. Defendant contends that under federal law, which both parties concede to govern, *see Cargill, Inc. v. Commodity Credit Corp.*, 275 F.2d 745, 751–753 (2 Cir. 1960), the "practical impossibility" of completing the contract excused its defaults in performance.

[5] We find persuasive the defendant's suggestion of looking to the Uniform Commercial Code as a source for the "federal" law of sales. The Code has been adopted by Congress for the District of Columbia, 77 Stat. 630 (1963), has been enacted in over forty states, and is thus well on its way to becoming a truly national law of commerce, which, as Judge L. Hand said of the Negotiable Instruments Law, is "more complete and more certain, than any other which can conceivably be drawn from those sources of 'general law' to which we were accustomed to resort in the days of *Swift v. Tyson*." *New York, N.H. & H.R. Co. v. Reconstruction Finance Corp.*, 180 F.2d 241, 244 (2 Cir. 1950). When the states have gone so far in achieving the desirable goal of a uniform law governing commercial transactions, it would be a distinct disservice to insist on a different one for the segment of commerce, important but still small in relation to the total, consisting of transactions with the United States.

[6] Section 2–615 of the UCC, entitled "Excuse by failure of presupposed conditions," provides that:

> Except so far as a seller may have assumed a greater obligation . . . delay in delivery or non-delivery . . . is not a breach of his duty under a contract for sale if performance as agreed has been made impracticable by the occurrence of a contingency the nonoccurrence of which was a basic assumption on which the contract was made. . . .

[7] The latter part of the test seems a somewhat complicated way of putting Professor Corbin's question of how much risk the promisor assumed. Recent Developments in the Law of Contracts, 50 *Harv.L.Rev.* 449, 465–66 (1937); 2 Corbin, Contracts § 1333, at 371. We see no basis for thinking that when an electronics system is promoted by its manufacturer as a revolutionary breakthrough, the risk of the revolution's occurrence falls on the purchaser; the reasonable supposition is that it has already occurred or, at least, that the manufacturer is assuring the purchaser that it will be found to have when the machine is assembled. As Judge Graven said: "The Board in its invitation for bids did not request invitations to conduct a development program for it. The Board requested invitations from manufacturers for the furnishing of a computer machine." Acceptance of defendant's argument would mean that though a purchaser makes his choice because of the attractiveness of a manufacturer's representation and will be bound by it, the manufacturer is free to express what are only aspirations and gamble on mere probabilities of fulfillment without any risk of liability. In fields of developing technology, the manufacturer would

thus enjoy a wide degree of latitude with respect to performance while holding an option to compel the buyer to pay if the gamble should pan out. We do not think this the common understanding—above all as to a contract where the manufacturer expressly agreed to liquidated damages for delay and authorized the purchaser to resort to other sources in the event of non-delivery. If a manufacturer wishes to be relieved of the risk that what looks good on paper may not prove so good in hardware, the appropriate exculpatory language is well known and often used.

[8] Beyond this the evidence of true impracticability was far from compelling. The large sums predicted by defendant's witnesses must be appraised in relation not to the single computer ordered by the Federal Reserve Board, evidently for a bargain price, but to the entire ALWAC 800 program as originally contemplated. Although the record gives no idea what this was, even twenty-five machines would gross $10,000,000 if priced at the level of the comparable IBM equipment. While the unanticipated need for expending $1,000,000 or $1,500,000 on redesign might have made such a venture unattractive, as defendant's management evidently decided, the sums are thus not so clearly prohibitive as it would have them appear. What seemingly did become impossible was on time performance; the issue of whether, if defendant had offered prompt rectification of the design, the Government could have refused to give it a chance and still recover not merely damages for delay but also the higher cost of replacement equipment, is not before us.

Affirmed.

NOTES AND QUESTIONS

1. As stated in paragraph [2], in the August 30 letter, the defendant characterized the $100 per day provision as a "penalty." This was probably a little too clever, trying to characterize it as a penalty and then claim that the government acceded to that characterization when it didn't correct them. (Although a similar record was made in the *Dow Corning* case in Chapter 21 and seems to have worked, or at least not been judged "too cute.") This little trick may have cost them some sympathy with the court. Nevertheless, the government lawyers should have shot back a letter saying that it was liquidated damages and not a penalty and then warned the people administering the contract to watch out for more slick tricks.

2. The UNIDROIT principles address impracticability in articles 6.2.2 and 6.2.3, which establish a renegotiation process prior to commencement of court action. What do you think of this procedure and the standards enunciated?

PROBLEM 27-1

In 1965, Amalgamated Edison ("AmEd") was planning to build a new generating plant. Choosing between a nuclear plant and a fossil-fuel plant, it was leaning toward a fossil-fuel plant. As its CEO told representatives of Eastinghouse, which was trying to sell it a nuclear plant, "We are concerned that as more utilities start building nuclear plants, the price of nuclear fuels will go up more quickly than will the prices of fossil fuels." To get the sale, Eastinghouse agreed to sell AmEd all the fuel it needed to run its plant at a price equal to (a) the 1965 price multiplied by (b) the ratio of (i) the Producer Price Index for the year in which the fuel was to be delivered to (ii) the Producer Price Index for the year 1965. (The Producer Price Index is measure of inflation similar to the Consumer Price Index but based on the price of raw materials rather than the price of goods and services used by consumers.)

Things went well until 1976, when inspired by the success of the Organization of Petroleum Exporting Countries ("OPEC"), the countries where uranium was mined formed a cartel, and the price of nuclear fuel quadrupled. Eastinghouse refused to honor its contract with AmEd, claiming that the formation of the cartel made performance under the terms of its contract impracticable.

It is 1976. You are a clerk to a United States District Judge. Eastinghouse has filed in your court a declaratory judgment action seeking to have the court declare that Eastinghouse is not bound to perform under the terms of its contract.

Advise the judge as to the way she should rule on the issue of whether U.C.C. § 2–615 relieves Eastinghouse of its obligation to supply fuel at the contract price. *No, could have contracted provision to protect from rising nuclear fuel prices*

PROBLEM 27-2

(a)   Farmer and Broker enter into a contract under the terms of which Farmer agreed to sell and Broker agreed to buy 100,000 bushels of wheat at a price of $3.00 per bushel. Some time thereafter, Farmer's crop was wiped out by a dust storm, something that had never before happened in that area. Farmer did not deliver the wheat even though wheat was available on the open market at a price of $3.50 per bushel. Farmer claims that the doctrine of impracticability relieved her of her obligation to deliver the wheat. Is she correct? *No? Alternative avail*

(b)   Suppose that when Broker offered Farmer the contract, Farmer had asked to have it changed so that instead of "100,000 bushels of wheat," it read "100,000 bushels of wheat grown by Farmer on her land." How would that affect the outcome?   *Impossible to perform*

KRELL V. HENRY

Court of Appeal
2 K.B. 740 (1903)

[When Queen Victoria died in 1901 and her son ascended the throne as King Edward VII, the British public was looking forward to a spectacular coronation. Mr. Krell was going to be out of London and told his solicitor to rent his rooms while he was gone. The apartment overlooked the route of the coronation parade, so the solicitor put the place up for rent as a party suite for the two-day coronation. Mr. Henry took it for a price of £75 (equivalent to over $3,000 today) for the two days. He paid £25 before the coronation was postponed due to an attack of appendicitis by the heir to the throne. He refused to pay the remaining £ 50, and Krell sued.—Eds.]

facts

[1]   Appeal from a decision of Darling J. . . . [who] held, upon the authority of *Taylor v. Caldwell . . .* that there was an implied condition in the contract that the procession should take place, and gave judgment for the defendant on the claim and counterclaim.

The plaintiff appealed.

[2]   [Counsel for the plaintiff argued:] In the contract nothing is said about the coronation procession, but it is admitted that both parties expected that there would be a procession, and that the price to be paid for the rooms was fixed with reference to the expected procession. Darling J. held that both the claim and the counter-claim were governed by *Taylor v. Caldwell . . .* , and that there was an implied term in the contract that the procession should take place. It is submitted that the learned judge was wrong. If he was right, the result will be that in every case of this kind an unremunerated promissor will be in effect an insurer of the hopes and expectations of the promissee. . . . There was, of course, the risk that the procession, the anticipation of which gave the room a marketable value, might, from some cause or other, never take place; but that risk passed to the defendant by the contract. On entering into the contract with the defendant the plaintiff put it out of his power to let the room to anyone else: he passed the right and the risk at the same time. No implied condition can be imported into the contract that the object of it shall be attained. There can be no implied condition that the defendant shall be placed in the actual position of seeing the procession . . . The contract here is absolute, and the defendant has not, as he might have done, guarded himself against the risk by suitable words.

not protected in contract though

[3]   [Counsel for the defendant argued:] The defendant abandons his counter-claim for £25, so that the sole question is as to his liability for the £50. . . . The price agreed to be paid must be regarded: it is equivalent to many thousands a year. What explanation can be given of that, except that it was agreed to be paid for the purpose of enabling the defendant to see

the procession? It was the absolute assumption of both parties when entering into the contract that the procession would pass. . . .

[4] VAUGHAN WILLIAMS L.J. read the following written judgment:— The real question in this case is the extent of the application in English law of the principle of the Roman law which has been adopted and acted on in many English decisions, and notably in the case of *Taylor v. Caldwell* . . . Thus far it is clear that the principle of Roman law has been introduced into the English law. The doubt in the present case arises as to how far this principle extends. The Roman law dealt with obligations *de certo corpore*. Whatever may have been the limits of the Roman law, the case of *Nickoll v. Ashton* . . . makes it plain that the English law applies the principle not only to cases where the performance of the contract becomes impossible by the cessation of existence of the thing which is the subject matter of the contract, but also to cases where the event which renders the contract incapable of performance is the cessation or nonexistence of an express condition or state of things, going to the root of the contract, and essential to its performance. It is said, on the one side, that the specified thing, state of things, or condition the continued existence of which is necessary for the fulfillment of the contract, so that the parties entering into the contract must have contemplated the continued existence of that thing, condition, or state of things as the foundation of what was to be done under the contract, is limited to things which are either the subject matter of the contract or a condition or state of things, present or anticipated, which is expressly mentioned in the contract. But, on the other side, it is said that the condition or state of things need not be expressly specified, but that it is sufficient if that condition or state of things clearly appears by extrinsic evidence to have been assumed by the parties to be the foundation or basis of the contract, and the event which causes the impossibility is of such a character that it cannot reasonably be supposed to have been in the contemplation of the contracting parties when the contract was made. In such a case the contracting parties will not be held bound by the general words which, though large enough to include, were not used with reference to a possibility of a particular event rendering performance of the contract impossible. I do not think that the principle of the civil law as introduced into the English law is limited to cases in which the event causing the impossibility of performance is the destruction or nonexistence of some thing which is the subject matter of the contract or of some condition or state of things expressly specified as a condition of it. I think that you first have to ascertain, inferences, drawn from surrounding circumstances recognized by both contracting parties, what is the substance of the contract, and then to ask the question whether that substantial contract needs for its foundation the assumption of the general words, and in such case, if the contract becomes impossible of performance by reason of the nonexistence of the state of things assumed by both contracting parties as the foundation of the contract, there will be no breach of the contract thus

limited. Now what are the facts of the present case? The contract is contained in two letters of June 20 which passed between the defendant and the plaintiff's agent, Mr. Cecil Bisgood. These letters did not mention the coronation, but speak merely of the taking of Mr. Krell's chambers, or, rather, of the use of them, in the daytime of June 26 and 27, for the sum of 75£, 25£ then paid, balance 50£[10] to be paid on the 14th. But the affidavits, which by agreement between the parties are to be taken as stating the facts of the case, show that the plaintiff exhibited on his premises, third floor, 56A, Pall Mall, an announcement to the effect that the windows to view the Royal coronation procession were to be let, and that the defendant was induced by that announcement to apply to the housekeeper on the premises, who said that the owner was willing to let the suite of rooms for the purpose of seeing the Royal procession for both days, but not nights of June 26 and 27. In my judgment the use of rooms was let and taken for the purpose of seeing the Royal procession. . . . I think that the coronation procession was the foundation of this contract, and that the non-happening of it prevented the performance of the contract; and secondly, I think that the non-happening of the procession, to use the words of Sir James Hannen in *Baily v. De Crespigny* . . . , was an event "of such character that it cannot reasonably be supposed to have been in the contemplation of the contracting parties when the contract was made, and that they are not be held bound by general words which, though large enough to include, were not used with reference to the possibility of the particular contingency which afterwards happened." The test seems to be whether the event which causes the impossibility was or might have been anticipated and guarded against. It seems difficult to say, in a case where both parties anticipate the happening of an event, which anticipation is the foundation of the contract, that either party must be taken to have anticipated, and ought to have guarded against, the event which prevented the performances of the contract. . . . I myself am clearly of the opinion that in this case, where we have to ask ourselves whether the object of the contract was frustrated by the nonhappening of the coronation and its procession of the days proclaimed, parol evidence is admissible to show that the subject of the contract was rooms to view the coronation procession, and was so to the knowledge of both parties. When once this is established, I see no difficulty whatever in the case. It is not essential to the application of the principle of *Taylor v. Caldwell* . . . that the direct subject of the contract should perish or fail to be in existence at the date of performance of the contract. It is sufficient if a state of things or condition which fails and prevents the achievement of that which was, in the contemplation of both parties, the foundation of the contract, is not expressly mentioned either as a condition of the principle of *Taylor v. Caldwell* . . . ought to be applied. This disposes of the plaintiff's claim for £50 unpaid balance of the price agreed to be paid

---

[10] [50£ in 1903 pounds is roughly the equivalent of 5,274£ in 2019 pounds using the CPI and the GNP Deflator.—Eds.]

for the use of the rooms. The defendant at one time set up a cross-claim for the return of the £25 to be paid at the date of the contract. As that claim is now withdrawn it is unnecessary to say anything about it. . . . I think this appeal ought to be dismissed.

[5] ROMER L.J. With some doubt I have also come to the conclusion that this case is governed by the principle on which *Taylor v. Caldwell* . . . was decided, and accordingly that the appeal must be dismissed. The doubt I have felt was whether the parties to the contract now before us could be said, under the circumstances, not to have had at all in their contemplation the risk that for some reason or other the coronation procession might not take place on the days fixed, or, if the processions took place, might not pass so as to be capable of being viewed from the rooms mentioned in the contract; and whether, under this contract, that risk was not undertaken by the defendant. But on the question of fact as to what was in the contemplation of the parties at the time, I do not think it right to differ from the conclusion arrived at by Vaughan Williams L.J. in his judgment, and I do not desire to add anything to what he has said so fully and completely.

[6] STIRLING L.J. said he had had the opportunity of reading the judgment delivered by Vaughan Williams L.J., with which he entirely agreed. Though the case was one of very great difficulty, he thought it came within the principle of *Taylor v. Caldwell.*

Appeal dismissed.

LLOYD V. MURPHY

Supreme Court of California
25 Cal.2d 48, 153 P.2d 47 (1944)

TRAYNOR, J.

[1] On August 4, 1941, plaintiffs leased to defendant for a five-year term beginning September 15, 1941, certain premises located at the corner of Almont Drive and Wilshire Boulevard in the city of Beverly Hills, Los Angeles County, "for the sole purpose of conducting thereon the business of displaying and selling new automobiles (including the servicing and repairing thereof and of selling the petroleum products of a major oil company) and for no other purpose whatsoever without the written consent of the lessor" except "to make an occasional sale of a used automobile." Defendant agreed not to sublease or assign without plaintiffs' written consent. On January 1, 1942, the federal government ordered that the sale of new automobiles be discontinued. It modified this order on January 8, 1942, to permit sales to those engaged in military activities, and on January 20, 1942, it established a system of priorities restricting sales to

persons having preferential ratings of A-1-j or higher. On March 10, 1942, defendant explained the effect of these restrictions on his business to one of the plaintiffs authorized to act for the others, who orally waived the restrictions in the lease as to use and subleasing and offered to reduce the rent if defendant should be unable to operate profitably. Nevertheless defendant vacated the premises on March 15, 1942, giving oral notice of repudiation of the lease to plaintiffs, which was followed by a written notice on March 24, 1942. Plaintiffs affirmed in writing on March 26th their oral waiver and, failing to persuade defendant to perform his obligations, they rented the property to other tenants pursuant to their powers under the lease in order to mitigate damages. On May 11, 1942, plaintiffs brought this action praying for declaratory relief to determine their rights under the lease, and for judgment for unpaid rent. Following a trial on the merits, the court found that the leased premises were located on one of the main traffic arteries of Los Angeles County; that they were equipped with gasoline pumps and in general adapted for the maintenance of an automobile service station; that they contained a one-story storeroom adapted to many commercial purposes; that plaintiffs had waived the restrictions in the lease and granted defendant the right to use the premises for any legitimate purpose and to sublease to any responsible party; that defendant continues to carry on the business of selling and servicing automobiles at two other places. Defendant testified that at one of these locations he sold new automobiles exclusively and when asked if he were aware that many new automobile dealers were continuing in business replied: "Sure. It is just the location that I couldn't make a go, though, of automobiles." Although there was no finding to that effect, defendant estimated in response to inquiry by his counsel, that 90 per cent of his gross volume of business was new car sales and 10 per cent gasoline sales. The trial court held that war conditions had not terminated defendant's obligations under the lease and gave judgment for plaintiffs, declaring the lease as modified by plaintiffs' waiver to be in full force and effect, and ordered defendant to pay the unpaid rent with interest, less amounts received by plaintiffs from re-renting. Defendant brought this appeal, contending that the purpose for which the premises were leased was frustrated by the restrictions placed on the sale of new automobiles by the federal government, thereby terminating his duties under the lease.

[2] Although commercial frustration was first recognized as an excuse for nonperformance of a contractual duty by the courts of England (*Krell v. Henry* [1903] 2 K.B. 740 [C.A.]) its soundness has been questioned by those courts, arguing that *Krell v. Henry, supra,* was a misapplication of *Taylor v. Caldwell,* 3 B. & S 826 [1863], the leading case on impossibility as an excuse for nonperformance, and they have refused to apply the doctrine to leases on the ground that an estate is conveyed to the lessee, which carries with it all risks. Many courts, therefore, in the United States have held that the tenant bears all risks as owner of the estate, but the

modern cases have recognized that the defense may be available in a proper case, even in a lease. As the author declares in 6 Williston, Contracts (rev. ed. 1938), § 1955, pp. 5485–87,

> The fact that a lease is a conveyance and not simply a continuing contract and the numerous authorities enforcing liability to pay rent in spite of destruction of leased premises, however, have made it difficult to give relief. That the tenant has been relieved, nevertheless, in several cases indicates the gravitation of the law toward a recognition of the principle that fortuitous destruction of the value of performance wholly outside the contemplation of the parties may excuse a promisor even in a lease. . . .

Even more clearly with respect to leases than in regard to ordinary contracts the applicability of the doctrine of frustration depends on the total or nearly total destruction of the purpose for which, in the contemplation of both parties, the transaction was entered into.

[3]   The principles of frustration have been repeatedly applied to leases by the courts of this state and the question is whether the excuse for nonperformance is applicable under the facts of the present case.

[4]   Although the doctrine of frustration is akin to the doctrine of impossibility of performance since both have developed from the commercial necessity of excusing performance in cases of extreme hardship, frustration is not a form of impossibility even under the modern definition of that term, which includes not only cases of physical impossibility but also cases of extreme impracticability of performance (*see Mineral Park Land Co. v. Howard,* 172 Cal. 289). Performance remains possible but the expected value of performance to the party seeking to be excused has been destroyed by a fortuitous event, which supervenes to cause an actual but not literal failure of consideration. *Krell v. Henry, supra.*

[5]   The question in cases involving frustration is whether the equities of the case, considered in the light of sound public policy, require placing the risk of a disruption or complete destruction of the contract equilibrium on defendant or plaintiff under the circumstances of a given case and the answer depends on whether an unanticipated circumstance, the risk of which should not be fairly thrown on the promisor, has made performance vitally different from what was reasonably to be expected. The purpose of a contract is to place the risks of performance upon the promisor, and the relation of the parties, terms of the contract, and circumstances surrounding its formation must be examined to determine whether it can be fairly inferred that the risk of the event that has supervened to cause the alleged frustration was not reasonably foreseeable. If it was foreseeable there should have been provision for it in the contract, and the absence of such a provision gives rise to the inference that the risk was assumed.

[6] The doctrine of frustration has been limited to cases of extreme hardship so that businessmen, who must make their arrangements in advance, can rely with certainty on their contracts. The courts have required a promisor seeking to excuse himself from performance of his obligations to prove that the risk of the frustrating event was not reasonably foreseeable and that the value of counterperformance is totally or nearly totally destroyed, for frustration is no defense if it was foreseeable or controllable by the promisor, or if counterperformance remains valuable.

[7] Thus laws or other governmental acts that make performance unprofitable or more difficult or expensive do not excuse the duty to perform a contractual obligation. It is settled that if parties have contracted with reference to a state of war or have contemplated the risks arising from it, they may not invoke the doctrine of frustration to escape their obligations.

[8] At the time the lease in the present case was executed the National Defense Act (Public Act No. 671 of the 76th Congress [54 Stats. 601], § 2A), approved June 28, 1940, authorizing the President to allocate materials and mobilize industry for national defense, had been law for more than a year. The automotive industry was in the process of conversion to supply the needs of our growing mechanized army and to meet lend-lease commitments. Iceland and Greenland had been occupied by the army. Automobile sales were soaring because the public anticipated that production would soon be restricted. These facts were commonly known and it cannot be said that the risk of war and its consequences necessitating restriction of the production and sale of automobiles was so remote a contingency that its risk could not be foreseen by defendant, an experienced automobile dealer. Indeed, the conditions prevailing at the time the lease was executed, and the absence of any provision in the lease contracting against the effect of war, gives rise to the inference that the risk was assumed. Defendant has therefore failed to prove that the possibility of war and its consequences on the production and sale of new automobiles was an unanticipated circumstance wholly outside the contemplation of the parties.

[9] Nor has defendant sustained the burden of proving that the value of the lease has been destroyed. The sale of automobiles was not made impossible or illegal but merely restricted and if governmental regulation does not entirely prohibit the business to be carried on in the leased premises but only limits or restricts it, thereby making it less profitable and more difficult to continue, the lease is not terminated or the lessee excused from further performance. Defendant may use the premises for the purpose for which they were leased. New automobiles and gasoline continue to be sold. Indeed, defendant testified that he continued to sell new automobiles exclusively at another location in the same county.

[10] Defendant contends that the lease is restrictive and that the government orders therefore destroyed its value and frustrated its purpose. Provisions that prohibit subleasing or other uses than those specified affect the value of a lease and are to be considered in determining whether its purpose has been frustrated or its value destroyed (*see* Owens, The Effect of the War Upon the Rights and Liabilities of Parties to a Contract, 19 California State Bar Journal 132, 143). It must not be forgotten, however, that "The landlord has not covenanted that the tenant shall have the right to carry on the contemplated business or that the business to which the premises are by their nature or by the terms of the lease restricted shall be profitable enough to enable the tenant to pay the rent but has imposed a condition for his own benefit; and, certainly, unless and until he chooses to take advantage of it, the tenant is not deprived of the use of the premises." (6 Williston, Contracts, op. cit. supra, § 1955, p. 5485; *see, also, People v. Klopstock,* 24 Cal.2d 897, 901 [151 P.2d 641].) In the present lease plaintiffs reserved the rights that defendant should not use the premises for other purposes than those specified in the lease or sublease without plaintiffs' written consent. Far from preventing other uses or subleasing they waived these rights, enabling defendant to use the premises for any legitimate purpose and to sublease them to any responsible tenant. This waiver is significant in view of the location of the premises on a main traffic artery in Los Angeles County and their adaptability for many commercial purposes. The value of these rights is attested by the fact that the premises were rented soon after defendants vacated them. It is therefore clear that the governmental restrictions on the sale of new cars have not destroyed the value of the lease. Furthermore, plaintiffs offered to lower the rent if defendant should be unable to operate profitably, and their conduct was at all times fair and cooperative.

[11] The consequences of applying the doctrine of frustration to a leasehold involving less than a total or nearly total destruction of the value of the leased premises would be undesirable. Confusion would result from different decisions purporting to define "substantial" frustration. Litigation would be encouraged by the repudiation of leases when lessees found their businesses less profitable because of the regulations attendant upon a national emergency. Many leases have been affected in varying degrees by the widespread governmental regulations necessitated by war conditions.

* * *

[12] No case has been cited by defendant or disclosed by research in which an appellate court has excused a lessee from performance of his duty to pay rent when the purpose of the lease has not been totally destroyed or

its accomplishment rendered extremely impracticable or where it has been shown that the lease remains valuable to the lessee.

The judgment is affirmed.

NOTES AND QUESTIONS

1. In paragraphs [2] and [3] the court addresses the question of whether the doctrine of frustration of purpose applies to leases. What was the basis for thinking that it might not?

2. In *Alabama Football, Inc. v. Greenwood*, 452 F. Supp. 1191 (W.D. Pa. 1978), L.C. Greenwood was sued because he had repudiated his contract to play for a start-up football league and returned to the Pittsburgh Steelers football team. At trial, Greenwood showed that the team had, in effect, folded. Its uniforms had been repossessed and its franchise had been terminated. The court said: "This would appear to be an appropriate situation for the application of the doctrine of commercial frustration recognized in Section 288 the Restatement of the Law of Contracts." It cited another case in which a court in Texas had applied the doctrine in favor of another player in the same league. Nevertheless the court refused to apply the doctrine because it had not yet been recognized by the courts of Alabama, under whose law the case was being decided. (Greenwood did win on other grounds, though.)

PROBLEM 27-3

Farmer and Ginning Company entered into a contract under the terms of which Farmer agreed to sell, and Ginning Company agreed to buy, 100,000 pounds of cotton at a price of 65 cents per pound. After the contract was made, India and Pakistan got into a war and India's cotton fields were nuked. Then most of the American cotton crop was destroyed by a newly mutated insecticide-resistant boll weevil. Farmer, who expected to be able to harvest 400,000 pounds of cotton on her land, was only able to harvest 100,000 pounds.

There is a silver lining to all this, however. Because cotton is in extremely short supply and because the tense international situation has caused the military to order much more cotton for uniforms, the market price of cotton has gone from 65 cents a pound to $3.00 a pound. Farmer has asked your opinion as to whether she can get out of her contract with Broker on the basis of (i) impracticability or (ii) frustration of purpose. Assume it is clear that no one could have foreseen the war, the boll weevil, or the increased demand for cotton. Note, also, that there is another fact you need to get from Farmer. *See* U.C.C. § 2–615(b).

CHAPTER 28

GOOD FAITH

∎ ∎ ∎

A Few Rules About Good Faith

The following is a list of statements about the obligation of good faith that have been articulated in the cases that follow. The rules are not consistent with each other, and almost every one of them has been rejected in at least one of the cases. Nevertheless, they probably provide the best framework for analyzing the law in this area because courts not only fail to agree on a standard for good faith, they fail to agree on what the issues are.

1. There is a general obligation of good faith that applies to all contracts.

2. A party to a contract has a duty to avoid doing anything that will injure the ability of the other party to receive the contemplated benefits.

3. It is impossible to say exactly what good faith is, but it consists of avoiding conduct which does not conform to accepted notions of decency, fairness, and reasonableness. (This formulation is generally credited to Professor Summers and seems to have been adopted in R2d § 205.)

4. Good faith means avoiding "opportunistic behavior," which is in turn defined as using a contract term to get an unbargained-for advantage, usually because of circumstances not contemplated when the contract was made.

5. The obligation of good faith does not override the express terms of the contract.

6. The obligation of good faith should not be used to protect parties from things they should have protected themselves from when they negotiated and drafted the contract.

With that orientation, we turn to the fuzzy doctrine of the duty of good faith and fair dealing, whose existence is clear but whose parameters are ill defined. As Ernest Hemingway is reported to have said: "What is moral is what you feel good after and what is immoral is what you feel bad after." This is a largely subjective area of contract law, and it is fair to say it differs not only jurisdiction-to-jurisdiction but judge-to-judge.

SCHOOLCRAFT V. ROSS

Court of Appeal of California
81 Cal. App. 3d 75, 146 Cal. Rptr. 57 (1978)

HOPPER, ASSOCIATE JUSTICE.

[1] We here consider the issue of application of proceeds from fire insurance under the terms of a deed of trust as between the trustor and the beneficiary. We hold that the right of a beneficiary to apply insurance proceeds to the balance of a note secured by a deed of trust must be performed in good faith and with fair dealing and that to the extent the security is not impaired the beneficiary must permit those proceeds to be used for the cost of rebuilding.

[2] In April 1974 the plaintiffs purchased a home from defendant Ross and executed a promissory note secured by a deed of trust naming her as beneficiary with defendant Modesto Title Guaranty as trustee. The purchase price was $14,500, and the terms of the note require plaintiffs to pay $100 monthly installments. The house was destroyed by a fire in January 1975. At that time $13,585.01 was owed on the house.

[3] Plaintiffs had purchased a fire insurance policy from the Hartford Insurance Company that provided them with two options if a loss occurred. The options were that the plaintiffs had a choice of collecting the cash value of the house at the time of the loss, which was $8,250, or, alternatively, they could rebuild the house and receive reimbursement from the insurance company of up to $14,100.

[4] The deed of trust provided in part:

A. To protect the security of this deed of trust trustor agrees:

> 1. . . . to complete or restore promptly and in good and workmanlike manner any building which may be constructed, damaged or destroyed thereon and to pay all claims for labor performed and materials furnished. . . .
>
> 2. To provide to Beneficiary fire insurance satisfactory to and with loss payable to Beneficiary. The amount collected under any fire insurance policy may be applied by Beneficiary upon any indebtedness secured hereby or at the option of the Beneficiary, the entire amount so collected or any part thereof may be released to Trustor.

[5] After the fire the plaintiffs decided to rebuild the house. They contacted Hartford Insurance Company, informed it of their decision, and later received a check for $8,250. The check was payable to defendant Ross and plaintiffs, thereby requiring the endorsement of all parties before it

could be negotiated. The insurance company informed the plaintiffs that the balance of the $14,100 would be paid upon completion of the new house.

[6] Defendant Ross refused to permit the proceeds to be used for rebuilding the house. Instead, she invoked the clause in the trust deed allowing her to retain insurance proceeds. Since the plaintiffs did not have a place to live, they could not afford to make the $100 monthly payments and rent an apartment also. Consequently, they were forced to cease payment on the note. Defendant Ross instructed the trustee to begin foreclosure proceedings and the property was ultimately sold at a private sale to defendant Ross for $600. She later resold it for $6,000.

[7] At trial the plaintiffs introduced evidence that a new home could have been constructed for $14,100 that would have had a fair market value of $20,000 upon completion because of the rise in property values. They also indicated that they were willing to sell the new home as soon as it was completed, remit the balance of the note to defendant Ross and keep their own equity of approximately $6,000. Their lawsuit asked for the damages they incurred because of defendant Ross' refusal to permit the rebuilding of the home. Judgment was awarded in favor of the plaintiffs for $4,500[1] plus costs. Attorney fees for plaintiffs were denied. Defendant Ross appeals from the judgment against her; plaintiffs appeal from the denial of attorney fees.

[8] This appears to be a case of first impression in California. The cases in other jurisdictions are in conflict.

[9] The trial court in this case, relying upon *Milstein v. Security Pac. Nat. Bank,* 27 Cal.App.3d 482, 103 Cal.Rptr. 16 (1972), concluded that the deed of trust was subject to an implied covenant requiring good faith and fair dealing on the part of the beneficiary, Maude Ross; that the beneficiary breached that implied covenant and awarded damages to plaintiffs in the sum of $4,500. We agree.

[10] In *Milstein*, the County of Los Angeles condemned 10 feet off the front of a commercial building and placed the estimated value of the condemned property into court. That building was owned by Milstein, who had given a deed of trust to Security Pacific. Security Pacific claimed that, under the terms of the deed of trust, it was entitled to enough of the condemnation proceeds to satisfy the outstanding promissory note and deed of trust. Milstein took the position that since Security Pacific's security was not impaired by the condemnation, it could not have a right to exercise its option under the deed of trust.

[11] The *Milstein* court held that the beneficiary was bound by an implied covenant to exercise his option reasonably and to claim the award

---

[1] [$4,500 in 1978 dollars is roughly the equivalent of $17,300 in 2019 dollars using the CPI and the GNP Deflator.—Eds.]

only to the extent his security was impaired. That same principle should apply to insurance proceeds. While the language in the deed of trust in this case differs slightly from the instrument in *Milstein*, in both situations the provisions were designed to accomplish the same ends.

[12] "In every contract there is an implied covenant of good faith and fair dealing that neither party will do anything which injures the right of the other to receive the benefits of the agreement." *Brown v. Superior Court* (1949) 34 Cal.2d 559, 564, 212 P.2d 878, 881, also quoted with approval in *Murphy v. Allstate Ins. Co.* (1976) 17 Cal.3d 937, 940, 132 Cal.Rptr. 424, 553 P.2d 584. The implied covenant imposes upon each party the obligation to do everything that the contract presupposes they will do to accomplish its purpose.

[13] As *Milstein* points out, the purpose of a deed of trust is that the borrower will have the use of funds loaned on specific terms and the lender will have the right to a specified repayment that is secured by the deed of trust. The lender does not have the right to unilaterally cut off the borrower's right to use the loaned funds unless he can show that his security is impaired. Here there is no evidence that the security was impaired by the fire nor is there any evidence that plaintiffs were unwilling or unable to continue making payments on the property. The sole reason advanced for defendant Ross' conduct was that she was old and sick and needed the money immediately to take care of her medical needs.

[14] The trial court in this case properly concluded on substantial evidence that the security was not impaired and that the beneficiary failed to act in accordance with the implied covenant of the deed of trust, all to plaintiffs' damages in the sum awarded.

[15] As in *Milstein*, the two clauses in the deed of trust must be construed to avoid the unintended acceleration of the note. The parties intended that the purchase price would be paid in the ordinary course of events to the end that plaintiffs could enjoy the full use of the house, subject to the required monthly payments. Forcing the buyer to pay off in advance would result in a buyer losing certain property rights contemplated by the parties, among them the benefit of a long-term loan which permits the buyer to spread the purchase price of the property over a long time.

[16] Counsel for defendant Ross' reference to his client having acted in good faith misses the mark. The covenant in this case does not mean good faith in the abstract, but, instead, refers to the purpose of the particular contract. To reiterate: To the extent the security was not impaired, defendant Ross had no right to the funds.

———

NOTES AND QUESTIONS

1.   If your house burned down and you went to the bank to borrow money to rebuild it, they wouldn't give you all the money all at once. They would give you enough to clear away the rubble and rebuild the foundation. When that was done, an inspector would come around and look at the property. If she was satisfied that the work so far had been up to standards, she would report that fact to the bank and they would give you the money for the next phase of construction. The process would be repeated (four or five times in the case of a small house, many more times in the case of a larger project) until construction was complete. The purpose is to keep the bank from giving out all the money and finding that what they have for security is a half-built house (construction projects are notorious for going over budget) or one that is shoddily built. How could Ms. Ross protect herself against these risks?

2.   As you can imagine, *Schoolcraft* caused considerable consternation among California (and other) lawyers who represented lenders. They pulled out their standard trust deed forms and started drafting. What would you say in such a document to be sure your lender client was protected?

3.   A general duty of good faith and fair dealing in all contracts is not universally recognized. The Texas Supreme Court, for example, rejected the *Schoolcraft* approach in *English v. Fischer*, 660 S.W.2d 521 (Tex. 1983), a case with facts almost identical to *Schoolcraft*. The court said:

> This concept is contrary to our well-reasoned and long-established adversary system which has served us ably in Texas for almost 150 years. Our system permits parties who have a dispute over a contract to present their case to an impartial tribunal for a determination of the agreement as made by the parties and embodied in the contract itself. To adopt the laudatory sounding theory of "good faith and fair dealing" would place a party under the onerous threat of treble damages should he seek to compel his adversary to perform according to the contract terms as agreed upon by the parties. The novel concept advocated by the courts below would abolish our system of government according to settled rules of law and let each case be decided upon what might seem "fair and in good faith," by each fact finder. This we are unwilling to do.

MARKET STREET ASSOCS. LTD. PARTNERSHIP V. FREY

United States Court of Appeals, Seventh Circuit
941 F.2d 588 (1991)

POSNER, CIRCUIT JUDGE.

[1]   Market Street Associates Limited Partnership and its general partner appeal from a judgment for the defendants, General Electric Pension Trust and its trustees, entered upon cross-motions for summary

judgment in a diversity suit that pivots on the doctrine of "good faith" performance of a contract. Cf. Robert Summers, " 'Good Faith' in General Contract Law and the Sales Provisions of the Uniform Commercial Code," 54 *Va. L. Rev.* 195, 232–43 (1968). Wisconsin law applies—common law rather than Uniform Commercial Code, because the contract is for land rather than for goods, and because it is a lease rather than a sale and Wisconsin has not adopted UCC art. 2A, which governs leases.[2] But before we can get to the substance of the dispute we need to consider a jurisdictional and a procedural question.[3]

* * *

[2]   We come at last to the contract dispute out of which the case arises. In 1968, J.C. Penney Company, the retail chain, entered into a sale and leaseback arrangement with General Electric Pension Trust in order to finance Penney's growth. Under the arrangement Penney sold properties to the pension trust which the trust then leased back to Penney for a term of 25 years. Paragraph 34 of the lease entitles the lessee to "request Lessor [the pension trust] to finance the costs and expenses of construction of additional Improvements upon the Premises," provided the amount of the costs and expenses is at least $250,000. Upon receiving the request, the pension trust "agrees to give reasonable consideration to providing the financing of such additional Improvements and Lessor and Lessee shall negotiate in good faith concerning the construction of such Improvements and the financing by Lessor of such costs and expenses." Paragraph 34 goes on to provide that, should the negotiations fail, the lessee shall be entitled to repurchase the property at a price roughly equal to the price at which Penney sold it to the pension trust in the first place, plus 6 percent a year for each year since the original purchase. So if the average annual appreciation in the property exceeded 6 percent, a breakdown in negotiations over the financing of improvements would entitle Penney to buy back the property for less than its market value (assuming it had sold the property to the pension trust in the first place at its then market value).

[3]   One of these leases was for a shopping center in Milwaukee. In 1987 Penney assigned this lease to Market Street Associates, which the following year received an inquiry from a drugstore chain that wanted to open a store in the shopping center, provided (as is customary) that Market Street Associates built the store for it. Whether Market Street Associates was pessimistic about obtaining financing from the pension trust, still the lessor of the shopping center, or for other reasons, it initially sought financing for the project from other sources. But they were unwilling to lend the necessary funds without a mortgage on the shopping center, which

---

2   [U.C.C. Art. 2A would not apply even if Wisconsin had adopted it. U.C.C. Art. 2A governs only leases of *goods*.—Eds.]

3   [The court's discussion of these questions is omitted.—Eds.]

Market Street Associates could not give because it was not the owner but only the lessee. It decided therefore to try to buy the property back from the pension trust. Market Street Associates' general partner, Orenstein, tried to call David Erb of the pension trust, who was responsible for the property in question. Erb did not return his calls, so Orenstein wrote him, expressing an interest in buying the property and asking him to "review your file on this matter and call me so that we can discuss it further." At first, Erb did not reply. Eventually Orenstein did reach Erb, who promised to review the file and get back to him. A few days later an associate of Erb called Orenstein and indicated an interest in selling the property for $3 million, which Orenstein considered much too high.

[4] That was in June of 1988. On July 28, Market Street Associates wrote a letter to the pension trust formally requesting funding for $2 million in improvements to the shopping center. The letter made no reference to paragraph 34 of the lease; indeed, it did not mention the lease. The letter asked Erb to call Orenstein to discuss the matter. Erb, in what was becoming a habit of unresponsiveness, did not call. On August 16, Orenstein sent a second letter—certified mail, return receipt requested— again requesting financing and this time referring to the lease, though not expressly to paragraph 34. The heart of the letter is the following two sentences: "The purpose of this letter is to ask again that you advise us immediately if you are willing to provide the financing pursuant to the lease. If you are willing, we propose to enter into negotiation to amend the ground lease appropriately." The very next day, Market Street Associates received from Erb a letter, dated August 10, turning down the original request for financing on the ground that it did not "meet our current investment criteria:" the pension trust was not interested in making loans for less than $7 million. On August 22, Orenstein replied to Erb by letter, noting that his letter of August 10 and Erb's letter of August 16 had evidently crossed in the mails, expressing disappointment at the turn-down, and stating that Market Street Associates would seek financing elsewhere. That was the last contact between the parties until September 27, when Orenstein sent Erb a letter stating that Market Street Associates was exercising the option granted it by paragraph 34 to purchase the property upon the terms specified in that paragraph in the event that negotiations over financing broke down.

[5] The pension trust refused to sell, and this suit to compel specific performance followed. Apparently the price computed by the formula in paragraph 34 is only $1 million. The market value must be higher, or Market Street Associates wouldn't be trying to coerce conveyance at the paragraph 34 price; whether it is as high as $3 million, however, the record does not reveal.

[6] The district judge granted summary judgment for the pension trust on two grounds that he believed to be separate although closely

related. The first was that, by failing in its correspondence with the pension trust to mention paragraph 34 of the lease, Market Street Associates had prevented the negotiations over financing that are a condition precedent to the lessee's exercise of the purchase option from taking place. Second, this same failure violated the duty of good faith, which the common law of Wisconsin, as of other states, reads into every contract. In support of both grounds the judge emphasized a statement by Orenstein in his deposition that it had occurred to him that Erb mightn't know about paragraph 34, though this was unlikely (Orenstein testified) because Erb or someone else at the pension trust would probably check the file and discover the paragraph and realize that if the trust refused to negotiate over the request for financing, Market Street Associates, as Penney's assignee, would be entitled to walk off with the property for (perhaps) a song. The judge inferred that Market Street Associates didn't want financing from the pension trust—that it just wanted an opportunity to buy the property at a bargain price and hoped that the pension trust wouldn't realize the implications of turning down the request for financing. Market Street Associates should, the judge opined, have advised the pension trust that it was requesting financing pursuant to paragraph 34, so that the trust would understand the penalty for refusing to negotiate.

[7] We begin our analysis by setting to one side two extreme contentions by the parties. The pension trust argues that the option to purchase created by paragraph 34 cannot be exercised until negotiations over financing break down; there were no negotiations; therefore they did not break down; therefore Market Street Associates had no right to exercise the option. This argument misreads the contract. Although the option to purchase is indeed contingent, paragraph 34 requires the pension trust, upon demand by the lessee for the financing of improvements worth at least $250,000, "to give reasonable consideration to providing the financing." The lessor who fails to give reasonable consideration and thereby prevents the negotiations from taking place is breaking the contract; and a contracting party cannot be allowed to use his own breach to gain an advantage by impairing the rights that the contract confers on the other party. Often, it is true, if one party breaks the contract, the other can walk away from it without liability, can in other words exercise self-help. But he is not required to follow that course. He can stand on his contract rights.

[8] But what exactly are those rights in this case? The contract entitles the lessee to reasonable consideration of its request for financing, and only if negotiations over the request fail is the lessee entitled to purchase the property at the price computed in accordance with paragraph 34. It might seem therefore that the proper legal remedy for a lessor's breach that consists of failure to give the lessee's request for financing reasonable consideration would not be an order that the lessor sell the property to the lessee at the paragraph 34 price, but an order that the

lessor bargain with the lessee in good faith. But we do not understand the pension trust to be arguing that Market Street Associates is seeking the wrong remedy. We understand it to be arguing that Market Street Associates has no possible remedy. That is an untenable position.

[9] Market Street Associates argues, with equal unreason as it seems to us, that it could not have broken the contract because paragraph 34 contains no express requirement that in requesting financing the lessee mention the lease or paragraph 34 or otherwise alert the lessor to the consequences of his failing to give reasonable consideration to granting the request. There is indeed no such requirement (all that the contract requires is a demand). But no one says there is. The pension trust's argument, which the district judge bought, is that either as a matter of simple contract interpretation or under the compulsion of the doctrine of good faith, a provision requiring Market Street Associates to remind the pension trust of paragraph 34 should be read into the lease.

[10] It seems to us that these are one ground rather than two. A court has to have a reason to interpolate a clause into a contract. The only reason that has been suggested here is that it is necessary to prevent Market Street Associates from reaping a reward for what the pension trust believes to have been Market Street's bad faith. So we must consider the meaning of the contract duty of "good faith." The Wisconsin cases are cryptic as to its meaning though emphatic about its existence, so we must cast our net wider. We do so mindful of Learned Hand's warning, that "such words as 'fraud,' 'good faith,' 'whim,' 'caprice,' 'arbitrary action,' and 'legal fraud' . . . obscure the issue." *Thompson-Starrett Co. v. La Belle Iron Works*, 17 F.2d 536, 541 (2d Cir. 1927). Indeed they do. The particular confusion to which the vaguely moralistic overtones of "good faith" give rise is the belief that every contract establishes a fiduciary relationship. A fiduciary is required to treat his principal as if the principal were he, and therefore he may not take advantage of the principal's incapacity, ignorance, inexperience, or even naivete. If Market Street Associates were the fiduciary of General Electric Pension Trust, then (we may assume) it could not take advantage of Mr. Erb's apparent ignorance of paragraph 34, however exasperating Erb's failure to return Orenstein's phone calls was and however negligent Erb or his associates were in failing to read the lease before turning down Orenstein's request for financing.

[11] But it is unlikely that Wisconsin wishes, in the name of good faith, to make every contract signatory his brother's keeper, especially when the brother is the immense and sophisticated General Electric Pension Trust, whose lofty indifference to small (less than $7 million) transactions is the signifier of its grandeur. In fact the law contemplates that people frequently will take advantage of the ignorance of those with whom they contract, without thereby incurring liability. *Restatement, supra*, § 161, comment d. The duty of honesty, of good faith even expansively conceived,

is not a duty of candor. You can make a binding contract to purchase something you know your seller undervalues. *Laidlaw v. Organ*, 15 U.S. (2 Wheat.) 178, 181 n. 2, 4 L. Ed. 214 (1817); *Teamsters Local 282 Pension Trust Fund v. Angelos*, 762 F.2d 522, 528 (7th Cir. 1985); *United States v. Dial, supra*, 757 F.2d at 168; 1 *Farnsworth on Contracts, supra*, § 4.11, at pp. 406–10; Anthony T. Kronman, "Mistake, Disclosure, Information, and the Law of Contracts," 7 J. Legal Stud. 1 (1978). That of course is a question about formation, not performance, and the particular duty of good faith under examination here relates to the latter rather than to the former. But even after you have signed a contract, you are not obliged to become an altruist toward the other party and relax the terms if he gets into trouble in performing his side of the bargain. Otherwise mere difficulty of performance would excuse a contracting party—which it does not.

[12] But it is one thing to say that you can exploit your superior knowledge of the market—for if you cannot, you will not be able to recoup the investment you made in obtaining that knowledge—or that you are not required to spend money bailing out a contract partner who has gotten into trouble. It is another thing to say that you can take deliberate advantage of an oversight by your contract partner concerning his rights under the contract. Such taking advantage is not the exploitation of superior knowledge or the avoidance of unbargained-for expense; it is sharp dealing. Like theft, it has no social product, and also like theft it induces costly defensive expenditures, in the form of over-elaborate disclaimers or investigations into the trustworthiness of a prospective contract partner, just as the prospect of theft induces expenditures on locks. *See generally* Steven J. Burton, "Breach of Contract and the Common Law Duty to Perform in Good Faith," 94 Harv. L. Rev. 369, 393 (1980).

[13] The form of sharp dealing that we are discussing might or might not be actionable as fraud or deceit. That is a question of tort law and there the rule is that if the information is readily available to both parties the failure of one to disclose it to the other, even if done in the knowledge that the other party is acting on mistaken premises, is not actionable W. Page Keeton *et al.*, Prosser and Keeton on the Law of Torts § 106, at p. 737 (5th ed. 1984). All of these cases, however, with the debatable exception of *Guyer*, involve failure to disclose something in the negotiations leading up to the signing of the contract, rather than failure to disclose after the contract has been signed. (*Guyer* involved failure to disclose during the negotiations leading up to a renewal of the contract.) The distinction is important, as we explained in *Maksym v. Loesch*, 937 F.2d 1237, 1242 (7th Cir. 1991). Before the contract is signed, the parties confront each other with a natural wariness. Neither expects the other to be particularly forthcoming, and therefore there is no deception when one is not. Afterwards the situation is different. The parties are now in a cooperative relationship the costs of which will be considerably reduced by a measure

of trust. So each lowers his guard a bit, and now silence is more apt to be deceptive.

[14] Moreover, this is a contract case rather than a tort case, and conduct that might not rise to the level of fraud may nonetheless violate the duty of good faith in dealing with one's contractual partners and thereby give rise to a remedy under contract law. Burton, *supra*, at 372 n. 17. This duty is, as it were, halfway between a fiduciary duty (the duty of *utmost* good faith) and the duty merely to refrain from active fraud. Despite its moralistic overtones it is no more the injection of moral principles into contract law than the fiduciary concept itself is. Summers, *supra*, at 204–07, 265–66. It would be quixotic as well as presumptuous for judges to undertake through contract law to raise the ethical standards of the nation's business people. The concept of the duty of good faith like the concept of fiduciary duty is a stab at approximating the terms the parties would have negotiated had they foreseen the circumstances that have given rise to their dispute. The parties want to minimize the costs of performance. To the extent that a doctrine of good faith designed to do this by reducing defensive expenditures is a reasonable measure to this end, interpolating it into the contract advances the parties' joint goal.

[15] It is true that an essential function of contracts is to allocate risk, and would be defeated if courts treated the materializing of a bargained-over, allocated risk as a misfortune the burden of which is required to be shared between the parties (as it might be within a family, for example) rather than borne entirely by the party to whom the risk had been allocated by mutual agreement. But contracts do not just allocate risk. They also (or some of them) set in motion a cooperative enterprise, which may to some extent place one party at the other's mercy. "The parties to a contract are embarked on a cooperative venture, and a minimum of cooperativeness in the event unforeseen problems arise at the performance stage is required even if not an explicit duty of the contract." *AMPAT/Midwest, Inc. v. Illinois Tool Works Inc., supra*, 896 F.2d at 1041. The office of the doctrine of good faith is to forbid the kinds of opportunistic behavior that a mutually dependent, cooperative relationship might enable in the absence of rule. " 'Good faith' is a compact reference to an implied undertaking not to take opportunistic advantage in a way that could not have been contemplated at the time of drafting, and which therefore was not resolved explicitly by the parties." *Kham & Nate's Shoes No. 2, Inc. v. First Bank, supra*, 908 F.2d at 1357. The contractual duty of good faith is thus not some newfangled bit of welfare-state paternalism or (*pace* Duncan Kennedy, "Form and Substance in Private Law Adjudication," 89 *Harv. L. Rev.* 1685, 1721 (1976)) the sediment of an altruistic strain in contract law, and we are therefore not surprised to find the essentials of the modern doctrine well established in nineteenth-century cases, a few examples being *Bush v. Marshall*, 47 U.S. (6 How.) 284, 291, 12 L. Ed. 440 (1848); *Chicago, Rock*

Island & Pac. R.R. v. Howard, 74 U.S. (7 Wall.) 392, 413, 19 L. Ed. 117 (1868); *Marsh v. Masterton*, 101 N.Y. 401, 410–11, 5 N.E. 59, 63 (1886), and *Uhrig v. Williamsburg City Fire Ins. Co.*, 101 N.Y. 362, 4 N.E. 745 (1886).

[16] The emphasis we are placing on postcontractual versus precontractual conduct helps explain the pattern that is observed when the duty of contractual good faith is considered in all its variety, encompassing not only good faith in the *performance* of a contract but also good faith in its *formation*, Summers, *supra*, at 220–32, and in its *enforcement. Harbor Ins. Co. v. Continental Bank Corp.*, 922 F.2d 357, 363 (7th Cir. 1990). The formation or negotiation stage is precontractual, and here the duty is minimized. It is greater not only at the performance but also at the enforcement stage, which is also postcontractual. "A party who hokes up a phony defense to the performance of his contractual duties and then when that defense fails (at some expense to the other party) tries on another defense for size can properly be said to be acting in bad faith." *Id.* At the formation of the contract the parties are dealing in present realities; performance still lies in the future. As performance unfolds, circumstances change, often unforeseeably; the explicit terms of the contract become progressively less apt to the governance of the parties' relationship; and the role of implied conditions—and with it the scope and bite of the good-faith doctrine—grows.

[17] We could of course do without the term "good faith," and maybe even without the doctrine. We could, as just suggested, speak instead of implied conditions necessitated by the unpredictability of the future at the time the contract was made. Farnsworth, "Good Faith Performance and Commercial Reasonableness under the Uniform Commercial Code," 30 U. Chi. L. Rev. 666, 670 (1963). Suppose a party has promised work to the promisee's "satisfaction." As Learned Hand explained, "he may refuse to look at the work, or to exercise any real judgment on it, in which case he has prevented performance and excused the condition." *Thompson-Starrett Co. v. La Belle Iron Works, supra*, 17 F.2d at 541. That is, it was an implicit condition that the promise examine the work to the extent necessary to determine whether it was satisfactory; otherwise the performing party would have been placing himself at the complete mercy of the promisee. The parties didn't write this condition into the contract either because they thought such behavior unlikely or failed to foresee it altogether. In just the same way—to switch to another familiar example of the operation of the duty of good faith—parties to a requirements contract surely do not intend that if the price of the product covered by the contract rises, the buyer shall be free to increase his "requirements" so that he can take advantage of the rise in the market price over the contract price to resell the product on the open market at a guaranteed profit. *Empire Gas Corp. v. American Bakeries Co.*, 840 F.2d 1333 (7th Cir. 1988). If they fail to insert an express condition to this effect, the court will read it in, confident that the parties

would have inserted the condition if they had known what the future held. Of similar character is the implied condition that an exclusive dealer will use his best efforts to promote the supplier's goods, since otherwise the exclusive feature of the dealership contract would place the supplier at the dealer's mercy. *Wood v. Duff-Gordon*, 222 N.Y. 88, 118 N.E. 214 (1917) (Cardozo, C.J.).

[18] But whether we say that a contract shall be deemed to contain such implied conditions as are necessary to make sense of the contract, or that a contract obligates the parties to cooperate in its performance in "good faith" to the extent necessary to carry out the purposes of the contract, comes to much the same thing. They are different ways of formulating the overriding purpose of contract law, which is to give the parties what they would have stipulated for expressly if at the time of making the contract they had complete knowledge of the future and the costs of negotiating and adding provisions to the contract had been zero.

[19] The two formulations would have different meanings only if "good faith" were thought limited to "honesty in fact," an interpretation perhaps permitted but certainly not compelled by the Uniform Commercial Code, *see* Summers, *supra*, at 207–20—and anyway this is not a case governed by the UCC. We need not pursue this issue. The dispositive question in the present case is simply whether Market Street Associates tried to trick the pension trust and succeeded in doing so. If it did, this would be the type of opportunistic behavior in an ongoing contractual relationship that would violate the duty of good faith performance however the duty is formulated. There is much common sense in Judge Reynolds' conclusion that Market Street Associates did just that. The situation as he saw it was as follows. Market Street Associates didn't want financing from the pension trust (initially it had looked elsewhere, remember), and when it learned it couldn't get the financing without owning the property, it decided to try to buy the property. But the pension trust set a stiff price, so Orenstein decided to trick the pension trust into selling at the bargain price fixed in paragraph 34 by requesting financing and hoping that the pension trust would turn the request down without noticing the paragraph. His preliminary dealings with the pension trust made this hope a realistic one by revealing a sluggish and hidebound bureaucracy unlikely to have retained in its brontosaurus's memory, or to be able at short notice to retrieve, the details of a small lease made twenty years earlier. So by requesting financing without mentioning the lease Market Street Associates might well precipitate a refusal before the pension trust woke up to paragraph 34. It is true that Orenstein's second letter requested financing "pursuant to the lease." But when the next day he received a reply to his first letter indicating that the pension trust was indeed oblivious to paragraph 34, his response was to send a lulling letter designed to convince the pension trust that the matter was closed and could be

forgotten. The stage was set for his thunderbolt: the notification the next month that Market Street Associates was taking up the option in paragraph 34. Only then did the pension trust look up the lease and discover that it had been had.

[20] The only problem with this recital is that it construes the facts as favorably to the pension trust as the record will permit, and that of course is not the right standard for summary judgment. The facts must be construed as favorably to the nonmoving party, to Market Street Associates, as the record permits (that Market Street Associates filed its own motion for summary judgment is irrelevant, as we have seen). When that is done, a different picture emerges. On Market Street Associates' construal of the record, $3 million was a grossly excessive price for the property, and while $1 million might be a bargain it would not confer so great a windfall as to warrant an inference that if the pension trust had known about paragraph 34 it never would have turned down Market Street Associates' request for financing cold. And in fact the pension trust may have known about paragraph 34, and either it didn't care or it believed that unless the request mentioned that paragraph the pension trust would incur no liability by turning it down. Market Street Associates may have assumed and have been entitled to assume that in reviewing a request for financing from one of its lessees the pension trust would take the time to read the lease to see whether it bore on the request. Market Street Associates did not desire financing from the pension trust initially—that is undeniable—yet when it discovered that it could not get financing elsewhere unless it had the title to the property it may have realized that it would have to negotiate with the pension trust over financing before it could hope to buy the property at the price specified in the lease.

[21] On this interpretation of the facts there was no bad faith on the part of Market Street Associates. It acted honestly, reasonably, without ulterior motive, in the face of circumstances as they actually and reasonably appeared to it. The fault was the pension trust's incredible inattention, which misled Market Street Associates into believing that the pension trust had no interest in financing the improvements regardless of the purchase option. We do not usually excuse contracting parties from failing to read and understand the contents of their contract; and in the end what this case comes down to—or so at least it can be strongly argued—is that an immensely sophisticated enterprise simply failed to read the contract. On the other hand, such enterprises make mistakes just like the rest of us, and deliberately to take advantage of your contracting partner's mistake during the performance stage (for we are not talking about taking advantage of superior knowledge at the formation stage) is a breach of good faith. To be able to correct your contract partner's mistake at zero cost to yourself, and decide not to do so, is a species of opportunistic behavior that the parties would have expressly forbidden in the contract

had they foreseen it. The immensely long term of the lease amplified the possibility of errors but did not license either party to take advantage of them.

[22] The district judge jumped the gun in choosing between these alternative characterizations. The essential issue bearing on Market Street Associates' good faith was Orenstein's state of mind, a type of inquiry that ordinarily cannot be concluded on summary judgment, and could not be here. If Orenstein believed that Erb knew or would surely find out about paragraph 34, it was not dishonest or opportunistic to fail to flag that paragraph, or even to fail to mention the lease, in his correspondence and (rare) conversations with Erb, especially given the uninterest in dealing with Market Street Associates that Erb fairly radiated. To decide what Orenstein believed, a trial is necessary. As for the pension trust's intimation that a bench trial (for remember that this is an equity case, since the only relief sought by the plaintiff is specific performance) will add no illumination beyond what the summary judgment proceeding has done, this overlooks the fact that at trial the judge will for the first time have a chance to see the witnesses whose depositions he has read, to hear their testimony elaborated, and to assess their believability.

[23] The judgment is reversed and the case is remanded for further proceedings consistent with this opinion.

REVERSED AND REMANDED.

———

NOTES AND QUESTIONS

1.   On remand, Judge Reynolds conducted a bench trial and took testimony. After considering all the evidence, he entered findings of fact and conclusions of law substantially identical to those in his original decision of the summary judgment motion that the Posner panel of the 7th Circuit had reversed. *See Market Street Assocs. Ltd. Partnership. v. Frey*, 817 F.Supp. 784 (E.D. Wis. 1993). On appeal, again, the trial court's decision stood. *See Market Street Assocs. v. Frey*, 21 F.3d 782 (7th Cir. 1994). Judge Posner had laid out the legal standard, which the trial court had documented in application at trial, and, faced with a fully developed factual record, which is reviewed on appeal under an abuse of discretion standard, the Seventh Circuit affirmed.

2.   If you were counsel for Market Street Associates, upon discovering the paragraph 34 option, how would you go about triggering it so as to maximize the chances that General Electric Pension Trust would refuse to negotiate while still meeting or exceeding the basic standards of good faith and fair dealing as described by Judge Posner?

———

CENTRONICS CORPORATION V. GENICOM CORP.

Supreme Court of New Hampshire
132 N.H. 133, 562 A.2d 187 (1989)

SOUTER, JUSTICE.

[1] A contract between the buyer and seller of business assets provided for arbitration of any dispute about the value of the property transferred, to which the purchase price was pegged, and required an escrow deposit of a portion of the price claimed by the seller pending final valuation. The seller has charged the buyer with breach of an implied covenant of good faith in refusing, during arbitration, to release a portion of the escrow fund claimed to be free from "dispute." The Superior Court (Hollman, J.) granted summary judgment to the buyer, which we affirm.

[2] The agreement between the plaintiff-seller, Centronics Corporation and corporations related to it (Centronics), and the defendant-buyer, Genicom Corporation (Genicom), sets the purchase price at the consolidated closing net book value (CCNBV) of the assets plus four million dollars. CCNBV is defined as the value reflected in Centronics's consolidated balance sheet as of the closing date, minus certain liabilities. Because CCNBV could not be stated definitely in advance, the parties agreed to derive it by a series of steps that we describe here in a somewhat simplified distillation of their contract documents.

[3] As a basis for calculations (albeit subject to later challenge), they selected the consolidated net book value to be determined from Centronics's consolidated balance sheet as of September 28, 1986, a date prior to the closing. Within thirty days of the closing, Centronics was obliged to revise the September balance sheet to reflect the results of operations from September 29 through the closing date, and, on the basis of the revision, to compute a consolidated closing net book value and consequent purchase price. Although Centronics was bound to follow "generally accepted accounting principles" in preparing both the September balance sheet and the subsequent revision, and although Centronics was required to review the latter with the Boston office of Coopers & Lybrand before delivering the revised figure to Genicom, the agreement provided that the revised balance sheet would nonetheless be unaudited and certified only by Centronics's president or principal accounting officer.

[4] After Genicom's receipt of the revised balance sheet, the Richmond, Virginia, office of Coopers & Lybrand then had thirty days to review it on Genicom's behalf and either to accept the revision as conclusive of CCNBV and the consequent purchase price, or to propose adjustments. If the Richmond office proposed no such adjustments on Genicom's behalf, the balance sheet as revised by Centronics would determine CCNBV. If the Richmond office did propose adjustments, Centronics would then have thirty days to object to them, in default of which the balance sheet with

Genicom's proposed adjustments would be conclusive. The parties agreed that any timely dispute about the consolidated closing balance sheet or the computations based upon it would be referred to a New York accounting firm for final and binding "determination in accordance with the terms of [the] Agreement," a process that each party now describes as arbitration.

[5]   Although the parties agreed to use their best efforts to promote the resolution of disputed issues within fifteen days of their submission to the arbitrator, even on the optimistic assumption that arbitration would conclude that soon the parties faced a potential delay of more than one hundred days between closing and final calculation of the purchase price. Instead of deferring all payment for such a time or longer, they agreed that upon closing Genicom would pay Centronics an amount equal to the purchase price based on the September balance sheet, less $5,000,000 to be placed in escrow. They also agreed that if Centronics proposed revisions to the September balance sheet indicating a higher purchase price Genicom would promptly increase the escrow deposit by the difference, to be known as the Adjustment Amount.

[6]   Distribution from the escrow fund was to be governed by two sets of provisions. Insofar as the escrow agreement relates to the issue before us, it simply provided that "[i]n accordance with Section 2.07 of the Purchase Agreement, the Escrow Agent shall hold the Escrow Fund in its possession until instructed in writing" by respective New York counsel for Centronics and Genicom "to distribute the same or some portion thereof to Centronics or [Genicom] as the case may be," whereupon the escrow agent was to make the distribution as ordered. Section 2.07 of the Purchase Agreement, entitled "Final Payment of Purchase Price," began with a provision that "[f]inal settlement and payment of the Purchase Price shall be made not later than ten days after determination of [CCNBV] and computation of the Purchase Price," whether by agreement of the parties or decision of the arbitrator. There followed detailed instructions for payment out of escrow and final settlement between the parties, which are of no significance in the matter before us, being intended to provide for the payment to Centronics of whatever balance it might be owed on the purchase price, and the distribution to Genicom of any amount it might be found to have overpaid.

[7]   The parties took the first step in applying these valuation and payment provisions at the closing held on February 13, 1987. Centronics's consolidated September balance sheet showed a net book value of $72,529,000 for the assets to be transferred, to which amount $4,000,000 was added, to give a preliminary purchase price of $76,529,000. Genicom placed $5,000,000 in escrow and paid Centronics the balance of $71,529,000.

[8]   On March 30, 1987, Centronics delivered a revised balance sheet to reflect operations for the four and one-half months before the closing. The revised net book value was $83,396,000, and Genicom accordingly increased the escrow by depositing the required Adjustment Amount of $10,867,000, representing the difference between the earlier and later figures. Genicom's accountants then proposed downward adjustments to the revised figures, which would reduce the net book value, and purchase price, by $10,213,164, almost back to the earlier figure. Centronics objected, and the dispute was submitted to the arbitrator.

[9]   The arbitration had begun to drag by the summer of 1987, when Centronics sought a distribution of $5,653,836[4] from the escrow fund, being the difference between the total fund of $15,867,000 and the $10,213,164 in downward adjustments Genicom had proposed. Centronics described the amount requested as free from dispute and complained of a loss of economic opportunity to use the funds for its corporate purposes. Genicom replied that the purchase agreement provided for no distribution from escrow prior to determination of CCNBV and the final purchase price, which, as it turned out, would presumably be at the close of arbitration.

[10] Centronics responded by bringing this two-count action to recover the amount in question and consequential damages. Count one alleged that Genicom had breached implicit terms of the agreement by delaying arbitration and refusing to release the presently undisputed amount from escrow. The second count characterized Genicom's action as the tortious breach of a legally-implied covenant of good faith and fair dealing (which we will speak of simply as one of good faith).

[11] Although count two was ill-pleaded, given this jurisdiction's clear law that a breach of contract does not sound separately in tort, *see Lawton v. Great Southwest Fire Ins. Co.*, 118 N.H. 607, 613, 392 A.2d 576, 580 (1978), the trial court treated the covenant of good faith mentioned in count two as the term said to have been breached under count one, and we will accept that merger of pleading. Centronics's allegations have undergone further refinement by dropping any claim that Genicom acted to delay the arbitration, the sedate progress of which is now acknowledged to be neither party's fault. (Slow as it was, the arbitration may well have concluded before this decision, although Centronics's claims for interest and consequential damages suffice to stave off the threat of mootness.)

[12] Genicom moved for summary judgment on the theory that, given the dispute over CCNBV, the terms of the parties' agreements required payments out of escrow only upon completion of arbitration, thus barring the implication of any duty to authorize a distribution before that event. Centronics objected and sought its own summary judgment, grounded on

4   [$5,653,836 in 1989 dollars is roughly the equivalent of $11,400,000 in 2019 dollars using the CPI and the GNP Deflator.—Eds.]

affidavits said to indicate that Genicom's refusal was meant to pressure Centronics into conceding a disputed item worth a substantial amount.

[13] The trial court ruled for Genicom, after construing the contract to provide that the

> "only way funds can be released is upon final determination of the purchase price, which, as the parties agree, is in the hands of the arbitrator.

> "The instant suit is no more than [an] attempt on the part of [Centronics] to rewrite the contract. Essentially, [Centronics] asks this Court to read between the lines of § 2.07 and insert therein a provision regarding partial disbursal of funds from escrow in light of the protracted arbitration. While it is true that the parties contemplated a short time period for resolution of disputes through binding arbitration, the Court cannot insert a provision in the contract for partial payments where such provision does not exist.

> "[Centronics] should have demanded a mechanism for partial payments from the Escrow Fund if the arbitration process lagged, or if the factual situation regarding adjustments to the final purchase price occurred as it did. The Court will not renegotiate the contract between the parties to obtain this result. To the extent [Centronics] made a less advantageous contract, it must now abide by the terms of that contract as originally agreed."

[14] Centronics reads the foregoing order as denying that any obligation of good faith is implied in the parties' contract. We read it differently, as concluding that the express terms of the contract are inconsistent with the claim that an obligation of good faith and fair dealing, or any other sort of implied obligation, either requires Genicom to agree to an interim distribution or bars Genicom from refusing to agree except in return for Centronics's concession on a disputed item. We consequently view this appeal as raising the related questions of whether the trial judge misunderstood the implied obligation of good faith or misconstrued the contract. We conclude that he did neither.

[15] Although an obligation of good faith is imposed by statute in the performance and enforcement of every contract or duty subject to the Uniform Commercial Code, *see* RSA 382–A:1–203; 382–A:1–201(19), the parties before us have addressed the implied contractual obligation of good faith at common law, and our first concern in this case is to identify the jurisdiction whose common law is to be applied. Although the parties agreed that their contractual relations were to be governed by New York law, and although Centronics's brief cites two cases from the Second Circuit applying the law of that State, Centronics's principal reliance is on New Hampshire cases. Since the New York decisions are not at odds with our

own, as we will indicate below, and since neither party has suggested that the relevant substantive law differs between the two jurisdictions, we will assume that to whatever extent the governing foreign law has not been proven it is identical to our own.

[16] Our own common law of good faith contractual obligation is not, however, as easily stated as we might wish, there being not merely one rule of implied good faith duty in New Hampshire's law of contract, but a series of doctrines, each of them speaking in terms of an obligation of good faith but serving markedly different functions. Since the time of our first contract decision couched in terms of good faith, *Griswold v. Heat Incorporated*, 108 N.H. 119, 229 A.2d 183 (1967), we have relied on such an implied duty in three distinct categories of contract cases: those dealing with standards of conduct in contract formation, with termination of at-will employment contracts, and with limits on discretion in contractual performance, which is at issue in the instant case. Although decisions in the first and second categories are not directly relevant here, a short detour through their cases will serve clarity by indicating the categorical distinctions.

[17] In our decisions setting standards of conduct in contract formation, the implied good faith obligations of a contracting party are tantamount to the traditional duties of care to refrain from misrepresentation and to correct subsequently discovered error, insofar as any representation is intended to induce, and is material to, another party's decision to enter into a contract in justifiable reliance upon it. In *Bursey* and *Dawe*, the continuing good faith bar to misrepresentation is antecedent to the agreement itself, a circumstance recently echoed in *Realco Equities, Inc. v. John Hancock Mut. Life Ins. Co.*, 130 N.H. 345, 350, 540 A.2d 1220, 1223 (1988), where dictum suggested that breach of an independently existing duty of good faith may be a way to explain the voidability of a contract found to be unconscionable. *Cf.* Restatement (Second) of Contracts § 205, comment e.

[18] By way of contrast, the good faith enforced in the second category of our cases is an obligation implied in the contract itself, where it fulfills the distinctly different function of limiting the power of an employer to terminate a wage contract by discharging an at-will employee. Under the rule evolved from *Monge v. Beebe Rubber Co.*, 114 N.H. 130, 316 A.2d 549 (1974) through *Howard v. Dorr Woolen Company*, 120 N.H. 295, 414 A.2d 1273 (1980), and *Cloutier v. A. & P. Tea Co., Inc.*, 121 N.H. 915, 436 A.2d 1140 (1981), an employer violates an implied term of a contract for employment at-will by firing an employee out of malice or bad faith in retaliation for action taken or refused by the employee in consonance with public policy. Although good faith in this context has not been rigorously defined, bad faith has been spoken of as equivalent to malice, and treated virtually as a subject of equitable estoppel in labor relations. Indeed, the

concepts of good and bad faith applied in these cases are best understood not as elements of general contract law as such, but as expressions of labor policy.

[19] The differences between the obligations of good faith exemplified even in these first two groups of cases are enough to explain why the commentators despair of articulating any single concept of contractual good faith, even after the more than fifty years of litigation following in the wake of the American common law's first explicit recognition of an implied good faith contractual obligation in *Kirke La Shelle Co. v. Paul Armstrong Co.*, 263 N.Y. 79, 87, 188 N.E. 163, 167 (1933).

[20] Even within the narrower confines of the third category of cases, those governing discretion in contractual performance, the one notable attempt to conceptualize implied good faith in a single, general definition, Burton, *Breach of Contract and the Common Law Duty to Perform in Good Faith*, 94 Harv. L. Rev. 369 (1980), discussed infra, is opposed by the view that the obligation of good faith performance is better understood simply as excluding behavior inconsistent with common standards of decency, fairness, and reasonableness, and with the parties' agreed-upon common purposes and justified expectations, see Summers, 67 Cornell L. Rev. at 820, 826; Restatement, *supra* at § 205, comment a. This view is consonant with our own cases in the third category, a canvass of which should inform our consideration of what good faith may or may not demand of Genicom in the circumstances before us.

[21] New Hampshire's seminal case on the implied obligation of good faith performance, *Griswold v. Heat* Corporation, 108 N.H. 119, 229 A.2d 183, held that a contract to pay $200 a month for " 'such [personal] services as [the plaintiff], in his sole discretion, may render' " required the plaintiff to provide a level of services consistent with good faith. The court sought out the inadequately articulated objectives of the contracting parties by examining their contractual language, their prior dealings, and the commercial context in which they dealt, and found a mutual intention to be bound by a contract for actual services. The court then indicated its readiness to vindicate what it inferred to have been the parties' reasonable expectations, and so saved the agreement from the unenforceability that would have followed from finding the plaintiff's undertaking to have been as illusory as the contract literally gave him the discretion to make it. Thus, a contracting party with expressly conferred discretion to do nothing at all was denied the right to frustrate the other party's expectation of receiving some reasonable level of performance.

[22] The discretion to refrain from acting, articulated in the *Griswold* contract, had been left unexpressed in the agreement litigated in the next case, where it resulted simply from the parties' failure to address any standard of enforceable performance on the point at issue. In *Seaward*

Constr. Co. v. City of Rochester, 118 N.H. 128, 383 A.2d 707 (1978), the city was obliged to pay for construction work only to the extent it received federal funds for that purpose, and the contract expressed no duty on the city's part to seek the funds. When, however, the parties fell into dispute over amounts due, and the city blocked what it believed was the contractor's demand for excessive payment by the simple expedient of refusing to ask for any federal money, this court held that the city could not rely on a lack of federal funds in defending against the contractor's claim for payment, without also proving it had honored an implied obligation to make a good faith effort to obtain the money. Thus, once again, the court imposed a limitation on one party's apparent discretion to thwart a reasonable expectation of the other party, going to the essence of the contract.

[23] The next case arose from discretion over the timing of performance. *Lawton v. Great Southwest Fire Ins. Co.*, 118 N.H. 607, 392 A.2d 576, held that an insurance company would violate an implied obligation of good faith if it delayed payment owed to its own insured for the purpose of coercing the insured into accepting less than the full amount due. Under the contractual circumstances illustrated by *Lawton*, the company's discretion to set the time for payment resulted neither from express provision (as is *Griswold*) nor from simple failure to address the subject (as in *Seaward*), but from the practical impossibility of identifying the moment in advance when a reasonable person would be satisfied of the insurer's obligation to pay the policy's proceeds. Although *Lawton* is to this extent distinguishable from the preceding cases, the court's response to the risk of unlimited discretion was consistent with *Griswold* and *Seaward*, and *Lawton* may be seen as holding that under a contract leaving the time for performance unspecified, good faith limits discretion under a standard of commercial reasonableness. *See also Albee v. Wolfeboro Railroad Co.*, 126 N.H. 176, 179, 489 A.2d 148, 151 (1985) (duty of good faith limits unspecified contract price to what is commercially reasonable). Since the timeliness of payment is often essential to the value of insurance, the insured in *Lawton*, like the corporation in *Griswold* and the contractor in *Seaward*, could otherwise have been effectively deprived of consideration for his own prior performance (i.e., in paying the premiums due).

[24] *Lawton*, to be sure, spoke also of the insurer's improper motive to coerce the insured into accepting less than the true amount owed. But once the time for performance has arrived, it would seem that any motive for withholding payment would be improper; e.g., withholding simply to enjoy continued use of the money would be wrong. If, then, any motive to withhold payment beyond the reasonable time is wrong, *Lawton* is best understood as a case in which good faith was held to require that discretion over the timing of payment be subjected to a test of commercial reasonableness.

[25] To this revisitation of *Griswold, Seaward,* and *Lawton,* which form the foundation of our law on good faith performance, we should add a somewhat less extended review of three other cases addressed in the briefs, which are to the same effect. Each party has cited *Atlas Truck Leasing, Inc. v. First NH Banks, Inc.,* 808 F.2d 902 (1st Cir. 1987), resting on New Hampshire law for holding that the lessee under a contract for the hire of specified automobiles for its business needs, but obligating it to pay only at a rate per mile of actual use, was bound in good faith to make reasonable efforts to use the lessor's cars in the conduct of the lessee's ordinary business. Absent such a construction, the contract would have obligated the lessor to make vehicles available to the lessee, but without any right to receive consideration in return except at the lessee's unfettered sufferance in choosing to drive the lessor's vehicles, instead of obtaining needed transportation some other way. The case reflects the law developed in the preceding performance cases in narrowing an otherwise unlimited discretion to deprive another party of reasonably expectable consideration.

[26] The remaining two cases have been cited by Centronics as stating relevant New York law. In *Wakefield v. Northern Telecom, Inc.,* 769 F.2d 109 (2d Cir. 1985), an employer was held to have violated good faith in firing an employee for the sake of taking advantage of a contract clause extinguishing the employee's right to accrued commissions upon discharge. Here, too, we see an otherwise unregulated right to discharge limited so as to preclude the employer from depriving his employee of contract consideration to which the employee had already become entitled by virtue of his own performance.

[27] Similarly, in *Zilg v. Prentice-Hall, Inc.,* 717 F.2d 671 (2d Cir. 1983), *cert. denied,* 466 U.S. 938, 104 S.Ct. 1911, 80 L.Ed.2d 460 (1984), a book publisher, whose contract with an author contained no restriction on its discretion to spend much or little in promoting the author's book, was held to be bound in good faith to make enough effort to give the book a reasonable chance of commercial success. Absent such a construction, the publisher would have been free to decline to publicize the book and so to deprive the author of virtually the entire value of the contract.

[28] Despite the variety of their fact patterns, these cases illustrate a common rule: under an agreement that appears by word or silence to invest one party with a degree of discretion in performance sufficient to deprive another party of a substantial proportion of the agreement's value, the parties' intent to be bound by an enforceable contract raises an implied obligation of good faith to observe reasonable limits in exercising that discretion, consistent with the parties' purpose or purposes in contracting.

A claim for relief from a violation of the implied covenant of good faith contractual performance therefore potentially raises four questions:

1.   Does the agreement ostensibly allow to or confer upon the defendant a degree of discretion in performance tantamount to a power to deprive the plaintiff of a substantial proportion of the agreement's value? Contracts may be broken in a multitude of ways and theories of relief are correspondingly numerous, but the concept of good faith in performance addresses the particular problem raised by a promise subject to such a degree of discretion that its practical benefit could seemingly be withheld.

2.   If the ostensible discretion is of that requisite scope, does competent evidence indicate that the parties intended by their agreement to make a legally enforceable contract? In many cases, such as *Lawton* and *Seaward*, this question will not pose a serious issue, and it surely would not call for any extended consideration in the case before us. *Griswold*, however, illustrates why the question must at least be recognized, for the very breadth of discretion necessary to predicate a claim of bad faith can also raise doubt about the parties' intent to be bound.

3.   Assuming an intent to be bound, has the defendant's exercise of discretion exceeded the limits of reasonableness? The answer to this question depends on identifying the common purpose or purposes of the contract, against which the reasonableness of the complaining party's expectations may be measured, and in furtherance of which community standards of honesty, decency and reasonableness can be applied.

4.   Is the cause of the damage complained of the defendant's abuse of discretion, or does it result from events beyond the control of either party, against which the defendant has no obligation to protect the plaintiff? Although this question is cast in the language of causation, it may be seen simply as the other face of question three. Suffice it to say here that its point is to emphasize that the good faith requirement is not a fail-safe device barring a defendant from the fruits of every plaintiff's bad bargain, or empowering courts to rewrite an agreement even when a defendant's discretion is consistent with the agreement's legally contractual character.

[29] Applying this analytical sequence to the instant case takes us no further than the first of the four questions, whether the agreement effectively confers such discretion on Genicom over the timing of distributions from the escrow fund that, in the absence of some good faith limitation, Genicom could deny Centronics a substantial proportion of the contract's benefit. Was Genicom, that is, given authority to deprive

Centronics indefinitely of a portion of the agreed consideration for the business assets previously transferred? The answer is obviously no. Unlike the contract in *Lawton*, for example, this one contains express and unequivocal provisions governing the timing of payment, which must occur no later than ten days after final resolution of the purchase price, presumably on conclusion of the mandatory arbitration. Genicom has no discretion to withhold approval for pay-out beyond that time, or to affect the timing of the arbitration itself. If, indeed, either party were dragging its heels in the conduct of the arbitration, it should go without saying that the dilatory conduct would be seen as a breach of contract, whether expressed in the language of bad faith or in traditional terms of the obligation to act within a reasonable time. *See* Restatement, *supra* at § 205, comment d. In short, because contractual provisions mandating payment on conclusion of the valuation process determine the date on which Centronics will get its due, it is clear that what Centronics claims to be Genicom's discretion over the timing of distribution is in reality a power that each party may exercise, but only jointly with the other, to agree to remove some or all of the escrowed funds from the ambit of the otherwise mandatory pay-out provisions.

[30] Although this discussion reflects the analytical structure of the prior good faith performance cases cited by Centronics and followed here, we should also note that the same result would obtain from applying an alternative analysis proposed by Professor Burton, referred to above, which Centronics has also urged us to employ. Burton's functional analysis of the obligation to observe good faith in discretionary contract performance applies objective criteria, *see* Burton, 94 Harv. L. Rev. at 390–91, to identify the unstated economic opportunities intended to be bargained away by a promisor as a cost of performance, and it identifies bad faith as a promisor's discretionary action subjectively intended, to recapture such an opportunity, thereby refusing to pay an expected performance cost. Centronics argues that its uncontradicted summary judgment affidavits establish that Genicom showed bad faith in Burton's sense, because its refusal to authorize distribution of the socalled undisputed amounts was an "attempt to recapture [the] degree of control concerning the amount of the final purchase price [which] it had agreed to place in the arbitrator's hands and thereby unjustifiably attain funds to which it was not entitled."

[31] Genicom, of course, denies the uncontradicted evidentiary force that Centronics claims for its affidavits. But even assuming, arguendo, that the affidavits are uncontradicted and tend to prove what Centronics asserts, there are two respects in which the facts would fail the Burton test of bad faith as an exercise of discretion meant to recapture an opportunity foregone at the creation of the contract.

[32] It is significant, first, that Genicom's refusal to consent to the distribution from escrow neither recaptures nor gains Genicom anything.

In and of itself, the refusal removes no issue from the contingencies of arbitration and gives Genicom no present or future right to the money it wishes to obtain. Genicom's behavior thus contrasts sharply with examples of bad faith given by Burton, in which the discretionary delay preserved the actual use of funds or other valuable resources to the party exercising the discretion. *See* Burton, 94 Harv. L. Rev. at 394–402. The point is that only when the discretionary act recaptures an economic opportunity does the exercise of discretion pass from the realm of applying leverage for the sake of inducing further agreement into the sphere of bad faith, in which no agreement is necessary to realize the offending party's advantage.

* * *

[33] A second and more fundamental flaw infects Centronics's reliance on the Burton analysis, however. It will be recalled that Burton's conception of bad faith in performance is the exercise of discretion for the purpose of recapturing opportunities foregone or bargained away at the time of contracting, with the identification of such foregone opportunities depending on objective analysis of the parties' "[e]xpectations [as they] may be inferred from the express contract terms in light of the ordinary course of business and customary practice. . . ." Burton, 94 Harv. L. Rev. at 389. Hence, if an objective basis exists to infer that the parties never bargained away the right of either of them to condition any distribution on completing the arbitration of any disputes, then Genicom cannot be guilty of bad faith by so insisting, whatever its subjective motive may be. We infer that the opportunity for such insistence never was bargained away.

[34] Although the contract documents do not concisely state there will be no interim distribution, the texts come very close to such a provision. We have previously quoted the language of the escrow agreement that "[i]n accordance with Section 2.07 of the Purchase Agreement," the escrow agent shall hold the fund until instructed by the buyer's and seller's counsel to make a distribution. Section 2.07 was also quoted above. Its topic heading is "Final Payment of Purchase Price," and it provides that final payment and settlement shall be made within ten days of the final determination of net book value and purchase price, which will presumably be at the close of arbitration. "Final Payment" is apparently so called to distinguish it from the "Payment to Sellers on Closing Date," required by § 2.03 of the agreement, since there is no other provision calling for any payment or distribution. The text thus supports the claim that the parties intended the escrow agent to leave the fund intact until the point of the final payment, if any, that would be due to Centronics ten days after the final price determination.

[35] This reading is confirmed by an understanding of the evident business purposes to be served by such a restriction on pay-out. We explained above that the original escrow of $5,000,000 was to be increased

by Genicom's deposit of an Adjustment Amount, which in effect was equal to the amount of Centronics's proposed revision of the final purchase price in excess of the preliminary purchase price. Although Centronics was obligated to follow accepted accounting procedures when it revised the balance sheet to calculate any adjustment, the revision was to be unaudited and Genicom had no control over the setting of this amount.

[36] Genicom, however, was not left entirely subject to Centronics's natural temptation to state a higher, rather than a lower, Adjustment Amount. It is reasonable to suppose each party appreciated that the extent of disagreement and the resulting duration of arbitration would be roughly proportional to the size of the Adjustment Amount. If Centronics had to wait upon the outcome of arbitration before it received any escrowed funds, then Genicom would be able to rely on Centronics's own self-interest to limit the probable length of arbitration by limiting the amount of the adjustment potentially subject to arbitration.[5]

[37] It is also reasonable to assume that neither party expected the other to emerge from arbitration with the whole escrow fund. Each therefore had reason to seek some mechanism for inducing the other side to promote speedy arbitration and the prompt distribution of escrowed money. Such a mechanism would be provided by a scheme conditioning any distribution on completing arbitration, since each would thus be induced to hasten the process for their common benefit.

[38] The probability is, therefore, that each party expected the escrow to remain intact throughout arbitration, as the reason for Genicom's agreement that Centronics would have discretion to state the amount of the adjustment, and as the inducement to a prompt effectuation of their common object of obtaining whatever would be due to each from the fund so escrowed. Whether, therefore, we rely on the analysis underlying our own prior cases, or on the rule as espoused by Burton, we affirm the trial judge's conclusion that Centronics is seeking a revision of the contract, not the enforcement of good faith in its performance.

Affirmed.

———

[5]   [If they had had the foresight to realize this, do you think they would have expressly stated that there would be no distributions until the arbitration was completed?—Eds.]

TAYLOR EQUIPMENT, INC. V. JOHN DEERE CO.
United States Court of Appeals, Eighth Circuit
98 F.3d 1028 (1996)

LOKEN, CIRCUIT JUDGE.

[1]   Deere & Company (formerly John Deere Co.) and its subsidiary, John Deere Industrial Equipment Company (collectively, "Deere"), appeal a judgment in favor of Deere's former industrial equipment dealer, Midcon Equipment Company ("Midcon"). The judgment was entered after a jury found that Deere breached the implied covenant of good faith and fair dealing when it refused to approve Midcon's proposed assignment of its dealership to a willing buyer, forcing Midcon's owners to sell the business to other approved buyers for $1,715,000 less. The dealer contract provided that Midcon could not assign its dealership "without the prior written consent of [Deere]." Because the implied covenant cannot override this express term of the contract, and because there was no proof that Deere failed to exercise "honesty in fact," we reverse.

I.   Factual Background

[2]   Deere manufactures construction and industrial equipment which it sells to independent dealers who sell or lease the equipment to end users. Deere dealers buy and sell parts and used equipment and service customer equipment. Because construction and industrial equipment is expensive, Deere provides its dealers "floor plan" financing—the dealer must take title to a piece of equipment, such as a $100,000 road grader, upon its delivery into inventory, but the dealer does not pay Deere until it sells or leases the equipment, and it pays no interest on this credit transaction for the first nine months after delivery. Given this financial stake in its dealers, Deere screens prospective dealers for financial strength and adequate capitalization.

[3]   Midcon was a long time Deere dealer in Sioux Falls, South Dakota, and Sioux City, Iowa. This controversy began in 1990 when Deere discovered that Midcon had sold $370,000 in equipment "out of trust" by failing to timely pay Deere after the sales.[6] The dealer contract between Deere and Midcon provided that Deere could terminate immediately for cause (defined to include defaults such as selling equipment out of trust), and that either party could terminate without cause upon one hundred twenty days written notice. Deere notified Midcon's owners, Paul and Cecelia Taylor, that Midcon would be terminated because of these serious defaults. However, in lieu of immediate termination, Deere advised that it would allow Midcon to continue as a dealer in good standing for up to

---

[6]   [The loan agreement between Deere and Midcon would have provided that Midcon would immediately pay Deere upon the sale of the piece of equipment. Most states have statutes making failure to pay under such an arrangement a criminal offense, but these statutes are seldom enforced.—Eds.]

eighteen months while the Taylors attempted to locate a buyer. The contract further provided that it "cannot be assigned by the Dealer without prior written consent of [Deere]."

[4] In the fall of 1991, Midcon entered into an "agreement in principle" to sell nearly all its assets to Interstate Companies of Minnesota, Inc. ("Interstate"). This tentative agreement was subject to a number of contingencies, including Deere's consent to the assignment of Midcon's dealer rights to Interstate. Though Deere had approved Interstate's acquisitions of Deere dealers in Montana and Des Moines, Iowa, in 1987 and 1989, Deere notified Interstate that it would not approve this assignment unless Interstate enhanced its financial strength with additional equity capital. Interstate declined to do so, Deere refused to approve the assignment, and Midcon's sale to Interstate fell through. In 1992, with Deere's approval of the purchasers as successor dealers, the Taylors sold most of Midcon's Sioux Falls assets to Midwest Machinery, Inc. ("Midwest"), and most of the Sioux City assets to Swaney Equipment Co. ("Swaney"), on substantially less favorable terms than Interstate had previously offered.

II.   Procedural History

[5] Midcon then commenced this action, alleging wrongful cancellation under the South Dakota equipment dealer statute, S.D.C.L. §§ 37–5–3 and –4, and breach of the implied covenant of good faith and fair dealing, when Deere refused to approve the assignment to Interstate. Deere counterclaimed, alleging that Midcon had fraudulently obtained government customer discounts.

[6] The district court summarily dismissed Midcon's wrongful cancellation claim because the dealership was not cancelled, but it denied Deere summary judgment on the breach of covenant claim. Prior to trial of that claim, the court severed Deere's fraud counterclaim for separate trial. It also granted Midcon's motion in limine to preclude evidence regarding Midcon's sales out of trust and Deere's intended termination on the ground that this evidence was irrelevant and unfairly prejudicial after dismissal of the wrongful cancellation claim. The court ruled that the sole issue at trial would be whether Deere acted in good faith when it refused to approve assignment of Midcon's contract to Interstate.

[7] Although Deere had not told Paul Taylor why it refused to approve the proposed assignment,[7] discovery revealed Deere correspondence conditioning approval on Interstate agreeing to enhance its equity capital. At trial, Midcon's theory was that this demand was pretextual—in fact, Deere had forced Midcon to sell its businesses to two "key dealers,"

---

[7]   When pressed by Taylor, Deere representatives told him to ask Interstate why it was not approved. This was an appropriate response since Deere's communications with Interstate had involved that company's confidential financial information.

Midwest and Swaney, to further Deere's secret plan to "rationalize" its dealer network by eliminating fifty to one hundred small dealers during the 1990's. Deere countered that the refusal was in fact based upon its good faith, rational concern over Interstate's financial ability to expand in this fashion. Midcon responded with evidence that Deere's equity capital demand was unusual and unreasonable. The jury obviously credited Midcon's pretext theory.[8]

[8] The jury awarded Midcon $1,715,710[9] in compensatory damages. The district court awarded $381,240.55 in prejudgment interest and denied Deere's alternative motions for judgment as a matter of law or a new trial. On appeal, Deere argues (1) it is entitled to judgment as a matter of law on Midcon's implied covenant claim; (2) the district court erred in excluding evidence of Midcon's sales out of trust and government discount fraud, and Interstate's subsequent financial woes; (3) error in the jury instruction on "good faith"; and (4) improper damages. In its conditional cross-appeal, Midcon argues that we should reinstate the claim for wrongful cancellation if we reverse the judgment for breach of the implied covenant. Given our interpretation of controlling South Dakota law, we need only address the first and last issues.

II. The Implied Covenant Claim

[9] The district court concluded that "the South Dakota Supreme Court would impose on [Deere] a duty to act reasonably in deciding whether to consent to a proposed dealership transfer." We review the court's construction of state law de novo. Application of the implied covenant is a matter of contract interpretation, a question we also review de novo.

A

[10] The Supreme Court of South Dakota recently held that South Dakota law implies a covenant of good faith and fair dealing into every contract. *See Garrett v. BankWest, Inc.*, 459 N.W.2d 833, 841 & n. 7 (S.D.

---

[8]   Early in the trial, Paul Taylor testified: "when Deere had put a certain amount of pressure on me, I decided that I would sell the business." Deere argued that Midcon thereby opened up the issue of its sales out of trust, but the district court adhered to its earlier motion in limine ruling. This ruling left the jury free to infer that Deere "pressured" Taylor as part of its secret plan to eliminate small dealers, not because Midcon had breached its dealer contract. The ruling also precluded Deere from explaining why Taylor did not have the option of refusing to sell the business if he found the Midwest and Swaney purchase offers unattractive. Finally, the ruling foreclosed Deere from putting its own actions in context, which is critical when a party's "honesty in fact" is at issue. Indeed, the district court even barred Deere from introducing evidence of Interstate's later financial troubles, evidence that would have substantiated the concerns that Deere contended were the reason for its refusal to approve assignment of the Midcon dealerships to Interstate. These evidentiary rulings left Deere to defend a claim of bad faith with one hand tied behind its back. Had we not concluded that Midcon's breach of covenant claim fails as a matter of law, we would have reversed and remanded for a new trial on this ground.

[9]   [$1,715,710 in 1996 dollars is roughly the equivalent of $2,750,000 in 2019 dollars using the CPI and the GNP Deflator.—Eds.]

1990). This covenant affords only contract remedies; there is no independent tort for its breach. Moreover, "good faith is not a limitless duty or obligation. The implied obligation must arise from the language used [in the contract] or it must be indispensable to effectuate the intention of the parties." *Id.* at 841–42 (quotation omitted). The Court in *Garrett* adopted for all contracts the definition of "good faith" found in South Dakota's uniform commercial code—"honesty in fact in the conduct or transaction concerned." S.D.C.L. § 57A–1–201(19).

[11] Though every contract includes the implied covenant, it does not affect every contract term. The covenant is "a method to fill gaps" in a contract. It has "nothing to do with the enforcement of terms actually negotiated" and therefore cannot "block use of terms that actually appear in the contract." *Continental Bank, N.A. v. Everett,* 964 F.2d 701, 705 (7th Cir.), *cert. denied,* 506 U.S. 1035, 113 S.Ct. 816, 121 L.Ed.2d 688 (1992). Where parties have addressed an issue in the contract, "no occasion to divine their intent or supply implied terms arises." *Cambee's,* 825 F.2d at 175 n.13.

[12] In *Garrett,* the Court declined to apply the implied covenant to compel a lender to extend credit when the contract's express terms did not require such action. Similarly, that Court has refused to "transplant[ ] the covenant of good faith and fair dealing into the foreign soil of the employment-at-will doctrine." *Breen v. Dakota Gear & Joint Co.,* 433 N.W.2d 221, 224 (S.D. 1988). A claim that an employee was terminated in bad faith is fundamentally inconsistent with the concept of at-will employment. Therefore, the implied covenant may not be used to restrict the employer's freedom to terminate.

[13] Applying similar reasoning, many courts have held that the implied covenant may not be applied to limit a clear contractual provision allowing termination of the contract without cause. The Deere-Midcon dealer contract was terminable by either party without cause. This suggests that Deere's right to disapprove an assignment of the contract was intended to be absolute, because Deere in any event would be free to terminate an unwanted successor without cause.[10]

[14] This appeal involves a no-assignment-without-approval clause, rather than a termination clause. However, courts have also been reluctant to apply the implied covenant to block a party's exercise of its contractual right to withhold approval. In *James v. Whirlpool Corp.,* 806 F.Supp. 835, 839 (E.D. Mo. 1992), for example, the contract provided that "[n]one of the rights or obligations under th[e] agreement shall be subject to assignment

---

[10] In *Cambee's,* we held that a distributor contract silent as to duration contained an implied covenant that the distributor would not be terminated without cause "for a period sufficient to allow [the distributor] to recoup its investment." 825 F.2d at 175. However, the Deere-Midcon agreement was not silent as to duration. Moreover, Midcon had many years as a Deere dealer in which to recoup its initial investment.

. . . without the prior written consent of [the manufacturer]." The court held that the implied covenant did not "override the express terms of the agreement" which "unmistakably" granted an unlimited right to disapprove assignments. *Id.* at 843–44. *See also In re Bellanca Aircraft Corp.*, 850 F.2d 1275, 1285 (8th Cir. 1988) (U.C.C. good faith obligation imposes no duty not to unreasonably withhold consent to assign a contract right).

[15] Similarly, in *Hubbard Chevrolet Co. v. General Motors Corp.*, 873 F.2d 873, 877–78 (5th Cir.), *cert. denied*, 493 U.S. 978, 110 S.Ct. 506, 107 L.Ed.2d 508 (1989), the court held that the implied covenant had "no role to play" in a dispute over the manufacturer's refusal to approve a dealer's relocation. "[The contract] gave GM the authority to approve or disapprove relocation for its own reasons," the court explained; "we decline to allow a jury to reevaluate the wisdom of the parties' choice to leave relocation decisions to GM." *Id.* at 878. *See also Tidmore Oil Co. v. BP Oil Co.*, 932 F.2d 1384, 1391 (11th Cir.) (no breach of the implied covenant where supplier refused to approve a jobber's expansion under a contract stating that the supplier "must approve each outlet"), *cert. denied*, 502 U.S. 925, 112 S.Ct. 339, 116 L.Ed.2d 279 (1991).

[16] Were the Supreme Court of South Dakota to apply the holdings in these cases to this fact setting, it is clear that Midcon's implied covenant claim would fail as a matter of law. The purpose of the implied covenant is to honor the parties' justified expectations. Absent contractual limitation, Deere has an absolute right to choose its equipment dealers. Midcon's dealer contract granted Deere an express, unrestricted right to disapprove a proposed assignment of Midcon's contract rights. This contract term gave Midcon no justified expectation that Deere was agreeing to surrender its absolute right to choose Midcon's successor. Instead, the no-assignment-without-Deere-approval term preserved that right. *Cf. Massey v. Tandy Corp.*, 987 F.2d 1307, 1309–10 (8th Cir. 1993); *Abbott v. Amoco Oil Co.*, 249 Ill. App. 3d 774, 189 Ill. Dec. 88, 619 N.E.2d 789, 796 ("the dealers cannot complain when Amoco merely exercises the discretion the dealers allowed Amoco to possess"), *appeal denied*, 153 Ill. 2d 557, 191 Ill. Dec. 616, 624 N.E.2d 804 (1993).

B

[17] There is another line of cases that suggest some role, albeit a limited role, for the implied covenant in a dispute involving exercise of a contractual right to disapprove assignment of a dealer contract. In *Kham & Nate's Shoes No. 2, Inc. v. First Bank of Whiting*, 908 F.2d 1351, 1357 (7th Cir. 1990), the court explained: " 'Good faith' is a compact reference to an implied undertaking not to take opportunistic advantage in a way that could not have been contemplated at the time of [the contract's] drafting, and which therefore was not resolved explicitly by the parties." The

Seventh Circuit further explained this concept in *Original Great Amer. Chocolate Chip Cookie Co. v. River Valley Cookies, Ltd.*, 970 F.2d 273, 280 (7th Cir. 1992):

> Contract law imposes a duty, not to "be reasonable," but to avoid taking advantage of gaps in a contract in order to exploit the vulnerabilities that arise when contractual performance is sequential rather than simultaneous. Suppose A hires B to paint his portrait to his satisfaction, and B paints it and A in fact is satisfied but says he is not in the hope of chivvying down the agreed-upon price. . . . This . . . would be bad faith, not because any provision of the contract was unreasonable and had to be reformed but because a provision had been invoked dishonestly to achieve a purpose contrary to that for which the contract had been made. The same would be true here, we may assume, if . . . the Cookie Company had tried to appropriate the value [the Sigels] had created by canceling the franchise on a pretext . . . utterly trivial violations of the contract that the company would have overlooked but for its desire to take advantage of the Sigels' vulnerable position. (Citations omitted.)

[18] Under this interpretation of the implied covenant, Deere would be liable if it dishonestly withheld approval of a proposed assignment, but not if its decision was simply unreasonable. This interpretation is consistent with *Garrett*'s adoption of the U.C.C. standard, "honesty in fact." It is inconsistent with the district court's imposition of a duty to act "reasonably."[11]

[19] We are frankly uncertain whether the Supreme Court of South Dakota would hold that the implied covenant may not restrict an unlimited contractual right of approval, following cases such as *Grand Light & Supply* and *James v. Whirlpool*, or whether it would follow the above-quoted Seventh Circuit decisions and hold that the implied covenant does bar dishonest exercise of an otherwise absolute right to disapprove. But we need not resolve that uncertainty in this case because Midcon presented no evidence that Deere acted dishonestly when it disapproved the proposed assignment to Interstate.

[20] Midcon's case was built upon pretext and unreasonableness. Deere's stated reason for disapproving—Interstate's inadequate equity capital—and the alleged secret reason—a long term plan to consolidate

---

[11] The district court instructed the jury that the implied covenant required Deere "to act fairly and reasonably," and that "[s]ubterfuge and evasions violate the obligation of good faith even though the actor believes its conduct to be justified." These instructions erroneously expanded the implied covenant far beyond "honesty in fact." In particular, the instruction regarding "subterfuge and evasions" has no place in a case of this kind. Deere's dealer strategies and its evaluation of Interstate's financial statements involved sensitive business information. The court should not have permitted the jury to find Deere guilty of "subterfuge and evasions" because it failed to disclose such information when it disapproved the assignment to Interstate.

dealerships in the hands of key dealers—are both legitimate business reasons for not approving Interstate as Midcon's successor. Midcon had no evidence of Deere's "dishonesty in fact"—an intent to take "opportunistic advantage" of Midcon's need to sell for any reason other than Deere's business interests in choosing its dealers, interests expressly protected in the contract. Thus, Deere is also entitled to judgment as a matter of law under this interpretation of the implied covenant.

C

[21] The district court relied upon *Larese v. Creamland Dairies, Inc.*, 767 F.2d 716 (10th Cir. 1985), for its conclusion that the implied covenant imposed a duty on Deere to act reasonably. In *Larese*, a franchise agreement prohibited assignment "without the prior written consent of" Creamland and declared any unapproved transfer "null and without effect." *Id.* at 717. Applying Colorado law, the court held that the implied covenant required that the franchisor not unreasonably withhold consent. In a passage quoted approvingly by the district court, the court in *Larese* opined that "the franchisor must bargain for a provision expressly granting the right to withhold consent unreasonably, to insure that the franchisee is put on notice." *Id.* at 718. We disagree.

[22] The normal meaning of the approval clause in the Deere-Midcon agreement is that Deere has an unrestricted right to withhold approval, at least if it acts honestly. As review of any contract drafting treatise will confirm, if the parties to a contract agree that the discretion granted under such an approval clause should be more limited, their draftsman will insert a provision stating that "consent to assignment shall not be unreasonably withheld," like the contract at issue in *Anheuser-Busch, Inc. v. Natural Bev. Distribs.*, 69 F.3d 337, 345 (9th Cir. 1995). *See generally* R.A. FELDMAN, DRAFTING EFFECTIVE CONTRACTS: A PRACTITIONER'S GUIDE § 5–J.2[a] (1996 Supp.). Unlike litigation, drafting a contract is a positive exercise among parties contemplating beneficial, harmonious relations. No experienced draftsman would think of inserting a provision to the effect that "this clause permits Party A to act unreasonably." Thus, we decline to follow *Larese* because it would impose an unrealistic drafting burden on parties who intend to create an unrestricted approval clause whose exercise will not be supplanted by a jury's notion of reasonableness.

[23] "[I]n commercial transactions it does not in the end promote justice to seek strained interpretations in aid of those who do not protect themselves." *James Baird Co. v. Gimbel Bros.*, 64 F.2d 344, 346 (2d Cir. 1933) (L. Hand, J.). Paul Taylor was an experienced businessman who had no justified expectation that Midcon's dealer contract would permit him to second-guess Deere's choice of Midcon's successor. Accordingly, Midcon's claim for breach of the implied covenant of good faith and fair dealing fails

as a matter of law under any reasonable application of the implied covenant defined in *Garrett*.

* * *

[The dissent of JUDGE GIBSON is omitted.—Eds.]

NOTES

1. Rather than saying "the contract cannot be assigned by Dealer without the prior written consent of Deere," it would be better to say "the contract cannot be assigned by Dealer." If Deere wanted to allow assignment, it could always waive this provision when the issue arose. So why do lawyers continue to use "without the prior written consent" language? One reason is just habit. Some attorneys do it until they read about a case like the one discussed in paragraph [21] where a court held that this language *does* create an obligation not to unreasonably withhold consent. Another reason may be that the language is "softer," and makes the contract seem less one-sided, helping to sell the deal to the other side. Still another reason is that the drafter may want to hold out the hope that consent will be granted. She may expect that the other lawyer will be more likely to try to negotiate a change in the draft if it flatly says there will be no assignment. But of course if this is the situation, then there *would* be a basis for implying an obligation not to unreasonably withhold consent.

From a purely lawyerly point of view, what the dealer's lawyer should do of course, is negotiate for a clause that says: "This contract cannot be assigned without the written consent of Deere, which consent will not be unreasonably withheld." This gets the issue raised and resolved before the parties get into a contract, when they can both back out without litigation.

Business people, however, are often so anxious to make the deal that they don't want their lawyers to raise potentially divisive issues. When the lawyers do, they complain about "deal-killing lawyers;" they believe that everything will work out. So you'll often feel under pressure not to raise points you know should be raised. Remember, though, when the client gets into trouble over language in the contract, the blame is going to fall on the lawyers who negotiated and drafted the contract. What you do in these situations depends on the circumstances, the client, and your relationship with the client. You will develop a feel for it as you get experience in practice. Usually, the best thing to do is explain the risks to the client and let her make the decision. But in many cases there are so many of these risks and the likelihood of any one of them resulting in a major problem is so small that going over them all with the client is time-consuming and irritating to the client. On the other hand, there are situations where the risk is so large or the client is so untrustworthy that the only safe course is to write a "CYA" letter to the client explaining the risk and noting that the client chose to assume it. This keeps your malpractice carrier happy, but it doesn't make for good client relations. Clients sometimes become unhappy when they realize their lawyer is charging them $250 (or $500) an hour to write a letter to protect *the lawyer*.

These comments illustrate a three-way tension that is present when documenting a deal. There are three underlying goals at work. First, the drafter is attempting to present a contract that the other party will accept. Second, the contract should be one that, once in effect, convinces the other party to perform according to its terms because of the consequences it provides for non-performance. Third, the contract must be one that a court will enforce once voluntary performance has ceased. These three "sales" goals, as discussed in the introduction, are somewhat inconsistent and only experience can teach you the right balance in any particular situation. But understanding the three goals should help you focus on finding that balance.

2.   Deere continues to consolidate its dealer network. A front page story in The Wall Street Journal put it in very blunt terms.

> For more than a century, Deere & Co. has relied on dealers to sell its iconic John Deere tractors and other farm equipment. Deere dealers like to brag that they "bleed green," the company's trademark color.
>
> But even as the farm boom helps Deere harvest record profits, dozens of North American dealerships are getting sent out to pasture, including some that have passed through families for generations. Chief Executive Robert Lane says times have changed. In an age where tractors use satellites to track the location of every seed, he says, dealers must match the sophistication and size of agribusiness customers.
>
> "For years we talked about Deere as a family," says Mr. Lane, a former banker. "The fact is we're not a family. What we are is a high-performance team. . . . If someone is not pulling their weight, you're not on a high-performance team anymore."

Ilan Brat & Timothy Aeppel, *Why Deere Is Weeding Out Dealers Even as Farm Booms*, WALL ST. J. Aug. 14, 2007, at A-1, col. 4.

––––––––––

INDUSTRIAL REPRESENTATIVES, INC. V. CP CLARE

United States Court of Appeals, Seventh Circuit
74 F.3d 128 (1996)

EASTERBROOK, CIRCUIT JUDGE.

[1]   CP Clare Corporation, a manufacturer of electrical components such as relays and surge arrestors, engaged Industrial Representatives, Inc. (IRI) in April 1991 to solicit orders for its products in Northern Illinois and Eastern Wisconsin. As its name implies, IRI touts the products of many firms; its sales staff offers a menu of goods, achieving economies of scale for

manufacturers too small to support a dedicated sales staff. Successful manufacturers eventually reach that critical size, however, and may elect to change distribution channels. By fall 1994 CP Clare's sales in IRI's territory exceeded $6 million annually, a tenfold increase since IRI's engagement. CP Clare decided to take promotion in-house and sent IRI a letter terminating its role at the end of October 1994. CP Clare gave IRI 42 days' notice; the parties' contract required only 30. The contract established a further obligation: CP Clare had to pay IRI a commission for all products, ordered before the terminal date, that were delivered in the next 90 days. CP Clare kept this promise. But IRI believes that it has not been paid enough for the work it did in boosting CP Clare's sales. It filed this suit under the diversity jurisdiction seeking commissions for all products delivered through 1999, plus $5 million[12] in punitive damages.

[2]   IRI acknowledges that CP Clare did not need good cause to bring their dealings to a close. The contract provides that Illinois law governs, and in Illinois a contract without a fixed term may be ended for any or no reason. Nonetheless, IRI insists, CP Clare was not entitled to take opportunistic advantage of the situation created by the parties' dealings. By "opportunistic" IRI means any decision by which, after one party has made investments, the other breaks off the transactions to appropriate more of the gain these investments brought into being. IRI's services created goodwill for CP Clare's products, and anticipated future sales were like an annuity that CP Clare decided to capture. An obligation to avoid opportunistic advantage-taking is part of the duty of good faith read into every contract in Illinois, IRI submits. The district court disagreed and dismissed the complaint under Fed. R. Civ. P. 12(b)(6) for failure to state a claim on which relief may be granted.

[3]   "Opportunism" in the law of contracts usually signifies one of two situations. First, there is effort to wring some advantage from the fact that the party who performs first sinks costs, which the other party may hold hostage by demanding greater compensation in exchange for its own performance. The movie star who sulks (in the hope of being offered more money) when production is 90% complete, and reshooting the picture without him would be exceedingly expensive, is behaving opportunistically in this sense. *See Alaska Packers' Ass'n v. Domenico*, 117 F. 99 (9th Cir. 1902). Second, there is an effort to take advantage of one's contracting partner "in a way that could not have been contemplated at the time of drafting, and which therefore was not resolved explicitly by the parties." *Kham & Nate's Shoes No. 2, Inc. v. First Bank of Whiting*, 908 F.2d 1351, 1357 (7th Cir. 1990). For example, we concluded in *Jordan v. Duff & Phelps, Inc.*, 815 F.2d 429 (7th Cir. 1987), that a firm and its employees had neither contemplated nor resolved by contract the question whether

---

[12] [$5,000,000 in 1996 dollars is roughly the equivalent of $8,000,000 in 2019 dollars using the CPI and the GNP Deflator.—Eds.]

news of an impending merger would be provided to employees considering whether to leave the firm, and that the common law rule requiring disclosure of information pertinent to securities transactions in closely held firms therefore remained in force. The court did not doubt in *Jordan* that an express agreement would control.

[4]   IRI does not allege that CP Clare acted opportunistically in either of these fashions. CP Clare did not seek to improve the deal to take advantage of IRI's sunk costs; rather it sought to enforce the bargain. And it did not take unexpected action against which IRI could not have defended. That a manufacturer will want to reassess its sales structure as volume grows must be understood by everyone—especially by a professional sales representative such as IRI. No one, least of all IRI, could have thought that a contract permitting termination on 30 days' notice, with payment of commissions for deliveries within 90 days thereafter, entitled the representative to the entire future value of the goodwill built up by its work. Goodwill (beyond the 90-day residual) was allocated to the manufacturer. The terms on which the parties would part ways were handled expressly in this contract, and IRI got what it bargained for. Contracts allocate risks and opportunities. If things turn out well, the party to whom the contract allocates the upper trail of outcomes is entitled to reap the benefits.

[5]   Allocating risks by contract is no easy matter, and only a long process of experimentation in the marketplace reveals the best terms. Consider the variables in a sales agency such as this one. The parties must select the length of the relationship, the commission rate, any bonuses for meeting objectives, and post-termination compensation. A long term, with termination only for cause, will assure the agent that it can reap the benefits of success in procuring repeat buyers for the goods—but disputes about "cause" may lead to costly litigation, and the longer term eventually may stifle effort. As the end of the term approaches, the agent cannot obtain much of the gain and may begin to take it easy, the "last-period problem" well known to contracting parties. Instead of rewarding the agent through a longer term, the parties may choose a higher commission rate. This increases the agent's incentive to work hard, but the higher rate also may over-reward the agent for sales that would have occurred without the agent's efforts; and a high commission rate gives the principal a greater reason to replace the agent. That incentive may be alleviated by paying the agent a bonus for defined levels of success, such as landing a big contract, but a bonus is risky for both sides—and as most people want to avoid risk, the prospect of a large bonus may be worth less to the agent than the cash outlay to the principal. Thus the parties may prefer to compensate the agent by a share of the profits over time, even after the agency is over. Stock options may do this; so do post-termination commissions. But backloading of the compensation, like a long-term contract, creates

incentives to shirk; for if the agent makes a big sale he can collect his residuals and invite the principal to fire him so that he can turn to other projects. All of the provisions for creating incentives and allocating risks have their advantages and disadvantages; all are well known to professionals such as IRI and CP Clare; no one combination of these terms is right for all people at all times.

[6] CP Clare and IRI addressed most of these issues explicitly in their contract. IRI received a minimum term of one year; either party could walk away on 30 days' notice thereafter. The contract set a commission rate of 6% for some products and 4% for others, but it provided a lower 2% rate on sales exceeding $500,000 per year to a single customer—except in the first year of sales to that customer, when IRI would collect its full commission rate. The contract did not provide for bonuses, and it tackled residuals by providing that IRI got its full commission on all deliveries within 90 days following its termination—unless IRI breached the contract, in which case it would receive no residuals. This agreement provides explicitly for what has come to pass: termination with substantial outstanding business. It allocates to IRI three months' worth of commissions. By demanding five years' worth after the fact, IRI has behaved opportunistically.

* * *

[7] When the parties are free to specify price and duration, a court cannot improve matters by intervention after the fact. It can only destabilize the institution of contract, increase risk, and make parties worse off. "The idea that favoring one side or the other in a class of contract disputes can redistribute wealth is one of the most persistent illusions of judicial power. It comes from failing to consider the full consequences of legal decisions. Courts deciding contract cases cannot durably shift the balance of advantages to the weaker side of the market. They can only make contracts more costly to that side in the future, because [the other side] will demand compensation for bearing onerous terms." *Original Great American Chocolate Chip Cookie Co. v. River Valley Cookies, Ltd.,* 970 F.2d 273, 282 (7th Cir. 1992). Parties to contracts are entitled to seek, and retain, personal advantage; striving for that advantage is the source of much economic progress. Contract law does not require parties to be fair, or kind, or reasonable, or to share gains or losses equitably. It does require parties to avoid taking advantage of the opportunities that arise from sequential performance, when the contract itself does not cover a particular subject. But the subject of this case—how long IRI's stream of commissions would last after termination—was covered explicitly. IRI was the repeat player in this arrangement, CP Clare the newcomer with small initial sales. IRI knew, or should have recognized, that the 90-day period created a risk; and it could have responded by demanding a higher commission rate to compensate. For all we know, the commission rate in this contract was higher than it would have been, had the period of post-termination

residuals been longer. But whether the commission rate adjusted or not, a deal's a deal.

AFFIRMED.

———

QUESTIONS

1.   Why does Judge Easterbrook mention the fact that CP Clare gave IRI 42 days' notice when the contract required only 30?

2.   Consider what Judge Easterbrook meant when, in paragraph 7, he said:

> The idea that favoring one side or the other in a class of contract disputes can redistribute wealth is one of the most persistent illusions of judicial power. It comes from failing to consider the full consequences of legal decisions. Courts deciding contract cases cannot durably shift the balance of advantages to the weaker side of the market. They can only make contracts more costly to that side in the future, because [the other side] will demand compensation for bearing onerous terms.

Original Great Am. Chocolate Chip Cookie Co. v. River Valley Cookies, Ltd., 970 F.2d 273, 282 (7th Cir. 1992) (internal citations omitted).

———

PROBLEM 28-1

Pat O'Reilly operated the most popular pizza parlor in Smalltown. Pat's place was so popular that nobody wanted to go into competition with him. When he turned 65, Pat decided to sell his place to Marcia Smith. Neither Marcia nor Pat was represented in the transaction by a lawyer, and the contract that they signed did not contain a "non-compete clause," a clause common in business sales whereby the seller agrees not to go into competition with the buyer. After a couple of years, Pat grew bored with retirement and decided to open up a new pizza parlor across the street from Marcia's place. Marcia comes to you and wants to know if she can sue Pat. What do you tell her? No, could have contracted for non-compete

PROBLEM 28-2

Mohammad Habib is an immigrant from Egypt. He holds a Ph.D. in history from the University of Cairo, and he is fluent in English, but he is not familiar with the American legal system, nor does he have any experience in business, either in Egypt or the United States. Unable to find a satisfactory teaching job in the United States, he took his $25,000 savings, borrowed an additional $75,000 from friends and relatives and purchased a Shamrock Pizza franchise. He was not represented by a lawyer in the transaction.

On the whole, the Shamrock franchise agreement is fairer to the franchisee than are most similar agreements, but it does lack one protection common in franchise agreements—it doesn't contain any territorial protection, i.e., there is nothing to prevent Shamrock from opening another restaurant right across the street. Shamrock's standard form franchise agreement has written across the top in large letters: "CONSULT A LAWYER BEFORE SIGNING THIS AGREEMENT" but Mr. Habib signed the agreement during his initial interview with the Shamrock salesperson who neither encouraged him to consult a lawyer nor discouraged him from doing so.

For the first two years, Mr. Habib did reasonably well, netting about $65,000 a year before taxes for six ten-hour days a week. In the third year, Shamrock decided that Mr. Habib's location was in fact a truly prime location and Mr. Habib's failure to earn large profits was due to his introverted personality and his failure to deal forcefully with a group of disreputable-looking (but actually quite harmless) teenagers who frequented his restaurant and detracted from its otherwise upscale (for a pizza restaurant) atmosphere. Shamrock officials therefore decided to open a "company store" (a restaurant owned by Shamrock itself, rather than by a franchisee) directly across the street from Mr. Habib's restaurant. Mr. Habib's net profit immediately dropped almost to zero, and he consulted you. Can you successfully argue that Shamrock breached the implied covenant of good faith and fair dealing?

Possibly argue unconscionability
procedural

by taking advantage of an unsophisticated
party

CHAPTER 29

NON-PARTY RIGHTS: ASSIGNMENT, DELEGATION, NOVATION, AND THIRD PARTY BENEFICIARIES

■ ■ ■

Prior chapters of this book examined the rights of parties to a contract. They began with issues of contract formation like offer, acceptance, and consideration. Next, they moved to selected formation defenses. Then, the rules that govern interpreting a writing that represents all or part of the contract were covered. After that, damages. Then the mechanics of the contract, including express or implied conditions and the nebulous duty of good faith and fair dealing. All these subjects were presented largely in the context of the parties to the original contract, the promissor and the promisee.

This chapter deals with the rights and obligations of third parties that were *not* the original promissor or promisee. The first group of subjects is assignment, delegation, and novation. "Assignment," classically, refers to a transfer of the right to receive the benefit of a contract, and "delegation," classically, refers to the transfer of the duties under a contract. In modern usage the two concepts are often lumped together under the term "assignment," probably reflecting the practical reality that contracts, unless one side has fully performed and the contract is no longer executory as to that party, are mixtures of benefits and burdens for each party. Thus, taking on one side of an executory contract will necessarily involve taking on duties as well as claiming the benefits. That said, it is certainly possible for parties to assign only the benefits or delegate only the duties under the original contract.

For example, if A enters into an option contract to purchase B's land for $100,000 in the next 180 days, A may be able to assign that option contract to C, a developer, who would then have the option to purchase the land for the stated sum during the given time period. If B refused to sell the land on the terms of the option, C could have the right to sue A and B for damages or specific performance. C's right to sue A on the assignment of the option contract is fairly straightforward; the assignment is a simple two party contract between A and C. C's right to sue B is a matter that will depend on whether the option was legally assignable (or, in our second group of concepts in this chapter, whether C was an intended third party beneficiary of the original option).

Closely related to assignment and delegation is the notion of a "novation" or a release of the original party who is assigning or delegating the contract (or has done so in the past). Imagine that ABC Corp. has a contract with a service that supplies and takes care of ABC's flowers and plants in the office that ABC leases from its landlord. Imagine further that ABC Corp. decides to relocate, assigning its lease and the plant servicing contract to a replacement tenant. When the replacement tenant doesn't pay the service, can the service look to ABC Corp. for payment under the contract? Generally, unless the plant service took actions that could be construed as releasing ABC Corp. from its contract, which would constitute a "novation," ABC remains liable on the contract even after the assignment.

If ABC desires to no longer be liable on the contract that it assigns, it needs to obtain a novation from the plant service in connection with the assignment to the replacement tenant. Think of a novation as a release of the original obligor from the original obligee when the original obligor transfers the contract to a new obligor. A novation theory may also provide a means to escape liability under a contract that appears to have been modified orally by conduct despite an all-modifications-must-be-in-writing clause.

The final issues for assignment and delegation revolve around whether the contract is assignable as a matter of law. The parties can provide that assignment is permitted, is permitted only in certain circumstances, or is prohibited. Sometimes, state law regulates what conditions on assignment are permissible. For example, the California Supreme Court has held that, in commercial real property leases, the landlord may not unreasonably withhold consent for assignment. *Kendall v. Ernest Pestana, Inc.*, 40 Cal.3d 488, 220 Cal.Rptr. 818, 709 P.2d 837 (1985). Thus, whether the law will enforce the provisions as the parties draft them is one set of issues.

Another set of issues involves whether, if the parties do not expressly provide for assignment or delegation in the contract, it will be permitted. If a world famous opera singer contracts to give a performance, can the opera singer delegate her performance duties to someone else, say, you? Probably not. The services are very specific, very personal to the opera singer. On the other hand, can an industrial cleaning service that cleans offices at night assign its contracts to a third party cleaner for a fee? Barring issues of security and confidentiality, the answer is "probably."

The cases that follow illustrate these principles and highlight the issues involved. Keep in mind that in practice just about every contract drafted by modern, competent counsel contains a clause addressing assignment and delegation. Assuming this clause is enforceable in the jurisdiction involved, this clause will specify the parties' rights in this regard and should end the inquiry. Examples of provisions dealing with assignment and delegation include:

> Neither party to this agreement may assign any of its rights or delegate any of its duties under this Agreement without the prior written consent of the other party, which may not be unreasonably withheld. Further, despite consent to the assignment, no assignment or delegation shall release the assigning or delegating party from any of its obligations under this Agreement or modify those obligations unless the release or modification is expressly contained in the written consent to the assignment or delegation.

-or-

> Each party to this Agreement may assign all or any part of its rights under this Agreement and may delegate all or any of its duties under this Agreement provided that *[insert relevant condition here, if any]*.

After covering assignment and delegation, this chapter turns to the subject of third party beneficiary contracts, that is, those made by A and B that benefit C.

A. ASSIGNMENT AND DELEGATION

SHORELINE COMMUNICATIONS, INC. v. NORWICH TAXI, LLC

Appellate Court of Connecticut
70 Conn. App. 60, 797 A.2d 1165 (2002)

PETERS, J.

[1] This appeal concerns the rights of an assignee to terminate a license agreement when it discovers, after the assignment, that it had been mistaken in its assumption that the licensed property would suit its commercial needs. The trial court held that the assignee had assumed the risk of its unilateral mistake because it had failed to inspect the licensor's premises before assuming the license agreement. Having assumed the risk, the assignee was obligated to pay license fees during the unexpired term of the license agreement. We agree and affirm the judgment of the trial court.

[2] The plaintiff, Shoreline Communications, Inc., the owner of a radio communications tower, sued the defendant, Norwich Taxi, LLC, to recover unpaid license fees due under a license agreement with the defendant's assignor, Eagle Cab Corporation (Eagle). Eagle had assigned its contractual rights to use space on the tower to the defendant, which

unconditionally assumed Eagle's obligations to the plaintiff. The defendant declined to pay the license fees once it became evident that, contrary to its expectations, its equipment could not make profitable use of the tower space. Characterizing the defendant's disappointment as a unilateral mistake, the court held that the defendant's mistake did not authorize its unilateral rescission of the license agreement. Accordingly, the court rendered judgment in favor of the plaintiff, awarding it damages in the amount of $12,600[1] for the unpaid license fees, as well as interest of $273.92 and costs. The defendant has appealed.

[3] The trial court's memorandum of decision recites the relevant facts, which are undisputed. On October 30, 1997, the plaintiff and Eagle entered into a five year license agreement that enabled Eagle to use its radio equipment at a designated space on the plaintiff's radio transmission tower in order to pursue its taxicab business. The license agreement granted Eagle the right to use the space without restriction to any particular usage. In return, Eagle undertook to pay stipulated monthly payments to the plaintiff. Eagle encountered no problems in its use of the transmission tower and promptly made license payments as they became due.

[4] On May 20, 1999, Eagle assigned the license agreement to the defendant. Without reserving any additional rights, the defendant informed the plaintiff that it had assumed the rights and obligations stated in the license agreement. As assignee, it made payments to the plaintiff until the end of October of that year.

[5] Between May, 1999, and October, 1999, the defendant made a good faith effort to install its radio equipment on the plaintiff's tower. Because Eagle's installation had encountered no difficulties, the defendant had not anticipated that its own installation would be problematic.

[6] At the time of the assignment, the defendant did not know whether it could use Eagle's equipment but it did know that its own taxi service differed from Eagle's because its service area was wider and its business was conducted at a location further away from the plaintiff's tower. Despite this uncertainty, the defendant unconditionally assumed the rights and duties set out in the license agreement. From May to October, 1999, the defendant attempted, unsuccessfully, to use the tower space. It discovered that its use of the plaintiff's tower space would have required the services of two different telephone companies, with unacceptable uncertainties about prompt detection and remediation of transmission failures.

[7] When these facts came to light, the defendant informed the plaintiff that the licensing agreement was terminated. The plaintiff

---

[1]   [$12,600 in 2002 dollars is roughly the equivalent of $17,600 in 2019 dollars using the CPI and the GNP Deflator.—Eds.]

promptly replied that the defendant had no right to terminate the
agreement unilaterally. The plaintiff reminded the defendant of the
provision of the agreement that required the payment of license fees until
the expiration of the agreement on October 31, 2002. It demanded prompt
payment of the fees already overdue. Nevertheless, the defendant stopped
making payments as of November 1, 1999.

[8]   At the time when the defendant assumed liability under the
licensing agreement, it had taken no steps to ascertain whether
installation of its equipment would be feasible. The defendant assumed
that Eagle's favourable experience with Eagle's equipment would carry over
to the defendant's own operations. Despite known differences between its
business operations and that of Eagle, the defendant did not avail itself of
the opportunity to arrange for a preassignment inspection of the tower
space.

[9]   On the basis of these findings of fact, the court concluded that, as
a matter of law, the defendant had failed to establish that its mistaken
assumptions entitled it to terminate the license agreement without the
assent of the plaintiff. Relying on 1 Restatement (Second), Contracts §§ 153
& 154, pp. 394, 402 (1981), the court held that the defendant had assumed
the risk of a misfit between the plaintiff's tower space and the defendant's
equipment. It had assumed that risk, the court held, because prior to
becoming Eagle's assignee, it had relied on Eagle's experience without
ascertaining whether its own greater needs might encounter difficulties
that Eagle had not experienced.

[10] The defendant challenges the court's conclusion on three grounds.
Conceding that it made a unilateral mistake, the defendant maintains that
the mistake terminated the licensing agreement because (1) it did not bear
the risk of that mistake, (2) enforcement of an agreement that is of no
benefit to the defendant is unconscionable and (3) prompt repudiation of
the agreement did not injure the plaintiff because it could be restored to
the rights it had before the assignment.

[11] Because the claims that the defendant has raised challenge the
trial court's conclusions of law, our review is plenary. We conclude that
none of these claims is persuasive.

I.   The Risk of Unilateral Mistake

[12] The defendant argues that it falls within various exceptions to the
general rule that a unilateral mistake is not a viable basis for rescission of
a bilateral contract. The defendant maintains that it did not assume the
risk of incompatibility between its equipment and the plaintiff's tower
because it had no reason to expect any such incompatibility and, therefore,
was acting in good faith when it delayed its inquiry into such matters to a
time subsequent to the assignment. We do not agree that, under the

circumstances of this case, the defendant was entitled unilaterally to set aside its contract obligation to pay license fees.

[13] As the trial court noted, the principles governing the law of mistake are set out in 1 Restatement (Second), *supra*, §§ 53 and 154. Under § 153, a unilateral mistake may make a contract voidable if the mistaken party "does not bear the risk of the mistake under the rule stated in § 154. . . ." 1 Restatement (Second), *supra*, § 53, p. 394. Under § 154, "A party bears the risk of a mistake when . . . (b) he is aware, at the time the contract is made, that he has only limited knowledge with respect to the facts to which the mistake relates but treats his limited knowledge as sufficient. . . ." 1 Restatement (Second), *supra*, § 154, pp. 402–03.

[14] The court, in its careful and comprehensive memorandum of decision, concluded that the defendant bore the risk of its unilateral mistake because, when it assumed the licensing agreement, it was aware of significant differences between its own planned operations and that of Eagle. Relying on § 154 of the Restatement (Second) of Contracts, the court held that, because of this awareness, the defendant bore the risk of mistake when it nonetheless undertook to become an assignee, without conditioning its assigned duties in any way.

[15] The defendant argues, to the contrary, that its knowledge of these differences was insufficient to assign the risk of loss to it because, relying on Eagle's favorable experience, it was entitled to assume that its operations would likewise be able to make use of the plaintiff's tower site. The defendant maintains that it did not have the kind of "limited knowledge" that would require it to bear the risk of its mistake. It was not, therefore, "consciously" aware of treating "[its] limited knowledge as sufficient."

[16] One difficulty with the defendant's view of the law of mistake is that its argument rests entirely on the defendant's subjective state of mind at the time of the assignment. The defendant concedes that its position finds no support in the terms of the license agreement. The agreement did not make a licensee's obligation to pay license fees contingent on the licensee's ability to make profitable use of the designated space on the plaintiff's radio tower. Neither in writing nor orally did the plaintiff undertake *any* contractual obligation other than to make tower space available.

[17] Apart from the agreement, the plaintiff had no reason to anticipate an assignment of any kind and consequently had no reason to anticipate the difficulties that an assignee might encounter. The plaintiff's operations bore no resemblance to a business such as the construction business, in which unilateral mistakes are known to occur as a result of the pressure of last minute preparation of competitive bids. In short, the plaintiff did not contribute to the defendant's mistake in any way.

[18] The record does not show that the defendant revealed to anyone, in advance of the assignment, that it had specific expectations about its use of the tower space. Negation of a contract obligation in these circumstances would place a risk on the plaintiff that the plaintiff could have neither foreseen nor avoided. It is the rare case in which contract rights are so ephemeral. "Where the language of the contract is clear and unambiguous, the contract is to be given effect according to its terms. A court will not torture words to import ambiguity where the ordinary meaning leaves no room for ambiguity ... Similarly, any ambiguity in a contract must emanate from the language used in the contract rather than from one party's subjective perception of the terms." *Tallmadge Bros., Inc. v. Iroquois Gas Transmission System, L.P.*, 252 Conn. 479, 498, 746 A.2d 1277 (2000) (internal quotation marks omitted).

[19] A second difficulty with the defendant's position is that the proven facts demonstrate that the defendant assumed the risk of its unilateral mistake as that risk is defined in § 154 of the Restatement. Before the assignment, the defendant knew that its use of the tower space would differ from that of Eagle because the defendant's taxi business covered a larger geographical area and was located further away from the tower. It did not ascertain whether Eagle's equipment would be suitable for its own needs. It made no effort to determine the suitability of the plaintiff's tower space. The defendant could as readily have discovered possible problems before the assignment as after the assignment. The defendant cannot avoid its contractual obligation when it could have taken steps to check out the accuracy of its expectations.

[20] On the basis of the facts found by the trial court and the law that it correctly stated and applied, we conclude that the defendant has not established that it was excused from the consequences of its unilateral mistake. Contrary to its arguments, we conclude that it bore the risk of loss attributable to its mistake.

II. Unconscionability

[21] The defendant further argues that, even if it bore the risk of mistake, enforcement of the license agreement would be unconscionable because it should not be required to pay for space that it cannot use. We disagree.

[22] The text of the Restatement does not support the defendant's argument. Although § 153 speaks of unconscionability, that provision applies only in the absence of an assumption of risk by the party that has made a unilateral mistake.

[23] As a general matter, we know of no case, and the defendant has cited none, in which a party may invoke unconscionability without a showing of some kind of relevant misconduct by the party seeking enforcement of a contract. The usual case concerns the liability of a

No misconduct by the P

consumer who assumed unexpectedly onerous contract obligations that were not fully disclosed by a commercial seller.

[24] Many of the unconscionability cases arise in the context of some kind of misleading conduct that comes close to being fraudulent. Under the law of procedural unconscionability, such contracts may be voidable by an innocent party who has been misled about the advisability of entering into a contract.

[25] The defendant does not claim that its duty to pay licensee fees should be set aside because the plaintiff engaged in misleading conduct. Instead, the defendant maintains that the license agreement should be set aside on the ground of substantive unconscionability. The leasing agreement is substantively unconscionable, according to the defendant, because of a "gross disparity in the values exchanged" by the parties. The defendant argues that it should not have to pay for tower space that is useless.

[26] The defendant's argument is unpersuasive for two reasons. The defendant fails to distinguish between personal lack of utility and general lack of utility. It fails to explain why an assignee has rights of termination that are greater than those of its assignor. It is important to restate that the tower space is not defective or valueless. It had value for some licensees, such as Eagle, and not for others, such as the defendant. So long as the plaintiff did not undertake to warrant the suitability of the tower space, it is inaccurate to describe the tower space as useless.

[27] Further, it bears remembering that the defendant's rights and obligations are derived from those undertaken by Eagle. The licensing agreement was fully enforceable before the assignment. There was no novation or modification of the license agreement. The defendant does not allege that Eagle, the assignor, had any right to terminate the agreement before expiration of its five year term. Eagle successfully made use of its assigned space on the plaintiff's tower. Eagle never made a unilateral mistake of any kind. In effect, the defendant asserts that, because its equipment differs from that of Eagle, it has a greater right to terminate than Eagle had.

[28] The defendant nonetheless claims the right to add a new condition to the license agreement to accommodate its own uncommunicated needs. It is hornbook law, however, that an assignee "stands in the shoes of the assignor." *Rumbin v. Utica Mutual Ins. Co.*, 254 Conn. 259, 277, 757 A.2d 526 (2000) (internal quotation marks omitted); *National Loan Investors Ltd. Partnership v. Heritage Square Associates*, 54 Conn. App. 67, 73, 733 A.2d 876 (1999); 3 E. Farnsworth, Contracts (1998) § 11.8, p. 105–07; 3 S. Williston, Contracts (3d Ed. 1960) § 404, p. 5, and § 432, pp. 181–83. An assignee has no greater rights or immunities than the assignor would have

had if there had been no assignment. *Fairfield Credit Corp. v. Donnelly*, 158 Conn. 543, 552, 264 A.2d 547 (1969).

[29] We can find no support for the proposition that, by dint of an assignment, an enforceable agreement has become unconscionable. To the contrary, it would be unreasonable to allow an assignment to deprive the plaintiff of its unconditional contractual right to license payments. The terms of the leasing agreement did not change. The plaintiff did not solicit the assignment. Standing in the shoes of the assignor, the defendant had no authority to rewrite the contract for which it has assumed full responsibility.

[30] We are not persuaded that the defendant was empowered, as a result of its own mistake, to change absolute contractual obligations into provisional contract obligations. Contrary to the defendant's argument, this case does not exemplify a "gross disparity in the values exchanged by the parties."

[31] In its argument for "gross disparity," the defendant underscores the cost of making license payments for space that, for its purposes, has no value. That cost must, however, be compared to the cost to the plaintiff if it does not receive such payments, because that is the other side of the equation.

[32] The trial court analyzed the consequences to the plaintiff of failing to receive license fees. In its discussion of the plaintiff's right to damages, the court considered whether such damages should be reduced as a result of the plaintiff's failure to search for other users for the defendant's tower site. The court concluded that such a reduction would be inappropriate because the plaintiff's tower had many vacant spaces. The defendant's nonpayment would not give the plaintiff the opportunity to profit from a new license agreement of the defendant's tower space. In this appeal, the defendant has not challenged the validity of the court's analysis.

[33] It follows from the court's conclusion that, in the event of nonpayment by the defendant, the plaintiff cannot be made whole. It cannot be restored to its situation before the leasing agreement unless it has forfeited its rights to payment because of the defendant's mistake. Put differently, the question of "gross disparity" devolves into the question of whether the innocent plaintiff or the mistaken defendant should be $12,600 out of pocket. It would turn contract principles on their head to put this burden on the plaintiff when, as we have decided earlier in this opinion, the defendant bore the risk of its mistake.

[34] We conclude, therefore, that enforcing the licensing agreement is not unconscionable. Two commercial parties, presumably with access to attorneys, entered into an agreement that the plaintiff has honored fully. There is nothing inherently unfair in an agreement that unambiguously and unconditionally requires one of the parties to assume the risk that its

use of the licensed space might be unprofitable. If such an agreement, in retrospect, seems harsh to the defendant, the defendant could have refused to become an assignee. Having undertaken the assignment without discussion with the plaintiff and without inspection of the tower site, the defendant cannot rely on a defense of unconscionability.

III. Consequences of a Rescission

[35] Underlying the defendant's final argument for rescission is that, even if it bore the risk of unilateral mistake, its mistake was the result of good faith expectations and therefore gave it an equitable claim, apart from unconscionability, to rescind its obligations under the license agreement. We disagree with this argument as well.

[36] Part of the defendant's claim is its contention that the agreement is rescindable because the plaintiff can be returned to the contractual rights that it had before the assignment. We have already addressed and rejected that contention. In *Milford Yacht Realty Co. v. Milford Yacht Club, Inc.*, 136 Conn. 544, 549, 72 A.2d 482 (1950), our Supreme Court held that "[a] court of equity is always reluctant to rescind, unless the parties can be put back in *statu quo*. If this cannot be done, it will give such relief only where the clearest and strongest equity imperatively demands it." (Internal quotation marks omitted).

[37] The other part of the defendant's claim is that rescission is proper because the plaintiff's rights are adequately protected by the fact that the plaintiff can seek recovery from Eagle. The defendant correctly notes that, as a matter of law, an assignor's obligations are not extinguished by an assignment. Despite Eagle's assignment of its contract rights and duties to the defendant, Eagle could not and did not unilaterally discharge its duties to pay license fees to the plaintiff. "When a duty is delegated . . . the delegating party . . . continues to remain liable. . . . [Delegation] does not free the obligor . . . from [its] duty to see to it that performance is rendered, unless there is a novation." *Gateway Co. v. DiNoia*, 232 Conn. 223, 233, 654 A.2d 342 (1995) (internal quotation marks omitted), citing J. Calamari & J. Perillo, Contracts (3d Ed. 1987) § 18–25, p. 757; *cf. Carrano v. Shoor*, 118 Conn. 86, 95–98, 171 A. 17 (1934). There was neither an allegation nor a finding that the assignment constituted a novation that would have relieved Eagle from liability.

[38] As a matter of fact, however, a judgment against Eagle would likely be unenforceable. As the defendant acknowledges in the opening paragraph of its appellate brief, it "bought the assets of Eagle Cab." There is no suggestion in the record that Eagle ever acquired other assets or, for that matter, that it stayed in business.

[39] It is anomalous that a party seeking equitable relief from the consequences of its own mistake should seek to justify its failure to make

license payments by pointing the innocent party to an alternate source of relief that is illusory. As far as the record shows, Eagle no longer exists.

[40] The defendant, therefore, has no right to rescind the licensing agreement. It has not made a persuasive case that "the clearest and strongest equity imperatively demands" such a rescission. The defendant must fulfill the obligations that it assumed when it became an assignee of the licensing agreement.

The judgment is affirmed.

In this opinion the other judges concurred.

NOTES AND QUESTIONS

1.   The *Shoreline Communications* case, besides being well organized and well written, illustrates that assignees "stand in the shoes of their assignor" and take only those rights that the assignor had, subject to the assignor's duties. This is the contract corollary to the property principle that one cannot receive more property rights than one's grantor(s) had.

2.   The case also illustrates the common reaction of courts to an attempt by a not unsophisticated party to change the terms of its contract using the doctrines of mistake, unconscionability, rescission, and broad equitable powers. It bears repeating: In general, a contract means what it says. Caveat emptor. Buyers and assignees should read the contract and inspect the goods, services, or premises before entering into the assignment. Counsel should advise them accordingly.

3.   Note how, although Norwich Taxi is said to have become "an assignee of the licensing agreement," *see* paragraph [40], the court holds it is bound to perform duties under the contract, thus being a classic delegatee. This illustrates the use of the term "assignment" to cover assignment and delegation of the benefits *and* burdens of a contract.

4.   A delegation of duties under a contract has no effect upon the delegator's duties to the original promissee absent a novation, i.e., a release by the original promissee of the duties of the delegator, the original promisor.

5.   The following case reviews standards relating to a contract, here a lease of commercial property, that provide for its conditional assignment, as well as the successful application of the doctrine of unconscionability to defeat what the court perceives as an overreaching provision. Further, the case illustrates how a novation theory may be used to support a modification of the parties' deal even when the original contract contains an all-modifications-must-be-in-writing clause.

FANUCCHI & LIMI FARMS V. UNITED AGRI PRODUCTS

United States Court of Appeals, Ninth Circuit
414 F.3d 1075 (2005)

W. FLETCHER, CIRCUIT JUDGE.

[1] Fanucchi & Limi Farms, Larry Fanucchi, and Richard Limi (collectively "Fanucchi") sued United Agri Products Financial Services, Inc. ("United") for breach of contract and promissory fraud. The district court granted summary judgment to United. Fanucchi appeals from the grant of summary judgment, and from an associated grant of attorneys' fees. We conclude that the novation theory providing one basis for Fanucchi's breach of contract claim should have survived summary judgment.

[2] Accordingly, we reverse and remand to allow the breach of contract claim to go forward on a novation theory. We otherwise affirm the summary judgment. Because we reverse part of the summary judgment, we vacate the order granting attorneys' fees.

I. Background

[3] Larry Fanucchi, Richard Limi, and Linda Limi were general partners in Fanucchi & Limi Farms, in Kern County, California. Fanucchi financed its farming operations by borrowing against its future crop proceeds. In December 1994, United lent money to Fanucchi to finance its operating costs for 1995 ("the 1994 Loan"). The 1994 Loan was memorialized in several documents, including an Agricultural Loan Agreement, a Promissory Note, an Agricultural Security Agreement, separate Commercial Guarantees personally executed by Larry Fanucchi, Richard Limi, and Linda Limi, and a Notice of Final Agreement. These documents set out the terms of the loan in considerable detail. The Agricultural Loan Agreement outlines the disbursement schedule, repayment terms, and circumstances under which the loan may be renewed in future years. The Agricultural Security Agreement establishes United's security interest in Fanucchi's crops. The Commercial Guarantees are individual loan guarantees by Larry Fanucchi, Richard Limi, and Linda Limi in the event United's security interest in the crops fails to cover the loan. The Notice of Final Agreement provides that the 1994 Loan incorporates all of the above documents. The 1994 Loan documents contain language describing how the parties may modify the agreement. Both the Agricultural Loan Agreement and Agricultural Security Agreement have an integration clause that reads:

> **Amendments.** This Agreement, together with any Related Documents, constitutes the entire understanding and agreement of the parties as to the matters set forth in this Agreement. No alteration of or amendment to this Agreement shall be effective unless given in writing and signed by the party or parties sought to be charged or bound by the alteration or amendment.

[4] The three Commercial Guarantees also contain integration clauses requiring modifications to be in writing. Finally, the Notice of Final Agreement provides that (1) "the written loan agreement represents the final agreement between the parties," (2) "there are no unwritten oral agreements between the parties," and (3) "the written loan agreement may not be contradicted by evidence of any prior, contemporaneous, or subsequent oral agreements or understandings of the parties."

[5] After Fanucchi and United entered into the 1994 Loan agreement, United increased the amount of the note from $700,000 to $800,000 on January 30, 1995; to $900,000 on March 1, 1995; and to $1,475,000 on September 18, 1995. All increases were made in writing and provided that "[t]he terms and conditions of [the original Promissory Note] will remain in full force and effect for this increase." Fanucchi's 1995 crops failed. As a result, Fanucchi was unable to repay the 1994 Loan, and owed more than a million dollars to United.

[6] Fanucchi consulted with a United representative, Wayne Keese, and with bankruptcy counsel. According to the depositions of Larry Fanucchi ("Larry") and Richard Limi ("Richard"), Keese persuaded Fanucchi not to file for bankruptcy, but rather to continue farming. According to Larry and Richard's depositions, Keese orally promised to subordinate United's debt to new crop financing loans from other lenders for up to five years.[2] During this period, United's 1994 Loan would be repaid from the crop proceeds available after new crop loans were paid off. These proceeds were to be split on a 60/40 basis, with 60 percent going to United and 40 percent going to Fanucchi's other creditors. According to Larry's deposition, Keese said that if Fanucchi had paid its debt on the 1994 Loan down to $300,000 or $400,000 at the end of the five-year period, United would forgive that amount. Keese testified in his deposition that "[w]e discussed pretty openly possibilities, options, of which bankruptcy was one." He stated, "[M]y approach always has been to—if you can work out an arrangement where they can continue to pay their debt in a reasonable period of time, I'm open and willing to listen to it." Keese confirmed that there was an oral agreement that after the new crop loans were paid off the remaining money would be split 60/40, but his recollection was that this was done only on a year-to-year basis. Keese stated that he did not recall discussing a five-year term during which Fanucchi could try to pay down its debt to United. Nor did he recall promising that United would forgive the debt at the end a five-year period should Fanucchi succeed in paying it down to a certain level: "I don't remember having any discussion of that nature" (ellipsis in original).

---

[2]   [Without the alleged subordination United would have had a first priority security interest (the functional equivalent of a first mortgage) on the 1995 crop and later crops and no other lender would have been willing to finance these crops until United was paid.—Eds.]

[7] The agreement operated as described by Larry and Richard for the crop years 1996 and 1997. New secured lenders were found for those years; those lenders were paid from the crop proceeds; and the remaining proceeds were divided 60/40 between United and Fanucchi's other creditors. There is ample undisputed evidence in the record to show this. For example, a January 5, 1997 letter from a United representative, Bruce Carter, to Southern California Cotton Financing ("Southern California Cotton") details United's agreement to subordinate its debt to enable Fanucchi to obtain other sources of crop financing for that year. The secured lenders for that year include Southern California Cotton, as well as the parents of Larry and Richard. The letter provides in part:

> [A]ccording to the attached "Acknowledgment and Agreement," on behalf of United Agri Products Financial Services, I give the authority to Southern California Financing to pay the above mentioned sums to first, Southern California Cotton Financing, secondly to Mr. & Mrs. Fanucchi and thirdly to Mr. & Mrs. Limi, prior to funds coming to United Agri Products Financial Services, Inc. All funds in excess of the Southern California Cotton Financing, Fanucchi and Limi funds should come to United Agri Products Financial Services, Inc.

[8] A May 12, 1997 letter from Carter to Daniel Rudnick, Fanucchi's attorney, similarly describes United's agreement:

> This letter is to advise you that United Agri Products has agreed to split the profits from the 1997 Fanucchi-Limi Farms Partnership #2 farming operations on a basis of 60% for United Agri Products and 40% for Fanucchi-Limi Farms. Profits should be defined as those monies left after the repayment of all 1997 operating loans, including interest, to Southern California Cotton Financing, and to both sets of parents[.]

[9] Keese's employment at United terminated in early 1998. His last day on the payroll was March 31. Beginning in the spring of 1998, United was no longer willing to perform in accordance with the agreement described by Larry and Richard. Instead of subordinating to all of the lenders for the 1998 crop, United was willing to subordinate only to Southern California Cotton. On April 17, 1998, Denise Fitzgerald wrote on behalf of United to Southern California Cotton, confirming that United had assigned its interest in the proceeds of the 1998 crop to Southern California Cotton up to the amount of its loan, and indicating that all the remaining proceeds from the 1998 crop were to be paid to United. Unlike in 1996 and 1997, United refused to subordinate to the parents of Larry and Richard. Jerry Simmons, who had been hired by United as the new credit manager in February or March 1998, testified at his deposition that it was his decision not to subordinate to the parents: "I don't subordinate to family

members." In August 2000, Fanucchi sued United in California Superior Court for breach of contract and promissory fraud. The gravamen of Fanucchi's breach of contract claim is that by promising substantially to change the terms of the 1994 Loan agreement, United induced Fanucchi not to declare bankruptcy after the failure of the 1995 crops. In return for Fanucchi's not declaring bankruptcy, United agreed in 1995 to subordinate its lien to crop loans by new lenders for the next five years, to take only 60 percent of the crop proceeds remaining after the new crop lenders were paid off each year, and to forgive between $300,000 and $400,000 of the outstanding loan at the end of five years if Fanucchi were able to pay it down to that level. United breached this new agreement in 1998 by refusing to subordinate its lien to the two sets of parents, who had made crop loans for that year, and by taking all of that year's excess crop proceeds for its own account. United's actions prevented Fanucchi from obtaining financing for future crop years, effectively forcing it out of business. United removed to federal district court based on diversity of citizenship. The district court granted summary judgment and attorneys' fees to United. Fanucchi has timely appealed. We review the district court's grant of summary judgment de novo. *Olsen v. Idaho State Bd. of Med.*, 363 F.3d 916, 922 (9th Cir. 2004). Viewing the evidence in the light most favorable to Fanucchi, we must determine whether there are any genuine issues of material fact and whether the district court correctly applied California's substantive law. *Id.*

II.   Breach of Contract

[10] Fanucchi makes two breach of contract arguments. First, it argues that the subsequent oral agreement between Fanucchi and United modified the original 1994 Loan. Second, it argues that the subsequent oral agreement novated the 1994 Loan. We affirm the district court's grant of summary judgment to United on the modification argument. However, we reverse on the novation argument.

A.   *Modification*

[11] Fanucchi first argues that the 1994 Loan agreement was modified through subsequent oral agreements pursuant to California Civil Code §§ 1698(b) and (c), which provide:

(b) A contract in writing may be modified by an oral agreement to the extent that the oral agreement is executed by the parties.

(c) Unless the contract otherwise expressly provides, a contract in writing may be modified by an oral agreement supported by new consideration.

The statute of frauds (Section 1624) is required to be satisfied if the contract as modified is within its provisions. The district court rejected this argument. We agree with the district court.

[12] Section 1698(b) allows modification of a written contract by an oral agreement to the extent the oral agreement is executed. "Executed" in § 1698(b) has the normal meaning of that term in contract law. That is, the agreement must have been fully performed. *Lockheed Missiles & Space Co. v. Gilmore Indus.*, 135 Cal. App. 3d 556, 559 (Ct. App. 1982) (relying on Black's Law Dictionary to define "executed" as "completed; carried into full effect" (internal quotations omitted)); *see also* Cal. Civ. Code § 1661 ("An executed contract is one, the object of which is fully performed"). Fanucchi's own argument defeats its claim under § 1698(b), for it argues that United breached its obligation under the oral agreement because it failed to perform the *un*executed part of the agreement.

[13] Section 1698(c) allows oral modification of a written contract only if the written contract does not provide otherwise. *See also Marani v. Jackson*, 183 Cal. App. 3d 695, 704 (Ct. App. 1986) (noting that oral modification of a written contract is allowed only if "the written contract does not contain an express provision requiring that modification be in writing"). The 1994 Loan provides that "the written loan agreement may not be contradicted by evidence of any prior, contemporaneous, or subsequent oral agreements or understandings of the parties." Fanucchi therefore cannot rely on § 1698(c) in support of its oral modification claim.

B.   Novation

[14] Fanucchi next contends that the 1994 Loan agreement was novated. Taking the evidence in the light most favorable to Fanucchi, we agree. That is, if Fanucchi's evidence is believed, the 1994 Loan agreement was novated, and the subsequent oral agreement governs the relationship between Fanucchi and United.

California Civil Code § 1698(d) provides:

> Nothing in this section precludes in an appropriate case the application of rules of law concerning estoppel, oral novation and substitution of a new agreement, rescission of a written contract by an oral agreement, waiver of a provision of a written contract, or oral independent collateral contracts.

[15] United does not argue that novation is unavailable because the subsequent agreement was oral. Rather, it argues Fanucchi has failed properly to plead novation, and that, even taking Fanucchi's evidence in its most favorable light, the subsequent oral agreement does not fulfill the substantive requirements of novation under California law. We disagree.

[16] Novation is "the substitute of a new obligation for an existing one." [Cal. Civ. Code § 1530]. Novation may be accomplished either by the substitution of a new debtor or a new creditor, California Civil Code § 1531(2)–(3), or "[b]y the substitution of a new obligation between the same parties, with intent to extinguish the old obligation[.]" *Id.* § 1531(1).

Whereas a modification of a term or a provision of a contract alters only certain portions of the contract, novation wholly extinguishes the earlier contract. "The intention of the parties to extinguish the prior obligation and to substitute a new agreement in its place must clearly appear." *Hunt v. Smyth*, 25 Cal. App. 3d 807, 818 (Ct. App. 1972). The existence of a new oral agreement replacing a prior written agreement must be shown with "clear and convincing" evidence. *Columbia Cas. Co. v. Lewis*, 14 Cal. App. 2d 64, 72 (Ct. App. 1936).

[17] In deciding whether an agreement was meant to extinguish the old obligation and to substitute a new one, California courts seek to determine the parties' intent. *See, e.g., Alexander v. Angel*, 37 Cal. 2d 856, 860 (1951) ("The question whether a novation has taken place is always one of intention").

[18] Determining the parties' intent is a highly fact-specific inquiry. Such inquiries are not generally suitable for disposition on summary judgment. Courts examining a novation claim first look to the agreements themselves, and, specifically, the substance of the change or changes between the old and new agreements. Courts may also take into consideration the conduct of the parties, particularly where, as here, the subsequent agreement is oral. Indeed, "it is not necessary to meet and state either in writing or orally that the original contract was rescinded. 'If the intent to abandon can be ascertained from the acts and conduct of the parties the same result will be attained. Abandonment may be implied from surrounding facts and circumstances.' " *Id.* (citations omitted).

[19] Assuming the truth of Fanucchi's evidence, United argues that there has been no novation. Specifically, United argues that the changes between the original 1994 Loan agreement and the later oral agreement were insufficient to evidence an intent to extinguish the 1994 Loan agreement and to replace it with a new agreement. The strongest case in support of United's argument is *Davies Machinery Co. v. Pine Mountain Club, Inc.*, 39 Cal. App. 3d 18 (Ct. App. 1974). In *Davies Machinery*, the Smiths entered into a security agreement under which they agreed to purchase heavy earthmoving equipment from Davies Machinery ("Davies") for slightly over a million dollars. The contract provided that the Smiths would pay $43,574 per month for 24 months. The contract further provided that payments not made when due would accrue interest at a rate of 12 percent. About a year later, the Smiths had fallen behind in their payments and owed over $100,000 under the contract. *Id.* at 21. Davies agreed with the Smiths that they could keep the equipment in order to generate income from their contracting business, and that they would pay for it at a specified rate based on the actual hours the equipment was used in the business. Nothing was said about terminating the original purchase contract. While the Smiths were performing work for the Pine Mountain Club, they fell behind in the newly arranged payment schedule. Davies

repossessed the equipment and sold it. Davies then sought to impose a mechanic's lien on the Pine Mountain Club. Under California law, Davies was entitled to a lien against Pine Mountain Club if the equipment had been rented to the Smiths, but not if it had been sold to them. No one disputed that the original agreement constituted a sale of the equipment. However, Davies contended that the change in the payment scheme after the Smiths fell behind in their payments constituted a novation of the original contract, by virtue of which the Smiths became renters rather than owners of the equipment.

[20] The Smiths' accountant testified at trial that the purpose of the new arrangement was "to arrange lower monthly payments on the purchase contract so that the equipment could ultimately be paid off." *Id.* at 25. Davies's manager testified that neither Davies nor the Smiths ever "released their equity in the equipment." *Id.* The Court of Appeal noted that the parties had explicitly agreed only that the manner and timing of the payments should be changed. On these facts, the court held that the original contract had not been novated, and that a mechanic's lien was improper.

[21] If Fanucchi's evidence is believed, the new agreement in this case did more than simply alter the timing and amount of the payments to United. For example, unlike the agreement in *Davies Machinery*, United agreed to "release its equity" (to use the phrase employed in *Davies Machinery*) in Fanucchi's crops in order to permit Fanucchi to obtain new crop financing after 1995. Further, under the new agreement, United would forgive between $300,000 and $400,000 at the end of five years. By contrast, Davies never agreed to forgive any part of the Smiths' obligation to pay for the equipment. This case more closely resembles *Alexander v. Angel*, 37 Cal. 2d 856 (1951), and *San Gabriel Valley Ready-Mixt v. Casillas*, 142 Cal. App. 2d 137 (1956), where the California Supreme Court and the Court of Appeals found novation. In *Angel*, the Alexanders sold a business to Angel and took back two promissory notes secured by a chattel mortgage. Each note was for $2,150. One note was due in one year, the other in two years. Neither note bore interest. Prior to the maturity of either note, Angel sold the business to the Hawses. Upon this sale, the Alexanders and the Hawses agreed that the Alexanders would not enforce the original notes, but would, instead, take back a new note from the Hawses. The new agreement was different from the old agreement in three respects: (1) Unlike the original notes, which were to be paid off on a lump-sum basis at the end of one and two years, the new notes would be paid at a rate of $150 per month until the entire $4,300 was paid off. (2) Unlike the original notes, the new notes bore interest. (3) Unlike the original notes, the new notes contained an acceleration clause in the event of nonpayment of the monthly obligation. When the Hawses fell behind in their payments, the Alexanders sued Angel to enforce the obligation under the original

notes. Angel defended on the ground that the agreement between the Alexanders and the Hawses was a novation, and that the obligation under the original notes was extinguished. The California Supreme Court held that the changed agreement between the Alexanders and the Hawses was a novation, extinguishing the old obligation "by the substitution of a new debtor in place of the old one" under California Civil Code § 1531(b). Even though the Court was addressing a novation in which there had been a change of parties to the agreement under § 1531(b), the Court's analysis was the same as that required for novation between the same parties under § 1531(a). That is, the Court's inquiry was whether the changes between the old and new obligations were sufficiently substantial to show an "extinguishment" of the old obligation and a replacement by the new one. 37 Cal. 2d at 861. Characterizing the changes between the old and new obligations as "drastic," the Court held that there had been a novation. *Id.*

[22] If Fanucchi's evidence is believed, the changes between the 1994 Loan agreement and the new agreement were more "drastic" than the changes at issue in *Angel*. In *Angel*, the only changes between the old and new notes was the difference in payment schedule, the added obligation to pay interest, and the addition of an acceleration clause. The old and the new notes were both secured by the same underlying chattels, and the amount of principal under the two notes was the same. In the case now before us, not only was the payment schedule different, United also agreed to give up part of its security interest by subordinating its lien to new crop lenders. Further, United agreed that the principal amount owed by Fanucchi would be reduced by between $300,000 and $400,000 at the end of five years if Fanucchi sufficiently paid down the debt. In *San Gabriel Valley Ready-Mixt*, the San Gabriel Valley Ready-Mixt Company ("Ready-Mixt") agreed with Casillas to supply 6,140 cubic yards of concrete at $9.45 per yard. For a short time, Ready-Mixt delivered concrete at that price. After a few months, however, Ready-Mixt informed Casillas that, due to a cement shortage, it would not be able to supply the rest of the promised concrete at the promised price. Casillas said, "To hell with it; I will get it from someone else." *Id.* at 139. After about two weeks of purchasing concrete elsewhere, Casillas told Ready-Mixt that he would buy additional concrete from Ready-Mixt if they would sell it at $11.52 per cubic yard. Ready-Mixt then delivered 800 cubic yards of concrete.

[23] After the concrete had been delivered, Casillas refused to pay the higher price, insisting on the old contract price. The Court of Appeal held that there had been a novation. A provision to pay the increased price alone "would have been insufficient to effect a novation." *Id.* at 140. But "[i]f there was a mutual understanding that defendant could and would buy his concrete elsewhere and that neither party would demand further performance of the contract by the other, this would have effected an abandonment of the contract. Entering into a new oral contract under these

circumstances would have effected an abandonment of the contract." *Id.* at 141.

[24] The changes between the first and second contracts in *San Gabriel Valley Ready-Mixt* are no more substantial than the changes between the 1994 Loan agreement and the later oral agreement in this case. In *San Gabriel Valley Ready-Mixt*, external conditions made it impossible for Ready-Mixt to fulfill the terms of the original contract without losing money; after a short hiatus, Casillas agreed to purchase less concrete at a higher price. In this case, external conditions made it impossible for Fanucchi to pay off the amount of the loan from the 1995 proceeds. If Fanucchi's evidence is believed, United then agreed to be paid over a longer period of time with less security, and, if certain conditions were fulfilled, to accept a substantially reduced amount.

[25] Another important factor in determining whether there has been novation, besides the nature of the changes between the old and the new contracts, is the conduct of the parties. In both *Angel* and *San Gabriel Valley Ready-Mixt*, the courts concluded that the parties' conduct indicated that they considered the new contracts to have extinguished and replaced the old contracts. In this case, the parties' conduct during crop years 1996 and 1997 supports Fanucchi's contention that the 1994 Loan was novated. It is undisputed that during those two years United subordinated its lien to the new crop lenders, and took only 60 percent of the proceeds remaining after the secured crop lenders had been paid off.

[26] In sum, we conclude that if Fanucchi's evidence is believed, the 1994 Loan agreement was novated. Summary judgment in favor of United was therefore improper on the issue of novation.

III. Judge Beezer's Concurrence

[27] Judge Beezer has written a separate concurrence to express his "understanding of novation under California law." Concurrence at 8206. To the extent Judge Beezer's concurrence is at variance from our majority opinion, it is, of course, a dissent. We disagree with Judge Beezer in three respects.

A.   *Alexander v. Angel*

[28] First, Judge Beezer contends that we mistakenly rely on *Alexander v. Angel* in concluding that the changes between the 1994 Loan agreement and the later oral agreement were substantial enough to constitute novation. Judge Beezer contends that *Angel* is inapt because, unlike in this case, there was a substitution of parties under California Civil Code § 1351(b) rather than a substitution of agreements between the same parties under § 1351(a). Judge Beezer is correct that *Angel* is a substitution-of-parties case. But he is incorrect in putting the case to one side. As Judge Beezer himself recognizes in a paragraph in which he

discusses *Angel*, the fundamental issue is whether "the parties intended to *extinguish* rather than merely modify the original agreement." Concurrence at 8210. The question the Court answered in *Angel* was whether the changes between the two contracts were sufficiently "drastic" such that there was an "extinguishment" of the earlier contract. *See* 37 Cal. 2d at 861. That is exactly the question at issue in this case.

B. Distinction Between Novation and Accord

[29] Second, Judge Beezer contends that we have conflated novation and accord. Under California law, an accord is defined as "an agreement to accept, in extinction of an obligation, something different from or less than that to which the person agreeing to accept is entitled." Cal. Civil Code § 1521. Once "the something different" has been delivered, there has been satisfaction of the accord. *See* Cal. Civ. Code § 1523; *Moving Picture Mach. Operators Union Local 162 v. Glasgow Theaters, Inc.*, 6 Cal. App. 3d 395, 402–03 (1970). Until performance by the obligor, the accord is executory, and the old obligation has not been extinguished. *Gardiner v. Gaither,* 162 Cal. App. 2d 607, 620 (1958). That is, when two parties enter into an accord, "the [original] obligation is not extinguished until the accord is fully executed, even though the parties to the accord are bound to execute it." *Id.* at 621 (citation and internal quotation marks omitted). A novation, on the other hand, is a substituted contract that extinguishes the previous agreement as soon as the parties enter into the new agreement, even if the new agreement is executory. *Davisson v. Faucher*, 105 Cal. App. 2d 445, 447 (1951); *Eckart v. Brown*, 34 Cal. App. 2d 182, 187 (1939); *Beckwith v. Sheldon*, 165 Cal. 319, 323–24 (1913). Put succinctly,

> [A]novation extinguishes one obligation by accepting for it another, that is, the creditor agrees to accept the second promise for his existing claim. But this is not true of an accord. Here it is not the new promise that is accepted in lieu of the existing claim, but the performance of that new promise.

Gardiner, 162 Cal. App. 2d at 620. In distinguishing between an executory accord and a novation, the determinative factor is the intent of the parties. *See, e.g., id.* at 619–20, *Rankin v. Miller,* 179 Cal. App. 2d 133, 138–39 (1960).

[30] Judge Beezer reads California law to contain an automatic across-the-board presumption in favor of accord and against novation. This is an overreading of the California case law. Judge Beezer relies heavily on *Gardiner* to support his argument for an across-the-board presumption. Judge Beezer quotes the first two sentences of a long paragraph from that opinion, the second of which states that there is a presumption against the conclusion that the parties intended that an executory contract would replace the old obligation. Concurrence at 8212–13. But a more extensive

quotation makes clear that the presumption comes from the overall circumstances of the case. The Court of Appeal wrote:

[31] In the instant case there is no evidence that respondent, on behalf of his clients, agreed to accept Gran-Wood's promise to complete three of the five structures as satisfaction of the pre-existing debts. *Certainly, the presumption is against any such conclusion.* The most reasonable and sensible interpretation of the correspondence is that the creditors were willing to accept performance of the agreement to finish three of the five houses in satisfaction of their existing claims, but extinguishment of those claims was conditional upon performance of the second promise. The correspondence in question between Gardiner and Selinger was a practical attempt at a practical solution by which creditors would get back some or all of their money, and Gran-Wood would be relieved of personal liability by salvaging the three buildings, which Gran-Wood obviously thought could be profitably done. But Gran-Wood found it to be unprofitable, and did not perform. Obviously, the whole agreement was prospective. What respondent's assignors wanted was performance of the second agreement. This they did not get. Thus, the original obligation was not extinguished and may be enforced. 162 Cal. App. 2d 607, 621 (emphasis added).

[32] The only other California case in which any kind of a presumption against novation is mentioned is *Brown v. Friesleben Estate Co.*, 148 Cal. App. 2d 720, 730 (1957), also cited by Judge Beezer. Concurrence at 8213. The court in *Brown* quoted § 419 of the Restatement (First) of Contracts, which provides that "if the pre-existing duty is an undisputed duty . . . to make compensation," "the interpretation *is assumed in case of doubt*," that only actual performance or execution of the duty prescribed in a new contract will discharge the pre-existing duty (emphasis added). Comment a to that section, also quoted by the *Brown* court, stated that in such a case, "the creditor *generally* will not enter into a bargain for an immediate cancellation of his claim without obtaining satisfaction and not merely a promise of it." *See* 148 Cal. App. 2d at 730 (emphasis added). We have been unable to discover in the California cases any other reference to any kind of presumption against novation.

[33] *Gardiner*, *Brown*, and the Restatement infer a presumption against novation from the particular circumstances of the facts or example before them. They do not state a general principle that in all cases where the choice is between accord and novation, accord is to be presumed. Rather, any presumption is inferred from the circumstances of the parties. Under *Gardiner*, *Brown* and the Restatement, the question is whether Fanucchi and United were likely to have agreed that the executory contract described by Fanucchi's evidence would extinguish and replace the old contract. This question is not an across-the-board presumption, to be applied in all cases without regard to their factual context. Rather, it is a tool to help the court ascertain the intent of Fanucchi and United in the

particular circumstances in which they found themselves after the failure of Fanucchi's 1995 crops.

[34] If Fanucchi's evidence is believed, Fanucchi was seriously considering declaring bankruptcy after the crop failure. At United's urging, Fanucchi agreed not to declare bankruptcy and, instead, to continue farming. In return, United agreed to subordinate its secured debt to new crop lenders for five years, to accept only 60 percent of the proceeds left over after the new crop lenders were paid, and to forgive between $300,000 and $400,000 if it had been paid down to that amount at the end of five years. According to Fanucchi's evidence, the new agreement imposed new obligations on both parties that were binding as soon as the parties entered into it. According to Fanucchi's evidence, there was nothing in the new agreement that allowed United simply to abandon the new agreement at its pleasure, and to enforce the old agreement instead. *Gardiner*, *Brown*, and the Restatement instruct the district court as part of its factfinding process on remand to consider the likelihood that Fanucchi and United, in the circumstances in which they found themselves, would have intended to enter into the novated contract described in Fanucchi's evidence.

C.   *Williams v. Reed*

[35] Finally, Judge Beezer relies on *Williams v. Reed*, 113 Cal. App. 2d 195 (1952), apparently for the proposition that an executor agreement cannot be a novated contract. He writes that "a central aspect of Fanucchi's novation claim rests on a theory of novation rejected by *Reed*." Concurrence at 8215. Judge Beezer misreads *Reed*.

[36] Defendant Reed failed to pay promissory notes of $30,000 and $10,000 when they came due. Reed then entered into an agreement with Williams, under which Williams agreed to accept $35,000 and five percent interest as full payment. The language of the settlement specifically made the settlement agreement contingent upon Reed's fulfillment of his obligation:

> "*Upon receipt of said payment in full*, W.E. Williams will execute any and all documents required to evidence full satisfaction of said obligation."

Id. at 198 (emphasis added). The trial court held that the settlement agreement was a novation, but the Court of Appeal reversed. Under the explicit terms of the settlement agreement, the old obligation was not extinguished unless and until Reed fulfilled the executory contract to pay off the $35,000 note, which meant that the new agreement did not of itself extinguish the old obligation. Rather, the old obligation was extinguished only if and when the new obligation to pay $35,000 was fulfilled. In other words, according to its explicit terms, the new agreement was an accord rather than a novation.

[37] Judge Beezer somehow reads *Reed* to contradict the novation theory of Fanucchi. But *Reed* is entirely consistent with Fanucchi's theory. *Reed* only tells us what we already know from black-letter California law distinguishing accord and novation: (1) If the obligation contained in the old agreement is extinguished only upon execution of the promise contained in the new agreement, the new agreement is an accord. (2) However, if the new executory agreement extinguishes the old agreement as soon as the new agreement is entered into, the new agreement is a novation. That is the standard definition of novation, contained in *Reed* and in all the other California cases.

[38] If Fanucchi's evidence is believed, United agreed that the new executory agreement would extinguish the old agreement when the new agreement was entered into. The fact that the new agreement was executory is not fatal to Fanucchi's theory of novation. As the Court of Appeal wrote in *Davisson v. Faucher*, 105 Cal.App.2d 445, 447 (1951): [*T*]*he written contract was a complete novation* of all obligations of the parties, one to the other, which existed prior to the execution of the written contract and in particular the obligations arising out of the oral contract. *The fact that the written contract was executory is of no moment.* (Emphasis added.)

IV. Promissory Fraud

[39] Even assuming that the 1994 Loan agreement was extinguished by the novated contract, the district court properly dismissed Fanucchi's promissory fraud claim. "Under California law, the indispensable elements of a fraud claim include a false representation, knowledge of its falsity, intent to defraud, justifiable reliance, and damages." *Vess v. Ciba-Geigy Corp. USA*, 317 F.3d 1097, 1105 (9th Cir. 2003) (internal quotation and citation omitted). Fanucchi asserts in its complaint that United had a "secret intention" not to perform on the contract. It does not, however, present any evidence supporting its claim that United intended to defraud. Affirmative evidence is necessary to avoid summary judgment because mere nonperformance is not enough to show intent to defraud. *Tenzer v. Superscope, Inc.*, 39 Cal.3d 18, 30 (Cal. 1985) ("[S]omething more than nonperformance is required to prove the defendant's intent not to perform his promise." (quoting *People v. Ashley*, 42 Cal.2d 246, 263 (1954)) (internal citations omitted)).

V. Attorneys' Fees

[40] The district court awarded attorneys' fees to United based on a provision in the Agricultural Loan Agreement providing:

> **Costs and Expenses.** Borrower agrees to pay upon demand all of Lender's out-of-pocket expenses, including without limitation attorneys' fees, incurred in connection with the preparation, execution, enforcement and collection of this Agreement or in connection with the Loans made pursuant to this Agreement.

California Civil Code § 1717(a), deems any contract that allows attorneys' fees to a prevailing party to one party to apply equally to the other party. Because we reverse summary judgment on Fanucchi's novation claim, we vacate the district court's award of attorneys' fees to United. Once the novation claim has been resolved, the district court will be in a position to revisit the question of attorneys' fees.

Conclusion

[41] We reverse the district court's grant of summary judgment on Fanucchi's novation claim. We otherwise affirm the district court's grant of summary judgment. We vacate the court's award of attorneys' fees. We remand for further proceedings consistent with this opinion. Each party shall bear its own costs.

AFFIRMED in part, REVERSED in part, VACATED in part, and REMANDED.

[JUDGE BEEZER's concurrence, discussed above, is omitted.—Eds.]

———

B. THIRD PARTY BENEFICIARY CONTRACTS

The second group of subjects in this chapter is the rights of purported "third party beneficiaries." Third party beneficiaries are parties other than the contracting parties that may be benefitted by the contract. Think of a life insurance contract, which is necessarily a third party beneficiary contract: The contract is between the insurer and the insured, the latter of whom will be dead when the performance (payment) is due to the third party beneficiary. Another example would be a contract between a law student's parents and a contracts tutor to provide tutoring services for their child the law student. The parents and the tutor are the parties to the contract; the law student is the third party beneficiary.

The individual who is the third party beneficiary need not be identified specifically in the contract and a description of attributes may be enough to suffice. Putting aside the alternative structure of using trust law, if a law professor contracts with her dean to provide a trophy to the highest scoring first year contracts student, that student, when finally identified after the end of the semester, may qualify as a third party beneficiary.

There are only two real issues in the third party beneficiary subject area: (1) when can a third party to the contract sue to enforce the contract and (2) when, if ever, can the parties to the contract change its terms as they affect the third party?

With regard to when third parties can sue, the common law, historically, was hostile to allowing suits by non-party beneficiaries. Gradually this position eroded. In modern contract law, largely through the efforts of the late Professor Corbin, the categories of intended beneficiaries and incidental beneficiaries have emerged. Intended beneficiaries can enforce the contract, incidental ones can not. *See* R2d §§ 302 and 304.

As to the modification of a third party beneficiary contract, the modern rule has emerged that the parties are free to modify the contract until the third party beneficiary has sued on the contract or has reasonably and materially changed position in reliance upon the contract. *See* R2d § 311. After that point, the parties may not modify, unless the contract itself permits this later modification. An example of a provision dealing with third party beneficiary status by purporting to eliminate it is:

> This Agreement is made solely for the benefit of the Parties and their successors and assigns and [except as provided herein] no other entity has or shall have any rights under or due to this Agreement.

As you read the cases below, keep in mind that, in most of the cases, the courts are dealing with contracts that did not have an enforceable provision dealing with the subject at issue. All of these issues can be dealt with in the language of the contract, and competent counsel in the modern age will ensure that the contract will specify who has the right to enforce it and how and when it can be modified. Provisions like this can narrow or broaden the results that would be obtained by application of the default legal rules that apply in their absence. These cases also demonstrate the intertwined nature of subjects like assignment and delegation with formation, interpretation, enforcement, and damage issues from prior chapters, generally in a modern commercial context.

The following case is one of the classics regarding the emergence of third party beneficiary rights.

LAWRENCE V. FOX

Court of Appeals of New York
20 N.Y. 268 (1859)

[1] Appeal from the Superior Court of the city of Buffalo. On the trial before Mr. Justice Masten, it appeared by the evidence of a bystander, that one Holly, in November, 1857, at the request of the defendant, loaned and advanced to him $300, stating at the time that he owed that sum to the plaintiff for money borrowed of him, and had agreed to pay it to him the then next day; that the defendant in consideration thereof, at the time of receiving the money, promised to pay it to the plaintiff the then next day. Upon this state of facts the defendant moved for a nonsuit, upon three several grounds, viz.: That there was no proof tending to show that Holly

was indebted to the plaintiff; that the agreement by the defendant with Holly to pay the plaintiff was void for want of consideration, and that there was no privity between the plaintiff and defendant. The court overruled the motion, and the counsel for the defendant excepted. The cause was then submitted to the jury, and they found a verdict for the plaintiff for the amount of the loan and interest, $344.66[3], upon which judgment was entered; from which the defendant appealed to the Superior Court, at general term, where the judgment was affirmed, and the defendant appealed to this court. The cause was submitted on printed arguments.

[2]   H. Gray, J. The first objection raised on the trial amounts to this: That the evidence of the person present, who heard the declarations of Holly giving directions as to the payment of the money he was then advancing to the defendant, was mere hearsay and therefore not competent. Had the plaintiff sued Holly for this sum of money no objection to the competency of this evidence would have been thought of; and if the defendant had performed his promise by paying the sum loaned to him to the plaintiff, and Holly had afterwards sued him for its recovery, and this evidence had been offered by the defendant, it would doubtless have been received without an objection from any source. All the defendant had the right to demand in this case was evidence which, as between Holly and the plaintiff, was competent to establish the relation between them of debtor and creditor. For that purpose the evidence was clearly competent; it covered the whole ground and warranted the verdict of the jury. But it is claimed that notwithstanding this promise was established by competent evidence, it was void for the want of consideration. It is now more than a quarter of a century since it was settled by the Supreme Court of this State—in an able and pains-taking opinion by the late Chief Justice Savage, in which the authorities were fully examined and carefully analyzed—that a promise in all material respects like the one under consideration was valid; and the judgment of that court was unanimously affirmed by the Court for the Correction of Errors. *Farley v. Cleaveland*, 4 *Cow.*, 432; same case in error, 9 *id.*, 639.

[3]   In that case one Moon owed Farley and sold to Cleaveland a quantity of hay, in consideration of which Cleaveland promised to pay Moon's debt to Farley; and the decision in favor of Farley's right to recover was placed upon the ground that the hay received by Cleaveland from Moon was a valid consideration for Cleaveland's promise to pay Farley, and that the subsisting liability of Moon to pay Farley was no objection to the recovery. The fact that the money advanced by Holly to the defendant was a loan to him for a day, and that it thereby became the property of the defendant, seemed to impress the defendant's counsel with the idea that because the defendant's promise was not a trust fund placed by the plaintiff

---

[3]   [$344.66 in 1859 dollars is roughly the equivalent of $10,700 in 2019 dollars using the CPI and the GNP Deflator.—Eds.]

in the defendant's hands, out of which he was to realize money as from the sale of a chattel or the collection of a debt, the promise although made for the benefit of the plaintiff could not enure to his benefit.

[4]   The hay which Cleaveland delivered to Moon was not to be paid to Farley, but the debt incurred by Cleaveland for the purchase of the hay, like the debt incurred by the defendant for money borrowed, was what was to be paid. That case has been often referred to by the courts of this State, and has never been doubted as sound authority for the principle upheld by it. (*Barker v. Bucklin*, 2 *Denio*, 45; *Hudson Canal Company v. The Westchester Bank*, 4 *id.*, 97.) It puts to rest the objection that the defendant's promise was void for want of consideration. The report of that case shows that the promise was not only made to Moon but to the plaintiff Farley. In this case the promise was made to Holly and not expressly to the plaintiff; and this difference between the two cases presents the question, raised by the defendant's objection, as to the want of privity between the plaintiff and defendant. As early as 1806 it was announced by the Supreme Court of this State, upon what was then regarded as the settled law of England, "That where one person makes a promise to another for the benefit of a third person, that third person may maintain an action upon it." *Schermerhorn v. Vanderheyden*, 1 *John. R.*, 140, has often been re-asserted by our courts and never departed from.

[5]   The case of *Seaman v. White* has occasionally been referred to (but not by the courts) not only as having some bearing upon the question now under consideration, but as involving in doubt the soundness of the proposition stated in *Schermerhorn v. Vanderheyden*. In that case one Hill on the 17th of August, 1835, made his note and procured it to be indorsed by Seaman and discounted by the Phoenix Bank. Before the note matured and while it was owned by the Phoenix Bank, Hill placed in the hands of the defendant, Whitney, his draft accepted by a third party, which the defendant indorsed, and on the 7th of October, 1835, got discounted and placed the avails in the hands of an agent with which to take up Hill's note; the note became due, Whitney withdrew the avails of the draft from the hands of his agent and appropriated it to a debt due him from Hill, and Seaman paid the note indorsed by him and brought his suit against Whitney. Upon this state of facts appearing, it was held that Seaman could not recover: first, for the reason that no promise had been made by Whitney to pay, and second, if a promise could be implied from the facts that Hill's accepted draft, with which to raise the means to pay; the note, had been placed by Hill in the hands of Whitney, the promise would not be to Seaman, but to the Phoenix Bank who then owned the note; although, in the course of the opinion of the court, it was stated that, in all cases the principle of which was sought to be applied to that case, the fund had been appropriated by an express undertaking of the defendant with the creditor. But before concluding the opinion of the court in this case, the learned

judge who delivered it conceded that an undertaking to pay the creditor may be implied from an arrangement to that effect between the defendant and the debtor. This question was subsequently, and in a case quite recent, again the subject of consideration by the Supreme Court, when it was held, that in declaring upon a promise, made to the debtor by a third party to pay the creditor of the debtor, founded upon a consideration advanced by the debtor, it was unnecessary to aver a promise to the creditor; for the reason that upon proof of a promise made to the debtor to pay the creditor, a promise to the creditor would be implied.

[6]   And in support of this proposition, in no respect distinguishable from the one now under consideration, the case of *Schermerhorn v. Vanderheyden*, with many intermediate cases in our courts, were cited, in which the doctrine of that case was not only approved but affirmed. *The Delaware and Hudson Canal Company v. The Westchester County Bank*, 4 *Denio*, 97. The same principle is adjudged in several cases in Massachusetts. I will refer to but few of them. *Arnold v. Lyman*, 17 *Mass.* 400; *Hall v. Marston, id.*, 575; *Brewer v. Dyer*, 7 *Cush.*, 337, 340. In *Hall v. Marston* the court say: "It seems to have been well settled that if A promises B for a valuable consideration to pay C, the latter may maintain assumpsit for the money;" and in *Brewer v. Dyer*, the recovery was upheld, as the court said, "upon the principle of law long recognized and clearly established, that when one person, for a valuable consideration, engages with another, by a simple contract, to do some act for the benefit of a third, the latter, who would enjoy the benefit of the act, may maintain an action for the breach of such engagement; that it does not rest upon the ground of any actual or supposed relationship between the parties as some of the earlier cases would seem to indicate, but upon the broader and more satisfactory basis, that the law operating on the act of the parties creates the duty, establishes a privity, and implies the promise and obligation on which the action is founded."

[7]   There is a more recent case decided by the same court, to which the defendant has referred and claims that it at least impairs the force of the former cases as authority. It is the case of *Mellen v. Whipple*, 1 *Gray*, 317. In that case one Rollins made his note for $500, payable to Ellis and Mayo, or order, and to secure its payment mortgaged to the payees a certain lot of ground, and then sold and conveyed the mortgaged premises to the defendant, by deed in which it was stated that the "granted premises were subject to a mortgage for $500, which mortgage, with the note for which it was given, the said Whipple is to assume and cancel." The deed thus made was accepted by Whipple, the mortgage was afterwards duly assigned, and the note [e]ndorsed by Ellis and Mayo to the plaintiff's intestate. After Whipple received the deed he paid to the mortgagees and their assigns the interest upon the mortgage and note for a time, and upon refusing to

continue his payments was sued by the plaintiff as administratrix of the assignee of the mortgage and note.

[8] The court held that the stipulation in the deed that Whipple should pay the mortgage and note was a matter exclusively between the two parties to the deed; that the sale by Rollins of the equity of redemption did not lessen the plaintiff's security, and that as nothing had been put into the defendant's hands for the purpose of meeting the plaintiff's claim on Rollins, there was no consideration to support an express promise, much less an implied one, that Whipple should pay Mellen the amount of the note. This is all that was decided in that case, and the substance of the reasons assigned for the decision; and whether the case was rightly disposed of or not, it has not in its facts any analogy to the case before us, nor do the reasons assigned for the decision bear in any degree upon the question we are now considering. But it is urged that because the defendant was not in any sense a trustee of the property of Holly for the benefit of the plaintiff, the law will not imply a promise. I agree that many of the cases where a promise was implied were cases of trusts, created for the benefit of the promiser.

[9] The case of *Felton v. Dickinson*, 10 Mass. 287, and others that might be cited, are of that class; but concede them all to have been cases of trusts, and it proves nothing against the application of the rule to this case. The duty of the trustee to pay the *cestuis que trust*, according to the terms of the trust, implies his promise to the latter to do so. In this case the defendant, upon ample consideration received from Holly, promised Holly to pay his debt to the plaintiff; the consideration received and the promise to Holly made it as plainly his duty to pay the plaintiff as if the money had been remitted to him for that purpose, and as well implied a promise to do so as if he had been made a trustee of property to be converted into cash with which to pay. The fact that a breach of the duty imposed in the one case may be visited, and justly, with more serious consequences than in the other, by no means disproves the payment to be a duty in both.

[10] The principle illustrated by the example so frequently quoted (which concisely states the case in hand) "that a promise made to one for the benefit of another, he for whose benefit it is made may bring an action for its breach," has been applied to trust cases, not because it was exclusively applicable to those cases, but because it was a principle of law, and as such applicable to those cases. It was also insisted that Holly could have discharged the defendant from his promise, though it was intended by both parties for the benefit of the plaintiff, and therefore the plaintiff was not entitled to maintain this suit for the recovery of a demand over which he had no control. It is enough that the plaintiff did not release the defendant from his promise, and whether he could or not is a question not now necessarily involved; but if it was, I think it would be found difficult to maintain the right of Holly to discharge a judgment recovered by the

plaintiff upon confession or otherwise, for the breach of the defendant's promise; and if he could not, how could he discharge the suit before judgment, or the promise before suit, made as it was for the plaintiff's benefit and in accordance with legal presumption accepted by him, *Berly v. Taylor*, 5 Hill 577–584, *et seq.*, until his dissent was shown. The cases cited, and especially that of *Farley v. Cleaveland*, establish the validity of a parol promise; it stands then upon the footing of a written one.

[11] Suppose the defendant had given his note in which, for value received of Holly, he had promised to pay the plaintiff and the plaintiff had accepted the promise, retaining Holly's liability. Very clearly Holly could not have discharged that promise, be the right to release the defendant as it may. No one can doubt that he owes the sum of money demanded of him, or that in accordance with his promise it was his duty to have paid it to the plaintiff; nor can it be doubted that whatever may be the diversity of opinion elsewhere, the adjudications in this State, from a very early period, approved by experience, have established the defendant's liability; if, therefore, it could be shown that a more strict and technically accurate application of the rules applied, would lead to a different result (which I by no means concede), the effort should not be made in the face of manifest justice.

The judgment should be affirmed.

[12] JOHNSON, CH.J., DENIO, SELDEN, ALLEN and STRONG, JS., concurred. JOHNSON, CH.J., and DENIO, J., were of opinion that the promise was to be regarded as made to the plaintiff through the medium of his agent, whose action he could ratify when it came to his knowledge, though taken without his being privy thereto.

[13] COMSTOCK, J. (Dissenting.) The plaintiff had nothing to do with the promise on which he brought this action. It was not made to him, nor did the consideration proceed from him. If he can maintain the suit, it is because an anomaly has found its way into the law on this subject. In general, there must be privity of contract. The party who sues upon a promise must be the promisee, or he must have some legal interest in the undertaking. In this case, it is plain that Holly, who loaned the money to the defendant, and to whom the promise in question was made, could at any time have claimed that it should be performed to himself personally. He had lent the money to the defendant, and at the same time directed the latter to pay the sum to the plaintiff. This direction he could countermand, and if he had done so, manifestly the defendant's promise to pay according to the direction would have ceased to exist. The plaintiff would receive a benefit by a complete execution of the arrangement, but the arrangement itself was between other parties, and was under their exclusive control. If the defendant had paid the money to Holly, his debt would have been discharged thereby. So Holly might have released the demand or assigned

it to another person, or the parties might have annulled the promise now in question, and designated some other creditor of Holly as the party to whom the money should be paid. It has never been claimed, that in a case thus situated, the right of a third person to sue upon the promise rested on any so and principle of law. We are to inquire whether the rule has been so established by positive authority.

[14] The cases which have sometimes been supposed to have a bearing on this question, are quite numerous. In some of them, the dicta of judges, delivered upon very slight consideration, have been referred to as the decisions of the courts. Thus, in *Schermerhorn v. Vanderheyden,* 1 John., 140, the court is reported as saying, "We are of opinion, that where one person makes a promise to another, for the benefit of a third person, that third person may maintain an action on such promise." This remark was made on the authority of *Dalton v. Poole,* Vent., 318, 332, decided in England nearly two hundred years ago. It was, however, but a mere remark, as the case was determined against the plaintiff on another ground. Yet this decision has often been referred to as authority for similar observations in later cases.

[15] In another class of cases, which have been sometimes supposed to favor the doctrine, the promise was made to the person who brought the suit, while the consideration proceeded from another; the question considered being, whether the promise was void by the statute of frauds. Thus, in *Gold v. Phillips,* 10 Johns., 412, one Wood was indebted to the plaintiffs for services as attorneys and counsel, and he conveyed a farm to the defendants, who, as part of the consideration, were to pay that debt. Accordingly, the defendants wrote to the plaintiffs, informing them that an arrangement had been made by which they were to pay the demand. The defense was, that the promise was void within the statute, because, although in writing, it did not express the consideration. But the action was sustained, on the ground that the undertaking was original and not collateral. So in the case of *Farley v. Cleaveland*, 4 Cow., 432; 9 *id.*, 639, the facts proved or offered to be proved were, that the plaintiff held a note against one Moon; that Moon sold hay to the defendant, who in consideration of that sale promised the plaintiff by parol to pay the note. The only question was, whether the statute of frauds applied to the case. It was held by the Supreme Court, and afterwards by the Court of Errors, that it did not. Such is also precisely the doctrine of *Ellwood v. Monk*, 5 Wend., 235, where it was held, that a plea of the statute of frauds, to a count upon a promise of the defendant to the plaintiff, to pay the latter a debt owing to him by another person, the promise being founded on a sale of property to the defendant by the other person, was bad.

[16] The cases mentioned, and others of a like character, were referred to by Mr. Justice Jewett, in *Barker v. Bucklin*, 2 Denio, 45. In that case, the learned justice considered at some length the question now before us.

The authorities referred to were mainly those which I have cited, and others, upon the statute of frauds. The case decided nothing on the present subject, because it was determined against the plaintiff on a ground not involved in this discussion. The doctrine was certainly advanced which the plaintiff now contends for, but among all the decisions which were cited, I do not think there is one standing directly upon it. The case of *Arnold v. Lyman*, 17 Mass. 400, might perhaps be regarded as an exception to this remark, if a different interpretation had not been given to that decision in the Supreme Court of the same State where it was pronounced. In the recent case of *Mellen, Administratrix v. Whipple*, 1 Gray, 317, that decision is understood as belonging to a class where the defendant has in his hands a trust fund, which was the foundation of the duty or promise in which the suit is brought.

[17] The cases in which some trust was involved are also frequently referred to as authority for the doctrine now in question, but they do not sustain it. If A delivers money or property to B, which the latter accepts upon a trust for the benefit of C, the latter can enforce the trust by an appropriate action for that purpose. *Berly v. Taylor*, 5 Hill 577. If the trust be of money, I think the beneficiary may assent to it and bring the action for money had and received to his use. If it be of something else than money, the trustee must account for it according to the terms of the trust, and upon principles of equity. There is some authority even for saying that an express promise founded on the possession of a trust fund may be enforced by an action at law in the name of the beneficiary, although it was made to the creator of the trust. Thus, in *Comyn's Digest Action on the case upon Assumpsit*, B. 15, it is laid down that if a man promise a pig of lead to A, and his executor give lead to make a pig to B, who assumes to deliver it to A, an assumpsit lies by A against him. The case of *The Delaware and Hudson Canal Company v. The Westchester County Bank*, 4 Denio, 97, involved a trust because the defendants had received from a third party a bill of exchange under an agreement that they would endeavor to collect it, and would pay over the proceeds when collected to the plaintiffs. A fund received under such an agreement does not belong to the person who receives it. He must account for it specifically; and perhaps there is no gross violation of principle in permitting the equitable owner of it to sue upon an express promise to pay it over. Having a specific interest in the thing, the undertaking to account for it may be regarded as in some sense made with him through the author of the trust. But further than this we cannot go without violating plain rules of law. In the case before us there was nothing in the nature of a trust or agency. The defendant borrowed the money of Holly and received it as his own. The plaintiff had no right in the fund, legal or equitable. The promise to repay the money created an obligation in favor of the lender to whom it was made and not in favor of any one else.

[18] I have referred to the dictum in *Schermerhorn v. Vanderheyden*, 1 *Johns.*, 140, as favoring the doctrine contended for. It was the earliest in this State, and was founded, as already observed, on the old English case of *Dutton v. Poole*, in Ventris. That case has always been referred to as the ultimate authority whenever the rule in question has been mentioned, and it deserves, therefore, some further notice. The father of the plaintiff's wife being seized of certain lands, which afterwards on his death descended to the defendant, and being about to cut £1,000 worth of timber to raise a portion for his daughter, the defendant promised the father, in consideration of his for bearing to cut the timber, that he would pay the said daughter the £1,000. After verdict for the plaintiff, upon the issue of non-assumpsit, it was urged in arrest of judgment, that the father ought to have brought the action, and not the husband and wife. It was held, after much discussion, that the action would lie. The court said, "It might be another case if the money had been to have been paid to a stranger; but there is such a manner of relation between the father and the child, and it is a kind of debt to the child to be provided for, that the plaintiff is plainly concerned." We need not criticize the reason given for this decision. It is enough for the present purpose, that the case is no authority for the general doctrine, to sustain which it has been so frequently cited. It belongs to a class of cases somewhat peculiar and anomalous, in which promises have been made to a parent or person standing in a near relationship to the person for whose benefit it was made, and in which, on account of that relationship, the beneficiary has been allowed to maintain the action. Regarded as standing on any other ground, they have long since ceased to be the law in England.

[19] Thus, in *Crow v. Rogers,* 1 Strange, 592, one Hardy was indebted to the plaintiff in the sum of £70, and upon a discourse between Hardy and the defendant, it was agreed that the defendant should pay that debt in consideration of a house, to be conveyed by Hardy to him. The plaintiff brought the action on that promise, and *Dutton v. Poole* was cited in support of it. But it was held that the action would not lie, because the plaintiff was a stranger to the transaction. Again, in *Price v. Easton,* 4 Barn. & Adolph., 433, one William Price was indebted to the plaintiff in £13. The declaration averred a promise of the defendant to pay the debt, in consideration that William Price would work for him, and leave the wages in his hands; and that Price did work accordingly, and earned a large sum of money, which he left in the defendant's hands. After verdict for the plaintiff, a motion was made in arrest of judgment, on the ground that the plaintiff was a stranger to the consideration.

[20] *Dutton v. Poole,* and other cases of that class, were cited in opposition to the motion, but the judgment was arrested. Lord Denman said, "I think the declaration cannot be supported, as it does not show any consideration for the promise moving from the plaintiff to the defendant."

Littledale, J., said, "No privity is shown between the plaintiff and the defendant. The case is precisely like *Crow v. Rogers*, and must be governed by it." Taunton, J., said, "It is consistent with all the matter alleged in the declaration, that the plaintiff may have been entirely ignorant of the arrangement between William Price and the defendant." Patterson, J., observed, "It is clear that the allegations do not show a right of action in the plaintiff. There is no promise to the plaintiff alleged." The same doctrine is recognized in *Lilly v. Hays*, 5 Ad. & Ellis, 548, and such is now the settled rule in England, although at an early day there was some obscurity arising out of the case of *Dutton v. Poole*, and others of that peculiar class.

[21] The question was also involved in some confusion by the earlier cases in Massachusetts. Indeed, the Supreme Court of that State seem at one time to have made a nearer approach to the doctrine on which this action must rest, than the courts of this State have ever done. 10 Mass. 287; 17 *id.*, 400. But in the recent case of *Mellen, Administratrix v. Whipple*, 1 Gray, 317, the subject was carefully reviewed and the doctrine utterly overthrown. One Rollin was indebted to the plaintiff's testator, and had secured the debt by a mortgage on his land. He then conveyed the equity of redemption to the defendant, by a deed which contained a clause declaring that the defendant was to assume and pay the mortgage. It was conceded that the acceptance of the deed with such a clause in it was equivalent to an express promise to pay the mortgage debt; and the question was, whether the mortgagee or his representative could sue on that undertaking. It was held that the suit could not be maintained; and in the course of a very careful and discriminating opinion by Judge Metcalf, it was shown that the cases which had been supposed to favor the action belonged to exceptional classes, none of which embraced the pure and simple case of an attempt by one person to enforce a promise made to another, from whom the consideration wholly proceeded. I am of that opinion.

[22] The judgment of the court below should therefore be reversed, and a new trial granted.

GROVER, J., also dissented.

––––––––

NOTES AND QUESTIONS

1. Who was the promissor, the promissee, and the third party beneficiary?

2. Who could have sued and recovered against whom under the contract? Why?

3. The court discusses "privity" and "privity of contract." Privity is an older, formalist notion of a direct, in this case contractual, relationship between

the parties that gave rise to the right to sue to enforce the contract. Although notions of privity are still in use, the modern trend is to avoid or gloss over the concept in performing third party beneficiary analysis. It is still useful, however, especially in understanding where the rules in this area began—as exceptions to the strict requirement of privity. Although formalists would differ, privity is more a conclusion than a fact.

PROBLEM 29-1

Old Nettie, in the belief that she was dying, asks her husband Albert to draft her a will. When she reviews it she is unhappy because it does not provide that her house should go to her favorite niece, Marion. Instead, under the will, it goes to Albert during life and then to a charity. Albert offers to write a new will, but Nettie thinks that her time is drawing near and there is no time to lose. So Nettie has Albert promise her that if she signs the will as drafted he will modify his own will to take care of Marion.

As you by now expect, when Albert dies, shortly after Nettie, his will makes no provision for Marion whatsoever.

Can Marion enforce the agreement between Nettie and Albert? *See Seaver v. Ransom*, 224 N.Y. 233, 120 N.E. 639 (1918).

———

SCHAUER V. MANDARIN GEMS OF CALIFORNIA, INC.

Court of Appeal of California
125 Cal. App. 4th 949, 23 Cal. Rptr. 3d 233 (2005)

IKOLA, JUDGE.

[1] IKOLA, J.—Sarah Jane Schauer (plaintiff) appeals from a judgment of dismissal in favor of Mandarin Gems of California, Inc., doing business as Black, Starr & Frost (defendant) after the court sustained defendant's demurrer to plaintiff's second amended complaint without leave to amend. Plaintiff sought to recover on various theories based on her discovery that a diamond ring given to her as an engagement gift prior to her marriage to her now former husband, Darin Erstad, allegedly was not worth the $43,000[4] he paid defendant for it in 1999. Erstad is not a party to this action.

[2] We reverse the judgment and remand. We conclude plaintiff has standing as a third party beneficiary of the sales contract between Erstad and defendant, and she has adequately pleaded a contract cause of action based on allegations of defendant's breach of express warranty. Defendant

---

[4] [$43,000 in 1999 dollars is roughly the equivalent of $64,800 in 2019 dollars using the CPI and the GNP Deflator.—Eds.]

must answer to that claim. In all other respects, the pleading is defective and cannot be cured by amendment.

Facts

[3]   Our factual summary "accepts as true the facts alleged in the complaint, together with facts that may be implied or inferred from those expressly alleged." (*Barnett v. Fireman's Fund Ins. Co.*, 90 Cal. App. 4th 500, 505 [108 Cal. Rptr. 2d 657] (2001).)

[4]   Plaintiff and Erstad went shopping for an engagement ring on August 15, 1999. After looking at diamonds in premier jewelry establishments such as Tiffany and Company and Cartier, they went to defendant's store, where they found a ring that salesperson Joy said featured a 3.01 carat diamond with a clarity grading of " 'SI1.' " Erstad bought the ring the same day for $43,121.55. The following month, for insurance purposes, defendant provided Erstad a written appraisal verifying the ring had certain characteristics, including an SI1 clarity rating and an average replacement value of $45,500. Paul Lam, a graduate gemologist with the European Gemological Laboratory (EGL), signed the appraisal.

[5]   The couple's subsequent short-term marriage was dissolved in a North Dakota judgment awarding each party, "except as otherwise set forth in this Agreement," "the exclusive right, title and possession of all personal property . . . which such party now owns, possesses, holds or hereafter acquires." Plaintiff's personal property included the engagement ring given to her by Erstad.

[6]   On June 3, 2002, after the divorce, plaintiff had the ring evaluated by the "Gem Trade Laboratory," which gave the diamond a rating of " 'SI2' quality," an appraisal with which "multiple other [unidentified] jewelers, including one at [defendant's store]" agreed. That was how plaintiff discovered defendant's alleged misrepresentation, concealment, and breach of express warranty regarding the true clarity of the diamond and its actual worth, which is—on plaintiff's information and belief—some $23,000[5] less than what Erstad paid for it.

[7]   Plaintiff sued defendant on several theories. Three times she attempted to plead her case. In the first cause of action of the second amended complaint, she sought to recover under the Consumers Legal Remedies Act (the Act, Civ. Code, § 1760 *et seq.*), stating, inter alia, that had the true clarity of the diamond been known, plaintiff would not have "acquired said diamond by causing it to be purchased for her." Thereafter, if the written verification of the clarity value sent to Erstad one month after the purchase had revealed the truth, plaintiff would have "immediately

---

[5]   [$23,000 in 2005 dollars is roughly the equivalent of $29,600 in 2019 dollars using the CPI and the GNP Deflator.—Eds.]

rescinded the sale based on a failure of consideration." The second cause of action, for breach of contract, alleged Erstad and defendant had a written contract under which Erstad agreed to purchase the ring "for the sole and stated purpose of giving it [to] Plaintiff," making plaintiff a third party beneficiary of the sales contract. Defendant breached the contract by delivering an engagement ring that did not conform to the promised SI1 clarity rating.

[8] In her third cause of action, for constructive fraud, plaintiff claimed the existence of a special confidential relationship in which defendant was aware plaintiff and her "predecessor in interest," presumably Erstad, "were not knowledgeable and ... were relying exclusively on the Defendants' integrity," but defendant falsely represented the clarity of the diamond with the intent to defraud "[p]laintiff and her predecessor in interest" to make the purchase at the inflated price. The fourth cause of action for fraud alleged defendant's malicious and deceitful conduct warranted punitive damages. In the fifth cause of action, plaintiff sought rescission under Civil Code section 1689 for defendant's alleged fraud in the inducement, mistake, and failure of consideration.

[9] Appended to the pleading was a redacted copy of a North Dakota court's judgment filed July 19, 2001, granting Erstad and plaintiff a divorce pursuant to their "Stipulation and Agreement," entitling each party, as noted *ante*, "to the exclusive right, title and possession of all personal property of the parties, joint or several, which such party now owns, possesses, holds or hereafter acquires [*except as otherwise provided in the agreement*]," and awarding the parties their respective "personal effects, clothing and jewelry."

[10] In its general demurrer to the second amended complaint and each cause of action, defendant asserted plaintiff had no viable claim under any theory because: (1) plaintiff was neither the purchaser of the ring nor a third party beneficiary of the contract between defendant and Erstad, who was not alleged to have assigned his rights to plaintiff; (2) the statute of limitations had expired for defendant's alleged violations of the Act; (3) plaintiff was not a buyer, and the ring tendered to Erstad conformed entirely to the contract; (4) defendant owed no special confidential or fiduciary duty to plaintiff upon which to predicate a fraud cause of action; (5) any alleged fraud was the act of EGL, not attributable to defendant; and (6) fraud was not pleaded with the required specificity.

[11] The court again sustained the demurrer, this time without further leave to amend. The judgment of dismissal followed, and plaintiff appeals. As we will explain, the court erred. Although the complaint is fatally defective in some respects, plaintiff is entitled as a matter of law to pursue her contract claim as a third party beneficiary.

Discussion

Standard of Review

[12] The trial court's decision to sustain a demurrer is a legal ruling, subject to de novo review. "[W]e give the complaint a reasonable interpretation, and treat the demurrer as admitting all material facts properly pleaded, but not the truth of contentions, deductions or conclusions of law. We reverse if the plaintiff has stated a cause of action under any legal theory. [Citation.]" *Barnett v. Fireman's Fund Ins. Co., supra,* 90 Cal. App. 4th at 507.

[13] The issue before us is whether, on well pleaded facts, plaintiff may maintain an action to recover the $23,000 difference between what Erstad paid for the diamond ring and what that gift was really worth, given its alleged inferior quality.

[14] We begin with the rule that "[e]very action must be prosecuted in the name of the real party in interest, except as otherwise provided by statute." Code Civ. Proc., § 367. Where the complaint shows the plaintiff does not possess the substantive right or standing to prosecute the action, "it is vulnerable to a general demurrer on the ground that it fails to state a cause of action." *Carsten v. Psychology Examining Com.,* 27 Cal.3d 793, 796 [166 Cal. Rptr. 844, 614 P.2d 276] (1980); *Cloud v. Northrop Grumman Corp.,* 67 Cal.App.4th 995, 1004 [79 Cal. Rptr. 2d 544] (1998).

[15] The second amended complaint alleges "[d]efendant entered into a written contract with [Erstad] to purchase the subject engagement ring." The attached exhibit shows defendant issued a written appraisal to Erstad. Erstad is clearly a real party in interest, but he has not sued.

[16] Plaintiff contends she, too, is a real party in interest because the North Dakota divorce judgment endowed her with all of Erstad's rights and remedies. As we will explain, this theory is wrong. However, as we will also discuss, plaintiff is correct in asserting she is a third party beneficiary of the sales contract. That status enables her to proceed solely on her contract claim for breach of express warranty. For the remainder, plaintiff is without standing to recover under any legal theory alleged, and the equitable remedy of rescission is also unavailable to her.

Transfer of Erstad's Rights and Remedies to Plaintiff

[17] Plaintiff alleges and argues the North Dakota divorce judgment granted her "the exclusive right, title and possession of all [of her] personal property," including the engagement ring, and the judgment automatically divested Erstad of his substantive rights and transferred or assigned them to her by operation of law. Such is not the case.

[18] Plaintiff undoubtedly owns the ring. *See* Civ. Code, § 679 ("The ownership of property is absolute when a single person has the absolute

dominion over it, and may use it or dispose of it according to his [or her] pleasure, subject only to general laws"); *see also* North Dakota Century Code, section 47–01–01 (2003) ("The ownership of a thing shall mean the right of one or more persons to possess and use it to the exclusion of others. In this code the thing of which there may be ownership is called property"). But ownership of gifted property, even if awarded in a divorce, does not automatically carry with it ownership of the rights of the person who bought the gift. As will be seen, contrary to plaintiff's hypothesis, the divorce judgment did not give plaintiff the ring embellished with Erstad's rights under the contract or his choice in action.

[19] A cause of action for damages is itself personal property. *See* Civ. Code, § 953 ("A thing in action is a right to recover money or other personal property by a judicial proceeding"; *Parker v. Walker,* 5 Cal.App. 4th 1173, 1182–1183 [6 Cal. Rptr. 2d 908] (1992) ["A cause of action to recover money in damages . . . is a chose in action and therefore a form of personal property"]; *see also Iszler v. Jordan,* 80 N.W.2d 665, 668–69 [a chose in action is property] (N.D. 1957).) At the time of the divorce judgment, all causes of action that could have been asserted against the jeweler by a buyer of the ring were Erstad's personal property. He was, after all, the purchaser of the ring. The divorce agreement awarded to each party his or her respective personal property, *except as otherwise expressly provided.* The disposition of the ring was expressly provided for in the agreement, i.e., plaintiff was given her jewelry. Any extant choice in action against defendant, however, were *not* expressly provided for in the agreement; therefore, they were *retained* by Erstad as part of his personal property.

[20] To be sure, Erstad could have transferred or assigned *his* rights to legal recourse to plaintiff (*see, e.g., Dixon-Reo Co. v. Horton Motor Co.,* 49 N.D. 304 [191 N.W. 780, 782] (1922) [a right arising out of an obligation, i.e., a thing in action, is the property of the person to whom the right is due and may be transferred]), but there are no allegations Erstad either did so or manifested an intention to do so.

Third Party Beneficiary

[21] The fact that Erstad did not assign or transfer his rights to plaintiff does not mean she is without recourse. For although plaintiff does not have Erstad's rights by virtue of the divorce judgment, she nonetheless has standing in her own right to sue for breach of contract as a third party beneficiary under the allegation, inter alia, that "[d]efendant entered into a written contract with Plaintiff's fiancee [*sic*] to purchase the subject engagement ring for the sole and stated purpose of giving it [to] Plaintiff."

[22] Civil Code section 1559 provides: "A contract, made expressly for the benefit of a third person, may be enforced by him [or her] at any time before the parties thereto rescind it." Because third party beneficiary status is a matter of contract interpretation, a person seeking to enforce a

contract as a third party beneficiary " 'must plead a contract which was made expressly for his [or her] benefit and one in which it clearly appears that he [or she] was a beneficiary.' " *California Emergency Physicians Medical Group v. PacifiCare of California,* 111 Cal.App.4th 1127, 1138 [4 Cal. Rptr. 3d 583] (2003).

[23] " '[E]xpressly[,]' [as used in the statute and case law,] means 'in an express manner; in direct or unmistakable terms; explicitly; definitely; directly.' [Citations.] '[A]n intent to make the obligation inure to the benefit of the third party must have been clearly manifested by the contracting parties.' " *Sofias v. Bank of America,* 172 Cal. App. 3d 583, 587 [218 Cal. Rptr. 388] (1985). Although this means persons only incidentally or remotely benefitted by the contract are not entitled to enforce it, it does not mean both of the contracting parties must intend to benefit the third party: Rather, it means the promissor—in this case, defendant jeweler—"must have understood that the promissee [Erstad] had such intent. [Citations.] No specific manifestation by the promissor of an intent to benefit the third person is required." Lucas v. Hamm, 56 Cal.2d 583, 591 [15 Cal. Rptr. 821, 364 P.2d 685] (1961); *see also Johnson v. Superior Court,* 80 Cal.App.4th 1050, 1064–1065 [95 Cal. Rptr. 2d 864] (2000).

[24] We conclude the pleading here meets the test of demonstrating plaintiff's standing as a third party beneficiary to enforce the contract between Erstad and defendant. The couple went shopping for an engagement ring. They were together when plaintiff chose the ring she wanted or, as alleged in the complaint, she "caused [the ring] to be purchased for her." Erstad allegedly bought the ring "for the sole and *stated* purpose of giving [the ring]" to plaintiff. (Italics added.) Under the alleged facts, the jeweler *must* have understood Erstad's intent to enter the sales contract for plaintiff's benefit. Thus, plaintiff has adequately pleaded her status as a third party beneficiary, and she is entitled to proceed with her contract claim against defendant to the extent it is not time-barred.

* * *

Breach of Contract/Breach of Express Warranty

[25] Plaintiff's breach of contract claim is based on allegations of defendant's breach of express warranty in representing the engagement diamond was of an SI1 clarity rating, when in actuality it was of an inferior quality. Other than noting the breach of express warranty claim is adequately pleaded, and that plaintiff is entitled to pursue it as a third party beneficiary, we express no opinion on its ultimate viability. It will be for the fact finder to determine from all the circumstances whether defendant's statements regarding the clarity rating of the diamond constituted an express warranty under California Uniform Commercial Code section 2313 or were merely nonactionable expressions of opinion. In

any event, this is the only cause of action on which plaintiff may proceed, as we discuss more fully, *post*.

Rescission

[26] Plaintiff has attempted to plead a separate cause of action for rescission. She is not entitled to that remedy. Civil Code section 1559 provides, "A contract, made expressly for the benefit of a third person, may be *enforced* by him [or her] at any time before *the parties thereto rescind it*." (Italics added.) But only the parties to the contract may rescind it. Civil Code section 1689 provides, in pertinent part, "(a) A contract may be rescinded if all the *parties* thereto consent. (b) A *party to a contract* may rescind the contract in the following cases: (1) If the consent of the *party* rescinding, or of any *party jointly contracting* with him [or her], was given by mistake, or obtained through duress, menace, fraud, or undue influence, exercised by or with the connivance of the *party* as to whom he [or she] rescinds, or of any other *party to the contract jointly interested with such party*. (2) If the consideration for the obligation of the rescinding *party* fails, in whole or in part, through the fault of the *party* as to whom he [or she] rescinds." (Italics added.)

[27] We have found no cases specifically holding the rescission remedy unavailable to a third party beneficiary, but the proposition is self-evident to a degree that might well explain the absence of precedent. Civil Code section 1559 grants a third party beneficiary the right to *enforce* the contract, not rescind it, and Civil Code section 1689 limits its grant of rescission rights to the contracting parties. Not only do the relevant statutes demand making rescission unavailable to a third party beneficiary, but common sense compels the conclusion. The interest of the third party beneficiary is as the intended recipient of the *benefits* of the contract, and a direct right to those benefits, i.e., specific performance, or damages in lieu thereof, will protect the beneficiary's interests. Rescission, on the other hand, extinguishes a contract between the parties. (Civ. Code, § 1688.) Plaintiff, not having participated in the agreement, not having undertaken any duty or given any consideration, is a stranger to the agreement, with no legitimate interest in voiding it. As a matter of law, without an assignment of Erstad's contract rights, plaintiff cannot rescind the sales contract to which she was not a party.

Statutory Remedies for Consumers or Buyers

[28] Plaintiff argues she has remedies under the Act because she is a "consumer." Unfortunately for plaintiff, by statutory definition Erstad was the consumer because it was he who purchased the ring. (*See* Civ. Code, § 1761, subd. (d) [" 'Consumer' means an individual who seeks or acquires, by purchase or lease, any goods or services for personal, family, or household purposes"].) Plaintiff's ownership of the ring was not acquired as a result of her own consumer transaction with defendant, and without

an assignment of Erstad's rights, she does not fall within the parameters of consumer remedies under the Act.

Actual and Constructive Fraud

[29] Further, the absence of an assignment of rights from Erstad precludes plaintiff from maintaining a cause of action for actual fraud. It is axiomatic that plaintiff must allege she "actually relied upon the misrepresentation; i.e., that the representation was 'an immediate cause of [her] conduct which alter[ed] [her] legal relations,' and that without such representation, '[she] would not, in all reasonable probability, have entered into the contract or other transaction.'" 5 Witkin, Summary of Cal. Law (9th ed. 1988) Torts, § 711, p. 810. Here, Erstad allegedly relied on the representation and entered into the contract of sale. As we have explained, he retained the right, if any, to sue for actual fraud.

[30] As for constructive fraud, the complaint fails to plead facts establishing the requisite fiduciary or special confidential relationship between plaintiff and defendant. *See, e.g., Tyler v. Children's Home Society*, 29 Cal.App.4th 511, 548 [35 Cal. Rptr. 2d 291] (1994); *Peterson Development Co. v. Torrey Pines Bank*, 233 Cal. App. 3d 103, 116 [284 Cal. Rptr. 367] (1991) ["It is essential to the operation of the doctrine of constructive fraud that there exist a fiduciary or special relationship"]. And even assuming plaintiff could overcome the standing hurdle, fraud causes of action must be pleaded with specificity, meaning "(1) general pleading of the legal conclusion of fraud is insufficient; and (2) every element of the cause of action for fraud must be alleged in full, factually and specifically, and the policy of liberal construction of pleading will not usually be invoked to sustain a pleading that is defective in any material respect." *Wilhelm v. Pray, Price, Williams & Russell, supra*, 186 Cal. App.3d at 1331. Plaintiff's complaint utterly fails the specificity test, not because she is an inartful pleader, but because those facts that are well pleaded necessarily negate the existence of the facts supporting the requisite elements of fraud.

Disposition

[31] The judgment is reversed. The case is remanded with directions to the trial court to overrule defendant's demurrer to plaintiff's cause of action for breach of contract and order defendant to answer. In all other respects, the demurrer has been properly sustained without leave to amend. Plaintiff shall recover her costs on appeal.

RYLAARSDAM, ACTING P. J., and BEDSWORTH, J., concurred.

———

NOTES

1.   The next case illustrates the evolution of third party beneficiary law in the context of multi-party commercial agreements that are meant to provide for mutual cooperation and benefit in order to avoid the "tragedy of the commons." The "tragedy of the commons" describes what is otherwise known as the public goods problem: It is hard to coordinate and pay for public goods, i.e., those that are owned or used collectively. Think of the "commons" as a pasture owned by the community and used by a group. Each user owns sheep and has the incentive to put more and more sheep on the pasture to gain, privately. The overall effect of many individuals doing this overwhelms the carrying capacity of the pasture and the sheep cannot all survive.

2.   In the case that follows, a group of food vendors has banded together to assess fees to clean and maintain the common food court area. One of the vendors was not happy with the method of allocating fees between the businesses.

————

GOURMET LANE, INC. V. KELLER
Court of Appeal of California
222 Cal. App. 2d 701, 35 Cal. Rptr. 398 (1963)

DESMOND, JUDGE.

[1]   Action on a contractual obligation by defendant to pay his agreed share of certain expenses in a joint food purveying operation. Plaintiff, after a court trial, recovered a money judgment in an action based upon a contractual obligation by defendant to pay his agreed share of certain expenses in a joint food purveying operation.

[2]   Defendant's appeal is on the ground that neither of the two theories of plaintiff's complaint was established. These theories were: (1) a direct agreement between plaintiff, an incorporated association, and defendant, one of its members, whereby the latter agreed to pay at the rate charged by plaintiff's board of directors for services admittedly received; and (2) defendant's obligation under a third party beneficiary contract to pay at such rate. The findings and holding of the trial court are in favor of plaintiff on both counts. We agree.

[3]   Plaintiff has seven shareholder-members, all of whom are directors. The seven are operators of food-dispensing concessions under separate leases with Kassis Building Corporation in the concourse of a large Sacramento market owned by the lessor. This concourse is known as Gourmet Lane.

[4]   The lessor furnished a dining area, kitchen, dishwashing and garbage disposal facilities used in common by these seven tenants.

[5] Each lease contains the following provisions: "Lessee promises and agrees, together with such other tenants as there may be of the other concourse shops, to maintain and operate in a sanitary businesslike manner the said dining area at no cost or expense of any nature to lessor. Lessee shall enter into an association and cooperate with such other tenants in the operation of said dining area. This obligation is to be joint and several among all of said tenants. *A decision of the majority of said tenants with regard to the details of the operation and maintenance of said area and allocating the costs thereof shall be binding upon lessee and all of the other tenants.*" (Italics supplied.)

[6] The tenants first operated as a voluntary unincorporated association, but soon decided to incorporate and plaintiff corporation was organized. The bylaws, approved by defendant, provide that a majority of directors shall constitute a quorum. They also provide: "Every act or decision done or made by a majority of the directors present at a meeting duly held at which a quorum is present shall be regarded as the act of the board of directors. . . ."

[7] At an early meeting the directors discussed the method to be adopted to defray the community expenses. One member preferred a "dish count" as a basis of allocation. This would have afforded a fair distribution of dishwashing costs which were apparently a major item of expense. Defendant operated a doughnut shop, including the dispensing of coffee and doughnuts to be eaten on the premises. He would have had a higher dish count per dollar volume than some of the others. He, with others, objected to this method of cost apportionment, since dishwashing was but one of the joint operating expenses. Apportionment on the ratio which the taxable sales of each bore to the taxable sales of all with a minimum charge to be fixed was the method finally agreed to by all the members. At the first meeting after the opening of the market $100 per week was agreed to by resolution of the directors as the fixed minimum. Defendant voted for this resolution. This was on December 6, 1958. By February 1959 all members but defendant had shown, and were paying charges based upon, sales tax returns in excess of the minimum. Defendant objected to the $100 minimum and, upon his request, the directors voted to reduce the weekly minimum to $75. At the February 16, 1959, meeting Keller again requested that the minimum be dropped; this time to $50 per week. The directors refused this request. Defendant testified he "went along with" that position. Defendant continued to take an active part in the affairs of the corporation. He was its treasurer and handled all of its finances. For a short time, he actively managed the maintenance operations.

[8] Defendant throughout this period continued to pay the $75 per week minimum. Commencing June 1, 1960, he refused to make further payments. The directors had refused his requests to abolish or lower the minimum charge. Although defendant contends the charge is unfair and

discriminates against his operation, plaintiff argues otherwise. It points out that when he pays the weekly minimum defendant's share is but 6.54 per cent of the total expenses, the percentages of the others running from 11.99 per cent to 23.75 per cent. Defendant's total gross receipts on the other hand are in line with the others and even exceed those of one other member. It was also shown that defendant's expenses are less than he would have had to pay operating alone.

[9] When defendant discontinued paying the $75 per week he discontinued all payments, although continuing to enjoy the community services furnished. He has continued so to use the facilities and is still a member of the association.

[10] It seems clear from the testimony of all the witnesses that no perfect method of apportioning the joint expenses of an enterprise of this type could be evolved. An accountant employed by the corporation to study the matter and investigate the method of allocation adopted by food purveyors in similar markets in other localities reported they used the same basis. In any event it was the method to which a majority of the group had agreed and defendant had agreed with his associates to be bound by the decision of a majority. The trial court, moreover, has found that the "basis established by the Board of Directors for allocating the costs of operating the community kitchen and dining room facilities among each of the purveyors of food is fair, equitable, and just and binding upon defendant. . . ." Evidence supports these findings and we cannot disturb them.

[11] Determination of the appeal could rest upon this alone. However, it is not the sole reason for affirming the judgment of the trial court.

[12] The second theory of the complaint was that a third party beneficiary contract existed under which plaintiff was the beneficiary giving it a legal right to sue thereunder. The trial court accepted this theory and its holding is sound.

[13] The lease provision which we have quoted above (1) creates a joint and several liability in, and between, the several tenants of the concourse to defray the maintenance costs of the dining and kitchen areas; to insure the collection of these costs in an expeditious and orderly manner the tenants (2) are required to organize themselves into an association to administer the joint operation and (3) to adopt "majority rule" in fixing maintenance cost allocation.

[14] Under these contracts the tenants (promisors) agree with the lessor (promisee) to pay money for maintenance costs to plaintiff association (third party beneficiary). Since the plaintiff was not a party to the agreement, in fact was not then even in existence, it may be true—if courts must be obeisant to the privity rule—that we must bring ourselves

within an exception to it. One exception is in Civil Code section 1559. It provides:

> "A contract, made expressly for the benefit of a third person, may be enforced by him at any time before the parties thereto rescind it."

[15] Courts have found difficulty sometimes determining when a contract is made "expressly" for the benefit of a third party. *See* discussion in *Lucas v. Hamm*, 56 Cal.2d 583 [15 Cal.Rptr. 821, 364 P.2d 685]. However, as is stated by Chief Justice Gibson, *id.* at 590: "The effect of the section is to exclude enforcement by persons who are only incidentally or remotely benefitted." Here plaintiff is more than incidentally or remotely benefitted.

[16] The whole *raison d'etre* for plaintiff was the creation of an entity (whether incorporated or not) which could efficiently maintain the dining and kitchen area. This the tenants, of whom defendant was one, promised to accomplish. Having also promised to bear the maintenance costs jointly and severally, they agreed to a "majority rule" allocation of these costs and obviously, since an association was to be organized, it was the parties' intent that the expression of majority rule would be through governance of that entity. Granted this is not the usual form of third party beneficiary contract, since the plaintiff was not a creditor-beneficiary (i.e., it was not a creditor of the promisee) and was not [a]donee-beneficiary in the sense that a gift was intended to be made to plaintiff. It was, however, [a]donee-beneficiary as defined by the Restatement, the purpose of the promisee in obtaining the promise being "to confer upon [the beneficiary] a right against the promisor to some performance neither due nor supposed or asserted to be due from the promisee to the beneficiary." Rest., Contracts, § 133(1) (a). In *El Rio Oils v. Pacific Coast Asphalt Co.*, 95 Cal.App.2d 186, 192, it was held that a preincorporation agreement made by one of the incorporators (as promisor) with another (as promisee) for the benefit of the corporation to be formed could be enforced and sued on by the [corporation, once formed] as a third party beneficiary. Plaintiff was therefore entitled to sue on the contract as a third party beneficiary.

The judgment is affirmed.

NOTES AND QUESTIONS

1.   Note how California's statute on third party beneficiary status (quoted in paragraph 12) makes no explicit mention of creditor and donee beneficiaries or the distinction between intended or incidental beneficiaries. Those distinctions are supplied by the courts in that state. This provides a good example of the continued common law tradition of judge-made law based upon and elaborating upon statutes that purport to codify the law in a quasi-civil law format.

2.   Review R2d § 133. In applying the standard of this section to the facts of the case, do you think that the court in *Gourmet Lane* got it right? Why or why not?

DOLAN V. ALTICE USA, INC.
Court of Chancery of Delaware
C.A. No. 2018–0651–JRS, 2019 WL 2711280 (2019)

* * *

I.   FACTUAL BACKGROUND

[1]   I draw the facts from the allegations in the Complaint, documents incorporated by reference or integral to the Complaint and judicially noticeable facts available in public Securities and Exchange Commission filings. For purposes of this motion to dismiss, I accept as true the Complaint's well-pled factual allegations and draw all reasonable inferences in Plaintiffs' favor.

A.   The Parties

[2]   Plaintiff, Charles F. Dolan, is the founder and former CEO of Cablevision Systems Corp. Prior to the Merger, he held a 14.1% interest in Cablevision. His wife, Helen A. Dolan, also held a 14.1% interest. One of their sons, James L. Dolan, held a 3.3% interest and is a former CEO of Cablevision. Another son, Patrick F. Dolan, held a 1.8% interest and was President of News12 at the time of and after the Merger.

[3]   Plaintiffs, Colleen McVey and Danielle Campbell, are current employees of News12, but both are slated to be terminated. McVey, an Emmy award-winning news anchor, has worked at News12 for over 30 years. She regularly appears on air at News12's leading network, News12 Long Island. Campbell, also an Emmy and Edward R. Murrow award-winning news anchor, has worked at News12 for almost 30 years. Viewers rate Campbell above average as compared to other Long Island reporters and she earns a high awareness score among the viewing public.

[4]   Defendants, Altice USA and Altice Europe, are cable, fiber, telecommunications, content and media companies. Altice USA, a Delaware corporation, operates in the United States. Altice Europe, a Dutch *naamloze vennootschap* (i.e., a Netherlands public limited liability company), is the parent of communications companies that operate in Europe, Israel and the Dominican Republic. Both Altice USA and Altice Europe are successors in interest to Altice N.V.

[5]   Nominal Defendant, Cablevision, a Delaware corporation, is wholly-owned and operated by Altice. The Dolan family founded and led Cablevision until Altice acquired Cablevision in 2015.

[6] Nominal Defendant, News12, a Delaware limited liability company, is a local television network that provides 24-hour "hyper-local" news coverage concentrating on distinct geographic areas including New Jersey, Connecticut and New York City. Altice acquired News12 as part of the Merger.

B. The Merger

[7] In 2015, Altice and the Dolan family began discussing Altice's possible acquisition of Cablevision. Initially, the Dolan family declined to include News12 in the transaction, proposing instead to spin off the asset to an entity they controlled. After intense negotiations with Altice, the Dolan family relented and agreed to include News12 in the Merger in exchange for assurances in the Merger Agreement that Altice would operate News12 in a manner that preserved its employee base, quality reporting and programming.

[8] The Dolan family, all of whom were members of Cablevision's "controlling stockholder group," were not named as parties to the Merger Agreement, but were represented by Debevoise & Plimpton LLP in the transaction negotiations. As negotiations continued, Altice determined that it would be useful to lock up the Dolan family's shares in favor of the Merger. Here again, comforted that Altice had committed to preserve the News12 asset, the Dolan family relented and committed by Written Consent to vote their substantial Class B shares "in favor of adoption of the Merger Agreement."

[9] Cablevision, Altice N.V. and Neptune Merger Sub Corp. entered into the Merger Agreement on September 16, 2015. The Merger consideration totaled $17.7 billion. Of that amount, the Dolan family received over $2.2 billion, or approximately 20% of the cash component of the Merger consideration. The transaction closed on June 21, 2016.

C. The Merger Agreement

[10] As noted, in exchange for the Dolan family's agreement to include News12 in the Merger, Altice agreed to include a covenant in the Merger Agreement (Section 6.4(f)) that it would operate News12 in accordance with the station's then-existing business plan:

> (i) Parent will operate News12 Networks LLC ("News12") from and after [June 21, 2016] [("]the Closing["])] substantially in accordance with the existing News12 business plan (the "News12 Business Plan"), a true and complete copy of which is included in Schedule 6.4(f) of the Company Disclosure Letter, as the same may be adjusted as provided in Scheduled 6.4(f), through at least the end of plan year 2020 within the current News12 footprint as of the date of this Agreement.

(ii) The Company will operate News12 in accordance with the existing News12 Business Plan through the Closing.

(iii) Either party may make reference to Section 6.4(f) and to Schedule 6.4(f) of the Company Disclosure Letter in connection with securing franchise and other regulatory approvals.

[11] As referenced in Section 6.4(f), the Merger Agreement incorporated the News12 Business Plan in Schedule 6.4(f). Among other things, that plan provides for News12 to employ a full-time equivalent headcount of 462 employees for a five-year period-plan years 2016 through 2020. The Business Plan also confirms that Altice will not materially modify News12's content or decrease any of the budgeted expenses, unless News12 should sustain a loss of $60 million or more, in which case Altice would be free to modify the plan as needed.

[12] Although, as a practical matter, the Dolan family and News12 employees are the beneficiaries of Section 6.4(f), the Merger Agreement, at Section 9.8, disclaims the existence of third-party beneficiaries:

> Except (i) as provided in Section 6.10 (*Director and Officer Liability*) or Section 9.15 (*Financing Sources*) and (ii) for the right of holders of Shares as of the Effective Time, after the Effective Time, to receive the aggregate consideration payable pursuant to Article IV of this Agreement, which rights set forth in clauses (i) and (ii) of this Section 9.8 are hereby expressly acknowledged and agreed by Parent and Merger Sub, **Parent and the Company hereby agree that their respective representations, warranties and covenants set forth in this Agreement are solely for the benefit of the other party hereto, in accordance with and subject to the terms of this Agreement, and this Agreement is not intended to, and does not, confer upon any Person other than the parties hereto any rights or remedies hereunder**, including the right to rely upon the representations and warranties set forth herein . . . . The representations and warranties in this Agreement are the product of negotiations among the parties hereto and are for the sole benefit of the parties hereto.

[13] The Merger Agreement also contains a survival provision at Section 9.1:

> This Article IX and the agreements of the Company, Parent and Merger Sub contained in Article IV and Sections 6.8 (*Employee Benefits*), 6.9 (*Expenses*) and 6.10 (*Director and Officer Liability*) shall survive the consummation of the Merger and the Transactions. This Article IX and the agreements of the Company, Parent and Merger Sub contained in Section 6.9 (*Expenses*), Section 6.11 (*Financing*), Section 6.12 (*Indemnification Relating*

to Financing) and Section 8.5 (*Effect of Termination and Abandonment*) and the Confidentiality Agreement shall survive the termination of this Agreement. **All other representations, warranties, covenants and agreements in this Agreement shall not survive the consummation of the Merger and the Transactions or the termination of this Agreement**.

[14] As the provision clearly reflects, the Parties agreed that only certain covenants, representations, warranties and agreements would survive the consummation or termination of the Merger. Section 6.4(f) was not among them.

[15] Finally, the parties agreed in Section 6.8(e), entitled "Employee Benefits," that:

> **Nothing contained in this Agreement is intended to** (1) be treated as an amendment of any particular Company Plan, (2) prevent Parent, the Surviving Corporation or any of their Affiliates from amending or terminating any of their benefit plans or, after the Effective Time, any Company Plan in accordance with their terms, **(3) prevent Parent, the Surviving Corporation or any of their Affiliates, after the Effective Time, from terminating the employment of any Continuing Employee, or (4) create any third-party beneficiary rights in any employee of the Company** or any of its Subsidiaries, any beneficiary or dependent thereof, or any collective bargaining representative thereof.

D. News12 after the Merger

[16] In the spring of 2017, after the Merger closed, Altice terminated approximately 70 employees, allegedly "in direct violation of Section 6.4(f)." At the time, Patrick Dolan was President of News12 and opposed the layoffs to no avail. The layoffs decreased News12's salary spend by about $7 million—dropping Operating Expenses to levels under the allocations in Section 6.4(f).

[17] After the 2017 layoffs, Altice developed a plan to lay off 10% of News12 employees each year. On August 21, 2018, Altice's controlling stockholder, Patrick Drahi, wrote to Patrick Dolan to confirm the planned layoffs. The downsizing plan contemplates that McVey and Campbell will be among the first of the News12 employees to lose their jobs. Michael Schreibner, President of Altice USA News, explained that the layoffs were necessary to give News12 a "fresh look." According to Plaintiffs, the termination of long-time, beloved news anchors, coupled with the planned structural changes, will negatively affect News12's ability to maintain its historic level of quality and hyperlocal news content.

E. Procedural Posture

[18] On September 4, 2018, Plaintiffs initiated this action specifically to enforce Section 6.4(f) and to enjoin Altice from terminating any News12 employee other than "for obvious cause" or otherwise operating News12 in deviation of the News12 Business Plan as incorporated in the Merger Agreement. Plaintiffs amended their Complaint to add Danielle Campbell as a plaintiff on October 1, 2018. Defendants then moved to dismiss. By stipulation of the parties, Plaintiffs filed the now-operative Verified Second Amended Complaint (the "Complaint") on March 12, 2019, to include a request that the Court appoint a monitor to enforce Altice's specific performance of Section 6.4(f) and to enhance the allegations in support of their breach of the implied covenant of good faith and fair dealing claim.

[19] In the Complaint, Plaintiffs assert six causes of action: breach of contract, breach of the implied covenant of good faith and fair dealing, equitable fraud, promissory estoppel, negligent misrepresentation, and declaratory relief. Plaintiffs seek specific performance, injunctive relief, monetary damages, recoverable costs, attorneys' fees and pre-judgment and post-judgment interest.

[20] Plaintiffs filed a Motion for a Temporary Restraining Order on October 9, 2018, along with their initial complaint. After several hearings to consider that motion were adjourned, the parties submitted a proposed status quo order. The Court entered that order on February 13, 2019, prohibiting Altice from terminating any News12 employee during the pendency of this litigation, except for actual, *bona fide* cause or upon approval of the Court.

II. ANALYSIS

[21] In considering a motion to dismiss, "(i) all well-pleaded factual allegations are accepted as true; (ii) even vague allegations are 'well-pleaded' if they give the opposing party notice of the claim; [and] (iii) the Court must draw all reasonable inferences in favor of the non-moving party[.]" This is to say, "Delaware follows a simple notice pleading standard." "To meet this standard and survive a Rule 12(b)(6) motion to dismiss, a plaintiff must make allegations in its complaint which provide the defendant with sufficient notice of the basis for the plaintiff's claim." The court may grant a motion to dismiss only if the "plaintiff would not be entitled to recover under any reasonably conceivable set of circumstances susceptible of proof."

[22] Questions of contractual interpretation generally are questions of law well suited for a motion to dismiss. With that said, the Court cannot select one reasonable interpretation of a contract provision over another as a basis for dismissal. Rather, "[d]ismissal, pursuant to Rule 12(b)(6), is proper only if the defendants' interpretation is the only reasonable construction as a matter of law."

A.   Have Plaintiffs Adequately Pled A Breach of Section 6.4(f)?

[23] Not surprisingly, as with most contracts, the Merger Agreement features some boilerplate, some bespoke provisions and some bespoke boilerplate. The question presented here is whether the boilerplate and bespoke boilerplate should be construed, as a matter of law, to render a bespoke provision superfluous. I consider that question, in parts, below.

1.   The Dolan Family Have Adequately Pled They Are Third-Party Beneficiaries; McVey and Campbell Have Not

[24] As a threshold matter, the parties dispute Plaintiffs' standing to bring contractual claims as third-party beneficiaries to the Merger Agreement. Since Plaintiffs were not parties to the Merger Agreement, they must demonstrate they have standing to enforce the contract as third-party beneficiaries. To do so at this stage, Plaintiffs must plead facts that allow a reasonable inference that:

> (i) the contracting parties [ ] intended that the third party beneficiary benefit from the contract, (ii) the benefit [was] intended as a gift or in satisfaction of a pre-existing obligation to that person, and (iii) the intent to benefit the third party [was] a material part of the parties' purpose in entering into the contract.

[25] For the first element, Plaintiffs have adequately pled the parties intended that Plaintiffs benefit from Section 6.4(f) of the Merger Agreement. As for the Dolan family, they allege they would not have agreed to include News12 in the transaction if Altice had not agreed to operate the stations in accordance with the News12 business plan, as promised in Section 6.4(f). As for McVey and Campbell, they allege the News12 business plan contains expenditures for newsgathering and production— the bulk of which goes to employee salaries. The News12 business plan protects these salaries with particular line items by department and an incorporated estimate of $60 million in losses over five years.

[26] The Dolan family also adequately allege that Section 6.4(f) was intended to meet a preexisting commitment made to them and that Altice intended "to give the[m] (as beneficiar[ies]) the benefit of the promised performance." Here again, the Dolan family alleges they agreed to sell News12 only because Altice made the commitment that it would operate News12 within clearly expressed parameters. They then agreed by Written Consent to vote their Class B shares "in favor of adoption of the Merger Agreement" in reliance upon that commitment.

[27] McVey and Campbell part ways with the Dolan family in the third-party beneficiary analysis on this second element. The Complaint contains no well-pled facts that Altice made any commitment or owed any "pre-existing obligation" to either McVey or Campbell prior to the Merger Agreement from which they could claim third-party beneficiary status with

respect to Section 6.4(f). This would explain why Section 6.8(e) of the Merger Agreement makes clear that Altice is not "prevent[ed] . . . from terminating the employment of any Continuing Employee (by definition including McVey and Campbell)." While the Dolan family may be able to advance an argument that the termination of McVey and Campbell's employment with News12 would constitute a breach of Section 6.4(f) as to them, McVey and Campbell have no standing to assert that claim of breach either as parties to, or third-party beneficiaries of, the Merger Agreement.

[28] Lastly, it is alleged that Section 6.4(f) was included in the Merger Agreement to induce the Dolan family to sell their Cablevision stock, merge Cablevision and News12 into Altice and sign the Written Consent in favor of the Merger Agreement. Under the circumstances, it is reasonably conceivable that "the intent to benefit the third party [was] a material part of the parties' purpose in entering into the contract."

[29] The Dolan family has well pled each of the three requisite elements to establish third-party beneficiary status. But, of course, the inquiry cannot end there. Section 9.8 of the Merger Agreement states, in part, that the parties "agree that their respective representations, warranties and covenants set forth in this Agreement are solely for the benefit of the other party hereto, in accordance with and subject to the terms of this Agreement, and this Agreement is not intended to, and does not, confer upon any Person other than the parties hereto any rights or remedies hereunder." While Section 9.8 is not absolute, it clearly does not identify the Dolan family as third-party beneficiaries. Recognizing this, the Dolan family invoke the canon that a specific provision of a contract trumps a general one in order to argue that Section 6.4(f) trumps Section 9.8. That canon does not fit here, however, because both sections are specific. Section 6.4(f) is specific in providing detailed rights that expressly benefit non-parties to the contract; Section 9.8 is specific in identifying who is and who is not intended to be a third-party beneficiary of the contract. Canons of contract construction, alone, cannot render unambiguous two specific and yet conflicting contractual provisions.

[30] The goal of contract construction in instances like this is to "harmonize" related contractual provisions. That simply cannot be done here by looking only within the four corners of the Merger Agreement. Extrinsic evidence will be needed to determine what Section 6.4(f) was intended to mean and how, if at all, it is to be enforced.

2. Plaintiffs Adequately Allege Section 6.4(f) Survived the Closing of the Merger

[31] For the Dolan family's claims under the Merger Agreement to survive Defendants' motion, it must be reasonably conceivable that Section 6.4(f) survived the Closing. Specifically, it must be reasonably conceivable that Section 9.1, the survival provision, did not apply to Section 6.4(f).

Defendants assert that, even if the Dolan family has standing, Section 6.4(f) did not survive Closing because it was not one of the sections designated for survival in Section 9.1.

[32] The parties offer conflicting interpretations of Section 6.4(f). The Dolan family reads Section 6.4(f) as clearly surviving Closing—why else would such a detailed, heavily negotiated provision with an accompanying schedule and five-year life span be included in the Merger Agreement? Defendants counter that Section 6.4(f) was simply a goodwill gesture and was in no way meant to bind Altice before or after the Merger closed. In reply, the Dolan family point out that Section 6.4(f) is not drafted as an expression of good will. Instead, it is drafted to state an obligation—"Parent *will operate* News12 in accordance with the existing News12 business plan . . . ."

[33] For Defendants to prevail on their motion to dismiss, theirs must be the only reasonable constructions of Section 6.4(f) and Section 9.1 as a matter of law. That definitive construction is not possible here. Defendants' construction fairly tracks the plain language of Section 9.1, but their construction of the interaction between Section 9.1 and Section 6.4(f) renders Section 6.4(f) superfluous in the sense that it is entirely unenforceable—by anyone. That result is inconsistent with the contractual cannon that discourages the court from construing a contract in a way that results in "mere surplusage." It also creates an arguably "absurd result" by rendering meaningless the protections the Dolan family allege they bargained for with respect to News12.

* * * * * *

[34] The Merger Agreement is ambiguous with respect to whether Section 6.4(f) is: (a) enforceable by the Dolan family as third-party beneficiaries, and (b) enforceable as a covenant that survived the Closing of the Merger. Accordingly, the motion to dismiss Counts I and VI must be denied as to the Dolan family. As neither McVey nor Campbell have standing to enforce the Merger Agreement, however, Counts I and VI must be dismissed as to them.

B. Plaintiffs Have Not Stated A Claim for Breach of the Implied Covenant of Good Faith and Fair Dealing

[35] Plaintiffs allege that Altice breached the Merger Agreement's implied covenant of good faith and fair dealing by promising pre-Closing to perform obligations to Cablevision and its stockholders while attempting to avoid this obligation after obtaining control of Cablevision, thereby "frustrating the essential purpose of Section 6.4(f)." The implied covenant is a "limited and extraordinary" legal remedy. It adheres only when "the contract is truly silent with respect to the matter at hand, and only when

the court finds that the expectations of the parties were so fundamental that it is clear that they did not feel a need to negotiate about them."

[36] Plaintiffs have not adequately identified any "gap" in the Merger Agreement that the Parties failed to anticipate and address. According to Plaintiffs, the alleged "gap" is revealed in the Merger Agreement's failure to identify who has standing to enforce Section 6.4(f) in the event of breach. I reject this argument as a matter of law. Section 9.8 clearly addresses standing under the Merger Agreement. This Court "will not rewrite contractual language covering particular topics [under the guise of the implied covenant] just because one party failed to extract as complete a range of protections as it, after the fact, claims to have desired during the negotiation process." Thus, Count II must be dismissed because it is duplicative of Plaintiffs' breach of contract claim. If the Dolan family is to have a right to enforce Section 6.4(f), that right will have to flow from parol evidence that allows the Merger Agreement reasonably to be construed to provide for that right.

C. The Dolan Plaintiffs Have Not Stated A Claim For Equitable Fraud Or Negligent Misrepresentation

[37] The claims for equitable fraud and negligent misrepresentation are not well pled both because they are bootstrapped improperly to the breach of contract claim and they rest on a flawed premise—that there was some sort of legally cognizable special relationship between Altice and the Dolan family.

[38] Conclusory allegations that a party to a contract did not intend to perform at the time of the contract's making do not state a claim for equitable fraud and negligent misrepresentation. These types of allegations, instead, reflect nothing more than a plaintiff's improper attempt to "bootstrap" breach of contract claims with fraud-based claims.

[39] Moreover, the Dolan family's equitable fraud/negligent misrepresentation claims fail as a matter of law because, in the context of a commercial arm's-length transaction, there is no "special relationship" between Altice and the Dolan family as required by Delaware law. "[A] plaintiff claiming equitable fraud must sufficiently plead a special relationship between the parties or other special equities, such as some form of fiduciary relationship or other similar circumstances." Cablevision and the Dolan family are sophisticated parties represented by sophisticated counsel. They bargained with Altice at arm's-length. There is no special relationship here. Therefore, Counts III and V must be dismissed.

D. The Dolan Plaintiffs Have Stated A Claim For Promissory Estoppel

[40] The Dolan family allege that Altice promised to operate News12 in accordance with the News12 Business Plan and, in doing so, induced Cablevision to include News12 in the Merger. Under the so-called *"Lord* test," promissory estoppel requires clear and convincing evidence that: "(1) a promise was made; (2) it was the reasonable expectation of the promisor to induce action or forbearance on the part of the promise; (3) the promisee reasonably relied on the promise and took action to his detriment; and (4) such promise is binding because injustice can be avoided only by enforcement of the promise."

[41] Typically, "[p]romissory estoppel does not apply . . . where a fully integrated, enforceable contract governs the promise at issue;" rather, the Court "must look to the contract as the source of a remedy[.]" But where a defendant denies that she is contractually bound to the plaintiff, or asserts that the contract is unenforceable, the plaintiff may plead promissory estoppel as an alternative to breach of contract. Here, if the Merger Agreement does not bind Altice to the Dolan family, then the Dolan family have adequately pled: (1) a definitive extra-contractual promise (to run News12 in accordance with its business plan); (2) intended to induce action (the sale of News12 and support for the Merger Agreement); (3) reasonable and detrimental reliance (the agreement to sell News12 and support the Merger Agreement); and (4) that injustice will result (the gross deviation from the News12 business plan) if the promise is not enforced. "Determining whether the elements for promissory estoppel are met will require a fact intensive inquiry into the details of the parties' dealings." Defendants' motion to dismiss Count IV as to the Dolan family is denied.

III. CONCLUSION

[42] For the foregoing reasons, Defendants' motions to dismiss must be DENIED with respect to Counts I, IV and VI as to the Dolan family, and GRANTED with respect to Counts I, IV and VI as to McVey and Campbell and Counts II, III and V as to all Plaintiffs. Counsel shall contact chambers to arrange for a scheduling conference with the Court.

INDEX

References are to Pages

895